Himalayan Art in 108 Objects

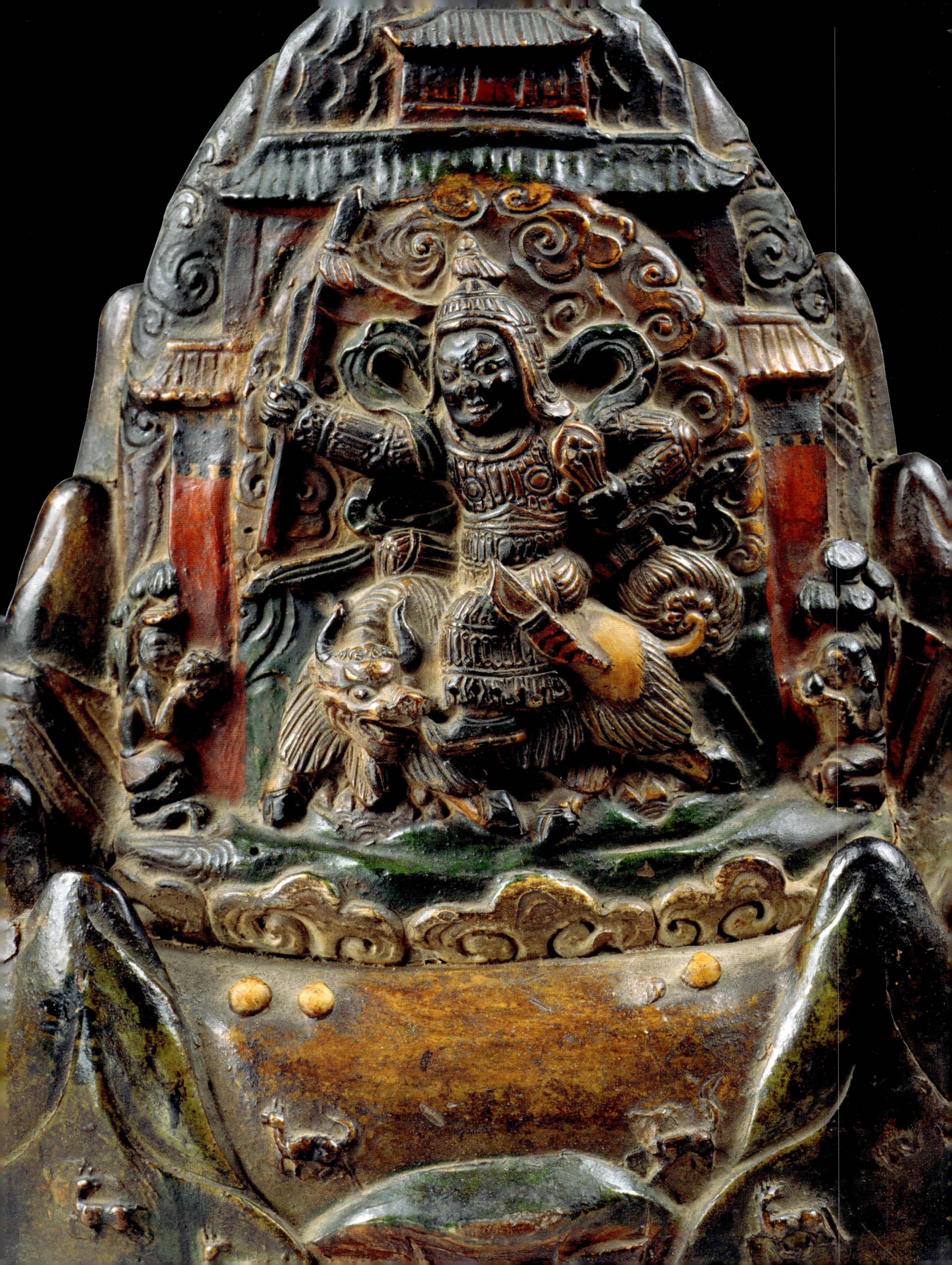

Himalayan Art in 108 Objects

Edited by Karl Debreczeny and Elena Pakhoutova

THE RUBIN MUSEUM OF ART

SCALA

RUBIN MUSEUM OF ART
IN ASSOCIATION WITH
SCALA ARTS PUBLISHERS, INC.

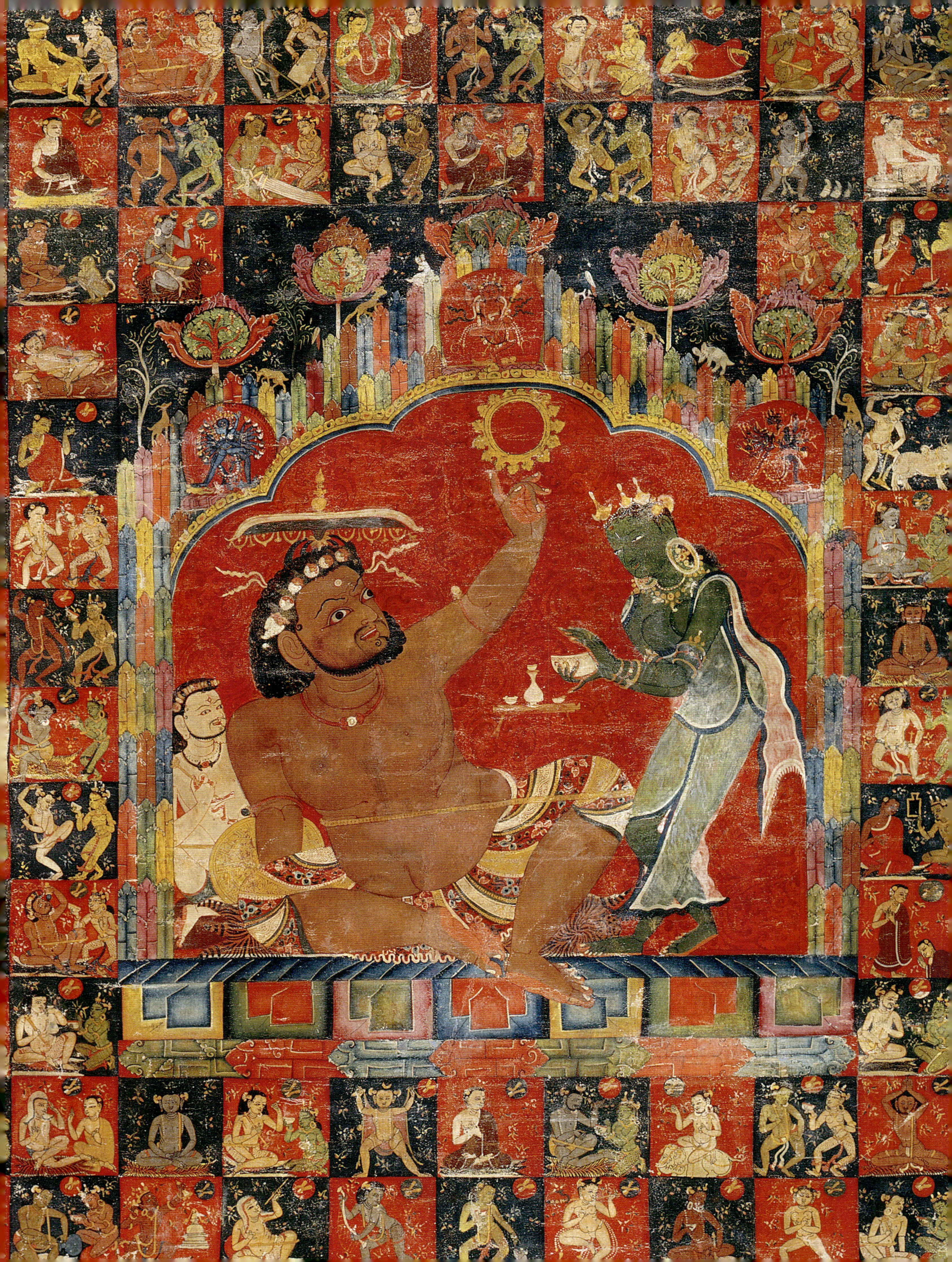

Contents

18TH CENTURY

19TH CENTURY

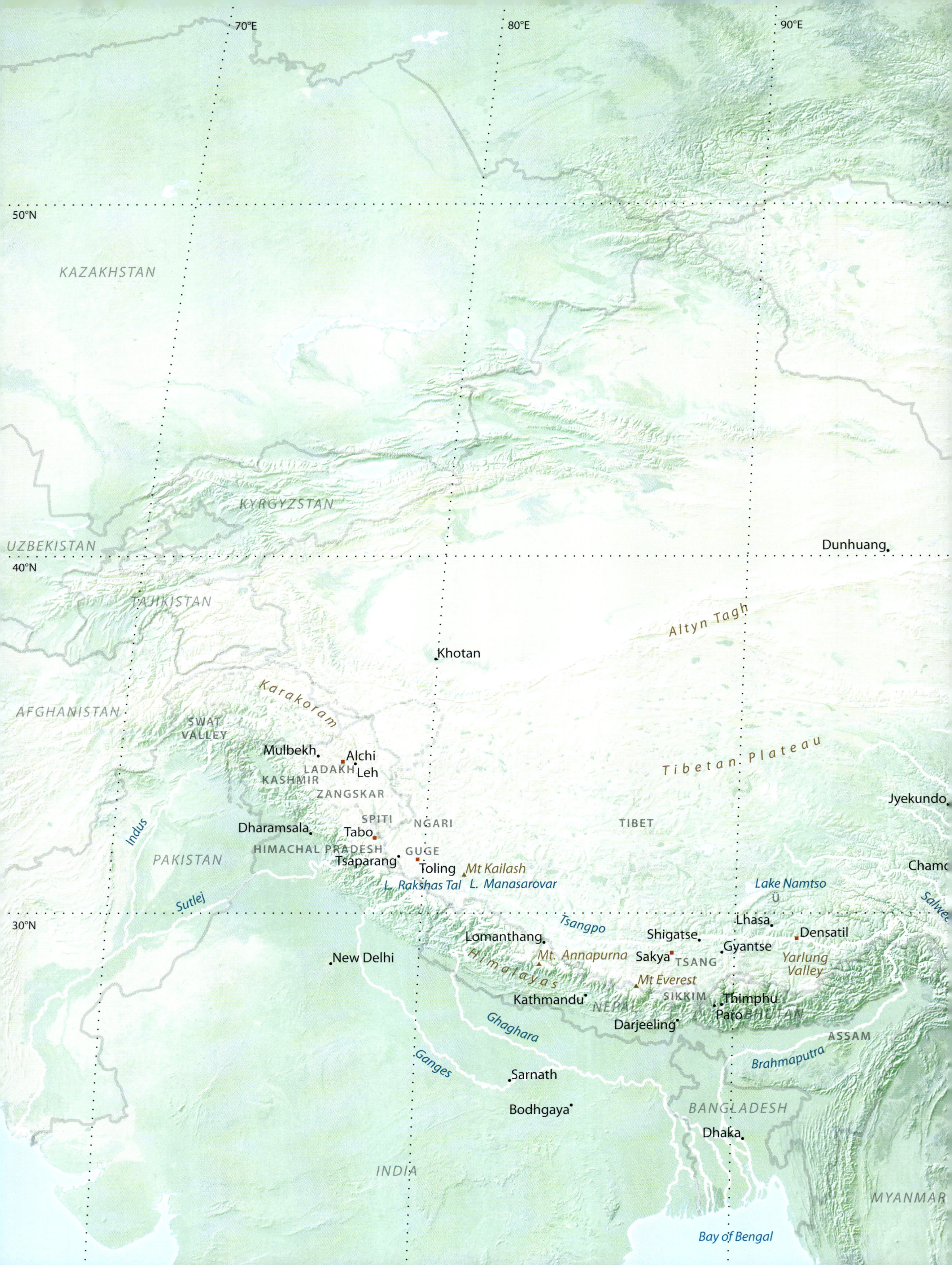
70°E
80°E
90°E
50°N
40°N
30°N
KAZAKHSTAN
KYRGYZSTAN
UZBEKISTAN
TAJIKISTAN
AFGHANISTAN
PAKISTAN
INDIA
NEPAL
BHUTAN
BANGLADESH
MYANMAR
Dunhuang
Altyn Tagh
Khotan
Karakoram
SWAT VALLEY
Mulbekh
Alchi
LADAKH
Leh
KASHMIR
ZANGSKAR
SPITI
NGARI
Dharamsala
Tabo
HIMACHAL PRADESH
GUGE
Tsaparang
Toling
Mt Kailash
L. Rakshas Tal
L. Manasarovar
Tibetan Plateau
TIBET
Jyekundo
Chamdo
Lake Namtso
Ü
Salween
Indus
Sutlej
Tsangpo
Lhasa
Shigatse
Densatil
Lomanthang
Gyantse
Sakya
TSANG
Yarlung Valley
Mt. Annapurna
Himalayas
Mt Everest
New Delhi
Kathmandu
SIKKIM
Thimphu
Paro
Darjeeling
ASSAM
Ghaghara
Brahmaputra
Ganges
Sarnath
Bodhgaya
Dhaka
Bay of Bengal

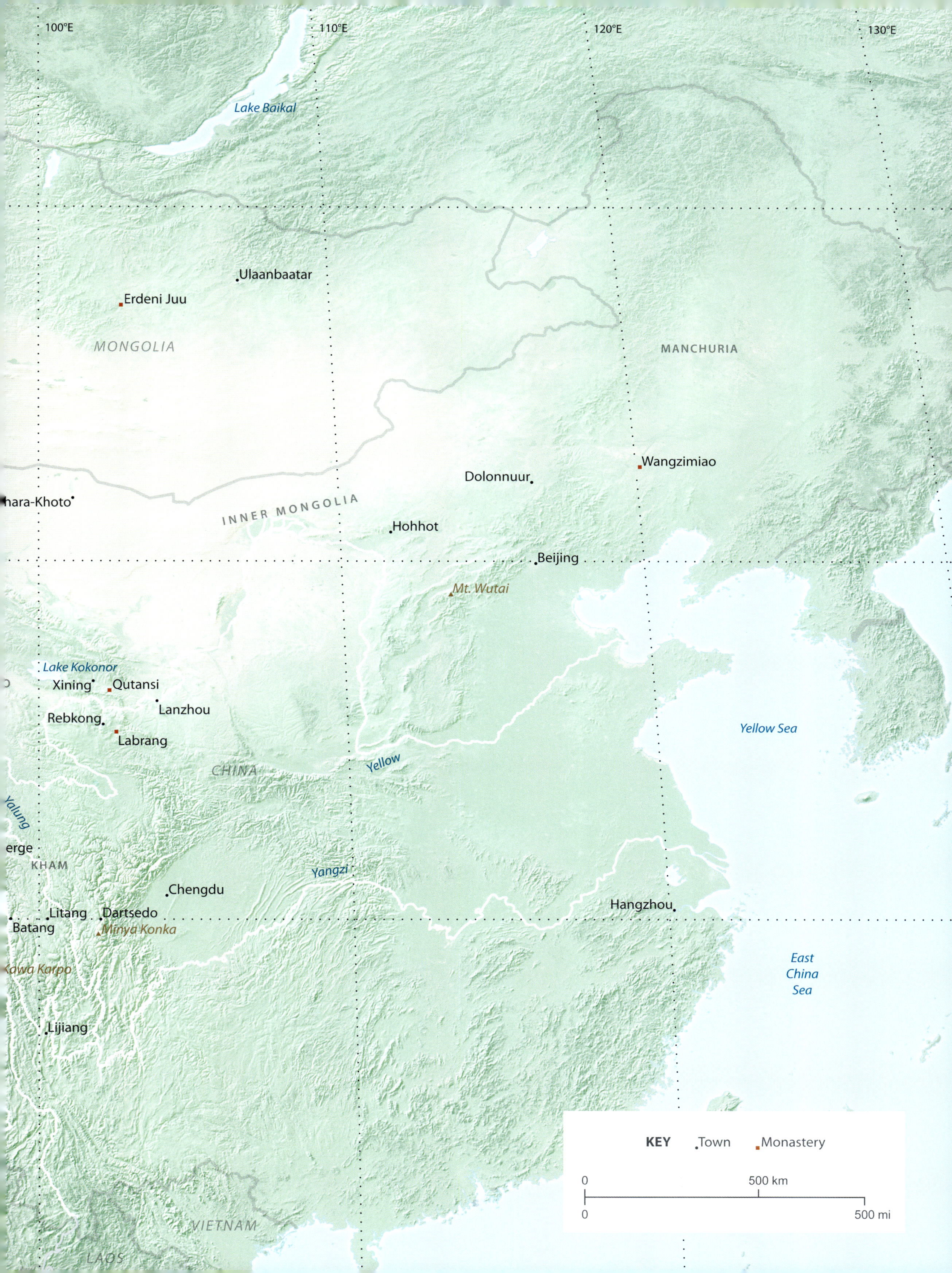
100°E
110°E
120°E
130°E
Lake Baikal
Ulaanbaatar
Erdeni Juu
MONGOLIA
MANCHURIA
Wangzimiao
Dolonnuur
hara-Khoto
INNER MONGOLIA
Hohhot
Beijing
Mt. Wutai
Lake Kokonor
Xining
Qutansi
Lanzhou
Rebkong
Labrang
Yellow Sea
Yellow
CHINA
Yalung
erge
KHAM
Yangzi
Chengdu
Hangzhou
Litang
Dartsedo
Batang
Minya Konka
East
China
Sea
Kawa Karpo
Lijiang
KEY
Town
Monastery
0
500 km
0
500 mi
VIETNAM
LAOS

Foreword

THE RUBIN MUSEUM OF ART is honored to present *Himalayan Art in 108 Objects* to readers interested in Himalayan art and cultures specifically, as well as those fascinated by the art and cultures of Asia more broadly.

This accessible introduction traces the art and material culture of the Tibetan, Himalayan, and Inner Asian regions with a focus on cross-cultural exchange. The object-centered approach is loosely modeled after the British Museum's *A History of the World in 100 Objects* and features contributions from seventy-two international scholars, who explore 108—an auspicious number—objects and sites from the perspectives of a wide range of fields and disciplines. It provides multiple access points for a deeper understanding of the region and its art and cultures.

The book presents objects from international holdings and the Rubin Museum's collection along with sites, architectural monuments, and works in situ that illuminate cross-cultural exchange centered on Tibetan art and culture. The essays foreground the connections and movement of things, people, traditions, ideas, and styles to and from Tibetan regions through paintings, sculptures, drawings, pilgrimage maps, sites, structures, ritual objects, textiles, and more, dating from Neolithic to contemporary times. It thereby seeks to highlight a complex web of connections across time and space.

This ambitious publication is part of an even larger three-part initiative, Project Himalayan Art, which aims to encourage the widespread incorporation of Tibetan, Himalayan, and Inner Asian art and cultures into liberal arts curricula. Our multifaceted approach comprises a traveling exhibition, digital platform, and the book you're holding in your hands. Project Himalayan Art seeks to remedy the underrepresentation of Himalayan art, due in large part to the lack of introductory resources for teaching. We've worked with specialists to create content for teaching on Asia across a wide range of disciplines, including history, religion, art, anthropology, and more. Our goal is to emphasize cultural connectivity and exchange, demonstrating that these connected traditions extend well beyond the Himalayan mountain range and even the Tibetan Plateau to play a significant role in Asia.

Informed by a wide-reaching survey of two hundred and fifty Asian-studies faculty, this publication along with the digital platform and traveling exhibition serve to ensure Himalayan art is not only taught but also understood in the context of broader Asia. We're honored to contribute resources to fill this teaching resources gap.

We recognize that the realities of choosing a focus on Tibet necessitate leaving out some things that could also be representative of the subject. This volume does not try to tell the entire story of the region and bordering areas; rather, it aims to draw connections through select objects. Any selection process also entails omissions, and the short format of the essays does not allow for the fullest possible explorations of these sites and objects. Our hope is that over time the Project Himalayan Art digital platform will allow for greater discussion of many more themes and topics, including contemporary art, cultural activism, colonialism, and issues of provenance, as well as highlight further intersections with other regions and religious traditions, enabling us to weave an even more interconnected fabric.

Himalayan Art in 108 Objects—and the larger project—has been informed by the work of our Humanities Advisory Group, comprising Kerry Lucinda Brown, Isabelle Charleux, Wen-shing Chou, Rob Linrothe, Christian Luczanits, Ariana Maki, Annabella Pitkin, Andrew Quintman, and Gray

Tuttle. This group was instrumental in conceptualizing the publication from the very beginning, from determining its format and selecting objects and contributing writers to suggesting the thematic focus of the essays. Thanks to the members of this group for tirelessly contributing expertise and supporting this endeavor.

Many hands have helped shape this monumental project. Without naming all the wonderful individuals who contributed to it, we are pleased to share our gratitude to all Rubin staff who have worked diligently on Project Himalayan Art over several years. Launching a project with this scope and complexity has entailed hard work—conducted simultaneously with other large-scale institutional initiatives taking place in New York City, Venice, Bilbao, and beyond. This work that can now reward the world. The board of trustees has generously supported the project as part of the Rubin's growing global portfolio advancing knowledge and understanding of the Himalayan regions.

Lastly, the best of ideas cannot take flight without generous supporters, including the individual and institutional donors listed in the acknowledgments. Thank you all for sharing and supporting the vision of this project!

JORRIT BRITSCHGI

EXECUTIVE DIRECTOR

RUBIN MUSEUM OF ART

Acknowledgments

The Rubin Museum's most ambitious and broad-reaching initiative to date, Project Himalayan Art, which encompasses this publication, a traveling exhibition, and a digital platform, would not have been possible without the generous support of many foundations, institutions, and individual donors.

Leadership support for Project Himalayan Art is provided by the Henry Luce Foundation. Lead support is provided by the Ellen Bayard Weedon Foundation, Bob and Lois Baylis, Barbara Bowman, the E. Rhodes & Leona B. Carpenter Foundation, Noah P. Dorsky, Fred Eychaner, Christopher J. Fussner, Matt and Ann Nimetz, the Randleigh Foundation, and Shelley and Donald Rubin. Major support is provided by the Edward & Elizabeth Gardner Foundation, Mimi Gardner Gates, the Monimos Foundation, Rossi & Rossi, Eric and Alexandra Schoenberg, Eileen Caulfield Schwab, and Sandy Song Yan. Special support is provided by Dr. Bibhakar Sunder Shakya to honor the memory and legacy of Professor Dina Bangdel, art historian, curator, cultural activist, and educator from Nepal, and Samphe and Tenzin Lhalungpa to honor the memory and works of L. P. Lhalungpa, Tibetan scholar, broadcaster, and educator. This project is supported, in part, by the National Endowment for the Arts. Project Himalayan Art has also been made possible, in part, by a major grant from the National Endowment for the Humanities: Democracy demands wisdom.

Himalayan Art in 108 Objects—and the larger Project Himalayan Art—has been greatly informed by the time and expertise of the specially assembled Humanities Advisory Group, comprising Kerry Lucinda Brown, professor of art history, Savannah College of Art and Design; Isabelle Charleux, director of research, CNRS (National Centre for Scientific Research); Wen-shing Chou, associate professor of art history, Hunter College and the Graduate Center, City University of New York; Rob Linrothe, associate professor and department chair, Department of Art History, Northwestern University; Christian Luczanits, David L. Snellgrove Senior Lecturer in Tibetan and Buddhist Art, Department of History of Art and Archaeology, SOAS, University of London; Ariana Maki, associate director of the UVA Tibet Center and Bhutan Initiative at the University of Virginia Tibet Center; Annabella Pitkin, associate professor of Buddhism/East Asian religions and director of Asian studies, Lehigh University; Andrew Quintman, associate professor of religion and East Asian studies, Wesleyan University; and Gray Tuttle, Leila Hadley Luce Professor of Modern Tibetan Studies, Department of East Asian Languages and Cultures, Columbia University.

Additional feedback in the development of our list of 108 objects was provided by Ian Alsop, Amy Heller, Alexander von Rospatt, Gautama V. Vajracharya, and Ulrich von Schroeder.

People who helped in the initial stages and in sourcing difficult to obtain materials, such as images and reproduction permissions, include Lauran Hartley at Columbia University; Rob Linrothe of Northwestern University; Luo Wenhua of the Palace Museum; Pratapaditya Pal; Karma Phuntsho at Loden Foundation; Shawo Khacham; Uranchimeg Tsultemin at the Herron School of Art and Design, Indiana University; Xie Jisheng of Zhejiang University; Xiong Wenbin at Sichuan University; and many others.

We would like to express special appreciation to the seventy external contributing authors, who are named individually in the Contributors section of the book, especially those who wrote or coauthored multiple essays, including Christian Luczanits, Rob Linrothe, Amy Heller, Ian Alsop, Kerry Lucinda Brown, Isabelle Charleux, Charles Ramble, Uranchimeg Tsultemin, John Vincent Bellezza, Jane Casey, Wen-shing Chou, David Jackson, Donald J. La Rocca, Ariana Maki, Katherine Anne Paul, Karma Phuntsho,

Alexander von Rospatt, Alice Travers, and Roberto Vitali. Thanks also to translators Tenzin Gelek, Xinhui Yang, and Guoying (Stacy) Zhang for allowing a wider range of voices to be represented.

For their perseverance, patience, and diligence thanks to project manager Erin Barnett; copyeditors Lory Frankel and Joe Hannan; foreign language consultants Dotno Dashdorj Pount, William Dewey, and Kristina Dy-Liacco; designer Phil Kovacevich; cartographer Anandaroop Roy; indexer and bibliographer Patrick Booz; image acquisitions assistant Stacey Sherman; project research assistant Hannibal Taubes; and interns Gabriela Espinosa, Yian (Emily) Ren, Xinhui Yang, and Muhan Zhang.

Thanks also to our partners in publishing this book at Scala, Director of Publications Jennifer Norman and Senior Editor Claire Young.

The development of the traveling exhibition, *Gateway to Himalayan Art*, was shaped by the work of an Exhibitions Advisory Group, including Benjamin Bogin, associate professor and director of Asian studies, Skidmore College; Wen-shing Chou, associate professor of art history, Hunter College and the Graduate Center, City University of New York; Sienna Craig, professor, Department of Anthropology, Dartmouth College; Ariana Maki, associate director of the UVA Tibet Center and Bhutan Initiative at the University of Virginia Tibet Center; Annabella Pitkin, associate professor of Buddhism/East Asian religions and director of Asian studies, Lehigh University; and Brenton Sullivan, associate professor of religion, Colgate University.

For their work on the traveling exhibition, we also thank project collections manager and installation specialist Danielle Butterly; exhibition design consultant Melinda Zoephel; bronze casting collective Foundry Foundation Nepal; bronze artist Tejesh Man Shakya; thangka painter Buchung Nubgya; and members of the Himalayan and Inner Asian communities who lent their voices to the exhibition and Project Himalayan Art at large.

The creation of the digital platform involved expertise and creative thinking from many collaborators. We thank Digital Designer Dan Shields and Digital Developer Adam Squires of CHIPS and Project Himalayan Art Digital Humanities Apprentice Grace Anne Marotta, as well as data specialist Stephanie Fischer, interpretive specialist consultant Jenna Madison, photographer and filmmaker Pranab Joshi, filmmaker Tsewang Lhamo, and filmmaker Tsejin Khando.

We are also grateful to Cecilia Garibay of Garibay Group whose work informed both the traveling exhibition and digital platform.

Heartfelt thanks to staff at the Rubin Museum of Art whose dedication over the last few years has made Project Himalayan Art possible, with unprecedented levels of collaboration and support from Collections Management; Curatorial; Development; Exhibition Design and Implementation; Marketing and Communications; Publications and Editorial; and Visitor Experience and Interpretation.

KARL DEBRECZENY AND ELENA PAKHOUTOVA

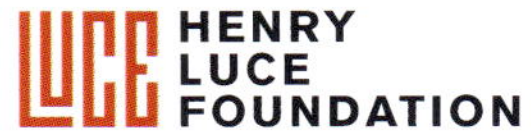

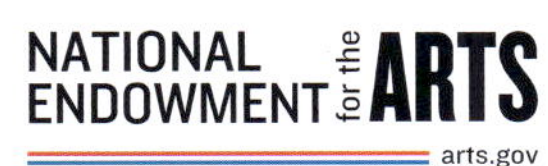

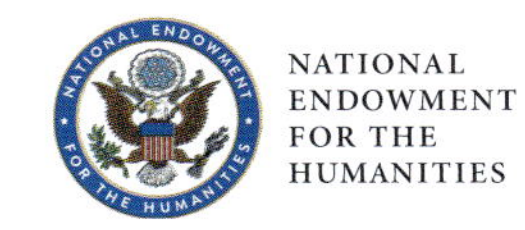

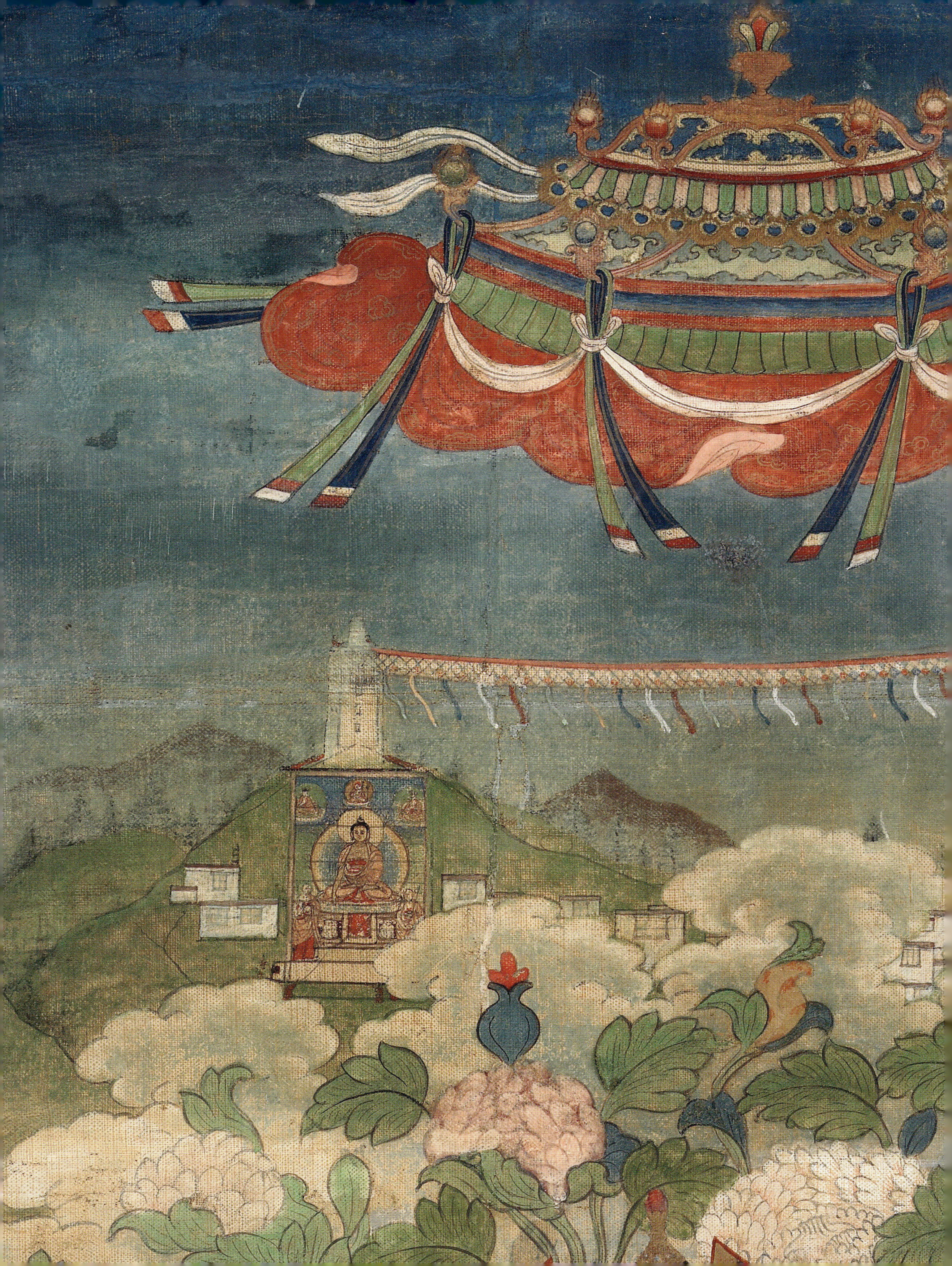

How to Use This Book

The essays in this publication are organized chronologically. Each object has a number, name or identification, location, date, and thematic essay topic. For portable objects, the location indicates where the object was made or found. For permanent sites and structures, the historical location appears first, followed by the present-day designation where applicable.

The object cross-references in the margins indicate linkages among objects within the book, emphasizing cultural connections and exchange. Each essay features further reading suggestions to encourage more exploration on the given topic.

For accessibility, the book employs phonetic spelling systems for foreign languages, including Tibetan, Sanskrit, Newari, and Mongolian. The Tibetan spelling follows the conventions established by The Treasury of Lives (www.treasuryoflives.org/standards-and-guidelines), with some exceptions for Dzongkha (used in Bhutan), Ladakhi, and other local variations; Chinese is in Pinyin romanization; Sanskrit and Newari follow the Rubin Museum house style; and Mongolian follows Christopher Atwood's *Encyclopedia of Mongolia and the Mongol Empire* (2004).

The index provides transcriptions with diacritics, Chinese characters, alternative names or spellings for people and places, and dates (life dates, reign dates, empire dates, etc.).

Common abbreviations include:

BDRC: Buddhist Digital Resource Center (www.bdrc.io)
HAR: Himalayan Art Resources (www.himalayanart.org)
PRC: People's Republic of China
TAR: Tibet Autonomous Region of the People's Republic of China

Digital Platform

The expanded digital platform, Project Himalayan Art, features additional contextual images and related multimedia for each essay, along with a glossary, theme pages, and content from the traveling exhibition *Gateway to Himalayan Art*. The interactive map geographically and temporally locates most of the objects from this book.

Visit http://rubinmuseum.org/projecthimalayanart/.

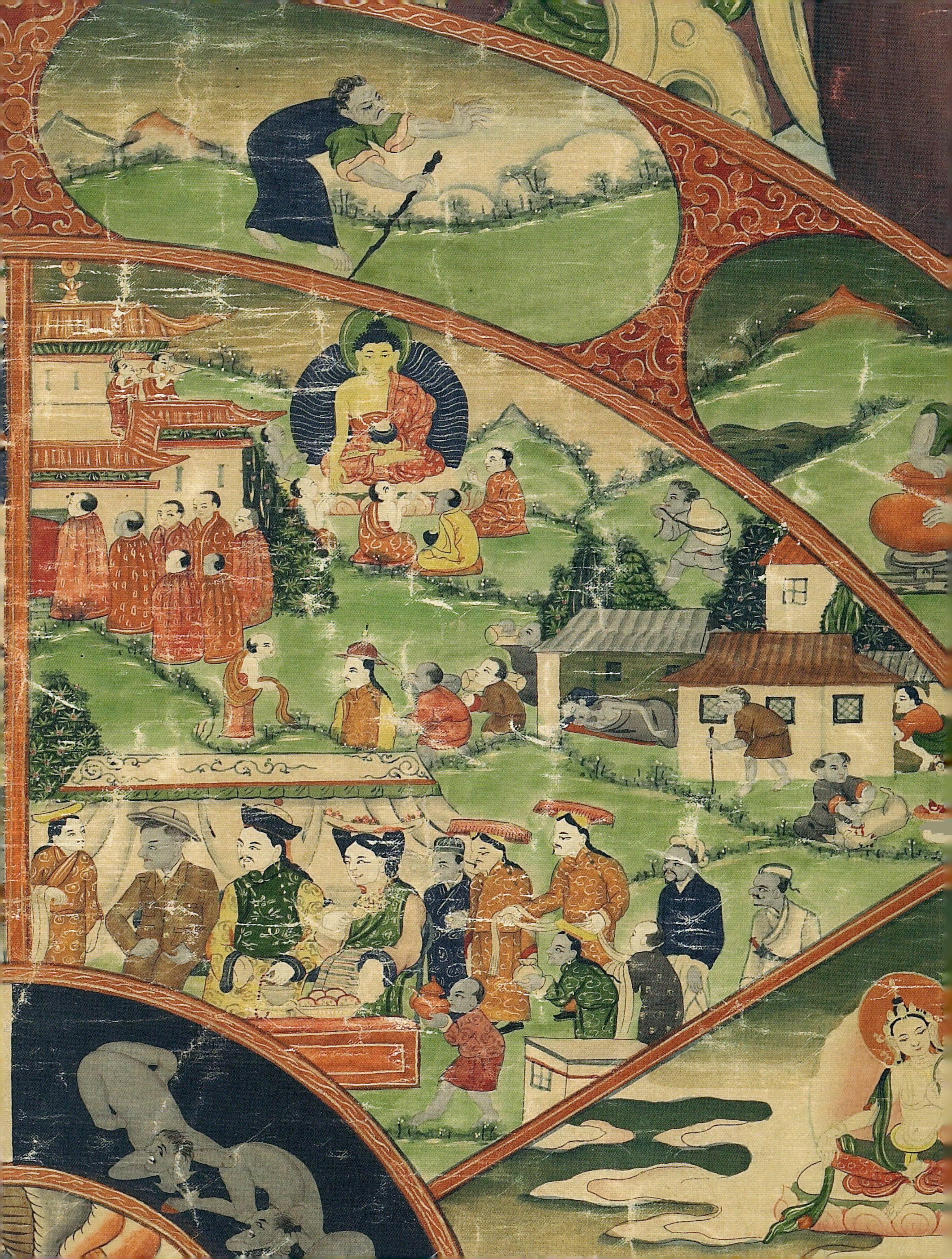

Himalayan Art and Cross-Cultural Exchange

BY KARL DEBRECZENY AND ELENA PAKHOUTOVA

THIS BOOK PRESENTS 108 OBJECTS as entry points to the world of Himalayan visual art, material culture, and religion. It features hanging scroll paintings, sculptures, drawings, pilgrimage maps, architectural sites, ritual items, textiles, and more, ranging from the Neolithic to contemporary times. The number 108 is auspicious, rooted in the ancient Indian Vedic tradition and its reverence for sound, as represented by the letters of the Sanskrit alphabet. As part of religious practice, the fifty letters are repeated twice, along with the letters representing the eight sections of the alphabet, totaling 108. This "garland of sounds" is believed to generate blessings and permeate them throughout the world. The number is therefore considered sacred in Hindu and Buddhist traditions; there are 108 prayer beads, 108 volumes of the Buddhist canon, and so forth.

Defining Himalayan Art in This Publication

Objects from Tibet and Nepal were first seen, collected, and presented in the West in the nineteenth century, initially as ethnographic curiosities and gradually as examples of artistic traditions.[1] In comparison to Chinese, Japanese, Korean, Indian, and other fields of Asian art, the study of Himalayan art is still a young, developing area.

Himalayan art has often been grouped with Indian and South Asian art or with Chinese and, by extension, East Asian art. In actuality it bridges and traverses the regional spaces defined by these somewhat arbitrary academic divisions,[2] and it disrupts fixed labels of regional groupings of Asian art, such as East Asian or South Asian art. In this volume we use the term "Himalayan art" to highlight cross-cultural exchanges between various regional cultures. Within this broader framework, Himalayan art encompasses artistic production from the greater Himalayan mountain range, the Tibetan Plateau, and connected Mongolian areas of Inner Asia.[3] This publication aims to use this more expansive definition to emphasize cultural connectivity and exchange between these related traditions.

Himalayan art visually expresses the religious cultures of Buddhism, Hinduism, and Bon, as well as integrating indigenous beliefs from these regions. Traditional areas of cultural production were in northeastern India, Nepal, the western Himalayas, and Tibetan and Mongolian regions, as well as Buddhist Central Asia and imperial centers of China. The scholarship of the past century has continuously built on previous advances in the study of the art, religion, and history of these diverse lands,[4] making it increasingly evident that Himalayan art reflects uninterrupted cross-cultural exchange in which artists and their works, forms, and methods have traveled and transformed in each area, supported by the patronage of rulers, aristocrats, religious teachers, and ordinary people.

The objects in this book represent cross-regional connections and engagements with ritual and visual expressions of Hindu and Buddhist tantric traditions,[5] which persist over significant time spans and continue to this day across culturally diverse areas. These artistic expressions trace their origins to Indic traditions and regional centers of Buddhist culture, such as the Himalayan kingdoms of Gilgit, Swat, Kashmir, and Ladakh, the Kathmandu Valley, and Buddhist Central Asia. Tibetans first sought, cultivated, and patronized these visual idioms. As Tibetan religious and artistic traditions flourished in close dialogue with their neighbors, Tibetan Buddhist culture inspired foreign patronage and expanded to the courts of Tangut, Mongolian, Chinese, and Manchu rulers, initiating the creation of distinctive new forms of Buddhist art.

The religious diversity of these regions includes the intersection of Hindu, Buddhist, and Bon belief systems, as well as local indigenous traditions.[6] Yet Buddhism is the common thread that ties these different cultures together, and it is the main focus here.

Cultural Exchange Across Regions

Buddhist visual culture initially flourished due to the patronage of artists, the construction of Buddhist institutions, and translation projects initiated by rulers who sought to fortify their polities and power. Lay people and monastics also contributed to this flourishing through their pursuit of Buddhist teachings, practices, and pilgrimage. Even though kingdoms and empires rose and fell, and their boundaries changed over time, Buddhist cultural production continued across these areas. Objects embodying Buddhist religious concepts and material culture were transmitted to and adopted in the ancient Tibetan kingdom, spurring Tibetan Buddhist culture to rapidly mature and extend across the breadth of the Himalayas, the entire Tibetan Plateau, and into Inner Asia. These movements and connections are represented in the art objects, architectural sites, and material technologies highlighted in this publication.

Bringing Buddhism Home from Northeastern India

As the cradle of Buddhism, where Buddha Shakyamuni taught and traveled, northeastern India is home to many Buddhist sacred pilgrimage sites, the most important being Vajrasana at Bodhgaya, the place of the Buddha's awakening. In the ancient past, when Buddhism in India was supported by kings and laity, Buddhist culture flourished, leading to the subsequent establishment of great Buddhist universities. The Indian emperor Ashoka (third century BCE), who supported and helped spread Buddhism with the expansion of his realm, became the exemplar of universal kingship (chakravartin), by which rulers across Asia would later claim political legitimacy.

Until the late thirteenth century, India was the source of much Buddhist material and visual culture in the form of texts, portable sculptures, and mementos from sacred sites. Buddhist teachers, visiting monks, traders, and pilgrims carried these objects to their own lands, including Tibet, western Himalayan regions, Nepal, and beyond.

For an example of a Painted Manuscript Cover from Greater Kashmir, see no. 12. For an example of the kind of Kashmiri sculpture collected and emulated, see Buddha on the Cosmic Mountain, no. 10.

For an example of a site reflecting Kashmiri imagery in Ladakh, see Rock Carving of Four-Armed Bodhisattva Maitreya, no. 17.

For examples of this Kashmiri cultural legacy in western Tibet, see Stupa at Toling Monastery, no. 19; Avalokiteshvara at Khartse, no. 20.

For an example of a Hindu tantric goddess, see Siddhi Lakshmi, no. 67.

Networking Buddhist Kingdoms: Kashmir and Western Himalayas

Kashmir, a fertile valley nestled between the highest ranges of the Himalayan mountains, was a revered land of Buddhist learning, arts, and culture up to the end of the thirteenth century, attracting Tibetan Buddhist travelers. Kashmir's position as a major destination on trade routes that traversed the neighboring western Himalayas and connected western and Central Asia facilitated their travels. Until the fourteenth century, Kashmir was an important center of Tantric Buddhism, where Tibetan and Himalayan Buddhists went to study, collected books and images, and invited Kashmiri teachers and artists to decorate newly established temples in the western Himalayan kingdoms, such as Ladakh. The legacy of Kashmir and its close cultural connections remained an important aspect of Buddhist visual culture in the western Tibetan Kingdom of Guge long after Buddhism declined in Kashmir.

Centers of pilgrimage focused on both Hindu and Buddhist tantric goddesses linked Kashmir with the greater sacred geography of the Himalayas, which is also a prominent feature of religious culture in Nepalese regions.

For a major center of Buddhist culture in the Kathmandu Valley, see the Svayambhu Chaitya of Kathmandu, no. 4.

On Newar seasonal festivals, see Bunga Dya, no. 6.

Nepalese Cultural Sphere: A Power Source of Artistry

Other major centers of Buddhist culture included Himalayan kingdoms of the Kathmandu Valley, which became especially significant with the decline of Buddhism in India and Kashmir. Tibetan Buddhists went to Nepal in search of teachers and instruction in tantric practices, as many Indian scholars moved to Nepal where Buddhism remained a thriving tradition. Hindu and Buddhist cultures coexisted in Nepal, and the same artists often produced images for both communities, creating a shared visual culture that continues today. Seasonal festivals and major rituals involved the participation of entire communities in the

For more on Newar Buddhist institutions, see Central Shrine Image of Kwa Baha, no. 22.

On Newar artists working for Tibetan patrons, see Jivarama's Sketchbook, no. 56.

city-kingdoms of Patan, Kathmandu, and Bhaktapur. Nepalese kings sponsored Hindu and Buddhist religious sites, including Buddhist institutions (*bahas*), and laity patronized the vibrant art guilds.

The arts of the Kathmandu Valley were well-known in Tibetan areas and beyond. Based on their skill and willingness to travel, Newar artists from the Kathmandu Valley have always been in high demand throughout Tibetan regions and Inner Asia. Historical accounts and artistic evidence testify to the important role of Nepalese artists in Tibet under the patronage of Tibetan religious institutions and rulers for the development of artistic traditions across the Himalayan range and further east.

Tibetans as Agents of Cultural Exchange

For an early Tibetan royal site associated with the ancient line of Tibetan kings, see Yumbu Lagang Castle, no. 5.

For an example of early Central Asian–Tibetan cultural exchange, see Silver Jug, no. 15.

For one of the earliest and most important Buddhist sites in Tibet, see Jokhang Temple, no. 7.

For an example of the conflation of deity and ruler, see Imperial Carvings of Vairochana, no. 13.

For more on Yungdrung Bon, see Bon Deity Trowo Tsochok Khagying, no. 60.

The kingdom of Tibet came into existence on the fertile valleys of the central Tibetan Plateau. From these lands Tibetan rulers expanded their domain into an empire that absorbed parts of Central Asia including important trade routes. They established military alliances and competed with their eastern neighbors, and encountered Buddhist, Islamic, and Christian cultures. They also actively traded with the surrounding regions and controlled major trade routes, increasing cultural exchange. At the height of the Tibetan Empire (ca. 608–866),[7] during the rule of Tri Songdetsen (742–ca. 800), Tibetan military advanced deep into areas held by the Chinese Tang Empire (618–907), capturing much of its northwestern territory, even briefly the capital Chang'an.

There are often gaps between traditional accounts and historical evidence. Traditional accounts give the Tibetan emperor Songtsen Gampo (ca. 605–649) a prominent role in establishing Tibet as a Buddhist kingdom, while historical evidence tends to point to later emperors. Surviving early sites testify to the royal engagement with Buddhist visual representations of power, and early translation efforts lay the groundwork for the flourishing of Buddhism in Tibetan regions. The indigenous religious beliefs, the foundation of the non-Buddhist tradition later referred to as Bon, coexisted with the nascent Buddhist establishment. Following the initial power struggle for influence, during the second dissemination of Buddhism in Tibet in the tenth through the thirteenth century, the indigenous belief system defined itself in relation to Buddhist traditions.[8]

After the assassination of Emperor Langdarma in about 842, the Tibetan Empire fragmented, and Tibetan Buddhist institutions declined with the loss of aristocratic patronage. Yet Buddhist tradition continued, especially in the eastern areas of the former Tibetan Empire, where a few Tibetans revived the practice of Buddhist ordination with the help of Chinese monks. They gradually reintroduced monastic Buddhism to central Tibetan areas.

Tibetan royal descendants fled to different regions and established local centers of authority. Kyide Nimagon, a scion of the ancient Tibetan imperial house, founded a kingdom that included Ladakh in the western Himalayas and western Tibetan areas (Ngari) in about 912. He intentionally fostered close ties with his neighbor to the west, the kingdom of Kashmir, a center of arts, learning, and commerce. After his death (ca. 930), his sons divided the realm and ruled in three Himalayan kingdoms—Ladakh (known as Maryul in Tibetan), Guge-Purang, and Zanskar. One of the imperial descendants, the prince-monk Yeshe Wo (947–1019/1024), was instrumental in the second diffusion of Buddhism in western Tibetan areas that ultimately affected the rest of Tibetan regions. His patronage of the arts, such as at Tabo Monastery, testifies to artistic engagement with Kashmir and the fostering of a thriving Buddhist culture.

See Goddess Dharmameghabhumi in the Tabo Main Temple, no. 21.

To revive Buddhism, Tibetans traveled to India, invited Buddhist teachers to Tibet, and upon return, established new monasteries with patronage from their followers and local rulers. One such important Indian teacher was Atisha Dipamkarashrijnana (ca. 982–1055), who stayed in the Kathmandu Valley before traveling widely in Tibetan areas. He worked with Tibetan translators, laying foundational teachings of the Kadam Tibetan Buddhist tradition. Another prominent Indian scholar, Shakyashribhadra (1127–1225), the abbot of the famous Nalanda Monastery in northeastern India, instructed his many Tibetan students—themselves known scholars—on all Buddhist topics, including *Vinaya* (monastic discipline), philosophy, tantric practice, and insight.

For an object associated with Atisha and his teachings, see Tara Who Protects from the Eight Great Fears, no. 27.

For an object once owned by Shakyashribhadra, see Illuminated Pages of the *Prajnaparamita Sutra* Manuscript, no. 23.

For an image copied at Nalanda Monastery, see Crowned Buddha, no. 16.

The tenth through thirteenth century is often referred to as the Tibetan Buddhist Renaissance, a time when Tibetan Buddhists not only received, translated, and codified Buddhist teachings, but also defined their own systems for structuring this knowledge and created a vibrant Buddhist culture. Extant murals of the early temples from this era, such as at Dratang, exemplify cultural and aesthetic connections, as well as a local cosmopolitan environment. Tibetans founded their own lineages of transmission directly from teachers to disciples, often centered around monastic centers of learning and at numerous hermitages. These new lineages, known as the New Transmissions (Sarma), are distinct from the Ancient (Nyingma) tradition.

On the local cosmopolitan environment at Dratang, see Maitreya and Manjushri Mural, no. 26.

This period also saw the consolidation of the ancient tradition's textual production, with the compilation of the early biography of the legendary Indian master Padmasambhava and the emergence of the associated treasure (*terma*) tradition. According to the legendary accounts, Padmasambhava identified specific locations as Hidden Lands (*beyul*), such as Sikkim, that would be safe havens for Buddhist communities in times of need.

See Padmasambhava and His Manifestations, no. 43.

For an example of *terma*, see *Dorje* Discovered by Dorje Lingpa, no. 51.

Some new lineages became known by the fundamental characteristic of their teachings; for instance, Kadam (Instructional Precepts) and Kagyu (Precept Transmissions). Often the new traditions assumed names after the monasteries where they originated—Sakya, Drigung, Zhalu—or after the place of origin of their founder—Dakpo Kagyu and Shangpa Kagyu. Most of the teachers of these traditions were also patrons of the arts, leading to emergence of local artistic traditions.

Major luminaries of these times included translators (*lotsawa*), such as Marpa Lotsawa (1012–1097), Bari Lotsawa (1040–1112), and Rinchen Zangpo (958–1055), as well as legendary practitioners, such as the Tibetan yogi Milarepa (1040–1123).

For more on Bari Lotsawa's activity, see Cave 3 at Yulin Cave Temples, no. 31.

See the Earliest Extant Printed Edition of Milarepa's Life Story, no. 62.

During this period Tibetans also introduced the means of religious succession using the Buddhist concept of reincarnation (*tulku*),[9] which was later systematized and employed to ensure religious and political stability. This system spread beyond Tibetan regions, implemented by the Bhutanese, Mongolians, and Manchus.

Around 1247 the Mongol Empire incorporated Tibetan areas, dividing its patronage of Tibetan teachers and their traditions among Mongol princely houses. As a result, Buddhist monasteries, such as Sakya and Zhalu, flourished as never before, becoming centers of cultural production. Instead of ruling directly, the Mongols granted suzerainty of central Tibet to the Sakya hierarchs raised in the Mongol court, upheld by Mongolian garrisons. Tibetans who resisted Sakya-Mongol rule, like those at Drigung Monastery, were suppressed. Mongolian support included maintaining a postal relay communication and travel system that connected Tibetan regions to other parts of the Mongol Empire, and many Tibetans ventured east to the Mongol Yuan courts in China and Inner Asia.

See Mural Painting at Zhalu Monastery, no. 47.

See Mongol Messenger's Badge, no. 42.

As a result of these exchanges, Chinese art entered Tibetan monastic collections, gradually inspiring Tibetans to adopt certain Chinese artistic conventions, such as landscape, into Tibetan painting. In the fifteenth century, the famous central Tibetan artists Menla Dondrub and Khyentse Chenmo incorporated Chinese-inspired landscape elements, including blue-and-green color schemes, into their painting, initiating a Tibetan artistic revolution once dominated by Indian, Kashmiri, and Nepalese aesthetics.

On Khyentse Chenmo's painting tradition, see Murals of Gongkar Chode, no. 58.

The seventeenth century was a turbulent time in central Tibet. In 1642, the Fifth Dalai Lama (1617–1682), aided by monasteries of the Geluk tradition and Mongol military force, became the first of the theocratic rulers of a unified Tibet, which had been fractured since the collapse of the Tibetan Empire. As part of his claim to power, the Great Fifth promoted himself as an emanation of the bodhisattva Avalokiteshvara, identifying himself as the Tibetan emperor returned, and thus the rightful inheritor of the ancient Tibetan state. The Potala Palace in Lhasa stands as a monument to this idea. Those perceived as being on the losing side of the civil conflict, including the Jonang, Karma Kagyu, and Bon traditions, were suppressed in central Tibet and largely relocated to the eastern Tibetan regions of Amdo and Kham.

See Potala Palace, no. 71.

One important initiative of the Great Fifth's government was the centralized systematization of institutional knowledge in key fields of learning, such as history, medicine, astrology, and the arts, through collection, codification, and production. These systems were widely disseminated through printing, networking, and the founding of medical colleges and artist guilds.

See Desi Sanggye Gyatso's Medical Paintings, no. 73. On Tibetan astrology, see *The White Beryl* Illuminated Manuscript, no. 86.

Bhutanese Consolidation and Fortification of Transmission Lineages

The earliest temples in what is now the Himalayan kingdom of Bhutan (Druk) are said to be contemporaneous with the seventh-century introduction of Buddhism in Tibet. Buddhist transmission lineages, in

On one of these early Bhutanese temples, see Maitreya Statue at Jampa Lhakhang, Bhutan, no. 9.

For an example of a Bhutanese Nyingma storytelling aid, see Portable Shrine, no. 88.

particular the Drukpa Kagyu and Nyingma traditions, fostered close ties between Bhutan and Ladakh, Nepal, and Tibet. In the seventeenth century, facing pressure from Mongol-backed Geluk authorities in central Tibet, many Kagyu teachers moved to Bhutanese areas where they had supporters. The Drukpa Kagyu teacher Zhabdrung Ngawang Namgyel (1594–1651) unified these disparate lands under his religious and temporal authority, establishing a system of governance and defending Bhutan from Tibetan and Mongol military incursions. His successors further codified religious education and ritual practices, including cultural production. Temples and establishments in Bhutan associated with Geluk and Sakya traditions were ceded to new Drukpa ownership and redecorated. Some communities in the eastern region retained Bon practices or followed hybrid Buddhist-Bon traditions, many of which survive. The institution of the regent (Druk Desi) controlled temporal matters through the late nineteenth century. A particularly effective leader, Druk Desi Jigme Namgyel (1825–1881), consolidated significant influence and power. His son, Urgyen Wangchuck (1862–1926), rose to prominence, becoming the first king of Bhutan in 1907.

For more on Bhutanese history and institutions, see Tamshing Temple, no. 61; Taktsang, the Tiger's Lair, no. 76.

Central Asian Crossroads Connecting Civilizations

Traveling merchants, monks, pilgrims, local populations, and even armies of various empires mixed and integrated at the oasis centers along the trade routes connecting Asia and the West. They were among the donors, visitors, and artists who created and contributed to the famous caves at Dunhuang, located at the juncture of the trade routes of the so-called Silk Road. The caves were decorated from the fourth until around the fourteenth century, when overland routes were largely abandoned in favor of sea trade, and the site lost its vibrant patronage.

The diverse visual traditions, belief systems, and languages found in murals, statues, and texts testify to these rich cross-regional and cultural connections. Tibetans were among the powers who ruled the area during the height of the Tibetan Empire, and their presence is documented in the material culture of Dunhuang. Tanguts formed a cosmopolitan state, known in Tibetan as Minyak and in Chinese as Xixia, which had a significant impact on the artistic production in the area and on Tibetan and Inner Asian religious culture, despite the Xixia state's destruction in 1227. Woodblock printing was one means by which texts and images were produced and widely disseminated. The status of Buddhist teachers in the Tangut Empire consolidated the priest-patron relationship. This model came to be especially consequential for Tibetan teachers and Mongolian emperors of the Yuan dynasty in China and Mongolia, ultimately affecting the Tibetan religious and political landscape.

On Tibetans at Dunhuang, see Bhaishajyaguru, no. 14.

On Tangut impact on artistic production, see Achala Silk Tapestry, no. 36.

For more on woodblock printing, see A *Pancharaksha* Print from Khara-Khoto, no. 32.

Mongolians Connecting through Conquest and Conversion

Mongolians have been widely active in the political, religious, and artistic life of the Tibetan Buddhist world, especially the western Mongols, or Zunghar, with former territories in present-day Xinjiang Province, China; the eastern Khalkha Mongols in the current state of Mongolia; various groups in modern-day Inner Mongolia;[10] and the Buryat and Kalmyk Mongols in areas that are now part of Russia.

For examples of Tibetan visual culture in the Chinese heartland, see Relief Carving of a Nine-Deity Ushnishavijaya Composition, no. 41; Juyong Guan Stupa Gate, no. 48.

In the thirteenth century, the Mongols conquered most of Asia and established the largest contiguous empire in world history, facilitating the spread of Tibetan visual culture to the Chinese heartland. When Qubilai Khan (r. 1260–1294) founded the Yuan dynasty in 1271, he established a government modeled on a Chinese system, but he relied heavily on peoples from other areas of his empire, such as the Uyghurs, Tanguts, and Tibetans. Qubilai Khan took special interest in Tibetan Buddhism, appointing Tibetan teachers as the highest religious authorities in the land. The relationship between the Mongol emperor Qubilai and his first Tibetan Imperial Preceptor Pakpa (1235–1280), often characterized as a priest-patron relationship, became a model invoked by subsequent imperial courts and Tibetans for centuries.

For a surviving example of Anige's work for the Mongol court in Beijing, see White Stupa, no. 40.

For more on the sixteenth-century renaissance of Buddhism in Mongolia, see Erdeni Juu Monastery, no. 65.

Under Mongol rule, skilled artisans were sought from all over the empire, and the head of the Yuan imperial atelier was a Nepalese artist, Anige (1245–1306). Although little by his hand survives, many luxury objects in Chinese media of lacquer, porcelain, and silk bear a distinct Nepalese aesthetic.

In the late sixteenth century, a massive second conversion of the Mongols to Tibetan Buddhism was more deeply rooted, a conversion so thorough that the religion became essential to Mongolian

On Zanabazar and one of his most famous compositions, see Maitreya, no. 75.

identity. Tibetan Buddhism became a cultural and political rallying point for the fractured Mongols and other Inner Asian groups. Zanabazar (1635–1723), Khalkha Mongol's incarnate lama, leader of Mongolian Buddhism, and direct descendant of Chinggis Khan, was also a famous artist who embodied these aspirations. From the seventeenth century to modern times, the Mongols once again played a key role in Tibetan culture and politics and Tibetan relations with China. In fact, the lingua franca among these cultures was often Mongolian. The Dalai Lamas, in turn, gained the authority to confer the title of "khan" on Mongol leaders.

Emulating Qubilai Khan's Imperial Model

In the centuries following the fall of the Yuan, Qubilai Khan's model of rulership was recognized widely across Asia.

After the collapse of the Mongol Empire and the establishment of the Ming dynasty, the Chinese court continued to use Mongol imperial Buddhist vocabulary symbolic of divine rule. The Yongle emperor (r. 1402–1424), whose power base was the former Yuan capital of Beijing, took a special interest in Tibetan Buddhism, fostering a great deal of cultural production at court, including the first printing of the Tibetan Buddhist canon in 1410. Tibetan religious masters selected some of the gifts given to them from the Yuan and Ming courts as models for the development of a new Tibetan artistic tradition in the sixteenth century.

On early Ming cultural production of Tibetan Buddhist art, see Pensive Bodhisattva Avalokiteshvara, no. 53; Qutan Monastery, no. 52.

On the rise of this new artistic tradition, see Portrait of the Ninth Karmapa, no. 66.

The Manchus, like the Mongols, were a people from north of the Great Wall who conquered China. The Manchu elite also assumed Tibetan Buddhism as a means for political legitimacy to rule their vast multiethnic empire. Positioning themselves as the rightful inheritors of Qubilai Khan's legacy as rulers of a united Buddhist Inner Asia was a key strategy to bring the various Mongolian confederations, who had their own aspirations for Buddhist state building, under the Qing domain. Workshops of Mongolian and Chinese artisans in artistic centers, such as in Dolonnuur, produced images and objects on a large scale, including monumental sculptures, which were sent all over the Tibetan Buddhist world.

On Tibetan Buddhism at the Qing Court, see The Qianlong Emperor as Manjushri-Chakravartin, no. 84.

On Dolonnuur sculptural production and its impact across the Tibetan Buddhist world, see Vajrapani, no. 82.

Persisting and Evolving with Modern Times

For more on the effect of Western encounters on Tibetan material culture, see Gendun Chopel's Woman Applying Kohl, no. 102; Photograph of the Thirteenth Dalai Lama, no. 98. For an Englishman in the Wheel of Existence, see no. 97.

For a sword captured by a British officer during the Opium Wars, see Sword, Scabbard, and Sword Belt, no. 68.

A forced encounter between Tibetans and the West occurred in 1903 to 1904 when the British military invasion from India reached Lhasa, and the disintegration of the Qing Empire in 1911 following the encroachment of European colonial powers coincided with the 1911 Mongolian and 1913 Tibetan declarations of independence. These events had profound consequences. The founding of the People's Republic of China in 1949 and the annexation of Tibetan cultural regions into it resulted in many Tibetans fleeing into exile. One practical outcome was the study and flourishing of Tibetan Buddhism internationally. However, the communist revolutions in Mongolia and China, the terrible persecutions of the 1930s socialist period in Mongolia and Russia, the forced reforms of the 1950s in Tibet, and the Cultural Revolution of 1966 to 1976 across China decimated religious and cultural institutions, especially Buddhist monasteries. These violent disruptions led to the dispersal of many artworks to collections around the world.

On the prominent role of Rebkong painters in post-Cultural Revolution monastic and artistic revival, see Shambhala Kings Mural, no. 99.

In China, after regulations on religious practice were relaxed in the 1980s, Tibetans revived traditional cultural production and restored many monasteries. This led to the wider popularization of Tibetan Buddhism and its visual culture, sparking commercial interest in China and abroad. There was a similar rise in popularity for other forms of cultural production, including modern and contemporary art.

On the intersection of contemporary pilgrimage, politics, tourism, and image making in Sikkim, see Monumental Statue of Guru Rinpoche, no. 104.

Other Himalayan regions, such as Sikkim, which was absorbed into India in 1975, created opportunities to promote not only religious but also political and business interests by establishing popular Buddhist tourist sites. Likewise, Ladakh, Mustang, and other cultural regions combined their cultural and economic interests to maintain their communities, often with the help of foreign investments and tourism.

In the Kathmandu Valley, art and craft production continued as part of generations of caste-related traditions. Metalworking, wood carving, stone carving, and painting still thrive in the region today. With Nepal's opening to the world in the 1950s, its art, culture, and natural landscape became the focus of foreign interest, and tourism became the main source of the country's economy. Nepalese artists embraced modernism and gained support from not only regional patrons but also international tourists and collectors. An appreciation of Nepalese traditional art created a demand in collecting and contributed to the theft and removal of art objects from Nepal, some of which entered private or museum collections abroad. Increasingly, museums have started returning such objects to Nepal as part of the recent repatriation movement.

See Ice Buddha, no. 108.

Artistic and religious traditions of these cultural regions continue to flourish locally and internationally. Artists who create modern art that builds on local traditional forms while engaging with global contemporary developments carry on the cross-cultural connections and movement of people, ideas, and objects.

Thank you to the Humanities Advisory Group members who provided valuable feedback for this essay: Kerry Lucinda Brown, Isabelle Charleux, Wen-shing Chou, Ariana Maki, Annabella Pitkin, Andrew Quintman, and Gray Tuttle.

Notes

1 Ethnology museums in Europe contained Tibetan and Nepalese objects acquired by explorers in the nineteenth century. Important early exhibitions in the United States included *Art of Nepal* at Asia Society in 1964 and *The Art of Tibet* at Asia House in 1969. Early publications include *Antiquities of Indian Tibet* by August Hermann Franke (in two parts: 1914 and 1926) and *Tibetan Paintings* by George Roerich (1925). A Tibetan temple was built in the Russian capital in 1909 with the inauguration and ritual services coinciding with the Tibetan New Year of 1913.

2 Although such divisions may be useful, they convey an external, Eurocentric perspective on Asia, which is limiting, divisive, and outdated. These divisions are also a product of postwar American geopolitics.

3 On different opinions regarding this inclusive definition, especially with regards to the inclusion of Mongolian art, see for instance Tsultemin 2018.

4 Some of the foundational authors and works from the twentieth century include Pelliot 1914; Tucci 1932–41, 1949; Snellgrove and Richardson 1968; Pal 1969, 1984b, 1985; Stein 1972; H. Karmay 1975; Shakabpa 1976; Macdonald and Imaeda 1977; Klimburg-Salter 1982; Slusser 1982; Tsultem 1982; Gega Lama 1983; Chayet 1985a; H. Richardson 1985; Snellgrove 1987; Petech 1990; Vitali 1990; Aubin and Béguin 1993; Béguin and Dashbaldan 1993; Ricca and Lo Bue 1993; Berger and Bartholomew 1995; Giès 1995; D. Jackson 1996; Lopez 1998; Harris 1999; A. Heller 1999; and many others.

5 Both Hindu and Buddhist esoteric traditions gave rise to the visual religious representations across the regions.

6 The early goddess cults connected to the formation of Buddhist and Hindu tantric traditions, as seen in the western Himalayas and Nepal, even transcend religious divisions.

7 Scholars use varying dates for the Tibetan Empire; some use ca. 600–859.

8 As a collection of indigenous traditions, Bon includes ancient pre-Buddhist religious practices in Tibet; Yungdrung Bon, an organized monastic system developed in a dialogue with Buddhist traditions; and various cults with mythic narratives and rituals for the protection and prosperity of local communities.

9 Lama Zhang (1123–1194), the founder of the Shangpa Kagyu tradition, declared himself a reincarnation of Tibetan emperor Songtsen Gampo (ca. 605–649). Kagyu hierarch Rangjung Dorje (1284–1339) asserted that he was the third reincarnation of the first Karmapa, the founder of the Karma Kagyu tradition.

10 The term "Inner Mongolia" (Mongolian: Dotogadu Monggol; Chinese: Nei Menggu) stems from the distinction under the Qing dynasty (1644–1911) between the "inner" *zasag*s (*jasag*s, or rulers) of Inner Mongolia and the "outer" *zasag*s of Outer Mongolia (the present-day state of Mongolia), Kokonor, and Xinjiang. See Atwood 2004, 240–52, 617–18.

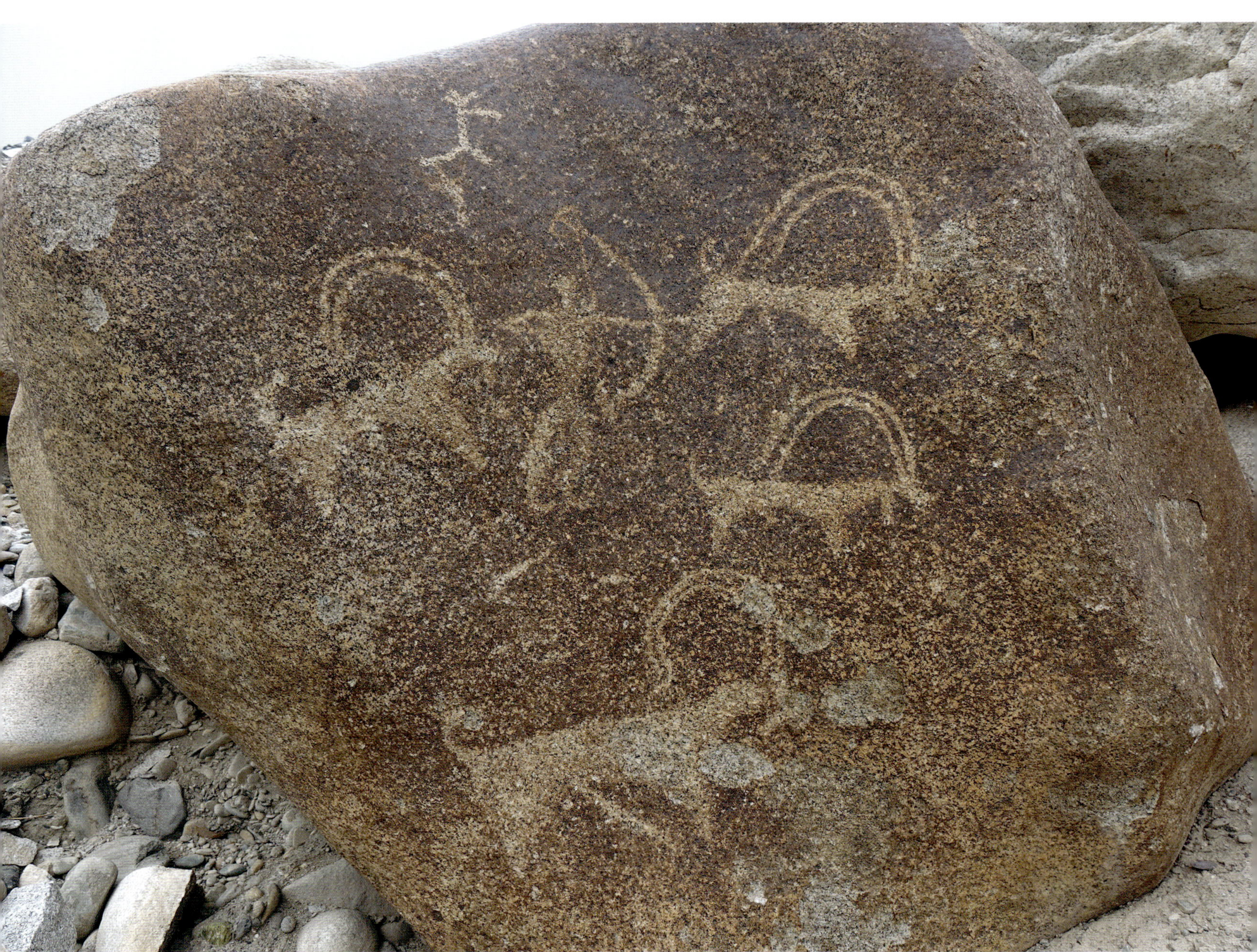

No 1

Alchi Petroglyph Field

Ladakh, India, Iron Age (ca. 700–100 BCE)

Early Himalayan Rock Art

JOHN VINCENT BELLEZZA

The Prototypic Hunter

In this rock art composition dating from the Iron Age (ca. 700–100 BCE), we see a hunting scene etched in stone featuring the ibex, a large and powerful wild goat species widely distributed in the highlands of west and Central Asia.[1] This evocative scene is found in Ladakh, a crossroads region in the northwest corner of the Tibetan Plateau. Ladakh commands a highly strategic position in the Himalayas, joining Tibet with the Central Asian, Persian, and Indian realms. Archaeological and art historical evidence clearly shows that Ladakh has been a meeting point for peoples and a hub of trade and exchange for millennia.

Creating art in one form or another is a fundamental human impulse found in all societies. Naturally occurring stone surfaces offer one of the oldest and most universal picture-making mediums. This enduring means of expression rewards archaeologists with unparalleled insights into the cultural composition, social structure, and economic functions of ancient peoples worldwide. In Himalayan regions, including the Tibetan Plateau, artists began to leave their mark in stone during the Bronze Age (ca. 2000–700 BCE) by carving and painting cave walls, cliffs, and boulders, and they continued to do so until well into the second millennium CE.[2] This unbroken tradition of rock art production records many routine activities and conceptions, ranging from hunting and martial scenes to ceremonial life and symbolic information. As Himalayan rock art developed over a period of more than two thousand years, it serves as an index of human progress beginning with archaic religious cults and culminating in the spread of the prevailing religions of the Tibetan world: Buddhism and Bon. No other Himalayan art form has proven as durable or encompassing as that set down in stone.

For more about the Bon religion, see Bon Deity Tsochok Khagying, no. 60.

In the Alchi composition, a solitary archer stands among four ibexes, each of which sports a large pair of horns arching over the spine. The human figure wielding a bow and arrow has a modified bi-triangular torso, a popular style of anthropomorphic depiction in the rock art of Ladakh and Tibet to the east. These human and animal figures, competently executed by means of abrading the surface of the boulder, possess a bold, well-balanced appearance, endowing the composition with a fine pictorial effect. The hunter is shown taking aim at the ibex directly in front of him, clearly poised to slay it. This unambiguous signal of success has a metaphoric dimension, for shooting an arrow so close to a game animal is impractical. Rather, the perspective used in the work stresses the prowess of the hunter as a provider of sustenance, while at the same time articulating various social and religious calculations that accompanied this most basic of human activities. In fact, hunting scenes throughout the vast Asian hinterland often present hunters with bows and arrows in very close quarters to their prey (ibexes, deer, wild sheep, wild yaks, and so on), the literal documentation of the hunt assuming second place to a set of grandstanding social considerations and ritualized demonstrations.

Hunting Scenes More Broadly

A rock art composition featuring a lone archer coming in for the final kill of ibexes; Alchi, Ladakh, India; Iron Age (ca. 700–100 BCE); photograph by J. V. Bellezza

The hunting of game animals is the single most common rock art theme in Ladakh. Ibex hunting scenes number in the thousands, carved in a variety of styles relying on a number of techniques for cutting and grinding the surface of boulders and outcrops.[3] The pursuit of ibex is also prominent in the rock art of the adjoining Trans-Himalayan region of Spiti in India, as well as in many other Inner Asian territories, comprising Mongolia, Gansu, Inner Mongolia, Kyrgyzstan, and southeastern Kazakhstan.

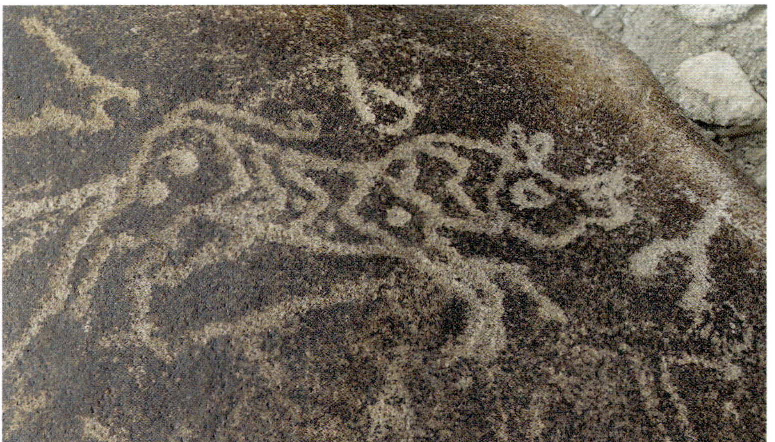

One of three striped carnivores carved on a boulder; Alchi, Ladakh, India; Iron Age (ca. 700–100 BCE); photograph by J. V. Bellezza

Farther west, ibex hunting is well known in the rock art of the Middle East. In lower-lying locales on the Tibetan Plateau, where agriculture came to be practiced, hunting was relegated to a subsistence venture of secondary importance for the bulk of the population by the Iron Age.[4] Although the overall economic importance of hunting had diminished in Ladakh and other parts of the Tibetan Plateau by the time the composition of the lone hunter was fashioned, the sheer number of such scenes offers evidence that hunting pursuits retained their high prestige and cultural centrality. The critical social and religious values that hunting articulated in the Bronze and Iron Ages appear to have been derived from an even more remote era, when hunting and foraging served as the economic bedrock for inhabitants of the Tibetan Plateau.

Other Rock Art at Alchi

See Stupa at Toling Monastery, no. 19.

Most of the rock art found in Alchi was made on boulders scattered along a shelf rising above the south bank of the Indus River, approximately one and a quarter miles (two kilometers) northwest of the village of Alchi and its renowned Buddhist temple complex. Carvers favored boulders covered in a shiny dark purplish patina for embellishment. In addition to ibex hunting scenes, petroglyphs at the site display ibexes engraved together with spotted carnivores resembling snow leopards, facsimiles of stepped architectural structures, including elaborate stupas (a Buddhist religious monument), a menagerie of animals, groups of swastikas, and combat or martial contests.[5] Rock art with the same types of subjects and compositions rendered in analogous styles can be seen all along a sixty-two-mile (a hundred-kilometer) stretch of the Indus River extending from Alchi to Dah. Some of the boulders with rock art in Alchi and nearby sites contain Tibetan inscriptions composed during the Tibetan Imperial period (ca. 600–850 CE).[6] Inscriptions and rock art in Ladakh made as late as the fourteenth century CE signal the death throes of the ancient tradition of rock carving (although engraving rocks for religious and more informal reasons has continued in the region to the present day). A long line of earthen stupas and a ruined fortress located on the same shelf demonstrate the enduring attraction of the Alchi rock art site. Old gold mines in the vicinity underline the economic significance of the area.

A Conveyor of Interregional Exchange

Prowling striped carnivores (probably tigers) comprise another category of iconic rock art at Alchi. Of special note are three striped carnivores found on a single boulder, which has become unmoored and is now precariously perched above the Indus River. The complete petroglyph of one of these tigrine animals covered in chevronlike stripes (seen with part of another striped carnivore and other petroglyphs) undeniably makes a strong impression with its pointed ears, gaping jaws, large round eye, flexed legs, and tail curling over the back. The form and design of the carnivore are emblematic of the "Eurasian animal style," which features peculiar modes of zoomorphic portrayal in various metals, stone, and textiles diffused across much of the continent in the Iron Age.

For a related depiction of wild herbivores on a Tibetan gold death mask, see Gold Burial Mask with Engraved Figures, no. 2.

The distinctive Eurasian animal style is well represented in the rock art of the Tibetan Plateau and other parts of Inner Asia, which typically boasts graceful and sinuous wild sheep, deer, and wild yaks with fancy horns standing on the tips of their hooves.[7] Both wild herbivores and carnivores typically bear volutes or scrolls as body decoration (in the petroglyph of the striped carnivore, these curvilinear motifs are replaced by interconnected dots). The styles of tigrine creatures vary from region to region, as individual cultures selectively adopted elements of the Eurasian animal style to conform to their own purposes and inclinations. However, this body of rock art also has much in common. A shared legacy

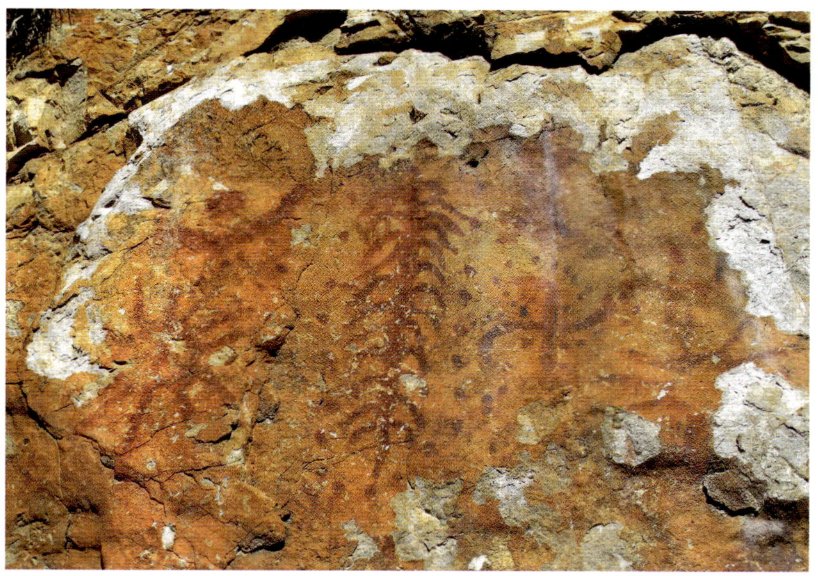

Rock paintings in red ocher of a conjoined sun and moon, two sunbursts, a tree, and two swastikas; Chukargyam, Rutok, Tibet; Iron Age (ca. 700–100 BCE) or Protohistoric period (ca. 100–600 CE); photograph by J. V. Bellezza

in form, presentation, and execution followed from far-reaching artistic, intellectual, and technological exchanges among diverse peoples. Participant cultures on the Tibetan Plateau and those in northwest China, northern Pakistan, Mongolia, southern Siberia, and southeastern Central Asia drew from a wellspring of allied ideas and sensibilities, contributing to the formation of a transcultural sphere in Iron Age Inner Asia. This emergent order anticipated by a millennium the cosmopolitan era that arose along the Silk Road in the first millennium of the Common Era (partially facilitated by the spread of Buddhism).

The Abstract and the Religious

On the Tibetan Plateau figurative art showcasing humans, animals, architectural structures, implements, and other objects is richly supplemented by subjects having symbolic value.[8] The image on the left highlights an array of rock paintings or pictographs consisting of special characters that probably represented far more than their outward appearance alone suggests. To this day, the same symbols are used in the Bon and Buddhist religions to signify a wide range of ritual processes, philosophical teachings, and mystic notions. Even though we cannot know precisely what the long-lost artist working at Chukargyam was attempting to communicate with his intriguing set of pictographs, archaic mytho-ritual texts written in Tibetan between the eighth and eleventh centuries CE furnish clues regarding their potential meaning. For instance, we know that the conjoined sun and moon epitomized major priestly lineages and that the swastika was synonymous with the sun, while the tree was a major cosmological motif. Analogous sets of symbols are found in the rock art of Ladakh and Spiti, which indicates that these adjoining regions of the Tibetan Plateau were closely connected religiously to western Tibet well before the rise of Bon and Buddhism and widespread literacy in the eighth century CE.

In brief, rock art is one of the most potent tools available to us for understanding the way of life of early peoples residing in the loftiest lands on earth. Moreover, Tibetan and Himalayan rock art confirms that its ancient makers did not live an isolated existence but for millennia strove to relate to other peoples of Eurasia.

Further Reading

Bellezza, John V. 2020b. *Drawn and Written in Stone: An Inventory of Stepped Structures and Early Rock Inscriptions in Upper Tibet (ca. 100 BCE to 1400 CE)*. British Archaeological Reports International Series 2995. Oxford: BAR.

Linrothe, Rob. 2016b. *Seeing into Stone: Pre-Buddhist Petroglyphs and Zangskar's Early Inhabitants*. Berlin: Studio Orientalia.

Suolang Wangdui (Bsod nams dbang 'dus). 1994. *Art of Tibetan Rock Paintings*. Introduction by Li Yongxian and Huo Wei. Chengdu: Sichuan People's Publishing House.

Notes

1 I want to heartily thank Quentin Devers and Viraf Mehta for detailed information and photograhs of the Alchi rock art site prior to my own visit there in August 2021.
2 Rock carvings are commonly known as petroglyphs and rock paintings as pictographs. For a discussion of these techniques and output in western Tibet, see Bellezza 2002a and 2008.
3 On ibexes in the rock art of Ladakh, see Bruneau 2010; Francfort, Klodzinski, and Mascle 1992. On other rock art featuring the hunt, see Bellezza 2002b.
4 Questions concerning the prehistoric cultural composition of Ladakh and western Tibet are addressed in Bellezza 2018 and 2020a; Bruneau and Bellezza 2013.
5 According to Bruneau 2010, the Alchi site consists of 24 anthropomorphic figures, 91 zoomorphic figures, and 328 stepped structures, as well as 131 rock inscriptions.
6 For surveys of Tibetan rock inscriptions in Ladakh, see Denwood 1980; Orofino 1990; Takeuchi 2012.
7 For a detailed study of Tibetan rock art and objects in the Eurasian style, see Bellezza 2020c.
8 On symbols in the rock art of Ladakh and adjoining regions of Tibet, see Bellezza 2017 and 2000.

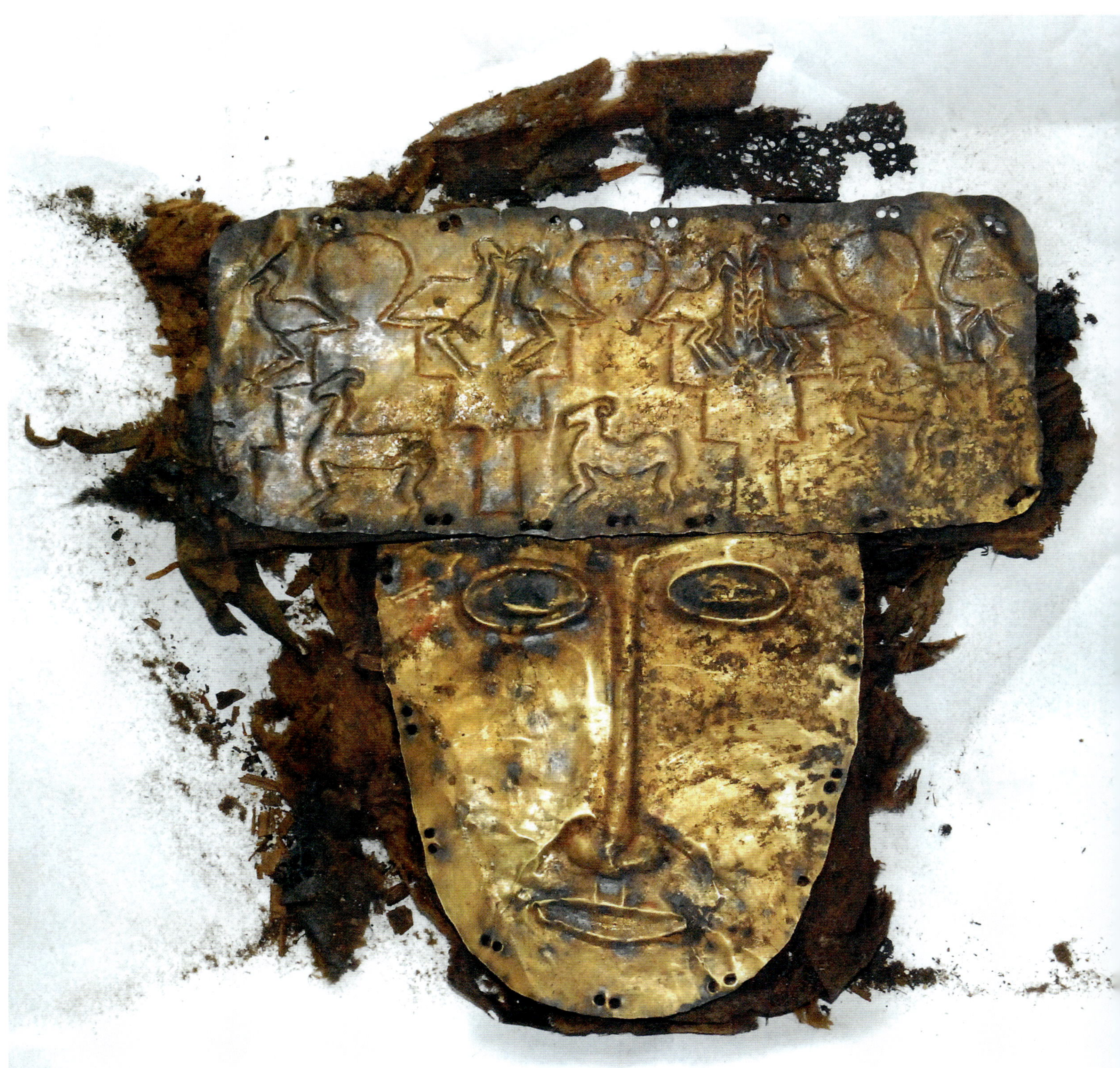

№ 2

Gold Burial Mask with Engraved Figures

Guge, Ngari region, western Tibet, Protohistoric period (ca. 2nd or 1st century BCE)

A Window onto Early Himalayan Artistic and Mortuary Practices

JOHN VINCENT BELLEZZA

See Murals at Toling Dukhang, no. 54.

For later examples of repoussé, see Plaque Commemorating the *Bhimaratha* Old Age Ritual, no. 85; Vajrapani, no. 82; Pitcher, no. 90.

Burial Mask with a Human Face in Repoussé, crowned by an engraved headdress; discovered in a tomb in Zone I of the Chutak cemetery, Guge, Ngari region, western Tibet; Protohistoric period (ca. 100 BCE to 600 CE), ca. 2nd or 1st century BCE; parcel-gilt silver, silk, wood; 5⅝ × 5½ in. (14.2 × 14 cm); Zhada County Cultural Relics Bureau, Ngari Prefecture, TAR; photograph by Li Linhui

THIS GOLD BURIAL MASK, also known as a death or funerary mask, is the most elaborate example of more than a dozen such objects discovered in western Tibet and adjacent Himalayan tracts in the last decade. The use of these masks, signifiers of high rank and status, was reserved for those who merited extravagant funerals. The pictured burial mask was unearthed in 2011 by Chinese archaeologists from a shaft tomb at Chutak (Water Mill), not far from Toling, an old capital of Guge (a region in western Tibet famous for its Buddhist monasteries and frescoes).[1] The Chutak mask is made in two parts, joined together by silk laces and reinforcing wood slats. It is fabricated from silver; the front side is coated in a fine layer of gold (parcel gilt), a technique employed in many regions of the ancient world. The rear of the object is sheathed in layers of silk material decorated with knotted lace.[2] The silk was fastened to the mask through a series of paired perforations along its edge. The diminutive size of the Chutak mask (most of the others are even smaller) indicates that it was not used as an actual adult face covering but rather placed in the tomb with symbolic purposes in mind.

The two slightly overlapping sheets of the Chutak mask were ornamented using different techniques. A sharp cutting tool was used to incise the figures on the bandlike crown, while the facial features were made in relief by bearing down on the reverse side of the mask with a hammer and punch, a method of metalworking known as repoussé. The lineaments of the face are difficult to read, save to say that the countenance is both delicate and dignified. The sides of the head taper inward toward a broad, rounded jaw. The elliptical eyes with wide pupils are set below a gently arching brow. The very long and narrow nose bridge terminates in bulbous nostrils, dividing much of the face into two longitudinal sections. The crescent-shaped mouth of the mask is connected to the nose by two ridges that simulate the medial cleft.

The upper half of the Chutak burial mask is adorned with a rich array of iconic figures, consisting of birds, wild herbivores, a tree, and stepped structures. The length and breadth of the crown is dominated by a trio of stepped structures, each composed of three graduated platforms surmounted by a globular upper section. The lower portion of each of the stepped structures bears an engraved standing herbivore. Their body forms and especially the short, tightly curling horns set behind the head are most reminiscent of sheep. The complement of birds on the crown hints that the herbivores may also be undomesticated animals, in which case they may represent one of two species of wild sheep native to the region, the blue sheep (*Pseudois nayaur*) and argali (*Ovis ammon*).[3] Across the upper tier of the crown appear six engraved birds, the four birds in the middle forming two pairs. Between the pair of birds on the right is a motif resembling a tree, as also depicted in the rock art of western Tibet and Ladakh. The identity of the long-legged birds is unclear. They may possibly depict aquatic species.

The Symbolism of the Mask

Unlike other gold masks discovered in western Tibet and the Himalayan rimland that display only human faces, this mask offers an array of iconic forms that lend themselves to comparison and interpretation. The birds and herbivores of the mask's crown are zoomorphic depictions (along with the horse) that predominate in Tibetan archaic funerary rituals.[4] Although the earliest Tibetan funerary texts were not composed before the eighth century CE, they preserve with varying degrees of fidelity a number of more ancient death themes, mortuary customs, and death rituals. The information they reveal is

Figurine of a Wild Sheep; closely associated with western Tibet; Protohistoric period (ca. 100 BCE to 600 CE); copper alloy; 1¼ × 1⅛ in. (3.2 cm by 2.8 cm); Private collection; photograph by J. V. Bellezza

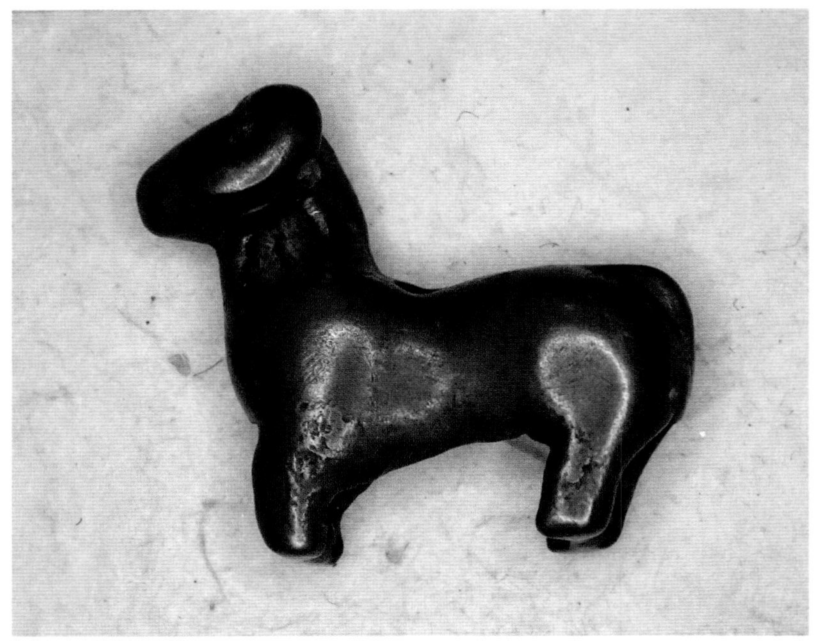

probably germane to archaeological evidence like that presented by the gold burial masks. It is still not very feasible, though, to correlate lore in the texts with specific objects and art; rather, they supply us with tools for a generalized understanding of the archaeological materials and processes underpinning ancient burial in Tibet.

In Tibetan archaic funerary texts dating to about the eighth to the twelfth century CE, birds and feathers are key components of harm-reducing and evocatory rites performed on behalf of the deceased. For example, it is recorded that feather headdresses symbolizing the power of flight were placed on horses called *doma*, which were entrusted with mystically transporting the dead to the afterlife. Sheep known as *kyibluk* occur in many archaic funerary texts as guides of the departed, showing the way over the mountains and rivers of the land of death to the celestial realm of the ancestors. In a collection of early Yungdrung Bon death ritual texts entitled *Muchoi Tromdur* (The Multitude of Funerary Rituals of Mucho), trees functioned as vessels to enshrine and protect the consciousness of the dead; the tree was thus referred to in this collection of death rituals as the "soul fortress." A soul evocation text of the *Muchoi Tromdur* describes a yellow golden visage (*zhel*) that serves as a receptacle or "soul-circle" for the deceased, in preparation for their journey to the afterlife.[5] Samten Karmay equates the yellow golden visage with the gold burial masks of Tibet, affirming that it served as the physical support for the soul of the deceased and probably also as a likeness of the interred.[6] The stepped structures engraved on the Chutak mask have actual architectural and artistic counterparts throughout western Tibet and Ladakh.[7] According to Yungdrung Bon literature, these functioned as repositories for deities, but how this conception of their use might inform the engravings on the burial masks remains unclear.

For more about Bon, see Bon Deity Trowo Tsochok Khagying, no. 60.

By virtue of their placement on the gold burial mask, the herbivores, birds, tree, and stepped structures are directly relatable to traditions and beliefs surrounding death and the afterlife. However, analogous figures and symbols materializing as objects and rock art occur in western Tibet in the Protohistoric period (ca. 100 BCE to 600 CE), supporting their status as cultural icons with multivalent meanings and functions. A copper alloy figurine of a wild herbivore (probably a sheep species) with horns that curl around the sides of the head and two pairs of legs (each pair joined by a crossbar) is one of a small group of zoomorphic figurines attributable to the Protohistoric period, reportedly found by farmers and herders in western Tibet. They have assumed talismanic value, but how they might have been worn and used originally is enigmatic.[8] The bird pictographs from Lake Namtso and the petroglyph of a stepped structure from Kabren Pungri, Rutok, are typical of rock art in western Tibet. Such rock paintings and rock carvings demonstrate that the iconography of the Chutak mask was not an isolated case; instead, these forms reoccur in various cultural and social contexts in the same era. By examining ever more examples of this art, a picture of the development of civilization in Protohistoric-period Tibet can gradually be built up.

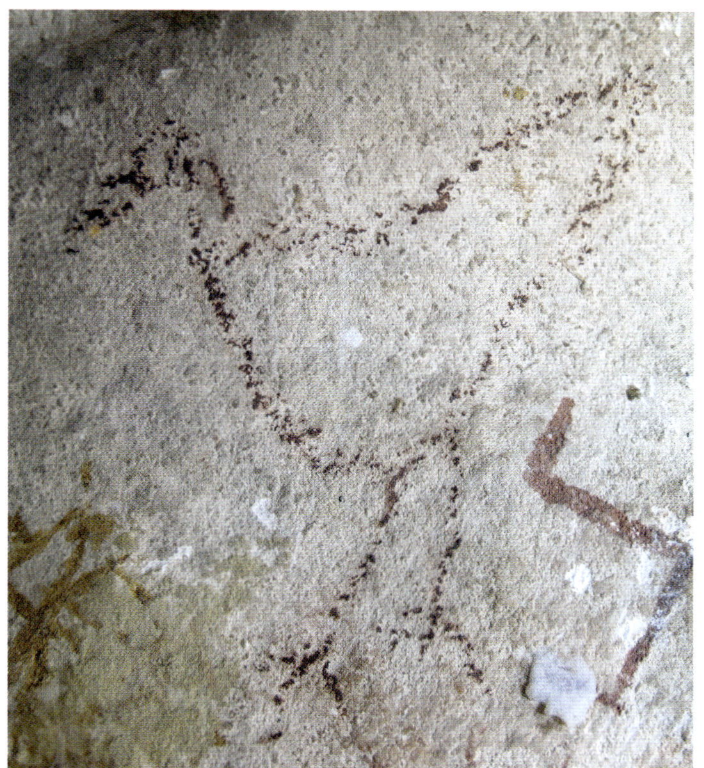

Rock Painting of a Bird; Che Do, Lake Namtso, Tibet; Protohistoric or Early Historic period (ca. 600–1000 CE); red ocher; length 2⅜ in. (6 cm); photograph by J. V. Bellezza. The other two pictographs near it are attributed to the Iron Age (ca. 700–100 BCE)

Other Gold and Silver Burial Masks

All of the known burial masks of the Tibetan Plateau and Himalayan rimland were recovered from tombs at five different ancient cemeteries excavated by archaeologists in Tibet, India, and Nepal. Initial analyses of organic materials deposited in tombs in Guge (western Tibet), Malari (Uttarakhand, India), and Mustang (Nepal) indicate that these masks were produced between about the second century BCE and the seventh century CE, spanning the entire Protohistoric period in western Tibet and adjoining Himalayan tracts. This was an era in which rock inscriptions in foreign languages were made in certain far western locales of the plateau but before the development of an indigenous system of writing in the region. Until the discovery of the gold burial masks, the Protohistoric period was best known for a line of thirty-two kings celebrated in Tibetan literature. The emergence of the masks in recent years brings an entirely new perspective on pre-Buddhist civilization concentrated in western Tibet, a territory traditionally known as Zhangzhung. These objects demonstrate the high level of ideological and material sophistication of the native cultures, putting them on a par with the achievements of other Eurasian civilizations. This observation is supported by other artifacts situated in the same tombs as these masks, which include silk and woolen fabrics, gold and silver ornaments, bronze vessels, wooden vessels and constructions, iron tools, and stone and glass beads, as well as by the extensive residential and ceremonial monuments and diverse agricultural system that existed on the western portion of the plateau during this period.

Further Reading

Karmay, Samten G. 2018. "The Gold Masks Found in Shang Shung and the 'Five Supports of the Soul *(rten lnga)*' of the Bon Funerary Tradition." In *Ancient Civilization of Tibetan Plateau: Proceedings of the First Beijing International Conference on Shang Shung Cultural Studies*, edited by Tsering Thar Tongkor and Tsering Dawa Sharshon, 330–44. Xining: Mtsho sngon mi rigs dpe skrun khang.

Massa, Giovanni, Mark Aldenderfer, and Marcos Martinón-Torres. 2019. "Of Gold Masks, Bronze Mirrors and Brass Bracelets: Analyses of Metallic Artefacts from Samdzong, Upper Mustang, Nepal 450–650 CE." *Archaeological Research in Asia* 18, 68–81.

Tong, Tao, and Linhui Li. 2016. "The Himalayan Gold Masks from the Eurasian Perspective." *Chinese Archaeology* 16, no. 1, 85–90.

Notes

1 On this mask, see Bellezza 2020c, 44, 45; Bellezza 2013, 157–59; Bellezza 2011–17, Oct. 2011, Nov. and Dec. 2013, Nov. 2017, *Flight of the Khyung*; Tong and Li 2016; Lü 2015, 88–93; S. Karmay 2018; A. Heller 2018.

2 Tong and Li 2016, 86.

3 Tong and Li 2016, 85, identifies these animals as goats. A. Heller 2018, 4, equates them with antelopes or deer. However, the horns of the figures are not indicative of goats, antelopes, or deer.

4 Bellezza 2008, pt. 3; 2013, pts. 2, 3.

5 Bellezza 2013, 156, 157.

6 S. Karmay 2018, 336–39.

7 On rock art facsimiles, see Bellezza 2020b. For actual built examples in ancient times, see Bellezza 2014a, 24, 25; 2014b, 521–27.

8 For another example (antelope), see John 2006, 131, fig. 306.

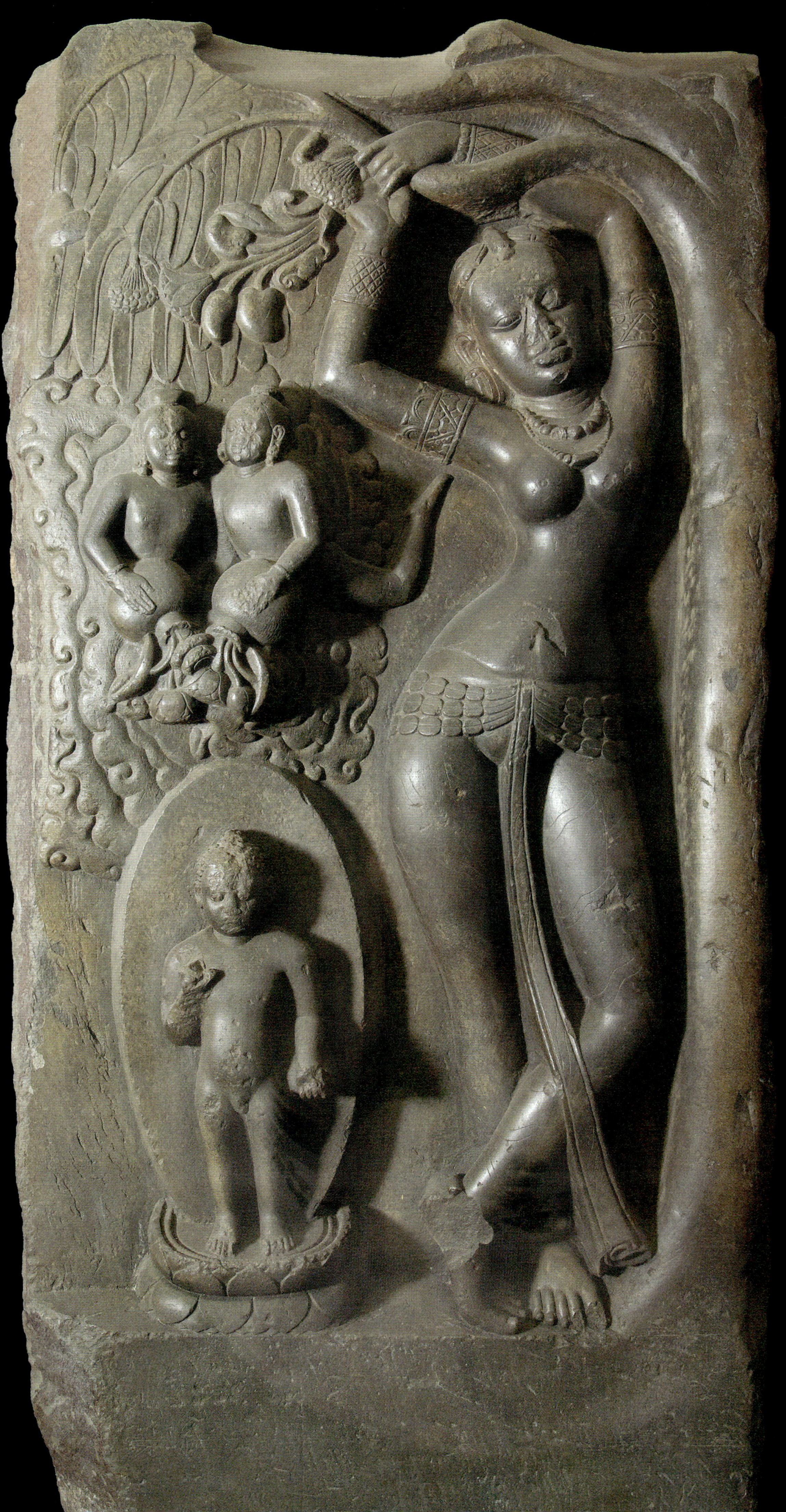

No 3

Mayadevi Giving Birth to Siddhartha

Nepal, Varman or Licchavi period, 4th–5th century

The Birth of the Buddha

ULRICH VON SCHROEDER

THE POLISHED STONE SCULPTURE illustrated here depicts Queen Mayadevi, wife of King Shuddhodana of Kapilavastu of the Shakya clan, giving birth to Siddhartha in the grove at Lumbini. It is one of the most famous artworks of Nepal. This stone relief was earlier installed inside the Jayavagishvari Sundhara fountain in Deopatan. It was likely moved there from a nearby Buddhist site in Chabahil, such as the Dharmadeva Chaitya (Charumati Stupa) or the Charumati Maharajavihara, with a number of stone sculptures from the Licchavi period (ca. 400–750 or 879) still left in situ. Queen Mayadevi stands in an exceedingly bent posture with one foot crossed in front *(padasvastika)*. As characteristic with representations of Mayadevi giving birth to Siddhartha, her lifted hands hold the branch of a tree, variously identified as Sal, Ashoka, or Plaksha tree, for support. This is known as the "tree posture" (*vrikshasana*), or as the "breaking a branch of a Sal tree" (*shalabhanjika*) posture. Mayadevi's garment, rendered in a transparent manner and only sparsely decorated with double incised lines, is secured by a broad cowrie-shell girdle from which a long sash hangs down between her legs. Her upper body is nude except for an ornate headdress, a pair of earrings, bejeweled necklaces, and bracelets and armlets.

Beside Mayadevi stands the newborn naked Siddartha on a double lotus. Immediately after his birth he took seven steps in the four directions, signifying his spiritual sovereignty. His right hand is raised in the gesture of reassurance (*abhaya* mudra), while the left hand is lowered, reminiscent of images of standing buddhas holding the hem of a monastic robe. Above the infant two cloud gods (*devaputras*), shown embedded in clouds, pour elixir from full vases (*purnakalasha*) filled with lotus flowers. In association with the rainy season, they are also known as *varsavalahaka devaputras*. The two gods Indra and Brahma, often included in Siddhartha's nativity scene, are not depicted here. This Jayavagishvari Sundhara stone carving is unique in its style among the surviving sculptures of the Kathmandu Valley. The earliest known representation of the birth of Siddhartha, generally dated to the third or fourth century, was discovered at Lumbini in the Nepal Terai region. The taller than life-size, very damaged red sandstone relief, carved by an Indian artist, however, bears little resemblance to the Jayavagishvari Sundhara image.[1]

For more on the eight great events, see Cave 3 at Yulin Cave Temples, no. 31; Illuminated Pages of the *Prajnaparamita Sutra* Manuscript, no. 23.

Buddha's Eight Great Miraculous Events

The nativity scene is the first of Shakyamuni's "eight great miraculous events" (*ashtamahapratiharya*). These took place at the "eight great places" (*ashtamahasthana*), which became popular as sites of pilgrimage. The eight events are the birth of Siddhartha—the future Buddha Shakyamuni—at Lumbini; the defeat of Mara (*maravijaya*) and subsequent enlightenment under the bodhi tree at Bodhgaya; the first sermon, known as "setting in motion the wheel of the doctrine" (*dharmachakra-pravartana*), in the Deer Park at Sarnath; the multiplication and fire and water miracles, known as the "great miraculous event" (*mahapratiharya*) of the *yamakapratiharya* and the *buddhapindi* at Shravasti; the descent from the Heaven of the Thirty-Three (Trayastrimsha) Gods (*devavatara*) at Sankashya; the taming of the wild elephant Nalagiri at Rajagriha; the gift of honey by a monkey at Vaishali; and the death of Shakyamuni (*mahaparinirvana*) at Kushinagara. Among the stone sculptures of northeastern India and Burma (present-day Myanmar) are quite a few depicting the eight great miraculous events. The only one known in Nepal was actually made in northern India during the Pala dynasty (ca. 750–1200).[2]

Apart from this sculpture, depictions of only individual great miraculous events have become known in the Kathmandu Valley. They include the birth of Siddhartha, the defeat of Mara (*maravijaya*), the first sermon, and the descent from the Heaven of the Thirty-Three Gods.

Mayadevi Giving Birth to Siddhartha; Nepal; Varman or Licchavi period, 4th–5th century; provenance Jayavagishvari Sundhara fountain; Cabahil, Deopatan, Kathmandu, Nepal; polished stone; 33⅛ × 13¾ in. (84 × 35 cm); National Museum Kathmandu, Nepal

For more about these events in relation to pilgrimage sites, see Mahabodhi Temple Model, no. 25.

For other images related to the Buddha's enlightenment, see Buddha on the Cosmic Mountain, no. 10; Jowo Shakyamuni, no. 8; Central Shrine Image of Kwa Baha, no. 22.

The historical Buddha Shakyamuni is the prime focus in the countries practicing the ancient Theravada forms of Buddhism. In the regions where Mahayana/Vajrayana Buddhism is popular, which include Nepal and Tibet, the transcendental buddhas or *tathagatas* are more important. This explains the scarcity of stone sculptures in the Kathmandu Valley illustrating the eight great miraculous events or eight great illusory displays (*ashtamahapratiharya*) of the life of Buddha Shakyamuni.[3]

Disputed Dating

There are few Nepalese stone sculptures that have caused so much disagreement regarding the date of manufacture as the Jayavagishvari Sundhara carving. The range of opinions covers a wide spectrum. According to John Huntington and Dina Bangdel, this work dates from the fifth to the sixth century,[4] disputing Pratapaditya Pal's dating of it from the tenth to the thirteenth century.[5] However, comparisons with early Nepalese stone carvings bearing undisputed dates lead to valid arguments for an attribution as early as the Varman period (until ca. 400) or the Licchavi period (ca. 400–879). The lotus pedestal on which the newborn Siddhartha took his first steps closely resembles the lotus pedestal of the earliest known Nepalese standing stone Buddha at the Vajrayogini Temple compound, dating from about the fourth century.[6] In addition, many stylistic similarities with the two Vishnu Vikranta stone carvings from Lazimpat in Kathmandu and Tilganga near Pashupatinatha, both consecrated in 467 by Licchavi King Manadeva I (r. ca. 464–505), support an early attribution.[7] The high polish is another characteristic of many stone carvings made during the Varman and Licchavi periods.

Buddha's Eight Great Miraculous Events in Nepalese and Tibetan Paintings

Nepalese paintings (*paubha*) tell a different story. Some paintings in small square cartouches arranged as narrative panels on the border present the life of Buddha Shakyamuni, including the eight great miraculous events. Such compositions are not restricted to paintings in which Buddha Shakyamuni is the principal image, although they do contain two additional vertical registers portraying the sixteen arhats together with Hwa shang and Dharmatala.[8] Illustrations of the life of Buddha Shakyamuni appear also on the inner side of wooden manuscript covers of some Nepalese manuscripts.

For more about arhats, see Arhats Viewing a Painting of Birds by the Tenth Karmapa, no. 72.

The only representations of Shakyamuni's eight great miraculous events discovered in Tibet are small steles carved in yellowish-beige stone. They originate from northeastern India and Burma and date from the eleventh to twelfth century.[9] It can be assumed that some of the miniature stone carvings were presumably manufactured in Bodhgaya, while others may be replicas produced elsewhere. No Tibetan cast images are known that illustrate any of the Buddha's great events. This is not surprising, because the subject is far better suited to the medium of painting. Two illustrated thangkas are among the few Tibetan paintings that take the birth cycle as the principal subject.

The first of these thangkas bearing scenes from the early life of the Buddha originates from western Tibet or western Nepal and dates from the fourteenth century. Between the eleventh and fourteenth century, this region was ruled by the Khasa Malla Kingdom. The principal subject depicts Mayadevi giving birth to Siddhartha. But unlike in the Jayavagishvari Sundhara stone carving, Mayadevi here is attended on her proper right side by the gods Brahma and Indra. On the proper left side are Mahaprajapati Gautami, the sister of Mayadevi and stepmother of Shakyamuni, together with a companion. Above on either side, some divinities are embedded in clouds, among them two cloud gods pouring elixir from full vases (*purnakalasha*). As pointed out by Pal, this painting likely belonged to a series of four paintings. The other events would include the enlightenment under the bodhi tree at Bodhgaya, the first sermon in the Deer Park at Sarnath, and the death of Shakyamuni (*mahaparinirvana*) at Kushinagara. In the lower registers are some narratives of the life of Siddhartha that would have continued on the other three thangkas of this series.[10] The very colorful second thangka, adapted from a Derge xylograph, was painted in the late nineteenth century. It also features Mayadevi giving birth to Siddhartha as its principal subject. Indra and Brahma, shown here with only one head instead of four, receive the newborn Siddhartha in a white blanket. The painting, like the Khasa Malla thangka, additionally includes other events in the life of Shakyamuni.[11]

For more about Tibetan depictions of the Life of the Buddha, see Murals of Gongkar Chode, no. 58; A Monumental Life of the Buddha Mural, no. 69.

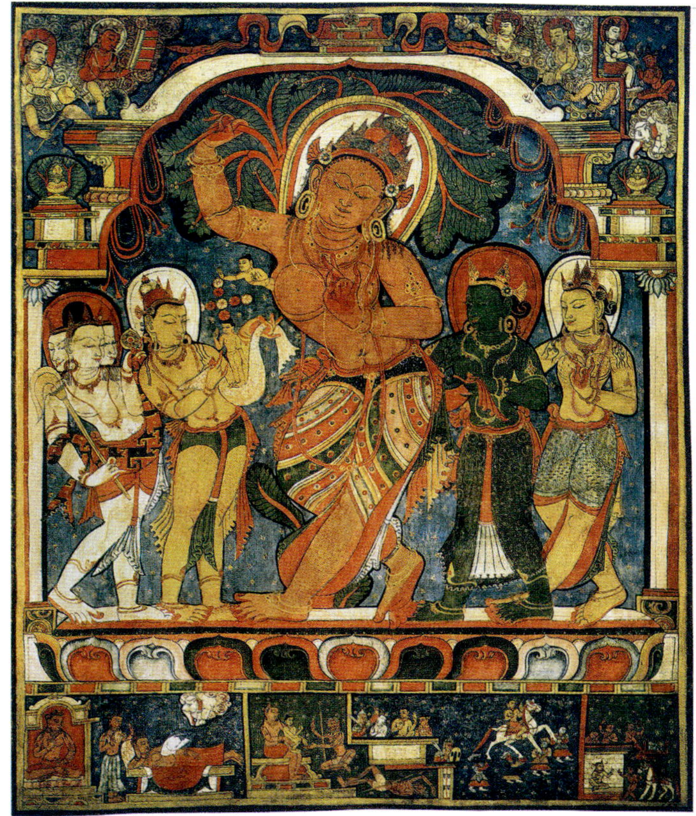

Scenes from the Early Life of the Buddha; western Tibet or western Nepal; 14th century; ink and pigment on cotton; 32⅓ × 21½ in. (82 × 67 cm); Private collection

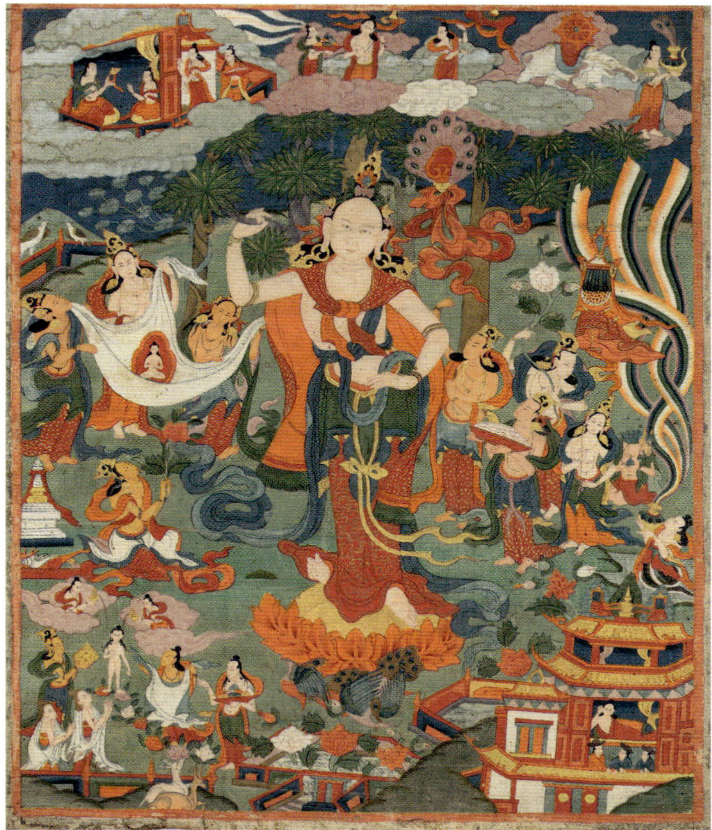

Birth of Buddha; Tibet; 19th century; pigments on cloth; 25¼ × 20¾ in. (64.1 × 52.7 cm); Rubin Museum of Art; C2004.14.6 (HAR 65342)

Further Reading

Bangdel, Lain S. 1982. *The Early Sculptures of Nepal*. New Delhi: Vikas.

Pal, Pratapaditya. 1974. *The Arts of Nepal*, pt. 1, *Sculpture*. Leiden: Brill.

von Schroeder, Ulrich. 2019. *Nepalese Stone Sculptures*. 2 vols. Weesen: Visual Dharma Publications.

Notes

1 von Schroeder 2019, vol. 2, 968, pl. 306A.
2 von Schroeder 2019, vol. 2, 974–75, pl. 309C.
3 von Schroeder 2019, vol. 2, pls. 250E, 253C, 253E, 256E, 263A, 264A, 309A–B, 309D–E, 310A, 310E, 313D.
4 Huntington and Bangdel 2003, 60–61, pl. 1.
5 Pal 1974, fig. 87.
6 von Schroeder 2019, vol. 2, 880, pl. 272A.
7 von Schroeder 2019, vol. 1, 382–83, pls. 120B–C.
8 Pal 1978, pls. 22, 24, 47–48, 204; Pal 2003, 50–51, pl. 25; von Schroeder 2009, 14–17, pl. 2.
9 von Schroeder 2001a, vol. 1, 394–405, fig. V-3, pls. 128–31.
10 Pal 2003, 154–55, no. 101.
11 Chogye Trichen Rinpoche 2021, 17, fig. 1.6.

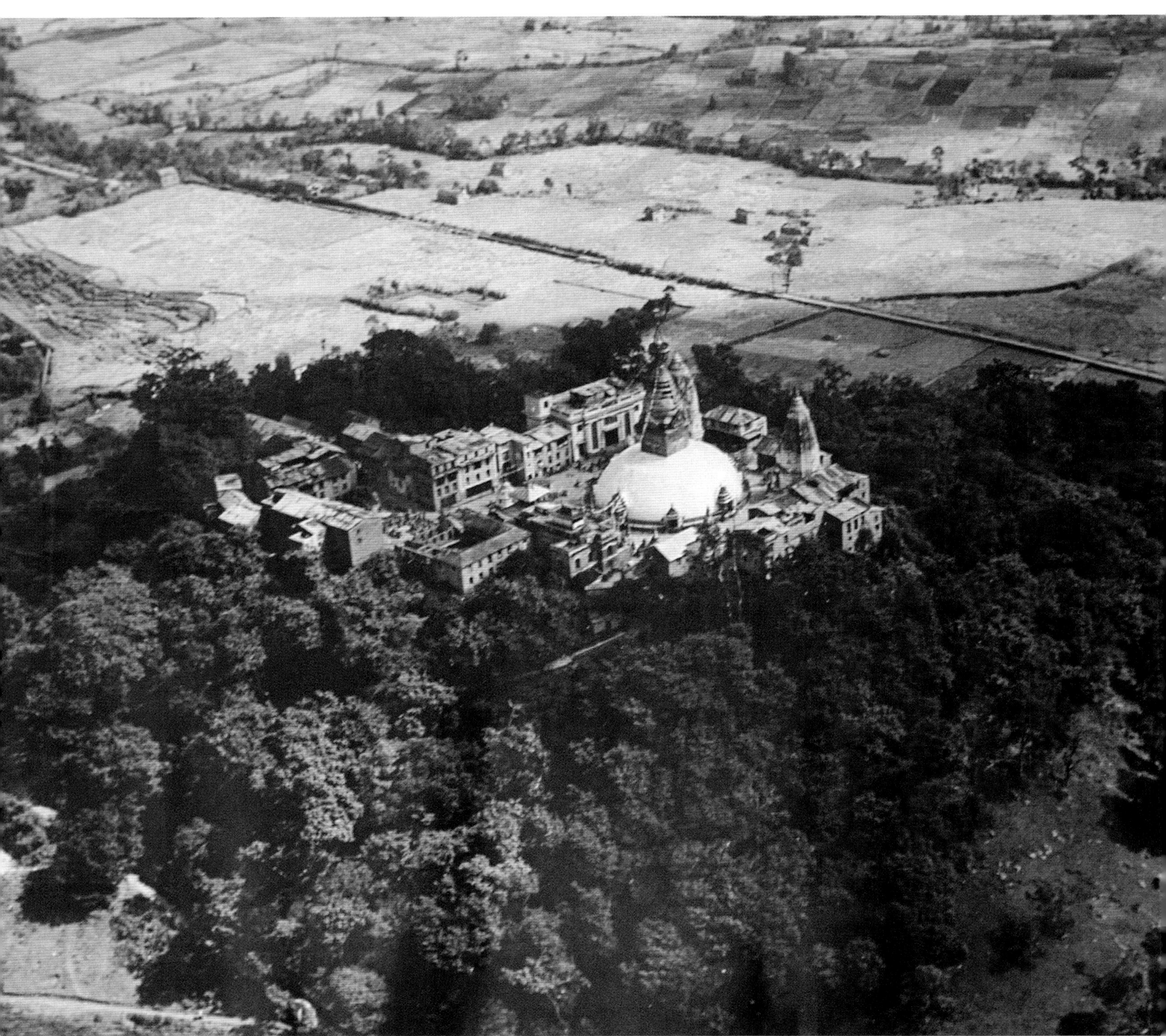

No 4

The Svayambhu Chaitya of Kathmandu

Kathmandu, Nepal, founded ca. 5th century or earlier

Shrines as the Focal Point of Buddhist Communities

ALEXANDER VON ROSPATT

THE SVAYAMBHU CHAITYA (in modern times also known as Svayambhu-nath) is the most important shrine for the tradition of Indian Buddhism that survives in the Kathmandu Valley among the original inhabitants, the Newars—a unique survival on the South Asian subcontinent, where otherwise Mahayana Buddhism had all but disappeared by the thirteenth century. (Chaitya is the term commonly used in the Nepalese tradition instead of "stupa," the standard term for the massive, hemispherical buildings enshrining the relics of the Buddha and worshipped through circumambulation.) Svayambhu, located about a mile west of Kathmandu on top of a hillock, is accepted by all Newar Buddhists, beyond the borders imposed by locality and caste, as the center of their religion.

The Kathmandu Valley is located on the southern flank of the Himalayas, sandwiched between the Gangetic plane of India and Tibet, along major trade routes—a situation that made it an important conduit for the transmission of Indian Buddhism to Tibet. Across the centuries Tibetan pilgrims and translators of Buddhist scriptures have stayed at Svayambhu. The chaitya repeatedly attracted major donations from Tibetan Buddhists, including sponsorship of renovations, the most recent example being the regilding of the chaitya's spire and niches undertaken by the Nyingma Institute of Berkeley, California, from 2008 to 2010.[1] Since at least the early nineteenth century the Tibetan tradition has also been present in the form of Drukpa Kagyu and Karma Kagyu monasteries in the immediate vicinity of the chaitya.

The Structure of the Svayambhu Chaitya

Despite the role Tibetan sponsors have played in its history, the Svayambhu chaitya has retained through the ages its characteristic Nepalese form and appearance.[2] The massive dome, almost 28 feet (8.5 meters) high, is surmounted by a cuboid structure (*harmika*) some 16½ feet (5 meters) high. From the center of the *harmika* rises the upper part of the massive wooden pole (*yashti*) that extends through the whole structure vertically, from the dome through the *harmika*, and through the series of thirteen gilded rings (*chakravali*) up to the structure supporting the finial (*gajur*) and crowning parasol (*chattra*). The portion of the yashti rising above the *harmika* measures nearly 40 feet (12 meters), giving the chaitya a total height of more than 82 feet (25 meters). Each side of the *harmika* is adorned by a pair of eyes; the nose-like curl, a derivative of the tuft of hair between the eyes of the Buddha (*urna*) and the light it emits, was not added until the early twentieth century.[3] These eyes are often identified with the Buddha and his compassionate and all-knowing gaze, and the copper shields mounted above the *harmika*'s sides, which give the impression of headgear crowning the *harmika*, reinforce this identification. Fittingly, the Newari language designates the dome as belly (*pvata*), and the *yashti* can be equated with the spine, as happens in the Tibetan tradition, which refers to it as life tree (*sok shing*). However, such an identification of the structure with the body of the Buddha, including his eyes, is not presumed in the corresponding mythological narratives, nor is it enacted in ritual, where the eyes are instead equated with the sun and moon—as are the sides of the *harmika* elsewhere in the Buddhist world.[4]

Inside the dome, the *yashti* rests on a rock protruding 11 feet (3.3 meters) above the otherwise level surface of the hilltop. This rock, entirely encased by the dome, is invisible, but architectural drawings and ritual chronicles attest to its existence, as do measurements of the overall length of the *yashti* (that is, just over 72 feet, or 22 meters), which bear out that it does not reach all the way down to the level of the ground. The chaitya attained the measurements given here only in the seventeenth century, when it was

Svayambhu Chaitya, Kathmandu, Nepal, aerial photograph taken from the southwest, with surrounding shrines, residential buildings, and the Drukpa Kagyu and Karmapa Karma Kagyu monasteries, summer 1955; photograph by Ganesh Man Chitrakar

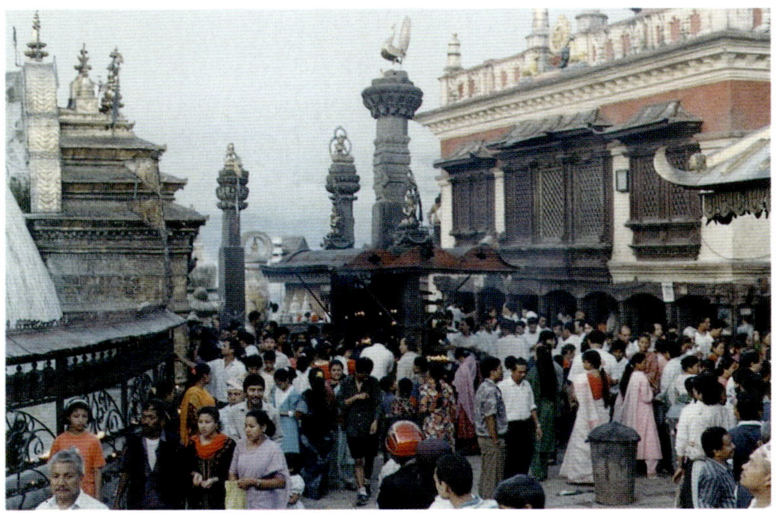

Buddhist devotees in the early hours for their daily worship of Svayambhu, Kathmandu, Nepal, during the "month of virtue" (*gumla*), dedicated to the pursuit of meritorious action, August 1996; the Drukpa Kagyu monastery is seen at right, facing the western side of the chaitya; photograph by Alexander von Rospatt

enlarged by roughly a third,[5] but the rock has always been encased in the dome. Given the sanctity the Nepalese attribute to rocks, particularly those in a prominent position, we may conjecture that the protruding rock had been worshipped even before the advent of Buddhism, and that the chaitya was built above it so as to incorporate this autochthonous site into the fold of Buddhism.[6] Certainly the site is much more than a holy place dedicated to Buddhahood. Adjacent to the chaitya is a temple dedicated to the mother goddess Hariti, whom the Newars worship here to assure the health of their children. Also, the chaitya is supplemented by a tantric temple and surrounded by four shrines dedicated to the elements, namely, earth, wind, fire, and water, which are propitiated to gain protection and prosperity.

The Myth of Svayambhu's Origins

The Svayambhu chaitya serves as the archetype of chaityas in the Newar tradition,[7] which typically bear marks of the iconography of Svayambhu through the eyes and in other ways. Similarly, scroll paintings and other images generally render chaityas in the likeness of Svayambhu as a default. Besides alluding to the iconic eyes on the *harmika*, these show the chaitya as resting on a lotus blossom floating on a lake, which references the myth narrated in the *Svayambhupurana*, a work of seminal importance for the Newar Buddhist tradition.[8] It relates that in prehistoric times the Kathmandu Valley was a sacred lake on which the primordial buddha principle (*dharmadhatu*) manifested (*bhu*) itself spontaneously (*svayam*) in the form of a light or a luminous crystal atop a thousand-petaled, jeweled lotus blossom. In order to make this sacred manifestation of Buddhahood accessible for worship, Manjushri (who had come for this purpose from "Maha China") drained the lake, enabling the settlement of the Valley. This left the *dharmadhatu* exposed, and in order to protect it from spoliation at the onset of the period when people become wicked (*kaliyuga*), a physical structure, the chaitya, was built over the self-manifesting *dharmadhatu*. While the enshrined *dharmadhatu* of the mythological narrative might be identified with the rock encased by the dome, nothing in the *Svayambhupurana* suggests that the chaitya houses the physical relics (*asthi-dhatu*) of the (or a) Buddha or other Buddhist saint, as do stupas. Moreover, the historical records make no mention of any relics or relic chambers. Rather, they bear out that on the ritual plane, the principle of Buddhahood is made manifest by performing elaborate tantric rituals that imbue the chaitya—principally by configuring it as a mandala and infusing it with mantras (*nyasa*)—with the presence of the Five Buddhas of the Yogatantras.[9] These deity-like buddhas are depicted in niches set in the dome, Akshobhya in the east, Ratnasambhava in the south, Amitabha in the west, and Amoghasiddhi in the north. In addition, the buddha at the center of this configuration, Vairochana, eventually came to be depicted in a niche of his own, installed just to the south of Akshobhya, which defies the logic of the mandala.[10]

For more on Manjushri's earthly abode in China, see Panoramic Map of Mount Wutai, no. 91.

For an example of a Nepalese mandala, see Chakrasamvara Mandala with Newar Donors, no. 29.

See The All-Knowing Buddha Vairochana Visualization Album, no. 87.

The presence of these five buddhas turns the chaitya into a "buddha abode" (*buddha-alaya*); collectively, they embody the qualities of Buddhahood and render it present, just as the self-manifesting, luminous *dharmadhatu* of the *Svayambhupurana* does. In this, the Svayambhu chaitya represents not an exception but the rule. For, in tantric Buddhism (*vajrayana*), chaityas (and stupas) are imbued with the presence of Buddhahood mainly through the employment of elaborate rituals and not (or less so) through the enshrining of relics.

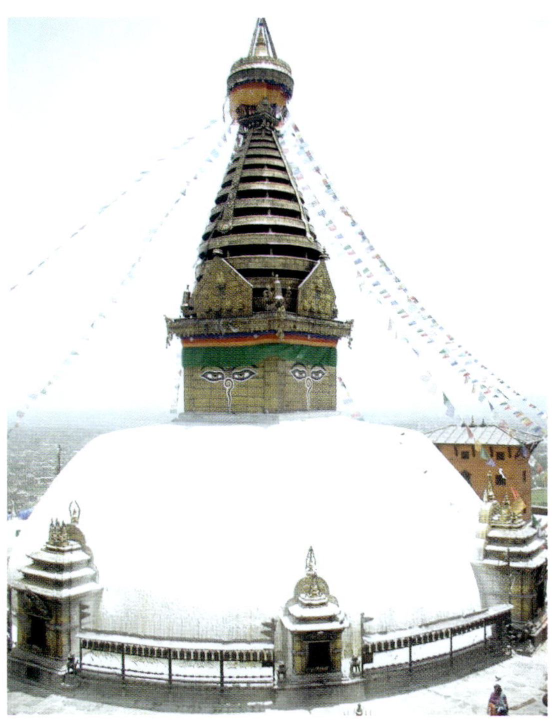

The northwestern face of the Svayambhu chaitya, Kathmandu, Nepal, with the niches of the Buddha Amoghasiddhi in the north, Amitabha in the west, and the goddess Aryatara in between, 2002; photograph by Manika Bajracharya, Lotus Research Centre, Lalitpur

Periodic Renovations of the Svayambhu Chaitya

The dependence on rituals for the sanctification of chaityas calls for their (more or less regular) reenactment, since the charge they deliver is understood to wane over time—arguably, in contrast to the Buddha's relics, which are commonly believed to be immune to decay, persisting unchanged until the end of the present age. In addition to daily worship (*nitya puja*) and annual anniversary rituals, such recharging may include the occasional physical renovation (*jirnoddhara*) of the chaitya, consisting in the extensive refurbishing or even rebuilding of much of the structure, accompanied by the appropriate rituals that culminate in the reconsecration of the chaitya at the end.

Over the course of the one to two millennia of its existence, the Svayambhu chaitya was rebuilt frequently, and at times in the process also modified and enlarged.[11] Records beginning in the thirteenth century bear out that between then and the nineteenth century the chaitya was extensively renovated on average twice a century, at irregular intervals. In the course of these renovations, the entire structure of the chaitya above the dome was dismantled and discarded, the dome itself cut open in order to allow for the replacement of the *yashti*, and the chaitya, stripped down in this manner, was then rebuilt with new materials. Such complex and labor- and time-intensive operations included the procurement of the gigantic hardwood (*sal*) tree, some 82 feet (25 meters) tall, to serve as new *yashti* from the subtropical valley of the Trishuli Ganga River, or one of its tributaries, a few miles to the northeast of the Kathmandu Valley (where such trees do not grow). The enormous trees needed to furnish a new *yashti* were exceedingly rare already two hundred years ago, so that the renovations at the beginning of the twentieth and twenty-first centuries did not entail replacing the *yashti* installed in 1817.

Given the small scale of Kathmandu's traditional economy, these costly renovations proved difficult to fund. As a result, Tibetan lamas, with varied backgrounds and different traditions, often played a dominant role as donors and even instigators of renovations, alongside the local Nepalese population, especially between the thirteenth and sixteenth centuries and between the mid-eighteenth and twenty-first centuries, in the process often drawing on their extensive network of contacts, ranging from the western Tibetan regions all the way to Sikkim, Kham, and Bhutan. This transformed these renovations into Trans-Himalayan events that drew different Tibetan Buddhist traditions together and brought them into conversation with Newar Buddhism as well as the kings of Kathmandu, who, while Hindus themselves, bore the ultimate responsibility for Svayambhu, as for all other public religious sites on their territory.

Further Reading

Gellek, Tsering Palmo, and Padma Dorje Maitland, eds. 2011. *Light of the Valley: Renewing the Sacred Art and Traditions of Svayambhu*. Cazadero, CA: Dharma Publishing.

Gutschow, Niels. 1997. *The Nepalese Caitya: 1500 Years of Buddhist Votive Architecture in the Kathmandu Valley*. Stuttgart: Edition Axel Menges.

Swoyambhu Stupa. 2019–22. https://swoyambhustupa.com/.

Notes

1 Gellek and Maitland 2011.
2 Gutschow 1997, 96–96, 194ff.
3 Kölver 1992, 129ff.
4 Rospatt 2013, 103.
5 Rospatt 2013, 97–99.
6 Rospatt 2009, 36ff.
7 Gutschow 1997.
8 Rospatt 2015, 1:827.
9 Rospatt 2010, 201ff.
10 Rospatt 2013, 100–104.
11 Gellek and Maitland 2011, 157–206.

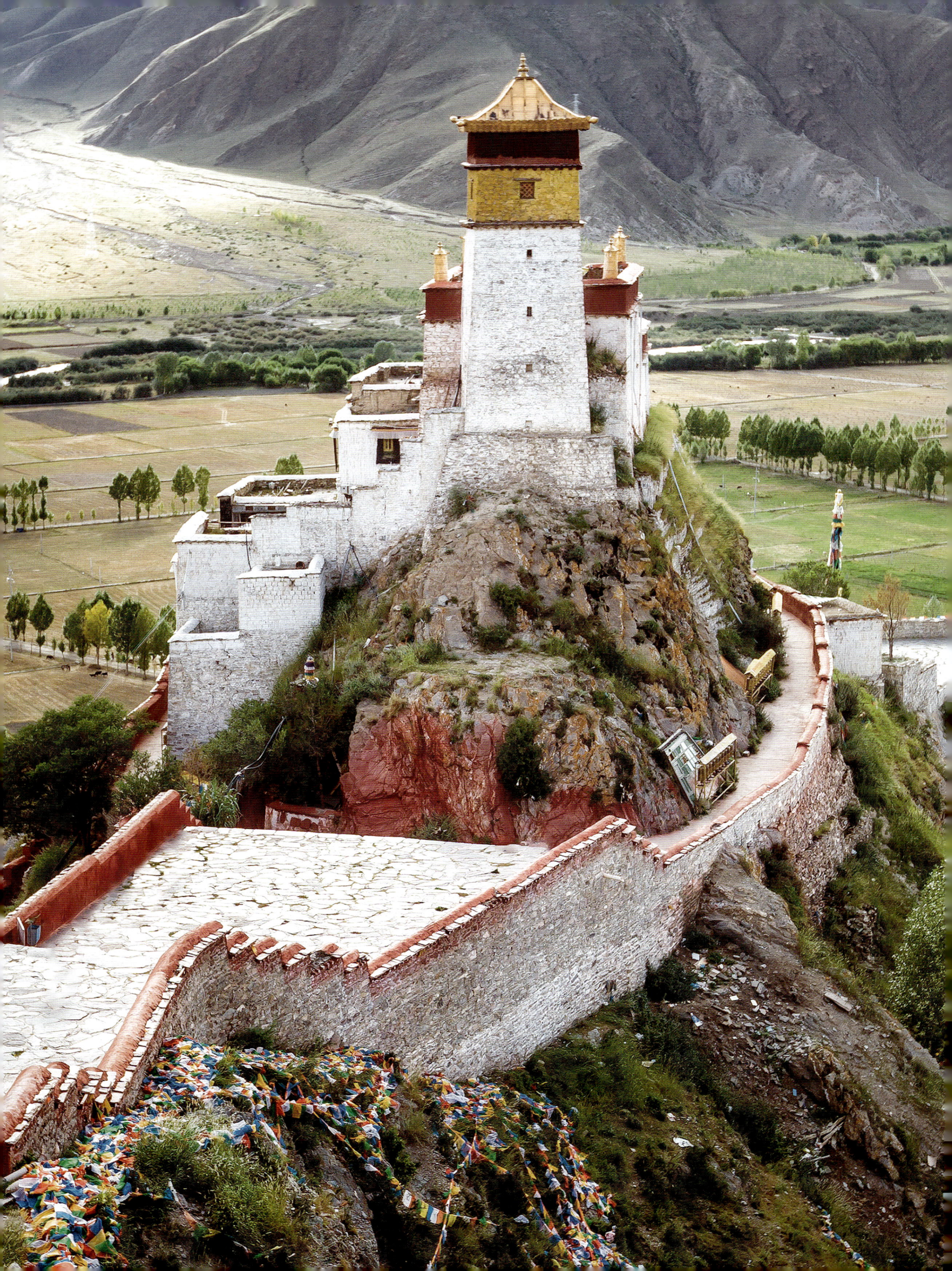

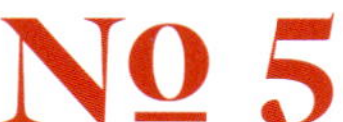

Yumbu Lagang Castle

Yarlung Valley, U region, central Tibet (present-day TAR, China), founded ca. 6th century

Residence of the Early Tibetan Kings and Sacred Shrine

GUNTRAM HAZOD

THE FAMOUS CASTLE OF YUMBU LAGANG[1] is located in Yarlung, the valley in southern central Tibet that, together with the western side valley of Chongpo, formed the core area of the early Yarlung Kingdom. From this area, the unification of the Tibetan territories began under the Yarlung king Tri Lontsen (also known as Namri Lontsen; d. ca. 618), which ultimately led to the formation of the Tibetan Empire (ca. 600–850).

The castle is situated prominently on a cliff, a spur of Mount Tashitseri, on the east side of Lower Yarlung, overlooking much of the fertile valley where the Yarlung River and the Chongpo River converge. Legend has it that the wide valley floor was once covered by a lake, probably a reminder of the regular flooding that hit the area before the water was tamed by canals. In this legend the flood is the work of a naga monster who was overwhelmed by a bird of prey; this was the "thundering falcon" (*trandruk*), which gave its name to the temple. Built in the middle of the former lake, under Emperor Songtsen Gampo (ca. 605–649), even before the Lhasa Jokhang, it is considered Tibet's first *vihara*, or Buddhist temple. It is alleged that a shrine was also established in Yumbu Lagang at this time.[2]

See Jokhang Temple, no. 7.

The story of Trandruk is part of a series of "first events" that Buddhist history locates in Yarlung—the "oldest of (Tibet's) lands" (*yulla ngaba*): the origin of "Tibet's first human beings," the development of the "first (agricultural) field" (situated below Yumbu Lagang), and, not least, the arrival of "Tibet's first king," Nyatri Tsenpo; he is said to have built the Yumbu Lagang residence, Tibet's "first castle" (*kharla ngaba*), following his heavenly descent onto a hill in the west of the valley. A parallel and probably older tradition contradicts this legend and describes Yumbu Lagang as one of four "personal castles" (*kukhar*) of the early kings of the Yarlung house, which were built on the four sides of the valley. Only Yumbu Lagang, the latest of the four residences, remained; it was the *kukhar* of the king named Lha Totori Nyentsen.[3]

Under this king, who is ranked in the royal genealogy five generations before Songtsen Gampo, another first event is said to have happened in Lower Yarlung: the first contact with Buddhism, known in classical Tibetan Buddhist history as the "advent of the sublime dharma" (*dampei chokyi unye*).

The "Advent of the Sublime Dharma"

The story goes that one day a set of Buddhist (basically Avalokiteshvara-specific) objects fell from the sky onto the roof of this king's castle—a cubit-sized golden chaitya (stupa), a drinking bowl with jewels, and texts of sutras, including the *Karandavyuha Sutra* and the somewhat obscure prayer text *Pangkong chakgyapa*.[4] At the same time, a voice from heaven announced that after five generations a king would understand the meaning of these items and texts—a reference to Songtsen Gampo, the celebrated emperor and Buddhist king under whom the texts were supposedly translated.[5] Lha Totori Nyentsen called these foreign objects "secret Nyenpo" (Nyenpo Sangwa), with *nyenpo* apparently being an allusion to the *nyen* spirits commonly associated with the mountain and with ancestry.[6] And although the king did not understand the objects and texts, he kept them in a separate place resembling a sanctuary inside the castle, the "*nyen* treasury," and made regular offerings to them. This prolonged his life in a miraculous way, perhaps leading to further miracles: later, a prince born blind followed the advice of his father and worshipped the Nyenpo Sangwa, which reportedly gave him the ability to see.

The Castle and Temple of Yumbu Lagang, Yarlung Valley, U region, central Tibet (present-day TAR, China); founded ca. 6th century; photograph by Vladimir Zhoga

The story, which has been in circulation in written form since the eleventh century, used the old motif of heavenly descent as exemplified in the legend of the arrival of the progenitor king (Nyatri

For more about the Bon religion, see Bon Deity Trowo Tsochok Khagying, no. 60.

For more about the Fifth Dalai Lama, see Potala Palace, no. 71.

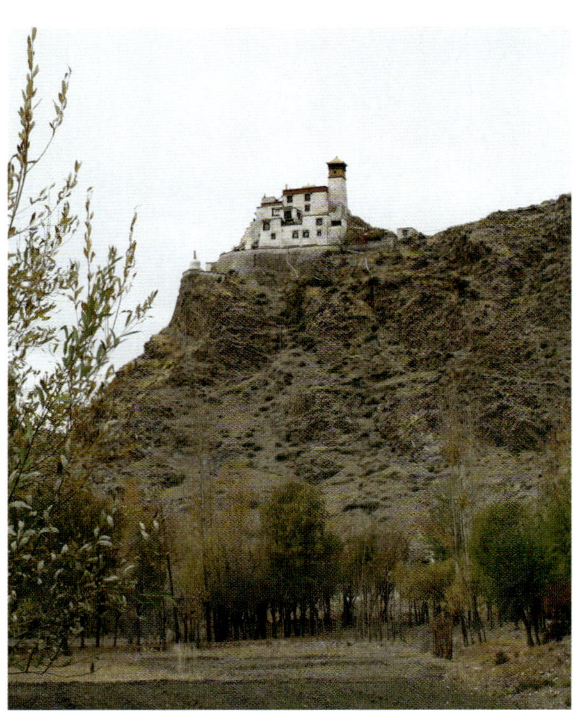

Tibet's "first field" below the castle of Yumbu Lagang, south side; photograph by G. Hazod, 2008

Tsenpo), a phenomenon that not all Tibetan Buddhists accepted. A well-known chronicle from the thirteenth century names this origin polemically as a falsification on the part of the Bonpos and asserts instead that an Indian *pandita* brought the texts to Tibet. The latter, however, could not teach the king because there was no knowledge of writing in Tibet at that time, so he moved on to China, leaving the objects with the king. Later authors also tended toward this version of the Nyenpo Sangwa origin, before the Fifth Dalai Lama (1617–1682), in his authoritative chronicle, declared the original (miraculous) version to be the correct one.[7]

It is not implausible to see a historical early contact with India and Buddhism in the fifth century CE behind the Nyenpo Sangwa story, although the figure of King Lha Totori Nyentsen cannot be ascertained as a historical figure. He remains in the semidarkness of the "mythical period" of the royal genealogy.

The Temple of Yumbu Lagang and Its Treasures

Yumbu Lagang has been restored many times in its long history, but it is believed that the basic structure has essentially been preserved: a square tower with four lookouts in the upper part, to which a residential building was attached, which was later rebuilt and expanded to become a temple (*lhakhang*) with adjoining monastic accommodation. A very similar, albeit somewhat smaller building is the still preserved Gyelpo Khang in Gyama (east of Lhasa), where Emperor Songtsen Gampo is said to have grown up.

Yumbu Lagang Castle was apparently continuously used as a (temporary) residence for members of the royal family during the empire, finally by Tri Wosung, the last pretender to the throne (ca. 843–ca. 893), who was born in Yumbu Lagang. After the death of Tri Udumtsen (the last emperor, popularly known as Langdarma, d. 842), Tri Wosung sought to maintain a remnant of the former imperial power from Yarlung. Even in the postimperial period the castle functioned as a royal residence, until the late thirteenth century, as one of the seats of the Yarlung Jowo, descendants of Tri Wosung, before its transformation into a temple gradually took place under the subsequent rule of Pakmodrupa (1350–1481). Associated with this was its establishment as a place of pilgrimage with the status of a national symbol, which was further strengthened under the Fifth Dalai Lama, not least externally, through the attachment of the characteristic golden canopy roof.[8] This led to the tradition of the temple's care being taken over by lamas from Riwo Cholung, the neighboring Gelukpa monastery, founded in the fifteenth century.

What we see today goes back to the reconstruction of castle and temple in 1982, which largely removed the destructive traces of the Cultural Revolution in the 1960s and included a restoration and partial replication of the original inventory. Some new components, such as the spacious driveway to the castle, and other adaptations were added to the site as a tourist attraction.

The temple is a three-story building, with the central shrine, an eight-pillar chapel, situated on the lower floor. The main statue is the crowned buddha known as the "Lord of the wish-granting jewel" (Jowo Norbu Sampel). The head of the original statue was made of stone, the rest of clay, and it had sported a jewel the size of a bird's egg in the chest area. Emperor Songtsen Gampo supposedly offered the gilt-bronze ornaments. The statue is flanked by clay statues of King Nyatri Tsenpo (left) and Emperor Songtsen Gampo (right), followed by statues of other representatives of the glorious royal past, such as Minister Tonmi Sambhota, Emperor Tri Songdetsen, Lha Totori Nyentsen (left wall); Emperor Tri Relpachen, Tri Wosung, and Minister Gar (right wall). The temple's murals include the legend of

King Lha Totori Nyentsen Paying Homage to the Objects of the Nyenpo Sangwa; mural in the Potala Palace, Lhasa; 1645–48; image after Lading 2000, 59

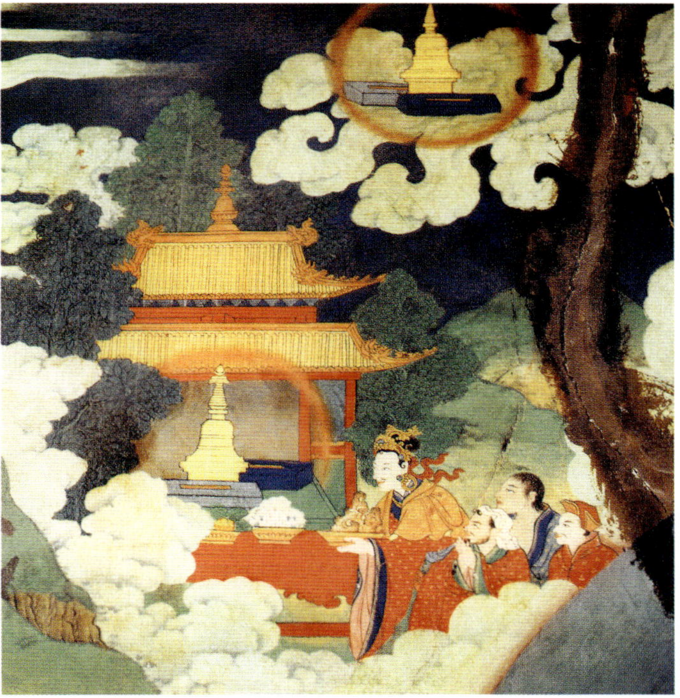

Nyatri Tsenpo's arrival in Yarlung, the story of the Nyenpo Sangwa, and other key events of early Tibetan Buddhist history. Among other things, the floor above housed a sandalwood statue of Lokeshvara almost twenty inches (fifty centimeters) high, reportedly from the seventh century, which was stolen in a burglary in 1999. The third floor has a passage to the tower, with an entrance for pilgrims to the central pillar, locally known as the "world pillar" (*sikyi kawa*).[9]

The original chamber (*drub-khang*) of Nyatri Tsenpo is said to have been situated behind the altar in the first-floor chapel. It is assumed that the old treasury of the castle, of which the sources speak—the *norbu bangso* ("sepulchre with the precious objects")—was found below it. The treasury included royal heirlooms related to kings before the time of Lha Totori Nyentsen, which were resealed as "hidden treasures" (*terma*) under Mutik Tsenpo (that is, Emperor Tri Desongtsen, d. 815)—described as the "thirteen precious treasures of the (Yarlung) kings" (*gyelpo korcha rinchen chusum*). They were under the special protection of Yarlha Shampo, the ancient territorial god of Yarlung and protector of the early kings. The objects of the Nyenpo Sangwa, the contents of the stated original sanctuary of Yumbu Lagang, are not mentioned among these objects. They appear in Trandruk, in *terma* lists related to events of the early ninth century, where they were said to have been hidden in one of this temple's treasure caves.[10] It is quite possible that the myth of the Nyenpo Sangwa and its association with Yumbu Lagang was first formulated at this time—at the height of the empire's Buddhist period—in the local milieu of Trandruk and Lower Yarlung.

For more about *terma*, see *Dorje* Discovered by Dorje Lingpa, no. 51.

For a mountain god of similar origin and function, see Mountain God Kula Khari, no. 92.

Further Reading

Akester, Matthew. 2016. *Jamyang Khyentsé Wangpo's Guide to Central Tibet*, 417–18. Chicago: Serindia.

Richardson, Hugh E. 1998. *High Peaks, Pure Earth: Collected Writings on Tibetan History and Culture.* Edited and with an introduction by Michael Aris, 319 and passim. London: Serindia.

Sørensen, Per K., and Guntram Hazod, in cooperation with Tsering Gyalbo. 2005. *Thundering Falcon: An Inquiry into the History and Cult of Khra-'brug, Tibet's First Buddhist Temple*, 99–102, 149–54. Vienna: Verlag der Österreichischen Akademie der Wissenschaften.

Notes

1 There are several spellings and interpretative variants in the sources. The most common is Yumbu Lagang (*yum bu b(r)la sgang*), cf. Sørensen and Hazod 2005, 101; Akester 2016, 417.

2 See Chan 1994, 539.

3 For variants of the "first castle" tradition, the founding history of Trandruk, and the historical geography of Lower Yarlung in general, see Sørensen and Hazod 2005, 101, 217ff., and Hazod 2022.

4 For *Pangkong chakgyapa* (*Pang kong phyag rgya pa*), see van Schaik 2022, 153–54.

5 The description of the objects and texts varies slightly depending on the version; see Sørensen 1994, 150, 534–35.

6 Rendered in the literature as "secret power" or also (but grammatically rather problematic) as "awesome secret."

7 See most recently van Schaik 2022.

8 See Akester 2016, 417–18; Sørensen and Hazod 2005, 102, 312, 318.

9 See Akester 2016, 418. For more details of the temple's inventory, see the Tibetan guide by Karma rgyal mtshan 1999; see also Tenzin (Bstan 'dzin) 1992.

10 For the royal heirlooms and the *terma* (hidden treasures) history of Trandruk and Yumbu Lagang, see Sørensen and Hazod 2005, 102, 149–54.

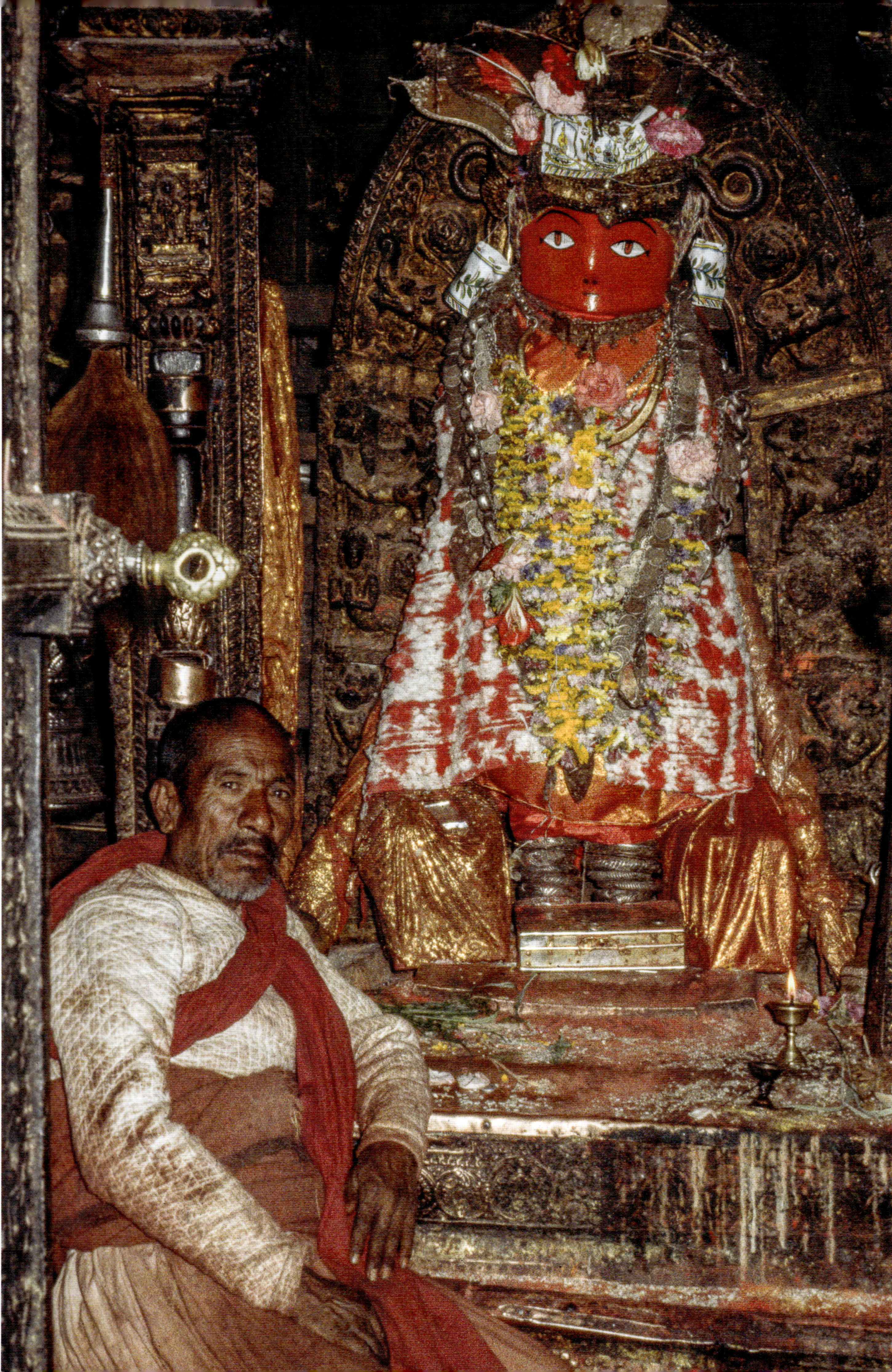

No 6

Bunga Dya
(Bunga Lokeshvara, Karunamaya, Rato Macchendranath)

Nepal, from the 7th century on

Seasonal Travels of the Valley God

IAN ALSOP

For more about the Bodhisattva of Compassion, see Avalokiteshvara at Khartse, no. 20.

Bunga Dya (the god of Bunga) is the quintessential god of the Newars of the largely Buddhist city of Patan in the Kathmandu Valley. His cult is clearly ancient, going back as far as the seventh century, and perhaps even before. His identity is threefold. He is thought to be an ancient rain god of the original inhabitants of the valley, who are most closely associated with the Jyapus, the farmers and agricultural workers of Newar society. He is also the great Buddhist bodhisattva Arya Avalokiteshvara, and through that association is often called Bunga Lokeshvara (a variant is the oldest historically recorded name for him) or Karunamaya, "full of compassion," an epithet of this bodhisattva. Finally, in the seventeenth century he became associated with the Hindu Nath yogi Matysendranath as Rato Macchendranath, or Red Macchendranath. This name, now popularly used by the non-Newar population of Nepal, is found in guidebooks and, thus, on the lips of guides and tourists. This last iteration of his identity brought the Hindu Nepalese into the fold of his devotees, and his yearly *jatra*, or festival, while run by Buddhist officiants, is celebrated by Buddhists and Hindus alike.

The Bunga of his Newar name is associated with his home village of Bungamati, where he resides for half the year. He is the only god in Nepal to have two home temples, his main temple in Bungamati, now under repair after being almost entirely destroyed in the 2015 earthquake, and another later temple in Ta Baha of Patan.

Bunga Dya's Annual Chariot Festival

Bunga Dya's chariot festival is undoubtedly the most elaborate festival in Nepal, spanning a period of about two months in the spring and early summer, with the end of the chariot's journey often coinciding, as expected, with the beginning of the monsoon rains. The timing of the festival and the enthusiastic participation of the farmer populations of the valley give testimony to the origins of Bunga Dya as above all a god of rain, and, thus, abundance.[1] The chariot procession travels through the old city of Patan, but every twelfth year it begins and ends in Bungamati itself, some four and a half miles south of Patan.

The usual yearly festival begins with the god being taken from his Patan temple and ritually bathed; he then returns to the temple precincts to be cleaned, repaired, and repainted. The god is ritually invited to reside in a silver jar while the image is attended to. While these rituals are being performed a towering chariot is constructed at the entrance to the city of Patan.

The *rath jatra*—the pulling of the chariot by a crowd of one hundred or more excited young devotees—is an exciting and somewhat riotous affair. The huge and unwieldy chariot is pulled through the narrow streets of Patan and makes stops, lasting from a day to several weeks, at several important places as it slowly wends its way to the field of Jawalakhel. Here, the festival culminates in the ritual showing of a shirt associated with the god, with the highest officials of the government—in former times, including the king of Nepal—in attendance.

Bunga Dya; Nepal; date uncertain; wood, metal (silver?), clay, pigments; height approx. 36 in. (92 cm); Ta Baha, Patan, and Rato Macchendranath Temple, Bungamati, Nepal; photograph by Bruce McCoy Owens, showing Bunga Dya newly reinstalled in temple sanctum of Ta Baha after repainting, May 11, 1983

Bunga Dya's Image

Bunga Dya's physical form is unusual. Since his image is almost always draped with clothing and elaborate jewelry, few are able to see the figure uncovered. Bruce Owens, who had the chance to observe the image, describes it as "slightly over three feet high, with silver arms and feet protruding from a relatively

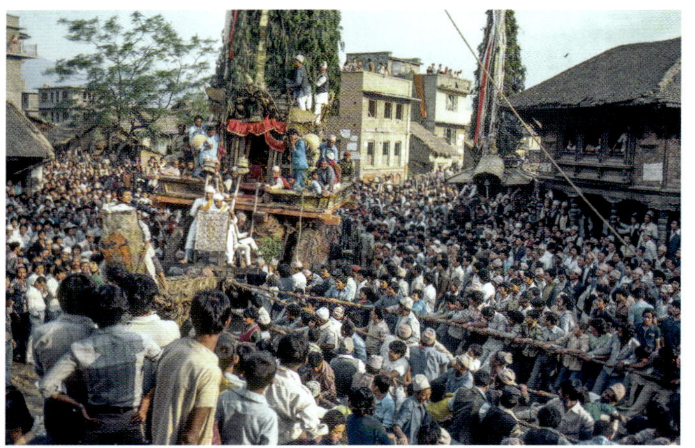

Bunga Dya chariot procession; Pode tol, Patan, Nepal; May 27, 1982; photograph by Bruce McCoy Owens

For Newar sculpture, see Central Shrine Image of Kwa Baha, no. 22; Goddess of Prosperity, Vasudhara, no. 34; Siddhi Lakshmi, no. 67.

formless standing body. The outermost layers of the torso and head clearly consist of caked paint and clay."[2]

This is a very strange depiction of the great bodhisattva in a culture abounding with skilled artists and artisans. Certainly, when compared with images from the same period, such as a wonderful sculpture of a white Avalokiteshvara in wood from the Pritzker Collection, the image of Bunga Dya lacks the elegance and fine workmanship we associate with Newar sculpture. The explanation surely lies in the rough treatment the idol must endure. One can imagine that if the god originally resembled the graceful figure of the white Lokeshvara, after not too many years of the tumultuous chariot *jatra*, it would be entirely destroyed. Each year the present sculpture must be repaired and repainted by specialists, and a photograph of that operation in progress shows that even after a single year there is much to be done.

The legend of the arrival of Bunga Lokeshvara in the valley describes the efforts of a great king, Narendradeva, to end a disastrous multiyear drought by bringing the great god from afar—either Kamarup or Mount Potalaka[3]—to the valley to remove the causes of the drought. In this quest he calls on the aid of a great teacher (*acharya*), Bandhudatta, and a Jyapu farmer, Lalita. After numerous tribulations and adventures, this team succeeds in finding the god, capturing him in a silver vessel, and bringing him back to the valley, where he is installed in his temple in Bungamati.[4]

History and Traditional Narratives of the Cult of Bunga Lokeshvara

The antiquity of the cult of Bunga Lokeshvara is attested by several historical sources. A Buddhist manuscript dated 1071 CE in the collection of the Asiatic Society, Kolkata, has a note describing a miniature illustration as "Bugama Lokeshvara in (of) Nepal."[5] Dharmasvamin, the thirteenth-century Tibetan translator and pilgrim who spent eight years in Nepal (1226–1234), left a detailed account of the cult of "Arya Bu-kham."[6] The *Gopalarajavamsavali*, an authoritative fourteenth-century Nepalese chronicle, mentions the god and his cult many times. The first citation records that King Narendradeva, with the help of the *acharya* Bandhudatta, initiated the festival of Lord Shri Bugma Lokeshvara, confirming the main protagonists in the story that has been handed down to the present.[7] This was almost certainly the seventh-century Licchavi king Narendradeva (r. 643–679).

For more about the Licchavi, see Central Shrine Image of Kwa Baha, no. 22; Mayadevi Giving Birth to Siddhartha, no. 3.

For more about Songtsen Gampo and his connection to the cult of Avalokiteshvara in Tibet, see Bodhisattva Avalokiteshvara and the Buddha's Footprints, no. 33.

In a popular fourteenth-century Tibetan religious and royal history, Bunga Dya is connected with another king, the great Tibetan emperor Songtsen Gampo (r. 618–649), and in this history we see glimmerings of a possibly close connection between the origins of the cult of Avalokiteshvara in Nepal and Tibet, the paramount bodhisattva of both countries.

The Tibetan chronicle recounts how Songtsen Gampo, meditating on how to bring Buddhism to his kingdom, determined that an emanated form lay hidden inside a tree of white sandalwood in the southern part of Nepal. He sent a magically emanated mendicant to fetch these "supports of the dharma." When the mendicant found the tree and cut into it, four emanations spoke, announcing where they were destined to go, and then appeared, all four in the form of the two-armed Avalokiteshvara.

The first and third can be identified respectively as the "noble Wati," who would become famous as the Kyirong Jowo in southern Tibet;[8] and the "noble Jamali," known to the Newars as Janbahadya, the white Avalokiteshvara of Kathmandu (also known as Seto Macchendranath), who has his own chariot festival.

The second announced that he would go to the city of Yambu Yagel, or Kathmandu/Patan, and the noble "Bu kam" appeared, our Bunga Dya or Bunga Lokeshvara.[9]

See Potala Palace, no. 71.

The fourth announced that he would go to the snowy kingdom of Tibet as King Songtsen Gampo's tutelary deity. That is the Pakpa Lokeshvara of the Potala Palace, who presides there to this day, in a

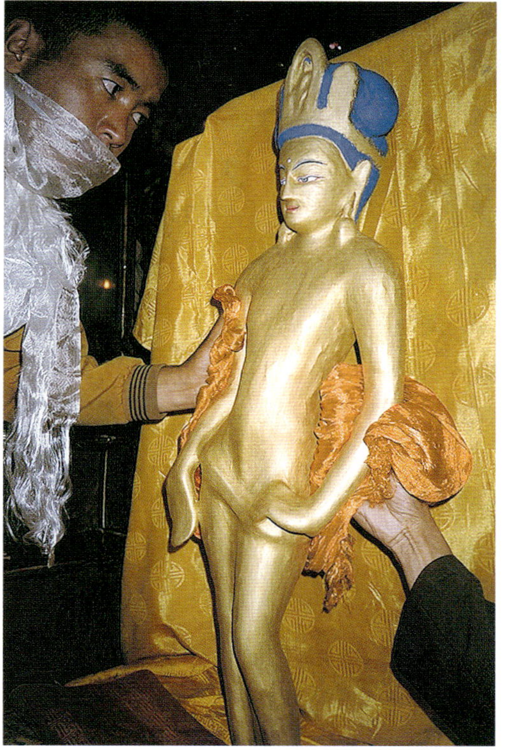

Pakpa Lokeshvara; Nepal; 7th century; wood, gold paint; height 32¼ in. (82 cm); Pakpa Lhakhang, Potala Palace, Lhasa; photograph by Ian Alsop

distinctive form as an elegant bodhisattva, with an unusual high, three-peaked crown, the central peak adorned with a standing buddha, two buns of hair cascading on either side, and distinctive bell-shaped earrings.[10]

Connections to Tibet

The two kings who play leading roles in these stories, the Nepalese Narendradeva and the Tibetan Songtsen Gampo, are connected in many ways. Narendradeva's father was the victim of a usurpation, and Narendradeva, forced to flee the Kathmandu Valley, went to Tibet, where he took refuge in Lhasa. He spent many years in Tibet, perhaps from 624 until his return to the throne in Nepal in 641. Twelve years of Narendradeva's stay in Lhasa coincided with Songtsen Gampo on the throne, and it may have been Songtsen Gampo who aided his return and the ousting of the usurpers.[11]

It was during the time of Narendradeva's sojourn in Tibet that the Newar contribution to the art there blossomed; the decoration of Jokhang temple, built during this period, clearly shows the hand of Newar sculptors.[12] The sculpture of Pakpa Lokeshvara, the tutelary deity of Songtsen Gampo, displays the Newar aesthetic even when covered with layers of gold offered by the devout.

See Jokhang Temple, no. 7.

The elegant figure of the Potala Pakpa Lokeshvara and the rustic *jatra*-worn idol of Bunga Dya share one other distinctive trait. They are both images of such renown and sanctity that the sculptures themselves have become sacred images, and have been reproduced for the faithful over the centuries, as sculptures and in paintings.

In spite of the mystery that shrouds these figures, the legend and history surrounding Bunga Dya and Pakpa Lokeshvara and the available stylistic evidence suggest that both are indeed precious relics of the early years of Mahayana Buddhism in the Himalayas. These two share characteristics unique to their cults: stories of royal introduction, peculiarities of iconography and style, and the very rare custom of manufacturing copies not of an iconographic type but rather of a specific sacred image.

Further Reading

Locke, John K. 1980. *Karunamaya: The Cult of Avalokitesvara-Matsyendranath in the Valley of Nepal*. Kathmandu: Sahayogi Prakashan.

Slusser, Mary Shepherd 1982. *Nepal Mandala: A Cultural Study of the Kathmandu Valley*, esp. 367–80. Princeton, NJ: Princeton University Press.

Vajracharya, Gautama V. 2016. *Nepalese Seasons: Rain and Ritual,* esp. 60–65, pls. 14, 15. Exhibition catalog. New York: Rubin Museum of Art. ttps://issuu.com/rmanyc/docs/nepalese_seasons_-_combo-_96_ppi.

Notes

1 Vajracharya 2016 elucidates the importance of the seasons to the religions of the Kathmandu Valley; see esp. 62.
2 Owens 1989, 155.
3 For Kamarup, Mount Kapotala, see Owens 1989, 149n15; for Mount Potalaka, see Locke 1980, 281.
4 For the various accounts, see Locke 1973, 39ff., and 1980, 281ff.; Owens 1989, 148ff.
5 Slusser 1982, 371, pl. 594; Locke 1980, 327.
6 Roerich 1959, 54–55.
7 Vajracarya, Dhanavajra, and Malla 1985, 31, 126, also 129–30, 145.
8 Sørensen 1994, 194 and n551.
9 Sørensen 1994, 194, and see 194n552 for all the versions of the name of the god in the Tibetan texts.
10 Alsop 1990, 58–59. See also Sørensen 1994, 193–95.
11 Vitali 1990, 71nn27, 28.
12 Vitali 1990, 71–72.

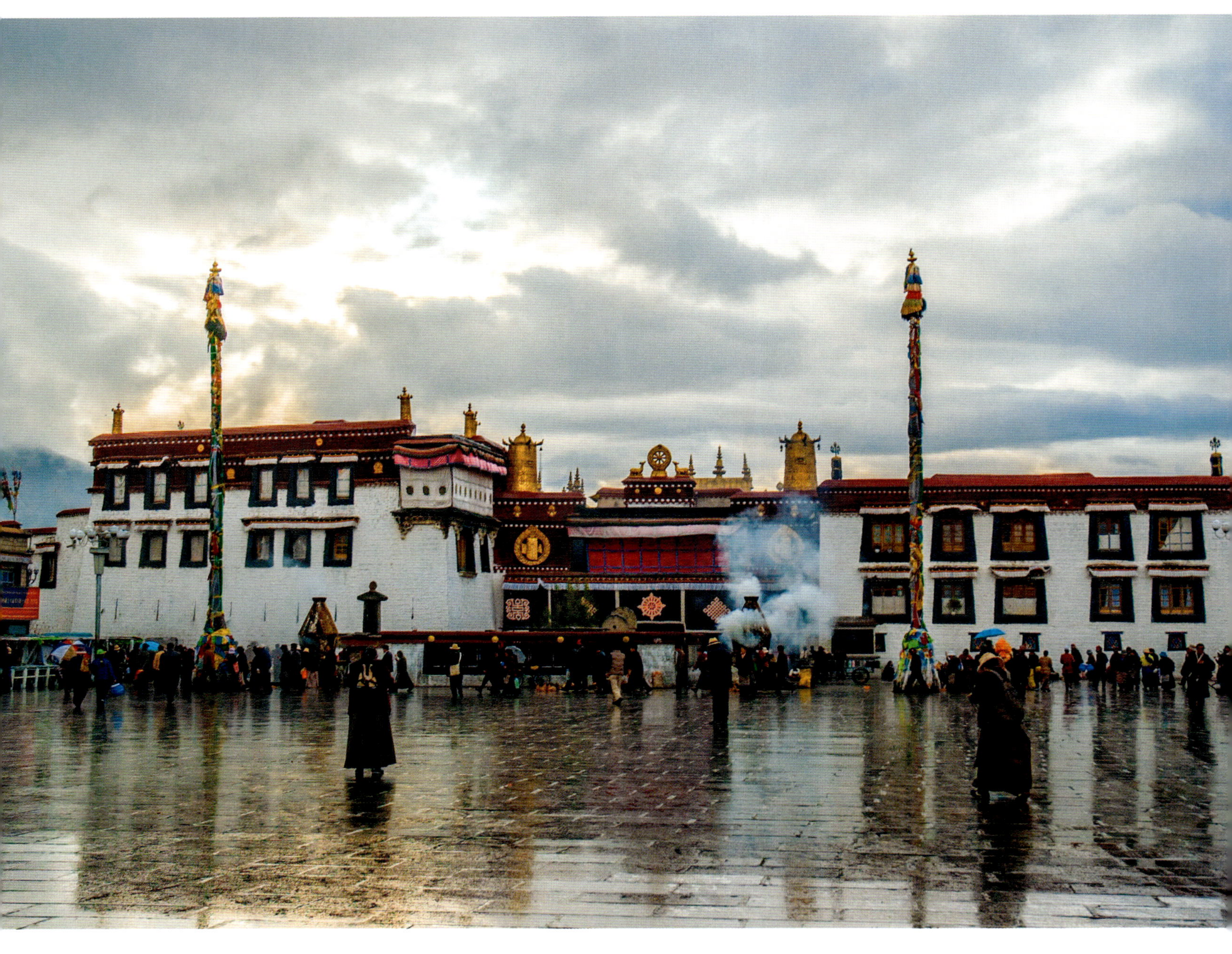

Jokhang Temple in 2005; Lhasa, U region, central Tibet (TAR, China); photograph by Meiqianbao

Nº 7

Jokhang Temple, Lhasa

Lhasa, U region, central Tibet (present-day TAR, China), ca. 620–640

Tibet's Most Sacred Temple

AMY HELLER

THE JOKHANG is undoubtedly the most revered temple in Lhasa, even in all of Tibet. Its role is so crucial that the urban development of Lhasa has centered around the Jokhang for over a millennium. Today the Jokhang is an extensive complex of temple buildings with courtyards, monks' quarters, offices, and kitchens. It has been constructed in several stages since Lhasa became the Tibetan capital during the seventh century after Emperor Songtsen Gampo (ca. 605–649), through numerous military campaigns to unify Tibet and expand Tibetan territory, managed the feat of confederating tribes.

Construction Phases of the Jokhang

Although shrouded in entangled myths and traditions, the history of the successive construction phases of the Jokhang may be clarified by a comparison with the architecture of Trandruk, Thundering Falcon, Tibet's earliest temple in the Yarlung Valley; Ramoche in Lhasa; and the Katsel temple just north of Lhasa. What is striking in these three temples attributed to the imperial period is the tall trapezoid structure at the center: the principal chapel with a roof twenty to twenty-three feet (six to seven meters) high. The inclined walls of the sides of the trapezoid afford protection in the earthquake-prone zone of the Himalayas, for such walls are broader and heavier at the base. Each trapezoid structure is surrounded by a narrow corridor for circumambulation (*kora*).

For the central image enshrined in the Jokhang, see Jowo Shakyamuni, no. 8.

The construction of this central structure destined to become the Jowo chapel, with the procession corridor forming the two adjacent chapels, initially extended eastward and upward to another floor, doubling it in volume.[1] Then, surrounding this inner square, the *nangkor*, or inner procession corridor, was added between the tenth and thirteenth centuries. During the thirteenth to fourteenth centuries, the inner courtyard was converted into an assembly hall, a third floor was added, and three of the four gilded copper roofs were constructed. In the seventeenth and eighteenth centuries, the Jokhang was completed with two more outer courtyards, four new entrances, a new main entrance porch, and an outdoor assembly square.[2]

Political and Religious History

Reflecting on these phases, it is apparent that the Jokhang evolved toward the architecture of a *vihara*, a square Indian temple with a cloistered courtyard, fifty-nine by fifty-nine feet (eighteen by eighteen meters), surrounded by small chapels or monks' cells.[3] Precisely when this occurred is not certain. Was this during the period of the reign of Songtsen Gampo or later generations? No data from Songtsen's lifetime confirms his role as a Buddhist sovereign. Historic records describe his military prowess and political acumen.

On King Narendradeva and his connection to Tibet, see Bunga Dya, no. 6.

In 641, Songtsen effectively installed the Licchavi King Narendradeva (r. 643–679) on the throne of Nepal.[4] Following a coup d'état in Nepal, Narendradeva and his court had taken refuge in Lhasa since about 624. According to later Tibetan tradition, the foundation of the Jokhang is attributed to Songtsen assisted by a Nepalese princess, known in Tibetan as "royal lady" Tritsun, who may have been with Narendradeva's court in Tibet.[5] Although the historical existence of the Nepalese princess has long been questioned, ample evidence supports active exchanges—political, cultural, and commercial—between Tibet and Nepal at this time. The earliest wooden carved lintels of the Jokhang are to be understood as a concrete reflection of Newar artists and artisans working in Tibet during the seventh to eighth century.

For an example of later Nepalese carving, see Torana of the Main Shrine at Yetakha Baha, no. 24.

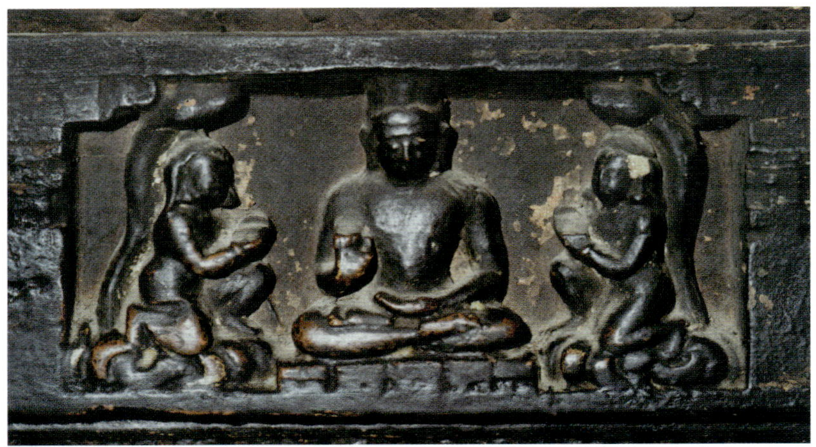

Buddha Sheltered by Nagaraja Muchalinda, with Two Nagini Attendants in Adoration, lintel panel of the doorway of Maitreya chapel, ground floor, adjacent to the Jowo chapel, Jokhang Temple; Lhasa, U region, central Tibet (present-day TAR, China); attributed to Nepalese carvers; 7th–8th century; wood panel; approx. 11¾ × 4¾ in. (30 cm × 12 cm); image after von Schroeder 2001, 417, fig. 133C

Later Tibetan historical tradition magnifies the promotion of Buddhism by Songtsen, the Nepalese princess, and a very young Chinese princess who arrived in Lhasa in 641 and married Songtsen in 646, three years before he died.[6] The early construction of several Buddhist temples in Tibet has been related to geomantic criteria attributed to the Chinese bride, who survived long after Songtsen's death; her funeral is recorded in 683–684 CE.[7]

Analysis and surveys by architectural historians confirm that ancient models of temples such as Tibet's first Buddhist temple, Trandruk, evolved into a *vihara* structure like the Jokhang.[8] The *vihara* was a model in Gupta India (320–600), Cave 2 at Ajanta (late sixth century), and still in use under the Pala dynasty (750–1161). Other early temples like the Ramoche, attributed to the Chinese bride, and Katsel also conform to the early architectural models.[9] Trandruk and Katsel figure among the thirteen temples mapped on an elaborate geomantic schema of concentric zones centered around the Jokhang—even extending as far southeast as present-day Bhutan and east to Kham—all attributed to Songtsen by later tradition.[10]

Luckily, a clear picture emerges by virtue of historic edicts and, above all, the Tibetan inscriptions carved on stone pillars erected at the founding of temples in the eighth and ninth centuries, such as Samye in 779 and Karchung (ca. 800–815), which record the existence of many Buddhist institutions throughout Tibet at the time.[11] Emperor Tri Songdetsen (742–ca. 800) declared Buddhism the official religion of the Tibetan Empire in 781, swearing to preserve Buddhism and actively support Tibetan monks.[12] *The Old Tibetan Chronicle*, probably compiled around 800–840, was the first to describe the flourishing of Buddhism in reference to the reign of Tri Songdetsen: "The incomparable religion of the Buddha had been received and there were sanctuaries in many parts of the land."[13]

See Stupa at Toling Monastery, no. 19.

Civil disorder in the mid-ninth century led to the dissolution of the Tibetan Empire, and the scions of the dynasty fled central Tibet. In about 1000 a revival of Buddhism was promoted at Toling in western Tibet. The flame of Buddhism was rekindled in central Tibet in the mid-eleventh century, when Tibetans coming from both western and eastern Tibet, as well as Indian and Nepalese monks and scholars, resumed teaching.

Zangkar Lotsawa, the Translator of Zanskar, studied Buddhism in Toling. After studies in Kashmir, he traveled toward Lhasa, where in 1076 he initiated a program of major renovation inside the Jokhang resulting in the present layout of the ground floor and second floor.[14] He organized renovations inside the Jowo chapel, including the addition of the twenty-foot-tall (six meters) enthroned Vairochana in clay, called Tubpa Gangchen Tsogyel (Vairochana of the Glacier Lake), accompanied by six male and six female bodhisattvas[15] standing behind him against the walls. The "Jowo," the cast-metal sculpture of Shakyamuni, is enthroned in the middle of the chapel. Mural paintings, such as that of Vasudhara, reflecting the style of Pala India, are also from that time.

For more about the style of Pala India in Tibet, see Tara Who Protects from the Eight Great Fears, no. 27.

Although much damaged, the mural shows compositions with a main central deity, and scrolling floral/vegetal motifs accommodating the seated attendants in the lower register are lively. In a very different palette is a mural of Jambhala as well as Vairochana and attendants on the walls of the Zhelre Lhakhang (literally, the chapel to revere the countenance of the Jowo Shakyamuni sculpture), situated on the upper level of the Jokhang. The bodhisattva seated below Vairochana shows the Pala characteristics of tiered crown with high piled chignon, the three-quarter view of the face with extended eye, the dip of the upper eyelid, and the elongated slender body proportions.

During a period of religious factionalism and great civil disturbance in Lhasa, the temple was damaged by a major fire in 1160. In the mid-thirteenth century, the Jowo sculpture was adorned by a sculpted throne back made by the Nepalese artist Anige (1245–1306) at the request of Shakya Zangpo, then acting abbot of Sakya Monastery.[16] Subsequently, the Pakmodrupa, ruling from Nedong, continued fervent support of the Jokhang in the fourteenth century. During their reign, the rulers of the Yatse Kingdom in western Nepal commissioned gilt-copper roofs over two portions of the Jokhang, undoubtedly the work of Nepalese artisans.

For more about Anige, see White Stupa, no. 40.

For more on the Yatse Kingdom, see Queen Dipamala as the Goddess Prajnaparamita, no. 49.

Plan of the Jokhang Temple, Lhasa, U region, central Tibet (present-day TAR, China); image after Larsen and Sinding-Larsen 2001, 114

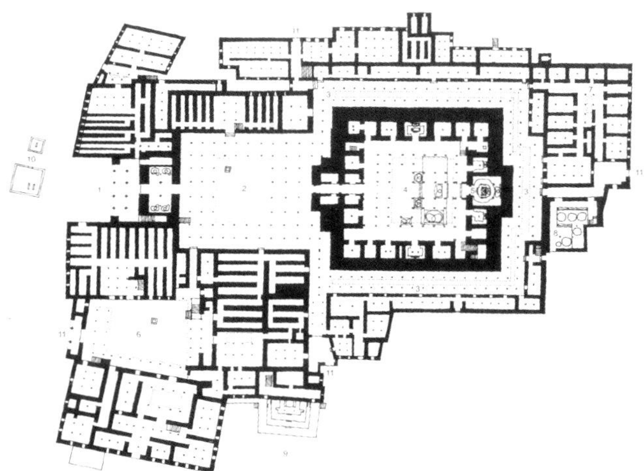

Although Lhasa lost its status as the capital after Zhang Rinpoche's demise, it regained prominence with the establishment of the Geluk tradition by Tsongkhapa (1357–1419) and the founding of the three major monasteries, Ganden, Sera, and Drepung, all of which supported the Jokhang. The next phase of renovation in the Jokhang was led by the Fifth Dalai Lama (1617–1682), whose government attracted many cosmopolitan visitors and instituted major annual ritual celebrations in Lhasa. The wealth of the Geluk government during the Fifth Dalai Lama's reign and the great influx of pilgrims to the Jokhang brought donations of sculptures as well as renovations, notably the refurbishment of the Jowo's throne by Newar artisans. The following Dalai Lamas and the great lay-ruler Polhane (1689–1747) all made donations of special sculptures and maintained the Jokhang throughout the period of the eighteenth and nineteenth centuries.

See Photograph of the Thirteenth Dalai Lama, no. 98.

See Potala Palace, no. 71.

The early twentieth century witnessed the arrival of the British Younghusband expedition in 1904 and Chinese armed forces led by Zhao Erfeng (1845–1911). During the battles, artillery damaged the Jokhang's gilded copper roofs, but with the expulsion of the troops, the Thirteenth Dalai Lama (1876–1933) rapidly restored the temple to its former splendor as pilgrims once more thronged the site. The Reting Regent and the Fourteenth Dalai Lama (b. 1935) likewise contributed to the glory of the Jokhang. Subsequently, the upper apartments were renovated and a new gilded copper roof fabricated. The Cultural Revolution (1966–1976) brought much destruction, notably due to extensive fires.[17] Sweeping renovations were made before Tibet opened to foreign tourists in about 1980, bringing the monument to world attention. In 2000 the Jokhang was nominated to the UNESCO World Heritage List of Monuments as part of the Potala Palace. On February 17, 2018, as Lhasa started Losar celebrations, a giant fire that broke out in the upper story of the Jokhang imperiled the Jowo Shakyamuni. In spring 2018, the Jokhang reopened to pilgrims and devotees, and like a phoenix, the Jowo Rinpoche emerged in full glory, as if unscathed by the flames.

Further Reading

Dorje, Gyurme, Tashi Tsering, Heather Stoddard, and André Alexander. 2010. *Jokhang: Tibet's Most Sacred Buddhist Temple.* London: Hans-Jörg Mayer.

von Schroeder, Ulrich. 2001b. "Nepal: Licchavi Period; Wood Carvings of the Jokhang of Lhasa." In *Buddhist Sculpture in Tibet*, 1:407–31. Hong Kong: Visible Dharma Publications.

Notes

1 Sørensen and Hazod, with Gyalbo 2005, 17; Larsen and Sinding-Larsen 2001, 115.
2 Larsen and Sinding-Larsen 2001, 116.
3 Larsen and Sinding-Larsen 2001, 116–17.
4 Dotson 2009, 82, translates the record of 641–642 CE in *The Old Tibetan Annals.*
5 Lo Bue 2011a, 27–28.
6 Dotson 2009, 82.
7 Dotson 2009, 94, and for the Table of royal events, 240.
8 Alexander 2008, Site 8 Khra 'brug.
9 Sørensen and Hazod with Gyalbo 2005, 17; A. Heller 2008.
10 Aris 1979, 12–31; Gyatso 1987, 37 passim.
11 H. Richardson 1985, 27 passim.
12 Halkias 2017, 131.
13 Bacot and Toussaint 1940, 153.
14 Dorje 2010, 11.
15 Dorje 2010, translating Shakabpa, 73.
16 Lo Bue 2011a, 40 and n87.
17 Dorje 2010, 21–24.

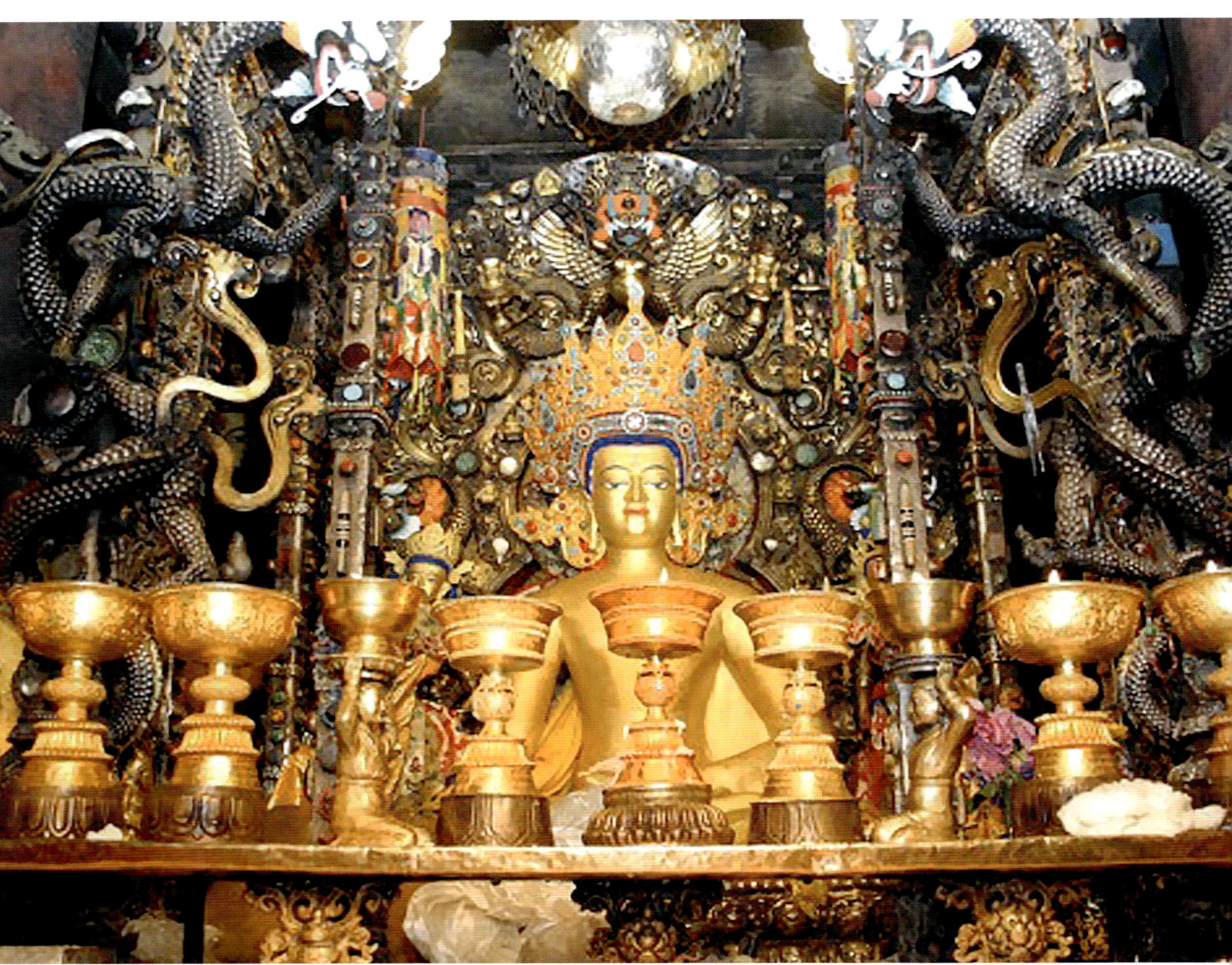

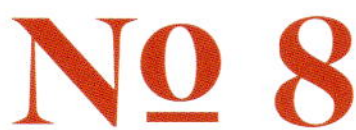

Jowo Shakyamuni of the Rasa Trulnang Tsuklakhang (Jokhang Temple)

Northern India or Tibet, 500 BCE? or 11th century CE

The Most Famous Religious Object in Tibet

CAMERON DAVID WARNER

See Jokhang Temple, no. 7.

It could be said that the Jowo Shakyamuni of the Rasa Trulnang Tsuklakhang, or Jokhang Temple, is the most famous and least understood object in this book. Despite its long history and ubiquity throughout Tibetan culture, as well as current popularity, many misperceptions of it abound, fundamental questions are unanswerable, and more often than not, it serves as a mirror of the investigator more than the source of new knowledge.

The Jowo

In Tibetan, the term *jowo* can mean "older brother" or "Lord" (in both the secular and religious senses), but most often, the term refers to the Jowo Shakyamuni of the Rasa Trulnang Tsuklakhang: that Jowo is Buddha Shakyamuni depicted in his celestial form, dressed in royal garments, not the wandering mendicant we are more used to seeing.[1]

However, there have been many Jowos in Tibetan history. Some were men. Some were Buddhist statues. Of the Buddhist statues, some have little to no connection with the one in the Rasa Trulnang Tsuklakhang. Others have their own features and histories, but they are connected to this Jowo through Tibetan mythological texts of the eleventh through thirteenth centuries CE that explain each statue's purpose for existence and genealogy.[2]

For a Jowo in Mongolia, see Erdeni Juu Monastery, no. 65.

Many Jowos are copies made of this Jowo, whether they be the same or different size, whether they be in Tibet or in another country, whether they are statues or photographs. For example, many ancient copies of the Jowo can be found hundreds of miles from Lhasa in parts of eastern Tibet, such as at the Sakya monastery called Ba Lhagang in the Ganzi Tibetan Autonomous Prefecture, Sichuan Province. Copies can be found in other countries, such as at Tharig Monastery in Kathmandu, Nepal, or the Drigung Meditation Center in Arlington, Massachusetts, in the United States.

Photographs of the present Jowo are ubiquitous across the Tibetan Plateau on home shrines, in restaurants, and over the cash registers in businesses. A unique and notable photograph can be found in the alcove next to the Dalai Lama's throne in the Tekchen Choling Tsuklakhang, the temple that serves as a national cathedral for exiled Tibetans in McLeod Ganj, Dharamsala, Himachal Pradesh, India. Taken in the early 1950s by a team of Czech photographers, Vladimír Sís and Josef Vanis, it is the last known photograph of the Jowo made before the Dalai Lama fled into exile in 1959. In the Sís and Vanis photograph, the Jowo's face is very thick and uneven, caked over with centuries of gold paint (*drangser*), which was allegedly removed in the 1960s by Red Guards during the Cultural Revolution.[3]

In European languages, when one refers to "the Jowo," it designates the Jowo Shakyamuni, the subject of this essay. In Tibetan, he would most often be referred to as "Jowo Rinpoche," meaning "the Precious Lord," but also the Jowo Shakyamuni, the Jowo Chomdende, even "the elder brother," or simply "the Lhasa Jowo," in order to distinguish the template from all of its scattered copies. Never using the many Tibetan words for statue, Tibetans have written and spoken about the Jowo as equivalent to a very holy person, not as an object. Countless miracles have been attributed to the Jowo in Tibetan biographies and autobiographies, mainly in the form of dreams or visions of him speaking, shining light rays, or moving. Some of these miracles serve as narratives to explain points of Buddhist doctrine, such as the power of faith; others have changed the course of Tibetan history, such as the Jowo explaining to the Fifth Dalai Lama (1617–1682) that he was a reincarnation of the Tibetan emperor Songtsen Gampo (ca. 605–649).

Jowo Shakyamuni; northern India or Tibet, 500 BCE? or 11th century CE; about life-size; Rasa Trulnang Tsuklakhang (Jokhang Temple), Lhasa; photograph by Sarah Schorr

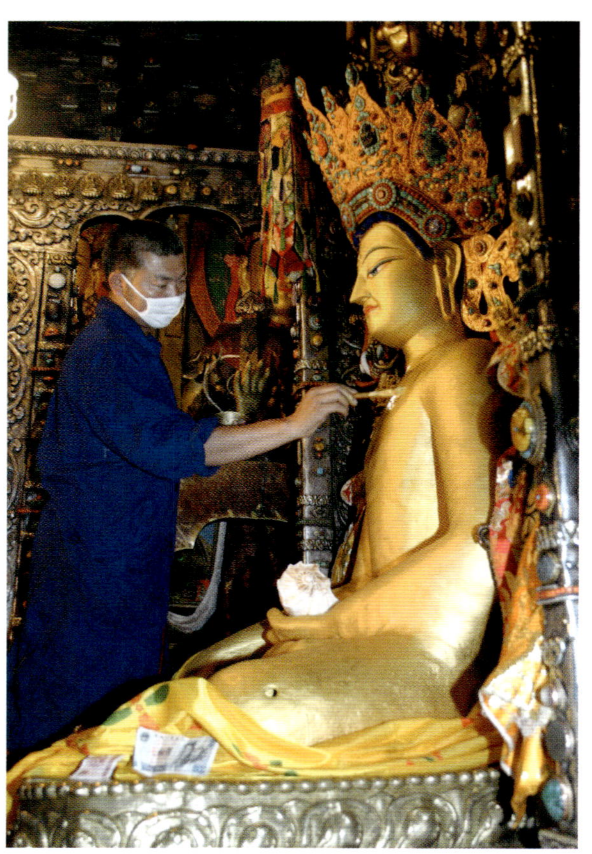

The caretaker (*konnyer*) applying gold paint (*drangser*) to the Jowo Shakyamuni; Rasa Trulnang Tsuklakhang; photograph by Sarah Schorr

But what or who is the Jowo? According to biographies of the Jowo that emerged in Tibetan literature around the eleventh through thirteenth centuries CE, he is a portrait-from-life of the historical Buddha Shakyamuni executed by Vishvakarma, the divine craftsman of Indian cosmology, during the Buddha's lifetime (ca. 500 BCE) and at the Buddha's command, and yet not a portrait, as the size of the Jowo comes from the memory of what Siddhartha Gautama (the man who became the Buddha) looked like at age twelve according to the memory of his nursemaid.[4] According to those biographies, the historical Buddha Shakyamuni intended for a proxy (*kutsab*) with his likeness and powers to reside in Tibet in his stead, in order to subdue Tibetans and help Avalokiteshvara guide them on the Buddhist path.[5] In that sense, elements of the Jowo Shakyamuni's biography resemble the biographies of other supposed "first" images of the Buddha found in nearly every Buddhist country in Asia, such as Xuanzang's Uddiyana Buddha, the Seiryoji Shaka in Japan, or the Emerald Buddha of Thailand.

The Jowo as Agent of Change: The Perspective of Tibetan Hierarchs

A judicious reading of Tibetan historiography would conclude that the mythopoetic biography of the Jowo and the physical object arrived in Tibet separately. That is, we know much more about what Tibetans have written regarding the Jowo Rinpoche than we know about the statue itself. While the physical object might have arrived about 641, it was not called "the Jowo" or treated as a portrait of the Buddha until at least the eleventh century CE.[6]

Perhaps the earliest signs of what later came to be known as the Jowo appear in *The Testament of Ba*, which records that a Chinese "princess," Wencheng Gongzhu (d. 680), brought a "golden god" to Lhasa in 641 as part of her dowry for her marriage to Songtsen Gampo.[7] Not only is that golden god not called "the Jowo," but also the descriptions of its physical form and miraculous activities do not accord with the later Jowo Shakyamuni. For example, the present Jowo is slightly larger than life-size, but *The Testament of Ba* states that Wencheng Gongzhu's retinue brought "the golden god" from China "in the lap of one horseman." And in another passage, the death of an anti-Buddhist government official is attributed to "the Chinese God" being angry.[8] Centuries later, across a range of texts, Tibetan religious historiographers presented a fully formed biography of the Jowo Shakyamuni identified with that same dowry image from Wencheng Gongzhu.[9] The complex of beliefs and practices around the Jowo described in those texts, such as making offerings, painting the face with gold, and associating him with Avalokiteshvara and the rulers of Tibet, later grew as nearly all prominent religious leaders in Tibet paid homage to the Jowo and reconceptualized their own position in Tibetan society vis-à-vis visionary experiences they reported to have received from him.

Early Kadampa and Kagyupa hierarchs wrote of the Jowo's importance to Lhasa, as well as his connection to the former Tibetan Empire (ca. 608–866) and the conversion of Tibet to Buddhism. One of them, Zangkar Lotsawa Pakpa Sherab Pel, in the late eleventh century renovated the Rasa Trulnang Temple, placing the Jowo in the Central Chapel, called the Jokhang (literally, house of the Jowo). His disciples and their later followers continued to add to the temple and received visions from the Jowo while simultaneously tightening their grip on Lhasa and the governance of central Tibet. The pattern of lamas pairing veneration of the Jowo with political rule of Tibet continued for centuries. For example, the founder of the Gelukpa tradition, Tsongkhapa (1357–1419), placed a crown on the head of the Jowo in 1409 and instituted the annual celebration of the Great Prayer Festival. Placing a crown on the Jowo's head controversially changed the Jowo's iconography, which later generations deemed an extreme act of sectarianism.[10] And later, when the Fifth Dalai Lama promulgated his new Ganden Podrang government, he recorded in his autobiography a series of visions he received from the Jowo confirming him as the latest birth in a line of embodiments of Avalokiteshvara that stretched back to Songtsen Gampo.

See Crowned Buddha, no. 16.

See Bodhisattva Avalokiteshvara and the Buddha's Footprints, no. 33; Potala Palace, no. 71.

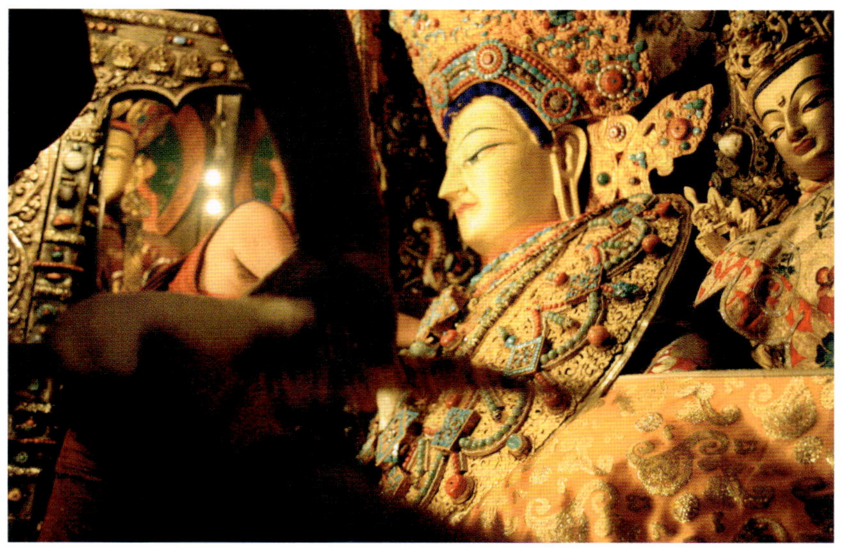

Jowo Shakyamuni being dressed in a monk's patched robe (*sanghati/namjar*); Rasa Trulnang Tsuklakhang; photograph by Sarah Schorr

The Jowo's Present Popularity and Significance

Each time someone has paid homage to the Jowo, it has reinforced him as the imprimatur of authenticity bar none. Even when the Communist Party of China officially selected Gyaincain Norbu to be the Panchen Lama in 1995, lamas performed the Golden Urn ceremony in front of the Jowo to confer legitimacy on the proceedings.[11] From the perspective of the Communist Party, the Jowo symbolically and indexically represents China's long benevolent relationship toward Tibet beginning with Wencheng Gongzhu and continuing today.[12] Therefore, because of its immense significance for the narrative Communist authorities desire to project, independent material analysis of the Jowo is impossible.

The Materiality of the Jowo

Some of the most compelling questions Tibetans have asked about the Jowo are those regarding the nature of materiality itself, the role it ought to play in Buddhist practice, and the part it has played in Tibetan politics and governance. For example, as the Buddha's *portrait* made-from-life and his *proxy*, what is the relationship between his appearance and his powers? If one were to change the Jowo's appearance, would that affect his powers? If he is a portrait-from-life, should not all paintings and statues of Buddha Shakyamuni in Tibet look like the Jowo, that is, share his iconometric measurements? Can average people even see the "real" Jowo, or does one have to be an advanced practitioner of tantric Buddhism? The only information we know for certain about the physical object currently in the Rasa Trulnang Tsuklakhang is that frequently performed rituals of both veneration and physical restoration, such as the application of gold paint and the regular changing of the crown, ornaments, and clothing, have morphed the outer appearance of the Jowo. The current popularity of these rituals among increasingly wealthy pilgrims who want to generate religious merit (*sonam*) means the Jowo's appearance is still shifting in front of our eyes. Though historical sources preserve testimony to multiple attacks on the site every few centuries, as well as periodic restorations of the temple, there is no way to determine whether the present Jowo is the one Wencheng brought with her, a later replacement, or was newly fabricated after the end of the Cultural Revolution. However, we can say for certain that based on his presence in pop culture and the number of visits to his temple, the Jowo's popularity has not diminished.

Further Reading

Warner, Cameron David. 2008. "The Precious Lord: The History and Practice of the Cult of the Jowo Śākyamuni in Lhasa, Tibet." PhD diss., Harvard University.

Notes

1 Zhang Yisun 1993, 878.
2 Sørensen 1994.
3 A comparison of the changes to the Jowo's face and analysis of the placement of the Sís and Vanis photograph of the Jowo can be found in Warner 2011a.
4 Warner 2008.
5 Warner 2011b.
6 Warner 2008, 146.
7 Multiple editions of this text exist. For the most recent translation, see Gonkatsang and Willis 2021.
8 Warner 2008, 82–84.
9 Warner 2008, 170–210.
10 Warner 2011b.
11 Walsh 2020.
12 Warner 2011c.

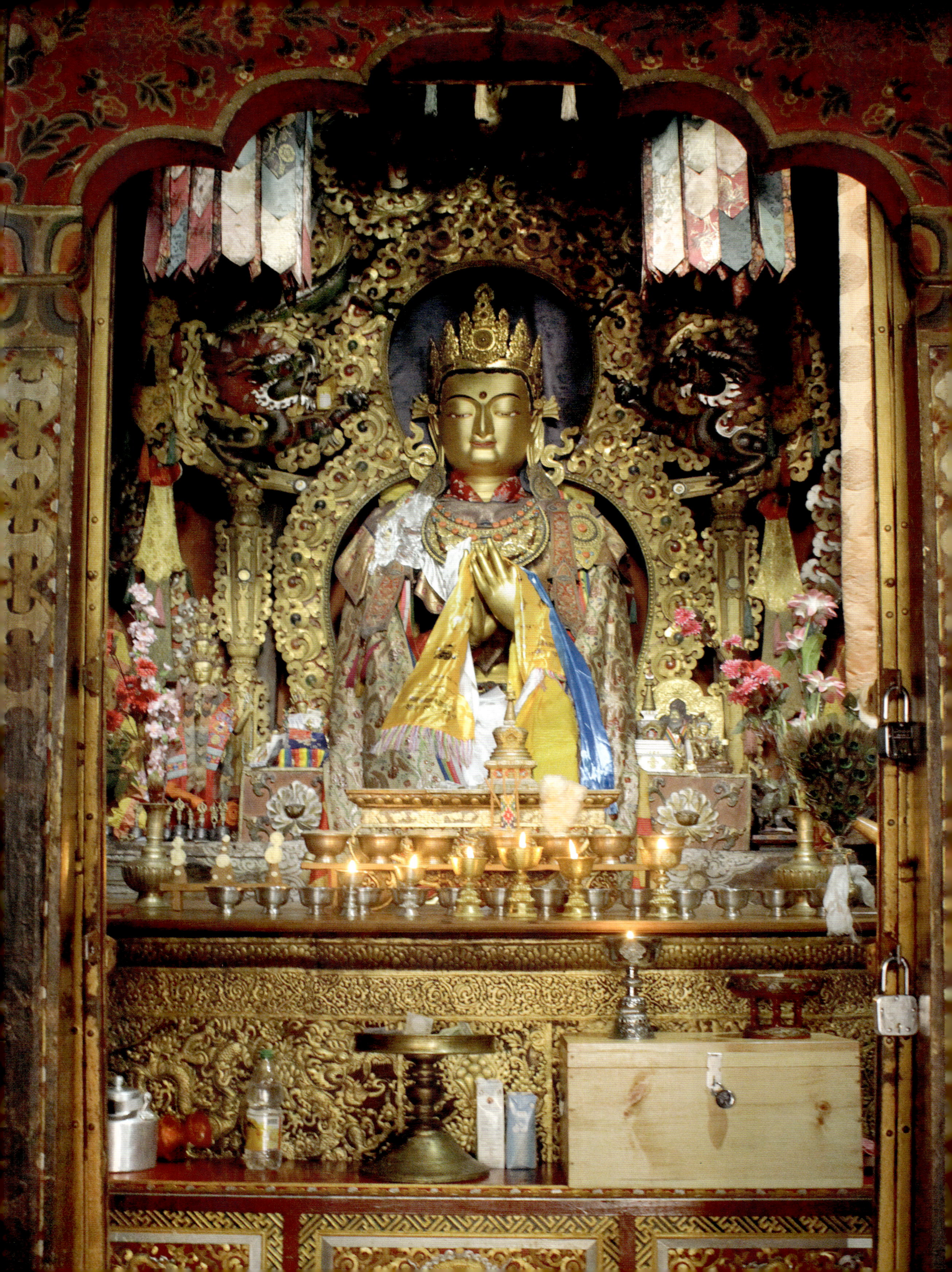

Nº 9

Maitreya Statue at Jampa Lhakhang, Bhutan

Jampa Lhakhang, Chokhor, Bhutan, ca. 7th century

The Earliest Grand Buddhist Clay Sculpture in Bhutan and the Bhutanese Tradition of Clay Sculpting

KARMA PHUNTSHO, ARIANA MAKI, AND ELENA PAKHOUTOVA

For a painted image of Maitreya in Tibet, see Maitreya and Manjushri Mural at Dratang, no. 26; for a standing Maitreya created in Mongolia, see Maitreya, no. 75.

The main image of Maitreya, the buddha of the future, in Jampa Temple in Bumthang is probably the earliest grand Buddhist clay sculpture made in Bhutan. The temple, or *lhakhang*, is named after this statue of Maitreya, who is known as Jampa in Tibetan, and is one of the thirteen temples said to have been built by Songtsen Gampo (ca. 605–649), the Tibetan king of the Yarlung dynasty. The temples were believed to have been built to subdue a supine demoness who embodies the Himalayan landscape. A list of the temples describes Jampa Lhakhang as pinning down the left knee of the supine demoness, while Kyerchu Lhakhang, a second of these early temples located in Bhutan, pins down the demoness's left foot. The main images of both temples, Maitreya in Jampa Lhakhang and Buddha Shakyamuni in Kyerchu Lhakhang, are flanked by sculpted sets of the Eight Great Bodhisattvas, a feature common to early temples throughout the Himalayas.[1]

There are no extant records to identify who made the statues or confirm their seventh-century date, but the practice of working with clay was likely thriving in many parts of Bhutan by the time Songtsen Gampo commissioned these statues. People in this region commonly used its rich deposits of clay minerals for making fireplaces and pottery. Clay was also used for construction as a binder in stone masonry and in building rammed mud walls, as well as for fashioning cultural decorative motifs, figures that adorn houses, and clay masks. The advent of clay as a medium for religious sculpture may not have begun until the construction of Buddhist monuments, including the Maitreya and Shakyamuni statues. A century later, the Tibetan king Tri Songdetsen (742–ca. 800) is said to have built many temples, including the Chokhor Lhakhang.[2] Its Vairochana sculpture is close in style to the Maitreya in Jampa Lhakhang.

For other Vairochana images, see Imperial Carvings of Vairochana, no. 13; The All-Knowing Buddha Vairochana Visualization Album, no. 87.

Buddhist cultural activity in Bhutan seems to have waned concurrently with the decline of the Tibetan Empire around the middle of the ninth century, but in the twelfth to fifteenth centuries Buddhist traditions reemerged and expanded. During this time, many Bhutanese and Tibetan Buddhist masters traveled to and within Bhutan, actively cultivated patrons, and founded temples throughout the region. These establishments often included clay statues as significant objects in their shrines, as seen with the central buddha figure in the Samarzingkha Lhakhang in Thimphu and Khewang Lhakhang in Phobjikha. The earliest datable clay works of this period are the clay sculptures in Tamshing Lhakhang; texts identify the dates of their creation as 1502 and 1503, when the temple founder hired artists from central Tibet.[3]

See Tamshing Temple, no. 61.

Formation of the Tradition

The art of clay sculpture gained new importance after the unification of Bhutan in the middle of the seventeenth century by Zhabdrung Ngawang Namgyel (1594–1651), who was considered to be both the incarnation of Tsangpa Gyare (1161–1211), the founder of the Drukpa Kagyu tradition of Tibetan Buddhism and a scion of the Ralung monastic establishment, which Tsangpa Gyare founded.[4] Embroiled in a conflict with the Tsangpa ruler of Tibet, Zhabdrung left his vibrant religious center of Ralung in 1616 and went into exile, building his base for Drukpa faith and culture in the western valleys of Bhutan. Zhabdrung learned the art of sculpting through his teachers, among them Lhawang Lodro and Taktsepa Pekar Wangpo, whom he invited to join him in his new base. He also founded workshops where monastics were taught clay and metal sculpture production alongside other arts. When

Maitreya, Buddha of the Future; Jampa Lhakhang, Bumthang, Bhutan; ca. 7th century, with later overpainting and adornments; painted clay; height including lotus seat 10 ft. 10 in. (3.3 m); photograph courtesy Bhutan Cultural Library, Shejun, University of Virginia, and Arcadia Fund

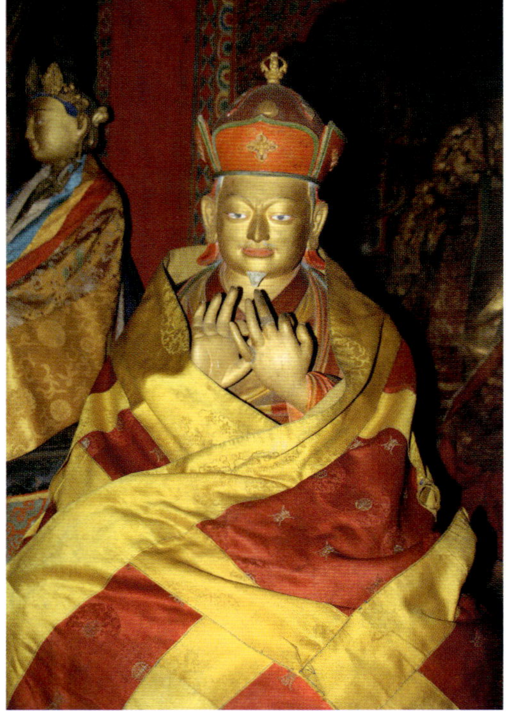

Sculpted Image of Nyephu (Hephu) Trulku Sangag Gyeltsen (ca. 1600–1661); Neyphu Temple; Paro, Bhutan; date unknown; painted clay, height approx. 30 in. (76 cm); photograph by Shejun

Zhabdrung took control of a preexisting fortress in Thimphu in 1641, he commissioned a sculptor named A'u Drung to help enlarge it and prepare its inner contents;[5] the new building was named Tashicho Dzong, and it became the heart of Bhutanese religious and secular administration.

After the founder's passing, the Fourth Druk Desi Tenzin Rabgye (1638–1696) further systematized the thirteen traditional arts and crafts (*zorik chuksum*), integrating some of the arts into the state monastic curriculum. A trained artist himself, Tenzin Rabgye was also a major patron of the arts and oversaw the renovation and establishment of many key historical sites. He supervised commissions of both local and regional artists to create clay shrine images. To craft images for the shrines at Punakha Dzong, Seula Gonpa, and Bondey Lhakhang, the master sculptor Trulku Zing (d. ca. 1674) was invited to Bhutan from Tibet, where he had received commissions from the Tenth Karmapa Choying Dorje (1604–1674). Considered to be an artist emanation of Maitreya, Trulku Zing was said to create sculptures so efficacious as not to need consecration. Although his clay works survive, including the sculptures attributed to him at Tango Monastery, historians are divided on whether he passed down his artistic tradition to any students.

For objects related to the Tenth Karmapa, see Arhats Viewing a Painting of Birds by the Tenth Karmapa, no. 72.

Yet the names of many important Bhutanese sculptors of the past survive.[6] Chumey Choje, Druk Chophel, Tenzin Gyeltsen, Ngawang Sherab, and Ngawang Phuntsho are all said to have propagated the art of clay sculpture, especially by creating Buddhist statues under state patronage in the eighteenth and nineteenth centuries. Bhutan's foremost clay artist, Hephu Trulku Sangag Gyeltsen (ca. 1600–1661), established clay sculpture as a distinct skill of the Hephu religious community in Paro.

Despite a catastrophic fire that destroyed Hephu Monastery in the 1860s, Bhutanese clay sculpture continued to thrive through the Hephu lineage and the surrounding community. In the twentieth century, two Hephu artists, Damchoe and Pelden, were commissioned as the primary sculptors for an elaborate Buddhist *tshokshing*, a three-dimensional depiction of an assembly of masters and deities as objects of refuge, now housed in the National Museum at Paro.[7] The Third King of Bhutan instructed Damchoe (1921–1995) and Pelden to set up a sculpture academy in Tashigang in 1967. This academy elevated the Bhutanese art of clay sculpture to a new level and produced many great contemporary sculptors, including Omtong (1945–2001), Chagdor Tshering, Karma, and others. In 1969, the academy moved to Thimphu, where it continues to flourish as a center for training young Bhutanese clay sculptors, many of whom have exercised their talents in other parts of the world, including Pelden's son, Nyima Dorji. Students also learn clay sculpting at the Trashiyangtse Institute of Zorig Chusum, founded in 1997, and on a more limited basis at the privately run Choki Traditional Arts School in Thimphu, established in 1999.

For images of the Buddha, see Buddha on the Cosmic Mountain, no. 10; Standing Buddha Shakyamuni Donated by Lundeva, no. 59; Crowned Buddha, no. 16; Central Shrine Image of Kwa Baha, no. 22; Jowo Shakyamuni, no. 8.

Iconographic Programs

Reflecting the religious and cultural trends, the subjects of clay sculptural works in Bhutan have also gone through significant changes. While early clay imagery focused on a buddha figure surrounded by eight bodhisattvas, by the first half of the second millennium clay compositions increasingly portrayed Guru Padmasambhava with two consorts, the Eight Manifestations of Padmasambhava, and religious masters. The twentieth century also witnessed a significant increase in the construction of gigantic clay figures of Padmasambhava, intricate images of tantric deities, and lineage masters. Today, it is quite common to find new shrines that house a central figure of Buddha Shakyamuni flanked by Padmasambhava and Zhabdrung Ngawang Namgyel.

For an example of Padmasambhava and His Manifestations in stone, see no. 43. For a mask of one of Padmasambhava's manifestations, see Ritual Dance Mask of Guru Dorje Drolo, no. 94.

For a monumental Padmasambhava sculpture, see Monumental Statue of Guru Rinpoche, no. 104.

The Process of Making Clay Sculptures

For another kind of clay image, see Molded Clay Image (*Tsatsa*) of Amoghapasha, no. 28.

For more on merit, see Prayer Wheel, no. 79.

Unfired clay was formerly the most common material for sculpture in Himalayan cultural areas.[8] In the traditional Bhutanese method, artists make sculptures from clay mixed with paper usually made from daphne plant and water. To increase the potency, longevity, and auspiciousness of the image, sometimes they add medicinal and sacred substances, such as saffron and camphor, to the mix. Some patrons also include precious stones such as coral, turquoise, and pearls, which are powdered and added to the clay in order to generate greater merit from the creation of the statue. Paper provides fiber that holds the unfired clay together. Sculptors distinguish various types of clay depending on its qualities, usually referred to as basic, medium, and high-quality clay. Artists use coarser clay for creating a basic form of the statue and finer clay for the thin outer layer to articulate more refined shapes and surface details.

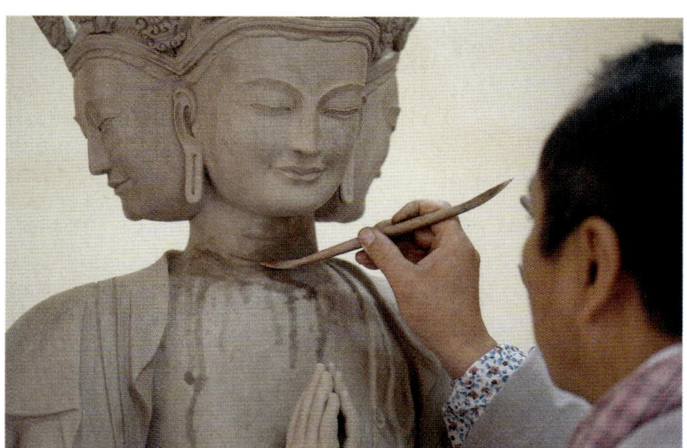

Clay sculptor at work in the Department of Culture, Thimphu, Bhutan; photograph courtesy Loden Foundation

They gradually build a hollow inner form of a statue with coiled clay strips, shaped and thinned by hand. Each strip is air-dried, and a new coil is built up until the basic figure, without arms and a head, is complete. Sometimes, a lotus base is made separately, especially if the sculpture is large. Artists use special wooden tools to produce surface details, polishing the fine clay until it looks like a burnished surface.

Then the artists create arms, inserting a metal wire like an arm bone into a clay shape, and mold fingers by the same method, shaping them using their wooden tools, and attach the arms to the figure. If the sculpture is large, they traditionally use a wooden armature to secure the arms to the sculpture.

Employing iconometric proportions, similar to the proportions applied in thangka painting, the artists shape the figure's head separately. The process for modeling the head is the same as for the basic figure. The sculptors first shape the form of the face, then work on the finer surface details and polish it with tools. They mold the rest of the head and attach it to the body of the sculpture, smoothing the seam to eliminate any unevenness. The artists make ornaments such as crowns, armlets, bracelets, necklaces, and lotus petals for the throne base separately, often using beeswax molds to ensure uniformity, and then attach them to the statue.

For more about consecration, see the Svayambhu Chaitya of Kathmandu, no. 4; Amulet Box (*Gau*) with Its Contents, no. 107; Prayer Wheel, no. 79.

Finally, a painter completes the sculpture, with the face and the eyes as the last steps in the painting process. The statue's hollow cavity is filled with consecrated materials (*zung*). This signifies the activation of the image, usually accompanied by a consecration ritual.

All clay statues follow specific iconographic models and are traditionally decorated and painted. Large statues are raised on a base formed from clay bricks, and a wooden armature secures them to the wall. Important large sculptures are usually dressed in brocade garments and serve as a temple's central image and the focus of ritual and worship activities.

Further Reading

Bartholomew, Terese Tse, and John Johnston, eds. 2008. *The Dragon's Gift: The Sacred Arts of Bhutan*. Exhibition catalog. Honolulu and Chicago: Honolulu Academy of Arts in association with Serindia.

Luczanits, Christian. 2004. *Buddhist Sculpture in Clay: Early Western Himalayan Art, Late 10th to Early 13th Centuries*. Chicago: Serindia.

Phuntsho, Karma. 2013. *The History of Bhutan*. London and Noida: Random House.

Notes

1 Vitali 1990, 50–76.
2 Padma gling pa 2014, 2.
3 Phun tshogs (Phuntsho) 2015, 242–43.
4 For more about Zhabdrung and his political activities, see Phuntsho 2013, 207–54.
5 Mkhan po phun tshogs bkra shis 2003, 99–100.
6 Bstan 'dzin chos rgyal 1759, fol. 115v.
7 Yablonsky 2002.
8 Luczanits 2004, 2–15.

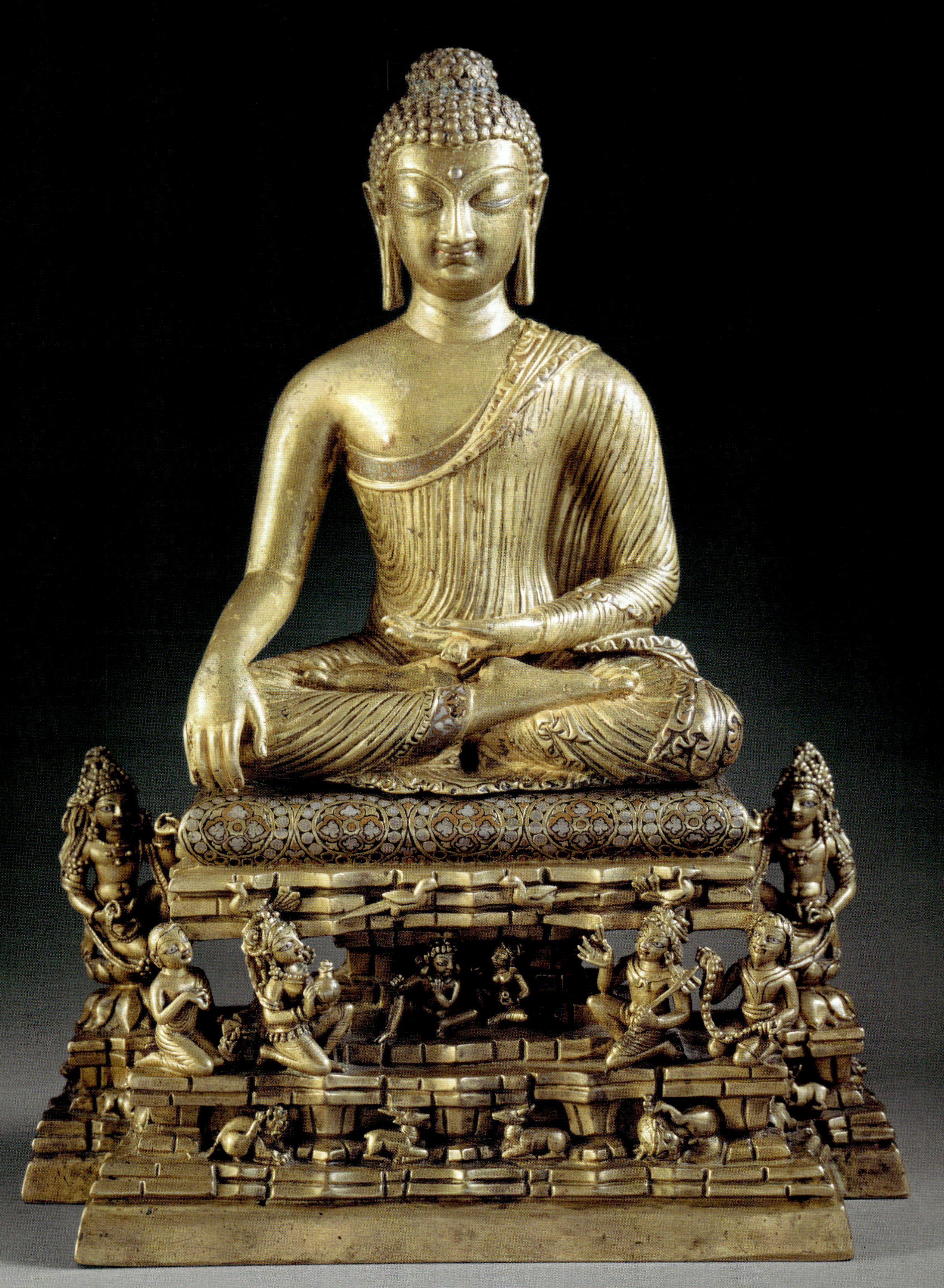

No 10

Buddha on the Cosmic Mountain

Kashmir, India, ca. 720

The Distinct Artistic Tradition of Kashmir and Its Impact in Tibet

CHRISTIAN LUCZANITS

THE DEPICTION OF THE BUDDHA IN THE NORTON SIMON MUSEUM is an extremely fine example of a Kashmir-style bronze. The wider region of Kashmir is well known for the high-quality artworks it produced in the second half of the first millennium. Combining idealized rounded forms with intricate detail, this school of art had a decisive impact on the artistic production of the western Himalayas, as represented in this publication by the temples of Tabo, Alchi, and Toling, as well as portable artworks related to them. Many of the Buddhist sculptures of the Kashmir region were preserved in Tibetan monasteries, where they partially remain.[1]

See Goddess Dharmameghabhumi in the Tabo Main Temple, no. 21; Monumental Manjushri with Mahasiddha-Adorned Robe at Alchi, no. 35; Murals at Toling Dukhang, no. 54.

In this account, the term "Kashmir" signifies an area that goes beyond the Srinagar Valley, whose ruined monuments form the basis for our understanding of the artistic development of the region.[2] Further, among Kashmir-style bronzes, an important subgroup can be distinguished whose inscriptions assign them to the small Buddhist kingdom of the Palola Shahi, centered on the area of Gilgit. As these bronzes, the so-called Gilgit manuscripts, and rock engravings along the river valleys indicate, this kingdom flourished from about 600 CE to about 820 CE, when Tibetan imperial troops arrived in the region.[3] More important, their inscriptions name the rulers in a way that makes it possible to align the associated artworks in their relative succession and allow for the construction of an absolute chronology. The dates provided by these inscriptions refer to the so-called Laukika era in two-digit numbers only, leaving the century attribution to stylistic and paleographic assessment.[4]

See Painted Manuscript Cover, no. 12.

Buddha on the Cosmic Mountain

The Buddha depiction in the Norton Simon Museum closely relates to the latest production of the Palola Shahi Kingdom. It is remarkable for the abundance of extremely fine inlay work and the crowded area around the Buddha's throne, both of which also appear in some Palola Shahi works. To appreciate the work fully, we must imagine an additional magnificent halo framing the main image that once was attached to the sculpture's back. It may have looked like a halo today preserved in a private collection.[5]

In this bronze, the Buddha and his pedestal have been cast separately, with tenons holding the image in place. The Buddha is seated cross-legged, with his right hand in the earth-touching gesture (*bhumisparsha* mudra). As is typical for Kashmir bronzes, his robe appears to cling to the body and falls in parallel folds, the hem expanding in a V shape on the covered shoulder and settling in a wide bow around the proper left thigh. Both the folding of the robe and the Buddha holding one end of the robe in his left hand are inherited from Gandharan depictions of the Buddha.

The pedestal is topped by a finely inlaid cushion that rests on an hourglass-shaped rock throne symbolizing Mount Meru, at the center of the Buddhist conception of the universe. At the sides of the throne, two bodhisattvas on double lotuses kneel with one leg, their inner hands directed palm up toward the Buddha. They may tentatively be identified as Maitreya, the future Buddha, and Avalokiteshvara, based on the flask standing in front of the left lower leg of the former and the jewel held in the left hand of the latter.

Buddha on the Cosmic Mountain; Kashmir; ca. 720; bronze with silver and copper inlay; height 13¼ in. (33.7 cm); The Norton Simon Foundation, Pasadena; F.1972.48.2.S; photograph courtesy The Norton Simon Foundation

Directly underneath the right hand of the Buddha kneels the earth goddess holding a vase with both hands, confirming that the Buddha is here shown at the moment of his awakening. At the same time, the female figure may also be the principal donor of the bronze, with her husband kneeling opposite her. The kneeling monk behind her would then need to be understood as their son, and the bearded

Standing Buddha; Kashmir; late 10th to early 11th century; brass with silver and copper inlay; height overall 38⅝ in. (98.1 cm), base 11⅛ in. (28.2 cm); Cleveland Museum of Art; John L. Severance Fund; 1966.30; CC0 1.0 Universal (CC0 1.0) Public Domain Dedication

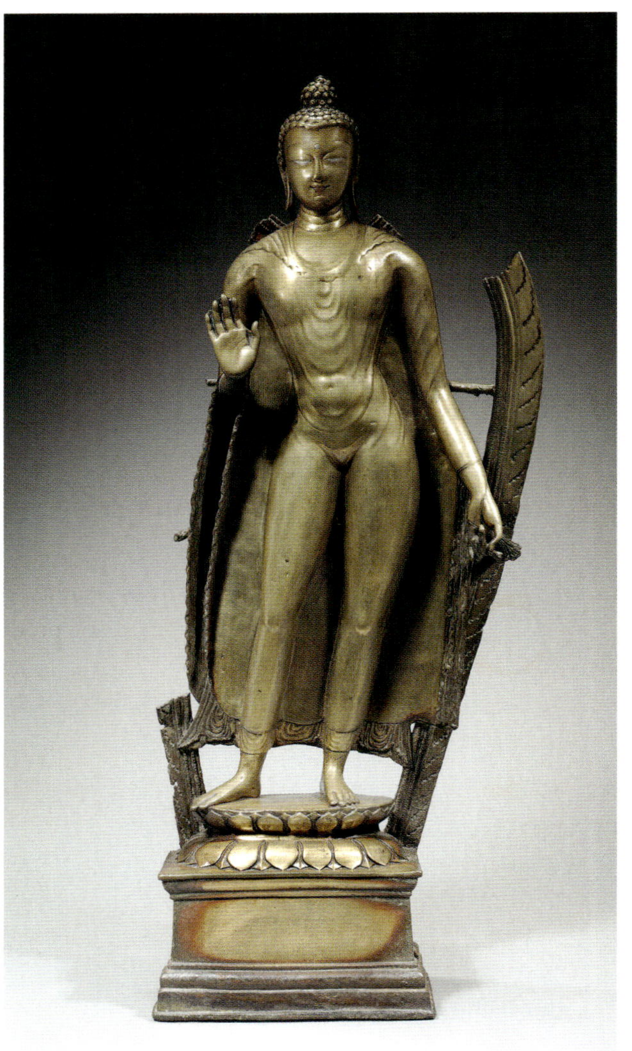

elder man with a garland on the right as the father of one of the couple. Among the attributes held by the principal male figure, a short band forming a loop in the right hand and a staff with three projections in the left are puzzling, but they are shared by the figure engraved in the same position on the comparable halo illustrating the same event. Two musicians celebrating the event by playing a flute (not preserved) and cymbals sit between the donors. Obviously, this is only one potential reading of this group; others have been suggested in the literature.[6] As such, this bronze presents the Buddha's awakening as a cosmic and eternal event, and thus alludes to a higher nature of Buddhahood.

A delightful element often found on Kashmir bronzes are the animals depicted among the rocks. Forming couples, they symbolize auspiciousness and, representing natural enemies side by side—the lions demonstratively cleaning themselves in the presence of deer—they also signal the calming effect of the Buddha's presence and teaching.

In comparison with inscribed bronzes of the Palola Shahi rulers, this piece lacks the specific details of the donors' dress characteristic of the latter. Moreover, analysis of the halo surrounding the etched Buddha points to a Kashmir Valley origin for it. The same comparisons also indicate a date of about 720 for the Norton Simon Buddha and the related halo.[7] Regardless of the precise attribution, that the Norton Simon Buddha's folds fall off center links it closely to the Palola Shahi production. Ultimately, this feature may have derived from Gandhara and communicated via the Swat region.

Kashmir Bronzes and Tibet

Probably since the earliest Tibetan conquests of the region in the second quarter of the eighth century, bronzes like this one became collectibles in Tibetan areas. Exceptionally, we have a record of one such collector, Prince Nagaraja, one of two sons of the western Tibetan king Yeshe Wo (947–1019/1024). We know this from a substantial number of bronzes to which inscriptions were added that assigned them to his personal collection. A famous example in this regard is a standing Buddha today in the Cleveland Museum of Art. Unusually, this elegant Buddha image shows extensive wear from daily ritual action. While this fact has been used to suggest an Indian usage of the image before it reached the western Tibetan kingdom, stylistic comparisons with other images likely from the early eleventh century indicate otherwise. Nagaraja, thus, may not only have carried an Indian name but also have followed Indian ritual procedures with this exceptional image. His bronzes were eventually distributed further across various Tibetan monasteries.[8]

Throughout the history of Tibetan art, Kashmir bronzes have been admired for their fine workmanship. The Tenth Karmapa, Choying Dorje (1604–1674), cited them in his paintings and sculptures, and they even inspired his distinctive sculptural style. In fact, the composition of the bronze today in the Norton Simon Museum or a very similar bronze is seen in a pedestal of one of the paintings attributed

For more about the Tenth Karmapa, see Arhats Viewing a Painting of Birds by the Tenth Karmapa, no. 72.

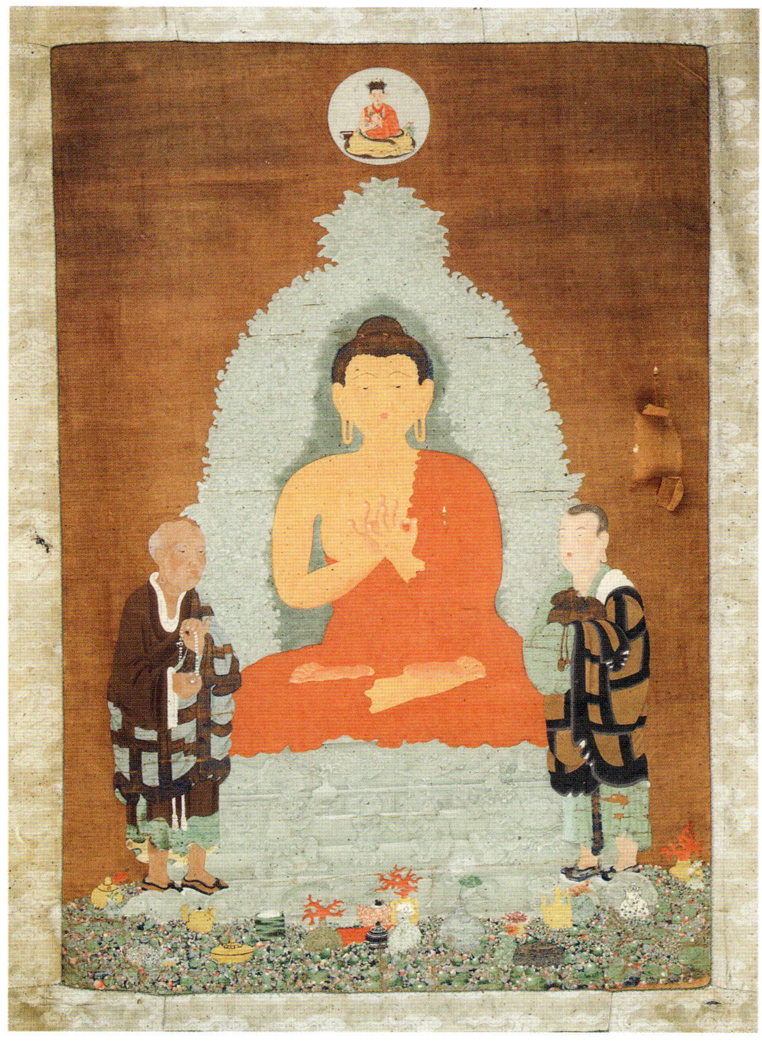

to the Karmapa's workshop in the Lijiang Municipal Museum. In this painting only the inner four figures have been reproduced in reinterpreted form. Here, both donors are female, but the earth goddess is faithfully reproduced—the vase serving to hold a coral tree as offering—as is the figure opposite holding a short sticklike attribute in the same way as the male donor on the bronze. The musician couple is also directly comparable, as are the paired animals, birds on top and deer and lions at the bottom, the latter of different typology. Moreover, the robe of the Buddha represented in this painting is inspired by Kashmir bronzes, and his throne back resembles the halo from Kashmir.[9]

Of course, Kashmir bronzes have been copied throughout the history of Tibetan art, with examples known from the western Himalayas and as far away as the Qing imperial court in Beijing. The impact of the art of Kashmir on Tibetan artistic production thus has been persistent and varied.

Further Reading

Linrothe, Rob. 2015b. "Introduction." In *Collecting Paradise: Buddhist Art of Kashmir and Its Legacies*, by Rob Linrothe, with essays by Melissa R. Kerrin and Christian Luczanits, 1–27. Exhibition catalog. New York: Rubin Museum of Art.

Siudmak, John. 2013. *The Hindu-Buddhist Sculpture of Ancient Kashmir and Its Influences*. Leiden: Brill.

Tenth Karmapa's workshop; Shakyamuni Flanked by His Main Disciples; Lijiang, Yunnan Province, China; 17th century; ink and color on silk; 30¾ × 20½ in. (78 × 52 cm); Lijiang Municipal Museum; no. 2387-II; photograph by Lijiang Municipal Museum

Notes

1 See Linrothe 2015 for the impact of the art of Kashmir on the Himalayas. For Kashmir sculpture in monasteries, see Khanchen Tsewang Rigzin, n.d.; and von Schroeder 2001, vol. 1, 53–209. The dates provided for the Kashmir bronzes may differ from those of the respective museum, but are explained in the narrative.

2 See Siudmak 2013 for a recent study on the stylistic development of the sculptural art of Kashmir.

3 See von Hinüber 2004 and numerous articles on individual bronzes by the same author for foundational work on the inscriptions from this small kingdom.

4 On the cyclical (astronomical) Laukika, respectively, Saptarsi, era used in the wider northwestern Indian region, see Salomon 1998, 196–97. To arrive at a date in the Common Era, twenty-four (twenty-five) years must be added to the number provided in the inscription.

5 Given their close stylistic and thematic association, the two objects have been tested to see if they fit together, but the halo turned out to be a bit too small for the bronze (Pal 2007, 99n21, fig. 97).

6 See, for example, the descriptions in Pal 2003, no. 62, or Siudmak 2013, 322–27.

7 A slightly earlier date, about 715, has been proposed in Siudmak 2013, 322–27.

8 For a list of bronzes once in the collection of Nagaraja, see von Schroeder 2001, 84–87.

9 For a detailed study of the relation of the Tenth Karmapa's work to western Himalayan art, see Luczanits 2016a.

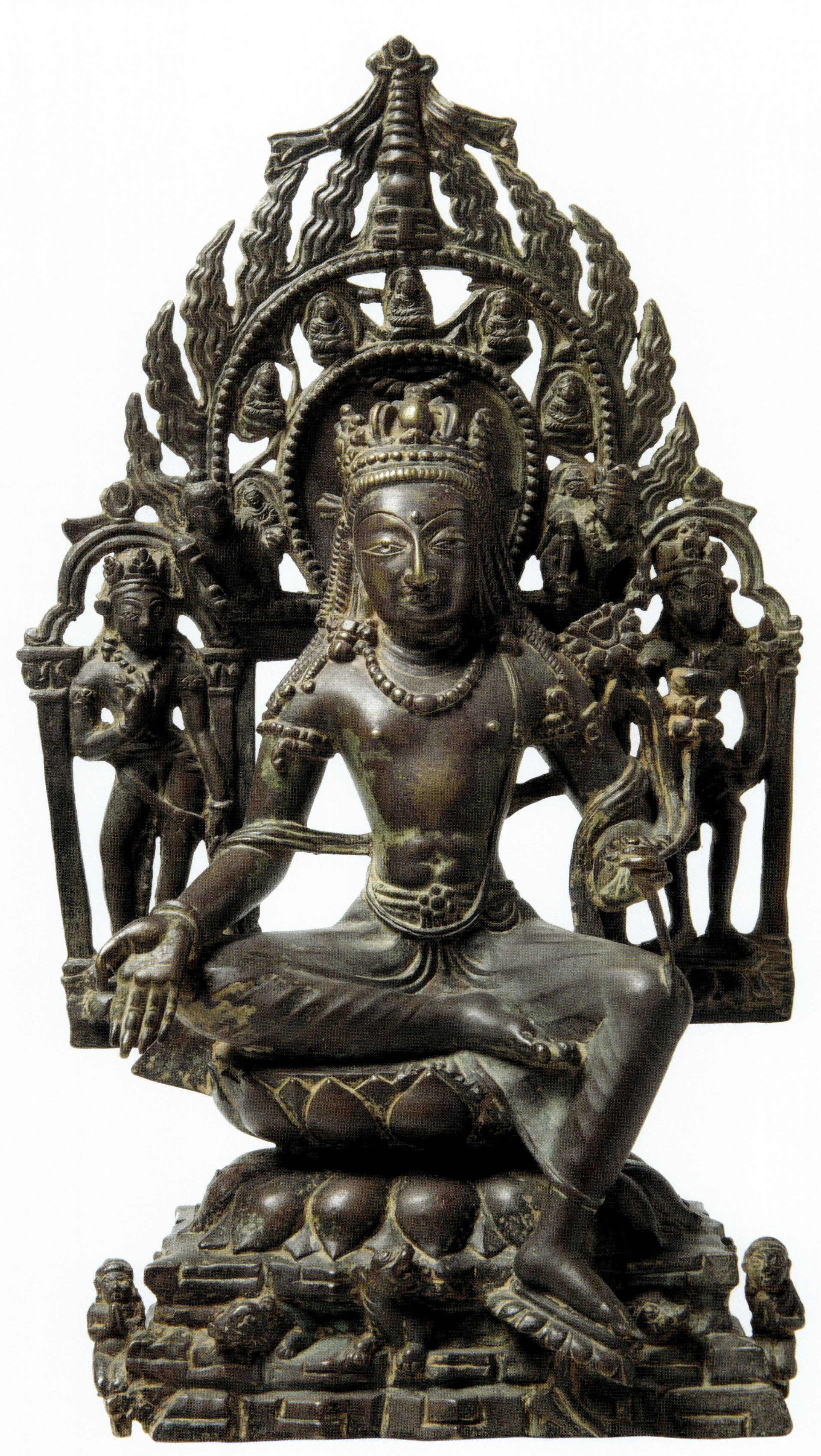

№ 11

Bodhisattva Bhaishajyaraja, the Healing King

Swat Kingdom (present-day Swat District, Pakistan), 8th–9th century

Intertwined Religious Cultures: Buddhism and Hinduism

LUCA MARIA OLIVIERI AND ANNA FILIGENZI

See Padmasambhava and His Manifestations, no. 43.

The Swat region, a valley at the foot of the Karakorum mountain range in Pakistan, is known for its special place in the sacred geography of Buddhism. Some episodes of the Buddha's previous lives took place there, and Swat (ancient Uddiyana) is believed to be the birthplace of Padmasambhava, the revered teacher to whom the first diffusion of Buddhism in Tibet is attributed. In the first millennium CE, the landscape of Swat housed a tight network of Buddhist monasteries and monuments, which greatly contributed to the doctrinal and visual culture of Buddhism. Its strategic position between China, Central Asia, and India made Swat a prominent zone of transit and pilgrimage. Swat was visited by Chinese pilgrims such as Faxian, Song Yun, and Xuanzang in the fifth to seventh century, and even later, when Buddhism was no longer practiced there, by Tibetan pilgrims from the thirteenth to the early twentieth century. It is therefore not surprising that many portable objects, including small votive bronzes and manuscripts, have left Swat, brought home by pilgrims, and have been lately rediscovered in Tibet and China, as well as in Western collections.

Swat was an important artistic center of the Buddhist art of Gandhara, which can be broadly dated between the first and the fourth century. At the end of the seventh century, when the region was disputed among the rulers of Kabul (Turki Shahi and then Hindu Shahi), the Tibetans, and the Chinese imperial forces,[1] it began experiencing a new artistic phase.[2] This is evidenced by sophisticated rock sculptures, mainly representing bodhisattvas connected with the Mahayana tradition, such as Avalokiteshvara and new iconographies of Maitreya, but also with the incipient Vajrayana, the esoteric form of Buddhism that seems to have had in Swat one of its major centers of elaboration. Moreover, these rock sculptures show interesting manifestations of intertwining between Buddhist and Hindu iconographies. A cognate production of this art, sharing the same visual forms, is represented by a class of portable bronze statues, among which this bronze is possibly one of the most magnificent examples.

This bronze sculpture, like all contemporary productions, is evidence of an artistically lively period during which strong ideological impulses started coalescing into new visual models. The bronze probably pictures Bhaishajyaraja, the Healing King or Healing Bodhisattva to whom several early Mahayana scriptures, including the *Lotus Sutra*, make allusion.

A Buddhist Triad

The bronze represents a haloed sitting bodhisattva flanked by auxiliary figures. It belongs to a class of hollow bronze sculptures made by the lost-wax method.[3] It consists of two parts—made separately using different techniques—that can be disassembled for ease of transport. The main part is the hollow central statuette and its throne, in the round, with a low-relief halo frame fixed to the back by means of two removable pins.

Bodhisattva Bhaishajyaraja; Swat Kingdom (present-day Swat District, Pakistan); 8th century; bronze with silver inlay; height 14⅛ in. (36 cm); Museo delle Civiltà–Museo di Arte Orientale, Rome; accession no. 651; inv. no. 5810; photograph © Museo delle Civiltà – MAO "G. Tucci"

The Central Bodhisattva

The bodhisattva, his feet resting on an open lotus with one leg pendent (*ardhaparyankaasana*), is seated on a throne in the form of a double lotus on a rock-shaped base. The right hand is in boon-granting pose (*varada* mudra), while the left hand holds a stem with three inflorescences; the most visible one, with reversed and upturned petals, bears a bowl.

The bodhisattva, adorned with bangles, necklace, armlets, and a tripartite jeweled tiara, tied

Bodhisattva Avalokiteshvara/Padmapani; Arabkhanchina (present-day Swat District, Pakistan); 7th–8th century; photograph courtesy the ISMEO Italian Archaeological Mission in Pakistan

See Pensive Bodhisattva Avalokiteshvara, no. 53; Maitreya, no. 75.

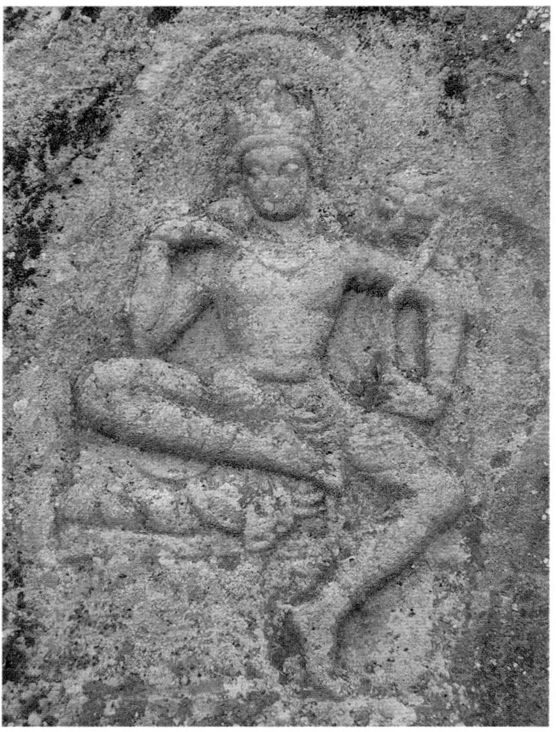

with ribbons knotted at either side, wears a long skirt (*paridhana*) held by a girdle with a central clasp in the form of a rosette. A narrow scarf (*uttariya*) passes behind his waist and over the crooks of his elbows. His torso is nude, with a soft rendering of the anatomy.

The headdresses worn by bodhisattvas usually contain elements that are distinctive of specific personalities, such as the buddha effigy for Avalokiteshvara and the miniature stupa for Maitreya. Here, the tiara features a central spherical jewel clasped by two arched lobes, and pointed crests at the sides, with a central motif composed of a squared gem surmounted by two concentric disks, surrounded by a petaled pattern. It is perhaps worth recalling that Indian medicine assigns to gems a therapeutic role, for they are believed to be sources of radiations capable of adjusting the inner light of the subtle body.

The Halo Frame

The frame, which accommodates the ancillary figures, seen from the front features two open shrines at the sides (housing the two attendant bodhisattvas), composed of trilobed arches resting on pillars. On the top of each arch is a sun/moon symbol, with fluttering ribbons. The upper part of the halo frame constitutes the nimbus of the central bodhisattva. It is formed of three oval concentric sections. The central section presents an open vegetal scroll running clockwise with seven buddhas surrounded by body halos, in meditation pose, with the monastic overrobe, or mantle, covering hands and feet. The outer part shows pointed flames converging upward. A miniature stupa at top center has a finial's tip in the shape of a sun/moon emblem, from which two ribbons flutter outward.

Attending Bodhisattvas

The two symmetrical standing bodhisattvas under arches at the sides are characterized by some divergent details. The figure on the right wears a short skirt (dhoti) and holds in his left hand the stem of what looks like a lotus flower. He also displays the usual bodhisattvas' ornaments and a tripartite tiara decorated with solar symbols: the central jeweled crest features a vertically open lotus flower at the top, while the lateral crests are seemingly composed of disks within crescents. The figure on the left wears a long skirt and the typical ornaments, with the remarkable exception of the short necklace, made of cowrie shells (*Cypraea moneta*), an emblem of fertility also connected with water and the moon. His tripartite tiara also contains lunar allusions, evident in a half lotus open vertically in the central crest and half flowers within crescents at the sides.

Two small, nearly frontal busts spring from the base of the bodhisattva's nimbus. Slightly inclined, they look toward the central figure. The pair's role as attendants is explicitly indicated by the fly whisk (*chamara*) they hold in their right hands. Surprisingly, though, the figure to the left has the appearance of a buddha, with right shoulder uncovered and (perhaps) an attribute in his left hand; the figure on the right holds an upright vajra (thunderbolt) in his left palm.

The Figures on the Base

The rocky base of the throne shows a recess sheltering three animals: two small boars, at the sides, and a roaring lion with jaws opening upward, at the center.

On either side of the rock kneel two simplified figurines of worshippers, possibly the donors. They are probably a male-female couple. Their ornaments and headdresses, though of simplified form, are revelatory of their high rank.[4]

The Interpretation

The bronze probably pictures Bhaishajyaraja, the Healing King or Healing Bodhisattva. The vegetal stem with three inflorescences (not be confused with the single-flower lotus) serves as the physical/mystical support of what we may consider to be the bodhisattva's main attribute, that is, a bowl. The tripartite stem might well represent the flowering branch (often of a myrobalan, highly extolled by ancient Indian physicians for its medicinal virtues) carried by Bhaishajyaraja. It is worth noting, indeed, that the artist represents the plant while having in mind the model of the lotus, which he was evidently more familiar with.

The combination of the bowl, the healing plant, and the gem on the headdress strongly evokes the notion of medicine, with which Buddhism engaged from its earliest days, being involved with the alleviation, prevention, and eradication of all suffering. The idea of the healing dharma is embedded in many Buddhist texts, which also exemplify the multilayered historical processes of absorbing and integrating medical knowledge, practices, orientations, and rituals into a "Buddhist path" to healing.

See Bhaishajyaguru, no. 14. For more on medicine, see Desi Sanggye Gyatso's Medical Paintings, no. 73.

The emergence in the iconography of well-defined Buddhist healing figures was partly due to competitive interaction with other religious systems. Similarities with Vishnu have been noted by scholars. Vishnu's connection with physical and spiritual health care, naturally embedded in his role as Preserver, is expressed by the miraculous gem (*kaustubha*) that Vishnu bears on his chest and is believed to emit healing light. Likewise, our bodhisattva is given a cosmic dimension, expressed both by the flaming halo with the Seven Buddhas and by the combined sun disk/crescent moon repeated on the top of the halo, on the top of the side arches, and in the crowns of the two side bodhisattvas. The presence of the boars and lion inside the rocky throne's recess further stresses the analogy with Vishnu's cosmic nature. The different crowns of the two ancillary bodhisattvas are suggestive of their respective identities, Suryaprabha (the sun, to the right side) and Chandraprabha (the moon, to the left side), two characters that often accompany Bhaishajyaraja.

See Vishnu Riding on Garuda, no. 18.

If we consider Swat to be the area of provenance of this sculpture, its relation to Vishnu may be seen in a well-defined historical background, whose most spectacular feature is the Vishnuite temple at Barikot, dating to the seventh century.[5] The presence of this and other pieces of archaeological and art historical evidence testify to the penetration of Hinduism into a stronghold of Buddhism such as Swat (ancient Uddiyana), supported by the powerful Shahi patronage. Rather than producing a clash between two opposing systems, this arrangement fostered a stimulating encounter in a period of great cultural and artistic innovations. Seen together, the rock and bronze sculptures represent the most direct and unquestionable affirmation of the incipient Vajrayana, with abundant implications for the rereading and understanding of the legendary accounts of Uddiyana and Padmasambhava from a historical perspective.[6]

Brief mention should also be made of the overall appearance of this sculpture, which is transformed into a veritable portable shrine by its aureole. Whether such compositions were inspired by large-scale versions is difficult to say. Given their ready mobility, they must certainly have been inspirational models for architectural structures and decorations of the kind found in later Himalayan temples.

It seems reasonable to conclude that the piece almost certainly comes from Swat,[7] and that its date,[8] in view of the art of the Palola Shahi,[9] can be no later than the eighth century.

For more on the art of the Palola Shahi, see Buddha on the Cosmic Mountain, no. 10.

Further Reading

Pal, Pratapaditya. 1975a. *Bronzes of Kashmir*. Graz: Akademische Druck- und Verlagsanstalt.

Reedy, Chandra. 1997. *Himalayan Bronzes: Technology, Style and Choices*. Newark: University of Delaware Press.

von Schroeder, Ulrich. 1981. *Indo-Tibetan Bronzes*. Hong Kong: Visual Dharma Publications.

Notes

1 See Tucci 1977, 74–77; Olivieri 2010.
2 See Filigenzi 2015.
3 See Barrett 1962; Pal 1975a; Reedy 1997; von Schroeder 1981.
4 Cf. the Buddha of Shamkarasena and Devashri, dated to 714/5 (Fussman 1993, 43–47, pl. 31).
5 See Olivieri 2010, with references. The excavation at the temple is still ongoing.
6 Filigenzi 2015, esp. 134ff.
7 Cf. the smaller Avalokiteshvara bronze from the National Museum in Karachi (NM 1959.444); see Pal 1975, no. 75; Zhiguan Museum of Fine Art 2018, no. 3; as well as Filigenzi 2015, figs. 25–27, 29–31.
8 Cf. the fragment of a halo frame, Udegram Castle, Swat, Shahi-Ghaznavid levels (Swat Museum, UD 250). Cf. also National Museum, Karachi, NM 1959.444 (Filigenzi 2015, fig. 28); The Metropolitan Museum of Art, New York, 1983.507.1.
9 See Hinüber 2005.

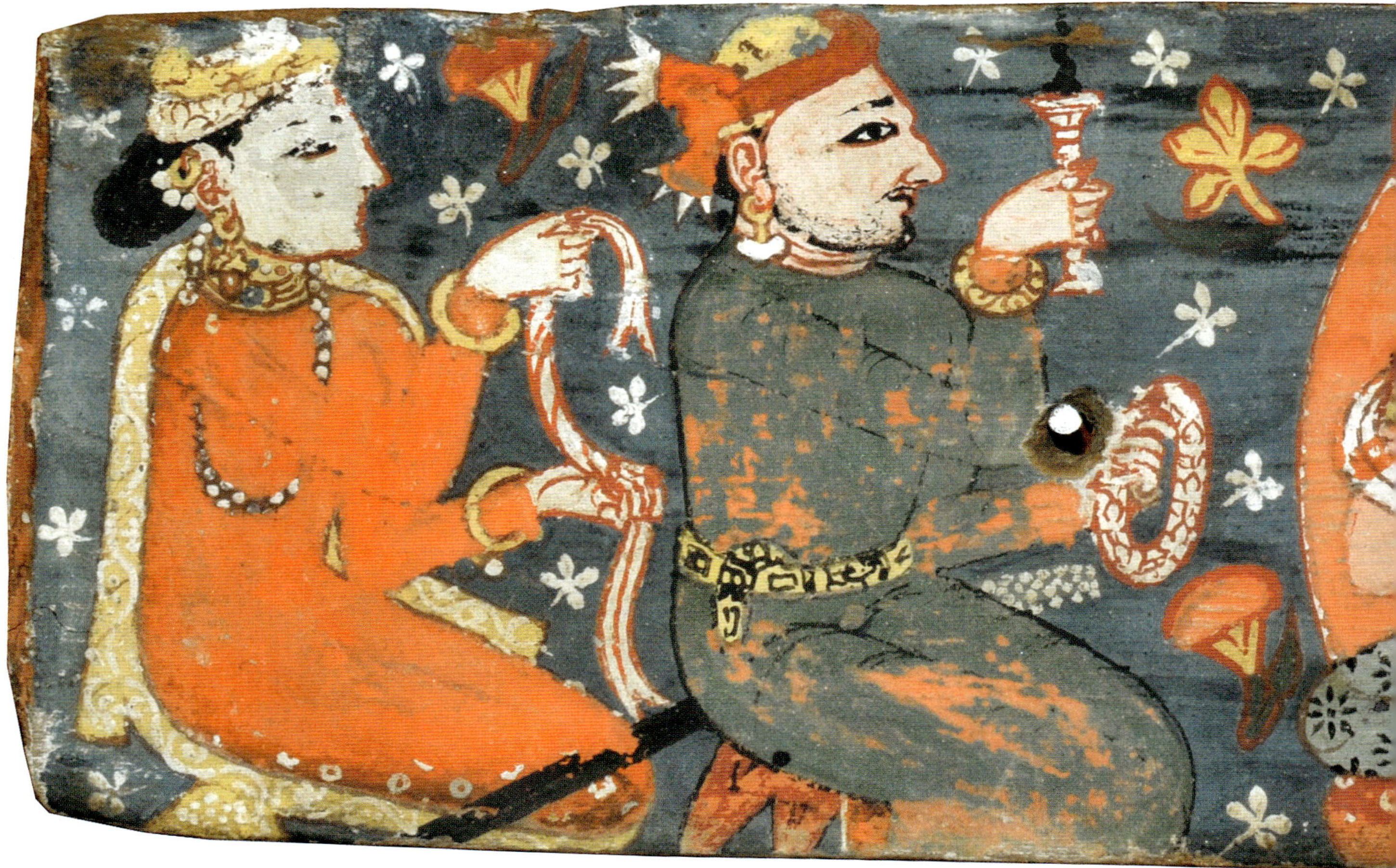

Nº 12

Painted Manuscript Cover

Gilgit Kingdom, Greater Kashmir (present-day Baltistan, Pakistan), ca. late 8th or early 9th century

Buddhist Painting in Greater Kashmir: An Early Inspiration for Tibet?

ROB LINROTHE

For examples of Indian and Tibetan book formats, see Illuminated Pages of the *Prajnaparamita Sutra* Manuscript, no. 23; Earliest Extant Printed Edition of Milarepa's Life Story, no. 62.

THIS PAINTING OF BODHISATTVAS MAITREYA AND AVALOKITESHVARA with patrons is on one of a pair of wooden boards clinching and protecting a stack of birch-bark pages constituting a handwritten Buddhist text. When found in 1938, it was on the underside of the top cover. (The bottom cover depicts three buddhas.) It is one of three sets of painted manuscript covers excavated in 1938 in the area north of Kashmir known as Gilgit. The other two sets, with vertical painted compositions, appear to be earlier, one from the seventh and the other from the early eighth century. Collectively, the three pairs offer not only the earliest but also, for all intents and purposes, the only excavated Buddhist paintings from the Greater Kashmir area. But what do they have to do with Tibet? Actually, quite a bit. The taller rectangular shape of the pages of the texts enclosed by the covers resembles those used later by Tibetans, strikingly different from the long, narrow format used in eastern India and Nepal. Along with similarities in the way that the exteriors of book covers were painted a little later in Tibet, this has led some to suggest a substantial role in the transmission of the "cult of the book" in its physical form from Greater Kashmir to Tibet.[1] Additionally, the aggressive,

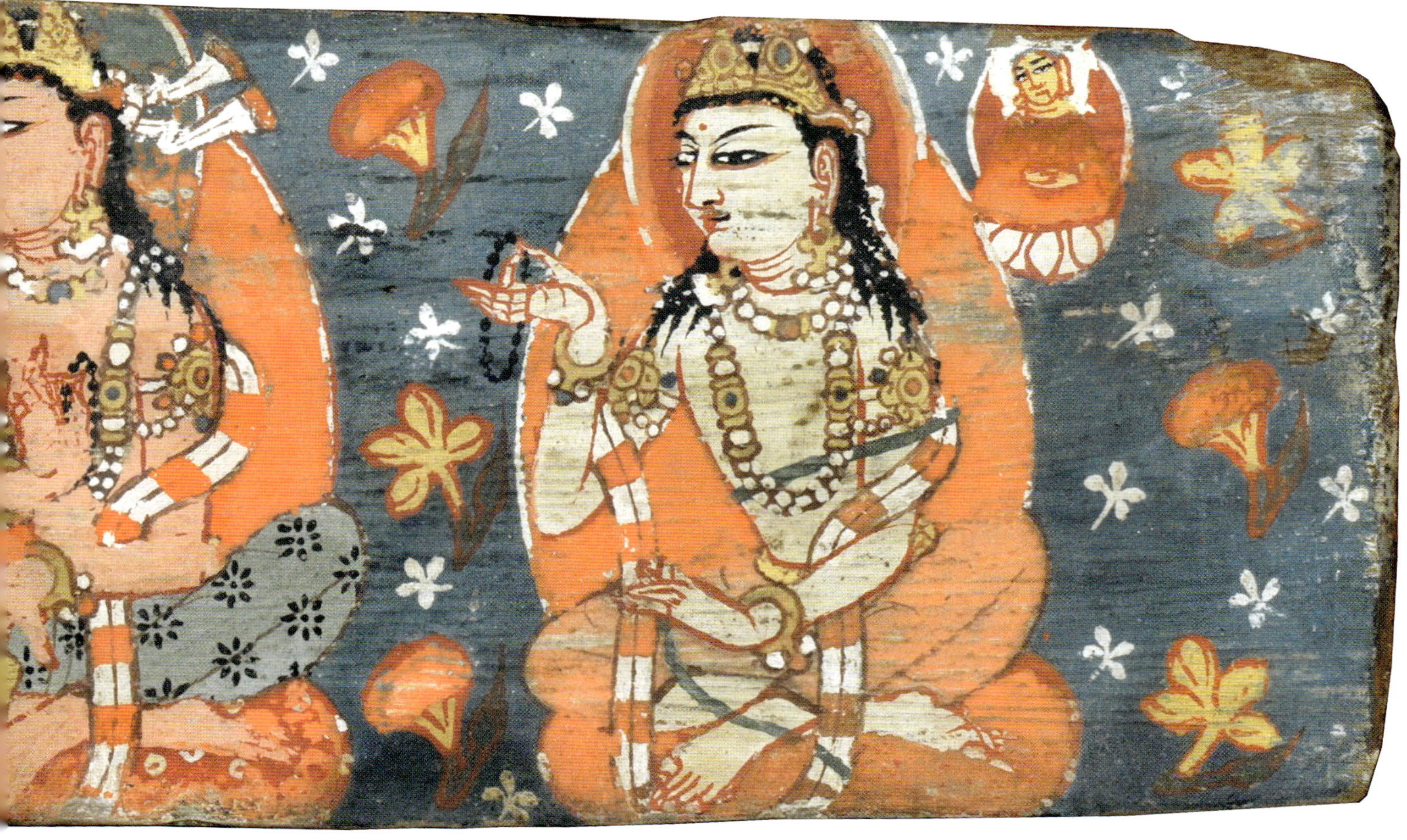

expansionist rulers of the Tibetan Empire (ca. 600–850) invaded and occupied Gilgit in the early eighth century and were instrumental in the destruction of the Patola Shahi rulers who had been fervent patrons of Gilgit's Buddhist art.

The Gilgit painted covers were found as part of a cache of manuscripts in the 1930s near the village of Naupur, north and slightly west of Kashmir, which culturally if not politically dominated the Gilgit rulers. The Patola Shahi dynasty oversaw this area between the late sixth century through at least the eighth. The Gilgit rulers, who identified themselves by name and with sponsor portraits, commissioned a number of spectacular silver-inlaid brass Buddhist images, probably from Kashmiri ateliers, as all display a distinctively Kashmiri style.[2] At times, the local rulers were at odds with the dynasties of Kashmir, but in the eighth century both were allies with the Tang Chinese against the invading and occupying Tibetan armies.[3]

For an example of the Kashmiri style, see Buddha on the Cosmic Mountain, no. 10.

The Tibetans temporarily occupied Gilgit in the early eighth century after the Shahi kings neither submitted to the Tibetan invaders nor allowed their troops to transit their state freely. The local ruler, Surendraditya (720–737), sent missions to the Tang court, which dispatched troops to help drive out the Tibetans. However, there seem to have been setbacks for both the Tibetans and the alliance of the Tang court, the Kashmiris (both the Karokota [ca. 625–855] and Utpala dynasties [ca. ninth–tenth centuries]), and the local Gilgit rulers, until the latter were finally defeated in the mid-eighth century. Some kind of Tibetan military presence was maintained until the early or mid-ninth century, when the Tibetan dynasty collapsed. Nonetheless, a late tenth-century itinerary between Central Asia and Kashmir mentions the city of Gilgit and eight Buddhist monasteries, evidence that Gilgit Buddhism survived or even thrived at least into the tenth century.[4]

Bodhisattvas Maitreya and Avalokiteshvara with Patrons, painted on the inside of the top of a pair of manuscript covers; Gilgit Kingdom, Greater Kashmir (present-day Baltistan, Pakistan); ca. late 8th or early 9th century; wood; 3½ × 1⅛ in. (9 × 3 cm); Shri Pratap Singh Museum, Srinagar, Kashmir; photograph by R. Linrothe

Of the three excavated sets of wooden book covers—now in the Shri Pratap Singh Museum in Srinagar, Kashmir—two of them protected copies of the *Samghata Sutra*, of which multiple copies were identified among the Gilgit manuscripts. They were written in Sanskrit in the script in common use in

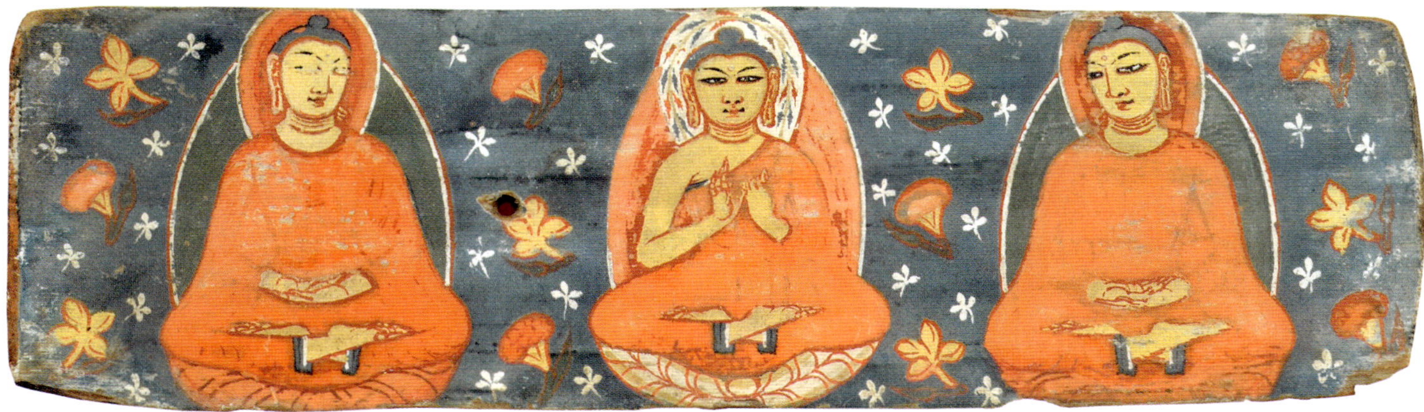

Three Buddhas, painted on the inside of the bottom of a pair of manuscript covers; Gilgit Kingdom, Greater Kashmir (present-day Baltistan, Pakistan); ca. late 8th or early 9th century; wood; 3½ × 1⅛ in. (9 × 3 cm); Shri Pratap Singh Museum, Srinagar, Kashmir; photograph by R. Linrothe

Greater Kashmir at the time, called Proto-Sharada. The sutra was translated into Chinese in the sixth century[5] and into Tibetan in the ninth century. It is a text that among other things describes the process of bodily death, advises the ways to avoid the hells and other karmic consequences for actions that harm others, and consoles family members of the deceased. In recent times, it has been recited in memorials for the victims of the 9/11 attacks and of the tsunami of 2004.[6]

The sutra features two bodhisattvas: Sarvashura (Universal Hero), and Bhaishajyasena (Medicine Son). A third, Maitreya, is briefly mentioned. Although it is tempting to see the two bodhisattvas painted on the inside top cover as Sarvashura and Bhaishajyasena, the bodhisattvas actually can be identified as the two-armed bodhisattvas Maitreya and Avalokiteshvara. This reminds us that the manuscripts, written on paper and birch bark, and the wooden covers were not necessarily made for each other or even at the same time. The covers in particular could have been shifted to other manuscripts or made to protect older manuscripts that may not originally have had such a cover. In the present instance, the manuscript found inside the covers is dated to the early seventh century, while the painted covers were created more than a century later.[7]

For more about images of Maitreya, see Rock Carving of Four-Armed Bodhisattva Maitreya, no. 17; Maitreya and Manjushri Mural at Dratang, no. 26; Maitreya, no. 75.

The inside of the top cover was painted with the two bodhisattvas and the sponsor couple in an undifferentiated space with flowers of different sizes and colors floating in the background. Maitreya is the pinkish bodhisattva in the middle holding a golden vase. The white Padmapani, a form of Avalokiteshvara, is on the right. At his left shoulder is an image of Buddha Amitabha on a lotus. Most intriguing is the kneeling sponsor couple on the far left. The woman dressed in orange holds a white scarf reminiscent of the offering scarf (*khatak*) ubiquitous in Tibet even today. The slightly larger male, in a belted robe with a sword buckled on his left, offers a lamp and a garland or wreath to the two bodhisattvas. Portraits of sponsors are quite common at the very bottom of compositions in later Nepalese and Tibetan art, but what is unprecedented in this composition is that here they are depicted the same size as the deities. The bodhisattvas each have a head and body nimbus, which the lay couple making offerings do not, but they look as if they are either in front of large sculptures of the bodhisattvas or sharing the same space with the deities themselves. Perhaps the latter is the intention. According to one of the Gilgit manuscripts recovered, the *Splendid Vision Sutra* (the Sanskrit title is *Sarvatathāgatādhisthāna-satvāvalokana-buddhakṣetrasandarśana-vyūha*), Avalokiteshvara says that those who hear, honor, and copy one of the prayers included in the sutra "will receive visions of buddhas and visions of bodhisattvas." As he spoke the prayer, "Heavenly flowers showered down," and he promised that through the right conduct and ritual actions, practitioners would be "seeing me face-to-face."[8]

For other donor depictions, see Buddha on the Cosmic Mountain, no. 10; Chakrasamvara Mandala with Newar Donors, no. 29; Vajrabhairava Mandala, no. 46; Mandala of Manjuvajra of the *Vajravali* Set, no. 50.

There remains some controversy about the function of the mounds in which the manuscripts and the covers were discovered. In 1931 local shepherds found a few texts in a wooden box. In 1938 the site was hastily excavated by an official attached to the government of the maharaja of Kashmir. If the main mound was a stupa, as many believe, the manuscripts placed in it were consecration deposits—powerful relics of the dharma taught by the Buddha—or else the manuscripts were ritually "retired" there. Others, however, believe that the dilapidated mound was the library of Buddhist ritualists, full of "inherited books, books they used in their daily vocation, gifts of books from grateful clients."[9] That it was a

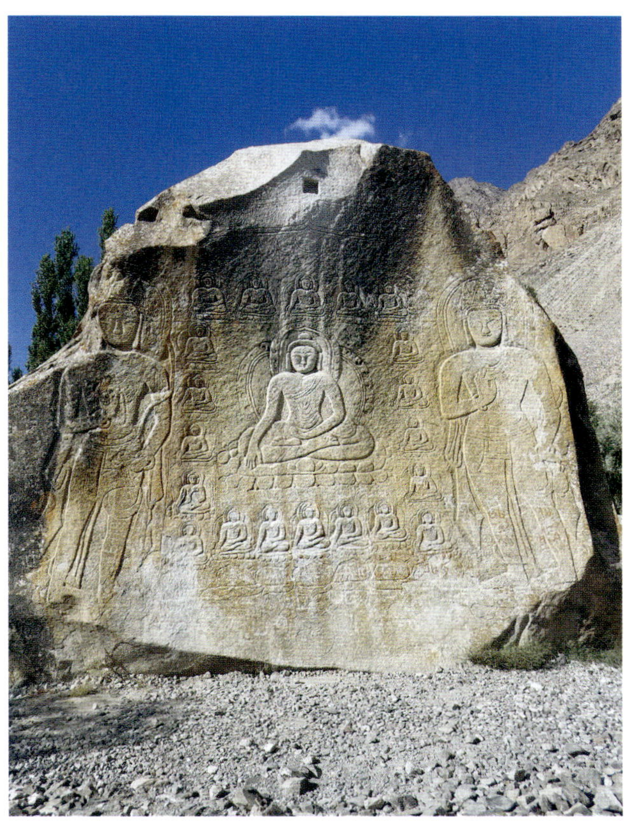

Stone carving of twenty-one buddhas and two bodhisattvas; Manthal village of Skardu, Pakistan; ca. late 8th century; photograph by Daniel Majchrowicz

For a rock carving in the Kashmiri style, see Rock Carving of Four-Armed Bodhisattva Maitreya, no. 17.

copying workshop or scriptorium is not out of the question, though the fact that the site contained multiple, incomplete, and worn texts found together is more indicative of ritual discarding.

Only a quarter of a mile (four hundred meters) from the excavation site is a cliff-carved standing buddha, almost ten feet (three meters) in height, within a pediment-like frame in the Kashmiri style.[10] Not far to the east, in Skardu, another complex rock carving can be seen; comparing it with the similarly dated but much smaller book cover set demonstrates the different skills or origins of the painters versus the sculptors that the Gilgit sponsors could call on. The seated buddha in the carving has a stiff upright posture, swelling shoulders, square face, and artificially splayed toes on his crossed feet. The central buddha on the bottom manuscript cover is much more relaxed and natural looking, with an egg-shaped face common to Kashmiri sculptures. The standing bodhisattvas on the carving, including Maitreya on the buddha's right, somewhat awkwardly dwarf the buddha and have similarly plastic faces. Kashmir was a few days walk south of the main Gilgit capital. Small metal sculptures and paintings were probably commissioned in the more cosmopolitan centers of the contemporary Kashmiri dynasties.[11] Available stone sculptors willing to work on site for days or weeks were probably local.

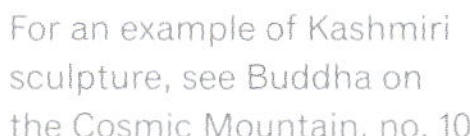

For an example of Kashmiri sculpture, see Buddha on the Cosmic Mountain, no. 10.

Further Reading

Klimburg-Salter, Deborah. 2015. "Along the Pilgrimage Routes between Uḍḍiyāṇa and Tibet: The Gilgit MSS Covers and the Tibetan Decorated Book Cover." In *Tibet in Dialogue with Its Neighbors: History, Culture and Art of Central and Western Tibet, 8th to 15th Century*, edited by Erica Forte, Liang Junyan, Deborah Klimburg-Salter, Zhang Yun, and Helmut Tauscher, 392–406. Vienna: China Tibetology Research Center and Arbeitskreis für Tibetische und Buddistische Studien Universität Wien.

Linrothe, Rob, with essays by Melissa R. Kerin and Christian Luczanits. 2015a. *Collecting Paradise: Buddhist Art of Kashmir and Its Legacies*, esp. 39–54. Exhibition catalog. New York: Rubin Museum of Art.

Notes

1 Klimburg-Salter 2015.

2 For examples of such images, see Linrothe 2015a, figs. 1.27, 1.28; also Virginia Museum of Fine Arts, *Crowned Buddha Touching the Head of a King*, https://www.vmfa.museum/piction/7898216-8393026/ and Asia Society, *Crowned Buddha Shakyamuni*, http://museum.asiasociety.org/collection/explore/1979-044-crowned-buddha-shakyamuni.

3 See Denwood 2008 and 2009.

4 Bailey 1936.

5 For the Chinese version of the *Samghata Sutra*, see Taishō Tripiṭaka, T.13.423.

6 Finnegan 2006, 113.

7 For a detailed discussion of these assigned dates, see Linrothe 2015a, 42–51.

8 Cohen 2012, 30.53, 31.57, 31.58.

9 Cohen 2012, 3.

10 Dar 1985.

11 Xuanzang writes that he saw a buddha image seven feet in height in Khotan in Central Asia that was said to have been brought from Kashmir, much farther away than Gilgit. See Xuanzang 1996, 379. While such a large image is rather implausible, a circa eighth-century seated metalwork buddha from Kashmir, 16½ inches (42 centimeters) in height, was excavated in the 1990s in Xinjiang, China. See Leidy 1997, figs. 1, 2.

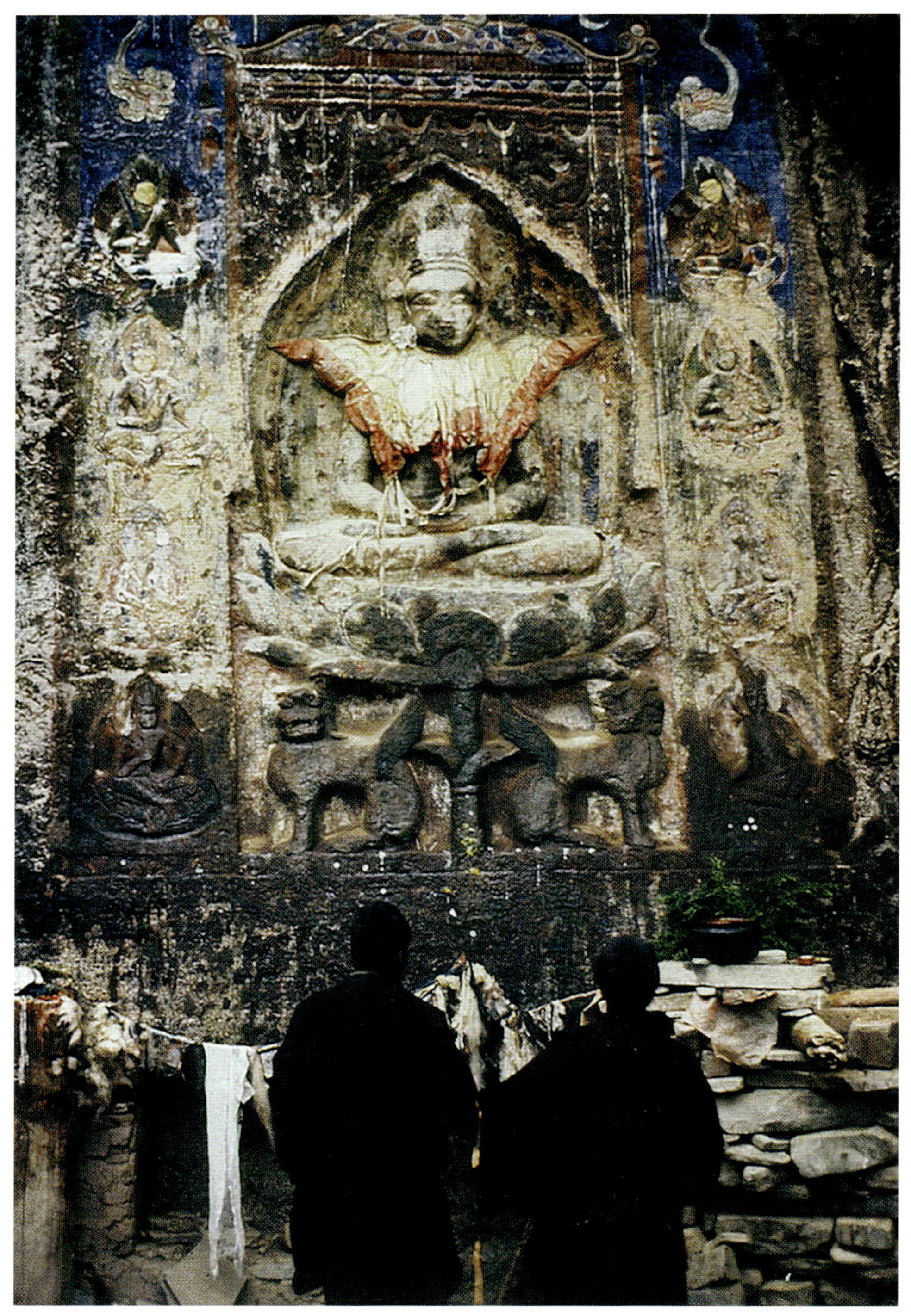

Yuk Nyak Dre Shab, Shok Lek Kong, and Dummagam, Tibetan stone carvers, Hun Bong Tseng Pe and Hwa Hou Jin, Chinese artists; Enthroned Buddha Vairochana Surrounded by Eight Bodhisattvas; Denma Drak, Kham region, eastern Tibet (present-day TAR, China); 804; stone; approx. 11 ft. 6 in. × 9 ft. 10 in. (3.5 × 3 m); photograph by Elisabeth Benard and Nima Dorjee Ragnubs, 1983

No 13

Imperial Carvings of Vairochana

Denma Drak, Kham region, eastern Tibet (present-day TAR, China), 804

Vairochana and the Eight Great Bodhisattvas Represented as the Tibetan Sovereign and His Courtiers

AMY HELLER

In the years 804 and 806, Yeshe Yang, Master of Meditation at the Tibetan Triga Monastery near Lake Kokonor (in present-day Qinghai Province), commissioned two series of stone carvings of a crowned buddha, seated on a lion throne, surrounded by eight bodhisattvas.[1] The first was carved at Denma Drak, some 186 miles (300 kilometers) to the south in what is present-day Chamdo, Tibet Autonomous Region; the second was carved at the Bimda Temple near Jyekundo (in present-day Qinghai Province). Authentic ancient Tibetan inscriptions in stone beside the images describe the historical circumstances of the carvings, the artists' names, and Buddhist prayers in relation to Buddha Vairochana in the concluding section of the *Gandavyuha Sutra*.[2] These sculptures document the preeminence of the Vairochana cult in the Tibetan imperial period (ca. 608–ca. 686). Furthermore, by virtue of the inscribed dates and the artists' names, these images are the earliest dated examples of Tibetan art known at present.

See Jokhang Temple, no. 7.

During the ninth century, there is a wide-ranging association between Vairochana and the royal cult; Vairochana is intended to represent the imperial presence of the Tibetan emperor, the *tsenpo*. This concept of the conflation of deity and ruler is given visual emphasis in Buddha Vairochana and the Eight Bodhisattvas, represented wearing the garments of Tibetan royalty—ample ankle-length robes in heavy fabric with overlong sleeves and double collar—in the Bimda and Markham County rock carvings. Numerous Tibetan prayers among the Tibetan manuscripts in Dunhuang document the importance of the cult of Vairochana during the late eighth to ninth century. Vairochana's emblem is the wheel, which refers to two distinct phenomena in Buddhist iconology: Shakyamuni's discourse, in which he initially "set the wheel of dharma in motion" by his teaching, and the Buddhist legend of the chakravartin, the wheel-turning sovereign who establishes social harmony and ensures utopia. This latter role certainly coincided with the position attributed to the *tsenpo*, according to Tibetan royal cults.

Stylistic Characteristics of the Carvings

For an example of painting at Dunhuang, see Bhaishajyaguru, no. 14.

For examples of art at Yulin Cave temples, see Cave 3 at Yulin Cave Temples, no. 31.

Aesthetically, the two series are quite distinctive. Although much damaged, the composition of the seated Vairochana in Denma Drak, flanked by two vertical registers containing four superimposed bodhisattvas, recalls portable paintings from Dunhuang and the mural painting of Cave 25 in the Yulin Cave temples.[3] The body proportions of the Denma Drak Buddha are much more slender and the elongated legs are perfectly smooth, lacking any muscular definition. The buddha is not represented with a squared face and jaw inside a circular halo, the conventional characteristics of Tang period (618–906) Chinese images. Instead, the broad forehead contrasts with the triangular jawline with prominent chin. The eyes appear long and narrow rather than round, with thin brows slightly arched. The bodhisattvas surrounding him are all shown seated, wearing crowns and dhotis. Their arms are in various gestures, giving dynamic motion to the static seated postures of their iconography.

In contrast, the crowned Buddha Vairochana at Bimda sits in meditation on a lotus cushion, with a horseshoe-shaped halo adorning his head. Recently repainted, the figure's golden body is dressed in elaborate robes, painted to give the impression of thick silk. The top robe, in deep red with a pattern of Buddhist emblems, has a pointed green collar with lapels crossed above the heart. Another (blue) collar's lapels meet at the collarbone. The shoulders have no apparent seams, and the creases of the sleeves are stiff. The folds radiating from the bent elbows gradually widen to almost double their length at the edge

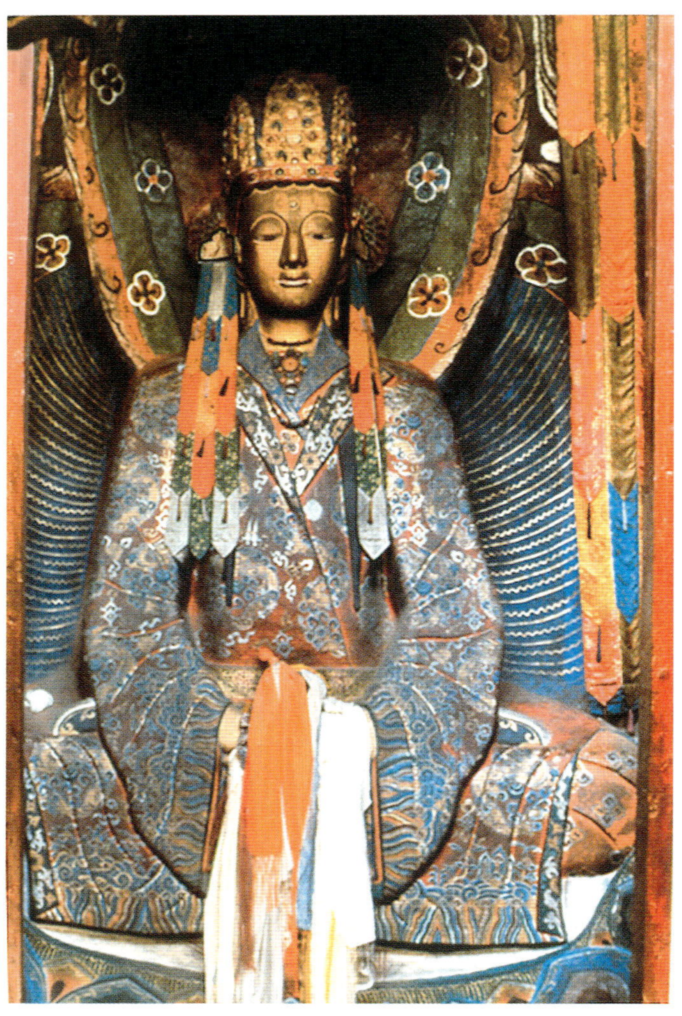

Buddha Vairochana; Bimda Temple; near Jyekundo (present-day Qinghai Province, China); 806; stone with painted and textile decoration; height approx. 63 in. (160 cm); photograph by Liu Lizhong

of the cuffs, which are embellished with a different pattern. A belt is indicated by a pattern of very diminutive flowers with long, thin tendrils and stalks in green and red on a gold background. Beneath the belt, the lower part of the top robe is draped over the buddha's lap and crossed legs, with the front panels hanging down. The tips of his boots—painted deep blue with gold fleurs-de-lis—contrast with the orange undergarment whose cloth is cut as if clinging to the leg in the form of trousers. The use of double collars has been previously noted as a characteristic of the representation of Tibetan royal robes in Cave 159 at Dunhuang.[4] The lotus cushion is supported by two lions, with manes very similar in shape to those of the stone lions at the Yarlung dynasty tombs.

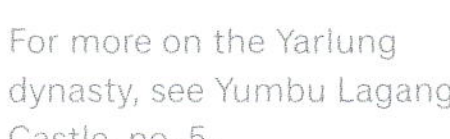

For more on the Yarlung dynasty, see Yumbu Lagang Castle, no. 5.

Iconography and Composition

The eight bodhisattvas surrounding the Buddha Vairochana at Bimda stand symmetrically in four groups on both sides of the buddha. Their faces and hands are all painted gold. Their bodies are mostly hidden by thickly rendered robes with double collars and widening sleeves that extend to just above the feet, which are notably shod in black boots. Each bodhisattva holds a distinctive attribute and has a name inscribed in Tibetan. It would appear, however, that the iconography comes from a specific ritual description that has not yet been identified and is different from the usual attributes of each bodhisattva. For example, Avalokiteshvara holds a water vase,[5] which is usually an emblem of Maitreya, while the opposite image on the other side inscribed Manjushri holds a pink and yellow lotus instead of a book.

Other Examples of Stone Imperial Carvings of Vairochana

Another focus on stone carvings of the imperial period comes from south of Denma Drak, where two important rock carvings of Vairochana have been documented. These reflect a different iconographic basis, derived from the *Vairochana-Abhisambodhi Tantra* instead of the *Gandavyuha/Avatamsaka Sutra* corpus, in which Vairochana is surrounded by the two bodhisattvas Vajrapani and Avalokiteshvara, who respectively represent the Vajra family and the Lotus family. Initially attributed to the reign of Tri Songdetsen (742–ca. 800), they appear to have been executed one reign later, in the early ninth century.[6]

Also, in the context of a different liturgical tradition, in the vicinity of Markham there is a newly discovered site of Vairochana and the Eight Bodhisattvas again dressed in the robes of the emperor, a Tibetan *tsenpo*, and his courtiers. Thanks to the Tibetan scholar Tsering Gyalpo, the discovery of this site of carvings of Vairochana and the Eight Bodhisattvas has been analyzed.[7] One may appreciate the fine carving, seen clearly on this rock face, and evidence of the Tang aesthetic, with square faces and hefty bodies.

Among the Dunhuang caves commissioned during the Tibetan period, the Tibetan emperor is represented prominently in Cave 158. The Tibetan emperor and his attendants wear long pale robes that close left to right with triangular lapel collars in contrasting color; the emperor's high turban has crown panels, while his two attendants wear the fabric turban only. In contemporary portraits of the Tibetan emperor and his entourage in Cave 159 and Cave 231, he is again depicted beneath the parasol, wearing similar garments and a high turban.[8] Moreover, the emperor extends his hand to give his attendant a small silver cup with a handle, ostensibly Sogdian silver, the most sophisticated metalwork of the period. This shows how the royal portraits conveyed the idea of Tibet as a link between east and west along the Silk Roads, accumulating cosmopolitan influences that emerged from the complex network of trade as well as the development of Tibetan aesthetics blending secular and Buddhist symbolism. In the imperial rock carvings of Vairochana, the iconological basis is understood to be the *Avatamsaka Sutra*, with the culmination in the *Gandavuyha Sutra*, although the individual attributes of the bodhisattvas in the entourage vary.[9] These rock carvings are among the earliest documents of Tibetan art. In subsequent times, at the Samye Monastery, and Dratang Monastery modeled on Samye, similar groups are documented as well.[10]

For an example of Sogdian silver in a Tibetan context, see Silver Jug, no. 15.

See Maitreya and Manjushri Mural at Dratang, no. 26.

Further Reading

Heller, Amy. 1997. "Buddhist Images and Rock Inscriptions from Eastern Tibet, Part IV." In *Tibetan Studies: Proceedings of the Seventh Seminar of the International Association for Tibetan Studies*, edited by H. Krasser, M. T. Much, E. Steinkellner, H. Tauscher, 385–403. Vienna: Verlag der Österreichischen Akademie der Wissenschaften.

Karmay, Heather. 1975. *Early Sino-Tibetan Art*. Warminster: Aris and Philips.

Kapstein, Matthew. 2009. "The Treaty Temple of the Turquoise Grove." In *Buddhism between Tibet and China*, edited by Matthew Kapstein, 21–72. Boston: Wisdom.

Notes

1 For Denma Drak, S. Karmay 1997, 480, confirmed the chronology of 804 as the monkey year in the reign, rather than 804 or 816, as initially proposed (A. Heller 1994a, 74). Imaeda 2012, 115, confirmed the date of 804.

2 A. Heller 1994b gives full translations of the inscriptions at Denma Drak, which relate to the concluding verses of the *Gandavyuha Sutra*; S. Karmay 1997 translates the Bimda inscriptions, 482, and identifies Vairochana as Vairochana of the Glacier Lake (thub pa gangs chen mtsho rgyal), 478.

3 Heller 1994a, fig 2, Yulin Cave 25, and fig. 9, British Museum 0A1919.1–1.050, Vairochana with the Eight Great Bodhisattvas, ink and colors on silk, 37⅜ × 25⅜ in. (95 × 64.5 cm), early 9th century (with Tibetan name inscriptions for the bodhisattvas).

4 H. Karmay 1977, 72.

5 Wong 2007, 154, describes an aspect of Avalokiteshvara with water vase in one of his six arms in Dunhuang Cave 384 attributed to the late eighth to early ninth century. However, the lack of lotus emblem of the Bimda Avalokiteshvara is highly unusual.

6 Sha bo mkha' byams 2021, correcting the chronology of the inscription as analyzed in A. Heller 1997, 389–90.

7 S. Karmay 1997 had provided some information but had not been able to situate the carvings, which was accomplished by Tsering Gyalpo in 2015, 181–87. See also Yang, Lu, and Zhang 2017.

8 The Tibetan emperor and his entourage are often portrayed in Dunhuang as part of the theme of Vimalakirti debating Manjushri, in Caves 159, 231, 196, as well as in portable scrolls such as British Museum 1919,0101,0.55 (ch.00350 IDP). Tibetans figure prominently also in the Shariputra debate; see Musée Guimet Pelliot chinois 4524. Murals of the Tibetan emperor and his entourage are seen in Dunhuang Caves 9, 359, 360; Yulin Cave 25. Cf. the pioneering studies by H. Karmay 1975, 14–16; H. Karmay 1977, 70–75; most recently, Debreczeny 2019a, 20–23.

9 A. Heller 2007, 85–86 passim.

10 S. Karmay 1997, 483.

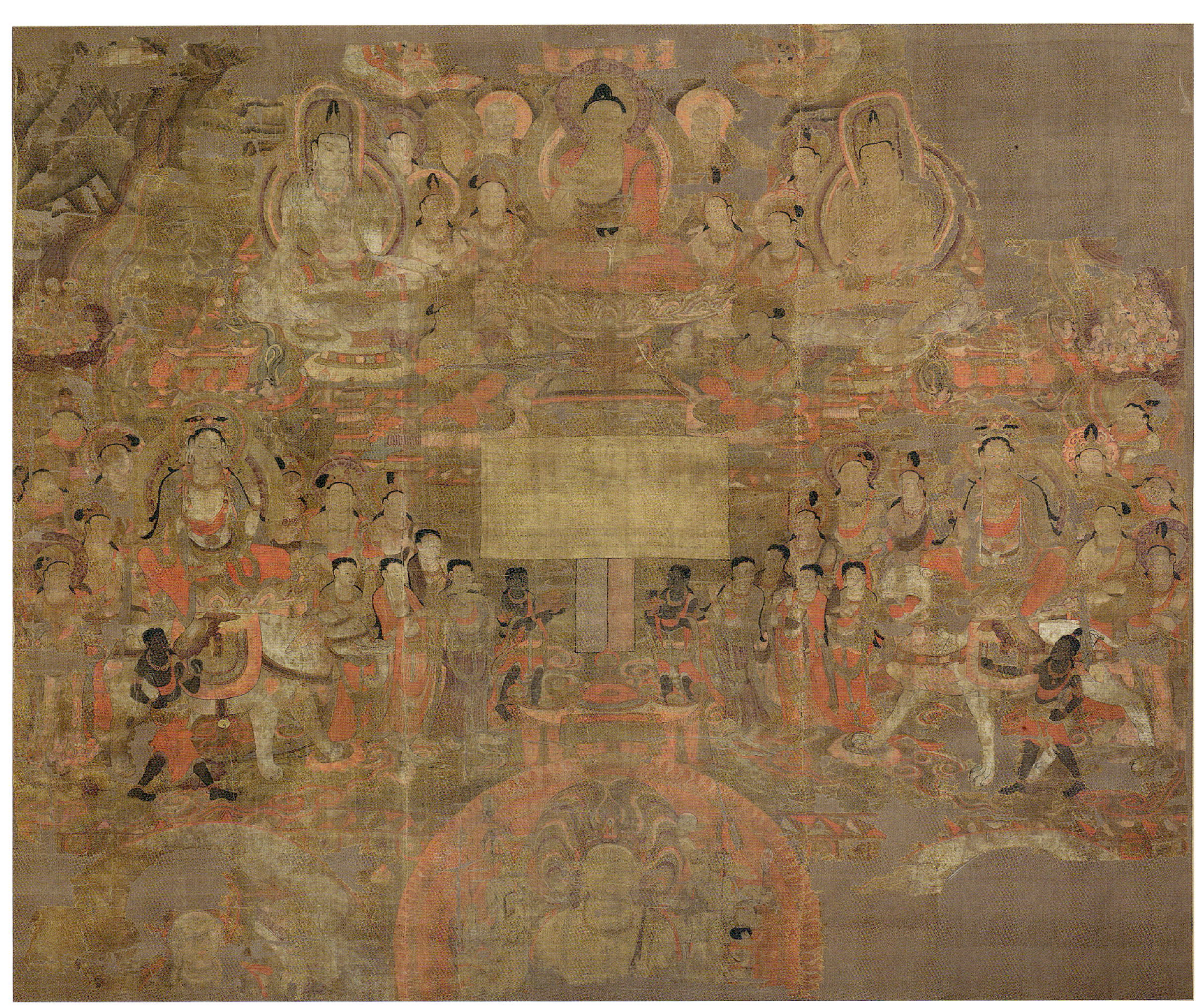

№ 14

Bhaishajyaguru, the Buddha of Healing

Dunhuang, Gansu Province, China, 836

Tibetan Visual Models on the Silk Road

AMY HELLER

For a sculpture of Bodhisattva Bhaishajyaraja, see no. 11.

THIS PAINTED SCROLL ON SILK represents the Paradise of Bhaishajyaguru (the Buddha of Healing, also known as the Medicine Buddha), set in a mountain landscape with the bodhisattvas Manjushri and Samantabhadra, numerous attendants, celestial musicians, and minor deities. Bhaishajyaguru, seated on a lotus pedestal above a dais that bears a dedication inscription written in Tibetan and Chinese, is positioned at the center of the upper register, emphasizing the spiritual and visual importance of the dedication. The large letters of the Tibetan alphabet make the Tibetan cultural matrix clear. The Chinese characters are aligned horizontally, rather than vertically (the conventional arrangement), but the Chinese inscription gives more information than the Tibetan text. The Buddha is flanked by his two principal attendants: at his right, the white Bodhisattva of the Moon (Chandra), and at his left, the golden Bodhisattva of the Sun (Surya). This iconography relates to early representations of the Buddha of Healing in Central Asia and China, notably in Dunhuang, the crossroads of the Silk Road. Dunhuang is best known for the hundreds of Buddhist grottoes in the nearby Mogao Caves that were embellished from the fourth to the fourteenth centuries. Among the Dunhuang murals, this subject was so popular that ninety-seven images of Bhaishajyaguru paradises have been identified, from the Sui dynasty (581–618) to the Xixia period (1038–1227).[1] In these murals, the buddha's body is most frequently pictured with a blue or a pale flesh tint, occasionally white or, more rarely, red, while extant portable paintings from Dunhuang and Central Asia tend to represent his body as beige or gold, as seen here.

The triad is surrounded by numerous small-scale bodhisattvas and *gandharvas* (celestial musicians) making offerings. The lower register depicts the two principal bodhisattvas—Manjushri mounted on his lion and Samantabhadra on his elephant beside the orchestra—above the Thousand-Armed Avalokiteshvara at the center of the lower register. It is striking that the Buddha of Healing as well as Samantabhadra and Manjushri are all rendered following Chinese aesthetic models, with round faces, their bodies clothed in voluminous fabrics and robes, while the two bodhisattvas flanking the Buddha of Healing reflect Indo-Tibetan aesthetic models of agile bending slender bodies lightly garbed in diaphanous shawls and patterned dhoti, which became popular during the Tibetan rule over Dunhuang (787–866).

Historic Significance

This is one of the largest portable paintings from Dunhuang, although major portions of the lower register are missing. Historically, this painted scroll, recovered during the field mission of archaeologist Sir Aurel Stein to Dunhuang in 1917, is highly significant: the colors and silk are well conserved due to Dunhuang's dry climate. It was also concealed for several centuries, allowing the bilingual Tibetan-Chinese inscriptions to remain legible. This is the earliest extant dated portable painting, a commission by Pelyang, a Tibetan monk then living in Dunhuang,[2] with a Tibetan inscription, corresponding to 836. The dedications read, "In the year of the dragon, I, the monk Pelyang, for the benefit of my health and to transfer merit, commissioned in a group the images of Bhaishajyaguru; Samantabhadra; Manjushri-Kumara; a thousand-armed thousand-eyed Avalokiteshvara. . . ." The Chinese text indicates the date—the full moon, on the fifteenth day of the ninth month of the *bing chen* year (October 28, 836)—and that it was requested for merit on behalf of Pelyang's deceased parents to be reborn in the peaceful celestial realm, the Dharmadhatu.

Paradise of Bhaishajyaguru; Dunhuang, China; 836; ink and color on silk; 60 × 70 in. (152.3 × 177.8 cm); The British Museum, London; 1919,0101,0.32; photograph © The Trustees of the British Museum.

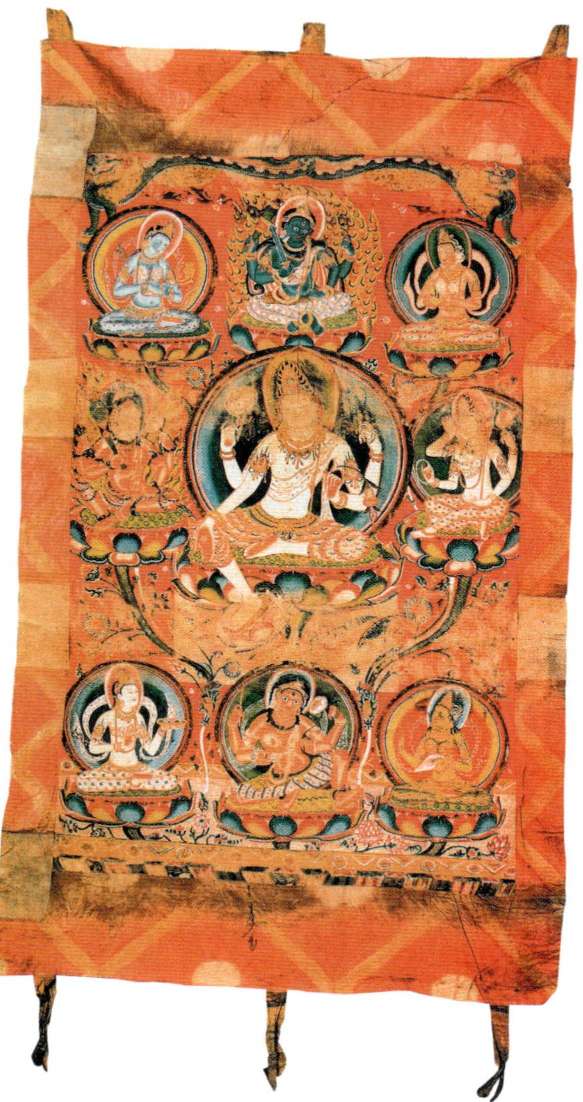

Mandala of Bodhisattva Avalokiteshvara in Several Different Aspects: Padmapani, Thousand-Armed Avalokiteshvara, Chintamanichakra Avalokiteshvara, and Amoghapasha at center; Dunhuang, China; period of Tibetan rule (ca. 781–848); ink and colors on silk; 56⅛ × 34¼ in. (142.5 × 87 cm); Musée national des arts asiatiques–Guimet, Paris; MG 26466; photograph © RMN–Grand Palais/Art Resource, NY

Iconography and Visual Conventions

Rather than a typical paradise of the Medicine Buddha, this group of deities reflects the personal preferences of the monk who commissioned the painting. The iconography of the buddha is distinctive: his right hand is raised toward his heart with the open palm facing right, a gesture reminiscent of the *vitarka* mudra, the gesture of argumentation, simultaneously clasping a golden leaf of a medicinal plant between the thumb and forefinger. His left hand rests in his lap, holding a bowl of nectar. Later Tibetan representations typically portray this buddha as seated and dressed in monastic robes, with his right hand extended toward the ground, palm up, in the *varada* mudra of generosity and boon-bestowing, holding a myrobalan, a medicinal fruit, to present to those in need. In portable paintings the buddha's body color may be beige or blue, the latter clearly linked to the lapis lazuli radiance attributed to the Buddha of Healing as described in his primary text, the *Bhaishajyaguru Sutra*, and in his ritual descriptions among the Dunhuang Tibetan documents: "The Buddha of Healing, the sovereign with the radiance of lapis lazuli."[3]

In this painting, the buddha's physiognomy, garments, and posture correspond to aesthetic codes of Chinese Buddhist painting. His two attendant bodhisattvas are composed with the explicit asymmetry of posture seen in Indian treatises:[4] seated with one leg pendent; their bodies as if in motion, implied by the angle of the head in contrast to the body bent slightly to one side; the head lengthened on one side and foreshortened on the other. This mode of dynamic representation as well as the visual contrast between the buddha's round halo and the elliptical halos of his attendant bodhisattvas—depicted with narrow waists, slightly elongated limbs, and garments reflecting Indian printed fabrics—appear to be at variance with the Chinese aesthetic mode, yet the painting techniques are the same. The figures are drawn in pale ink, with the white or gold of the skin color, along with slight shading to give volume, added. Above this base, outlines of facial features and the garments' fabrics are drawn in darker ink.[5] This paradise of Bhaishajyaguru reveals the flourishing of Buddhist art during Tibetan rule precisely by its juxtaposition of two different modes of aesthetic depiction. The identical technique of line and coloring indicates that the same artists were responsible for the entire painting.

Comparative Examples from Dunhuang of the Tibetan Period

See Imperial Carvings of Vairochana, no. 13.

Many painted scrolls on linen, silk, or hemp made during the Tibetan rule of Dunhuang represent Buddhist deities and ritual diagrams that reflect the newly evolving Indo-Tibetan aesthetic as well as iconographies stemming from Mahayana and Vajrayana Buddhist rituals among the Tibetan Dunhuang manuscripts. There is special focus on Buddha Vairochana, due to new translations of his tantra and rituals, as in a drawing of Vairochana and his entourage of buddhas and guardian deities. Images of bodhisattva Avalokiteshvara in several different aspects abound: Padmapani, Thousand-Armed Avalokiteshvara,

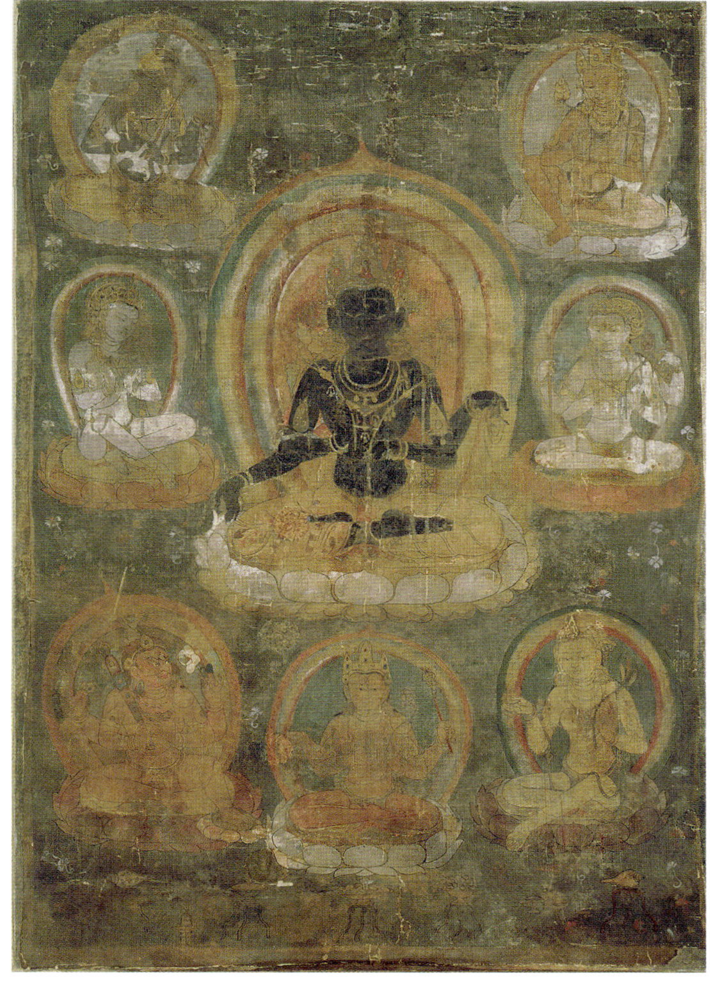

Deities of the Padmakula Mandala; Dunhuang, China; period of Tibetan rule (ca. 781–848); pigments on silk; 35¼ × 25⅝ in. (89.6 × 60 cm); Mission of Paul Pelliot, 1906–1908; Musée national des arts asiatiques—Guimet, Paris; EO 1131; photograph © RMN-Grand Palais/Art Resource, NY

Chintamanichakra Avalokiteshvara, and Amoghapasha. A painting of the mandala of the Padmakula featuring eight deities of the Lotus (Padma) family, is centered on the dark, four-armed Amoghapasha, seated and holding the noose for which he is named, used to save beings from suffering. Regal with his triple-panel crown and a makara earring, multiple thin gold necklaces, and a sumptuous dhoti, he is surrounded by seven male and female deities, all seated within elliptical rainbow haloes. Their precise identification remains enigmatic. Two of them, holding a lotus in two arms and four arms, might be aspects of Avalokiteshvara. The protector Hayagriva can be recognized by the horse head in his crown; the White Tara, to the left of Amoghapasha, holds a lotus in front of her chest; and perhaps the goddess Yasodhara, seated in the lower right corner, like Amoghapasha holds a noose and wears a makara earring on her right ear, as well as gold hoops on her left ear.[6] There is extreme delicacy in the rendering of their expressive faces, naturalistic body poses, sinuous draping of the sacred thread (*yajnopavita*), and lithe bodies seated on the simplest of lotus pedestals. This composition reflects the inspiration of India, eschewing the aesthetic of Chinese Buddhist painting to a degree hitherto unknown among the portable paintings attributed to the period of Tibetan rule at Dunhuang. There is a blending of diverse elements of Indian, Central Asian, and Chinese Buddhist aesthetic modes that characterizes the majority of the murals and portable paintings of Dunhuang during Tibetan rule.

Further Reading

Stoddard, Heather. 2008. *Early Sino-Tibetan Art*, 2nd ed. Bangkok: Orchid Press. Reprint of Karmay, Heather. 1975.

Whitfield, Roderick. 1982. *The Art of Central Asia: The Stein Collection in the British Museum, Vol. 1, Paintings from Dunhuang*. Tokyo: Kodansha International.

Notes

1 I thank Roderick Whitfield for this information and discussion of the Dunhuang representations of the Buddha of Healing (personal communications March 2014 and August 2014), notably citing his student's dissertation: Chih-hung Yen. "Bhaiṣajyaguru at Dunhuang." PhD diss., SOAS University of London, 5.

2 H. Karmay 1975, 10, first translated the Tibetan and Chinese inscriptions, understanding the monk Pelyang to be both painter and donor, as well as a translator of bilingual texts. Whitfield 1982, pl. 16, subsequently modified the translation after additional infrared photography of the Chinese inscription revealed the monk Pelyang as sponsor, not as painter.

3 "Sman gyi bla be du rya 'od gyi rgyal po," in Pelliot tibétain 247, Bibliothèque nationale de France, Paris, http://idp.bl.uk/database/oo_scroll_h.a4d?uid=3594404465;recnum=58640;index=1. See also Pelliot tibétain 248, Bibliothèque nationale de France; both texts are discussed in Lalou 1939, 68–69.

4 In his discussion of plate 47, perhaps featuring Padmapani, Whitfield 1982 (pl. 16, figs. 43–46) cites Bussagli 1963, 32, for the Indian aesthetic principle of *kshayavriddhi*, "increase and decrease," which results in the three-quarter view of the face, with the face turned to the left. The receding parts of the face are contracted and the nearer parts are enlarged. See also British Museum 1919,0101,0.102, a banner painting: https://www.britishmuseum.org/collection/object/A_1919-0101-0-102.

5 Whitfield 1982, pl. 16. Whitfield's description is quoted on the website of the British Museum, London, https://www.britishmuseum.org/collection/object/A_1919-0101-0-32.

6 See https://www.britishmuseum.org/collection/object/A_1919-0101-0-32; Vandier-Nicolas 1974, 159–62; Hambis 1976, pl. 86, "Mandala d'Amoghapasa (?)," for the first and most extensive discussion to date. It is also reproduced in Tanaka 1995, 400–401; Debreczeny 2019, fig. 3.6.

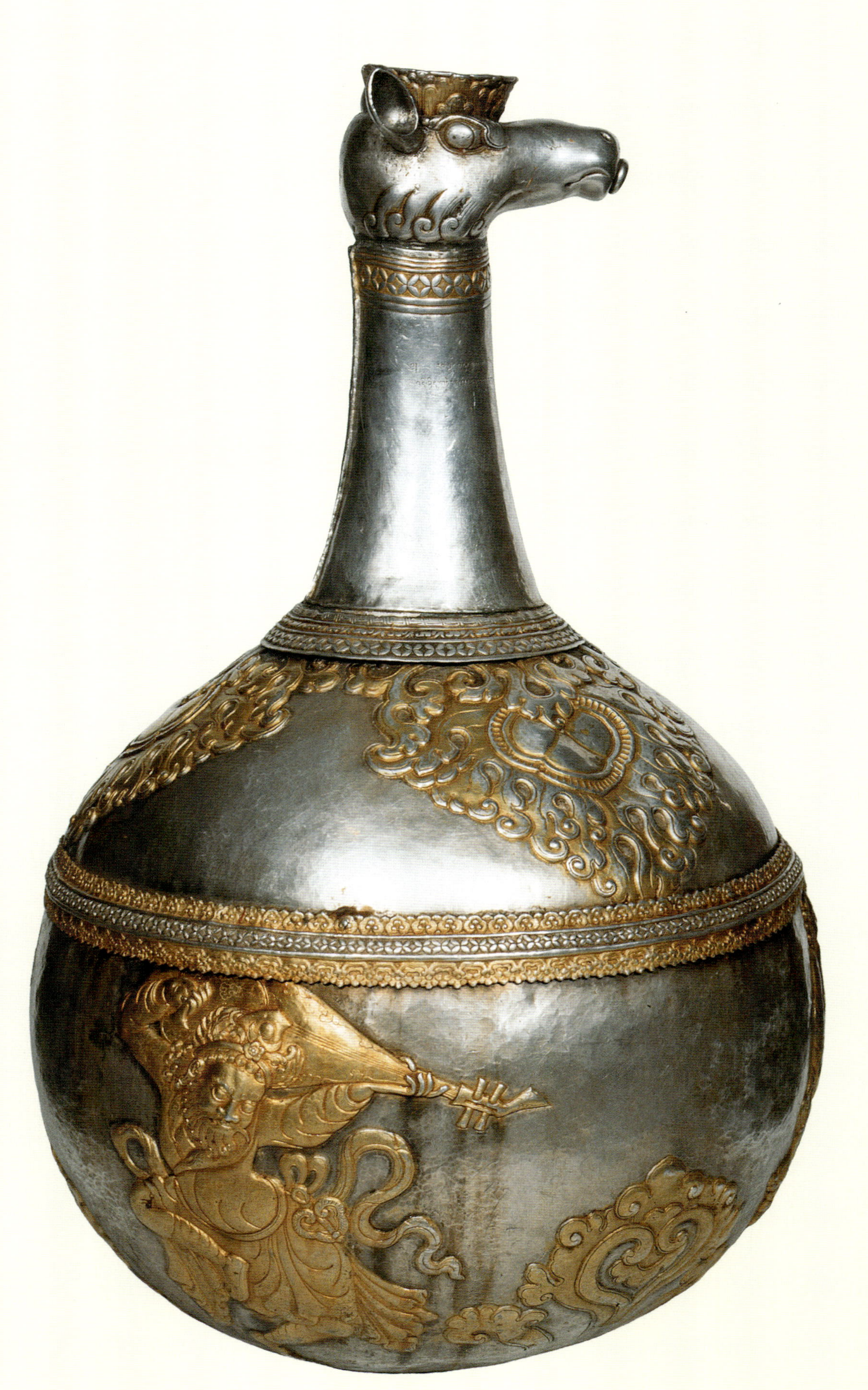

No 15

Silver Jug

Tibet, 9th–10th century, based on Sogdian or Uyghur prototypes

Ceremonial Banquet Vessels in Silver and Gold

AMY HELLER

See Jokhang Temple, no. 7.

TODAY, THIS SILVER JUG STANDS IN A WOODEN FRAME in a chapel of the Lhasa Jokhang, one of the oldest temples in Tibet. The tall ewer was hammered from silver sheets, cut and assembled in four parts, with two hemispherical sections joined at the diameter of the circle, and a long, thin neck surmounted by an animal head with round mouth from which liquid can be poured. At the nape of the neck, a necklace is formed of small metal circles in repoussé, each with a square cut out at the center, their shapes adapted from Tang Chinese coins. The jug weighs seventy-seven pounds (thirty-five kilograms) when full of liquid, and monks fill it daily with offerings of *chang*, Tibetan barley beer. The jug's upper bowl features raised designs in gilded heart-shaped medallions, and the lower bowl presents three scenes representing Central Asian people. These figures, two lively solo dancers and three men in drunken revelry, reflect Tibetan familiarity with their neighbors' appearance and customs. The animal head of the jug has variously been identified as a horse, a camel, a sheep, or a deer. The *Kings' Chronicle* (*Gyelpo Katang*), written in about 1345, described ten silver *chang* jugs hidden in the Jokhang in ancient times, of which three had camel heads and seven had duck heads, while the Fifth Dalai Lama's account of the Jokhang refers to the jug as "the great silver vessel with a horse head."[1]

Imperial Treasures as Symbols of Power

For more about the Tibetan Empire, see Yumbu Lagang Castle, no. 5.

For Jokhang's main image, see Jowo Shakymuni, no. 8.

Reputed to be associated with the Tibetan emperors, particularly Songtsen Gampo (ca. 605– 649), the first Tibetan ruler of historical record, this ewer is conserved in the chapel that bears his name.[2] This sovereign is traditionally revered for his foundation of the Jokhang Temple, although he is better known for his numerous military campaigns to unify Tibet and expand Tibetan territory, which proved crucial to the establishment of the Tibetan Empire in Central Asia. During the more than two centuries that the empire lasted, it carried on communications and trade with the outside world via the lucrative and multicultural Silk Roads threading between China and the Mediterranean world. These conquests are important to consider because they help explain the foreign connections and inspirations formative to Tibetan art and civilization during the imperial period, which this ewer reflects. Notably, the Sasanian Persian aesthetic had a profound impact on Tibetan art and culture. In Dunhuang, Turfan, and the Silk Road oases, Tibetans encountered the populations of Sogdian colonies—merchants, weavers, or artisans of silver and gold—who emulated Sasanian models of design for armor, metalwork, and textiles, leading Tibetans to import textiles and silver with animals, birds, and hybrid creatures in Iranian styles.[3] The Tibetan aristocracy even adopted the customs and vessels of the Iranian wine banquet, such as wine bowls, rhytons with animal heads, decanters, cups, and animal-headed ewers,[4] with the help of a partially gilt-silver rhyton, wine decanter, and cup inscribed with Tibetan letters.[5]

Silver Jug; Tibet; 9th–10th century, based on earlier Sogdian or Uyghur prototypes; hammered silver with gilding; height approx. 31½ in. (80 cm); Jokhang Temple, Lhasa; image after von Schroeder, 2001, 793, fig. 190A

Tibetan trade and diplomatic missions were important corollaries of these conquests. According to the Chinese *Tang Annals*, Tibet made the spectacular gifts in 641 of a goose-shaped golden ewer seven feet high, capable of holding almost sixteen gallons (sixty liters) of wine, and in 648, a miniature golden city decorated with animals and men on horseback.[6] The tribute continued, including in 658, a large bowl or basin of gold; in 727 hundreds of silver and gold vessels to be exhibited outside the imperial palace in Chang'an; in 728, a vase, a bowl, a duck, all in gold; in 824, a yak, a sheep, a bull, and a rhinoceros of silver.[7] Were these creations of Tibetan goldsmiths or imports via the Silk Road?[8] Comparison with Tibetan artifacts may help us to understand their provenance as well as inform an assessment of what Tibetan artisans then produced.

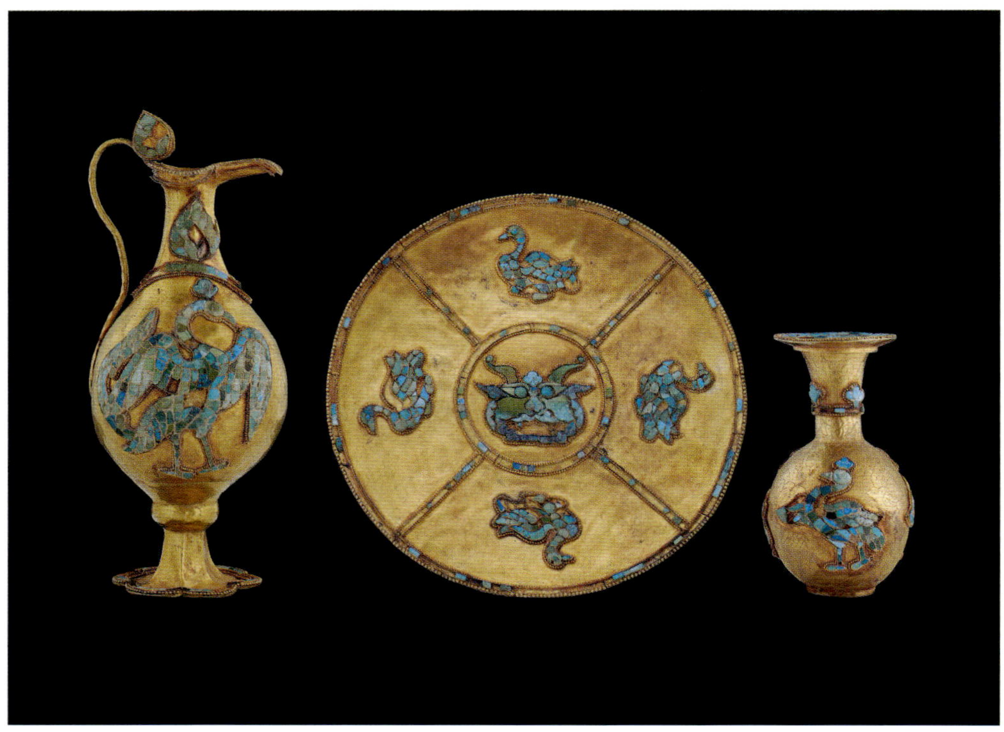

Banquet Set with Ewer, Decanter, and Plate; Tibet; Yarlung dynasty, 600–800; hammered gold, turquoise; ewer height 12⅝ in. (32.2 cm), diam. body 5⅛ in. (12.9 cm), diam. foot 3⅞ in. (9.7 cm), weight 1,114.6 g, decanter height 7 in. (17.7 cm), diam. mouth 3⅛ in. (8 cm), diam. body 4 in. (10.2 cm), weight 504.4 g, plate height 1⅛ in. (3 cm), diam. 10⅝ in. (27 cm), weight 913.2 g; Al Thani Collection; ATC1025a; photograph © The Al Thani Collection, 2019. All rights reserved; photograph by Prudence Cuming Associates Ltd.

Techniques and Materials

By their techniques and materials, these artifacts, a banquet set with ewer, decanter, and plate, clearly show the workmanship of a single atelier. Aesthetically, they are characterized by a spacious composition emphasizing the brilliance of pure gold, embellished by large-scale decorative motifs of birds and/or fantastic creatures. Each creature has raised sections of gold into which the turquoise was inset, with the bodies outlined in beads of gold granulation.[9] The prominence of the bird designs was linked to the ancient Sasanian and Sogdian political and religious concept of the bird as a symbol of royal power, particularly royal charisma, in Sogdian iconography;[10] when later incorporated into Buddhism, the bird acquired connotations as a symbol of rebirth. The plate has four ducks framing a central medallion of a *kirtimukha*, an ancient Indian motif that found its way to the Sogdian world as well as Tibet and Nepal. Since the insignia of rank in Tibet attributed gold and turquoise exclusively to the sovereign and his immediate family, it is understood that these gold artifacts reflect the highly sophisticated taste of the Tibetan court. The ewer and plate both have brief Tibetan inscriptions as well as small punched circle marks indicative of the weight of gold.[11] According to David Pritzker's research, the vessels with their "sleek linear forms . . . point to a Sogdian master goldsmith." Although no vessels like these have been found in the Sogdian world, he suggests that they "were fashioned by a Sogdian craftsman in western Central Asia and subsequently imported to Tibet in an undecorated state to be embellished locally, probably under direct imperial commission." Indeed, several plain gold decanters of similar dimensions have been excavated from the royal Azha tombs in Qinghai, tending to support his analysis.[12]

Aesthetics

Rather than animals or birds, the bowl of the Lhasa silver jug has three figural scenes in gilt repoussé, separated by thick scrolls with a heart in the center of the scrollwork. An inert hefty man with thick eyebrows, long beard, mustache, and curly hair is carried by two younger men, in a state of drunken revelry. Their hair, long curls, and beards might indicate Central Asian or Mediterranean ethnic groups. The man being carried wears a short cape over his robe, whose long sleeves hang far beyond the wrist. Such attire was already represented among Tibetan costumes in Dunhuang. The other two scenes, in gilt silver, show men wearing long-sleeved robes of thick fabric performing the dance known in China as the Sogdian whirl. Each dancer holds above his head a large lute recalling *kinnara*, celestial musicians, and musicians in the divine orchestra painted on Tibetan coffins, as well as in murals of Dunhuang and Yulin.[13] According to the *Tang Annals*, a caravan set out from Samarkand in 718 for Xi'an, carrying carpets, brass, precious rings, mats, lions, and dancers—female performers of the Sogdian whirl.[14] The dance was so fully assimilated to China that a dancer performs the Sogdian whirl in Amitabha's paradise in Yulin Cave 25 (ca. 820). Painted coffins from Tibetan tombs consistently illustrate musicians and the dancer of the Sogdian whirl in their vision of the paradise for the deceased, revealing Tibetan adaptation of the foreign motifs.[15]

For such costumes in Dunhuang murals, see Imperial Carvings of Vairochana, no. 13.

The aesthetic motifs of this ewer show complex cross-cultural relations. Perhaps the most telling evidence is a drawing by the German archaeologist Alfred Grünwedel copying a mural of about the

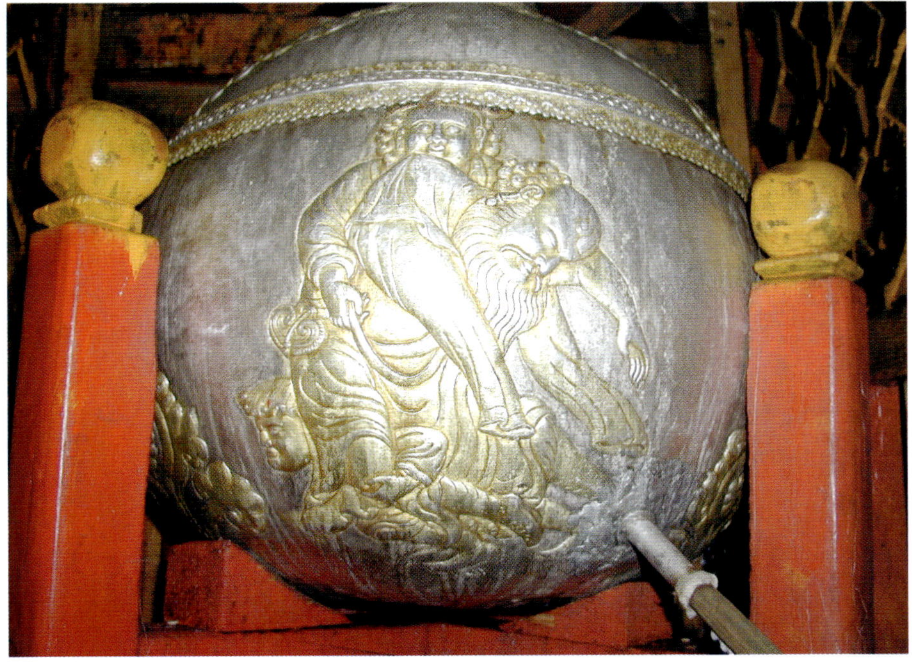

Inebriated man wearing a short cape over a robe with very long sleeves, detail of Silver Jug; Tibet; Jokhang Temple, Lhasa; photograph by David Pritzker

ninth century he observed in the Uyghur palace in Gaochang (near present-day Turfan, China).[16] He drew two grandiose ewers, with elongated necks, one with a bird-head finial and one with a celestial deer. These were the models that may have inspired the shape of the silver jug now in Lhasa, while the motifs have multiple origins. An alternative interpretation attributes the manufacture of the Lhasa silver jug to "Sogdian or other foreign silversmiths from Western Central Asia about in the 8th century."[17] Most probably it was made far from Lhasa, in the realms of the Tibetan Empire in Central Asia.

Further Reading

Heller, Amy. 2013b. "Tibetan Inscriptions on Ancient Silver and Gold Vessels and Artefacts." *Journal of the International Association for Bon Research* 1: 259–91. http://himalaya.socanth.cam.ac.uk/collections/journals/jiabr/pdf/JIABR_01_13.pdf.

Pritzker, David, and Wang Xu Dong 王旭东. 2020. Sizhou zhi lu de wenhua jiaoliu—Tubo shiqi yishu zhenpin zhan 丝绸之路上的文化交流—吐蕃时期艺术珍品展 / *Cultural Exchange along the Silk Road: Masterpieces of the Tubo Period (7th–9th Century)*. Exhibition catalog. [In Chinese.] Beijing: Zhingguo Zangxue chubanshe. English edition forthcoming.

Huo, Wei. 2012. "A Study of Ancient Tibetan Gold and Silver Ware," translated by Suzanne Cahill and Ye Wa. *Chinese Archaeology* 12, no. 1, 165–74. https://doi.org/10.1515/char-2012-0020.

Notes

1 Vitali 1990, 84n4.
2 Tsongkapa, founder of the Gelukpa monastic school (see https://treasuryoflives.org/biographies/view/Tsongkhapa-Lobzang-Drakpa/8986), fortuitously discovered the hidden silver jug and offered it as homage to Songtsen Gampo in the Jokhang, according to the Fifth Dalai Lama's history of the Jokhang, cited by H. Richardson (1977) 1998, 254.
3 A. Heller 1998.
4 See Melikian-Chirvani 2011, 97–101, for discussion of characteristic Iranian vessels.
5 See Melikian-Chirvani 2011, 101–3, for discussion of the cup, decanter, and rhyton, 103–4 for discussion of the Lhasa silver jug.
6 H. Karmay 1975, 3–4, citing Demiéville 1952, 203.
7 These dates and objects are quoted from the translation by Paul Pelliot of the *Jiu Tang shu* compiled in 945 (Pelliot 1961, 1–78), complemented by the *Xin Tang shu*, completed in 1060 (Pelliot 1961, 79–144).
8 One may refer to Edward Schafer, cultural historian par excellence of the Tang dynasty, who wrote about Tibet as a formative influence on China during this period. See Schafer 1963, 250–57.
9 Comparable in technique to two pectorals of parrots and flowers attributed to Sogdian artisans in Tibet, seventh to eighth century; see A. Heller 2018, figs. 8, 9.
10 Marshak 2002, 254.
11 Pritzker and Wang 2020, 216; Pritzker 2021.
12 Tong 2021, pl. 3-2-40, illustrates two plain gold decanters, 7¾ in. (19.7 cm) and 8 in. (20.2 cm) high, as well as fragments of a gilt-silver reliquary (pl. 6-2-7) attributed to Sogdian artisans by virtue of the distinctive Sogdian technique of gilded-foil cladding rather than mercury gilding, excavated at the principal Tibetan tomb in Dulan, Qinghai, attributed to the eighth century.
13 A. Heller 2003b.
14 Mahler 1959, 71.
15 A. Heller 2016a, detail of painted coffin with dancer and lute player, 197, fig. 17.
16 Grunwëdel 1912.
17 von Schroeder and Karsten 2009.

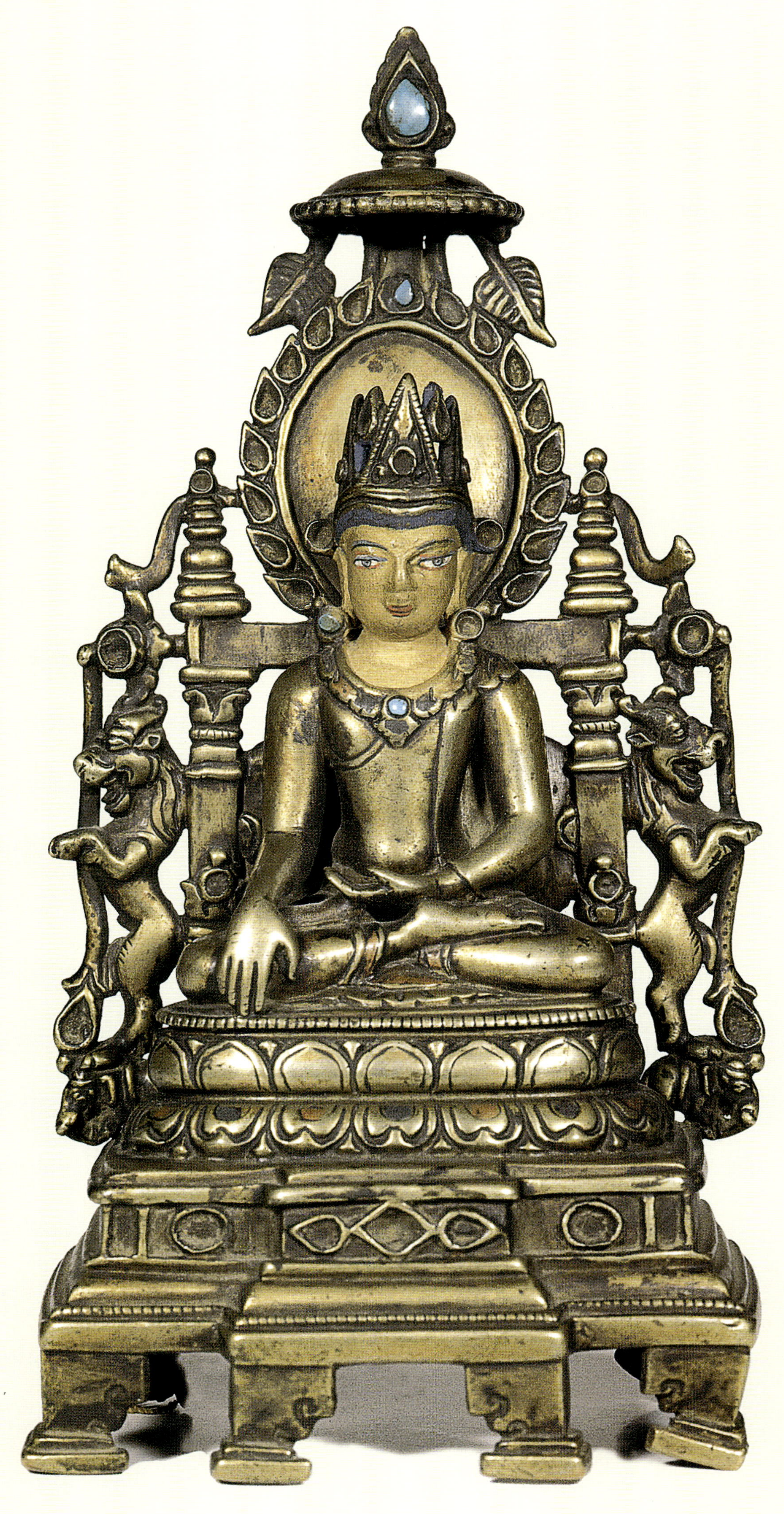

Nº 16

Crowned Buddha

Nalanda Monastery, northeastern India, 10th century

Intriguing Relations between India, China, and Tibet

CHRISTIAN LUCZANITS

AMONG THE BRONZES that Ulrich von Schroeder documented in some of the major monuments of Tibet, this Crowned Buddha stands out for the questions it poses.[1] Of Indian origin, it features a Chinese inscription on its back, and today it is in the Potala Palace in Lhasa, Tibet. This object raises a number of intriguing issues relating to the transmission of Buddhism from India.

East Asian Pilgrims to India

Much of what we know about Indian Buddhism in the second half of the first millennium CE stems from the reports Chinese and Korean pilgrims wrote for their home audiences. Their presence in India covers the emergence of esoteric Buddhist teachings, a development that can be approximated on the basis of dated Chinese translations of Indian texts. This bronze speaks directly to these connections through the Chinese inscription found on its back. The main parts of this inscription, to be read in vertical rows from left to right, have been translated as follows:

> The dharma master Huichao [of the] Kaiyuansi [-monastery in] Anxi [has this statue] made on his tour [through India], vowing [that] all groups of living beings of the dharma realm may reach enlightenment [literally: become Buddha] and realize the way [of the Buddha]. Copied [in the] monastery of Nalanda in the middle of the kingdom of East-India. . . . [reach] high age, father and mother [may be] reborn in heaven. . . . happiness.[2]

Taken literally, the inscription informs us that the dharma master Huichao, of Kaiyuan Monastery in Anxi, had this bronze made in Nalanda Monastery in northeastern India for the sake of his parents. Huichao is also the Chinese name of the Korean pilgrim Hyecho, of whom a fragmentary pilgrimage report has been found in the Dunhuang Library Cave. According to this report, he visited India from 724 to 727 before arriving via Central Asia in Anxi, on the western end of the Gansu Corridor, late that year.[3] However, trying to bring these facts together is far from straightforward, and Max Deeg thus asks in his study of the bronze if Hyecho (Huichao) had later gone back to India. The issue is that Hyecho reached Anxi only at the end of his trip, and that the system of Kaiyuan state monasteries was not established until 738. But can such an overlap in information between the bronze and the biography of this eminent monk be accidental?

An Informative Back

On the back of the nimbus, the bronze has a second inscription, the commonly applied consecration verse (*ye dharma* . . .), in the northeastern Indian Gaudiya or Siddhamatrika script. But the execution of the script differs remarkably from that of the Chinese text. Deeg has already assumed that the Chinese text must have been executed by somebody not familiar with the script but merely copying it. I want to add to this that given the gradation of strokes achieved with the Indic script and the absence of such gradation in the Chinese text, it is unlikely that the copyist had seen the text painted with a brush.

Observing the back of this sculpture provides direct insight into its production. The parts of the throne appear to have been molded separately in wax and then joined together, often using additional wax to strengthen the connection. We can observe this at the back of the two bodhi leaves on top of the

Crowned Buddha; Nalanda Monastery, northeastern India; 10th century; brass with inlays of silver, copper, semi-precious stones; height 7¼ in. (18.5 cm); Sasum Lhakhang, Potala Palace, Lhasa; 2013; photograph by Ulrich von Schroeder, 1997

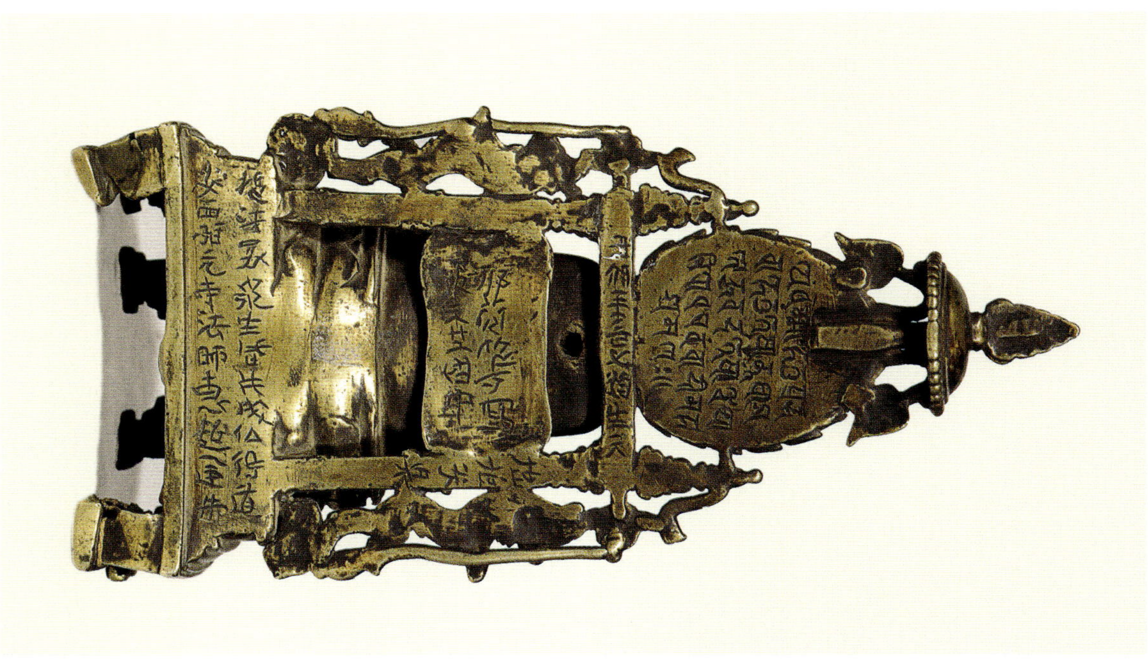

Back of Crowned Buddha, shown sideways; Sasum Lhakhang, Potala Palace, Lhasa; 2013; photograph by Ulrich von Schroeder, 1997

nimbus, the frame of the throne, the back cushion placed between the two uprights of the throne, the throne animals, and, in particular, the strings of pearls hardly recognizable as such hanging at the sides of the throne. While the object was expertly cast, the fact that some of the rougher patches were not smoothed out hints at a workshop production.

Seen from the front, the bronze produces a similar impression of an object finely made, but not exceptionally so. The minimalist modeling contrasts with the exuberant use of inlays, whether copper and silver for the lotus petals, dress, and presumably also eyes and mouth, or semiprecious stones along the periphery of the bronze. Of the latter, only the setting remains in most cases.

Esoteric Awakening

For more about the tantric interpretation of complete enlightenment, see The All-Knowing Buddha Vairochana Visualization Album, no. 87.

In this bronze, the Buddha, performing the earth-touching gesture (*bhumisparsha* mudra), is bejeweled and crowned, an iconography that alludes to his esoteric awakening. According to tantric sources, the awakening under the bodhi tree, two leaves of which are placed on top of the nimbus, does not represent the actual awakening of the Buddha. The latter takes place in Akanishtha heaven in the form of a tantric initiation by the Buddhas of the Ten Directions. The crown initiation is part of this esoteric initiation, and the rich set of inlays found on the bronze can be seen as signifying a miraculous event.

The Buddha sits on a throne executed in fine detail with a back cushion fitted between the uprights of the throne back. The two horned lions standing on elephants are part of the traditional throne ornamentation. The two somewhat abstracted stupas on top of the throne back can be read as hints toward the past and future Buddha and the continuation of the Buddha's teaching.

Northeastern Indian Bronzes

The chronology of northeastern Indian art is a complex issue. It largely relies on inscriptions mentioning the regnal years of different Pala dynasty rulers, some names of which are repeated multiple times, and the development of the diverse scripts used within the realm that can also be related to manuscripts. They make it possible to assess the development of the stone sculptures of a site on the basis of provenanced objects and the interrelations between these sites. Given the flourishing of artistic production in the entire northeastern Indian region, much of it related to major monastic or pilgrimage sites, such as Nalanda, Vikramashila, or Bodhgaya, this results in a complex picture that is increasingly refined.[4] It is more difficult to attribute bronzes to a site, as they are generally rarer, yet more diverse.[5]

Based on their art historical judgment in this light—and supported by Gourishwar Bhattacharya's assessment of the Gaudiya (that is, Siddhamatrika) script as belonging to the tenth or eleventh centuries—art historians have dated this bronze to the tenth century, much later than the Chinese inscription implies.[6] Indeed, comparing any of the details of this bronze with dated or roughly datable bronzes of the region, the tenth century is the most likely production date. Some details, like the cushion between the throne uprights, seem comparable to earlier examples, while others, such as the Buddha's crown, the shape of the bodhi leaves, and the rich inlay, relate to bronzes produced under rulers of the tenth and eleventh centuries. This attribution relies on stylistic features and is independent of the iconography, which would also be relevant to the mid-eighth century.

Northeastern India and Tibet

For depictions of the life of the Buddha, see Mayadevi Giving Birth to Siddhartha, no. 3; Mahabodhi Temple Model, no. 25; A Monumental Life of the Buddha Mural, no. 69.

See Goddess Dharmameghabhumi in the Tabo Main Temple, no. 21.

Stylistically, the bronze can be considered typical of northeastern India's high-quality sculptural production during the time in which Tibetans adopted Buddhism. But although numerous Tibetans traveled to the holy places and monasteries of India on pilgrimage and to receive teachings, there are only a few instances when Tibetan artistic creation can be directly linked to the artistic production of northeastern India. Depictions of the life of the Buddha based on the concept of the eight great events provide probably the most prominent example of such a direct impact.[7] In this connection, it is interesting to note that the crowned Buddha appears not to have been employed for such compositions in early Tibetan art, even though the esoteric awakening has, for example, been used to guide the iconographic program of the Tabo Assembly Hall.

Likely Scenario

Given its Chinese inscription, the bronze has been lauded as the only material confirmation of the presence of any East Asian pilgrims in India,[8] which is doubtlessly the case. But taking the different disciplinary viewpoints considered above into account, this evidence appears not to be as direct as one would hope. The most likely scenario is that this bronze was produced for a Chinese monk, of whom we have no record, with the same name as the one used by the famous Korean pilgrim. Another possibility would be that it replicates an earlier bronze and its inscription, which may well have been considered auspicious.

How the bronze ended up in the Potala Palace is another intriguing question. If the Chinese monk took it to his home monastery, it may have reached Tibet from there. In the second scenario, a Tibetan pilgrim may well have acquired it in India and taken it back to Tibet. The bronze thus documents the complex network of Buddhist travels at the time Tibet adopted Buddhism. The collections of Tibetan monasteries preserve plenty of evidence in this regard, but none of them quite literally brackets Tibet in the way this bronze does.

Further Reading

Bloom, Rebecca, Kevin Carr, Chun Wa Chan, Donald S. Lopez, Carla Sinopoli, and Keiko Yokota-Carter. 2018. "Hyecho's Journey." http://hyecho-buddhist-pilgrim.asian.lsa.umich.edu/index.php.

Deeg, Max. 2010. "Has Huichao Been Back to India? On a Chinese Inscription on the Back of a Pāla Bronze and the Chronology of Indian Esoteric Buddhism." In *From Turfan to Ajanta: Festschrift for Dieter Schlingloff on the Occasion of His Eightieth Birthday*, edited by Eli Franco and Monika Zin, 197–213. Lumbini: Lumbini International Research Institute.

von Schroeder, Ulrich. 2001. *Buddhist Sculptures in Tibet*, 1:210–320. Hong Kong: Visual Dharma Publications.

Notes

1 von Schroeder 2001, 234–75, pls. 70A–B.
2 Deeg 2010, 202, the fragmentary last section being a traditional transfer of merit.
3 Yang, Jan, Iida, and Preston 1984.
4 See for example the recent study on the production of Kurkihar by Bautze-Picron 2014.
5 For this assessment I mainly used von Schroeder 1981 and Ray, Khandalavala, and Gorakshkar 1986.
6 von Schroeder 2001, 218, 234–35 (citing Battacharya), pl. 70A–B; Bautze-Picron 2014, 190, 643, fig. B43.
7 The most detailed account of this is offered in a two-part study by Bautze-Picron 1995–96 and 1998.
8 Deeg 2010, 197.

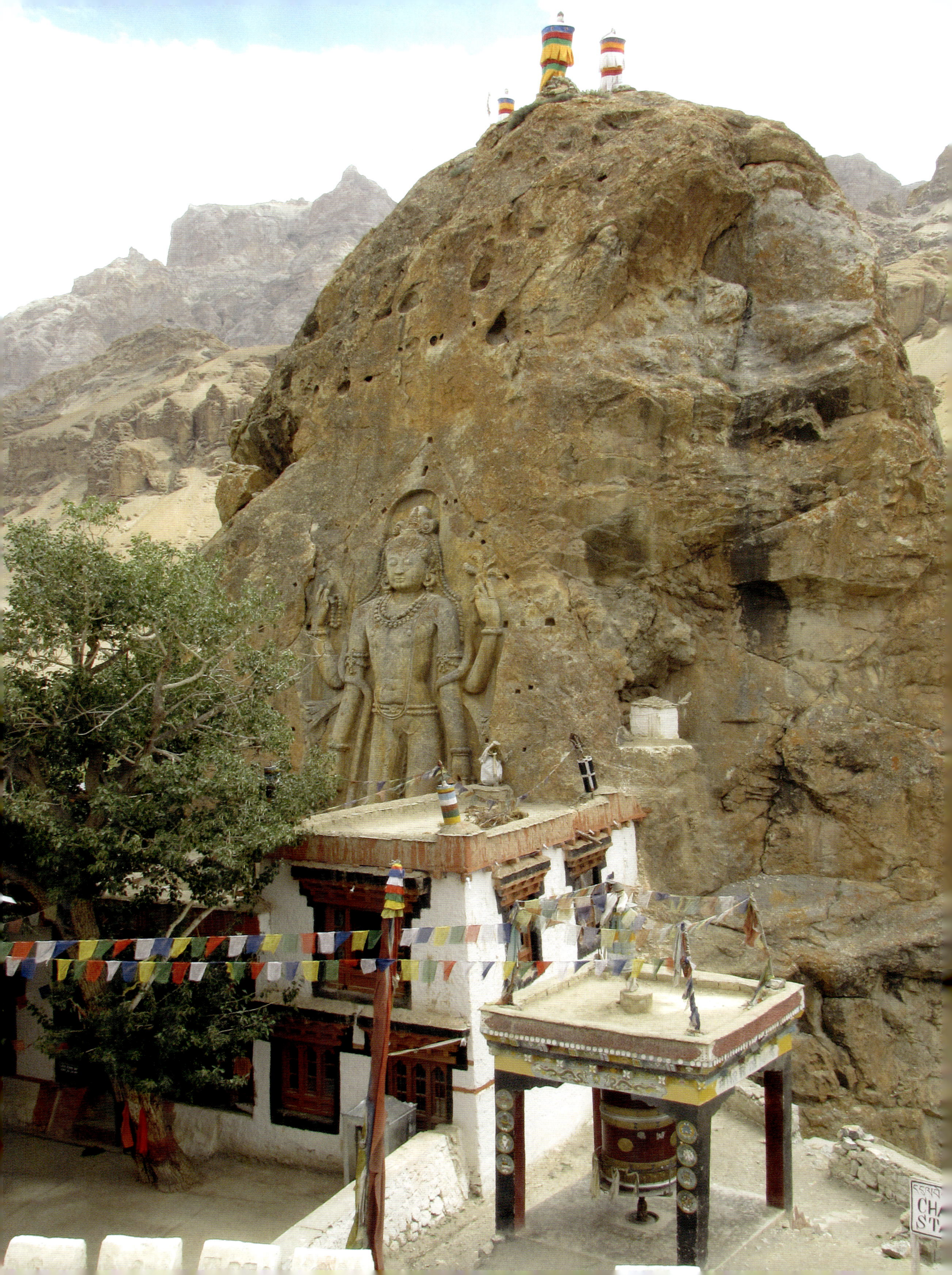

No 17

Rock Carving of Four-Armed Bodhisattva Maitreya

Mulbekh, Ladakh, India, ca. 10th–11th century

Kashmiri "Loving-Kindness" in Ladakh: A Tall Order?

ROB LINROTHE

For more on the importance of Kashmiri arts in the western Himalayas, see Goddess Dharmameghabhumi in the Tabo Main Temple, no. 21; Monumental Manjushri with Mahasiddha-Adorned Robe at Alchi, no. 35.

On the continued role of Kashmiri art in western Tibet into the fifteenth century, see Murals at Toling Dukhang, no. 54.

THIS SCULPTURE AT THE WESTERN EDGE of the greater Tibetan cultural horizon illustrates a stage in Buddhism's transmission to Tibet in which Kashmir played a large role. The kingdoms of Ladakh and Zangskar (Zanskar, now in northernmost India) were within the circuit of traveling Kashmiri painters and sculptors, a number of whose spectacular works survive on their western edges and interiors. Before gradually making their way to Tibet proper, the highly developed Kashmiri Buddhist teachings and art first made themselves deeply felt in the western Himalayas, extending also to the regions of Spiti and Ngari, on either side of the present border between India and Chinese-controlled Tibet, respectively.

Kashmir's visual inheritance was dominant in the western Himalayas between the eighth and twelfth centuries, and it remained important there in the fifteenth and sixteenth centuries, after Kashmir itself had turned away from Buddhism.[1] The monumental sculpture at Mulbekh, about twenty-five feet (seven and a half meters) in height, was carved into an isolated rock along a major route between the capitals of Ladakh (Shey and Leh) and Kashmir. The most well-known, handsome, and accessible of several life-size or larger rock carvings of Maitreya, the bodhisattva who will appear as the next Buddha, on the border region between Kashmir and the western Himalayas, it constitutes an impressive landmark of the Kashmir style's diffusion into the western Himalayas.[2]

Unlike most other stone carvings of Maitreya in the western Himalayas, the Mulbekh sculpture is four-armed. He holds a string of prayer beads and the *nagapuspa* flower in his ringed upper hands. The *nagapuspa* flower is a reference to the tree under which Maitreya will eventually sit when, like Buddha Shakyamuni under the bodhi tree, he attains enlightened Buddhahood. In his lower left hand he holds a *kundika*, a pure-water vase, signifying that in Maitreya's final life, he will be born into the Brahman caste, not, like Shakyamuni, into the warrior aristocracy. Maitreya's lower right arm extends in a gesture of giving, reminder of the meaning of his Sanskrit name, which is based on *maitri* (Tibetan: *jampa*), meaning "loving kindness." The stupa nestled against the high chignon on his head unmistakably signals that the carving at Mulbekh is the Future Buddha Maitreya, its shape in a distinctively Kashmiri form.

For an example of a stupa monument, see Stupa at Toling Monastery, no. 19.

The stupa has a trapezoidal stepped base, a small dome, and a superstructure with a stack of umbrella-like disks above a platform with slanting struts on top of the dome. This characteristic form goes back at least to Kanishka, the famous Kushana dynasty king and promoter of Buddhism from about the second century CE. Another feature of the Maitreya at Mulbekh in line with earlier Buddhist art is the elaborate arrangement of his hair. Curling "butterfly" loops tied to the ends of his chignon recall double-bow topknots featured in western Kushana dynasty Maitreya images.[3]

For more about Kashmiri metal sculpture, see Buddha on the Cosmic Mountain, no. 10.

Further unmistakable Kashmiri visual features are the tripartite structure of the torso, diamond-shaped scoring around the navel, large beaded jewelry with rosette medallions on his belt and necklace, the relaxed hip-slung pose, as well as the thick garland hanging from Maitreya's shoulders, wrapping around his arms, and ending above his ankles. All these features are found on stone and metal sculptures known to be Kashmiri. Dates from the seventh through the twelfth century have been proposed for the Mulbekh sculpture. Close comparison with other sculptures and with studies of the development of Kashmiri art provides some guidance in the absence of inscriptive or textual documentation.[4] The rendering of the slender and elongated limbs without sacrificing the articulation of a nuanced body structure suggests a working date of the late tenth or early eleventh century.[5]

Rock Carving of Four-Armed Bodhisattva Maitreya; Mulbekh, Ladakh, India; ca. 10th–11th century; stone, height approx. 25 ft. (7.62 m); photograph by R. Linrothe

Also revealing of the sculpture's Kashmiri origins is the triangular pediment-like framing device enclosing the tight trefoil niche in which the bodhisattva stands. This was the preferred architectural

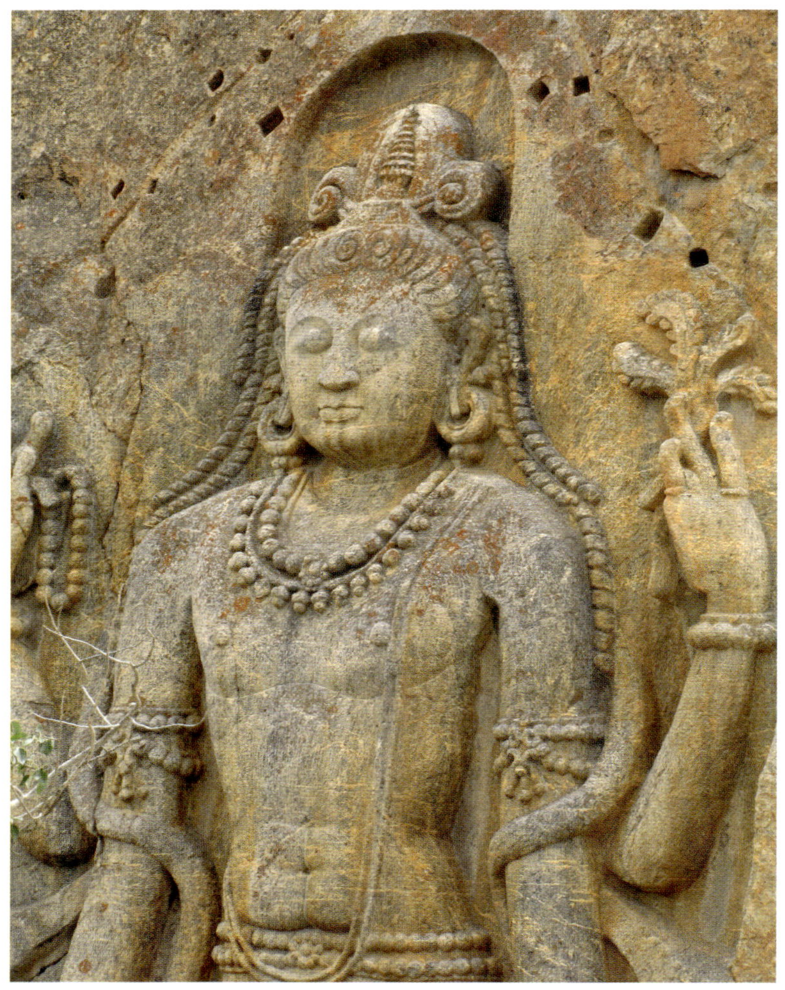

Detail of Rock Carving of Four-Armed Bodhisattva Maitreya; Mulbekh; photograph by R. Linrothe

form for Buddhist and Hindu shrines in Kashmir at the time. Square and rectangular sockets chiseled into the rock apparently stabilized one end of wooden beams for a slightly projecting porch or facade. Shrines built in front now control and accommodate roadside reverence. They block unobstructed views of the entire sculpture and hide seven archaic-looking figures standing at the level of Maitreya's feet. Among them might be the four directional guardians (*lokapalas*), hoisting swords and other objects, but damage sustained by the figures over the years precludes full identification. The group probably also includes donor figures, dressed in belted robes.

The fact that so many monumental sculptures—not just in Ladakh—depict Maitreya has occasioned speculation based on traits described in early Buddhist texts:

> In the future age of Maitreya, beings will not only have extremely long lifespans, but will also be physically enormous; Maitreya's own body is described in such terms. . . . The enormous size of Maitreya's body has been connected by some scholars with the many monumental sculptures of him either extant or referred to in textual sources.[6]

Importance conveyed through size also organically lends itself to expressions of rulership. "The monument imposes order on the landscape or the city . . . the monument signals the authority of the state over resources and skills as well as over time itself."[7] These concepts may help explain why some Asian political dynasties tried to associate themselves with Maitreya and produced such sculptures. Christian Luczanits has noticed that Maitreya veneration was popular in elite circles around the time of Kanishka within the ruling family of the Kushana dynasty (ca. first–third century CE).[8] André Alexander and Sam van Schaik emphasize "Maitreya worship during the imperial period in central Tibet." The latter wish to deduce from an impressive number of large images found in Leh, Shey, and the borderlands of Kashmir, including the Mulbekh sculpture, the "revival" of the central Tibetan pattern using forms from "regions to the west" within "the early domains of the western Tibetan kings."[9]

Intriguing as that suggestion might be, it runs the danger of accepting central Tibetan narratives of the invasion and dominion of the western Himalayas and the imposition of a reconstituted rulership as historically accurate. To be sure, later western Himalayan accounts also claim for themselves a measure of legitimacy through continuity with imperial Tibet. One wonders, however, what is meant when various places in the eighth or early ninth century in the western Himalayas are said to be "in the hands of the Tibetans."[10] Existing evidence mainly concerns their control of passes, bridges, or fords with garrisoning troops to rebuff enemies from invading and disenfranchising local rulers. However, those actions should not obscure the local and regional ties and enduring relationships between Ladakh and Zanskar with Greater Kashmir before the twelfth century. The timing and process of the reorientation of the western Himalayas toward Tibetan culture is called into question by the presence of Kashmiri sculptures such as the Mulbekh standing bodhisattva, particularly when, as is acknowledged for the inscribed Maitreya in Leh, the Tibetan inscription was added to a preexisting sculpture at an unknown date.[11]

See Imperial Carvings of Vairochana, no. 13.

See Avalokiteshvara at Khartse, no. 20.

Challenging both of those interpretations—that sculptures of Maitreya express textual claims of monumentality and reflect dynastic cults—is an inconvenient fact: in Tibet and the western Himalayan kingdoms, there are plenty of large early sculptures of other Buddhist deities, including Shakyamuni and Vairochana Buddhas and various forms of Avalokiteshvara. Another puzzle is the fascinating tendency

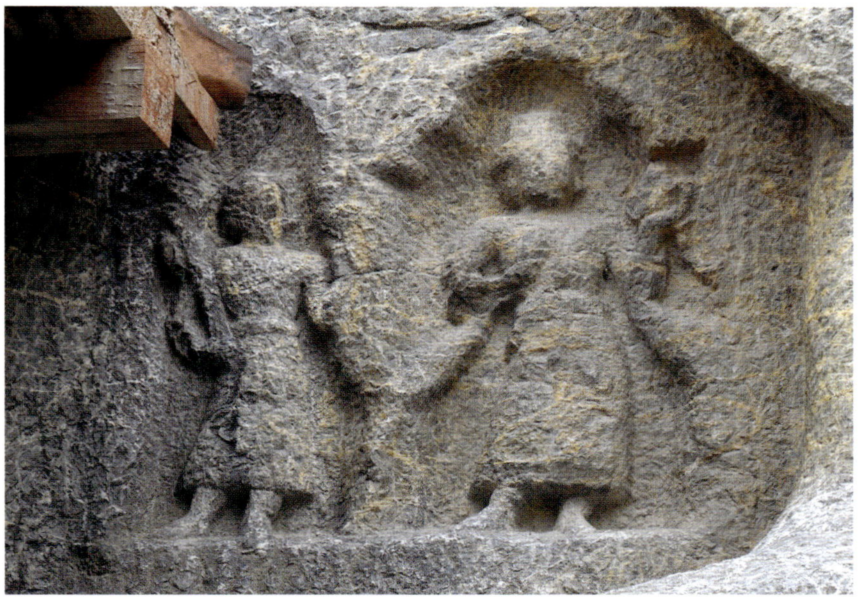

Detail of Rock Carving of Four-Armed Bodhisattva Maitreya showing two of the seven figures at the feet of Maitreya; Mulbekh; photograph by R. Linrothe

of recent and contemporary observers to misconstrue the gender of early Tibetan and Himalayan deities. The Maitreya carving at Mulbekh is one such example. A contemporary archaeologist describes it as having a "feminish" face and pelvic region, triggering the desire to "take the figure to be that of a female."[12] In the early nineteenth century, William Moorcroft described a Maitreya in Leh thus: "[A]lthough the person is male, the countenance is female, and the whole appears to be an androgynous type of the powers of nature."[13] Janice Leoshko noticed a similar tendency in nineteenth-century British observers of art in India: "Male figures were often mistaken for females in early accounts of eastern Indian sculptures."[14] I notice many of my undergraduate students, intelligent and interested as they are, often misread different secondary sexual characteristics in Tibetan art. It is a tendency that one should expect to encounter in the study of Tibetan art, which, among its rewards, offers to bring home the pertinence of the oft-repeated axiom that gender is socially constructed and thus culturally relative, not biologically given. Though the Bodhisattva Maitreya sculpture at Mulbekh has long hair, elaborate jewelry, soft fleshy features, and a line demarcating the upper chest with nipples, interpreting the sculpture as female is a misreading.

Further Reading

Alexander, André, and Sam van Schaik. 2011. "The Stone Maitreya of Leh: The Rediscovery and Recovery of an Early Tibetan Monument." *Journal of the Royal Asiatic Society* 21, no. 4, 421–39.

Linrothe, Rob. 2016a. "Origins of the Kashmiri Style in the Western Himalayas: Sculpture of the 7th–11th Centuries." In *Transfer of Buddhism across Central Asian Networks (7th to 13th Centuries)*, edited by Carmen Meinert, 147–88. Leiden: Brill.

Linrothe, Rob, with essays by Melissa R. Kerin and Christian Luczanits. 2015a. *Collecting Paradise: Buddhist Art of Kashmir and Its Legacies.* Exhibition catalog. New York: Rubin Museum of Art.

Notes

1 See Linrothe 2015a.
2 These include Dras, Kartsé, and Apati on the border areas and a few sculptures in Leh and Shey, all sites in greater Ladakh. See Linrothe 2016a; Alexander and van Schaik 2011; Denwood 2007.
3 See Luczanits 2008, 245, fig. 4, and 250, fig. 1; also Linrothe 2016a, 172.
4 Siudmak 2013.
5 Linrothe 2016a, 179–80.
6 Bowring et al. 2019, 305. Akira Miyaji, who gives the height of the Maitreya at Mulbekh as nine meters, connects the "cult of Maitreya" to "the divinity of the Cakravartin" and "adoration for emperors related to the enormous Buddhas"; Miyaji 2004, 91, 98; Julia Shaw also points to "the Dharma being easily appropriated by kings who sought to draw on analogies between themselves and the Buddha as Dharmaraja and Cakravartin"; J. Shaw 1999, 10.
7 Wood 2019, 22.
8 Luczanits 2008, 250–51.
9 Alexander and van Schaik 2011, 438.
10 Denwood 2008, 9.
11 "The inscription is probably not a formal record of the creation and dedication of the image, but a later graffito"; Alexander and van Schaik 2011, 428. Inscriptions recorded by A. H. Francke at Mulbekh are all fifteenth-century or later; see Francke 1906.
12 Dar 1985, 192.
13 Wilson 1841, 1:343.
14 Leoshko 2003, 81, 99.

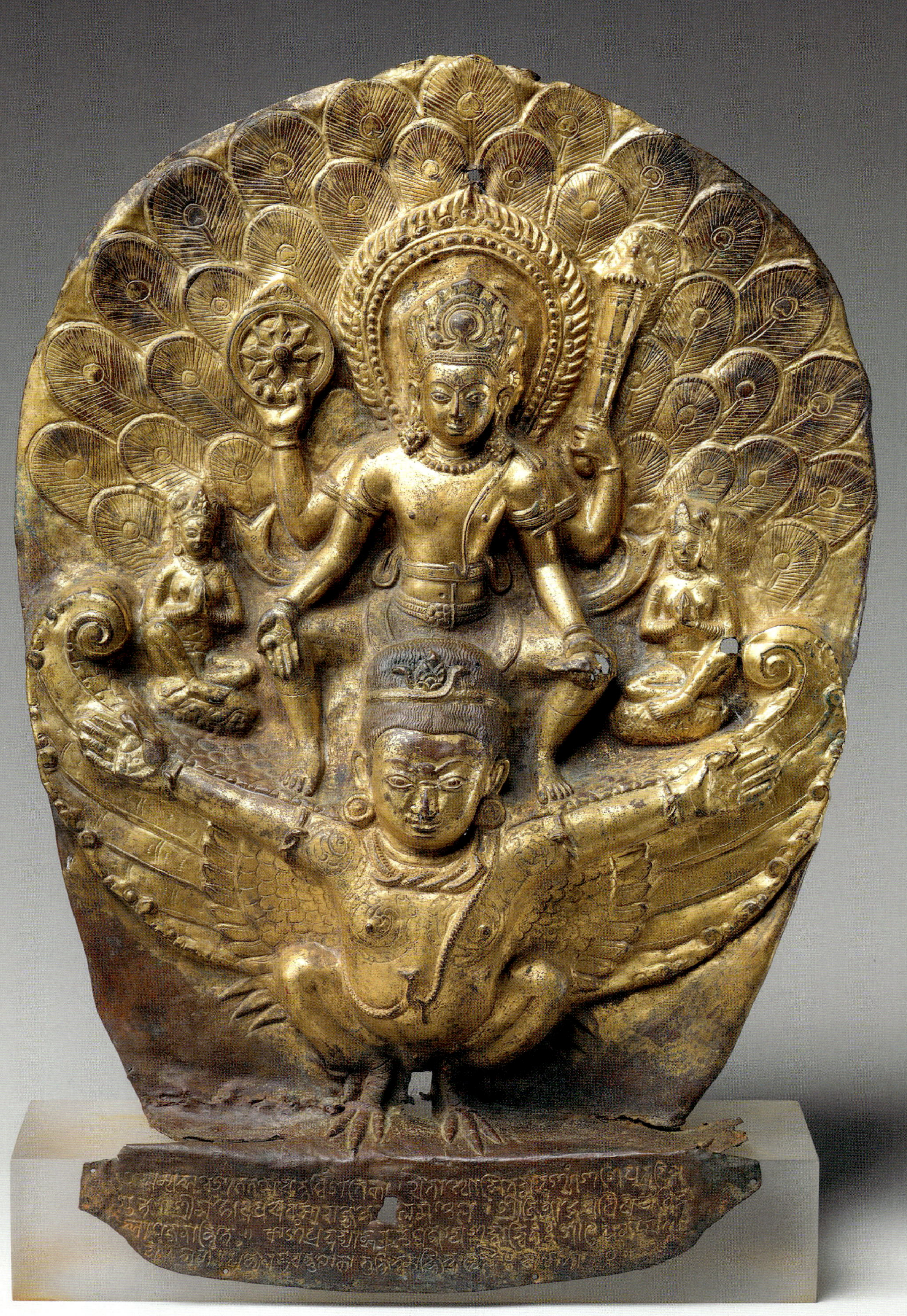

Nº 18

Vishnu Riding on Garuda

Nepal, dated 1004

Divine Kingship in Nepal Mandala

KERRY LUCINDA BROWN

FOR THE INHABITANTS OF THE KATHMANDU VALLEY, Buddhism and Hinduism have been practiced side by side since the earliest periods of recorded history. Adherents of both faiths patronized temples and monastic complexes, in addition to erecting sculptures across the valley as statements of religious devotion. These works gave physical form to the gods believed to inhabit the area, constituting the region referred to as Nepal Mandala, the historical name for the confederation of Newar kingdoms that ruled the valley. According to Buddhist belief systems, sculptures serve as public statements of religious devotion, while also generating significant spiritual merit (*punya*) for the patron. Archaeological evidence suggests that Buddhist and Hindu visual culture was well established in the region by the start of the Licchavi period (ca. 300–ca. 879 CE). Indeed, the surviving material remains from this period attest to active veneration of the primary Hindu gods, including Shiva, Vishnu, and the Goddess, with strong visual parallels with Indian kingdoms to the south. Whereas the power of the Licchavi rulers waned during the Transitional or Thakuri period (ca. 878 to ca. 1200), Newar artistic developments flourished. Inspired by stylistic traditions from northern India, most notably from the Gupta and Pala Empires, artistic production in the Kathmandu Valley thrived.

Vishnu Riding on Garuda

Dated to 1004 CE, Vishnu Riding on Garuda is one of the finest examples of Newar repoussé from the eleventh century. Vishnu, an important Hindu god associated with preservation and cosmic order, emerged as an important deity in the Kathmandu Valley by the fifth century. Vishnu's mythological narratives and iconographic features derive from Sanskrit Vedic texts and great Indian epics like the *Mahabharata*, which describe his heroic actions and divine powers. Made of gilt-copper repoussé, this piece was originally fabricated as a covering for a separate stone or metal sculpture of Vishnu seated on his half-man, half-bird mount (*vahana*), Garuda. However, with the original sculpture lost, the covering has become an image in its own right. This particular form is also known as Garudasana Vishnu. An inscription at the bottom of the piece reads, "In the year 1004 . . . in the Jichchodgesu district of the Nepal Mandala, the devout Sri Lipa gave (this) covering [*kosa*] to Garudadhaja."[1] The title Garudadhaja is a reference to Vishnu Garudadhvaja (One Whose Banner Is Garuda), a form of Vishnu riding on the back of Garuda, who literally becomes a throne for the god (*Garudasana*).[2] Historically, this title is significant because the Gupta rulers of northern India, who were contemporaries of the Licchavi kings, used this symbol as their dynastic emblem. Similarly, the Licchavi rulers of Nepal Mandala patronized numerous monuments and temples dedicated to Vishnu during their reign, demonstrating shared notions of divine kingship and ritual authority that endured through later generations. Thus, Vishnu Riding on Garuda provides an opportunity to understand how individuals in the eleventh century asserted their religious beliefs through the continued adornment of earlier sculpted works. Further, Vishnu Riding on Garuda allows us to contextualize the larger cultural significance of divine kingship and cosmic order in Nepal Mandala, a notion with lasting significance into the Malla period (ca. 1200–1769) and Shah dynasty (1769–2008).

Vishnu Riding on Garuda; Nepal; dated 1004; gilt-copper repoussé; 16½ × 11⅝ × 3⅜ in. (41.9 × 29.5 × 8.6 cm); The Metropolitan Museum of Art, New York; Zimmerman Family Collection, Purchase, Lila Acheson Wallace, Jeffrey B. Soref and Natalie Soref Gifts, 2012; 2012.463; CC0 - Creative Commons (CC0 1.0)

Vishnu and the Kings of Nepal Mandala

Vishnu and Garuda are the primary focus of this visual narrative. The vertical arrangement of forms, with Vishnu seated astride Garuda, expresses the vital supporting role Garuda plays in assisting Vishnu

For a parallel goddess of wealth in Nepal, see Goddess of Prosperity, Vasudhara, no. 34.

as he fulfills his dharmic duties. Garuda's outstretched arms are unwavering in their power. Vishnu's feet rest directly on Garuda's wings. They support Vishnu and his two wives, Bhu Devi and Lakshmi, shown tucked between Vishnu and the spirals of Garuda's wings on each side of the piece. These two goddesses, portrayed with their hands pressed together in a gesture of reverence (*anjali* mudra), are associated with the earth and abundance, reiterating Vishnu's duty to maintain order to support the cultivation of material and spiritual wealth. Vishnu has four arms and wears an elaborate crown, with his head surrounded by a flaming halo of a style typical for this period. His upper arms are associated with power and protection. The discus (*chakra*), grasped in his upper right hand, and the mace (*gada*), held in his upper left hand, are powerful weapons that reaffirm Vishnu's divine power and ritual authority. More pacific in nature, his lower hands hold a conch shell (*shankha*) in his left and a lotus seed (*padma*) in his right, both in a gesture of bestowal, with attributes associated with creation and spiritual transformation.

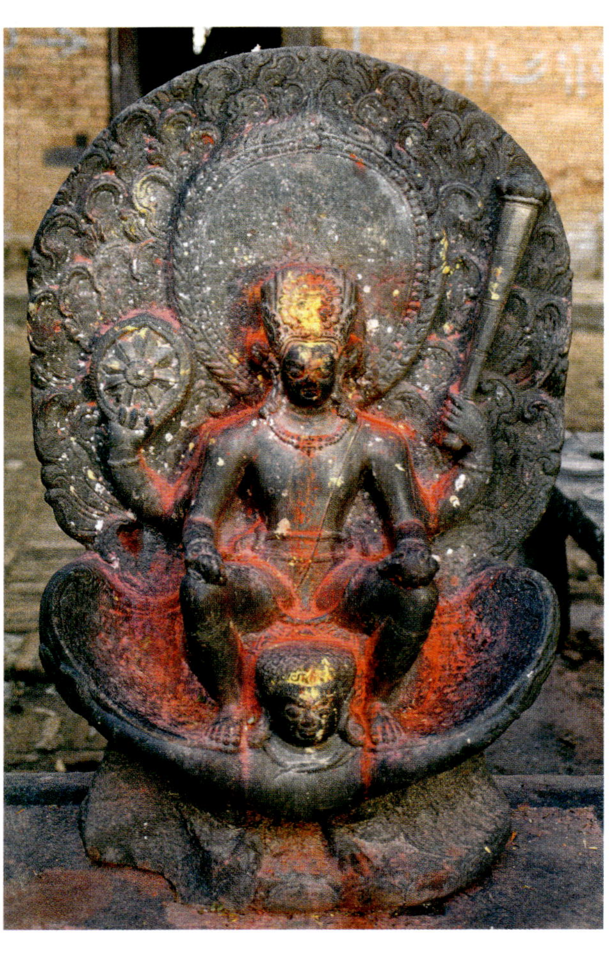

Garudasana Vishnu; Changyu Narayan Temple; Nepal; ca. 7th–8th century; stone; photograph by John C. Huntington, courtesy the John C. and Susan L. Huntington Photographic Archive of Buddhist and Asian Art

The importance of Vishnu to the rulers of Nepal is attested by the continued patronage of religious buildings, monuments, and sites dedicated to Vishnu and his incarnations (*avatars*).[3] One of the oldest surviving sites dedicated to Vishnu in Nepal Mandala is the hilltop temple complex of Changyu Narayan, located on the eastern edge of the Kathmandu Valley. An inscription installed at the site by King Manadeva (r. 464–506 CE) dated to 464 describes the revered position of kings within Newar society and, more importantly, the parallels established between the living ruler and the celestial divine embodied by Vishnu.[4] The site contains several sculptures of Vishnu, including a circa seventh–eighth-century carving of Garudasana Vishnu. A similar sculpture would have likely served as the original image for the repoussé piece currently under discussion. This composition remained quite popular during the Licchavi and Transitional or Thakuri periods and continued to appear during the Malla period and Shah dynasty.

While he serves as the seat for the gods above him, Garuda is in fact the largest figure in the composition. Presented crouching, with his talons tucked tightly below his body, Garuda wears snake (naga) jewelry, attesting to his control over snakes and the bodies of water they control.[5] His outstretched arms reveal multiple layers of feathers, with swirled details chased into his chest that weave together his human and avian features. Garuda's plumage extends across the lower register, with his tail feathers rising behind the divine triad, framing them in an elaborate peacock plumage. The stacking of deities to convey a visual hierarchy is a popular compositional device used in Nepalese art to establish relationships between personas. Vishnu Riding on Garuda reiterates the importance of the Hindu god Vishnu and his divine mount, Garuda, to serve and protect the inhabitants of the kingdom.

For more on snakes and the control of water, see Golden Fountain of Bhaktapur, no. 74.

For more on the stacking of deities to convey visual hierarchy, see Siddhi Lakshmi, no. 67.

By the Malla period and continuing into the Shah dynasty, the kings of Nepal, considered living incarnations of Vishnu, incorporated Garuda imagery into their thrones. A fantastic example is seen in the throne given to King Srinivas Malla in 1666. The gilt-copper throne is attached to a wood frame. Two elements emerge from the base of the throne, each featuring a pair of elephants surmounted by a lion, with a large image of Garuda in the base between them. Here, the use of visual devices clearly conflates the kings of Nepal with the Hindu god Vishnu. When seated on the throne, the king assumes the same position as Vishnu from Vishnu Riding on Garuda and similar Garudasana Vishnu forms. The composition displays a clear understanding of the connection between Vishnu, Garuda, and the kings of Nepal Mandala.

Similarly, the appearance of this visual format in later Tibetan works attests to the cross-cultural exchange in the region. For example, in the Hariharihari Lokeshvara painting presented to the Qianlong emperor (r. 1735–1796) by the Sixth Panchen Lama, the Nepalese stacked composition is utilized with

For more on Qianlong, see The Qianlong Emperor as Manjushri-Chakravartin, no. 84.

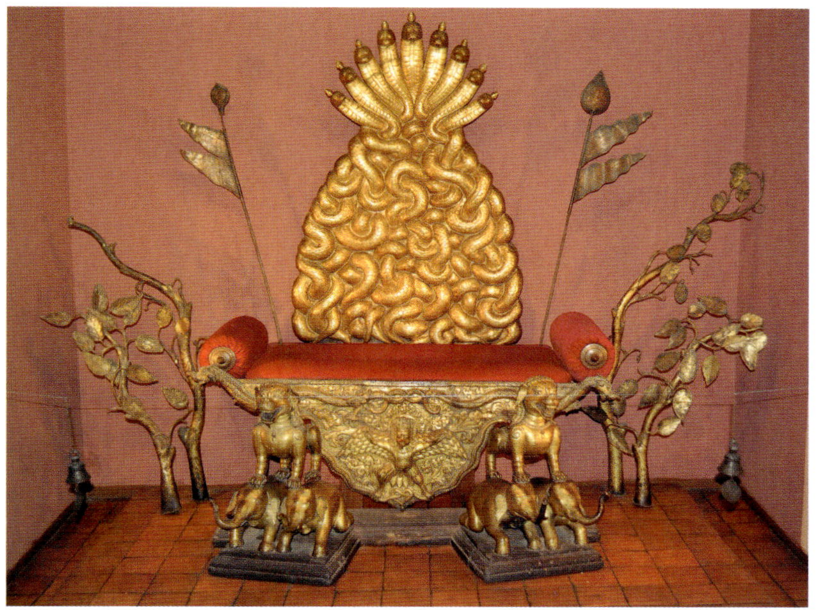

Throne of the Patan Kings; Patan, Nepal; 1666; gilt copper, wood, modern upholstery; 74 × 57½ × 57½ in. (188 × 146 × 146 cm); Patan Museum; photograph © Kerry Lucinda Brown

a Buddhist deity in a Tibetan context.[6] Again, we see how vertical hierarchies establish relationships and reaffirm cultural dominance. With this example, Buddhism asserts its authority over Hinduism: bodhisattva Avalokiteshvara sits on the shoulders of Vishnu, who in turn sits on Garuda, who stands on the back of a snow lion, yet the interdependent relationship cannot be overlooked.[7]

Repoussé as Offerings to the Gods

Repoussé has a rich history in the Kathmandu Valley, and Newar artisans were prized for their metalworking capabilities throughout the Himalayas and Inner Asia. The technique requires the delicate handling of metal sheets that are hammered from the reverse side to create a three-dimensional relief on the front. Within Newar religious traditions, clay, wood, and stone deities may be covered with repoussé fittings as adornments. The metal sheath can serve as a complete dress, armor, or ornaments applied to the deity.[8]

With Vishnu Riding on Garuda, the metal sheath once covered an older sculpture that would have served as the base for the repoussé. No doubt the importance of Vishnu and Garuda to the ritual and cultural heritage of Nepal Mandala was on the mind of the devout Sri Lipa in the eleventh century when they commissioned the copper repoussé covering. Covers such as these were offered to the deity as a gift (*dana*) to cultivate spiritual merit for the donor. In addition to protecting the original carving, these metal covers further beautified and ornamented the image. The new layer of repoussé became a way for the donor to connect their merit to the living history of the original sculpture. It activated the form, renewing the deity for a new generation of patrons. When the devout Sri Lipa gave this new covering to Garudadhvaja, they were attesting to the importance and value that this deity had for the community. The new layer of repoussé acknowledges the power of the sacred image for those who worship in its presence.

Further Reading

Slusser, Mary Shepherd. 1996. “Lord Vishnu and the Kings of Nepal.” *Asian Art & Culture: The Himalayas* 9, no. 3, 9–29.

Slusser, Mary Shepherd, Nutan Sharma, and James A. Giambrone. 1999. “Metamorphosis: Sheet Metal to Sacred Image in Nepal.” *Artibus Asiae* 58, nos. 3–4, 215–52.

Vajracharya, Gautama V. 2014. “Kirtimukha, the Serpentine Motif, and Garuda: The Story of a Lion that Turned into a Big Bird.” *Artibus Asiae* 74, no. 2, 311–36.

Notes

1 The Metropolitan Museum of Art, n.d., https://www.metmuseum.org/art/collection/search/78185.
2 Vajracharya 2014.
3 Pal 2004, 47–50.
4 Riccardi 1989, 611, 616–17.
5 Gail 2004.
6 Zhang Yajing 2014, 25.
7 Zhang Yajing 2014, 25.
8 Slusser, Sharma, and Giambrone 1999, 221.

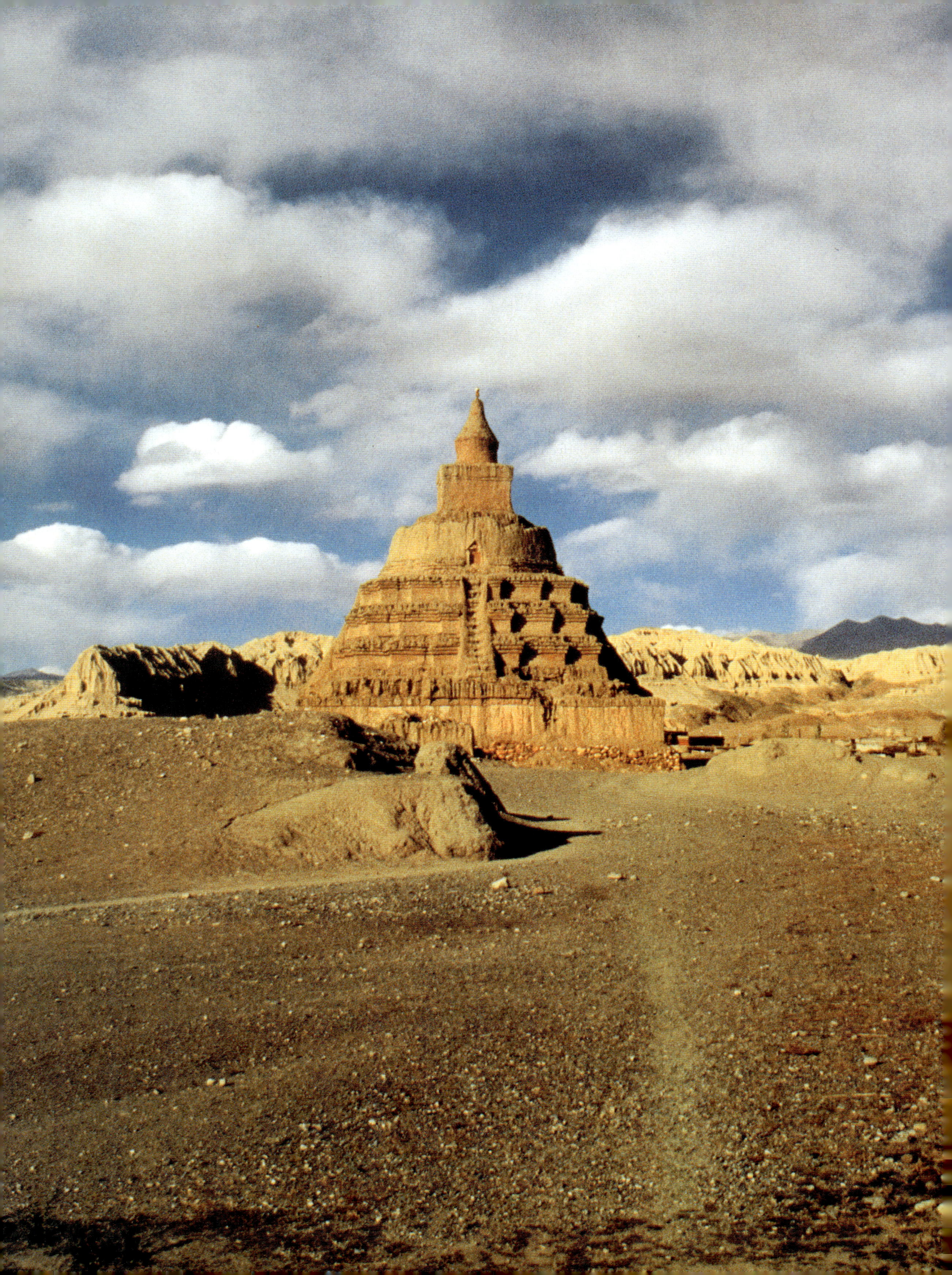

№ 19

Stupa at Toling Monastery

Ngari region, western Tibet (present-day TAR, China), early 11th century

Kashmiri Aesthetics at the Royal Monastery in Western Tibet

AMY HELLER

For another example of art at Toling, see Murals at Toling Dukhang, no. 54.

The royal monastery of Toling, at the center of the former capital of the kingdom of Guge, is singularly important in the history of political authority, religion, and art in the Ngari region of western Tibet. Its founding is attributed to Yeshe Wo (947–1024), then sovereign ruler of Guge. Although the circumstances of its construction remain to be studied, according to later Tibetan historical sources, he established Toling in 996, with his personal chaplain Rinchen Zangpo (958–1055), the renowned Tibetan translator.[1] Yeshe Wo issued a royal edict calling for local workshops to create Buddhist art of aesthetic perfection.[2] To this end, he invited artists and Buddhist scholars (*pandita*) to bring Buddhist texts and Buddhist art to Toling. Rinchen Zangpo traveled to monastic universities in India and Kashmir in search of Buddhist texts to take to Tibet. It is believed that the first temples in Toling were embellished by a team of thirty-two Kashmiri artists who accompanied Rinchen Zangpo to Guge from Kashmir.[3]

The stupa of Toling is located to the northwest of the main temple and was left in a ruined state following the destruction of religious institutions during the Cultural Revolution. It was subsequently studied and resealed. Recent excavation inside the stupa shows the impact of the Kashmiri aesthetic in western Tibet, as seen in the distinctive iconographic program centered on Vairochana in its sculptures and mural paintings. Pages from an illuminated *Perfection of Wisdom* (*Prajnaparamita*) *Sutra* manuscript produced during this time within the same artistic environment help contextualize these murals and sculptures.

See Imperial Carvings of Vairochana, no. 13.

The stupa's iconographic program is clearly related to the ritual practices for Vairochana popular in the early eleventh century. This program emerged from the translations and retranslations by Rinchen Zangpo, based in part on rituals translated into Tibetan during the eighth to ninth century. The stupa statues correspond to the *Mahavairochana Tantra*, with emphasis on Buddha Vairochana (gold body color) accompanied by bodhisattva Avalokiteshvara (white) and Vajrapani (blue). The paintings represent the eight offering goddesses and sixteen great bodhisattvas of the Vajradhatu mandala of Vairochana.

Kashmiri Aesthetics

The paintings and sculptures of the stupa are characterized by a brilliant palette of bright colors, thickly applied to create an opaque yet lustrous effect. On top of the base color of the body, shading adds the perception of chromatic modeling and volume. On some goddesses, a broad field of pale color was applied to enhance the sense of volume, further accentuated through the repeated use of red or black outlines. Juxtaposed rich colors, such as the crimson and yellow of the fabric clinging to the body of the deep blue statue and the deep yellow body aura against white behind the painted bodhisattvas and goddesses and their lavish gold crown and hair ornaments generate a sense of opulence. The feet of the standing buddha (on the left) demonstrate that artists innovated with gold leaf, goldfields near Toling providing the source. His elongated body and asymmetrical stance, with one foot forward on the lotus pedestal, correspond to the aesthetic seen in the Khartse Avalokiteshvara, adapted to represent the standing buddha in monastic robes. In the small mural paintings, the surrounding bodhisattvas are represented frontally, while all the goddesses are presented in three-quarter profile, displaying the elongated eye characteristic of Kashmiri sculpture, their eyelids thickly outlined in black, as if wearing eyeliner (kohl). The goddesses' faces have slightly puffed cheeks and small pointed chins, also associated with Kashmiri style.

See Avalokiteshvara at Khartse, no. 20.

Stupa at Toling Monastery; Ngari region, western Tibet (present-day TAR, China); 11th century; mud bricks and wood; photograph by Lionel Fournier

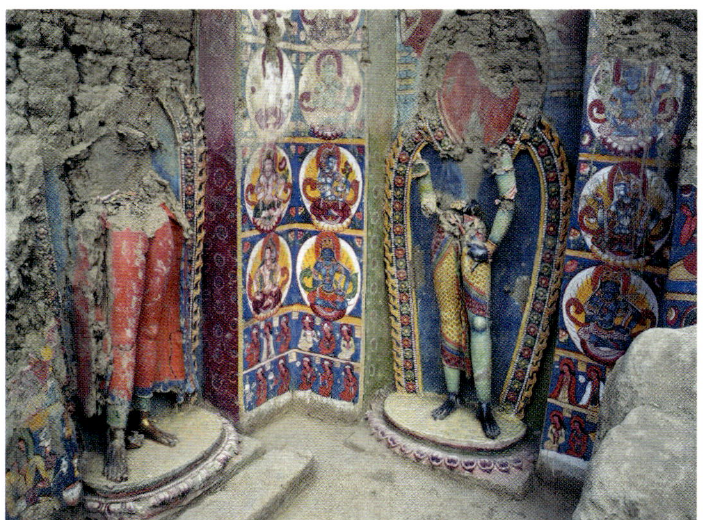

Interior of Stupa at Toling Monastery; Ngari region, western Tibet (present-day TAR, China); 11th century; clay, wood, straw, pigments, and gold leaf; height approx. 78¾ in. (200 cm); photograph by Zong Tongchang

The bodies of the bodhisattvas exhibit the strong muscular torso and defined waist typical of Kashmiri art. The twists of the goddesses' lithe bodies and their varied arm positions create a dynamic sense of motion. Although portrayed as immobile, the painted bodhisattvas echo the varied arm positions. The goddesses wear veils behind their hair, in front of the ovoid halo (*prabha*), and two sets of earrings: a small gold ring on the upper earlobe and a hoop with concentric pearls and gems suspended from the lower lobe. The veil is typical for both goddesses and female donor figures in Kashmiri sculpture. The double earrings are also found in the roughly contemporary Kashmiri sculpture of Lakshmi, so one may presume that it constituted a fashionable element for women in the northwestern region of the Indian subcontinent.[4] Furthermore, the veil and the double earrings adorn the goddess Prajnaparamita in a manuscript collected by Giuseppe Tucci at Toling whose illumination is traditionally attributed to Kashmiri artists at the beginning of the eleventh century.[5] The thick ringlets of curly black hair framing the goddess's forehead also reflect Kashmiri fashion, as does the fit of the goddess's lower garment (dhoti) to emphasize the lower belly, two features also apparent in a fragmentary page from a *Prajnaparamita Sutra* manuscript from Toling.

A seated silver Manjushri in the Ashmolean Museum, Oxford, is a helpful comparison for the seated bodhisattvas of Toling stupa's murals. The silver Manjushri is sculpted in the Kashmiri aesthetic mode, with three-leaf crown, flowing upward scarf, elongated eyes, and other characteristic features. The sculpture's very small scale and light weight indicate that it was probably used for the rituals involving a group of such sculptures such as initiation into a mandala, as its highly portable nature made it possible for teachers to carry it on their travels.

Contextual Considerations of Illuminated Manuscripts from Toling

For another example of an illuminated *Prajnaparamita Sutra* manuscript, see no. 23.

In the fragmentary page of a *Prajnaparamita Sutra* manuscript, the apparel, coiffure, and jewelry of the two offering goddesses accompanying six-armed Prajnaparamita correspond closely to the goddesses' images in the stupa. Their garments' floral roundels on red background also closely resemble the painted decor of the standing buddha sculpture alcove, making the buddha look as if he were surrounded by textiles. In addition, one of the main designs of the dhoti of the standing bodhisattva sculpture is comparable to that of the dhotis in the illuminations. Thus, it is quite probable that this manuscript was produced in the ateliers of Toling.

The production and dissemination of Buddhist manuscripts—particularly illuminated manuscripts of the *Prajnaparamita Sutra* literature—lay at the crux of intense multicultural religious transfer and artistic transformations, as these stemmed from the cult of the book practiced in Mahayana Buddhism. The practice of donating embellished manuscripts of Mahayana sutras was intended to generate additional merit for the donors and for the community. The richly illuminated manuscripts of the *Prajnaparamita Sutra* made in Toling are the tangible products of the royal edict to foster the implantation of Buddhism through the promotion of artistic and scribal excellence.

The Tibetan translations faithfully retain the wording of the Indian antecedents of the text, but the manuscripts of the *Prajnaparamita Sutra* found at Toling are written in Tibetan, in an elegant and stylized calligraphy of the highest quality. Rather than the long and narrow birch bark, palm leaves, and clay-coated paper used in their Indian antecedents, these manuscripts were created on wider large sheets of smooth beige paper.[6] The elaborate illuminations in the Toling *Prajnaparamita Sutra* manuscripts of the late tenth

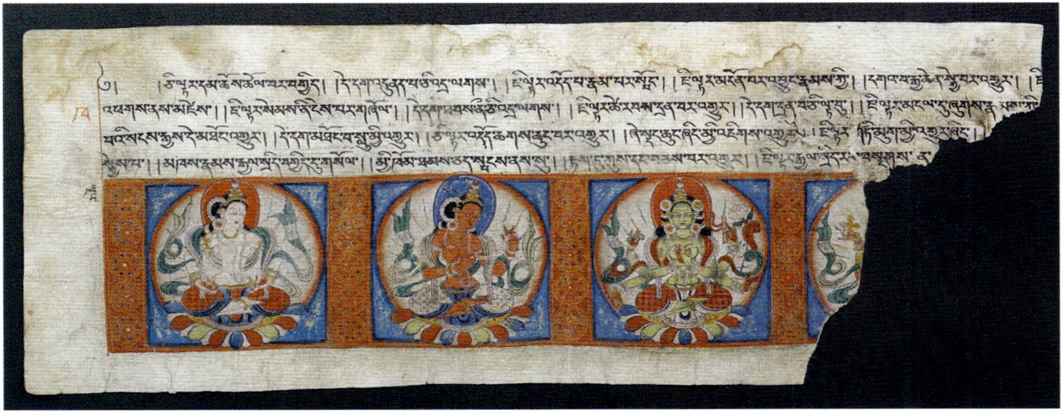

Fragmentary page from a *Prajnaparamita Sutra* manuscript; Toling, Ngari region, western Tibet; 11th century; 7⅛ × 19⅛ in. (18 × 48.6 cm); Private collection, Switzerland

See Goddess Dharmameghabhumi in the Tabo Main Temple, no. 21.

to eleventh century proceeded from the use of this large-scale and finely finished Tibetan paper, which afforded the painters a support that allowed a new degree of artistic refinement, following Yeshe Wo's edict.

Reflections on Chronology

One element of the jewelry represented in the wall paintings may help to provide chronological context. In Tibet, it is customary for aristocratic men to wear earrings,[7] but none adorn any of the donor figures, male or female, in the Toling stupa. Although we do not know when this custom started, it is interesting that the goddesses all display a small gold ring on their upper lobes and very ostentatious earrings on their lower lobes, while the bodhisattvas have no earrings on their upper lobes. This contrasts with the mural paintings made in 1041 in the Tabo Ambulatory, where all the great bodhisattvas sport a small gold ring in their upper earlobes as well as large earrings suspended from their lower lobes, though none of the clay sculptures produced at the same time have this upper earring.[8] This may be an indication that the paintings of the Toling stupa were creations of artists coming directly from Kashmir, such as those said to accompany Rinchen Zangpo. As Kashmiri artists, they would be more likely to faithfully represent the Kashmiri/Indian jewelry traditions, while in Tabo, the presence of the upper earring for the painted bodhisattva may indicate an adaptation of the original Kashmiri/Indian jewelry model to suit the taste of their Tibetan patrons. In comparison with the Tabo murals, those of the Toling stupa display a much thicker application of paint, which may reflect a different primer technique for the wall prior to painting. This results in a striking opulence of color, calling to mind the lustrous Kashmiri manuscript illuminations.

Considering the magnificence of the sculptures and paintings within this exceptional stupa and the iconographic program with its emphasis on Vairochana, the deity traditionally associated with the Tibetan sovereigns, it is probable that this stupa was made to honor the memory of a highly important person at Toling, one whose devotion to the ideals of Buddhism was equaled by his spiritual inspiration and aesthetic appreciation. This person may indeed have been Yeshe Wo, whose work to establish Toling as an epicenter of Buddhist learning and art in Tibet ceased with his death in 1024. Therefore, this stupa may have been created about 1025 to honor the memory of Yeshe Wo on the anniversary ceremonies a year after his death.

Further Reading

Heller, Amy. 2010b. "Preliminary Remarks on the Donor Inscriptions and Iconography of an 11th-Century Mchod rten at Tholing." In *Tibetan Art and Architecture in Context*, edited by Erberto Lo Bue and Christian Luczanits, 43–74. Andiast: International Institute from Tibetan and Buddhist Studies.

Heller, Amy. 2016b. "Three Ancient Manuscripts from Tholing in the Tucci collection, IsIAO, Roma, Part I. Manuscript 1329 E." In *Studi in Onore di Luciano Petech, Rivista degli Studi Orientali* 89, 125–32.

Klimburg-Salter, Deborah E., ed. 1982. *The Silk Route and the Diamond Path: Esoteric Buddhist Art on the Trans-Himalayan Trade Routes*, esp. 24–37, 64–81. Los Angeles: UCLA Art Council.

Notes

1 Cf. Vitali 1999, 19–20, on the foundation of Toling.
2 Vitali 1996, 111.
3 Harrison 2007, 235.
4 A. Heller 1999, 123, fig. 64; Foucher 1913, fig. 63.
5 Pal 1990, LACMA M81.90.6; Tucci and Ghersi 1996.
6 The page dimensions were approximately 7⅞–10⅝ by 26¾ in. (20–27 by 68 cm).
7 Reynolds 1978, fig. 20.
8 Luczanits 2004, 52–53, figs. 44–45.

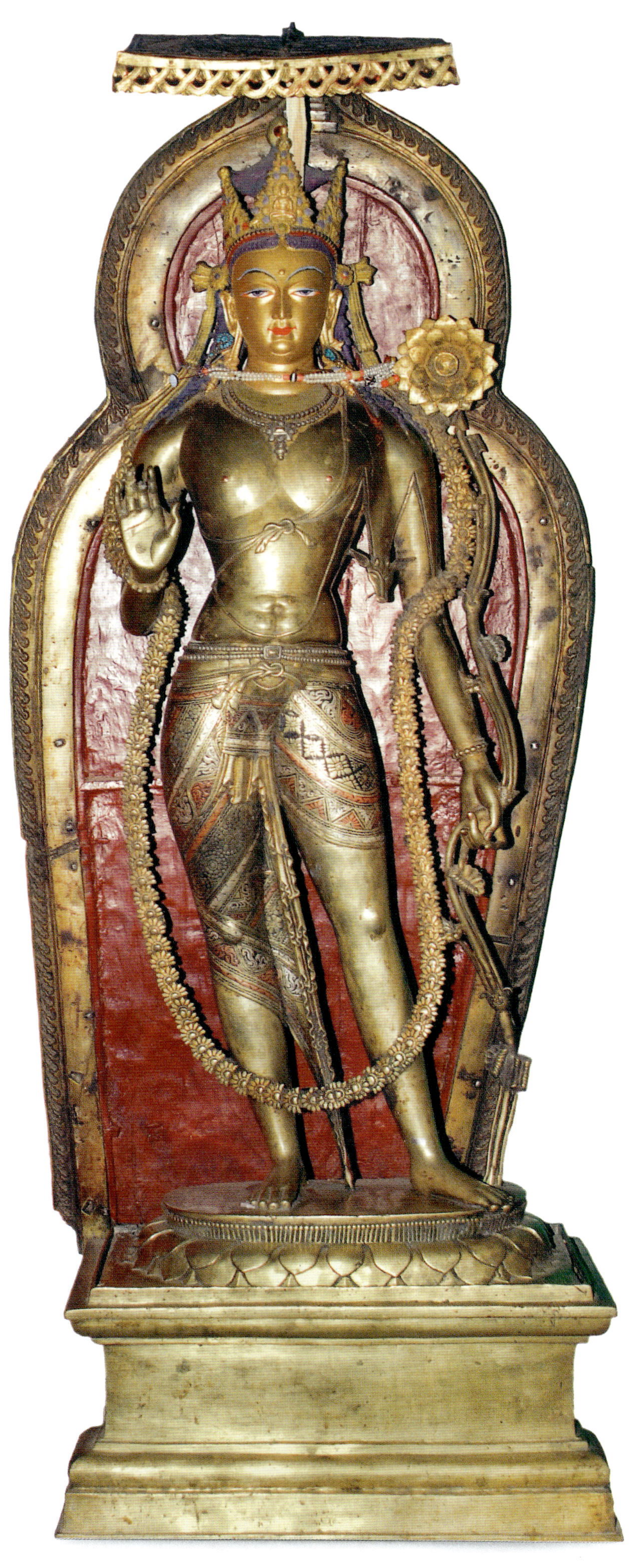

№ 20

Avalokiteshvara at Khartse

Ngari region, western Tibet, ca. early 11th century

Kashmir's Visual Legacy in the Western Himalayas

ROB LINROTHE

For more on another Jowo, see Jowo Shakyamuni, no. 8.

THIS TALL, ELEGANTLY DETAILED AND PROPORTIONED brass (not bronze, as is commonly assumed) sculpture is inlaid with silver and copper, enhancing its impressive presence at the center of a shrine in western Tibet near the village of Khartse. It is locally known as the Khartse Jowo (revered Lord) and is believed to have been commissioned in 998 by one of the most famous personages in western Himalayan history, the Great Translator (Lotsawa Chenpo) Rinchen Zangpo (958–1055). Datable to the early eleventh century, it retains its original base as well as the unusual full-size nimbus. Although the nimbus was uniquely built for this work, the original outline is now solidly backed or filled in. In some photographs, a canopy, indicating auspiciousness, is suspended overhead, but it is probably not original. The head and torso face forward, but the hips sway to the standing figure's right, while the left arm moves away from the body. This active movement is accommodated only somewhat successfully by the symmetrical body nimbus. Six feet (nearly two meters) in height, the figure with its backdrop is "the largest known [metal] statue cast in the Kashmir style to have survived."[1] "Technical accomplishment," so clearly manifested here, "is unanswerable."[2]

Legendary Origins

For a monastery founded during this time in the Guge Kingdom, see Murals at Toling Dukhang, no. 54.

For more about Avalokiteshvara, see Bodhisattva Avalokiteshvara and the Buddha's Footprints, no. 33; Pensive Bodhisattva Avalokiteshvara, no. 53.

For more about stupas, see Stupa at Toling Monastery, no. 19.

For more about Maitreya, see Maitreya and Manjushri Mural at Dratang, no. 26; Maitreya, no. 75.

According to a biography of Rinchen Zangpo written after his death, the sculpture was made at his expense for a fee of five ounces of gold he brought from his home in western Tibet.[3] He is said to have traveled to Kashmir at least twice, once at the behest and with the support of the Royal Lama Yeshe Wo (947–1019/1024), ruler of Guge. During that yearlong period of study in Kashmir, the Great Translator commissioned an artisan in Kashmir whose name is recorded as Bhidhaka. The sculpture was then consecrated by Shraddhakaravarman, "one of his earliest and main teachers and co-translators,"[4] who also received five ounces of gold, for the formal ritual animation of the sculpture.[5] Later, it was brought to and installed in the Gokhar Shrine in Khartse, western Tibet, a Buddhist sanctuary that Rinchen Zangpo is said to have founded,[6] where it (hopefully) remains today. According to some of the biographies of Lochen (the "Great Translator," as Rinchen Zangpo is often called), it takes the form of Avalokiteshvara known as Mahakarunika, or "The Great Compassionate One." The bodhisattva, beloved in Tibet, has a small image of Amitabha in his crown and a fully open lotus blossom at his left shoulder. The identification as Avalokiteshvara is therefore certain, as these are among his key attributes, even though a stupa sits at the pinnacle of his nimbus. When a stupa-reliquary appears in the crown of a bodhisattva, it generally signifies Maitreya, but here it apparently contributes an alternative significance, possibly a reminder of the commemorative function of the work.

Avalokiteshvara; Khartse, Ngari region, western Tibet; possibly commissioned by Rinchen Zangpo, possibly created by Bhidhaka; ca. early 11th century; brass with silver and copper inlay, gold, pigments; height of figure 51 in. (129.5 cm), with nimbus 72 in. (183 cm); Gokhar Shrine, Khartse; photograph courtesy D. Pritzker, 1994

Some versions of Rinchen Zangpo's biographies state that while he was in Kashmir, he had this sculpture made on hearing, or recalling, the passing away of his father.[7] His sorrow and gratitude to his parent prompted him to make a tributary image of his late father. It was not so much a portrait likeness as a kind of idealized memorial token, and purportedly matched the height of his father. The Great Translator then sent or brought it back with him to Khartse, the ancestral home of his family.[8] According to the biographical narrative, on the way back from Kashmir, the sculpture hit a rock and the ring finger of the right hand broke off. In 1994, Thomas Pritzker and his son David saw the sculpture at Khartse and confirmed its "missing ring finger."[9] The left hand is complete, its long, elegantly tapered fingers finished with fingernails either inlaid with copper or bearing an applied reddish pigment.

Bringing such a major work of metal sculpture from Kashmir to western Tibet, over a number of Himalayan passes exceeding sixteen thousand feet, involves a considerable degree of difficulty. Naturally, one wonders if it could not instead have been made by a Kashmiri sculptor in western Tibet, like the Mulbekh sculpture in Ladakh. This is especially relevant, since another famous episode included in the Great Translator's biographies states that when he returned to western Tibet from Kashmir, he brought with him thirty-two Kashmiri artists in order to fill the shrines which he is said to have founded—rather fantastically, 108 of them, an auspicious number not to be taken literally. Most scholars accept that the imposing Khartse sculpture was indeed made in Kashmir and was certainly not made by Tibetan artisans either inspired by Kashmiri art or even trained by the latter. But could it have been made in western Tibet by a Kashmiri artist who traveled there? After considering the matter closely, the art historian Christian Luczanits concludes the following:

On the Mulbekh sculpture, see Rock Carving of Four-Armed Bodhisattva Maitreya, no. 17.

> Despite its large size, the Khartse Avalokiteśvara is the best example of a commission that was produced in Kashmir and brought to Western Tibet, as suggested by the story associated with this work. In my reading of the art, a Kashmiri origin for the sculpture is plausible.[10]

Comparison with an Inscribed Sculpture from Kashmir

Support for this conclusion may be found in its similarity with another sculpture that was most definitely made in Kashmir, now in a major monastery of Ladakh known as Hemis.[11] The fact that the Hemis sculpture has an inscription on its base in Proto-Sharada script, in use in Kashmir, means that it would only have been crafted in Kashmir to be read by a Kashmiri sponsor, not a Tibetan-speaking one. To be sure, Kashmiri works eventually were "collected" by religious figures and institutions in the western Himalayas, especially after Buddhism died away in Kashmir.[12] Several important works of art were made in Kashmir and later brought to the western Himalayas, so what is most distinctive about the case of the Khartse Avalokiteshvara is the known Tibetan sponsor and the relative simultaneity of the making and the transporting, as well as the purported textual documentation.

For another example of Kashmiri sculpture, see Buddha on the Cosmic Mountain, no. 10.

The Hemis sculpture, which also depicts the two-handed Avalokiteshvara, is nearly identical in terms of posture, gestures, jewelry and adornments, inlay on the dhoti (wrap-around skirt worn by males in India), and the stupa-reliquary at the pinnacle of the back nimbus. Even the shape of the lotus on which the bodhisattva stands is comparable. However, it is slightly over a third of the size of the figure (17¾ inches, or 45 centimeters, versus 51 inches, or 129.5 centimeters), though the even more elaborate aureole extends relatively higher, for a total height of just over 35 inches, or nearly 90 centimeters (compared with the Khartse's 72 inches, or 183 centimeters). One of the distinctive features of both of these forms of Avalokiteshvara is the fact that the head of the antelope skin he wears as a kind of shawl hangs between his left arm and the ribcage in both examples. Another is the similarity of each level of the hourglass-shaped base below the lotus on which he stands. In the case of the Khartse sculpture, the narrowed middle section is solid and plain, while in the Hemis sculpture it is perforated with recumbent animals carved on it. Below is the Proto-Sharada inscription, which gives the so-called consecratory verse (the *pratityasamutpada-giti*), and the following dedication:

> This is the pious gift (and) that was ordered to be made by the Śākayabhikṣu Puṇyajaya. Whatever merit (was made) here, that should go to Śrī Vasantarāja together (with) all beings.[13]

In other words, it too was commissioned by a Buddhist monk, but probably a Kashmiri rather than one from western Tibet.

Both of the dhotis, as already mentioned, are inlaid with copper and silver. In addition, the Khartse sculpture has inserted black niello, a silver sulfide that sets off the metal colors. The skirt is decorated with stripes of different motifs, including pearl-bordered roundels, diamond-shaped lozenges, alternating upward- and downward pointing triangles, and a curling tendril vine pattern. The kneecap protrudes visibly beneath the cloth-covered right leg in a subtle mastery of volume and bodily structure. On both sculptures, the dhoti extends below the knee on the right leg and ends at the thigh on the left. The long

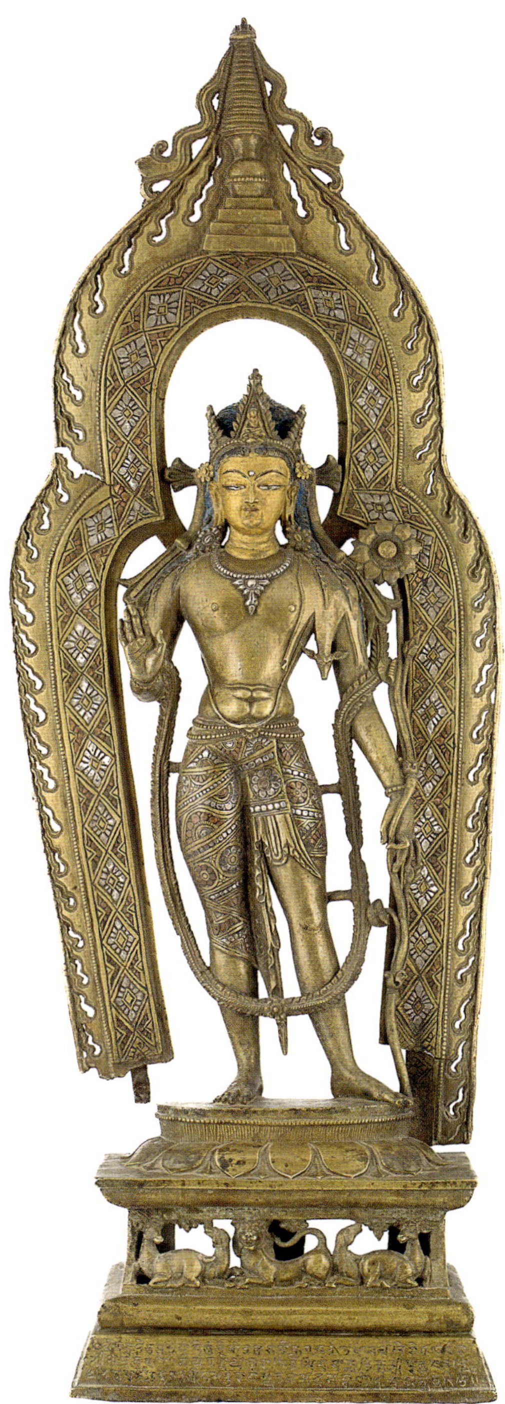

Avalokiteshvara; Kashmir; early 11th century; brass or metal alloy with copper and silver inlay; height of figure 17¾ in. (45 cm), with aureole approx. 35⅜ in. (90 cm); Hemis Monastery, Ladakh, India; photograph courtesy C. Luczanits

strands of hair painted blue lie over the upper shoulders, and the scarves tying the crown to the head stand out horizontally above the ears. The mouth is small but pursed, the chin prominent, and a reverse widow's peak marks the hairline at the middle of the forehead. The upper chest of the smaller Hemis sculpture is disproportionately inflated. The feet, however, are placed in the identical splayed positions, the left foot's toes just barely extending beyond the edge of the lotus-calyx base. The two metal sculptures could have been made in the same workshop. The Khartse sculpture, however, surpasses its Hemis cousin—and most if not all other known Kashmiri sculptures in Tibet and the western Himalayas—in its scale and plausible historical associations.

Further Reading

Luczanits, Christian. 2015b. "From Kashmir to Western Tibet: The Many Faces of a Regional Style." In *Collecting Paradise: Buddhist Art of Kashmir and Its Legacies*, edited by Rob Linrothe, with essays by Melissa R. Kerin and Christian Luczanits, 108–49. Exhibition catalog. New York: Rubin Museum of Art.

Pritzker, David. 2000. "The Treasures of Par and Kha-tse." *Orientations* 31, no. 7 (September): 131–33.

Tucci, Giuseppe. (1932) 1988. *Rin-chen-bzan-po and the Renaissance of Buddhism in Tibet around the Millenium*. Translated by Nancy Kipp Smith and edited by Lokesh Chandra. *Indo-Tibetica* 2. Reprint, New Delhi: Aditya Prakashan.

Notes

1 von Schroeder 2001, 70. On the same page, von Schroeder provides the total height, including the aureole, as 183 centimeters, and the figure as 129.5 centimeters. The sculpture is reproduced on p. 70, fig. II-5.
2 Wood 2019, 74.
3 Snellgrove and Skorupski 1980, 92.
4 Van der Kuijp 2018, 427.
5 Snellgrove and Skorupski 1980, 92.
6 Tucci (1932) 1988, 71.
7 See Snellgrove and Skorupski 1980, 83–116. Not all of them mention this, but many are quite hagiographic; see Rigzin 1984.
8 Jahoda et al. 2012, 50; Tucci (1932) 1988, 66; Kalantari and Gyalpo 2011.
9 Pritzker 2000, 133. There are questions about the literal accuracy of this. In some photographs, the ring finger appears to have been damaged or repaired above the first knuckle, while the middle finger is still missing above the second knuckle. See for example van Ham 2016, 30; von Schroeder 2001, 71.
10 Luczanits 2015b, 118.
11 Published in Hemis Museum 2011, 17.
12 On the collecting of Kashmiri art in the western Himalayas, see Linrothe 2015, 3–11.
13 Von Hinüber 2015, 3.

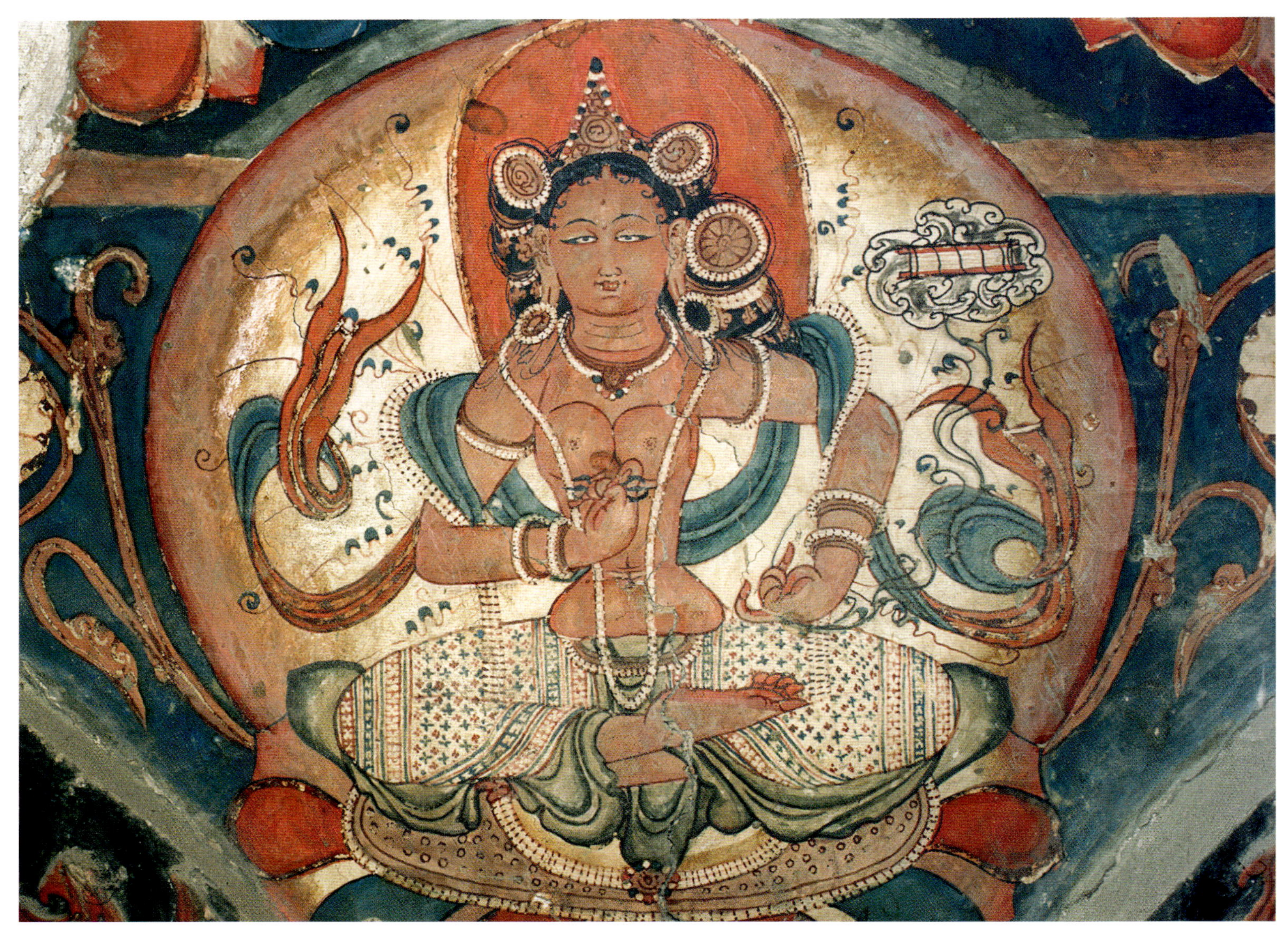

Goddess Dharmameghabhumi (Dharma Cloud Stage); Tabo Monastery, Spiti, Himachal Pradesh, India; ca. 1040; mineral colors on clay; height approx. 9⅞ in. (25 cm); photograph by Jaroslav Poncar, 1984

Nº 21

Goddess Dharmameghabhumi in the Tabo Main Temple

Tabo Monastery, Spiti, Himachal Pradesh, India, ca. 1040

The Iconographic Program of a Mid-Eleventh Century Monument

CHRISTIAN LUCZANITS

ARGUABLY, THE MAIN TEMPLE of Tabo Monastery in the Spiti Valley of Himachal Pradesh, India, is the earliest Tibetan Buddhist monument preserved in its entirety, as its content fully reflects its renovation finished in 1042 CE. We know from its identifying captions and inscriptions that Tabo was founded forty-six years earlier under the auspices of King Yeshe Wo, while its renovation was commissioned by his grandnephew Jangchub Wo. Both are portrayed in the temple's murals, Yeshe Wo flanked by his sons on the south wall of the entry hall, and Jangchub Wo at the access to the ambulatory above the renovation inscription, which provides the crucial twelve-year cycle date.[1] Given that both represent the ruling elite of the Purang-Guge Kingdom established at that time in western Tibet, the structure can be called a state temple. Its construction and refurbishment align with major state support of a conservative form of monastic Buddhism in the western Himalayan area, the ambivalence of which is demonstrated here by the goddess Dharmameghabhumi (Dharma Cloud Stage) painted between the main sculptures on the south wall of the main temple's assembly hall.

Contested Forms of Buddhism

For more about the Bon religion, see Bon Deity Trowo Tsochok Khagying, no. 60.

Buddhism arrived in the Himalayan areas in many different forms. In fact, numerous strands of esoteric Buddhism, most commonly classified in four categories of tantra, competed with older traditions, native beliefs, and some form of Bon religion. It was Yeshe Wo who promoted the use of esoteric Buddhism—in particular, in the form of the more conservative Yogatantra, as a means of state formation across the newly established Purang-Guge Kingdom. The Tabo Main Temple must have constituted an integral part of this effort, complementing the major foundations of Toling (Guge), Khorchak (Purang), and Nyarma (Ladakh).[2]

Historical sources convey the selective approach of the western Tibetan royal house to Buddhism and religion more broadly. In particular, unorganized village Tantrism and Bon were persecuted. The sources also make clear that the Indian derivation of Buddhist teachings was valued, and that the secrecy of the more controversial highest Yogatantra teachings was adhered to.[3] What this meant for the public presentation of Buddhism can best be gathered from the Tabo Main Temple.

Iconographic Program

All three structural units of the main temple at Tabo—a small entry hall, a spacious assembly hall, and a large sanctum surrounded by an ambulatory—date to the foundation of the monument in the late tenth century, but most of the decoration dates to the renovation finished in 1042.

For more about the wheel of life, see Wheel of Existence, no. 97.

The entry hall preserves most of the foundation period decoration—a wide range of the protective deities, fragments of the wheel of life and the cosmos, as well as a donor depiction headed by Yeshe Wo and his two sons. As this last image retains the names of all the prominent monks, we can be sure that the famous translator Rinchen Zangpo was not directly involved in the foundation. Instead, Dulwa Jangchub, shown among the top row of monks in the entry hall and, as abbot of the monastery, above the renovation inscription, has a central position. That the entry hall was not renovated indicates that its program did not need to be updated.

The assembly hall is dominated by the thirty-three life-size sculptures of the Vajradhatu mandala, which forms the dynamic center of the iconographic program of this room. Two narratives are painted

For more about Buddha Vairochana, see Imperial Carvings of Vairochana, no. 13; The All-Knowing Buddha Vairochana Visualization Album, no. 87.

underneath them. On the south side, the narrative of Sudhana's pilgrimage to different teachers according to the *Gandavyuha Sutra* culminates in Sudhana's assimilation of Samantabhadra in the presence of Vairochana and all the buddhas. Thereby Vairochana is Buddha Shakyamuni's glorified aspect, and he is also the main buddha of the Vajradhatu mandala. This ascending movement is counterbalanced by the descending movement of Vairochana displaying the Buddha's life on the north side of the assembly hall. The multiplicity of buddhas across space is manifest in the Buddhas of the Ten Directions, occupying the top level on the south and north walls.

Recent research has further revealed that most of the sculptures are part of a second mandala assembly, the assembly of the Dharmadhatu mandala, which takes up much of the remaining space above the sculptures.[4] The main deities of this assembly are represented in the northwestern corner of the assembly hall, while the rest of the deities are spread across the room in a distribution that builds on that of the Vajradhatu mandala. This mandala introduces the notion of the Buddha's consorts into the Yogatantra corpus, and more broadly presents a comprehensive system that integrates Mahayana concepts, such as the ten stages of a bodhisattva's career, into a tantric environment, as does the assembly hall program in its entirety.

The presence of two intertwined mandala assemblies in the assembly hall also explains the doubling of the Sixteen Bodhisattvas of the Fortunate Aeon (*bhadrakalpa*) in the ambulatory surrounding the sanctum or cella. Even though their iconography is not yet fully understood, the upper bodhisattvas can be interpreted as complementing the Dharmadhatu mandala assembly, while the lower ones complement the Vajradhatu mandala assembly. Their presence supplements the thousand Buddhas of the Fortunate Aeon that, together with the group of eight Buddhas of Past and Future, occupy the remaining space of the ambulatory. Thus, while the assembly hall emphasizes the spatial spread of the buddhas, the ambulatory focuses on the temporal spread from the past into the future. Underneath the buddhas and bodhisattvas is a third narrative, Sadaprarudita's search for the Perfection of Wisdom, the symbolic mother of all buddhas.

The main sculpture in the sanctum is again Vairochana, who presides over a bodhisattva and goddesses retinue looked over by further buddhas. The flanking bodhisattvas are Avalokiteshvara on the left and Vajrasattva on the right, who together with the central buddha form a three-family configuration that symbolically counters the three poisons that keep sentient beings in the cycle of existence (samsara).

Goddess Dharmameghabhumi

The goddess Dharmameghabhumi (Dharma Cloud Stage), part of the Dharmadhatu mandala assembly, represents one of the stages (*bhumi*) of a bodhisattva's career. As one of the personifications of these stages occupying the eastern quarter of the middle palace of the mandala, the goddess is found between the sculptures representing the eastern assembly. Her main attribute, the vajra, signifies her affiliation with the eastern family of Buddha Akshobhya, which has the vajra as its symbol. Her identifying attribute is a book surrounded by a cloud, the book representing Buddhist teaching (dharma).

The stages of a bodhisattva's progression toward awakening constitute a primary Mahayana concept. Usually, ten such stages are enumerated, with the ultimate leading to the awakening of the bodhisattva. The goddess Dharmameghabhumi, however, represents the penultimate stage in a twelve-fold system that is unique to the Dharmadhatu mandala. Symbolically, she stands for the realization of the all-pervading nature of the Buddha's teachings, including the esoteric ones.

For an example of Kashmiri sculpture, see Buddha on the Cosmic Mountain, no. 10.

The painting of the goddess also exemplifies the highest-quality murals of the temple's decoration, employing an artistic style that is commonly associated with Kashmir. Most of the renovation-period murals, including the much larger bodhisattvas in the ambulatory, display this sophisticated style, with round features, soft outlines, and fine shading in particular colors. As these were also executed in the highest-quality materials, they have remained largely unaltered since their creation in the mid-eleventh century.

Buddhist Path

Overall, the sophistication of the Tabo Main Temple is stunning. The identification of the full Dharmadhatu mandala assembly has made clear that the temple must be read as an integrated whole across the three spatial units. While the core of the two mandala assemblies is in the assembly hall, the

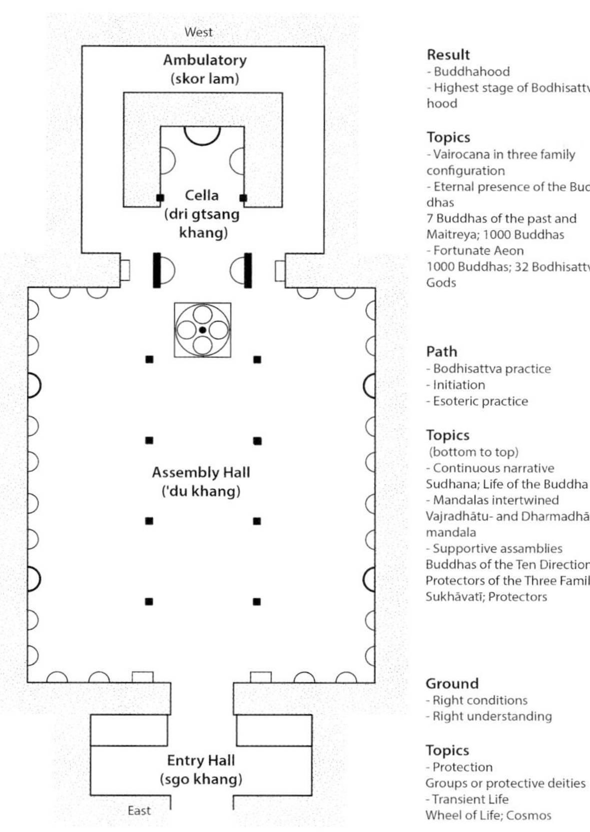

Plan of the Tabo Main Temple, Tabo Monastery, Spiti, Himachal Pradesh, India, with a listing of its iconographic program after the renovation was completed in 1042; drawing by C. Luczanits, 2021

pan-Indian protective deities in the entry hall represent their outer perimeter. On the other side of the temple, the Bodhisattvas of the Fortunate Aeon stretch the assembly into the ambulatory. This complex program supersedes the three-family configuration seen in the sculptures of the foundation period in the sanctum and two protectors in the entry hall.

Given the increasing sanctity of the three spatial units, the temple itself can also be read as a representation of the Buddhist path. In this reading, the entry hall designates the ground for Buddhist practice, the correct understanding of the nature of the samsara, and the conditions required to eventually overcome it. The assembly hall presents the actual path, the diverse practices of a bodhisattva, and the initiation into the esoteric Buddhist practice in the presence of the Buddhas of the Ten Directions, as well as its implementation. Finally, the sanctum and its ambulatory stand for the result, the attainment of the Perfection of Wisdom, the presence of the buddhas and Buddhahood itself.

Wider Relevance

The multivalent decoration of the Tabo Main Temple may appear exceptional, but it is typical of Tibetan Buddhist art and architecture. As Tabo demonstrates, by the time of the so-called Later Diffusion of Buddhism in the late tenth and eleventh centuries, a broad range of Buddhist sources had already been translated and systematized. The temple constitutes an instance in this process, fusing a broad Mahayana base with esoteric Buddhist teachings, whose ultimate forms were only hinted at through the Dharmadhatu mandala. This cautiousness is a direct result of the conservative attitude of the temple's founders toward esoteric Buddhism.

The conservative nature of the iconographic program of the Tabo Main Temple is also indicated by the fact that the stupa of Borobudur in Java, which is thought to have been built between the late eighth and mid-ninth centuries, already used the same principal sources for its decoration. However, the decoration in Borobudur utilized these sources in a different manner and placed less emphasis on esoteric Buddhist practice. With the Dharmadhatu mandala superseding the Vajradhatu mandala, the program of the Tabo Main Temple goes far beyond that of Borobudur.

Further Reading

Klimburg-Salter, Deborah E. 1997. *Tabo: A Lamp for the Kingdom: Early Indo-Tibetan Buddhist Art in the Western Himalaya.* Milan: Skira; New York: Thames and Hudson.

Petech, Luciano, and Christian Luczanits, eds. 1999. *Inscriptions from the Tabo Main Temple: Texts and Translations.* Rome: Istituto italiano per l'Africa e l'Oriente.

Luczanits, Christian. n.d. "Tabo Main Temple." Accessed December 7, 2022. http://www.luczanits.net/sites/Tabo/MainTemple.html.

Notes

1 Foundational works on the Tabo Main Temple are Klimburg-Salter 1997 and Petech and Luczanits 1999. Theoretically, the temple could also have been renovated twelve years earlier or later, but the dates provided here fit best with other historical information.

2 On the state support of organized Buddhism, see Jahoda and Kalantari 2015.

3 The most important primary sources in this regard are two ordinances issued by members of the ruling house; see S. Karmay 2009a; S. Karmay 2009b.

4 Luczanits, forthcoming(a). While the core deities of the Dharmadhatu mandala had been recognized earlier, its full representation and integration into the entire iconographic program of the temple has only been established with this forthcoming article.

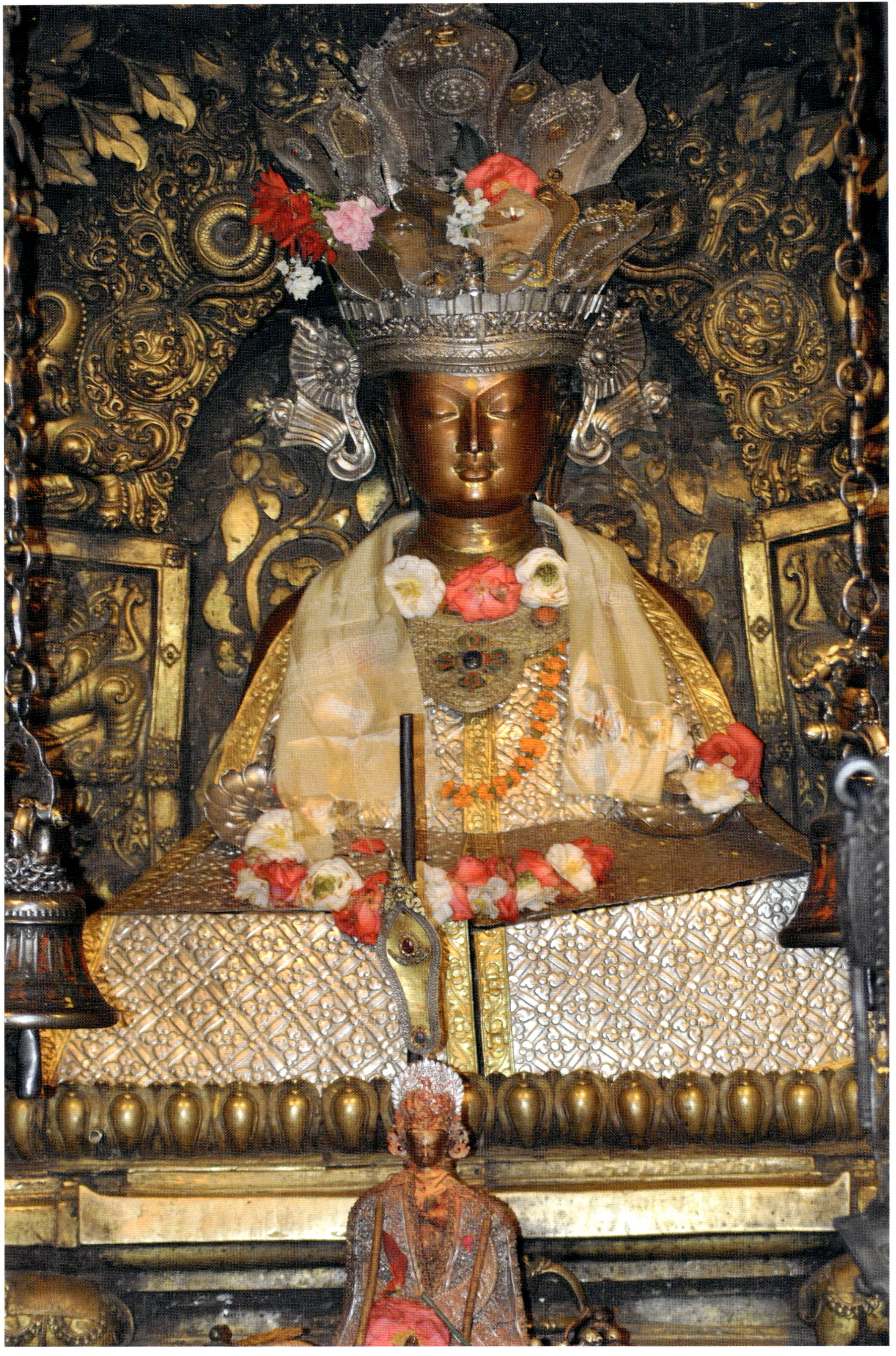

Nº 22

Central Shrine Image of Kwa Baha (Hiranyavarna Mahavihara)

Patan (Lalitpur), Nepal, ca. 11th century

In the Presence of the Buddha

KERRY LUCINDA BROWN

In the densely packed spaces of Nepal's Kathmandu Valley, hundreds of Buddhist monastic structures dot the urban landscape. These monastic centers utilize complex visual systems that reiterate the religious beliefs and practices of the Newar Buddhist community. While popular Buddhist culture in the Kathmandu Valley engages in public acts of veneration rooted in Mahayana Buddhist teachings, Newar monasticism is layered with esoteric tantric practices associated with Vajrayana Buddhism.[1] Initiation is limited to male members of the Shakya and Vajracharya castes, whose historical titles such as Shakyavamsa (of the Shakya lineage) or Shakyabhikshu (Buddhist monk) reiterate connections to the historical Buddha.[2] The architectural components of monastic structures display elaborate iconographic programs that are activated by daily ritual performance to create dynamic environments for spiritual attainment and communal engagement. Newar monasteries are primarily divided into two architectural types. *Bahis* are the oldest type and were built as living quarters for celibate renunciants. With the rise of tantric Buddhism, *bahas* emerged to house new communities of married householder monks who wanted to distinguish themselves from their celibate counterparts.[3] While the *bahis* emphasized worldly renunciation, members of the *bahas* married and remained engaged with temporal concerns. In having families and initiating their sons into the lineage, these householder monks preserved their monastic heritage with each subsequent generation.[4] Despite the end of celibate monasticism in the fifteenth century, the terms *bahi* and *baha* remain as references to these historical differences.

The History of Kwa Baha

Established in the mid-eleventh century, Kwa Baha is one of the most important monastic complexes in the Kathmandu Valley. Its official Sanskrit name, Bhaskaradeva Samskarita Hiranyavarna Mahavihara, reiterates its position as one of the great monastic centers (*mahavihara*) of the valley. Located in the city of Patan, Kwa Baha was established by the Thakuri king Bhaskara Deva (r. 1045–1048) to house a metal image of the Buddha discovered in the ruins of an ancient monastery that now serves as the main shrine image of the complex.[5] Affectionately called Kwabaju, the Buddha image is adorned with elaborate repoussé ornaments. The *Kvabahaya Vamshavali* chronicles the history of the site, asserting that the statue came to the king in a dream and requested a space be built for its veneration.[6] The Buddha provided the king with a specific set of requirements for his preferred location, including a pond that had not dried up since Manjushri drained the valley's lake and a place where rats chase cats. In the end, the king came upon a golden rat chasing a cat and proclaimed the site as the location for the Buddha's new shrine. While the actual origins of the image are not fully known, these narratives provide insight into the importance of sacred space, the agency of religious imagery, and the role of the community in caring for the divine. The agency of the image to secure a location of their choosing, while remarkable, is not particularly unique in Newar culture, as there is a universal belief that the sculpted form serves as a vessel for the divine and can act for the benefit of the embodied divine spirit. In examining the shrine image at Kwa Baha, we can understand how Newar Buddhists have positioned their Buddhist identity within the larger context of Himalayan ritual culture.

For more on repoussé, see Vishnu Riding on Garuda, no. 18.

For another example of a sculpture having agency, see Jowo Shakyamuni, no. 8.

Buddha Akshobhya, Kwa Baha (Hiranyavarna Mahavihara); Patan (Lalitpur), Nepal; ca. 11th century; metal with gilt-copper repoussé coverings, inlaid stone, adornments; photograph © Kerry Lucinda Brown

The Layout of the Baha

Newar monastic architecture is incredibly localized, with members generally living in the immediate vicinity of their family's monastic complex. The layout of Kwa Baha includes the three mandatory

See Vajracharya Priest's Crown, no. 30.

See the Svayambhu Chaitya of Kathmandu, no. 4.

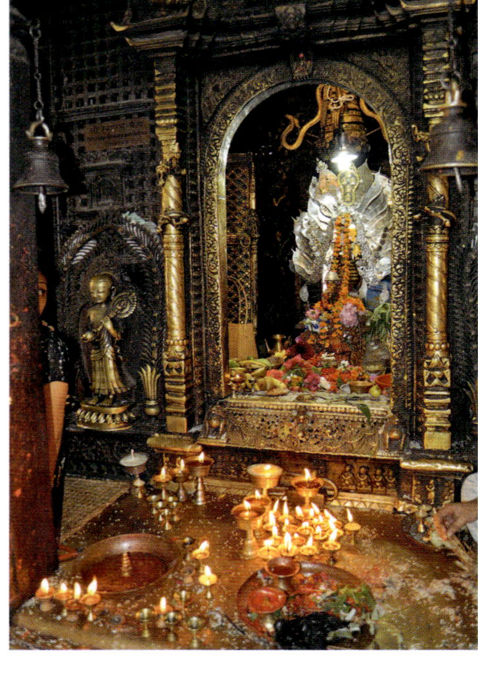

The western side of the votive stupa of Svayambhu Mahachaitya at Kwa Baha, Patan, Nepal, associated with the Buddha Amitabha, faces the main shrine entrance and is where numerous offerings are displayed; photograph © Kerry Lucinda Brown

See Chakrasamvara Mandala with Newar Donors, no. 29.

elements of *baha* architecture—namely, a votive stupa (chaitya), a public shrine deity (*kvahpah dyah*), and a secret esoteric shrine (*agam*). For Newar Buddhists, the married householder monks of the Vajracharya and Shakya castes are responsible for caring for the main shrine deity, in addition to conducting tantric rituals in the esoteric shrine. At Kwa Baha, these elements are built around a central courtyard, with its entrance on the east side and a large three-tiered pagoda on its western side. At the center is a large open pagoda housing a votive stupa of the Svayambhu Mahachaitya. The stupa generates the sacred geography of the space, serving as the center of the mandala, just as the Svayambhu Stupa generates the sacred geography of the Kathmandu Valley.[7] This votive stupa serves as the lineage deity (Newar: *digu dyah*; Sanskrit: *kula devata*) for the monastery, meaning the members of the community acknowledge this deity as their common lineage ancestor and see themselves as descendants.[8]

An axial arrangement governs the space of this architectural mandala, with the entrance located across from the main shrine. Directly above this public shrine is the secret shrine dedicated to the tantric deity Chakrasamvara and his consort, Vajravarahi. Access to this shrine is limited to the most senior members of the community (Ajus) who have received tantric initiation (*diksha*). In the cells surrounding the central courtyard are small subsidiary shrines dedicated to other deities of the Buddhist pantheon.

The Main Shrine Image

At Kwa Baha, the physical form of the main shrine image is often obscured by layers of offerings adorning the image, which include elaborate repoussé covers, inlaid jewelry, flower garlands, and offering scarves. During rituals and celebrations, offerings to the Buddha are managed by attendants, who place them at the base of the throne. When unadorned, the form of the metal image emerges, along with iconographic features of the throne that allow for a proper identification of this buddha. The seated figure wears monastic robes that tightly cling to his body. Small curls form his hair and cranial bump (*ushnisha*) on the top of his head. His right hand is outstretched in the earth-touching gesture (*bhumisparsha* mudra), while his left rests in his lap, holding an offering bowl. Although the visual features are similar to those of Buddha Shakyamuni, the appearance of elephants and a vajra in the throne base identify him as Buddha Akshobhya. As one of the five celestial buddhas that comprise the Five Buddha mandala, Akshobhya symbolizes the beginning of the path to enlightenment. Buddhist texts describe how seeing the Buddha can foster devotion and lead one on the bodhisattva path. As the main shrine deity, Akshobhya provides an opportunity for practitioners to engage in acts of worship and veneration; they can see the Buddha, be inspired by his presence, and accrue spiritual merit.

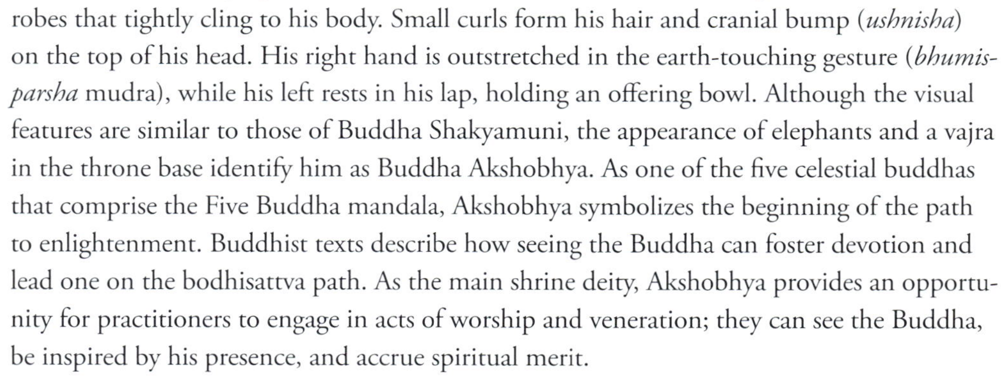

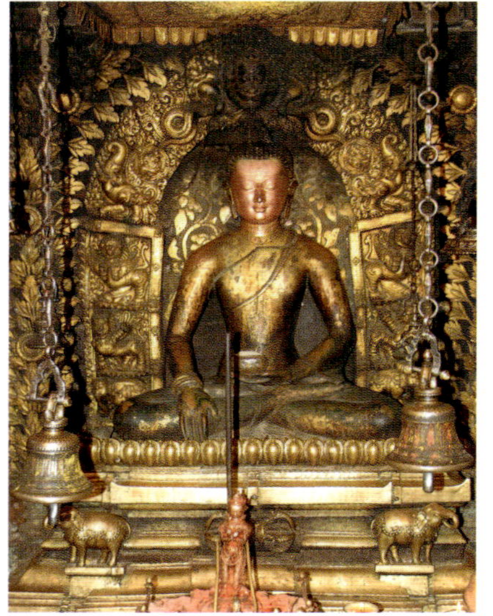

The main shrine image at Kwa Baha, Patan, Nepal, without its covering, revealing the body of Buddha Akshobhya; photograph © Suman Ratna Dhakwa

Stylistic and Dating Considerations

From the sixth century on, Newar Buddhist art developed in response to cultural contact with northern Indian dynasties. Visual features notable in Gupta art would inform Newar art from the fifth to ninth centuries. By the Transitional or Thakuri period (ca. 878–ca. 1200), the Kathmandu Valley was a destination for those wanting to engage with the Mahayana-Vajrayana teachings practiced by Newar ritual masters from India, who brought with them new artistic styles. While Gupta influences continued into the ninth and tenth centuries of the Thakuri period, forms became stiffer, reflecting influence from Pala artistic developments from northeastern India. The wide chest, elongated torso, slim waist, and round face of the seated image at Kwa Baha are characteristic of Gupta and later Pala visual conventions. The Buddha's full face, large lips, well-defined eyebrows, and posture recall crowned Buddha images from the eleventh-century Pala period. However, here the rounder face and elongated torso demonstrate Newar stylistic aesthetics.

Most scholars accept an eleventh-century date for the Kwa Baha Buddha, yet both the *Kvabahaya Vamshavali* chronicles and local narratives describe the work as predating the building of the monastic complex. If we accept that King Bhaskara Deva established the monastery during his reign, it would place the founding of the *baha* between 1045 and 1048, which would give the mid-eleventh century as the latest possible date for this sculpture. Conversely, the *Kvabahaya Vamshavali* recounts that the metal sculpture, one of the finest ever made, was hidden by earlier sculptors for fear it would be stolen.[9] After being lost to time, it was discovered by farmers and pulled from the ground, when it was ultimately presented to King Bhaskara Deva. This could place the origin of the image several centuries earlier. Similarly, some at Kwa Baha described the shrine image as the brother to Jowo Mikyo Dorje, the seventh-century buddha image at the Ramoche Temple in Lhasa. This image is believed to have been brought to Lhasa from Nepal by the Newar princess Bhrikuti Devi when she married King Songtsen Gampo in 632 CE.[10] In placing the history of this image in the distant past, these narratives also connect Newar Buddhism in the Kathmandu Valley to important Tibetan dynasties. Although an earlier date for the Kwa Baha shrine image is not certain, surviving material and epigraphic evidence at Kwa Baha suggests that the site had Licchavi (ca. 300–ca. 879 CE) foundations but was rebuilt and restored to follow the present Vajrayana iconographic program in the eleventh century under the direction of King Bhaskara Deva.[11]

For more on Songtsen Gampo, see Bunga Dya, no. 6; Jokhang Temple, no. 7; Bodhisattva Avalokiteshvara and the Buddha's Footprints, no. 33.

Shrine Complex as Architectural Palimpsest

The attention given to Kwa Baha and its elaborate monastic complex is owed in part to the continued patronage and active monastic community that has cared for the site for the last millennium. The organizational structure of membership, initiation rituals, and utilization of trusts (*guthi*) to sustain economic support of material and ritual practices weave together ancient traditions with contemporary cultural practices. Generations have maintained the art and architectural heritage of the site through renovations and expansions. This upkeep of the site has created layers of visual culture representing hundreds of years of development, allowing this space to function as an architectural palimpsest. Sites like Kwa Baha, where medieval origins engage with ancient narratives in ever-changing definitions of contemporary ritual veneration, demonstrate that these spaces are not fixed in the ancient past. They have an active living history that evolves, expands, and reaffirms Buddhist ritual and cultural identity with each generation.

Further Reading

Brown, Kerry Lucinda. 2017. "Adorning the Buddhas: The Ceremonial Regalia of the Daśa Sthavira Ājus from Kwā Bahā, Nepal." *Ars Orientalis* 47, 266–302. https://doi.org/10.3998/ars.13441566.0047.012.

Gellner, David N. 1992. *Monk, Householder, and Tantric Priest: Newar Buddhism and Its Heirarchy of Ritual.* Cambridge: Cambridge University Press.

Shakya, Min Bahadur. 2004. *Hiraṇyavarṇa Mahāvihāra: A Unique Newar Buddhist Monastery*. Lalitpur: Nagarjuna Publication.

Notes

1 Lewis 1994, 2–4.
2 Gellner 1989, 5–7.
3 Gellner 1992, 189–97; Brown 2017, 267.
4 Gellner 1989, 6, and 1997, 661–62, 673.
5 Locke 1985, 39.
6 M. B. Shakya 2004, 17–18.
7 Slusser 1982, 3–7.
8 D. Bangdel 1999, 138.
9 M. B. Shakya 2004, 13–14.
10 M. B. Shakya 1997, 35–37, 85; A. K. T. L. Tenzin 1982, 84.
11 D. Bangdel 1999, 220–22.

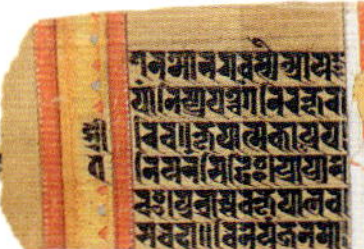
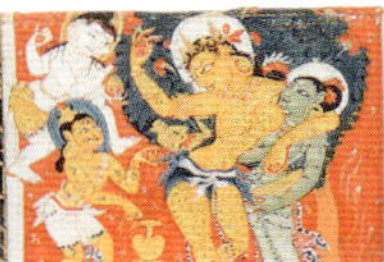
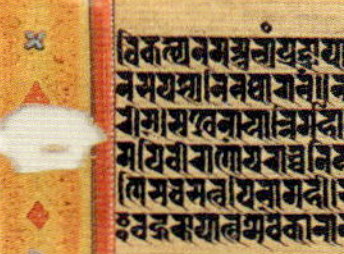
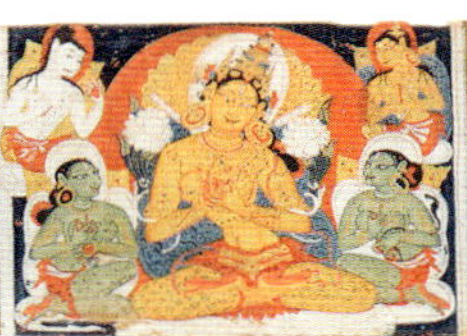
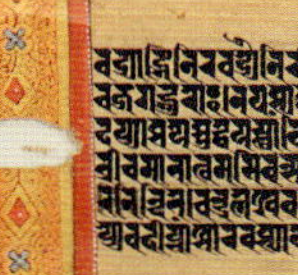
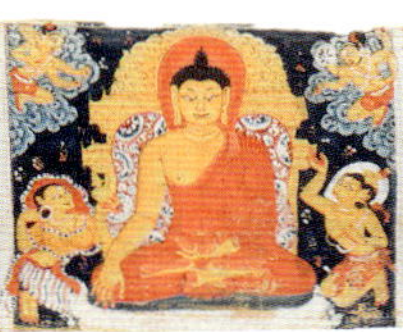
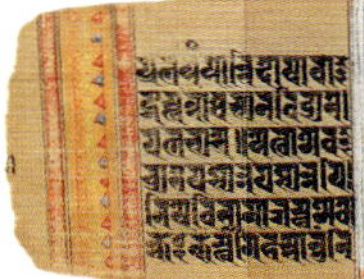
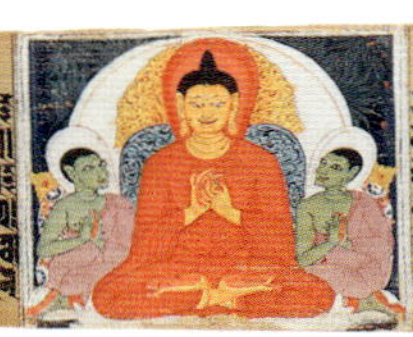
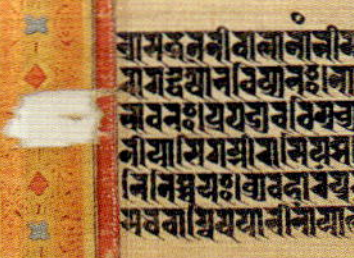
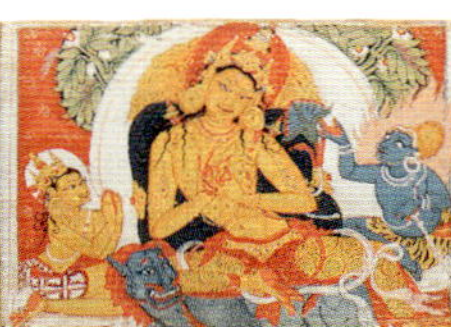
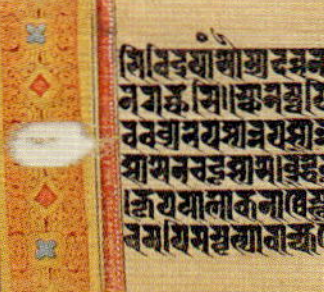
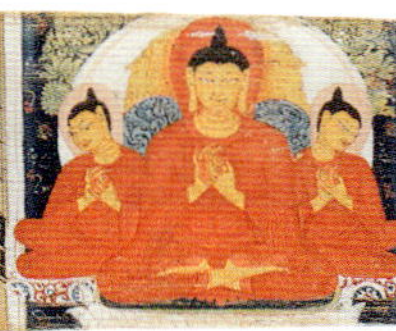
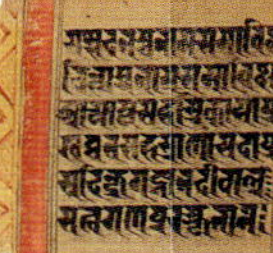
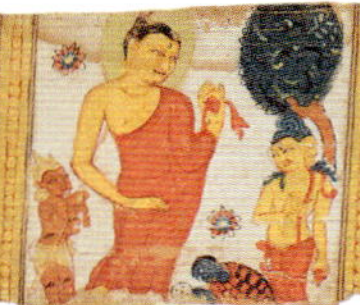
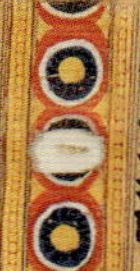
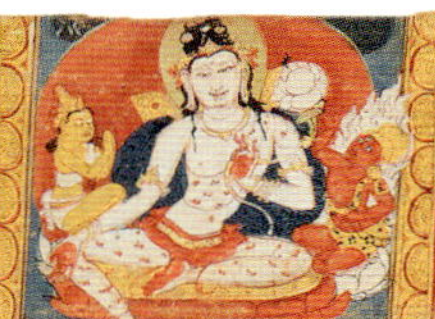
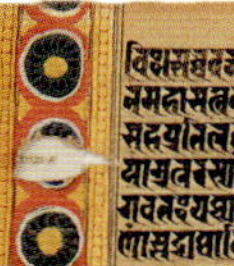
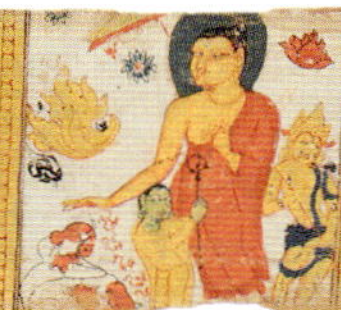
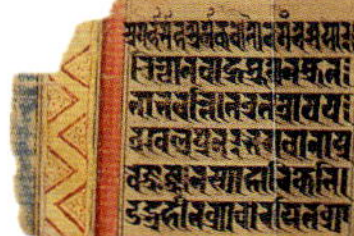
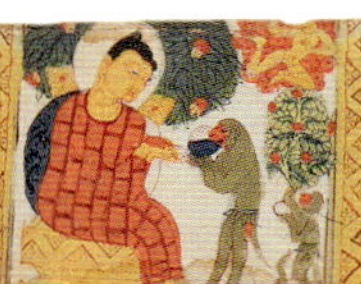
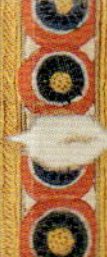
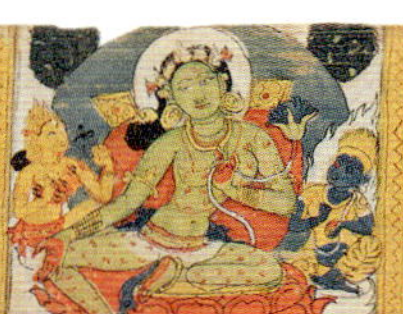
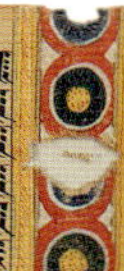
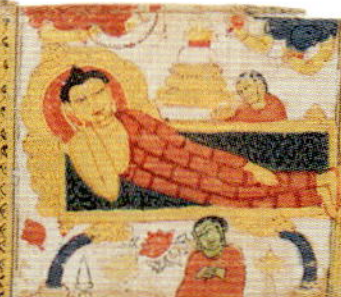
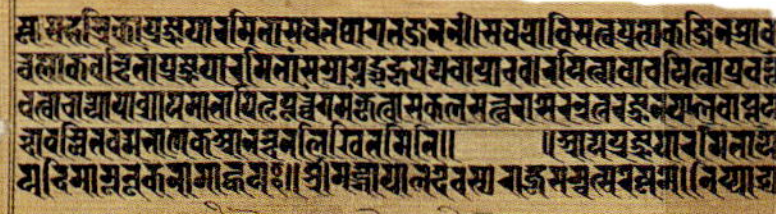

Leaves from *The Perfection of Wisdom (Prajnaparamita) Sutra* manuscript; Nalanda Monastery, Bihar, India; 1073, 1151; ink and opaque watercolor on palm leaf; each approx. 2⅞ × 22⅜ in. (7.3 × 56.8 cm); Asia Society, New York; Mr. and Mrs. John D. Rockefeller 3rd Acquisitions Fund; 1987.1; image courtesy Asia Society

№ 23

Illuminated Pages of the *Prajnaparamita Sutra* Manuscript

Nalanda, India, 1073, 1151

Embodying the Words of the Buddha

ELENA PAKHOUTOVA AND AGNIESZKA HELMAN-WAZNY

THESE ILLUMINATED PAGES contain text written in ink on palm leaves and images rendered in mineral pigments. The text of the Sanskrit manuscript presents the teachings of *The Perfection of Wisdom in Eight Thousand Verses (Ashtasahasrikaprajnaparamita) Sutra*, known as *Prajnaparamita*, which is thought to have been developed over two centuries, from the first century BCE to the first century CE.

The Buddha's teachings were first communicated as oral recitations, and only later were written down and envisioned in images. "Thus have I heard, at one time" is the phrase that begins the texts known as sutras. These words launch the story describing an occasion when the Buddha gave the teaching that is the subject of this manuscript. This sutra's narrative is structured as a dialogue between the Buddha and one of his disciples, the elder (arhat) Subhuti.

For more about arhats, see Arhats Viewing a Painting of Birds by the Tenth Karmapa, no. 72.

As one of the earliest and important sutras, *Prajnaparamita* reflects the developments in Buddhist thought and practice of that time. It conveys the core principles of the Greater Vehicle, or Mahayana movement, communicating the Buddhist philosophical notion of no-self as the means to understand the emptiness of all things and perfect the wisdom that comprehends reality. As physical objects, *Prajnaparamita* manuscripts represent the words of the Buddha and the teachings themselves.

Illuminations

The painted images in *Prajnaparamita* manuscripts created in India do not illustrate the text but represent contemporaneous Buddhist teachings and reflect the preferences of the patrons who commissioned them. The illuminations form a consistent group depicting the Eight Great Events of the Buddha's Life and images of bodhisattvas and deities. Manuscripts usually feature twelve figural images, as in this example, or eighteen.[1] Typically, a page, or folio, is decorated with three panels, with the central panel displaying a bodhisattva or a deity and the two side panels showing scenes of the Buddha's life. The illuminated folios are commonly placed in the beginning, middle, and end of the manuscript, but the arrangement can vary. In this manuscript the eight episodes of the Buddha's life begin in the left panel of the first folio, followed by the right panel, and they recur in the same order on the other three leaves, depicting the Buddha's birth at Lumbini; his enlightenment at Vajrasana in Bodhgaya; the first teaching at Sarnath; the multiplication miracle at Shravasti; the descent from the Heaven of the Thirty-Three Gods at Samkashya; the taming of a mad elephant at Rajgir; accepting a monkey's gift of honey at Vaishali; and his passing away (parinirvana) at Kushinagara.

See Mayadevi Giving Birth to Siddhartha, no. 3. For more on the Buddha's enlightenment, see Mahabodhi Temple Model, no. 25.

The central panels, from the first to the fourth leaves, portray the goddess Prajnaparamita, bodhisattvas Manjushri and Avalokiteshvara, and the goddess Tara. The images display the established iconography also found in contemporaneous and later representations of the Eight Great Events in sculpture and other forms of painting in India, Tibet, and beyond.[2]

For examples of these deities, see Maitreya and Manjushri Mural at Dratang, no. 26; Avalokiteshvara and the Buddha's Footprints, no. 33; Pensive Bodhisattva Avalokiteshvara, no. 53; Tara Who Protects from the Eight Great Fears, no. 27.

Objects of Devotion and Accumulation of Merit

Wealthy patrons commissioned scribes and artists to create elaborately decorated manuscripts considered physical containers of wisdom and the words of the Buddha. Such valuable commissions were devotional objects intended to generate merit—an investment of positive karma to ensure good present and future lives. It is believed that the text of this sutra, read aloud on special occasions, purifies the space wherever

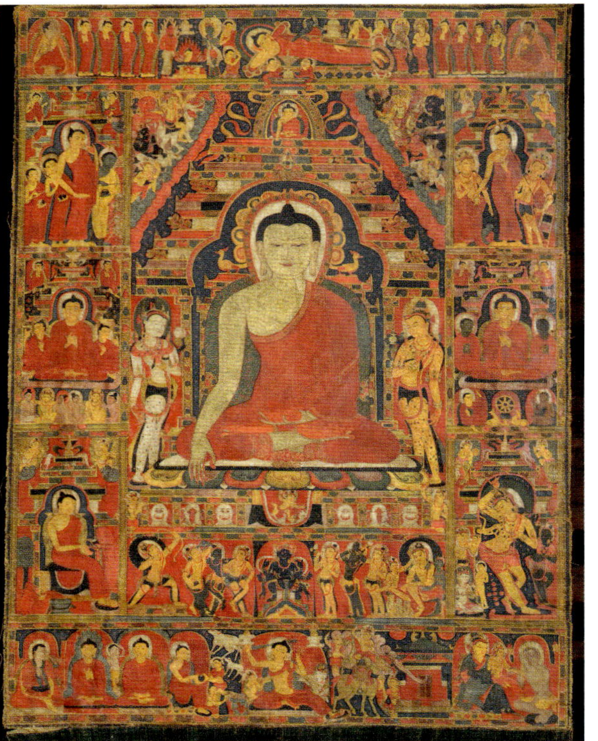

The Eight Great Events of the Buddha's Life; Tibet; ca. 13th century; pigments on cloth; 41¾ × 30¾ in. (106 × 78 cm); Private collection, Switzerland

it is heard, generates positive karmic links with the teachings in the minds of all gathered, and brings well-being and prosperity to the whole region.[3]

Format and Materials

Indian Buddhist books such as this, known as *pustaka* in Sanskrit, were the most treasured items that traversed the Himalayan regions, and were held as valued assets in Tibetan monasteries. The term used for describing books of loose leaves in rectangular landscape format is *pothi*, which means "book" in Indian languages. These Indian manuscripts made from palm leaves became a model for the paper manuscripts known as Tibetan long books, *pecha*, as palm leaves were not available in Tibet.

The loose leaves of Indian palm-leaf books are gathered by a cord pulled through holes drilled into the leaves and two wooden covers. The holes in such books also served to attach bookmarks. This *Prajnaparamita* manuscript from the Asia Society, New York, has two holes symmetrically located within painted vertical bands. Early Tibetan books often include drawn circles to faithfully represent this practical feature of palm-leaf manuscripts.

For more about manuscript covers, see Painted Manuscript Cover, no. 12.

The Process

To create support for writing, palm leaves were cut from a tree and their twigs sliced off. The leaves came from two types of palm trees, the talipot and the palmyra,[4] which differed in size and quality. The talipot type was employed until the fifteenth century in northern and western India and until the eighteenth century in Bihar and Sri Lanka. The palmyra type was used in eastern India from the sixteenth to the nineteenth century. The leaves were boiled in water or milk to make them soft and durable, dried, and then trimmed to two lengths, long or short.

The leaves were flattened and polished with sand until smooth,[5] then cut to the desired size. The string holes were drilled, and the space for text and miniatures laid out. Scribes usually worked independently from painters, first marking the lines for text and choosing a script. In the talipot manuscripts from northern India, Central Asia, and Nepal, they wrote characters in ink with a reed pen, as in this manuscript, a good example of that type, written in Ranjana script.[6]

Composed of soot mixed with oil or animal glue, the inks in palm-leaf books resembled inks for writing on paper.[7] Before the nineteenth century most painting pigments came from natural minerals; synthetic pigments followed later.[8]

Palm leaves were readily available in tropical climates, and although they are more durable and resistant to insects than paper, the oldest examples do not survive. A few rare, dated examples are in the collections of the National Archives and the Kaiser Library in Kathmandu, Nepal, the University of Cambridge, and the British Museum, London.[9] During the early second millennium Tibetan monks studying in India produced palm-leaf manuscripts made from regional materials and written in Tibetan language.[10] Although palm leaves were not available for making books in Tibet, many Indic palm-leaf manuscripts have been preserved in Tibet's dry climate.[11]

Materials and Patronage

The materials used in a book's production were determined by regional availability and the patron's preferences, reflecting their aesthetic choices as well as the book's status and function. Materials were carefully selected for their qualities and suitability for specific types of writing and decorations.

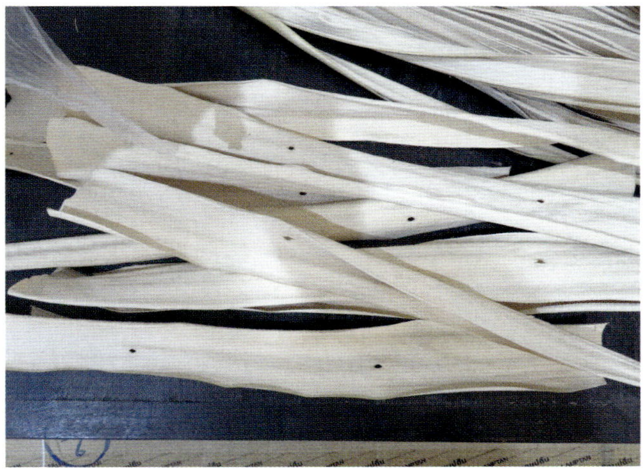

Prepared palm leaves before they become supports for writing; photograph by Agnieszka Helman-Ważny, 2020

For another example of art from Nalanda, see Crowned Buddha, no. 16.

See Mural Painting at Zhalu Monastery, no. 47.

In most instances the last part of the text, called the colophon, recorded patrons, scribes, and the location where the manuscript was created.

Patronage and History of Ownership

In addition to illuminations, this manuscript contains an interesting record of its ownership.

The manuscript's Sanskrit and Tibetan colophons state that it was produced at Nalanda Monastery in 1073 CE and restored and rededicated in 1151 CE.[12] This monastery in eastern India was well known to Tibetans as the major center of Buddhist learning. The book's two Tibetan colophons translate the Sanskrit and indicate that it was once owned by the renowned Kashmiri scholar Shakyashribhadra (1127 or 1145–1225), educated at Nalanda. Invited to Tibet to teach, he traveled extensively in Tibetan regions from 1204 to 1214. Thereafter, the manuscript belonged to Buton Rinchen Drub (1290–1364), the famous Tibetan scholar and editor of the first Tibetan canon and the founder of Zhalu Monastery. The last Tibetan inscription documents dedicatory use of this book for the benefit of Kunga Gelek Wangchuk.[13] These inscriptions reveal networks and connections from the manuscript's creators and patrons to famous Indian and Tibetan teachers, who treasured the book and passed it down in their turn.

Other preserved manuscript colophons reveal that an especially high number of Nepalese and Tibetan patrons commissioned such books in India in the first half of the eleventh century, the period when Tibetans were actively acquiring Buddhist culture from India.[14]

Further Reading

Allinger, Eva. 2001. "Narrative Paintings in 12th–13th Century Manuscripts: An Examination of Photographs Taken by Rahula Sankrtyayana at the Ngor Monastery, Tibet." *Journal of Bengal Art* 6, 101–15.

Helman-Ważny, Agnieszka. 2014. *The Archaeology of Tibetan Books*. Brill's Tibetan Studies Library 36. Leiden: Brill.

Jamieson, R. C. 2000. *The Perfection of Wisdom: Extracts from the Aṣṭasāhasrikāprajñapāramitā*. New York: Viking Studio.

Notes

1 Losty 1982, 20.
2 For example, a large stone stele at Jagdispur, India, in Leoshko 1993–94, 262; one in the British Museum collection, OA 1942.4-15.3; small stone stele in the Potala Palace collection. See von Schroeder 2001, fig. V-3, 129 A, B, C, D; in the Rubin Museum C2005.4.2 and elsewhere; and early Tibetan thangkas depicting the Eight Great Events of the Buddha's Life. See Bautze-Picron 1995–96, 255–408.
3 See for instance Padmakara Translation Group, trans. 2018. "*The Transcendent Perfection of Wisdom in Ten Thousand Lines (Daśasāhasrikāprajñāpāramitā)*" 84000: Translating the Words of the Buddha. 33.70. (Toh 11. Degé Kangyur, vol. 31 [shes phyin, ga], fols. 1b–91a, and vol. 32 [shes phyin, nga], fols. 92.b–397.a.), http://read.84000.co/translation/UT22084-031-002.html.
4 *Corypha umbraculifera* or *C. taliera* and *Borassus flabellifer*. Konishi 2013, 3.
5 Agrawal 1984, 24–62.
6 In South India and Southeast Asia letters were usually incised on the surface of the palm leaf with special tools and then filled in with a black, sooty pigment. See Losty 1982, 7.
7 Agrawal 1984, 31–36.
8 Pal and Meech-Pekarik 1988.
9 One of the oldest manuscripts, the *Skandapurāṇa* (National Archives, NAK 2/229 / NGMPP B 11/4), is dated Mānadeva Saṃvat 234, or 810–811 CE. The *Suśrutasaṃhitā* manuscript containing an Āyurvedic text (the Kaiser Library, KL 699 / NGMPP C 80/7), is dated Mānadeva Saṃvat 301, or 878 CE; Harimoto 2017, 355–76, 363–64, Bhattarai 2020, 18.
10 Yonezawa 2020, 65–84.
11 Steinkellner 2004.
12 Huntington and Huntington, 1990, 186–89.
13 My reading of what is visible in the currently framed folio—Ze Ring (bzad ring), Buton (bus ston kha che—an alternative spelling, his primary name with the nickname "Big mouth"), and Chopel Zangpo (chos dpal bzang po)—confirms an anonymous translation in Leidy and Lee 1994, 66; Huntington and Huntington, 1990, 87.
14 J. Kim 2013, 226–27.

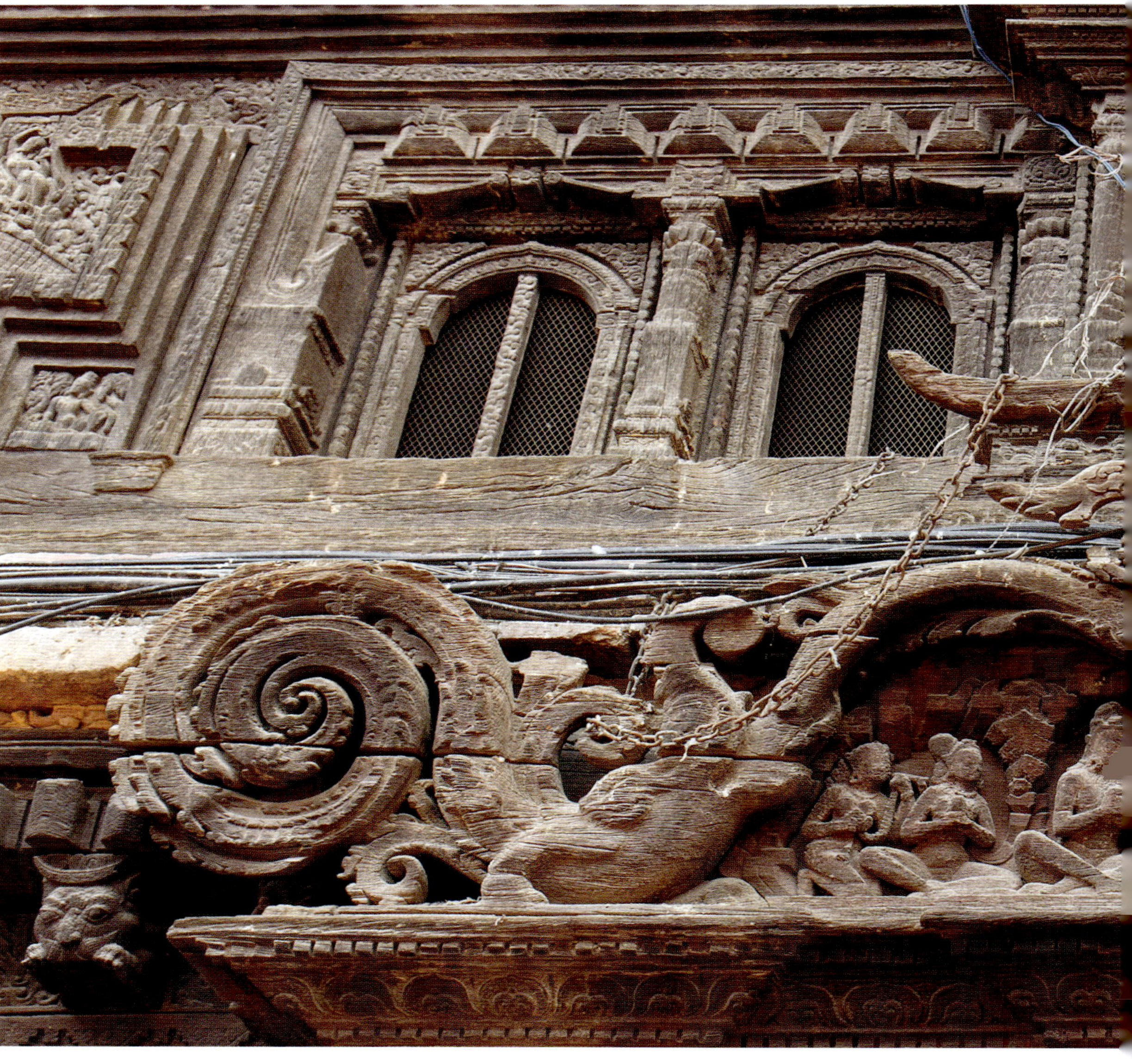

Nº 24

Torana of the Main Shrine at Yetakha Baha

Kathmandu, Nepal, 10th–11th century

A Marvel of Newar Woodworking

KASHINATH TAMOT AND IAN ALSOP

The most celebrated examples of Newar woodworking in the Kathmandu Valley are the roof struts, almost always depicting curvaceous tree dryads (*shalabhanjikas*), that decorate and reinforce the pagoda roofs and the toranas that guard and embellish the entrances to the main shrines of temples and Buddhist monasteries (*bahals*).

The main shrine of the spacious square known as Yetakha Baha, not far from the royal palace of the city of Kathmandu, boasts stunning examples of these two important genres of Newar wood carving. The four carvings of lovely dryads entwined in trees mounted on the third floor and supporting the roof are prime examples in the valleywide corpus of remarkable early struts.[1] But the torana topping the gateway to the main shrine is particularly important for its great age, wonderfully elegant composition, and the rarity of its design.

For another example of torana ornamentation, see Juyong Guan Stupa Gate, no. 48.

Torana is a Sanskrit word usually referring to the entire gateway; in Nepalese usage, however, it is primarily reserved for the upper panel.[2] The torana of Yetakha Baha is the oldest such wooden

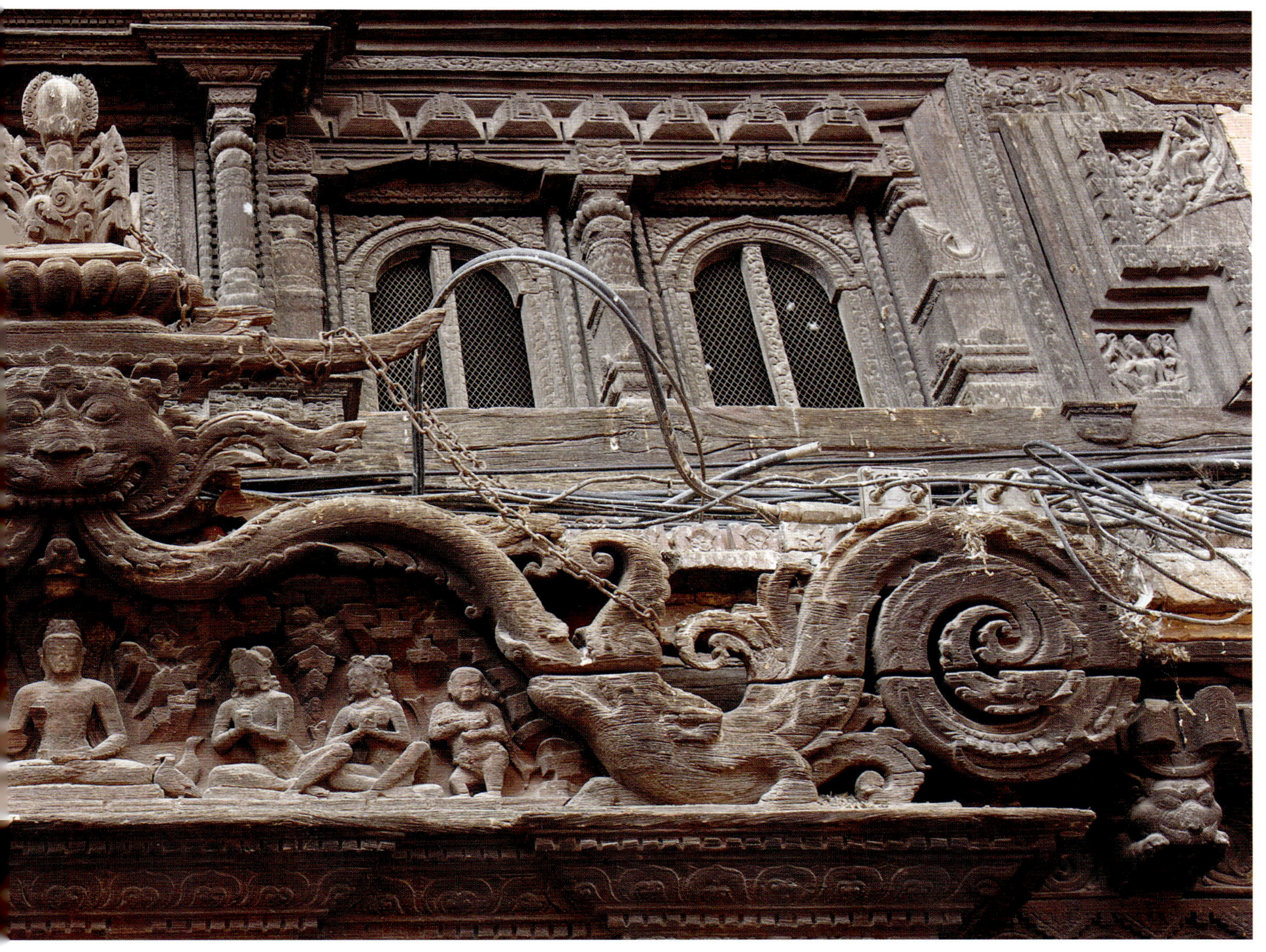

architectural element known in the Kathmandu Valley, radiocarbon-dated between 900 and 1030 CE.[3] It takes the form of an elongated horizontal, unlike most other toranas gracing Nepalese Hindu temples and Buddhist *bahals* in the valley, which are semicircular, such as the spectacular one embellishing the entrance to Chusya Baha in Kathmandu.

Unusual Composition

The Yetakaha Baha torana is also unique for its composition, which features the Buddha in the center preaching to an assembly of two men and two women (or divine beings), all seated with their legs loosely crossed and their hands held together in the gesture of attentive adoration and respect. The Buddha is seated serenely in full lotus position, his left hand in his lap and his right hand raised before his chest in the gesture of teaching. His hair is adorned, piled up in a chignon fronted by a crown ornament, like that of a bodhisattva.

This group is augmented at either end by smaller attendant figures: on the left, a kneeling woman or goddess holding a garland in offering, and on the right, a small, rotund dwarflike male looking out from the scene and holding an offering of some kind in his crossed arms. An array of geometrically defined rocks forms the background to this peaceful scene of religious discourse, each figure set into a recess as if in caves in a vertical face. At the Buddha's knees are a deer and a pair of birds, while other creatures—a monkey, a child, and a pair of lions—cavort or peer out from the rocks above. This rocky scene evoking the mountains that dominate the Kathmandu Valley skyline on a clear day is the only torana so far known "showing a Himalayan scene."[4]

Torana of the Main Shrine of Yetakha Baha; Kathmandu, Nepal; 10th–11th century; wood; total width approx 8 ft. 5 in. (2.57 m); photograph by Sameer Tuladhar, 2021

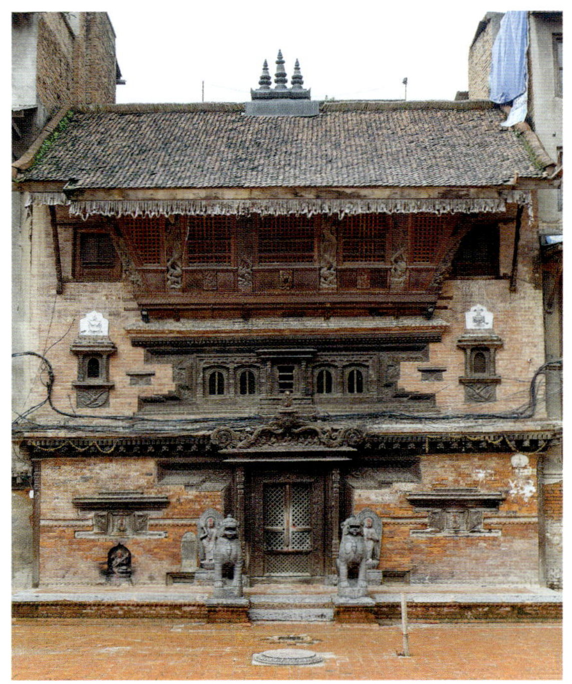

The entire scene is surrounded by a dynamic frame of three mythological creatures: two makaras—aquatic-footed creatures with an elephant-like trunk and extravagant curling tails—to left and right and the awesome grimacing leonine face of a *chepu* or *kirtimukha* above center.[5] These three familiar figures in Newar art and design are joined by the sinuous coils of serpents—resembling tendrils of an enormous vine—which emerge from the chepu's mouth and disappear into the maws of the makaras on either side. The interplay of the peaceful contemplative scene of the Buddha and his acolytes surrounded by the energy of these creatures produces an unrivaled tour de force of Newar wood carving.

The History of Yetakha

Considering the great age of the wonderful torana, surprisingly little inscriptional or documented evidence of the place name Yetakha can be found prior to the sixteenth century,[6] and all of the on-site inscriptions belong to the eighteenth and nineteenth centuries. A nineteenth-century inscription gives the name of the *bahal* as Bhaskara Malla Mahavihara, "the great monastery of (King) Bhaskara Malla," a Kathmandu king who reigned from 1700 to 1722.[7]

The Main Shrine of Yetakha Baha; Kathmandu, Nepal; 9th–12th century; photograph by Sameer Tuladhar, 2021

Some local legends attribute the *bahal* to an earlier king, Bhaskara Deva of the eleventh century, which has led to the name Sri Bhaskarakirti Mahavihara (the monastery of the glory of [king] Bhaskara). The age of the wooden torana and the struts above it lend some credence to this earlier attribution, and largely because of this evidence several scholars have endorsed the connection with the earlier king.[8] An oral tradition holds that the queen of the earlier Bhaskara Deva (r. ca. 1045–1048) founded the *bahal* sometime after the nearby Itum Baha was founded.[9] These two *bahals* have long been linked: Itum Baha is one of the most important of the main monasteries of Kathmandu, and Yetakha Baha is usually counted as a branch of Itum Baha, a relationship often confirmed by Itum Baha residents, but disputed by the residents of Yetakha.[10]

The Udas Community of Yetakha

The community in which this remarkable carving is found is as unusual as the work itself. The residents of Yetakha Baha are from the Newar group known as the Udas or Uray.[11] The Udas community in Kathmandu can be traced back to quite ancient times. It seems that eventually they moved into the areas of medieval Kathmandu, and some came to the locality later called Etakha or Yetakha; it is possible that the Udas adopted Buddhism at the time of these migrations.

The Udas community in Kathmandu is large and influential, comprising various groups of families who traditionally followed a specific trade or practiced a craft. The largest single group is the Tuladhar (the holders of the scales), who are traditionally businessmen and historically have played an important role in trade with Tibet. It is possible that the original founder of the shrine now known as Yetakha Baha was a wealthy Lhasa trader, a devout Buddhist who commissioned the torana with its remarkable Himalayan theme, perhaps partially to remind him of his second home in the Land of Snows. Dhanasimha Tamrakar, the Udas founder of a small subsidiary nineteenth-century shrine in Yetakha, was known as a merchant who prospered in the Tibet trade. Most of the other Udas groups are artisans, including the Tamrakar, workers in copper, Kansakar, workers in bronze, and, notably, the Sthapit, builders and wood-carvers. It is likely that the Yetakha torana was made by a Sthapit wood-carver.

The name Bhaskara Malla Mahavihara, which refers to Yetakha Bahal, is found in the nineteenth-century dedicatory inscription commemorating the establishment of Dhanasimha Tamrakar's private shrine, which has since become known as Dhanasimha Baha. This shows the relative looseness of the term *baha*, which normally is associated with the *viharas* (monasteries) but can also mean "any courtyard having a Buddhist shrine." The term *bahal*, related to the Sanskrit *vihara*, is normally reserved for communities of Shakya or Vajracharya residents, initiated Newar Buddhists who are considered the descendants of the original monks and priests of an earlier time. Although the Shakyas and Vajracharyas

See Vajracharya Priest's Crown, no. 38.

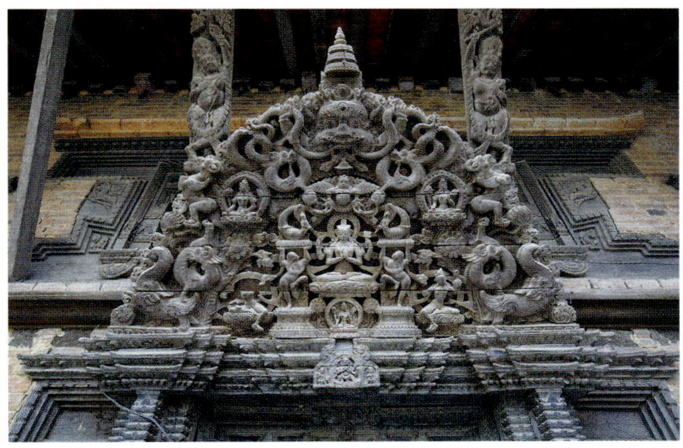

Torana over the Main Entrance of Chusya Baha; Kathmandu, Nepal; 1663; wood; photograph by Sameer Tuladhar, 2021

are now all married householders, they still are initiated in their youth into the Buddhist monkhood or priesthood, in a ritual that is usually followed by a brief period of symbolic monkhood, and their community is still known as a sangha, the community of monks that is one of the traditional three pillars of Buddhism—Buddha, dharma, and sangha (the Buddha, his teachings, and the community of monks).

The Udas community of Yetakha Baha cannot be considered a sangha because its members, though considered the respected laymen of the traditional Buddhist hierarchy, do not go through the ritual initiation into the monkhood, which is experienced by all young Shakya and Vajracharya men. Rather, the community of Yetakha Baha is defined by membership in a *guthi*, the main Newar social grouping; the Yetakha *guthi* is dedicated to the recitation of the *Namasamgiti*, an essential Vajrayana Buddhist text.[12] Up until recent times, the daily worship of the central deity of the Yetakha Baha shrine was performed by a Vajracharya priest from nearby Itum Baha, but after a recent dispute, since the early 2000s the daily worship has been taken up by a group of Udas elders from the Yetakha community itself.

Wood-carvers

See Jokhang Temple, no. 7.

The renowned business skills of the Udas trading families were matched in the arts by the skills of the Sthapits, wood-carvers and architects. Likely from ancient times, these master wood-carvers, like the traders, often traveled north to pursue their craft, most spectacularly evidenced in the wonderful carvings of the Lhasa Jokhang. Their skills are on display elsewhere in the Yetakha neighborhood as well, as in the tour de force known as the Window without an Equal (Deshay Maru Jhya) in a house on a street outside the Yetakha square. Members of these two groups of the Udas community collaborated, to paraphrase Hemraj Shakya, as the artist who created . . . and the donor who financed[13] the torana and the struts of Yetakha, at a time long ago, when it was not yet known as Yetakha Baha, but already represented the wealth and skills of the Newar Buddhist lay community of traders and artisans.

Further Reading:

Gutschow, Niels. 2011. *Architecture of the Newars: A History of Building Typologies and Details in Nepal,* esp. 244–47. Chicago: Serindia.

Slusser, Mary Shepherd, with Paul Jett. 2010. *The Antiquity of Nepalese Wood Carving: A Reassessment*, esp. 66–78, 207–26. Seattle: University of Washington Press.

Vajracharya, Gautama V. 2016. *Nepalese Seasons: Rain and Ritual.* Exhibition catalog. New York: Rubin Museum of Art. https://issuu.com/rmanyc/docs/nepalese_seasons_-_combo-_96_ppi.

Notes

1 Slusser 2010, 128, examines the "woman and tree" motif, and in 66ff., figs. 64–69, dates the Yetakha Baha struts.
2 The term *tympanum*, a word derived from Greek or Latin, refers specifically to the decorative element above the doorway, and is used by Gutschow 2011, 246, and Vajracharya 2016, 57, while Slusser 2010, 207, prefers the term *torana*, used in Nepal.
3 Slusser 2010, 208, fig. 194.
4 H. Shakya 1978, 15.
5 Slusser 2010, 212ff., and Vajracharya 2014, 311ff., fig. 22, examine the history and meaning of this motif.
6 The oldest mention of Yetakha is a legal document from 1573; Pant 2013, 64, 67.
7 H. Shakya 1978, 19ff.
8 H. Shakya 1978, 20–23; see also Locke 1985, 293; Slusser 2010, 66.
9 H. Shakya 1978, 20–23.
10 Locke 1985, 293.
11 The Udas in Kathmandu are overwhelmingly Buddhist, while the equivalent group in Patan are Hindu.
12 The full name is *Manjushrinamasangiti* (*The Litany of the Names of Manjushri*), a foundational Buddhist tantra.
13 H. Shakya 1978, 15.

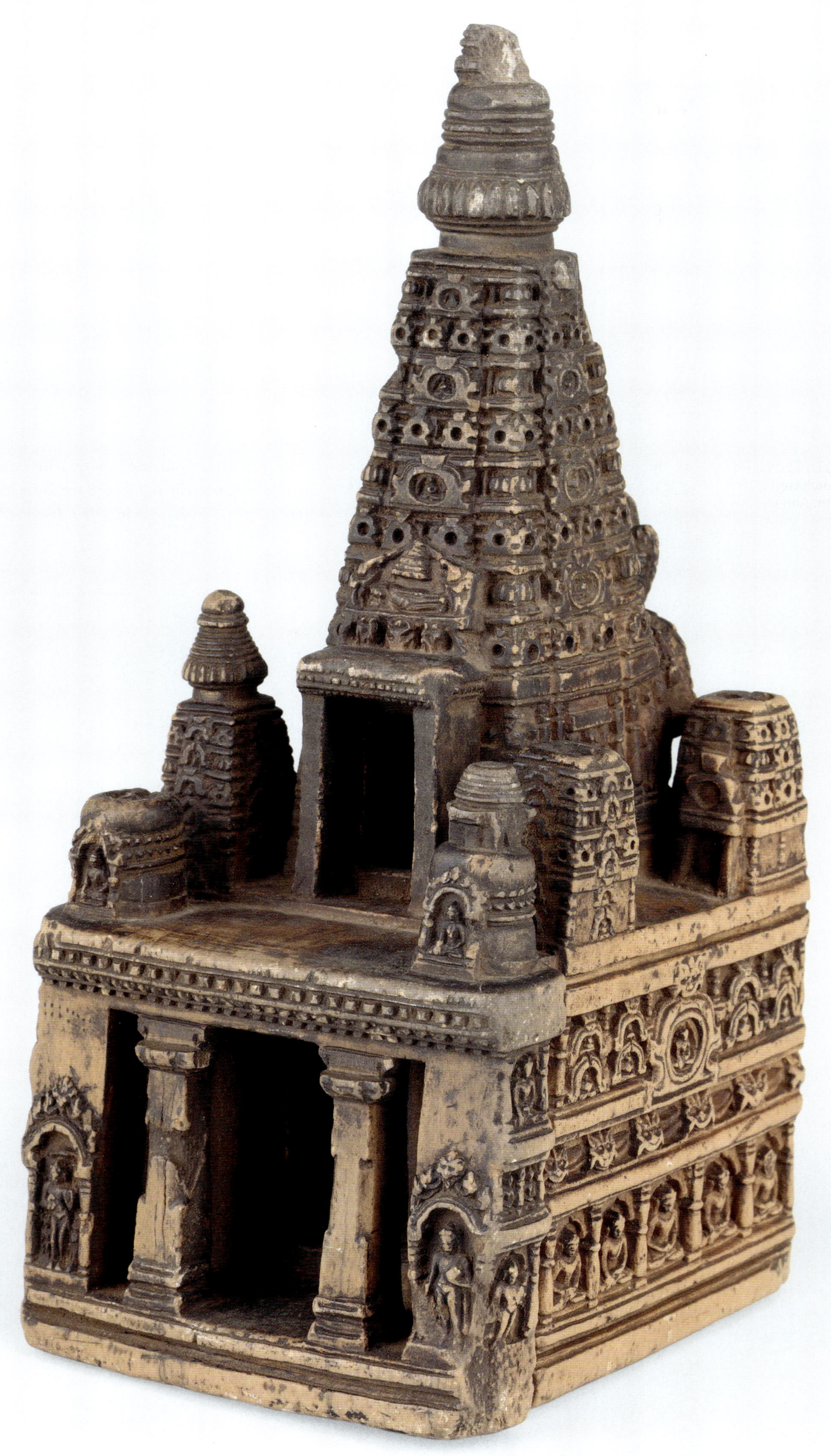

№ 25

Mahabodhi Temple Model

Eastern India, ca. 11th century

Representing the Sacred Site of the Buddha's Awakening

ELENA PAKHOUTOVA

Model of the Mahabodhi Temple; eastern India, probably Bodhgaya; ca. 11th century; stone (serpentinite); 6⅞ × 3½ × 4 in. (17.5 × 8.9 × 10.2 cm); Rubin Museum of Art; Purchased with funds from Ann and Matt Nimetz and Rubin Museum of Art; C2019.2.2 (HAR 68417)

For an example of a Buddhist text that traveled, see Illuminated Pages of the *Prajnaparamita Sutra* Manuscript, no. 23.

THIS SMALL CARVED RENDERING OF THE MAHABODHI TEMPLE is one of many portable objects that were produced and exchanged within the Buddhist world in relation to pilgrimage and the site of Bodhgaya. The Mahabodhi Temple marks the place known as Vajrasana, or the Adamantine Seat, in Bodhgaya, India, where Prince Siddhartha Gautama sat in unwavering contemplation under the bodhi tree until he became the Buddha, meaning the Awakened. Vajrasana, along with centers of Buddhist learning such as the nearby Nalanda Monastery, was especially significant for Tibetans during the tenth to the thirteenth century, a period of Buddhist cultural renaissance in Tibet. In this climate, during the active accumulation and assimilation of the latest Buddhist teachings, Tibetans traversed the Himalayas to India, most often via Nepal, in search of texts and to invite Indian masters to Tibetan areas to teach. They also commissioned and carried back to their temples objects that symbolized Indian sacred sites and invoked the Buddha's life, representing and literally conveying Buddhist teachings.

See Potala Palace, no. 71.

Material mementos of sacred places have always been an important element of Buddhist pilgrimage. Pilgrims brought models of the Mahabodhi Temple, which directly referenced the sacred site of the Buddha's awakening, or enlightenment, back to Tibet. A few models in stone and wood survive in museum collections and Lhasa's Potala Palace.[1] With varying degrees of accuracy, these models reflect the changes the temple underwent throughout its history of renovations. They date to the period around the eleventh century, when Tibetan Buddhists ventured to India in search of teachings and on pilgrimage, through the thirteenth century,[2] possibly even up to 1305, when the Burmese restored the temple.[3]

For an example of the Buddha with the earth-touching mudra, see Buddha on the Cosmic Mountain, no. 10.

For examples of important Buddhist sites with such a Buddha image, see Jokhang Temple, no. 7; Central Shrine Image of Kwa Baha, no. 22; Cave 3 at Yulin Cave Temples, no. 31.

The overall composition and decoration of the models express symbolic Buddhist meanings of the edifice, serving as faithful representations of the temple's general configuration rather than exact copies. For instance, the bodhi tree is not part of the temple's structure, but the miniature replicas include the tree within the building itself. Likewise, an image of the seated Buddha in a niche under the tree, with his right hand touching the ground, a gesture known as the *bhumisparsha* mudra, is prominent in the models but not part of the temple. Its inclusion references the moment of the Buddha's awakening, emphasizing the event as well as the site's significance.

See Crowned Buddha, no. 16.

For more about tantric enlightenment, see The All-Knowing Buddha Vairochana Visualization Album, no. 87.

The temple itself enshrines the main stone image of the seated Buddha touching the ground, and the sanctum of this model originally may have also contained such an image.[4] Images of the Buddha displaying this mudra are found across Buddhist cultures, including at important sites in Nepal and Tibet. Some show the Buddha crowned, following tantric Buddhism's interpretation of Enlightenment, but still refer to Vajrasana Buddha, the main image at the Mahabodhi Temple and the event of the Buddha's awakening.[5]

Scenes of the Buddha's Life

See Mayadevi Giving Birth to Siddhartha, no. 3.

Representations of the Mahabodhi Temple are not uniformly decorated, but many depict scenes of the Buddha's life in relief.[6] The most commonly featured scenes are the birth of the Buddha at Lumbini and his *parinirvana*, or passing, at Kushinagara.[7]

The present-day structure at Bodhgaya does not contain such reliefs. These inconsistencies suggest that besides representing the temple the Mahabodhi models may have signified the major sacred sites tied to the Buddha's life. The life scenes evoke these locations, with the Buddha's enlightenment at Vajrasana being the central and most important site.

Mahabodhi Temple at Bodhgaya, India; photograph by Christian Luczanits

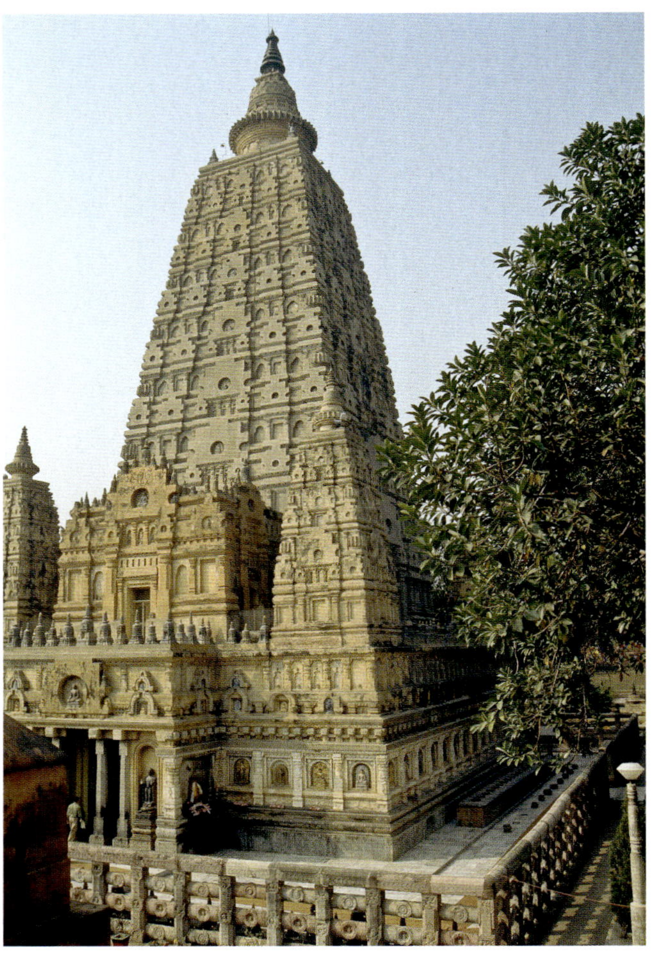

Structure and Symbolism

The small models of the Mahabodhi Temple embody its characteristic features: the stupa atop the central tower, which signifies it is a Buddhist temple; the sculptural images of the bodhi tree; the directional buddhas inhabiting the four corner towers; and images of buddhas and bodhisattvas in registers all around the structure. The tall central tower is of the Indian *sikhara* type—"mountain peak" in Sanskrit—a common architectural element of Indian architecture. The notable structural layout of four smaller towers placed around a central one identifies it as the sacred site of the enlightenment. According to the *Mahavairochana-Abhisambodhi-Tantra*, Buddha Shakyamuni at the moment of his great awakening is also the tantric Buddha Vairochana, who resides at the center of his mandala, or sacred realm.[8] The five-tower structure references Buddha Vairochana's three-dimensional mandala. This layout appears in Tibetan images, objects, and sites.

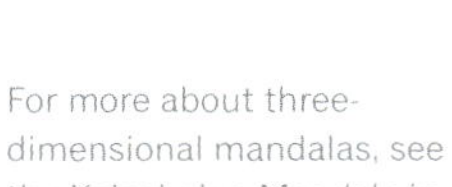

For more about three-dimensional mandalas, see the Kalachakra Mandala in the Potala Palace, no. 77.

See Murals at Toling Dukhang, no. 54.

See Monumental Manjushri with Mahasiddha-Adorned Robe at Alchi, no. 35.

See the Svayambhu Chaitya of Kathmandu, no. 4.

In tenth- to eleventh-century western Tibet, the famous Tibetan translator Rinchen Zangpo (958–1055) built the main temple of Toling Monastery, the so-called Red Temple, with four stupas marking its corners. A large five-tower stupa at Alchi, Ladakh, in the western Himalayas displays a similar structural arrangement, with four stupas at the corners placed around the central, taller stupa. This particular building is not a temple but a shrine, or chaitya. In both buildings the structural organization follows that of Vajrasana's symbolic representation of a Vairochana mandala. Tibetan Buddhists employed this layout as the basis for several early temples and religious edifices, seemingly reinventing the Indian architectural models known to them at the time, if not in their original materials and technologies then in their symbolism and definition of space.

In the late nineteenth century, British archaeologists, Buddhist scholars, and entrepreneurs used Mahabodhi models to reconstruct the actual Mahabodhi Temple in Bodhgaya, which was in ruins, half buried and fully neglected.[9] Their efforts may not have restored the precise historical form of the temple, but they succeeded in resurrecting the site, which resumed its status as the central, most visited pilgrimage site in the Buddhist world.

Re-creations of the Mahabodhi Temple beyond India

Historically, the importance of Bodhgaya and the Mahabodhi Temple for Buddhist pilgrims cannot be underestimated. Buddhists believe a visit to Vajrasana can erase negative karma and ensure future enlightenment. It is therefore not surprising that the Mahabodhi Temple was replicated as large architectural structures in locations outside of India, establishing a local sacred place that by proxy evoked the same sentiment and power as the original.

The Mahabuddha Temple at Patan in Nepal, conceived and founded in 1564 by a Buddhist priest, Abhaya Raj of Uku Baha Monastery, remains a part of that monastery to this day, drawing pilgrims and tourists alike. Built over several decades, the temple was completed by Raj's descendants in 1601.[10]

Nepal remained a destination for Tibetan Buddhists especially after Buddhist institutions in India

For examples of artworks by Nepalese artists commissioned by Tibetans, see Densatil Monastery, no. 30; Mural Painting at Zhalu Monastery, no. 47.

fell into decline by the late thirteenth century. Tibetans continued to commission Nepalese artists and artisans to work on projects for new temples in Tibet. Tibetan patrons also maintained close cultural connections with local Nepalese centers of cultural production as well as with political and regional rulers. From the thirteenth century to the present day, they have engaged with the important Buddhist sites of the Kathmandu Valley. Prominent Tibetan Buddhist teachers, such as Tsangnyon Heruka (1452–1507) and Katok Rigzin Tsewang Norbu (1698–1755), among others, initiated and sponsored renovations of the famous Svayambhu and Boudhanath chaityas and worked with Newar artisans of the Kathmandu Valley and local communities on these projects.[11] Most recently, from 2008 to 2010 Tarthang Rinpoche organized the fifteenth renovation of Swayambhu, engaging local artisans and the communities of Patan and Kathmandu.

The Zhenjue Temple, also known as the Five Pagoda Temple, in Beijing, is yet one more rendering of Vajrasana outside of India. Its five pagodas represent the towers of the Mahabodhi Temple, and the outside decorations recall the reliefs. It was constructed in 1473 and fashioned after a stone model of the Mahabodhi Temple brought to the Yongle emperor (r. 1402–1424) by an eminent Indian monk.[12]

In Hohhot, Inner Mongolia, where Tibetan Buddhism was spread and supported by regional rulers, another replica of the Mahabodhi Temple was built during Qing rule in 1732, this time following Beijing's Five Pagoda Temple.[13]

Representing or re-creating sacred sites remains an active practice in Buddhist cultures, including in Tibet and other Himalayan regions.[14] This practice underscores important ideas inherent in Buddhist traditions, such as the accumulation of merit, in this case through pilgrimage, commissioning Buddhist objects that directly reference the most sacred site of the Buddha's awakening, and ongoing visits to the site—be it with one's mind or body.

For more about merit, see Prayer Wheel, no. 79.

Further Reading

Geary, David. 2017. *The Rebirth of Bodh Gaya: Buddhism and the Making of a World Heritage Site*. Seattle: University of Washington Press.

Huber, Toni. 2008. *The Holy Land Reborn: Pilgrimage and the Tibetan Reinvention of Buddhist India*. Chicago: University of Chicago Press.

Leoshko, Janice. 1988. *Bodhgaya: The Site of Enlightenment*. Bombay: Marg Publications.

Notes

1 For the sandalwood Mahabodhi Temple in the collection of the Potala Palace, Lhasa, see von Schroeder 2001, 328–30, pl. 111A, figs. 113A–C.

2 Vitali 2009–10, 161–63; Gonkatsang and Willis 2013, 434–37.

3 On the Burmese restorations of the Bodhgaya temple, see Woodward 1981, 21; Guy 1991, 361; Leoshko 1996, 573–97; Asher 2008, 24–27.

4 See more on this in Leoshko 2020.

5 Manuals of tantric visualization and rituals (*sadhana*) translated from Sanskrit into Tibetan during this period describe how to envision the Buddha at the seat of awakening, the Vajrasana, and read as descriptions of an actual image. See Rdo rje gdan gyi sgrub thabs (1724), P 3969, Thu, fols. 210b2–212b8; P 3970, Thu, fols. 213a1–214a4; P 4223, Du, fols. 85b1–87b3; P 4224, Du, fols. 87b3–88b3; P 4225, Du, fols. 88b3–89b2; Dpal rdo rje gdan gyi sgrub thabs (1724), P 4127, Du, fols. 1b–4a6. Western scholars who studied these texts include Foucher (1900) and Mallmann (1975).

6 As also seen in the Potala Palace example. See von Schroeder 2001, fig. 113.

7 See von Schroeder 2001, fig. 113 A, C. The Rubin Museum's model also includes these scenes on the north face. The standing figure with an outstretched hand could represent the Descent from the Heaven of the Thirty-Three Gods or the Taming of the Elephant episodes.

8 *The Mahā-Vairocana-Abhisaṃbodhi-Tantra with Buddhaguhya's Commentary*, trans. Hodge 2003, 14, 47. *The Mahavairochana Tantra* was compiled in India about the seventh to eighth century.

9 Cunningham (1892) 1961; Trevnick 1999, 635–56.

10 For more on connections between Bodhgaya and Nepal, see Slusser 1988, 125–42.

11 Rospatt 2011, 157–74, 189–206.

12 Charleux 2006a, 120–42.

13 Charleux 2006a, 120–42.

14 Among the many representations of the Vajrasana Mahabodhi Temple are well-known examples in Burma, Thailand, and India, as well as one in Japan, one in Korea, and two in the United States, in Florida and Las Vegas.

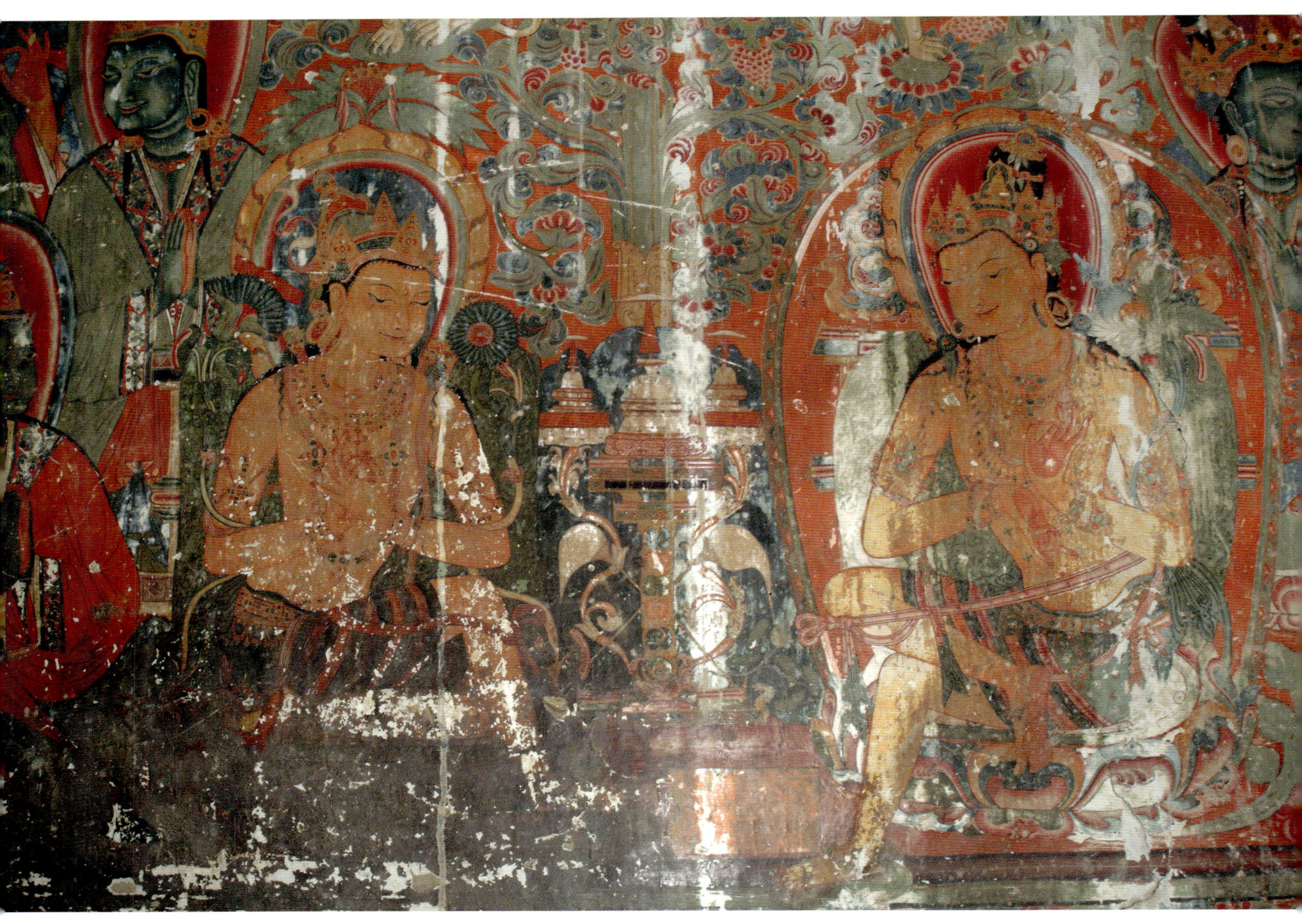

№ 26

Maitreya and Manjushri Mural at Dratang

Dratang Temple, U region, central Tibet (present-day TAR, China), ca. 1081–1093

Cosmopolitanism in a Local Tibetan Environment

ROBERTO VITALI

THE TEMPLE OF DRATANG with its awesome murals is a telling sign of the fertile context responsible for their execution.[1] A product of the culture of eleventh-century central Tibet (U-Tsang) that transcended local boundaries, Dratang is a representation of cosmopolitanism in an environment that was local. The people of the land opened themselves to a wider Buddhist world that created the conditions for the introduction of the Later (and definitive) Diffusion of Buddhism in U-Tsang.

The temple near the bank of the Brahmaputra—midway between Samye and Yarlung, the cradle of the ancient Tibetan kings' dynasty—was the *opus magnum* of the great master Drapa Ngonshe (1012–1091). Its murals, including the "conversation" between Maitreya and Manjushri depicted here, are firmly attributed to his patronage.

The Background

For more about the Tangut Kingdom, see Cave 3 at Yulin Cave Temples, no. 31; Achala Silk Tapestry, no. 36; A *Pancharaksha* Print from Khara-Khoto, no. 32.

Cosmopolitanism was the outcome of the import of Buddhist practice based on monastic observance—and thus on the bestowal of the vow—from the lands of northeast Tibet and beyond, where the Tangut Kingdom was a prosperous center of the religion.

A few antecedents favored the rebirth of Buddhism in U-Tsang, where the religion was languishing at the time. One was the activity of Gongpa Rabsel, a propagator of the religious resurgence in Kham and Amdo (eastern Tibet) in the tenth century. He availed himself of the teachings he received from Tibetan expatriates and the instructions on "Monastic Observance" (*Vinaya*) under Gorong Senggedrak at a holy place outside the plateau in the future Tangut Kingdom.[2]

An ancient manuscript from Central Asia proves that the region that became the Tangut Kingdom—known then as the land of the Bhata Hor—was a center of uninterrupted Tibetan Buddhist practice from the mid-eighth century until when Buddhism was brought back to central Tibet.[3] Local practice was the precondition for the future integration of Buddhism into the heart of the Tibetan highlands.

Another antecedent was the return from Kham and Amdo to central Tibet of the masters (the Men of U-Tsang) who had traveled as far as the limits of the highlands in the northeast to study Buddhism under Gongpa Rabsel. The event marked the reintroduction of Buddhism and its monastic practice in U-Tsang. Its date is disputed, year 978 being a serious possibility,[4] but the diffusion of the second wave of Buddhism was slow. It took off around the time when Drapa Ngonshe, the founder of Dratang, was born in 1012.[5] Lume, the most important of the Men of U-Tsang, built his first temples in the area around Lhasa—the sphere of his activity—from 1009 on,[6] about thirty years after he returned from the east. The delay was due to difficulties the Men of U-Tsang faced locally.[7]

The Life and Deeds of Drapa Ngonshe

The "Conversation" between Maitreya and Manjushri; Dratang Temple; U region, central Tibet (present-day TAR, China); ca. 1081–1093; mural; photograph by R. Linrothe

Drapa Ngonshe did not receive an education as a child. He was an illiterate shepherd for five years in his youth, which gives the wrong impression that he was of humble origins. In fact, Drapa Ngonshe hailed from a noble family. His uncle Zhangton Chobar (993–1055) later trained him in the knowledge of the sutras and tantras, so that his education eventually reached the highest peaks.

Drapa Ngonshe's monastic initiation gives evidence of the heights he reached in his education. The initiation was administered by Yangshu Gyelwawo,[8] a close disciple of the great Lume and a major propagator of monastic observance that came from northeast Tibet and beyond. This led Drapa Ngonshe

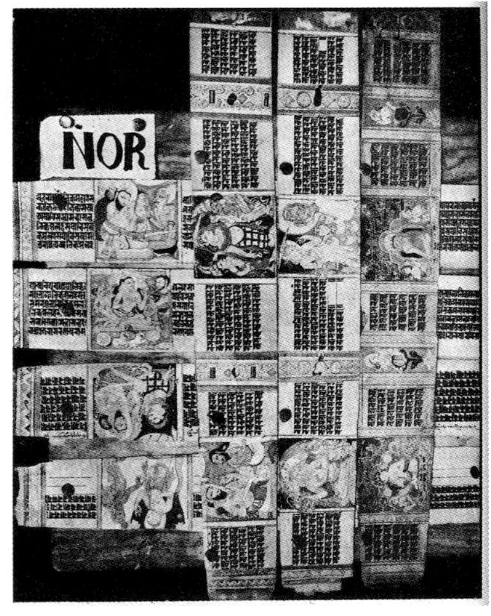

Pala manuscripts photographed by Rahul Sankrityayan in Ngor during one of his visits to Tibet in search of palm-leaf specimens in the 1930s; image after Pathak, S.K., ed. 1986. *The Album of the Tibetan Art Collections*. Patna: Kashi Prasad Jayaswal Research Institute

For more about *terton*, see *Dorje* Discovered by Dorje Lingpa, no. 51.

For more about *Four Medical Tantras*, see Desi Sanggye Gyatso's Medical Paintings, no. 73.

to work with his teacher Yangshu Gyelwawo to maintain the monastic centers they established, like other major masters of their tradition. He and his disciples contributed several of them. The literature includes Dratang among the impressive network of *vinaya* temples founded, owing to the impetus from Kham, Amdo, and the Tangut region.[9]

Cosmopolitanism was one trait of Drapa Ngonshe's personality. His work, like that of other great masters of the period, stands out for his eclecticism, too. He was an expert on the theory and practice of medical science, which he studied under Zhu, a great master of the discipline[10] and a *terton* ("textual archaeologist"). His rediscovery at Samye of the *Four Medical Tantras* (*Gyuzhi*), the fundamental text of Tibetan medical science, was epochal.[11]

Later in his life Drapa Ngonshe perfected under the Indian sage Somanatha the *Guhyasamaja Tantra* and the knowledge of *Kalachakra* imparted to him by his uncle in his youth. He was an adept of the "Pacification Method" (*Zhije*), for he was a disciple of Padampa Sanggye, the extraordinary Indian personality who visited Tibet three or five times to impart the doctrine he personally devised.[12] As the teacher of Machik Labdron, Drapa Ngonshe gave indirect impetus to "Cutting of the Ego" practice (*chod*).[13]

For more about *chod*, a ritual implement used in this practice, and an image of Machik Labdron, see Double-Sided Skull Drum, no. 93.

Legends hold that Drapa Ngonshe founded 108 holy sites in expiation of the death of his teacher Zhu. He practiced piercing Zhu's heart—a form of ancient angioplasty—because medications did not solve the medical problem. The surgery went wrong and Zhu died.[14] In any event, he kept pursuing the common task of diffusing Buddhist practice by building monuments. One of them, the little-known Cheye,[15] was renowned for the purity of its monastic observance.

The Temple of Dratang

Despite the conspicuous number of holy institutions built in central Tibet during the Later Diffusion, Dratang is a lone survivor of several temples in eleventh-century U. Decay caused by time and ravages has emptied the land of practically all of them.

Dratang, too, had its share of disruption. Its temple was reduced to an empty shell during the Cultural Revolution (1966–1976). Its statues have been destroyed. But the murals have survived, although with damages, because the temple was transformed into a granary for the local commune, the last to have existed in U until the end of the 1980s, when the authorities discovered the potential of Dratang to attract scholars and tourists.

Drapa Ngonshe founded Dratang in 1081. It took thirteen years (1081–1093) to complete the religious complex.[16] Most work was directed by Drapa Ngonshe himself. On his death in 1091, his great opus was on the verge of completion. The last touches were given by his two nephews.

His death was caused—the legends say—by a demonstration to his medical students of the practice of piercing the heart with a golden needle that—a baffling recurrence of fate—went wrong. It is more likely that the demise of his medical teacher Zhu was transferred to him (or vice versa).

Hints on the Source of the Dratang Murals

The temple of Dratang reflects the religious developments of the period. Its wall paintings are not the outcome of a single cultural situation. Art and architecture accompanied the diffusion of Buddhism to central Tibet. The model for a number of temples in eleventh-century central Tibet was Namgyi Theu, a holy building in Amdo, associated with the Tangut,[17] whose description echoes the structure of Dratang.

Three lines of diffusion to central Tibet of the idiom born in Gangetic India during the time of the Pala dynasty (750–1162) gave stylistic substance to the religious cycles popular in these regions of the highlands during the eleventh century:

For a Pala example, see Illuminated Pages of the *Prajnaparamita Sutra* Manuscript, no. 23.

- One moved directly from Gangetic India to central Tibet;[18]

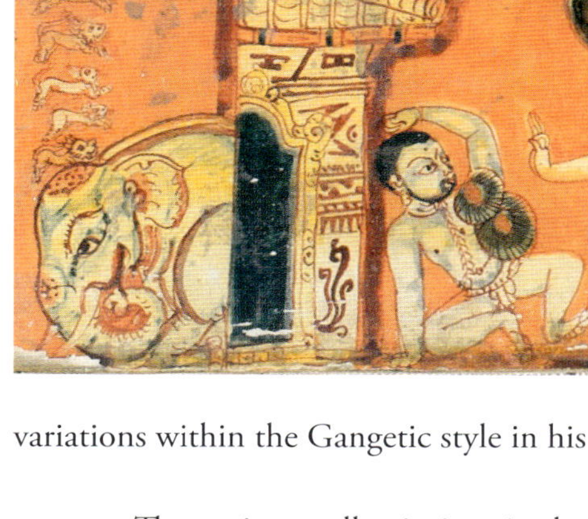

Detail from Cover of a *Prajnaparamita* manuscript (Scenes from the Life of Buddha Shakyamuni), Covers of an *Ashtasahasrika Prajnaparamita (The Perfection of Wisdom in Eight Thousand Verses)*; Newar, Kathmandu Valley, Nepal; dated 1054; opaque watercolor on wood; 2⅛ × 22⅛ × ½ in. (5.4 × 56.2 × 1.3 cm); Los Angeles County Museum of Art, from the Nasli and Alice Heeramaneck Collection, Museum Associates Purchase; M77.19.1a–b; photograph © Museum Associates/ LACMA, www.lacma.org

- Another was the peculiar rendition of the style that prospered in the Kathmandu Valley and transferred from there to central Tibet;
- A third traveled from Gangetic India toward the southern regions of Central Asia before reaching central Tibet; it also went eastward to the kingdom of Pagan.

Situ Chokyi Gyatso (1880–1923/1925) was right in detecting an amalgam of the various variations within the Gangetic style in his description of Dratang:[19]

> The ancient wall paintings in the style of Bel[yul] (the Kathmandu Valley) are of excellent quality and with ornamental motifs. In the middle floor, they are likewise in the manner of Bel[yul]. The figures are executed in the rendition of China.

Could this Nyingma master's "rendition of China" point toward the transfer of the Gangetic style in its Newar version to the Chinese protectorates near the border of northeastern Tibet, where the Tangut Kingdom was located?

The rendition of the images at Dratang is neither Newar nor Gangetic. It reflects the physiognomies adopted in the style of Central Asia.[20] Situ Chokyi Gyatso sensed this stylistic aspect, which he attributed to an amalgam of the Newar and Chinese idioms.

For more about the Nepalese artist Arniko (Anige), see White Stupa, no. 40.

The theme of the mural depicting the "conversation" between Maitreya and Manjushri found on a wall of Dratang endured during successive periods. A well-known "conversation" is on the first floor of Zhalu Serkhang, painted in the first quarter of the fourteenth century by a Tibetan artist trained at the school of the great artist Arniko (Anige). An earlier and not so well-known "conversation" between Maitreya and Manjushri is found inside the Jokhang of Pasho Monastery in Kham, executed during the Kagyupa phase—its murals depict saints of the school, including a portrait of Milarepa in his typical cotton attire—before the Gelukpa took over this monastic institution.

Further Reading

Henss, Michael. 2014. *The Cultural Monuments of Tibet: The Central Regions*, 1:353–62. Munich: Prestel.

Vitali, Roberto. 1990. *Early Temples of Central Tibet*, 37–68. London: Serindia.

Notes

1 See J. Watt, 2018–19; Miller 2022.
2 See Roerich (1949) 1979, 90, lines 8–10, for the statements of On Bici, an obscure personality expert in the history of the Later Diffusion in central Tibet.
3 Ch. 0021, vol. 31, fol. 116b, in Thomas 1935–63, 2:85–86.
4 Roerich (1949) 1979, 1086.
5 Roerich (1949) 1979, 95.
6 Roerich (1949) 1979, 74; Dpa' bo gtsug lag phreng ba (1545–64) 1986, 474, lines 2–4.
7 Vitali 2020, 856–61.
8 Byams pa 'phrin las 1990, Gso rig bstan pa'i nyin byed rnam thar, 93, lines 7–10.
9 Ne'u pandi ta 1990, 43, lines 17–18.
10 Byams pa 'phrin las, 93, line 11.
11 Byams pa 'phrin las, 94, lines 7–8.
12 Roerich (1949) 1979, 96.
13 Roerich (1949) 1979, 97.
14 Byams pa 'phrin las, 93, 17, 94, 4.
15 Roerich (1949) 1979, 96.
16 Roerich (1949) 1979, 96–97.
17 Padma rdo rje, n.d., 7, lines 12–20.
18 See Indian illuminated manuscripts cataloged and photographed by Rāhulji Sāṅkṛityāyana in Sāṅkṛityāyana 1937.
19 Si tu Chos kyi rgya mtsho 1999, 123, lines 19–124, 1.
20 Vitali 1990, pls. 30, 32–33.

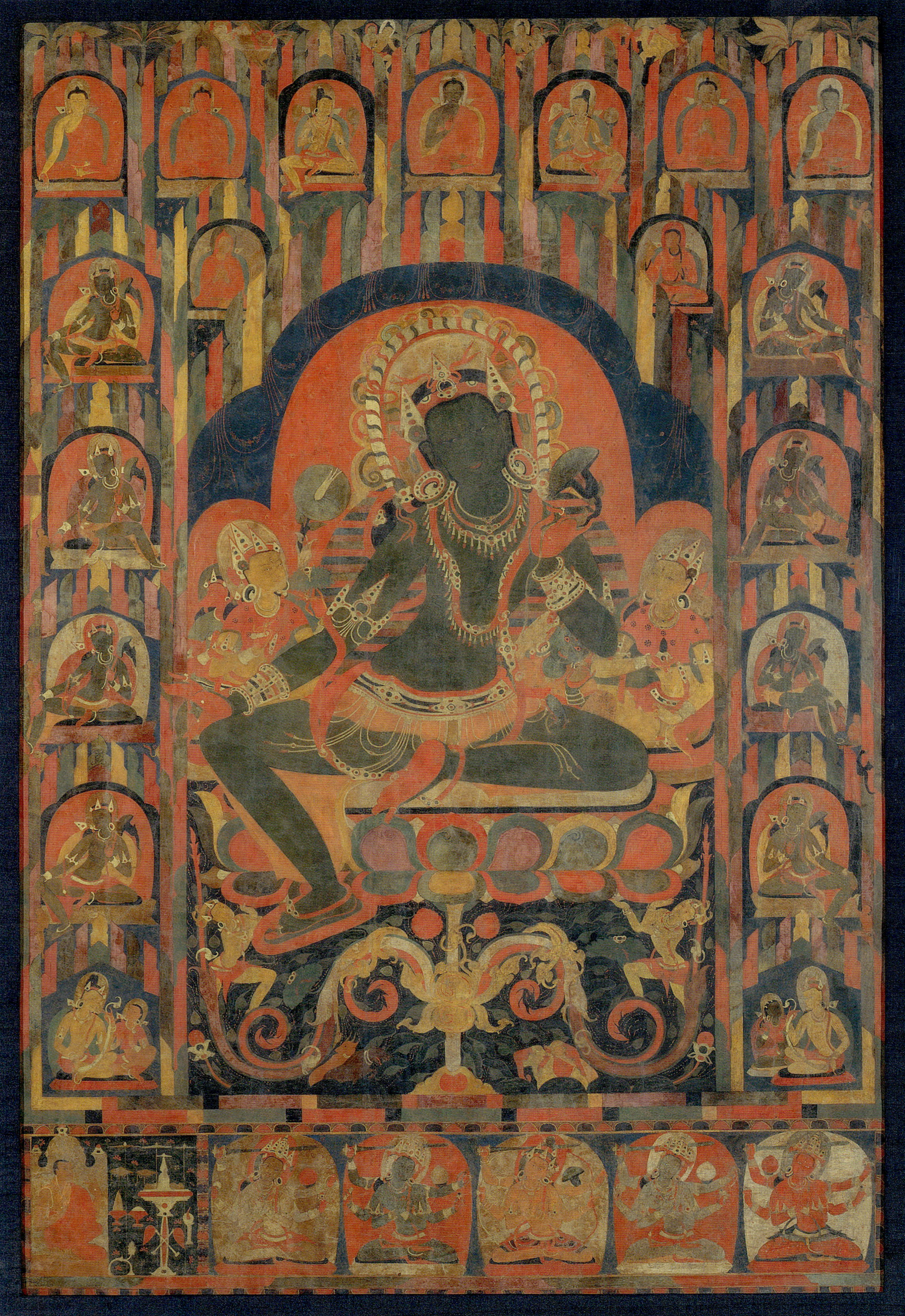

Nº 27

Tara Who Protects from the Eight Great Fears

Reting Monastery, U region, central Tibet, ca. 1056–1189

On the Origins and History of an Early Tibetan Masterwork

JANE CASEY

Tara, the Buddhist goddess of compassion, is the subject of this painting. It is one of the finest examples of early Tibetan art, remarkable for its elegant composition and aesthetic refinement.

It has a distinguished, if still somewhat mysterious provenance. Although it has been the subject of a few brief studies, fundamental questions remain about when it was commissioned, and by whom. Analysis of the painting's iconography, lineage of teachers, inscriptions, and style provides evidence of its origins and early history.

Iconography

The painting presents the beloved goddess within a mountain cave. Tara's languid body is adorned with an array of jewels. A fine orange gauze gathers on her lap and falls almost undetected along her lower limbs. She sits on a lotus supported by two snake deities, in a natural setting dense with vegetation and inhabited by elephants and other wild animals. At the top of the painting, saintly beings make their way through a forest likewise filled with dangerous predators. The side registers present eight additional images of Tara within smaller mountain caves. In each, the goddess offers an open hand to a supplicant. The iconography of the painting is known as Ashtamahabhaya Tara, "Tara Who Protects from the Eight (*ashta*) Great Fears (*mahabhaya*)." A text from about the seventh century describing this iconography was composed by the Indian philosopher Chandragomin. His text describes Tara's setting as "on a lake, in a jewel cavern."[1] In this form, Tara was patron and guide to traveling Buddhist merchants and pilgrims. The eight perils described in Chandragomin's account were very real dangers to medieval travelers: attacks by the demons who cause disease or by bandits, stampeding elephants, lions, and poisonous snakes; being caught in forest fires or in floods (perhaps drowning in failed attempts to cross rivers or streams); and false imprisonment in foreign lands.

The Lineage of Teachers

Three historical figures appear in the painting, constituting a lineage of revered teachers who transmitted teachings connected with this form of Tara from one generation to the next. The Indian monk in a red-peaked cap represents Atisha (ca. 982–1054), the celebrated Buddhist master whose presence in Tibet between 1042 and 1054 helped to establish a firm foundation for the practice of Buddhism. Tara was Atisha's tutelary deity, and he and his Tibetan disciple Naktso translated Chandragomin's text on the Eight Great Fears Tara into Tibetan in the eleventh century.[2] On the other side is Atisha's chief Tibetan disciple Dromton (1005–1064), dressed in the robes of a lay practitioner because he was never ordained as a monk. The painting's patron appears in the lower left corner. The monk wears the uniquely Tibetan short-sleeved yellow vest under the red robe, indicating he was a Tibetan. A lineage of teachers can be helpful in assigning dates to Tibetan paintings, for they are sometimes continuous to the period of the painting's patron.[3] If that were the case in this painting, the patron would be a disciple of Dromton, who founded Reting Monastery north of Lhasa in 1056 and died in 1064.[4]

Tara; Reting Monastery, U region, central Tibet; ca. 1056–1189; distemper on cloth; 48 × 31½ in. (122 × 80 cm); The Walters Art Museum, Baltimore; John and Berthe Ford Collection; F.112; photograph by John Bigelow Taylor

The Inscriptions

Two Tibetan inscriptions appear near the top on the back of the painting. One states, "Reting Deity," an indication that the painting was once associated with Reting Monastery.[5] Dan Martin, a leading historian of Tibet, understands the inscription to be a mark of "ownership" by Reting and acknowledges "it could have become a part of that impressive *thang-ka* collection any time since the monastery's founding in 1056."[6] The second inscription, written in a different hand, states (in part) that the painting is "the 'high aspiration' [*tukdam*] of Jatson Druwo" and that it was "consecrated by Sechilpuwa (1121–1189) of Chekhawa."[7] The second inscription indicates that at some point, the painting was associated with Jatson Druwo (dates unknown), who deemed the painting his "high aspiration"; this too is in some sense an indication of ownership.[8] Leaving aside the ambiguities in the second inscription, one can confidently state that the painting was [re-]consecrated no later than 1189, the year Sechilpuwa died.

These inscriptions shed light on the painting's early history, but their implications are open to interpretation. Martin interprets the statement that the painting is the "high aspiration" of Jatson Druwo as evidence that the latter had commissioned the painting. While this is possible, it is by no means a certainty. Paintings accrue inscriptions over time. This painting's visual lineage, which may indicate the painting was commissioned by a disciple of Dromton, and the first inscription stating "the Reting Deity" may indicate that the painting was first at Reting, where it was commissioned, and that it later came into the hands of Sechilpuwa, who reconsecrated it sometime before his death in 1189.

In support of this interpretation is evidence in paintings associated with Taklung Monastery. Thirty-eight twelfth- and thirteenth-century Taklung paintings bear an inscription stating they were consecrated by Sanggye Won (d. 1296), interim fourth abbot (1272–1273) of Taklung. Of these paintings, perhaps only a quarter were also commissioned by him. The great majority were reconsecrations of earlier paintings. Moreover, six Taklung paintings bear an inscription asserting that they are the "high aspiration [*tukdam*]" of Sanggye Won. Of these paintings, five are certainly older paintings inherited by Sanggye Won; only one painting bearing this inscription *may* have been commissioned by him. In the Taklung paintings, the *tukdam* inscription appears on paintings that were inherited from a teacher, a teacher's teacher, and sometimes, a teacher's teacher's teacher.[9]

Tara's Connection with Atisha and Reting Monastery

While in Tibet, Atisha had a vision of Tara, which he described to his disciples: "Jowo said, 'I visualize Tārā even in dreams with the idea she is a mother. The Jomo is clearly in this, and she will be my witness [to the truth of this].' They asked him where the Jomo [Holy One, in feminine form] was and he replied, 'She is in a thangka of Eight Fears Tārā. This is the one.' That thangka is even now to be found in Reting."[10] A descriptive catalog of Reting Monastery describes an abbot of Reting, Neljor Chenpo Jangchub Rinchen (1015–1078; abbot 1065–1078), who was sent to India to commission a painting of the Eight Fears Protector Tara. He presented it to Atisha, then residing at Netang Monastery, who performed consecrations of the painting.[11]

Style and Summary

For objects from Nalanda collected in Tibet, see Crowned Buddha, no. 16; Illuminated Pages of the *Prajnaparamita Sutra* Manuscript, no. 23.

For Indian-inspired Buddhist architecture in Tibet, see Mahabodhi Temple Model, no. 25.

The style of the painting is closely related to eastern Indian art of the period.[12] Around the turn of the eleventh century, Tibetan Buddhists looked to eastern India, the Buddhist homeland, as a crucial source of Buddhist culture. For over two centuries, they apprenticed themselves to tantric masters and enrolled as students in the great monastic universities of eastern India such as Nalanda, Odantapuri, and Vikramashila. While there, they experienced the ritual use of Buddhist images and were inspired by the art and architecture of Buddhist India.[13] They also commissioned and otherwise procured perhaps thousands of sculptures and paintings, which they brought back to Tibet.[14] The aesthetic and iconographic canons of eastern India formed the foundation of one of the two major artistic styles in central Tibet from the eleventh until the beginning of the fifteenth century.

Some early Tibetan paintings so closely resemble Indian art that scholars have begun to explore whether any of the surviving early Tibetan paintings, like this Tara, might in fact have been commissioned in India. Aside from observing the aesthetic and iconographic norms of eastern India (such as the proportions of figures, the architectural and iconographic forms, the jewelry and costume design, and the tropical jungle references, all of which find antecedents in the art of eastern India), this painting is remarkable because it has presence. The central figure of Tara expresses a gentle, transcendent presence. Her fine, tapering fingers hold the stem of a lotus on her left, while her right hand offers a gracious gesture of renunciation (*shramana* mudra). Note the poise of her right hand, its ringed finger raised slightly as she presents an open palm, and the fall of the gem-encrusted gold pendants of her girdle over her left calf, observing the fall of gravity. A diaphanous shawl, now just barely evident across her upper arms and chest, bears an elegant circle motif. Her form is languid, poised, relaxed, but alert. All of these aspects suggest an artist of exceptional skill and sophistication. Regardless of the uncertainties surrounding its early provenance, the painting remains one of the great masterworks of Tibetan art, one that will richly reward additional investigation.

Further Reading

Casey, Jane. Forthcoming. *Taklung Painting: A Study in Chronology*. Chicago: Serindia.

Martin, Dan. 2001b. "Painters, Patrons and Paintings of Patrons in Early Tibetan Art." Tiblical. https://sites.google.com/site/tiblical/painters-patrons-and-paintings-of-patrons-in-early-tibetan-art.

Singer, Jane Casey. 1998b. "An Early Tibetan Painting Revisited: The Ashtamahabhaya Tara in the Ford Collection." *Orientations Magazine* 29, no. 10 (October): 65–73.

Notes

1 Willson 1986, 340. See also Allinger 1995; M. E. Shaw 2006, 318–22.

2 *Ārya Tārā aṣṭabhaya trāta nāma sādhanaṃ* (Tibetan: *'Phags ma sgrol ma 'jigs pa brgyad las skyob pa zhes bya ba'i sgrub thabs*). In D. T. Suzuki, ed., *The Tibetan Tripitaka*, Peking edition, *Bstan 'gyur rgyud 'grel*, 1955–61, vol. 81, 74 1.1–5.4, DU 373a–375a, as cited in Allinger 1995, 667. English translation in Willson 1986, 337–42. Dan Martin notes that they translated the text while at the Jokhang in Lhasa. D. Martin 2018, 13n14.

3 See D. Jackson 2011, 104–31; D. Jackson 2010, 23–49; and Casey, forthcoming.

4 Reting became the seat of the Kadam order and is located in Penyul valley about thirty-seven miles (sixty kilometers) north of Lhasa.

5 *Ra sgreng ba'i lha*. Transliterations of the inscriptions appear in Kossak and Singer 1998, 54–59; photographs and transliterations appear in D. Martin 2001a, 17–19, figs. 3, 4.

6 D. Martin 2001a, 18.

7 *Bya brtson 'grus 'od kyi thugs dam se phyil phu ba'i {mchad kha ba'i} rab gnas bzhugs spyil phu ba'i chos skyong la gtad do.* Other inscriptions on the verso, of less relevance to the present discussion, are discussed in Kossak and Singer 1998, 57–59; Singer 1998, 67–73; D. Martin 2001a, 18–23. Dan Martin corrects my mistaken identification of Jatson Druwo.

8 See D. Martin 2001a, 19–22, for various interpretations of the consecration inscription. Dan Martin notes my translation, above, as a possible interpretation in D. Martin 2001a, 19 and n39.

9 Casey, forthcoming.

10 D. Martin 2018, 14–15. See a different version of this episode, recounted in Tsuklak Trengwa's chapter on the Kadampas, in Singer 1994, 108n60.

11 See D. Martin 2001a, 10–11n21, for additional information on other early paintings of Tara commissioned by eleventh- and twelfth-century Tibetans.

12 For further discussion and specific comparisons with eastern Indian art, see earlier discussions by Singer 1998b; Kossak and Singer 1998a, 54–59. See also Huntington and Huntington 1990, 318–20; Pal 1984, appendix.

13 Chak Lotsawa and other Tibetan pilgrims to eastern India describe images that speak, cry, and impart wisdom. See Roerich (1949) 1959, xx, 92–93; Dpa' bo gtsug lag phreng ba (1545–64) 1961, 290.

14 Singer 1998, 68–73; Weldon and Singer 1999, 54–55; Singer 1998a, 12–13.

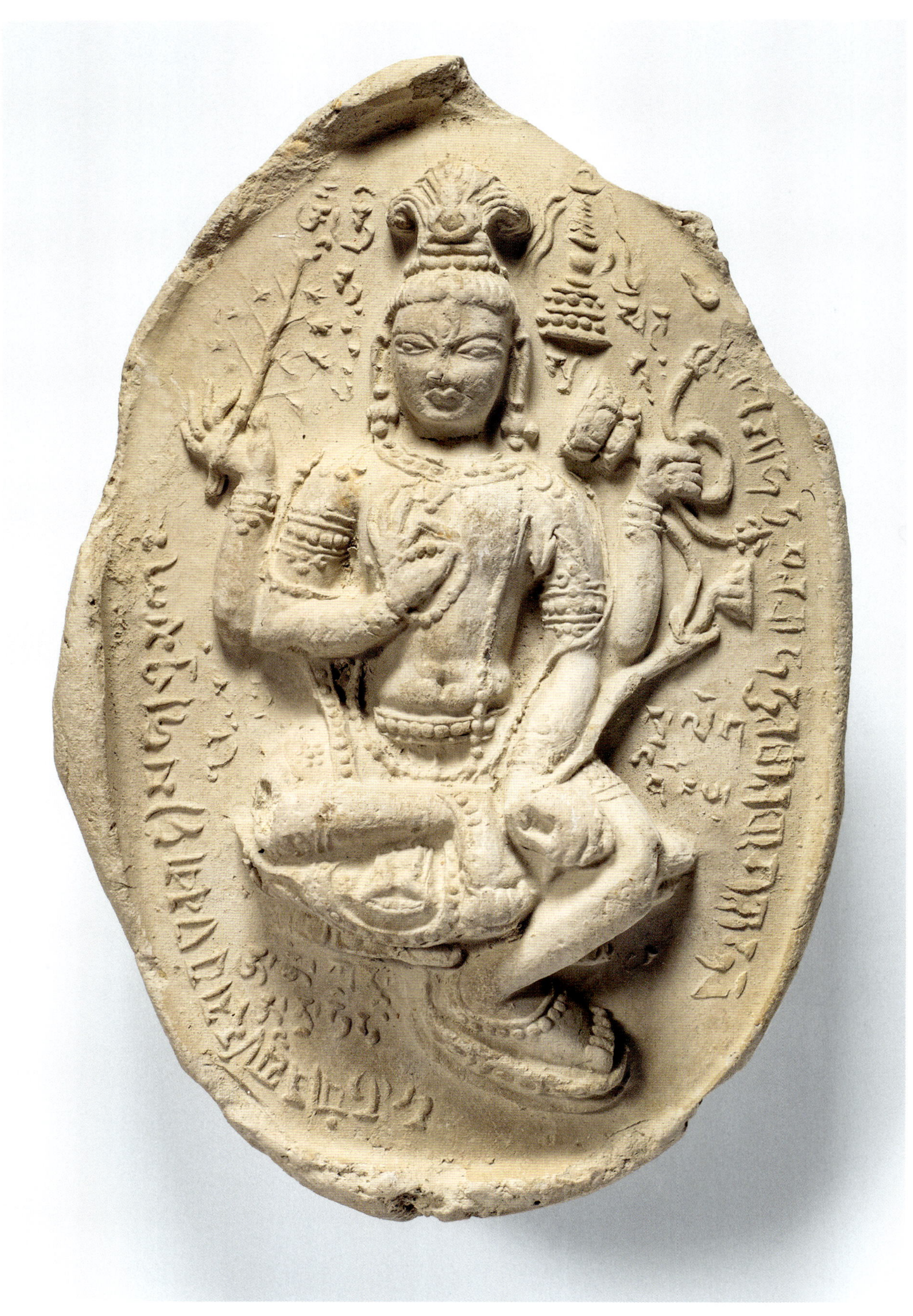

Molded Clay Image (*Tsatsa*) of Amoghapasha; Guge, Ngari region, western Tibet; 11th–12th century; sun-dried clay; 3¼ × 2½ × 3¼ in. (9.5 × 6.3 × 3 cm); Private collection; photograph by Rémi Chaix

№ 28

Molded Clay Image (*Tsatsa*) of Amoghapasha

Guge, Ngari region, western Tibet, 11th–12th century

Mass Production of Images as a Ritual Practice

KUNSANG NAMGYAL-LAMA

THIS CLAY PLAQUE, RECOVERED FROM WESTERN TIBET, constitutes a particularly noteworthy example of a *tsatsa* from the later spread of Buddhism (*tenpa chidar*, late 10th–13th century). Made using a mold, this type of image was abundantly produced in the Tibetan world. The ritual of making *tsatsas* spread to Tibet beginning in the second half of the eighth century.[1] However, it was only at the end of the tenth century that this practice of Indian origin underwent major developments in Tibet, as evidenced by archaeological findings and by the copious ritual literature.[2] According to later Tibetan traditions, the great Indian teacher Atisha (ca. 982–1054) played a central role in developing the practice of making *tsatsas* in Tibet.[3]

For more about Atisha, see Tara Who Protects from the Eight Great Fears, no. 27.

For more about accumulation of merit, see Prayer Wheel, no. 79.

Canonical texts primarily advocate making *tsatsas* as part of ritual practices associated with the production and accumulation of merit (*tsoksak*), as well as with the purification of negative deeds and obscurations (*dikdrib jang*). Though *tsatsas* have been generally produced to serve as consecration deposits to be placed inside stupas or for the final stage of funerary rituals, the reasons for making them and their uses in the Tibetan context have largely varied over the centuries. Parallel to ritual and textual developments, images depicted on *tsatsas* display rich iconographic diversity and evidence the same stylistic trends as those that influenced every other Tibetan artistic production.

For more and later images at Guge and Purang, see Murals at Toling Dukhang, no. 54.

The earliest *tsatsas* made in western Tibet during the later spread of Buddhism, initiated by the rulers of Guge and Purang at the end of the tenth century, provide relevant and particularly rich documentary resources for the study of Tibetan art history.

Iconography of Amoghapasha and Kashmiri Aesthetics

For more about Avalokiteshvara, see Avalokiteshvara at Khartse, no. 20; Bodhisattva Avalokiteshvara and the Buddha's Footprints, no. 33.

This sun-dried *tsatsa* depicts an aspect of Avalokiteshvara called Amoghapasha, the one with the "unfailing lasso," a characteristic attribute that the bodhisattva holds here in his upper left hand. The Tibetan inscription of his mantra, scattered around his image, further helps to establish the identification. In this unusual and rare four-armed form, Amoghapasha is depicted sitting in a relaxed pose, his left leg pendent, the foot resting on a lotus pad. The first right hand, raised in the gesture of argumentation (*vitarka* mudra), holds a rosary, while the second one grasps the branch of an unidentified plant bearing small flowers. The first left hand, placed on his thigh, holds the stalk of a fully open lotus flower that is level with his face, right next to the lasso, each extremity of which ends with a half vajra. A third eye is visible on his forehead, and a small effigy of Buddha Amitabha appears against his towering coiffure. He wears an antelope skin over his left shoulder. Like several other Indian sculptures or paintings from Dunhuang depicting Amoghapasha (see image on p. 83), this one does not conform exactly to the various iconographic descriptions given in textual sources.[4]

For more about Kashmiri aesthetics, see Buddha on the Cosmic Mountain, no. 10; Rock Carving of Four-Armed Bodhisattva Maitreya, no. 17.

For more about Tabo, see Goddess Dharmameghabhumi in the Tabo Main Temple, no. 21.

On stylistic grounds, this small image reflects a strong Kashmiri aesthetic, specifically, in the treatment of the physiognomic and facial features, the tall ascetic chignon, and the jewelry, which are also found on existing Kashmiri bronzes.[5] Under the patronage of the Guge and Purang rulers, the Kashmiri style deeply inspired the art of the western regions of the Tibetan Plateau during the later spread of Buddhism. The invitation of Indian religious masters and artists to work in newly built temples, such as Toling and Tabo, and the creation of numerous Buddhist receptacles (stupas, paintings, sculptures) contributed to the diffusion and adoption of foreign iconographic and stylistic elements.

The molds were either brought from India or created in the Tibetan context. Note that several molds were engraved after their production with new inscriptions. For example, on this *tsatsa* of

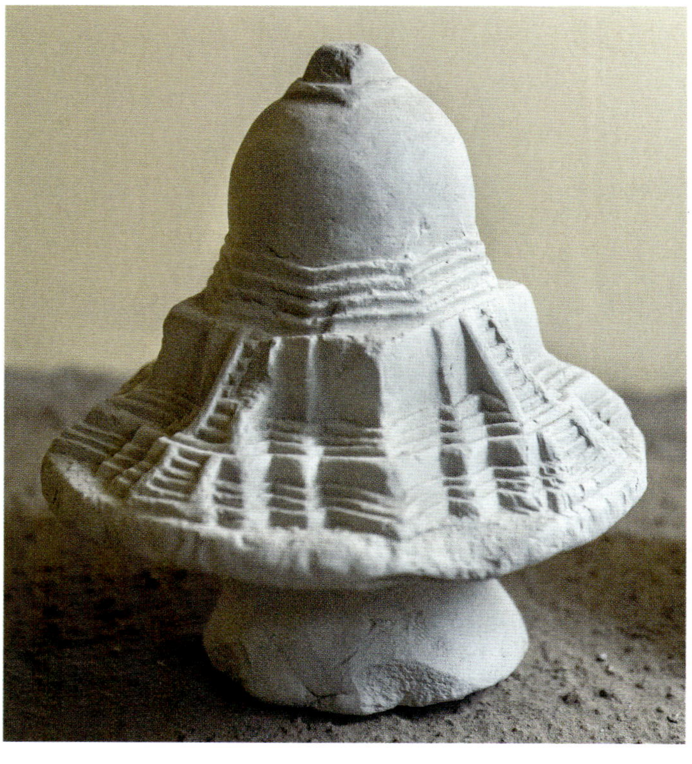

Molded Clay Image (*Tsatsa*) of a Stupa Molded in the Round; Toling Monastery, Ngari region, western Tibet; 11th–12th century; sun-dried clay; height approx. 4 in. (10 cm); Toling Monastery; photograph by Rémi Chaix

For an example of a stupa monument, see Stupa at Toling Monastery, no. 19.

Amoghapasha, the layout of his mantra, which is displayed vertically in a discontinuous manner on the available space around the deity, suggests a later inscription in Tibetan *uchen* script, while the "verse of Interdependent origination" (*Pratityasamutpadagatha*), in an Indian script, occupies the periphery and appears to be original.

Tsatsas as Images of Stupas

While most of the major deities of the Tibetan Buddhist pantheon and the main historical figures are represented on these objects, ritual texts primarily advocate the making of miniature stupa-shaped *tsatsas*. This directive finds its origin and justification in canonical texts that prescribe depositing certain effective formulas (dharanis), such as the *Pratityasamutpadagatha*, inside stupas, even tiny ones.[6] Such *tsatsas* shaped as stupas, reproducible in mass, have been considered privileged receptacles for these "sacralizing" formulas. These formulas can be written on various materials (tree bark, palm leaves, paper, cloth) or impressed on small clay seals and inserted into the miniature stupas.[7] The introduction of these formulas into the moldings is one of the essential ritual steps in the manufacturing process.[8] Thus consecrated, they can be deposited inside newly built stupas or other receptacles to serve in turn as consecration deposits.

In western Tibet, a large number of *tsatsas* depicting stupas with various architectural shapes were produced between the tenth and thirteenth centuries. They feature some of the distinctive characteristics of the Eight Stupas of the Tathagata (*Deshek Chorten Gye*) as described by Tibetan scholars, at least from the end of the twelfth century or the beginning of the thirteenth century.[9] Miniature stupas molded in the round are mostly of a cruciform shape, with two flights of stairs at the center of each of the four main sides, under a central dome. This is a model that has sometimes been described as being of the type "Descent from the Heaven of the Thirty-Three Gods" (*Lhabab Chorten*). However, given their similarity with the remains of monuments built in earlier periods and located in different regions of northwestern India (Kashmir, Afghanistan) and Central Asia (Rawak), we cannot make this identification definitive. Nevertheless, the figuration of the Eight Stupas seems more evident on plaque-shaped *tsatsas*, where we find not only the "Descent from Heaven" type, with the flight of stairs or the ladder, but also other types, often including the stupa of the "Many Auspicious Doors" (*Tashi Gomang Chorten*) or of the "Heaped Lotuses" (*Pepung Chorten*).[10] The latter is easily identifiable by the ornamentation of lotus petals on its four circular steps, evoking those that miraculously appeared under the very first steps the future Buddha took after his birth. The existence of *tsatsas* depicting stupas with these architectural features suggests that these models may certainly constitute prototypes for the set of the Eight Stupas of the Tathagata that was standardized about the thirteenth century in Tibet. Interestingly, one *tsatsa* from Guge produced about the twelfth or thirteenth century illustrates a set of eight different stupas, of which at least five clearly feature the standardized characteristics.[11]

For an example of the "Many Auspicious Doors" type of stupa, see Gyantse Kumbum, no. 55.

See Mayadevi Giving Birth to Siddhartha, no. 3.

The Functions and Status of *Tsatsas*

Tsatsas are mainly manufactured during the erection of stupas to serve as consecration deposits and at the end of funerary rituals. Besides these two main contexts, they can be made for other specific purposes in connection with apotropaic, prophylactic, or therapeutic rituals. Their function and status

Molded Clay Image (*Tsatsa*) of the "Heaped Lotuses" Stupa; Guge, Ngari region, western Tibet; 11th–12th century; sun-dried clay; 3⅜ × 3⅛ × 1½ in. (8.5 × 8 × 3.7 cm); Private collection; photograph by Rémi Chaix

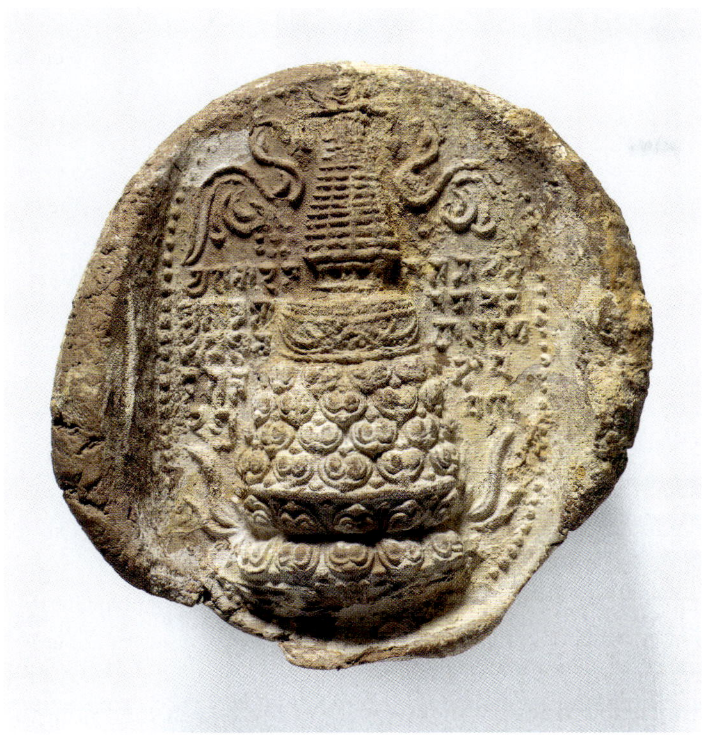

See Amulet Box (*Gau*) with Its Contents, no. 107.

See Portable Shrine, no. 88.

See Monumental Manjushri with Mahasiddha-Adorned Robe at Alchi, no. 35; Mural Painting at Zhalu Monastery, no. 47.

differ depending on the context and purposes for which they are made and may determine the places where they are deposited. They are primarily placed inside stupas or special edifices built to house them (*tsakhang*), around sacred sites, in holy caves, or inside rock cavities. *Tsatsas* produced in a funerary context have a different status depending on whether they contain the mortuary remains of an ordinary lay person or of a religious master, in which case they are considered relics and placed inside funeral stupas, reliquaries (*gau*), or statues. Finally, *tsatsas* have been used as images for portable shrines, including *tashi gomang*, or as wall decorations (Alchi and Zhalu).

In the Tibetan world, *tsatsas* are very common objects, and the ritual for making them is performed, individually or collectively, by religious specialists as well as by lay practitioners.[12] This practice was envisaged as a simple and efficacious ritual means to accumulate merit and improve one's karma. Most of the great Tibetan scholars, such as Nyangrel Nyima Wozer (1124–1192), the Fifth Dalai Lama (1617–1682), and Jamgon Kongtrul (1813–1899), composed ritual texts, some of which are still used today as basic manuals. With the propagation of Tibetan Buddhism, this practice spread to other countries, such as China and Mongolia, where it underwent remarkable developments in the eighteenth and nineteenth centuries.

Further Reading

Namgyal-Lama, Kunsang. 2013b. "*Tsha tsha* Inscriptions: A Preliminary Survey." In *Tibetan Inscriptions: Proceedings of a Panel Held at the Twelfth Seminar of the International Association for Tibetan Studies, Vancouver 2010*, edited by Kurt Tropper and Cristina Scherrer-Schaub, 1–41. Brill's Tibetan Studies Library 32. Leiden: Brill.

Tucci, Giuseppe. 1988b. *Stupa: Art, Architectonics and Symbolism*. New Delhi: Aditya Prakashan.

Xiong Wenbin 熊文彬 and Li Yizhi 李逸之. 2016. *Xizang Guge caca yishu* 西藏古格擦擦艺术 [Art of *tsatsa* from Guge, Tibet]. Beijing: Zhongguo zangxue chubanshe.

Notes

1 The sojourn in central Tibet of Indian Buddhist masters, authors of ritual texts about the making of *tsatsas*, such as Shantigarbha, suggests that this practice spread around this period. By the ninth century Tibetans were already performing it, as attested by several Tibetan manuscripts mentioning *tsatsas* that were discovered in Dunhuang (Gansu), as well as by records of *tsatsa* texts in the inventories of imperial libraries.

2 Concerning archaeological findings, see Tucci 1988b, 53–109; Huo and Li 2001, 153–72; Jin 2001; Xiong and Li 2016. For ritual texts, see Namgyal-Lama 2013a, 18–34.

3 Mchims nam mkha' grags 1994, 110, 163; Huber 1992, 496.

4 For Indian or Dunhuang images, see respectively Donaldson 2001, 200–206; Giès and Cohen 1995, 400–405; for further details, see also Chandra 1999, 290–309. Concerning canonical texts related to Amoghapasha, see Wong 2007; Tuladhar-Douglas 2007, 164–66. For other contemporary *tsatsas* showing Amoghapasha found in Guge, see Xiong and Li 2016, 114–22.

5 Pal 1975a, 140–49.

6 Concerning dharanis and the *Pratityasamutpada* stanza, see Namgyal-Lama 2013b, 15n59.

7 See Namgyal-Lama 2013b, 5, 17. These formulas can be substituted by a seed deposit (a few grains of either barley or wheat) over which dharanis have been recited beforehand.

8 Concerning the stages in the ritual, see Tucci 1988b, 57–60; Namgyal-Lama 2013a, 132–49.

9 Bentor 1995a, 31–37.

10 For examples, see Xiong and Li 2016, 202–43.

11 See Jin 2001, 56n97; Xiong and Li 2016, 227n232.

12 Note that *tsatsas* can also be made with the three other elements (water, wind, and fire).

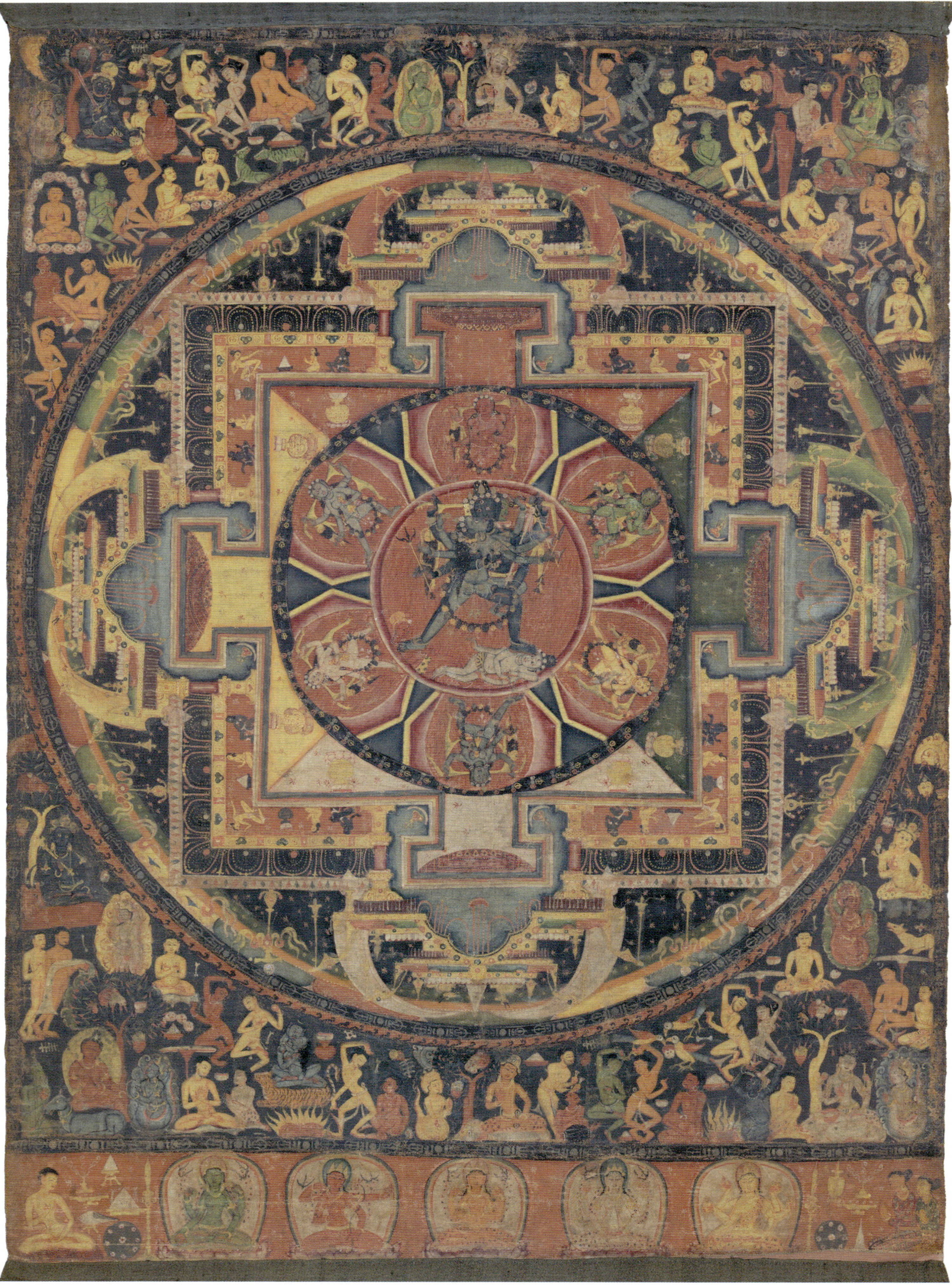

№ 29

Chakrasamvara Mandala with Newar Donors

Kathmandu Valley, Nepal, ca. 1100

The Art of Transgression and Transformation

JINAH KIM

For examples of sites in the Kathmandu Valley, see the Svayambhu Chaitya of Kathmandu, no. 4; Bunga Dya, no. 6; Torana of the Main Shrine at Yetakha Baha, no. 24.

For more about this process, see The All-Knowing Buddha Vairochana Visualization Album, no. 87.

THIS BRILLIANT PAINTING contains a mandala of a powerful tantric Buddhist deity, Chakrasamvara, and his consort, Vajravarahi. Hailing from the Kathmandu Valley of Nepal, this painting on cloth, called *paubha* in Newari (the language of Newars, one of the oldest inhabitant groups of the valley), was most likely created around the turn of the twelfth century. A mandala in the most basic sense of the term in Sanskrit means a circle. Imagine a drop of water hitting a calm pond: with the central point of impact and rippling rings, this is easily a core image of a mandala. A mandala is often understood to be a spiritual diagram or a mind map for meditation. In the esoteric or Vajrayana Buddhist ritual practice, a mandala is a tool of transformation that can help an initiate become one with her chosen deity. A painting like this one pictorializes the experience of transformation instructed in textual and verbal sources.[1] A group of ritual texts elaborates on the process of identification with one's chosen deity. One such *sadhana* (literally, accomplishment, propitiation; means of conjuring up a deity), the *Saptaksharasadhana*, or the *sadhana* of the Seven-Syllabled one, describes a form of six-armed Chakrasamvara in sexual embrace with his consort surrounded by the entourage of six yoginis on six spokes of a wheel.[2] This instruction comes very close to what we see in the central sphere of the painting.

The Mandala

For examples of other mandalas, see Mandala of Manjuvajra of the *Vajravali* Set, no. 50; Kalachakra Mandala in the Potala Palace, no. 77

Inside a circle bordered by a row of flame and a row of vajras (meaning "thunderbolt," the quintessential symbol of esoteric teachings, considered indestructible) is a square with four cardinal gateways marked by jewel-studded palatial architecture with prongs of vajra emerging at the four sides, indicating that the lord of the mandala is situated in the intersection of a double vajra (called *vishvavajra*). This square is divided diagonally, with each cardinal direction marked by four different colors: white, yellow, red, and green, designating east, south, west, and north (clockwise from bottom, which is the eastern direction in the pictorial space).[3] A second circle inside the square bordered by a ring of double vajras contains a red lotus with six petals, uniquely shaped as if to help visualize the spokes of a wheel (*chakra*) on which deities emerge. The very center of this lotus-wheel is the third circle of the mandala, the innermost seed, if you will, from which emanates a fantastic vision of the lord of the mandala.

For more on vajra, see *Dorje* Discovered by Dorje Lingpa, no. 51.

With three heads, six arms, holding up a flayed human skin in his uppermost hands and a trident (*trishula*) and a skull-topped staff (*kapalakhatvanga*) in his lowermost hands, the dark-blue male deity, Chakrasamvara, embraces his consort with his main arms, his interlocked hands holding a vajra and a bell (*ghanta*). Vajravarahi, also six-armed, ecstatically wraps her right leg around Chakrasamvara's bent thigh, holding in her left hand, wrapped around his neck, a skull cup and in her right hand, raised in a threatening gesture (*tarjani* mudra, with her index finger held up), a vajra. In her remaining four hands, she holds a bell, a trident, a bow, and an arrow.

Chakrasamvara Mandala; Nepal; ca. 1100; mineral and organic colorants on cotton; image: 26½ × 19¾ in. (67.3 × 50.2 cm); The Metropolitan Museum of Art, New York; Rogers Fund, 1995; 1995.233;

As if the human skin dripping blood behind them and the flame around them are not terrifying enough, the couple is also adorned with ornaments made of bones and a garland of severed heads. The couple tramples on two Hindu deities, Bhairava and Kalaratri, in unison while kissing and sharing a drink from the skull cup in Vajravarahi's left hand. The appearance of these two tantric Shaiva deities, Bhairava (a wrathful form of the Hindu god Shiva) and Kalaratri (a dark, bloodthirsty goddess), acknowledges the importance of Shaiva tradition in the development of the Buddhist tantras while articulating the superiority of the Buddhist path. The six yoginis who surround the couple occupying each petal-spoke of the wheel are equally terrifying; all are four-armed, clasp a human skin in their raised hands, and hold a hand drum (*damaru*) and a bell. Between the swaying bells, rattling drums, and snarly flames encircling them, one can almost hear the ecstatic shrills and loud ringing of the bells that would frighten any ordinary human.

See Double-Sided Skull Drum, no. 93.

The Charnel Grounds

This powerful mandala is surrounded by a frightening charnel ground, haunted by jackals and vultures, where those seeking supreme attainment and supernatural powers engage in transgressive activities. Each corner of the outer space is marked by eight directional deities, or guardians of directions (*dikpala*): three in the top section (Nritti-southwest, Varuna-west, and Vayu-northwest) and five in the bottom section (Yama-south, Agni-southeast, Indra-east, Ishana-northeast, and Kubera-north). Each deity is clearly identifiable by his directional placement and the distinct vehicle or mount (*vahana*).

What is unusual in this painting is how well these deities are integrated into the charnel ground setting: each sits under a tree whose leaves seem to drip with blood. From each tree a head of a figure peeks out, six of them animal-headed, like the mounts of the deities, with two hands holding a dagger and a skull cup. In the top left-hand corner of the painting, Nritti, sitting on a man lying flat, holds a sword and a severed head. Two siddhas (literally, perfected ones, see mahasiddhas below) sit in front of him, exchanging gazes with him. Next to this group are a slender male holding a dog and a slender female adorned with nothing but her bone ornaments. They dance in unison side by side. The dancing male with a dog and his consort alludes to Kukkuripa, one of the canonized mahasiddhas (literally, great perfection, referring to tantric masters who achieved supernatural power and supreme insight). Although such a terrifying backdrop is not described in the *Saptaksharasadhana*, the charnel grounds are the literal and imagined space in which the *Samvara Tantra* texts, a group of tantric texts that explicate some of the most esoteric Buddhist practices and teachings, arose.

For images and discussion of mahasiddhas, see Monumental Manjushri with Mahasiddha-Adorned Robe at Alchi, no. 35; Virupa, no. 37; Lukhang Murals, no. 80.

The Human World

Despite its gruesome contents, at first glance the painting, with its vibrant colors—saturated yellow, green, blue, red, and white—appears almost cheerful. The unnamed Newar artist(s) masterfully executed every line and animated each character of the charnel ground drama with dynamic expressions, postures, and diversely appointed colors. Even the expressions of the deities seem individualized, especially their eyes, adding to the dramatization of the powerful vision.[4] Among Chakrasamvara mandalas that survive from Nepal and Tibet, this painting is most brilliant in terms of not only its polychromatic qualities but also its articulation of individual characters and components.

Another extraordinary aspect of this painting lies in the depiction of the human world below the mandala. In the left corner of the bottom register, a shaven-headed man in a diaphanous white garment sits cross-legged with ritual implements and offerings in front of him, while two women dressed in fine textiles kneel with their hands folded together with another set of offerings in the far-right corner. Between them are five goddesses: Prajnaparamita in the center with Green Tara (a form known as Dhanada-Tara) and Kurukulla to her right, and Chunda and Vasudhara to her left. Sharing the same flower-strewn red space as the human figures, the five goddesses occupy the human world, as if they were in a shrine space. Although no known textual sources link these five goddesses to the *Chakrasamvara Tantra,* the five color-coded goddesses are the visual and spiritual conduits between the human realm and the transcendent realm of Chakrasamvara.[5]

For more about the goddess Tara, see Tara Who Protects from the Eight Great Fears, no. 27.

The identity of the human figures remains elusive, as no inscription survives. It is possible that the man is related to the women as conjugal partners, especially in the context of the Kathmandu Valley, where the Newar Buddhist system of married householder monks and tantric Buddhist masters (Vajracharyas and Shakyas) developed.[6] Whatever their relationship, these finely dressed women may have been the sponsors of this exquisite painting.[7] The man's bare attire is unusual for a Vajracharya, which we expect in this position in a mandala painting.[8] Is it possible that this painting records his initiation into this special form of Seven-Syllabled Samvara? Inscriptional evidence on surviving Tibetan thangkas of similar age suggests that a painting like this one may have been consecrated as a personal

For more about Vajracharya, see Vajracharya Priest's Crown, no. 38. For a depiction of a ritual with a Vajracharya priest, see Plaque Commemorating the *Bhimaratha* Old Age Ritual, no. 85.

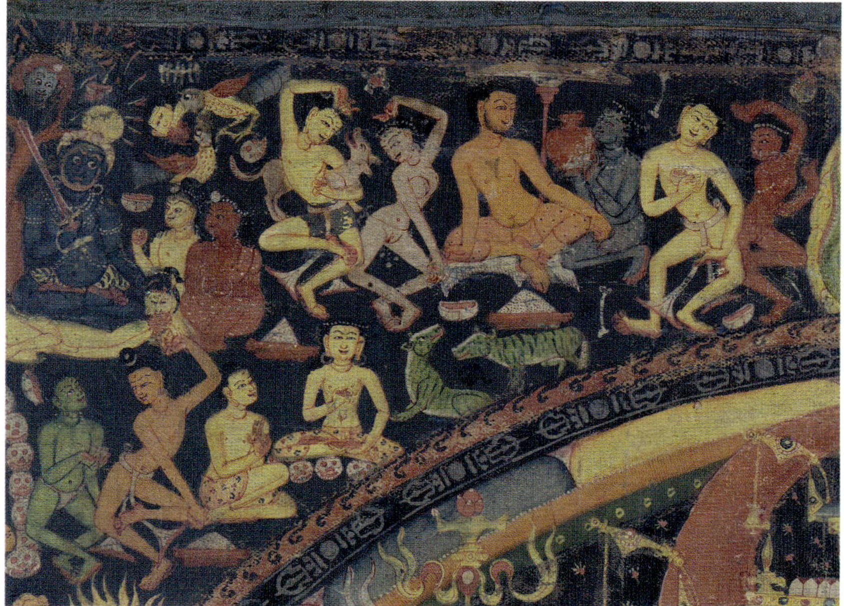

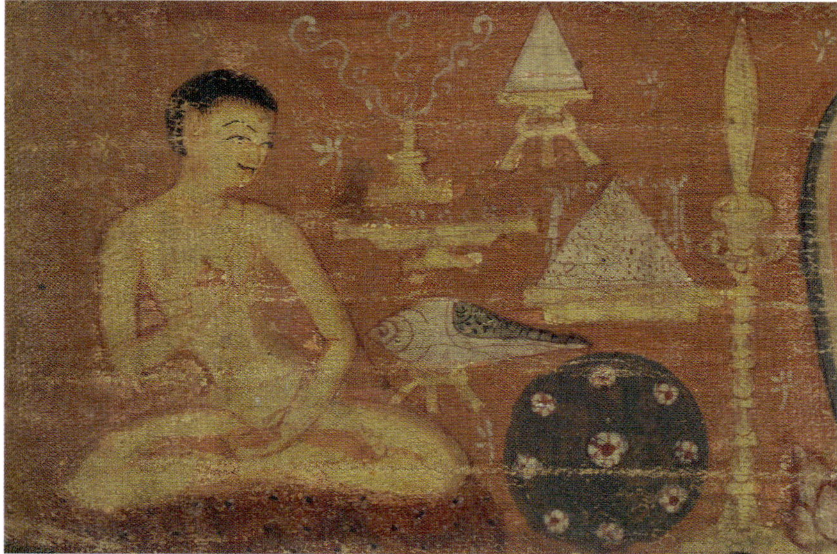

(top) Detail of Chakrasamvara Mandala, northeastern corner (top left), showing the charnel ground with Nritti and siddhas and yogis (including Kukkuripa?); Nepal; The Metropolitan Museum of Art, New York; Rogers Fund, 1995; 1995.233; CC0 - Creative Commons (CC0 1.0)

(bottom) Detail of Chakrasamvara Mandala, bottom left corner, showing an esoteric Buddhist practitioner or patron of the Chakrasamvara mandala; Nepal; The Metropolitan Museum of Art, New York; Rogers Fund, 1995; 1995.233; CC0 - Creative Commons (CC0 1.0)

meditation deity.[9] At least one fourteenth-century Chakrasamvara mandala painting from Nepal suggests that a commemorative ritual for a deceased Vajracharya offered another occasion to commission a painting of the Chakrasamvara mandala.[10] This painting may represent a phase of Newar Buddhism before a strict codification and institutionalization of Vajrayana practices, when personal and individual aspects of esoteric Buddhist practices were tolerated and encouraged in the art of transformation.

Further Reading

Gray, David. 2007. *The Cakrasamvara Tantra: The Discourse of Śrī Heruka (Śrīherukābhidhāna)*. New York: American Institute of Buddhist Studies at Columbia University.

Sinclair, Iain. 2014. "Envisioning Durjayacandra's Saptākṣarasādhana: On the Sources and Sponsors of a Twelfth-Century Painting of Seven-Syllabled Saṃvara." In *Himalayan Passages: Tibetan and Newar Studies in Honor of Hubert Decleer*, edited by Benjamin Bogin and Andrew Quintman, 205–50. Boston: Wisdom.

Sugiki, Tsunehiko. 2003. "Five Types of Internal Maṇḍala Described in the Cakrasamvara Buddhist Literature: Somatic Representations of One's Innate Sacredness," *Tōkyō Daigaku Tōyō Bunka Kenkyūjo* 東洋文化研究所紀要 [Notes of the Institute of Oriental Culture of Tokyo University] 144, 276–202 [157–203]. Tokyo: Institute of Oriental Culture, University of Tokyo.

Notes

1 In the esoteric Buddhist tradition, the most crucial instruction necessary for one's transformation into the enlightened body is transmitted only within an initiate lineage within a strictly sanctified ritual context. On secrecy, see Gray 2005.

2 See Sinclair 2014.

3 The eastern direction is typically signaled by blue, the color of Akshobhya, the eastern buddha. But in mandalas of the mahayoga and yogini tantras, in which the center is occupied by powerful blue deities, blue and white are swapped in terms of their directionalities. On the mahayoga and yogini tantras, see Isaacson 1998.

4 The tantric Buddhist iconography became increasingly schematic and canonized in later centuries.

5 On the esoteric Buddhist five-color system, see J. Kim 2021, 155–74.

6 See Gellner 1992.

7 See J. Kim 2020, 11–12.

8 Sinclair 2014, 219. See Brown 2017.

9 See for example the Vajravarahi mandala that was a personal meditation deity, or *yidam*, discussed in Kossak and Singer 1998, 96—99.

10 Huntington and Bangdel 2003, 260–63.

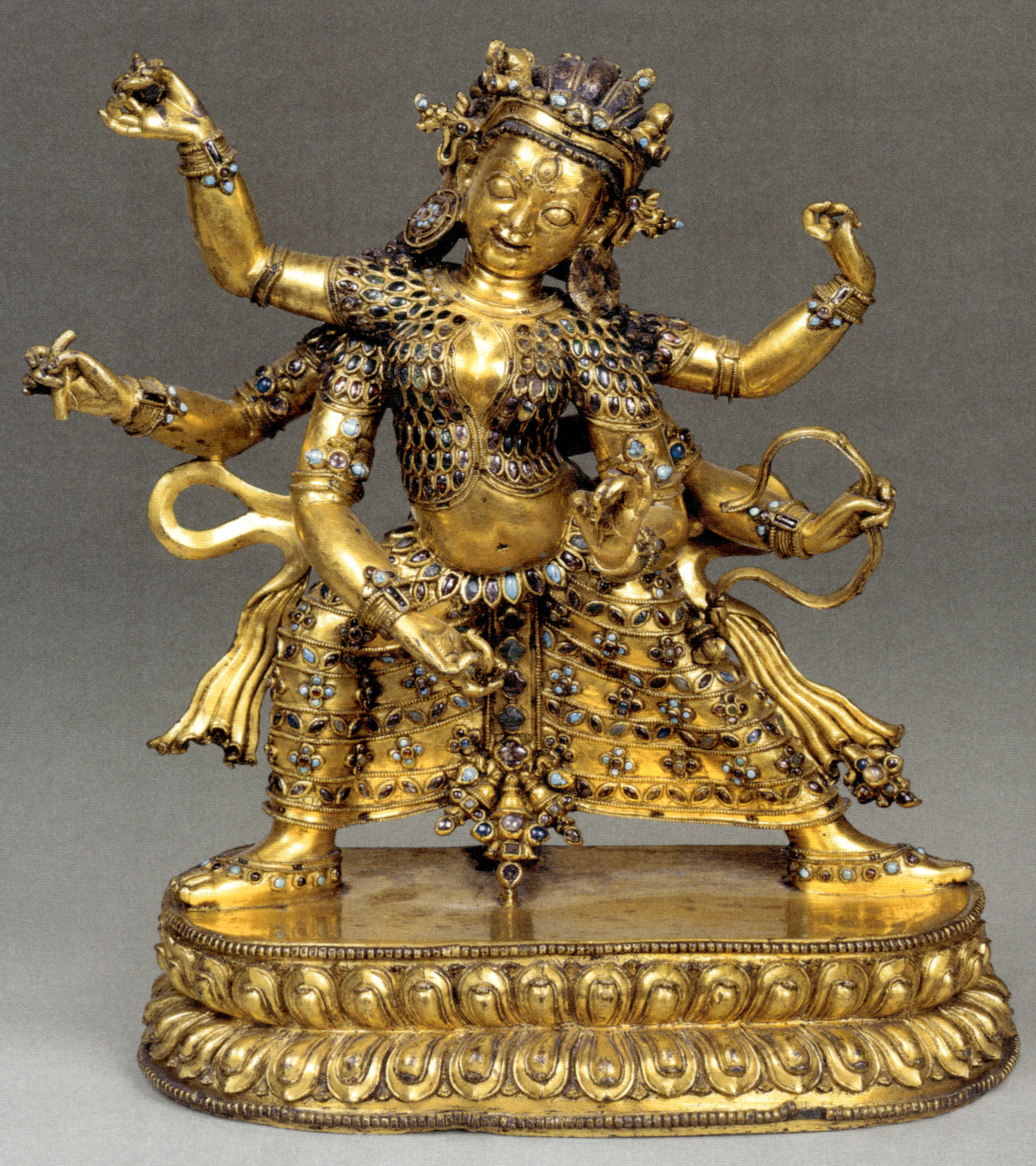

№ 30

Densatil Monastery

Pakmodru, U region, central Tibet (present-day TAR, China), founded 1158

The Commemorative Stupas of the Lang/Pakmodrupa Dynasty

JEAN-LUC ESTOURNEL

THE STUDY OF PUBLIC AND PRIVATE COLLECTIONS of Tibetan art has made it possible to identify a group of objects of uncommon quality, often of larger than normal sizes, and above all presenting superb gilding and very rich inclusions of semiprecious stones. It is only since the 1990s that, by comparing such objects with photographs taken in 1948 by P. F. Mele, they could be identified as elements of the large commemorative stupas (height approximately sixteen feet, or five meters) built at the Densatil Monastery between 1267 and 1435.

Densatil Monastery

Densatil Monastery developed from 1198 onward around the hut that the monk Dorje Gyelpo built in 1158 at a place called Pakmodru overlooking the Yarlung Tsangpo River, in the present Neudong District. Its fame rests on the eighteen stupas erected between 1170 and 1570, housing the relics of a long lineage of abbots of the Lang/Pakmodrupa dynasty, and mainly on the eight great, elaborately ornamented ones partially visible in the photographs taken in 1948 by Mele. These eight very specific monuments are undoubtedly among the most complex and precious ever built in Tibet.

A Brief History of the Eight Monumental Stupas of Densatil

The first of the eighteen stupas once at Densatil was cast in 1170 to house the heart of Pakmodrupa Dorje Gyelpo (1110–1170), which remained intact after cremation, together with other relics. This stupa was called Tashi Wobar, or Radiating Light of Auspiciousness.[1] It was a huge *mahaparinirvana*-type stupa associated with the Buddha's passing, created in the Kadampa style, as was common practice at the time.[2] In the years following the construction of the monastery, the Tashi Wobar lay at the heart of an incredible political and artistic adventure due to Jikten Gonpo (1143–1217), who served as second abbot of Densatil from 1177 to 1179 before leaving for his own monastery in Drigung.

After the construction of the main hall of Densatil in 1198, Jikten Gonpo went to meditate at Gampo in the Dakpo area and there had a vision of the "pure crystal mountain" of Tsari with the deity Chakrasamvara in his palace, the whole surrounded by twenty-eight hundred deities, organized as a monumental Stupa of Many Auspicious Doors, or *tashi gomang*–type stupa.

For more about this deity and his palace, see Chakrasamvara Mandala with Newar Donors, no. 29.

For more about this stupa type, see Portable Shrine, no. 88; Gyantse Kumbum, no. 55.

On his return to Drigung, in order to pay homage to his master, he undertook to build the multi-chapel monument he had visualized to serve as a pedestal for the Tashi Wobar stupa of Pakmodrupa, which he brought to Drigung from Densatil. The construction work on this monument, organized in six levels supporting hundreds of deities in gilt copper alloy and precious materials on all its faces, seems to have lasted ten years, until 1208.[3]

This particular type of *tashi gomang* stupa, which must be considered as the Reliquary Stupa of Many Auspicious Doors for Pakmodrupa, would then be reproduced to commemorate selected deceased abbots of Drigung and Densatil, since they were the holders of the direct lineage of the master.

To sum up, the *tashi gomang* stupa model created by Jikten Gonpo must be considered, as Christian Luczanits phrased it in an essay title, a "mandala of mandalas," a veritable tangle of universes of deities (twenty-eight hundred in total);[4] Luczanits in turn was referring to Giuseppe Tucci's description during his visit to Densatil in 1948: "The whole Olympus of Mahayana seemed to have been assembled on those monuments."[5]

Parnashavari; Tibet; ca. 1370; metal, precious stones; 12½ × 11½ × 8 in. (31.8 × 29.2 × 20.3 cm); Private collection; HAR 32081; image after Czaja and Proser 2014, 121

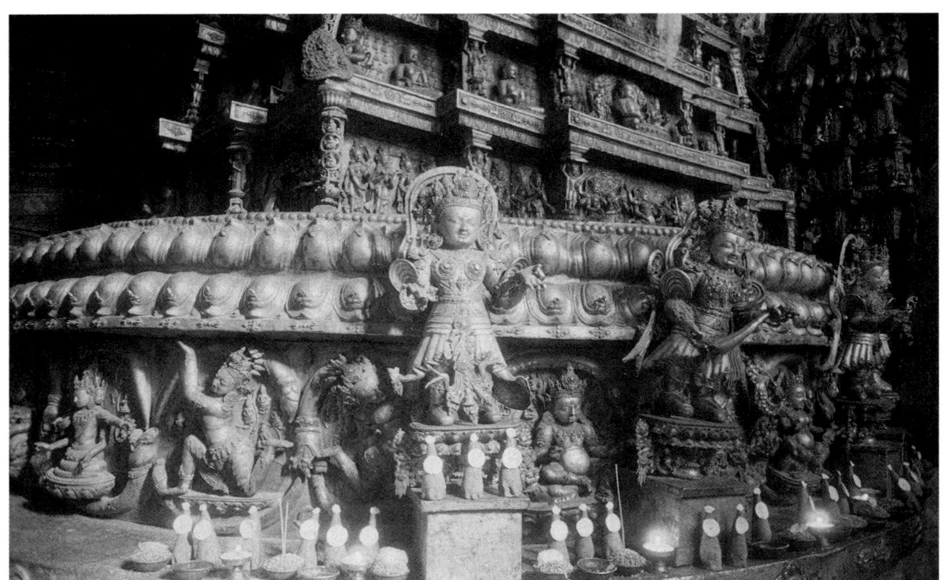

Pietro Francesco Mele (Italian, b. ca. 1924); Detail of Second *Tashi Gomang*; Densatil Monastery, U region, central Tibet (present-day TAR, China); erected from 1360 for Drakpa Gyeltsen; gelatin silver print, 1948; Ethnographic Museum at the University of Zurich; VMZ-402-00-0513; photograph courtesy Ethnographic Museum at the University of Zurich

The fact that Jikten Gonpo chose to build this memorial stupa to his master in his own monastery rather than in Densatil, which would have been its logical location, is historically interesting. Indeed, it may suggest that the abbot of Drigung attempted to shift the power of Densatil's spiritual center from its abandoned location to his own monastery, to gain political advantage over other powerful contemporary Buddhist traditions. It seems that from the outset, the *tashi gomang* stupas of Drigung (totally destroyed during the repression of the Drigung revolt against the Sakya/Mongol rule in 1290) and then Densatil were created with political aims in addition to a sacred function, which explains their unusual magnificence.

The departure of the Tashi Wobar stupa from Densatil having caused troubles among the local population, Jikten Gonpo judged it preferable to return it there in 1208, with Drakpa Jungne (1175–1255), one of his main disciples, as the new abbot. A member of the powerful Lang family, he took care in 1235 to place his brother Drakpa Tsondru (1203–1267) on the throne of Densatil before returning to Drigung to become the new abbot, thus initiating a shift of dependence, which took Densatil from the tutelage of Drigung to that of his clan.

For more about the Khasa Malla Kingdom, see Queen Dipamala as the Goddess Prajnaparamita, no. 49.

The extent of Drakpa Tsondru's fame brought him many offerings from as far away as the Khasa Malla Kingdom of western Nepal and Ceylon. The decision by the Lang clan to erect the first *tashi gomang* stupa in Densatil, on the model of the ones in Drigung to honor the memory of Drakpa Tsondru after his death, took place at a key moment in the history of the Lang/Pakmodrupa clan.

On the Pakpa-Qubilai alliance and Sakya-Mongol rule, see Mahakala Stone Sculpture, no. 39; White Stupa, no. 40; Mongol Messenger's Badge, no. 42; Juyong Guan Stupa Gate, no. 48.

With the definitive seizure of power by the Sakya tradition over Tibet through Qubilai (Kubilai) Khan's nomination of Pakpa (1235–1280) as the ruler of Tibet, the Sakya administration divided the territory into thirteen myriarchies, one of which fell to the Lang, already strong with the prestige of their monastery of Densatil. The Mongolian takeover of Tibet then placed Densatil and the surrounding area under the protection of Hülegü (1217–1265), grandson of Chinggis (Genghis) Khan and founder, in 1256, of the Mongol Il-Khan dynasty in the Middle East, who is said to have made important offerings to the monastery.[6] It is conceivable that at the time the Lang clan was in a prosperous financial position to decide to undertake this exceptional construction in order to affirm the greatness of its temporal and spiritual power over his myriarchy and beyond.

The second *tashi gomang* stupa was built in 1360 for Drakpa Gyeltsen (1293–1360), the eighth abbot of the monastery from 1310 to 1360. All sources unanimously confirm that his brother Jangchub Gyeltsen (1302–1364), who succeeded in taking temporal power over the country from the Sakyapas, had a commemorative *tashi gomang* stupa erected for Drakpa Gyeltsen. Given that the Lang/Pakmodrupa clan now reigned over Tibet, Jangchub Gyeltsen, as head of one of the most prestigious and richest monasteries, had no choice but to revive this prestigious tradition to affirm the power of his family.

Six more *tashi gomang* stupas were built for the next six abbots, in 1370, 1386, 1407, 1408, 1431–1432, and 1434. While remaining at very high levels of quality, the works from the Densatil *tashi gomang* stupas are a perfect reflection of the political rise and fall of the Lang/Pakmodrupa dynasty. From 1360 to 1408, the sculptures are decorated with rich inlays of semiprecious stones, following a typology that characterizes the style of Densatil and therefore of the Lang/Pakmodrupa dynasty.

Description of a Reliquary Stupa of Many Auspicious Doors for Pakmodrupa

The analysis of the *tashi gomang* stupas of Densatil allows us to note that if the general iconographic plan globally remained the same over time, variations exist. The numbers of divinities indicated by the texts

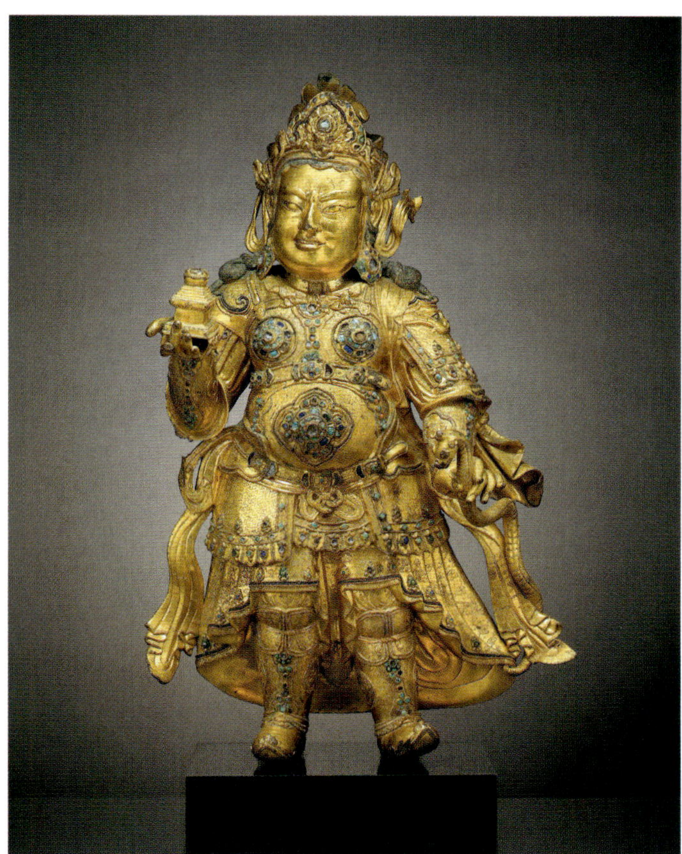

Virupaksha, the guardian of the West, one of the Four Guardian Kings of the four directions of the universe; Tibet; 15th century; copper gold and semiprecious stones (lost-wax method); 28 × 17 in. (71 × 43 cm); Musée des Arts Asiatiques-Guimet, Paris (HAR 32070); photograph by Thierry Ollivier © RMN-Grand Palais / Art Resource, NY

imply that some mandalas constituting certain tiers have been modified or replaced by more complex ones, while perhaps retaining the same basic divinities. These variations are probably due to the particular tantric texts studied by the concerned abbots.

We will here simply refer to the six-tiered structure of the archetype described in various texts, from top to bottom:

—At the top, tier 1, around a huge Kadampa-style *mahaparinirvana* stupa, are arranged masters lineages, two representations of Vajradhara to the east and south, Chakrasamvara to the west, and Hevajra to the north. Three aspects of Vajrayogini/Vajravarahi are indicated to be placed in front of each of these four main deities.

—Tier 2 presents various texts of the Highest Yogatantras, including the *Anuttarayoga Tantra*, with the seventy-two-deity mandala of Guhyasamaja in the east, the assembly of Vajrakila in the south, that of Hevajra in the west, and the sixty-two-deity mandala of Chakrasamvara in the north. An aspect of Avalokiteshvara is arranged at each of the four corners.

—Tier 3 presents on the east face the Vajradhatu mandala in forty-seven deities, on the south the assembly of Buddhakapala, on the west the assembly of Prajnaparamita, and on the north the mandala in fourteen deities of Chakrasamvara. An aspect of Achala is arranged at each of the four corners.

—Tier 4 presents in the center of each side a Buddha surrounded by two of the eight bodhisattvas of the Bhadrakalpa and two wrathful deities on each side. They are surrounded on each side by two hundred and fifty representations of the *tathagata* of their respective directions. A gate guardian (*dvarapala*) is arranged at each of the four corners.

—Tier 5 is dedicated to goddesses. On each side are three central goddesses flanked by the group of the sixteen goddesses of sensual enjoyment bearing offerings. The four main goddesses occupying the center of each side are Parnashavari in the east, Eight-Armed Tara in the south, Dhvajagrakeyura in the west, and Vasudhara in the north.

—Tier 6 is the lowest level. On each face, on either side of a central lotus stem, we find an aspect of Mahakala and one of the goddess Lhamo, themselves flanked by two deities of wealth and two *nagarajas* closing the section. They are all arranged in the foliage of scrolls supporting the lotus flower from which the rest of the monument seems to emerge.

At the front of the monument were placed the Four Guardian Kings of Space (*lokapalas*).

Further Reading

Czaja, Olaf. 2014. *Medieval Rule in Tibet: The Rlangs Clan and the Political and Religious History of the Ruling House of Phag mo gru pa*. Vienna: Verlag der Österreichischen Akademie der Wissenschaften.

Czaja, Olaf, and Adriana G. Proser. 2014. *Golden Visions of Densatil: A Tibetan Buddhist Monastery*. Exhibition catalog. New York: Asia Society.

Estournel, Jean-Luc. 2020. "About the 18 Stupas and Other Treasures Once at the Densatil Monastery." Asianart.com. Published September 29, 2010. https://www.asianart.com/articles/densatil/index.html.

Notes

1 Roerich (1949) 1976, 563.
2 See examples at Himalayan Art Resources, such as https://www.himalayanart.org/items/8377, https://www.himalayanart.org/items/50255, and https://www.himalayanart.org/items/64904.
3 Czaja 2014, 380, 381.
4 Luczanits 2010, 281–310.
5 Tucci 1956b, 128.
6 See Sperling 1990, 145–57.

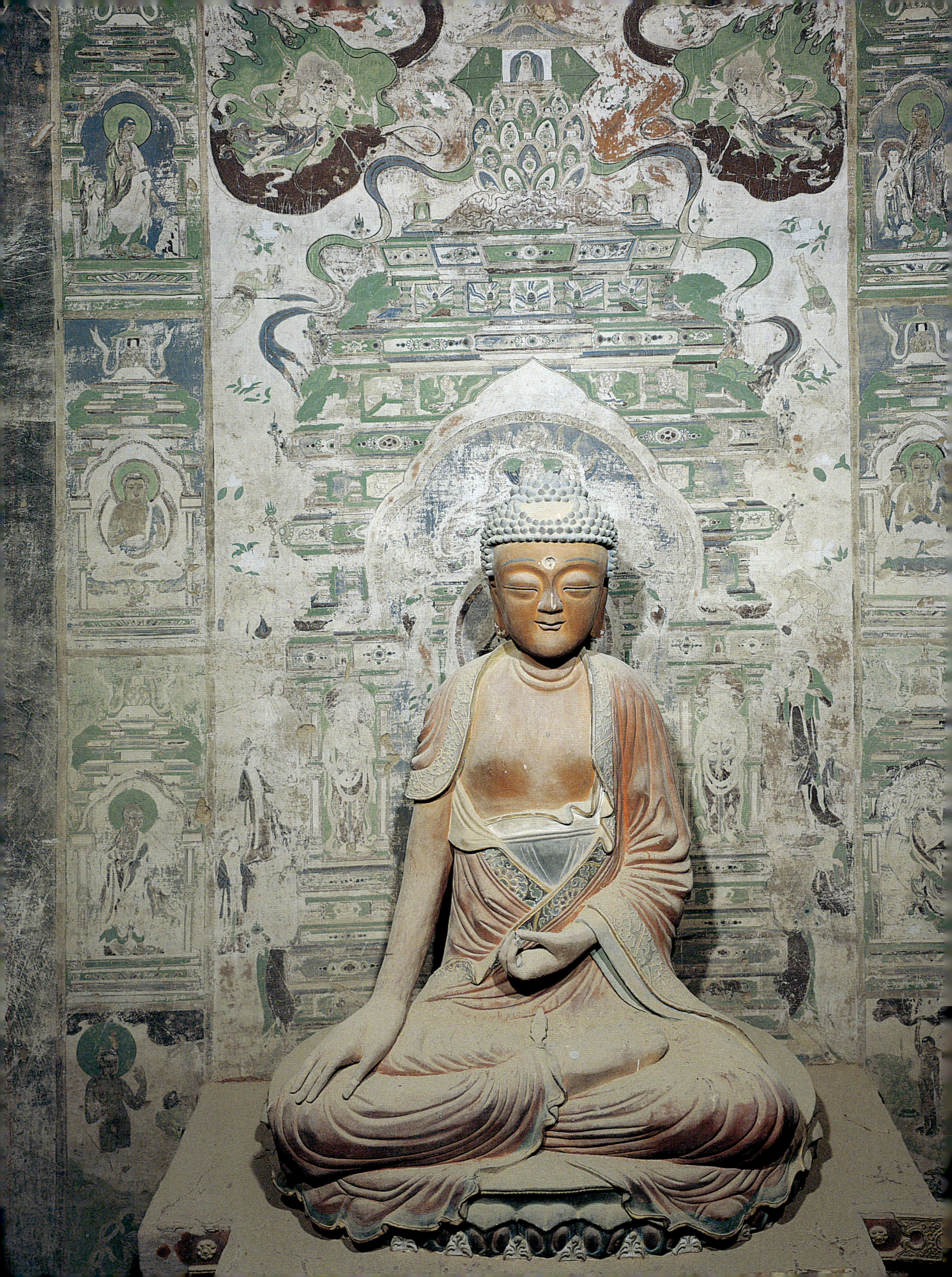

No 31

Cave 3 at Yulin Cave Temples

Yulin, Tangut Kingdom (Xixia) (present-day Anxi, Gansu Province, China), ca. late 12th century

Tangut Patrons' Embrace of Buddhist Sacred Sites and Cosmopolitan Teachings

ELENA PAKHOUTOVA AND JIA WEIWEI

For an example of Dunhuang painting, see Bhaishajyaguru, no. 14.

THE MURAL OF THE EIGHT GREAT EVENTS OF THE BUDDHA'S LIFE serves as the focal point, or the main image, of Cave 3 at the Yulin cave temples, located near present-day Anxi, Gansu Province, in northwestern China, not far from the famous Dunhuang cave temples. This late twelfth-century cave is among the most remarkable of the forty-two decorated caves at Yulin.[1] It is known for its large size, presumed royal patronage, the exceptional quality of its murals, and distinctive combination of Chinese and so-called Himalayan visual conventions.[2]

For another example of Tangut (Xixia) art, see A *Pancharaksha* Print from Khara-Khoto, no. 32.

Like the Dunhuang caves, the Yulin caves were maintained and decorated over centuries, most actively during the time when the Tangut people populated the area, from the mid-eleventh century to 1278.[3] The Tangut Xixia state (1038–1227) was one of the thriving Buddhist empires in Central Asia[4] contemporaneous with the Song dynasty (960–1279), the rise of the Mongols, and the Buddhist revival in Tibetan areas. It had close religious ties with Tibetan Buddhist teachers, who even rose to become imperial preceptors.[5]

The cave's visual program suggests a strong emphasis on the representation of sacred places, territories, and themes of rebirth and the removal of obstacles. Individual murals, employing iconographic conventions of Buddhist representations during this time in Central Asia and Tibet, articulate this emphasis in their composition and in their spatial arrangement within the cave.

The Buddha at Vajrasana with Scenes of His Life as the Central Image

For other representations of these events, see Mayadevi Giving Birth to Siddhartha, no. 3; Mahabodhi Temple Model, no. 25.

See the painting of The Eight Great Events of the Buddha's Life on page 118.

The mural of the Eight Great Events of the Buddha's Life is on the east wall that faces the entrance and occupies a central position of the main image, as it would in a temple. The painting is iconographically and compositionally consistent with eastern Indian and Tibetan examples.[6] The panel follows the Indian convention developed during the fifth to the ninth century to represent the main events of Buddha Shakyamuni's life. Eastern Indian stone steles, stupas, and portable objects—as well as illuminated manuscripts, clay and stone plaques found in India, Burma, Tibet, and Central Asia dated to the tenth to thirteenth century, and Tibetan paintings on cloth—all bear compositions and iconography similar to this central panel.[7]

Tibetan hanging scroll paintings (thangkas) from the late eleventh to the thirteenth century depicting the Eight Great Events of the Buddha's Life are the closest comparatives.[8] The iconographic and visual organization of the mural and thangka paintings directly reference these events: the Buddha's enlightenment at Bodhgaya; his birth at Lumbini; his multiplication miracle at Shravasti; his descent from the Heaven of the Thirty-Three Gods at Samkashya; his passing (*mahaparinirvana*) at Kushinagara; his taming of the mad elephant at Rajagriha; his first sermon at Sarnath; and the gift of honey at Vaishali. They also reference the commemorative stupas marking the assumed locations of these events in India.

Yulin Cave 3, east wall center, Eight Pagodas, Tangut Kingdom (Xixia), (present-day Anxi, Gansu Province, China); ca. late 12th century; image courtesy Dunhuang Research Academy, photograph by Wu Jian

The arrangement of the events around the main image of the enlightenment at Bodhgaya is dictated by symmetry, not chronology. Just as in the thangka paintings and sculptural examples, the composition is both a narrative depiction of these episodes and an iconic image structured in a way similar to figural mandala arrangements. The central panel's composition is comparable to a thirteenth-century Tibetan thangka of the Mandala of Amitabha (Amitayus) from a private collection.[9] The mandala's central figure and the six surrounding smaller figures are seated within architectural structures that represent stupa shrines—maintaining the visual convention while emphasizing the mandala's spatial hierarchy of center and periphery.

Thus, the central panel of the Cave 3 east wall represents the place where the Buddha was born, attained enlightenment, taught, performed various miracles, and passed away—that is, India, with Vajrasana in Bodhgaya as its central, most important location. Although the panel's iconography parallels the Indian and Tibetan examples, its painting style displays the Tangut preference for using Chinese pictorial conventions for flowing scarves, the royal attire of the figure at the Buddha's feet in the *parinirvana* scene, and the type of monks' robes.

For more on Vajrasana, see Mahabodhi Temple Model, no. 25.

Cosmopolitan Visual Program of the Cave: Avalokiteshvara Murals

Two images of Avalokiteshvara, the deity of compassion, flank the central panel. The White Thousand-Armed Avalokiteshvara is on the left. The arrangement of his eleven heads follows Tibetan conventions, but his hundreds of attributes follow traditional Chinese depictions, with the Sun and Moon disks held aloft near Avalokiteshivara's main head as the key distinction.

See Avalokiteshvara at Khartse, no. 20.

See Bodhisattva Avalokiteshvara and the Buddha's Footprints, no. 33.

The dark Avalokiteshvara with fifty-one heads to the right of the central panel is the only recorded image of this form. Neither textual nor visual materials refer to this specific deity; he was likely envisioned by this cave's patrons,[10] inspired by interpretations of the deity's protective or redemptive powers and the emergence of culturally adapted, irregular forms in the Song empire.[11]

Pure Land of Buddha Amitabha
Vajradhatu mandala
Marichi mandala
Manjushri
Vimalakirti
Eleven-Headed Thousand-Armed Avalokiteshvara
N
Ceiling
Vajradhatu mandala
Buddha Shakyamuni and the Eight Great Events
Xuanzang, return from India
Fifty-One-Headed Avalokiteshvara
Samantabhadra
Durgatiparishodhana mandala
Ushnishavijaya mandala
Pure Land of Buddha Amitabha

Plan of Yulin Cave 3 showing the layout of the murals; drawing by the authors

Mandala Murals

The cave integrates both esoteric, or tantric, iconography and imagery derived from Mahayana sutras. Two mandalas of deities Ushnishavijaya and Marichi at the east ends of the south and north walls match the iconographic structure of Tibetan mandalas. The Chinese and Tibetan translations of the *Ushnishavijayadharani vitarka* texts are almost identical except for the Indian god Indra's attribute: a bow in the Chinese version and a parasol in the Tibetan one. The inner circle of the Ushnishavijaya mandala includes thirteen deities. Indra, shown as a man with a parasol in front of a stupa, is a clue to this mandala's Tibetan textual source.[12]

In the Marichi mandala, eight-armed Marichi is three-faced with a blue sow face on the proper left. She stands in a stupa, and her four retinue figures occupy the four quadrants. Two wheels flanking the lotus pedestal represent her chariot drawn by seven sows. In this region, beginning in the tenth century, this image replaced a royal woman with two attendants, Marichi's iconography described in a Chinese sutra.

Two mandalas at the west ends of the south and north walls also face each other. One is a Vajradhatu mandala centered on Buddha Vairochana, and the other is a mandala centered on Buddha Shakyamuni described in the *Durgatiparishodhana Tantra*.[13] Numerous Tibetan dharani texts, initiation rituals, practice manuals, and mandalas found at nearby Dunhuang are directly related to these mandalas.[14] In Xixia society of the time, Tanguts believed that rituals focused on these mandalas could liberate all beings from hells and lead to their rebirths in a Pure Land.

For an example of dharani and their use, see A *Pancharaksha* Print from Khara-Khoto, no. 32.

Translator Bari Lotsawa

Most of the esoteric images in this cave link to Bari Lotsawa Rinchen Drak (1040–1111), a Tangut monk of Tibetan ordination who was a prominent translator and master of the Sakya Tibetan tradition. He received many tantric empowerments and teachings in India. His best-known work, "One Hundred Sadhanas of Bari" (*Bari gyatsa*), compiled texts on deity meditations (*sadhanas*) drawn from all types of tantras known at the time. Images of the Ushnishavijaya and Marichi mandalas in Yulin Cave 3 follow Bari Lotsawa's textual descriptions. It seems that the Indian Buddhist traditions he introduced had a direct, significant impact on Tangut Buddhist iconography.

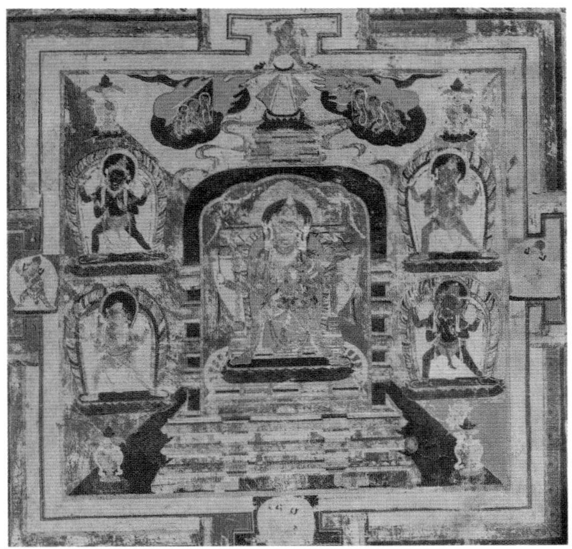

Yulin Cave, Cave 3, Main Chamber, Northern Wall, Marichi Mandala; image produced by the Institute of Culture Relics Digitization

Mahayana Sutra Depictions

Two panels of the Pure Land of Buddha Amitabha represented in Chinese painting conventions—scenes of sixteen contemplations and the story of Prince Ajatashatru—occupy the central panels of the north and south walls.

A small panel illustrating the lay scholar Vimalakirti meeting bodhisattva Manjushri, a popular theme in Chinese Buddhism, sits above the cave's entrance. Two panels of Manjushri and Samantabhadra flank the entrance. Within the Samantabhadra mural the famous scene of the Chinese monk Xuanzang returning from his travels in India depicts the luminous bag on the back of his white horse, indicating he brought with him Buddhist texts. Eight images below this panel depict scenes of the Chinese monk Tanyi contemplating Samantabhadra appearing as a female.[15] The murals are rendered in a purely Chinese stylistic mode related to Chinese Buddhist tradition.

The inclusion of Xuanzang with his companions is a common element of the Water-Moon Avalokiteshvara depictions in eleventh- to thirteenth-century China, but the connection with Samantabhadra is rare and relates to the miracles in which Samantabhadra imparts sutras to monk-translators. Although Xuanzang's story originated in much earlier Chinese historical texts,[16] images of Xuanzang with his monkey-headed protector and a horse depicted in Song (960–1035) and Tangut period (1036–1278) caves acquired a symbolic meaning beyond the original context. As historical figures in Chinese Buddhism gradually transformed into protagonists of miraculous stories, monks were worshiped as saints. With the Buddhist renewal in the late tenth century, Xuanzang, a famous scholar, traveler, and translator, gained a new, venerated status among Chinese Buddhists.[17]

Overall, the patrons of the cave purposefully unified iconographic forms and Buddhist belief systems of Indian, Tibetan, Tangut, and Chinese Buddhist traditions of the time.

Further Reading

Dunnell, Ruth W. 1996. *The Great State of White and High: Buddhism and State Formation in Eleventh-Century Xia*. Honolulu: University of Hawai'i Press.

Kimiaki, Tanaka. 2014. Kimiaki, Tanaka. 2014. "On the So-called Garbhadhātu Maṇḍala in Cave 3 of Anxi Yulin Caves." In *Han Zang Fojiao meishu yanjiu: Disi jie Xizang kaogu yishu guoji xueshu taolun wenji* 汉藏佛教美术研究：第四届西藏考古与艺术国际学术讨论会论文集 / *Study on Sino-Tibetan Buddhist Art: Essays of the Fourth International Conference of Tibetan Archaeology and Art*, edited by Xie Jisheng 谢继胜, Luo Wenhua 罗文华, and Shi Yangang 石岩刚, 155–60. [Primarily in Chinese, with some English.] Shanghai: Shanghai guji chubanshe.

Notes

1 The cave was dated on stylistic and historical considerations. See Linrothe 1996, 1998. Other sources attribute it to the Tangut period rule, from the early eleventh to the late thirteenth century. Sculptures in the cave are later additions and are not discussed here.
2 Fan 1999; Klimburg-Salter 2001.
3 The dates of the Tangut conquest of the area vary from 1036 to a later 1072/1073, when the Gansu Corridor, including the Yulin caves, fully came under Tangut domain. It is accepted that the Tanguts remained in the area and their habitation did not end when the Mongols conquered the Xixia state in 1227.
4 J. Shi 2021, 8–23.
5 Sperling 2004a, 7; Sørensen and Hazod 2007, 2: app. 1, 370–74.
6 Another example is Cave 76 at Dunhuang, but the murals' placement, composition, and style are quite different. See Toyka-Fuong 1998.
7 See Pakhoutova 2009, figs. 1.10, 1.11; 2.8–2.10, 2.16, 2.17; Bautze-Picron and Bautze 2003.
8 Pakhoutova 2009, 88–112.
9 Kossak and Singer 1998, fig. 29; Pal 2003, pl. 133.
10 See Pakhoutova 2009, 155–87.
11 See Jia 2020, 180–83.
12 "lha rnams kyi dbang po brgya byin lag na gdugs thogs pa dang." See Si tu chos kyi 'byung gnas 1985, 90: 474–83.
13 After *Compendium of Principles* (*Tattvasamgraha*) *tantra* and *Purification of All Bad Rebirths* (*Sarvadurgatiparishodana*) *Tantra*. See also Pakhoutova 2013, 39–40.
14 See Jia 2020, 242–43, 276–77.
15 See Zhang Shubin 2019, 22–30.
16 大慈恩寺三藏法师传 [*Daci'ensi sanzang fashi zhuan*]. Taishō Tripiṭaka, T.2053.
17 See Wong 2002; Jia 2020, 145–51.

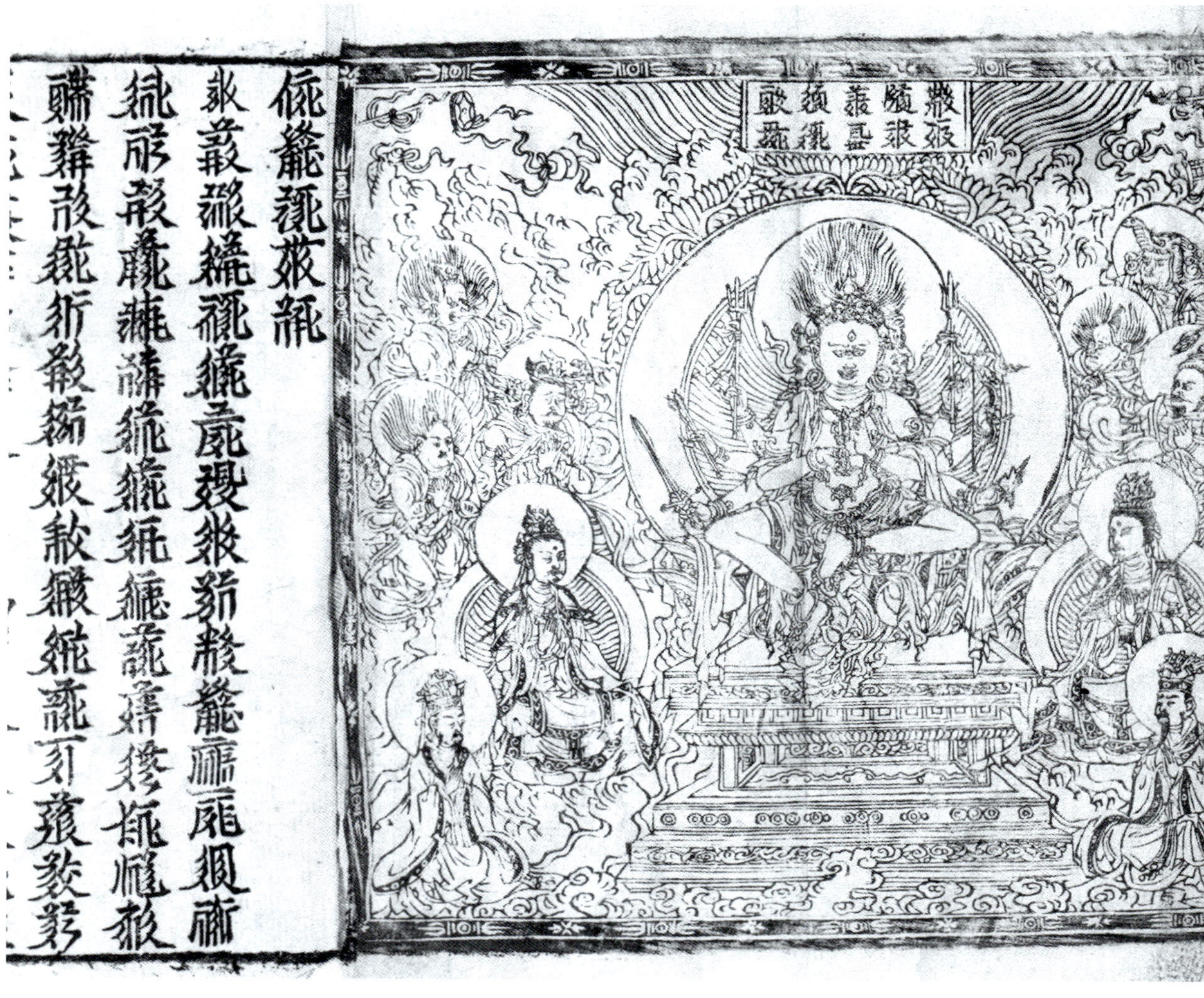

Nº 32

A *Pancharaksha* Print from Khara-Khoto

Khara-Khoto, Tangut Kingdom (Xixia), Gansu Province, China, ca. late 12th century

Woodblock Printing and State Protection in the Inclusive Buddhist Culture of the Tanguts

KIRILL SOLONIN AND ELENA PAKHOUTOVA

THIS PRINTED IMAGE AND A TEXT IT ILLUSTRATES offer one example of many prints from carved woodblocks produced in the Tangut state of Xixia and excavated from the ancient city of Khara-Khoto. The multiethnic state formed by the Dangxiang, a Tibeto-Burman-speaking people, was known in Chinese sources as Western (Xi) Xia. Its Tangut name means the Great State of White and High, and its territory stretched west of the Yellow River's (Huang He) northern bend known as Hexi Corridor (Hexi, "west of the river"), flanked by the Mongolian and Tibetan Plateaus. The area served as an important link along the so-called Silk Road, the trade routes connecting cultural regions of Central and Inner Asia with the Western world.

Chinese records indicate that the Tangut state was established in 1038, when the Tangut emperor Li Yuanhao (r. 1032–1048) officially informed the Northern Song court of his new status, but Tangut texts count the state's chronology from Yuanhao's grandfather Li Jiqian (963–1004).[1] Tangut script was created not long before 1038.[2] Mongol invasions of 1215 and 1227 destroyed the Tangut state; its population was assimilated into the Mongol Empire or integrated into Tibetan areas.[3]

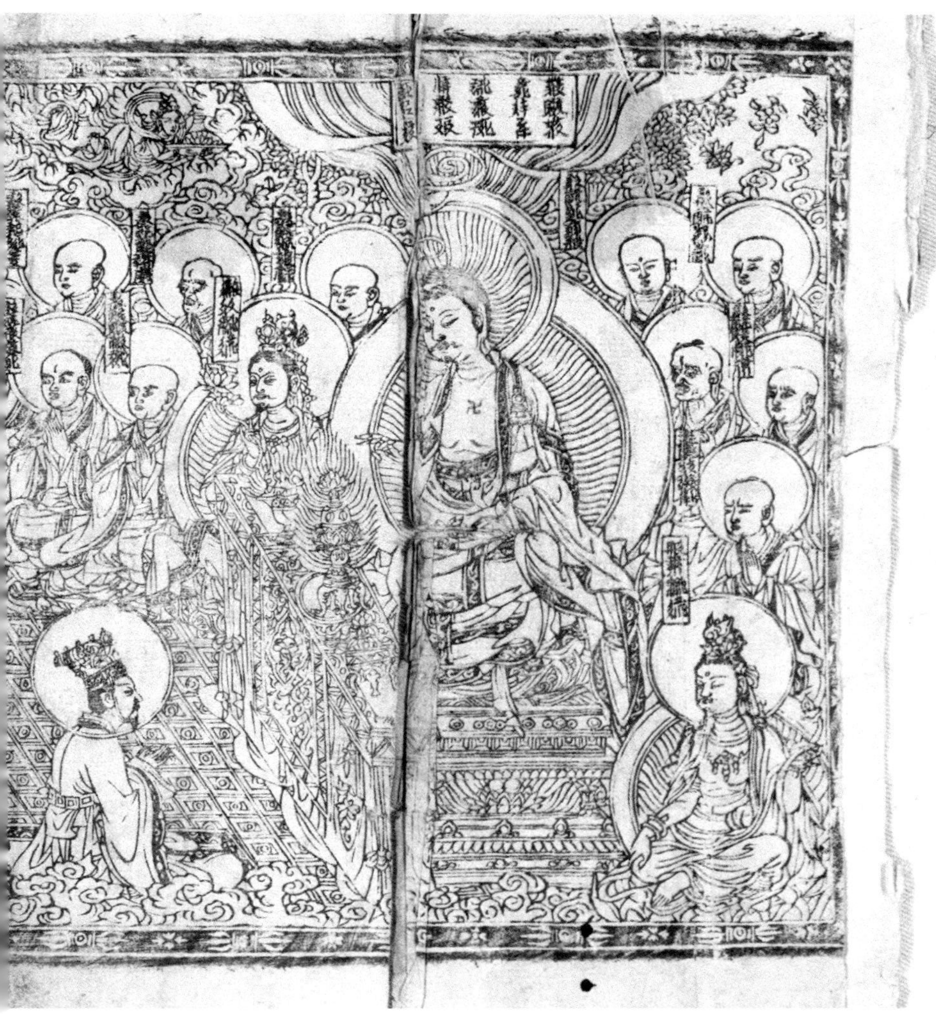

A *Pancharaksha* Text with Frontispiece Illustrations; excavated from Khara-Khoto, Tangut Kingdom (Xixia), Gansu Province, China; ca. late 12th century, reign period of the emperor Renzong (1124–1193, r. 1139–1193); xylographed ink on paper, concertina binding, 60 pages of text and 4 illustrated pages; 1⅞ × 4⅜ in. (27.5 × 11 cm); Institute of Oriental Manuscript Research; P. K. Kozlov Collection; Russian Academy of Sciences, Saint Petersburg, Russia; Tang 214, n40–41/1

Khara-Khoto

The city of Khara-Khoto was an important northern outpost of the Xixia state through the mid-fourteenth century and remained populated even after the state's demise in 1227.[4] Studies of a large cache of multilingual printed and written Buddhist texts, documents, and printed and painted images offer insights into the Tanguts' history, religion, art, literature, economy, and cross-cultural connections.[5]

Buddhism was crucial for unifying and protecting the Tangut realm and maintaining its prosperity. The state propagated Buddhist teachings by acquiring Buddhist texts, inviting foreign monks to assist in translation projects, building temples, and importing relics.

Tangut Buddhism

Chinese texts served as the initial source of Buddhism among the Tangut elite, as confirmed by acquisitions of the Buddhist canon in Chinese and its translation into Tangut. The cosmopolitan Tangut state embraced diverse sources of Buddhist culture—Indian, Tibetan, Chinese, and Khitan (Liao)—and systematically integrated them into its own cultural production. Several tantric Buddhist texts were translated from Tibetan and some probably from Sanskrit.[6]

The Tanguts' expansion westward brought them into direct contact with Tibetans of the eastern Tibetan region (Amdo) and facilitated connections with central Tibet, increasing exchanges with Tibetan Buddhist traditions.[7] Kadam, Kagyu, and Sakya Buddhist lineages spread in Xixia alongside Chinese Buddhist traditions. Tibetan and Tangut sources indicate that some Tibetan monks served as Imperial and State Preceptors in the Xixia court.[8]

Tangut Buddhist hierarchy was headed by the State Preceptor, a position of "supreme" rank, according to Tangut legislation. Another important figure was the imperial preceptor. It seems that in

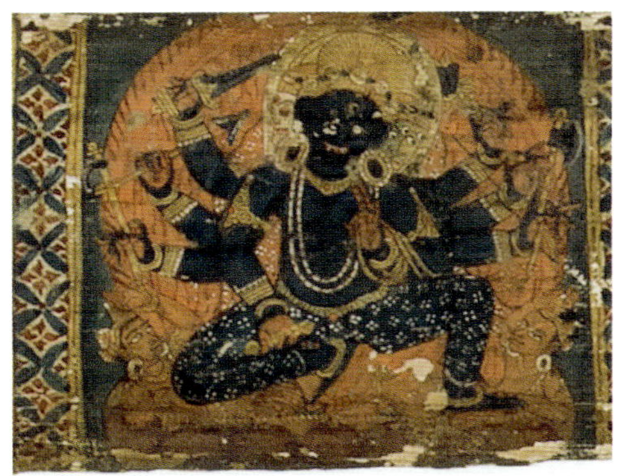

Goddess Mahasahasrapramardani, detail of a folio from a *Pancharaksha* (Five Protections) illuminated manuscript; Nepal; 1138; ink and opaque watercolor on palm leaf; 2¼ × 23⅝ in. (5.6 cm × 60 cm); San Diego Museum of Art; Edvin Binney 3rd Collection; 1990.156.1; photograph courtesy the San Diego Museum of Art

practice, the imperial preceptor's single duty was to perform tantric empowerment (*abhisheka*) rituals for the emperor, and the highly prestigious position included an assigned temple.[9]

Triggered by the inflow of Tibetan texts during the reign of Renzong Renxiao (r. 1139–1193), new translations of canonical scriptures continued, with the focus shifted to revise earlier translations. The arrival of the Indian translator Sumatikirti in the late eleventh century and the Kashmiri Buddhist scholar (*pandita*) Jayananda with his Tibetan disciples in the 1140s perhaps enabled the Tangut transcription of invocation spells (dharani) and mantras to more closely reflect Sanskrit sounds.[10]

The Amended and Revised Legal Code of the Tiansheng Reign Period, promulgated in the mid-twelfth century, stipulated regulations for monastic ordination as well as the curriculum of Buddhist doctrinal learning and mandatory texts for monastic communities' recitations. The list included several *Pancharaksha* texts associated with the protection of the state and the well-being of sentient beings, as indicated by the Tangut imperial preface to the publication.[11]

Woodblock Prints (Xylographs)

For an example of a Tibetan woodblock-printed book, see Earliest Extant Printed Edition of Milarepa's Life Story, no. 62.

The method of printing text and images by pressing paper to carved wooden blocks that have been inked and the movable-type method were well documented in the region. Tanguts made a significant contribution to the development of printing technology as early as the beginning of the twelfth century. In Khara-Khoto, texts in Tibetan and translated into Tangut and Chinese had been printed from woodblocks by the mid-twelfth century.[12]

The printing of images was widely practiced, and images often served as frontispieces of the printed Buddhist texts, as in this example. The origins of the printed images' compositions remain in question, but portable scroll paintings and illuminated manuscripts were among the sources of the prints' iconography. Mass-produced printed images, in turn, helped to propagate the iconographies, visual conventions, and messages these images and texts conveyed.

Most of the printed publications in Xixia were distributed by the imperial court for several statewide Buddhist assemblies in the eleventh and twelfth centuries, but some texts may have been published through alternative venues. The names of the temples mentioned in the publications' colophons indicate the translators' affiliations and, possibly, publication sites.[13]

Many of the materials discovered throughout the former Tangut territory, especially the texts of tantric instructions, were not listed in the legal regulations for the monasteries. This suggests that Buddhism in the Tangut state performed two functions. "Popular" Buddhism utilized various manuscripts and printed esoteric instructions (*upadesha*). Worship of Maitreya, broadly popular in Xixia, may have been expressly intended for the well-being and good rebirths of the royal family. Though not officially sanctioned, Maitreya-related sutras were published and widely distributed during Buddhist assemblies. "Official" Buddhism employed the sanctioned canonical texts, including the state protection texts of Tibetan and Chinese origin.[14]

The Illustrated Buddhist Text for Protection of the State

For another *Pancharaksha* protector goddess, see Dabaojigong Temple, no. 64.

This printed work of the *Five Sutras* was published on the order of the Tangut emperor Renzong for nationwide distribution. Its title and the opening line of a preface, composed by Qi Qiu, appear to the left of the image. The sutras, known as Five Protections (*Pancharaksha*), are associated with Five Protector Goddesses and their specific mantras. Chinese and Tibetan traditions include translations of the *Pancharaksha* texts with dharani and instructions for their use, and various Tangut texts have similar content.

This Tangut translation of the Buddha's discourse (sutra) from Tibetan,[15] printed in a folded (concertina) format, sets up the text's narrative. The Buddha and the Four Great Kings offer protection in the aftermath of an earthquake at Vaishali.[16] The frontispiece combines two images rendered in a seemingly Chinese mode. The left frame shows a semiwrathful deity seated on a large throne with left leg pendent, surrounded by her retinue. Dressed in Indic fashion, she has four heads, each with three eyes; her hair is standing on end; and her eight arms hold various implements.[17] This is one of the five goddesses,

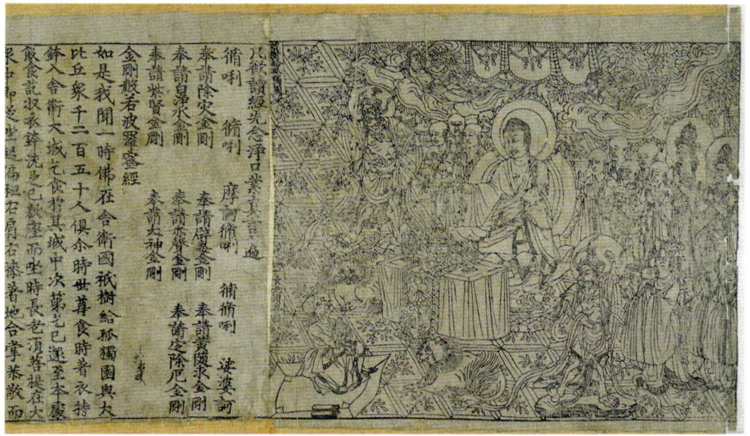

Frontispiece of the Chinese translation of *Vajracchedika Prajnaparamita Sutra (Diamond Sutra)*; Dunhuang, present-day Gansu Province, China; 11 May 868 CE; woodblock print, ink on paper; fully unrolled 10⅞ × 196¼ in. (27.6 × 499.5 cm); British Library, London; Or.8210/P.2 recto, detail; image from British Library / Granger. All rights reserved

Mahasahasrapramardani. The cartouche reads, "Root Dharani Heavenly Mother 'protecting the Great Thousands of States.'" The tantric iconography of the deity stems from Indian and Nepalese models, as in the illuminated manuscripts of *Pancharaksha* in the National Museum in Delhi and San Diego Museum of Art.[18] In the lower corners of the image, two figures in Tangut royal attire sit with their hands in supplication, and the whole tableau is framed by a vajra fence. The image diverges from earlier prints of *Pancharaksha* dharanis found in Dunhuang.[19]

The right frame image follows the previous modes of Chinese sutra frontispieces in printed form.[20] A kneeling royal figure in front of Buddha Shakyamuni replaces the elder Subhuti, depicted in another sutra. To the right of the Buddha are Ananda and Bodhisattvas Manjushri and Samantabhadra, identified by cartouches. The convention of depicting royal figures as participants inserted into the scenes in Tangut Buddhist images indicates imperial patronage. The whole group faces the goddess and the text, denoting their importance.

For another instance of Tangut royal donors, see the top register of Cave 3 at Yulin Cave Temples, no. 31.

During the two hundred years of the Xixia state's existence and well after its destruction in 1227 by the expanding Mongol Empire of Chinggis Khan, the Tangut people and their Buddhist culture, with material objects like this print, produced a lasting sociopolitical legacy in Central Asia, including in their conqueror's culture, religious authority, and state rituals.

Further Reading

Galambos, Imre. 2015. *Translating Chinese Tradition and Teaching Tangut Culture: Manuscripts and Printed Books from Khara-Khoto*. Berlin: De Gruyter.

Piotrovsky, M. B., ed. 1993. *Lost Empire of the Silk Road: Buddhist Art from Khara-Khoto (X-XIIIth Century)*. Exhibition catalog. Milan: Electra.

Solonin, Kirill. 2015. "Local Literatures: Tangut/Xixia." In *Brill's Encyclopedia of Buddhism*, edited by Jonathan A. Silk et al., 1:844–59. Leiden: Brill.

Notes

1 Russian scholars date the Tangut state from 982 to 1227. Kychanov 1999, 49–58; Galambos 2015, 102–8.
2 See Galambos 2015, 120–28.
3 See Shen 2005, 189.
4 Galambos 2015, 17–96.
5 Solonin 2008, 64–74, and 2020, 129–35; Shi 2021.
6 van der Kuijp 1993; Solonin 2013a. On the complexity of the Buddhist sources in Xixia, see Solonin 2008, 67–70; Kornicki 2012, 85; Kychanov 1999.
7 On Tangut texts of Tibetan origin, see Solonin 2015.
8 Sperling 1987; Dunnell 1992.
9 Kychanov 2013, 227.
10 Wei 2013, 317–18.
11 See Solonin 2015. An early monument of Tangut epigraphy, the "Inscription Commemorating the Renovation of Ganying Stupa of the State Protection Monastery" marks the importance of this function of Buddhism. See Dunnell 1996.
12 Bogdanov 2012, 78n26; Galambos 2015, 178–82; Kornicki 2012, 84–88; Helman-Ważny 2014, 121–23, 68, fig. 28.
13 Such as the temples Daduminsi 大度民寺 and Xiansheng Wuming Jingshe 顯生五明精舍.
14 See Solonin 2013b and 2015.
15 Kychanov 1999, 245–46. The title's Tangut transcription is from the original Sanskrit title, generally thought to represent a translation from Tibetan.
16 Hidas 2020, 237–40; 2013, 225–32.
17 Her front right hand holds a vajra, the other three hold a sword, arrows, and a goad/trident. Her front left hand holds a noose, displaying a gesture of vigilance (*tarjani* mudra), and the other three hold a jewel, a bow, and a trident. J. Kim 2010, 265–66; Bhattacharyya (1928) 2017, 2: 406.
18 See Bhattacharyya 1958, fig. 197; J. Kim 2010, fig. 1.
19 The *Mahapratisara dharani* print is discussed in Formigatti 2016, 79–80, fig. 6.1; Copp 2008, 243–44, 257–58.
20 See *Vajracchedikā Prajñāpāramitā Sūtra* in the British Library, London, Or.8210/P.2 recto. For examples of the Yuan and Ming periods, see Huang 2014, figs. 6, 13, 14, 18, 35.

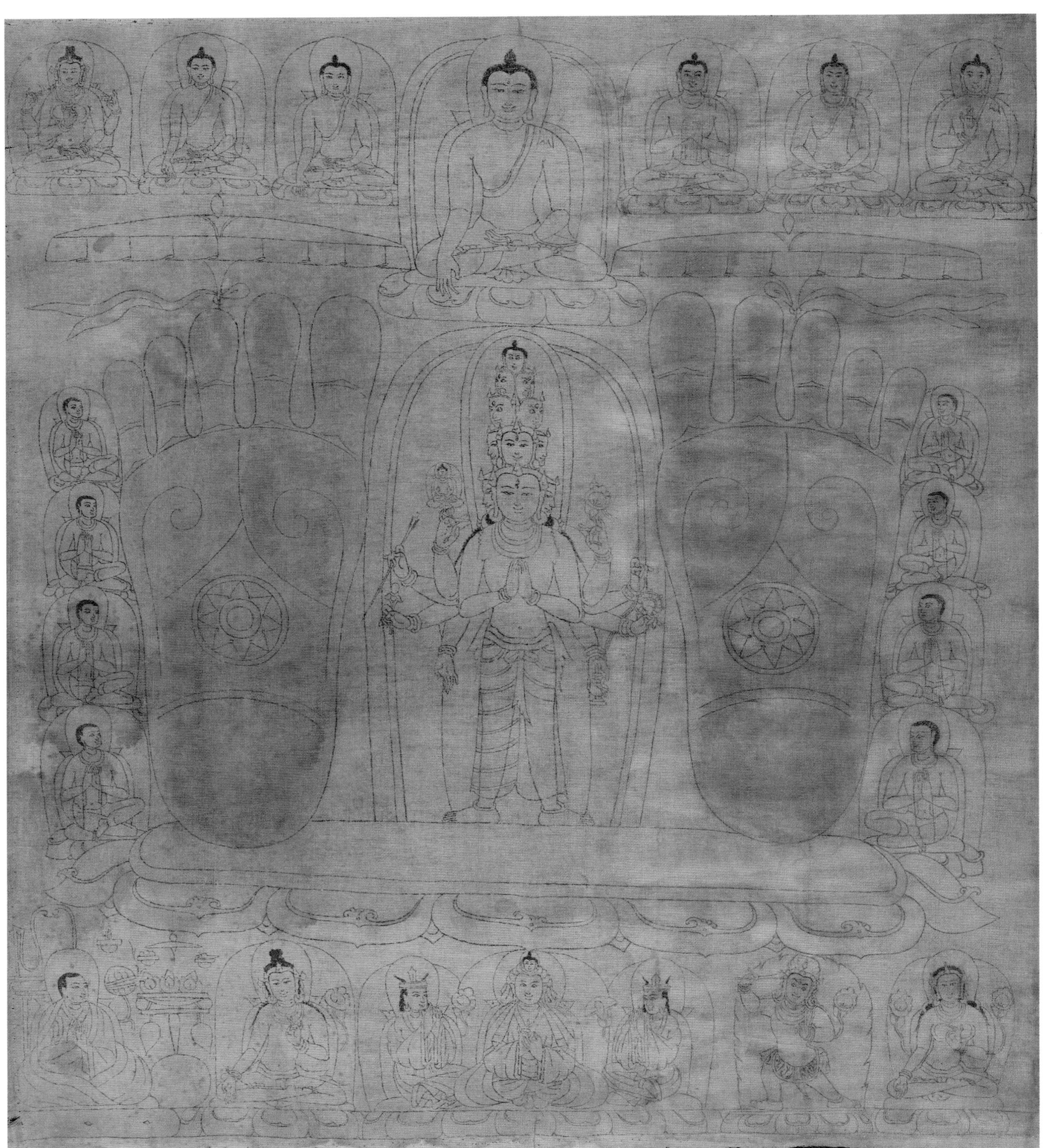

№ 33

Bodhisattva Avalokiteshvara and the Buddha's Footprints

Central Tibet, 12th century

Presence and Power: Footprints in Tibetan Art

KATHRYN SELIG BROWN

FOOTPRINTS ARE ONE OF CIVILIZATION'S MOST POTENT SYMBOLS. Simultaneously mysterious and familiar, they convey the immediacy of physical contact and the poignancy of absence. Often associated with magic and power, footprints are venerated in many of the world's religions: footprints made by Vishnu, Jesus, Mohammed, and the Buddha are all worshipped today.

Displayed on a lotus pedestal in the central area of this twelfth-century painting is a pair of larger-than-life-size footprints flanking an eleven-headed form of Avalokiteshvara, the bodhisattva of compassion and the patron deity of Tibet.[1] The depiction of Buddha Shakyamuni, the historical Buddha, above Avalokiteshvara, and of Songtsen Gampo (ca. 605–649), who began the expansion of what later became the Tibetan Empire, directly beneath Avalokiteshvara creates an axis of imagery imbued with layers of meaning.

Indian Worship of the Buddha's Footprints

According to tradition, Buddha Shakyamuni lived roughly twenty-five hundred years ago, but until some four hundred years after his death, he was not portrayed in human form. Instead, he was represented by a variety of symbols, including footprints, which soon became one of the most popular modes of signaling his presence.

Called *buddhapada* (footprints of the Buddha) in ancient Indian texts, footprints continued to be created and worshipped in India even after images of the Buddha became prevalent. Venerated from roughly the second century BCE on, superhuman-sized *buddhapada* in stone appeared in numbers at Buddhist sites around the country.[2] There are numerous examples of such footprints at one of Buddhism's holiest sites, Bodhgaya, where the Buddha attained enlightenment, including a famous pair that still attracts streams of worshippers. An imprint of these *buddhapada* remains a favored souvenir of modern pilgrims to Bodhgaya.

On Bodhgaya, see Mahabodhi Temple Model, no. 25.

It is possible that the footprints on this thangka represent those from an Indian site like Bodhgaya and are perhaps a souvenir taken back to Tibet by the thangka's patron, a Tibetan lama who appears in the lower left corner, holding a smoking censer. This hypothesis is supported by the fact that the outline of the right foot overlaps Avalokiteshvara's aureole, suggesting that the footprints on the thangka were produced first and then the drawing overlaid afterward. Additionally, the footprints are not placed exactly, as they would be if an artist had created them from the beginning on a grid; the right foot is positioned a little higher than the left.[3]

In Buddhism, as in other religions, when a revered person has touched or come into contact with something, that object reverberates with a residue of their presence and power and becomes a relic. And as relics, footprints represent important loci for worship because they establish an earthly presence of their maker, who may have passed away into nirvana. Literary evidence indicates that this concept applies to both real (from the perspective of the devout) and man-made footprints of Buddha Shakyamuni. The Buddha (or another holy person) is actually manifest in his or her print, and anything that comes into contact with the print is blessed. And because the prints represent contact with a holy person, they are not viewed as merely passive and unresponsive objects of worship but are thought to emit blessings or possess other miraculous capabilities. Thus, a thangka such as this one, which displays *buddhapada*, would have been treated as if it had come into contact with the Buddha himself.

Bodhisattva Avalokiteshvara and the Buddha's Footprints; central Tibet; 12th century; pigments on cloth; 22 × 19⅜ in. (55.9 × 49.2 cm); Rubin Museum of Art; Gift of Shelley and Donald Rubin; C2003.50.5 (HAR 271)

See Standing Buddha Shakyamuni Donated by Lundeva, no. 59.

Buddha Shakyamuni's presence in this thangka is amplified by his depiction in the center of the top register, a figure larger than the other deities in the row. His footprints, too, are the largest objects on the thangka, indicating their placement at the apex of the Tibetan artistic hierarchy, in which the largest item is the most important. The footprints are each topped by an honorific parasol, an ancient Indian sign of respect and honor. The round mark in the center of each foot, a stylized wheel symbolizing the Buddhist doctrine, the *dharmachakra*, is one of the thirty-two congenital marks (*lakshana*) that distinguish a buddha from a mortal.[4]

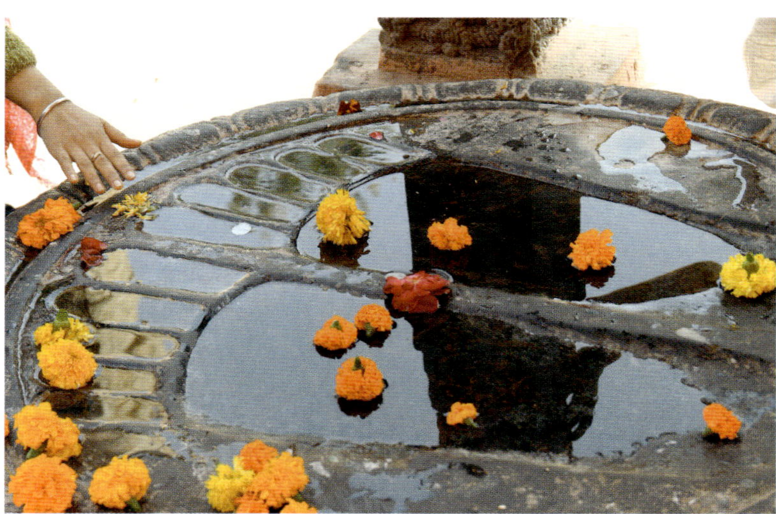

Buddhapada; Bodhgaya, India; photograph by Janice Leoshko

Feet and footprints play polar roles in Indian culture because the feet are considered to be lowest in the bodily hierarchy. By touching or worshipping the feet, one humbles oneself beneath that person or deity. This inherent humbling layer of symbolism also underlies the worship of footprints.

Tibetan Buddhist Worship of Footprints

The *buddhapada* tradition traveled across Asia, appearing in varied forms in China, Japan, Sri Lanka, Burma, Thailand, Laos, and Cambodia, the footprints achieving a noteworthy popularity as symbols in Tibet.[5] The worship of footprints on cloth is said to have been brought to Tibet by the Bengali Buddhist master Atisha (ca. 982–1054) and the translator Marpa (1012–1097), among others,[6] but many Tibetans visited India and witnessed the worship of *buddhapada* firsthand. In 1234, roughly around the same time that this thangka was created, Chak Lotsawa (1197–1263/4), a Tibetan monk and translator, visited Bodhgaya and viewed the main pair of footprints. The *buddhapada* were so popular with pilgrims that he noted a chapel was supposed to have been built over the footprints to protect them; in the end it was not constructed because the resulting entry fee would have reduced the number of devotees who could worship there.[7]

For more on Atisha, see Tara Who Protects from the Eight Great Fears, no. 27.

During the eleventh and twelfth centuries, the Tibetan *buddhapada* tradition expanded to include the footprints of Tibetan Buddhist lamas and other revered holy figures, such as Atisha, whose footprints were once housed at Reting Monastery, in central Tibet.[8] According to twelfth- and thirteenth-century Tibetan texts, a lama's footprints are so imbued with his presence that they can act as a stand-in for the teacher and can even give teachings in the teacher's absence. The renowned scholar Pakmodrupa (1110–1170), who wrote a text called "Requesting Footprints," commented that receiving Buddhist teachings via the footprints, such as those in an object from the Rubin Museum of Art,[9] is no different from hearing "whatever practice, explanation, or teaching" from the real lama,[10] an esoteric capability implying the prestige and power inherent in owning such a footprint thangka.

Avalokiteshvara and His Incarnations

See Avalokiteshvara at Khartse, no. 20; Pensive Bodhisattva Avalokiteshvara, no. 53.

For more on Songtsen Gampo, see Yumbu Lagang Castle, no. 5; Jokhang Temple, no. 7; Jowo Shakyamuni, no. 8.

The *buddhapada* on this thangka flank Avalokiteshvara, the most popular bodhisattva in Buddhism, particularly in Tibet, where he is part of the country's founding mythology and his mantra, *om mani padme hum*, is recited universally. Depicted directly below an eleven-headed image of Avalokiteshvara is Songtsen Gampo, the first monarch of the Tibetan Empire, who is also credited with bringing Buddhism to the country. This axial placement visually cues the viewer to the famous story of Songtsen, who, along with his two wives, dissolved into light in the midst of prayer and was then absorbed into a statue of an eleven-headed sculpture of Avalokiteshvara. Although this legend dates to at least four hundred years after Songtsen's death, his association with this particular form of Avalokiteshvara, whose eleven heads are stacked in a particular manner, has become an integral part of the nation's identity. Images such as this thangka bear witness to the ways in which art can project ideas such as the first emperor, a fearsome warrior, being an emanation of Tibet's most widely worshipped bodhisattva of compassion.[11]

For more on the Fifth Dalai Lama's conflation with Songtsen Gampo, see Potala Palace, no. 71.

Although Songtsen was already being identified with Avalokiteshvara by the end of the early dynastic period (ca. 608–866), it was Atisha and his team of disciples and translators in the eleventh century who advanced the cult of Songtsen as a manifestation of Avalokiteshvara, aligning this conquering ruler with the favored bodhisattva.[12] Over the succeeding centuries, many others followed suit, using a link to this deity to further themselves or their particular tradition of Tibetan Buddhism politically.[13] The Fifth Dalai Lama (1617–1682), for example, who united Tibet, asserted his divine right to rule by presenting himself as an emanation of both the country's patron deity and the empire-building emperor, Songtsen Gampo. To glorify this status, he widely publicized a list of his previous incarnations, commissioning a series of paintings with his handprints and footprints surrounding each incarnation (see image on p. 310), emphasizing his presence and his identification with each one.[14]

Consecration

The act of consecration ensures that a deity takes up residence in an object, and all religious sculptures and paintings undergo this enlivening process before they can be used for devotion and meditation. On this thangka, as on most Tibetan paintings, evidence of consecration can be seen on the reverse, represented by the Sanskrit seed syllables *om ah hum* written behind the major figures. The typical dedicatory formula known as the Buddhist creed is also written here.

Unadorned drawings such as this are often among the consecratory materials inserted into sculptures.[15] A number of such footprint thangkas have fold marks that indicate they were originally part of the consecration contents for a sculpture, including one with parallel iconography now in the Metropolitan Museum of Art, New York.[16]

The appearance of footprints on this thangka, combined with Avalokiteshvara and Songtsen Gampo, makes this object resonate on many levels. As Buddha Shakyamuni and his footprints protectively surround Avalokiteshvara, the patron deity of Tibet, Avalokiteshvara safeguards the Tibetan nation, founded by his emanation Songtsen Gampo, who brought Buddhism to his people. The footprints, too, conjure the eternal presence of their maker, humble the devoted, and continue to emanate blessings on a thangka with imagery that marries these ancient Buddhist symbols with the legendary inception of the Tibetan nation-state.

Further Reading

Dotson, Brandon. 2019. "The Emanated Emperor and His Cosmopolitan Contradictions." In *Faith and Empire: Art and Politics in Tibetan Buddhism*, edited by Karl Debreczeny, 69–81. Exhibition catalog. New York: Rubin Museum of Art. https://issuu.com/rmanyc/docs/faith_and_empire.

Selig Brown, Kathryn H. 2004. *Eternal Presence: Handprints and Footprints in Buddhist Art.* Exhibition catalog. Katonah, NY: Katonah Museum of Art.

Sørensen, Per K. 2019a. "In His Name: The Fake Royal Biography—Fabricated Prophecy and Literary Imposture." *Revue d'Etudes Tibétaines*, no. 52 (October): 284–335.

Notes

1 This painting has been carbon dated to 1100 plus or minus fifty years.
2 This material on introductory *buddhapada* is from Selig Brown 2004, 13–18, 34–37.
3 See Jackson and Jackson 1988, 45–73, for information on thangka composition.
4 For more on *lakshana*, see Lopez 2004b.
5 For examples, see Selig Brown 2004, 27–30, 63–67, and for their different appearances in Tibetan culture, 19–27.
6 Selig Brown 2004, 19n21, 22, citing Phag mo gru pa 1997, 299–303; Lhun grub chos 'phel 1994, 137; 'Bri gung skyob pa 'jig rten gsum mgon 1975, 525.
7 Roerich 1959, 72.
8 D. Martin 2001a, 147.
9 See Chakrasamvara and the Footprints of Drigungpa Jikten Sumgon (1143–1217), C2003.7.1 (HAR 65205).
10 Selig Brown 2004, 31n39.
11 For more on the "emanational nexus" of Avalokiteshvara, see Dotson 2019.
12 Sørensen 2019a, 296–99.
13 Sørensen 2019a.
14 Selig Brown 2004, 22, 24, 48–54; Sørensen 2014 and 2019.
15 Selig Brown 2004, 26–27, fig. 21.
16 Selig Brown 2004, 60, 60n65.

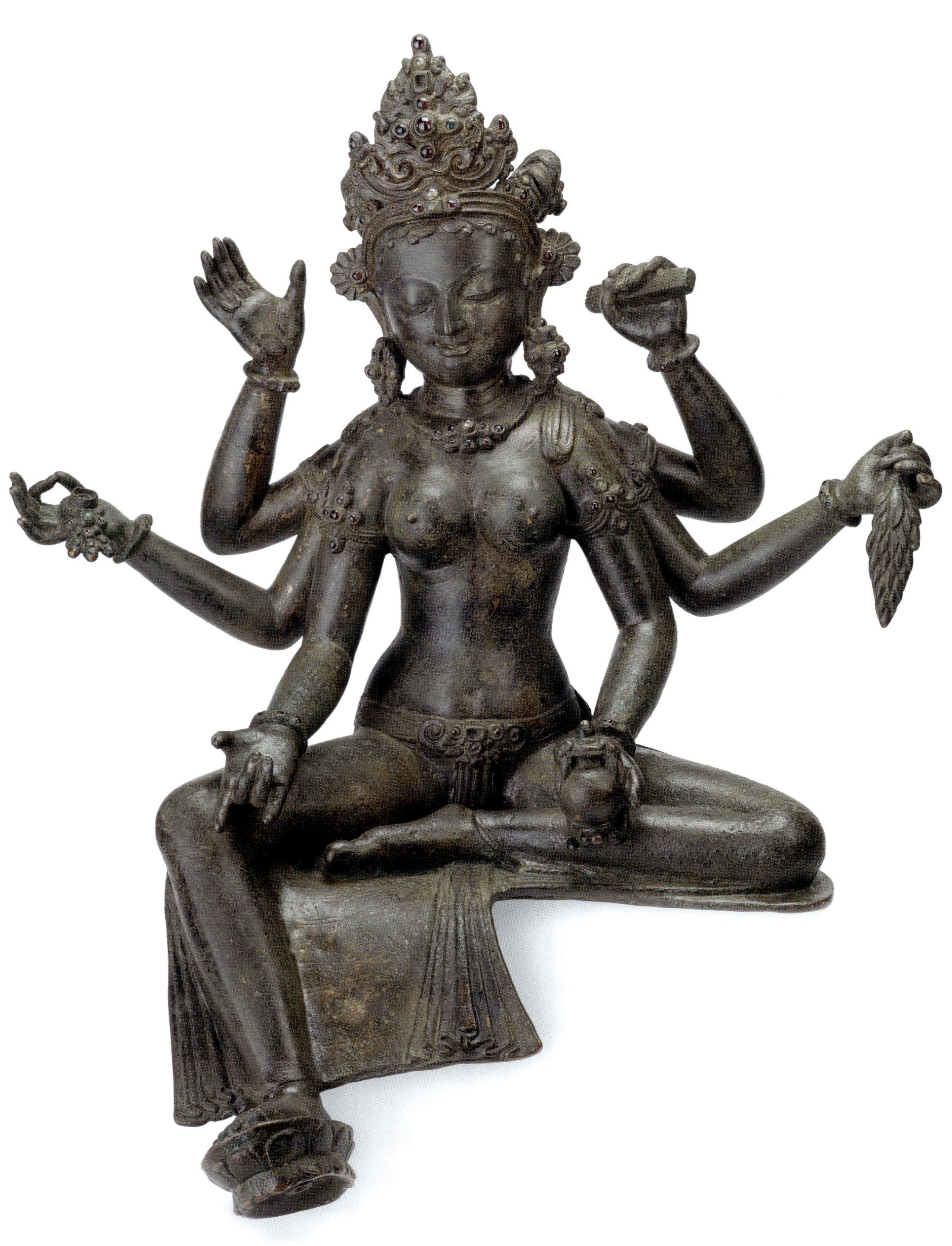

Nº 34

Goddess of Prosperity, Vasudhara

Nepal, ca. late 12th–early 13th century

Material and Spiritual Abundance in the Kathmandu Valley

KERRY LUCINDA BROWN

THROUGHOUT THE HIMALAYAS, the accumulation of material wealth has been important to the survival of spiritual and ritual practice. As the Buddhist goddess of prosperity, Vasudhara is associated with material and spiritual abundance. She shares parallels with Lakshmi, the Hindu goddess of wealth, in addition to the earth goddess, Bhu Devi. Her name, "Bearer of Treasure," associates Vasudhara with a host of deities who assist individuals with cultivating material and spiritual fortune. While her two-armed form more frequently appears in India and Tibet, it is her six-armed manifestation that is dominant among the Newar community of the Kathmandu Valley. For Newar Buddhists, this form of Vasudhara emphasizes her association with rice cultivation and the agricultural bounty provided by the fertile soil of the valley.[1] She is also one of the most popular deities worshipped by families in home shrines to ensure success in business and at home. Moreover, for Nepal's Newar Buddhist community, the six-armed form of Vasudhara emphasizes her close connection to agricultural wealth and spiritual abundance rooted in the sacred geography of the Kathmandu Valley. Completed in the late twelfth to thirteenth century, with some scholars suggesting an even earlier date in the eleventh or twelfth century, this bronze is a visual testimony to the exquisite metalworking traditions active in the Kathmandu Valley during this period.[2]

Newar Stylistic Considerations

Notable for its elegant form and graceful positioning of the torso and six arms, Vasudhara was created during the late Transitional or Thakuri period (ca. 878 to ca. 1200 CE) or Early Malla period (ca. 1200–1482). Her eyes, nose, and mouth are set low on the face, and her wide forehead supports a large bejeweled crown. The shell-like foliage motif (*samkhapatra*) behind her ears balances the large crown on her head.[3] Her hair is tied into two buns at the back. She wears a diaphanous garment that is gathered on her left shoulder and drapes across her torso. As typical for Newar sculptures from this period, she has a narrow waist, small bosom, and an elongated torso. A girdle hugs her hips, as the folds of her lower garment cascade down the front of the figure, framing her right leg. Larger than the earliest known dated depiction of Vasudhara from 1082, this piece allows for more refined details in the adornments. The goddess wears a short necklace, matching armbands, bracelets, and large multitiered inlaid earrings. She presents a sweetly smiling expression, with a full lower lip, slightly upturned mouth, and a full, round face. While signifying her youth and vitality, these visual traits of Vasudhara emerge as key stylistic features associated with Newar sculptural styles from this period. Most notably, the sweetly smiling expression and elongated torso distinguish Newar works from other regional styles.

Buddhist Goddess Vasudhara; Nepal; ca. late 12th–early 13th century; copper alloy with traces of gilding, inlaid with gemstones and glass; 19 × 15½ × 11 in. (48.3 × 39.4 × 28 cm); Los Angeles County Museum of Art; From the Nasli and Alice Heeramaneck Collection; M.81.8.2; photograph © Museum Associates/ LACMA, www.lacma.org

Iconographic Considerations: Material and Spiritual Abundance

Vasudhara is a golden goddess, usually depicted with a yellow or gold complexion.[4] While the original metal dominates her visual appearance, surviving traces of gold on this sculpture suggest it was once fully gilded. She sits in a posture of royal ease (*Lalitasana*), with her right leg outstretched and supported by a lotus pedestal base, with her left leg resting bent beneath her. The base that would have originally supported this image has been lost. The work was most likely originally installed on a metal or stone base and, judging from its size, would have served as a primary deity in a shrine.

Vasudhara's upper hands express spiritual bounty. The upper right hand is open and outstretched near her ear, making a gesture associated with praising or greeting the buddhas (*tathagata vandana*

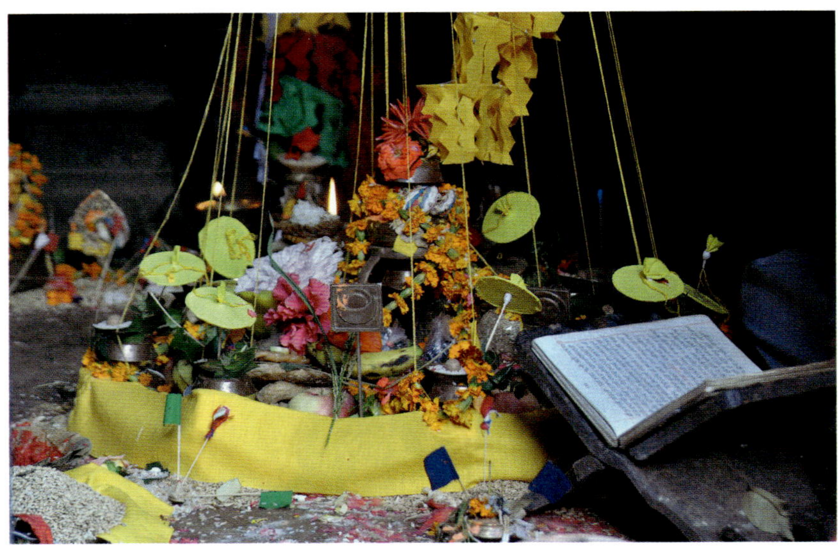

Mandala offering to the goddess Vasudhara at Ha Baha (Ratnakar Mahavihara) during a Gatila celebration in Patan, Nepal; photograph © Kerry Lucinda Brown, 2010

mudra), while the upper left hand holds a copy of *The Perfection of Wisdom* (*Prajnaparamita*) *Sutra*. This attribute connects Vasudhara with the Buddhist goddess Prajnaparamita, "The Mother of All Buddhas," and alludes to her role as the source of the dharma and upholder of the knowledge of all the buddhas (*Vidyadaneshvareshvari*).[5]

Her four lower hands are associated with the more secular aspects of her lay devotional worship in Nepal. Vasudhara's center left hand holds a sheath of rice (*dhanya manjari*), symbolizing the source of wealth, while the lower holds a vase filled with folige (*purna ghata kalasha*), symbolizing abundance. Her center right hand holds a sheath of cascading jewels (*ratna manjari*) and her lower left hand displays the gesture of bountiful giving (*varada* mudra). The wealth she grants to those who venerate her has implications in this lifetime and in lives to come. Further, this visual arrangement establishes a parallel between the cascading sheath of rice and the cascading sheath of jewels.

For Newars in the Kathmandu Valley, rice is wealth. Rice feeds the family, sustains the religious community, and facilitates the salt trade with Tibet. Rice is the primary offering given during ritual feasts and celebrations. The agricultural abundance of the Kathmandu Valley is directly tied to the cultivation of rice in the fertile lowlands of the valley floor, sustained by the summer monsoon rains. By the latter half of the Licchavi period (ca. 300–ca. 879 CE), the Kathmandu Valley and surrounding foothills were known regionally for their rich, fertile soil, which supported the production of rice, millet, and buckwheat. By the Thakuri period, well-established trade routes tied together trade between Tibet, Nepal, and northern India. Thus, when images of Vasudhara began to appear with more frequency in the Kathmandu Valley during the eleventh century, it coincided with the growing social and economic importance of rice cultivation. Vasudhara's connection to rice and the annual rice harvest fostered a rich devotional following related to the goddess in the Kathmandu Valley. A successful harvest of rice, transplanted to flooded fields in June and harvested in November, could establish an individual family's wealth and allow for surplus trade with communities living at higher elevations, most notably Tibet.[6]

Ritual Legacy

Because of Vasudhara's associations with the harvest, each fall she is honored during a two-day devotional ritual (*vrata*) known as Gatila or Tila, through both individual and collective veneration.[7] This event typically takes place in September, before the rice harvest in November, to ensure success and abundance. Elaborate mandala offerings to the goddess are part of her communal veneration in the courtyards of Newar monasteries (*baha*, *bahi*). While both men and women may participate in the observance of Gatila, the primary participants are women, who often wear yellow garments during these rites to affirm their connection to the golden goddess. Small images of Vasudhara commonly appear in home shrines, where her veneration is performed for the spiritual benefit (*punya*) of the family. There are also numerous shrines dedicated to Vasudhara throughout the Kathmandu Valley that reaffirm her central importance to the Mahayana-Vajrayana practices of the Newar community.

For more about Newar Buddhist monasteries, see Central Shrine Image of Kwa Baha, no. 22.

Among Vasudhara's epithets is "Perfectly Generous One" (*danaparamita*), directly attesting to her connection with acts of giving (*dana*) and cultivating generosity. From her earliest known appearance in Nepal in the eleventh century, her popularity continued to flourish throughout the Malla period (ca. 1200–1769) and Shah dynasty (1769–2008). The most common text associated with her veneration in the Kathmandu Valley is known as the *Vasundhararoddhesha*. This ritual manual outlines the role Vasudhara plays in sustaining the vitality of the Buddhist lineage. Buddhist merchants are encouraged to venerate Vasudhara annually during the Buddhist holy month of Gunla, typically in July or August, and members of the monastic community are also encouraged to participate in order to cultivate

Vasudhara Mandala; Nepal; dated 1777 (Samvat 897); distemper on cloth; 33¾ × 28½ in. (85.7 × 72.4 cm); The Metropolitan Museum of Art, New York; Gift of Stephen and Sharon Davies Collection, 2015; 2015.299; CC0 - Creative Commons (CC0 1.0)

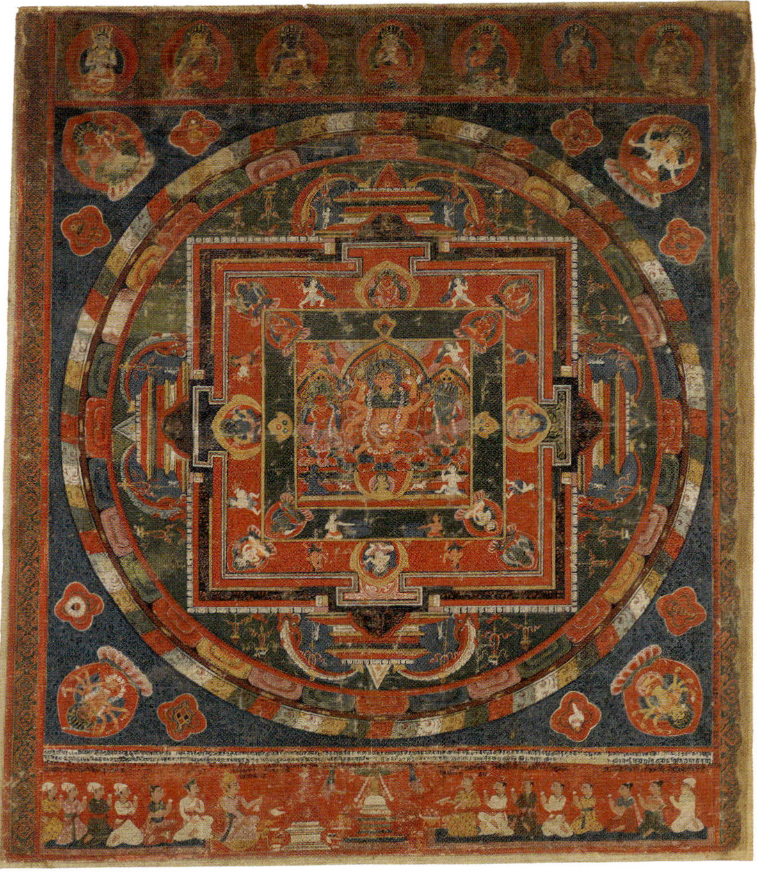

auspicious wealth. In some cases, monasteries establish trusts (*guthi*) to ensure the annual performance of Vasudhara rituals. Historical accounts of Vasudhara's power to provide for those that honor her illustrate the use of wealth to sustain Buddhist ritual traditions and support monastic institutions.[8]

The singular importance of Vasudhara to the Newar community is attested by the numerous recordings of her ritual worship illustrated in surviving Newar cloth paintings (*paubha*) that commemorate her veneration. One example, the Vasudhara mandala, dated 1777, demonstrates how the six-armed form of Vasudhara venerated in the Kathmandu Valley remains consistent, despite other variations of Vasudhara in Tibet that are two-armed or shown with an accompanying male deity. Here, Vasudhara, placed in the center, is surrounded by the deities of her mandala. Directly below the central mandala of the goddess, at the bottom of the painting, is a register of decoration depicting the ritual veneration (*vrata*) of Vasudhara. Here, worshippers flank a central white stupa. Noticeable to the left of the stupa is a Newar Buddhist Vajracharya priest wearing his distinctive gilt-bronze crown facilitating the rituals in front of a fire altar. The visual parallels between the venerative traditions of the past and present are striking. As Miranda Shaw has noted, "There is no inherent conflict between wealth and gnosis in the Buddhist worldview, for property may well serve the persons and institutions engaged in the pursuit of wisdom."[9] The stability of Vasudhara's form, which has remained a consistent presence in Newar artistic and ritual practice since the eleventh century, reaffirms her central importance to the Buddhist community in the Kathmandu Valley.

See Vajracharya Priest's Crown, no. 38.

Further Reading

Johne, Isabell. 2014. *Vasudhārā: A Study of the Origin, Development, and Diffusion of Artistic Representations of the Buddhist Goddess of Prosperity in Their Cultural Contexts.* Translated by Rachel Marks-Ritzenhoff. Aachen: Shaker Verlag.

Kim, Jinah, and Todd Lewis. 2019. *Dharma and Puṇya: Buddhist Ritual Art of Nepal.* Leiden: Hotei Publishing.

Shaw, Miranda Eberle. 2006. *Buddhist Goddesses of India.* Princeton, NJ: Princeton University Press.

Notes

1 Slusser 1982, 3–9.
2 Pal 1975b, 81, and 1985, 102.
3 Vajracharya 2016, 135.
4 Huntington and Bangdel 2003, 409.
5 Pal 1985, 102; Huntington and Bangdel 2003, 409.
6 A. Höfer 1978, 180; Hitchcock 1978, 120.
7 Lewis 2000, 93; Vajracharya 2016, 139–40; Kim and Lewis 2019, 2–3, 6.
8 M. E. Shaw 2006, 251.
9 M. E. Shaw 2006, 251.

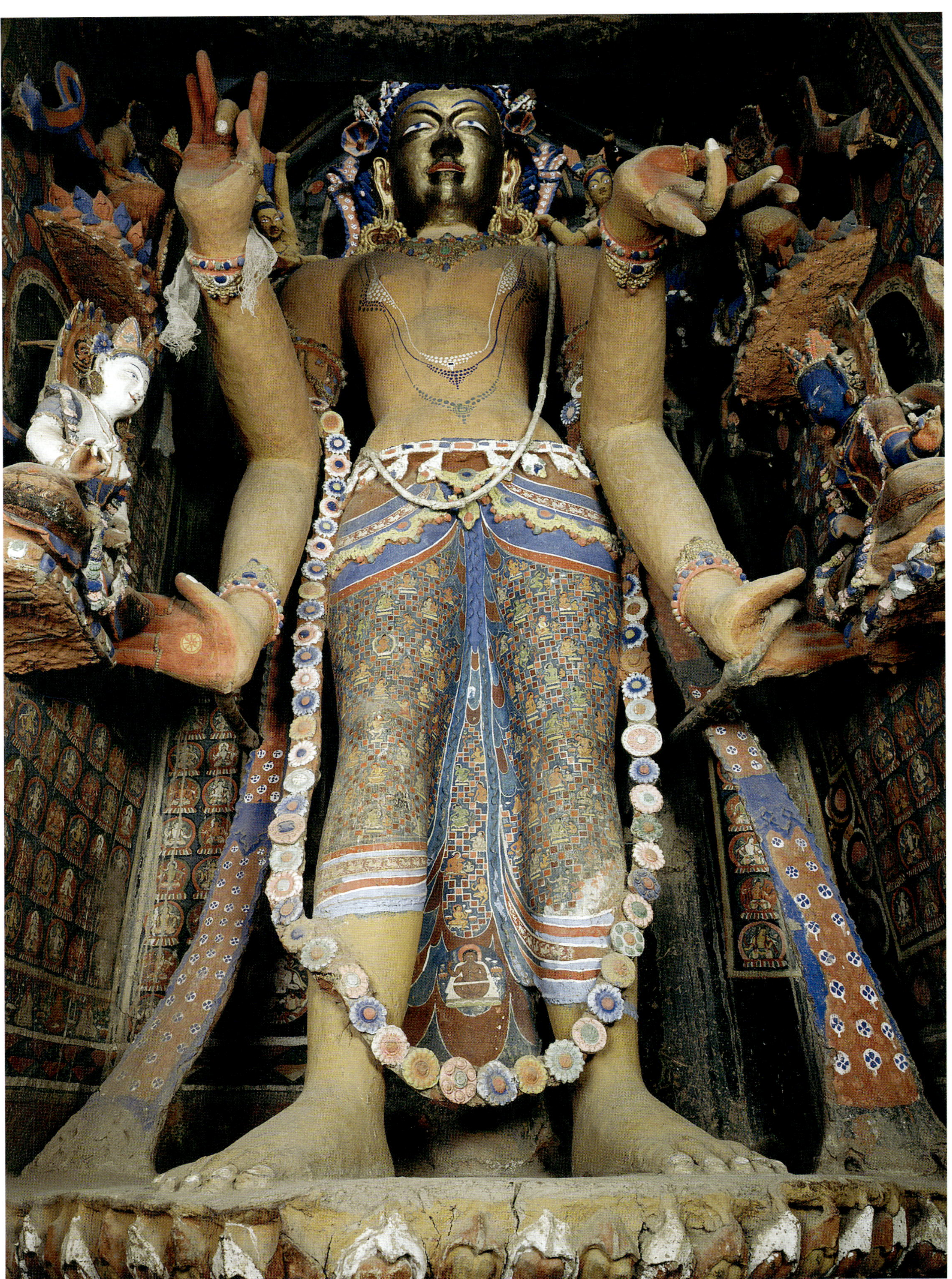

Nº 35

Monumental Manjushri with Mahasiddha-Adorned Robe

Alchi Sumtsek, Ladakh, India, ca. 1220

Alchi at the Threshold of a New Era in Tibetan Buddhist Art

CHRISTIAN LUCZANITS

THE ALCHI CHOSKHOR MONASTIC COMPLEX in Ladakh, northwestern India, is one of the jewels of world art. Within this complex housing five painted monuments dating from the late twelfth to the first quarter of the thirteenth century, the three-story Sumtsek Temple stands out in terms of conception, preservation, and quality.[1] Built in the memory of Jikten Gonpo Rinchen Pel (1143–1217), the Sumtsek can also be dated to about 1220. Although some scholars continue to date the monument earlier, internal evidence leaves no doubt about its historical context. Moreover, the Alchi monuments provide ample signs that they were constructed at the threshold of developments that make Tibetan Buddhist art distinctive.

Manjushri with Mahasiddhas

One of the depictions that demonstrate this development is the monumental clay sculpture of Manjushri with eighty-five mahasiddhas—adepts of esoteric Buddhist teachings—on his dhoti, that is, the painted cloth covering the hip and legs of the image. This representation of the Bodhisattva of Wisdom is orange and four-armed, and he is surrounded by the sculptures of the four outer offering goddesses, which personify the offerings of incense (*dhupa*), flower blossoms (*pushpa*), light (*dipa*), and fragrance (*gandha*).

The same bodhisattva, surrounded by tiny offering goddesses, is also shown in the main panels flanking this niche, and these depictions clarify the attributes that are now missing from the sculpture. As in the painting, the upper hands once held an arrow and a bow, while the lower hands held a sword and a book on top of a flower blossom, commonly a blue lily (*utpala*), as still preserved above the sculpture's left shoulder. This form of Manjushri is alluded to by a verse of the *Litany of Names of Manjushri* (*Manjushrinamasamgiti*), where Manjushri figures as the ultimate expression of the Buddha's wisdom:

> Dressed in the mail of loving kindness, equipped with the armor of compassion, with a volume of insight scripture, a sword, a bow and an arrow, he is victorious in the battle against defilements and unknowing.[2]

The *Litany of Names of Manjushri* derives from an esoteric Buddhist context and has inspired a rich literature commenting on it from both a Yogatantra and Highest Yogatantra perspective. The mahasiddhas on the dhoti stand for the transmission of the highest esoteric teachings and thus the latter perspective. Their depiction can be linked to the *Legends of the Eighty-Four Mahasiddhas* as narrated by the Indian scholar Abhayadatta to his Tibetan disciple in the early twelfth century.[3]

The dark-skinned figure at the bottom center of the dhoti can be identified as Padampa Sanggye, an Indian adept active in Tibet until his passing in 1117.[4] Although not part of Abhayadatta's group of mahasiddhas, he specifically signifies the transmission of the highest esoteric teachings to Tibet.

Manjushri with Mahasiddhas, right niche of the Sumtsek Temple; Alchi, Ladakh, India; ca. 1220; mineral pigments on clay; height approx. 13 ft. 1 in. (40 m); photograph by Jaroslav Poncar

Three Stories, Three Sculptures

The Sumtsek is a three-story building with central niches in the back and the side walls. The three niches house such tall clay sculptures that their heads look into the middle story. As encountered by the circumambulating visitors, these sculptures are the bodhisattvas Avalokiteshvara, Maitreya, and Manjushri,

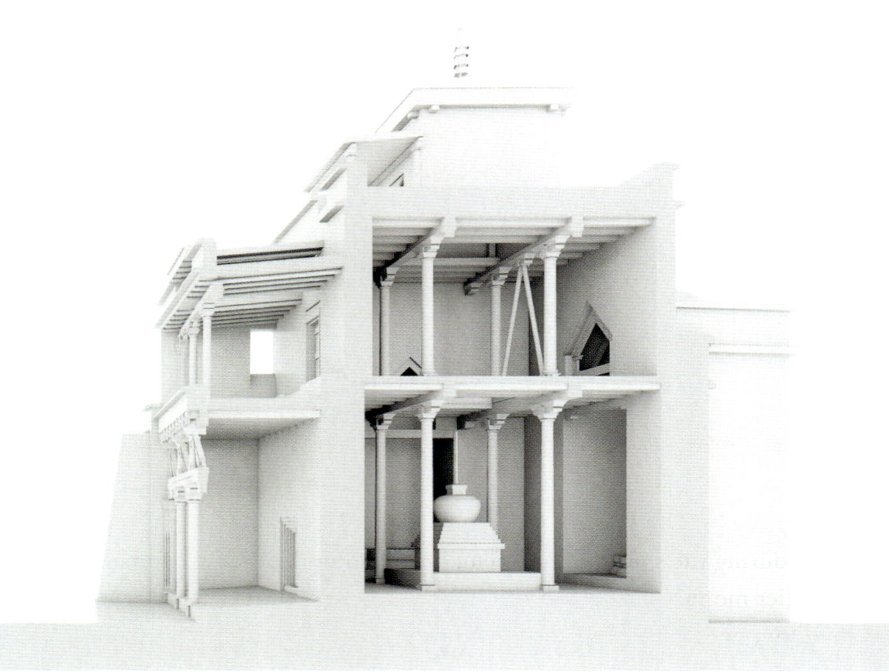

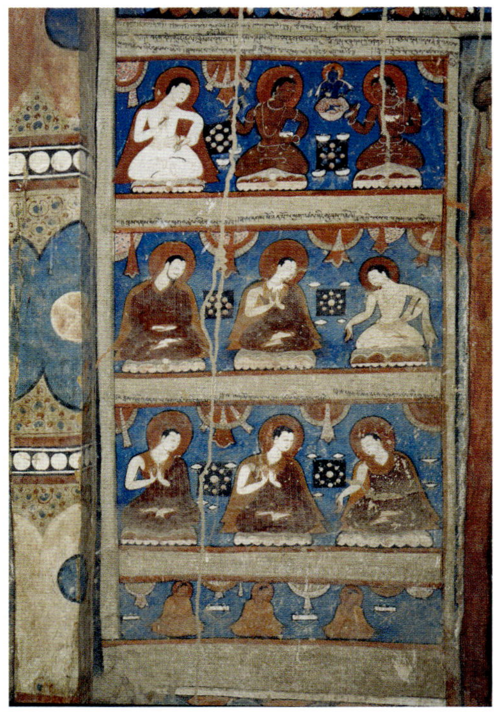

(left) Model of the three-story Sumtsek Temple as seen from the side of the figure of Manjushri; model by Holger Neuwirth and Carmen Auer

(right) The Drigung lineage in the top story of the Sumtsek, entry wall, left side; ca. 1220; mineral pigments on clay; photograph by Jaroslav Poncar

and their clothing is covered with paintings of the holy places of Kashmir, the life of a buddha, and the mahasiddhas.

As stated by inscriptions within the Sumtsek and a slightly later monument, the Pelden Drepung Chorten (previously referred to as Great Stupa), the temple was founded by the master (*lobpon*) Tsultrim Wo of the Dro family. In the top story of the Sumtsek, this master pays homage to a lineage of teachers ending with Drigungpa, that is, Jikten Gonpo Rinchen Pel (1143–1217), the founder of a branch of the Kagyu tradition named after the monastery he founded, Drigung. A close study of the inscription written by Tsultrim Wo for the Pelden Drepung Chorten further reveals that it is dedicated to Drigungpa as well, and that Tsultrim Wo, besides the Sumtsek, built a shrine for his relics.[5] This may well be a reference to the chorten (Sanskrit: stupa) originally placed in the center of the Sumtsek, the shape of the current chorten indicating that it is a more recent replacement.

Family Monastery

Combining the information from these two monuments with that of the earlier Main Temple founded by the master Kelden Sherab, it is clear that the Alchi Choskhor was a family monastery inherited from uncle to nephew. Such arrangements were common for Tibetan monasteries at the time.

The Dro clan was already prominent during the Tibetan Empire (seventh to ninth century), and during the later spread of Buddhism in Tibet (tenth to eleventh century) it established itself in western Tibet. As the recently identified foundation inscription of the Sumtsek establishes, the branch of the family that founded Alchi was based in Sumda, a village in the valley parallel to and south of Alchi.[6] The family likely controlled trade moving between the western Tibetan Plateau and the Kashmir Valley, giving them the means to establish their own monastery and sustain it for several generations.

The artists who painted the earlier monuments of the complex—the Main Temple, the Sumtsek, the Pelden Drepung Chorten, the Tashi Gomang Chorten (previously called Small Stupa), and the Jampel Lhakhang (or Manjushri Temple)—are thought to have come from Kashmir, while the structures established subsequently were likely decorated by local artists. The shift in workmanship, accompanied by changes in the material quality and the religious content of the monuments within and around the Alchi Choskhor, directly reflects changes in economic circumstances and the religious environment in which they were established. The moves from depictions of the Yogatantra to those of Highest Yogatantra themes—most notably, deities in sexual embrace—and from an independent western Tibetan tradition to one closely aligned with central Tibet are most remarkable. Representative of the latter is the so-called Lhakhang Soma, the New Temple, with images of the highest Yogatantra deities covering its main wall.

Religious Politics

Traditionally, the temples of Alchi—and many other monuments throughout the region predating the fifteenth century—are credited to the great translator (*lotsawa*) Rinchen Zangpo (958–1055). Within the Alchi Choskhor such credit is expressed by the Lotsawa Lhakhang ("Translator's Temple"), whose name directly refers to him. This naively painted temple dates between the early monuments and the Lhakhang Soma and features the portrait of a teacher to the left of Shakyamuni on the main wall. However, the same teacher is already portrayed in the two early chortens, where he can be identified as Drigungpa based on the contexts of these depictions.[7]

Today, the Alchi Choskhor is run by Likir Monastery, which is of the Geluk tradition founded by Tsongkhapa (1357–1419). An originally conservative tradition, it directly associated itself with the teachings of Atisha Dipamkarashrijnana (ca. 982–1054), who met Rinchen Zangpo in western Tibet before traveling to central Tibet. It is therefore not surprising that when the Geluk tradition established itself in the western Himalayas through pupils of Tsongkhapa in the fifteenth century, it directly linked back to Rinchen Zangpo. This is obvious in the Red Temple, or Dukhang Dzamlinggyen, in Toling, where a triad focused on Rinchen Zangpo to the left of the niche is balanced by a triad with Tsongkhapa in its center.[8] Thus, it must have been during the spread of the Geluk tradition in the western Himalayas from the fifteenth century on that earlier monuments in the region were credited to Rinchen Zangpo, sidelining the traditions, such as the Drigungpa, that flourished in between.

See Murals at Toling Dukhang, no. 54.

For the monuments of the Alchi Choskhor this meant that portraits of Drigungpa became identified as Rinchen Zangpo. Likir Monastery even today maintains the attribution, despite the fact that it contradicts the content of the monuments. The depiction of the eighty-four mahasiddhas on Manjushri's dhoti, for example, is based on a source that certainly dates after Rinchen Zangpo's time. Dating to about 1220, it remains the earliest image of this topic preserved anywhere in the Himalayas. Further, portraying the Tibetan teacher as an awakened being, as apparent in the paintings of Drigungpa in the two early chortens at Alchi, did not become prevalent until the early thirteenth century, once again positioning the Alchi depictions at the threshold of a new development.

For another thirteenth-century depiction of the eighty-four mahasiddhas, see Virupa, no. 37.

The more recent and modern understanding of the site is an expression of a sectarianism foreign to the time when Alchi was founded. Being a family monument, attributing the foundation of the Alchi Choskhor to any tradition is misguided. Instead, the Alchi Choskhor needs to be interpreted on the basis of the information it contains, and then it offers a uniquely detailed glimpse into a past for which we have very few reliable records. In this regard, too, the value of Alchi cannot be overestimated.

Further Reading

Linrothe, Robert N. 2006. *Holy Madness: Portraits of Tantric Siddhas*. Exhibition catalog. New York: Rubin Museum of Art.

Luczanits, Christian, and Jaroslav Poncar, eds. 2023. *Alchi: The Choskhor*. Chicago: Serindia.

Luczanits, Christian. "Alchi, Ladakh," including picture galleries. http://www.luczanits.net/sites/Alchi.html.

Notes

1 The Sumtsek has been published in Goepper and Poncar 1996, which is now part of Luczanits and Poncar 2023, covering all the ancient monuments of Alchi Choskhor.
2 Davidson 1995, stanza 150.
3 On this collection of stories, see Dowman 1985; on its relation to the Alchi depictions, see Linrothe 2001b. The Tibetan title is *grub thob brgyad bcu tsa bzhi'i lo rgyus*.
4 On this siddha, see D. Martin 2006.
5 See Luczanits, forthcoming(b).
6 For a translation of this inscription, see N. Martin 2023; a more detailed study by the same author is forthcoming.
7 For detailed studies of these depictions, see Luczanits 2006a and 2015a.
8 See also the accompanying inscription in Vitali 2012a, 131–33, which makes this continuation explicit.

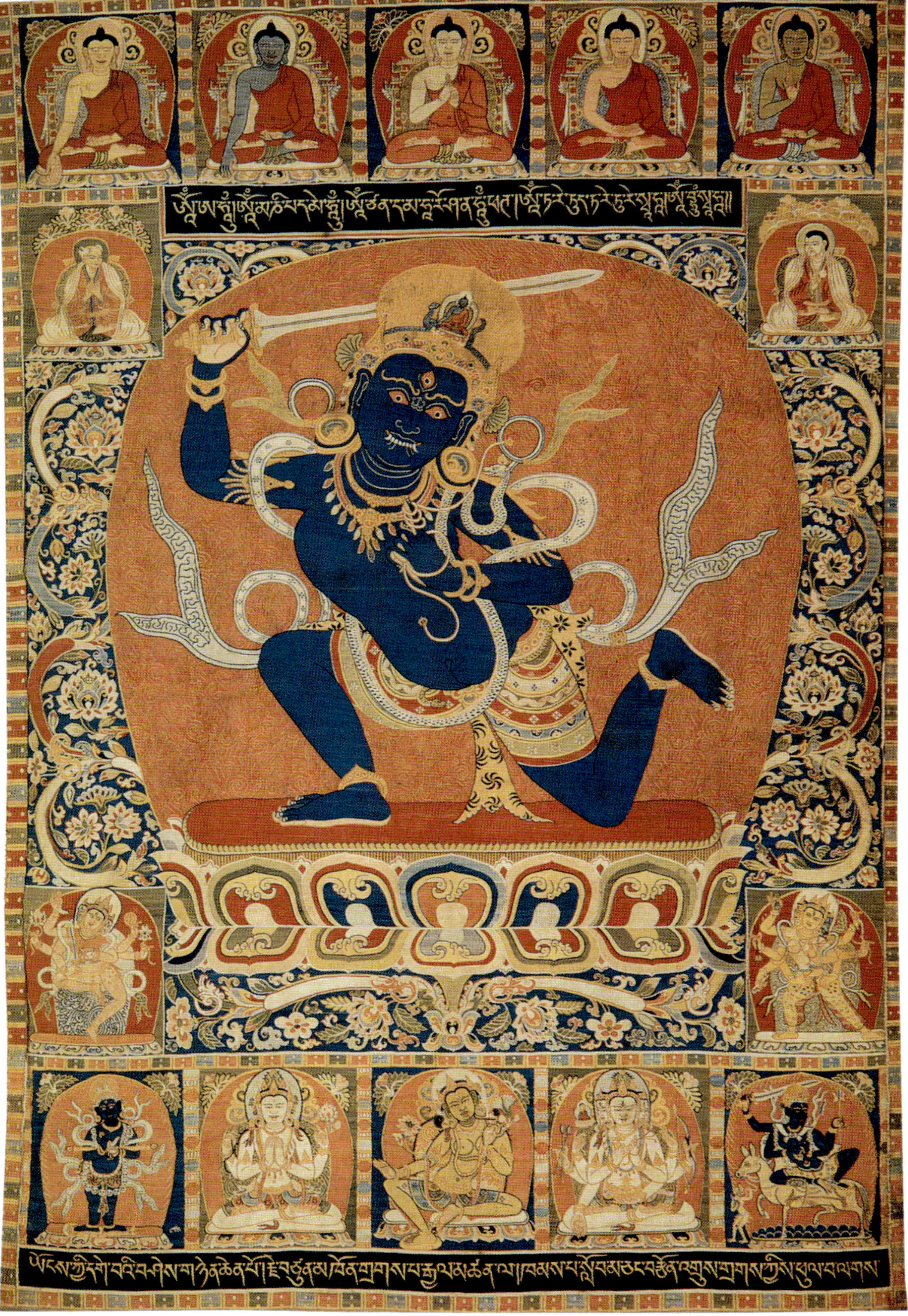

№ 36

Achala Silk Tapestry

Composition: Tangut Kingdom (Xixia), possibly produced in Dingzhou (present-day Baoding, Hebei Province, China); early to mid-13th century

Tibetan Buddhist Icons Produced in Silk

XIE JISHENG

TRANSLATED BY XINHUI YANG

Achala; composition designed in Tangut Xixia, possibly produced/woven in Dingzhou (present-day Baoding, Hebei Province, China); early–mid-13th century; *kesi* silk tapestry with seed pearl; 35⅜ × 22 in. (90 × 56 cm); Potala Palace Collection, Lhasa; image after *Tibet Museum*. 2001. Beijing: Encyclopedia of China Publishing House, 4

The Tangut Kingdom of Xixia (1038–1227) was a small but significant multiethnic kingdom that ruled the eastern end of the trade routes that connected east with west, known as the Silk Road.

Tangut patronage integrated Tibetan and Chinese religious and artistic traditions and established many practices, including the use of silk for the production of Tibetan Buddhist images. The thangka created with the technique known as *kesi* (carved silk) because of the effect it produced appeared as a special form of Tibetan art around the thirteenth century. The technique combined influences from Tibet, Tangut Xixia, and Chinese Song in the Amdo area, testifying to the exchange among different peoples during the period.

Achala

In esoteric Buddhist practice the primordial buddhas have in their retinue five deities (*vidyarajas*) to guard four cardinal directions and the center. Achala, one of the *vidyarajas*,[1] is an emanation of Vairochana and often served as guardian in early central Tibetan monasteries.[2] He seems to have been a popular deity among the Tanguts, as many depictions of Achala can be found among extant Xixia hanging scrolls (thangka).

Silk Tapestry

The *kesi* weaving technique, introduced to China from Central Asia during the Tang dynasty (618–907), was at first employed mainly for book decoration.[3] From the tenth century (Five Dynasties period), artisans began to produce works of calligraphy and painted compositions by means of this weaving technique. This method uses raw silk (*shengsi*) as the warp and boiled silk (*shusi*) of various colors as the weft. Wielding a shuttle, the artisan weaves the pattern based on a painted design specially prepared for this technique. As the finished surface produces a carved-like effect, giving the textile a three-dimensional quality, the technique became known as *kesi*, which literally means "carved silk." Many silk tapestries produced in the Tang and Song dynasties (960–1279) feature patterns of flowers and birds; figural images did not become popular until the Southern Song dynasty (1127–1279).[4]

The Tanguts innovatively produced silk tapestry featuring Tibetan Buddhist images, or thangkas, by employing Uyghur artisans (a people from today's Xinjiang region) who migrated to the Xixia territory. The Uyghur had learned the *kesi* technique in the Dingzhou region (in modern-day northwest Hebei Province) during the Northern Song (960–1127), where they had settled previously.[5] Their creative efforts generated a new artistic idiom that was followed in most silk tapestry thangkas of the Yuan (1271–1368) and Ming (1368–1644) periods, such as seen in the famous Vajrabhairava mandala silk tapestry (ca. 1329) now in the Metropolitan Museum of Art, New York. Examples of Tangut *kesi*, including the Green Tara excavated at Khara-Khoto, the portrait of Lama Zhang (1123–1194) preserved in the Potala Palace, and the Achala seen here, possess high artistic and historical value.

See Vajrabhairava Mandala, no. 46.

For more about Khara-Khoto, see A *Pancharacksha* Print from Khara-Khoto, no. 32.

Composition and Iconography

This Achala silk tapestry was based on an initial drawing or painting. The motifs of this relatively simple composition are highly decorative, with highly contrasting colors.

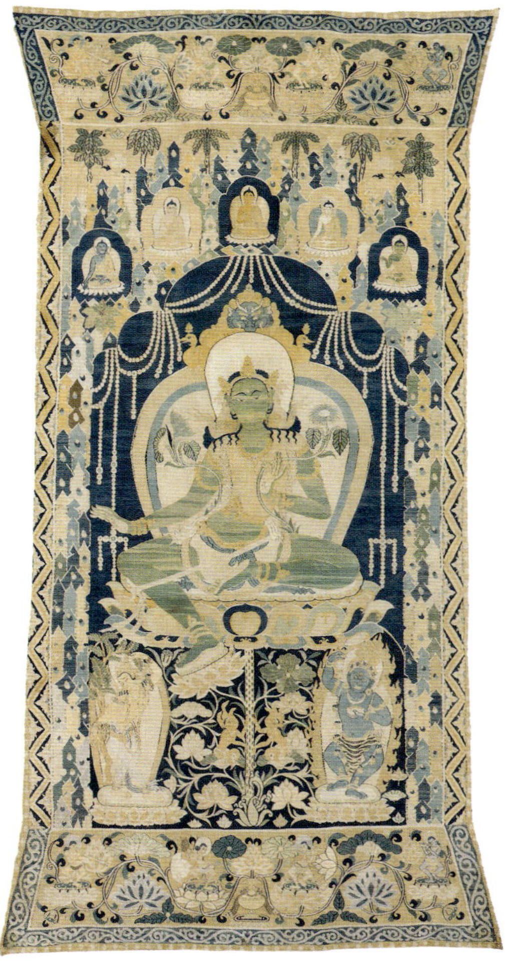

At the very top of the thangka sit the Five Tathagatas of the Vajradhatu (diamond realm): from left to right, Amoghasiddhi of the north, Akshobhya of the east, Vairochana of the center, performing the gesture of ultimate enlightenment (*uttarabodhi* or *bodhyagri* mudra), Amitabha of the west, and Ratnasambhava of the south. A large image of blue Achala, situated inside a red aureole, takes up the center of the thangka. He has one face and three eyes. His hair is tied up in a three-petaled crown commonly worn by bodhisattvas. An image of Akshobhya embellishes his hair bun. Achala is kneeling with one knee touching the ground, a position often seen in Xixia thangkas, termed *Achalasana*, or the "posture of Achala." Dressed in a lower garment (dhoti) with multicolored bands, he raises his right hand, holding a sword, while his left hand performs the threatening (*tarjani*) mudra with a lasso around his index finger.

Above Achala, a black cartouche is inscribed in gold Tibetan script with the Three-Syllable Root Mantra and mantras of bodhisattvas. From the left side: 1) the Three-Syllable Mantra, *Om a hum*; 2) the mantra of Avalokiteshvara, *Om mani padme hum*; 3) the mantra of Achala, *Om tsen da ma ha ro sha na hum pat*; 4) the mantra of Tara, *Om ta re tu ta re tu re swaha*; and 5) the mantra of the Buddha's Crown: *Om bhum swaha*.

In the lower corners adjacent to the primary deity's lotus are the three-faced, six-armed Vajrasarasvati and the three-faced, eight-armed Sitatapatra (White Parasol). Green Tara, at the center of the bottom register, is flanked by Four-Armed Avalokiteshvara and Ushnishavijaya (Victorious Crown Ornament). At the lower corners are two protective deities of the Sakya tradition: the standing two-armed Mahakala (left), who holds a *gandi* stick, and Palden Lhamo (right).

The combination of Achala and the Five Tathagatas symbolizes right effort in practicing the Buddha dharma. Vajrasarasvati and Sitatapatra indicate the guru's unhindered capacity of speech and auspiciousness, respectively. Green Tara, Avalokiteshvara, and Ushnishavijaya represent the salvation of sentient beings.

Green Tara; Tangut Xixia, excavated from Khara-Khoto; 12th–13th century; *kesi* silk tapestry; 39¾ × 20⅝ in. (101 × 52.5 cm); The State Hermitage Museum, Saint Petersburg; XX-2362; photograph by Vladimir Terebenin © The State Hermitage Museum

The Patron and Recipient

At the bottom of the composition, a golden inscription names both the patron and recipient: "The Khampa disciple Chang Tsondrudrak offers [this image] to Jetsun Khon Drakpa Gyeltsen, the great spiritual guide."[6] The recipient named here, Khon Drakpa Gyeltsen, refers to the famous third patriarch of the Sakya tradition, who lived from 1147 to 1216. The fact that the patron named in the inscription, Chang Tsondrudrak, was able to commission such an expensive silk tapestry thangka signals his high status. In the colophon of his *Precious Rosary of Religious Practice*, Drakpa Gyeltsen suggests, "The Sakya *upāsaka* (lay practitioner) Drakpa Gyeltsen received a request from Tsongkha's [Changton] *bhikṣu* (fully ordained monk) Tsöndrüdrak, by which [this text was] perceptively written after the foremost meritorious one."[7] Another text by the same author, *Noble Ornament of the Vajra Tent*, relates that "(a student named) Chenton Tsondrudrak delightfully participated in sutra copying in the sixth month, the year of male iron-horse (1210), at the Sakya Monastery in Tsang."[8] *Genealogy of the Sakya* contains a list of Drakpa Gyeltsen's disciples, among whom four had names with the element *drak*. One of them, Tsangton Tsondrubdrak, appears to be the name of this thangka donor, his name spelled slightly differently.[9]

It is interesting to note that the patron calls himself a Khampa. Before the thirteenth century, "Kham" often refers to the two regions of northeast and southeast Tibet, Do Kham, combined. The region of Tsongkha, where Drakpa Gyeltsen's colophon tells us that the patron was from, is near the Huang River and is a part of Do (northeast Tibet), called Dome during the Yuan period. In the eleventh and twelfth centuries, people of Tsongkha occasionally referred to themselves as Khampa.[10] The Tanguts who lived in Tsongkha were sometimes called Tanguts of Kham (*Kham Minyak*). For example, the two famous Xixia translators Tsami Lotsawa (twelfth century) and Ga Lotsawa (1110–1198) were both born in Tsongkha.[11]

For more about the Tibetan Empire on the Silk Road, see Bhaishajyaguru, no. 14; Imperial Carvings of Vairochana, no. 13.

The people of the kingdom of Tsongkha (1008–1104) were self-proclaimed inheritors of the Tibetan Empire in the east, their ruler Gyelse (Chinese: Gusiluo; 997–1065), a descendant of the Tibetan emperors, using the old Tibetan imperial dynastic title *tsenpo*.[12] Monastic Buddhism flourished in Tsongkha, and it played an important role in the revival of Buddhism in central Tibet as well as the transmission of Tibetan Buddhism to Tangut Xixia when they absorbed it.[13]

Dating

The figure depicted above Achala at right can be identified as the first Sakya patriarch Kunga Nyingpo (1092–1158), and the figure above him at left, the second patriarch Sonam Tsemo (1142–1182). However, it is rare that the recipient of this thangka as mentioned in the inscription, Drakpa Gyeltsen—who was the last of the Three Lay Patriarchs of Sakya—does not appear in the composition, which suggests that Drakpa Gyeltsen was still alive when the original design of the thangka was commissioned. This also corresponds well with the date 1210, when Chang Tsondrudrak reportedly joined the sutra copying event held by Drakpa Gyeltsen at Sakya Monastery. Thus, the original painting this silk tapestry is based on was likely created in the early thirteenth century.[14]

This Achala composition and other extant early *kesi* thangkas are related to the lamas of Sakya or Kagyu sect, roughly in the early to mid-thirteenth century. Just at this period, in Hangzhou and other Southern Song locations, no *kesi* technique for producing Tibetan Buddhist icons existed. From the ninth to the twelfth century, many Uyghur artisans migrated to the Gansu Corridor and North China, bringing new *kesi* skills with them, and the places where they settled became centers of *kesi* production. However, there was no tradition of *kesi* technique in the Tsongkha River basin or in central Tibet. Monk donors in the Xixia court who offered or donated a *kesi* thangka to his lama (guru) had to commission its weaving in the areas adjacent to Xixia. In the twelfth and thirteenth centuries, China's *kesi* centers included Dingzhou, which linked Tangut Xixia, Khitan Liao (916–1125)/Jurchen Jin (1115–1234), and Chinese Northern Song by trade routes.

Further Reading:

Xie Jisheng. 2019. "Tibetan Buddhism and Tibetan Buddhist Art in the Xixia Kingdom." In *Faith and Empire: Art and Politics in Tibetan Buddhism*, edited by Karl Debreczeny, 82–103. Exhibition catalog. New York: Rubin Museum of Art. https://issuu.com/rmanyc/docs/faith_and_empire.

Watt, James C. Y., and Anne E. Wardell. 1997. *When Silk Was Gold: Central Asian and Chinese Textiles*, esp. 53–63, 90–103, 202–9. Exhibition catalog. New York: The Metropolitan Museum of Art.

Sørensen, Per K., and Guntram Hazod. 2007. *Rulers on the Celestial Plain: Ecclesiastic and Secular Hegemony in Medieval Tibet; A Study of Tshal Gung-thang*, 2:253–380. Vienna: Verlag der Österreichischen Akademie der Wissenschaften.

Notes

1 Śubhakarasiṃha, *Uṣṇīṣa Vijaya Dhāraṇī Sūtra*, Tripitaka, vol. 18, no. 906, https://cbetaonline.dila.edu.tw/zh/T18n0906_p0912b07?q.

2 Achala and Hayagriva protected the ritual precinct of the mandala, as in Yulin Cave 29 and Cave 7 at the Eastern Thousand Buddha Caves complex; Xie Jisheng 2019, 88.

3 Hong Hao 2008, 117; Zhou Mi 2001, 210.

4 Cao 2012, 231; *Yuandai huasu ji* 2005, 1–3.

5 Dingzhou of the Northern Song (today's Baoding, Hebei Province) was not only a center of silk tapestry production but also a pathway connecting the Xixia and the Liao. Until the Hongzhi period of the Ming dynasty, there still were Xixia descendants living in this region. See Hong Hao 2008, 117; Zhuang 1983, 33.

6 yongs kyi dge ba'i bshes gnyen chen po/ rje btsun mkhon grags pa rgyal mtshan la/ khams pa slob ma cang brtson 'grus grags kyis phul ba lags/.

7 Tsangwang Gendun Tenpa 2019, 106; Grags pa rgyal mtshan 2007a, 241.

8 Sørensen and Hazod 2007, 2:367–68; Grags pa rgyal mtshan 2007b, 247–48.

9 For Tsangton Tsondrubdrak (Gtsang ston brtson 'grub grags), see Ngag dbang kun dga' bsod nams 1986, 83.

10 Sørensen and Hazod 2007, 2:368.

11 Sørensen and Hazod 2007, 2:368.

12 The kingdom of Tsongkha is primarily known through Chinese sources, such as the *Qingtang lu* 青唐录.

13 See Xie Jisheng 2001; Xie Jisheng 2019, 83–85.

14 For different opinions on the dating of this silk tapestry, see Su 1996, 375; Watt and Wardell 1997, 91–93; Xie Jisheng 2001, 106–7; Sørensen and Hazod 2007, 367–76; Broeskamp 2009; Tsangwang Gendun Tenpa 2019, 106–7.

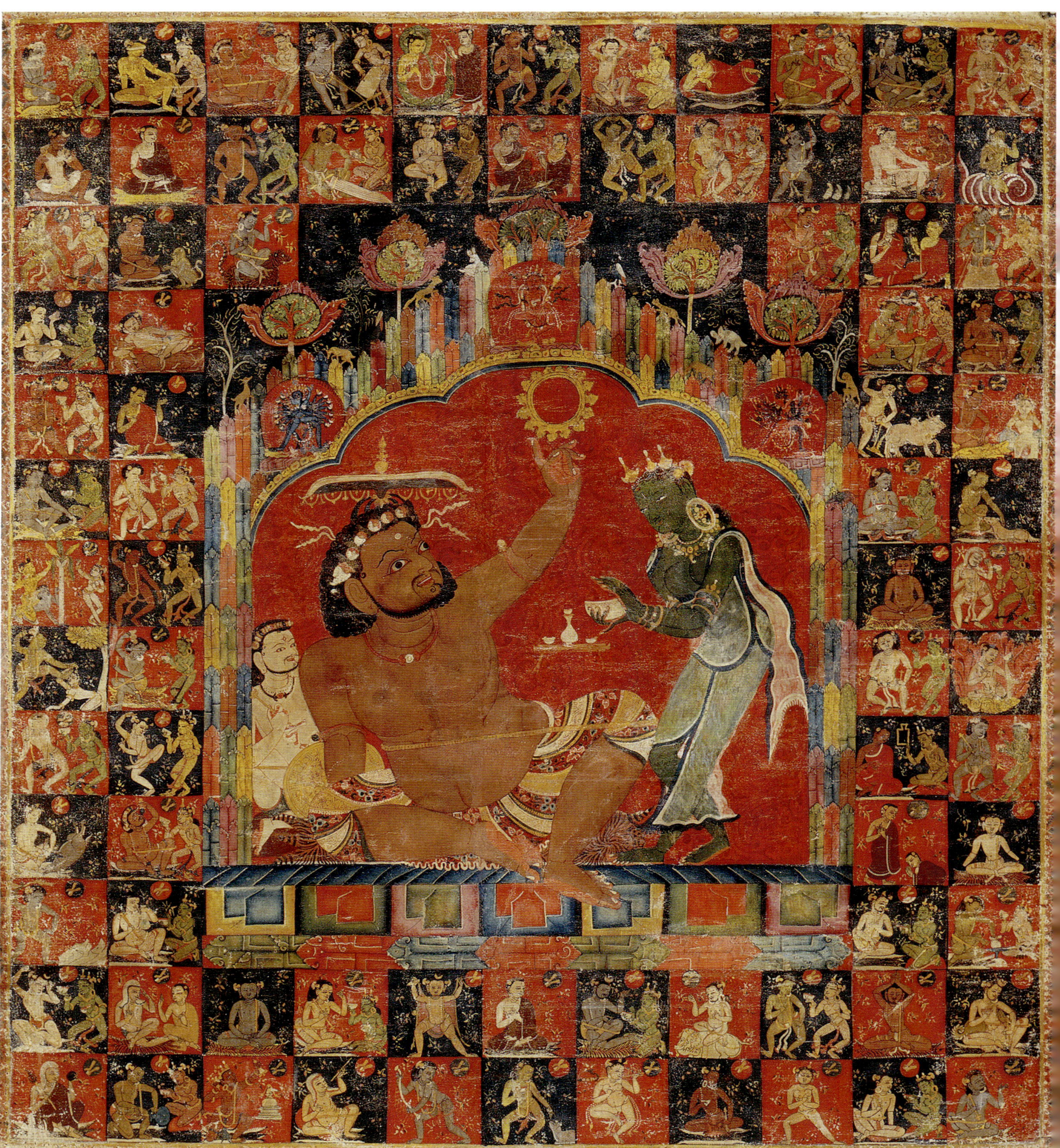

№ 37

Virupa

Sakya Monastery, Tsang region, central Tibet, ca. 1216–1244

A Masterwork Depicting Tantric Masters of the Sakya Tradition

JANE CASEY

The painting recounts an episode in the life of Virupa, an Indian yogi of about the tenth century.[1] Having resided for twenty-four years at Somanatha Monastery in eastern India, he was ejected for eating the monastery's pigeons.[2] He abandoned the life of a monk and embraced the life of a wandering yogi, performing miracles, engaging others in debate, and living off the land. One day he entered a tavern and feasted and drank until the barmaid asked him for payment. He responded by pledging to pay when the sun set. He then arrested the sun's motion, and continued to drink. The country was thrown into chaos by the endless days. King Kanasata sought a solution. In a dream, the Sun Goddess informed him that she was bound by Virupa's pledge to the barmaid. On waking, the king paid Virupa's debt, Virupa disappeared, and the sun continued in its course.[3]

In this painting, Virupa is shown at the moment of arresting the sun. A corpulent figure seated on a tiger pelt, he leans on his right hand as he raises his left arm, pointing to a golden orb above. He has large, mesmeric eyes, a full beard, and long, dark locks. A green goddess, likely Tara, the Buddhist goddess of compassion, offers him a drink in a skull cup. A tray behind them is set with cups and a libation urn. The scene refers to the episode in the tavern, although the setting is a mountain cave, above which appear the deities Nairatmya ("No Self"), directly overhead, Chakrasamvara, and Hevajra.[4] Surrounding the central scene are eighty-two cartouches, each with scenes of yogis, yoginis, and other Buddhist practitioners.

In medieval eastern India, a key archetype of Buddhist practice was the mahasiddha (great accomplished one), referring to individuals who often received formal training in the monastic universities of northern India but left these centers to pursue their tantric practice in seclusion, in nature, and on the margins of society. These maverick yogis attracted disciples, including Tibetans, because of their profound if unconventional wisdom. Virupa was one of the most celebrated mahasiddhas. That he could overcome the power of the natural world (arresting the sun) while consuming large amounts of alcohol demonstrates both his extraordinary power and his unconventional path.

Virupa and Tibet

For more about Tibetan involvement with the Mongol Empire, see Mahakala Stone Sculpture, no. 39; Mongol Messenger's Badge, no. 42; White Stupa, no. 40; Vajrabhairava Mandala, no. 46; Juyong Guan Stupa Gate, no. 48; Mural Painting at Zhalu Monastery, no. 47.

Virupa; Sakya Monastery, Tsang region, central Tibet; ca. 1216–1244; distemper on cloth; 22 × 19⅝ in. (55.9 × 49.8 cm); The Kronos Collections; photograph by John Bigelow Taylor

Virupa was particularly important to the Sakya tradition of Tibetan Buddhism. Sakya founder Khon Konchok Gyelpo (1034–1102) is said to have received teachings directly from Virupa, whom he saw in visions at Sakya Monastery over the period of a month.[5] Sachen Kunga Nyingpo (1092–1158) composed songs of praise to Virupa, from whom he also sought spiritual instruction. An inscription on the verso of the painting establishes its association with Sakya Monastery during the second quarter of the thirteenth century. The inscription states, "Sakya Pandita performed the rite of consecration of this [painting] of Virupa, the Great Lord of Yoga, together with his retinue of eighty [*sic*] mahasiddhas."[6] Kunga Gyeltsen (1182–1251), also known as Sakya Pandita because of his fluency in Sanskrit, served as Tibetan emissary to the court of the Mongol prince Köten (fl. 1235–1247). The Sakya tradition played a critical role in forging close relations with the powerful Mongol rulers of China. Sakya Pandita was a deft diplomat, securing a great deal of autonomy for Tibet in exchange for spiritual counsel and generous tribute. The consecration mentioned in the verso inscription would have occurred between 1216, when Sakya Pandita became abbot of Sakya on the death of his uncle Khon Drakpa Gyeltsen, and 1244, the year he left Sakya Monastery for the Mongol court in Liangzhou, former seat of the Tanguts,

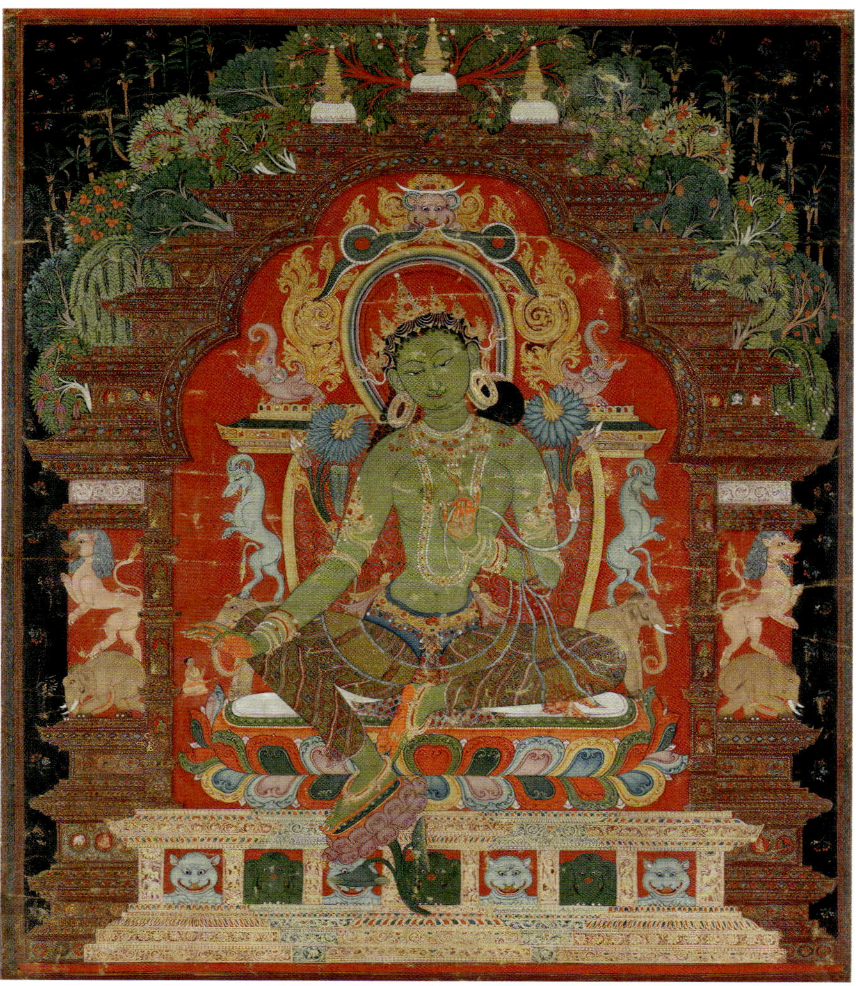

Tara; central Tibet; ca. 1300; distemper on cloth; 20⅝ × 17 in. (52.4 × 43.2 cm); The Cleveland Museum of Art; purchase from the J. H. Wade Fund, by exchange; 1970.156; CC0 - Creative Commons (CC0 1.0)

where he remained until his death. All Tibetan sacred objects are consecrated, usually soon after the object is created, although they can also be reconsecrated. After consecration, an object is thought to be the embodiment of the divine. The purpose of consecration rituals is to invoke the Wisdom Being (Sanskrit: *Jnanasattva*, Tibetan: *yeshe sempa*), invite it to dwell within the painting or sculpture, and ensure that it abides there.[7]

Virupa and other Indian mahasiddhas became recognized authorities for specific Buddhist teachings in Tibet. Indian authorities were of critical importance, particularly during the eleventh, twelfth, and thirteenth centuries, while Tibetans were assimilating Buddhist teachings from India. Lineages of teachers and teachings arose, always rooted in one or more Indian masters, many of whom are said to have themselves received teachings directly from a Buddhist divinity. Virupa, for example, is believed to have been instructed in the liberative teachings of the Hevajra Tantra by the deity Nairatmya. The teachings associated with Virupa, known as "Path and Result" (*Lamdre*),[8] became the central tantric system of the Sakya tradition in Tibet, involving both intellectual training and experiential cultivation of meditation techniques. The teachings were transmitted from one generation to the next by accomplished masters who ensured that a worthy disciple mastered the teachings and passed them on to the following generation.

Iconography and Style

The painting offers one of the earliest representations of Virupa in Himalayan art. Throughout the centuries, both painters and sculptors portrayed him in this iconographic form, as a corpulent seated figure pointing to the sun.[9] One of the most famous examples is seen in a gilt-copper alloy sculpture of Virupa produced under Yongle patronage in China (r. 1402–1424).[10] He also appears in this form in a painting of about the mid-fifteenth century depicting the transmission of Lamdre teachings from celestial deities Vajradhara and Nairatmya to Virupa and then to his disciple Kanha.[11]

The style of the painting indicates the artist was Newar, from the Kathmandu Valley in Nepal. Newars are descended from some of the earliest inhabitants of the Kathmandu Valley. Theirs was a particularly exalted aesthetic, refined over many centuries, coupled with exceptional technical skill in the arts of painting, sculpture, and architecture. Tibetans solicited Newar artists for special commissions, and beginning in the seventh century, Newar artists traveled to Tibet, seeking commissions from the rapidly developing Buddhist communities. The sketchbook by Newar artist Jivarama dated 1435 in this volume may have been created while he was traveling in Tibet to seek commissions. Newar artists left a lasting legacy in Tibet by fulfilling commissions at monasteries and temples throughout the country, often returning to Nepal after months or years of working in Tibet.

See Jivarama's Sketchbook, no. 56.

The inscription recording a consecration by Sakya Pandita provides a secure range of dates to the work, between 1216 and 1244, and helps to anchor in time related Tibetan paintings in the Newar style.[12] A superb painting of Tara within a jewel-like temple enveloped by trees is another example of Newar-style painting produced for Tibetan patrons.[13] Here, below Tara's right hand, a Tibetan patron is shown wearing the monastic short-sleeved vest unique to Tibetan Buddhist communities.[14] The painting of

Virupa, like that of Tara, favors a palette of deep vibrant red, jade green, and a pale but rich blue. Figures observe petite proportions, corresponding to the Nepalese people. Clothing and textile patterns follow Nepalese models, and the jewelry resembles that worn by the Nepalese. In the Virupa painting, Virupa sits on a mountain floor consisting of multicolored cubes, also a Nepalese convention.[15] Both paintings present the deity within a five-lobed arch. Beyond these elements, the Newar style can be distinguished from others flourishing in Tibet in this period by the line—thin, wiry, lyrical, and capable of conveying rounded volumes and convincing mass. Three compositions of celestial buddhas (*tathagatas*) are also to be considered in this group of thirteenth-century paintings produced for Sakya patrons by Newar artists.[16] A distinction can be made between paintings made by Newar artists for Tibetan patrons (all of the above-cited works) and Newar paintings produced for Nepalese patrons (an outstanding example can be found in a painting of Vajradhara and consort, dated 1488, in the Musée Guimet in Paris).[17] Nepalese works for Nepalese patrons often encompass Hindu iconography (less common in Tibetan art), Nepalese throne and temple architecture, and patronage narratives that include musicians, dancers, and local kings and their families. Tibetan artists also worked in the Newar style, although more research is needed to understand the history of this tradition in Tibetan painting.

See Chakrasamvara Mandala with Newar Donors, no. 29.

Further Reading

Dowman, Keith. 1985. *Masters of Mahamudra: Songs and Histories of the Eighty-Four Buddhist Siddhas.* Albany: SUNY Press.

Jackson, David P. 2010. *The Nepalese Legacy in Tibetan Painting: Early Beri to Ngor.* Masterworks of Tibetan Painting Series 2. Exhibition catalog. New York: Rubin Museum of Art. https://issuu.com/rmanyc/docs/nepalese_legacy_96.

Kossak, Steven M. 1997. "Sakya Patrons and Nepalese Artists in Thirteenth-Century Tibet." In *Tibetan Art: Towards a Definition of Style*, edited by Jane Casey Singer and Philip Denwood, 26–37. London: Laurence King Publishing.

Notes

1 The dates for Virupa are disputed. They range from circa eighth century to circa the last quarter of the tenth century. See Davidson 2005, 53; Dowman 1985, 44–46. Davidson argues that Virupa's late tenth-century date is grounded in his association with Somanatha Monastery, which was built by Mularaja I about 960–973 and then destroyed by Mahmud of Ghazna in 1026.

2 Dowman 1985, 44.

3 See Dowman 1985, 44–46.

4 This form of Hevajra is known as Kapaladhara. See Mallmann 1975, 185.

5 Tulku Thondup Rinpoche 1982, 33.

6 *rnal 'byor gyi dbang phyug chen po 'bi ru ba la 'khor 'grub chen brgyad bcus bskor ba 'di'i rab tu gnas pa'i cho ga chos rje sa skya pan dhi tas mdzod/*

7 See the work of Yael Bentor 1995b and 1996.

8 See Buswell and Lopez 2014, 464–65; Cornu 2001, 308–9.

9 Textual sources for this iconography are noted in Davidson 2002, 403n60.

10 Cleveland Museum of Art, 1972.96, https://www.clevelandart.org/art/1972.96.

11 Cleveland Museum, 1960.206, https://www.clevelandart.org/art/1960.206.

12 This term refers not only to Newar artists' work under Tibetan patronage but also to works created by Tibetan artists following and inspired by Newar painting traditions. More research is needed to clarify the Newar traditions in Tibetan art.

13 Cleveland Museum, 1970.156, https://www.clevelandart.org/art/1970.156.

14 Huntington and Huntington 1990, 329–33.

15 Compare with Pal 1975, no. 57.

16 Kossak and Singer 1998, 138–43. See also Kossak 1997; D. Jackson 2010.

17 Published in Auboyer and Béguin 1977, 120, 123, fig. 97.

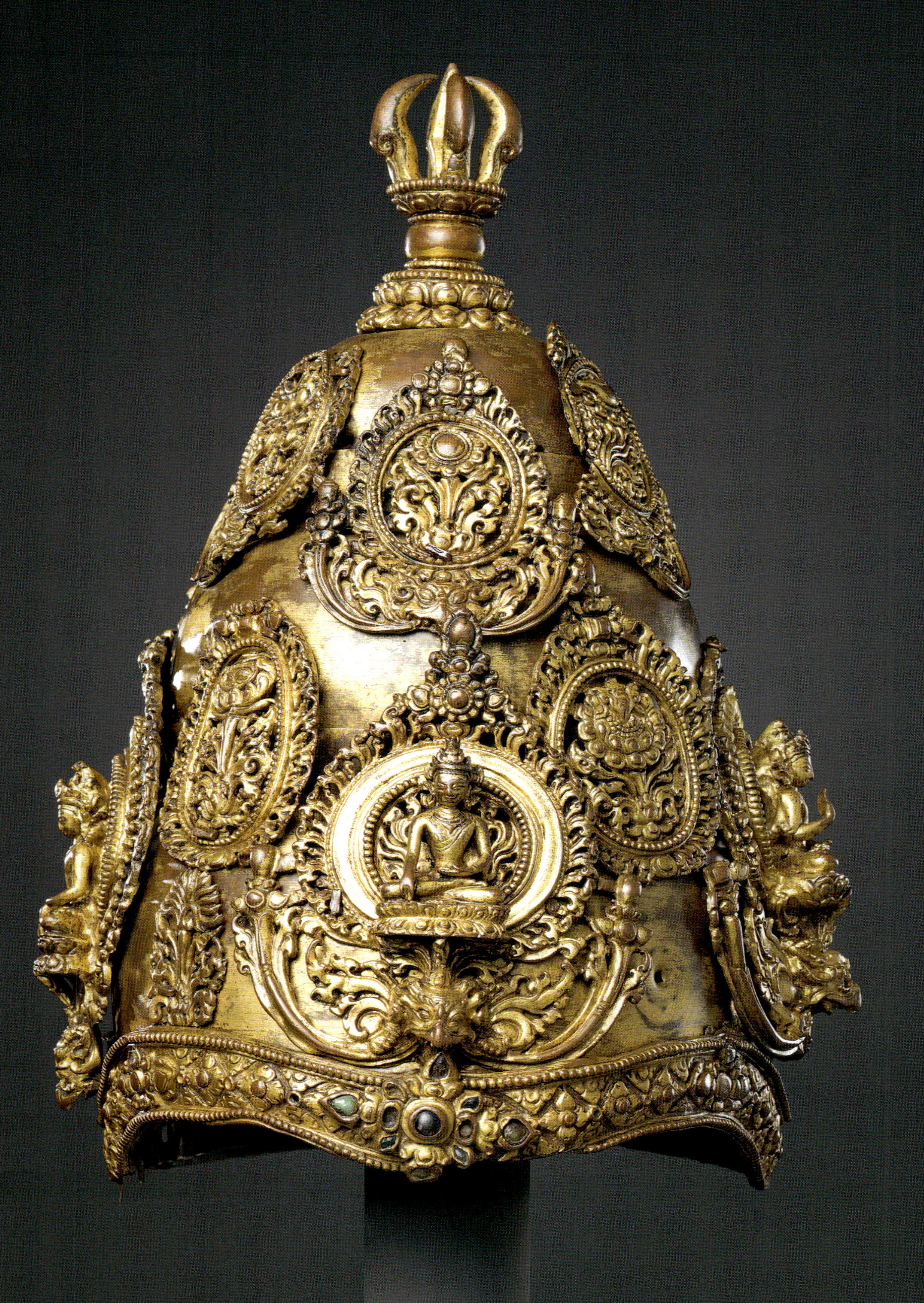

№ 38

Vajracharya Priest's Crown

Nepal, ca. 13th century

Cosmos, Empowerment, and Ritual Regalia

AURORA GRALDI

NEPALESE BUDDHISM REVOLVES AROUND RITUALS, and Vajracharya crowns are a visual manifestation of this elaborate system of rituals. Crowns such as this one, the main ritual regalia worn by Vajracharya priests at crucial moments of Vajrayana ceremonies, serve as potent symbols of the magical power of specialized priests and underscore their high status in the Newar social structure.

This crown has a singular iconographic configuration that makes it unique to the Nepalese Buddhist artistic tradition. In Nepalese Buddhism, Vajrayana refers to the esoteric tantric path followed by the Newars of the Kathmandu Valley to attain enlightenment. The Vajrayana path entails the worship of tantric deities and the fulfillment of an awakened state through the performance of esoteric rituals.

Vajracharya Crowns as Three-Dimensional Mandalas

The priest's crown has an oblong shape composed of three semispheres of decreasing size. Openwork medallions with different motifs and figures are evenly distributed on the crown. It is topped by a vajra, the prominent five-prong instrument with a stylized lotus flower and a central pearl at the base. On the lowest level of the helmet, four medallions depicting four of the Five Cosmic Buddhas are positioned in correspondence with the cardinal directions. Each crowned buddha, framed by a halo, sits cross-legged on a lotus pedestal atop a mythical golden-winged bird with a ferocious expression (*garuda*). The four Cosmic Buddhas seen here, Akshobhya, Amitabha, Amoghasiddhi, and Ratnasambhava, make hand gestures specific to each buddha. The fifth Cosmic Buddha, Vairochana, is symbolized by the half vajra at the top. The upper level of the helmet displays openwork medallions decorated with lotus flowers and foliate motifs and a celestial goddess holding a windblown sash.

For more about the *garuda*, see Vishnu Riding on Garuda, no. 18.

The components of this crown present the core iconographic elements of a mandala. Within the Vajrayana tradition, a mandala is a cosmic diagram of symbols representing the entire universe. Mandalas can be rendered in many visual forms: mural paintings, paintings on cloth, three-dimensional compositions, or temporary sand creations. The mandala of the Five Cosmic Buddhas is among the most common. The Vajracharya crown is a three-dimensional construction of this theme. The helmet embodies Mount Meru, which is the fulcrum of the universe. The four Cosmic Buddhas preside over pure realms in the south, north, west, and east and guide the Vajrayana practitioners in the path toward enlightenment. Vairochana is the ultimate deity of the Vajrayana system: he is placed at the center of the cosmic field, and in the figurative form holds a vajra with two five-prong finials in his right hand; in this crown he is denoted by the vajra itself. This pentad of Cosmic Buddhas is represented in a superb forehead ornament made of settings of precious stones: the four directional Buddhas flank the double-pronged vajra at the center, which is made of a setting of crystal and turquoise.

See Chakrasamvara Mandala with Newar Donors, no. 29; Mandala of Manjuvajra of the *Vajravali* Set, no. 50; Kalachakra Mandala in the Potala Palace, no. 77.

For more about Vairochana, see Imperial Carvings of Vairochana, no. 13.

Vajracharya Priest's Crown; Nepal; ca. 13th century; copper, gold, crystal, turquoise; 14 × 8½ × 9½ in. (35.6 × 21.6 × 22.9 cm); The Metropolitan Museum of Art, New York; Gift of Bashford Dean, 1906; 06.19; CC0 - Creative Commons (CC0 1.0)

Crowns: Ritual Regalia of Vajracharya Priests

In Sanskrit, the term "Vajrayana" means the "way of the vajra" or the "Diamond way," and "Vajracharya" means "Masters of the Diamond Way." The vajra is, indeed, the archetypal symbol of tantric Buddhism in Nepal and alludes to the adamantine state of existence of human beings who reach full enlightenment. It is represented in the three most important ritual regalia of Vajracharya priests: the vajra ritual scepter, the vajra bell, and the crown. Initially, the crown is gifted to young boys who descend from

Vajracharya families during the initiation ceremony.[1] This initiation ceremony consists of a complex series of rituals that consecrate boys as Vajra priests and invest them with the esoteric power to perform Vajrayana rituals. At the climax of this ceremony, the initiated boy wears the consecrated crown, while holding in his hands the consecrated vajra scepter and bell. Through this consecration, the crown acquires ritual agency: it empowers Vajracharya's high status. The act of wearing this crown evokes the priest's religious achievement: the head of the priest aligns with the central axis—corresponding to the half vajra at the top of the crown—and identifies with Buddha Vairochana himself. A direct visual parallel with Vairochana gives the priest authority to guide other practitioners on the path to enlightenment.

For more on vajra and its symbolism, see *Dorje* Discovered by Dorje Lingpa, no. 51.

The crown, the property of Vajracharya families, is often transmitted from generation to generation. After the performance of the initiation ceremony, it becomes an essential accoutrement in the rituals of the consecration and empowering of sacred images and monuments. Vajracharya priests officiate at these usually communal rituals for the salvation of all Buddhist devotees in public spaces, in the presence of donors who commissioned the ceremony.

Newar Buddhism constitutes an elaborate pluralistic religious system, which combines ancient forms of Mahayana and Vajrayana Buddhism of Indian origin. The Newar Buddhist community is organized in castes, whose classification relates to ritual, social, and economic allocations.[2] Within this socioreligious caste structure, Vajracharya occupy the highest position and are recognized by the entire Buddhist community as the officiating priests. Vajracharya have the duty to perform rituals and to guide the spiritual life of the community. They are married, householder monks; the observance of marriage rules and caste endogamy, as well the initiation ceremony of young Vajracharya boys, are pivotal to this system. Traditionally, Vajracharya and their families reside in compounds known as *baha* (*vihara*, in Sanskrit), likely former monasteries built around the main shrine and the courtyard where Vajracharya perform rituals. The architectural structure of the Nepalese monastery develops from ancient models in northeastern India, such as those found at Nalanda.

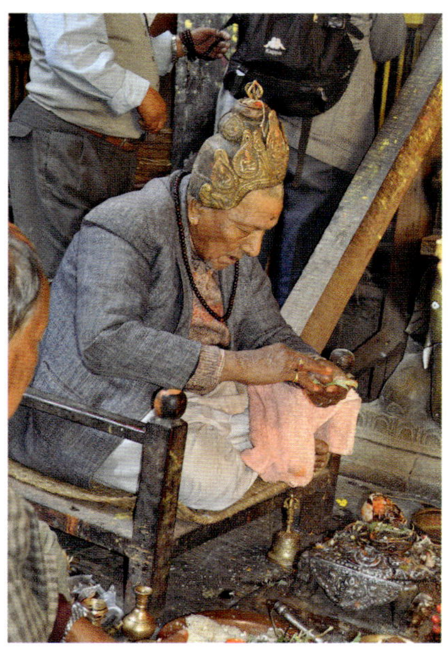

A Vajracharya priest wearing a crown with the Five Cosmic Buddhas performs a tantric ceremony, a vajra bell visible on the floor, in the monastery of Kwa Baha, Nepal, in 2011; photograph © Kerry Lucinda Brown

An Ancient Ritual Regalia, a Continuing Tradition

The usage of this type of crown in tantric ceremonies goes back to at least the twelfth century, when Nepal had close interactions with the religious and artistic traditions of the Buddhist Pala Kingdom (eighth to twelfth century).[3] Crowns from this period are rare; the earliest surviving crown dates to 1145, and a few other crowns dating from the thirteenth to the seventeenth century are now conserved in museum collections. The crown presented here is among the earliest surviving examples; the high quality of the craftsmanship, the elongated shape, the simple representation of figures and motifs allow one to ascribe this crown to the thirteenth century.

Nepalese scroll paintings (*paubhas*) give extensive insight into the usage of Vajracharya crowns and the associated ritual practices in ancient times. The lower register of these scroll paintings often portrays ritual scenes in which the officiating priest wears a crown of similar shape. In the Mandala of the Sun God Surya Surrounded by Eight Planetary Deities, a detail showcases a priest performing the fire ritual in front of his acolytes wearing elegant ritual garments and a multitiered crown of golden color.

This is a living tradition in the Kathmandu Valley, which persisted throughout the centuries and the complex social and doctrinal changes in Newar Buddhism. Vajracharya crowns are still produced by local artisans; the iconographic composition remains identical, while the shape and stylistic lexicon reflect modern manufacture and taste. While performing lavish tantric ceremonies, Vajracharya priests today sit cross-legged in monastic courtyards surrounded by votive lamps. Dressed in colorful silk garments with gold embroidery and wearing a crown, they hold a bell and a vajra scepter in their hands as they recite mantras in front of the Buddhist community.[4]

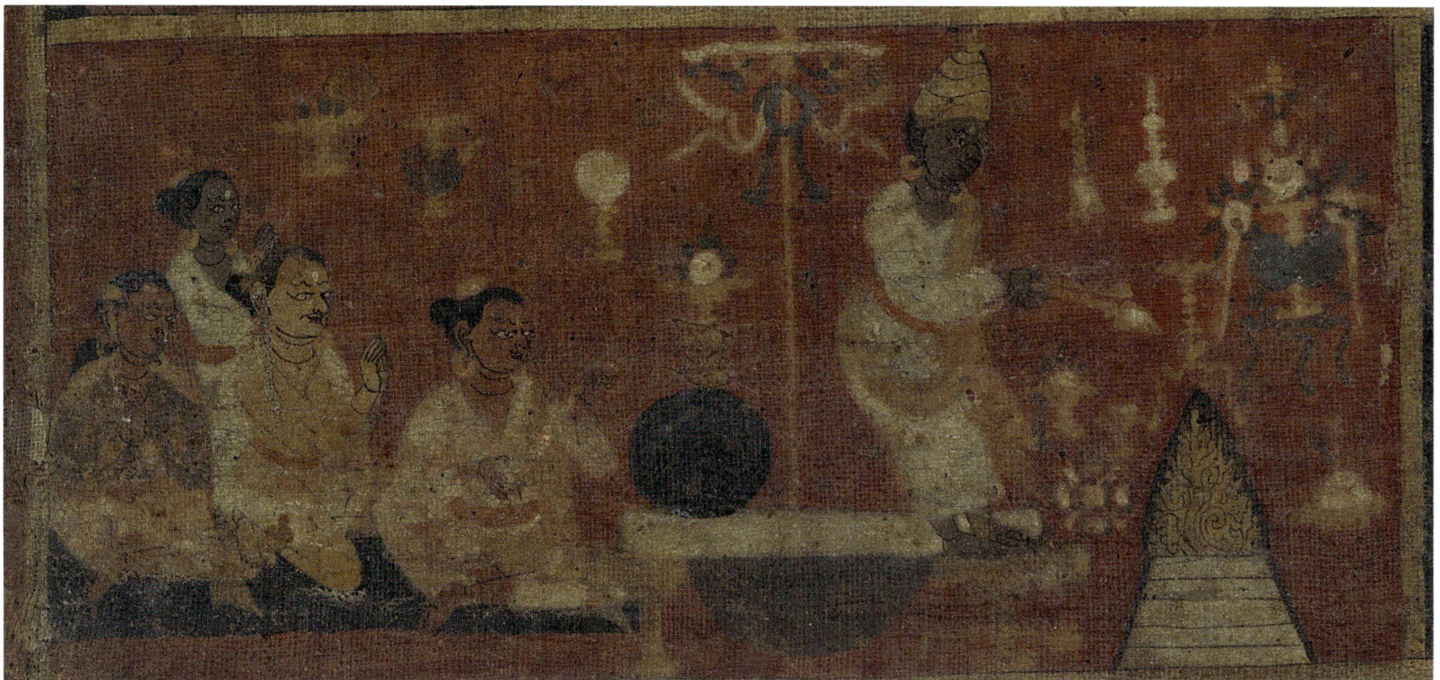

Detail of Mandala of the Sun God Surya Surrounded by Eight Planetary Deities showing a Vajracharya priest performing the fire ritual in the presence of the donor's family; Nepal; dated, likely 1379; The Metropolitan Museum of Art, New York; Zimmerman Family Collection; Purchase, The Vincent Astor Foundation and Friends of Asian Art Gifts, 2012; 2012.462; image © The Metropolitan Museum of Art, image source Art Resource, NY

Vajracharya Crowns: Masterpieces of Repoussé Technique by Newar Artisans

Vajracharya crowns exemplify the skills of Newar artisans working in the repoussé technique, which has thrived in the Kathmandu Valley since at least the seventh century. The central component of the crown is made from sheets of embossed copper. Medallions and other decorative elements are attached to it with rivets and split pins, expertly hidden in the elaborate design. The surface is then fire gilt with an amalgam of mercury and gold. Newar artisans are rightly considered among the most accomplished metalworkers in Asia, and the traditional repoussé technique, mastered in the workshops of the Kathmandu Valley, is still practiced today. Crystals and turquoise are inset into the front band of the crown, and other semiprecious stones are visible on the halos surrounding the four Cosmic Buddhas. The only cast element of the crown is the half vajra at the top.

Further Reading

Guy, John. 2018. "Crowns of the Vajra Masters: Tracing Nepalese Buddhist Ritual Art." *Orientations* 49, no. 2 (March/April): 90–101.

Huntington, John C., and Dina Bangdel. 2003. *The Circle of Bliss: Buddhist Meditational Art*, 560. Chicago: Serindia.

Kim, Jinah, and Todd Lewis. 2019. *Dharma and Punya: Buddhist Meditational Art*, 256. Leiden: Hotei.

Notes

1 The initiation ceremony (*acharyabhishekha*) consecrates young boys as Vajra masters. The many steps of this ceremony are thoroughly described by Gellner 1997.

2 The multifaceted aspects of the Newar Buddhist caste system have been thoroughly investigated by Gellner 1992.

3 Because of the paucity of early visual evidence, it is hard to determine the origin of these crowns and how they were deployed. Guy 2018 suggests that crowned deities of Indic Buddhist traditions provided the model for ritual crowns. Rospatt 2019 points out the difficulties in assessing the origin and the earlier development of the Vajracharya type of crown, as it is unique to Newar Buddhism of the Kathmandu Valley.

4 Two recent exhibitions, *Crowns of the Vajra Masters: Ritual Art of Nepal* at the Metropolitan Museum of Art, New York (2017– 18) and *Dharma and Punya: Buddhist Ritual Art of Nepal* at the Iris and B. Gerald Cantor Art Gallery at the College of the Holy Cross, Worcester, Massachusetts (2019), showcased the central role of ritual implements in the Nepalese context.

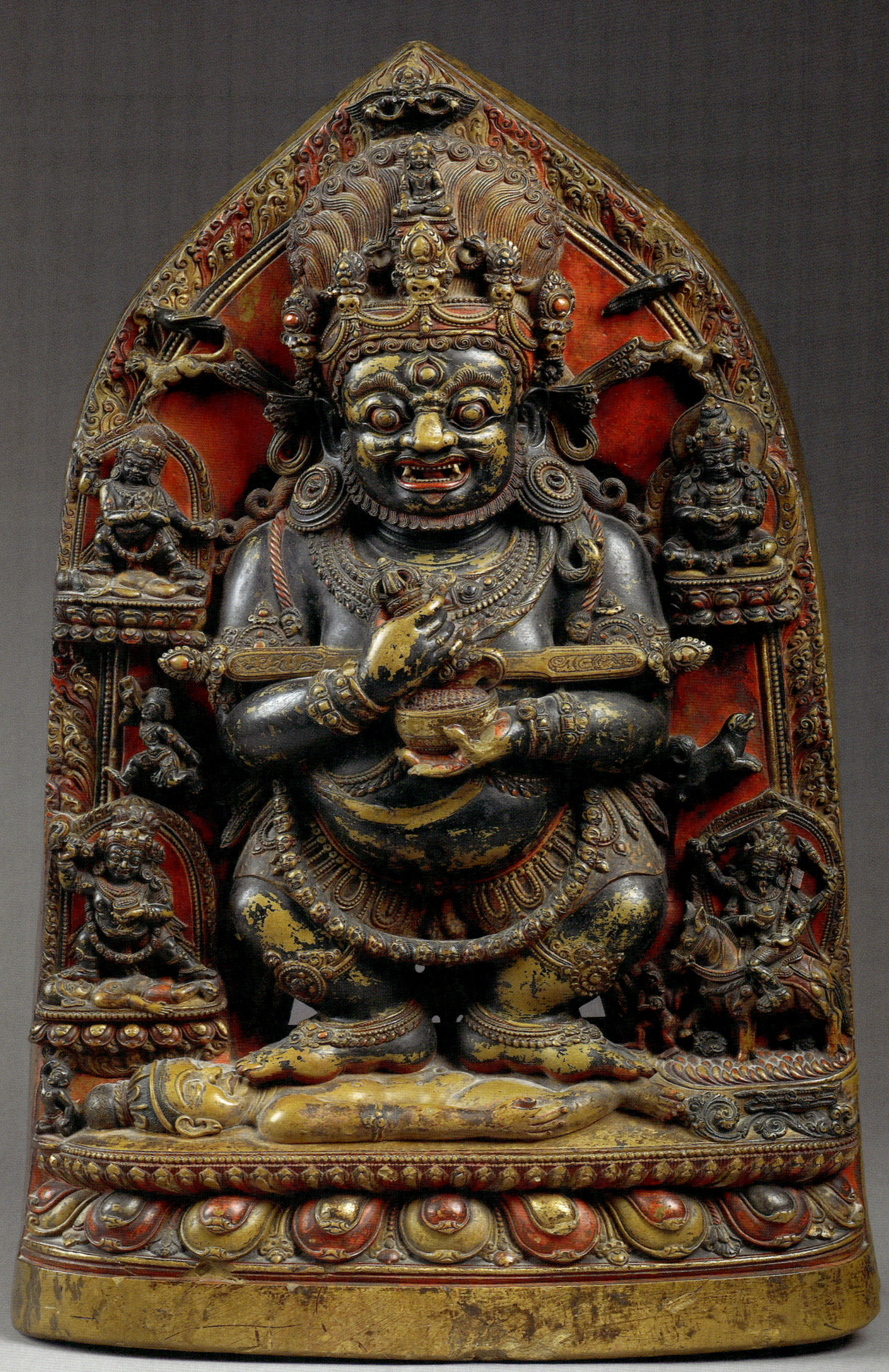

№ 39

Mahakala Stone Sculpture

Beijing, China, and Sakya Monastery, Tsang region, central Tibet, dated 1292

The Political Role of Tibetan Buddhism at the Mongol Court

KARL DEBRECZENY

A POWERFUL BUDDHIST PROTECTOR DEITY, Mahakala is a manifestation of divine wrath employed to remove internal and external obstacles. This wrathful deity is considered especially effective in military applications. Beginning in the thirteenth century, the Mongol state employed Tibetan Buddhism as a means to power, both symbolically, as a path to legitimation via sacral kingship, and literally, as a ritual technology to physical power through the use of magic, which was most clearly demonstrated in Mahakala rites. The Mongol court singled out the wrathful figure of Mahakala in his form as Panjaranatha ("Lord of the [Bone] Pavilion") as state protector and focus of the imperial cult. This form of Mahakala came to symbolize Qubilai Khan (1215–1294), the famous Mongol emperor and founder of the Yuan dynasty (1271–1368), as the wrathful destructive power of the universal sacral ruler (chakravartin). The Nepalese master artist and head of the Yuan imperial atelier Anige (1245–1306) made a sculpture of Panjaranatha Mahakala for Qubilai Khan's final conquest of China, and it became a potent symbol of both Qubilai's rule and the Yuan imperial lineage. The association was so strong that even four centuries later, when the Manchus, who conquered China in the seventeenth century, were positioning themselves as Qubilai's rightful inheritors, they installed what they claimed was the same statue of Mahakala in the Manchu imperial shrine at Mukden in 1635.[1]

For more about the Nepalese artist Anige, see White Stupa, no. 40.

For more about the Manchus' use of Tibetan Buddhism to claim inheritance of Qubilai's empire, see The Qianlong Emperor as Manjushri-Chakravartin, no. 84.

The Stone Sculpture Dated 1292

Although Qubilai Khan's Mahakala sculpture disappeared after the fall of the Qing dynasty (1644–1911), the limestone version in the Musée Guimet, dated 1292, is a product of the same context and reveals much about the tradition. Mahakala's power is conveyed through the deity's fierce appearance—bulging eyes, bared fangs, hair standing on end, a crown of skulls and bone ornaments—and his pose, squatting on a human corpse. Images of wrathful deities are commonly carved in black stone, a color closely associated with wrathful activity. Here, the stone figure of Mahakala was painted black, in keeping with the deity's iconography.

An inscription on the back of the sculpture names Qubilai Khan and his Tibetan Imperial Preceptor, Pakpa Lodro Gyeltsen (1235–1280), placing it at the very center of Mongol imperial interests:

> As for this sculpture, in order to spread the precious teachings of the Buddha far and wide and endure for a long time; to pacify obstacles to the lives of all the great patrons and priests; and to destroy all enemies, the one called Atsara Pakshi, close attendant and cared for by the kindness of the *dharmaraja* called Pakpa, eminent guru and second Buddha of [this] degenerate age, and protected by that widely renowned great khan called Qubilai, king who rules nearly all of the world, acted as patron. The master artist unrivaled in this field of knowledge (craft), called Konchok Kyab, having served, successfully accomplished it in the Water Male Dragon Year (1292). May you enjoy great prosperity!

Panjaranatha Mahakala; Beijing, China, and Sakya Monastery, Tsang region, central Tibet; dated 1292; lithographic limestone, partially gilded and polychromed; 18½ × 11¼ in. (47 × 28.5 cm); Musée national des arts asiatiques–Guimet, Paris; gift of L. Fournier; MA 5181; image © RMN-Grand Palais / Art Resource, NY; photograph by Thierry Ollivier

The Patron's Identity

There has been some speculation as to the identity of the patron of this famous statue.[2] Atsara Pakshi, mentioned in the inscription, is not a name but rather an epithet meaning the learned master or

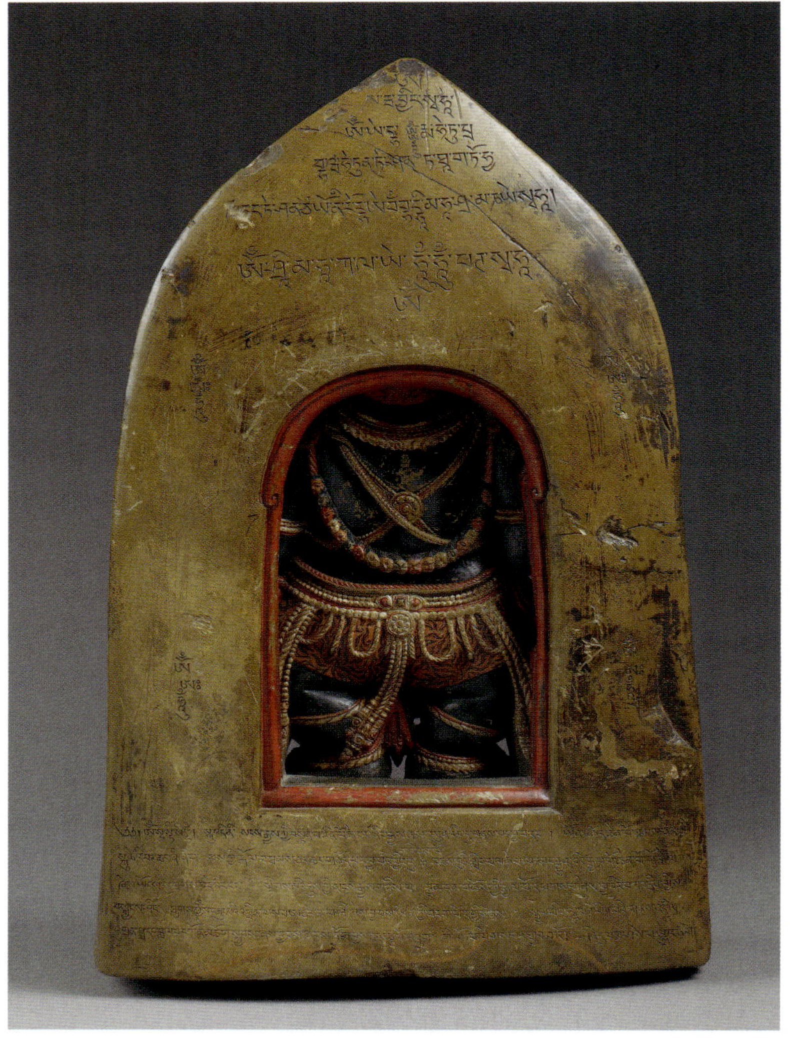

Back of Panjaranatha Mahakala showing the inscription; Musée national des arts asiatiques–Guimet, Paris; gift of L. Fournier; MA 5181; image © RMN-Grand Palais / Art Resource, NY; photograph by Thierry Ollivier

sorcerer.[3] One intriguing attribution that elucidates Tibetan Buddhism's political role in the Mongol court is Qubilai Khan's primary Mahakala ritual specialist at court, Ga Anyen Dampa Kunga Drak (ca. 1230–1303), a close disciple of Imperial Preceptor Pakpa and often described as *pakshi* in both Yuan Chinese and Tibetan sources.[4] Dampa, recognized as an emanation of Mahakala walking on earth, was credited with intervening in several key battles in Mongol military campaigns, including the momentous final fall of the Chinese Southern Song dynasty (1127–1279), and erected several imperially sponsored temples and images of Mahakala.[5]

Dampa served the Yuan imperial court and Qubilai Khan directly. The Persian historian Rashid al-Din, who wrote his famous history about 1300, specifically mentions Dampa as someone of great authority and importance in the great khan's eyes.[6] The calligraphy for Dampa's epitaph stele (1316) was written by the most famous Chinese artist of his time, Zhao Mengfu (1254–1322), and highlights Dampa's importance at the Mongol court.[7] It has even been suggested that Zhao Mengfu's famous painting *Red-Robed Monk of the Western Regions* (1304) commemorates him.[8]

Several historical sources attest to Dampa's applications of Mahakala in the service of the Mongolian military machine; in recognition, many temples and images dedicated to Mahakala were built throughout the empire. Numerous Mongol victories were attributed to Dampa's summoning of Mahakala. For instance, when the Mongol army first marched south, the Chinese petitioned their martial god Zhenwu to save them, but the Chinese god of war fled, leaving a message that he too had to hide from the Great Black God leading the Mongol army. In another battle Mahakala was sighted on the battlefield. Dampa's Chinese biography concludes, "This is proof of how he aided the state."[9]

Most famously, in 1275, when Qubilai asked his Imperial Preceptor Pakpa to induce the protector deity Mahakala to intervene against the Southern Song, the Nepalese artist Anige constructed the temple south of Beijing with its statue facing south (that is, facing the Song), and Dampa consecrated it.[10] The Song capital fell soon thereafter. When the captured Chinese emperor and his courtiers were brought north, they were astonished to see the image of Mahakala just as they had seen the deity among the Mongol troops.[11] These accounts of the fall of the Southern Song via the ritual intervention of Mahakala are recorded in both Chinese and Tibetan sources.[12]

The Artist's Identity

The artist Konchok Kyab is thus far unidentified. It has been variously suggested that the sculptor was a Tibetan trained in Anige's Newar-inspired workshops at the Yuan court, or that he might have been a Newar, or even Anige himself.[13] This sculpture in fact bears Newar artistic features, while also showing conservative eastern Indian/Pala aspects.[14] However, the horns placed on the *garuda* bird (Tibetan: *khyung*) at the top of the sculpture are a small yet very specific Tibetan cultural reference, which suggests that the sculptor Konchok Kyab was Tibetan.

For an example of a small portable carved stone stele, see Padmasambhava and His Manifestations, no. 43.

The kind of hard beige-green stone that composes the sculpture is known to have been used in Burma and eastern India.[15] Of those found in Tibet, most are believed to have originated from these places.[16] Such small stone sculptures often follow a stele, or plaque, format, with an image carved into the front of a slab of stone in deep relief, while the broad back remains flat. These sculptures were often painted, as seen here.

Extant Chinese stone sculptures of this deity reveal an entirely different aesthetic, as evident in one example related to the Yuan state cult of Mahakala and found at Baochengsi (dated 1322), a sculptural niche in Hangzhou, the cultural heartland of China.[17] This sculpture must have been made by a Chinese artist, for Mahakala resembles a bearded Chinese general.

Rethinking Yuan Dynasty Art

The sculpture of Mahakala featured here, and the inscription it bears, embodies the religio-political relationship at the heart of Tibetan involvement at the Mongol court. Two years before its creation, in 1290, Dampa was recorded sculpting images from clay with his own hands, which Chinese sources specifically described as "Indic" (*fanxiang*).[18] Tibetan sources also refer to Dampa as the principal sculptor directing a group of artists—some sources specify Chinese artists[19]—in creating large-scale images of the same form of Mahakala in 1284.[20] If Dampa was indeed the patron, could this sculpture have been produced by a Tibetan or Newar artist in Beijing in an "Indic" style under his direction? Considering the diversity of cultural traditions brought together by the Mongols, including the prominent role of Tibetans, Newars, and Tanguts in visual production (for example, Feilaifeng, the White Stupa, Juyong Guan, and more), this stone image signals a need to further rethink what characterizes Yuan dynasty art.

See White Stupa, no. 40; Juyong Guan Stupa Gate, no. 48. On Feilaifeng, see Relief Carving of a Nine-Deity Ushnishavijaya Composition, no. 41.

Further Reading

Berger, Patricia. 1994. "Preserving the Nation: The Political Use of Tantric Art in China." In *Latter Days of the Law: Images of Chinese Buddhism 850–1850*, edited by Marsha Weidner, 89–124. Exhibition catalog. Lawrence: Spencer Museum of Art, University of Kansas.

Charleux, Isabelle. 2008. "From the Yuan to the Qing Dynasty: The Career of a Famous Statue of Mahākāla, Lord of the Cemeteries." In *Han Zang Fojiao Meishu Yanjiu* 汉藏佛教美术研究 / *Studies in Sino-Tibetan Buddhist Art*, edited by Xie Jisheng 谢继胜, 183–207. Beijing: Shoudu shifan daxue chubanshe.

Debreczeny, Karl. 2019b. "Faith and Empire: An Overview." In *Faith and Empire: Art and Politics in Tibetan Buddhism*. 19–51. Exhibition catalog. New York: Rubin Museum of Art. http://issuu.com/rmanyc/docs/faith_and_empire.

Notes

1 Grupper 1984, 76n19; Charleux 2008, 188.
2 Stoddard 1985a, 281; Sperling 1991, 457n7; van der Kuijp 1995, 287; A. Heller 1999, 87–88; Vitali 2001, 37–38n45; Debreczeny 2015, 132–33.
3 Van der Kuijp 1995, 275, 287.
4 Sperling 1991, 457n7; Vitali 2001, 37–38n45; Debreczeny 2015, 132–33.
5 On Dampa, see Franke 1984; Chen and Zhou 1990; Sperling 1991; Huang Hao 1993; 'Jigs med bsam grub 1995; Shen Weirong 2004; Debreczeny 2015.
6 Franke 1984, 79, and 1996, 53–63.
7 Wang Yao 1994, 958; Franke 1996, 42–46, 175–217; Z. Sun 1999, 308.
8 Hong Zaixin 1995, 519–33; J. C. Y. Watt 2010, 198; McCausland 2014 (2015), 141.
9 *Fozu lidai tongzai*, chap. 22; Shen Weirong 2004, 204; Franke 1984, 161–62.
10 Wang Yao 1994, 958; Shen Weirong 2004, 204; Debreczeny 2015, 137.
11 Shen Weirong 2004, 204.
12 For instance, the *Fozu lidai tongzai*; the *Protection of the Nation Temple Stele* (*Huguosi beiming*); and the *Rgya bod yig tshang*. See Franke 1984, 158, 161–62, 175; Sperling 1991; Shen Weirong 2004, 204.
13 Stoddard 1985a, 281–82; A. Heller 1999, 87; Béguin 1990, 52–56; http://www.guimet.fr/collections/himalaya/mahakala-sous-son-aspect-gur-gyi-mgon-po/; Tsangwang Gendun Tenpa 2019, 115.
14 Thanks to Elena Pakhoutova, Gautama V. Vajracharya, Kerry Lucinda Brown, and Ian Alsop for sharing their thoughts on the Newar stylistic qualities of this work.
15 Stoddard 1985a, 278.
16 Other examples are largely made from a softer pyrophyllite, such as one in the Metropolitan Museum of Art, New York, 2015.500.4.23, and one in the Palace Museum, Beijing. See Luo (2009) 2012, 138–39, pl. 72.
17 Su 1996b, 368–72; Xiong 2003, 162–68; Debreczeny 2015, 138–40.
18 Song 1976, chap. 202, 4519; *Fozu lidai tongzai*, chap. 22; Franke 1984, 166.
19 *Hor chos rje sku phreng gong rim gyi rnam thar* 1983, 34 (fol. 17v); Khang dmar pa, n.d. fol. 11b, line 3.
20 *Sde mgon po'i dkar chag* 1996, 91 (fol. 245r); 'Jigs med bsam grub 1995, 158; Debreczeny 2015, 142.

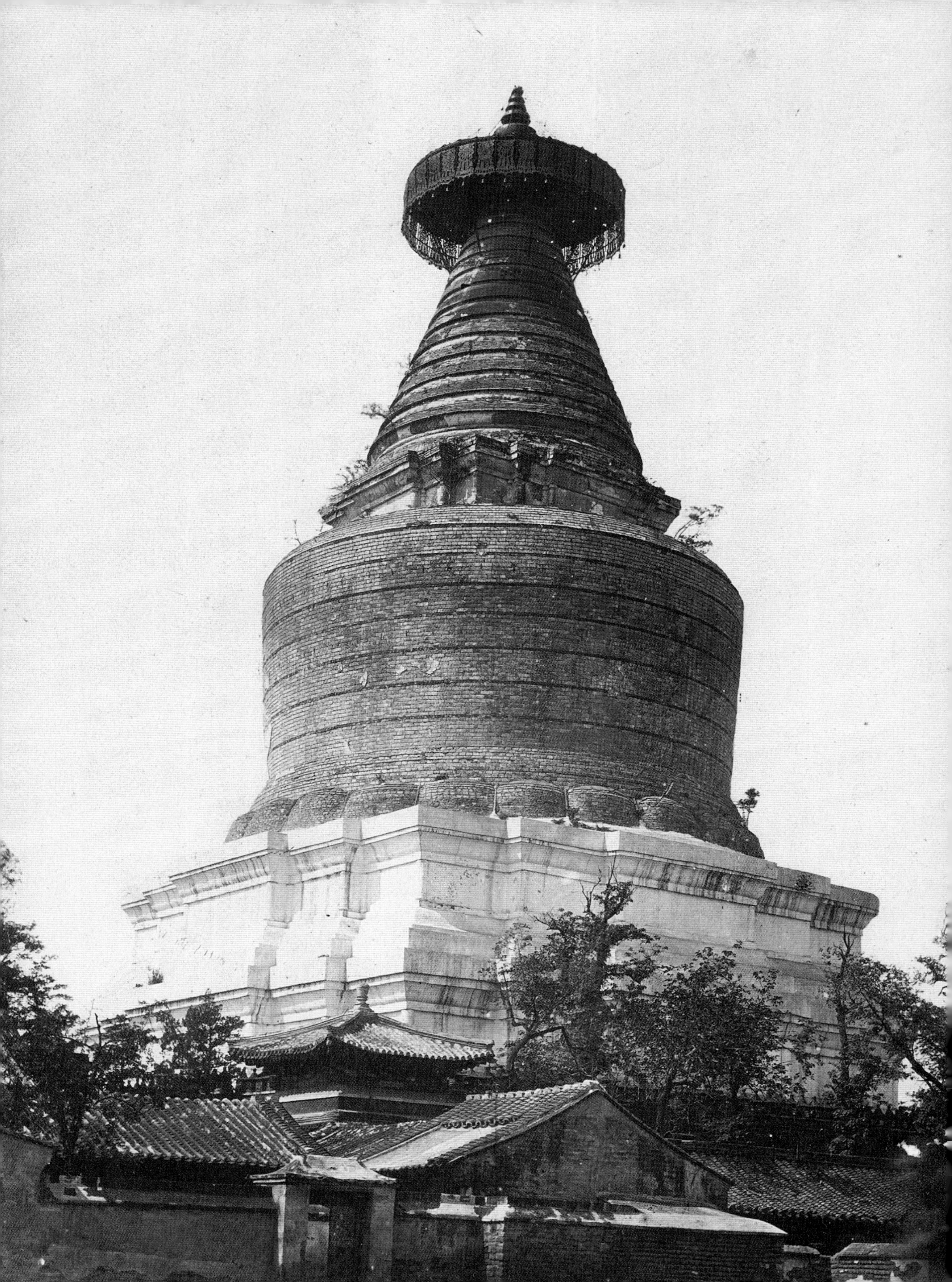

№ 40

White Stupa, Attributed to Nepalese Artist Anige

Beijing, China, 1279

Newar Artist's Buddhist Monument for the Mongol Emperor in Beijing

ISABELLE CHARLEUX

THE WHITE STUPA, located less than two miles (three kilometers) to the west of the imperial city of Beijing,[1] is one of the few architectural structures remaining in Mongol Daidu, capital of the Yuan dynasty (1271–1368).[2] For many centuries, this monument was probably the capital's most visually outstanding building.

The Mongols and Tibetan Buddhism

For more about Tangut Buddhism and the state, see Relief Carving of a Nine-Deity Ushnishavijaya Composition, no. 41.

The Mongols encountered Tibetan Buddhism among the Tangut (Xixia state, 1038–1227), whose kingdom Chinggis Khan destroyed in 1227, and in their campaign in Tibet. In 1260, Qubilai Khan (r. 1260–1294) proclaimed Tibetan Buddhism the official religion of the empire. Tangut Buddhism became the model for Qubilai's religio-political rulership. Qubilai designated Pakpa Lama (1235–1280), nephew of Sakya Pandita (1182–1251), a highly influential Buddhist scholar, as imperial preceptor and established a "priest-patron" (*choyon*) relationship with him.

In 1261, Pakpa invited Anige (or Araniko, 1244–1306), a young Newar artist, to the Yuan court, along with a group of twenty-four other Himalayan artisans. Anige spent almost all his life at the Yuan court as "director of all artisan classes." He was accorded high honors and embraced Chinese literati culture. His epitaph summed up his prolific career as artist, architect, and administrator at Qubilai Khan's court.[3]

The White Stupa of Daidu

In 1271, Qubilai heard that relics of Shakyamuni from the ruined pagoda of a Jin dynasty Buddhist monastery emitted miraculous lights by night. He gave orders to excavate the relics and erect on the ruins the White Stupa.

The White Stupa; Monastery of Miraculous Retribution, popularly known as White Pagoda Monastery, Beijing, China; Yuan dynasty (1279–1368), 1279; masonry; height 167 ft. (51 m); photograph attributed to Felice Beato (1825–1908), 1860; Los Angeles County Museum of Art. Gift of Mr. and Mrs. Philip Feldman (M.83.302.33); photograph © Museum Associates/ LACMA, www.lacma.org

Qubilai's decision to construct a Tibetan-style stupa (the first in the region) instead of a Chinese-style multistory pagoda in his main capital,[4] directly to the west of his palace, reflects the imperial support of Tibetan Buddhism. He acted as a universal Buddhist ruler (chakravartin) on the model of Indian emperor Ashoka (r. 273–232 BCE), who was said to have built eighty-four thousand stupas for Shakyamuni's relics throughout his empire. Previously, in 1267, Pakpa had advised Qubilai to erect a pillar crowned with a golden wheel, a symbol of the chakravartin, in front of the Imperial Palace.

Between 1270 and 1279, Anige and Rinchen Gyeltsen (1238–1282), Pakpa's brother, who succeeded him as imperial preceptor, were in charge of designing and supervising the construction of the stupa. Rinchen Gyeltsen consecrated the monument in 1279.[5]

The White Stupa has been repeatedly restored and was seriously damaged by the 1976 earthquake of Tangshan. It is a massive hollow structure that rises to a height of 167 feet (51 meters) and has a diameter of 98 ½ feet (more than 30 meters) at its base. With the stupas of Boudhanath and Swayambhu in Nepal, both about 131 feet (40 meters) in height, it is one of the biggest stupas in Asia. The White Stupa apparently follows the Indian Pala model known as "Kadampa stupa," recognizable by its bell-like shape, common at that time in Tibet.

See the Svayambhu Chaitya of Kathmandu, no. 4.

See Stupa at Toling Monastery, no. 19.

The White Stupa rests on a multifaceted (*ratha*) two-tiered base. Its domed body (*anda*) is made of rings of bricks piled one atop the other, marked by thirteen circular bands, on a base of lotus petals. Its surface is entirely covered by white lime. On its top is a stylized square fence (*harmika*) modulated by a series of cornices with a broken profile that reproduces the facets of the base, a conical spire of thirteen stacked disks, a wooden umbrella covered with copper adorned with thirty-six bronze bells hanging from its rim, and a stupa-shaped bronze finial filled with relics.[6] The umbrella and the bronze finial were made in 1753 under the Qianlong emperor (r. 1735–1796), to replace earlier ones.

The White Stupa was meant to be a three-dimensional mandala of the Five Tathagatas (or Five Cosmic Buddhas). According to a stele, the exterior of the "vase" (the *anda*?) was originally carved with the attributes of four of the Five Tathagatas (with the implicit presence of those of Vairochana at the center).

Although designed by Anige, it differs considerably from Nepalese models. Its sources of inspiration may have been stupas built in the Tangut realm: its shape and proportions resemble those of the 108 stupas of Qingtongxia.[7] It served as a model for later stupas of the Yuan.

For more on Bodhgaya, see Mahabodhi Temple Model, no. 25.

See Panoramic Map of Mount Wutai, no. 91.

See Molded Clay Image (*Tsatsa*) of Amoghapasha, no. 28.

See The Qianlong Emperor as Manjushri-Chakravartin, no. 84.

In addition, the White Stupa offers a unique case study of relics installed during the consecration ceremony; these were recorded in detail in a stele, and others were revealed after the stupa's opening following the earthquake. The items placed in 1279 in a crypt include relics of the Buddha, many images of deities and Buddhist texts, and miniature stupas made with earth taken from the sacred Buddhist sites of Bodhgaya in India and Mount Wutai ("Five Peak Mountain") in China. Additional items were inserted in the new bronze finial on the Qianlong emperor's order in 1753.

The Great Monastery of Eminent Longevity and Myriad Peace

Qubilai Khan had the Great Monastery of Eminent Longevity and Myriad Peace (Dashangshouwan'ansi) dedicated to Manjushri built around the stupa, with sumptuous Chinese-style temples modeled on halls of the Imperial Palace. Completed in 1288, it was the main imperial monastery of Daidu and served as a private temple for the imperial family.

See Mahakala Stone Sculpture, no. 39.

For more about the cult of kings, see Yumbu Lagang Castle, no. 5; Bodhisattva Avalokiteshvara and the Buddha's Footprints, no. 33; The Qianlong Emperor as Manjushri-Chakravartin, no. 84.

For a silk a tapestry depicting a giant mandala, see Vajrabhairava Mandala, no. 46.

In 1289, the Sandalwood or Uddiyana Buddha, the most precious Buddhist image of Chinese dynasties, revered by Tibetans and Mongolians alike, was installed in the rear hall.[8] Octagonal pavilions were built in 1313 to worship Mahakala, main protector of the Yuan state. The monastery became a center for Buddhist translations from Tibetan into Mongolian and Uyghur.

The monastery also had two Halls of Imperial Portraiture for deceased ancestors: for Qubilai and his empress Chabui (or Chabi, 1225–1281) to the west; and for their son and late heir apparent Jingim (1243–1285) and his empress, to the east. They enshrined their portraits in silk tapestry (*kesi*) together with, probably, a silk tapestry depicting a giant mandala.

The monastery was damaged by a fire in 1368 and rebuilt in the fifteenth century. In 1457 it was renamed Monastery of Miraculous Retribution (Miaoyingsi). It was restored in the Qing period and, thanks to the 1753 guidebook written by Changkya Khutugtu Rolpai Dorje, became a pilgrimage site for Mongols.

Other Stupas of the Yuan Period

See Juyong Guan Stupa Gate, no. 48.

Qubilai also ordered the construction of Tibetan-style stupas in the capital atop Chinese-style city gates. His descendant Toghan Temür (r. 1333–1367), the last emperor, erected two road-spanning stupas north and southwest of Daidu. Unlike the White Stupa, these were public monuments; located at strategic junctures, they symbolically protected the capital and its inhabitants.[9]

Twenty-two years after the consecration of Daidu's White Stupa, Emperor Temür (1295–1307) had its replica erected on Mount Wutai, the most important site of Tibetan Buddhist activity outside the Mongol capitals. Anige and Dampa (1230–1303), Qubilai's tantric ritual specialist, constructed the gigantic stupa on a ruined Tang-period octagonal pagoda that enshrined a relic of Shakyamuni allegedly brought there by Ashoka. It became the iconic monument of Mount Wutai. In 1407, at the request of the Fifth Karmapa (1384–1415), Ming emperor Yongle (r. 1402–1424) ordered that the stupa be restored and heightened.

The Great White Stupa at Mount Wutai stands on an octagonal platform with tiled eaves protecting prayer wheels. It was heightened to 185 feet (56.4 meters) during the 1407 restoration. Its dissimilarities with the Beijing White Stupa, such as the octagonal base and *harmika* and the slender shape of the *anda*, might date to the 1407 restoration.[10]

Following their predecessors, the Yuan emperors also sponsored Chinese Buddhist monasteries on Mount Wutai. One of these, attributed to Anige, the Myriad Saints Safeguarding the State Monastery (Wansheng Youguosi), built from 1295 to 1297, was the most extravagant construction of the Yuan period.

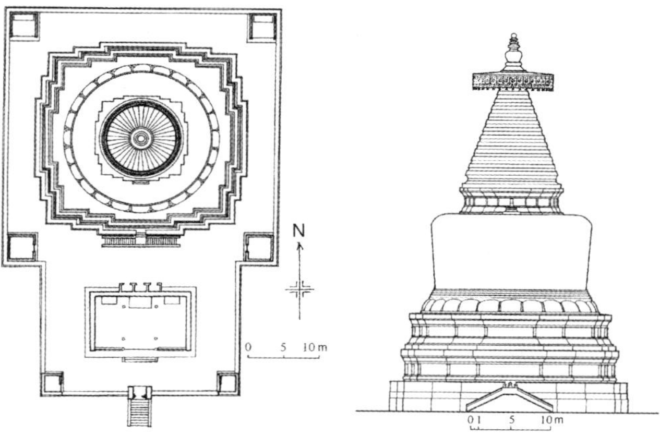

Ground plan and elevation of the White Stupa; Monastery of Miraculous Retribution, Beijing, China; image after Pan Guxi 潘谷西, ed. 2002. *Zhongguo gudai jianzhu shi: Yuan, Ming jianzhu* 中國古代建築史: 元明建築 [History of ancient Chinese architecture: Architecture of the Yuan and Ming]. New Haven: Yale University Press, 357

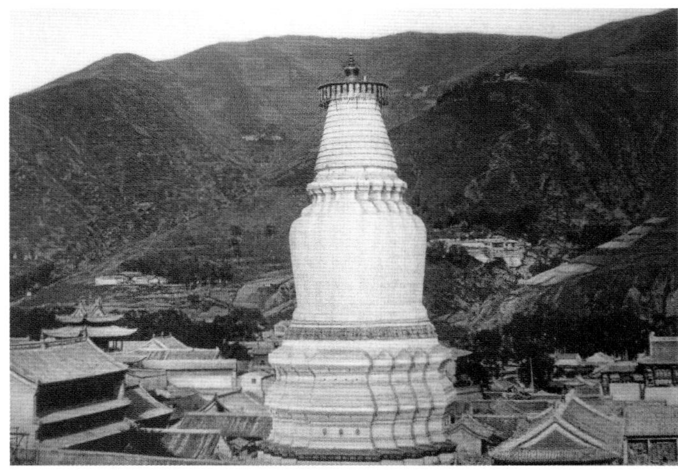

White Stupa, known as Precious Stupa of Great Compassion and Longevity, and its surroundings, photographed between 1906 and 1909; Great Precious Stupa Cloister Monastery, Mount Wutai, Shanxi Province, China; 1301, renovated in 1407; height after the 1407 restoration 185 ft. (56.4 m); image after Boerschmann, Ernst. 1923. *Picturesque China: Architecture and Landscape: A Journey through Twelve Provinces*. New York: Brentano's

Other Works Attributed to Anige

Anige's epitaph mentions "[the] construction of three stupas, nine great Buddhist temples, two Confucian shrines, one Daoist temple, and countless images and objects made for the emperor, his imperial family, the court, and private persons."[11] He directed tens of thousands of artisans (including Chinese) who produced luxury goods for the imperial household. Because he is the best-documented Himalayan artist of the time, a number of artworks are attributed to him, such as a dry lacquer bodhisattva that bears a distinct Nepalese style, a figure of Manjushri in the Palace Museum, a painting of Green Tara (see the image on p. 174), and bust portraits of Qubilai and Chabui.[12] Even if he may have supervised these artworks, to this day, none of them can be securely attributed to his hand.

Whatever the real role of Anige in integrating Tangut, Nepalese, and Chinese artistic conventions and aesthetics, Yuan patronage introduced a series of artistic and technical innovations that lasted long after the collapse of their dynasty, in painting, imperial portraiture, sculpture, and architecture. More research is needed on Yuan Buddhist artistic production that is often simply labeled with the umbrella terms of "Sino-Tibetan" or "Tibeto-Chinese," which mask its broad diversity.

Further Reading

Campbell, Aurelia. 2022. "The Consecrated City: Royal Stupas in Yuan Dynasty Dadu." *Journal of Song and Yüan Studies* 51, 207–243.

Jing, Anning. 1994. "The Portraits of Khubilai Khan and Chabi by Anige (1245–1306), a Nepali Artist at the Yuan Court." *Artibus Asiae* 54, nos. 1–2, 40–86.

Khokhlov, Yury. 2016. "The Xi Xia Legacy in Sino-Tibetan Art of the Yuan Dynasty." Asianart.com. Published September 15, 2016. https://www.asianart.com/articles/xi-xia/.

Notes

1 Not to be confused with the White Stupa, built in 1651 northwest of the Forbidden City.
2 Daidu (modern pronunciation: Dadu) or Khanbaliq was on the site of modern Beijing.
3 Anige's funerary stele is reproduced in Cheng 1970, 1:313–20; Anige's official biography is in the *Yuan shi* [History of the Yuan] 1976 (see Jing 1994). For Tibetan sources, see Tsangwang Gendun Tenpa 2019, 123n26.
4 Chinese-style pagodas were familiar to the Mongols. Their first capital, Qara-Qorum, had a five-story pagoda 295 feet (90 meters) high. Up to eighty pagodas from the Khitan-Liao dynasty (907–1125) have survived in Inner Mongolia and northern China, and many Liao and Jurchen Jin (1115–1234) pagodas were built around Daidu.
5 The stupa's history is told in a stele by Xiangmai, translated by Franke 1994, in imperial records, gazetteers of Beijing, and Changkya Khutugtu Rolpai Dorje (1717–1786)'s guidebook (1753). See Franke 1994; Jing 1994; 50–52; Campbell 2022.
6 The White Stupa does not have the pair of rings encircling the *anda* and the lotus bud–form pinnacle of the Kadampa stupa, and its *harmika* is different (Hatt 1980).
7 Khokhlov 2016.
8 The statue was moved to the Monastery of Vast Humaneness (Hongrensi) in the seventeenth century and disappeared in 1900 (Carter 1990).
9 Campbell 2022.
10 Boerschmann 1937; Charleux 2015.
11 Jing 1994, 66.
12 Jing 1994; McCausland 2014 (2015).

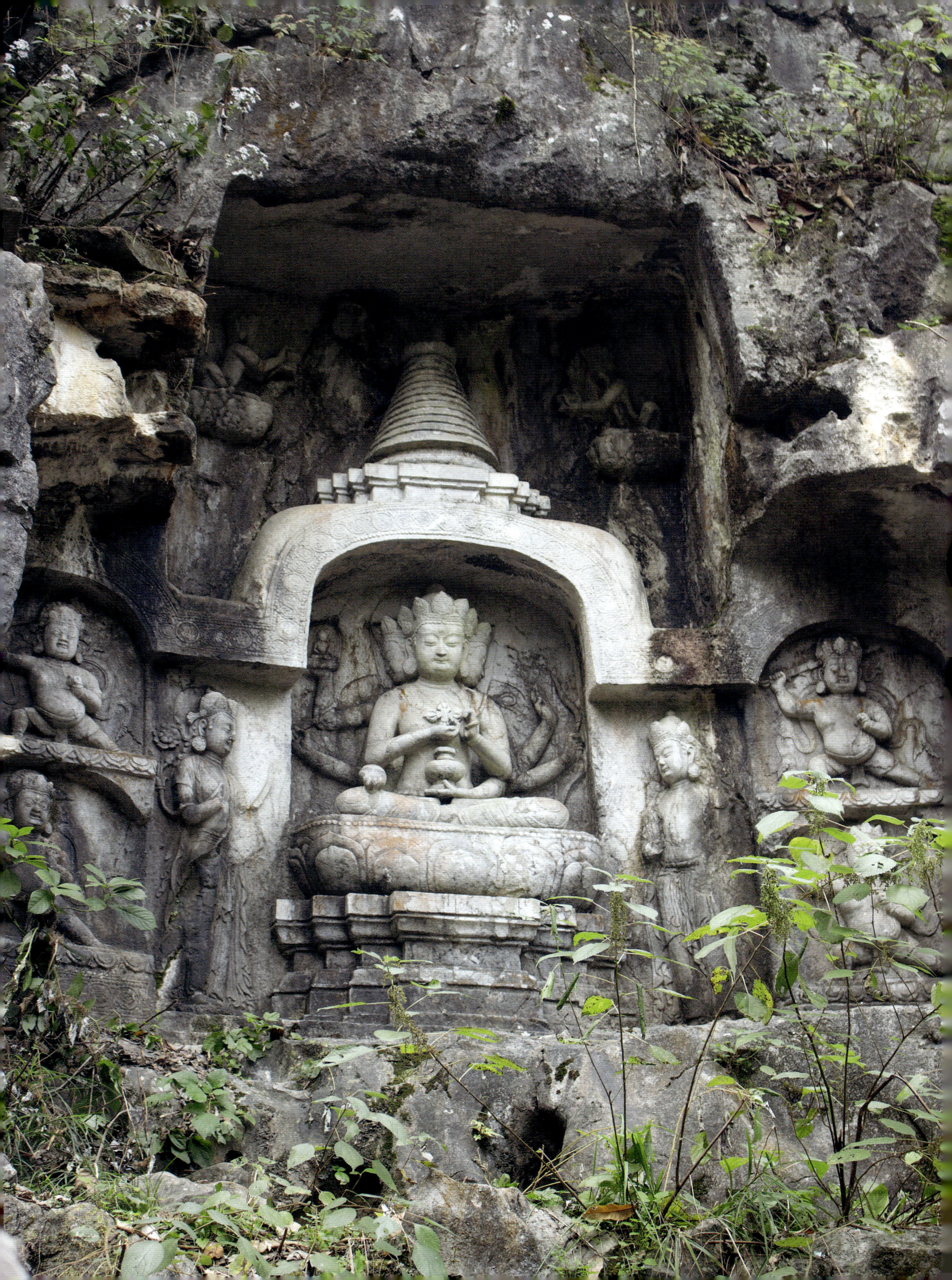

№ 41

Relief Carving of a Nine-Deity Ushnishavijaya Composition, Niche 84 at Feilaifeng Cliff

Hangzhou, China, ca. 1282–1292

Sculpture under Mongol Patronage: An Indian Buddhist Deity in a Nepalo-Tibeto-Chinese Form

ROB LINROTHE

In considering this relief, many themes intertwine. Carved into a cliff near the Lingyin Monastery in Hangzhou, China, it has as its central theme a personified prayer for long life and favorable rebirth. Its hybrid style, a combination of Nepalese and Tibetan artistic conventions filtered through the eyes of Chinese sculptors, visually documents the role of Tibetan Buddhists in multiethnic politics of Mongol rule over China. The sculptural work stands as testimony to tidal waves of culture breaking on the beaches of religious and political entities along the South, central, and East Asian inhabited spaces, and in the process depositing Indian knowledge systems strained through Himalayan nets. It silently illustrates the extended reach of Himalayan cultures in wider interchanges across Inner Asia, Mongolia, and western and eastern China.

Ushnishavijaya, Deity and Dharani

The deity depicted inside the stupa, surrounded by eight other deities, is Ushnishavijaya ("Victorious Crown Ornament"). She is the personification of a Sanskrit spell-like prayer (dharani) expounded by the Buddha according to an early text, translated into Chinese from the Sanskrit, but which transliterated the Sanskrit dharani. This version was popular in Tang dynasty (618–906 CE) China and in Japan during the same period.[1] The prayer promises to extend lifetimes and ensure favorable rebirth. The short version of her namesake speech is carved into the composition. The narrow ornamental band outlining the central niche of the stupa is carved in low relief in a scrolling vine pattern. Every third scroll depicts a disk with a so-called *ranjana* syllable of Sanskrit. Between each such disk with carved writing are two smaller scrolls clasping lotus flowers. The carved text starts one position to the left of center and moves toward the viewer's right, then continues, moving right to left this time, just to the left of where it started.[2] The first line, "om bhrum svaha," is Ushnishavijaya's heart mantra, and the last line, "om amritya ayur dade svaha," means "Om, Giver of Immortal life, svaha!" The *Ushnishavijaya Dharani* was also transliterated and carved in Tangut, Tibetan, Mongolian square script ("Pakpa script"), Uyghur, and Chinese scripts at the Juyong Guan.[3] The vase that she holds in her lap is filled with *amrita*, the nectar of deathlessness with which she is identified.[4]

See Juyong Guan Stupa Gate, no. 48.

The *Ushnishavijaya Dharani* is an early powerful protective prayer originating in India but widely promulgated in China and Japan. Then, there was no mention of a personification. Only later, in India, was the prayer personified and then transmitted to Tibet. She does not appear as a personification in East Asia except in Himalayan contexts such as the Achala *kesi*, where she is portrayed as a peaceful deity in the lower register. In the late twelfth century, Tanguts created many images of her derived from Tibet in various media, including woodblock prints. She seems to have been included in a dynastic cult to confer legitimacy, state protection, and personal welfare on the Tangut royal family.[5]

See Achala Silk Tapestry, no. 36.

For more about Tangut art, see Cave 3 at Yulin Cave Temples, no. 31; A *Pancharaksha* Print from Khara-Khoto, no. 32.

Nine-Deity Ushnishavijaya Composition; Feilaifeng Cliff, Niche 84, Hangzhou, China; ca. 1282–1292; stone; photograph by Karl Debreczeny

The Tangut background is not incidental to the Feilaifeng image, since some of its sculptures were sponsored by a Tangut employed by the Mongol court. Yang Lianzhenjia was a married Buddhist monk trusted by Qubilai Khan (r. 1260–1294), who appointed him commissioner of religious affairs in Hangzhou, the capital of the wealthy Southern Song state recently defeated by the Mongols.

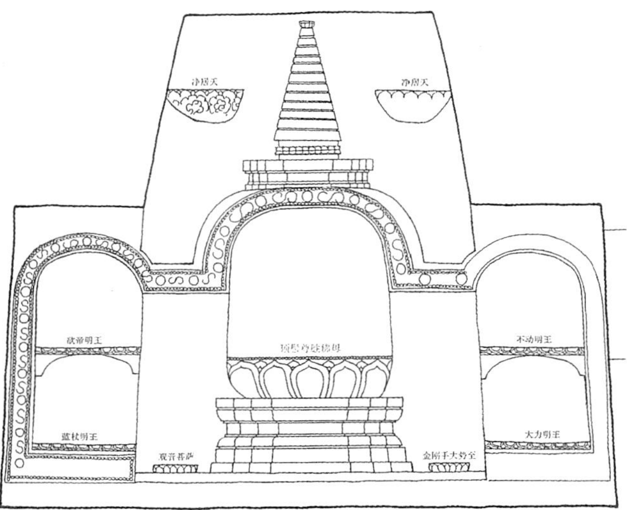

Diagram of the Nine-Deity Ushnishavijaya Composition, Feilaifeng Cliff, Niche 84, including the ornamental band with the dharani; image after Liao Yang 2014, fig. 95; used with permission

The Ushnishavijaya composition at Feilaifeng resembles others paid for by Commissioner Yang, including two dated to 1292 depicting Buddhist themes in the same hybrid Sinicized Himalayan manner.[6]

Rituals of Commemoration

See Plaque Commemorating *Bhimaratha* Old Age Ritual, no. 85.

See Molded Clay Image (*Tsatsa*) of Amoghapasha, no. 28.

Tibetan paintings of Ushnishavijaya commemorated recently deceased loved ones, and the merit thus accrued dedicated to their favorable rebirth. An Ushnishavijaya painting in the collection of the Rubin Museum of Art, New York, depicts the deceased reborn in white robes on a lotus in a Pure Land.[7] Two known rituals in Nepal involving Ushnishavijaya are carried out on attaining the age of sixty and, more rarely, seventy-seven. Both produce merit for extending one's lifetime and preparing for rebirth. One calls for the fabrication of (ideally) one hundred thousand mold-stamped stupas[8] and paintings with a large stupa in the center containing Ushnishavijaya surrounded by smaller stupas.[9] Such practices illustrate the Buddhist association of Ushnishavijaya with funerary and commemorative functions.[10] It raises the unanswerable question of whether or not Niche 84 had a related function late in the reign of Qubilai Khan.[11]

It is possible that this composition was also one of Commissioner Yang's productions. No readable donor inscription dates the sculpture, but several of the commissioner's inscriptions mention Qubilai Khan and other members of the Mongol court, including those dated to 1292. That year, after the commissioner was condemned to death for corruption, Qubilai rescinded the sentence and rehabilitated him—a narrow escape. The year 1292 also happened to be Qubilai's seventy-seventh, so it is not impossible that the sculpture of Ushnishavijaya was gratefully dedicated to him and for his long life. Alternatively, it may have commemorated the deceased emperor who died in 1294, to ensure his rebirth in auspicious circumstances. Yang Lianzhenjia's death date, which would have been after 1292, is not known.

Complex, Mandala-like Composition

See Vajrabhairava Mandala, no. 46.

Niche 84 at Feilaifeng is the most complex Yuan-period composition at a site dotted mainly with single deities. Among extant niches at the site, this one most closely approaches a mandala, though the composition is triadically, not pentadically, symmetrical. The complexity starts with the central deity: Ushnishavijaya has three heads and eight arms. Her upper right hand supports a small image of Buddha Amitabha. Other attributes are the vase of *amrita*, a bow and arrow, a noose to draw the suffering to safety, gestures of reassurance and generosity, and a double vajra held before her chest. As the personification of the dharani spoken by the Buddha, she is herself a kind of dharma relic animating the stupa.

Eight other beings surround Ushnishavijaya. At her sides are bodhisattvas, Avalokiteshvara holding an open lotus on her right, and Vajrapani on her left. Two pairs of wrathful protectors, or gate guardians, appear on the far edges of the composition.[12] Above, on either side of the stupa's superstructure (the mast [*yasti*] with umbrellas [*chhatri*]), a pair of *devaputras* (heavenly beings) offer more vases of *amrita*.

A Transcultural Form-Idiom

A final feature underscoring the transcultural nature of the Ushnishavijaya composition is its carving style. Later Chinese, responding to the non-Chinese elements, saw it as intrusively foreign, a reminder of Mongol rulers who patronized non-Chinese artists and Buddhism. Indeed, Mongol rulers were patrons of respected Tibetan Buddhist teachers who endorsed their own tastes in art, and they promoted a talented young Newar artist who had previously worked at Sakya Monastery in Tibet. This artist, supposedly named Balubu (literally, "The Nepalese") but known now as Anige (1245–1306), in 1273 became

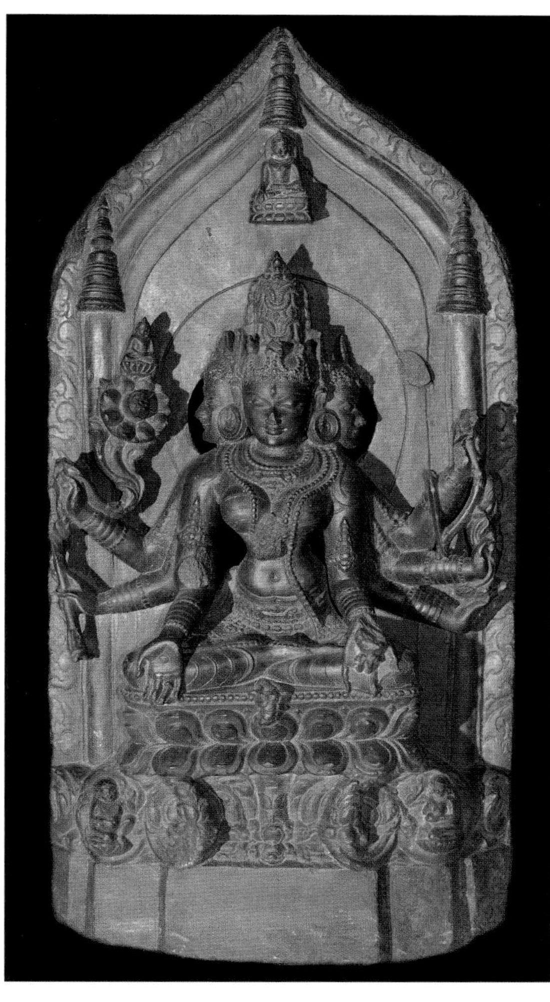

Ushnishavijaya; Nalanda, Bihar, India; ca. 11th–12th century; stone; height 26 in. (66 cm); Indian Museum, Kolkata; photograph by R. Linrothe

For more about Anige, see White Stupa, no. 40.

See for example Pensive Bodhisattva Avalokiteshvara, no. 53; The Qianlong Emperor as Manjushri-Chakravartin, no. 84.

Supervisor-in-Chief of All Classes of Artisans under the Mongols with thousands of artisans working for him.[13] While there is no evidence that Anige himself had a hand in the carving at the Feilaifeng sculptural complex, the sculptors employed by Commissioner Yang appear to have been familiar with the hybrid Nepalese-Tibetan mode of depiction and iconography that Anige is credited with advancing. However, the puffy eyes and cheeks, high eyebrows, and minimized secondary sexual characteristics of the female Ushnishavijaya reflect an undeniable admixture of Chinese sensibility. Contrary to later Chinese impressions of its "Tibetanness," Tibetans might remark on the sculpture's "Chineseness." In context, the niche is surrounded by many sculptures that would not shock Han Chinese observers. The commissioner seems to have endorsed artists working in both modes.[14] Indeed, from the Yuan period on, themes and forms related to Buddhism of Tibet became familiar at several Chinese courts of the succeeding Ming and Qing dynasties.

Further Reading

Edwards, Richard. 1984. "Pu-tai-Maitreya and a Reintroduction to Hangchou's Fei-lai-Feng." *Art Orientalis* 14, 5–50.

Linrothe, Rob. 2009. "The Commissioner's Commissions: Late Thirteenth Century Tibetan and Chinese Buddhist Art in Hangzhou under the Mongols." In *Buddhism between China and Tibet*, edited by Matthew Kapstein, 73–96. Boston: Wisdom.

Xie Jisheng, Xiong Wenbin, Liao Yang, and Rob Linrothe. 2014. *Jiangnan Zangchuan Fojiao Yishu: Hangzhou Feilaifeng shike zaoxiang yanjiu* 江南藏传佛教艺术：杭州飞来峰石刻造像研究 [Tibetan Buddhist art south of the Yangtse River: Collective research of Feilaifeng's Tibetan-style sculpture]. [In Chinese.] Beijing: Zhongguo Zangxue chubanshe.

Notes

1 Muller and Nanjio 1884.

2 It reads: *oṃ bhr(ū)ṃ svāhā / namaḥ bha(ga)vate (u)ṣṇīṣāya / oṃ bhagavaṃ jayatu viśuddhe svāhā / oṃ amṛta ayur dade svāhā*. This is after Liao 2014, 144–47, with the last line corrected on the basis of Willson and Brauen 2000, 286.

3 Bentor 1995a.

4 Usually *amrita* is translated as the ambrosia of "immortality," though the concept seems antithetical to basic Buddhist notions of no-self. Here I follow the literal meaning of "not dead" as found in Mallinson and Szántó 2021, 7.

5 Linrothe 1996 and 1998.

6 Linrothe 2009.

7 HAR 975 (Rubin Museum object C2006.66.507).

8 HAR 73827, 77231, 90540.

9 Further descriptions and references for these are found in Linrothe 1996.

10 Since at least the eighteenth century, Ushnishavijaya has been grouped with Amitayus and White Tara as the Three Deities of Longevity. This triad seems to have been formulated in Tibet, not in India; see Kapstein 2015.

11 For a succinct summary of Tangut and Mongol Yuan rule and interest in Himalayan Buddhism, see Debreczeny 2019, 28–39.

12 On the left, Takkiraja with a long-handled elephant goad (above) and Niladanda with a club (below); on the right, Achala with a sword (above) and Mahabala with a three-pointed vajra (below).

13 Jing 1996, 46–47.

14 This is in line with other initiatives that attempted to synthesize, not separate, Han Chinese and Tibetan Buddhism. For example, in 1285, Qubilai "gathered at his court a number of famous Tibetan, Han Chinese and Uygur Buddhist scholars of the time . . . and set them to the task of editing both the Chinese and the Tibetan versions of the Buddhist scriptures, checking one against the other, a task which took them three years to accomplish. . . . Their efforts opened up a wider field for the study of Tibetan and Han Chinese religion and culture." Sun 1988, 91.

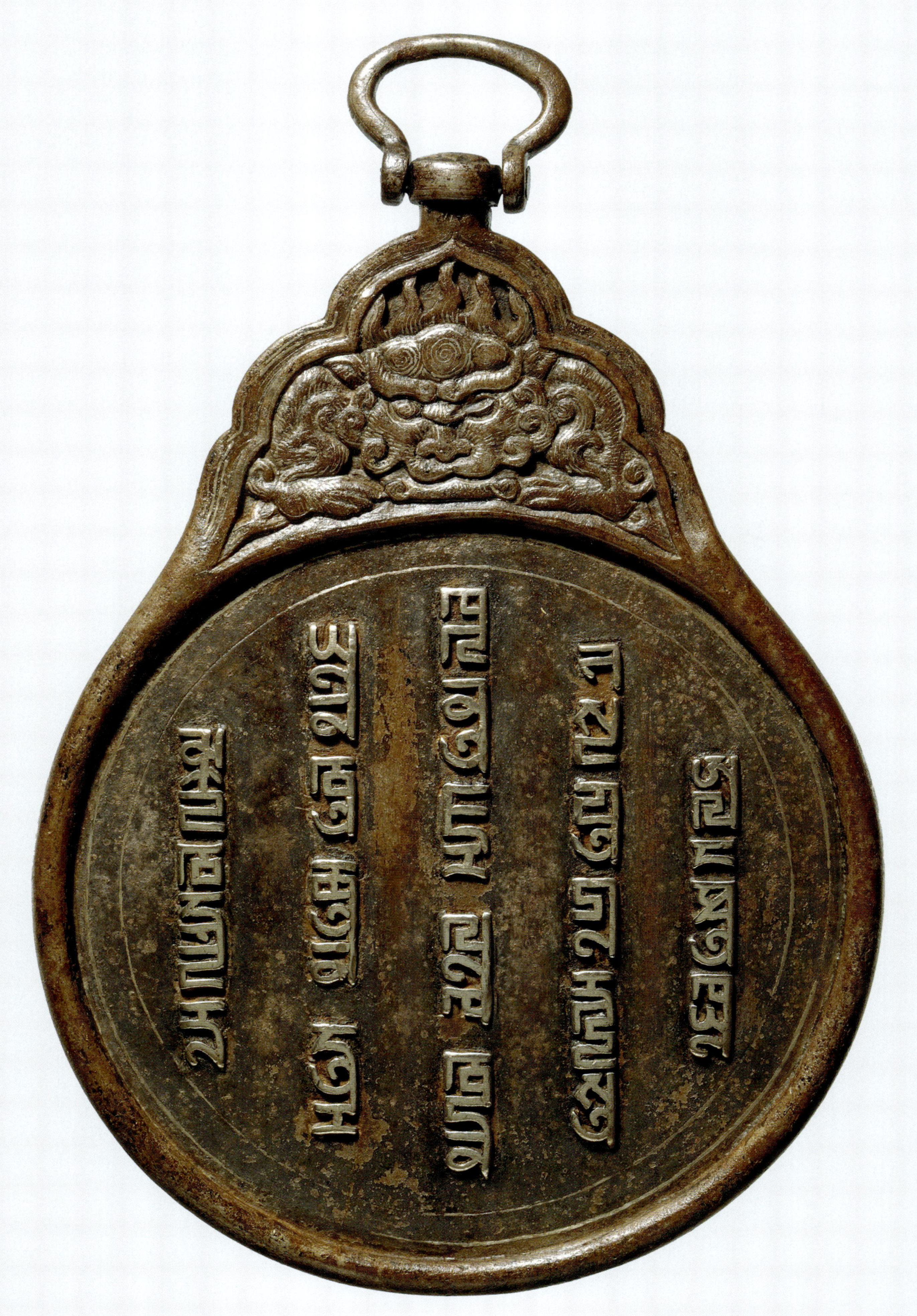

№ 42

Mongol Messenger's Badge (*Paiza* or *Gerege*) in Pakpa Script

Mongol Empire/Yuan dynasty, late 13th–early 14th century

Signs of Authority in the Mongol Empire

CHRISTOPHER P. ATWOOD

Tablets of authority, such as the one pictured here, served as one of the central institutions of the Mongol Empire, giving the bearer power to requisition resources. Together with the "exemption decree," or *darqan jarliq*,[1] which rendered the holder immune from requisitions by others, they were fundamental manifestations of governance under the Mongol Empire. These tablets were known most commonly in the Mongol Empire as *paizas*, a Persian reading of the Chinese *paizi*, "tablet." The Mongolian name, *gerege*, meaning "that which bears witness," is found only in Mongolian-language texts.[2]

Paizas in the Mongol Empire

The primary right granted by such *paizas* was the ability to requisition resources. The more basic type of *paiza* was issued to messengers (*elchin*) and was supposed to be used only on the Mongol Empire's famous post-road (or *jam*) system.[3] Such a *paiza*, as pictured here, gave the holder the right to receive room, board, fresh horses, and an escort while traveling from station to station on the *jam*.

The post-road system linked the entire empire together, enabling the famous level of cultural exchange achieved under the Mongol Empire. Despite the empire's decentralization under regional princes, or khans, its maintenance was one of the key functions that princes owed the central government. In the late thirteenth century, the area directly ruled by Qubilai Khan had more than 1,400 stations and bridges, serviced by 44,293 horses, 8,889 oxen, 6,007 asses, 4,037 carts, 378 sedan chairs, 5,921 boats, 1,150 pack sheep, and even 3,000 sled dogs in northern Manchuria. These statistics do not include Tibet; twenty-one major *jam* stations were established there from 1269 on.[4] Although expensive for the regime and burdensome for the peasants and herders who staffed it in rotation, the *ulagha*, or post-road duty, was preserved in Tibet and Mongolia into the mid-twentieth century.

Another, more prestigious, type of *paiza* was issued to military commanders (*noyat*) at various levels, non-Mongol tributary rulers and local civil administrators, and overseers (*darughas, darughachin*) appointed by the Mongols to supervise non-Mongol officials. "Partner" (*ortaq*) merchants trading with funds from imperial or princely funds and clergy of the empire's recognized religions—Buddhism, Christianity, Daoism, and Islam—also often received *paizas* as members of the imperial elite. These *paizas* granted the right to requisition goods and services not just from the *jam* but from the general civilian population as well. Such *paizas* were issued together with *jarliq*, or decrees,[5] stamped with a red seal (*al tamgha*), that gave the reasons why the holder was privileged with a *paiza* and the specific degree of power that it conferred.

The issuing authority for either type of *paiza* included the great khan, as well as princes, empresses, princesses, and imperial sons-in-law entrusted with jurisdiction over a given territory. In theory, issuing *paizas* was supervised by the great khan, and all were recalled on the death of one great khan and the enthronement of another. In practice, however, these rules were often not followed.[6]

The *paiza* system in the Mongol Empire developed out of the badges used by those on assignment in the Khitan Liao (907–1125) and Jurchen Jin dynasty of North China (1115–1234) and in previous Chinese dynasties. *Paizas* for commanders were ranked by materials and design, ranging from the highest, in gold with a tiger head (*bars terigütü*) inscribed on it, to the lower-ranked ones, in plain gold or silver. The tiger's head is depicted frontally, at the top end of the *paiza*, as can be seen in the molding on the object presented here, or else as incised decoration, as seen in the *paiza* for a commander issued by

Mongol Messenger *Paiza (Gerege)* in Pakpa Script; Mongol Empire/Yuan dynasty (1206–1368), late 13th–early 14th century; iron with silver inlay; 7⅛ × 4½ in. (18.1 × 11.4 cm); The Metropolitan Museum of Art, New York; 1993.256;

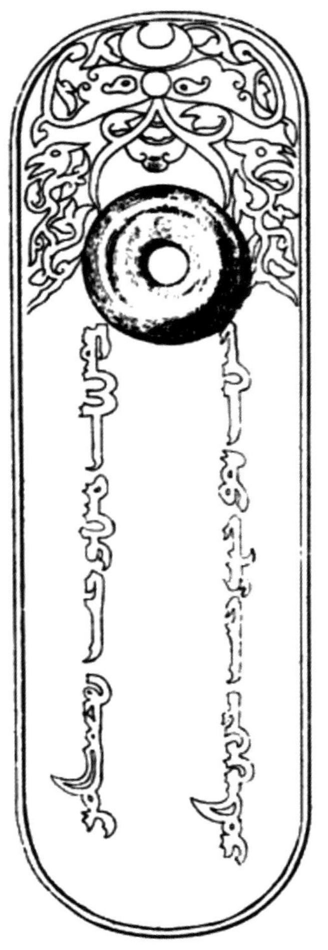
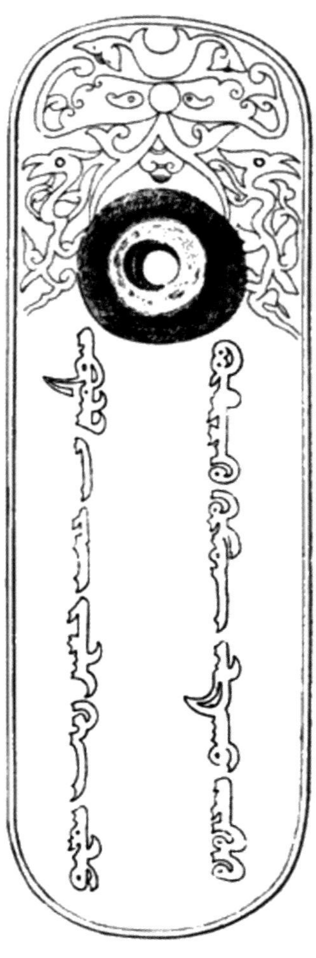

Paiza found in the former lands of the Golden Horde (Dnieper River, 1845); 13th century; Unknown 954 *Paiza* Golden Horde; The Picture Art Collection / Alamy Stock Photo / MNP4DJ

Abdulla, the khan of the Mongol Golden Horde (r. 1362–1370). In many cases, as in the example shown, they were actually composed of base metals, with at most silver or gold inlay.

During the reign of Chinggis Khan (1206–1227), the inscriptions on the *paiza* were in Chinese on the obverse and Khitan language on the reverse, reflecting their origin in the practices of the Jurchen Jin dynasty.[7] Soon, however, they were switched to Mongolian. The extant Mongolian examples for officials always began with the famous phrase, "By the power of eternal heaven" (*Möngke tngri-yin kücün-dür*). They conclude with the phrases, "The decree of the great khan [or whoever issued it]; any person whosoever who does not respect it shall be punished, shall die." In between those two lines of texts, *paizas* for those of official or military rank carried an additional line of text: "By the protection of the imperial good fortune." Those *paizas* only for use on the post roads, however, such as the one pictured here, did not include that phrase.

Reforms under Qubilai Khan

The *paiza* system was reshaped by the reforming zeal of the fifth Mongol khan, Qubilai (r. 1260–1294), as were virtually all other features of the Mongolian government. The first reform, initiated in 1261, established a new level of urgent post-road *paizas*, marked not by a tiger's head but by a gyrfalcon. Other reforms are visible in the *paiza* pictured. The inscription was simplified to no longer say "shall die." The shape of *paizas* for messengers was changed from oblong to round; these new-style *paizas* were called in Chinese "round tallies" (*yuanfu*). Post roads elsewhere in the Mongol Empire, however, retained the traditional oblong form and inscription.

Pakpa Lama and the Square Script

Another major reform visible in this *paiza* was in the script used to write the inscription. Between 1269 and 1271, after defeating his rivals and securing the throne but before planning the conquest of the Song dynasty in South China, Qubilai Khan carried out a number of reforms that promoted a new multi-ethnic style of universal rule. These included claiming the Chinese-style dynastic title of Yuan and building and renaming a new capital at the site of present-day Beijing. Another of these universalizing measures was to commission his Imperial Preceptor, the Pakpa Lama, Lodro Gyeltsen (1235–1280),[8] to create a script for the entire empire, suitable for writing Mongolian, Chinese, and Tibetan.

Pakpa Lama had entered the Mongol empire as a boy hostage in 1244 when the famous Sakya Pandita, his uncle (1182–1251), was summoned to the court of the Mongol prince Köten[9] in what is now Gansu Province. According to Mongol practice, every local ruler and official above a certain rank had to submit a son, younger brother, or nephew as hostage to serve in the bodyguard (*keshikten*) of the khan or of the local member of the imperial family in charge of the area. As a local ruler in Tibet, Sakya Pandita had to nominate Lodro Gyeltsen and his brother as his hostages, and they entered Köten's entourage. After Köten died, his cousin Qubilai, then a prince supervising all of North China, took over his bodyguard. Lodro Gyeltsen soon graduated from the bodyguard and was ordained as a monk in 1255. Within a few years he was making his mark as a debater, Sanskritist, and tantric guru to Qubilai and his wife Chabui. One year after Qubilai became great khan in 1260, he appointed his young chaplain, now known as Pakpa Lama, or "Noble Guru," as "State Preceptor" and head of all Buddhists in the empire.

For more about Tibetan Buddhism at the Mongol court, see Mahakala Stone Sculpture, no. 39.

Pakpa Lama used his philological knowledge to create a script called the square script in Mongolian[10] and the Pakpa script in the West. Up until this moment, the Mongols had been using the script of the Turkic-speaking Uyghurs, itself derived from the Sogdian and eventually the Aramaic script. Although well-adapted to Uyghur and Mongolian, the script was very poor at rendering Chinese or Tibetan. Pakpa Lama took the Tibetan letters, squared them off (hence the name), and reorganized them to be written vertically in columns left to right. With his training in traditional Indian philology, he added diacritical signs and special letters to handle the sounds of Mongolian and Chinese that were not available in the Tibetan script. The whole was proclaimed by Qubilai Khan in 1269 as the new script for the empire.

Although Qubilai established schools throughout the East Asian region of the Mongol Empire to promote the new script, it could not replace the Uyghur-Mongolian script, let alone Chinese or Tibetan, as the writing system of choice for scholars. Surviving samples of Pakpa script are mostly official pieces, such as the *paiza* shown here, or stone inscriptions, such as that at the Juyong Gate. Only a few pieces of printed literature are known. With the expulsion of the Yuan emperors from China, the Pakpa script fell out of use, except for occasional ornamental use in Tibet.

See Juyong Guan Stupa Gate, no. 48.

The most commonly preserved genre in Pakpa script writing is that of exemption decrees, or *darqan jarliq*. These decrees declare that in return for clerics saying prayers for the long life of the khan, this or that Tibetan Buddhist monastery, Eastern Orthodox church, Muslim Sufi lodge, or Daoist temple was exempt from any requisitions, whether demanded by messengers or by itinerant officials and commanders. These decrees were commonly bilingual, and in China, Mongolia, and Tibet, the Mongolian version was usually in the Pakpa script.[11] Such decrees are, along with the *paizas*, monuments to the privileges of the Mongol Empire's ruling class, privileges to requisition from others and to be free of requisitions themselves. Religious leaders were key members of this ruling class, using their prayers to preserve the lives of the khans and their learning to train the khans' heirs and improve the regime's governance.

Further Reading

Atwood, Christopher P. 2004a. *Encyclopedia of Mongolia and the Mongol Empire*, 258–59 (on post-road system), 519–20 (on square script). New York: Facts on File.

Dang, Baohai. 2001–3. "The Paizi of the Mongol Empire." *Zentralasiatische Studien* 30, 31–62; 32, 7–10.

György Kara. 2005. *Books of the Mongolian Nomads: More than Eight Centuries of Writing Mongolian*. Translated by John R. Krueger, 51–62. Bloomington: Research Institute for Inner Asian Studies, Indiana University Press.

Notes

1 Unless otherwise indicated, all terms are Mongolian.
2 See Doerfer 1965, 239–41; Cleaves 1953, 255–59.
3 Uyghur and Persian: *yam*. See Dang 2006; Shim 2014; Vér 2016 and 2017.
4 Petech 1990, 61–68.
5 Uyghur and Persian: *yarligh*.
6 See Atwood 2021, 148–49; Juvaini 1958, 2: 508–9, 598–99.
7 See Atwood 2021, 86–87, 112–13.
8 Mongolian: Pağba Blam-a Lodoi-Jaltsan.
9 Tibetan: Goden.
10 Mongolian: *Dörbeljin üsüg*.
11 Atwood 2004b, 238–43.

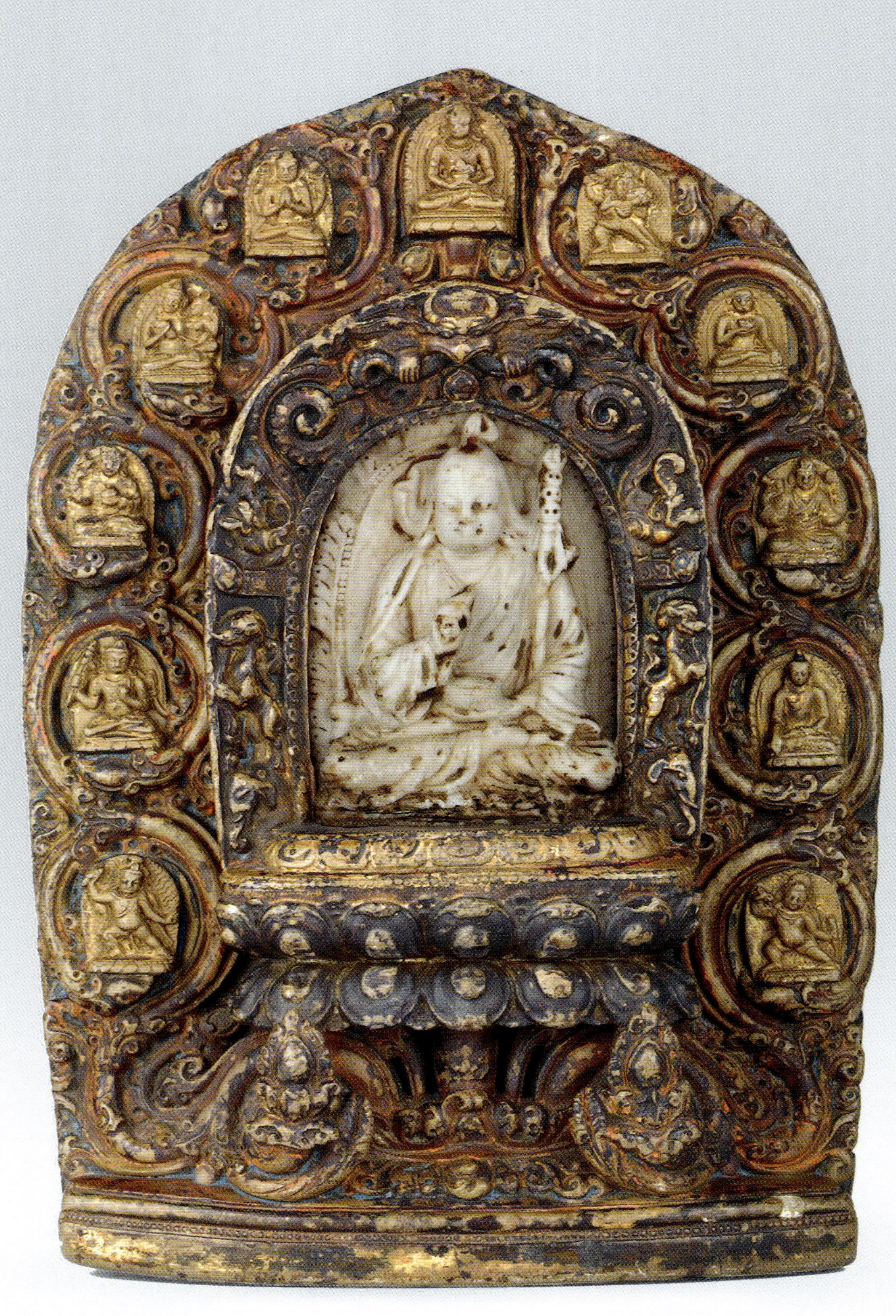

Nº 43

Padmasambhava and His Manifestations

Tibet, late 13th century or later

The Names that Encode Many Aspects of the "Lotus-Born" Guru

DANIEL A. HIRSHBERG AND ELENA PAKHOUTOVA

THIS UNUSUAL SCULPTURE CARVED FROM STONE is perhaps the earliest depicting Padmasambhava, the Precious Guru (Guru Rinpoche), in his eight manifestations. Among all the great masters who brought Buddhism to Tibet, Padmasambhava, whose name means "Lotus-Born," is unparalleled. Although the historical record makes scant mention of him, a vibrant biographical tradition developed in the centuries after the Tibetan Empire's collapse (ca. 842), establishing his place at the epicenter of Tibetan Buddhism, both figuratively and iconographically.[1] According to later histories, the Indian monastic Shantarakshita advised the Tibetan emperor Tri Songdetsen (742–ca. 800) to invite Padmasambhava, a tantric master, to accomplish what they could not: ritually subdue the local gods and demons so Buddhism could be established in Tibet.

The earliest surviving mentions of Padmasambhava seem to indicate that he operated under several aliases.[2] He became the focal point of the Ancient (Nyingma) tradition, which traces its lineages to his teachings. Regardless of sectarian affiliation, every Tibetan monastery contains statues and paintings of this cultural hero, for all of Tibet's traditions are thought to stem from Padmasambhava and his activities.

Aspects Revealed

For more about treasures (*terma*) and treasure revealers, see *Dorje* Discovered by Dorje Lingpa, no. 51.

For a representation of Padmasamhaba's pure realm, see Portable Shrine, no. 88.

For examples of mandalas, see Chakrasamvara Mandala with Newar Donors, no. 29; Mandala of Manjuvajra of the *Vajravali* Set, no. 50.

Nyangrel Nyima Wozer (1124–1192) was the first of the great Buddhist treasure revealers. These *tertons* claim to be reincarnations of Padmasambhava's eighth-century disciples who are empowered to recover his concealed texts and relics, known as treasures (*terma*) in later centuries. As the preeminent architect of this tradition, Nyangrel compiled the *Copper Island Biography of Padmasambhava* (*Namtar Zanglingma*).[3] The first text to structure a complete narrative of the Precious Guru's life, it began with his origin story of being discovered on the pistil of a lotus in northwest India and ended with his final departure from Tibet. Nyangrel incorporated the scattered threads of Padmasambhava lore, preserving the precedents of details available to him, including the multiple monikers that accumulate throughout the story. In the earliest surviving versions of the *Copper Island*—texts that are closest to Nyangrel's twelfth-century original—Padmasambhava goes by a dozen names and epithets.

Many years after completing the *Copper Island*, Nyangrel had a meditative vision in which he traveled to a pure realm and met eight distinct Padmasambhavas, each positioned at the cardinal and intermediate directions of a mandala.[4] The "eight names of the guru" *(guru tsen gye)* became a standard set, encoding key moments of Padmasambhava's life into monikers that inspired each aspect's iconography, despite scant descriptive details in textual references.

Iconography of the Eight Names

Padmasambhava and His Manifestations; Tibet; ca. late 13th century or later; stone with traces of pigment, 9¼ × 6½ × 2 in. (23.5 × 16.7 × 5 cm); Foundation of Alain Bordier–Tibet Museum, Gruyères, Switzerland; photograph courtesy Tibet Museum–Fondation Alain Bordier

This sculpture from the Alain Bordier collection represents the normative set of Padmasambhava's eight names in a typical composition. The central figure is his most popular form, named Padmasambhava in Sanskrit and Pema Jungne in Tibetan, also known as Lake-Born Vajra (Tsokye Dorje), referencing his miraculous birth on a lotus.

At bottom left and right are his two fierce aspects, Sengge Dradrok and Dorje Drolo, unmistakable with ferocious faces and corpulent bodies wreathed in flames. Nothing in the *Copper Island* suggests that these names should be depicted so monstrously. Dorje Drolo was the last of the Guru's names to be standardized. Here, he displays his characteristic iconography—a vajra in the right hand and three-sided

For other examples of this form, see Ritual Dance Mask of Guru Dorje Drolo, no. 94.

dagger, or *purba*, in the left—suggesting that the sculpture was created at a time when Padmasambhava's lore was already popularized by two expanded fourteenth-century biographies.[5] These texts repeat the eight names several times, further establishing them as the definitive set for Padmasambhava's aspects.[6]

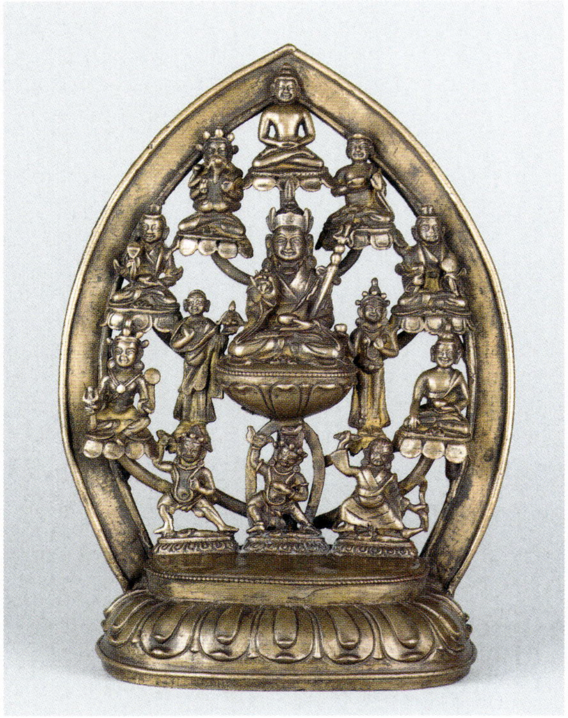

Directly above the fierce aspects are his manifestations as the tantrika Nyima Wozer and the monk Shakya Sengge, the latter of whom appears identical to renderings of Buddha Shakyamuni. Above them are the two king types, Loden Chokse and Pema Gyelpo, though only the latter is royalty. Loden Chokse is a tantrika who thrives in the charnel grounds; his royal attire adds symmetry to the visual pairing but lacks any precedent in narrative descriptions. The arrangement could also acknowledge an alignment of Nyima Wozer and Loden Chokse as transgressive tantric yogins, compared with the monk Shakya Sengge and king Pema Gyelpo, who are bound by social norms.

The final pairing below the triad at the apex includes Pema Jungne, wearing scholar's robes on the right, and Orgyen Dorje Chang, shown with his consort Mandarava at left. The depiction of a couple facing outward is unusual, reminiscent of Indic images of the Hindu deities Shiva and Parvati.

Padmasambhava and His Eight Manifestations, Hayagriva, flanked by Yeshe Tsogyel, and Shantarakshita; Tibet; 16th century; copper alloy, 9¼ × 6¾ × 4¼ in. (24.4 × 17.1 × 8.6 cm); Rubin Museum of Art; C2003.51.1 (HAR 65283)

Hierarchy of Padmasambhava's Three Bodies

Finally, the top triad includes Padmasambhava's most subtle and refined aspects. At the apex of the sculpture is Amitayus, who signifies his ultimate empty essence, known as the "truth body" (*dharmakaya*). Slightly below is the Four-Armed Avalokiteshvara, the bodhisattva of compassion, representing his blissful luminous nature as the "complete enjoyment body" (*sambhogakaya*). The figure at top right, portrayed with his consort in a dynamic standing posture and ensconced in flames, is less immediately recognizable. It is most likely Hayagriva, the fierce meditational deity of the lotus buddha family. He is appropriately placed in the position of Padmasambhava's "magically emanated body" (*nirmanakaya*). Hayagriva is also included in a similarly composed metal sculpture of Padmasambhava's aspects in the Rubin Museum. The iconography of Hayagriva seen here—with one face, two arms, and standing with his consort—is said to stem from the early treasure revealers, including Nyangrel.[7]

An early mandala painting shows the same form of Hayagriva at its center, surrounded by the manifestations of Padmasambhava on the lotus petals of the inner mandala.[8] It is dated to the fourteenth century on iconographic and stylistic grounds and provides a context for this carved image and its possible date.

Form and Material

The Padmasambhava sculpture featured here follows Indian compositions, most notably depictions of the Events of the Buddha's Life, in which a large central image is surrounded by smaller figures. Such portable reliefs made of soft stone phyllite and dated to the eleventh through thirteenth centuries are found across the Buddhist world.[9] Carved images of teachers with episodes from their lives in the same stone and format also survive but present different stylistic features.[10]

For another example of portable stone sculpture, see Mahakala Stone Sculpture, no. 39.

This sculpture also might have been carved from phyllite, a brown-beige-colored soft stone, but the central image is made from white stone, possibly soapstone. If so, it could explain the slightly worn features of the central figure's face and right hand, the elements that protrude the most on the sculpture. The rest of the central figure, set in shallower relief and protected by its placement in the niche, retains crisper details. Examples of miniature sculptures in soapstone portraying Tibetan teachers are rare.[11] Stone sculptures were typically painted, as traces of pigments here indicate.

For an image of an elaborate throne back, see Central Shrine Image of Kwa Baha, no. 22. For an image of a torana, see Torana of the Main Shrine at Yetakha Baha, no. 24.

Visual Conventions

The structurally common composition of the figures arranged around the main image includes a throne back reminiscent of Nepalese visual conventions. Such thrones, with elaborate torana-like arches,

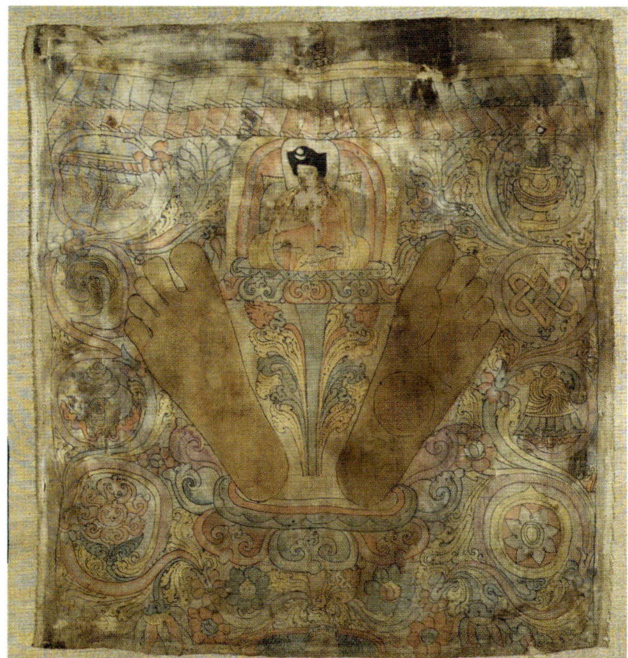

Karmapa with His Footprints; central Tibet; late 12th–early 13th century or later; pigments on silk, 21½ × 19 in. (54.61 × 48.26 cm); Rubin Museum of Art; gift of the Shelley and Donald Rubin Foundation; F1997.32.2 (HAR 508)

mythical *garuda* birds at the top, and stacked animals on either side of the throne, are often found in architectural settings—for instance, stone sculptures carved into the niches of stupas or fountains—as well as paintings.

Given the scarcity of stylistically equivalent sculptural examples, it is helpful to consider painted representations that parallel the sculpture's visual conventions. Possibly contemporary with this carving is an early thangka painting of Karmapa with His Footprints in the Rubin Museum collection.[12] It shares several visual elements with the sculpture: the throne back, an oval-shaped mandorla (body radiance), stacked animals on either side of the throne, entwining lotus vines that encircle each of the vignettes around the central figure,[13] and the arrangement of the teacher's lotus throne, including two small blooms at the lower forefront.

A distinct element in the painting is a parasol that replaces the *garuda*-topped torana-like arch. However, a painting from about the thirteenth century in a private collection that portrays another famous Indian master, Padampa Sanggye, exhibits the same style of throne as the sculpture, complete with the *garuda* at the throne's apex. It also displays all the other elements described above. Additionally, similar encircling single-figure vines painted around a focal point on the ceiling of the Luri stupa cave and generally dated to the thirteenth to early fourteenth century provide another temporal reference to this visual convention.

See the Chorten Cave of Luri, no. 44.

Teacher depictions appear to emerge from a shared cultural environment, in which Nepalese and Indian conventions were skillfully employed to create Tibetan Buddhist images. Unlike the earlier Indian sculptures, often treasured as portable souvenirs from sacred sites, these images seem intended to inspire devotional reverence in their patrons, who were disciples of the lineages represented by these masters.

Further Reading

Hirshberg, Daniel A. 2016. *Remembering the Lotus-Born: Padmasambhava in the History of Tibet's Golden Age.* Somerville, MA: Wisdom.

Pakhoutova, Elena, ed. 2018. *The Second Buddha: Master of Time.* Exhibition catalog. New York: Delmonico Books/Prestel.

Yeshe Tsogyal (Ye shes mtsho rgyal). 1991. *The Lotus-Born: The Life-Story of Padmasambhava.* Translated by Erik Pema Kunzang. Boston: Shambhala.

Notes

1 For an overview of Padmasambhava's historicity and mythology, see Hirshberg 2016, 1–31.
2 See Dalton 2020, passim.
3 For an English translation of a later nineteenth-century publication of the *Copper Island*, see Tsogyal 1991.
4 *Dri ma med pa*, in Chos kyi 'od zer, Myang ston Bsod nams seng ge, and Mi 'gyur rdo rje 1978, 150–60.
5 *Shel brag ma* (the *Crystal Cave*) and *Gser 'phreng* (the *Golden Garland*) are named after their places of discovery. A problematic early twentieth-century French translation of the *Crystal Cave* was later translated into English as the *Life and Liberation of Padmasambhava* (Yeshe Tsogyal [1978] 2007). Kazi Dawa Samdup translated excerpts of the *Golden Garland* into English (Evans-Wentz [1954] 2000).
6 Guru Chowang (1212–1270), who was intimately familiar with his claimed preincarnation's writings, dreamed of the eight names. By the fourteenth century, the eight names are praised repeatedly in the *Crystal Cave*, so the convention had become quite normalized by that time.
7 Jeff Watt, "Mandala of Hayagriva (Buddhist Deity)—Red with Consort (1 Face, 2 Hands)," Himalyan Art Resources, accessed June 29, 2021, https://www.himalayanart.org/items/30911.
8 Private collection, https://www.himalayanart.org/items/30911.
9 See Bautze-Picron 1999.
10 Compare with fig. 122D in von Schroeder 2001a, 1:382–83.
11 See a lama figure featured in the Christie's sale catalog New York, March 20, 2012, lot 105, https://www.christies.com/en/lot/lot-5538758.
12 The painting had been variously dated. Kathryn Selig Brown (2004, 60) dates it to the early fourteenth century. David Jackson gives two different dates, the late twelfth century (2011, 79) and the thirteenth century (2009, 73–74).
13 In the painting these are the Eight Auspicious Symbols.

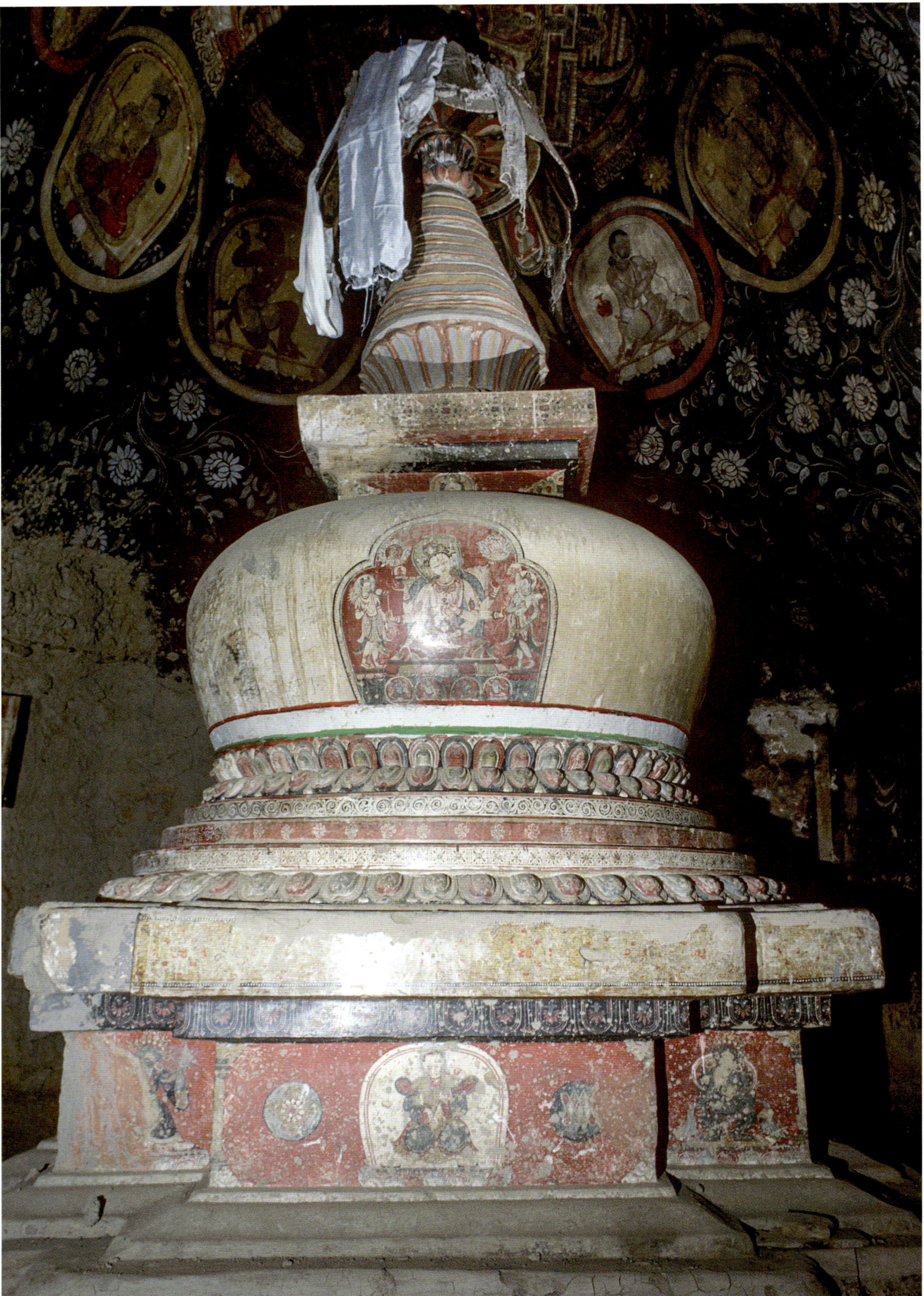

No 44

The Chorten Cave of Luri

Luri, present-day Mustang District, Nepal, ca. 1300

Commemorative Monument for a Charismatic Teacher

CHRISTIAN LUCZANITS

Mustang is well known for its caves containing a single large chorten, the Tibetan-style stupa. Most of them, spread across the country, are in ruins, but Luri's chorten is well preserved.[1] The small cave cut into the conglomerate rock contains paintings of exceptional quality, the chorten itself outstanding for its highly polished surface. Accordingly, the cave has gained considerable scholarly attention, but problems of attribution remain.[2] Further, attention on the cave's art has distracted from any attempt to explain its remote location and appearance.

Chorten of Victory

Despite its early date, the chorten already has a shape that takes precedence in Tibet from the fifteenth century on. A multicornered base forms the protective foundation of the structure. Its central surfaces are painted with the Four Great Kings flanked by two of the Eight Auspicious Symbols; Dhritarashtra, the protector of the East, flanked by the wheel and the endless knot, is seen here. The short faces on the corners feature two protective deities each, some of them challenging to identify precisely. A jewel-ornament pattern and a garland mark the projecting steps at the throne's top, indicating the distinguished nature of what comes above.

The chorten's distinctive base is formed by three stepped rings, each painted with a different pattern. They sit on a single row of lotus petals and identify the structure as Chorten of Complete Victory.[3] The dome, sitting on a double lotus base, features the long-life goddess Ushnishavijaya, who is represented together with her assembly. On the other three sides of the dome, in clockwise succession, are the Bodhisattvas Manjushri and Avalokiteshvara in four-armed forms and the protector Vajrapani. They form a group called the protectors of the three families, the term "family" here designating deities of similar symbolism.

For more about Ushnishavijaya, see Relief Carving of a Nine-Deity Ushnishavijaya, no. 41; Plaque Commemorating the *Bhimaratha* Old Age Ritual, no. 85.

The dome is crowned by the square stepped *harmika,* which carries the thirteen wheels of a conic spine surmounted by an umbrella and a sun and moon finial. The lower faces of the *harmika* feature four of the five esoteric buddhas, Vairochana facing the eastern direction. The fifth buddha, Akshobhya, is represented by the chorten itself, and also in the center of the mandala right above the chorten. In this nine-deity mandala, Akshobhya presides over the female personifications of the Eight Auspicious Symbols. The Eight Medicine Buddhas and eight offerings personified as goddesses are represented on the parasol and its sides, signifying a continuation of the life theme also on the level of the buddha representations.

Proponents of Highest Esoteric Teachings

The Akshobhya mandala above the chorten also centers the decoration of the cave itself, where it is surrounded by eight great siddhas within a common lotus scroll. These are, read from the east clockwise, Indrabhuti, Dombiheruka, Nagarjuna, Ghantapa, Padmavajra, Luyipa, Kukkuripa, and Saraha. They constitute a subgroup of the eighty-plus siddhas who symbolize the transmission of the highest esoteric Buddhist teachings to Tibet.[4] That Padmavajra takes here the position above the head of Buddha Akshobhya is significant, for it excludes a Sakya tradition context for the cave, as Virupa would be represented instead.

The lotus ring on which the mandala sits is also the central blossom of the scrollwork that expands toward the eight siddhas and then across the entire upper part of the cave against its black background, its predominantly white blossoms appearing like stars in the night sky.

The Luri Chorten, as seen from the entrance, showing Ushnishavijaya and Dhritarashtra; Mustang, Nepal; ca. 1300; photograph by Philip Lieberman, 1993

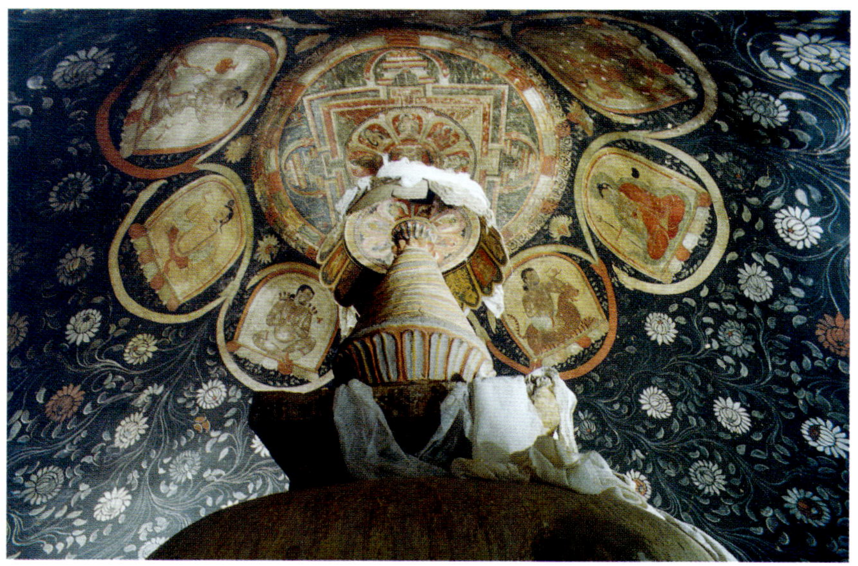

The top of the chorten showing some of the Eight Medicine Buddhas, and on the ceiling, the Akshobhya mandala surrounded by the eight siddhas; Luri chorten cave; Mustang, Nepal; ca. 1300; photograph by Jaroslav Poncar, 1996

The bottom part of the cave has straight walls, the back wall covered with further murals. If we assume that two panels are lost in the damaged left corner of the cave, then Shakyamuni flanked by his chief disciples forms the center of the composition. To his left is the portrait of a teacher wearing a rounded red hat, as is typical of but not exclusive to Sakya tradition portraits. On the right are Vajradhara, the primordial buddha of the highest esoteric teachings, Vajrasattva, and Achala. The composition is topped by a row of inscribed teachers forming a teaching transmission lineage, with a row of subsidiary deities and auspicious symbols below them. While the lineage cannot be identified precisely, the three lay and six monastic teachers indicate a derivation from one Marpa via a Ngok teacher, and thus a broader Kagyu context.[5]

The right side wall is covered with a succession of mantras on a common lotus base. The large six-syllable mantra referring to Avalokiteshvara occupies the left side of the panel. It is followed by the mantras of Shakyamuni, the Medicine Buddha Bhaishajyaguru, Vajrasattva, the five esoteric buddhas beginning with Akshobhya, Manjushri, Vajrapani, and Achala. Here, almost all deities depicted in the murals are referenced in their speech form.

Overall, the walls refer to the highest esoteric teachings and their earthly protagonists, the Indian siddhas surrounding the mandala on the ceiling and the Tibetan teacher within his teaching transmission.

A Stylistic Benchmark

The Luri murals are remarkable for their sophistication. Expertly drawn, proportionate outlines frame the finely shaded figures. Textiles are decorated with fine patterns, signaling their delicate nature, but their ends fall in thick, fleshy folds. The jewelry is delicate and built of multiple layers of color. Where appropriate, fine scrollwork covers the surfaces, and flower blossoms envelop the backgrounds.

Most of the shapes and details seen in the Luri paintings find their direct comparison in Kathmandu Valley painting, and they are thus considered exemplary for Tibetan patronage of the early Newar style, traditionally called the Nepalese style or Beri.[6] Most notable among the motifs are the clouds in the shape of a three-pointed leaf flanking the heads of Ushnishavijaya and the figures on the main wall. Technically, the highlighting of exposed areas through a white line is particularly noteworthy and results in a single or double white line on the nose ridge.

For examples of Beri-style scroll paintings in Tibet, see Virupa, no. 37; Mandala of Manjuvajra of the *Vajravali* Set, no. 50.

See Mural Painting at Zhalu Monastery, no. 47.

The Luri cave's attribution has to rely on stylistic comparison. Close similarities with the most pronounced Beri-style paintings for Tibetan patrons preserved on canvas and at Zhalu Monastery, in southwestern Tibet, and assumptions about the relative chronology and dates of the murals there resulted in an attribution of Luri to about 1300.[7] However, this is merely a hypothesis, as none of the comparators can be securely dated, and there are not enough dated Kathmandu Valley paintings around that time that could be used for comparison.

It is clear, though, that the Luri cave marks the moment when Beri-style murals in Mustang began to flourish, leading toward the earlier of the two large temples in the regional capital Lo Montang, the Jampa Lhakhang (Maitreya Temple). A local variant of this style is also documented in recently studied manuscript illuminations preserved locally, some of them predating the Luri cave.[8]

Commemorative Monument

Surveying the art of Mustang preceding the rise of its kingdom in the fifteenth century, it is remarkable that donor depictions on manuscripts and the stupa caves feature single monastic teachers. These must

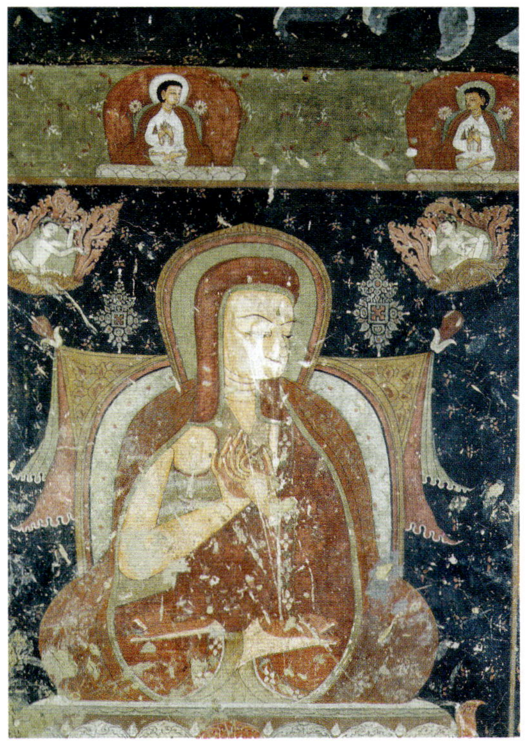

Tibetan Teacher, with two white-clad lineage figures in the row above, on the back wall of Luri chorten cave; Mustang, Nepal; ca. 1300; photograph by Jaroslav Poncar, 1996

have been charismatic teachers of great influence within the community. The Luri cave most likely is a commemorative monument constructed after the passing of such a charismatic teacher, the stupa plausibly containing his remains and the painting on the main wall of the cave representing him.

A nearby stupa cave called Tashi Gheling or Tashi Kabum reduces its decoration to the portrait of the teacher and Shadakshari Lokeshvara, the form of Avalokiteshvara named after and representing the six-syllable mantra *om mani padme hum*, which is also written on the wall. The comparison of the caves shows that besides the teacher portrait, Avalokiteshvara plays a special role, presumably because of the salvific powers ascribed to him. His prominence may well be early evidence for the practice of a so-called *mani dungchur*, the recitation of the mantra of this bodhisattva one hundred million times on behalf of the deceased. This, or a similar practice, may also explain the panel on the entry wall of the Luri chorten cave covered with stroke marks denoting the repeated completion of a certain religious task.

A local example of a chorten of the Luri type used to fulfill the intentions of a deceased teacher is preserved at Namgyal Monastery. This stupa, identified by inscription as Liberation through Seeing, is dedicated to Kunga Drolchok, 1507–1566, a prominent teacher of the Jonang tradition. It is likely that the Luri stupa is a precedent in this regard.

A commemorative purpose also fits the location and the black background of the Luri cave. High up on a cliff with originally no or very little light and almost no space for worship beyond circumambulation, the Luri cave certainly was not meant for group visits. One wonders if the cave was meant to be casually visited at all, a question that also applies to other Buddhist cave monuments.[9] As such, the sumptuous decoration of the cave is solely meant to create the most suitable backdrop for the initial entombment and accrual of merit, as well as the subsequent rituals. They qualify the teacher commemorated as an exceptional religious practitioner with an illustrious religious pedigree and backed by an affluent community. Local tradition holds that this teacher is a certain Kunzang Jalu, literally, "all-good rainbow body," but nothing is known about this individual.[10]

Further Reading

Neumann, Helmut F., and Heidi A. Neumann. 2010. "Early Wall Paintings in Lo: Luri Reconsidered." In *Wonders of Lo: The Artistic Heritage of Mustang*, edited by Erberto Lo Bue, 64–75. Mumbai: Marg Foundation.

Sharf, Robert H. 2013. "Art in the Dark: The Ritual Context of Buddhist Caves in Western China." In *Art of Merit: Studies in Buddhist Art and Its Conservation; Proceedings of the Buddhist Art Forum 2012*, edited by David Park, Kuenga Wangmo, and Sharon Cather, 38–65. London: Archetype.

Notes

1 A documentation of the Luri cave with photographs by Philip Lieberman and Jaroslav Poncar is found online: https://luczanits.net/sites/Luri.html. Without these photographs, generously provided, and a research grant from the Arts and Humanities Research Council (AHRC) for "Tibetan Buddhist Monastery Collections Today" (Grant Ref: AH/N00681X/1), which facilitated the last visit to the site, this study would not have been possible.

2 Studies directly focused on the cave are Gutschow 1994; Neumann 1994 and 1997; Neumann and Neumann 2010.

3 For different interpretations of this stupa type, see Bentor 1995a; Skorupski 2001.

4 On early representations of the eight great siddhas, see Luczanits 2006b.

5 The captions identifying the teachers are mentioned in Alsop 2004, 138n2, and briefly discussed in Vitali 2012b, 96–100. While the reading of the captions in the latter is partially erroneous, and more can be said about the depicted teachers, they do not provide conclusive information.

6 See D. Jackson 2010, 103, whose interpretation of the Tibetan teachers represented is erroneous.

7 In Neumann and Neumann 2010, 73–74, a late thirteenth-century date is proposed for the Luri cave, slightly earlier than in their previous publications.

8 See Luczanits 2021, 132–43.

9 See Sharf 2013.

10 See Vitali 2012b, 96–97.

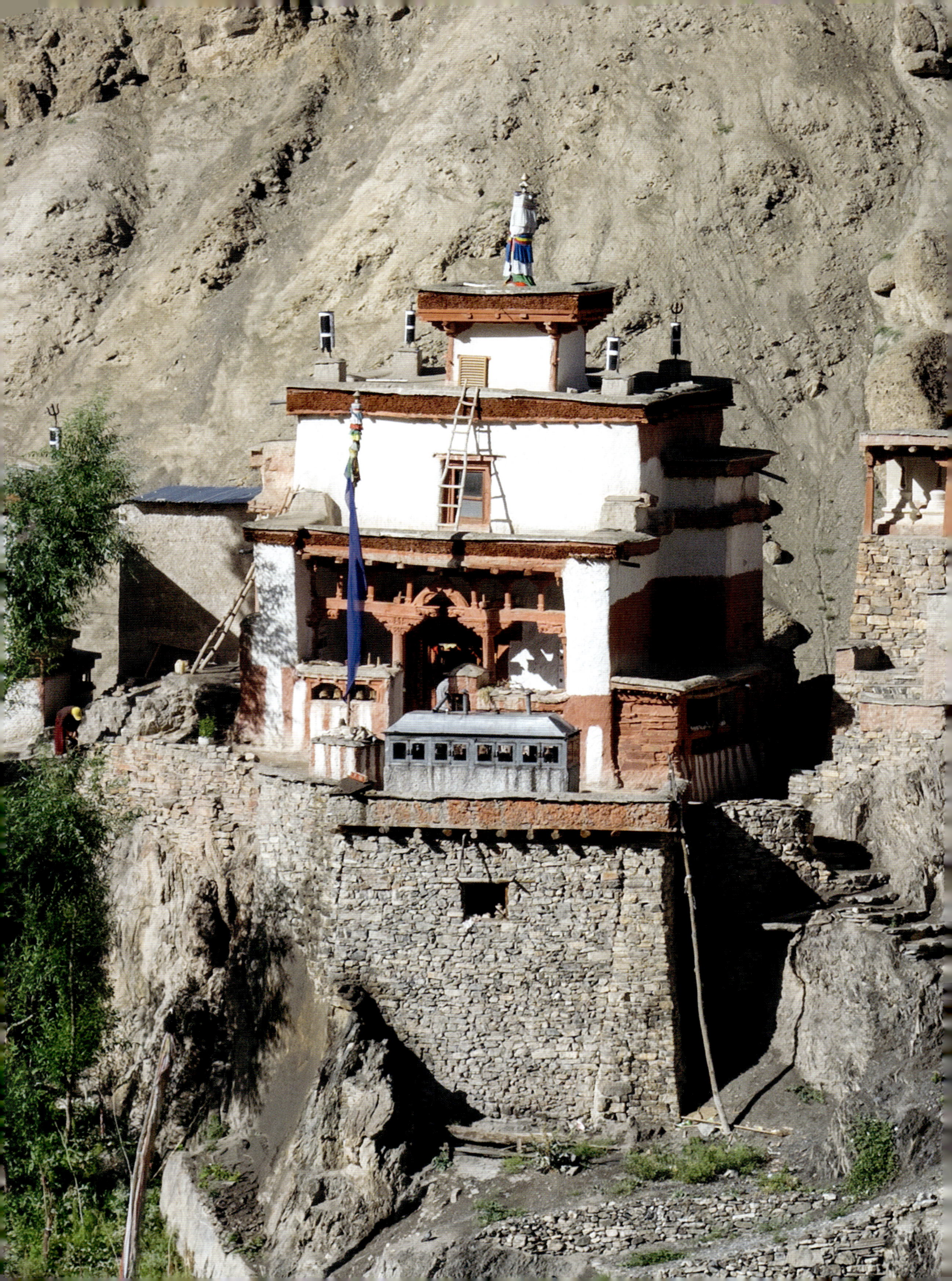

№ 45

The Temple of Wanla

Wanla, Ladakh, India, first half of the 14th century

A Landmark Monument in the Art History of Ladakh

NILS MARTIN

THE THREE-STORY TEMPLE OF WANLA holds a special place in the history and art history of the western Himalayan region of Ladakh and Tibet. It is the largest extant Buddhist monument of the mid-thirteenth to mid-fifteenth century in Ladakh and architecturally one of the most elaborate. It contains, moreover, an illuminating foundation inscription as well as vast original ensembles of sculptures and murals in relatively good condition.

The Foundation of a Local Chief

Through its location and its foundation inscription, the Wanla temple attests to a concentration of political, economic, and religious powers in a local chief of Ladakh around the first decades of the fourteenth century, a period otherwise little known in the history of the region.

Visible from afar, the temple overlooks the confluence of two rivers, along which used to run a profitable trade route connecting Ladakh to Tibet, the Tarim Basin, and northern India to the east, and to Kashmir and Central Asia to the west. It was built as the crowning jewel of an ancient fortified complex that also included a settlement and a three-story palace.[1] Prior to the foundation of the temple, the top floor of that palace, ornamented with wood carvings of Kashmiri style, probably served as a family shrine for the Wanla chiefs.

The foundation inscription of the temple recounts how its patron, a local chief bearing the partly non-Tibetan name Bhak Darskya, conquered several strategic sites around his ancestral estate before rising to regional prominence, presumably supported by nearby Kashmir. Later in his life, he founded the temple to accumulate merit for the awakening of all sentient beings and, in particular, for ensuring a good rebirth for his parents and himself, following a pattern typical of Buddhist art patronage.[2] This foundation marked Wanla as a significant place in Ladakh not only for politics and economics but for religious activities as well.

See Monumental Manjushri with Mahasiddha-Adorned Robe at Alchi, no. 35.

Viewed from outside, the temple recalls the famous three-story temple of Alchi (early thirteenth century), about eighteen and a half miles (thirty kilometers) east, also in Ladakh. Its architectural conception, its iconographic program, and the style of its artworks, however, differ considerably.

Both temples feature a square ground floor with an entrance hall at the front and three niches in the back and sides, a square gallery of about the same width as the ground floor, and a small cubic lantern.[3] Yet, unlike the Alchi temple, the Wanla temple appears from several perplexing architectural details to have undergone a gradual transformation from a one-story building to its present shape, presumably over a few decades.[4]

A Rich Iconographic Program Displaying Tantric Teachings

Temple of Wanla viewed from the northeast; Wanla, Ladakh, India; first half of the 14th century; stone masonry, adobes, and timbers; approx. 32 × 32 × 37 ft. (10 × 10 × 11.5 m); photograph by Nils Martin

Inside are found three large clay sculptures in the niches, a set of statues modeled in clay and manuscript paper on the back side of the gallery, and murals on all the walls. Together, these artworks compose an iconographic program so rich that the temple has been considered one of the earliest encyclopedic monuments of Tibet.[5]

The colossal fifteen-foot-tall clay statue of the main niche represents the eleven-headed form of Avalokiteshvara, the personal meditation deity of Bhak Darskya. The cult focused on this universal form

For another eleven-headed form of Avalokiteshvara following a different tradition, see Bodhisattva Avalokiteshvara and the Buddha's Footprints, no. 33.

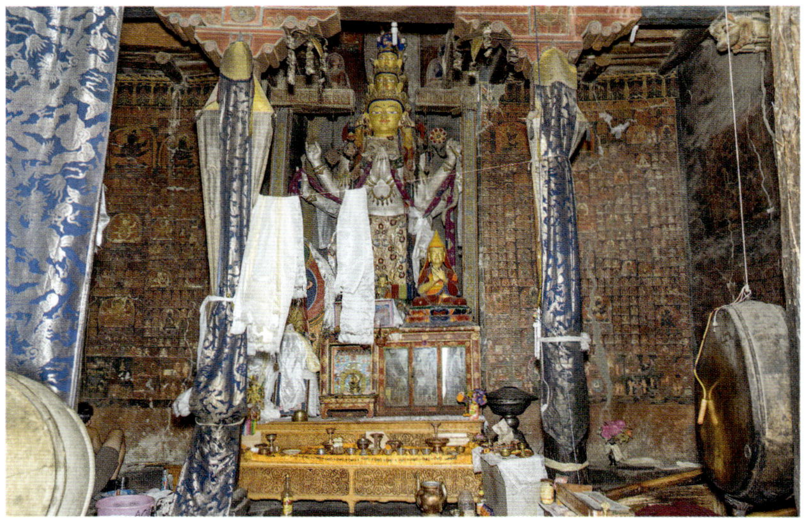

Temple of Wanla, the main wall of the ground floor, with the colossal statue of Eleven-Headed Avalokiteshvara enshrined in the main niche; Wanla, Ladakh, India; first half of the 14th century; photograph by Nils Martin

was considered by some the vehicle subsuming all other Buddhist practices. Eleven-Headed Avalokiteshvara is represented again in an admirable mural illustrating aspects of his iconography and practice that may have been difficult to achieve in sculpture. There, the deity is properly endowed with a thousand arms and hands showing various attributes and gestures. At his feet, Bhak Darskya, his family members, and a few monks are portrayed performing a ritual. The nearby representation of King Songtsen Gampo, recognized as an emanation of Avalokiteshvara since at least the eleventh century, may have served to relate the patron to him in terms of religious practice if not of enlightened political activities.

For more about this assembly and the iconography of the Ancient (Nyingma) tradition, see Padmasambhava and His Manifestations, no. 43.

For more about this assembly, see Chakrasamvara Mandala with Newar Donors, no. 29.

In general, the murals are arranged hierarchically from the more inclusive to the more tantric as one progresses from the entrance to the back of the temple and contemplates the walls from bottom to top and from their periphery to their center. Among them figure numerous tantric assemblies with deities in sexual union, which were rarely represented in western Tibet, if at all, before the late thirteenth century, as the associated teachings were not yet openly promoted. Some of these assemblies, including the Eight Forms of Padmasambhava and the Eight Pronouncements, relate to the teachings of the Ancient (Nyingma) tradition, allegedly obtained during the height of the Tibetan Empire (mid-eighth to early ninth century). Others, like the mandala of the deity Chakrasamvara, relate to the teachings of the New traditions (Sarma), obtained from India and Nepal over the course of the eleventh and twelfth centuries.[6] The combined practice of these teachings was common within different branches of the Kagyu tradition, which carried on the teachings of Gampopa and formed a large portion of the New traditions.

Several assemblies and all the lineages of transmission from master to disciple represented in the set of statues as well as on top of the walls relate, in particular, the Wanla temple to the Drigung branch of the Kagyu tradition,[7] which was firmly implanted in western Tibet since the early thirteenth century.[8] The foundation inscription specifies that the youngest son of Bhak Darskya received teachings from the hierarch of Drigung Monastery.

An Aesthetic Change from Kashmiri to Central Tibetan Art

The sculptures and murals of the temple are attributed in the foundation inscription to three artists with Tibetan names composing a familial workshop. However, the hands of at least ten painters, from masters to apprentices, can be recognized in the murals of the temple. These artists followed not the Kashmiri style characteristic of earlier western Tibetan art, but the styles in vogue in central Tibet at the time, which derived from northeastern Indian and Nepalese arts.

For a famous example of Sharri style, see Tara Who Protects from the Eight Great Fears, no. 27.

For famous examples of Beri style, see Mural Painting at Zhalu Monastery, no. 47; Virupa, no. 37.

The murals predominantly feature the repertoire of motifs associated with the northeastern Indian style (Sharri), while that of the Nepalese style (Beri) was reserved for a secondary stylistic mode. This mode served in part to bring variation to the thrones of the main deities and to convey a gradation from secondary "Nepalese" deities to principal "northeastern Indian" ones in a few assemblies.[9]

Together with the promulgation of highly tantric teachings, this aesthetic change may have reflected the gradual religious alignment of Ladakhi patrons with central Tibetan Buddhist schools over the thirteenth century. It may, however, have also become inevitable owing to a lack of available

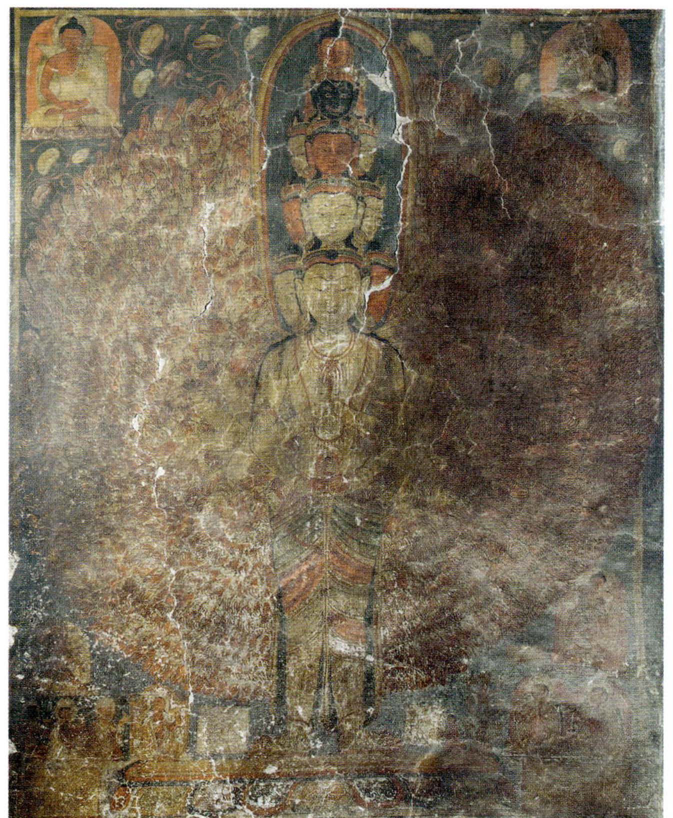

Eleven-Headed Thousand-Armed Avalokiteshvara surrounded by related divine figures, including King Songtsen Gampo (lower right corner), and donors performing a ritual (bottom); temple of Wanla, ground floor, left side wall of the left niche; Wanla, Ladakh, India; first half of the 14th century; natural pigments on painting plaster; approx. 5 × 4 ft. (1.5 × 1.2 m); photograph by Nils Martin

craftsmanship from Kashmir following the brutal conquest of that region by the Mongols in the mid-thirteenth century.[10]

The Wanla Group of Monuments

The Wanla temple is not the only Buddhist monument of Ladakh displaying the above-mentioned iconographic and stylistic features. In fact, they are also seen in at least five other temples and a gateway stupa. These were founded in areas under the political influence of Bhak Darskya, and most of their murals appear to have been executed by painters also active in Wanla.[11] In particular, the great gateway stupa of Nyoma, in Ladakh's Jangtang, enshrining an admirable upper painted chamber,[12] almost certainly corresponds to the commemorative stupa that was founded by the sons of Bhak Darskya after the passing of their father.

Epigraphic, art historical, and radiocarbon-dating evidence concur to suggest that the Wanla group of monuments developed over several decades from the first to the second half of the fourteenth century. It attests to the continuous influence of the Drigung tradition over Ladakh even during the period of Sakya-Yuan rule in central Tibet (1264–1354).

The foundation of the Wanla temple appears to have been crucial for the creation of this group of monuments. Presumably, some of the numerous artisans who were hired to build, decorate, and furnish this large monument with Buddhist images over the years continued to be active in the next decades under the patronage of the same group of nobles constituted around Bhak Darskya. The creation of the Wanla group, in turn, had a tangible influence on later mural painting in Ladakh, with some painters active in the first half of the fifteenth century carrying on the artistic principles associated with it.[13]

Further Reading

Luczanits, Christian. 2002. "The Wanla bKra shis gsum brtsegs." In *Buddhist Art and Tibetan Patronage, Ninth to Fourteenth Centuries. PIATS 2000: Proceedings of the Ninth Seminar of the International Association for Tibetan Studies, Leiden 2000*, edited by Deborah Klimburg-Salter and Eva Allinger, 115–26. Brill's Tibetan Studies Library 2/7. Leiden: Brill.

Luczanits, Christian. 2015c. "The Interior Decoration of Wanla (Draft)." Homepage of Christian Luczanits. https://luczanits.net/sites/Wanla.html.

Martin, Nils. 2022. "The Wanla Group of Monuments: 14th-Century Tibetan Buddhist Murals in Ladakh." PhD diss., École Pratique des Hautes Études.

Notes

1 On this site, see Howard 1989, 257–61; Neuwirth and Auer 2015, 15–27; Pabel 2014, 57–67; on the palace, see De Antoni, Vets, and Martin, 2021.
2 On this inscription, see Tropper 2007; N. Martin 2022, 127–39.
3 On the architecture of the temple, see Kozicz 2002; Pabel 2014, 68–135; Neuwirth 2015.
4 See Pabel 2014, 318–37.
5 See Luczanits 2015a, 244.
6 On the iconographic program of the temple, see Luczanits 2015a; N. Martin 2022, 149–68.
7 On the early iconography of this tradition, see Luczanits 2015a; D. Jackson 2015a.
8 On the history of the Drigung tradition in the region, see Petech 1978.
9 See N. Martin 2022, 174–77.
10 On this conquest, see Jahn 1956, 180; Li 2011, 207.
11 On these monuments, see Luczanits 2015a, 244–47; N. Martin 2022.
12 On this monument, see van Ham 2014; Devers, Bruneau, and Vernier 2014, 122–28. For its connection to Wanla, see N. Martin 2022, 299–324.
13 For an example of a mural site continuing some artistic principles of the Wanla group, see Lo Bue 2007. For an extensive discussion on the legacy of the Wanla group in the arts of Ladakh, see N. Martin 2022, 344–434.

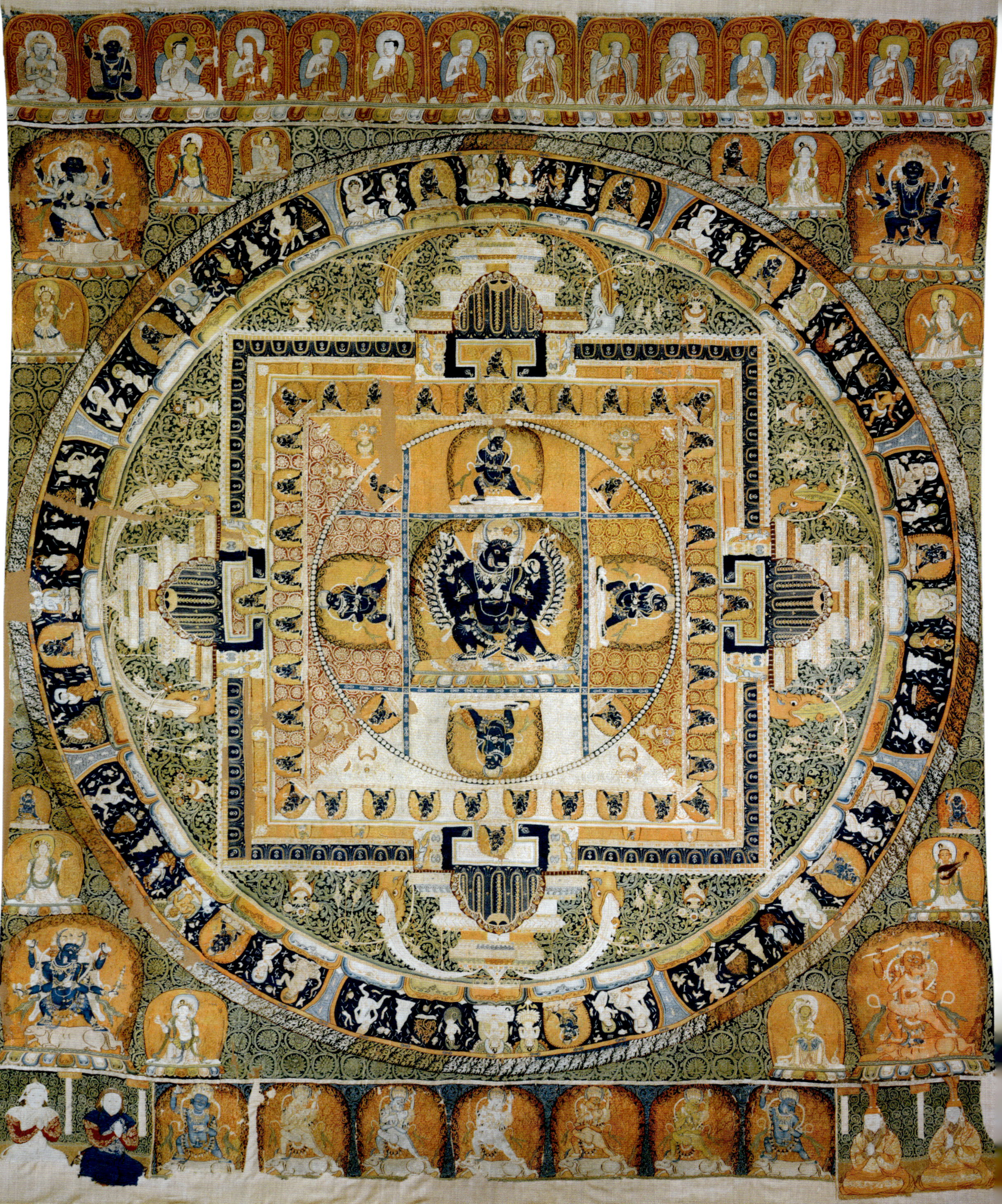

№ 46

Vajrabhairava Mandala

Mongol Empire/Yuan dynasty, probably Daidu (Beijing, China), ca. 1329

Woven Mandalas in the Mongol Imperial Court

YONG CHO

THE VAJRABHAIRAVA MANDALA is a large work, produced by weaving silk and gold threads using a highly sophisticated technique known in Chinese as "silk tapestry with slits (*kesi*)." The iconographic composition of this tapestry follows a standard pattern found in the Buddhist visual idioms of the wider Himalayan world. Dominating its pictorial program at the center is the mandala itself, which consists of a series of concentric circles and squares that create an architectural blueprint of a palatial structure. Vajrabhairava, the main deity of the mandala, occupies its central niche.[1] In the top row, weavers added portraits of Buddhist deities and monks who participated in the transmission of the iconographic and ritual knowledge associated with the Vajrabhairava mandala below. Along the bottom row, donor portraits clearly identify the work as a product of the imperial patronage during the Yuan period (1271–1368), the Mongol dynasty that ruled over eastern Eurasia.

For more about mandalas, see Chakrasamvara Mandala with Newar Donors, no. 29.

For more about the Mongol Empire, see Mongol Messenger's Badge, no. 42.

The Tibetan-language inscriptions provide names of each of these imperial donor figures. The white-robed figure in the bottom left corner is labeled "Emperor Tuq-Temür (Gyelpo Tuk Timur)" (Wenzong, r. 1328–1329, 1329–1332), while the blue-robed figure sitting next to him is his brother, labeled "Prince Qoshila (Gyelbu Koshala)" (Mingzong, r. 1329).[2] The two female donors, the respective wives of these two male figures, appear opposite them in the bottom row. "Budashiri Qatun (Ponmo Bhudhashri)" (1307–1340), the wife of Tuq-Temür, sits on the edge of the bottom right corner, and the wife of Qoshila, "Babusha Qatun (Ponmo Bhabucha)" (d. 1330), sits next to her.

Mandalas and Portraits

There are differing opinions about the intended function of this tapestry Vajrabhairava mandala.[3] One plausible theory is that it was originally produced to be hung inside one of the Yuan imperial portrait halls.[4] Starting in 1294, when the portrait hall was commissioned for the first Yuan emperor, Qubilai (Shizu, r. 1260–1294), and his principal wife, Chabui (Chabi, d. 1281), the members of the Mongol ruling house enshrined portraiture of their deceased family members in the imperially sponsored Buddhist monasteries.[5] These monasteries, established around the Yuan capital of Daidu (modern Beijing), had separate halls devoted to this purpose.[6]

For more on Daidu, see White Stupa, no. 40.

According to Chinese textual records, in each of these halls, the Mongol ruling house enshrined the portraits that captured the likeness of their deceased family members together with tantric Buddhist mandalas.[7] All of the imperial portraits and mandalas were completely woven in silk, rather than being painted or sculpted, as was previously the norm for imperial portraiture in eastern Asia. These woven images were large, comparable in dimensions to the Vajrabhairava mandala.[8]

Vajrabhairava Mandala; Mongol Empire/Yuan dynasty, probably Daidu (Beijing, China); ca. 1329; silk and gold, tapestry with slits (*kesi*); 96⅝ × 82¼ in. (245.5 × 209 cm); The Metropolitan Museum of Art, New York; 1992.54;

The iconographic choice of Vajrabhairava as the main deity, occupying the center of the mandala, was likely to have been related to the fact that Vajrabhairava is a wrathful emanation of the bodhisattva Manjushri. This bodhisattva was a particularly important figure for the members of the Mongol ruling house, so much so that the Yuan emperors fashioned themselves as bodily emanations of Manjushri.[9] An architectural inscription from 1345, for example, praised Qubilai as "the bodhisattva of wisdom," Manjushri's epithet.[10] Put another way, enshrining the Vajrabhairava mandala in proximity to the Mongol imperial portraiture was a way to layer the rhetoric of Buddhist kingship into the visual program of the Yuan imperial portrait halls.[11]

For more about this architectural structure, see Juyong Guan Stupa Gate, no. 48.

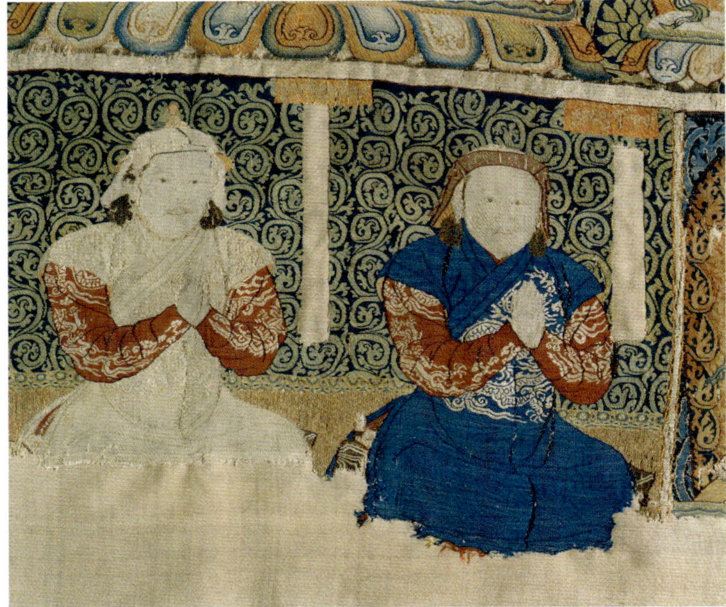

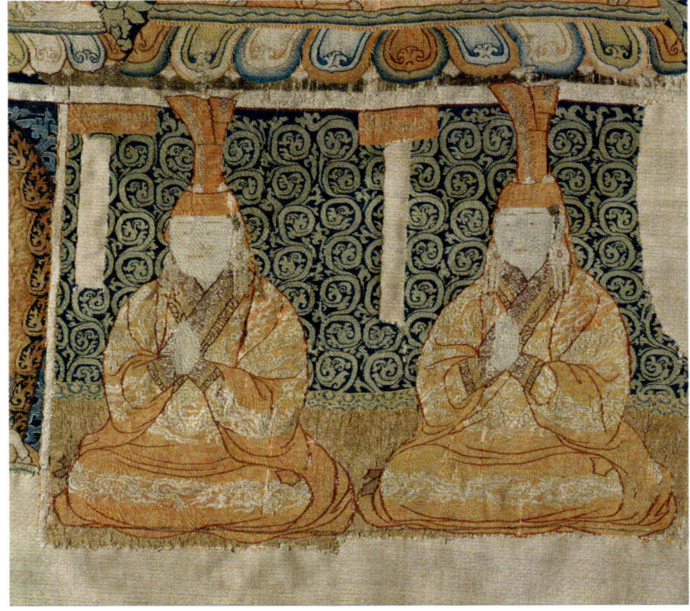

Male imperial donor portraits, Emperor Tuq-Temür and Prince Qoshila, detail from Vajrabhairava Mandala; The Metropolitan Museum of Art, New York; 1992.54 CC0 - Creative Commons (CC0 1.0)

Female imperial donor portraits, Budashiri Qatun and Babusha Qatun, detail from Vajrabhairava Mandala; The Metropolitan Museum of Art, New York; 1992.54 CC0 - Creative Commons (CC0 1.0)

For more about the relationship between the Mongol court and Tibetan Buddhism, see Mahakala Stone Sculpture, no. 39. On Pakpa's activities at the Mongol court, see Mongol Messenger's Badge, no. 42.

Judging from the inscriptions that accompany the donor portraits, one can deduce that this tapestry Vajrabhairava mandala was produced under the patronage of Emperor Tuq-Temür about the year 1329. Having usurped the throne after killing his half-brother Qoshila, Tuq-Temür sought to establish his political legitimacy by elevating the status of his deceased mother, for whom he conducted a posthumous coronation as Empress Wenxianzhaosheng. Unlike Qoshila's mother, who was of Mongol origin, Tuq-Temür's mother was a Tangut, and the posthumous coronation made her the first non-Mongol empress in Yuan history. During this process, Tuq-Temür commissioned a new portrait hall for his father and mother, and this Vajrabhairava mandala was likely enshrined inside this structure.[12]

Transmission Lineage

Around the thirteenth century, Vajrabahraiva was a relatively new deity in eastern Asia, with the associated tantric scriptures existing only in Sanskrit and Tibetan.[13] It was through the Mongol ruling house's close relationship with the wider Tibetan Buddhist world that the tantric iconographies and rituals of Vajrabhairava came to be transmitted to the members of the Yuan court.[14] The specific iconography of the Vajrabhairava mandala reveals the transmission lineage associated with what is known as the "forty-nine deity cycle."[15] Indeed, Pakpa Lodro Gyeltsen (1235–1280), the highest-ranking Tibetan monk working for the Yuan court during its early decades, also composed his own version of the Vajrabhairava liturgical hymn following in this cycle, titled *Sadhana of Forty-Nine Deity Vajrabhairava*.

Woven Images

Archaeological records suggest that the weaving technique "silk tapestry with slits" already existed in the Tarim Basin region (present-day Xinjiang) in the sixth to eighth century.[16] By the thirteenth century, this weaving technology had already become a mainstream component of the Chinese material culture. Even so, in eastern Asia before the Yuan period, the technique of silk tapestry was primarily used for the production of utilitarian items such as sartorial products or protective covers for scrolls and texts; there is no evidence that the technique was employed to produce figural images intended to fulfill devotional or other ritual functions.[17] In other words, the medium of the Vajrabhairava mandala—and all other images that were enshrined in the Yuan imperial portrait hall—was a major innovation that marked a significant development in the history of silk tapestry in eastern Asia.

For more about the Tangut visual culture, see Cave 3 at Yulin Cave Temples, no. 31; A *Pancharaksha* Print from Khara-Khoto, no. 32.

For more about the pre-Yuan silk tapestry Buddhist icons, see Achala Silk Tapestry, no. 36.

This new development was most likely linked to the Mongol ruling house's exposure to the visual culture of the Tangut state of the Western Xia (Xixia, 1038–1227), where earlier examples of the silk tapestry Buddhist icons have been preserved. At Khara-Khoto (Mongolian; Chinese: Heishuicheng), a site associated with the Western Xia, artists produced Buddhist icons in silk tapestry during the twelfth

For an example of the Tangut patronage of Buddhist art in the Yuan, see Relief Carving of a Nine-Deity Ushnishavijaya Composition, no. 41.

century.[18] The most famous example of the tapestry icon from Khara-Khoto is the image of the Green Tara now in the State Hermitage Museum, Saint Petersburg (see the image on p. 170). Considering the significant roles played by Tangut personnel and culture in the formation of Yuan imperial courtly culture, it is likely that the members of the Yuan court were aware of such a tradition and drew inspiration from it.[19]

Within the Yuan court, this choice of medium was also part of the larger shift in the hierarchy of artistic forms that the members of the Mongol ruling house promoted. The Yuan rulers maintained a close relationship with their pastoral nomadic roots and environmental surrounds, which included the abundance of animal fibers that constantly provided material for visual and material productions.[20] The ruling house preferred fiber arts over other forms of artistic expression, such as painting and calligraphy, previously considered the most prestigious in China.[21]

More broadly, the production of monumental woven images such as the Vajrabhairava mandala was representative of the larger trend in the Yuan court workshop to experiment with a variety of materials and techniques in making Buddhist icons. In addition to silk tapestry images, the Yuan court artists fabricated icons of Buddhist deities using a wide range of materials and technologies. Examples of Buddhist imagery fired as a porcelain or sculpted using lacquer survive in museum collections around the world, attesting to the creativity and flexibility of those who produced Buddhist imagery for the Yuan court.[22]

Further Reading

Charleux, Isabelle. 2010a. "From Ongon to Icon: Legitimization, Glorification and Divinization of Power in Some Examples of Mongol Portraits." In *Representing Power in Ancient Inner Asia: Legitimacy, Transmission and the Sacred*, edited by Isabelle Charleux, Grégory Delaplace, Roberte Hamayon, and Scott Pearce, 209–60. Bellingham: Center for East Asian Studies, Western Washington University.

Cho, Yong. 2020. "The Mongol Impact: Rebuilding the Arts System in Yuan China (1271–1368)." PhD diss., Yale University.

Tsangwang Gendun Tenpa. 2019. "Tibetan Buddhism in the Mongol Empire According to Tibetan Sources." Translated by Eveline Washul. In *Faith and Empire: Art and Politics in Tibetan Buddhism*, edited by Karl Debreczeny, 105–23. Exhibition catalog. New York: Rubin Museum of Art. https://issuu.com/rmanyc/docs/faith_and_empire.

Notes

1 For more information on Vajrabhairava and the Vajrabhairava tantras, see Siklós 1996; Ra Yeshé Sengé 2015.

2 "Wenzong" and "Mingzong" are Chinese titles of the respective emperors.

3 For various interpretations, see Berger 1994; Watt and Wardwell 2001; Shang 2009; Leidy 2010; Cho 2020.

4 For more on this theory, including a thorough reconstruction of the original context of the work's production, see Cho 2020, 74–108.

5 Song Lian et al. 1976, 75, 1875–78; 134, 3253–54.

6 For more on the history of imperial portraiture in the Yuan, see Charleux 2010a; Xu 2012; Cho 2020.

7 Zhao Shiyan and Yu Ji 2020, 841–47.

8 For example, see Zhao Shiyan and Yu Ji 2020, 842.

9 On the importance of Manjushri in the Yuan, see Farquhar 1978; Franke 1978; Debreczeny 2011.

10 Farquhar 1978, 12; Franke 1978, 52–69.

11 For the relationship between the idea of Buddhist kingship and the Yuan imperial portrait halls, see Dongyang Dehui 1338, T.2025: 1114c20–1114c22.

12 For an overview of the political history during this time period, see Hsiao 1994. For the role of the imperial ancestral halls and portraiture in Yuan political history, see Ma 2013; Cho 2020.

13 Siklós 1996.

14 For an overview of the relationship between the Mongol court and the Tibetan Buddhist world, see Petech 1990; Shen 2011; Tsangwang Gendun Tenpa 2019.

15 See Bsod nams rgya mtsho 1991, no. 57; Tsangwang Gendun Tenpa 2019. Also see Bryan Cuevas's introduction to Vajrabhairava lineages in Ra Yeshé Sengé 2015, ix–xliv.

16 For the origins of this weaving technique, see Sheng 1995; Sheng 1998.

17 For histories of silk tapestry prior to the Yuan period, see Malagò 1988; Malagò 1991; Tunstall 2012.

18 For an overview of the paintings excavated at Khara-Khoto, see Piotrovsky 1993. For an overview of Tibetan Buddhist art at Khara-Khoto, see Xie Jisheng 2019.

19 For the impact of Tangut culture in the Yuan court, see Dunnell 1992; Linrothe 2009; Shen 2011.

20 For the importance of fiber arts and textiles in the Mongol Empire, see Allsen 1997; Watt and Wardell 1997, 127–41.

21 Cho 2020, 38–73.

22 For an overview of the variety of Buddhist icons produced by the Yuan imperial workshop, see Jing 2004; Leidy 2010. For a deeper exploration of the reasons for this development, particularly with the medium of silk tapestry, see Cho 2020.

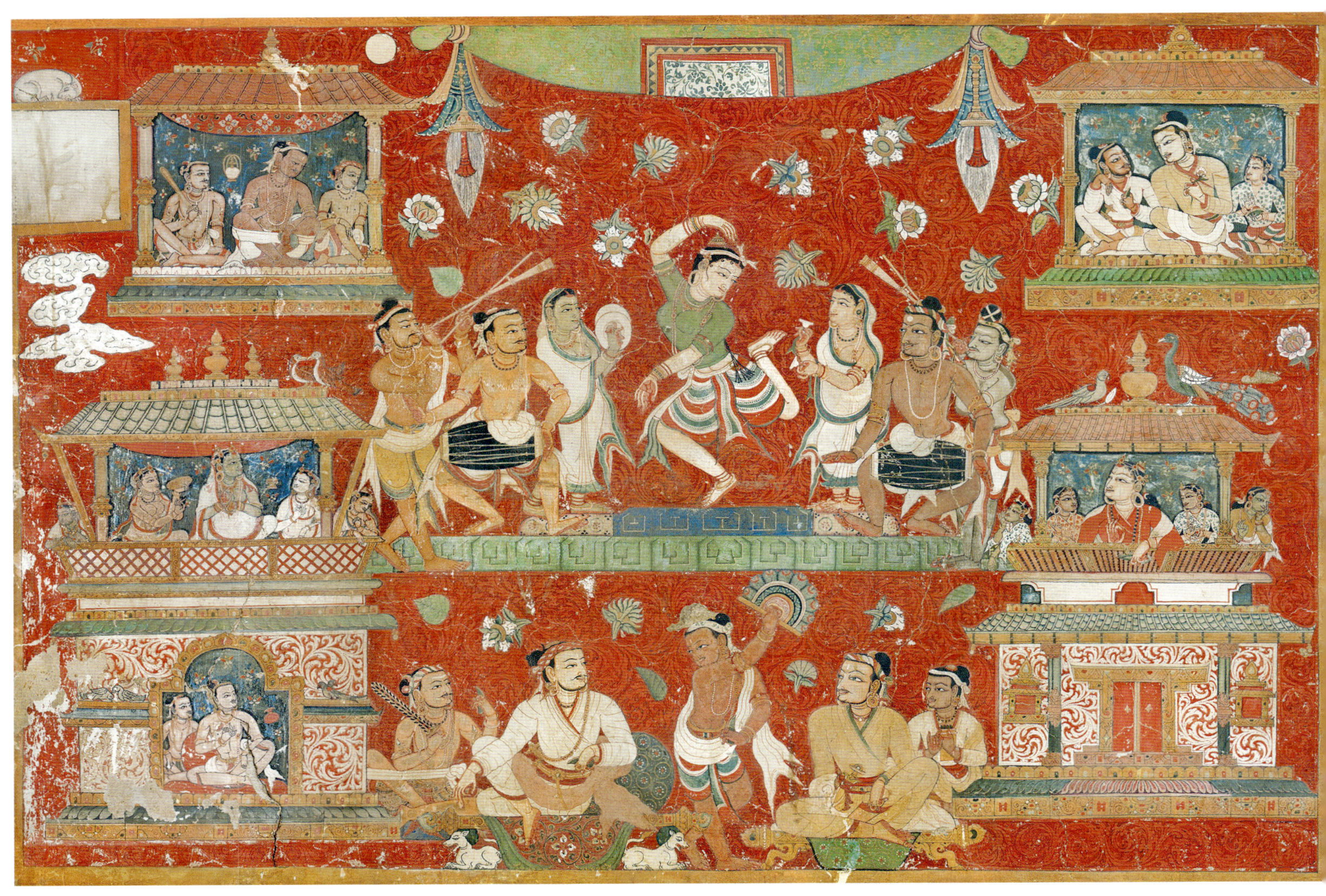

№ 47

Mural Painting at Zhalu Monastery

Zhalu Monastery, Tsang region, central Tibet (present-day TAR, China), ca. 1340

Mongol Patronage, Nepalese Artists, and Murals as a Public Marketing Strategy for Sacred Books

SARAH A. RICHARDSON

THIS PAINTING OF A PREVIOUS BIRTH of the bodhisattva before he became the Buddha, known as a jataka story, is among the one hundred individual stories of the Buddha's previous lives that were meticulously painted and inscribed in the Great Circumambulatory Passage (*korlam chenmo*) of Zhalu Monastery. These jataka paintings, among the many detailed murals from the fourteenth century that miraculously survive intact at the site, are notable for the intricate narrative details they display and the fact that they are the earliest known extant large and sequential set of paintings of this subject matter in Tibetan art. Like many of the other fourteenth-century murals at Zhalu, they are accompanied by extensive Tibetan inscriptions, and the combination of text and image painted together across the passageway creates a traversable mural representation of a book. Looking like books on walls, they convey to viewers the value of sacred books. At this time, the editing of the nascent Tibetan canonical collections was taking place at Zhalu under the supervision of the temple's most famous abbot, Buton Rinchen Drub (1290–1364).

Jataka Stories: The Story of the Dancer

Jataka stories are fantastic accounts of previous lives of the bodhisattva who would eventually become Buddha Shakyamuni. At Zhalu, a curated selection of one hundred of these stories are organized into sets of the ten perfections (*paramita*), the stages and skills or practices that bodhisattvas perfect on their path toward Buddhahood. These paintings, arranged as ten stories for each of the ten perfections, form a gridlike arrangement above their accompanying inscriptions across two registers disposed along the outer wall of the enclosed passageway, placed on an upper section of the wall above human height, in a venerable position usually maintained for sacred books. The stories, both painted and inscribed, narrate some of the bodhisattva's many manifestations, as a king, a peasant, a merchant, an elephant, a monkey, and once, even an enormous fish, in every case performing admirable and awe-inspiring selfless deeds.[1]

In the story of the dancer, number sixty-six in this enumerated set, the inscription relates that the bodhisattva was born as a male professional dancer and had a beautiful daughter called Drowai Pelmo (Most Glorious One), herself a skilled dancer. While the male is clearly named as the bodhisattva in this version, the textual story focuses exclusively on the female.[2] The painting here of this tale also places her higher in the composition. The text describes the girl's compelling qualities and details the lyrics of her songs. She is credited with the ability to draw in audiences through her skillful dancing and then using the opportunity to teach important Buddhist lessons, such as impermanence. The story can be read to make a statement about art in Buddhist contexts, arguing that creating or using beautiful things, like song, dance, and physical adornment, is justified if the intention of the teaching is itself noble.

Jataka of the Dancer (Story 66); west wall of the ground-floor circumambulatory passage, Zhalu Monastery; Tsang region, central Tibet (present-day TAR, China); ca. 1340; mineral and vegetal pigments on dry clay wall; 40 × 60 in. (104 × 155 cm); photograph © Thomas Laird, 2018 from *Murals of Tibet*, TASCHEN

This painting depicts both male and female dancers, with the male situated at the bottom center of the composition holding a fan and the female dancer in the higher register, portrayed in a dynamic dance posture with one foot kicked up behind her. Six musicians, including two white sari-clad women, frame the elegant female dancer. She is supported on a floating, geometrically stylized blue and green lotus pedestal, and a green canopy with oversize floral tassels hangs above her. Around the edges of the composition, four smaller architectural pavilions accommodate groups of courtly onlookers who direct their gaze toward her. Other scenes of jatakas at Zhalu also show the earliest Tibetan and Nepalese artistic experimentations with landscape depictions; here, the vignettes of this story are set against a flattened,

Inscription of a Jataka Story; west wall of the ground-floor circumambulatory passage, Zhalu Monastery; Tsang region, central Tibet (present-day TAR, China); ca. 1340; mineral and vegetal pigments on dry clay wall; photograph by Sarah Richardson, 2009

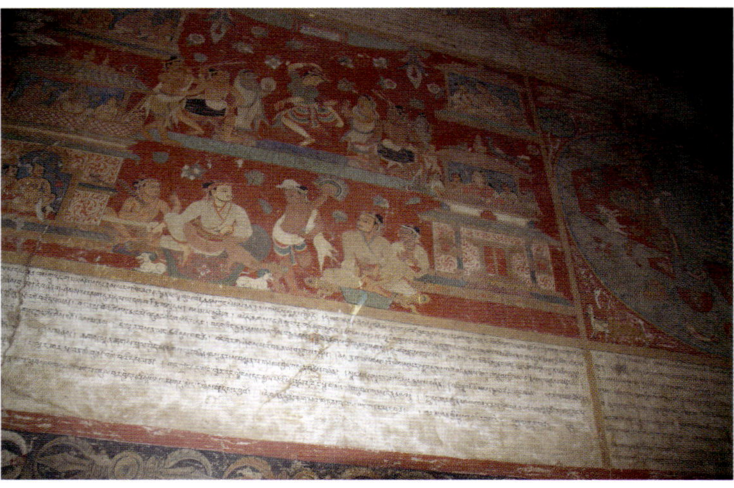

red-ground background that is covered with a delicate scrolling vine motif, a favorite pattern among Nepalese artists.

Nepalese Artists, Chinese Architects, Tibetan Context: Material Cultures that Meet and Mix

This painting is full of specific Nepalese details. The tiled pavilions with pitched roofs, the upper-story balconies with sloping beams and small windows, the women in saris with red tikka marks on their foreheads, the large skin-covered drums and other instruments, and the background design of red-on-red vine and tendril pattern all indicate that it was made by a Newar artist. Since no large mural paintings from Nepal survive from this period, Zhalu preserves the best and earliest surviving examples of Newar mural art, which was much valued across Asia during this period.[3]

For a Newar artist working for the Mongol court in Beijing, see White Stupa, no. 40.

For more on Newar artists working for Tibetan patrons, see Virupa, no. 37; Jivarama's Sketchbook, no. 56.

Approximately one quarter of the jataka murals in this passageway appear to have been painted by this Newar artists group, while the others display a more Tibetan style, with Chinese costumes and architecture throughout. Newar painters clearly worked alongside Tibetan artists at the site, but on different paintings, implying that there were likely multiple workshops of artisans working here at the same time.[4]

The Zhalu narrative murals also provide numerous depictions of ordinary people: male and female, young and old; and everyday worldly settings, such as markets and urban gatherings. This painting alone contains varieties of dress and architecture, printed cloth patterns, and musical instruments used in this period. The Zhalu murals prove a rich resource for information about what the world looked like in fourteenth-century Tibet, Nepal, and (Mongol-controlled) China.

Cosmopolitan Connections and Patronage

In the renovation that saw the addition of these murals, the members of the Zhalu Monastery were celebrating their inclusion in a wider network of global commerce, contact, and cosmopolitanism: their small and beloved temple was a beneficiary not only of Nepalese rulers to the south but also of prestigious and direct Mongol patronage from the Yuan court. Because of Zhalu's close alliance with the house of Sakya through matrimonial ties, Zhalu's ruling Che clan received significant gifts from the Yuan emperor Temür in the early fourteenth century, including funds as well as foreign artisans.[5] Subsequently, the much smaller temple at the site since the eleventh century was greatly expanded, with upper levels added to the entire structure that were topped with four elaborate Chinese-style tiled roofs. The murals that were painted in this fourteenth-century expansion preserve visual evidence of an explosively rich, creative synthesis in Tibetan art from this conjunction of Mongol patronage, direct contact with elite material objects from east, south, and Central Asia, and traveling itinerant artisans from the south and east. Newar artists were responsible for some paintings, and it is likely that Chinese artisans oversaw the addition of the Chinese-style tiled roofs.

Sources of Authority

For more related to Buton Rinchen Drub, see Illuminated Pages of the *Prajnaparamita Sutra* Manuscript, no. 23.

The Zhalu mural art produced following the fourteenth-century renovation clearly reflects Tibetan sources of authority. During the renovation period, Zhalu's new wealth and foreign favor attracted an important and brilliant author, editor, and lama to serve as abbot. The illustrious canon collector Buton Rinchen Drub came to Zhalu in 1320 and remained as acting abbot until 1356. During this time he oversaw the production of most of the new paintings, as well as the creation of his own massive edited and newly scribed versions of both Tibetan canonical collections, the Kangyur ("Words of the Buddha") and Tengyur ("Commentaries" or "Treatises").

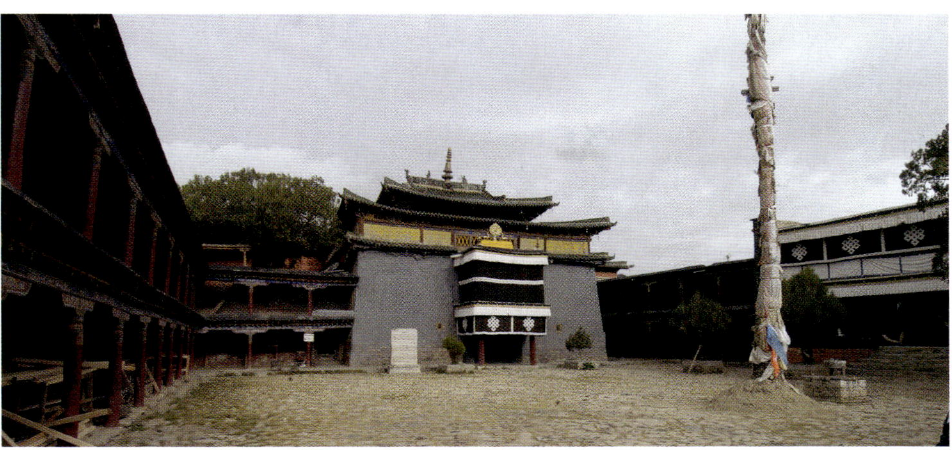

View of the Zhalu Monastery temple from the courtyard; Tsang region, central Tibet (present-day TAR, China); 14th century; photograph by OSU Trip/Eric Huntington, 2006

Reflecting Buton's interest in textual authority and correctly edited texts, the fourteenth-century paintings at Zhalu include a great volume of visible textual inscriptions. The *korlam* circumambulatory passageway is not the only new space at Zhalu whose walls were furnished with long Tibetan inscriptions. Other areas of the temple, including an upper-level circumambulatory passage and four rooms filled with Mandalas of the Yogatantras, also feature extensive inscriptions placed directly on the walls. Indeed, in the first of the four central shrines a pilgrim would have entered on the ground floor, two textual inscriptions were specifically chosen that concerned the important religious function of seeing paintings, evidence that the mural decorations and the textual inscriptions were mutually supportive efforts.[6] Paintings were described in these selected inscribed passages as important tools with which to prepare and train visions of divinity that would yield a good rebirth.

Textual Sources

For later depictions of the Buddha's life, see A Monumental Life of the Buddha Mural, no. 69; Murals of Gongkar Chode, no. 58.

At Zhalu, specific Tibetan books were chosen as the basis for the murals. The jatakas painted along the entire outer wall of the ground-floor passage are all taken from *The Life Stories of the Buddha* (Tibetan: *Sangs rgyas kyi skyes rabs*), a collection of one hundred jataka stories leading up to the story of Shakyamuni (the one-hundred-and-first story) that had been just recently collected or authored and arranged in 1314 by the Third Karmapa, Rangjung Dorje (1284–1339).[7] A slightly elder contemporary of Buton and another esteemed religious teacher, Rangjung Dorje was the first person to be recognized in his lifetime as a direct reincarnation (*tulku*) of his predecessor, Karma Pakshi (1204–1286).[8]

Zhalu contains many important surviving fourteenth-century paintings and a large number of inscriptions. While the monastery is best known for its images of deities, the detailed narrative jataka paintings admirably illustrate the prowess and creativity of the artists. Painted by Newar and Tibetan artists working on different sections, these murals show significant details of fourteenth-century life. Furthermore, the large volume of inscribed texts on the walls testify to the period's interest, exemplified by Buton, in authoring and editing sacred texts.

Further Reading

Richardson, Sarah A. 2021. "When Walls Could Talk: The Powers of Tibetan Paintings in a Buddhist Library." *Archives of Asian Art* 71, no. 2, 243–68.

Vitali, Roberto. 1990. "Shalu Serkhang and the Newar Style of the Yuan Court." In *Early Temples of Central Tibet*, 89–122. London: Serindia.

Notes

1 Some of the best published photographs of these difficult to access Zhalu murals are reproduced in Laird et al. 2018.

2 In some later Tibetan versions and references to this story, the bodhisattva is female. See Ronis 2017, 118. Nonetheless, most jataka literature in both Mahayana and Theravada traditions keeps the bodhisattvas as gendered male. See Appleton 2011.

3 For an example of Newar artists working across Asia in this period, see Jing 1996, 36.

4 Newar painters were credited with painting some of the new temples at the monastery of Sakya; D. Jackson 2010, 70–71.

5 For the earliest Tibetan written source referencing the patronage of Zhalu's renovation and noting the presence of foreign artisans at Zhalu, see Ruegg 1996, 89–90, Tibetan fols. 14b. 1–2.

6 S. Richardson 2021, 244. For a discussion of the placement and content of the ground-floor shrine inscriptions, see S. Richardson 2021, 243–68.

7 For reference to the date of composition at the end of Song number 58 from Rangjung Dorje's *mgur 'bum*, see Gamble 2013, 227, 368.

8 For more on the Third Karmapa and the institutionalization of his reincarnation lineage, see Gamble 2018.

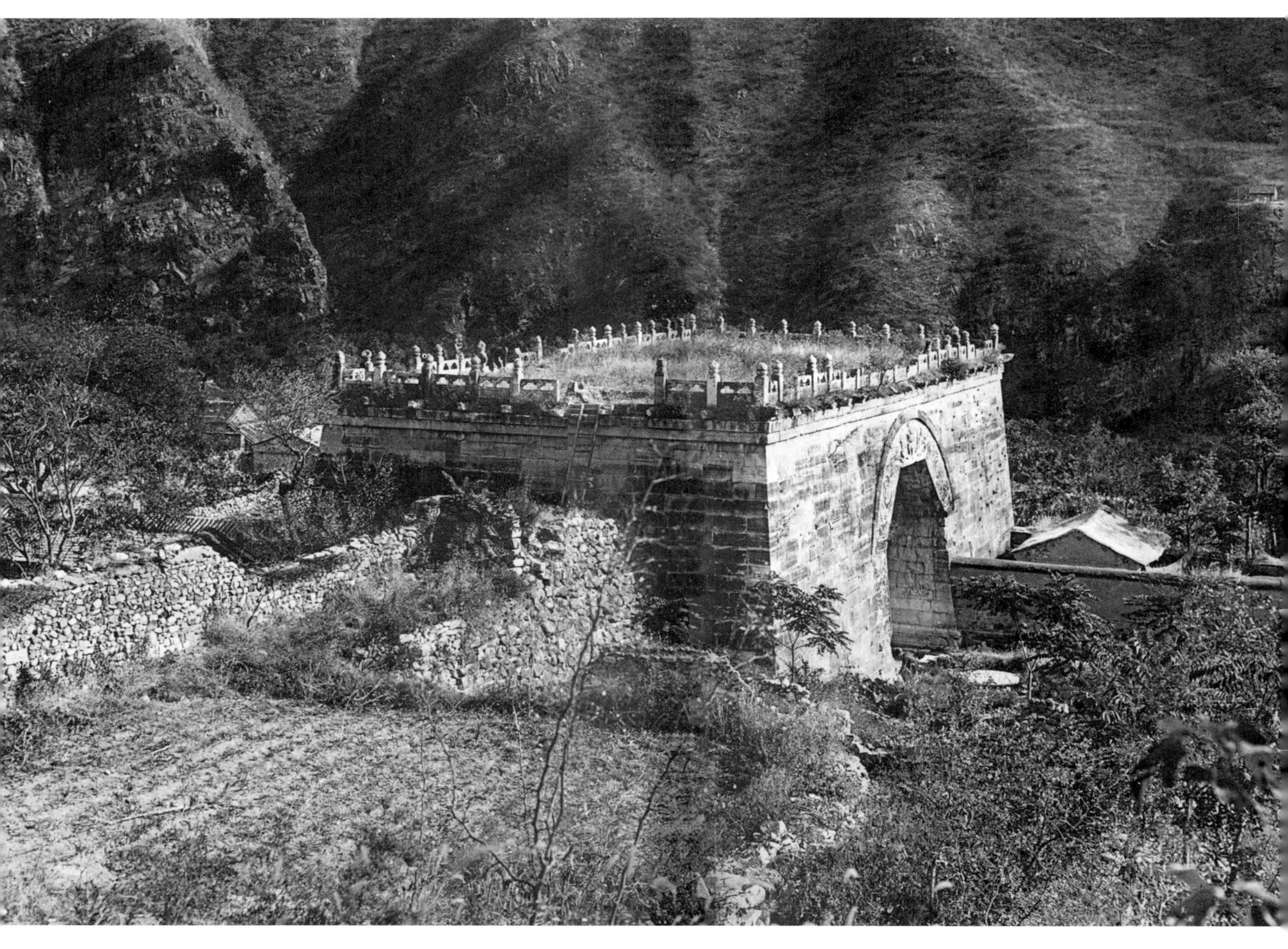

Juyong Guan Stupa Gate; Nankou Town, Changping District, Beijing, China; dated 1345; white limestone; 32 ft. 9½ in. × 88 ft. 7 in. × 59 ft. (10 × 27 × 18 m), gateway: 23 × 59 ft. (7 × 18 m); image after Murata 1958, pl. 1

№ 48

Juyong Guan Stupa Gate

Changping District, Beijing, China, 1345

Stabilizing Empire through Buddhist Monument, Text, and Image

KARL DEBRECZENY

THE GATE AT JUYONG GUAN, meaning "Dwelling in Harmony Pass" (Mongolian: Chabchiyal), is located at the foot of the famous Great Wall, about thirty-seven miles (sixty kilometers) northwest of Beijing. A strategically important hub on a pivotal route in the fourteenth century, Juyong Pass connected Daidu (modern-day Beijing), the winter capital, to the northern areas, including the summer capital, Shangdu—the two capitals of the Yuan dynasty (1271–1368). With the Mongol incorporation of Tibetan areas in 1247, Mongolian emperors came to embrace Tibetan Buddhism, through which they ruled. They constantly invited Tibetan lamas to their capitals, built royal monasteries, and set up official institutions to create Tibetan Buddhist art. Juyong Guan Gate is a monumental surviving testament of this artistic, cultural, and political legacy, its six-language inscriptions propagating imperial identity in a Buddhist framework.

Construction

The existing monument is a massive rectangular platform with a grand gateway in the center, facing north and south. Its magnificence is attributable to its grand scale. Historical records and inscriptions record that the original gate complex of the Juyong Guan Gate comprised the gate and Yongming Baoxiang Temple, and Juyong Guan Gate once supported three stupas on top of it. The temple and the three stupas no longer exist. A comparison with the stupa gate built in 1311 at Xijindu in Zhenjiang, Jiangsu Province, gives a sense of Juyong Guan Gate's original appearance.[1]

Juyong Guan Gate was constructed from 1342 to 1345, under the order of Toghan Temür Khan (1320–1370; r. 1333–70), the last emperor of the Yuan dynasty. Toghan Temür was such an avid follower of Tibetan Buddhism that later Confucian historians consider this one of the causes of the fall of the Yuan dynasty. Many important Mongolian, Chinese, Tibetan, and Tangut officials and monks were responsible for the gate's construction, including Tibetan monk-officials Namkha Sengge, who supervised the project, and Imperial Preceptor Kunga Gyeltsen Pel Zangpo (1310–1353), the highest religious authority in the land, who performed the consecration ritual after its completion.[2]

Images and Inscriptions

For more about toranas, see Torana of the Main Shrine at Yetakha Baha, no. 24. For more about *garudas*, see Vishnu Riding on Garuda, no. 18. For more about nagas and makaras, see Golden Fountain of Bhaktapur, no. 74.

On mandalas, see Chakrasamvara Mandala with Newar Donors, no. 29.

Relief carvings are engraved on the north and south facades of the platform around the gateway openings and the inner vaulted ceiling and walls. Six ornaments commonly found on Nepalese and Tibetan gateways, or *toranas*—mythical bird (*garuda*), snake spirit (naga), water monster (makara), leogryph, youth, and elephant—are carved on the north and south faces of the base, framing the gateway openings.

On the vaulted ceiling, five mandalas are engraved in shallow relief along the apex of the central axis, whose main deities are identified by Uyghur and Mongolian inscriptions as Akshobhya, Sarvavid Vairochana, Vajrapani, Amitabha, and Shakyamuni.[3] The inscriptions also identify the large Buddhas of the Ten Directions, which line the east and west sloping sides, surrounded by tiny reliefs of the Thousand Buddhas of the Fortunate Aeon (Bhadrakalpa).[4] The Four Guardian Kings, who traditionally guard the four cardinal directions at the entrances of Buddhist temples, are engraved on the east and west inner walls of the gateway near the north and south entrances.

In addition, the inner walls at the top are also inscribed, in large Lantsa (Sanskrit) script, with two dharani, Sanskrit formulas believed to have protective power through their sound and written physical

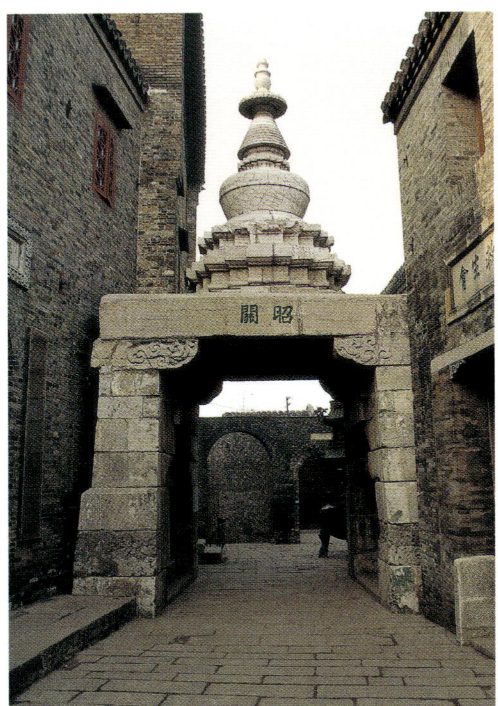

Xijindu Stupa Gate; Zhenjiang City, Jiangsu Province, China; dated 1311; photograph by Xie Jisheng

presence: the *Ushnishavijaya Dharani* and the *Tathagatahridaya Dharani*, which are associated with long life, purification, and protection/averting disaster.

Smaller inscriptions in Tibetan, Mongolian square script, Uyghur, Tangut, and Chinese transliterate these Sanskrit incantations and celebrate the merits of stupa construction.[5] The inscriptions in each language differ. For instance, the Tangut and Chinese inscriptions additionally provide a story from the *Tathagatahridaya Sutra* that helps explain the benefit of building such a stupa at a crossroads with the dharani in it to prevent shortening of life and to avoid unfortunate rebirths as an animal and in the hell realms.[6]

The Mongolian inscriptions articulate a Buddhist sacralization of Mongol rule, likening the founder of the Yuan dynasty Qubilai Khan (r. 1260–1294) to Ashoka, stupa builder and the archetypal Indian universal Buddhist ruler (chakravartin), and further glorifying Qubilai Khan and, by extension, his successors of the Yuan imperial line as long-prophesied bodhisattva rulers, establishing the sacral nature of their rulership and empire:

See Panoramic Map of Mount Wutai, no. 91.

> That blessed bodhisattva the Emperor Sečen [Qubilai], possessed of vast wisdom, about whom the prophecy was made that there would be someone named "the Wise one from the vicinity of Mount Wutai" [Manjushri] who would become a great emperor. . . . Commemorating in gold the marvelous deeds which have been brought about by those bodhisattvas destined by Heaven [to rule; that is: the Yuan emperors], [I] the Emperor Bodhisattva, the Son of Heaven and Master of Men [Toghan Temür], have caused this extensive and vast pagoda to be founded.[7]

This unusual language draws on one of the most important tantric authorities on prophecy, especially related to kings, the *Manjushrimula Tantra*.

For example, see Vajrabhairava Mandala, no. 46.

See Mural Painting at Zhalu Monastery, no. 47.

All the images at Juyong Guan Stupa Gate are in low relief. The depictions of the buddhas and bodhisattvas at the gateway follow Tibetan iconographic and visual conventions combined with distinct Nepalese aesthetics. Surrounding these buddhas is a scrolling flower pattern, a prominent stylistic feature of both Xixia and Yuan art that can also be seen in contemporaneous Yuan court production and in the early fourteenth-century renovations at Zhalu Monastery in central Tibet. Nepalese decorative motifs visible at Juyong Guan Gate appear in the decorative arch framing the entranceways, especially in the dramatically stylized scrolling foliate tails of the water monsters at the top.

For more on Tangut Buddhism and art, see Cave 3 at Yulin Cave Temples, no. 31; Achala Silk Tapestry, no. 36, A *Pancharaksha* Print from Khara-Khoto, no. 32.

Chinese artistic idioms are reflected in the faces, armor, implements, and attendant demons of the Four Guardian Kings at the gateway. Some subjects, such as "new mode" Manjushri and Water-Moon Avalokiteshvara decorating the armor worn by the Four Guardian Kings, are derived from Tangut Buddhism, originating in the Silk Road kingdom of Xixia, conquered and absorbed by the Mongol Empire in 1227.[8]

For other Yuan works drawing on Tangut Buddhist and artistic traditions, see Relief Carving of a Nine-Deity Ushnishavijaya Composition, no. 41.

See White Stupa, no. 40.

The entire relief at Juyong Guan Stupa Gate exemplifies a perfect fusion of Tibetan, Chinese, and Tangut art. This rich fusion of artistic traditions is closely related to the sophisticated cosmopolitan idiom of Tibetan Buddhist art created by the workshop of the royal court in the Yuan dynasty. The decoration with Buddhist images and dharanis in Juyong Guan Stupa Gate closely resembles that of the imperially sponsored White Stupa in Beijing, completed in 1279, which is attributed to the Nepalese artist Anige (1245–1306).

Function and Symbolism

It has been suggested that Juyong Guan Stupa Gate was built as a religio-political monument intended to revitalize Mongol rule through the articulation of an all-encompassing Buddhist vision of universal rulership, combined with its accompanying cosmology of religious imagery and magical dharani formulas.[9]

According to historical records, the construction of stupa gates in Beijing followed a precedent established by Qubilai Khan, who had a stupa erected on top of the south city gate (Zhangyi Gate) in

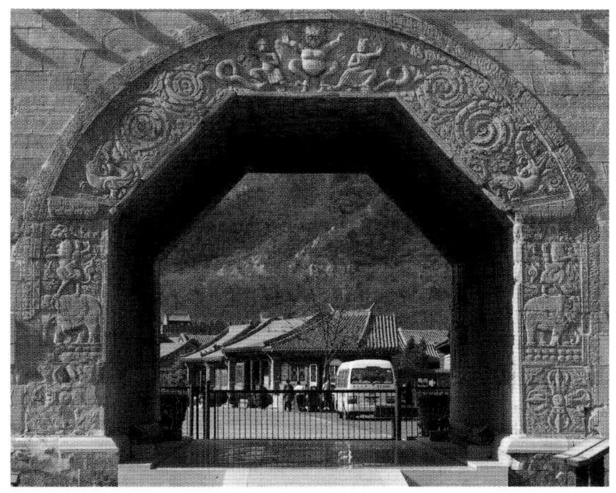

Juyong Guan Stupa Gate, showing six ornaments of the south face; photograph by Xie Jisheng

1294.[10] Regarding the origin of its architectural form, scholars have not yet come to a definitive conclusion. Stupa gates are found in Tibetan regions, and in Ladakh many gateway stupas are dated to the thirteenth to fourteenth century.[11] Most scholars thus assume that this form was introduced from Tibet and is closely related to the function of Buddha Akshobhya (meaning "unshakable") to provide stability, in the physical sense of geomantic protection and here, perhaps by extension, of the realm. The central mandala at Juyong Guan Gate is Akshobhya, with the surrounding deities personifying the Eight Auspicious Symbols, a specific form suggesting this monument is analogous to Kankani stupa gateways found in Ladakh.[12] The name Kankani refers to the dharani of Akshobhya, which commands that evils be cut off and obstacles dispelled.[13] Gateway stupas did not become widely popular until Akshobhya took over the central position in stupas, which in Ladakh appears to have occurred in the late thirteenth century.[14] The other four mandalas in this gate are the first four of the *Purification of All Bad Rebirths Tantra* (*Sarvadurgatiparishodhana Tantra*), and are all protective in nature.

Why was such a protective stupa gate needed at this place and time? Juyong Pass became increasingly important strategically when control over Mongolia was in question, which became true after 1323, when Yisün Temür Khan (r. 1323–1328), in a Mongolia-based coup d'état, seized power in Daidu. In 1326, he ordered Sanskrit dharanis carved on the walls of Juyong Pass.[15] However, this proved insufficient, as a short but intense civil war (1328–1329) soon followed between the two capitals on either side of the pass. Civil conflict was therefore a driving force in fortifying the pass.

For more about Tibetan Buddhism in Mongolia, see Erdeni Juu Monastery, no. 65.

Thus, by means of these images and multilingual inscriptions, the last Yuan emperor aspired to reinforce unity among the various ethnic groups under his rule, consolidate political power, and realize peace and stability. However, already in the 1330s and 1340s the dynasty had been rocked by a series of new crises, including disease and famine—disasters that the stupa gate was intended to suppress—and the Yuan collapsed soon after, unable to ritually stem the tide. In 1368 Toghan Temür fled north through Juyong Guan Gate, where his descendants continued to claim the Yuan title in Mongolian lands until 1634.[16]

Thank you to Xiong Wenbin for his help in developing an initial draft of this essay.

Further Reading

Campbell, Aurelia. 2022. "Consecrating the Imperial City: Tibetan Stupas in Yuan Dynasty Dadu." *Journal of Song-Yüan Studies* 51, 207–43.

Cho, Yong. 2022. "Juyong Gate: Wall Hangings in Stone." *Archives of Asian Art* 72, no. 2, 221–53.

Murata, Jirō 村田治郎, ed. 1955–58. *Kyoyōkan* 居庸關 / *Chü-Yung-Guan: The Buddhist Arch of the Fourteenth Century AD at the Pass of the Great Wall Northeast of Peking*, 1:325–59. [In Japanese, with a summary in English.] Kyoto: Faculty of Engineering, Kyoto University.

Notes

1 Wen Yucheng 2002. For a rendering of the three stupas, see Su 1996a, 355, fig.17–4.
2 Murata 1955–58, 1:225–322.
3 Murata 1955–58, 1:335; Poppe 1957, 61.
4 Murata 1955–58, 1:334.
5 See Bentor 1995a.
6 Murata 1955–58, 1:341.
7 Farquhar 1978, 12; Poppe 1957, 60–66; Nagao 1985.
8 Xie Jisheng 2014, 73.
9 Robinson 2009, 214, 285; Franke 1978, 68; Berger 1994.
10 Xie Jisheng 2014, 57; Murata 1955–58, 328; Campbell 2022.
11 Kozicz 2017, 234; Xie Jisheng 2014, 56.
12 Christian Luczanits, personal communication, October 29, 2021.
13 Luczanits 2023, 364; Linrothe 2006b, 171–74. Thanks also to Elena Pakhoutova for suggesting this connection.
14 Thanks to Christian Luczanits for this clarification.
15 Song 1976, chap. 30, 670. On the strategic importance of Juyong Pass, see Atwood 2004a, 281.
16 Atwood 2004a, fall of Yuan 609–11; Northern Yuan: 407–11.

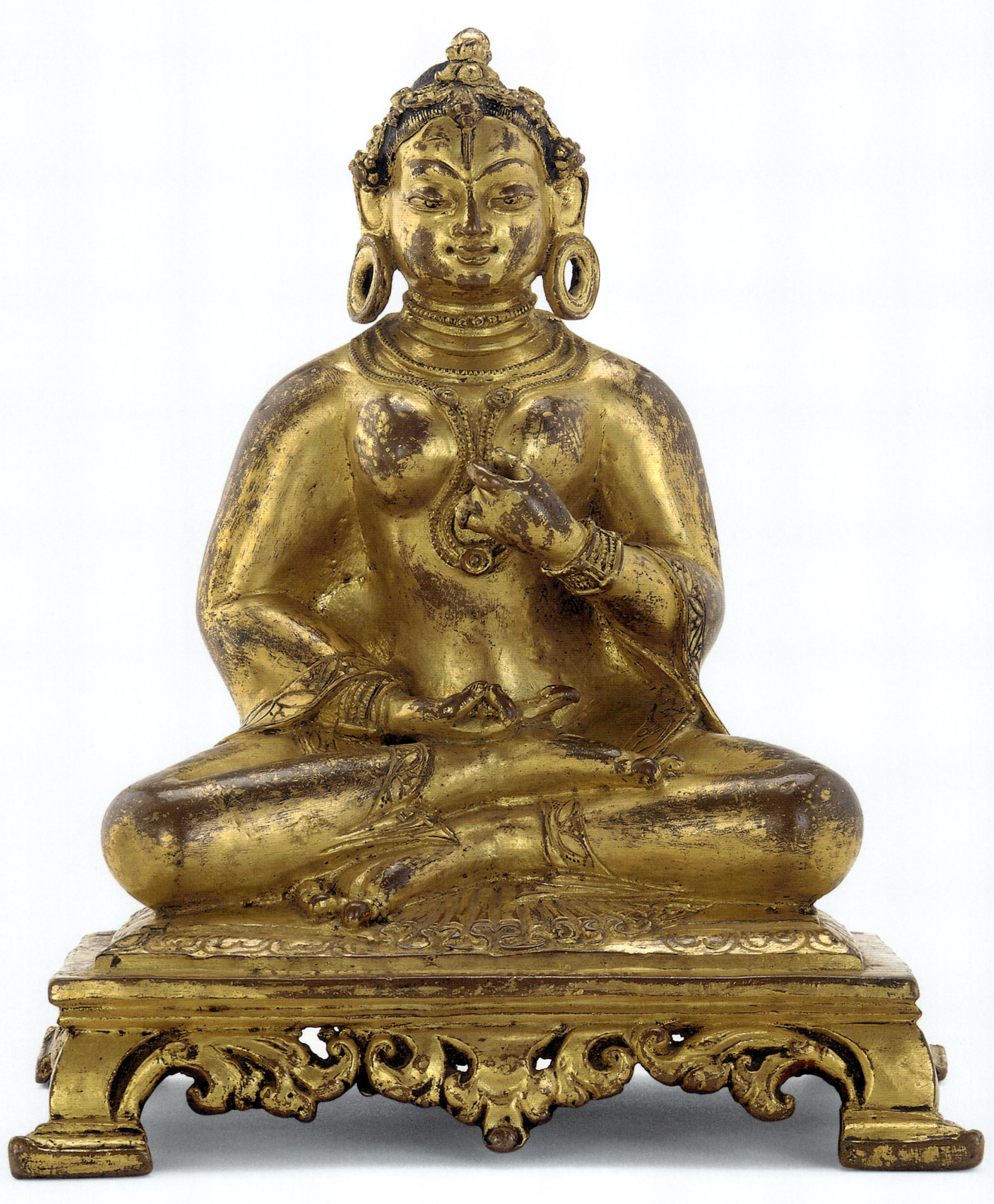

No 49

Queen Dipamala as the Goddess Prajnaparamita

Western Nepal/western Tibet, mid-14th century

A Sculpture from a Himalayan Cultural Contact Zone

IAN ALSOP

THIS SMALL BUT BEAUTIFULLY MODELED and impressively detailed gilt-copper figure of a robed woman or goddess has been tentatively identified as Dipamala, wife of the mid-fourteenth-century king Prithivi Malla of the Khasa Kingdom of western Nepal/western Tibet, perhaps in the guise of the great Buddhist goddess Prajnaparamita.

When it was illustrated and discussed in Himalayan art historical catalogs and studies several times since the late 1960s, the sculpture had been variously attributed to Tibet, Tibet under Indian influence, or Nepal.[1] Although it carries two brief inscriptions on the top of the base of the sculpture, they are difficult to interpret. One, in Tibetan script, is the simple word *yum*, or "mother," which was originally misread by several authors as Uma, one of the names of the spouse of the great Hindu god Shiva. This misreading caused confusion regarding the identity of the figure. The other inscription, in Sanskrit in the Devanagari script, reads "made by Dipamala," eventually leading scholars to realize this referred to one of Prithivi Malla's two queens, thus pinpointing the origin of the sculpture.[2]

The identity of the figure remains uncertain. *Yum*, or "mother," is part of a familiar Tibetan epithet of the great Mahayana goddess Prajnaparamita—"*yum chenmo*," or "great mother." This great goddess, the personification of a central Mahayana sutra, is usually depicted with four arms in Nepalese and Tibetan portrayals; she is rarely portrayed as two-armed, and the graceful arrangement of the hands does not correspond with known forms.[3] Also, the goddess is usually portrayed in full lotus position, whereas this figure displays the more relaxed half lotus. Moreover, it is unusual for any goddess to be shown draped in the full robe seen here. Another very small gilt sculpture, similarly robed and from the same sculptural tradition, can be definitively identified as a donor figure, leading us to conclude that this figure may likely portray the queen herself. Nevertheless, the inscribed *yum* strongly suggests identification with and conflation with the goddess Prajnaparamita.

For more on the Mallas of the Kathmandu Valley, see Vishnu Riding on Garuda, no. 18; Torana of the Main Shrine at Yetakha Baha, no. 24; Goddess of Prosperity, Vasudhara, no. 34; Nepalese *Paubha* Commemorating the Death of Pandita Vanaratna, no. 57.

The Khasa Kingdom

The Khasa Kingdom of western Nepal was a powerful but short-lived dynasty that in its heyday in the thirteenth and fourteenth centuries rivaled the medieval Mallas of the Kathmandu Valley in power and influence. Several times Khasa Malla kings invaded the three kingdoms of the Kathmandu Valley, while at other times, these kings visited the valley on peaceful religious pilgrimage.[4] Their reign was remarkable for its bicultural and bilingual characteristics, sometimes expressed in bilingual inscriptions such as the two short notes inscribed on the Dipamala sculpture. The kings of this dynasty ruled over a large area that was home to high-altitude Tibetan-speaking Buddhists and Nepali and Indian Nepali-speaking Khasa Hindus of the middle hills. Historical evidence indicates that the lineage of this dynasty was disrupted at several points; to this day it is still uncertain from which group the ancestors of the various kings of this dynasty originated.

Queen as the Goddess Prajnaparamita; western Nepal/western Tibet; mid-14th century; gilt copper; height 8 in. (20.5 cm); Freer Gallery of Art, Washington, DC; F1986.23; image courtesy Freer Gallery of Art, Smithsonian Institution

Distinctive Metal Sculpture

Over the years since 1981, when this sculpture was first linked with the Khasa Malla queen Dipamala, other cast-metal sculptures with similar inscriptions have emerged. It was noticed that all of these images tended to exhibit certain similar stylistic characteristics, allowing them to be considered part of a group, which has been called Khasa Malla.[5] Eventually, other sculptures, though lacking inscriptions, were

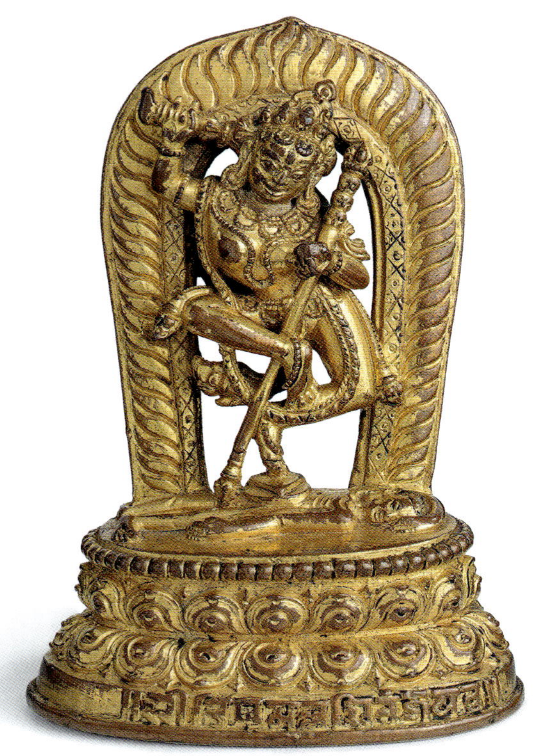

The Dakini Nairatmya; western Nepal/western Tibet; 1300–1325; gilt copper; 3½ × 2¾ × 1¼ in. (8.89 × 6.99 × 3.18 cm); Los Angeles County Museum of Art; Purchased with funds provided by Harry and Yvonne Lenart; M.85.221: photograph © Museum Associates/LACMA, www.lacma.org

included in this group because they also exhibited these stylistic characteristics, which set them apart from the well-known metal sculpture of the same period from the Kathmandu Valley.

Without exception, these sculptures present Buddhist subjects. They share materials and techniques with the metal sculptures of the Kathmandu Valley, specifically, castings in almost pure copper luxuriously gilded by the mercury fire-gilding process, and occasionally—less commonly than in Kathmandu Valley sculptures—they are further decorated with inlaid stones. This similarity of technique suggests that the original artisans of this school must have emigrated from the Kathmandu Valley to one of the centers, not yet ascertained, of the Khasa domain. An examination of the architectural and sculptural evidence in stone remaining in the western Nepal centers of the Khasa Kingdom reveals little that resembles the luxurious and delicate style of the metal sculptures.[6] That does not mean that a workshop cannot have existed there or in a nearby Buddhist center. Metal sculptors need very little to move from place to place: as long as there is beeswax and a good supply of metal available, a Newar metal sculptor can work anywhere.

For more examples of itinerant Newar artists working for patrons outside the Kathmandu Valley, see Virupa, no. 37; White Stupa, no. 40; Chorten Cave of Luri, no. 44.

Such migration on the part of the Newar artisans of the Kathmandu Valley has been going on for centuries. The Newar sculptors, painters, and architects and builders were renowned throughout the entire Himalayas for their skill, and they were willing to travel wherever there was demand and adequate funding to richly recompense them. In metal craft the Newar sculptors were considered the best, as asserted in one early Tibetan chronicle that listed the "Belpo" (Nepalese, or Newar) as the "*li gyel*" (king furnishers of bronze).[7]

As we will see, the Khasa Malla metal sculptures exhibit certain specifically idiosyncratic characteristics that set them apart from the parent style of the Kathmandu Valley. It is likely that one great master may have been responsible for this distinctive style. But who that master was in the Khasa tradition, and where exactly he worked, remains a mystery; none of the inscribed sculptures so far known bear the name of an artist.

Lost-Wax Casting Method

All of the Khasa metal sculptures were created using the lost-wax casting process, which was and is the process used throughout all of South Asia. In this technique, a wax version of the sculpture is encased within a clay mold, with the inner layer of the mold being a very fine clay to pick up all the details of the sculpture, and the outer layers increasingly coarse. Several wax pipes are added to the original to serve as conduits to empty the wax and then pour in the molten metal. When the clay mold is dry, it is heated in an oven and the wax is poured out through these conduits. While the mold is being heated, the metal is melted in a crucible in a furnace. When fully melted, it is poured into the mold, filling the space previously occupied by the wax, which has been "lost" when the mold was heated and emptied.[8]

Examples and Comparisons

Ripumalla (r. ca. 1312–1314) was a predecessor of Prithivi Malla in the Khasa Malla lineage, although likely of a different family line. A small metal figure of a *dakini,* the dancing female goddesses of Tibetan Buddhism, bears a cast (rather than carved) Sanskrit inscription in Devanagari characters with his

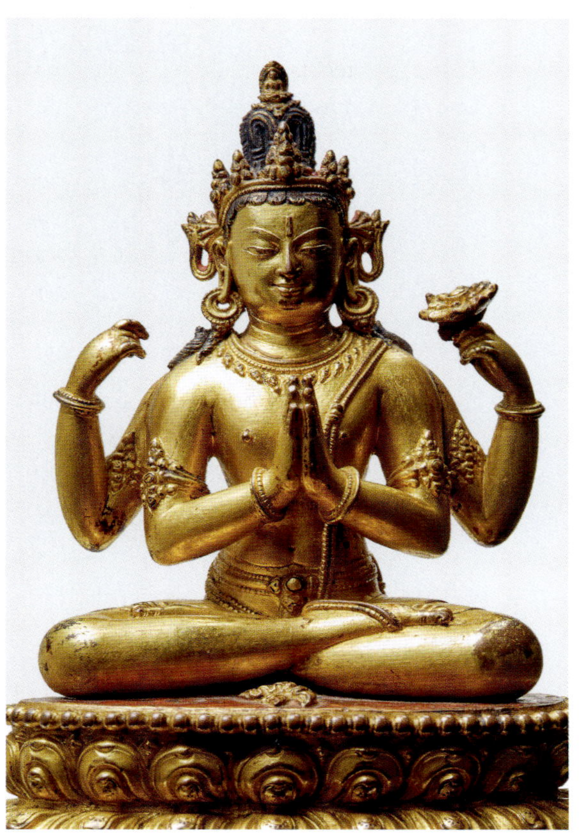

Avalokiteshvara; Yatse Kingdom (Khasa Malla Kingdom), western Nepal/ western Tibet; ca. 13th–14th century; gilt-copper alloy; height 7 in. (18 cm); ex-collection Yury Khokhlov; image courtesy Bonhams

name in a simple invocation, "May Ripumalla live long." Like the image of Dipamala, this diminutive sculpture is in glowing gilt copper.

Another sculpture with a connection to the rulers of the Khasa Malla Kingdom depicts the most popular figure of the Tibetan pantheon, the Four-Armed Avalokiteshvara, or Chenrezig in Tibetan. This form of the great bodhisattva is known in Sanskrit as Shadakshari Lokeshvara, the Lord of the Six Syllables; the name refers to his mantra, *om ma ni pad me hum,* the best-known mantra of all northern Buddhism. While relatively rare in the Kathmandu Valley, this figure is ubiquitous in Tibet. The sculpture carries a Tibetan inscription on the front of the lotus base, inscribed in the Tibetan *ume*, or cursive script. The ruler is not named, as the inscription merely states, "The Yatse sovereign has offered this to the monastery of Lhatong."[9] Yatse was the Tibetan name of the Khasa Malla Kingdom in Nepal, so we know that one of this lineage gave this lovely sculpture to a Tibetan monastery, although the monastery mentioned in the inscription also has yet to be identified.

We can see that this sculpture bears some significant stylistic similarities to both the little *dakini* figure and the Dipamala/Prajnaparamita figure. All three share a lusciously beautiful gilded surface, which is a hallmark of the Khasa Malla style, also seen in the work of the Kathmandu Valley from which the Khasa style surely developed. The *dakini* and the Avalokiteshvara display a similar treatment of the lotus base, notably in the shape of the leaves and a row of large pearls adorning the top rim. The Dipamala figure does not compare with this treatment of the base, as the footed throne is rarely found in the sculpture of Nepal or Tibet; it is more frequent in northern Indian Buddhist sculpture.

But there are hints of other stylistic vocabularies that set this tradition apart from that of Kathmandu. The bodies of both the Chenrezig and the queen/goddess figures are smoothly and fully modeled, and the hands are delicate and pliable. The faces in particular are fleshy and beautifully full, with similar treatment of chin, mouth, and eyebrows, and the pupils of the eyes are delineated in both. Further, the Chenrezig can be seen to display two interesting stylistic idioms found almost exclusively in the Khasa Malla figures: the back of the base is left relatively unfinished, ungilded and painted with red color; and the joints of the fingers are clearly delineated on the outside of the hands.

Numerous examples of Buddhist metal sculptures have come to light exhibiting these various idiosyncrasies, and we are gradually learning more about this stylistic tradition.

Further Reading

Alsop, Ian. 2005. "The Metal Sculpture of the Khasa Mallas of West Nepal/ West Tibet." Asianart.com. Published August 26, 2005. https://www.asianart.com/articles/Khasa/index.html.

Tucci, Giuseppe. 1956a. *Preliminary Report on Two Scientific Expeditions in Nepal.* Serie Orientale Roma 10; Materials for the Study of Nepalese History and Culture 1. Rome: Istituto Italiano per il Medio ed Estremo Oriente.

Tucci, Giuseppe 1962. *Nepal: The Discovery of the Malla.* London: Allen and Unwin.

Notes

1 Pal 1969, 32, 146–47, fig. 51; Béguin 1977, 70, fig. 16; von Schroeder 1981, 348, fig. 90B; Alsop 1994, 61; Alsop 1997, 68–69; Alsop 2005.
2 von Schroeder 1981, 348, fig. 90B.
3 Pal 1969, 146. For another two-armed image, also Khasa Malla, see Alsop 2005, fig. 10.
4 Vajrācārya and Malla 1985, for the religious visit, 145; for incursions and attacks, 147, 149, 151.
5 Alsop 1994.
6 See Sharma 1972; Andolfatto 2021.
7 Tucci 1956a, 86.
8 See Alsop and Charlton 1973, 22–49, reproduced in Alsop and Charlton 2021.
9 A. Heller 2013a.

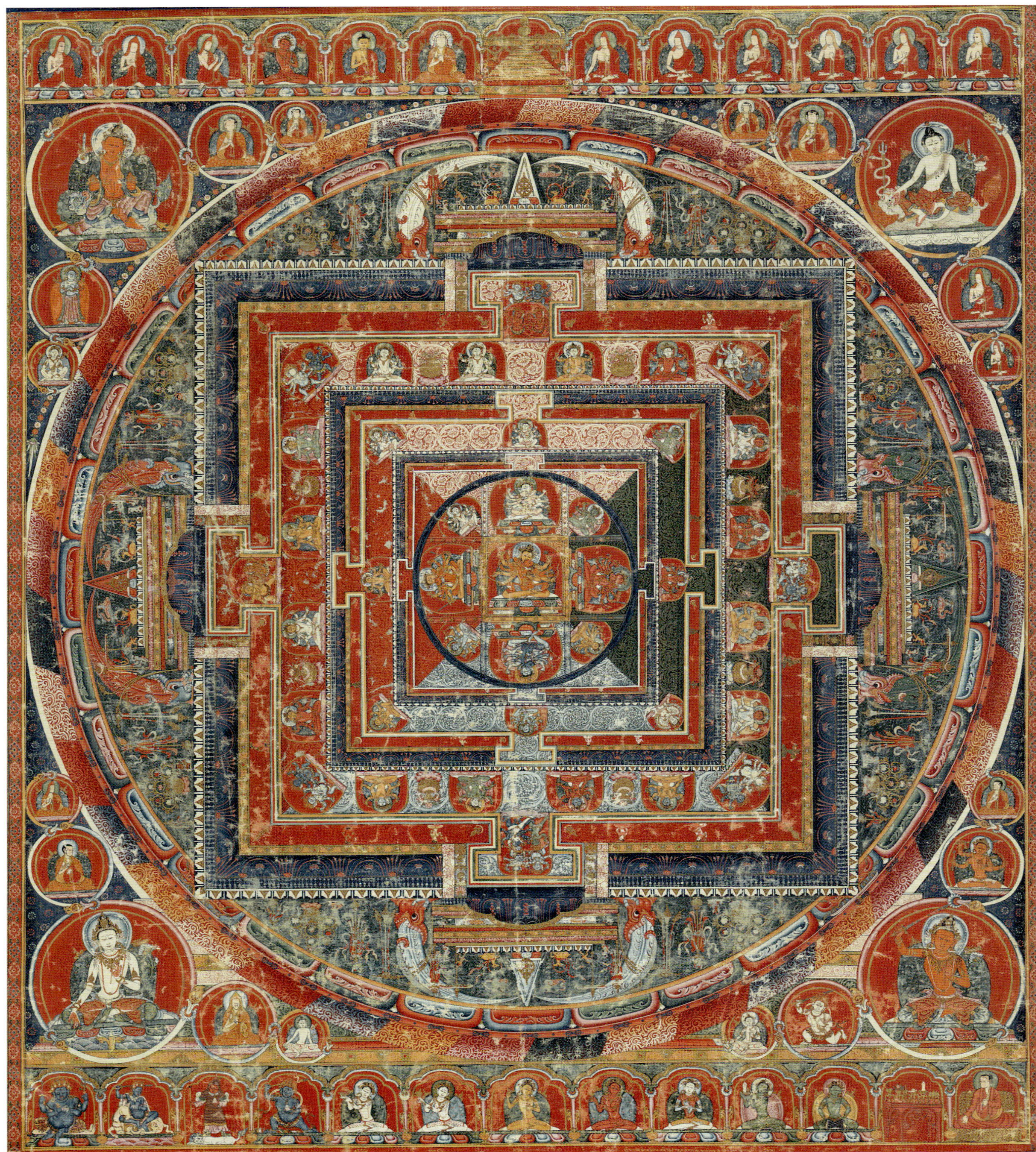

№ 50

Mandala of Manjuvajra of the *Vajravali* Set Commissioned in Memory of Lama Dampa

Central Tibet, 1375–1380

An Example of Court Patronage to Honor a Religious Master

DAVID JACKSON AND CHRISTIAN LUCZANITS

THIS EXQUISITE TIBETAN SCROLL PAINTING (thangka) depicts the three-headed and six-armed tantric deity Manjuvajra embracing his consort in the center of his forty-three-deity mandala. This painting once was part of a set depicting the mandalas of the *Vajravali* in the Nepalese-inspired Beri style. The paintings of this set are further remarkable for their informative captions, identifying most of their figures as well as their subject matter. Nevertheless, to establish the precise historical context of the creation of the set and its later usage based on the fragments that are now spread across Western museums and private collections remains challenging.

Mandalas of the *Vajravali*

The term *Vajravali* refers to the first and main part of a trilogy compiled by the late eleventh- to early twelfth-century Indian scholar Abhayakaragupta, the other parts being the *Nishpannayogavali* and the *Jyotirmanjari*. Whereas the *Vajravali* describes the rituals associated with twenty-six mandalas, such as their making, consecration, and initiation, the other two texts complement it by describing the visualization of their deities and the associated fire rituals.[1] The *Vajravali* was an attempt to bring order to the diversity of ritual procedures alluded to in esoteric Buddhist literature, and the comparative point of view used in discussing the mandalas may well have provided a model for Tibetan scholars of later periods. Today the *Nishpannayogavali*, which contains the iconographic details of the mandala deities, ranks among the most important primary sources on Indian Buddhist iconography transmitted to Tibet.

While the *Vajravali* focuses on twenty-six mandalas, passing remarks about different opinions and variants in texts describing them leave considerable scope for interpretation. Consequently, Tibetan interpretations of the *Vajravali* may contain considerably more mandalas.[2] In Tibet, these interpretations were handed down in distinct transmission lineages, and the painting set focused on here is an early witness of one such interpretation.

Forty-Three-Deity Mandala of Manjuvajra

This mandala of Manjuvajra, a form of Manjushri, the bodhisattva of wisdom, derives from the *Mayajala Tantra*, as the caption on the painting also confirms: "The twenty-second Mandala; the forty-three-deity Manjushri Mayajala mandala." The mandala is the twentieth described in detail in the text, and its iconography matches the *Nishpannayogavali* perfectly.[3] It shows the five buddhas embracing their consorts, with the central figure of Manjuvajra taking the place of Vairochana. Four goddesses complete the central circle, and eight more goddesses inhabit the second palace. The Sixteen Bodhisattvas of the Fortunate Aeon occupy the outer palace, along with the ten wrathful deities and their consorts. The latter protect the ten directions; those protecting the zenith and nadir explain the double occupancy in the western (top) and eastern (bottom) gates.

The paintings of this *Vajravali* set are easy to recognize; all have the same composition dominated by a mandala taking up the full width of the canvas. Furthermore, the same teacher is represented in the top center. In this painting, that teacher has been shifted to the left of center, as his position is taken by a golden finial. Close observation reveals that a fine white line, deriving from this finial and accompanied by a flower garland, is drawn along the outermost fire ring of the mandala, which then merges with a multilayered base represented in the bottom corners of the central panel behind the deities. Thus, in this

Forty-Three-Deity Mandala of Manjuvajra, the twenty-second painting of the *Vajravali* set commissioned in memory of Lama Dampa, detail showing the painting only; central Tibet; 1375–1380; distemper on cloth; 33 × 29⅛ in. (83.9 × 74 cm); The Metropolitan Museum of Art, New York; Rogers Fund, 1977; 1977.340; CC0 -Creative Commons (CC0 1.0)

For comparison, see White Stupa, no. 40.

case, the mandala is coequal with a stupa that is drawn directly behind it and encompasses the entire mandala. Indeed, the *Nishpannayogavali* mentions that the palace of this mandala is to be drawn within a white stupa.[4]

Each corner of the mandala is filled by five medallions; the smaller ones continue the teaching transmission lineage of this particular mandala in the top row, while the larger ones depict different forms of the bodhisattvas Manjushri and Avalokiteshvara. Finally, the bottom row contains four protective deities and seven goddesses personifying offerings, along with a portrayal of the receiver and practitioner of the depicted teaching, who is possibly also the donor, in the bottom right corner.

Historical Context of the Set

A characteristic of this set of mandala paintings is that many historical figures and deities are identified by tiny captions. Nevertheless, to precisely establish the historical context is challenging, and different opinions were offered in the past.[5] On this painting, the main teacher to the left of the stupa's top is vaguely referred to as "His excellency, the Lord of Dharma,"[6] and the likely donor of the painting in the bottom right corner has no caption at all.

Fortunately, the second painting of the set, depicting the thirty-two-deity mandala of Akshobhyavajra from the *Guhyasamaja Tantra*,[7] is more informative in this regard. There, the inscription for the main teacher reads, "Dharma Lord Sonam Gyeltsen"; and the bottom right figure is identified as "The donor Dzongji Chenpo."[8] Clearly, since these figures repeat on each painting, their names have not been repeated on all paintings of the set. After all, in their original context all paintings would have been viewed together.

For more on the Pakmodrupa regime, see Densatil Monastery, no. 30.

Accordingly, the top central teacher can be identified as Lama Dampa Sonam Gyeltsen (1312–1375), an idealist born in the Sakya Khon family who left the leadership of the great seat of Sakya and its political entanglements so that he could lead a more genuinely religious life.[9] In the early 1370s, his religious acclaim was so great and widespread that even the rulers of the Pakmodrupa court, which succeeded the government of the Sakya tradition, held him in high esteem. It is thus no surprise that the patron of this painting set is Dzongji Gyeltsen Zangpo, a powerful functionary of the Pakmodrupa regime in the 1370s and 1380s, when its rulers were comparably weak.

The most likely scenario is that Dzongji commissioned this painting in memory of Lama Dampa after his passing in 1375. A work of this quality and complexity would take some time to produce, especially considering the many paintings that make up the whole set. And, given his extreme modesty and saintliness, Lama Dampa would not have approved such a big project in his honor while he lived.

The Beri Painting Style

For eastern Indian style painting in Tibet, see Tara Who Protects from the Eight Great Fears, no. 27.

For another example of this Nepalese-inspired style in Tibet, see Virupa, no. 37.

Originating from the heartland of Buddhism, the art created in northeast India strongly impacted Buddhist art in Tibet, particularly down to the twelfth century. At that time, Tibet was experiencing a second revival of Buddhism, and patrons and artists avidly copied compositions from Pala-ruled northeastern India. However, from the thirteenth century on, following the destruction of the main monasteries in India, Tibetans turned more and more to Nepal's Kathmandu Valley, home to the exceptionally skilled Newar artists, for aesthetic inspiration and artisanship. Tibetans themselves quickly began to also employ the Beri style, a Newar or "Nepalese style," first mainly in Tsang region immediately north of the Kathmandu Valley. The Beri then became one of the country's most influential styles, flourishing from the thirteenth through the sixteenth century.

The *Vajravali* painting set is an extremely refined example of the Beri style, demonstrating the enduring artistic connections between Tibetan art and the art of the Kathmandu Valley. Hallmarks of this style as they appear in this set are the dominance of vermilion, used in all the nimbuses, the dark blue background filled with blossoms, the intricate lotus scroll backgrounds filling all spaces of the mandala palace, and the lotus column pillars that support lobed arches framing the figures in the upper and lower rows of the painting. In fact, many of the dress, jewelry, and throne motifs employed for the deities themselves can be linked to Newar art.[10] Furthermore, the sumptuous decorative motifs topping and

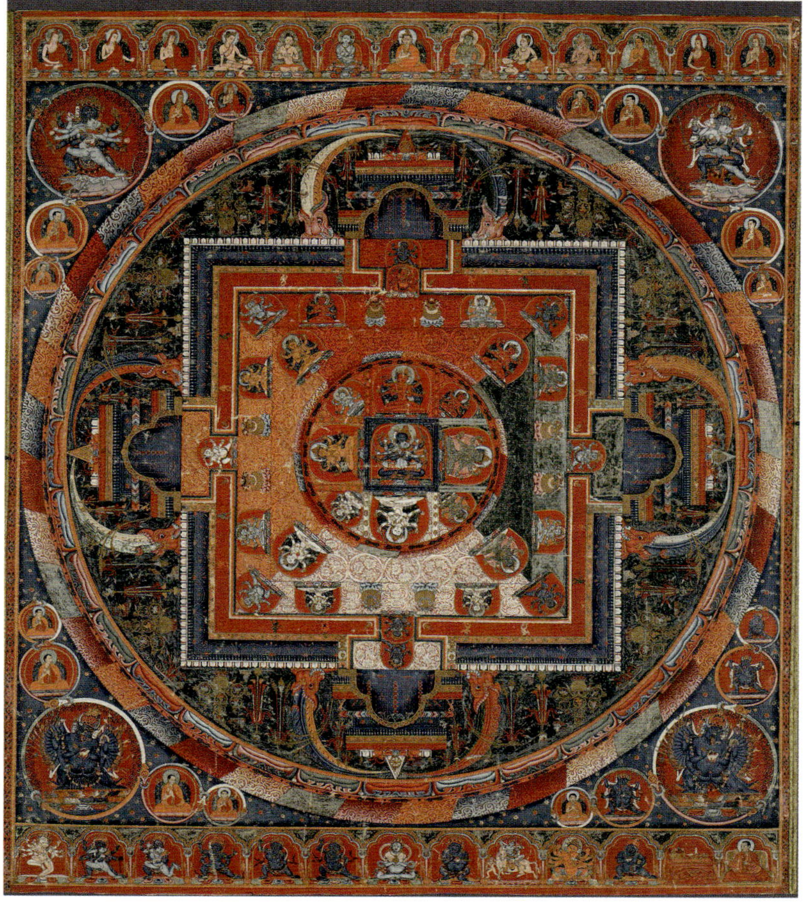

Thirty-Two-Deity Mandala of Aksobhyavajra, the second painting of the *Vajravali* set commissioned in memory of Lama Dampa; central Tibet, Sakya tradition; 1375–1380; distemper on cloth; Pritzker Collection

flanking the mandala gates, including representations of monkeys and vases crowned by a scroll forming seven flower medallions, confirm this connection.

Nevertheless, the set was painted in a Tibetan workshop, as evidenced by color notations—letters used to indicate the color to be filled in—many of which can be seen where the paint layer has been abraded.[11] A workshop production also accounts for the differences between the individual paintings in the set. This workshop may well have been located in or near Lhokha, in central Tibet, near the place where Lama Dampa passed away and near the seat of the government in which the donor served.

Usage and Dispersal

Pratapaditya Pal has proposed that the paintings later ended up in Ngor Monastery.[12] There is a scenario that could account for this. Ngorchen, its founder, might have received the set as an official gift from the Pakmodrupa government. When he visited central Tibet in 1441, Ngorchen was regally sponsored by the then ruler, Drakpa Jungne (1414–1445). One of his main dharma projects was to teach the *Vajravali* and sponsor a complete new set of its paintings.[13]

Such a scenario would also account for a later very limited usage of the set, which would explain its present excellent condition. This set would not have been displayed on the occasions that abbots of Ngor gave the teachings and initiations for the *Vajravali* set of mandalas, using instead the more recent set commissioned by the later abbot Namkha Pelzang or even the famous Ngorchen-sponsored set.

Further Reading

Estournel, Jean-Luc. 2021. "About the Portraits of Tibetan Masters." Asianart.com. Published February 28, 2021. https://www.asianart.com/articles/tibetan_masters/index.html.

Jackson, David P. 2010. *The Nepalese Legacy in Tibetan Painting*. Masterworks of Tibetan Painting 2. Exhibition catalog. New York: Rubin Museum of Art. https://issuu.com/rmanyc/docs/nepalese_legacy_96.

Notes

1 Bühnemann 1992; Mori 1997; Chandra and Sharma 2015.
2 Mori 2008.
3 See for example Mallmann 1986, 58–60; Chandra and Sharma 2015, 164–78.
4 While this is clear in the text (see Chandra and Sharma 2015, 165), such a detail gets lost in short iconographic summaries, such as those contained in Mallmann 1986, 58–60.
5 See for example Pal 1997, 147, pl. 73; Estournel 2021.
6 On this phrase, "drung chos kyi rje pa," see for example D. Jackson 2010, 134–35.
7 The painting is identified as "dkyil 'khor gnyis pa bsdus pa'i rim par gsungs pa gsang ba 'dus pa lha sum bcu so gnyis kyi dkyil 'khor/."
8 The relevant captions read, "chos rje bsod nams rgyal mtshan and sbyin pa'i bdag po dzong ji chen po."
9 D. Jackson 2010, 132.
10 See the detailed account of Beri characteristics in D. Jackson 2010, 81–97.
11 For example, on painting two of the set, light green is worn off in many areas, revealing the Tibetan color code *ja*. In the Manjuvajra painting most color degradations have occurred in the skin tones of the teacher portraits. That color was the least stable after all those years.
12 Here Pal (Pal 1997, 147, pl. 73) is following Stoddard.
13 See Heimbel 2017, 344–47.

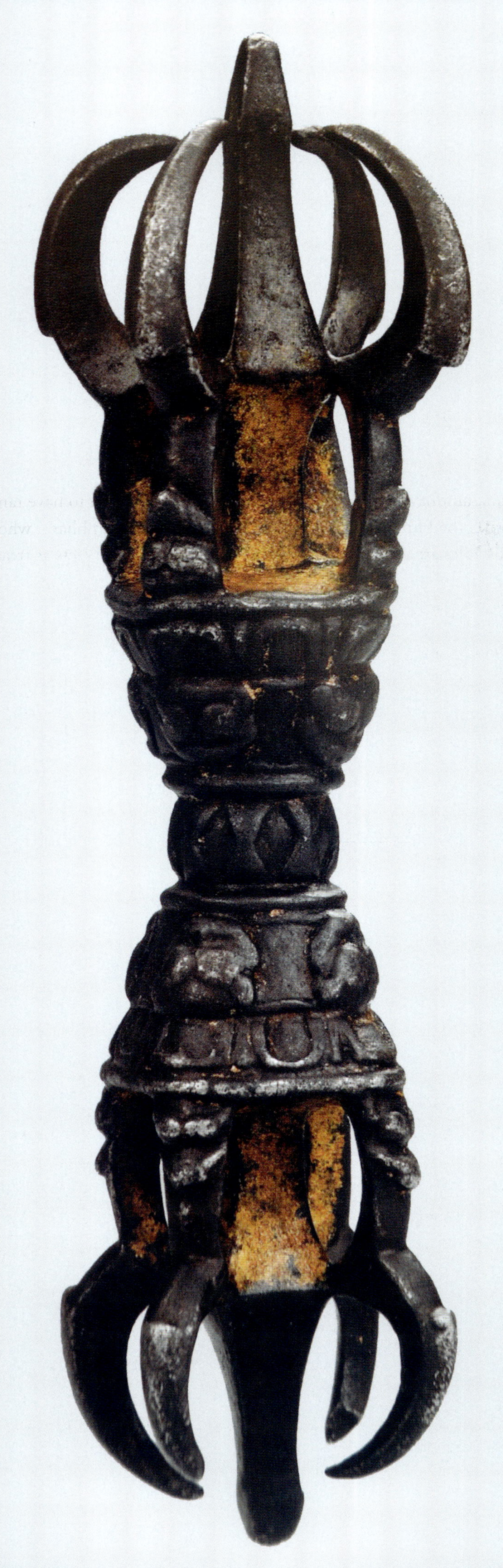

No 51

Dorje Discovered by Dorje Lingpa

Discovered in Senge Dzong, Bhutan, attributed to the 8th century, discovered in the 14th century

Sacred Art among Hidden Treasures

KARMA PHUNTSHO

For more on Padmasambhava, see Padmasambhava and His Manifestations, no. 43; Ritual Dance Mask of Guru Dorje Drolo, no. 94; Monumental Statue of Guru Rinpoche, no. 104.

THE *DORJE* (vajra in Sanskrit) is a very important ritual object prevalent in Vajrayana Buddhist communities in the Himalayas. Symbolizing the indestructible nature of reality and pristine awareness, it is widely used by priests as a ritual object and aid for meditation. This particular *dorje* belongs to a popular category of sacred objects known as rediscovered treasures, or *terma*, associated with Padmasambhava, the master from Oddiyana who is said to have tamed the wild spirits and spread Buddhism in the Himalayas in the eighth century. Padmasambhava, who wields a *dorje* in his right hand, and his disciples are said to have buried religious texts and objects as treasure, or *ter*, in the earth, rocks, lakes, and statues for safekeeping. Considered a sacred heritage discovered by later treasure discoverers with special connections to Padmasambhava, such *terma* artifacts are highly valued and venerated in the Himalayan Buddhist world. This particular *dorje*, currently housed in Trashigang Dzong in eastern Bhutan, is believed to have been discovered in the fourteenth century by Dorje Lingpa (1346–1405), a leading Tibetan treasure revealer, who, like many other figures through the centuries, frequented the Bhutanese valleys in search of religious treasures and economic patronage. Aja Lam Dorje, a patriarch in the tradition of Dorje Lingpa, claimed that this *dorje* was discovered at Senge Dzong cave in northeastern Bhutan, along with a bell and *purba* dagger.[1] According to his son, Lam Kesang Chophel, the *purba* dagger was lost in a temple fire, but the bell was retrieved and in his possession.

Terma Culture and Art

The Tibetan Buddhist treasure culture is a unique and skillful practice of religious preservation and regeneration that started in the eleventh century during the period of Tibetan Buddhist renaissance (late tenth through the thirteenth century). This practice may have begun as a practical endeavor to bury religious articles for safekeeping as the Yarlung dynastic power of the Tibetan Empire, which patronized the transmission of Buddhism in Tibet from the seventh to ninth centuries, crumbled in the middle of the ninth century and Tibet went through an era of political chaos and peasants' revolts. Hidden during such troubled times, the objects were then perhaps retrieved using guides and notes when the sociopolitical situation became conducive to their use from the beginning of the eleventh century, when Buddhism regained support and popularity. Thus, Tibet saw the emergence of the culture of treasure discovery, which focused on revealed knowledge in contrast to received tradition passed down from person to person.

It is quite likely that early treasure discoveries involved ordinary human procedures of recovering texts or artifacts, although the acts of retrieval may have been accompanied by some religious rituals and prayers. However, as the practice developed, it appears to have gone through a process of sacralization and ritualistic systematization, and it gradually evolved into a complex mystical and transcendental process involving specific sacred sites, secret codes, guides, rituals, miracles, and, above all, treasure discoverers with special connections to Padmasambhava. The objects, including texts and artifacts, came to be highly regarded as powerful pieces blessed and buried by Padmasambhava and his cohort in the eighth century, and the treasure discoverers came to be seen as exceptional beings who were associated with and predicted by Padmasambhava. By Dorje Lingpa's time, treasure discovery was not merely an ordinary practice of hiding and retrieving things but a transcendental revelation of religious knowledge and objects involving superhuman and prophetic abilities.

Terma Dorje Discovered by Dorje Lingpa (1346–1405); discovered in Senge Dzong, Bhutan; produced ca. 8th century, discovered 14th century; iron and cold gold; 6⅛ × 1⅜ in. (15.5 × 3.4 cm); Collection of Royal Government of Bhutan; photograph by Shuzu Uemoto, Honolulu Museum of Art, reproduced with permission from Ministry of Culture, Royal Government of Bhutan

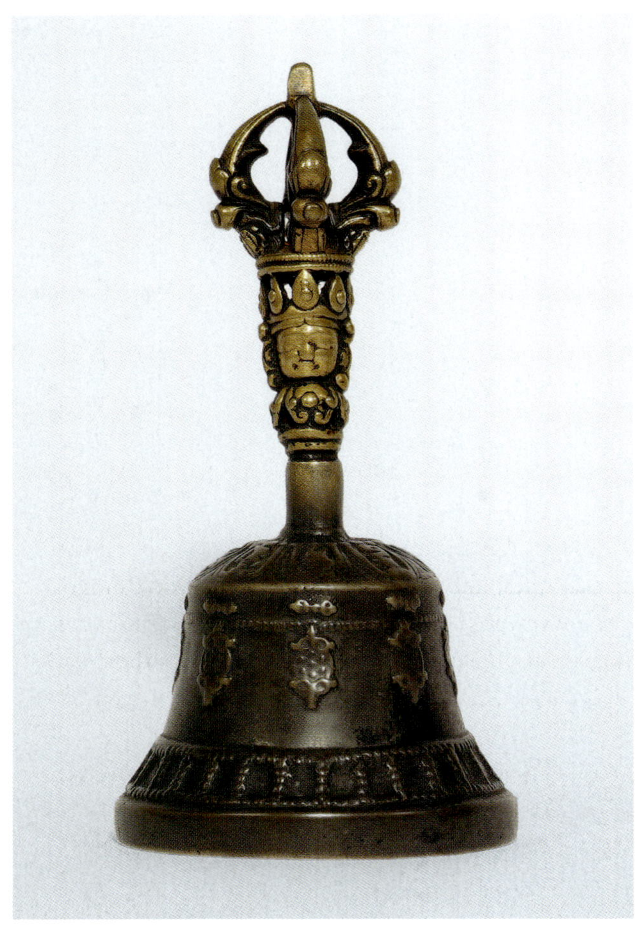

Dorje Lingpa, considered to be an incarnation of Vairochana, a translator and master in the eighth century who worked alongside Padmasambhava, was a leading treasure discoverer—in fact, one of the five so-called king treasure discoverers, who had many other treasure discoverers as their disciples. He left behind a large corpus of revealed teachings, important spiritual and family lineages in Tibet and Bhutan, and many artistic objects, such as this *dorje*, which are said to have been discovered by him. Another king treasure discoverer, and a figure influential particularly in Bhutan and southern Tibet a generation after Dorje Lingpa, was Pema Lingpa (1450–1521), the foremost spiritual figure Bhutan produced. Today, in addition to dozens of volumes of texts attributed to him, one can find many statues and ritual implements believed to have been revealed by him.[2] They are now highly revered and cherished as community relics or religious heirlooms.

There were numerous other treasure discoverers like Dorje Lingpa and Pema Lingpa. Kongtrul Lodro Taye (1813–1899), who compiled the biographies of these treasure discoverers up to the middle of the nineteenth century, enumerates some 230 treasure discoverers.[3] He also compiled most of their revealed teachings in *Treasury of Precious Terma Teachings*, but the *terma* artifacts attributed to them remain dispersed without a proper inventory and procedure for authentication, thus often leading to false claims. The culture of revealing texts and artifacts (*terma*) continues today and, given the special status *terma* objects enjoy as religious artifacts, many objects have been claimed to be rediscovered treasures.

Drilbu Bell Claimed to Have Been Discovered by Dorje Lingpa; Bhutan; discovered in the 14th century; bronze; Thimphu, Bhutan; photograph courtesy Loden Foundation

The Significance and Use of *Dorje*

The Tibetan word *dorje* literally means "lord of stone" and refers to diamond, thunderbolt, or an indestructible phenomenon. In the Indian Vedic religion, the vajra is a scepter associated with the Vedic god Indra, the king of gods. Indra wielded the vajra, believed to have been made from a sage's bone, as a powerful weapon against evil forces. In Buddhism, the vajra thunderbolt is presented as the handheld implement of buddhas and deities such as Akshobhya, Vajrapani, Vajradhara, Vajrasattva, and Mahakala, among others. The term *vajra* is also used as an adjective to refer to something that is adamantine, such as the vajra topic, vajra seat, vajra body, vajra speech, and vajra heart. As a corollary, the adjective *vajra* is attached to the names of many deities and gods.

In the tantric or Vajrayana form of Buddhism, which is named after it, the term *vajra* bears a much greater significance and role as both a spiritual concept and a ritual object. As a concept, *vajra* refers to the ultimate nature of reality, which is indestructible, and the pristine awareness of it. Any experience or phenomenon ensconced in such nature and awareness is described as *vajra*, or adamantine. As the tantric form of Buddhism is centered on the actualization of such adamantine reality and awareness, it is called Vajrayana, or the adamantine or diamond vehicle. The vajra as a religious object generally symbolizes such immutable ultimate nature of existence and pristine awareness of it. However, when juxtaposed with the bell with which it is normally paired, the vajra represents skillful method or compassion, while the bell represents wisdom. The vajra also symbolizes supreme bliss or appearance and male energy, while the bell signifies emptiness and feminine power. In this context, the term *vajra* is also used to refer to the male organ. Together, they represent the union of wisdom and compassion, emptiness and bliss, and male and female energy.

The vajra or *dorje* plays a prominent and ubiquitous role in Tibetan Buddhist rituals and practices and is normally, but not specifically, wielded by the leading priest. According to accounts, there are single-pronged *dorje*, *dorje* with three, five or nine prongs, and also crossed *dorje*, but the five-pronged type, known as *damtsik dorje*, and the nine-pronged, known as *yeshe dorje*, are most common.[4] There are

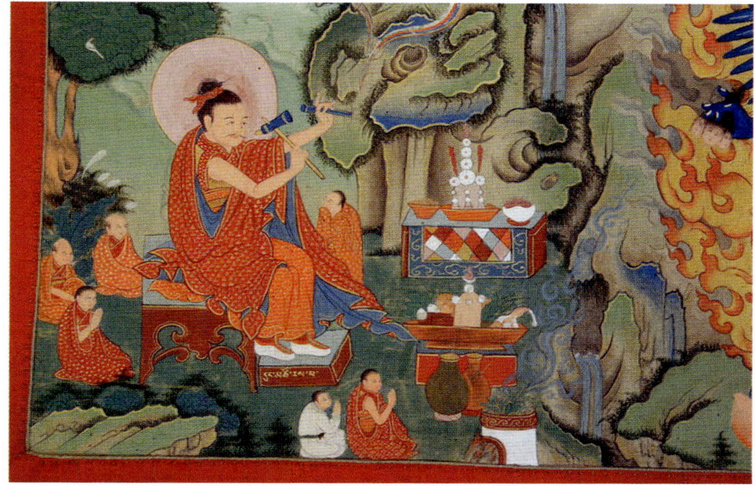

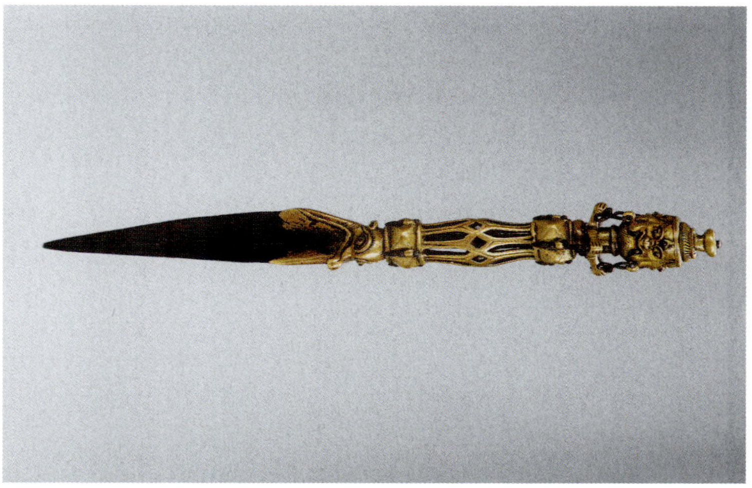

Dungtso Repa Extracting Treasure, detail of a thangka; Gangteng Monastery, Phobjikha, Bhutan; photograph courtesy Shejun

Purba Dagger Discovered by Pema Lingpa; date unknown; mixed metals and gilding; 13¾ × 1½ in. (35 × 4 cm); Collection of Royal Government of Bhutan; photograph by Shuzu Uemoto, Honolulu Museum of Art, reproduced with permission from Ministry of Culture, Royal Government of Bhutan

dorjes for peaceful activities as well as for fierce or wrathful practices. In the case of the common five-pronged *dorje*, of which this is an example, the five prongs at the top symbolize the Buddhas of the Five Families, or the buddhas associated with the center and four directions in a mandala configuration; the five prongs at the bottom symbolize the five types of pristine wisdom; the eight upper lotus petals the eight bodhisattvas; the eight lower lotus petals the eight female divinities; and the central hub Buddha Vajrasattva. In the same manner, every aspect of the *dorje* object bears spiritual symbolism. The accounts of the *dorje* also mention the ways in which it should be used together with the bell, and the benefits of possessing and using the *dorje*.[5]

As the *dorje* is widely used in Himalayan Buddhist rituals, they are produced and sold in great numbers, but some examples, like the one discovered by Dorje Lingpa shown above, are highly regarded for their antiquity, for their association with important figures, or for their status as rediscovered treasures. They are generally made of metal, sometimes plated in gold and also studded with precious stones. In Bhutan, one also finds *dorjes* called *damchen ledungma*, which are claimed to have been crafted by the protective deity Damchen Dorje Lekpa, using his thigh as an anvil and presented to Padmasambhava, who named him Garwa Nakpo, the dark blacksmith, in recognition of his work. The *dorjes* in Somthrang in Bumthang District and Dungkar in Lhuntse District are believed to have been made by Damchen Dorje Lekpa.

Further Reading

Doctor, Andreas. 2005. *Tibetan Treasure Literature: Revelation, Tradition, and Accomplishment in Visionary Buddhism.* Boulder, CO: Shambhala.

Ghosh, Bhajagovinda. 1997. "The Concept of Vajra and Its Symbolic Transformation," *Bulletin of Tibetology* 33, no. 2, 25–43.

Tulku Thondup Rinpoche. 1997. *Hidden Teachings of Tibet: An Explanation of the Terma Tradition of Tibetan Buddhism.* Boston: Wisdom.

Notes

1 Lam Kezang Chophel, personal communication with author, August 14, 2021.
2 Bartholomew and Johnston 2008, 304–5.
3 Kongtrul Lodöe Thaye 2021.
4 Jigme Lingpa 1985, 90.
5 See for instance Jigme Thinley Özer 2019.

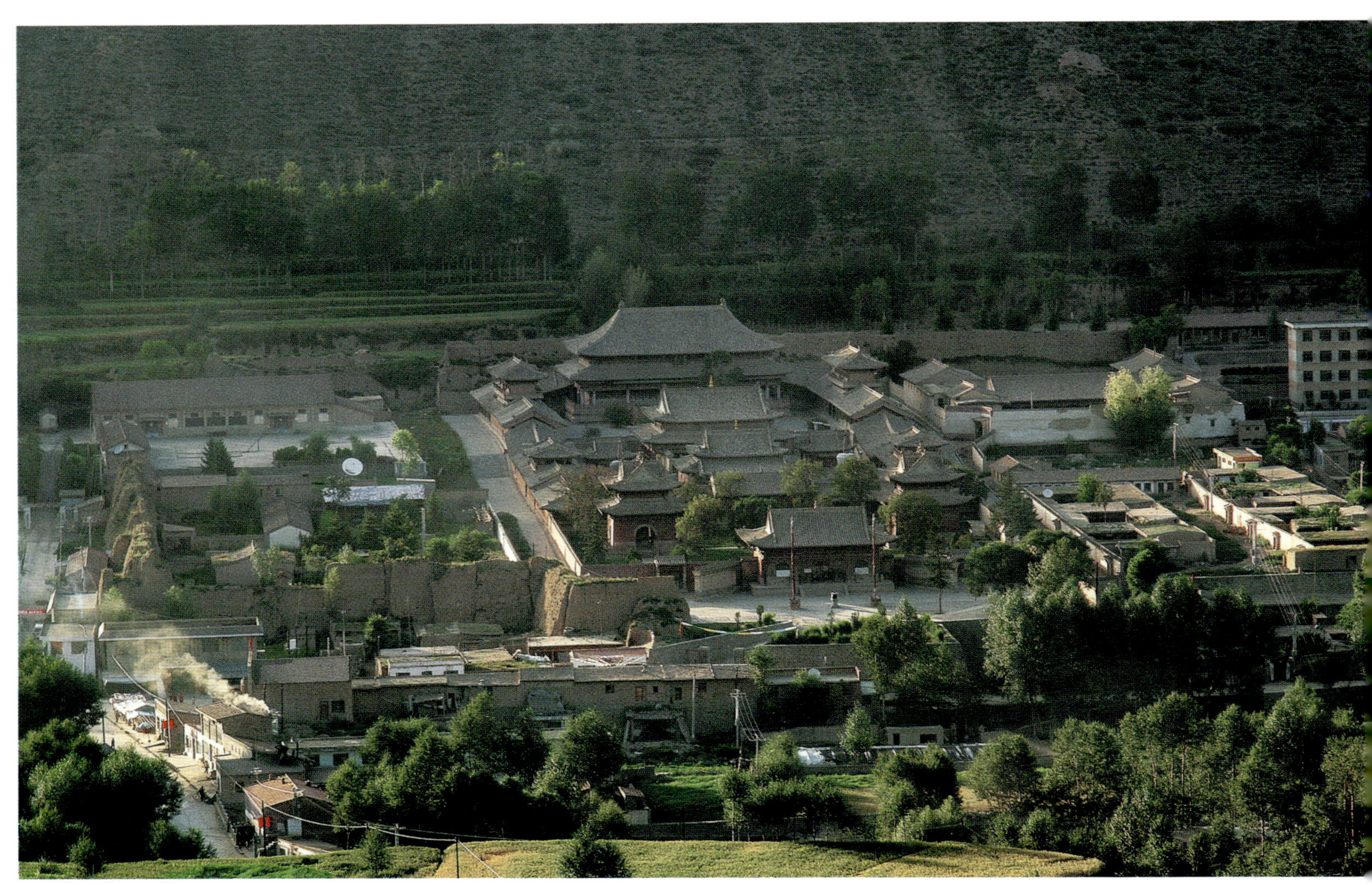

No 52

Qutan Monastery (Drotsang Dorje Chang)

Drotsang, Tsongkha, Amdo region, eastern Tibet (present-day Ledu County, Qinghai Province, China), 1392–1427

A Ming Dynasty Monastery at the Sino-Tibetan Frontier

AURELIA CAMPBELL

QUTANSI (GAUTAMA MONASTERY) is a well-preserved Tibetan Buddhist monastery located near Ledu in Qinghai, China, and Amdo, Tibet, a borderland region where Tibetan, Mongolian, and Chinese populations intersect. The monastery's name in Tibetan, Drotsang Dorje Chang, refers to Buddha Vajradhara, to whom the temple was dedicated. Founded by a Tibetan lama in about 1392, Qutansi was constructed over a period of approximately thirty-five years with support from three powerful early Ming dynasty (1368–1644) emperors, Hongwu (r. 1368–1398), Yongle (r. 1402–1424), and Xuande (r. 1425–1435). These emperors sent artisans from the imperial court to manage the construction and decoration of the monastery's sumptuous Buddha halls, along with numerous luxurious objects created in the imperial workshops to furnish them. They also had carvings made on stone stele of several edicts, in Chinese and Tibetan, outlining the terms of their support and reasons for their patronage, which still stand at the monastery.[1] Their main motivations for supporting Qutansi were to bring peace to and help control the politically unstable Sino-Tibetan borderlands, as well as to use it as an imperial lineage temple in which the resident lamas could pray for the long life of the dynastic line.[2] Qutansi was just one of several temples supported by the Ming court in the northern Amdo Sino-Tibetan frontier.[3] Taken as a whole, the buildings, objects, and murals at Qutansi constitute our most comprehensive surviving record of imperial Tibetan Buddhist art from the early Ming dynasty.

For more on the creation of Tibetan Buddhist objects in early Ming imperial workshops, see Pensive Bodhisattva Avalokiteshvara, no. 53.

Ming Imperial Patronage

Qutansi was founded shortly before 1393, when a Tibetan Buddhist lama named Sanggye Tashi (d. 1414) traveled from Amdo to the first Ming capital in Nanjing, bearing horses as tribute, in order to request imperial protection for his newly established Buddhist temple. Earlier, Sanggye Tashi had persuaded the disbanded followers of a Mongol Yuan dynasty loyalist in Gansu Province to submit to the Ming, thereby helping to stabilize the politically turbulent borderland area. Recognizing the lama's important role as a peacekeeper in the northwest, Hongwu granted him protection of the temple along with its name, Qutansi, which was carved in the emperor's calligraphy on a signboard that still hangs from the front eaves of the temple's founding hall, Qutandian (Gautama Hall).[4] Hongwu's support of Qutansi constitutes one of the earliest signs of the Ming court's interest in Tibetan Buddhism and reveals an awareness of Buddhism's potential for exercising political control in the Tibetan frontier.[5]

Ming imperial patronage of Qutansi reached its height in the reign of Yongle, a fervent supporter of Tibetan Buddhism. Yongle invited three of the highest-ranking Tibetan hierarchs from Tibet to the Ming capitals in Nanjing and Beijing to serve as his personal Buddhist masters and perform for him powerful esoteric rituals and consecrations.[6] He also hosted hundreds of lesser-ranking Tibetan lamas in Beijing, including Sanggye Tashi's eldest nephew, Pelden Zangpo, whom he appointed to the position of abbot of Qutansi in 1408.[7] Yongle seems to have developed a particular affinity for Pelden Zangpo, bestowing illustrious titles and lavishing high praise on him in three edicts that he sent to Qutansi. In the third edict, dated 1418, Yongle gifted Pelden Zangpo with a (now destroyed) "self-arisen" golden Buddha image created for a newly completed hall, Baoguangdian (Hall of Jewel Light), at the monastery.[8]

Imperial construction at Qutansi culminated in the reign of Xuande, Yongle's grandson, with the completion of the monastery's largest hall, Longguodian (Hall of Dynastic Prosperity), in 1427. This hall had been part of Yongle's vision for the temple, but he died before it was finished.[9] To furnish the hall,

Qutansi (Gautama Monastery), aerial view; Drotsang, Tsongkha, Amdo region, eastern Tibet (present-day Ledu County, Qinghai Province, China); 1392–1427; photograph by Xie Jisheng

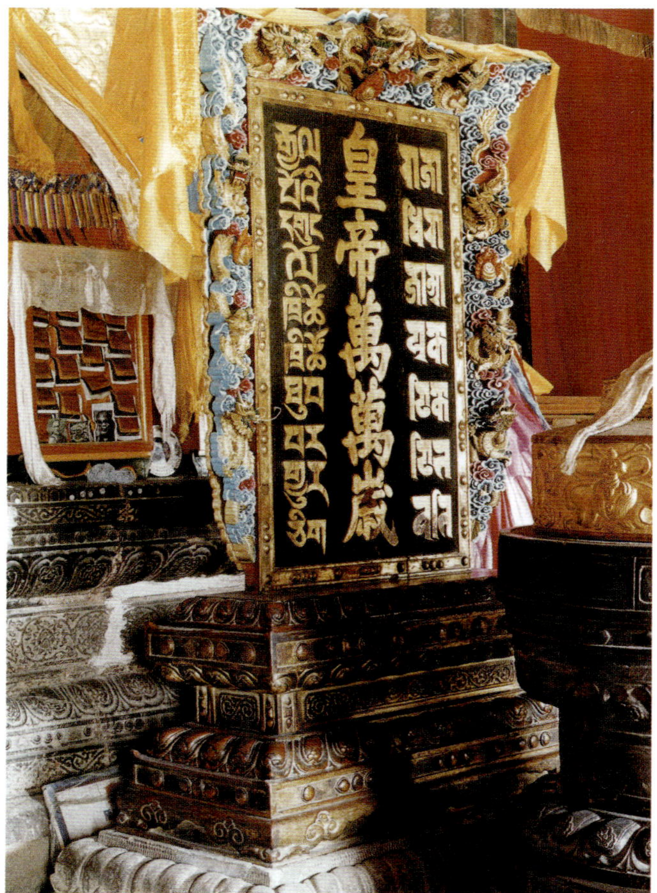

"Long Live the Emperor" Tablet; China; 1427; *nanmu* wood, lacquer, and stone; height 78¾ in. (200 cm); Longguodian (Hall of Dynastic Prosperity), Qutansi; Drotsang, Tsongkha, Amdo region, eastern Tibet (present-day Ledu County, Qinghai Province, China); image after Qinghai sheng wenhua ting, *Qutansi*, 195

Xuande sent a magnificent tablet inscribed with the words "Long Live the Emperor" in Chinese, Tibetan, and Sanskrit on the front and the names of three eunuchs who supervised the building project on the back.[10] Textual records indicate that he also sent a large statue of Buddha Vajradhara (no longer extant) to be installed as the hall's central image. Xuande was completing the architectural project according to his grandfather's wishes.[11]

Monastery Layout, Decorative Program, and Significant Objects

Qutansi follows a traditional Chinese architectural style, with timber-frame halls capped with ceramic tile roofs aligned along an axis. The first hall along the main axis, Jingangdian (Vajra Hall), formed the monastery's entrance for most of its history; in the twentieth century, a new main gate, along with two stele pavilions, was added in front of it. Aligned behind Jingangdian are Qutandian, Baoguangdian, and Longguodian. Longguodian is a magnificent structure of the highest order within the Ming architectural system, possessing a massive hipped roof, complex bracket sets, and corridors on both sides that connect to bell and drum towers. This form was generally used only in imperial palace halls, including Fengtiandian (Hall of Revering Heaven; later known as Taihedian, Hall of Supreme Harmony), the largest hall in the Ming Forbidden City.[12] The monastic complex is enclosed by a covered arcade and, until modern times, was surrounded with a thick earthen fortification to prevent attacks.[13]

One of Qutansi's most remarkable features is its more than five thousand square feet (five hundred square meters) of original wall paintings. The murals in the three main halls were mainly executed in a Sino-Tibetan style popular during the Mongol Yuan period (1271–1368) and depict deities belonging to the Sakya and Kagyu traditions. Of particular importance is a complete set of the forty-three deities of the Manjuvajra mandala from the eleventh-century collection of esoteric teachings *Vajravali* (Diamond Garland) in Qutandian—our earliest example of imagery related to this text in Amdo.[14] Baoguangdian contains the first ring of ten deities from the forty-three-deity Manjuvajra mandala, as well as rare portraits of the Second Zhamarpa, Khacho Wangpo (1350–1405); the Fifth Karmapa, Dezhin Shekpa (1384–1415); and Pelden Zangpo, who by painting himself alongside these two important hierarchs was claiming to belong to their illustrious lineage.[15] The walls of the arcade surrounding the monastic complex are covered in murals of the Buddha's life and past lives, done in the Chinese blue-and-green landscape style, which date to the Ming and Qing (1644–1911) dynasties.[16]

For more about Vajravali and Manjuvajra, see Mandala of Manjuvajra of the *Vajravali* Set, no. 50.

For nearly contemporary Tibetan murals of the lives of the Buddha, see Murals of Gongkar Chode, no. 58.

Unfortunately, nearly all of the monastery's original statuary program—including the "self-arisen" Buddha image gifted by Yongle and the large image of Vajradhara bestowed by Xuande—were destroyed during the Cultural Revolution (1966–1976). The only exception is an exquisite gilt-bronze statue of a bodhisattva inscribed on the lotus base with the words, "Donated in the reign of Yongle of the great Ming dynasty" in Sanskrit, Tibetan, and Chinese.[17] Several objects inscribed with the reign dates of later Ming emperors reveal that imperial patronage continued throughout the rest of the dynasty, though it never again reached the glory of the early fifteenth century.[18]

Qutansi after the Ming

By the Qing dynasty, Qutansi had fallen into significant decline, primarily suffering from the growing competition from the monasteries of Tsongkhapa's (1357–1419) Geluk tradition beginning in the sixteenth century.[19] At its height in the fifteenth and sixteenth centuries, the monastery housed more than five hundred monks; by the Qing, this number had been reduced to about three hundred; and in 1915 only sixty or so monks resided at the monastery.[20] It was not until the 1980s that Qutansi's buildings and furnishings were restored and the monastery was opened for tourism.

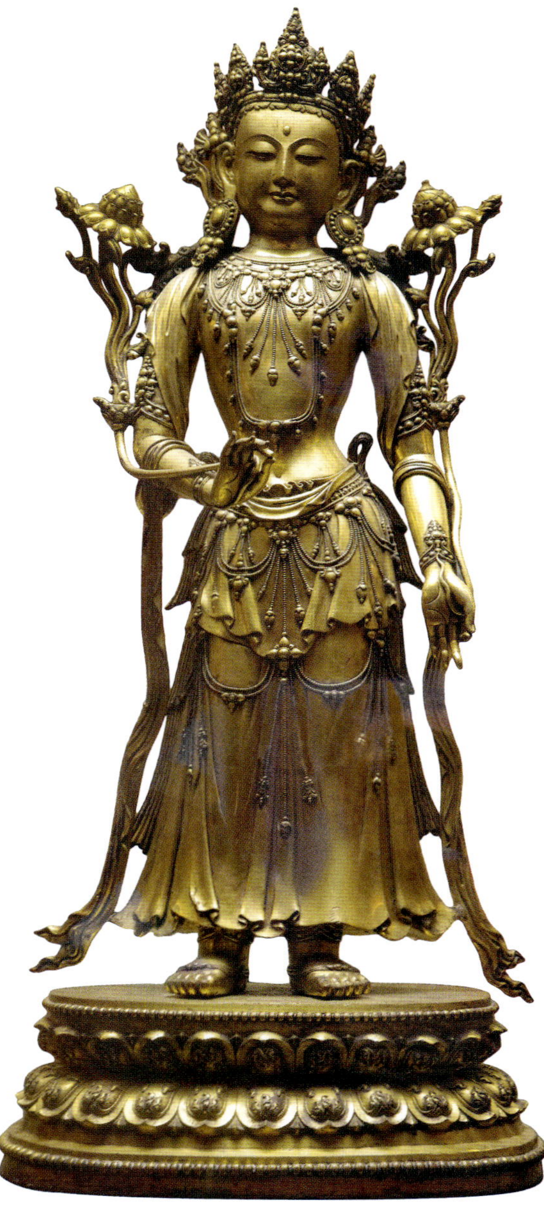

Standing Bodhisattva with a Yongle-period inscription in Chinese, Tibetan, and Sanskrit on the base; China; 15th century, Yongle period (1403–1424); gilt bronze; height 57 in. (145 cm); Qinghai Provincial Museum; photograph by Aurelia Campbell, 2017; edited by Jane Cassidy, 2019

Further Reading

Campbell, Aurelia. 2020. "From Mandala to Palace: Transforming Space and Site at Gautama Monastery." In *What the Emperor Built: Architecture and Empire in the Early Ming*, 127–64. Seattle: University of Washington Press.

Debreczeny, Karl. 2016a. "The Early Ming Imperial Atelier on the Tibetan Frontier." In *Ming China: Courts and Contacts, 1400–1450*, edited by Craig Clunas, Jessica Harrison-Hall, and Yu-ping Luk, 152–62. London: British Museum Press.

Sperling, Elliot. 2009. "Tibetan Buddhism, Perceived and Imagined, along the Ming-Era Sino-Tibetan Frontier." In *Buddhism between Tibet and China*, edited by Matthew Kapstein, 155–80. Boston: Wisdom.

Notes

1 Hongxi 洪熙 (r. 1424–1425) also sent an edict to the monastery during his short reign. The stele inscriptions are all transcribed in Wu Jingshan 2011.

2 Campbell 2020, 142–44; 159–63.

3 For instance, Xuande constructed a grand monastery called Dachongjiaosi 大崇教寺 (no longer extant) in Minzhou, Gansu Province, not far from Qutansi. See Campbell 2020, 161–62; Debreczeny 2003, 57–58. The Chenghua emperor (r. 1447–1487) patronized Honghuasi 弘化寺 in Minhe, Qinghai Province. According to Otosaka Tomoko, this monastery served as a local power base to defend against the Mongols, who were gaining power in the region.

4 *Ming Taizu Gao Huangdi shilu* 明太祖高皇帝實錄, *juan* 卷225. See Xie Zuo 1998, 10–12, for more on Sanggye Tashi.

5 Sperling 2009, 156.

6 The first was the Fifth Karmapa, Dezhin Shekpa (1384–1415), who stayed in Nanjing from 1407 to 1408; the second was Kunga Tashi (1349–1425), who stayed from 1413 to 1414; and the third was Shakya Yeshe (1354–1435), who stayed from 1415 to 1416. See Chen 2000; Sperling 1983.

7 "Qutansi Yongle liunian huangdi chiyu bei" 瞿曇寺永樂六年皇帝敕諭碑 (1408). Transcribed in Wu Jingshan 2011, 108.

8 "Yuzhi Qutan si jin foxiang bei 御制瞿曇寺金佛像碑" (1418). Transcribed in Wu Jingshan 2011, 110. See also Campbell 2020, 140–42.

9 In an edict Xuande sent to the monastery, he states that he built the hall in order to "fulfill the wishes of his grandfather." Xie Zuo 1998, 96–100.

10 Xie Zuo 1981, 56.

11 Wu, Mao, and Ma 1989, 168.

12 Campbell 2020, 156–58.

13 Following the completion of the monastery in the Xuande period, fifty-two soldiers were sent to guard it. In this respect, the monastery functioned as a kind of military garrison. Xie Zuo 1998, 105.

14 Chung 2014; Chung 2015.

15 Pelden Zangpo visited the Ming court in Nanjing in 1407, when the Fifth Karmapa was temporarily residing there at the invitation of the Yongle emperor. It is possible that he received teachings of the *Vajravali* from the Fifth Karmapa at this time. The Fifth Karmapa had, in turn, studied the *Vajravali* with the Second Zhamarpa since the age of four. Chung 2014, 193. See Roerich (1949) 1976, 507, for the record of the Fifth Karmapa being taught by the Second Zhamarpa.

16 The covered arcade around the second courtyard was probably constructed in the fifteenth year of the Yongle period (1418), alongside Baoguangdian, while the corridors around the rear courtyard were probably constructed in the second year of the Xuande period (1427), alongside Longguodian. Xie Jisheng and Liao 2006; Qian 1995; Debreczeny 2007, 191–205.

17 A similar statue survives in the Musée Cernuschi in Paris. Debreczeny 2016a, 160.

18 Chenghua 成化 (r. 1464–1487) granted a gold-plated bronze seal to the Tibetan abbot, and Wanli 萬曆 (r. 1572–1620) and Chongzhen 崇禎 (r. 1627–1644) both granted signboards to the temple. Xie Zuo 1981, 54–55.

19 Gruschke 2001, 44.

20 Schram 1957, 23.

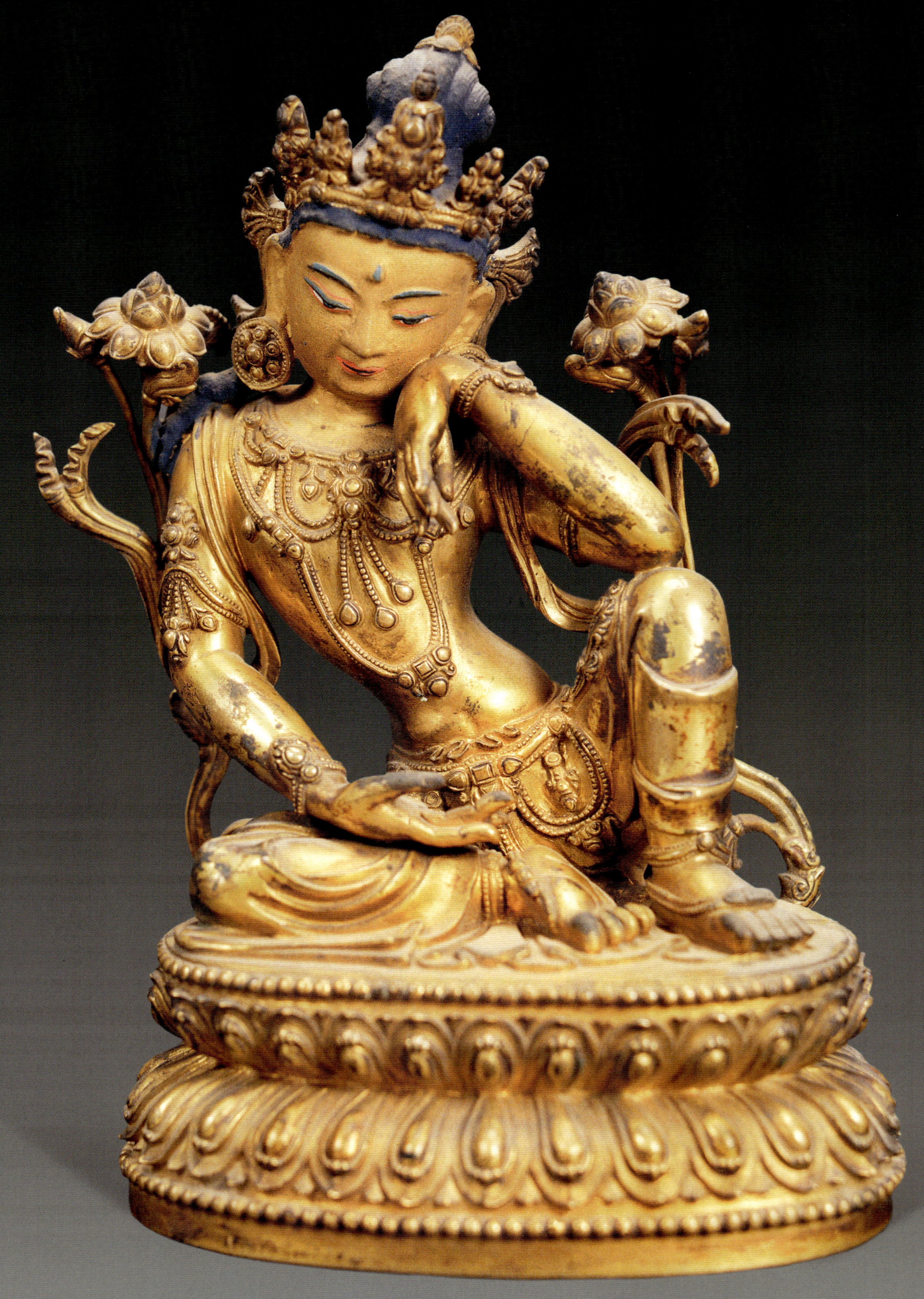

№ 53

Pensive Bodhisattva Avalokiteshvara

Nanjing or Beijing, China, Yongle period (1403–1424)

Imperial Tibetan Buddhist Statues under the Yongle and Xuande Reigns of the Ming Dynasty

LUO WENHUA

TRANSLATED BY GUOYING STACY ZHANG

THERE IS NO DOUBT that the making of Tibetan Buddhist statues at the Ming court was inspired by the preceding Yuan dynasty (1271–1368). Under the rule of Qubilai (Kubilai) Khan (1215–1294), the Nepalese artist Anige came to Beijing, on the recommendation of the Imperial Preceptor Pakpa, bringing authentic Himalayan imagery and techniques. This revitalizing art tradition was called *fanxiang* (Indian Images) and was further adopted by the Ming court. The Ming dynasty established its capital in Nanjing along the Yangtze River, while Beijing bolstered the northern frontier to keep residual Mongol forces on the defensive. During the reign of the first Ming emperor Zhu Yuanzhang (r. 1368–1398), Tibetan Buddhist statues do not seem to have been manufactured or circulated at the court. His fourth son Zhu Di was enthroned as a prince in Beijing in 1380, supervising military affairs in the north with a series of impressive achievements. In 1402 Zhu Di captured Nanjing with his troops and usurped the emperor's throne from his nephew. He was proclaimed Ming Chengzu and assumed the reign name Yongle (r. 1402–1424). It was from his reign until his grandson Xuande's reign (1426–1435) that Tibetan Buddhism and its arts gained favor at court. Owing to his extensive stay in the north, Zhu Di had a deep understanding of Tibetan Buddhism. He invited Dezhin Shekpa (1384–1415), the fifth "Black Hat" Karmapa of the Kagyu tradition; Kunga Tashi Gyeltsen (1349–1425), head of the Sakya tradition; and Shakya Yeshe, disciple of Tsongkhapa (1357–1419) who was the founder of the Geluk tradition, to Nanjing, and conferred on the first two respectively the titles of Dharma King of Great Treasure (*Rinchen chogyel*) and Dharma King of Great Vehicle (*Tekchen chogyel*). Shakya Yeshe was titled Dharma King of Great Compassion (*Jamchen chogyel*) in 1434 under Xuande's reign. At the request of Zhu Di, Dezhin Shekpa performed deliverance rituals for the emperor's deceased parents in Nanjing, which lasted for more than twenty days, and he also promulgated Tibetan Buddhist teachings among local followers. Moreover, Zhu Di commissioned the production of Kangyur—the Buddhist canon in Tibetan translation—in woodblock printing, which was the first complete block-printed edition of Kangyur in Tibetan history. He also ordered exquisite bronze statues, embroidered as well as painted thangkas, and ritual implements to bestow on Tibetan hierarchs at court or imperial monasteries, and frequently sent eunuch envoys to distribute imperial gifts among monasteries around Tibet.[1] To date, large numbers of gifts from the Ming court are still preserved in monasteries of various scales in Tibet, such as this pensive Avalokiteshvara statue, now in the Potala Palace in Lhasa.

For more about Anige, see White Stupa, no. 40.

For more about Himalayan art produced under the Mongol court of the Yuan dynasty, see Relief Carving of a Nine-Deity Ushnishavijaya Composition, no. 41; Vajrabhairava Mandala, no. 46; Juyong Guan Stupa Gate, no. 48.

For more about Ming court engagement with Tibetans, see Qutan Monastery, no. 52.

See Potala Palace, no. 71.

Unique Iconography

This bodhisattva Avalokiteshvara is an exemplar of Ming imperial statues. The top of the pedestal, in front of the figure's legs, is inscribed with the six-character Yongle mark "Da Ming Yong le nian shi."[2] Cast in brass with smooth gilt surfaces and a polished finish, the figure wears a five-leaf crown. An effigy of Buddha Amitabha is attached to the front of the high chignon, which is one of the identifiable features of Avalokiteshvara. The figure has a bare torso, wears a lower garment (dhoti), and is adorned with necklaces and jewels around the chest and the girdle. The rendering of the petals on the lotus pedestal is meticulous and orderly. The upper body sways to its right with exaggerated movement, while the head inclines toward the left, resting on the bent left wrist. The bodhisattva is seated in the royal ease posture (*rajalilasana*), left leg bent vertically and right leg horizontally, left elbow propped up by the left knee,

Pensive Bodhisattva Avalokiteshvara; Imperial Workshop, Nanjing or Beijing, China; Ming dynasty, Yongle period (1403–1424); gilt brass; height 8½ in. (21.5 cm); Potala Palace, Lhasa; photograph by Luo Wenhua

(left) Raktayamari; Imperial Workshop, South China; Ming Yongle period (1403–1424); silk embroidery; 11 × 7 ft. (3.35 × 2.13 m); Private collection; photograph provided by Long Museum, Shanghai

(right) Pensive Avalokiteshvara; Swat (present-day Pakistan); 7th century; brass; height 6⅞ in. (17.5 cm); Palace Museum, Beijing; g187473; image courtesy Palace Museum

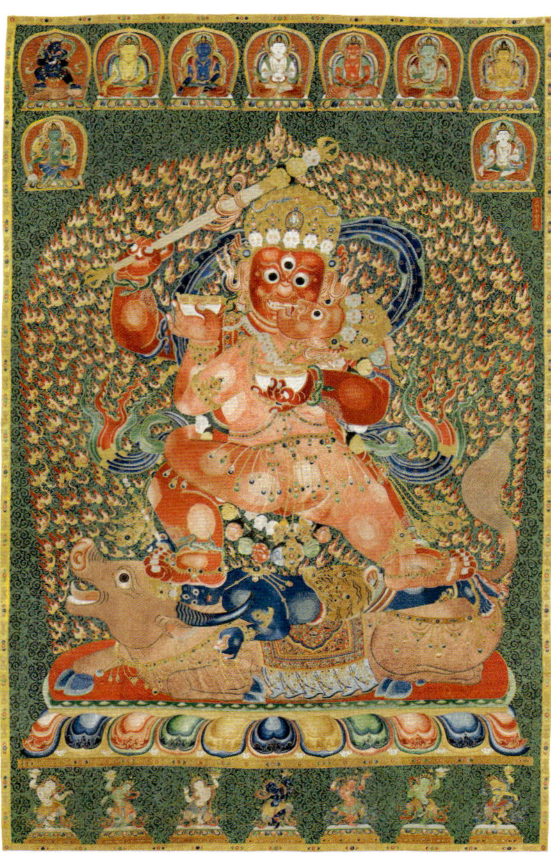

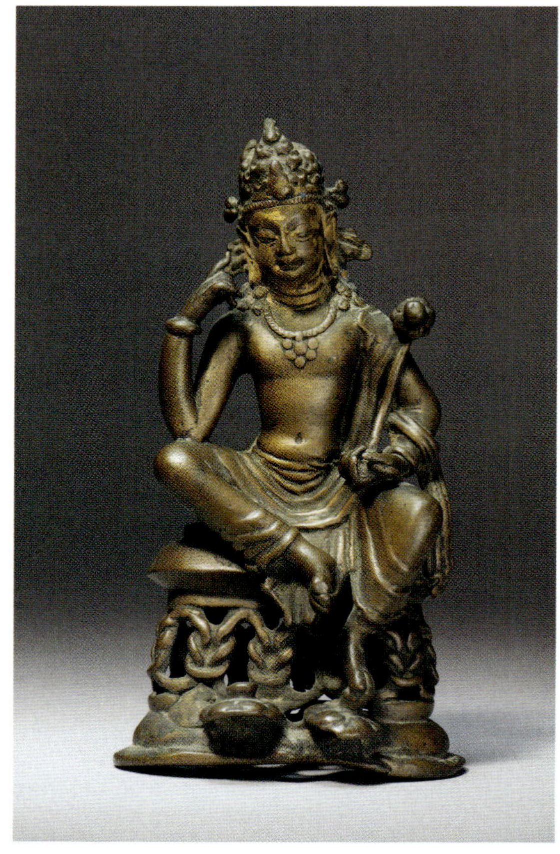

right hand held in the gesture of meditation (*dhyana* mudra). The dynamic yet well-balanced body posture exudes the mastery of craftsmanship. We know of two other Ming Yongle-period statues of pensive bodhisattva Avalokiteshvara. Others, however, do not bear the effigy of Amitabha, and therefore their identification is debated.[3] It has been suggested that the particular gesture of this object is a variant form of pensive gesture, but it does not have the common characteristic of index finger pointing to the cheek.[4]

Sculptures of pensive Avalokiteshvara could be found in ancient northwestern India. The iconography of the pensive bodhisattva was introduced from India to China between the third and fourth centuries. It became popular in Chinese Buddhist art, and the form of pensive Avalokiteshvara eventually came into being. The iconography of pensive bodhisattva, by contrast, is hardly found in Tibetan art, let alone its association with Avalokiteshvara. In the Chinese tradition, the pensive bodhisattva is usually interpreted as depicting Prince Siddhartha Gautama, founder of Buddhism, contemplating the meaning of life under a tree, usually seated in the *ardhaparyankaasana* posture (sitting with left leg dangling and bent right leg on the base or on the left knee), with his head tilted slightly to the right and his right index finger pointing to his face.[5] These features can be clearly seen in a pensive bodhisattva on the back of a white stone Maitreya produced in 547 and excavated in Hebei Province. The pensive Avalokiteshvara statue of the Yongle period, however, is seated in the royal ease posture, with the left cheek resting on the left wrist, instead of the usual composition with the right index pointing to the right cheek. These unique features must have synthesized other, currently unknown iconographies of that time. It has been argued, for example, that the Avalokiteshvara in the royal ease posture with the pensive mudra could be Chintamanichakra Avalokiteshvara in China.[6] In Chinese art, however, the prevalent forms of Chintamanichakra Avalokiteshvara include four arms or six arms instead of just two. Note also that the left hand of the pensive Avalokiteshvara is bent in a rather unnatural manner, which possibly betrays the lack of experience and knowledge of human anatomy of the Chinese artisans at the Ming court. Further features of the pensive Avalokiteshvara iconography are the two lotus flowers emanating from the pedestal, one on each side of the figure, and blossoming directly above its shoulders.

For more about this bodhisattva, see Avalokiteshvara at Khartse, no. 20; Bodhisattva Avalokiteshvara and the Buddha's Footprints, no. 33.

Pensive Avalokiteshvara on the back of a Maitreya statue; Yecheng, Hebei Province, China; 547; bas-relief, white stone; height 32⅜ in. (82.3 cm); Yecheng Museum; photograph by Luo Wenhua

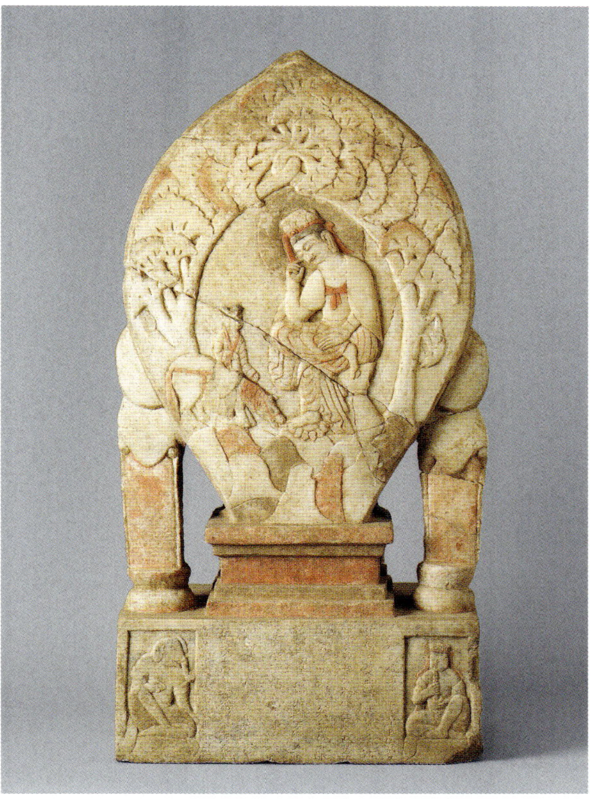

Artistic Style

The style of imperial Tibetan Buddhist statues under the Yongle and Xuande periods is eclectic. The quintessential Yongle and Xuande style includes wheel-shaped earrings, the necklace and ornamentation patterns, the folds of the dhoti, and the double lotus pedestal with round beaded borders, all very much standardized. The material of gilt brass is also characteristic of Ming imperial statues, which differs from Himalayan and Indian traditions, in which most brass statues are not gilded. Moreover, Ming imperial statues feature delicate details, elegant lines, finely polished surfaces, and bright gilding, but are not embellished with gems, in accordance with the artistry and aesthetics of the Ming imperial workshops. At the same time, they also borrow from Nepalese and Tibetan art traditions, with characteristics such as the wide shoulders, slender waist, supple posture, and gentle facial expression.

The Wider Impact of Yongle Sculpture

For more about the wider impact of Chinese images as artistic models in Tibet, see Portrait of the Ninth Karmapa, no. 66; Arhats Viewing a Painting of Birds by the Tenth Karmapa, no. 72.

The Buddhist statues of the Yongle and Xuande periods depicting Tibetan Buddhist images had a profound impact.[7] They established new traditions for Chinese sculpture of the fifteenth century and later, particularly in North China. Moreover, in areas of present-day Tibet, Qinghai, Yunnan, and western Sichuan, local artisans continue to emulate both the form and the style of Ming imperial statues.[8]

Further Reading

Sperling, Elliot. 2003. "The 5th Karma-pa and Some Aspects of the Relationship between Tibet and the Early Ming." In *The History of Tibet*, edited by Alex McKay, vol. 2, *The Medieval Period, c. 850–1895: The Development of Buddhist Paramountcy*, 473–82. London: Routledge Curzon.

Watt, James C. Y., and Denise Patry Leidy. 2005. *Defining Yongle: Imperial Art in Early Fifteenth-Century China*. Exhibition catalog. New York: The Metropolitan Museum of Art.

Wylie, Turrell V. 2003. "Lama Tribute in the Ming Dynasty." In *The History of Tibet*, edited by Alex McKay, vol. 2, *The Medieval Period, c. 850–1895: The Development of Buddhist Paramountcy*, 467–72. London: Routledge Curzon.

Notes

1 Stoddard 2008, 16–22, 50–58, 65–97; Sato 1986, 173–208; Watt and Leidy 2005, 92, pl. 37; Zhang, Su, and Luo 2012, 248–49.

2 大明永樂年施, "bestowed in the Yongle era of the great Ming."

3 The other statues: one without effigy of Amitabha is preserved in Norbulingka, Lhasa, Tibet; see von Schroeder 2001a, 2:1270–1271, pl. 353C (Prabhāketu). One with effigy of Amitabha is in the National Museum, Beijing, the same as the one in the Potala Palace; see China Cultural Heritage 2002, 2:338–339, pl. 153. Another with effigy of Amitabha was originally in the Tuyet Nguyet Collection, Hong Kong (*Arts of Asia*, September–October 1994, cover illustration) and was sold at Sotheby's Hong Kong, October 7, 2010, lot 2143. A fourth without effigy of Amitabha was sold at Nagel Auctions, Stuttgart, May 21, 2004, no. 747. See Henss 2008, 1–80, 215–16, figs. 39, 40.

4 von Schroeder 2001a, 2:1270–1271, suggests the bodhisattiva without effigy of Amitabha "probably formed part of a group flanking an image of Pranidhanamati, with a mirror-like image of Shantendriya flanking the other side." See also Olschak and Wangyal 1973, 150–51; Cangkya 1994, pls. 52, 222.

5 Miyaji 2010, 102–11.

6 Yixi 2013, 210–11; Henss 2008, 216, fig. 41.

7 Reedy 1997.

8 Luo 2014, 29–56.

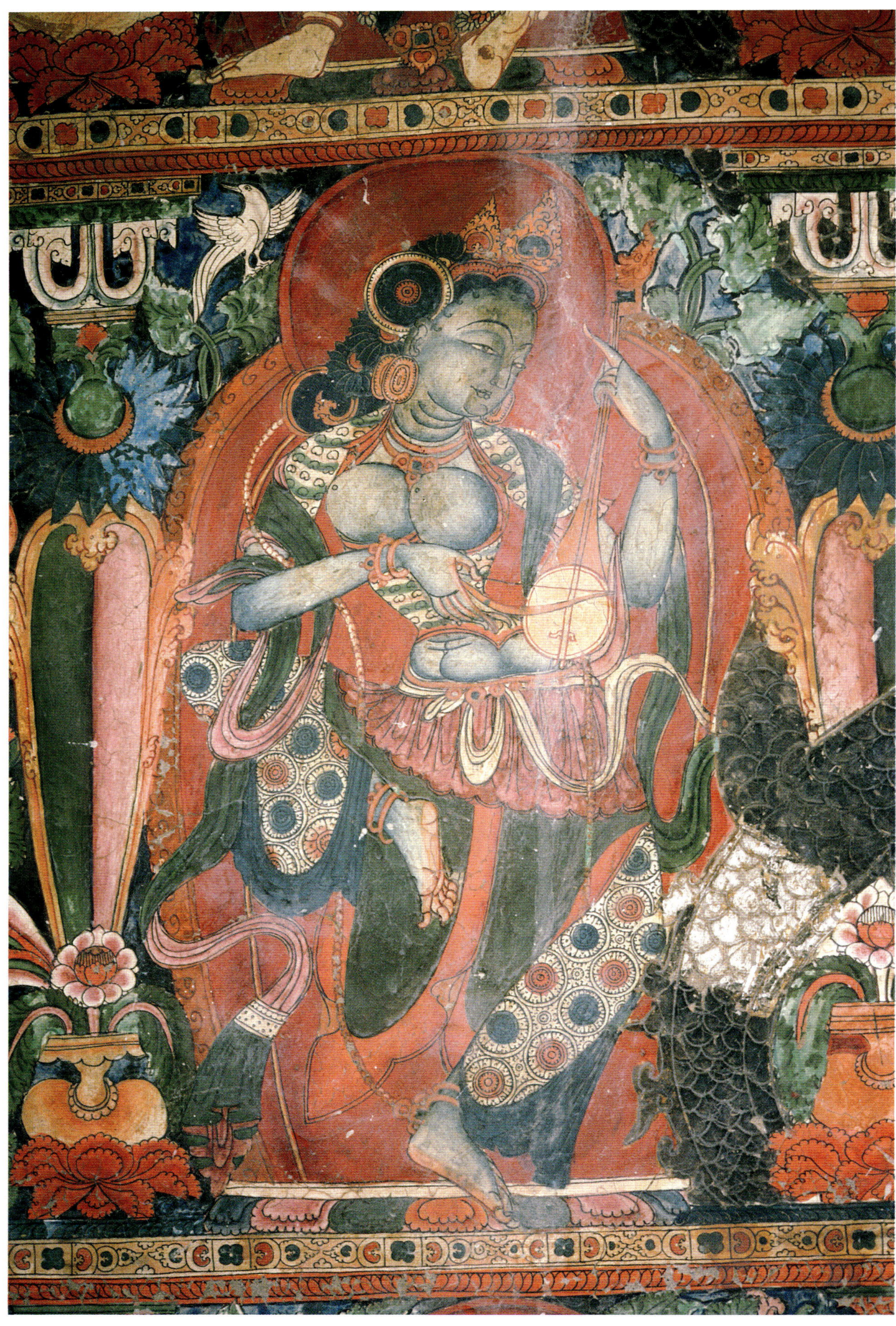

№ 54

Murals at Toling Dukhang, "Ornament of the World"

Toling Monastery, Guge Kingdom, Ngari region, western Tibet (present-day TAR, China), 15th century (ca. 1424–1458)

The Style of Upper Western Tibet under Gelukpa Patronage

ROBERTO VITALI

See Stupa at Toling Monastery, no. 19.

IN 1409, TSONGKHAPA (1357–1419), the founder of the Gelukpa tradition,[1] decided to send his disciples known as the "six flags of the borders" back to their native lands in the outskirts of the Tibetan Plateau to diffuse his teachings. One "flag," Ngawang Drakpa, returned to Toling in Guge—the land in upper western Tibet with a great past. He came back with the consent of the Guge kings. With the support of the local rulers—Namgyelde first and then his son Puntsokde—Ngawang Drakpa engaged in the promotion of the Gelukpa doctrine and carried out a building phase at Toling.[2]

The Gelukpa in Guge, Western Tibet

For more about the Pakmodrupa regime, see Mandala of Manjuvajra of the *Vajravali* Set, no. 50; Densatil Monastery, no. 30.

The end of the Yuan/Sakyapa domination of Tibet and the rise to power of the Pakmodrupa family in central Tibet in the second half of the fourteenth century brought a new status quo to the plateau.[3] Two factors contributed to the seminal presence of the Gelukpa in Guge:

- The Pakmodrupa, followers of the Kagyupa tradition for centuries, became supporters of Tsongkhapa.[4]
- The new lords of Tibet allowed the royal houses in upper western Tibet—from Mustang to Guge—to recover autonomy.[5]

The rulers of Guge could thus patronize the work of Ngawang Drakpa. They granted him supreme religious status, which they took away from the previous officiating lama of the Sakyapa tradition.[6]

Toling Monastery

See Jokhang Temple, no. 7.

In those days the temples of the ancient monastery, second in importance only to Lhasa Jokhang and Samye, occupied the western side of the plain, where the complex stood. Ngawang Drakpa and his successors extended the monastery to the plain's eastern side. The Gelukpa surrounded the sacred precinct with a boundary wall, now eradicated. The monastic complex assumed the shape it retained until recent times,[7] before being ravaged during the Cultural Revolution (1966–1976).[8]

Toling was founded by the great king-monk Lha Lama Yeshe Wo (947–1024)[9] in 996.[10] He built its lofty temple in the form of the fortress of a mandala, a unique architectural structure in Tibet.[11]

When Ngawang Drakpa reached Toling, the monastery had benefited from centuries of grand religious and secular achievements. The temple complex signaled a tradition of greatness. After the apogee of upper western Tibet during the late tenth and eleventh centuries, Toling continued to go through important phases marked by the tenure in the monastery of great religious traditions of Tibet. It belonged to the Drigungpa, the Tselpa, and, finally, the Sakyapa through their Zhalu associates.[12] These phases left significant cultural impacts, but they were not as important as the contributions to Toling by the Gelukpa.

Offering Goddess, detail of Buddha Shakyamuni Surrounded by the Sixteen Arhats, main wall of the niche from the throne frame; Toling Dukhang "Ornament of the World," (also known as the "Red Temple"), apse, west wall, Toling Monastery; Toling, Guge Kingdom, Ngari region, western Tibet (present-day TAR, China); ca. 1424–1458; photograph by Jaroslav Poncar, 1993, courtesy Western Himalayan Archive Vienna

Toling Dukhang (Assembly Hall)

Toling Dukhang (assembly hall), known as "Ornament of the World" (Dzamling Gyen), holds prime position among the Gelukpa foundations at Toling but was not the school's earliest congregation hall.

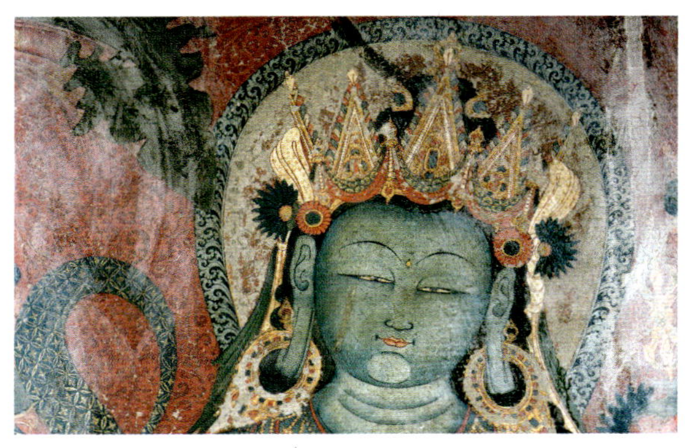

Deity Representative of the Gelukpa Style of Upper Western Tibet; Toling Dukhang "Ornament of the World," (also known as the Toling "Red Temple"), apse, north wall, Toling Monastery; Toling, Guge Kingdom, Ngari region, western Tibet (present-day TAR, China); ca. 1424–1458; photograph by Jaroslav Poncar, 1993, courtesy Western Himalayan Archive Vienna

Following Tsongkhapa's policy to convert preexisting monasteries, the ancient temple founded by Yeshe Wo was turned into that of the Gelukpa tradition. A first move was that the front part of the temple was transformed and expanded to form an assembly hall (Dukhang Tubwang Dudulma).

Dukhang "Ornament of the World" was built to congregate the growing monastic community. The mural I focus on here is found in this temple. Other building phases followed in the same (eastern) area of the monastery, first Toling Lhakhang Karpo ("White Chapel") and then Toling Serkhang ("Gold Chapel"). Toling Dukhang was meant to gather the monks from the territory of Guge south of the Langchen Khabab (Sutlej), and Lhakhang Karpo was for the monks from the northern side of the river.[13]

The foundation date of Toling Dukhang is nowhere found in the literature or epigraphs. It was built during the abbotship of Ngawang Drakpa. Possible construction dates range from after 1424 to before 1458.[14]

Toling "flew high" again under the Gelukpa—the Dukhang was a major step—to paraphrase the proclamation of Yeshe Wo. He threw his gong in the air, announcing that he would found a lofty temple wherever it landed. The gong flew (*ding*) high (*to*) in the sky. Toding (Tibetan: mtho lding) is the Gelukpa-period name in the tradition's literature, although Toling (Tibetan: tho ling) is preferable, being the original one.

A seventeenth-century text giving a description of the temples at Toling[15] says that the main statues of Dukhang "Ornament of the World" were the Buddhas of the Three Times—known as Tubpa Gandima—but they have been destroyed. The murals depict deities of the three lower tantra.[16] At the time of my first stay in 1985, the inner space of Toling Dukhang was devoid of shrines, monumental statues, and the paraphernalia commonly found inside a Tibetan temple. The emptiness of the interior conveyed a sense of immediacy to the murals.

Wall Paintings of the Dukhang

The work on the walls of the Dukhang goes beyond a mere transposition of iconographic themes. The double space of Toling Dukhang—a larger hall for the congregation and the smaller, connected inner sanctum—has a dual function. The assembly hall is for the mundane plane, the inner holy space is for the ultramundane. Mundanity is represented in the episodes of Buddha's life and a scene of the local court,[17] together with religious and secular inscriptions.[18]

The extraordinary size of the deities in the sanctum, coupled with an ascensional sensation, gives to the faithful the impression of being transported to the realm of the gods.

For more about *garudas*, see Vishnu Riding on Garuda, no. 18.

See Monumental Manjushri with Mahasiddha-Adorned Robe at Alchi, no. 35.

The painted wooden planks of the ceiling depict a variety of animals (lions, birds, *garudas*) and mythical beings (*kinnaras*), a theme adopted in other Gelukpa temples in Guge—an innovative development of the ornamented ceilings at Alchi (Ladakh), for instance, which reproduce precious fabrics.

The wall paintings of the Dukhang leave a stunning impression on anyone who has in mind the history of Toling, Guge, and upper western Tibet at large. The many religious phases in upper western Tibet, marked by excellence overall, brought to its lands various stylistic representations that substantiated the doctrinal systems that put roots in the region. Upper western Tibet for centuries was a showcase of the expressions typical of these stylistic elaborations. The sequence of representations in the lands of the west amounts to the idioms of Kashmir, the manner of Gangetic India born in the period of the Pala dynasty and imported to Tibet in its local interpretation,[19] the Newar alternative from the Kathmandu Valley, and the idiom of Zhalu,[20] brought to Mongol China by the Newar master Arniko (Anige) and reelaborated at its court.

See Mural Painting at Zhalu Monastery, no. 47.

For more about Anige at the Mongol court, see White Stupa, no. 40.

The "Gelukpa Style of Upper Western Tibet"

The confluence of these idioms—closer or more distant from the phase brought to Guge by Ngawang Drakpa—gave birth to what I call the Gelukpa style of upper western Tibet ("Geluk Tori," Tibetan: *dge lugs stod ris*) documented in Toling Dukhang. This distinctive stylistic conception adopted by the Gelukpa found application in successive murals in Toling Lhakhang Karpo and the Serkhang at Tsaparang inside Chokhang Marpo, at various other temples in Guge, and farther away in Spiti at Tabo and Lo Mentang in Mustang in Tubchen Lhakhang.

The deities in the Gelukpa style of upper western Tibet preserve the elliptical faces and slender torsos of the Kashmiri idiom. But the style in general is mellowed by the Zhalu representations that reflect the gentle Newar Pala idiom.

The color palette of the murals is richer than the restrained antecedents from Kashmir. All colors are used in deeper hues. Thrones are elaborate, with mythical beings, caryatids, and heraldic animals. Landscape is absent.

The genesis of the Gelukpa style of upper western Tibet is another tantalizing question if one looks at the last phase in the land before the advent of Tsongkhapa's tradition, characterized by few existing specimens of the idiom popular at Zhalu.

The style has no extant antecedents. It was developed before Toling Dukhang by a single artist or artists of a workshop, as shown by evidence inside this temple. The earliest application of the Gelukpa style of upper western Tibet, so accomplished that it did not need any further experimentation or development, is found in another temple at Toling. Its brilliantly developed expression is first met in the major temple founded by Yeshe Wo in 996. Various smaller sacred rooms in the structure were renovated when an area of the major temple was transformed into an assembly hall. The idiom adopted was the "Gelukpa style of upper western Tibet," shown in pictures taken by Western visitors before Toling's destruction during the Cultural Revolution.[21]

For more on Yeshe Wo and his construction projects, see Goddess Dharmameghabhumi in the Tabo Main Temple, no. 21.

The painted masterpieces in Toling Dukhang are credited to Sanggye Zangpo and Konchok Dorje by an inscription inside the temple,[22] one more denial of the stereotype in vogue with Tibetologists of the past generations that Tibetan art was strictly anonymous.

Further Reading

Vitali, Roberto. 1999. *Records of Tho-ling: A Literary and Visual Reconstruction of the "Mother" Monastery in Gu-ge*. New Delhi: High Asia.

Notes

1 Those known as the Gelukpa are practitioners of a philosophical system and members of the religious school established by Tsongkhapa around the end of the fourteenth century or the beginning of the fifteenth. Its founder developed a religious system from earlier traditions, especially the Kadampa and the Sakyapa. The Dalai Lamas belong to the Gelukpa. See Repo 2011.
2 Vitali 1996, 505–8, and Vitali 2012a, 147–52.
3 Vitali 2012a, 211–12.
4 Wylie 1980, 319–22.
5 For Mustang, see Vitali 2012b, 122–23; for Guge, see Vitali 1996, 477, 471–76.
6 Mkhar nag lo tsa ba, *Dga' ldan chos 'byung*, fols. 84b, 6–85a, 2.
7 A valuable description of Toling before it suffered lethal treatment is in Young 1918, the report of his 1912 visit to the monastery. It is the most brilliant and accurate description of Toling before it was too late.
8 In 1985, when I was first at Toling, I saw a wrecking ball, with an iron rod around it, abandoned inside Toling Lhakhang Karpo. It was used to destroy the statues.
9 See Cook 2018.
10 Gu ge Khyi thang pa Ye shes dpal 1977, *Rin chen bzang po'i rnam thar 'bring po* 89, lines 1–2.
11 The similarity with Samye, advocated by scholarship, does not stand. The temples of Samye overall formed a mandala. Toling's main temple alone was shaped as the core of a mandala.
12 Vitali 1996, passim.
13 Vitali 2012a, 189.
14 Vitali 2012a, 133–37.
15 Snying stobs rgya mtsho 2012, fol. 2b, 6–7.
16 Snying stobs rgya mtsho 2012, fols. 2b, 7–3a, 1.
17 *nTholing [sic] Monastery*, plates on 28–33.
18 *nTholing [sic] Monastery*, plates on 32–33.
19 Tucci Photographic Archive, Istituto Italiano per il Medio ed Estremo Oriente (IsMEO), acc. no. 6074/3.
20 Tucci Photographic Archives, Istituto Italiano per il Medio ed Estremo Oriente (IsMEO), acc. no. 6074/2.
21 See Tucci Photographic Archive, Istituto Italiano per il Medio ed Estremo Oriente (IsMEO), acc. nos. 6097/14, 6035/12, 6097/15, 6571/3.
22 Vitali 2012a, 131–33, 137.

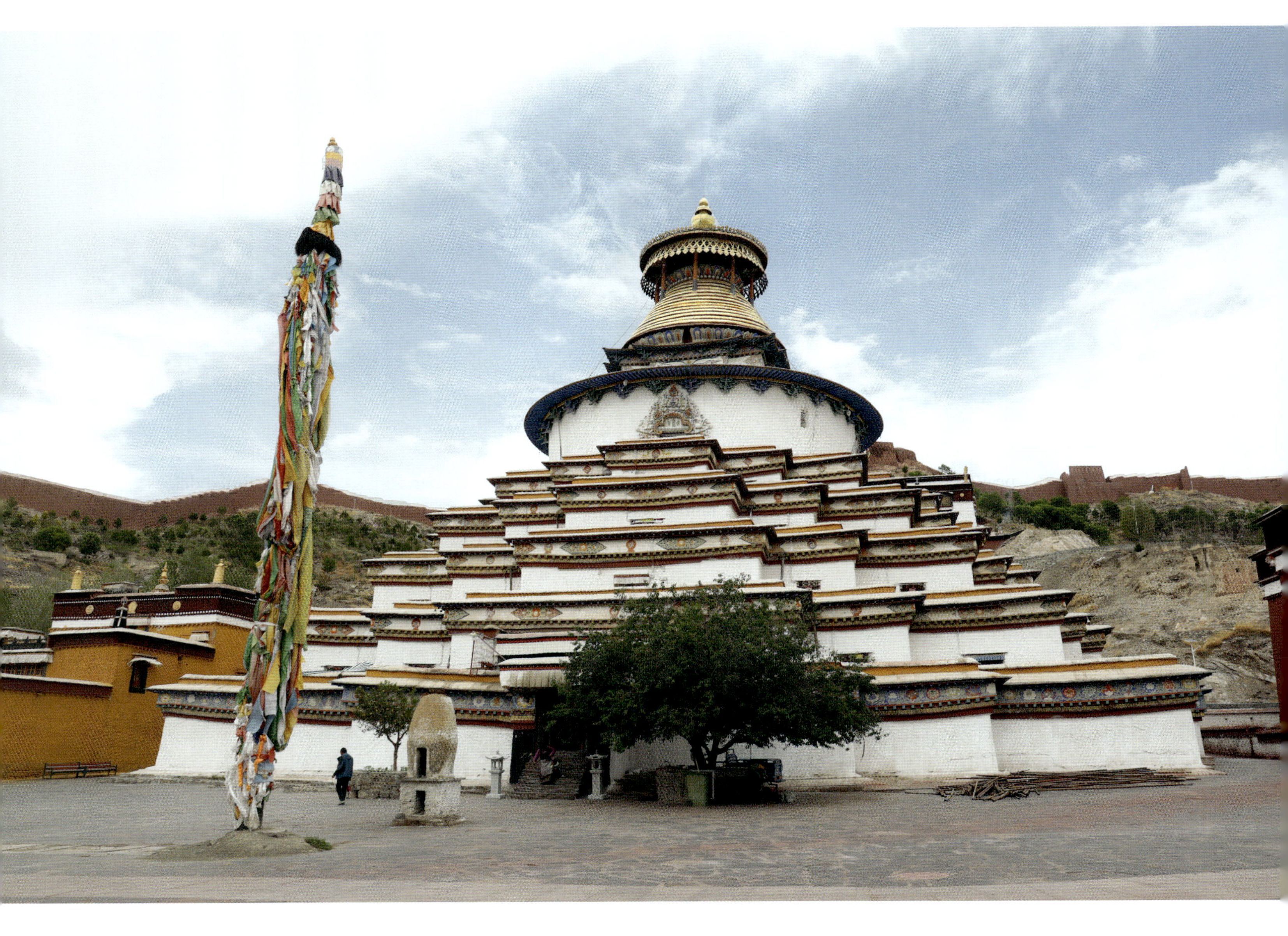

The Kumbum of Pelkhor Chode Monastery; Gyantse, Tsang region, central Tibet (present-day TAR, China); ca. 1427–1442; photograph by Shengnan Dong, 2021

No 55

Gyantse Kumbum

Pelkhor Chode Monastery, Gyantse, Tsang region, central Tibet (present-day TAR, China), ca. 1427–1442

An Architectural Representation of Complete Tantric Knowledge

SHENGNAN DONG

THE KUMBUM OF PELKHOR CHODE MONASTERY (ca. 1427–1442) is located in the heart of Gyantse County in upper Nyangchu Valley of the Tsang region. The name *kumbum* is commonly interpreted as "a hundred thousand images," denoting the great number of deities depicted inside. It is one of the biggest chortens in Tibet and the best-preserved example of its kind. The artistic splendor of the Kumbum, built during a time of political turbulence after the fall of the Sakya Yuan polity (1244–1354), attests to the peak of the Gyantse dynasty as a burgeoning new power in central Tibet. The statues and painted deities it houses provide a nearly complete representation of the Buddhist pantheon as it was understood in the fifteenth century. A grand construction project that lasted for decades, the Kumbum preserves rich visual evidence for an emerging era of indigenous artistic creation.

Structure, Prototype, and Symbolism

See the Svayambhu Chaitya of Kathmandu, no. 4.

See brackets also discussed in Qutan Monastery, no. 52.

The overall structure of the Kumbum displays some of the essential elements of a Tibetan chorten, including a four-tiered base, a cylindrical vase called a *bumpa*, a spire base *harmika*, and a conical spire on top. Yet the seventy-three chapels spanning eight stories, with more than twenty thousand deities represented,[1] make it stand out as a unique edifice, as chortens in the Himalayas are normally solid and can only be approached by circumambulating the outside. The exterior decoration shows a remarkably eclectic style, revealing cultural exchanges with neighboring regions, as exemplified by the painted eyes on the *harmika* that are typical for stupas in the Kathmandu Valley, as well as the corbel brackets under the roof, an element from the Chinese architectural tradition.

The four-tiered terrace is designed in a twenty-eight-corner plan. On each tier there are doors opening to individual chapels. Visitors enter these chapels via the open-air path surrounding each floor before reaching the *bumpa*, a round story with four main temples. Staircases lead further up into the *harmika*, where one can walk a two-story inner circumambulation path around the Central Pillar before climbing up to the topmost chapel inside the gigantic spire.

For more on Buddha Shakyamuni's life, see Mahabodhi Temple Model, no. 25.

See Molded Clay Image (*Tsatsa*) of Amoghapasha, no. 28.

The Kumbum of Gyantse takes the form of an Auspicious Stupa of Many Doors, or *tashi gomang*, one of the eight chortens in Tibetan Buddhist tradition commemorating the Eight Great Events in Buddha Shakyamuni's life. *Tashi gomang*, in particular, is a remembrance of the Buddha's exposition of dharma.[2] As explained by the third patriarch of Sakya, Khon Drakpa Gyeltsen (1147–1216), the numerous openings that adorn the four tiers symbolize the myriad doorways of the Buddhist teachings.[3] *Tashi gomang* became popular in western Tibet during the tenth to twelfth centuries and were found in much simpler designs on many *tsatsa* clay tablets, or as architectural units.[4]

For an example of such architecture units in western Tibet, see Stupa at Toling Monastery, no. 19. For mural paintings done in a later period, see Murals at Toling Dukhang, no. 54.

Immense *tashi gomang* like the Gyantse Kumbum emerged as early as the thirteenth century in central Tibet. Decorative niches of early *tashi gomang* were turned into actual entrances to chapels devoted to different tantras.[5] These large chortens likely evoke Buddha's third turning of the wheel, an occasion when tantras were first taught at the Glorious Stupa of Dhanyakataka, as widely believed in the Tibetan tradition.[6]

Iconographic Program, Style, and Artist Collective

For more on Buton Rinchen Drub, see Illuminated Pages of the *Prajnaparamita Sutra* Manuscript, no. 23.

From the lowest level to the top, chapels of the Gyantse Kumbum are arranged in a hierarchical order in accordance with the Four Classes of Tantras, as systemized by Buton Rinchen Drub (1290–1364).

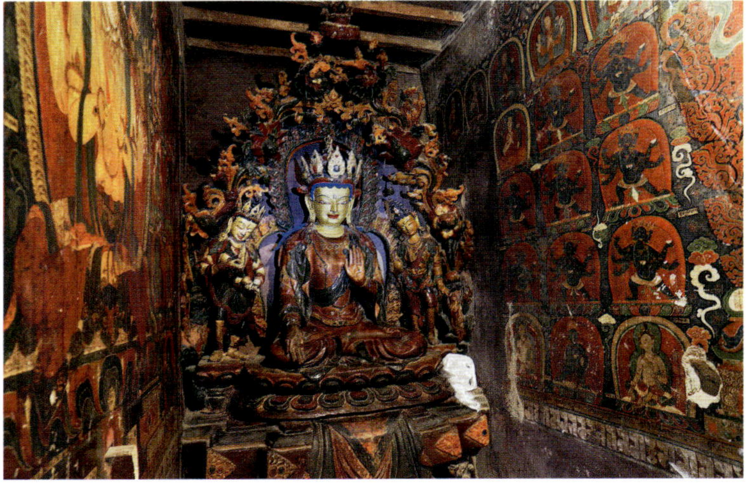

The Chapel of Purifying All Evil Rebirths, north side, third story, Gyantse Kumbum; Gyantse, Tsang region, central Tibet (present-day TAR, China); 1430–1435; photograph by Shengnan Dong, 2021

This fourfold scheme of categorizing tantric teachings belongs to the New Transmission Period traditions. The bottom two stories are mainly devoted to Kriya Tantra and Charya Tantra, the two lower classes of the system, while the chapels of the third story are mostly associated with Yogatantra. On the fourth story, various lineages of masters who contributed to the introduction of these tantric cycles to Tibet are represented, connecting the terrace to the *bumpa*, where devotion to Yogatantra continues in the four temples dedicated to Vairochana, Vajrasana (the diamond throne in Bodhgaya), Shakyamuni, and Prajnaparamita respectively. The double-story *harmika* is a space for two aspects of *Anuttarayoga Tantra,* the Father and Mother tantras. In the top chapel sits Vajradhara, the Adibuddha embodying the ultimate origin of the universes,[7] surrounded by masters of Kalachakra, representing the third aspect: the nondual tantras.[8]

For more on Kalachakra, see the Kalachakra Mandala in the Potala Palace, no. 77.

For other examples of clay sculpture, see Tamshing Temple, no. 61; Portrait of Ngadak Puntsok Rigdzin, no. 70; Maitreya Statue at Jampa Lhakhang, Bhutan, no. 9.

Although they were repainted over the centuries, almost all the large sculptures in the main chapels are the fifteenth-century originals. The sculptures are predominantly made of clay over an internal wooden structure.[9] The Vajradhara inside the top chapel and the Vairochana in the east temple of the *bumpa* are the only gilded-copper exceptions, underlining their higher status in the whole tantric system.

Encircling the sculptures are mural paintings of features drawn from both Indic and Chinese sources, showing a diversity that echos the designs of the Kumbum's outer structure. The prevalence of sumptuous vegetal curls and floral motifs suggests a dominance of Nepalese style in the overall rendering. Meanwhile, Chinese elements permeate in the stylistic design of clouds and a naturalistic treatment of the figures.

The grand project attracted a galaxy of talents, whose work was overseen by Rinchen Peldrub, the abbot of Nenying Monastery, a then prosperous teaching center near Gyantse. Inscriptions in different chapels document the names of at least thirty-nine painters from different regions of the Tsang region, which may explain the diverse styles coexisting in the Kumbum. The inscriptions also indicate that in most chapels the master artists worked in teams with their students instead of on their own.[10] Their work demonstrates the wide range of modes and styles available to the artists, and potentially how different ideas might have circulated among them.

Many scholars are of the opinion that the Gyantse Kumbum represents the maturation of a Tibetan style,[11] while some maintain that the art of the Kumbum still stands at a transitional point.[12] What is clear is that the art contained in the Kumbum is closely related to two major later Tibetan art schools. According to an artist manual attributed to the founder of the Menri style, Menla Dondrub, he once studied with Peljor Rinchen and Sonam Peljor, the master artists from Nenying who led the decoration at the Gyantse Kumbum.[13] Recent studies further propose that Khyentse Chenmo, the founder of the Khyenri style, might have once worked with Menla Dondrub as apprentices at Gyantse or Nenying. This means that the project at Gyantse may have played a direct part in the development of their own styles.[14]

For murals painted by Khyentse Chenmo, see Murals of Gongkar Chode, no. 58.

Patronage and Related Projects

Rabten Kunzang (1389–1442, r. 1414–1442), the prince of Gyantse, was the main donor of the Kumbum and the entire monastic complex.[15] During his reign, the principality thrived at an unprecedented level, so it was able to compete with other major powers like the Rinpungpa or even the Pakmodrupa establishment that superseded Sakya rule in the mid-fourteenth century.[16]

For projects supported by the Pakmodrupa establishment, see Densatil Monastery, no. 30.

For more on large-scale appliqué thangkas, see Monumental Appliqué of Begtse, no. 95.

The ruler embraced a nonsectarian attitude toward Buddhist teachings and sponsored a great number of other artistic and building projects. Besides the magnificent chorten, he famously commissioned a set of three giant appliqué thangkas, depicting the Buddhas of the Three Times,[17] which are the earliest

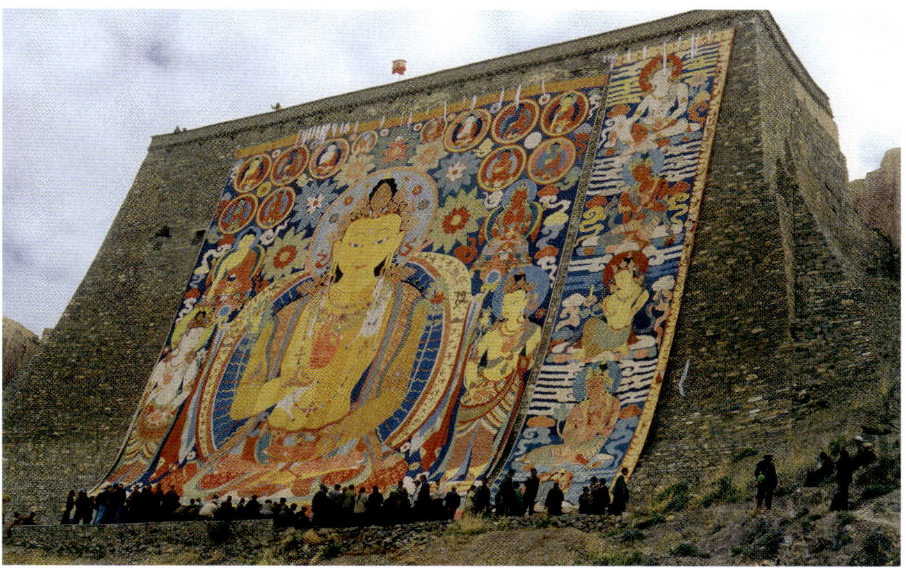

Appliqué Cloth Thangka of Maitreya, based on a sketch by Sonam Peljor; Gyantse; 1437–1439; colored silk embroidered on silk; 73 ft. 10 in. × 73 ft. 10 in. (22.5 × 22.5 m); image after Henss 2014, fig. 727

large-scale cloth thangkas that have survived to this date. The weaving of the Maitreya image, in particular, was based on sketches made by one of the Nenying master artists mentioned above, Sonam Peljor.[18] These thangkas were likely shown consecutively over three days during the Sagadawa festival, commemorating the enlightenment of the Buddha, similarly to how this is practiced at Tashilhunpo Monastery in Shigatse.[19] Considered as Liberation through Seeing images, they render the display an important occasion for viewing.[20] The wall specially designated for their exhibition sits on the mountain ridge above the monastic complex and is visible from miles away.

The Kumbum witnessed Gyantse's own grandeur as a local dominion and a high point in the history of Tibetan art. Even after the fall of the principality at the end of the sixteenth century, it has remained one of the most important pilgrimage sites of the Tibetan Buddhist world. The idea of opening doors to pictorial depictions of the Buddhist divinities continued in the portable *tashi gomang* shrines used by traveling monks, a Bhutanese cultural heritage dating to the seventeenth century.

See Portable Shrine, no. 88.

Further Reading

Lo Bue, Erberto, and Franco Ricca. 1990. *Gyantse Revisited*. Florence: Le Lettere.

Ricca, Franco, and Erberto Lo Bue. 1993. *The Great Stupa of Gyantse: A Complete Tibetan Pantheon of the Fifteenth Century*. London: Serindia.

Tucci, Giuseppe. (1932–41) 1989. *Gyantse and Its Monasteries*. Edited by Lokesh Chandra. Translated by Uma Marina Vesci. 3 vols. *Indo-Tibetica 4*. Reprint, New Delhi: Aditya Prakashan.

Notes

1 Tucci (1932–41) 1989, 1:172; Tucci 2009, 1:30n1.
2 Tucci 2009. The Chinese edition of *Indo-Tibetica 4* (Tucci 1941), provides full documentation of the inscriptions from different chapels of the Gyantse Kumbum, including about one-third of the text that was omitted in Tucci's original publication; see Tucci 2009, vol. 2. For wider discussions on the eight events in the Indo-Tibetan tradition, see Bagchi 1941.
3 Bentor 1995a, 35–39. A similar version of the eulogy is found at Juyong Guan Stupa.
4 Tucci 1932, 1: pls. 5, 6; Pakhoutova 2009, 55–56, fig. 2.7.
5 Many of these stupas were associated with influential masters. See Tucci 1949, 179–96; Vitali 1990, 123–36; Akester 2016, 487–90, 608–9, 615, 637–39, 653–56.
6 See Macdonald 1970; Hoffmann 1973.
7 The Adibuddha is the primordial buddha from which all other buddhas and deities emanated. This conception was promulgated mainly by the dissemination of the Kalachakra cycle of tantras after the eleventh century and is interpreted differently within the Tibetan tradition. The Nyingma tradition considers Samantabhadra as the Adibuddha, while for the New traditions, it is Vajradhara who sits in the center of the doctrinal universe.
8 For an iconographic description of each room, see Ricca and Lo Bue 1993, app., 225–313.
9 On the making of clay sculptures, see Luczanits 2003.
10 Lo Bue and Ricca 1990, 32.
11 Tucci 1949, 1:206–7; Ricca 1997, 198; Stoddard 1996, 41–43.
12 D. Jackson 2010, 148–50.
13 Sman thang pa sman bla don grub 1985, 177–88, quoted in D. Jackson 1996, 108.
14 Jackson and Fermer 2016, 7.
15 Lo Bue 1992.
16 For the political history of the Gyantse principality, see Everding 2017.
17 They depict Dipamkara, Shakyamuni, and Maitreya.
18 'Jigs med grags pa 1987, 241, 244, quoted in Henss 2011, 79.
19 Henss 2011, 73–74.
20 On his other projects, see Everding 2017; Lo Bue 1992. On the Tsuklakhang of Gyantse, see von Schroeder 2006.

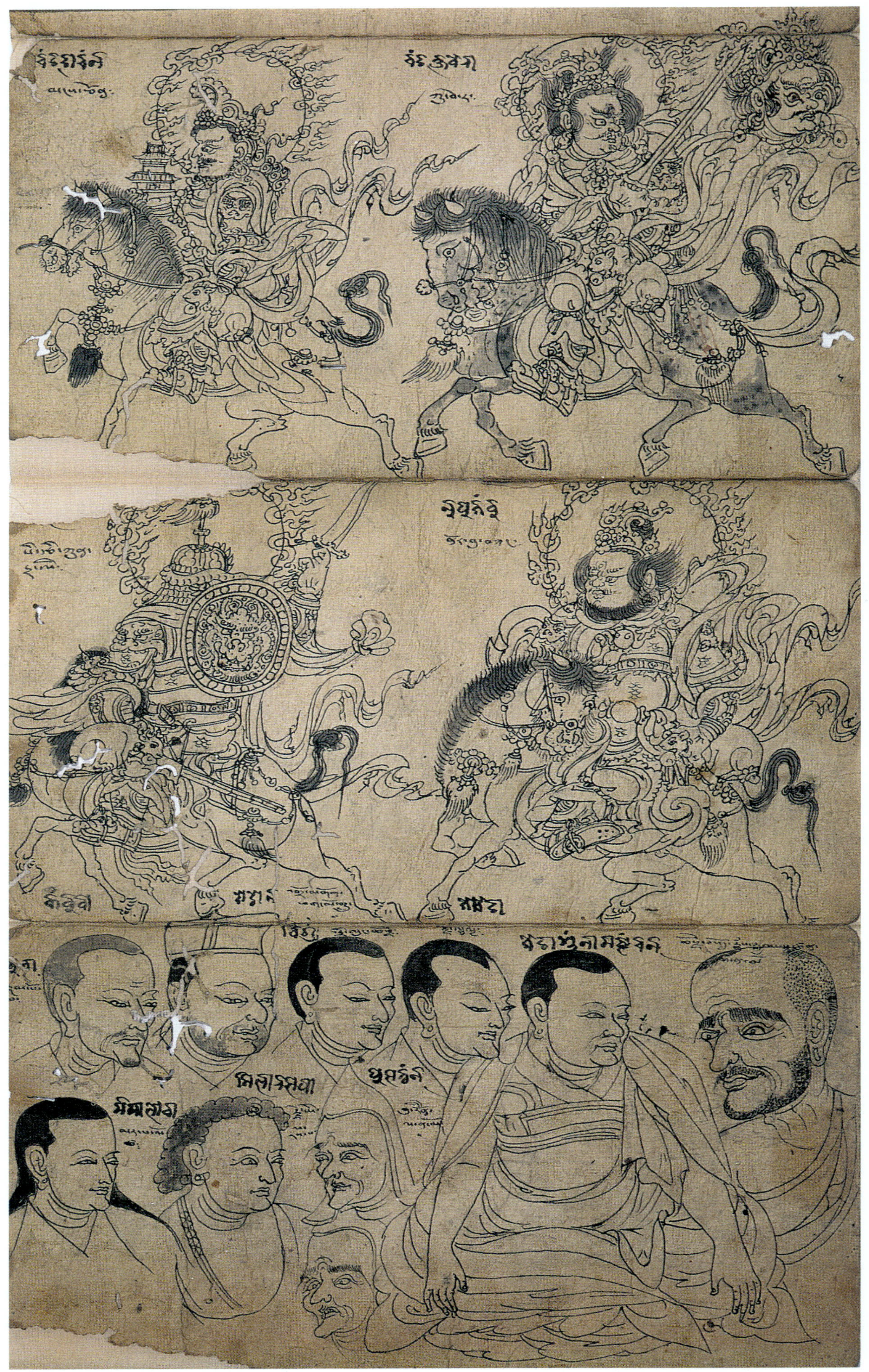

No 56

Jivarama's Sketchbook

Tibet (and Nepal?), 1435

The Earliest Dated Newar Artist's Sketchbook

IAN ALSOP AND ELENA PAKHOUTOVA

THE ITINERANT NEWAR ARTIST JIVARAMA made this accordion-like book with sketched drawings. Sometime in the first half of the fifteenth century, he left his home in the Kathmandu Valley and ventured north to Tibet to ply his trade as a painter of religious icons. Like many artists throughout the world, he used a sketchbook to copy models and practice his drawing. Nowadays, in the West, artists use bound albums for sketches, but in fifteenth-century Nepal and until quite recently, artists often used a folding book (*thyasaphu*) to record their sketches. Jivarama included a dated notation written in Newari in elegant characters to a page in the middle of the book. This inscription is difficult to fully interpret and has long puzzled scholars; the following version draws from three published translations:

> On the twelfth day of the dark fortnight of Vaisakha, in the year 555 [April–May 1435]: Jivarama himself went [to Tibet], and after consultations with *Gaya Chona* [*Bhota*], made this whole book himself. When further questions arose, he asked *Lalacunava*; then he returned [home] with it and continued work at *Nyaradvam*. [The book] was made according to Jivarama's idea.[1]

The date likely identifies when the inscription was added to the book to record the circumstances of its production. It does not state when Jivarama set off on his trip or finished the book. It simply marks the date of the inscription, as an unusual brief statement (colophon), about the book.

The colophon inscription leaves questions about the identity of mentioned personages and places, but we can still learn a lot from the book about Jivarama and the religious and artistic context at the time in Tibet.[2]

Seeing the Larger Picture

Sketchbooks are important to the study of art history because of what they reveal about artists, their techniques, and their working environments. Most religious art from the Himalayas originates from anonymous creators, yet this sketchbook gives us a name and a date related to the book's drawings.

Short captions to some images in both Tibetan and Newar script suggest that the artist collaborated with Tibetans, probably his patrons or fellow artists. The Tibetan labels, written in Tibetan cursive script, were likely added by a Tibetan collaborator, while Jivarama added labels in Newar script. Not all the images are labeled; perhaps Jivarama left those he was familiar with unmarked. His selection of images shows what he was seeing and learning to create—he recorded subjects not well known to him as material for his future work.

Jivarama (act. 15th century); pages from a sketchbook in a folding book (*thyasaphu*) format, with Lords of the Horse deities and Tibetan teachers portraits; upper two folios, four of the eight Lords of the Horse deities; bottom folio, heads of Tibetan teachers, including Marpa and Milarepa, bottom left corner; Tibet (and Nepal?); 1435; ink and colors on paper, 39 leaves of an unknown number; each folio 5 × 9½ in. (12.5 × 24 cm); Suresh Neotia Collection, Jnana-Pravaha Centre Museum, Varanasi, no. 102

Drawings of New Subjects

The figures represented in the sketchbook fall into several categories. Two sets of related images take up several pages of the book. One set comprises figures from the retinue of Jambhala, or Vaishravana, a god of wealth. This includes four of the eight mounted Lords of the Horse deities found on the first two pages and the Four Guardian Kings of the four directions on the following four pages. Jivarama's drawings show his mastery of picturing these kings or generals, traditionally depicted in Tibetan painting according to Chinese pictorial conventions, unfamiliar in his native Nepal. These protective figures are

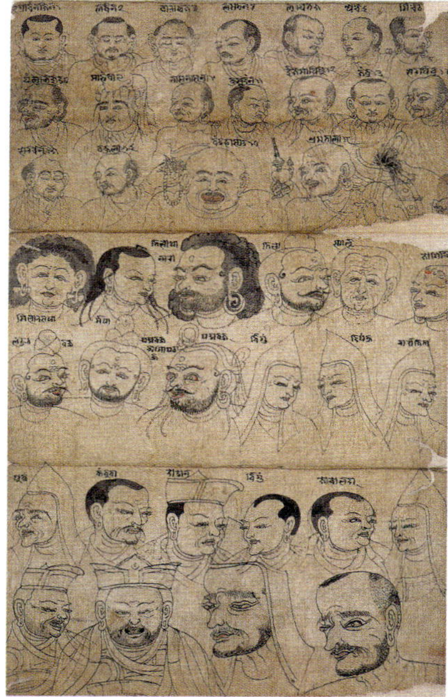

Jivarama (act. 15th century); details of Tibetan teacher portraits, pages from a sketchbook in a folding book (*thyasaphu*) format; Tibet (and Nepal?); Suresh Neotia Collection, Jnana-Pravaha Centre Museum, Varanasi; no. 102

often painted on the entry walls framing Tibetan monasteries' portals and as outer figures for sets of arhat paintings.

The sixteen arhats, or the awakened disciples of the Buddha, form another set of images common in Tibetan painting but relatively unknown in the Newar Buddhist context of the Kathmandu Valley. Jivarama first depicted the arhats in his sketchbook as a series of heads, annotated in Newar script but stating their Tibetan rather than Sanskrit names, which indicates he relied on Tibetan sources for identification. He portrayed them again, as full figures, later in the sketchbook, identified by labels in Newar script and Tibetan. Jivarama had confidently assimilated the distinct Chinese pictorial conventions adopted in the Tibetan tradition—complete compositions that include seats, attendants of each arhat, and washes of color.

For a unique Tibetan example, see Arhats Viewing a Painting of Birds by the Tenth Karmapa, no. 72.

Tibetan Buddhist Teacher Portraits

Perhaps the most intriguing drawings in the sketchbook are portrayals of the heads of various Tibetan teachers. Jivarama's focus on depictions of lineage masters is significant, as such portraits are very important in Tibetan thangkas but not in Newar paintings commissioned for Newar Buddhists.[3] This furthers the evidence that Jivarama was working for Tibetan patrons.

For other examples of painted Tibetan Buddhist teacher portraits, see Portrait of the Ninth Karmapa, no. 66; Portrait of Situ Panchen, no. 83.
For sculptural examples, see Portrait of Lowo Kenchen Sonam Lhundrup, no. 63; Portrait of Ngadak Puntsok Rigdzin, no. 70.

Most of the images in this four-page section depict teachers of the Kagyu tradition, leading some researchers to believe that Jivarama's patron and the monastery where he worked belonged to this tradition of Tibetan Buddhism.[4] The heads are masterpieces of idiosyncratic detail and emphasize specific physiognomy or distinctive features. There are often several views of the same teacher (lama). For instance, Jivarama made two portrayals of the great poet-yogi Milarepa next to his teacher Marpa. While Marpa looks similar in both portrayals, with a pleasant, well-defined face in three-quarter profile and long flowing hair, the portraits of Milarepa vary. In one depiction he looks to the right and appears younger, while in the other he looks straight on with concentration wrinkling his features. The artist confidently drew each head with great expression. Notably, the short captions in Newar script follow the Tibetan spelling, suggesting that whoever wrote the captions transcribed them from Tibetan, with Milarepa's name written as Mi-la–ras-pa. Another featured portrait is Pakmodrupa Dorje Gyelpo (1110–1170), a famous teacher of the Taklung branch of the Kagyu tradition.[5] Tibetan portrayals of this master often depict him in a three-quarter view facing right, with a shadow-beard, as seen in the earlier paintings.[6] In this sketch he is also drawn with a shadow-beard and facing right in three-quarter profile view. Jivarama likely sketched from existing examples, and the importance of these subjects may have inspired him to draw them more than once.

For another object related to Milarepa, see Earliest Extant Printed Edition of Milarepa's Life Story, no. 62.

Drawing Techniques and Visual Conventions

There is a difference between the drawing styles and techniques of Tibetan and Newar artists. In the Tibetan tradition, student painters study proportions and ratios laid out in grids (*tiktse*).[7] This system ensures that the deities, important figures, and symbolic forms are rendered with correct proportions in religious paintings. Students copy these prescribed iconometric conventions in sketchbooks to learn how to accurately draw the figures and then can draw them from memory. One especially authoritative iconometry handbook provides an example of standard Tibetan proportions, as in a page showing Vajravarahi, an important goddess in Nepalese and Tibetan Buddhism.[8] Newar artists usually drew freehand: this more relaxed technique, seen in two small, quick sketches of tantric goddesses (*dakini*) in Jivarama's sketchbook, is evident in most Newar sketchbooks, which may occasionally include a simple grid. Artists from both traditions relied on textual descriptions for the rules of proportions.

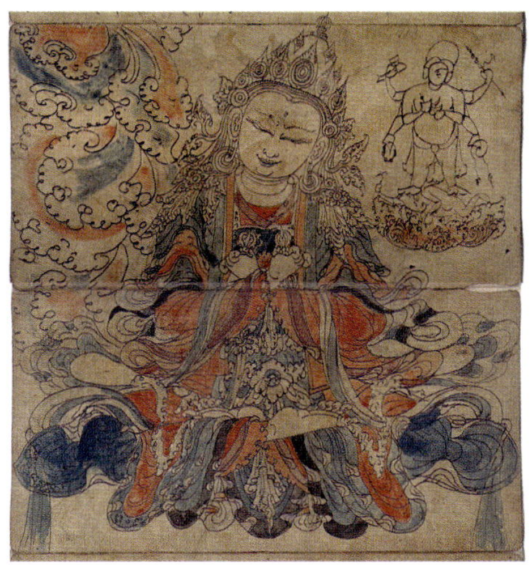

Jivarama's sketchbook is exceptional among Nepalese sketchbooks. It does not include many of the important standard figures of the shared Tibetan and Nepalese iconography. This absence implies that Jivarama was an experienced senior artist and had no need to reproduce images of the deities he already knew how to depict. He did include a two-page colored representation of Buddha Vajradhara, an important icon in both the Newar and Tibetan traditions. That sketch, however, presents the deity dressed in voluminous robes not found in Nepalese depictions, and, like the sketches of the arhats, the guardian kings, and Lords of the Horse, it shows Jivarama practicing the Chinese pictorial conventions he saw in Tibet. Among the most striking images in the sketchbook are the black and red sketches of floral patterns and mythological creatures—designs that decorated the thrones of deities in Newar and Tibetan painting. Extraordinarily dense, complex, and exuberant, these drawings embody the essence and virtuosity of Newar creativity.

Jivarama (act. 15th century); Buddha Vajradhara, pages from a sketchbook in a folding book (*thyasaphu*) format; Tibet (and Nepal?); Suresh Neotia Collection, Jnana-Pravaha Centre Museum, Varanasi; no. 102

Attributions

Jivarama's sketchbook is widely acknowledged as the finest and the earliest dated example of Newar draftsmanship in a book of this kind. The remarkable quality and the securely dated inscription has inspired scholars to connect Jivarama with well-known but unsigned masterpieces. In a comprehensive essay on one of the finest known paintings of the deity Chakrasamvara, Dina Bangdel assigned the painting to a Newar artist and suggested that Jivarama may have created this work for a Tibetan patron.[9] In an essay she wrote with John Huntington, they positively attributed a spectacular painting of the god Ganapati to Jivarama, relying on similarities between the sketchbook and the painting, and correlating the sketchbook's date with the dates of the patron who commissioned the painting of Ganapati.[10] This is a tantalizing but theoretical possibility absent Jivarama's name in the extensive inscriptions on the painting's front and reverse.

The sketchbook remains among the most interesting material objects of artistic practice that demonstrates close cultural connections between the art of Nepal and Tibet, Newar artists and Tibetan patrons, and their close collaboration, which continues today.

Further Reading

Jackson, David. P. 2010. *The Nepalese Legacy in Tibetan Painting*. Masterworks of Tibetan Painting Series 2. Exhibition catalog. New York: Rubin Museum of Art. https://issuu.com/rmanyc/docs/nepalese_legacy_96.

Huntington, John. 2006. "Nevar Artist Jīvarāma's Sketchbook." In *Indian Art Treasures: Suresh Neotia Collection*, edited by R. C. Sharma, Kamal Giri, and Anjan Chakraverty, 76–85. New Delhi: Mosaic Books.

Huntington, John, and Dina Bangdel. 2003. *The Circle of Bliss: Buddhist Meditational Art*, esp. 136, 190, 265–69, 495–97. Exhibition catalog. Columbus, OH: Columbus Museum of Art; Chicago: Serindia.

Notes

1 This composite translation of the inscription draws from: 1) Lowry 1977, 83, translation by Gautama Vajracharya; 2) Huntington and Bangdel 2003, 496, translation by Kashinath Tamot; and 3) Huntington 2006, 76, translation by Kashinath Tamot. Italics added to emphasize proper names that appear to be Tibetan, recorded phonetically. Given the unknown spelling, the names are uncertain.

2 This was a turbulent time in Tibet. From 1434 to 1435 Rinpungpa rulers overpowered the dynasty of Pakmodru in Tsang, central Tibet.

3 On portraits in thangkas, see D. Jackson 2010, 23.

4 Huntington and Bangdel 2003, 136.

5 Noted here in Tibetan as 'gro mgon phag mo gru. The note in Newar script reads *doṅona*, which could be read as a phoneticized shorthand for "dro gon [la] na [ma]."

6 See Rubin Museum objects C2005.16.38 (HAR 65461); C2002.24.3 (HAR 65119). On the Tibetan portrayals, see Singer 1995, 81–99.

7 See Cüppers et al. 2012.

8 Cüppers et al. 2012, pl. 70.

9 Huntington and Bangdel 2003, 268.

10 Huntington and Bangdel 2003, 495–97. Jane Casey Singer suggests that a highly skilled Tibetan artist may have created the painting. See Kossak and Singer 1998, pl. 49, as well as https://www.asianart.com/exhibitions/svision/i49.html.

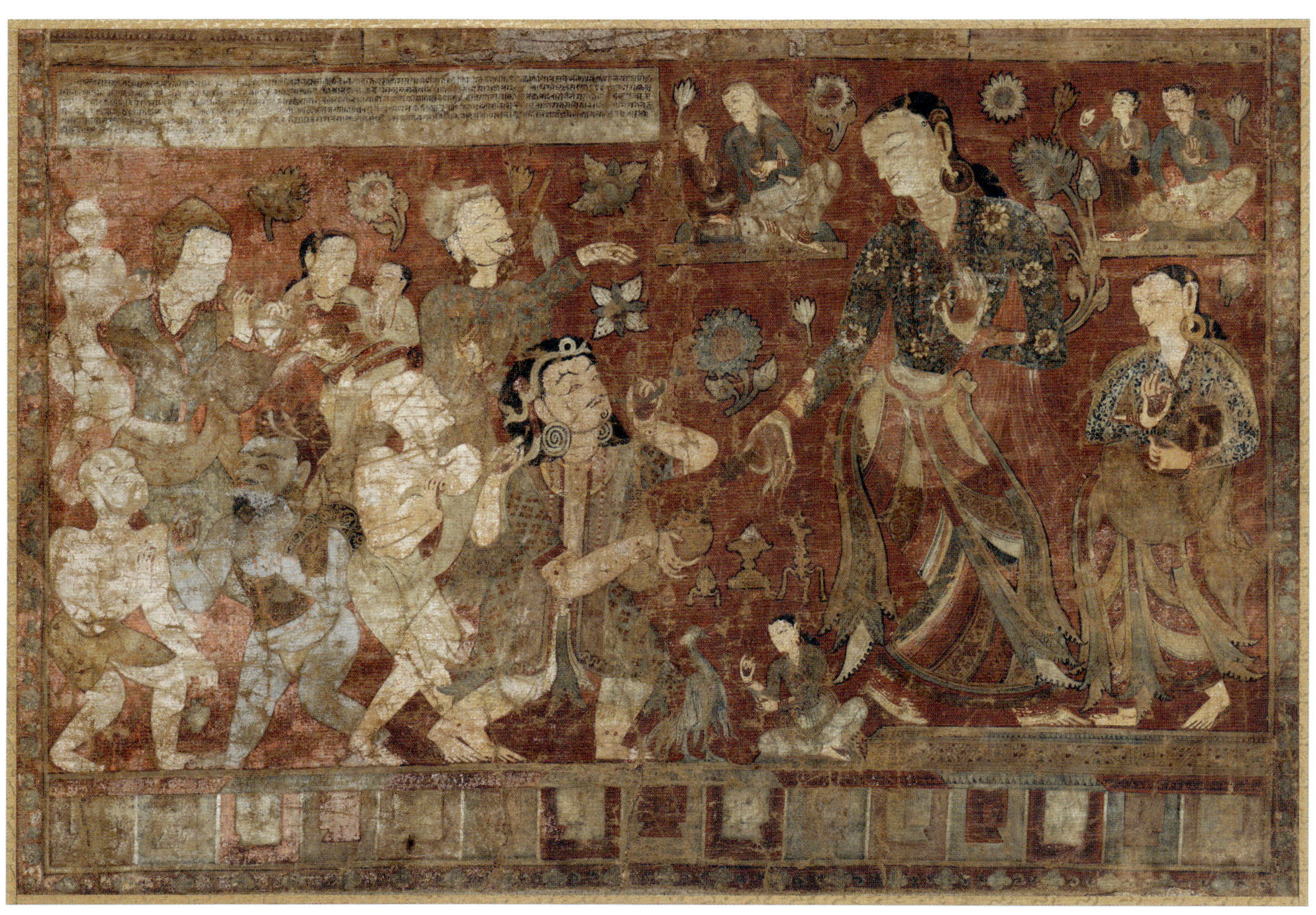

Nº 57

Nepalese *Paubha* Commemorating the Death of Pandita Vanaratna

Gopichandra Monastery, Patan, Nepal, 1469

Carrying Out Acts of Service in the Buddhist Community

RYAN DAMRON

In 1469 master artisans of the Kathmandu Valley put pigment to cloth to commemorate the life and passing of the Indian Buddhist monk, scholar (*pandita*), and teacher Vanaratna (1384–1468). The cloth painting (*paubha*), a masterful early example of Newar painting in the medieval Malla period (ca. 1385–1769), was likely commissioned by the community of Gopichandra Monastery, Vanaratna's seat in the city of Patan, shortly after his passing. The *paubha* bears a Newari inscription describing two large-scale alms distributions Vanaratna performed at Gopichandra, and provides us with the date and year of his passing. The main image presents a vibrant and detailed scene of one of these alms distributions, but instead of depicting Vanaratna, it features a large female figure flanked by two smaller women handing out alms to a diverse crowd of alms seekers. The inscription does not provide the names of the artists, but it bears clear stylistic similarities with another masterwork of fifteenth-century Newar artistry, a portrait of Gaganasim Bharo of Dolakha and his wives Ashayani Lakshmi and Jivatana.[1] These similarities strongly suggest that the *paubha* commemorating Vanaratna's passing was made by Adyayaraja Puna and Udrayarama Puna of Kathmandu, or in the atelier in which they worked.[2] The two artists made a number of important innovations in Newar art and specifically portraiture, some of which—including the depiction of the female form and the prominence given to human figures in relation to the divine—are evident in the unattributed *paubha* commissioned by the Gopichandra community.[3]

The Pandita Vanaratna

The painting is of great significance both as a work of high Newar art and for the historical data it offers us on its subject, the Buddhist master Vanaratna. Born in 1384 in the town of Sadnagara near what is now the border of Bangladesh and Myanmar (Burma), Vanaratna received his early training at the local Mahachaitya monastery. After completing his studies and taking full ordination, he traveled to Sri Lanka, where he spent six years studying at the island's leading Buddhist institutions. He then returned to India, first studying in the Krishna River valley before proceeding to the ancient heartland of the Buddhist world, Bodhgaya. Vanaratna remained there for six years, but the attenuation of the Buddhist community and the derelict condition of its once-great monuments left him dissatisfied, compelling him to leave India for the Himalayan kingdoms of Nepal and Tibet and their thriving Buddhist communities. He arrived in the Kathmandu Valley in 1423, and spent the remainder of his life traveling between Nepal and Tibet, becoming a teacher celebrated by the leading Newar and Tibetan Buddhist figures of the day and patronized by royal courts on both sides of the Himalayas. In roughly 1438, Vanaratna was given Gopichandra Monastery in Patan, known in Newari as Pintu Bahi, which became his home and spiritual seat. He died in his private chambers at Gopichandra in 1468.[4]

For more on Bodhgaya, see Mahabodhi Temple Model, no. 25.

Paubha Commemorating the Death of Pandita Vanaratna (1384–1468); Patan, Nepal; 1469; mineral pigments on cotton cloth; 27¼ × 39¼ in. (69.4 × 99.7 cm); Los Angeles County Museum of Art; The Nasli and Alice Heeramaneck Collection, Museum Associates Purchase; M.77.19.3; photograph © Museum Associates/LACMA, www.lacma.org

The Inscription and Image

In the upper-left corner of the painting, a Newari inscription records three important events in Vanaratna's later years at Gopichandra: his large alms distribution in 1455, a similar rite in 1467, and the date and year of his death. The food distributions are described in detail, including the diverse assembly of supplicants and the varieties of offerings made. These details are corroborated with remarkable consistency in the biography of Vanaratna composed by his Tibetan disciple and colleague Sonam Gyatso

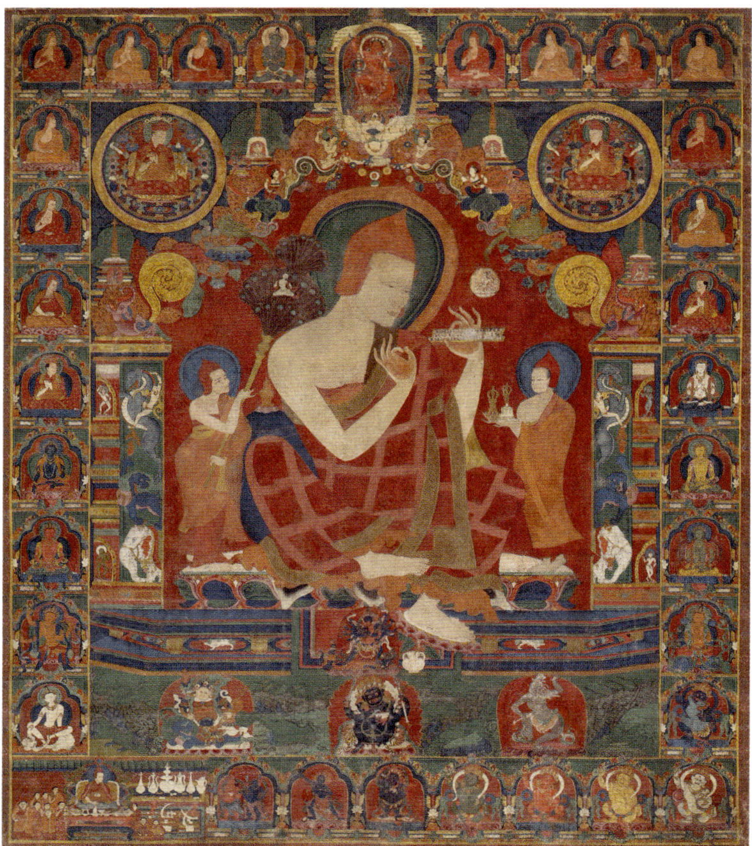

Portrait of Vanaratna (1384–1468); central Tibet; 15th century; distemper on cloth; 40¼ × 34½ in. (102.2 × 87.6 cm); Kronos Collections; photograph by John Bigelow Taylor

(1424–1482), who also confirms the date of Vanaratna's passing recorded in the inscription: midnight on Monday, the seventh day of the dark fortnight in the month of Margashirsha (November–December) in Nepala Samvat 589 (1468).

The image depicts an alms distribution at Gopichandra, though the inscription does not clarify if it is related to one of the events recorded there or a later distribution led by the Gopichandra community. The left half of the image is arrayed with a diverse group of supplicants approaching three women dispensing alms. The inscription, the details of the painting, and textual sources all concur that the crowd included Buddhist monastics, non-Buddhist mendicants, and lay people, among whom were musicians and beggars. The right half of the image is taken up by a large portrait of a woman distributing alms with her right hand and holding a lotus elegantly in her left. She is flanked by two women who, like the central figure, are dressed in fine garments. Four seated figures adorn the upper-right corner of the image, and though they are not identified by name, their position suggests them to be the patrons of the image or prominent members of the Gopichandra community. Interspersed between the figures are various flowers and ritual utensils that add to the festive imagery. The entire image is surrounded by a decorative border and sewn into a brocade frame. The painting is faded, worn, and incomplete, and its inscription is nearly illegible; however, a copy of the image commissioned by the Gopichandra community in 1862 clarifies many of the details of the original image, provides a more legible reading of the inscription, and demonstrates that the 1469 painting is likely missing an upper register that contained an image of an unidentified buddha surrounded by monastics and flanked by Buddhist adepts and other buddhas. That this upper register was included in the original image is suggested by traces of ornamental features still evident at the top of the original painting.

The identity of the large female figure is a matter of some debate that has been the primary focus of previous scholarship on this image. Some propose that the main figure is Vanaratna's widow distributing alms,[5] and cite Vanaratna's biographies to argue that Vanaratna abandoned his monastic status and took a wife while living in Kathmandu, a custom common among Newar Vajracharyas in more recent times.[6] This reading of Vanaratna's biography is inaccurate and incomplete, however, as it ignores substantial evidence that Vanaratna placed great importance on his monastic ordination, even if he did rely on a consort in specific esoteric ritual contexts.

See Vajracharya Priest's Crown, no. 38.

A more plausible, but ultimately unsatisfying argument is made by Dina Bangdel, who asserts that the main female figure is the white form of the female deity Tara.[7] Her argument is based on the figure's iconography and prominence, other minor details from the image, and proposed connections between Vanaratna and Tibetan lineages of White Tara practice. The textual and lineage connections Bangdel proposes are tenuous, however, as the sources she cites date four centuries after Vanaratna's passing and cannot be directly linked with Vanaratna's biography or extant writings. There is also little evidence to suggest White Tara was of specific relevance to either Vanaratna or the Gopichandra community. The key iconographic features and details that in Bangdel's argument identify the figure as Tara—specifically the figure's hand gestures and the ritual objects arrayed throughout the image—are in fact stylistic motifs also used in the previously mentioned secular portrait of Gaganasim Bharo and his wives, a portrait likely made by the same artists or in the same artist collective. While the prominence of the female figure in the image and the fact that she holds a lotus lends some support to Bangdel's claim, the evidence is insufficient to identify her as Tara.[8]

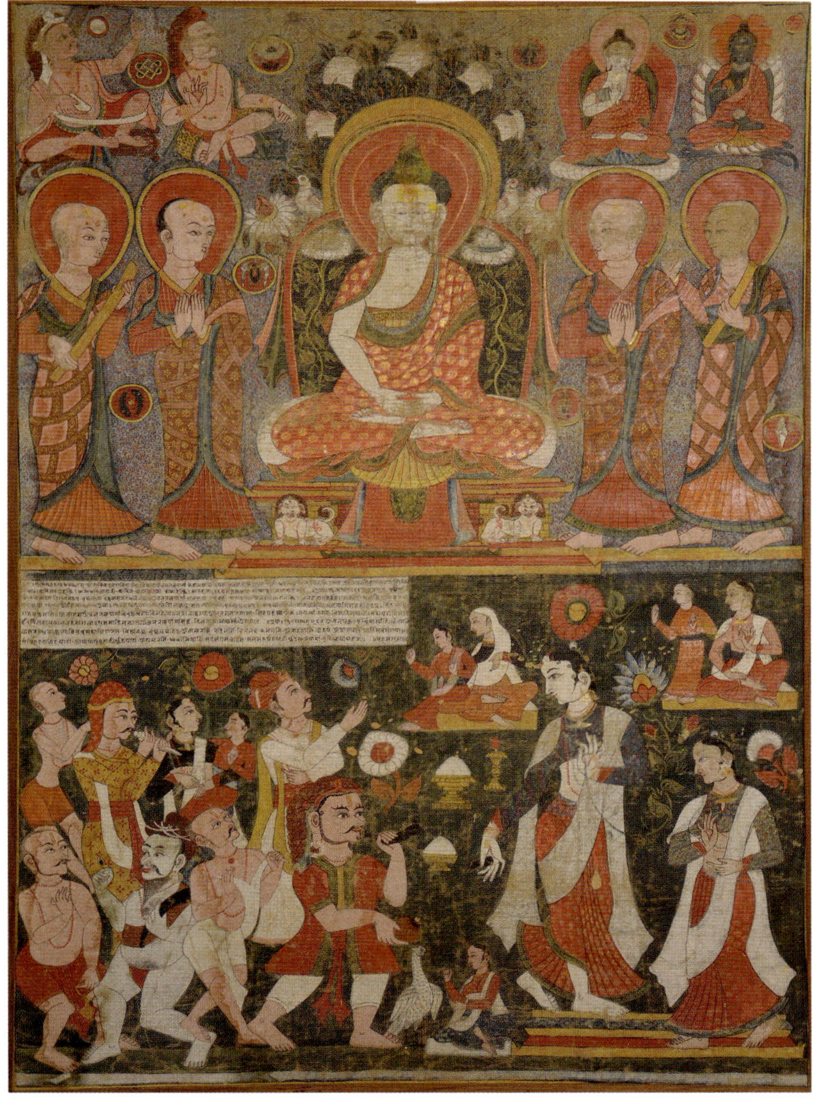

Nineteenth-Century Copy of the *Paubha* Commemorating the Death of Pandita Vanaratna (1384–1468); Patan, Nepal; 1862; opaque watercolors on cloth; dimensions unknown; Bharat Kala Bhavan, Benares Hindu University, Varanasi

While her scale and placement suggest she is someone of importance, it is notable that the woman is not mentioned in the inscription. It is also notable that Vanaratna himself is not pictured, despite the fact that his is the only name provided in the inscription that exclusively describes his activities at Gopichandra Monastery. If, as the 1862 copy of the image indicates, the alms distribution scene is in the lower frame of what was originally a two-frame image, then the painting discussed here would be subordinate to the missing image of a buddha above. It is therefore perhaps not intended to be the primary focal point of the painting.

If we leave the mystery of the woman's identity unsolved, a different interpretation comes into focus: the image is not meant to depict a specific individual, but rather represents the Gopichandra community as a whole. As we know from his biography, Vanaratna used the gold he amassed throughout his career to establish a food bank at Gopichandra that continued to serve the people of the Kathmandu Valley long after he passed away. The anonymity of the main figures focuses our attention not on an individual, but on the community carrying out the acts of service instigated and inspired by their spiritual leader. Thus, as this exceptional image attests, it was a dynamic depiction of the community, rather than a formal portrait of Vanaratna, that was selected to memorialize his passing and serve as a remembrance for the vital community he left behind.

Further Reading

Damron, Ryan C. 2021. "Deyadharma—A Gift of the Dharma: The Life and Works of Vanaratna (1384–1468)." PhD diss., University of California, Berkeley.

Pal, Pratapaditya. 1985. *Art of Nepal: A Catalogue of the Los Angeles County Museum of Art Collection*. Los Angeles: Los Angeles County Museum of Art and University of California Press.

Vajracharya, Gautama V. 2003. "Threefold Intimacy: The Recent Discovery of an Outstanding Nepalese Portrait Painting." *Orientations* 34, no. 4 (April): 40–45.

Notes

1 This painting is reproduced in Pal 2003, 68–69.
2 On the exceptional painting of Gaganasim Bharo and his wives and its stylistic similarities with the *paubha* discussed here, see Vajracharya 2003.
3 For more on the innovations introduced by Adyayaraja Puna and Udrayarama Puna, see Vajracharya 2003, 42–45.
4 Vanaratna's life story is preserved in two Tibetan biographies (*namtar*) composed by his close disciples, often with his direct input. Zhonnu Pel (gzhon nu dpal, 1392–1481) covers the years 1384–ca. 1438. Sonam Gyatso (bsod nams rgya mtsho, 1424–1482) covers the years ca. 1438–1468. For a study of the two biographies, Vanaratna's extant writings, and related art historical and material resources, see Damron 2021.
5 On this argument, see Pal 1985; Pal 1989, 194–95; Decleer 2005, 87; Vajracharya 2004, 69.
6 Gellner 1992, 162–7.
7 Huntington and Bangdel 2003, 143–45.
8 For a more detailed discussion of Pal's and Bangdel's arguments, see Damron 2021, 94–97, 237–40.

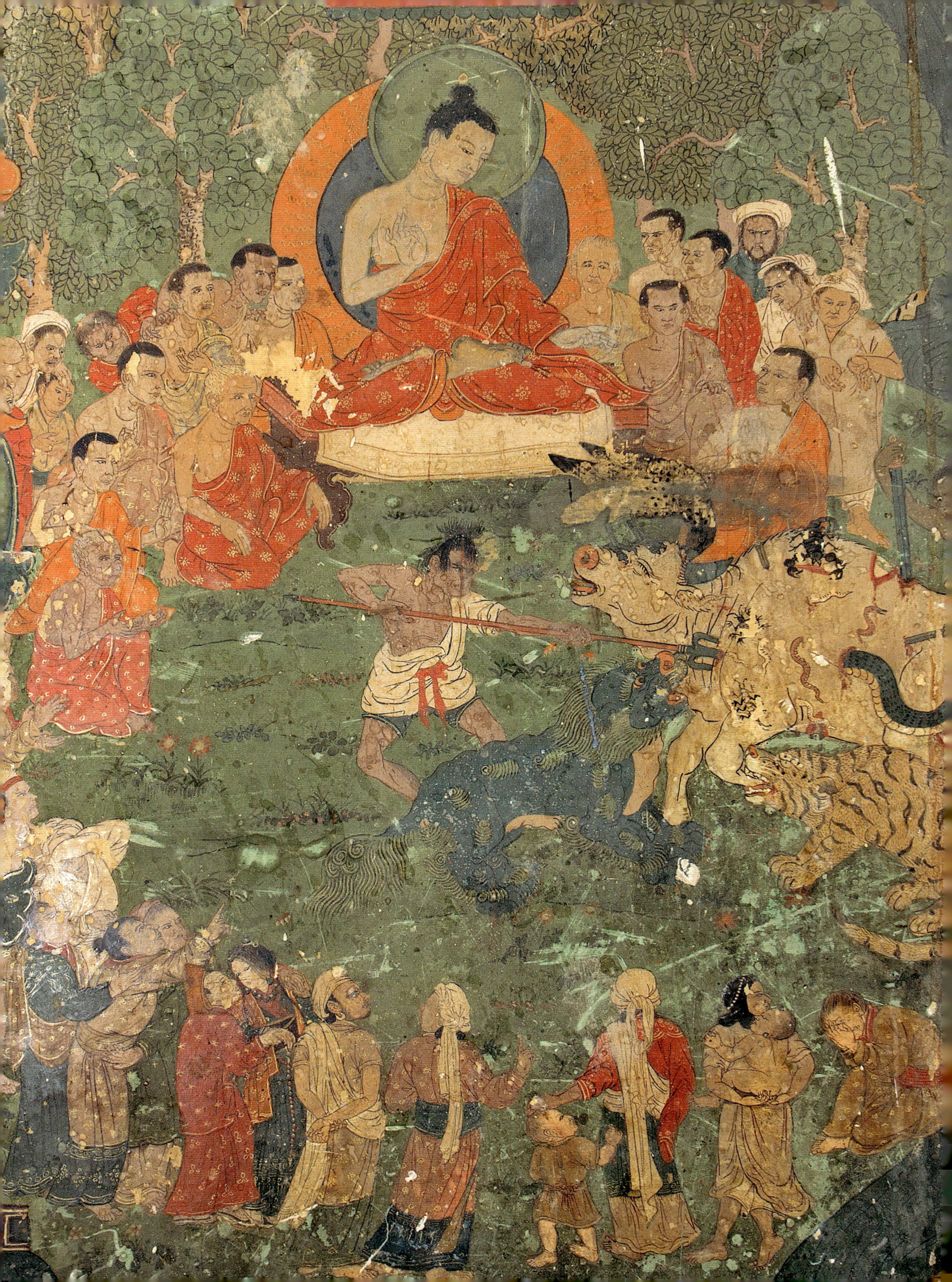

No 58

Murals of Gongkar Chode

Lhokha, U region, central Tibet (present-day TAR, China), 1464–1476

Reexamining Khyentse Chenmo and His Painting Tradition

TSECHANG PENBA WANGDU
TRANSLATED BY TENZIN GELEK

At the beginning of the fifteenth century, two new distinctive artistic traditions of Tibetan painting and sculpture arose in central Tibet: the Khyentse and Menla traditions.[1] The artist Khyentse Chenmo Genyen Nampar Gyelwa established the Khyentse tradition, which is named after him, including the Khyentse painting style (or Khyenri), exemplified by his surviving murals at Gongkar Chode Monastery.

Founded in 1464 by a master of the Sakya tradition, Kunga Namgyel (1432–1496), Gongkar Chode, or Gongkar Dorjeden, is located about thirty-seven miles (sixty kilometers) south of Lhasa. Khyentse Chenmo was responsible for creating paintings and sculptures throughout the monastery, including the ground, middle, and upper floors of the main temple, which took him twelve years, from 1464 to 1476.

Overview of the Murals

Ground floor: The main building has a total area of about 9,040 square feet (840 square meters), with each higher floor smaller than the one below it.[2] In the Main Assembly Hall, the walls are painted with the one hundred deeds of the Buddha, illustrating the popular narratives as told in the *Wish-Fulfilling Vine* (*Bodhisattvavadanakalpalata*). In the Great Protector Chapel, paintings depict charnel grounds, a common setting for the wrathful deities who are venerated there.

On depictions of the *Wish-Fulfilling Vine* narratives, see also A Monumental Life of the Buddha Mural, no. 69.

The wall paintings of the Inner Sanctum feature the Buddhas of the Three Times, including Kashyapa and seven successive buddhas. Flanking the entrance to the Inner Sanctum on the right are the Three White Ones (lay masters) of the Sakya school surrounded by lineage masters of the Lamdre teachings, and on the left side are the Three Red Ones (ordained masters)—Sakya Pandita (1182–1251), Pakpa Rinpoche (1235–1280), and Pelden Lama Dampa (1312–1375).

See also Mural Painting at Zhalu Monastery, no. 47.

The inner Circumambulation Corridor depicts the twelve great deeds of the Buddha, and the Great Tantric Chapel, or Vajrabhairava Chapel, includes scary scenes of charnel grounds.

See Virupa, no. 37.

Middle floor: The Protector Chapel features images of the great Sakya master Sachen Kunga Nyingpo (1092–1158) and the Indian mahasiddha Virupa, as well as charnel-ground scenes, with the *yaksha* Vaishravana and his Eight Horsemen. The highest tantric deities, including the nine deities of Hevajra, are painted in the Hevajra Chapel. The Lamdre Chapel has wall paintings of Vajradhatu, while the Vajradhatu Chapel features Maitreya and 996 other bodhisattvas.

Upper floor: On the roof, in the Guru Chapel, are paintings depicting the lineage masters of the Lamdre teachings, which are central to the Sakya tradition of Tibetan Buddhism.

Khyentse Chenmo (act. 15th century); Detail of Morality Tale of Vidura from chapter 76 in the *Wish-Fulfilling Vine (Bodhisattvavadanakalpalata)*; southern mural painting of the original Main Assembly Hall, ground floor, Gongkar Chode Monastery, Gangto Village, Gongkar County, Lhokha, U region, central Tibet (present-day TAR, China); ca. 1464–1476; photograph by Andrew Quintman, 2011

New Evidence on the Life of the Artist Khyentse Chenmo

Details about Khyentse Chenmo's life are sparse. Most scholars believe he was born around the third decade of the fifteenth century.[3] Yet an important source recently came to light, *A Note of the Uncommon Biography of Lhatsun Rinchen Gyatso* by Rinchen Tsultrim (ca. fifteenth century),[4] which is one of the earliest records mentioning Khyentse. According to this text, in 1428 Drongtse Chode Lhatsun Rinchen Gyatso constructed Genden Riwo Tarpa Ling,[5] a monastery consecrated by his famous teacher of the Geluk tradition Khedrubje Rinpoche (1385–1438) and Baso Chokyi Gyeltsen (1402–1473) in 1432. During

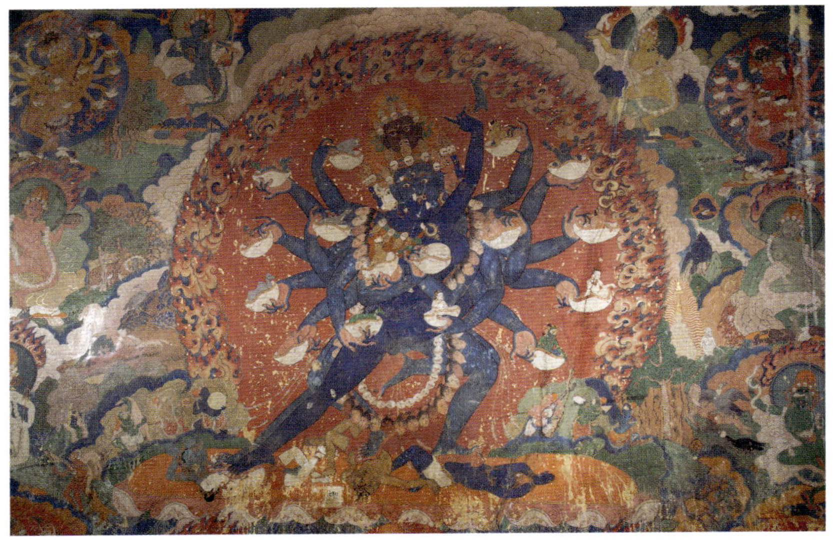

Khyentse Chenmo (act. 15th century); Hevajra; Northern mural painting in Hevajra Chapel, middle floor, Gongkar Chode Monastery, Gongkar County, Lhokha, U region, central Tibet (present-day TAR, China); ca. 1464–1476; photograph by Tsechang Penba Wangdu, 2018

this time, over thirty artists trained in the Khyentse tradition and Tibetan painters trained in Nepalese-style painting (Beri) painted the murals of the Assembly Hall and the temples. The murals of the Reconciliatory Stupa, designed by Lhatsun himself, were also painted according to the Khyentse artistic tradition. The text also states that Menla Dondrub was learning Nepalese-style painting in Nenying Monastery while the painting of the main temple mural was underway. Lhatsun suggested to Menla that it would be of great benefit to the Buddhist doctrine and all sentient beings to create a new tradition of Mentangpa painting (also known as Menri) by analyzing the Nepalese style and Chinese tradition, adopting the best practices from the two traditions, and relying mainly on the proportion system used for Chakrasamvara and Kalachakra tantras.

It is clear from this narrative that the Khyentse tradition existed before the Menla tradition was founded, a view also expressed by the Thirteenth Karmapa (1733–1797). It further suggests that Khyentse Chenmo was born at the beginning of the fifteenth century. In light of this new evidence, we must also reevaluate other commonly held beliefs about the artist, such as that Khyentse Chenmo, together with Menla and his students, carried out the painting of Yangpachen Monastery in 1505.[6] That was likely accomplished by followers of the Khyentse tradition, not Khyentse Chenmo himself.[7]

Characteristics of the Khyentse Painting Tradition

Most of what we know about Khyentse Chenmo's work comes from his surviving wall paintings at Gongkar Chode. The main characteristic of the Khyentse tradition, as pointed out by the Fifth Dalai Lama (1617–1682), is that it excels in the depiction of wrathful deities, whereas the Menla tradition excels in peaceful deities. After many trips to Gongkar Chode, I have perceived another characteristic of the Khyentse tradition: a strong sense of realism. For example, in the Assembly Hall, a mural section depicting the story of Vidura, as told in the seventy-sixth chapter of the *Wish-Fulfilling Vine*, is expressed through realistic impressions that mimic everyday life. As one can see from the main image here, the mural depicts humans, tigers, crocodiles, crows, insects, and other animals inflicting harm on a buffalo. The onlookers are crying; some point their fingers, while others are conversing.

In the Nepalese style, the bodies of Buddhist masters usually include a halo and body nimbus, but in the Khyentse tradition, there is a halo but no body nimbus. The face shapes, body types, and individual appearances are distinct and exquisitely represented. For instance, the physical characteristics of the root masters of the Lamdre teachings, flanking the entrance to the Inner Sanctum, are painted with such liveliness that they give the impression they are about to speak.

The paintings of charnel ground scenes in both the Protector Chapel and in the Vajrabhairava Chapel evoke the impression of being immersed in the charnel grounds. The appearance of scenes of figures eating human flesh is akin to depictions of otherworldly beings in Western films about alien planets. The paintings are realistic beyond expectation.

Figural Proportions of the Khyentse Tradition

The proportions of figures are determined by rules of measurement, or iconometry, as outlined in religious texts. These proportions are commonly expressed visually in artist manuals as iconometric grids. It is commonly assumed that the proportional measurements of the Khyentse and Menla traditions are the same. Yet when I examined the wall paintings at Gongkar Chode, I noticed the figures appear shorter than in the Menla tradition. My research into ancient iconometric texts revealed clear differences.

Khyentse's measurements closely match the iconometric guide written by Tsamo Rongpa Sonam Woser, a disciple of Drogon Chogyel Pakpa (1235–1280), *Source of Excellent Qualities: A Treatise on*

Khyentse Chenmo (act. 15th century); Vajrabhairava, Solitary Form of the Ra Lotsawa Tradition; western mural painting in Hevajra Chapel, middle floor, Gongkar Chode Monastery, Gongkar County, Lhokha, U region, central Tibet (present-day TAR, China); ca. 1464–1476; photograph by Tsechang Penba Wangdu, 2018

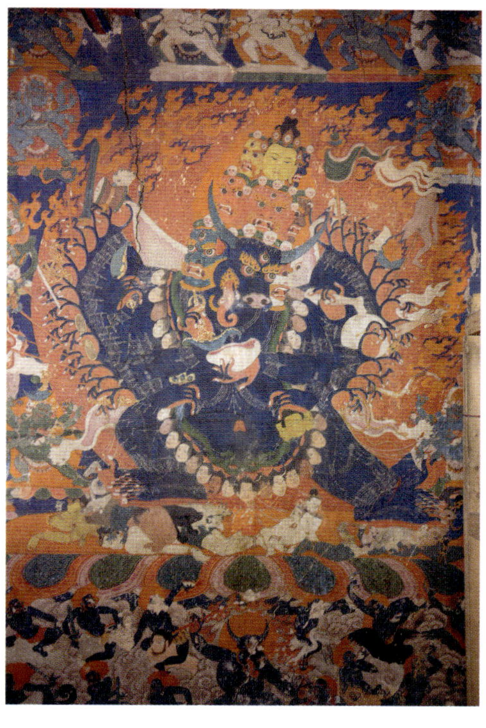

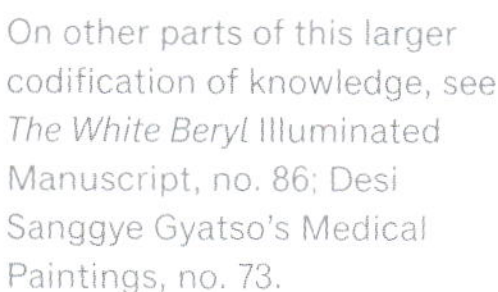

On other parts of this larger codification of knowledge, see *The White Beryl* Illuminated Manuscript, no. 86; Desi Sanggye Gyatso's Medical Paintings, no. 73.

Proportions for Making Three Representations and Their Abodes, and Bodong Tamche Khyenpa's (1376–1451) manual, *Entrance for the Experts*.[8] These two iconometry manuals were the popular standards during Khyentse and Menla's time. The basic unit of measure in this system of iconometry is one *zhel*.[9] This system of proportions has three main proportional classes or figural types; it gives a measurement of nine *zhel* for the body of a peaceful deity, six *zhel* for a fierce deity, and eight *zhel* for a semi-wrathful deity.

Menla's measurements are different in both the categorization of figures and their sizes. Generally speaking, Menla figures follow ten classifications of measurement, as described in his text, *The Wish-Fulfilling Jewel*.[10] Space does not allow a detailed explanation here, but, for example, the first four classes of figures in Menla's system include peaceful deities such as buddhas and bodhisattvas (ten *zhel*) and wrathful figures (eight *zhel*). Both are taller than the system Khyentse followed. The Fifth Dalai Lama's regent, Desi Sanggye Gyatso (1653–1705), later standardized all the traditions of painting proportions as part of a larger effort to systematize different fields of knowledge.[11]

Khyentse Chenmo's founding of the Khyentse tradition ended the spread of Nepalese and Indian painting traditions in Tibet and started a new direction of art traditions with Tibetan characteristics. Today it is rare to see his work; Gongkar Chode is the only monastery that preserves wall paintings by his hand. His paintings represent a unique style among the Tibetan traditions. The qualities that distinguish him from other artists include his ability to capture the nature and character of his subject matter, his realism, his great attention to detail, particularly in paintings of wild animals and birds, and the striking expression of wrathfulness in fierce deities. Upon seeing Khyentse Chenmo's painting of Vajrabhairava at Gongkar (see above), the famous Western Tibetologist Giuseppe Tucci (1894–1984) was overwhelmed with fear, which demonstrates the artistic quality and evocative power of Khyentse's work.

Further Reading

Jackson, David P. 2016. *A Revolutionary Artist of Tibet: Khyentse Chenmo of Gongkar*, 3–22; 67–80; 83–119. Masterworks of Tibetan Painting Series 6. New York: Rubin Museum of Art. https://issuu.com/rmanyc/docs/a_revolutionary_artist_96.

Tsechang Penba Wangdu. 2010. "Gong dkar sgang stod mkhyen brtse chen mo dge bsnyen rnam par rgyal ba dang mkhyen lugs kyi khyad chos skor rags tsam gleng ba." *Journal of Tibet University* 4, 112–17. Translated by David P. Jackson as "A Recent Introduction of Khyentse Chenmo and His Art," in *A Revolutionary Artist of Tibet: Khyentse Chenmo of Gongkar*, edited by David P. Jackson, 67–80. Masterworks of Tibetan Painting Series 6. New York: Rubin Museum of Art, 2016.

Notes

1 Editor's note: this essay was edited and shortened from its original length and more specialized scope. For more images of Gongkar Chode, see Luo and Qupei 2015.

2 This calculation of area is based on the monastery's 130 large pillars. In this monastery the two-pillar size is about 9 feet, 6 inches, to 11 feet, 2 inches, in width (2.92–3.4 meters), and 8 feet, 9 inches, to 11 feet, 3 inches, in length (2.68–3.43 meters).

3 See, for instance, D. Jackson 1996, 103; Tsechang Penba Wangdu 2005, 105–9; Yu 2006, 232; Yu 2021, 700.

4 Rin chen tshul khrims, ca. 15th century.

5 Geden Riwo Tarpa Ling, or Drongtse Chode Tarpa Ling, is in Drongtse Township, Gyantse county, Shigatse.

6 Dpa' bo gtsug lag phreng ba (1545–64) 1986, 1148.

7 Khyentsewa. The ending *pa/wa* added to a place or person's name can mean a person from a region, or the follower of a tradition.

8 Tsa mo rong pa bsod nams 'od zer, 14th century, 30–35; Bo dong paN chen phyogs las rnam rgyal 1981, 9:256–60.

9 *Zhel* (Tibetan: *zhal tshad*), literally means "face measure," which in the system Khyentse followed can be further divided into twelve *sor* ("finger measure"), a smaller unit of measure.

10 Sman bla don grub 1944.

11 Sde srid sangs rgyas rgya mtsho 2002. See also Cüppers, van der Kuijp, and Pagel 2012.

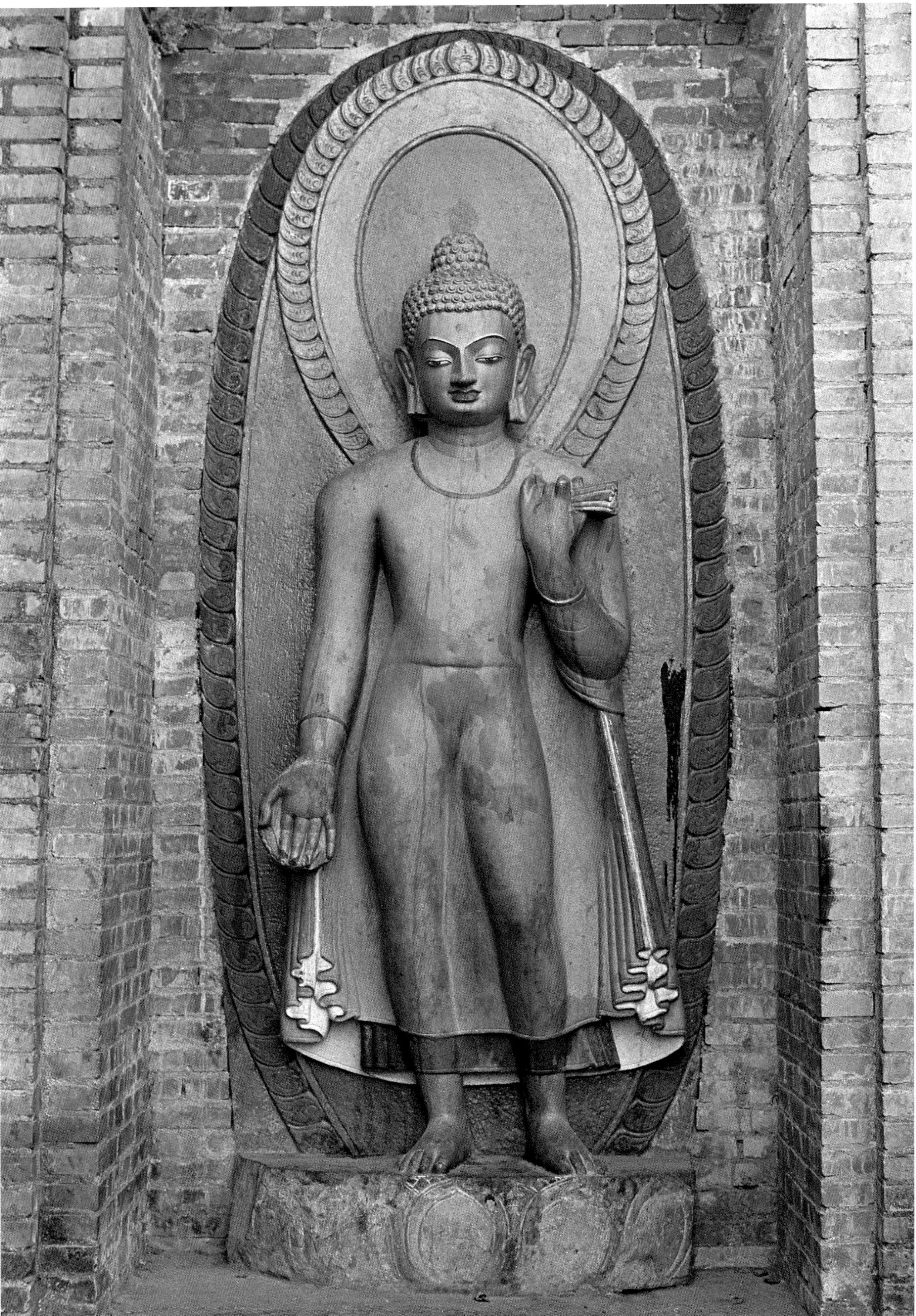

№ 59

Standing Buddha Shakyamuni Donated by Lundeva

Kathmandu, Nepal, 15th century, commissioned in a 9th–10th-century style

Challenges in Dating Nepalese Stone Sculpture

ULRICH VON SCHROEDER

THE ANCIENT SACRED HILL SITE of the Svayambhu Mahachaitya (stupa) at Kathmandu is filled with stone chaityas and several hundreds of stone sculptures, mostly of Buddhist deities. Very prominent among them is a tall stone carving of a standing Buddha installed west of the Svayambhu Mahachaitya that receives special attention from the numerous visitors. This Buddha, measuring 10½ feet (3.2 meters) high, is the tallest known Nepalese stone image of a Buddha.[1] Facing east, he stands inside an open shrine built with bricks, in a slightly sideways bent attitude on a single lotus pedestal characterized by large petals. The right hand, with clearly visible webbed fingers, is lowered in the gesture of charity (*varada* mudra), and the raised left hand holds the tip of the diaphanous monastic robe, rendered without pleats and covering both shoulders. The gesture of charity is known in Nepal also as mudra of prediction, which explains why this image is also known as the Buddha with the Gesture of Prediction. The edge of the lower garment is also visible. The image is set against an oval aureole and the head against an oval nimbus—both decorated with leaves.

See the Svayambchu Chaitya of Kathmandu, no. 4.

Intriguing Iconography

This buddha, here considered to represent the historical Shakyamuni, has also been differently identified as Maitreya—the future Buddha. However, there are no particular iconographic characteristics present that would endorse such an identification. Among Nepalese scholars in particular, this buddha is also often identified as Devavatara Bodhisattva, relevant to the descent of the Buddha from the Heaven of the Thirty-Three Gods (*Trayastrimsha*) at Sankashya.

For representations of the scenes of the Buddha's life, see Illuminated Pages of the *Prajnaparamita Sutra* Manuscript, no. 23.

Uncertain Dating of the Svayambhu Buddha

Like the Nepalese stone carving of Mayadevi giving birth to Siddhartha, this buddha has also caused much disagreement regarding the date of the sculpture's creation, which is variously dated between the fifth and the fifteenth century.[2] At a first glance, because it imitates an early style, the viewer is tempted to attribute the sculpture to the Licchavi period (ca. 300–879). Closer inspection, however, raises doubts regarding such an early date. According to a personal written communication by Swoyambhu Tuladhar, this buddha and the smaller one at the south facade of the Shantipura cave shrine[3] were commissioned by two of his ancestors, namely by Lundeva and Dhandeva, sons of Patindra Malla (about whom nothing is known), whose name appears on a painting on cloth made in Nepala Samvat 559 (1438).[4] This account is corroborated by the fact that even in recent times, according to Swoyambhu Tuladhar, when the Vajracharya priests go around during their daily prayer ritual (*puja*) ringing their handbells, they include in their praise the names of Lundeva and Dhandeva.[5]

See Mayadevi Giving Birth to Siddhartha, no. 3.

For another example of a commission on behalf by famous Nepalese donors, see Nepalese *Paubha* Commemorating the Death of Pandita Vanaratna, no. 57.

For more about Vajracharya priests, see Vajracharya Priest's Crown, no. 38.

Standing Buddha Shakyamuni Donated by Lundeva; Svayambhu, Kathmandu, Nepal; 15th century, commissioned in a 9th–10th-century style; stone; height 10 ft. 7 in. (324 cm); photograph by Ulrich von Schroeder, 1976

Broader Context

These two buddhas were modeled after an older standing stone buddha such as the one at Rajarajeshvari Ghat of Pashupatinatha, Kathmandu, Nepal, dating from about the tenth century,[6] or a slightly earlier buddha such as that of the Bhinche Baha in Patan, Nepal, made in the eighth to ninth centuries.[7] Although the monumental Svayambhu buddha was rendered in a style common in the late Licchavi period, its surface lacks the abrasions one would expect on an image that was for more than a thousand

Shakyamuni Donated by Dhandeva; Shantipura, Svayambhu, Kathmandu, Nepal; 15th century; photograph by Ulrich von Schroeder, 1976

Buddha Shakyamuni; Rajarajeshvari Ghat, Pashupatinatha, Kathmandu, Nepal; ca. 10th century; photograph by Jürgen Schick, 1980s

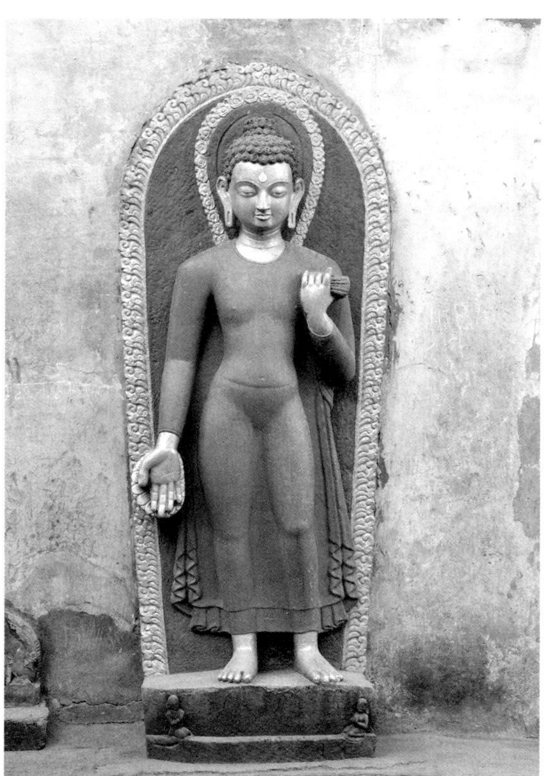

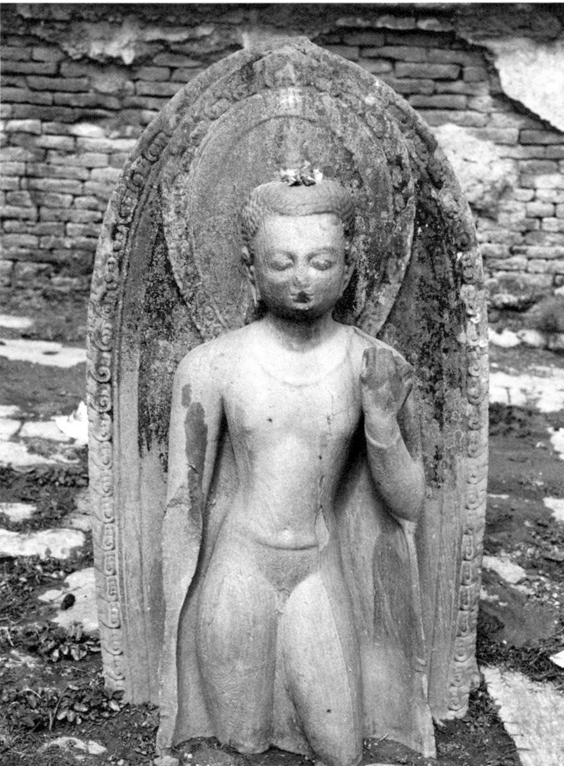

years subjected to weather and ritual wear. However, the present state of preservation is compatible with a fifteenth-century image. For a Licchavi period image the nimbus would proportionally also be much too large. There is thus a discrepancy between the date of manufacture and the style in which the sculpture was created. An attribution "carved in the fifteenth century in a ninth- to tenth-century style" would likely be the best compromise. My personal conclusion with regard to the age of this buddha, formed during numerous visits since 1965, always ruled out the possibility of its having been made during the Licchavi period.

Dating of Nepalese Stone Sculptures

In the best case, the dating of ancient sculptures may be achieved through comparisons with dated sculptures. However, this is not possible in the case of Nepalese standing buddha images carved in stone, because the earliest dated examples date from the seventeenth century.[8] Nevertheless, the importance of dated sculptures should not be overestimated for several reasons. The date, if correctly deciphered, just records when a particular image has been manufactured. Contrary to general acceptance, a dated inscription thus does not stipulate that images in a similar style were necessarily made around the same time. It is also not a given that all images manufactured in a particular period have to be similar in style. In retrospect it is unknown what image the artist was using for inspiration—a contemporary model or perhaps, on request of the patron, a particular older image. The margin of errors in attribution of dates of manufacture is therefore considerable.

To enable an overview about the stylistic spectrum within a particular period of time, the reader might consult groups of dated images of the same iconography all manufactured in the same centuries.[9] Such groupings illustrate the differences in style among dated images produced during a particular century and demonstrate that any attempt to pinpoint a style to a particular period of time is bound to fail. Especially in short articles discussing a few deliberately chosen examples that fit the agenda, the conclusions look at first reasonably well documented. However, when considering a wider selection of sculptures, it becomes clear that conclusions based on just a few sculptures are in a wider context often erroneous. Only in a strictly supervised and centralized environment such as the imperial workshops in China, all images created during a particular period of time are almost identical in style. From this it follows that images produced in different workshops according to individual agreements between artists

For more about Chinese imperial workshops, see Pensive Bodhisattva Avalokiteshvara, no. 53.

Buddha Shakyamuni; Bhinche Baha, Patan, Nepal; 8th–9th century; photograph by Ulrich von Schroeder, 2011

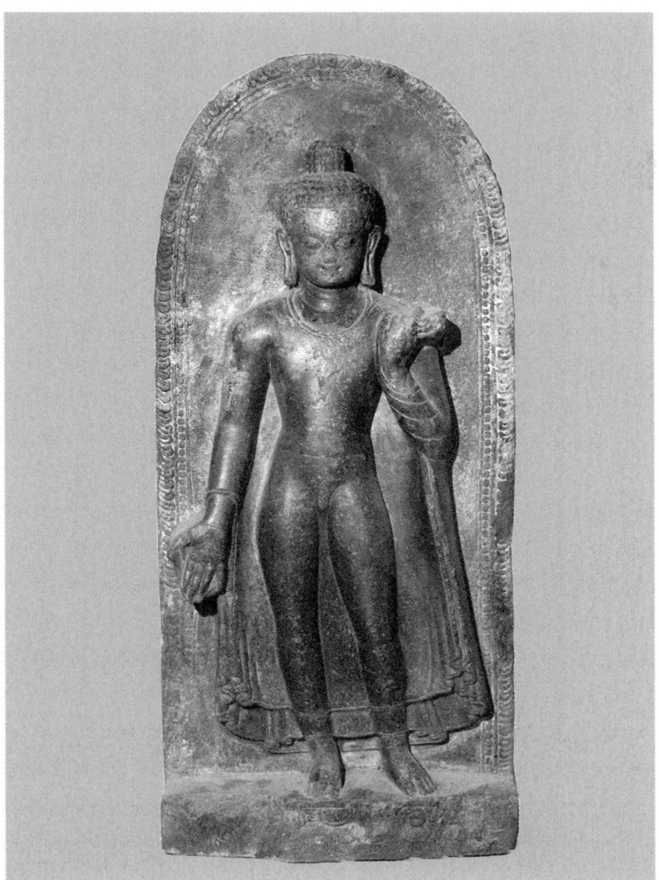

and patrons have a much larger spectrum regarding styles. One of the main purposes of history of art is to illustrate the evolution of styles. The merits of any particular sculpture become visible only in comparison with as many similar images as possible. If it would be predictable—it would not be art!

Further Reading

Bangdel, Lain S. 1982. *The Early Sculptures of Nepal.* New Delhi: Vikas.

Pal, Pratapaditya. 1974. *The Arts of Nepal*, pt. 1: *Sculpture*. Leiden: Brill.

von Schroeder, Ulrich. 2019. *Nepalese Stone Sculptures*. 2 vols. Weesen: Visual Dharma Publications.

Notes

1 von Schroeder 2019, 2:873, 878, 896, 897, pl. 280B, fig. VII–7. For other works on this sculpture, see Singh (1968) 1971; L. S. Bangdel 1995, 188–89, section 44, figs. 1, 3: Standing Buddha, circa 10th–11th century; plate 44-1, plate 44-3; L. S. Bangdel and Aryal 1996, 59, 77, plate 14; D. Bangdel 1999 and 2011; H. R. Shakya 2004; Hutt 2010; M. R. Shakya 2011.

2 von Schroeder, 2019, 2:896.

3 von Schroeder, 2019, 2:878, 896–97, pl. 280A.

4 According to Sukra Sagar Shrestha, the painting was stolen and its present whereabouts is unknown. No photograph exists.

5 von Schroeder, 2019, 2:SD card, pl. 280B.

6 von Schroeder, 2019, 2:873, 878, 896–97, pls. 279B–D.

7 von Schroeder, 2019, 2:888–89, pls. 276E–F.

8 von Schroeder, 2019, 2:900–901, pls. 282B–C.

9 von Schroeder, 2019, 2:1492–1504, 13 plates of dated images.

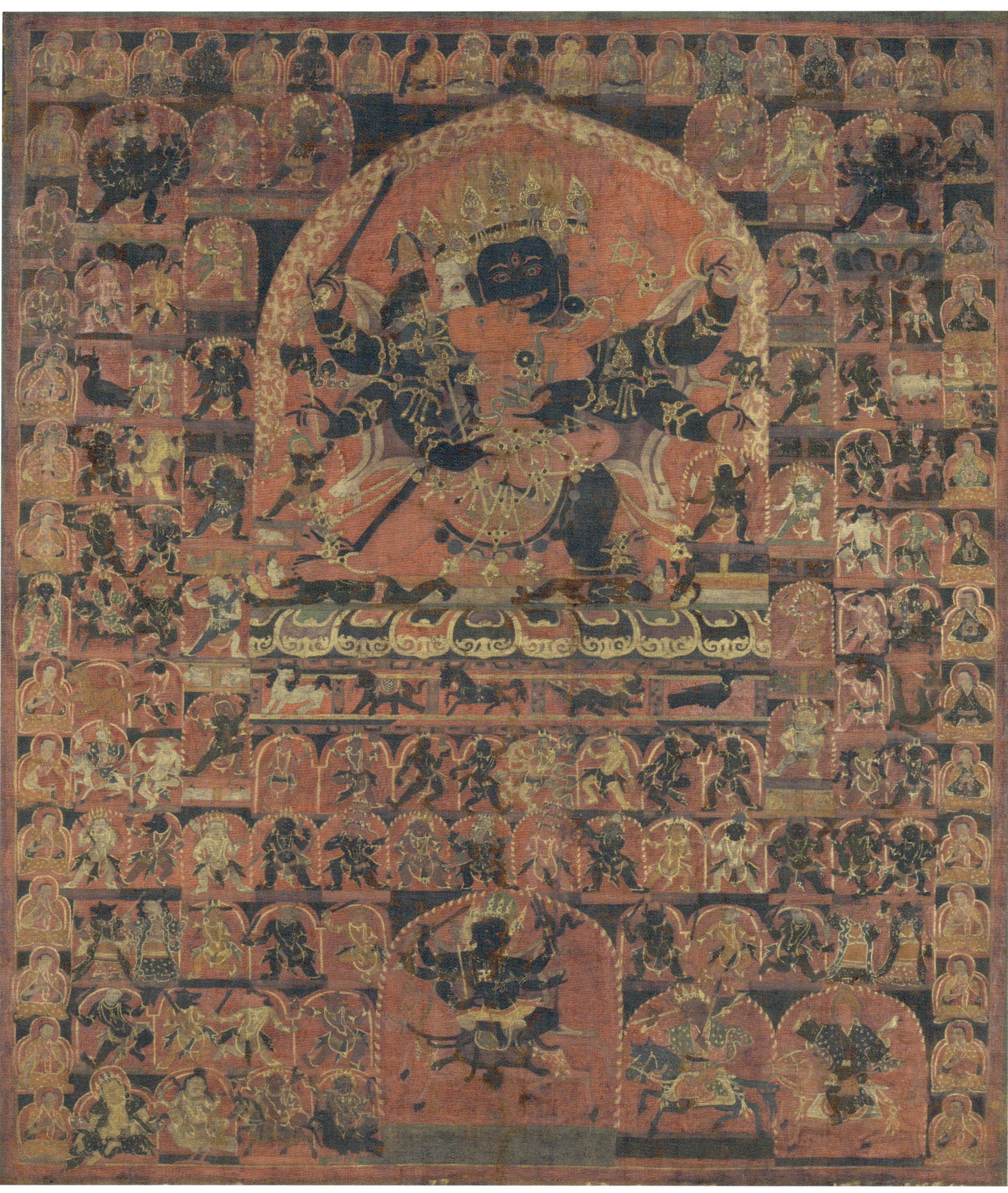

№ 60

Bon Deity Trowo Tsochok Khagying

Tibet, 15th century

A Microcosm of the Bon Religion

CHARLES RAMBLE

The central figure in this thangka (scroll painting) is one of the most important divinities of the Bon religion of Tibet: Trowo Tsochok Khagying, "The Wrathful One, the Supreme Lord Stretching across the Sky." He is in union with his consort, Khala Dukmo, "Fierce Lady in the Sky," surrounded by their entourage. While this arrangement suggests a typical tantric Buddhist configuration, a closer examination reveals that it is associated not with Buddhism but with the Bon religion. One immediate clue is the swastika on the chest of the figure in the center of the lowest row: the arms of the swastika point counterclockwise, which, in post-eleventh-century Tibetan iconography, is generally an indication that the image is associated with Bon. Before undertaking an examination of the thangka, however, a few words should be said by way of introduction to this religion.

What Is Bon?

As Per Kvaerne has pointed out, "Bon" denotes at least three different things: First, the religion that prevailed in Tibet before Buddhism became the official faith in the late eighth century; second, an organized system with a monastic component that emerged in the tenth to eleventh centuries, and generally referred to as Yungdrung ("Eternal") Bon; and third, a plethora of cults consisting of mythic narratives and rituals for the protection and prosperity of local communities.[1] These cults, which exhibit significant continuities with the earliest form of Bon, are found throughout Tibet but persist especially in the Himalayan borderlands. Since there is no indigenous term for this mosaic of local cults, we may call it "pagan" Bon, since each one is concerned with the well-being of a local territory (*pagus* in Latin, the origin of the term "pagan").[2] The followers of Yungdrung Bon, known as Bonpos, consider themselves the heirs of the pre-Buddhist religion. They do not, however, recognize any kinship with pagan Bon, which sometimes involves animal sacrifice, a practice anathema to Yungdrung Bon. Confusingly, the term *bonpo* is often also applied to priests and shamans of pagan Bon.

Bonpos believe that everything in Yungdrung Bon derives from the teaching of the religion's legendary founder, Shenrab Miwo, who is believed by followers of the religion to have lived sixteen thousand years ago, but for whom no historical sources are available. This name is understood to mean "the great man who is an excellent priest," but may also, with a slightly different orthography, mean "the great man of the Shen clan," a form that is found especially in older sources.

For more on the close relationship between Bon and the natural world, see Thread Crosses, no. 106.

Bon Deity Trowo Tsochok Khagying; Tibet; 15th century; distemper, ink, gold on cloth; 31 × 26 in. (78.7 × 66 cm); The Metropolitan Museum of Art, New York; Gift of Carlton Rochell, in honor of John Guy, and in celebration of the Museum's 150th Anniversary, 2018; 2018.890;

As different as these three types of Bon may be, they are not completely isolated from one another. Yungdrung Bon shares with Buddhism the techniques and principles that underpin their sutras, tantras, and philosophical systems. However, it has cosmological concepts and divinities that predate the arrival of Buddhism, and it shares with pagan Bon a range of non-Buddhist rituals. These rituals, as well as the animal divinities that they feature, are an enduring reminder of the close relationship between Bon and the natural world.

All the Buddhist schools look to India as the source of their fundamental tenets, and to Sanskrit as the main language from which their scriptures were translated. For the Bonpos, the land from which their teachings came was Zhangzhung, once an actual polity in the western part of the Tibetan Plateau and beyond, but accorded fantastic dimensions in Bon religious histories. The language from which the scriptures were translated is believed to have been not Sanskrit but the language of Zhangzhung. Historically, then, the complex system that Bonpos attribute to a single founder figure may be the

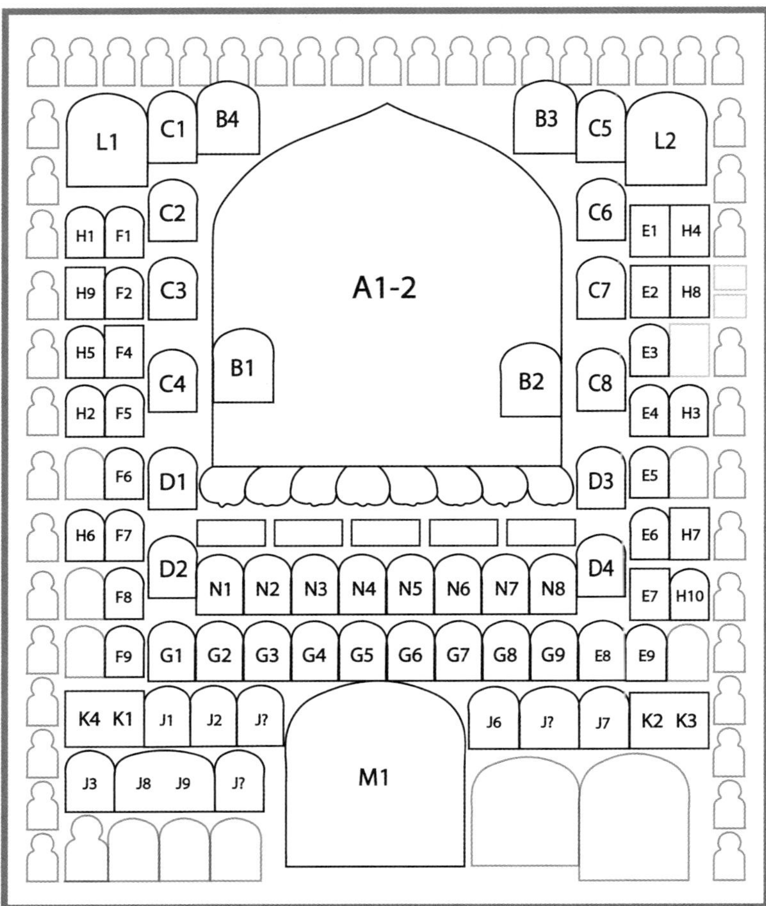

Key to the thangka of Bon Deity Trowo Tsochok Khagying; Tibet; drawing by Olga Helman

pooling of influences from several provenances: India, Central Asia, Tibet, and the Himalayan region, and also China, which was the source of certain divinatory traditions.

The Composition of the Thangka

The texts relating to Tsochok Khagying are broadly in agreement about the main figures represented in this thangka, which may be summarized briefly.[3] Tsochok himself (A1 in the key to the thangka) has three faces, six arms, and two legs, and his consort, Khala Dukmo, has two arms and two legs. The double triangle in her right hand is a golden thunderbolt, and with her left hand she feeds a heart to the lord. In the innermost circle (B) are four manifestations of the lord himself, the Four Wrathful Ones who Avert Evil. Outside these, in two columns (C), are eight further manifestations called the Wrathful Ones of Awareness. Below each of these columns are two figures who form a group known as the Manifested Wrathful Ones (D), identifiable by the half-man half-bird creature called *shangshang* that supports the throne of each. These are framed on three sides by twenty-seven divinities known as the Fierce Ladies, comprising three categories: the Nine Zema in a column to our right (E), the Nine Female Champions to the left (F), and the Nine Jinte in a row below them (G).[4] The names Zema and Jinte have no obvious translation. In two columns of five figures each outside these are the Ten Champions (H), who are paired with another set of female animal-headed divinities called the Ten Warlords (J), of whom seven are grouped to our left of the central figure at the base and three to the right, at the level of her head. The last group whose members belong to the entourage of Tsochok are four animal-headed figures in long robes, two to the far left and two to the far right of the row level with the head of the main figure at the base. These are the Four Steadfast Ones (K), who guard the cardinal directions. The other images in the thangka are not part of the Tsochok's retinue. In the Bon pantheon, Tsochok is one of a triad called Chipung, the "Universal Embodiment," the other two being Walse Ngampa (L1) and Lhago Tokpa (L2). The central figure below is Sipai Gyelmo, the "Queen of the Universe" (M1), in one of her numerous manifestations, here riding a red mule. Below the animals supporting the throne of Tsochok himself is a row of goddesses (N), each holding a sense offering.[5] The perimeter of the thangka, and a few locations in the interior, are occupied by unidentified divinities, saints, and lamas.

A Fusion of the Different Strands of Bon

This painting admirably represents the cluster of influences that constitute Yungdrung Bon. While the concept of a divinity with his consort and entourage is indebted to the Indian tantric tradition, there is much here that does not have such a straightforward attribution. Sipai Gyelmo was originally an ancestral Tibetan goddess, but over time her iconography and other attributes have converged with those of the Buddhist goddess Palden Lhamo. Most of the members of the entourage are unknown to Buddhism: although the three groups (E, F, and G) of the Twenty-Seven Fierce Ladies, whose chief is Sipai Gyelmo herself, have parallels in Buddhism, they are probably war gods of indigenous or Central Asian origin.[6] Tsochok and his entourage are sometimes pictured in other media: during rituals in which he is the main divinity, often with his benign (*zhiwa*) counterpart, he is portrayed as a dough-and-butter effigy (*torma*). Alternatively, he and his inner circle—including the Fierce Ladies—are depicted in an abstract

See *Tormas*, no. 105.

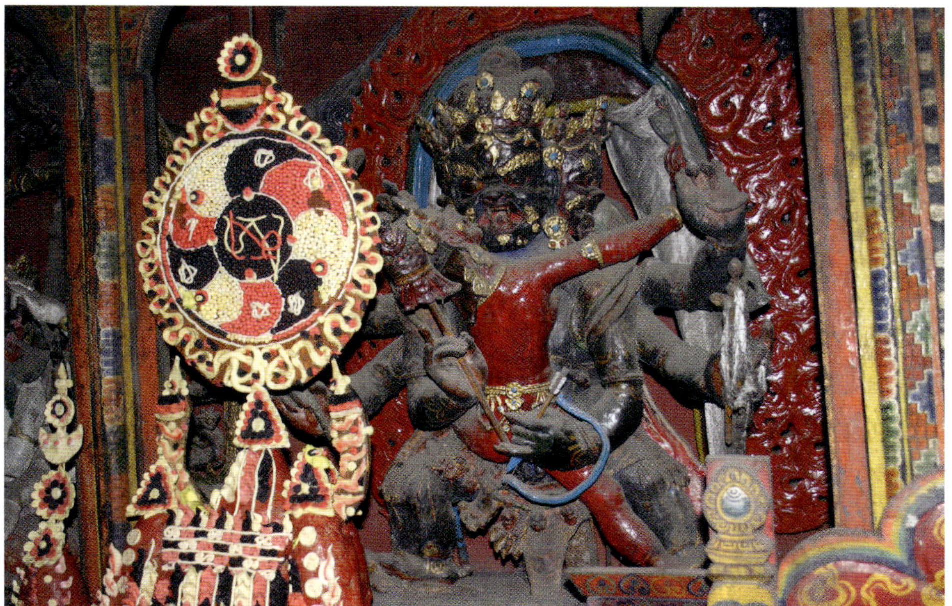

A large *torma* (dough-and-butter sculpture) representing Tsochok Khagying and his consort, standing on an altar in front of a clay image of the same pair of divinities, Lubrak Village, Mustang District, Nepal; photograph by Charles Ramble, 2008

geometric form as a mandala, where he and his consort are denoted at the center by the interlaced letters A and MA.[7] In another form of the mandala, Tsochok and his inner circle take the shape of ritual daggers and ritual claws, while the Zema, the Female Champions, and the Jinte are embodied respectively by hooks, arrows, and wooden plaques or tablets. All the members of the entourage who fall outside the Fierce Ladies—the Champions, the Warlords, and the Steadfast Ones, as well as others who are not featured in this thangka—do not appear in the inner mandala at all but have their own separate residence, known as the "outer support arrangement" (*chitenko*).[8] This is an assemblage comprising a long vertical spear surrounded by sets of objects: eight smaller spears, with the horns, fangs, and claws of different animals as spearheads; arrows fletched with feathers of different colors; sacks of various substances (grains, minerals, and so forth), posts, cairns, and banners that are all connected to the central spear with cords festooned with the forelegs of animals and stuffed groups of birds, among other things. All these components are the supports of the divinities in the outer reaches of Tsochok's entourage. Constructions resembling this outer support, sometimes known as "bird perches" (*jadang*),[9] are described in older Bon texts and feature in increasingly rare rituals for the propitiation of war gods, independently of any tantric ritual context. Clearly, the cult of Tsochok is a fusion of tantra with the divinities and associated rituals of indigenous divinities who have nothing to do with Buddhism but have been integrated into the complex of Yungdrung Bon.

Further Reading

Blezer, Henk. 2000. "The '*Bon' dBal-mo Nyer-bdun* (*/brgyad*) and the Buddhist *dBang-phyug-ma Nyer-brgyad*." In *New Horizons in Bon Studies: Proceedings of a Conference Held in Osaka, August 1999*, edited by Samten Karmay and Yasuhiko Nagano, 117–80. Osaka: National Museum of Ethnology.

Kvaerne, Per. 1990. "A Preliminary Study of the Bonpo Divinity Khro bo gTso mchog mkha' 'gying." In *Reflections on Tibetan Culture: Essays in Memory of Turrell V. Wylie*, edited by Lawrence Epstein and Richard F. Sherburne, 117–25. Lewiston, NY: Edwin Mellen Press.

Kvaerne, Per. 1995. *The Bon Religion of Tibet: The Iconography of a Living Tradition.* London: Serindia.

Notes

1 Kvaerne 1995, 9–10.

2 For a justification of the use of the term "pagan" in this context, see Ramble 1998, 124.

3 For two studies of the iconography of Tsochok Khagying based on a thangka and scriptural accounts, see Kvaerne 1990 and 1995. For a description of another thangka of this divinity, see A. Heller 2015, 225–32.

4 Note that the third of the Nine Zema, a "black female with the head of a chough, holding a claw," who would have been identified in the thangka as F3, has been omitted by the artist.

5 Tsochok is the main divinity in certain elaborate Bonpo rituals in which both he and members of his entourage are represented by masked dancers. For a film of one such performance from Mustang, in Nepal, see https://youtu.be/SqjN_owRXls.

6 Blezer 2000, 121.

7 For a reproduction of the mandala of Trowo Tsochok Khagying, see Namdak, Nagano, and Tachikawa 2000, 43.

8 Diagrams and a description of this construction are given in Tshangs pa bstan 'dzin et al. 2014, 16–20.

9 A description of a *jadang* and associated rituals is given in Lcags mo mtsho, n.d. I am grateful to Lcags mo mtsho, of the Northwest Minorities University, Lanzhou, for permitting me to consult and refer to this unpublished work.

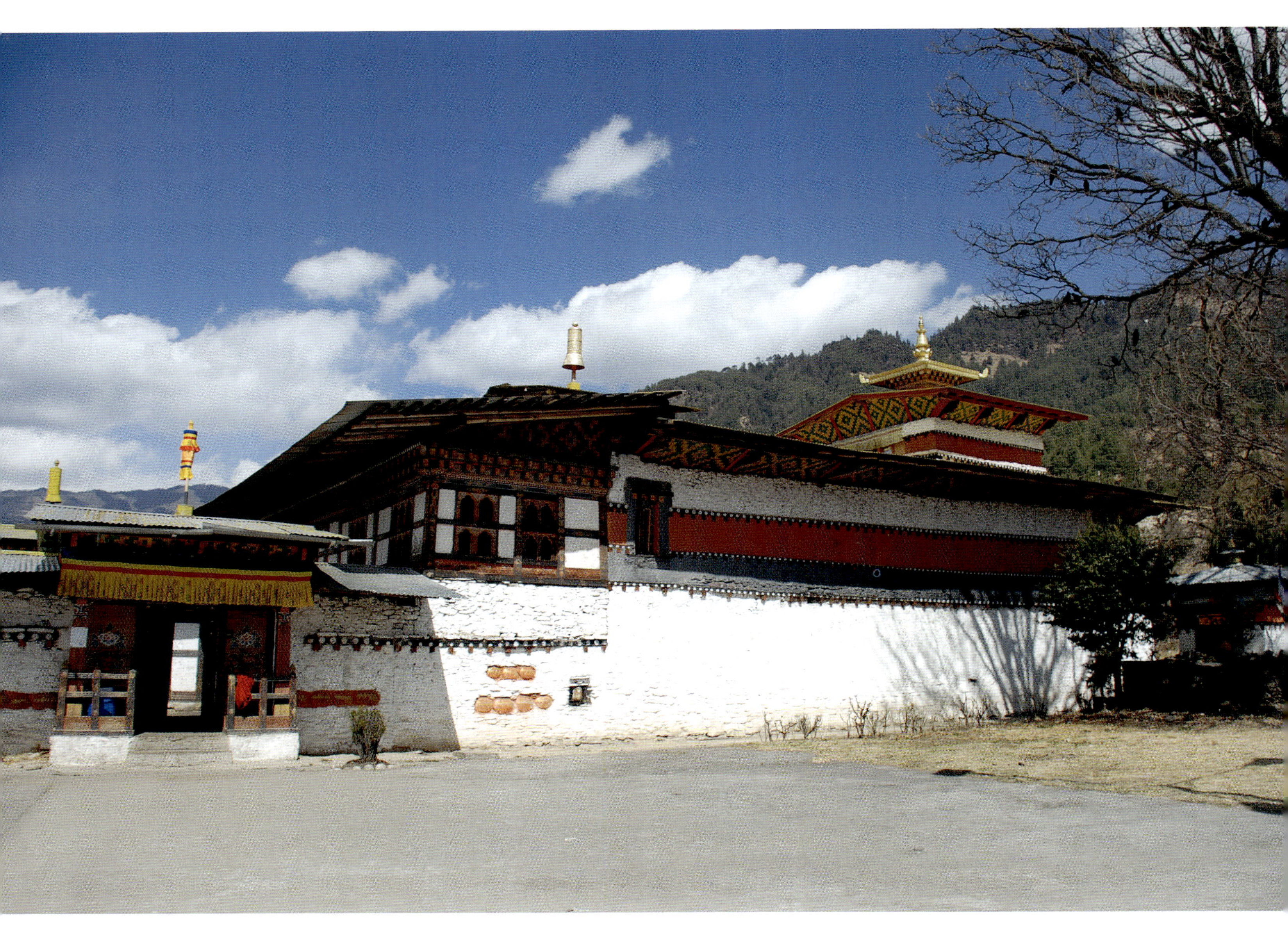

№ 61

Tamshing Temple

Bumthang District, Bhutan, 1501–1505

A Bhutanese Buddhist Master's Treasure House

ARIANA MAKI

In 1476, at the age of twenty-six, a blacksmith was foraging for mushrooms in the forest when he paused to rest. A monk wearing tattered robes awakened him, handing him a scroll with instructions to visit a nearby cliff on an upcoming full-moon night. After some consideration, the man decided to go. He arrived at the cliff edge, which overlooked a deep riverine pool. Suddenly overcome, the man plunged into the water and reemerged holding a chest he had retrieved from a submerged cave. This marked the first of scores of such discoveries he would make throughout Bhutan and southern Tibet, and he would ultimately become known as Pema Lingpa (1450–1521), one of the Five Great Treasure Revealers of the Ancient (Nyingma) tradition. His appearance in the world had been prophesied by the Indian master Padmasambhava (ca. eighth century).

See Padmasambhava and His Manifestations, no. 43.

For more on *terma*, see *Dorje* Discovered by Dorje Lingpa, no. 51.

As Pema Lingpa continued to reveal hidden treasures (*terma*), he also accrued more patrons and greater renown, and his sphere of influence expanded far beyond his birthplace in Bumthang's Tang Valley, reaching well into the Lhodrak region of southern Tibet, where he gave numerous teachings and conducted initiations and rituals. After nearly a quarter century of accumulating treasures and offerings, and despite having given away many tangible objects to his disciples, he shared in his autobiography that he still had significant holdings. In his words, "I realized that [having received] so many alms, I should assemble the necessary things to make a shrine."[1] The text describes his subsequent discussions with the local leader, wherein they came to an agreement on who would provide the labor. The local leader suggested a building site, saying, "Tamshing offers a good place for the consecration. The ground in front of it is a good place for horse races."[2] Local tradition attributes another actor in the temple's founding—the enlightened female deity Dorje Pakmo, who is believed to have manifested as a sow that began rooting in the ground, turning the earth to indicate where the temple cornerstone was to be placed.[3]

The foundation was laid in the female iron bird year (1501), and the temple would become the seat of Pema Lingpa's activities for the rest of his life. Tamshing serves as a storehouse for his legacy—it consolidates *terma* he withdrew from around the region, displays mural paintings of powerful deities unique to his tradition, holds sculptures consecrated with sacred substances provided by the master himself, and hosts ritual dance performances he received through visions. Local oral tradition maintains that his arm span was used as the building's unit of standard measurement, so that the structure itself reflects his physical proportions and, by extension, his continual presence within it.

Pema Lingpa's autobiography describes the artists commissioned to provide the temple's paintings and sculptures. The sculptor Lama Chogyam is credited with shaping statues in the ground floor shrine and inserting consecratory materials such as precious and semiprecious stones, medicinal herbs, and coins, while Pema Lingpa consecrated the main image, a skyward-gazing Padmasambhava. His biography lists over a dozen objects—among them texts, small sculptures, relics of other Buddhist masters, and pieces of clothing from Padmasambhava and his consort Yeshe Tsogyel—that he inserted within the sculpture.[4] Among the consecratory objects were *terma* that he had extracted locally as well as farther afield, for example, from Samye in central Tibet. Pema Lingpa is also credited with sculpting a self-portrait currently housed in Tamshing's upper story. By consolidating the treasures that he withdrew from throughout the region, Pema Lingpa was demonstrating his sphere of influence while also supporting his claims to legitimacy, as the objects directly connect him with the activities he undertook at many important sites.

Tamshing Lhundrub Choling Temple; Bumthang District, Bhutan; founded 1501, consecrated 1505; photograph by Ariana Maki

Pema Lingpa's autobiography describes the temple as a "palace of images" and the murals of the courtyard as the respective realms of the deities and masters depicted, imagery that he states is being

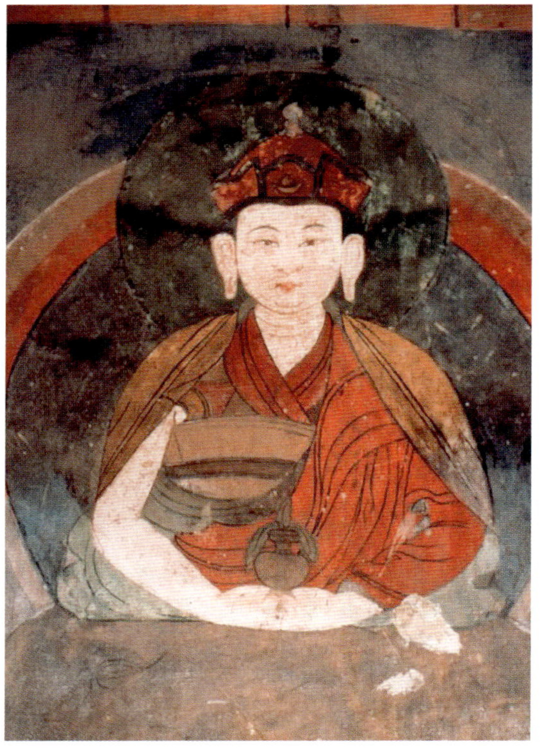

Detail of Pema Lingpa (1450–1521); Bhutan; date unknown; mural; dimensions unknown; photograph by Françoise Pommaret

provided to adherents to support their eventual liberation from the cycle of death and rebirth.[5] Multiple artists, including Tshepa Tshering, Kharwa Tshering, and Kuntrey, are credited with drawing and painting the murals, using pigments and materials that were gifts from Tibetans, including the Seventh Karmapa, Chodrak Gyatso.[6] Quite unusually, Pema Lingpa relates that he inserted consecratory scrolls into the plaster upon which the assembly hall murals were painted, an act rarely attested in the history of Himalayan architecture.[7] For followers, his vivifying the wall paintings and consolidating important treasures inside sculptures exponentially increases their spiritual power and efficacy.

The consecrated murals line the walls of the sutra courtyard, where monks and patrons assemble to receive the master's teachings. Originally painted between 1503 and 1505, the compositions provide their intended viewers—initiates into Pema Lingpa's tradition—with content Pema Lingpa selected, and may reflect what he considered the most salient practices from his teachings. Protective figures appear at the beginning and end of the circumambulatory path. Pilgrims enter and move clockwise past the first protective figures before turning right, where they encounter a mural of an enthroned Pema Lingpa surrounded by his previous incarnations. Following are successive compositions dedicated to the Seventh Karmapa Chodrak Gyatso (1454–1506), Yeshe Tsogyel (ca. eighth century), Padmasambhava (ca. eighth century), Garab Dorje (dates uknown), and Buddha Vajradhara, who together constitute an extremely condensed lineage of Great Perfection transmissions. The next subset of images begins with Vajrasattva, a deity whose practice is a purificatory step made prior to undertaking higher-level meditations. Following are the Five Buddha Families—Amoghasiddhi, Amitabha, Ratnasambhava, Vairochana, and Akshobhya—and a composition depicting the primordial buddha of the Nyingma tradition, Samantabhadra, in union with his consort Samantabhadri. This grouping provides initiates with a condensed map of the qualities that must be fully realized in order to experience enlightenment. In short, initiates may undertake the preparatory Vajrasattva practice prior to meditations associated with the Five Buddha Families, each of which provides avenues to cultivate specific insights and overcome particular obstacles, a process intended to facilitate higher levels of awareness. Should the meditators completely master all aspects of these practices, their nature becomes indistinguishable from that of the primordial Buddhas Samantabhadra and Samantabhadri; in other words, they reach enlightenment. This wall, therefore, provides initiates with both an accounting of Pema Lingpa's spiritual lineage and a path toward higher accomplishment.

For more on Great Perfection (Dzogchen), see Lukhang Murals, no. 80.

For other examples representing the qualities, in parallel to the Five Buddhas, see Chakrasamvara Mandala with Newar Donors, no. 29; Mandala of Manjuvajra of the *Vajravali* Set, no 50.

At this point, visitors may enter the main shrine or continue along the circumambulation path that passes around and behind it. The murals along the path show the sixteen arhats, their attendants, and the Seven Universal Buddhas, some of which reveal overpainting. Visitors emerge on the opposite side of the sutra hall, where the mural compositions include practices unique to Pema Lingpa's tradition. He described the paintings' creation in his autobiography, referring to several compositions as "heavens":[8]

For more on arhats, see Arhats Viewing a Painting of Birds by the Tenth Karmapa, no. 72.

> The lines [for the paintings] were added to the left side of the sutra hall. Senior artist Tshering began making the arrangement of the newly arisen [images]: the Buddhas of the Three Times, the heaven of the Great Compassionate One, the Lamp that Dispels Darkness. Starting from there [successively are] the Highest and Most Secret Buddha of Long Life, [and] the Highest and Most Secret Horse-headed One. After that, peaceful Samantabhadra with consort and the forty-two deities of [the mandala], the landscape of the Five Blood-drinking Heruka Families, [then, further is] Highest and Most Secret Vajra-holder. Then is the heaven of the Gentle-voiced

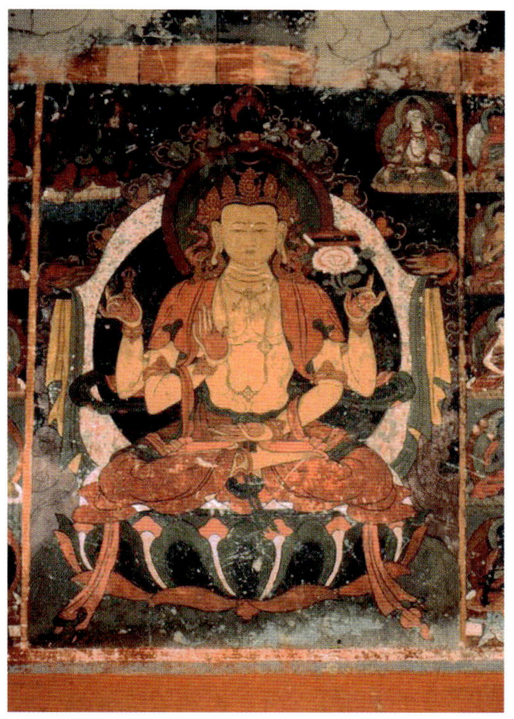

Prajnaparamita; Tamshing Lhundrub Choling Temple, Bumthang District, Bhutan; 1503–1505 with potential later interventions; mural; dimensions unknown; photograph by Françoise Pommaret

> One and his retinue, the Perfection of Wisdom, and the rest of the paradises of the Buddhas of the ten directions, and the Indestructible Dagger, the Most Secret and Unsurpassed Kila, with ten wrathful ones encircling [him].[9]

Ranging from exoteric (Manjushri and Prajnaparamita) to esoteric (deities in union), this side of the hall illustrates practices aimed at higher levels of accomplishment alongside those that provide protection, remove obstacles, and help navigate the state between death and rebirth. As a whole, the sutra hall mural program fulfills multiple functions: it ensures protection of the teachings, establishes sacred space, situates Pema Lingpa within the Nyingma tradition, and provides initiates with tools to address everyday concerns and enhanced practice. Pema Lingpa's autobiography attests that he selected the murals' content, carefully recording their creation along with his intent that they support generations of Buddhist adherents.

Throughout his life, even as Tamshing and its images were being created, Pema Lingpa continued to be called by his patrons nearby and farther afield to give initiations, conduct rituals, oversee funerals, and resolve disputes. With numerous demands on his time, Pema Lingpa consolidated many of his treasures and teachings at Tamshing, thereby providing future generations of adherents with a continual source of blessings, and scholars with a body of texts, objects, and images that offer a window into his motivations and intent. In 1521, after decades of activities throughout the region, Pema Lingpa passed away at Tamshing. In the late seventeenth century, many of his practices were incorporated into official Bhutanese state monastic curricula, including dances and rituals that continue to be performed throughout the country and beyond, reflecting the fact that Pema Lingpa's legacy has disseminated far beyond the walls of his home temple.

Further Reading

Gayley, Holly. 2007. "Patterns in the Ritual Dissemination of Padma Gling pa's Treasures." In *Bhutan: Traditions and Changes. PIATS 2003: Proceedings of the Tenth Seminar of the International Association for Tibetan Studies, Oxford 2003*, edited by John A. Ardussi and Françoise Pommaret, 97–120. Brill's Tibetan Studies Library 10/5. Leiden: Brill.

Harding, Sarah, trans. 2003. *The Life and Revelations of Pema Lingpa*. Ithaca, NY: Snow Lion.

Phuntsho, Karma. 2008. "Ogyen Pema Lingpa (1450–1521), His Life and Legacy." In *The Dragon's Gift: The Sacred Arts of Bhutan*, edited by Terese Tse Bartholomew and John Johnston, 66–77. Exhibition catalog. Honolulu and Chicago: Honolulu Academy of Arts in association with Serindia.

Notes

1. Phuntsho 2015, 210. See also a translation offered in Aris 1988, 33.
2. Phuntsho 2015, 210. See also Aris 1988, 33.
3. This event is regularly reenacted in a ritual dance called the Phag Cham during the temple's annual festival, the Tamshing Phala Choepa.
4. Phuntsho 2015, 215–16.
5. Aris 1988, 33.
6. Phuntsho 2015, 215–16. See also Aris 1988, 37.
7. Phuntsho 2015, 215.
8. In his autobiography, Pema Lingpa refers to the compositions as *zhing bkod* and *zhing khams*, which have an "otherworldly" sense of "buddha-field," "heaven," or "Buddha realm," as well as more "this-worldly" terms like *logs ris* (mural).
9. Phuntsho 2015, 216. See also Aris 1988, 36.

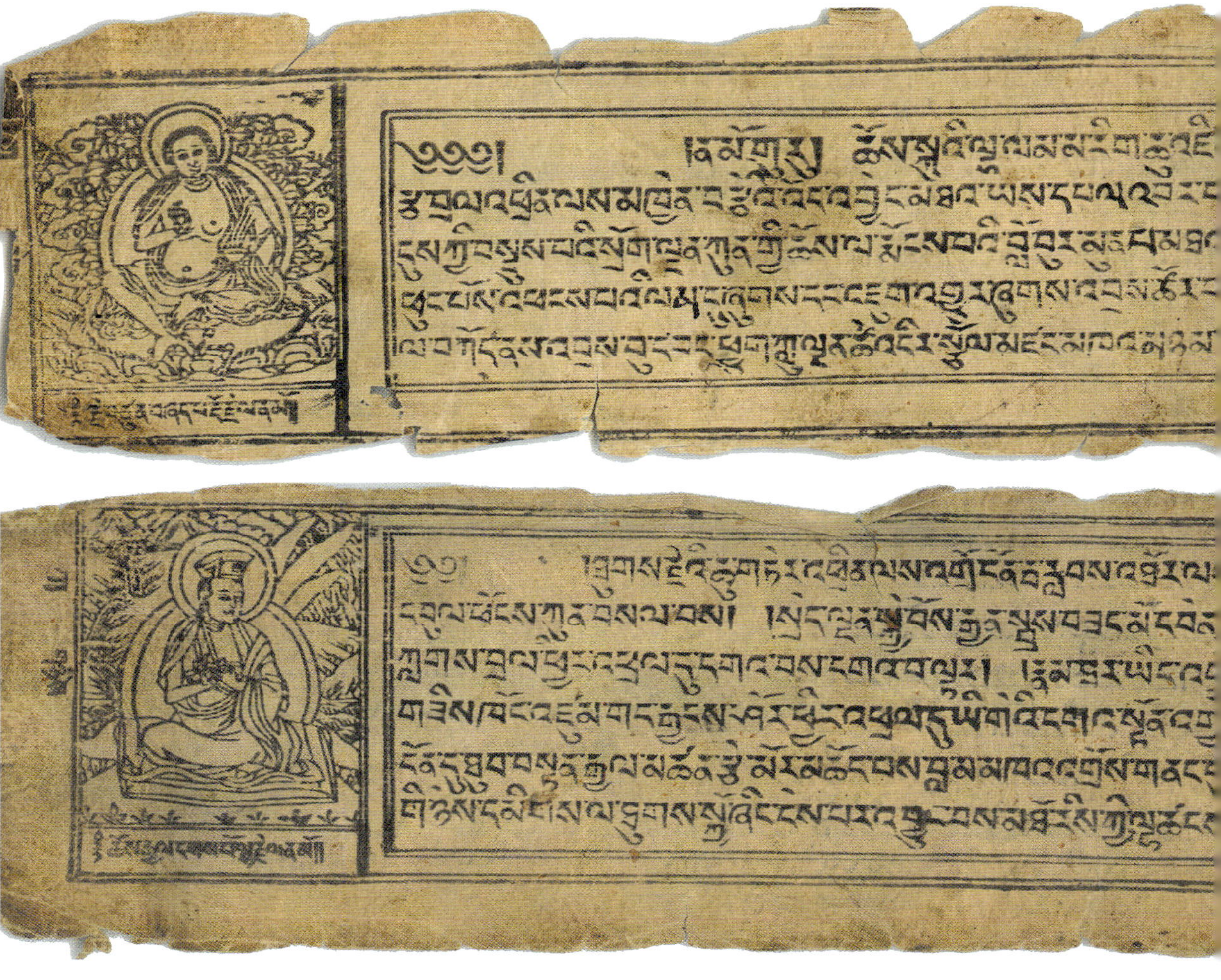

Nº 62

Earliest Extant Printed Edition of Milarepa's Life Story

Ron Wosel Puk, southwest Tibet, 1538

A Tibetan Liberation Tale Illustrated in Print and Manuscript

ANDREW QUINTMAN

Few religious figures have left as indelible a mark on the landscapes of Himalayan religion as Milarepa (ca. 1028–1111), the eleventh-century Tibetan saint acclaimed for his prowess in meditation and his poetic expressions of spiritual attainment.[1] The stories of his life, together with those describing the activities of the Indian tantric master Padmasambhava (ca. eighth century), transformed the contours of Buddhist practice, literature, and geography on both sides of the Himalayas. While accounts of Milarepa's deeds proliferated in the centuries after his death, the best-known version appeared only in the late fifteenth century through the compositions of Tsangnyon Heruka (1452–1507), the so-called Madman of Tsang. These singular works, known as *The Life of Milarepa* and *The Hundred Thousand Songs of Milarepa*, describe the yogin's childhood crimes of revenge, his repentance and search for a Buddhist master, his renunciation and solitary meditation retreats, and his eventual awakening and teaching through song. Together, these texts established a model for an exemplary spiritual life across the Himalayan world, one that emphasized devotion to the guru, dedication to solitary meditation, and perseverance through adversity. "Mi la" was his clan name; "repa" refers to the cotton robe worn by meditators in the high Himalayan region. The very name Milarepa thus marks his status as a religious virtuoso. *The Life of Milarepa* remains one of Tibet's most beloved narratives and arguably its most famous book.

See Padmasambhava and His Manifestations, no. 43.

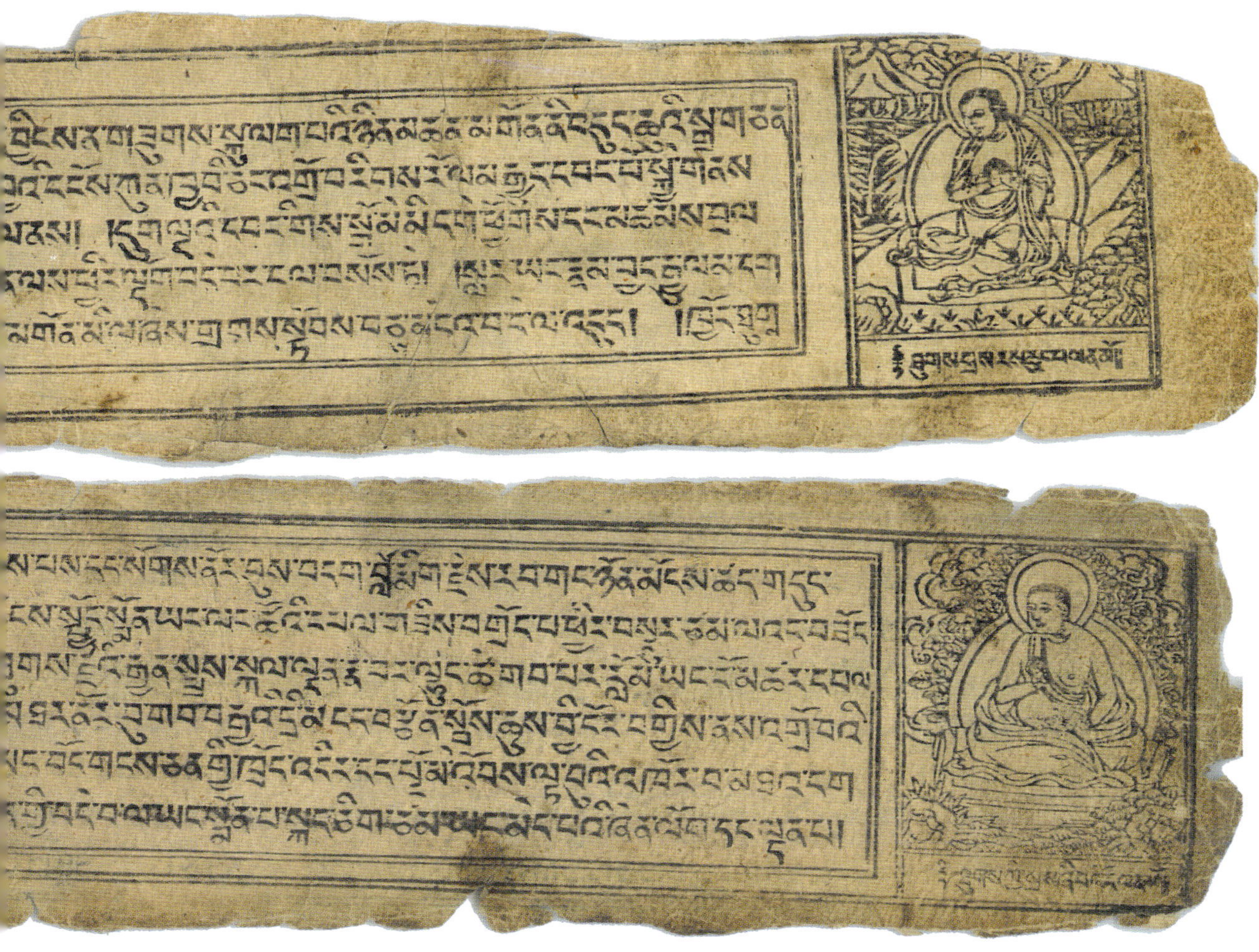

First two folios from *The Life of Milarepa*; Ron Wosel Puk, Tibet; 1538; xylographic print on paper; each approx. 3⅛ × 17¼ in. (8 × 44 cm); image after *A Brief Survey of the Evolution of Tibetan Printing Technology (Bod kyi shing spar lag rtsal gyi byung rim mdor bsdus)*, Bod ljongs bod yig dpe rnying dpe skrun khang, 2013

The stories of Milarepa's life record a tale of human pathos, transgression, transformation, and accomplishment on a grand scale. He was born to a wealthy family in the border region of Mangyul Gungtang on the cusp of a Buddhist renaissance in Tibet. His father died suddenly while Milarepa was still a child, leading a greedy aunt and uncle to steal his rightful patrimony, and thrusting the child, together with his mother and sister, into a life of poverty and servitude. At his mother's behest, Milarepa sought teachers of hail-casting and black magic in order to exact revenge on their avaricious relatives. His success in these pursuits led to the desolation of his ancestral village and the murder of more than three dozen people. Milarepa came to recognize the weight of his misdeeds, leading him to pursue Buddhist instruction and practice under the guidance of the acclaimed translator Marpa Chokyi Lodro (ca. 1012–1097). This guru, known equally for his great learning and short temper, subjected Milarepa to intense physical trials, such as constructing immense stone towers. Such activities were later revealed to be a method for purifying his past negative deeds. Milarepa eventually dedicated himself to extended meditation retreats and spent the remainder of his life wandering among solitary locations, teaching small groups of disciples through the medium of spiritual poems and songs of realization. Details of these encounters constitute *The Hundred Thousand Songs*.

Editions of the *Life* and *Songs* of Milarepa spread widely as both manuscripts and xylographic prints made from engraved woodblocks. Influential Mahayana Buddhist works such as the *Lotus Sutra* extoll the benefits of reproducing sacred texts, and this sentiment is echoed in the closing lines of *The Life of Milarepa*:

> Seeing the Life, one is freed from the eight worldly concerns.
> May it serve a feast for renunciates who've relinquished attachments.
>
> Hearing the Life, faith arises all on its own.
> May it serve a feast for the fortunate endowed with good karma.

Recollecting the Life, entanglements are forcefully severed.
May it serve a feast for the omniscient, accomplished in this life.

Touching the Life, the two aims are spontaneously achieved.
May it serve a feast for doctrine holders who benefit beings.

Preserving the Life, the intent of the lineage is realized.
May it serve a feast for lineage holders who practice their master's command.[2]

Print Editions of Milarepa's Life

See A *Pancharaksha* Print from Khara-Khoto, no. 32; Nartang Woodblock Prints and Their Painted Copies, no. 81; Panoramic Map of Mount Wutai, no. 91.

Woodblock printing originated in China during the seventh century, and by the twelfth and thirteenth centuries the first printed Tibetan materials had begun to appear in Khara-Khoto, Turfan, and eventually Beijing and elsewhere.[3] Yet, when Tsangnyon Heruka prepared the first xylographic edition of Milarepa's life in the late fifteenth century, print technology was still relatively new in central Tibet. Such projects were often major economic enterprises, requiring massive investments of capital, labor, and raw materials such as wood, paper, and ink. Tsangnyon Heruka overcame such obstacles with great difficulty, and his work represents a major innovation for the literary tradition of Milarepa's life.[4] For the first time, the narratives could be printed and disseminated in large quantities at relatively high speed. The combination of broad patronage and rapid and widespread distribution led, in part, to the ubiquity of his accounts.

The original xylograph edition has not yet come to light. The folios here present the first two pages from the earliest extant print edition of *The Life of Milarepa*, from Wosel Puk, a site associated with Milarepa's acclaimed disciple Rechungpa (1085–1161) near the village of Ron in the Gungtang Valley. This version was prepared under the direction of the Madman's disciple Tokden Chokyi Gyatso (sixteenth century). A print of the companion volume of the *Hundred Thousand Songs of Milarepa* was completed several years later.[5]

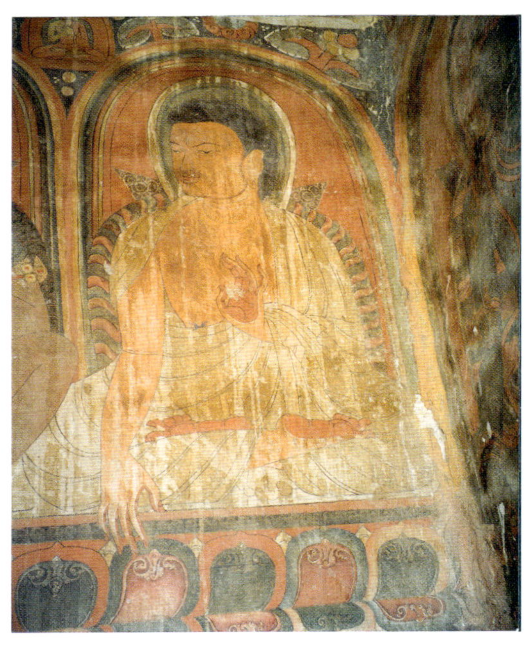

Milarepa (ca. 1028–1111); "Milarepa's Tower," Sekar Gutok, Lhodrak, southern Tibet; 1200–1250; color pigments on substrate; approx. 30 × 48 in. (76.2 × 122 cm); photograph by Andrew Quintman, 1994

As is common in many block-print editions, the text opens with illustrations in the left and right margins depicting the lineage of disciples descending from Milarepa, together with a short prayer of homage. In the upper left is Milarepa, identified by his honorific title and tantric initiation name Jetsun Zhepa Dorje. The images continue with the "heart disciple" Rechungpa (upper right), the Doctor from Dakpo (Dakpo Lhaje), better known as Gampopa (1079–1153) (lower left), and heart disciple Zhiwa Wo (lower right). All four figures are depicted in the gesture of teaching. Milarepa, Rechungpa, and Zhiwa Wo each wear the simple robe and meditation belt of an ascetic yogin, while Gampopa appears in more formal robes, reflecting his former status as an ordained Buddhist monk. Milarepa's two principal disciples—Gampopa and Rechungpa—are seated before the mountain peaks that served as preferred retreat locations for Milarepa's followers. The text concludes with two dharma protectors, four-armed Mahakala and Remati, who remain closely associated with the Kagyu tradition that stemmed from Milarepa. Representations of Milarepa in this fashion, seated with hands in the gestures of meditation or teaching, were common in early depictions, such as the painting in Sekar Gutok, perhaps the earliest extant mural portrait of Milarepa, preserved in the tower he famously constructed at his guru's command. Here, he is seated on a lotus throne, draped in the white cotton robe of an ascetic meditator, his hands in the gestures of teaching and touching the earth.

We might compare these depictions to those found in another reprint edition of Milarepa's *Life* and *Songs*, produced about a decade and a half later (between 1550 and 1555) by the Madman's disciple Lhatsun Rinchen Namgyel (1473–1557). These were prepared at the hermitage known as Drakkar Taso (White Rock Horse Tooth), situated high above the river valley in the Mangyul Gungtang Corridor. This site began as one of Milarepa's primary retreats, where he famously turned green from eating nothing but nettle porridge for many years. Drakkar Taso would become a small but influential monastery (and later, a nunnery) together with a printery. The Drakkar Taso print edition of the *Hundred Thousand Songs* depicts Milarepa

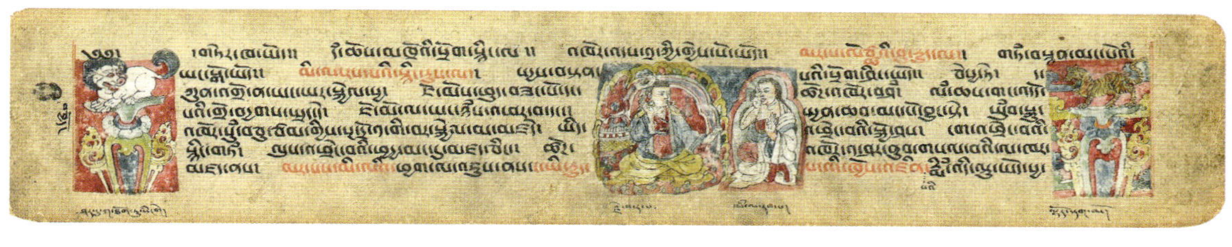

The Black Treasury Manuscript, Dream of the Four Pillars; Tibet; 16th century; ink and colored pigment on paper; each 4⅜ × 17¼ in. (8 × 42.5 cm); Tibet Museum/Fondation Alan Bordier, Gruyères, Switzerland; ABS 039

in a new way, forming what would become the yogin's most recognizable posture: legs loosely crossed, left hand in his lap holding a skull cup, and holding his right hand to his ear in a gesture of singing.[6] (A print edition from ten years earlier produced at Lande Langpuk to the south of Drakkar Taso depicts Milarepa with this singing gesture, but in this depiction he holds his left hand aloft).

Depictions of this classic hand-to-ear gesture are not witnessed prior to Tsangnyon Heruka's publication, and the Madman likely played a role in disseminating it for the first time. In the centuries that followed, however, this would become a distinguishing and widely recognized feature of Milarepa's iconography, replicated in text illustrations, scroll paintings, murals, and statues.

Milarepa in Illustrated Manuscripts

New xylographic editions of Milarepa's *Life* and *Songs* multiplied in the centuries that followed, with woodblock sets carved at nearly two dozen sites spanning western, central, and eastern Tibet, as well as Bhutan and Beijing. Although printed versions of these works would predominate, a culture of manuscript production continued to thrive. Some manuscripts were copies of the Madman's print undertaken as a pious act of merit-making. Others preserved works that predate Tsangnyon Heruka's version, and these were frequently illustrated with vignettes of Milarepa's activities and his disciples. The most widely illustrated Milarepa manuscripts belong to a cycle of texts informally known as the Black Treasury, named after a temple and repository built by the Karmapas in southern Tibet.[7] In one version, Milarepa is seated before his guru Marpa the Translator as he recounts a prophetic vision known as the Dream of the Four Pillars. A manuscript copy of the so-called *Twelve Great Disciples*, among the earliest Black Treasury texts, takes a different approach to illustrating Milarepa's life. Here, characters from the story move across and through the text, creating an integrated textual and visual narrative.

Further Reading

Quintman, Andrew, trans. 2010. *The Life of Milarepa*. New York: Penguin Classics.

Quintman, Andrew. 2014b. *The Yogin and the Madman: Reading the Biographical Corpus of Tibet's Great Saint Milarepa*. New York: Columbia University Press.

Stagg, Christopher, trans. 2016. *The Hundred Thousand Songs of Milarepa*. Boulder, CO: Shambhala.

Notes

1 Determining firm dates for Milarepa's birth and death has proved a vexing issue for both premodern Tibetan authors and contemporary scholars of Tibet. The dates used in this essay (1028–1111) follow prominent scholars of Milarepa's own Kagyu tradition, such as Situ Panchen Chokyi Jungne (1700–1774) and Katok Rigzin Tsewang Norbu (1698–1775). For an analysis of the complexities of Milarepa's dates, see Quintman 2013.

2 Milarepa, quoted in Quintman 2010, 233–34.

3 On the history, materials, techniques, and economics of woodblock printing in Tibet, see Dungkar and Tsering 2014; Helman-Ważny 2014; Diemberger, Ehrhard, and Kornicki 2016. For a survey of Tibetan book culture more broadly, see Schaeffer 2009.

4 On the creation of the first xylographic edition of the *Life* and *Songs*, see Quintman 2014b, esp. 125–34.

5 See Sernesi 2011; Ehrhard and Sernesi 2019.

6 Some interesting discrepancies in this first folio appear in the Drakkar Taso print held at the British Library (OPB 19999a3) and the one microfilmed by the Nepal German Manuscript Preservation Project (NGMPP Reel nos. L250/8–L251/1). These require further investigation.

7 On the Black Treasury text tradition, see Quintman 2014b, esp. chap. 3.

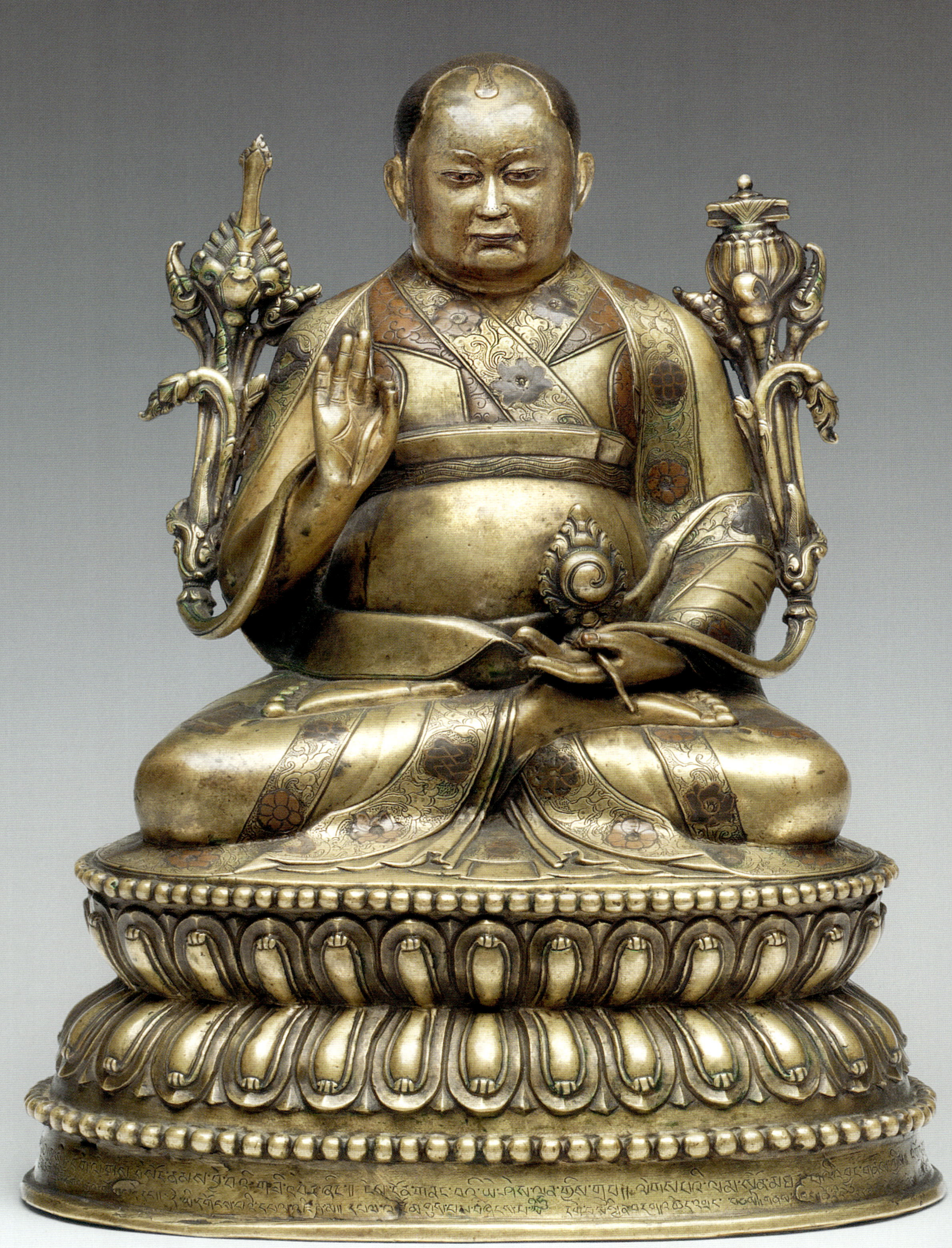

№ 63

Portrait of Lowo Khenchen Sonam Lhundrub

Mustang, Nepal, first half of the 16th century

A Royal Teacher and an Artist

JOWITA KRAMER AND CHRISTIAN LUCZANITS

A PRINCE OF THE RULING HOUSE OF LOWO (or Mustang) in the Nepalese-Tibetan borderlands, Lowo Khenchen Sonam Lhundrub (1456–1532) was a prominent teacher of the Sakya, one of the four main traditions of Tibetan Buddhism. The span of his life saw not only the heyday of scholasticism in fifteenth-century Tibet but also the apogee of his family's power in Mustang, situated on an important north-south salt route connecting the high-altitude plateau of Tibet with the northern Indian plains. Personifying both scholasticism and royalty, portraits of Lowo Khenchen are unusually abundant, in both Western collections and his home region of Mustang, and many are of high artistic quality. The portrait presented here even records the name of the artist responsible for the work.

Royal Scholar

In his autobiography, Lowo Khenchen links the origins of his family to the nomadic tribes of the Khyungpo clan in the northern plains of Tibet called Jangtang. The royal line of the family, which continues to the present day, was established in the early fifteenth century by Lowo Khenchen's grandfather, the fort commander (*dzongpon*) Amapel (1380–ca. 1440).

Lowo Khenchen was the third son of the ruler Amgon Zangpo (b. 1420) and his wife Pelkyong. While his brothers were raised to engage in worldly affairs, Lowo Khenchen was designated from birth for a religious career. Already at the age of one, he took refuge with his early teacher Jamyang Sherab Gyatso and received his first empowerments and transmissions of Buddhist teachings.[1] In his eleventh year he received his novice ordination and soon after began a six-year study of Buddhist discipline (*vinaya*) and philosophy. During these years he also came into contact with works of Sakya Pandita (1182–1251), one of the greatest figures of the Sakya tradition, and he developed a special devotion toward this master. In 1477 Lowo Khenchen received his full ordination from his teacher Kunga Wangchuk and was subsequently appointed abbot of the Tubten Dargye Ling Monastery of Mustang, which had more than one thousand monks at that time.

Lowo Khenchen was a prolific writer, and his collected works run to more than three hundred titles. His main contributions to Tibetan scholasticism were his commentaries on Sakya Pandita's major works. He also composed biographies, histories, praises, and manuals for rituals and meditative practice. Of particular interest are his writings that bear witness to the schism within the Sakya tradition caused by Shakya Chokden's composition of some provocative questions concerning one of Sakya Pandita's works.

In 1505 the region of Mustang and the whole western Himalayas were shaken by a great earthquake, which destroyed not only the natural environment but also many monasteries. Lowo Khenchen spent some of the following years in central Tibet, where he taught and wrote several of his works. In 1532 he passed away at Samdrub Ling Monastery in Mustang, where he had spent the last years of his life.

Royal Portrait

This portrait shows the scholar in the most frequently encountered form, as a corpulent, middle-aged master with distinct facial features and a rather stern expression. In the portrait Lowo Khenchen performs the gesture of argumentation (*vitarka* mudra) with the right hand while the left rests at the lap. Both hands also hold the stem of a flower, the blossoms of which carry a sword and a book, the symbols of the bodhisattva of wisdom, Manjushri. They thus signify his status as a major Buddhist scholar.

Namkha Drak (western Tibet, fl. first half of 16th century); Portrait of Lowo Khenchen Sonam Lhundrub; Mustang, Nepal, first half of 16th century; copper alloy with copper and silver inlays; 11¼ × 8⅜ × 6½ in. (28.6 × 21.3 × 16.5 cm); Philadelphia Museum of Art; Purchased with the Stella Kramrisch Fund, 2003; 2003-6-1; photograph courtesy Philadelphia Museum of Art

Further, a large flaming gem is placed on the palm of the left hand, representing the wish-fulfilling gem.

The two-line poetic inscription on the base of the bronze has been translated as follows:

> *Svasti*! With billions of shimmering merits and excellent virtues, he spontaneously accomplished the wisdom that bestows ultimate truth. I bow down to the excellent teacher, the source of liberation, who sets all migratory beings in a state of exalted wealth.
>
> The unequaled guru Manjushri, the Protector of the World [Avalokiteshvara], and the Vajra Holder [Vajrapani] are the body, speech, and mind of all the Victorious Ones, who have taken the form of this image.
>
> As for Tri Songdetsen's activities in the past, they too are being upheld in this day and age, by the descendant of Amapel, the foremost ruler of men and minister.[2]
>
> The one [named] Tsewang Gyelpo, whose aspirations [were fulfilled by] his glorious spouse Peldzom, commissioned [this image] respectfully.
>
> By this virtuous deed, may the benefactor together with his many relatives enjoy a long, healthy, and wealthy life for the time being, and, ultimately, attain perfect Buddhahood!
>
> The emanation artisan is Namkha Drak. May it be auspicious![3]

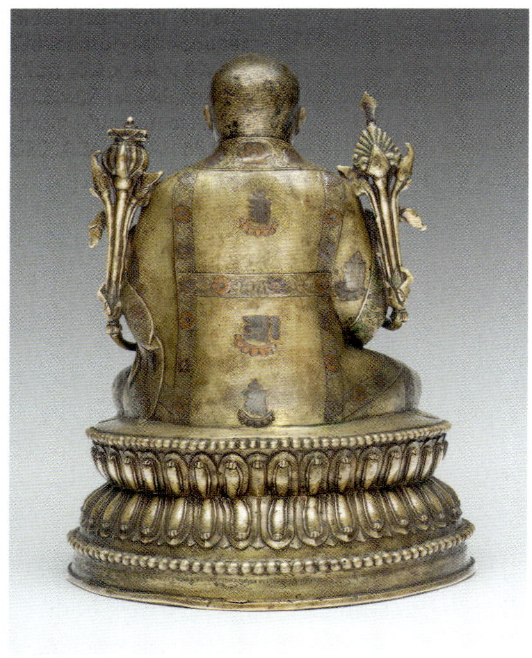

Namkha Drak (western Tibet, fl. first half of 16th century); Back of Portrait of Lowo Khenchen Sonam Lhundrub; Mustang, Nepal; Philadelphia Museum of Art; 2003-6-1; photograph courtesy Philadelphia Museum of Art

The inscription provides a good idea of the exalted position of the portrayed. It also fully accounts for the iconography, the gem standing for both wisdom and the royal origin of the depicted. While it is not entirely clear who the donors are, the spouse Peldzom commissioned the statue in commemoration of Tsewang Gyelpo, her late husband from a ruling family. Most remarkable is, however, the mention of the sculptor Namkha Drak, as the artists behind such works are rarely mentioned in a Tibetan context. The same name is mentioned in another bronze and in the records of a restoration of Khorchak Monastery in western Tibet.[4] Fine inlay work in copper and silver characterizes both bronzes, exemplified by the characters of the purification mantra *Om a hum* inlaid on the back, each resting on a copper lotus.

Precious Portraiture

It appears that in the late fifteenth and early sixteenth centuries, many portraits of religious masters were produced in Mustang, either as part of teaching transmission lineages or as stand-alone portraits of eminent local masters associated with the royal house. Thus, the richly inlaid sculptures, many of them depicting Lowo Khenchen, may well be the product of a regional workshop, as bronzes of this type are found in unusual abundance in Mustang.[5]

Many of the portraits of Lowo Khenchen can be recognized by his distinctive facial features. In fact, considering inscribed portraits only, his life can be followed from his appearance in his twenties to his seventies, the body becoming more corpulent, the hairline receding, and the facial features becoming increasingly stern.[6] There are also differences in facial expressions and hairline, not all featuring the central, increasingly thinner bush of hair. Depictions at earlier ages tend to show him with the hat of a scholar, while those of later years often feature the characteristic inlays. Further, work by several workshops can be distinguished. Given the abundance of the images, it seems that in the master's home region every wealthy household must have had a sculpture of this eminent royal scholar.

In contrast, most Tibetan portraiture was produced to depict oral teaching transmissions covering several centuries, and the actual features of many of the protagonists had long been lost by the time the lineages were created.[7] Thus, Tibetan masters are usually portrayed with indistinct idealized features in accordance with the representation of an awakened being. In such a case, the transmission of the teaching arguably is of greater import than the individual person transmitting it. The term "portrait," then,

See for example Portrait of the Ninth Karmapa, no. 66.

For likeness portraits, see Portrait of Situ Panchen, no. 83; The Qianlong Emperor as Manjushri-Chakravartin, no. 84.

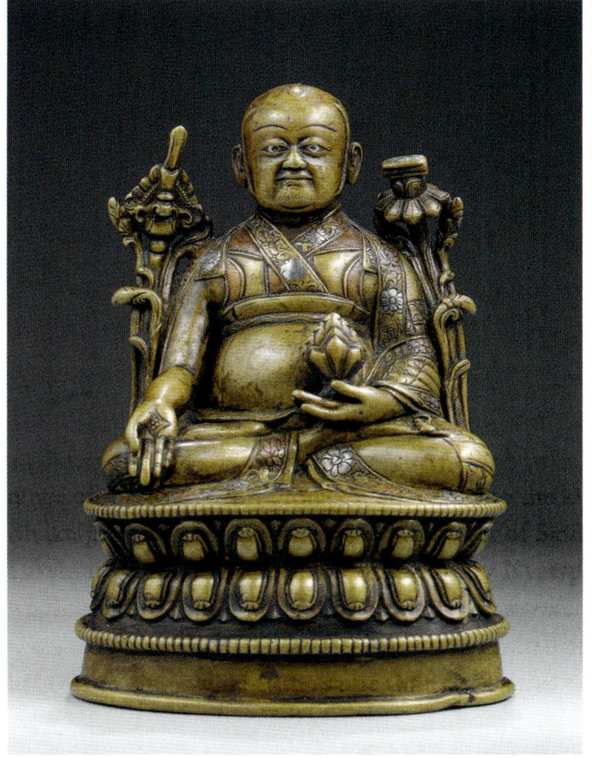

Uninscribed representation of Lowo Khenchen, identified on the basis of his distinct physical features and the workmanship; Lo (Mustang), Nepal; first half of 16th century; bronze with silver and red copper inlays; 4½ × 3⅛ × 2¼ in. (11.4 × 7.9 × 5.7 cm); Collection of Zhu Shijie 朱世杰; photograph © Bruce M. White, 2011

has a wide range of meanings in Tibet, among which likeness portraits, locally referred to as *ngadrama,* "looks like me," are rather rare.

Wider Context

Lowo's history was continually influenced by the political situation in the neighboring kingdoms of western Tibet (Ngari and parts of Tsang), which were closely interlinked with each other, not least through marriage alliances. The kingdoms of Guge, Purang, and Gungtang in western Tibet in particular were involved repeatedly in political conflicts with Mustang. Besides their political activities, the rulers of these kingdoms distinguished themselves as great supporters of Buddhism. Gungtang and Guge were both patrons of Lowo Khenchen, who gave teachings at their courts.

See Gyantse Kumbum, no. 55. For art in Guge, see Murals at Toling Dukhang, no. 54. For art in Lo, see the Chorten Cave of Luri, no. 44.

See Mandala of Manjuvajra of the *Vajravali* Set, no. 50.

Both the rivalries and the interconnection are also expressed in the Buddhist art of the time, each kingdom favoring styles that linked back to its own regional past. This is particularly apparent if one compares the art produced in the contemporaneous kingdoms of Gyantse, Guge and Lo (Mustang). The art of Mustang closely aligns with the development of Newar artisanship in south central Tibet (Tsang), a connection continually refreshed through invitations of master artists from the Kathmandu Valley. Literary accounts and inscriptions provide us with the names of a few such artists, but these are the exception rather than the rule.[8] Instead, we must assume that most of the art was produced by regional masters of considerable local fame, and Namkha Drak's name may have come down to us as he worked in both Guge and Mustang. The portrait of Lowo Khenchen, thus, is precious not only for its workmanship and likeness but also for offering a glimpse on how it came about.

Further Reading

Dinwiddie, Donald, ed. 2003. *Portraits of the Masters: Bronze Sculptures of the Tibetan Buddhist Lineages.* Chicago: Serindia.

Kramer, Jowita. 2008. *A Noble Abbot from Mustang: Life and Works of Glo-bo mKhan-chen (1456–1532).* Vienna: Arbeitskreis für Tibetische und Buddhistische Studien, Universität Wien.

Lo Bue, Erberto, ed. 2010b. *Wonders of Lo: The Artistic Heritage of Mustang.* Mumbai: Marg Foundation.

Notes

1 To take refuge indicates the ceremony of accepting the Buddhist way of life and the Three Jewels of the Buddha (the teacher), the Dharma (the Teachings), and the Sangha (Buddhist community) as the ultimate refuge and source of guidance.
2 Tri Songdetsen (742–ca. 800), one of the three Tibetan emperors who are considered emanations of bodhisattvas, in his case an emanation of Manjushri.
3 After Khokhlov and Laurent 2020, app. 1, with changes in formatting, the transcription of the names, the translation of untranslated terms as proposed in the respective footnote, and the translation of the auspicious formula at the end of the text.
4 Khokhlov and Laurent 2020 conclusively proposes that the copy of the three silver brothers at Khorchak Monastery in Purang, western Tibet, is the work of the same artist, who also worked at the monastery itself.
5 The documentation of these collections is part of an AHRC-funded research project, "Tibetan Buddhist Monastery Collections Today" (Grant Ref: AH/N00681X/1).
6 For published images of the master, see Dinwiddie 2003, nos. 75–77.
7 See Dinwiddie 2003 for a wide range of teacher portraits in Tibetan art.
8 Many of the artists' names are preserved at Gyantse; see Lo Bue 2000.

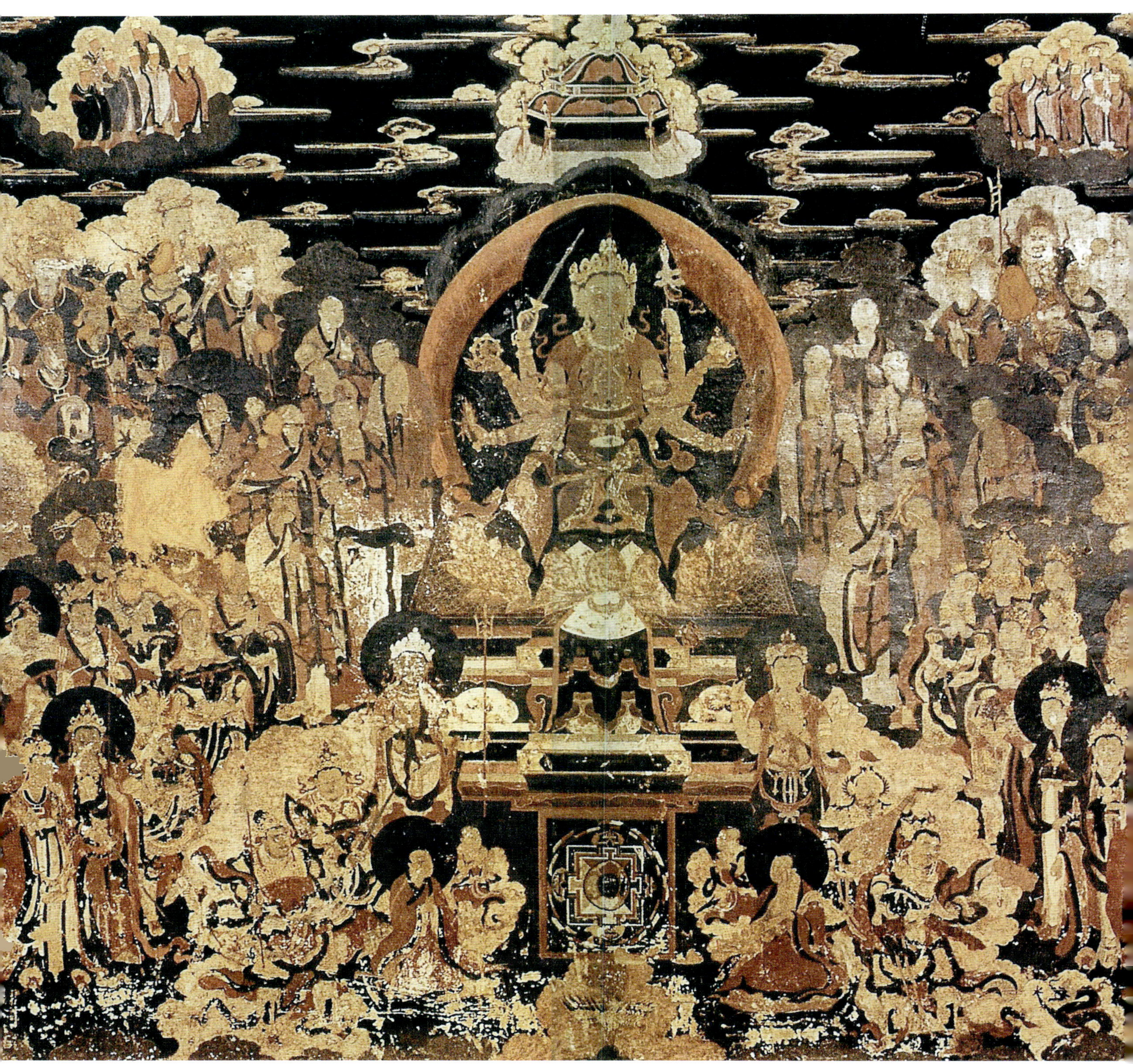

№ 64

Dabaojigong Temple

Lijiang, Yunnan Province, China, founded 1582

Agents of Religious and Artistic Dialogue along the Southern Sino-Tibetan Frontier

KARL DEBRECZENY

On Tanguts, see Achala Silk Tapestry, no. 36.

On Mongols, see Relief Carving of a Nine-Deity Ushnishavijaya Composition, no. 41; Vajrabhairava Mandala, no. 46; Juyong Guan Stupa Gate, no. 48.

On Manchus, see The Qianlong Emperor as Manjushri-Chakravartin, no. 84.

THIRD-PARTY INTERMEDIARIES, such as the Tangut, Mongol, and Manchu courts, often initiated intersections of Tibetan and Chinese religious and artistic culture. A similar pattern of patronage also took place on a smaller scale along the outer reaches of the Sino-Tibetan frontier. Dabaojigong is a small Buddhist temple located in Baisha Village, several miles outside of Lijiang in remote northwestern Yunnan Province, the southern meeting of Tibetan and Chinese areas.[1] The temple was built by the Naxi people, an ethnic group living in areas between Chinese and Tibetan regions that drew from both cultural spheres.[2] Dabaojigong is the earliest extant temple in Lijiang that gives evidence of a local workshop that had fully absorbed both Chinese and Tibetan religious and artistic traditions, and as such it exemplifies the wide range of cultural dialogue that took place on this frontier.

The Kingdom of Lijiang

In official Chinese Ming dynasty (1368–1644) histories, the kingdom of Lijiang (Tibetan: Jang Satam) was an area recognized as beyond direct imperial control. By the fifteenth century, the local Naxi inhabitants, while ethnically related to the Tibetans, had closely allied themselves politically and culturally with the Chinese. They depicted themselves as Chinese officials and kept records in Chinese. The rulers of Lijiang were also enthusiastic patrons of both Chinese and Tibetan Buddhism. Through military campaigns the kingdom of Lijiang expanded its domain into Tibetan territories, and the local ruling family took an increasing interest in Tibetan Buddhism. The main trade routes between Yunnan and Tibet all passed through Lijiang-controlled territory, giving the Naxi control over the Yunnan-Tibet tea-horse trade, which provided a great deal of revenue to support such construction projects.[3]

Dabaojigong Temple

Dabaojigong exemplifies the synthesis of Chinese and Tibetan traditions characteristic of the local Naxi rulers, and its wall paintings contain Chinese Buddhist, Daoist, and Tibetan Buddhist themes.[4] The architecture is Chinese, and the temple is roughly square in appearance, with a face three bays wide and a double-eaved, hip-gabled tile roof. Twelve panels of wall paintings measure a total of 661.7 square feet (61.48 square meters). A set of Chinese name boards record that in 1582 the local official Mu Wang (r. 1580–1596) built the temple.[5] Known in Tibetan sources as the king in Lijiang, in 1582 he also invited the Ninth Karmapa (1555–1603) to Lijiang, expressing his wish to commission a new woodblock edition of the Tibetan Tripitaka (Kangyur).[6]

See Portrait of the Ninth Karmapa, no. 66.

Mahamayuri Presiding Over a Water-Land Assemblage, detail of wall painting, south wall; Dabaojigong Temple, Baisha Village, Lijiang, Yunnan Province, China; ca. 1643; 79⅞ × 175½ in. (203 × 446 cm); image after Wang Haitao 2002, fig. 98

Painting Program: Front of the Hall

The wall paintings at the front of the hall contain a mixture of imagery derived from Buddhist, Daoist, and Confucian traditions, focused on worldly concerns and dominated by iconographic themes standard to Chinese Buddhist temples of the Ming dynasty. Nonetheless, Tibetan elements permeate these paintings. For instance, the main theme of the south wall is a painting of a water-land (*shuilu*) assemblage, a Chinese Buddhist ritual of universal salvation designed to feed the untended spirits of the dead, which cleverly co-opts Confucian concerns of ancestor worship and sets them in a Buddhist ritual framework.

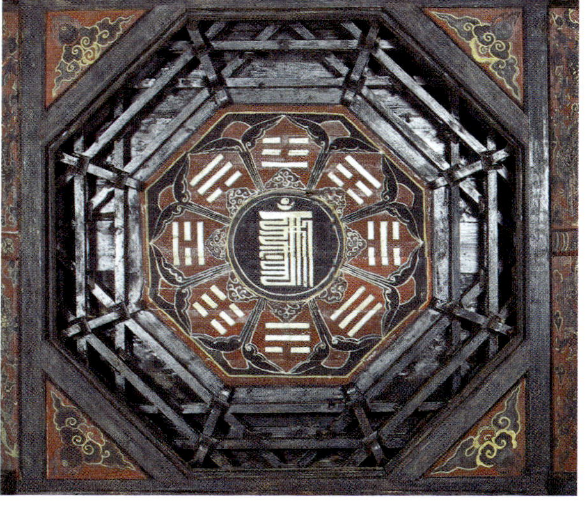

Kalachakra Mantra surrounded by the Eight Chinese Trigrams, ceiling painting; Dabaojigong Temple, Baisha Village, Lijiang, Yunnan Province, China; ca. 1643; photograph by K. Debreczeny

For more on the Five Protector Goddesses, see A *Pancharaksha* Print from Khara-Khoto, no. 32.

Presiding over this gathering of one hundred deities drawn from Chinese Buddhist and Daoist pantheons dressed in Chinese royal garb is a form of Mahamayuri, one of the Five Protector Goddesses (Pancharaksha), the magical reliever of suffering invoked to protect against poisons and calamities, as well as to bring rain and relieve drought. She represents the protective virtue of all the buddhas as she holds her identifying attribute, a peacock feather, drawn from Tibetan iconographic models and identified by a Tibetan inscription on her throne. In addition, a mandala following Tibetan conventions hangs from her throne, flanked on the right by a Tibetan monk, identifiable by his bare right shoulder, and on the left by a long-sleeved Chinese monk, giving visual expression to the Naxi ruling house's embrace of both Buddhist traditions. Tibetan color notations visible through the paint layer of this otherwise Chinese imagery suggest a mixed workshop.[7]

Flanking the east side of the front door is the Buddhist deity Marichi, also identified by a Tibetan inscription, surprisingly surrounded by Daoist gods, such as the Three Purities. Directly across the hall are the Daoist gods known as the Three Officials of Heaven, Earth, and Water. They are charged with keeping an equilibrium in the world through bureaucratic management of natural forces, and act as intermediaries between the living and the bureaucracy of the underworld. These are the only overtly Daoist figural themes found at Dabaojigong, and their presence is indicative of the religious syncretism prevalent across China at this time.

For more on Kalachakra, see the Kalachakra Mandala in the Potala Palace, no. 77.

On the ceiling above the central altar screen, in the center of a sunken well, the interlocked syllables of the Kalachakra mantra—known in Tibetan as "the ten syllables of power"—are surrounded by the eight trigrams[8] painted on the leaves of a lotus. In Chinese temples the eight trigrams would typically surround a yin-yang circle, forming a Daoist protective talisman. The presence of the Kalachakra mantra here combined with the trigrams makes for a fascinating hybrid of Tibetan and Chinese protective symbols.

Painting Program: Rear of the Hall

For more on the Tenth Karmapa, see Arhats Viewing a Painting of Birds by the Tenth Karmapa, no. 72.

The wall paintings at the rear of the hall are entirely Tibetan Buddhist in nature, devoted to inner practices and standard for temples of the Karma Kagyu tradition. Interestingly, almost all of the deities represented in the rear of Dabaojigong appear as meditational deities in the biographies of the Sixth Zhamar (1584–1630) and the Tenth Karmapa (1604–1674), two of the most influential lamas to visit Lijiang.

The south-central section of the rear wall depicts the Mahamudra transmission lineage, one of the two primary teaching lineages of the Kagyu tradition. The figures are all labeled in Tibetan, except the central figure, which makes it possible to trace the transmission of the teachings through the Ninth Karmapa.[9] It seems most likely that the unidentified central figure in a black hat is the Tenth Karmapa. If true, his teacher, the Sixth Zhamar, would be missing. One possible explanation might be that the Sixth Zhamar, who visited several times between 1610 and 1621, oversaw the composition and omitted himself out of modesty. This would place the execution of the painting after the date of the Tenth Karmapa's enthronement in 1611, and before the arrival of the Tenth Karmapa in Lijiang in 1646. Had the painting been executed after the Tenth Karmapa's arrival, it is unlikely that he would have consented to omit his own teacher, which would cut off his connection to this transmission.

Dating the Wall Paintings

Sites continuously evolve, and one should not assume that the wall paintings date to the temple's initial founding. A dated Tibetan inscription located in the front of the hall reads: "This great inconceivable temple which rivals the abode of the gods, of excellent Dharma, of the superior Dharmaraja called Dorje

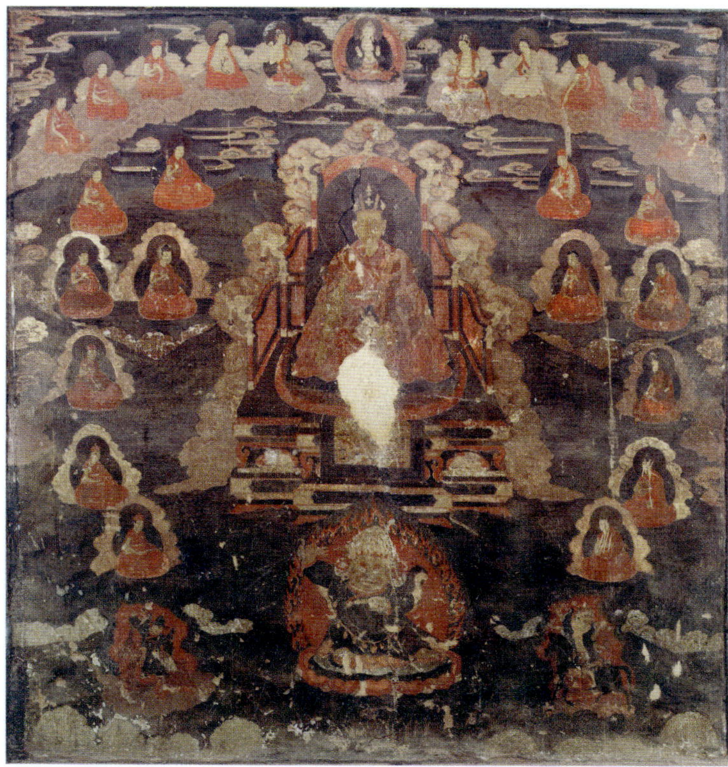

Mahamudra Lineage, detail of wall painting, rear wall; Dabaojigong Temple, Baisha Village, Lijiang, Yunnan Province, China; ca. 1643; 81⅞ × 76¾ in. (208 × 195 cm); image after He Shiyong, ed. 2011, 50

Demchok, was perfectly completed on the third day of the sixth month of the female water-sheep year."[10] Unfortunately, the identity of the ruler Dorje Demchok named in this inscription remains unclear, as it does not match any known Tibetan names of the local Naxi kings.[11] However, the anomaly in the Mahamudra lineage painting, taken together with the water-sheep year mentioned in this inscription, narrows the date to 1643, about three years before the arrival of the Tenth Karmapa.[12] Distinctive stylistic details, such as wispy flames and throne patterns, are consistent throughout the temple, suggesting the same workshop. This allows us to extend the dating to the wall paintings throughout the temple, roughly simultaneous to at least five other Buddhist construction projects sponsored by the founder's grandson Mu Zeng.

Patron of the Wall Paintings

Mu Zeng (1598–1646), known in Tibetan sources as the King of Lijiang Karma Mipam Tsewang Sonam Rabten, was the greatest supporter of Tibetan Buddhism among the Naxi rulers. In 1624 he abdicated the throne to act as monk-regent, and a number of portraits depict him in Chinese monastic robes beneath a Tibetan long-life deity.[13] One of the most important products of his patronage was the Jang Satam (Lijiang) edition of the Buddhist canon (Kangyur), completed by the Sixth Zhamar in 1621.[14] This massive literary undertaking established Lijiang's reputation as a major center of Tibetan Buddhist activity.[15]

The push to build or convert temples in Lijiang may have been intended in part to attract major Tibetan hierarchs to the local ruling family's court, and thereby to gain prestige within its newly conquered Tibetan territories.

Further Reading

Debreczeny, Karl. 2009. "Dabaojigong and the Regional Tradition of Ming Sino-Tibetan Painting in Lijiang." In *Buddhism between Tibet and China*, edited by M. T. Kapstein, 97–152. Boston: Wisdom.

Dy-Liacco, Kristina. 2005. "The Victorious Karma-pa Has Come to 'Jang: An Examination of Naxi Patronage of the Bka'-brgyud-pa in the Fifteenth to Seventeenth Centuries." Master's thesis, Indiana University.

Notes

1 This essay is largely drawn from Debreczeny 2009 and 2012, 64–95.
2 On the Naxi, see Rock 1947; Mathieu and Ho 2011.
3 Sperling 1988, 39; Booz 2011, 2016, 2018.
4 For a discussion of the complete iconographic program, see Debreczeny 2009. For images, see Lijiang Naxizu and Lijiang Naxi Dongba 1999, 20–67; Wang Haitao 2002, 96–167; He Shiyong 2011, 12–103.
5 萬曆壬午端陽圓滿拜書, 土官功德主木旺志.
6 Si tu and 'Be lo (1775) 1972, 180, ll. 1–2.
7 For instance, in the Mahamayuri water-land assemblage, the letters *ka* for white (*dkar po*) are visible. See He Shiyong 2011, 25.
8 Trigrams are the eight symbols composed of three broken or unbroken lines, used in Daoist cosmology and divination.
9 See Debreczeny 2009, fig. 15, app. 2, Painting Key 1; He Shiyong 2011, 51; Xiong 2014, 484–87.
10 *Gong ma chos rgyal rdo rje bde [m]chog zhes/ chos bzang lha gnas de dang 'gran nus pa'i/ gtsug lag khang chen bsam gyis mi khyab 'di: chu mo lug lo zla [ba] drug pa'i/ tshes pa gsum la bkra shis bde leg[s] grub/*
11 Debreczeny 2009, 105; Xiong, Shargan, and Habibu 2013, 68–69; Xiong 2014.
12 Xiong, Shargan, and Habibu 2013; Xiong 2014.
13 See Debreczeny 2012, 63, 80–82: Rock 1947, pl. 44.
14 Now known as the Litang Edition. See Imaeda 1982, 176.
15 Schaeffer 2009, 145; Imaeda 1977; H. Karmay 1975, 50–58; Harrison 1996, 70–94.

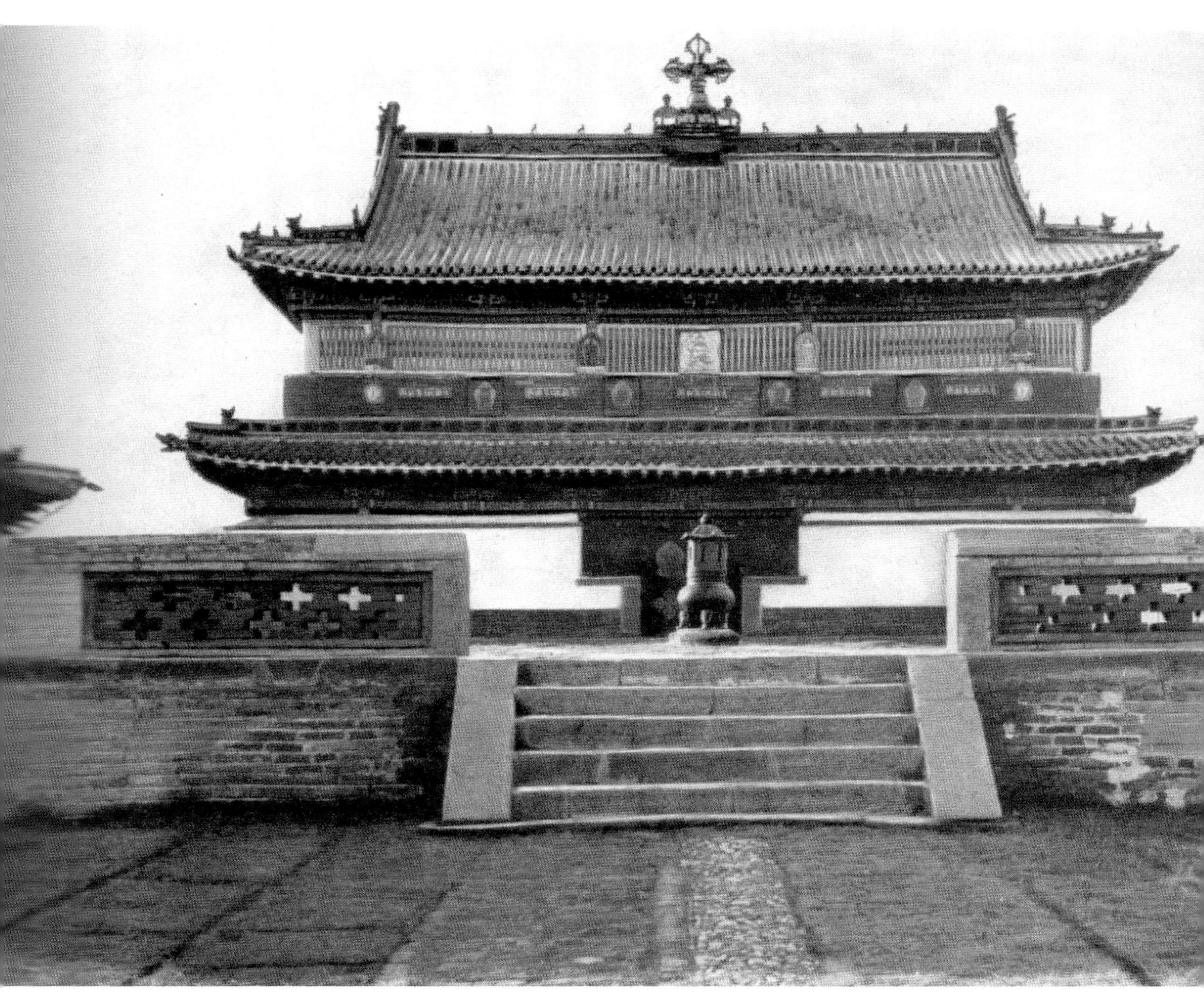

№ 65

Erdeni Juu Monastery

Övörkhangai Province, Mongolia, founded 1586–1587

The Sixteenth-Century Renaissance of Buddhism in Mongolia

ISABELLE CHARLEUX

ERDENI JUU IS THE OLDEST EXTANT TIBETAN BUDDHIST MONASTERY of Khalkha Mongolia (present-day Republic of Mongolia) and its holiest monastery, due to its prestigious origin, holy relics, and icons. It has a long history of construction and partially escaped destruction several times.[1]

It is located in the fertile valley of the Orkhon River, which was the center of former steppe empires. Not only it is located adjacent to the ruins of Qara-Qorum, capital of the Mongol Empire between 1235 and 1260 (razed to the ground by the Ming armies in 1388), but recent excavations have revealed that it was built directly above the palace of Emperor Ögedei (r. 1227–1241), son of Chinggis Khan.[2]

The Late Sixteenth-Century "Renaissance" of Mongol Buddhism

For more on Zanabazar, see Maitreya, no. 75.

Erdeni Juu was founded by Abatai Khan (1554–1588), a descendant of Chinggis Khan who ruled the Khalkha Mongols, and grandfather of First Jibzundamba Khutugtu Zanabazar (1635–1723).[3]

Abatai Khan converted to Tibetan Buddhism, following his cousin Altan Khan (1507/8–1582), ruler of the Tümed in Southern Mongolia (now Inner Mongolia, China), who had met Sonam Gyatso, the hierarch of the Geluk tradition, and granted him the title of Dalai Lama in 1578. This period of massive reconversion of Mongols to Buddhism was a time of cultural and artistic renaissance. In 1579–1580, Altan Khan had Chinese carpenters build a temple south of his palace of Hohhot (Inner Mongolia), to house a statue of twelve-year-old Shakyamuni modeled on the Jowo Rinpoche, the holiest icon of Lhasa. The statue and the temple were known in Mongolian as "Erdeni Juu," translating Jowo Rinpoche ("Juu" being the Mongolian pronunciation of Tibetan Jowo, "lord").[4] The temple, now known as Great Juu/Temple (Yekhe Juu), and its statue have been preserved. The Tümed monasteries developed a Chinese-style version of the large Tibetan main temple with a porch, an assembly hall, and a back shrine in one building, covered by a succession of three Chinese roofs. The back shrine is surrounded by a colonnade to allow circumambulation of the main icon from the outside. Most of the other monasteries were itinerant, in felt tents.

See Jowo Shakyamuni, no. 8.

The Three Juu Temples

Following Altan Khan's example, Abatai Khan met the Dalai Lama, who entrusted him the mission of founding the first Khalkha monastery. He commissioned a Shakyamuni statue to enshrine a relic given by the Dalai Lama and hired Chinese carpenters from Hohhot to erect his own Erdeni Juu monastery. The clay statue we observe today replaced an older one. According to oral tradition, the statue would be an old "true portrait" of the Buddha dating from the Uyghur Empire (744–840) or its copy.

Abatai Khan settled his palatial tent on the ruins of Ögedei Khan's palace and probably rebuilt the old walls. His temple, erected in 1586–1587, is located in the southwest corner of the square wall, maybe because the palace was in the middle. Erdeni Juu may first have been a Sakya tradition monastery (the school favored by the Mongol Yuan dynasty, 1271–1368), and converted to the Geluk tradition in the late eighteenth century.

Abatai Khan's temple (now known as the Central Juu) is a Chinese-style two-story pavilion with bracket sets supporting a double-eaved gable and hip roof covered with green tiles, standing on a terrace. It reused bricks and stones from Qara-Qorum. Several Tümed temples may have inspired Abatai Khan's construction, such as the Glazed [Tile] Hall of Maidari-yin Juu, located fifty-four miles (eighty-seven kilometers) west of Hohhot.

The Central Temple of Erdeni Juu Monastery, founded by Abatai Khan; Övörkhangai Province, Mongolia; 1586–1587; floor dimensions 48 ft. 9 in. × 37 ft. 3 in. (14.85 × 11.35 m); early 20th-century photograph; image after Maidar 1972, fig. 75

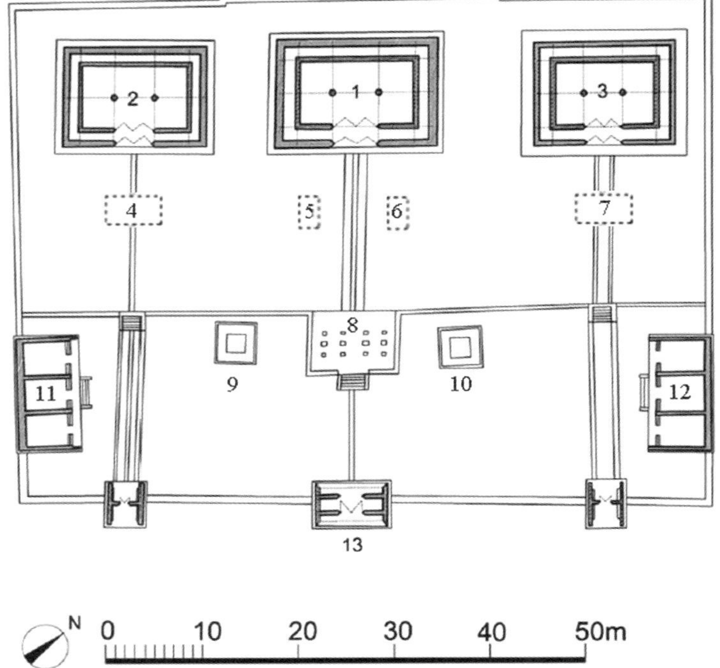

Plan of the Three Temples Complex, Erdeni Juu Monastery; Övörkhangai Province, Mongolia; built 1585–1630; 1. Central Temple, 2. Right Temple, 3. Left Temple, 4. Temple to the Maharajas, 5. Shrine to Avalokiteshvara, 6. Shrine to Maitreya, 7. Temple to the Maharajas, 8. Ceremonial Archway, 9. Tomb of Abatai Khan, 10. Tomb of Gombodorji, 11. Tsangpa Karpo Temple, 12. Amitayus Temple, 13. Entrance Gate; image after Brandt and Gutschow 2003

The Right Juu/Temple and the Left Juu/Temple, erected by Abatai's son and grandson on either side of the Central Juu, were completed around 1630. Each was a one-story pavilion with a gable and hip roof. Their original icons probably represented the Buddhas of the Past and Future Eras (Dipankara and Maitreya); around 1880 they were replaced by statues of Amitabha and Shakyamuni.[5] These statues are now said to represent Shakyamuni at two stages of his life: at eighty years and thirty-five years—flanking the twelve-year-old Shakyamuni of the Central Temple.

These three temples are unique in Mongolia. First, they stand in a line and face east, a configuration that is not seen in Tibet and China, but which appears to be a Mongol characteristic. A second distinction of the three temples is the presence of an inner circumambulation corridor surrounding the central shrine, as in Central Asian and Tibetan temples of the first millennium. The pilgrims' practice of circumambulating outside Erdeni Juu's wall and inside the corridors to worship the Juu statues recalls the concentric circumambulations around the Jowo Rinpoche at Jokhang Temple in Lhasa.

For the Kalachakra mantra, see Dabaojigong Temple, no. 64, p. 282.

The facades and roofs of the Three Temples are decorated with Buddhist symbols (Kalachakra mantra, double vajra, brass plaques depicting deities), consecration formulas in Lantsa script, and Chinese decoration. Their interiors have coffered ceilings and Chinese framework with red-lacquered columns circled by dragons. Additional structures were later added in the compound, surrounded by a wall, including the square-shaped tomb-stupas of Abatai and his son Gombodorji (1594–1655).

On Vajrapani and his importance in Mongolian regions, see Vajrapani, no. 82.

Abatai Khan also founded the small Blue Temple (Khökhe süme, rebuilt in 1970) to house an image of Vajrapani donated by the Third Dalai Lama. In 1675 his grandson and heir Chakhundorji (r. 1655–1698) built the small Dalai Lama Temple with a Tibetan-style door frame (preserved).

See Mongolian Map of Capital Yekhe Khüriye, no. 96.

After the death of its founder, Erdeni Juu became a funerary temple. In addition to the two tombs, it preserved mural paintings depicting Abatai Khan with his wife.[6] Abatai Khan's tent-palace with a capacity of three hundred people served as his ancestral shrine; it contained Abatai's throne, armor, and weapons, and wrathful statues of his marshals (Zanabazar moved the tent-palace to Urga/Yekhe Khüriye, where it was known as the Western Palace). Erdeni Juu can be compared to Maidari-yin Juu, also a fortified palace that was progressively converted into the funerary temple of Altan Khan's family, with a funerary stupa and a painting depicting two princesses and donors.[7]

Erdeni Juu in the Qing Period

The square-shaped fortified wall was rebuilt in the seventeenth and eighteenth centuries. Made of earth with brick cladding and painted white, it encloses an area of 1,540 by 1,360 feet (470 by 415 meters), with four monumental gates opening at the four directions. Four stupas were built at the corners, and ninety-six other stupas were erected between 1730 and 1804 (the lucky number of 108 was never reached). The stupas were of different shapes and sizes but were rebuilt as identical structures around 1970.

New temples were founded after the Khalkha joined the Qing dynasty (1644–1911) in 1691. In the nineteenth century, the site included twenty major temples and about forty smaller temples and administrative buildings. Fifteen hundred monks and novices lived in some five hundred yurts and houses within wooden fences, forming quarters divided by narrow alleys. A major restoration was made from

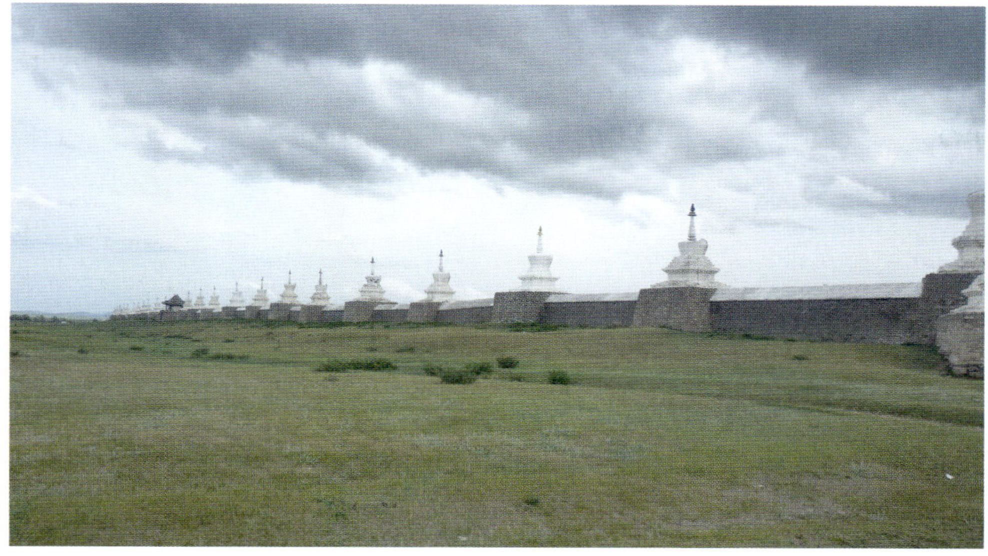

Fortified Stupa Wall, Erdeni Juu Monastery; Övörkhangai Province, Mongolia; wall rebuilt 17th–18th century; 1,558 × 1,365 ft. (475 × 416 m); photograph by Isabelle Charleux

1795 to 1798 by Chinese carpenters from Hohhot.

The heart of the monastery, near the center of the complex, was the three-story assembly hall. Its front courtyard served for *tsam* dances. The main temples were dedicated to the deities Avalokiteshvara, Vajradhara (private temple of the Jibzundamba), Mahakala, Geser, and Amitayus; there were also six academic colleges and many stupas. Most of the buildings adopted the Chinese style and construction techniques, but their Tibetan Buddhist identity was immediately recognizable from the outside by means of symbolic elements decorating the exteriors. Their interiors did not greatly differ from those of Tibetan temples.

About two-thirds of the structures were demolished in the antireligious persecutions of 1938 that destroyed the greatest part of the Mongolian Buddhist heritage; thirteen main temples and five smaller ones survived, but were heavily damaged.[8] The surviving structures include the Three Temple complex, the Dalai Lama Temple, the thirty-three-foot (ten-meter) Golden Stupa flanked by smaller stupas (built in 1799), and the residence (Labrang) of the reincarnated lama, in the northwest, built between 1780 and 1785. The Labrang is a flat-roofed, three-story building constructed of brick; its appearance is Tibetan, with decorations of dark friezes, brass mirrors, and Kalachakra mantra medallions.

On *tsam* dances, see Ritual Dance Mask of Guru Dorje Drolo, no. 94.

Erdeni Juu now operates both as monastery and museum, and is registered on the heritage list of UNESCO. The Labrang (partially rebuilt) serves as the assembly hall for the Gelukpa community that revived after 1990; in addition, a yurt-temple houses the only Sakyapa community of Mongolia. Erdeni Juu enshrines two miraculous images: a small statue of the Sandalwood Buddha, said to come from India, and a stone statue of Gur Gombo (Sanskrit: Panjara Mahakala), special protector of the Sakya tradition. These statues have been preserved, along with paintings and liturgical objects.

On this form of Mahakala and the Mongol Empire, see Mahakala Stone Sculpture, no. 39.

Further Reading

Charleux, Isabelle. 2017. "Circumambulating the Jowo in Mongolia: Why 'Erdeni juu' Must Be Translated as 'Jowo Rinpoche.'" In *Interaction in the Himalayas and Central Asia: Processes of Transfer, Translation and Transformation in Art, Archaeology, Religion and Polity*, edited by Eva Allinger, Frantz Grenet, Christian Jahoda, Maria-Katharina Lang, and Anne Vergati, 357–74. Vienna: Verlag der Österreichischen Akademie der Wissenschaften.

Pozdneev, Aleksei M. (1892, 1893) 1997. *Mongolia and the Mongols*, in one vol. Translated by J. R. Shaw and D. Plank. Reprint, London: Curzon Press.

Tulisow, Jerzy, Osamu Inoue, Agata Bareja-Starzyńska, and Ewa Dziurzyńska, eds. 2012. *In the Heart of Mongolia: 100th Anniversary of W. Kotwicz's Expedition to Mongolia in 1912*. Cracow: Polish Academy of Arts and Sciences (with DVD).

Notes

1 All but five of the thousand monasteries of Mongolia were destroyed during the late 1930s purges of the Communist period.
2 Brandt and Gutschow 2003; Gutschow and Brandt 2005; Barkmann 2010; Matsukawa and Ochir 2011.
3 The history of the monastery is recorded in Mongolian chronicles, biographies of Zanabazar, and a manuscript known in short as "History of Erdeni Juu" (1803) 1999. Two other main sources are Pozdneev (1896) 1971, 281–99, and Kotwicz, in Tulisow et al. 2012, 334. See also Khatanbaatar and Naigal 2005, 35–40; Matsukawa and Ochir 2011.
4 By metonymy, *juu* came to designate a temple, a monastery; Charleux 2017.
5 See Jamtsarano 2012, 335, for a description of the interior of the Three Temples in 1912.
6 They are known to us through copies at the Zanabazar Museum of Fine Arts in Ulaanbaatar.
7 Charleux 2014.
8 For period photographs from several collections, see Baasansüren 2011.

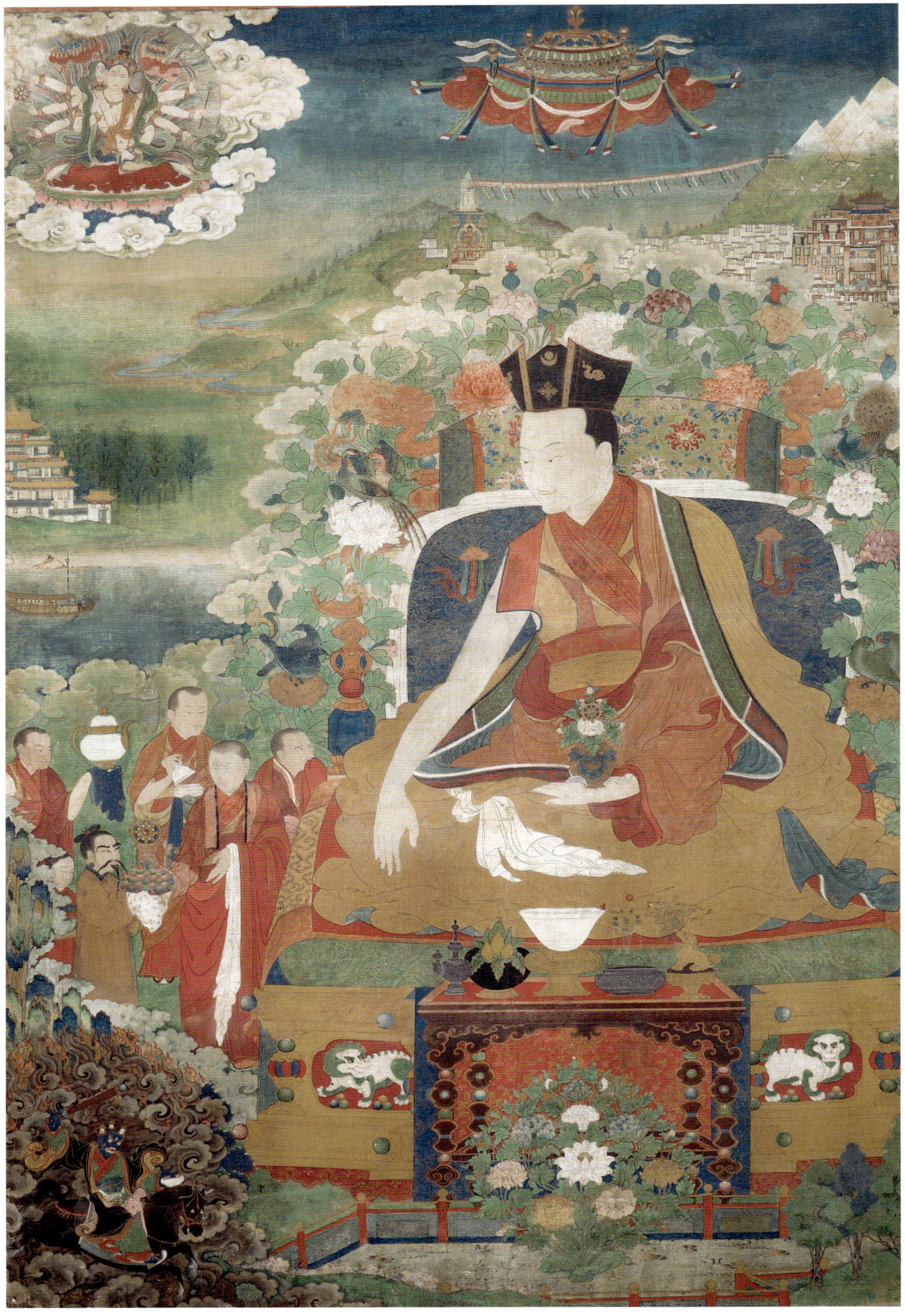

Nº 66

Portrait of the Ninth Karmapa

Central Tibet (possibly Tsurpu Monastery), ca. 1590

Rise of the Encampment Painting Tradition

KARL DEBRECZENY

THIS PORTRAIT DEPICTS THE NINTH KARMAPA, Wangchuk Dorje (1555–1603), head of the Karma Kagyu tradition of Tibetan Buddhism, with his seat, Tsurpu Monastery, in the distance behind him. The long-life vase in his lap and the long-life deity Sitatapatra floating in the top-left corner represent wishes for the Karmapa's longevity, suggesting this painting was created during his lifetime. The winding river and soft washes of blue and green create a sense of open, receding space, illustrating a new style that arose in the court of the Karmapas, inspired in part by Chinese court painting.

The Karmapas

Traditions of Tibetan Buddhism trace their origins through a lineage of teachers going back to India, the birthplace of Buddhism. Beginning in the twelfth century, the Karmapas were the first lineage to institutionalize succession through the mechanism of reincarnation. Each Karmapa is thought to be an emanation of the bodhisattva of compassion Avalokiteshvara, the patron deity of Tibet. Karmapas wear distinctive black hats that serve as both a crown and a badge of office. The hat depicted here, bearing a golden crossed vajra in front and a golden cloud motif called *garuda* wings on the sides, was a gift from the Chinese Yongle emperor (r. 1402–1424) in the fifteenth century.

See Avalokiteshvara at Khartse, no. 20; Bodhisattva Avalokiteshvara and the Buddha's Footprints, no. 33.

While most Tibetan artists were historically laymen, monastics were also trained in the arts. The Ninth Karmapa painted, including murals at Sungrab Ling Monastery, and made sketches for murals that other artists copied.[1] Yet he was not known for being particularly talented and was chided for his lack of skill, motivating him to predict that in his next life he would put those who criticized him to shame.[2] This underdeveloped ability is evident in one extant work of musical notations featuring charmingly naive marginalia.

For more on the Tenth Karmapa as an artist, see Arhats Viewing a Painting of Birds by the Tenth Karmapa, no. 72.

The Karmapa's Court, the Great Encampment

Starting in the fourteenth century, the Karmapas traveled in large monastic tent encampments, much like a prince's traveling court, consisting of portable temples, a community of monks, and skilled artists and artisans. This mobile court, known as the Great Karmapa Encampment (*Karma garchen*), produced its own distinctive painting tradition called the Karma Gardri, or "the style of the Karmapa Encampment."

According to Tibetan sources, the Encampment style was established—or more likely codified—in Central Tibet by the painter Namkha Tashi (act. ca. 1568–1599) in the court of the Ninth Karmapa in the second half of the sixteenth century. An early description of the Encampment style by the art theorist Deumar Geshe (b. 1665/72) in his *Manual of Brilliant Colors* characterizes the style as having color similar to Chinese painting, with dilute washes and soft shading, and layouts mostly conforming with Chinese paintings.[3]

Portrait of the Ninth Karmapa, Wangchuk Dorje (1555–1603); central Tibet (possibly Tsurpu Monastery); ca. 1590; pigments on cloth; 50 × 33½ in. (127 × 85.1 cm); Rubin Museum of Art; purchase from the Collection of Navin Kumar, New York; C2005.20.2 (HAR 90005)

Portrait of the Ninth Karmapa

No extant painting by the hand of Namkha Tashi has yet been reliably identified.[4] But this painting of the Ninth Karmapa is a promising representative example of this early court style.[5] A partially effaced inscription indicates that the composition was executed during the Karmapa's lifetime:

> This painting of [Wangchuk] Dorje, which was accomplished under the instructions of the Gyelwa [Karmapa] himself, by the nephew, the monk from Kong[po] in the east. Because of great fortune established [. . .], by this merit, may all beings be established in the level of Buddhahood![6]

The inscription identifies the patron of the work as a monk, called "nephew," from Kongpo in the east. The Ninth Karmapa had two important patrons with this title, and their life dates place the creation of this work in the 1590s.[7] One of these nephews, Won Gushri Karma Chogyel (d. 1602), is recorded as a sponsor of works by Namkha Tashi, founder of the Encampment style.[8]

Another internal clue to the dating of the painting is found in the background landscape, where a monumental thangka is unfurled on a mountainside adjacent to the Karmapa's seat, Tsurpu Monastery. This is a famous silk appliqué of Buddha Shakyamuni called *Beautiful Ornament of the World*. The artist Karma Sidrel made this appliqué at Tsurpu for the Ninth Karmapa in 1585, and its inclusion here provides the earliest possible date for this painting.

For more on appliqués, see Monumental Appliqué of Begtse, no. 95.

Founding of the Encampment Style

The founder of the Encampment style, Namkha Tashi, appears several times in the Ninth Karmapa's biography as an important artist. He painted murals of the sixteen arhats, inspired by Chinese models at the Karmapa's seat of Tsurpu, in 1582, shortly before this painting was made.[9] However, traditional accounts of this art history often begin with the previous Eighth Karmapa, Mikyo Dorje (1507–1554), who is remembered as a master of great scholastic learning and is said to have been influential in the founding of the Encampment style. The Eighth Karmapa wrote a treatise on art, *The Great Sun of Drawing Proportions*, but little is known about his role in founding this artistic tradition, with no mention of painting in his available biographies.[10] At the end of the Eighth Karmapa's biography, two artists are named as emanations of the Karmapa who manifested in order to continue his work:

> Regarding the extraordinary artist (*tulku*)[11] Namkha Tashi, he was born in Yartong. From the time he was a little child he admitted that he was an emanation of the [Eighth] Lord [Karmapa]. He was prophesied as the doer of actions of [the Karmapa's] religious activities in the sphere of religious images and, instructed by the Fifth Zhamar, he established the [painting] tradition of the Encampment style.
>
> As for the one known as Karma Sidrel also known as Gonyon, the head-man of Dakpo, he is [also] an emanation of the body of the Lord [Karmapa] himself and is the one who founded the practice of sculpting in the Encampment manner.[12]

A prominent court painter within this tradition, Tangla Tsewang (1902–1989), followed this traditional narrative in his history of Tibetan painting, written in the 1950s, but he pushed the initial founding of the Encampment style back to the time of the Seventh Karmapa (1454–1506). He suggests that already in the late fifteenth century Encampment artists were taking the figural forms of the Old Menri painting tradition of Menla Dondrub as their models, while drawing inspiration from the color and drawing of Chinese painting.[13]

Namkha Tashi's painting teacher was Konchok Pende of E, a master of the Menri painting tradition and an important artist active in the Ninth Karmapa's court, whose works are primarily known to us through later copies. These compositions reveal that Konchok Pende was already looking to Chinese models before the Encampment style was formally established.

Artistic Models

Two of the main religious masters of the Karma Kagyu, the Fifth Zhamar (1526–1583) and the Fourth Gyeltsab (1550–1617), played a significant advisory role, offering guidance for the creation of a new visual idiom for the Karmapa's court. They instructed Namkha Tashi to take famous Chinese paintings in Tibet as models, including products of the late Yuan and early Ming courts, to which the Karmapas had historical ties.[14] The only surviving named model is a monumental 163-foot-long handscroll, *Delivering*

For more on the Karmapa's ties to the early Ming court, see Qutan Monastery, no. 52.

For more on Ming Yongle court production as gifts to Tibetans, see Pensive Bodhisattva Avalokiteshvara, no. 53.

the Soul of Ming Taizu, made in the court of the Ming Yongle emperor in 1407. These religious masters urged Namkha Tashi to follow Indian Buddhist art, including sculpture, for the shape of the sacred figures, and to look to Chinese art for the coloring and shading. Lineage figure depictions from this tradition feature clear adaptations of visual conventions of Ming court arhat paintings, while other works are more loosely inspired.[15]

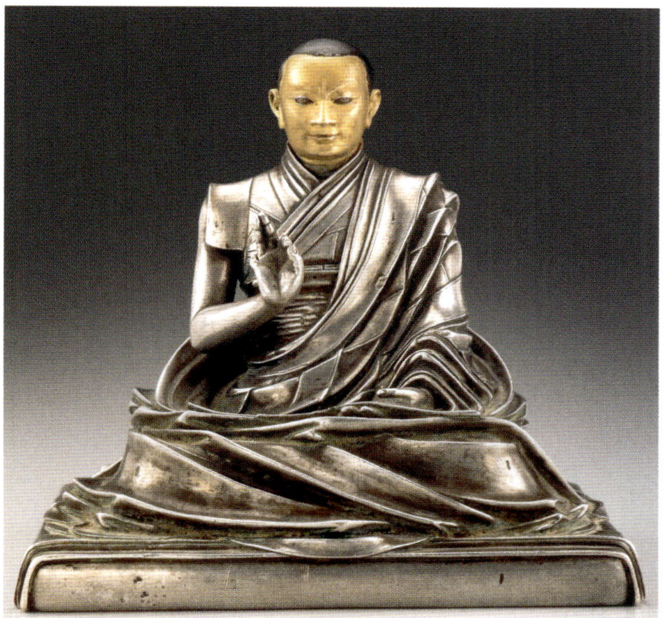

Karma Rinchen (act. late 16th century); Portrait Sculpture of the Ninth Karmapa Wangchuk Dorje (1555–1603); central Tibet; 1598; silver with pigment; 7½ × 8 × 5½ in. (19.1 × 20.3 × 14 cm); Private collection

Encampment Sculptural Tradition

The arts of the Karmapa's court also included a lesser-known sculptural tradition, founded by the artist Karma Sidrel (d. 1591/92) who, like Namkha Tashi, was also considered to be an emanation of the Eighth Karmapa. A talented sculptor, he also made murals, masks, and monumental appliqués, like the one depicted in this painting.[16] A portrait sculpture of the Ninth Karmapa with realistic physiognomy bears an inscription on the back of its base; it states that the artist Karma Rinchen made this sculpture when the Karmapa was forty-four years old (ca. 1598).[17] This is one of the few datable statues of the Karma Kagyu tradition that are contemporaneous with the founding of the Encampment artistic tradition. It reveals several distinctive features, including an intense interest in the layering of the robes, which gives a sense of weight and plasticity of form. The medium of silver itself also appears to be characteristic of these early portraits.

Forty years after the establishment of the Encampment style, bitter sectarian warfare came to a head in central Tibet, and in 1645 the Karmapa's court, the Great Encampment, was obliterated, placing the Karmapa's religious and artistic traditions in danger of extinction. Thus, most of what we know about the Encampment tradition is from its eighteenth-century revival engineered by Situ Panchen.

See Portrait of Situ Panchen, no. 83.

Further Reading

Jackson, David P. 1996. *A History of Tibetan Painting: The Great Painters and Their Traditions* 169–80. Beitrage zur Kultur- und Geistesgeschichte Asiens 15. Vienna: Verlag der Osterreichischen Akademie der Wissenschaften.

Gega Lama. 1983. *Principles of Tibetan Art: Illustrations and Explanations of Buddhist Iconography and Iconometry according to the Karma Gardri School.* 2 vols. Translated by Karma Chochi Nyima (Richard Barron). Darjeeling: Jamyang Singe.

Notes

1 Karma Nges don bstan rgyas (1891) 1973, 343, lines 3–4; KaH thog Si tu 2001, 103, line 5; D. Jackson 2009, 264n312.
2 Karma Nges don bstan rgyas (1891) 1973, 333–34.
3 A paraphrase of D. Jackson 1996, 50, 173–74, 387–90, who quotes the *Kun gsal tshon gyi las rim me tog mdangs ster ja' 'od 'bum byin*, chap. 10, verses 33–34.
4 Some attributions have been made; see Kang Gesang Yixi 2015, 21–31.
5 This essay largely follows text developed together with David Jackson for the 2009 exhibition *Patron and Painter.*
6 [effaced] . . . *rdo rje'i sku thang 'di/ rgyal ba nyid kyis ljags bkod pa*[s?] *grub pa'i/ dbon shar phyogs kong btsun gyis// skal ba bzang phyir u btsug* [effaced] *dge 'dis 'gro kun sangs rgyas sa dgod shog//*. Similarly translated in D. Jackson 2009, 101.
7 D. Jackson 2009, 101–2.
8 D. Jackson 2009, 101–2.
9 D. Jackson 1996, 176, quoting the biography of the Ninth Karmapa in Si tu and 'Be lo 1775, 182, line 2.
10 One painting has been attributed to the Eighth Karmapa; see Blezer 2015.
11 *Tulku* (*sprul sku*), literally "magical emanation body," refers to spiritual masters who reincarnate, but it can also be a figurative reference to artists of extraordinary talent. Here it seems to function both ways.
12 Si tu Pan chen and 'Be lo, fol. 65.
13 Dkon mchog bstan 'dzin et al. 2006, 217–18; for a translation, see Debreczeny 2012, 250–52, 308n786.
14 See Sperling 2004b; D. Jackson 1996, 173.
15 D. Jackson 2009, 107–8, figs 5.17, 5.18.
16 Dkon mchog bstan 'dzin et al. 2006, 217–18; D. Jackson 1996, 176–77.
17 A. Heller 1999, 188; Stoddard 2003, 33–34; D. Jackson 2009, 109, 265n329.

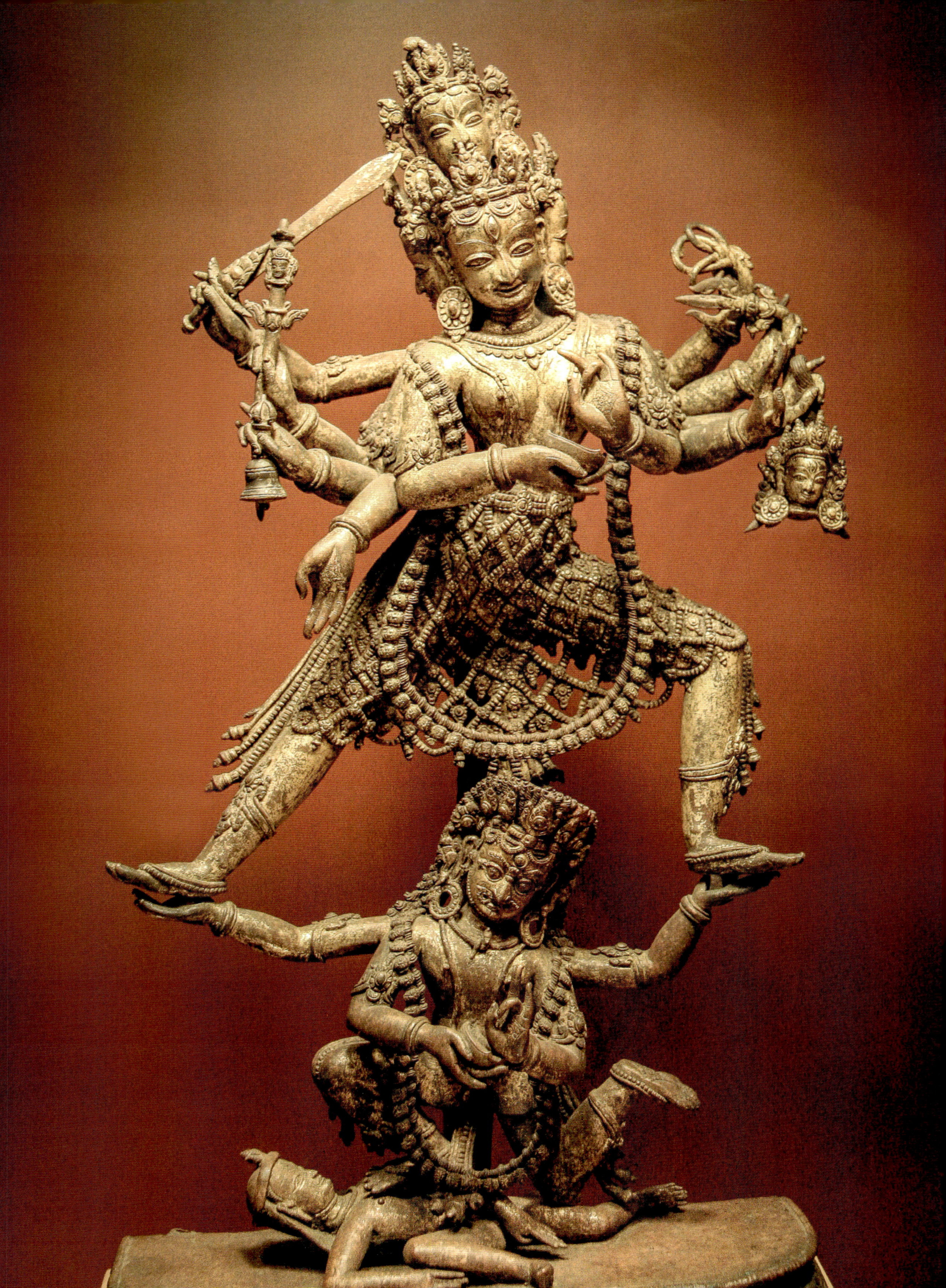

№ 67

Siddhi Lakshmi (Purnachandi)

Nepal, ca. 16th–17th century

The Goddess of Miraculous Power

KERRY LUCINDA BROWN

Siddhi Lakshmi (Purnachandi); Nepal; ca. 16th–17th century; gilt bronze with pigment; height 15¾ in. (40 cm); Patan Museum, Patan, Nepal; object 234; photograph by Erik Törner

GODDESSES PLAY A VITAL ROLE in establishing sacred geography and reaffirming the power of the rulers and kingdoms they protect. One of the most powerful tantric goddesses in the Kathmandu Valley is Siddhi Lakshmi, also known by her local name, Purnachandi. She is a secret form of Taleju, the tutelary goddess for the royal families of the Malla dynasty (ca. 1200–1769) and the self-chosen goddess (*ishtadevata*) of the king. After the death of King Yaksha Malla (r. 1428–1482) in the fifteenth century, the Newar kingdom fractured into three parts. In what is now known as the Three Kingdoms period (1482–1769), royal power was divided among the cities of Kathmandu, Patan (Lalitpur), and Bhaktapur. Rivalries between rulers for political and religious authority led to intense building campaigns that resulted in capital cities filled with elaborate palace complexes, temples dedicated to Buddhist and Hindu deities, and large public squares for communal celebrations. The rulers of the Three Kingdoms period used tantric systems to organize their kingdoms, with royal palaces and protective deities situated in the center of each kingdom.[1] Within this contentious environment, Siddhi Lakshmi emerged as a powerful, yet secret tantric deity for the Malla kings.

The veneration of Siddhi Lakshmi is part of a larger tantric system referred to as Sarvamnaya and is associated with the Secret Black Mother (Guhya Kali) tantras. She encompasses the totality of all the goddesses and their collective spiritual energy (*shakti*). As such, she is a manifestation of the supreme great goddess, Mahadevi.[2] Furthermore, the association with Taleju connects Siddhi Lakshmi with the Hindu goddess Durga, one of the most popular public goddesses of the Hindu pantheon. Siddhi Lakshmi is worshipped to destroy evil, repel negative forces, cultivate wisdom, and provide material and spiritual success. With these powers, it is no wonder she became one of the primary tantric deities venerated by the Malla kings.

Tantric Ritual Authority

Dated to the sixteenth or seventeenth century, the gilt-bronze image of Siddhi Lakshmi in the collection of the Patan Museum serves as one of the finest examples of Newar lost-wax casting from the Three Kingdoms Period. The delicate modeling of the form makes it easy to understand why Newar artists were highly prized by Tibetan and Inner Asian patrons. The stacked composition of the image establishes a clear visual hierarchy and reinforces the power and ritual authority of the goddess. Siddhi Lakshmi is positioned in an aggressive standing posture (*alidha sthana*), with her left leg bent and the right stretched to the side. She balances on the outstretched arms of Bhairava, a wrathful form of the Hindu god Shiva, whose palms support the feet of the goddess. Bhairava is in a kneeling posture astride a corpse that is splayed across the lotus pedestal base. The dynamic postures of the figures animate the form and enliven the deities, setting this piece apart from other depictions of Siddhi Lakshmi with static compositions.

For another example of stacked deities, see Vishnu Riding on Garuda, no. 18.

As the largest figure in the composition, Siddhi Lakshmi communicates a complex visual narrative that affirms her ability to bestow unwavering success and accomplishment. Each of her five heads has a third eye and wears a crown with skull ornaments and foliate motifs. While classified as dangerous and bloodthirsty, Siddhi Lakshmi has a sweetly smiling face, a stylistic feature typical in Newar art. The hand gestures (mudras) and attributes displayed in her ten arms reinforce her ability to protect and grant power. As part of her wrathful nature, she wears a bone apron and necklace of severed skulls, similar to the ritual regalia worn by the goddess Kumari. Each set of five arms delicately extends from

For more about the Kumari tradition in Nepal, see *Tayobizakani* Ritual Necklace, no. 89.

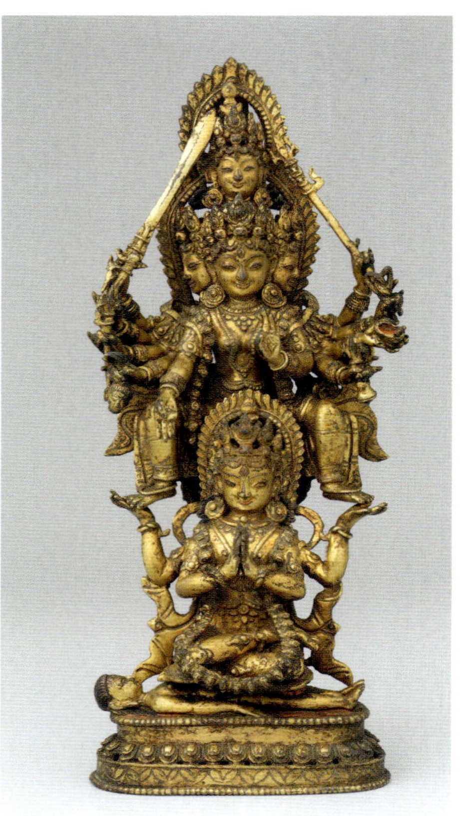

Siddhi Lakshmi; Nepal; 17th century; gilt-copper alloy; 10¾ × 4¾ × 5⅞ in. (27.3 × 12.1 × 14.9 cm); Rubin Museum of Art; C2004.34.4 (HAR 65402)

the shoulders, with each arm gracefully arranged around the torso. While holding a skull cup to her chest with her central right hand, her left hand makes the sprinkling gesture (*bindukapala* mudra), signifying the transmission of spiritual power to the practitioner. From top to bottom, her remaining right hands display a sword, a staff, and a bell, with the last hand outstretched in the gesture of giving (*varada* mudra), reinforcing her ability to bestow power. Her remaining left hands hold a noose, a trident, and a freshly severed head, with the lowest hand presenting the fear-not gesture (*abhaya* mudra). Together, these features reiterate her ability to overcome obstacles, wield power, and protect the faithful.

Bhairava is shown as subordinate to the goddess, yet also subjugating the corpse below his feet. He plays an important role in this visual narrative, as he literally supports and sustains the goddess above. His upper arms extend to bear the goddess, whose feet rest in his hands. Mirroring the goddess above, Bhairava stands in an aggressive stance, wears a necklace of skulls, holds a skull cup, and conveys the gesture of sprinkling (*bindukapala* mudra). His large eyes, fangs, mustache, flaming hair, and snake ornaments reaffirm his wrathful nature. The visual harmony of these two figures strengthens the overall visual narrative and reinforces the relationship between the deities. Here the male-female dichotomy in Hinduism is expressed by a delicate balance of male and female principles, yet the visual hierarchy asserts the dominance of the feminine divine.[3] This union expresses the duality of these principles in Nepalese tantric systems. The exalted status of Siddhi Lakshimi among the Malla kings is rooted in the notion that she embodies the collective spiritual energy (*shakti*) of all goddesses, thus she wields the combined power of all sacred abodes (*tirtha*) and seats (*pitha*) of the greater Kathmandu Valley.

Spiritual Power and Protection

The array of surviving paintings and sculptures of Siddhi Lakshmi suggests her veneration was popular among the royal elites and possibly extended beyond this circle to other tantric initiates. In Sanskrit, the word *siddhi* can mean accomplishment, knowledge, or attainment. As the supreme goddess of miraculous accomplishment, Siddhi Lakshmi was venerated by the kings of Nepal to protect their throne, their ritual authority, and their kingdom.

In the city of Patan, Siddhi Narasimha Malla (r. 1619–1661) consecrated the Purnachandi Temple in 1635.[4] The temple is the center of mother goddess (*matrika*) veneration in Patan. The main shrine and flanking deities at the Purnachandi shrine consist of river stones (*dhunga*), which identifies this site as the naturally arisen seat of the goddess (*shakti pitha*). She is venerated by both Buddhists and Hindus, demonstrating the importance of the goddess to Newar culture. Various rites and celebrations honor Purnachandi, including an annual pilgrimage (*yatra*) to the eight *shakti pitha* of Patan. This pilgrimage begins with the worship of all the goddesses in the courtyard in front of the Purnachandi Temple, followed by a daylong journey around Patan making offerings at each *shaki pitha*, culminating in a final communal offering back in front of the Purnachandi Temple. As a tantric goddess, she receives meat and alcohol offerings from participants. The popularity of these types of localized pilgrimage traditions in the Kathmandu Valley today speaks to the importance of the goddess traditions in contemporary practice. More important, this temple and the community rituals supported by the community provide opportunities for the public to gain access to the secret goddess, Siddhi Lakshmi, through the veneration of Purnachandi. Annual celebrations such as these reaffirm community support for the goddess and root these ritual systems in each new generation, affording Newar culture a tremendous amount of cultural continuity with each passing century.

For another deity venerated by Buddhists and Hindus, see Bunga Dya, no. 6.

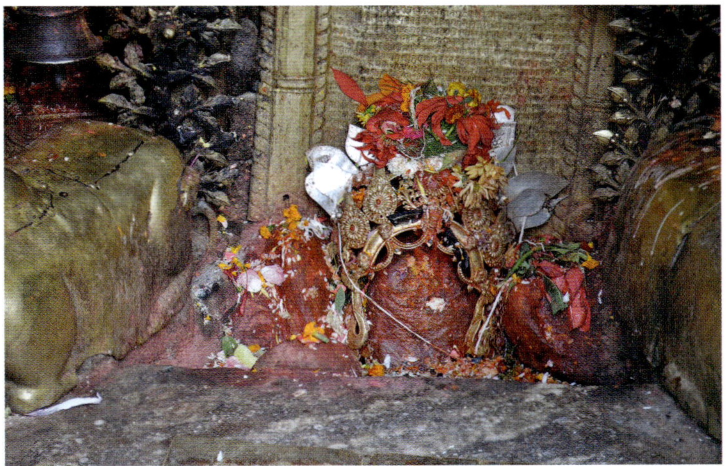

Detail of the crowned *dhunga* within the Purnachandi Temple, located to the left of the central shrine; Patan, Nepal; 2010; photograph © Kerry Lucinda Brown

For the Malla kings of Patan, the esoteric forms of this goddess, whether called Purnachandi, Siddhi Lakshmi, or Taleju, were important in validating their divine right to rule. Subsequent kings of Patan built elaborate temples to reaffirm the importance of goddess veneration to the kingdom. The Degutale Temple, built in 1661, and the grand multistory Taleju Temple, built in 1667 as part of the Patan Royal Palace, reiterate the central importance of these powerful protector goddesses to the kings and their successors. Similarly, the kingdom of Bhaktapur also saw temples erected in honor of Siddhi Lakshmi, such as the seventeenth-century Siddhi Lakshmi Temple and the eighteenth-century Nyatapola Temple. Access to the goddess at these temples was limited to royal tantric priests, known as *karmacharyas*.[5] Thus, while important for state protection, access to Siddhi Lakshmi at these sites was limited to the royal court. Her powers were reserved for use by the king, while at the same time alternative manifestations were provided for public veneration through goddesses like Taleju, Durga, Lakshmi, and Kumari. Siddhi Lakshmi represents the complete, unwavering power and success of the feminine divine. Her multivalent associations in the Kathmandu Valley concentrate her power, making her an important deity for any ruler seeking to wield tantric power. Her ritual veneration connects the dynamic, intertwined religious forces in the sacred geography of the valley.[6] Siddhi Lakshmi encompasses the power of all goddesses. She serves as a powerful tantric deity who provides protection, prosperity, and ritual authority to all who honor her, whether they venerate her secret or public manifestations.

For more on the sacred geography of the Kathmandu Valley, see the Svayambhu Chaitya of Kathmandu, no. 4.

The Malla period lasted until 1769, when Gorkhas from western Nepal, under the leadership of King Prithivi Narayan Shah (r. 1743–1775), conquered the last independent kingdom in the valley and established the Shah dynasty (1769–2008). This new dynasty set the modern political boundaries of Nepal, absorbing the Kathmandu Valley and Newar culture into a new kingdom of Nepal under Shah rule. While Siddhi Lakshmi was unable to bring success to the Malla kings, Newar cultural traditions continued despite political shifts in the valley. Most significantly, the veneration of the goddess was sustained by Shah kings. Their status as divine incarnations of the Hindu god Vishnu required that they maintain the ritual obligations to the state previously established by the Malla rulers. This legacy remains an important aspect of ritual and religious practice in the Kathmandu Valley to the present day.

To learn more about the kings of Nepal as manifestations of the Hindu god Vishnu, see Vishnu Riding on Garuda, no. 18.

Further Reading

Lidke, Jeffrey S. 2017. *The Goddess Within and Beyond the Three Cities: Śākta Tantra and the Paradox of Power in Nepāla-Maṇḍala*. New Delhi: DK Printworld.

Mocko, Anne. 2017. "Tolerance in Nepal Mandala: Communal Relations and Royal Religious Patronage in Malla-Era Kathmandu." In *Toleration in Comparative Perspective*, edited by Vicki A. Spencer, 121–39. Lanham, MD: Lexington Books.

Timalsina, Sthaneshwar. 2006. "Terrifying Beauty: Interplay of the Sanskritic and Vernacular Rituals of Siddhilakṣmī." *International Journal of Hindu Studies* 10, no. 1, 59–73.

Notes

1 Toffin 2007, 293.
2 Lidke 2017, 1–2.
3 Toffin 2007, 394.
4 S. Shrestha 2000.
5 Coyle 2004–5.
6 Slusser 1982, 7.

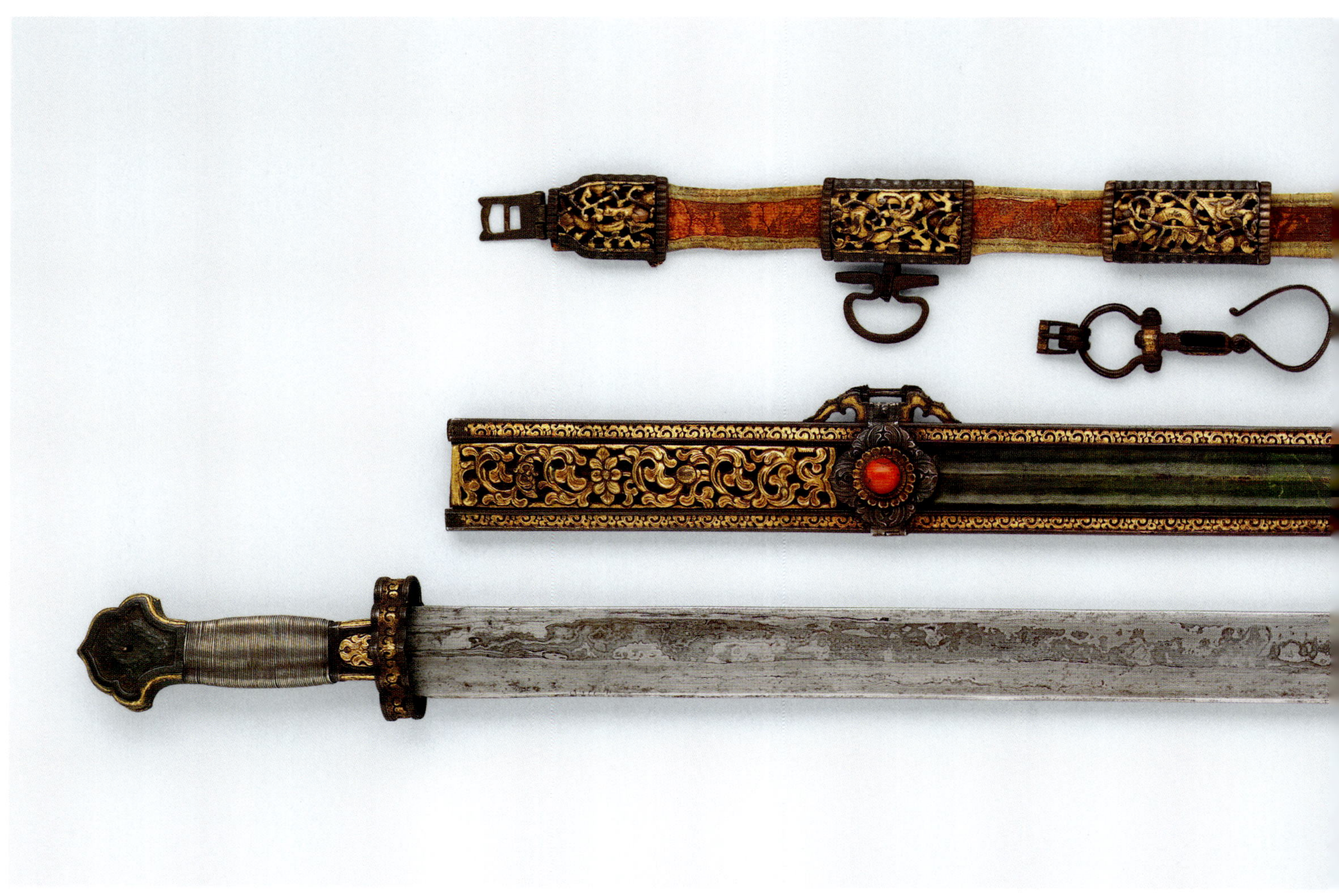

№ 68

Sword, Scabbard, and Sword Belt

Tibet, Blade: ca. 16th–17th century; Hilt, Scabbard, and Belt: ca. early 18th–mid-19th century

The History, Literature, and Art of Tibetan Swords

DONALD J. LA ROCCA

Tibetan armor and weapons were renowned for their quality and effectiveness from as early as the period of the Yarlung dynasty in the seventh century.[1] Swords (*reldri*) were one of the principal weapons and remained in use throughout Tibet for well over a thousand years, only being superseded by firearms in the early twentieth century.[2] Swords are still worn today as part of traditional dress in culturally Tibetan regions on festival occasions. In addition to their former martial function, swords also retain deep significance within Tibetan Buddhism as ritual objects, wielded by oracles or in sacred dances, and as a symbolic weapon of many deities, particularly the wrathful guardians of Buddhism (Tibetan: *gonpo*, Sanskrit: *dharmapala*), and as such are frequently rendered in sculpture, paintings, and other sacred images and texts. As the Sword of Wisdom (*sherab reldri*), for example, representing the ability to cut through spiritual ignorance, it is a chief attribute of bodhisattva Manjushri (Jampelyang). Aspects of this symbolic power are sometimes expressed in the form and decoration of actual swords, which can be complex and beautiful objects, combining expensive materials and fine craftsmanship.[3] However, the majority of Tibetan swords made prior to the modern era are simple and functional objects with minimal decoration, some of which bear signs of repairs or alterations that indicate their reuse over many years, if not generations.

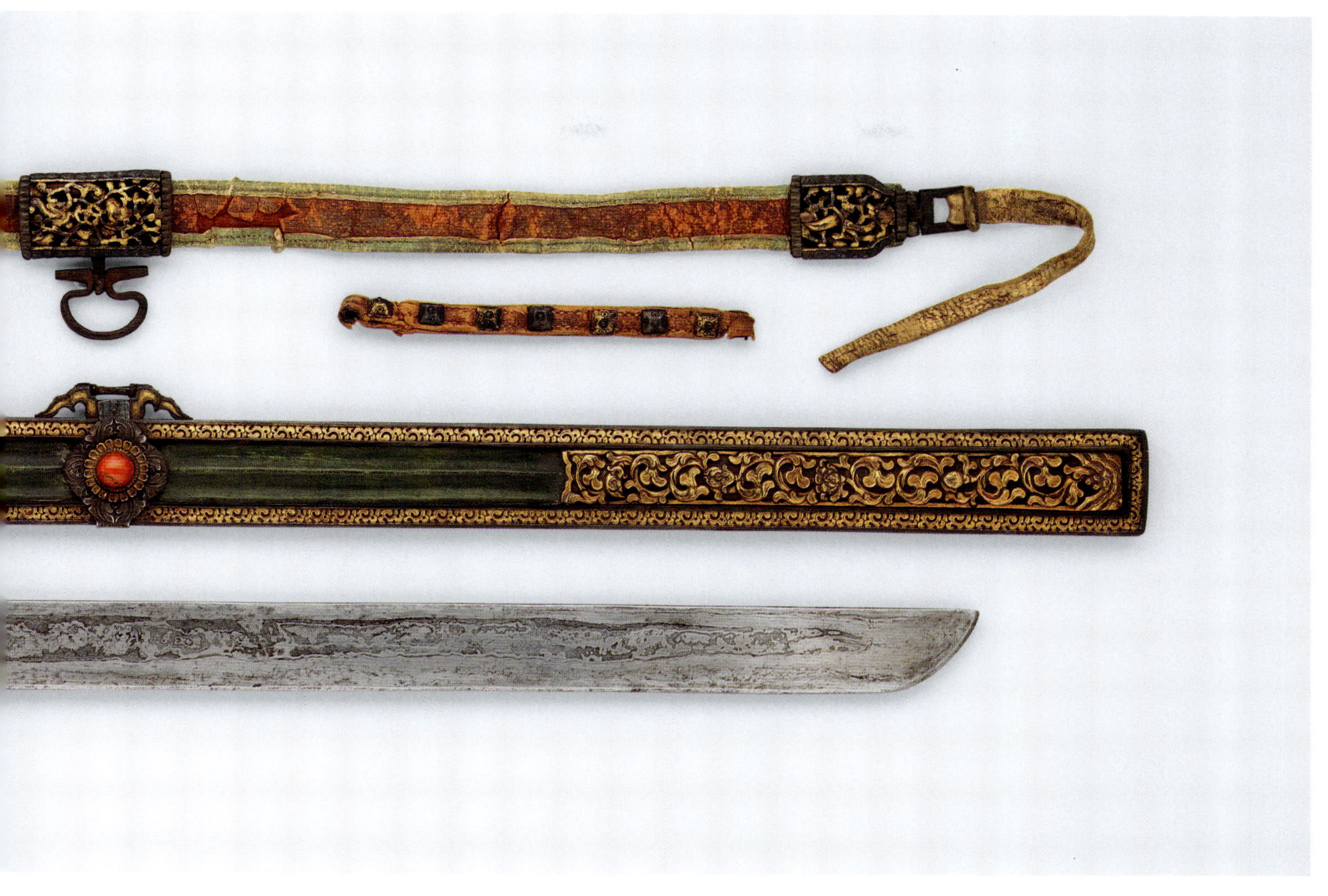

Sword, Scabbard, and Sword Belt; Tibetan; blade ca. 16th–17th century; hilt, scabbard, and belt ca. early 18th–mid-19th century; steel, silver, copper, gold, coral, wood, leather; sword length without scabbard 39 in. (99.1 cm), weight 2 lb. 9.4 oz. (1173.7 g); scabbard weight, 1 lb. 15.7 oz. (898.7 g); The Metropolitan Museum of Art, New York; Purchase, Arthur Ochs Sulzberger Gift, 2014; 2014.262.1a–c, 2014.262.2a, b; CC0 - Creative Commons (CC0 1.0)

Traditional Tibetan Texts and the Typology of Tibetan Swords

A small number of Tibetan texts devoted to arts and crafts (*zorik*) and the appraisal and appreciation of objects (*taktab*) include chapters outlining the connoisseurship of swords.[4] These texts, which date from the fourteenth century to the eighteenth or nineteenth century, ignore hilts, scabbards, or other fittings and focus on blades exclusively, dividing them into five canonical types, each with multiple subtypes. Their "defining characteristics" (*tsennyi*) and "invariable features" (*mingyur ngepai tak*), terms more familiar from Tibetan debate manuals and other textbooks involved with monastic education, are categorized and described in ways that are often poetic and metaphorical, rather than technical.[5] The five types that repeat in all of the texts, with some variations in spelling, are: *zhangma*, *sokpo*, *hupe*, *guzi*, and *jarel*. Explanations of the meanings of the five names vary among the texts and appear in part to be fanciful etymologies created to supply lost facts.[6] For instance, *zhangma* in one text is said to derive from the western Tibetan kingdom of Zhangzhung and in another to refer to the emperor's uncle (Tibetan: *zhang*), who created the type. The only unambiguous name, *sokpo*, connects the creation of this type to a branch of the Mongols (Tibetan: *sog po*). For each there is an origin story involving a legendary event or a mythological, legendary, or historical figure, the earliest starting in the reign of the semilegendary fifth- or sixth-century king Drigum Tsenpo (his name meaning, "to die by the sword").[7] While it is seldom possible through the texts to make direct correlations between the canonical types and existing Tibetan swords, the texts nevertheless demonstrate the importance accorded to swords historically and establish a literary foundation for their understanding and appreciation.[8]

The Art and Technology of Tibetan Blades

The blades of most extant Tibetan swords, those handmade prior to the twentieth century, have a "hairpin" pattern clearly visible on both sides, possibly what is sometimes referred to in the texts as being

Detail of the blade of a Tibetan sword showing a hairpin pattern; eastern Tibet; 18th–19th century; iron, copper alloy, wood, ray skin, leather, turquoise, coral, glass; The Metropolitan Museum of Art, New York; Bequest of George C. Stone, 1935; 36.25.1463a; CC0 - Creative Commons (CC0 1.0)

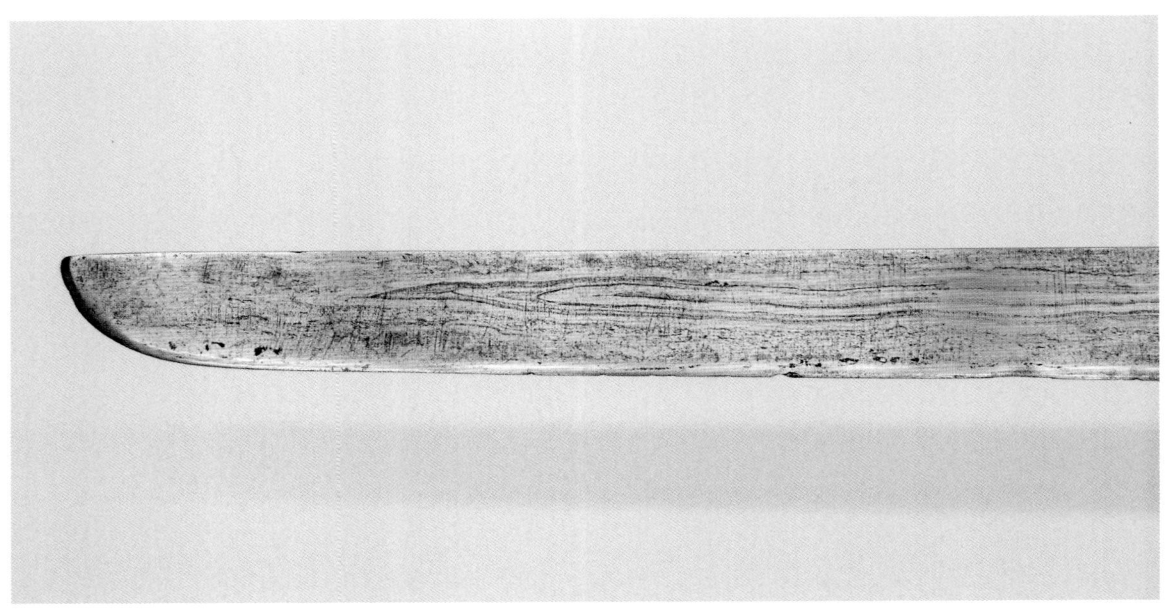

"like the Milky Way."[9] The pattern is formed of closely set, slightly wavy, alternating dark and light lines that meet in a point near the tip of the blade. It is created by a forging process known as pattern welding, in which rods of higher carbon and lower carbon iron or steel are folded over and hammered together. In the textual references the harder, whiter steel is generally called "male iron" (*pochak*) and the more ductile, darker steel is "female iron" (*mochak*).[10] Other less frequently encountered patterns include a series of wavy lines resembling tiger stripes, a series of concentrically rolled lines, and, rarest of all, a more complex variegated pattern that looks something like swirling water or burl wood.

One of the few known examples of this last type is preserved on the sword featured here. The blade ranks among the finest examples of Tibetan pattern welding, evoking ripples and eddies in swirling water, billowing clouds, flowing mist, and wood-grain designs, in some ways reminiscent of the ethereal forms of *hamon* (tempering patterns) seen on the famed samurai sword blades of Japan. The pattern on this blade fits a description by Tashi Namgyel, writing in the sixteenth century, of blades made from blending together "mixed iron" (*nadu, nadu dre,* or *chakdre*) to create "many flowing and swirling designs."[11]

Its hilt is an ornate example of the classic Tibetan form, with trefoil pommel, grip wrapped in silver wire, a short collar below the grip, and oval guard with downturned and cusped edges—the sides of the pommel, collar, and guard chiseled and gilt with matching designs. Unfortunately, the characteristic bead of turquoise or coral, usually mounted in a silver bezel on the front of the pommel, is missing.

A Tibetan sword, depending on the fittings of its scabbard, is generally worn in one of two ways. Many are designed to be carried diagonally across the front of the body, thrust through a waist belt or sash, with the hilt to wearer's right just above waist level. In the second method, often found with more elaborate swords, including this example, the scabbard is suspended from a sword belt and worn at the left hip in a style inspired by Chinese fashion that was also popular in Tibet and Mongolia. The scabbard of this sword comprises a wooden core sheathed in leather and framed with elaborately chiseled and gilt-iron mounts. It is one of the few swords that retains both its matching scabbard and sword belt, the latter also fitted with pierced and gilt iron mounts. The mounts are excellent examples of the type of ornamental pierced ironwork often seen on Tibetan ceremonial saddles and other fine metalwork. Those on the scabbard feature panels of lush flora scrolls skillfully rendered in a precise yet fluid manner that is a hallmark of the best ironwork from eastern Tibet and Mongolia.

See Saddle Made for Yuthok Tashi Dhondup, no. 101.

The style and treatment of the hilt, scabbard mounts, and belt fittings suggest they were made between the early eighteenth and mid-nineteenth century. The blade, a masterpiece of its kind, is probably earlier and may date from the sixteenth to seventeenth century. While it was typically not the custom in Europe to refit old blades, in Asia, it was not unusual for highly regarded sword blades, generations old, to be remounted with updated fittings, which appears to be the case here.

This sword, scabbard, and belt were reportedly captured by Lieutenant Edward Henry Lenon (1838–1893), a British soldier, at the Battle of North Taku (Dagu) Fort, Tianjin, China, on August 21, 1860.[12] The battle was a fierce engagement fought within the broader context of the Second Opium War,

Detail of the blade of a Tibetan sword showing pattern welding designs; The Metropolitan Museum of Art, New York; Purchase, Arthur Ochs Sulzberger Gift, 2014; 2014.262.1a; CC0 - Creative Commons (CC0 1.0)

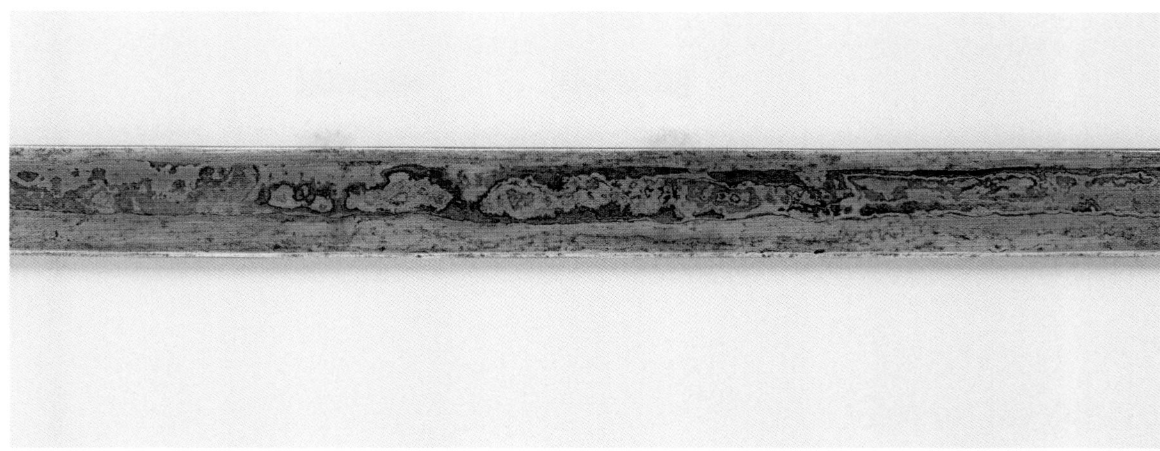

and Lenon was later awarded the Victoria Cross, Britain's highest military honor, for his part in it. The carnage that resulted from the devastating combined Anglo-French assault on the fortress was documented in a series of photographs by Felice Beato (1832–1909). The Qing garrison was commanded by General Sengge Rinchen (1811–1865), a Mongolian nobleman and experienced soldier with a prestigious record of imperial service, who had successfully repelled an Anglo-French attack on the same fort a year earlier.[13] The sword, taken by Lenon during or after the battle, is of a quality and style suitable for personal use by Sengge Rinchen or one of the Mongol officers serving under him, which would account for the presence of such an elaborate Tibetan sword in a Chinese fortress at the time.

Notes

1 Stein 1972, 62.

2 For an overview of the history and development of arms and armor in Tibet, see La Rocca 2006, 3–19, and for swords in particular, 146–73.

3 For examples of exceptional swords incorporating iconography of this kind, see a sword in the Royal Armouries, Leeds, UK (XXVIS.295) and a sword guard (formerly in a private collection) and a sword, both in the Metropolitan Museum of Art, New York (2014.533 and 1995.136), illustrated and discussed in La Rocca 2006, 148–53.

4 The texts are identified and discussed in La Rocca 2006, 146–48, 252–64; and La Rocca 2014.

5 Perdue 1992, 60–74.

6 On this point, see La Rocca 2006, 147–48; La Rocca 2014a, 92, 98–100.

7 Regarding Drigum Tsenpo and the stories of his death and how it purportedly relates to his name, see Stein 1972, 48–49, 232.

8 For examples of extant swords that possibly correspond to some of the canonical types, see La Rocca 2014, esp. 95–97.

9 Tib. *dgu tshigs skya mo 'dra.*

10 On the construction and metallurgy of the blades, see particularly La Rocca 2006, 146, 253–57, 264; La Rocca 2014, 89–94.

11 *lcags 'dres pa ni ri mo gya gyu mang.* Tashi Namgyel, cited in La Rocca 2006, 168, cat. 71, in a discussion of the most closely comparable blade of this kind, which is found on a sword in the Pitt Rivers Museum, Oxford (1989.1.1.1, .2). For one version of the quoted phrases, see British Library, Or 11,374, fol. 76b. Tibetan blades of "mixed iron" are also discussed in La Rocca 2014, 93–94.

12 Two old paper labels were still attached to the sword when it was acquired by the museum in 2014. The handwritten information on these labels describes it as "a rare Chinese Mandarin officer's sword . . . taken by Lt. E. H. Lenon . . . at battle of Taku Forts 1860 . . . purchased from descendants in 1964." Object files, Department of Arms and Armor, Metropolitan Museum of Art.

13 For the entry on Sengge Rinchen in Wikipedia, see https://en.wikipedia.org/wiki/Sengge_Rinchen, accessed July 16, 2021.

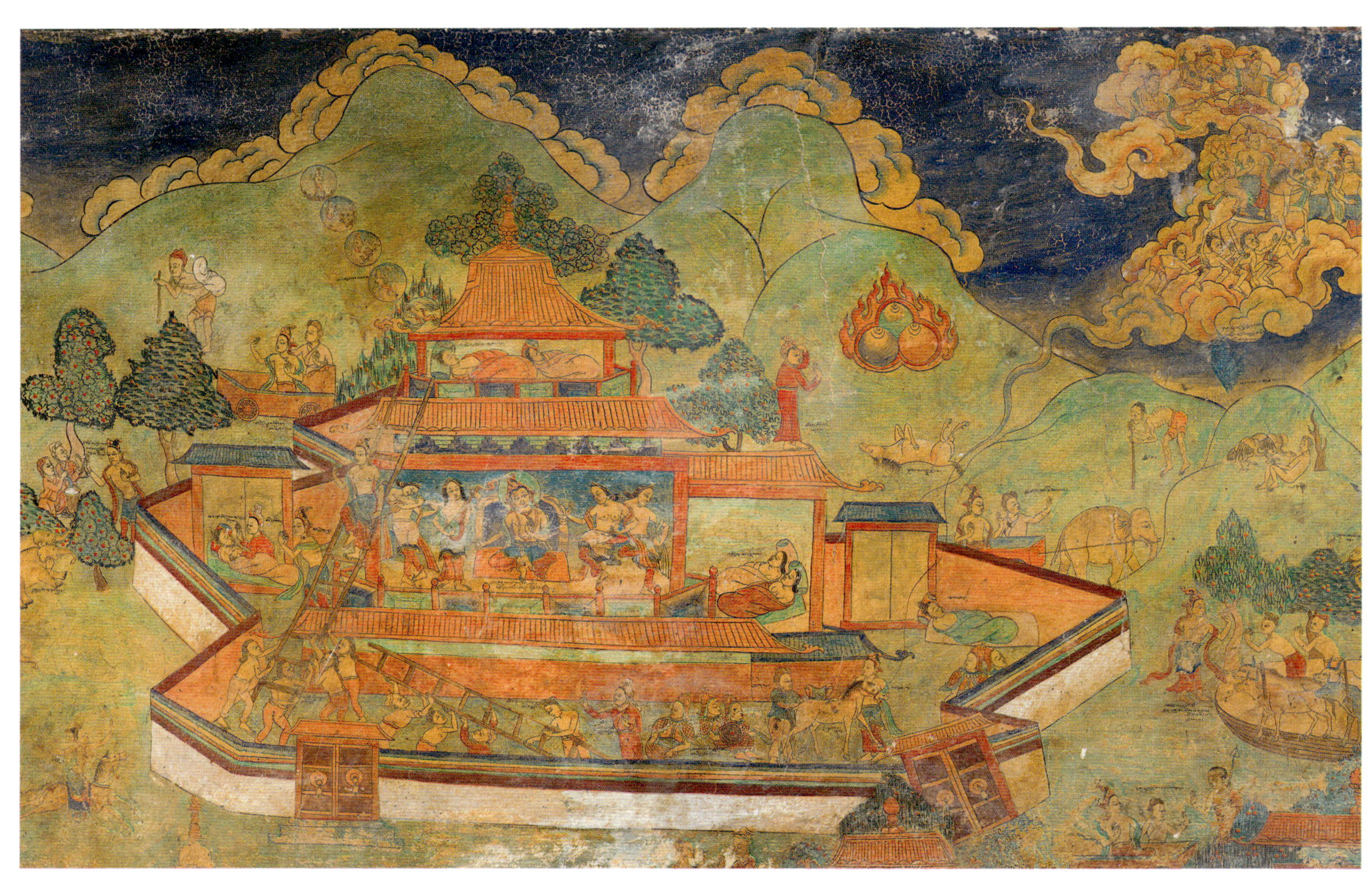

№ 69

A Monumental Life of the Buddha Mural

Puntsok Ling Monastery, Tsang region, central Tibet (present-day TAR, China), ca. 1615–1630

Taranatha's Vision of Shakyamuni's Quest

ANDREW QUINTMAN AND KURTIS R. SCHAEFFER

Visualizing the Story of the Buddha

THE STORY OF THE BUDDHA'S LIFE has been told and retold countless times throughout the history of Buddhism and across Asia. The story presents both a gripping tale of personal transformation and a dazzling vision of ultimate meaning in a vast cosmos of gods, demons, and humans. The tale of the prince who left home to discover the meaning of life, became enlightened, and spent the remainder of his life teaching others the contemplative and ethical ways of thinking is the founding narrative of Buddhism and a deep source of inspiration for Buddhists grappling with what it means to live a good life.

In Tibet, the Buddha's life was a popular topic for writers; dozens of versions exist throughout Tibet's rich literary history, from encyclopedic chronicles of the Buddha's every deed to brief stories meant for novice monks and nuns. The story was also a popular topic for large mural paintings that adorn Tibet's temples and monasteries. While many narrative murals depicting the Buddha's deeds feature his previous lives, some focus on his final life as Buddha Shakyamuni, the founder of Buddhism in our current era of life on earth. One of the most striking examples of the narrative of Buddha Shakyamuni to be found in Tibet is the monumental mural at a key institution of the Jonang tradition, Puntsok Ling Monastery.

The Mural Scene

This image shows a small detail depicting a prominent scene from the Buddha's life prior to his enlightenment: his renunciation of royal trappings and escape from the family palace. The complex arrangement presents several stages of narrative within a single visual field. Shakyamuni appears in courtly jewelry and clothing, indicating that he is not yet awakened as the Buddha, but rather still a young prince, a buddha-to-be, enmeshed in the mundane social world of palace life. In the upper left and right, the prince journeys beyond the palace walls, where he experiences, for the first time, the hard facts of human existence. In the upper right, he encounters an aging person, thereby discovering that, one day, he too will age. In the upper left he sees a corpse wrapped in a white cloth, according to traditional Tibetan custom, and carried on the back of an undertaker. He realizes, for the first time, that he too will die. These constitute two of the so-called "four sights" (together with a sick person and a wandering mendicant) that bring about an existential crisis in the young prince. The boy's father worries these grim realities of human life will prevent the prince from taking his rightful place as king, and so attempts to distract him with women and song. In the palace's large central room, the prince enjoys the music and dance of his harem, all staged by the king. But palace amusements are no longer of interest to the buddha-to-be. Instead, he decides to escape by night in search of liberation from suffering. The image signals his escape through the repetition of a single ladder. To the right sits a horizontal ladder, so heavy, the story tells us, that even five hundred men (represented here by only five) could not lift it. To the left stands the ladder now miraculously raised vertically by a single *yaksha*, an earthly spirit conspiring with the gods to ensure the prince's escape. The prince descends the ladder and joins his horse Kanthaka and charioteer Chandaka, who stand near the palace gate on the lower right. Then, as depicted in the upper right of the detail, all three ride away from the palace with the horse born on the shoulders of the gods, so as not to wake the palace guards with the sounds of hoofbeats. Kanthaka later returns, only to die just outside the palace walls, his heart broken by the prince's departure.

Designed by Taranatha Kunga Nyingpo (1575–1634); Detail depicting the Buddha's escape from life in the palace, Life of the Buddha Mural, panel 1; Puntsok Ling Monastery, Tsang region, central Tibet (present-day TAR, China); ca. 1615–1630; photograph by Andrew Quintman and Kurtis R. Schaeffer, 2011

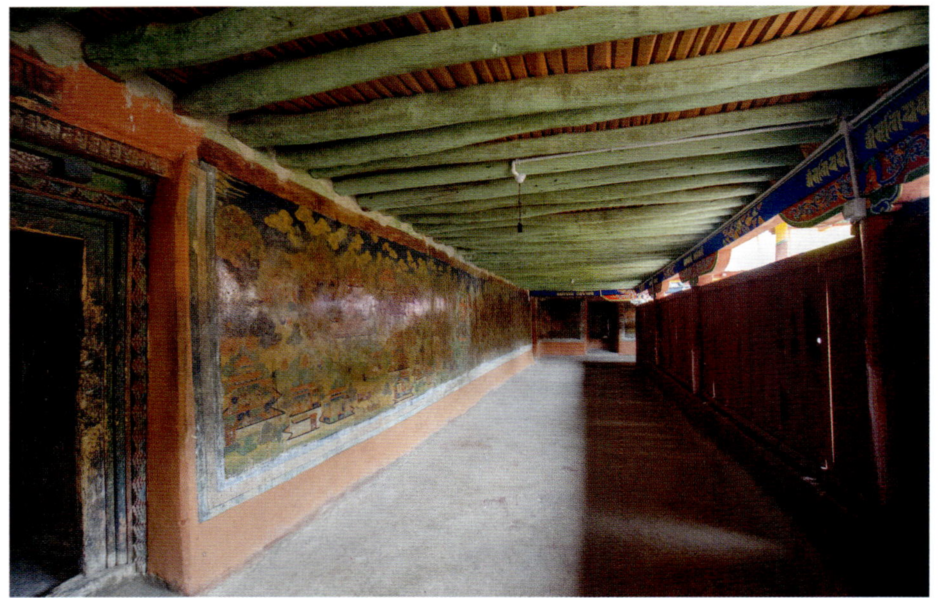

Ambulatory of Puntsok Ling Monastery, Tsang region, central Tibet (present-day TAR, China), showing the northern wall with Life of the Buddha Mural, panel 7; photograph by Andrew Quintman and Kurtis R. Schaeffer, 2011

The Context of Puntsok Ling Monastery: Synthesizing Text and Image

The seventeenth-century Tibetan luminary Taranatha (1575–1634) planned and commissioned this monumental life of the Buddha mural for his seat at Puntsok Ling Monastery in the Tsang region of central Tibet. The work presents the Buddha's life on a grand scale, at a level of detail and complexity rarely matched. The mural is roughly 5½ feet (1.7 meters) in height and runs nearly 277 linear feet (84.5 meters), divided into fifteen panels separated by doors or windows. In total, the visual narrative covers some 1,450 square feet (135 square meters) of painted surface. The murals extend along four walls of an external ambulatory space on the monastery's second floor. The resulting space allows the viewer to walk through the Buddha's deeds from beginning to end, while simultaneously being surrounded by the sum total of his life.

See Mayadevi Giving Birth to Siddhartha, no. 3.

On the Buddha's enlightenment, see Mahabodhi Temple Model, no. 25.

The designs were based largely on Taranatha's literary rendering of the Buddha's life entitled *The Sun of Faith*, which itself draws broadly from the classic Indian texts of Buddhist monastic law known as *Vinaya*. Tibetan accounts most commonly divide the life story into twelve discernable acts: 1) his descent to earth from Tushita Heaven; 2) his mother Queen Maya's dream of his impending birth; 3) his birth; 4) his skill in youthful sports; 5) his education as a prince; 6) his life of pleasure in the royal palace; 7) his renunciation of royal status (shown here); 8) ascetic practices; 9) his battle with demons; 10) his enlightenment; 11) his career as a spiritual teacher; and finally 12) his death. *The Sun of Faith* instead presents the Buddha's story in 125 chapters that incorporate all twelve acts, but also includes more than one hundred stories of the Buddha teaching, traveling, meeting gods, performing miracles, and overcoming demons in his effort to expand the Buddhist community of monks, nuns, and laypeople throughout northern India. These stories are not commonly illustrated in Tibetan texts or painting, yet constitute a majority of Taranatha's literary and visual narratives.

Taranatha also composed a painting manual with guidelines for translating his literary narrative into visual images. Painters would have used these guidelines to plan mural vignettes, though it is clear that they took creative license in mapping the layout of scenes. The result is a complex presentation, lacking formal chapter markers, although the artists made creative use of landscape and architectural features to designate breaks between narrative elements. Some stories extend across wide sections of mural space to suggest geographic movement. Viewers would have had to spend time interpreting the images to appreciate the action.

Comparisons and Contrasts

For an example of a portable scroll painting, see Portrait of Situ Panchen, no. 83.

See Murals of Gongkar Chode, no. 58; Jokhang Temple, no. 7.

While the Buddha's life story divided into twelve acts was popular in Tibet, perhaps the most common source for rendering visual depictions of the life is the work known as *The Wish-Fulfilling Vine of Bodhisattva Lives* (*Bodhisattvavadanakalpalata*), an eleventh-century composition of Sanskrit verse (translated into Tibetan in the thirteenth century) in 108 chapters and narrating episodes from the Buddha's previous rebirths as well as selected episodes of his final life on earth as Shakyamuni. These stories were rendered in portable scroll paintings (thangka) and woodblock prints, but are perhaps equally known through their presentation in murals adorning monastery temples and assembly halls. Some examples, such those found at the monasteries of Gongkar Chode, Drepung, and Tashilhunpo, as well as the Jokhang Temple in Lhasa, cover hundreds of square meters.

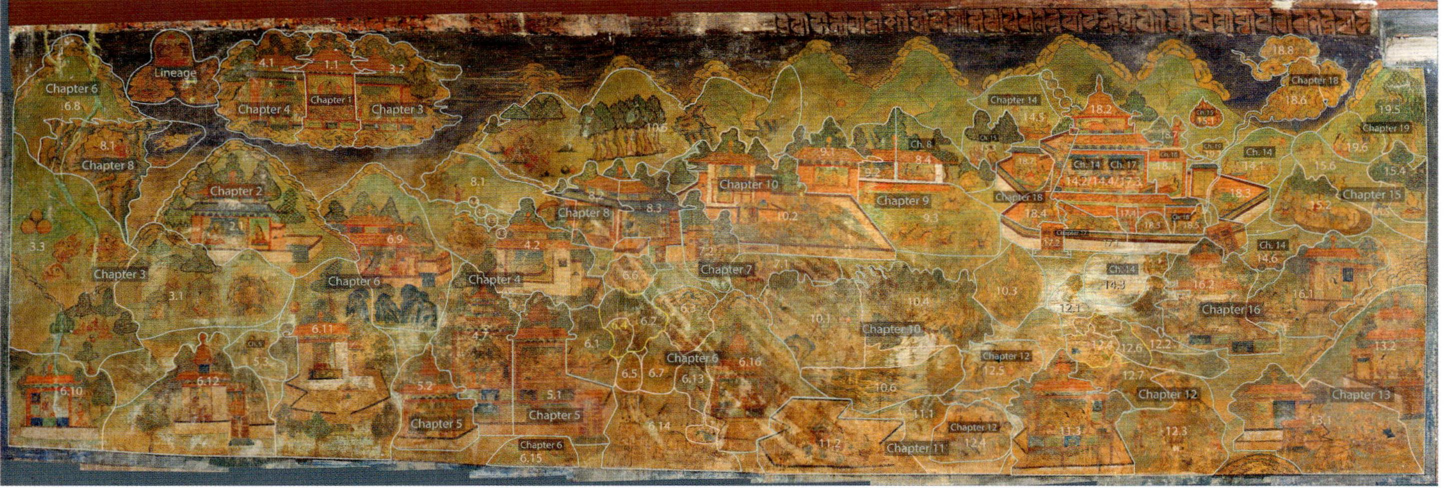

Designed by Taranatha Kunga Nyingpo (1575–1634); Detail with annotations showing outline for chapters 1–19 of *The Sun of Faith*, Life of the Buddha Mural, panel 1; Puntsok Ling Monastery, Tsang region, central Tibet (present-day TAR, China); ca. 1615–1630; photograph and annotations by Andrew Quintman and Kurtis R. Schaeffer, 2015

Taranatha also criticized the practice of dividing the Buddha's life into twelve acts, suggesting it mixed distinct types of Indian Buddhist literature. The first eleven acts come from the *Living Out of the Game Sutra* (*Lalitavistara Sutra*), a massive Buddha narrative of the Greater Vehicle tradition (the Mahayana), which does not include the Buddha's death. Tibetan writers drew an account of the Buddha's final days, Taranatha claims, from the *Vinaya*, which Tibetans consider to be from the so-called Lesser Vehicle tradition (the Hinayana). Taranatha rejects the mixing of these two traditions. For him, the Greater Vehicle emphasizes the miraculous and cosmic aspects of the Buddha's life, while the Lesser Vehicle version emphasizes the social, the ethical, and the earthbound details of the story. For him, the Buddha's life in the *Vinaya* forms the most useful version of the story; it provides what ordinary people who might view the mural are able to comprehend. It is for this reason that he spends so much time telling stories of the Buddha's travels among the people of India. His encounters with farmers, merchants, beggars, kings, and queens are what give the Buddha a human quality. In the mural, the Buddha walks among humans, and though he may transcend human foibles, in Taranatha's vision the Buddha traverses the world among its inhabitants. In this way, Taranatha's mural of the Buddha's life contrasts with the portraiture and statues that depict the Buddha solely as an enlightened figure, sitting high above and far removed from the activities of his disciples and devotees.

If there are doctrinal and pedagogical differences between the Buddha of the *Vinaya*-inspired narrative painting and the Buddha of more static, iconic presentations, these differences translate into the visual language of the narrative mural. The Buddha's encounters with manifold humans, gods, and demons occur in diverse landscapes and entail many types of action, from sailing the seas to scaling mountains, from talking with queens in palaces to meeting merchants on the road. Each of these uses a visual logic that would have taken time and attention for viewers to make the most of. Repetition, as we have seen in the case of the ladder, encourages the reader to move back and forth between spaces on the mural to work out the temporal flow of the story. The density of the many narratives, coming one right after the other, stacked vertically or winding back and forth among other episodes, holds the potential to arrest the viewer with its constant motion, the sustained activity that made the Buddhist teachings flourish. Here the Buddha is not sitting in meditation, he is in the world, talking with people, on the move. The viewer, too, must be in motion to follow the story; one must walk one hundred meters to get the whole story, to fully immerse oneself in the life of the Buddha.

Further Reading

Quintman, Andrew, and Kurtis R. Schaeffer. 2016. "The Life of the Buddha at Rtag brtan Phun tshogs gling Monastery in Text, Image, and Institution: A Preliminary Overview." *Journal of Tibetology* 13, 32–73.

Quintman, Andrew, and Kurtis R. Schaeffer. 2021. "The Life of the Buddha." http://www.lifeofthebuddha.org.

Tenzin Chögyel. 2015. *The Life of the Buddha*. Translated with an introduction by Kurtis R. Schaeffer. New York: Penguin Classics.

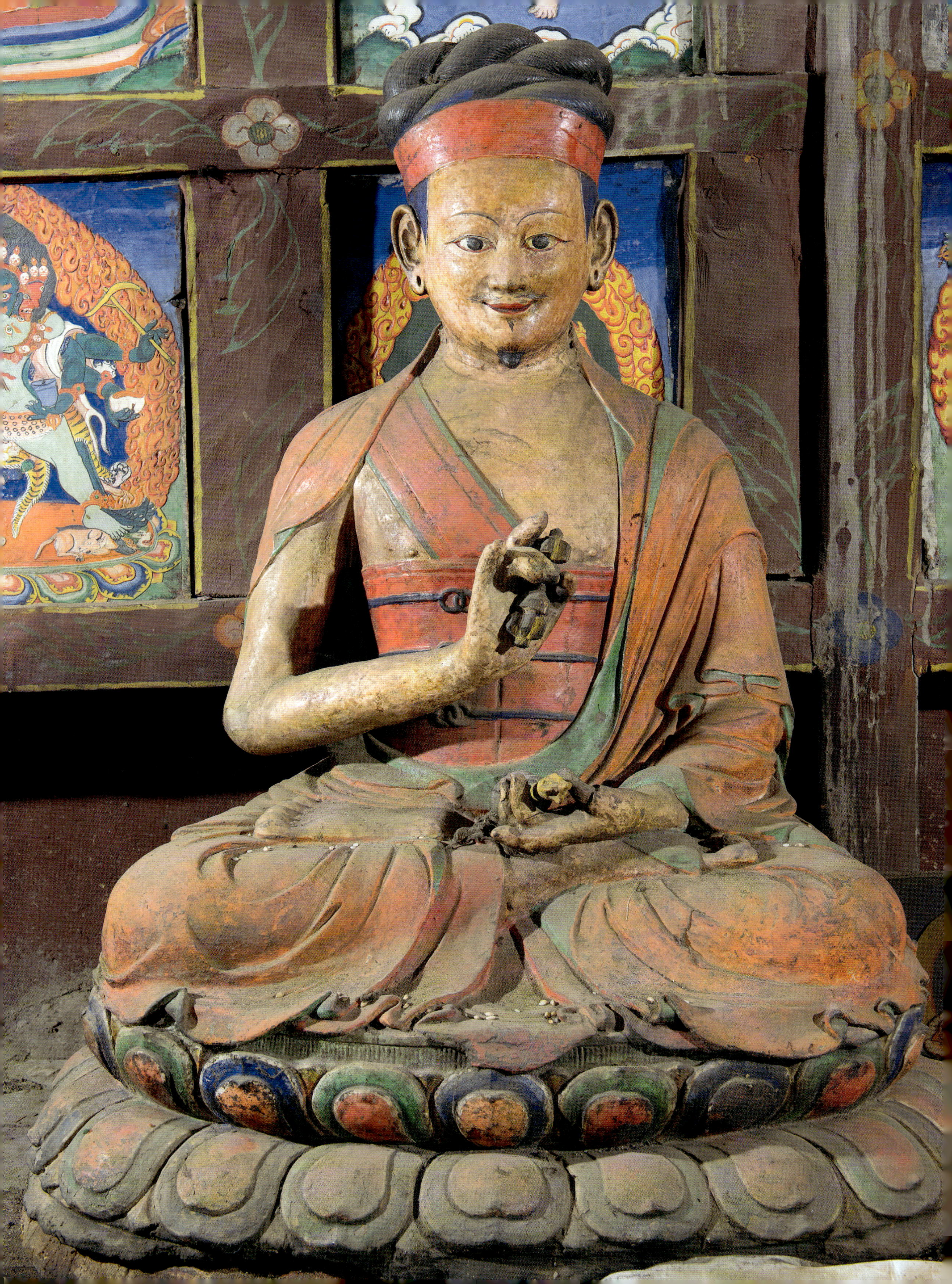

№ 70

Portrait of Ngadak Puntsok Rigdzin

Lo Gekhar, Mustang, Nepal, mid-17th century

Papier-Mâché Sculpture and the Nyingma School at the Periphery

CHRISTIAN LUCZANITS

Ngadak Puntsok Rigdzin (1592–1656); Lo Gekhar Monastery, Mustang, Nepal; mid-17th century; papier-mâché; height approx. 35½ in. (90 cm); photograph by C. Luczanits, 2014

This life-size portrait depicts Ngadak Puntsok Rigdzin (1592–1656), a Nyingma tradition master of the Ngadak family from western Tibet.[1] This teacher is best known for being one of the four yogins who opened the hidden land of Sikkim to Buddhism. The notion of a "hidden land" surrounded by mountains signifies an ideal ground for Buddhist practice, and Sikkim is described as such in Nyingma treasure literature. Meeting there, the four yogins enthroned its first Buddhist ruler in 1642.[2] In 1651 Puntsok Rigdzin visited Lowo (Mustang) at the invitation of the royal couple Aham Samdrub Rabten and his Ladakhi wife Ayum Nyida Gyelmo, where this image has been preserved at Lo Gekhar Monastery.

The identity of the depicted is clarified by an inscribed metal sculpture of the same yogin in nearby Tsarang Village. That the portrayed is the same teacher can be concluded from his distinctive hairstyle and unusual dress, especially the lower robe wrapped around the lower body and supported by three parallel strings. The inscription on the bronze reads:

> Worship to the teacher!
> This image of Todrengtsel source of all virtues [Puntsok],
> auspicious emanation of the Shakya clan [Rig-] and the Tibetan ruler,
> and upholder [-dzin] of the profound treasure teachings
> was made to generate faith and the nine desirables.
> Having completed the aspiration of the glorious teacher,
> may I along with my court be endowed with a long life free of disease,
> authority, prosperity, perfection, and the holy dharma.
> May this wish be fulfilled and protected in this life and in future.
> Made by Agon, born of the Ama clan, and his noble spouse Nyida.[3]

This metal sculpture, thus, must have been produced shortly after the visit of Ngadak Puntsok Rigdzin to Mustang, the vase in the teacher's hand symbolizing the wish for his long life. The papier-mâché portrait very likely also stems from about the same time. Considering the background of the portrayed master, the emphasis on the preservation of secular power and health in the inscription is less surprising.

These portraits offer a fascinating glimpse into the mid-seventeenth century, when the Nyingma tradition appears to have mushroomed along the southern border of the Himalayas. This is in part associated with the political instability in central Tibet at the time. Ngadak Puntsok Rigdzin himself founded Tashiding Monastery in Sikkim, and the monastery in which his sculpture is found, Lo Gekhar, must have seen a major restoration at that time.

Lo Gekhar Monastery

See Padmasambhava and His Manifestations, no. 43.

For more on hidden treasures and treasure revealers, see *Dorje* Discovered by Dorje Lingpa, no. 51.

The temple of Lo Gekhar, also known as Gar Gonpa, is considered the oldest Buddhist temple of Mustang and is contemporaneous with the first monastery of Tibet, Samye, which was founded in the late eighth century. The connection of these two monuments is recorded in the *Pema Katang*, a text containing the biography of Padmasambhava, the teacher credited with the taming of local deities across the Himalayas. This text was discovered by the treasure revealer Orgyen Lingpa (b. 1323), his date thus providing a *terminus ante quem* for the existence of Lo Gekhar. The relevant account is found in canto 62, recording the completion of Samye Monastery, and is translated as follows (with explanatory additions in square brackets):

> "At Lowo [Mustang], the place which is as if a *rakshasi* [a demoness] were lying on her back, place on her heart a monastery with nine floors, a stupa on her navel, another small and black one on her head, and one hundred and eight on her four limbs![4]
>
> In Meldro is the naga king called Shines in Meldro. He has great influence in Tibet; I will establish for him a naga treasure; I want his life philtre [life water]."
>
> And the Guru came along into Meldro. Keeping his promise, shaking the depths, giving solid explanations, and having given treasure and a place of worship for the nagas, he received the life philtre. However, no oath bound the mind of the nagas, so to keep them silent, he erected at Lowo the monastery of White Virtue.[5]

Accordingly, Lo Gekhar is this monastery of White Virtue, and the surrounding chorten and springs—referred to by the reference to the naga king, a serpent spirit associated with water—are part of the holy site. This account also explains why Lo Gekhar is of great cultural and religious importance to the Mustang region and to Tibetan Buddhism at large. Apart from its thick-walled core, the temple as it stands today is, of course, much more recent. The high-quality papier-mâché sculptures found at the site, the portrait of Ngadak Puntsok Rigdzin being one of them, indicate renewed attention to this monastery in the mid-seventeenth century.

Papier-Mâché Sculpture

See Portrait of Lowo Khenchen Sonam Lhundrup, no. 63.

For more on the production of clay images in the Himalayas, see Maitreya Statue at Jampa Lhakhang, Bhutan, no. 9.

For another work made of papier-mâché, see Ritual Dance Mask of Guru Dorje Drolo, no. 94.

Tibetan art is well known for its excellent metal sculpture, the portrait of Lowo Khenchen being a good example for an earlier sculpture of the same region. But at least half of the sculptural production preserved in the region today uses other materials, among them clay and different varieties of papier-mâché being the most prominent. Clay was used extensively in early Tibetan art for the main sculptures of monuments and has been researched to some extent,[6] but papier-mâché has not yet received similar attention. The designation of the material itself is an issue, as the term "papier-mâché" is used here for a wide variety of similar fibrous materials that enable lightweight, hollow, three-dimensional sculptures, the best of which are remarkable for their fine modeling.

The sanctum of Lo Gekhar predominantly features clay and papier-mâché sculptures, among them a set of the Eight Manifestations of Padmasambhava likely made under the same master artist responsible for the portrait of Ngadak Puntsok Rigdzin. Although partially cleaned, repaired, and repainted, these images share the same attention to detail resulting in an unusual degree of realism.

From the documentation of monastery collections throughout Mustang undertaken since 2012, we can now say that all major periods of sculptural production in the region also preserve excellent sculpture in papier-mâché, although of different technologies. Fifteenth- to sixteenth-century metal sculpture is accompanied by an equally refined school of papier-mâché sculpture of different sizes, Namgyal Monastery alone preserving parts of several sculpture sets.[7] Further, accomplished sculpture in this material is also found beyond the seventeenth century; a triad of Padmasambhava in the palace of Ghami is a particular compelling example preserved in the shrine made for it.

Nyingma Tradition

See Potala Palace, no. 71.

The life of Ngadak Puntsok Rigdzin, leading him from western Tibet to Sikkim, and including a short but impactful visit to Mustang, demonstrates the mobility of Nyingma protagonists and the decentralized character of this tradition before it established itself at the very heart of political power in Tibet through the support of the Fifth Dalai Lama Ngawang Lobzang Gyatso (1617–1682). Not only did the Fifth Dalai Lama reveal treasures himself, which he transmitted to the Nyingma master Terdak Lingpa (1646–1714), but he also supported the latter in establishing Mindroling Monastery.[8]

Guru Padmasambha, the scholar manifestations of Padmasambhava; Lo Gekhar Monastery, Mustang, Nepal; mid-17th century; papier-mâché; 26¾ × 22⅞ × 15¾ in. (68 × 58 × 40 cm); photograph by C. Luczanits, 2014

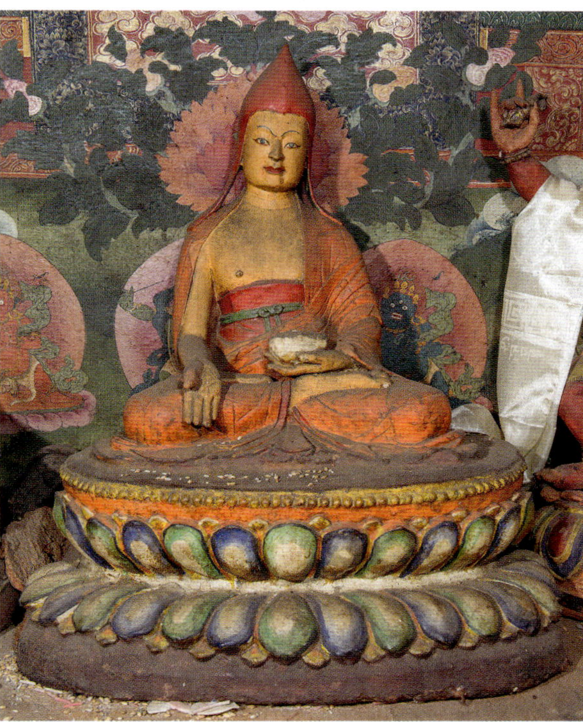

Mahasiddha Damarupa of a Lamdre lineage; Namgyal Monastery, Mustang, Nepal; 16th century; 13⅜ × 9½ × 5⅞ in. (34 × 24 × 15 cm); photograph by C. Luczanits, 2013

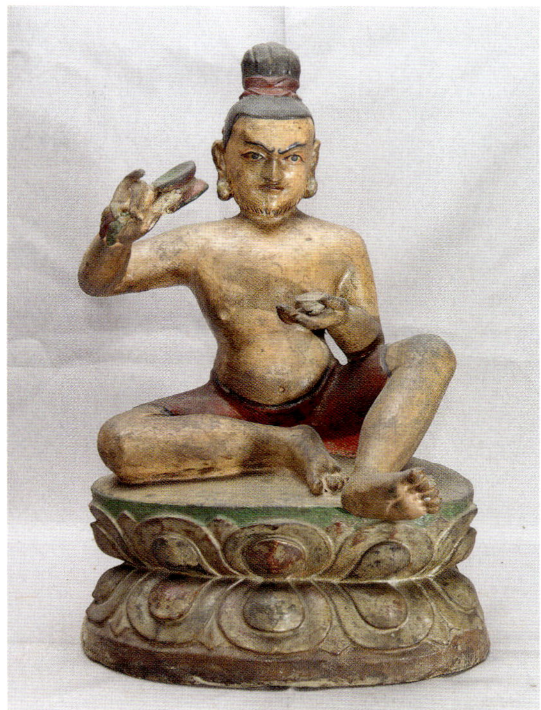

This development in central Tibet, too, directly reflects back on peripheral regions such as Mustang, where the monasteries of Kutsab Ternga and Gonpa Gang were established by Orgyen Pelzang (1617–1677) and his disciple and successor Kunzang Longyang (1644–1696) respectively.[9] Like Ngadak Puntsok Rigdzin, these teachers traveled widely and received teachings from numerous scholars and traditions, until establishing monasteries themselves under the support of local elites, in this case the rulers of Lower Mustang, a pattern that may be considered typical of the time.

Further Reading

Dorje, Gyurme, and Matthew Kapstein. 1991. *The Nyingma School of Tibetan Buddhism: Its Fundamentals and History.* Boston: Wisdom.

Ehrhard, Franz-Karl. 2005. "The mNga' bdag Family and the Tradition of Rig 'dzin Zhig po gling pa (1524–1583) in Sikkim." *Bulletin of Tibetology* 41, no. 2, 11–29.

Harrison, John, Christian Luczanits, Charles Ramble, and Nyima Drandul, eds. 2018. *A Blessing for the Land: The Architecture, Art and History of a Buddhist Nunnery in Mustang, Nepal.* Kathmandu: Vajra.

Notes

1 The documentation of this image and research on it are results of an AHRC-funded research project, "Tibetan Buddhist Monastery Collections Today" (Grant Ref: AH/N00681X/1).

2 See the most detailed account on his life in Ehrhard 2005.

3 The image has been published in A. Heller 2010a, 99–103, figs. 7.9a, 7.9b, its inscription transcribed in n. 14. She identifies the teacher based on a mention in the Tsarang Molla (D. Jackson 1984, 150, 155), without attempting to explore his background. Heller's reading has been amended on the bases of photographs on the Mustang DVD of Lionel Fournier. The Sanskrit text ending the inscription is not documented on these photographs and thus is not being reproduced here: *na mo gu ru/ phun tshogs dge legs kun 'byung thod phreng bstsal// skal ldan don du shag rigs bod rjer sprul// zab gter dam chos srid 'dzin gang de'i sku// dad ldan 'dod dgu 'byung ba 'di zhengs pas// dpal ldan bla ma'i thugs gongs rdzogs pa dang// bdag swogs 'khor bcas tshe ring nad med cing // mnga' thang dpal 'byor phan chogs dam chos ldan// bsam don 'grub cing 'di phyi kun du skyobs// A ma'i rigs skyes A mgon dang lha lcam nyi zla'i zhengs//*
In the translation, Todrengtsel, a common secret name of Padmasambhava, is taken as referring to the depicted master as Padmasambhava's successor. I am grateful to Yannick Laurent for his corrections and comments to my reading and translation.

4 This refers to the story of the Himalaya-size demoness that had to be pinned down by temples to make it a fertile ground of Buddhism; see Gyatso 1997.

5 Yeshé Tsogyel (1978) 2007, 385, with the spellings of Tibetan names adapted to the conventions used throughout this resource.

6 Luczanits 2003 and 2004.

7 On the collection of Namgyal Monastery, see Luczanits 2016a and 2016b.

8 Dorje and Kapstein 1991, 821–34.

9 See Harrison et al. 2018.

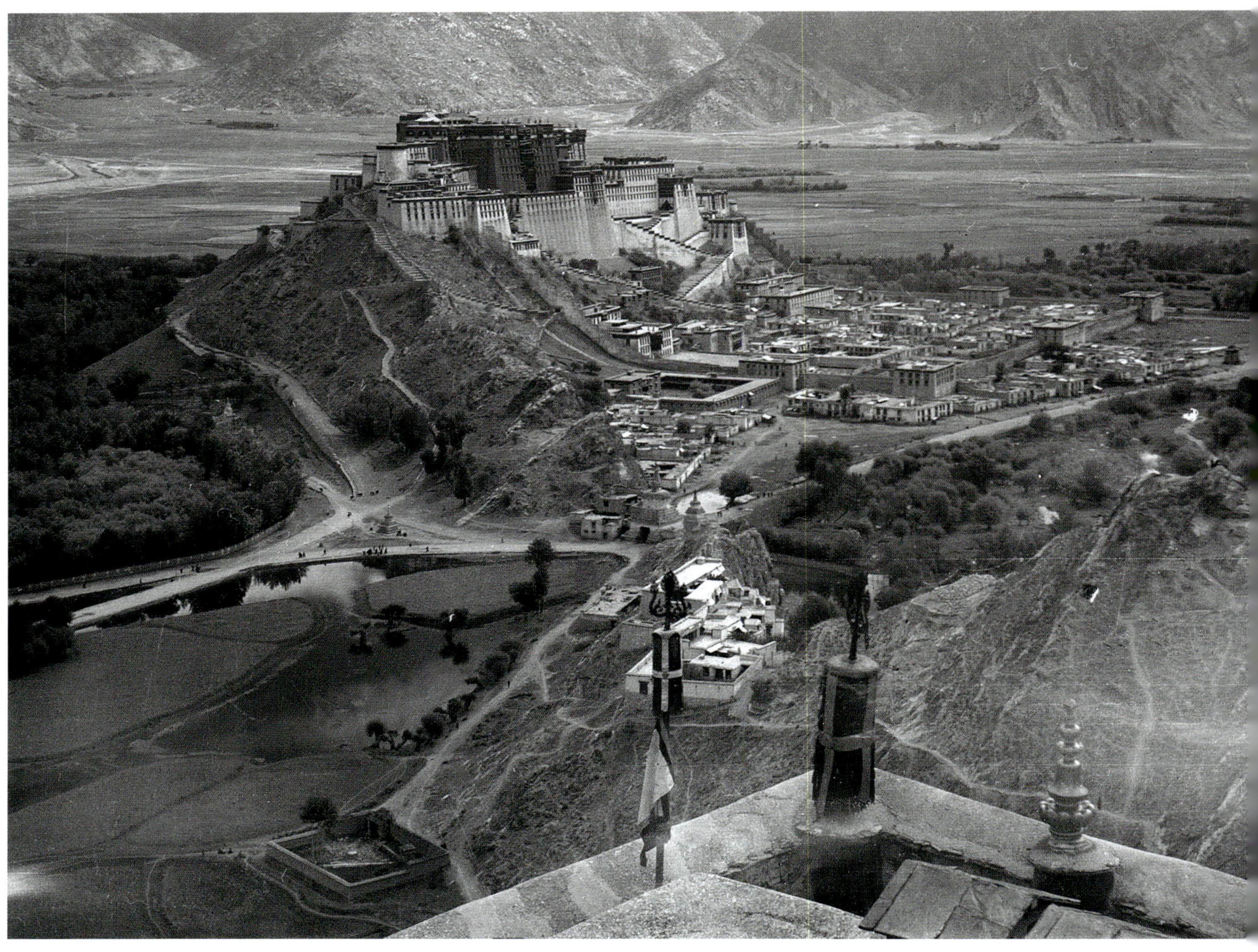

Photograph by Prodhan (Sikkimese; dates unknown); *The Potala Palace, Lhasa: The Seat of the Dalai Lamas*; 1948; film negative; courtesy Istituto Italiano per l'Africa e l'Oriente (Is.I.A.O.) in l.c.a. and Ministero degli Affari Esteri e della Cooperazione Internazionale; Neg. dep. 7710/02 + 8037/05; © Museo delle Civiltà

Nº 71

Potala Palace

Lhasa, U region, central Tibet (present-day TAR, China), 1645–1694

A Monument of Tibetan Cultural Identity

NATASHA N. KIMMET

The Potala Palace in Lhasa is Tibet's most iconic monument and symbol of Tibetan cultural and national identity. The palace's massive scale and prominent setting reflect the prestige and power of its charismatic inhabitants—the Dalai Lamas—from its construction in the seventeenth century to the end of the centralized Tibetan Ganden Podrang government in 1959.

In 1642, following decades of civil war, the "Great Fifth" Dalai Lama (1617–1682) and the Geluk tradition of Tibetan Buddhism consolidated their power through strategic alliances with Mongol leaders and unified Tibet. The Great Fifth relocated the seat of Tibetan government from nearby Drepung Monastery to Lhasa and undertook a massive nation-building campaign centered in the historical Tibetan capital and Potala. His imposing palace-fortress visually commands the entire Kyichu River valley from atop the Red Hill at the western periphery of Lhasa, a site selected for its associations with

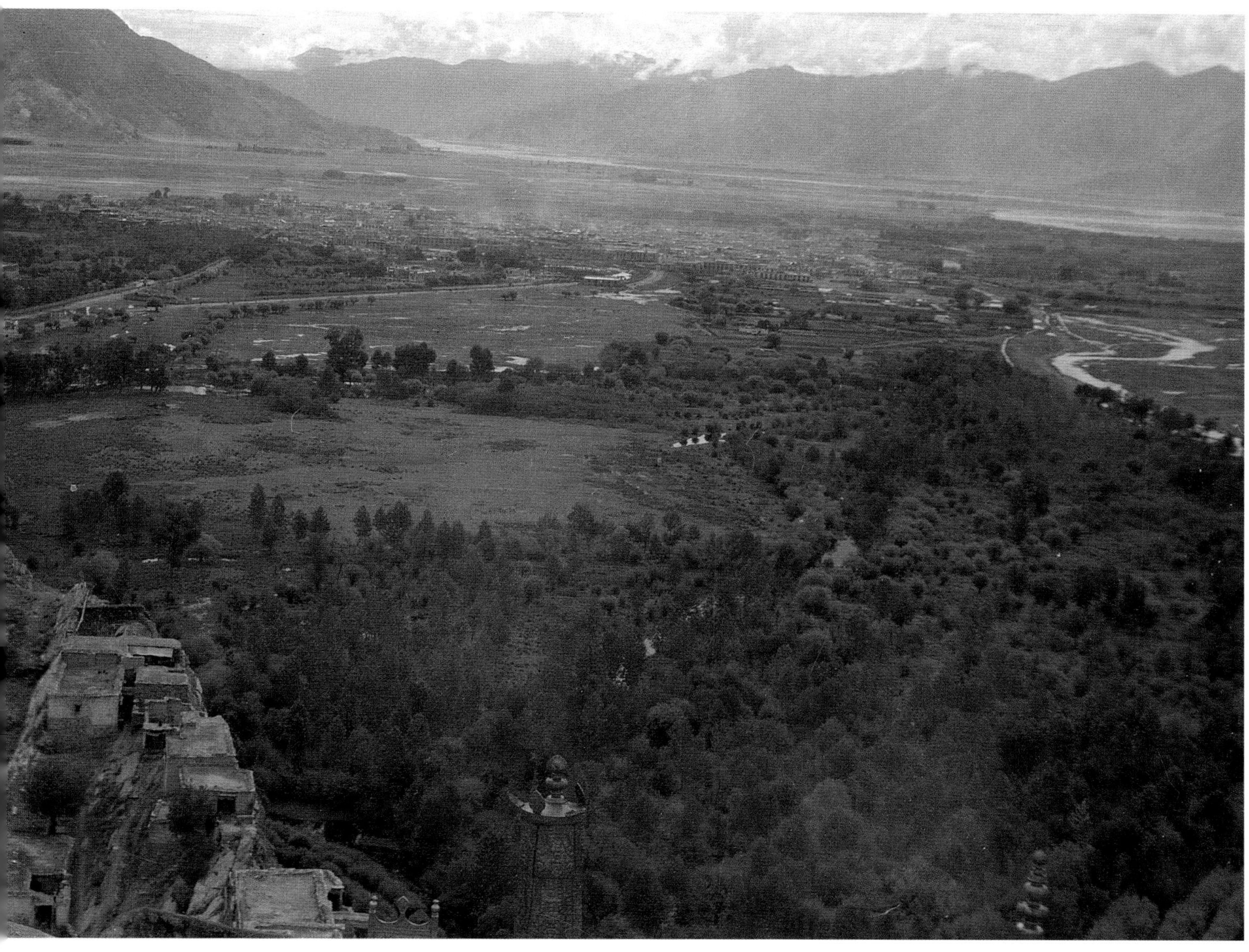

See Bodhisattva Avalokiteshvara and the Buddha's Footprints, no. 33.

bodhisattva Avalokiteshvara and the imperial kings of Tibet. The Dalai Lamas positioned themselves as emanations of Avalokiteshvara and incarnations of the first Tibetan emperor, and thus used the Potala to anchor and legitimize their identity as Tibet's supreme spiritual and temporal leaders.

An architectural masterpiece, the Potala is made more potent as a vast repository of cultural treasures revealing the wealthy patronage, mobility of artisans, and cross-cultural networks of exchange involved in its decoration. The landmark was pivotal to Lhasa's transformation into a vibrant social center, and increasingly attracted foreign dignitaries and pilgrims for state functions and Buddhist rituals. The Potala has been replicated in a variety of visual forms to convey religious, cultural, and political messages to diverse audiences.

The Monument: Art and Architecture

For an early Tibetan castle, see Yumbu Lagang Castle, no. 5.

For more on metal sculptures in the Potala collection, see Crowned Buddha, no. 16; Pensive Bodhisattva Avalokiteshvara, no. 53; Kalachakra Mandala in the Potala Palace, no. 77.

The thirteen-story Potala epitomizes classical Tibetan architecture.[1] It developed from early Tibetan castles and fortified settlements, with its modular structure embedded in the rocky landscape, and combines the functions of fortress, palace, and monastery. The battered rammed-earth walls and austere facade articulated by timber-framed windows and balconies contribute to the overall symmetry, order, scale, and proportions of the classical Tibetan order. The interior is lavishly decorated with wood carvings and textiles, mural paintings depicting important historical events and people, and exquisite movable objects, including scroll paintings (thangkas), sculptures, religious texts, and objects made of precious materials. The collection of thousands of metal sculptures represents workshops across Tibet, Nepal, India, Mongolia, and China, and spans a history of over one thousand years.[2]

The Potala was constructed in two major phases, beginning with the White Palace (1645–1648) under the direction of the Fifth Dalai Lama, and followed by the Red Palace (1690–1694) built by the Great Fifth's regent Desi Sanggye Gyatso (1653–1705). The Dalai Lama died in 1682, but his death was concealed by the regent to allow completion of the Red Palace and to maintain political continuity. The White Palace contains assembly halls, libraries, and private monastic residences. Notably, the tantric college and personal monastery of the Dalai Lamas, Namgyel Monastery, was relocated from Drepung Monastery to the western courtyard for performing prayers and rituals for the welfare of Tibet. The Red Palace, with its golden roofs, is integrated with the central portion of the White Palace. It houses chapels, assembly halls, and the reliquary stupas of eight Dalai Lamas. Long switchback staircases visually and functionally tether the palace to Zhol Village at its southern base, where administrative buildings and state-run craftsmen's workshops were established. Construction of such a monumental building required a workforce comprising thousands of master craftsmen, artisans, engineers, and conscripted laborers. Subsequent related buildings include the Lukhang Temple, built by Sanggye Gyatso and the Sixth Dalai Lama behind the Potala as a private esoteric meditation retreat, and the Norbulingka Palace, built as a summer residence during the life of the Seventh Dalai Lama.

See Desi Sanggye Gyatso's Medical Paintings, no. 73.

See Lukhang Murals, no. 80.

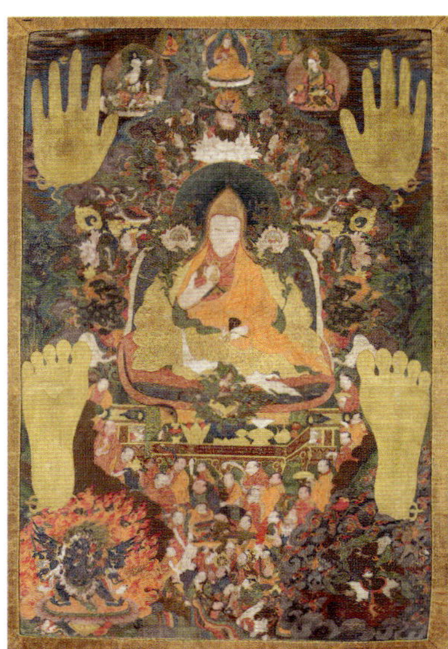

The Fifth Dalai Lama, with Hand- and Footprints; Tibet; late 17th century; pigments on cloth; 30½ × 19⅝ in. (77.5 × 50 cm); Musée national des arts asiatiques Guimet, Paris; MG19107; photograph by Thierry Ollivier © RMN-Grand Palais / Art Resource, NY

The Symbol: Placemaking and National Identity Construction

For many Tibetans, Tibetan political unity and identity are anchored by the charisma of the Dalai Lamas and the prestige of the monuments they promoted. In 1642, when the Fifth Dalai Lama assumed spiritual and temporal leadership of Tibet with the support of the Khoshud Mongol leader Güüshi Khan (Gushri, 1582–1655, r. 1642–1655), he commenced an ambitious project of placemaking and identity construction in Lhasa. He employed various tactics to aggrandize his identity as the spiritual protector and political unifier of Tibet. According to Tibetan tradition, Lhasa's Red Hill is the earthly manifestation of Avalokiteshvara's Buddhist paradise (Pure Land) Mount Potalaka. By selecting this location and name for his palace, the Great Fifth established the Potala as a paradise and himself as an incarnation of Tibet's protector bodhisattva. The Potala is further linked to the first emperor of the Tibetan Empire, Songtsen Gampo (r. 618–649), believed to be an incarnation of Avalokiteshvara and, despite the absence of archaeological evidence, to have built a palace in the same location.

For more on Choying Gyatso and the New Menri painting tradition, see Nartang Woodblock Prints and Their Painted Copies, no. 81.

This religio-historical lineage is strengthened through the writings of Sanggye Gyatso and mural paintings in the Potala.[3] The earliest murals—painted in the Great Eastern Assembly Hall in 1647/1648 by Choying Gyatso (1622–1665)[4]—narrate the history of Buddhism in Tibet up to the Fourth Dalai Lama. A mural series in the Great Western Assembly Hall visually testifies to the Great Fifth's reunification of Tibet, together with murals in the upper galleries illustrating the construction of the Potala and his other achievements.[5]

See Jokhang Temple, no. 7.

Lhasa's Jokhang Temple has attracted Buddhist pilgrims since the seventh century. The Potala was promoted as an equally prestigious monument in the Geluk-administered restructuring of Lhasa as a cosmopolitan ceremonial center with renewed appeal for pilgrims, merchants, scholar-diplomats, and artisans from Asia and distant locations. A network of new (predominantly Geluk) landmarks was established in relation to new circulation routes, creating a structured way of viewing and experiencing the capital.[6] Lhasa was reorganized around three arteries for circumambulation of its sacred sites: the inner circuit (*nangkor*) around the Jokhang, housing Tibet's most sacred image, the Jowo statue of Buddha Shakyamuni; the middle circuit (*barkor*) around the full temple complex, expanded under the Great Fifth's administration; and the outer circuit (*lingkor*) around most of Lhasa and its main religious monuments, notably the Potala. Additionally, new annual festivals and (ostensibly) religious ceremonies were introduced, with ritual processions highlighting the Geluk state and Dalai Lama lineage.[7] By visiting

See Jowo Shakyamuni, no. 8.

these monuments and engaging in pilgrimage, rituals, trade, and governance, Lhasa's inhabitants and visitors reinforced the new Tibetan national identity centered in Lhasa and its monuments.

For the related genre of pilgrimage maps, see Panoramic Map of Mount Wutai, no. 91; Mongolian Map of Capital Yekhe Khüriye, no. 96.

Representations of the Potala and the Cultural Transfer of a Symbol

Cross-cultural encounters in the Tibetan capital shaped the production and dissemination of Potala-centric images. In the eighteenth century, a unique genre of portable scroll paintings emerged featuring sacred Tibetan monuments, the majority of which depict Lhasa with the Potala—sometimes paired with the Jokhang—as the central subject.[8] The paintings are devotional, instructive, and promotional—they prescribe specific religious sites to be visited by Buddhist pilgrims to accrue merit, function as devotional objects conveying Lhasa's holy aura, and promote political and social order concentrated in Lhasa's major institutions. The patrons, artists, and audience came from across the Tibetan cultural region.

For more on photography in Tibet and the Himalayas, see Photograph of the Thirteenth Dalai Lama, no. 98.

Lhasa captured the attention of Christian missionaries, explorers, and political officers from Europe, Russia, the United States, and Japan who created their own images of the capital, particularly through photography. During the nineteenth century, foreign nations competed for control of trade and diplomatic relations across Central Asia, with Tibet at the center of the "Great Game" between the British and Russian Empires. As religious devotees, Buddhist pilgrims from Mongolian regions of Russia could still visit Lhasa. But Tibet's "closed door" policy—a reaction against encroaching imperialism—kept Lhasa largely inaccessible to Westerners from the late eighteenth century until 1903–1904, when the British Younghusband expedition forcefully entered the capital. In their sketches, photographs, and writing, British diplomat-officials used the same prominent monuments seen in indigenous paintings to convey Tibet as a unique, independent nation—distinct from China, yet requiring British protection.[9] The Potala was often replicated in images made for foreign audiences, bolstering its status as Tibet's preeminent landmark.

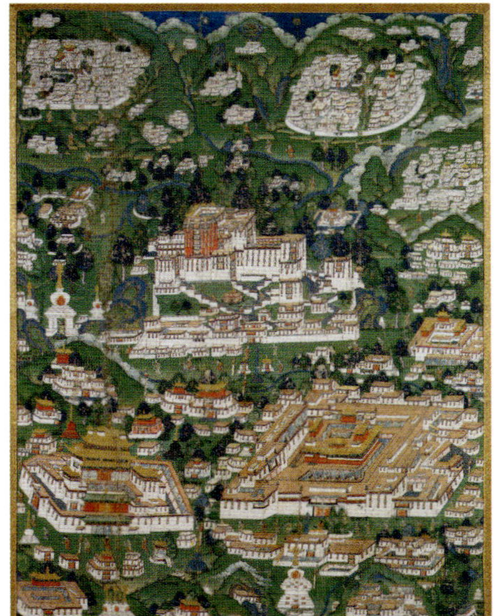

The Potala and the Principal Monuments of Central Tibet; Tibet; 19th century; distemper on cloth; 38¾ × 28⅜ in. (98.5 × 72 cm); Musée national des arts asiatiques Guimet, Paris; MG21248; photograph by Jean Schormans © RMN-Grand Palais / Art Resource, NY

The most significant three-dimensional "Potala" is the Putuo Zongcheng Temple in Chengde, China. Built around 1767–1771 during the Qing dynasty reign of the Qianlong emperor (r. 1735–1796), it draws on the Potala's associations with spiritual and secular authority.[10]

The Potala was designated a UNESCO World Heritage site in 1994. Today it is a museum and tourist attraction administered by the People's Republic of China.[11] It is integral to China's ongoing transformation of Lhasa, such as through elaborate performances at the palace that serve to reposition Tibetan historical narratives within the history of China. The palace has not been inhabited by the Dalai Lamas since 1959, when the Fourteenth Dalai Lama fled to India following the forceful annexation of Tibet by the PRC in 1950. But the cultural resonance of the Potala as a symbolic center of Tibet and Tibetan identity continues to be promoted and reinforced globally.

Further Reading

Brauen, Martin, ed. 2005. *The Dalai Lamas: A Visual History*. Chicago: Serindia.

Henss, Michael. 2014. *The Cultural Monuments of Tibet: The Central Regions*. 2 vols. Munich: Prestel.

Pommaret, Françoise, ed. 2003. *Lhasa in the Seventeenth Century: The Capital of the Dalai Lamas*. Leiden: Brill.

Notes

1 Alexander 2007; Kimmet 2018; Larsen and Sinding-Larsen 2001, 39; Meyer 1987, 32.
2 von Schroeder 2001a and 2008.
3 Schaeffer 2005.
4 Illustrated in Ping Cuo Ci Dan 2000, 51–82.
5 S. Karmay 2005; illustrated in Ping Cuo Ci Dan 2000, 83–102.
6 Schaeffer 2006.
7 H. Richardson 1993; Schaeffer 2006.
8 Arthur 2015 and 2016; see also Béguin 2003; Kimmet 2016.
9 Bishop 1994; Harris 2005 and 2007; Harris and Shakya 2003.
10 Chayet 1985b; Chou 2018, 134.
11 Harris 2012b discusses postcolonial politics and the making of this museum.

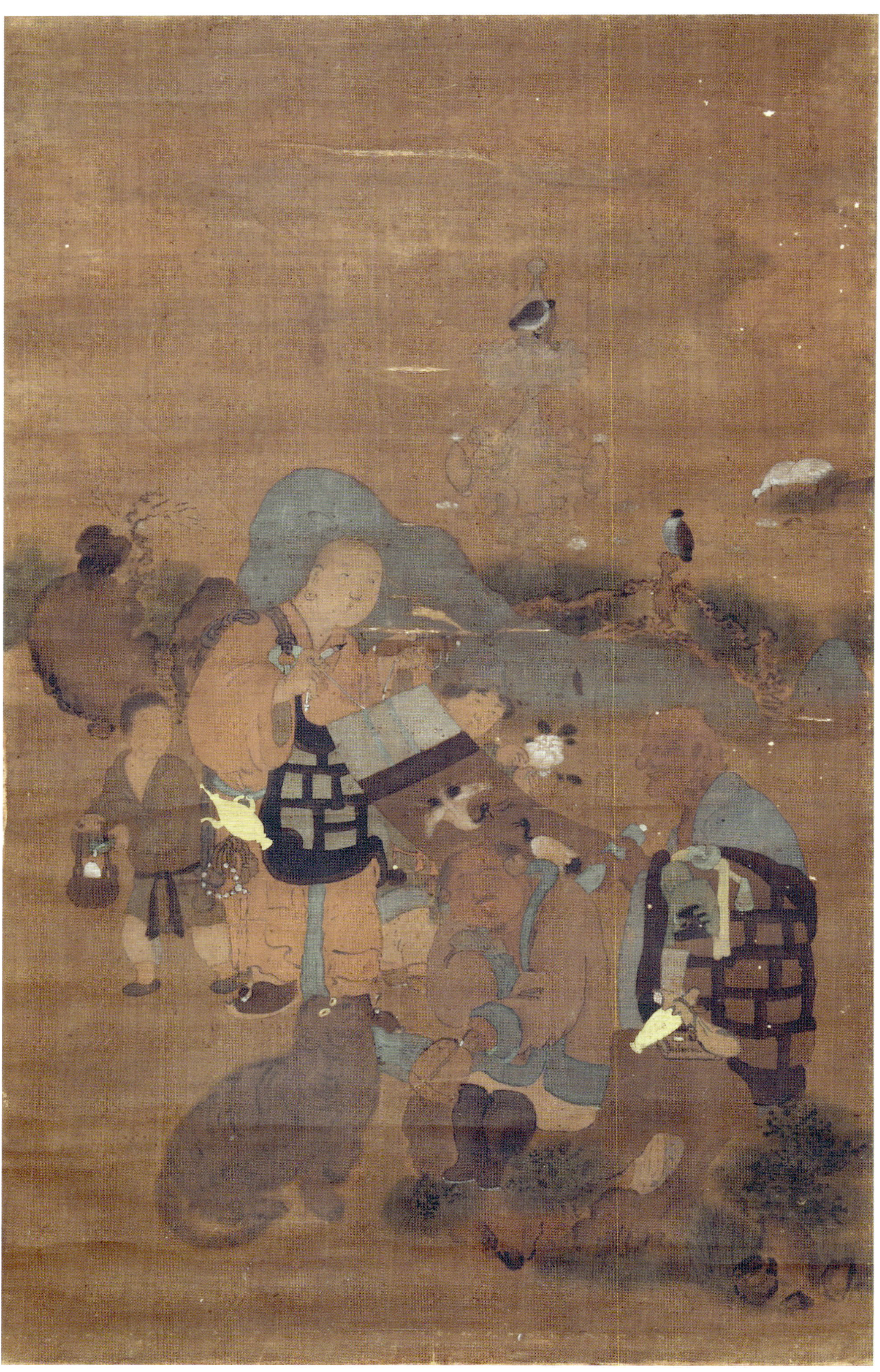

№ 72

Arhats Viewing a Painting of Birds by the Tenth Karmapa

Lijiang, Yunnan Province, China, 1660

A Tibetan Artist's Interest in Archaic Chinese and Kashmiri Art

KARL DEBRECZENY

The Tenth Karmapa, Choying Dorje (1604–1674), provides a rare glimpse into the life of a Tibetan artist. Little is known about the lives and works of most artists, but the Karmapa's importance as the head of the Karma Kagyu tradition of Tibetan Buddhism led to the production of extensive biographical material, giving us a wealth of information about his artistic career, including his early training, collecting interests, documentation of his artistic production, and models he sought for imitation.[1] He drew from a wide range of sources. According to Tibetan tradition his paintings were inspired by Chinese models and his sculpture by the Kashmiri tradition. A true connoisseur of the art of the past, the Tenth Karmapa was inspired by archaic models not practiced by other artists for centuries, as if harking back to a better time, a reaction to his own turbulent era. He did not just adopt styles and genres wholesale, but rather experimented with different compositional and figural models as well as styles, even mixing genres to create a personal visual idiom.

For more on the Karmapa incarnation lineage, see Portrait of the Ninth Karmapa, no. 66.

The Karmapa's Life and Authorship

The Tenth Karmapa was something of a child prodigy. By the age of seven he is said to have fully learned the art of painting, and by the age of eight he was already a prolific artist. His most quoted statement reveals his self-conception as an artist: "Regarding poetry and painting there is none greater than me in Tibet. I am one who pleases Avalokiteshvara. I am one who has come into this world to paint."[2]

Despite being a great incarnate lama, the Tenth Karmapa lived a challenging life. When the long-standing sectarian strife between the Karmapa's main patron, the ruler of Tsang in southwestern Tibet, and the Geluk monastic order and their Mongolian patrons boiled over into war, the Dalai Lamas rose to political power. In 1645 the Karmapa fled east to the distant lands of Yunnan on the Sino-Tibetan border, an area protected by the Karma Kagyu's longtime patrons, the Naxi kings of Lijiang. While the Tenth Karmapa's long twenty-five-year exile seems to have limited his wider activity as a religious leader, it also provided him with the opportunity to explore his creative affinity as an artist.

For more on the rise of the Dalai Lamas to political power, see Potala Palace, no. 71.

For more on the Naxi ethnic group and the kingdom of Lijiang, see Dabaojigong Temple, no. 64.

In Lijiang survives a set of seven paintings of Buddha Shakyamuni and the Sixteen Arhats dated 1660, executed and inscribed by the Tenth Karmapa's own hand. The end of a lengthy gold inscription at the top of the set's central painting makes his authorship clear:

> For the sake of the wishes of the Prince Karma Puntsok Wangchuk who possesses a wealth of faith, the one practiced in the arts called "Lokeshvara," and who is praised as the tenth to be blessed with the name "Karmapa," Choying Dorje, painted in their entirety by his own hand.[3]

Tenth Karmapa, Choying Dorje (1604–1674); Arhats Viewing a Painting of Birds, from a set of seven paintings; Lijiang, Yunnan Province, China; dated 1660; ink and pigment on silk; 26¾ × 16½ in. (68 × 42 cm); Lijiang Municipal Museum; no. 439.3

The modest, almost self-deprecating phrasing suggests the Tenth Karmapa wrote the inscription himself. Moreover, "Lokeshvara," meaning "Lord of the World," is an unusual epithet that the Tenth Karmapa used to refer to himself, which reaffirms his authorship. The name Lokeshvara references the Karmapas' identity as emanations of the bodhisattva Avalokiteshvara. Both Tibetan and Chinese sources corroborate that the recipient of this set of paintings named in the inscription was the Naxi crown prince of Lijiang, Mu Jing (1628–1671).

See Avalokiteshvara at Khartse, no. 20; Bodhisattva Avalokiteshvara and the Buddha's Footprints, no. 33.

The Arhat Genre

Most paintings identified as being in the style of the Tenth Karmapa depict arhats, the original followers of the Buddha, and biographical writings confirm that arhats were the Karmapa's favorite subject to paint. The arhat genre was imported from China, making it a rich vehicle for Chinese visual modes, which may have made it a convenient medium for the Karmapa to explore his artistic interests.

The paintings in this set feature small groups of arhats participating in social activities and mundane acts such as eating. In Arhats Viewing a Painting of Birds, two arhats are looking at a painting, a scholarly activity. Chinese convention would show the arhats looking at a religious icon such as Avalokiteshvara, but here the arhats view a secular theme of birds.[4] The Tenth Karmapa's love of birds was so well known that people gifted them in great profusion, inundating his court with avian creatures.[5] The Karmapa combined secular and religious artistic traditions, here merging the Chinese bird-and-flower painting genre and the arhat genre.

The arhat holding the top of the painting of cranes grasps a brush in his right hand, suggesting he painted these birds. This depiction therefore self-identifies the Karmapa, himself a monastic incarnation and painter of birds, with these arhats. Moreover, the Tibetan-style cap on the young boy attendant is likely a reference to the birth of the Tenth Karmapa's son, the Sixth Gyeltsab, Norbu Zangpo (1660–1698), that year. While the Karmapa was fully ordained, he lived an unconventional life in exile, taking a consort and having children.[6] These elements demonstrate that the paintings in this set are more than simple icons—they are personal paintings, quite unlike the usual Tibetan conventions of this genre.

His Painting Style

As seen in this inscribed set, the Tenth Karmapa's figural forms are idiosyncratic and spontaneously drawn. They share a whimsical naïveté recognizable by the fleshy abbreviated faces with tiny pursed red lips. These faces do not resemble contemporary Tibetan forms but seem to draw on ancient Chinese Tang dynasty (618–907) models. Following the conquest of China by the Manchus and the establishment of their new alien regime, the Qing dynasty (1644–1911), Chinese artists living through the social turmoil used such models to evoke a distant golden age. The Karmapa was likely exposed to these conventions while living in Yunnan.

For more on the Manchus and the Qing, see The Qianlong Emperor as Manjushri-Chakravartin, no. 84.

The Tenth Karmapa was also fascinated with a wide range of animals, especially birds, which he rendered sensitively and even playfully. His brushwork is especially distinctive; he skillfully employed subtle ink washes and often used a "boneless" technique combined with short, quick, controlled lines to evoke shape, a brush technique known in the Chinese tradition as "tremulous brush" (*zhanbi*).

The use of silk as a support, or canvas, is another unusual characteristic, as Tibetan painters usually preferred cotton. The Tenth Karmapa's biographies suggest some of the sources for his new "Chinese-style thangka painting." Shortly after arriving in Lijiang, for instance, he "examined many thousands of Chinese paintings on silk" in the king's palace.[7] Local tradition also recounts that the ruler invited the master painter Ma Xiaoxian from Ningbo to Lijiang, and the Tenth Karmapa is said to have greatly admired his work. Perhaps not coincidentally, the Karmapa's compositions most resemble extant twelfth-century paintings from Ningbo, a famous center of artistic activity on the east coast of China.

These stylistic observations enable us to identify other works by the Karmapa's hand. However, the Tenth Karmapa's biographies also record that he set up workshops for the production of images, and he worked collaboratively with other artists throughout his life. Several sets of paintings evidence his distinctive idiom but lack his telltale brushwork, as well as revealing the hands of multiple artists of varying skill. These characteristics indicate workshop production.[8]

The Tenth Karmapa was also fond of making painted copies of old famous statues, especially from Greater Kashmir, which he sometimes used to model his painted figures, such as images of the Buddha.[9] His own sculptural production featured figural forms largely inspired by the arts of Kashmir, while the faces of some of his sculptures seem to draw on ancient Chinese models.[10] The Karmapa's sculptures therefore also reflect a synthesis of stylistic sources from different cultures and time periods.

For a Kashmir sculpture close to some of the Karmapa's Buddha paintings, see Buddha on the Cosmic Mountain, no. 10.

Attributed to Tenth Karmapa, Choying Dorje (1604–1674); Padmapani Lokeshvara; Tibet; 17th century; ivory; height 11½ in. (29.2 cm); Cleveland Museum of Art; Sundry Purchase Fund; 1968.280; CC0 - Creative Commons (CC0 1.0)

See Portrait of Situ Panchen, no. 83.

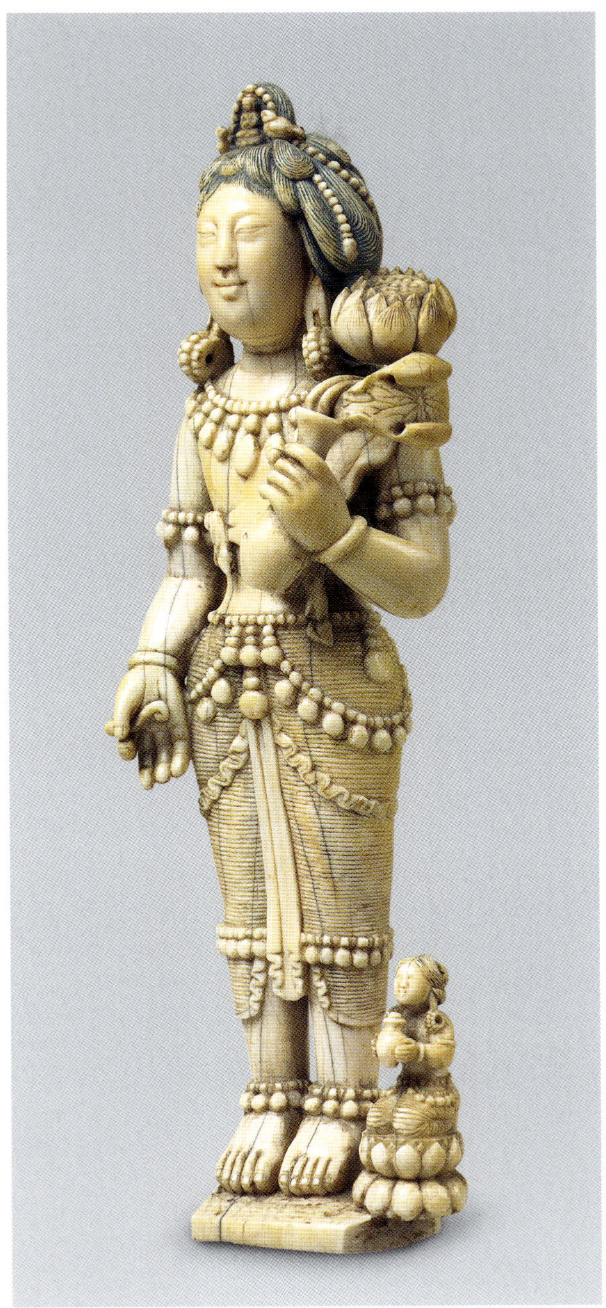

Impact and Later Followers

Some Tibetan scholars have suggested that the Tenth Karmapa's long exile in Lijiang may have limited the spread of his activity.[11] Yet others believe that the Tenth Karmapa's art forms one of the roots for the painting tradition founded by Situ Panchen (1700–1774) at Pelpung Monastery in Kham region, southeastern Tibet, in the eighteenth century.[12] There is even some confusion between the works of the Tenth Karmapa and those of Situ Panchen.[13] Strong textual and visual evidence shows later followers emulated the Tenth Karmapa's style into the nineteenth and twentieth centuries.[14]

Looking beyond the individual artist, workshop pieces suggest that teams of artisans were trained in the Tenth Karmapa's unusual style. Given the exalted status of the artist as one of the highest incarnate lamas, it is little wonder that his works were also copied. So far, the Tenth Karmapa marks the only instance in the history of Tibetan art where we can trace works from the hand of the master to workshop production and later copies.

Further Reading

Debreczeny, Karl. 2012. *The Black Hat Eccentric: Artistic Visions of the Tenth Karmapa.* Exhibition catalog. New York: Rubin Museum of Art. https://issuu.com/rmanyc/docs/6._black_hat_eccentric_96.

Debreczeny, Karl, and Gray Tuttle, eds. 2016. *The Tenth Karmapa and Tibet's Turbulent Seventeenth Century.* Chicago: Serindia.

Shamar Rinpoche. 2012. *A Golden Swan in Turbulent Waters: The Life and Times of the Tenth Karmapa Choying Dorje.* Lexington, VA: Bird of Paradise Press.

Notes

1 For instance, in English translation see Shamar Rinpoche 2012; Mengele 2012.
2 Si tu and 'Be lo 1775, fol. 184a, lines 7–184b, line 1.
3 For more on this inscription, see Debreczeny 2012, 97–103, 299n474.
4 See for instance Debreczeny 2012, 125, fig. 3.19.
5 Gtsang mkhan chen 1982, 210; Si tu and 'Be lo 1775, fol. 174b, lines 2, 6–7.
6 See Shamar Rinpoche 2012, xiv, 210, 219; Mengele 2012, 245.
7 Si tu and 'Be lo 1775, fol. 179b, line 3.
8 On these sets as workshop productions, see Debreczeny 2012, 128–69; Debreczeny 2020; Debreczeny 2021.
9 D. Jackson 2012a, 282–86; Luczanits 2016.
10 On his sculpture, see von Schroeder 2001a; Alsop 2012; Luczanits 2016a; Luo 2016.
11 Tangla Tsewang, quoted in Dkon mchog bstan 'dzin et al. 2006, 218.
12 Karma Gyeltsen, personal communication, October 20, 2010. Tangla Tsewang (written in the 1950s, reproduced in Dkon, mchog bstan 'dzin et al. 2006, 218) and Shakabpa 1976 propose similar theories.
13 D. Jackson 1996, 251–52; Debreczeny 2012, 263–72.
14 On later followers, see Debreczeny 2016b, 219–31.

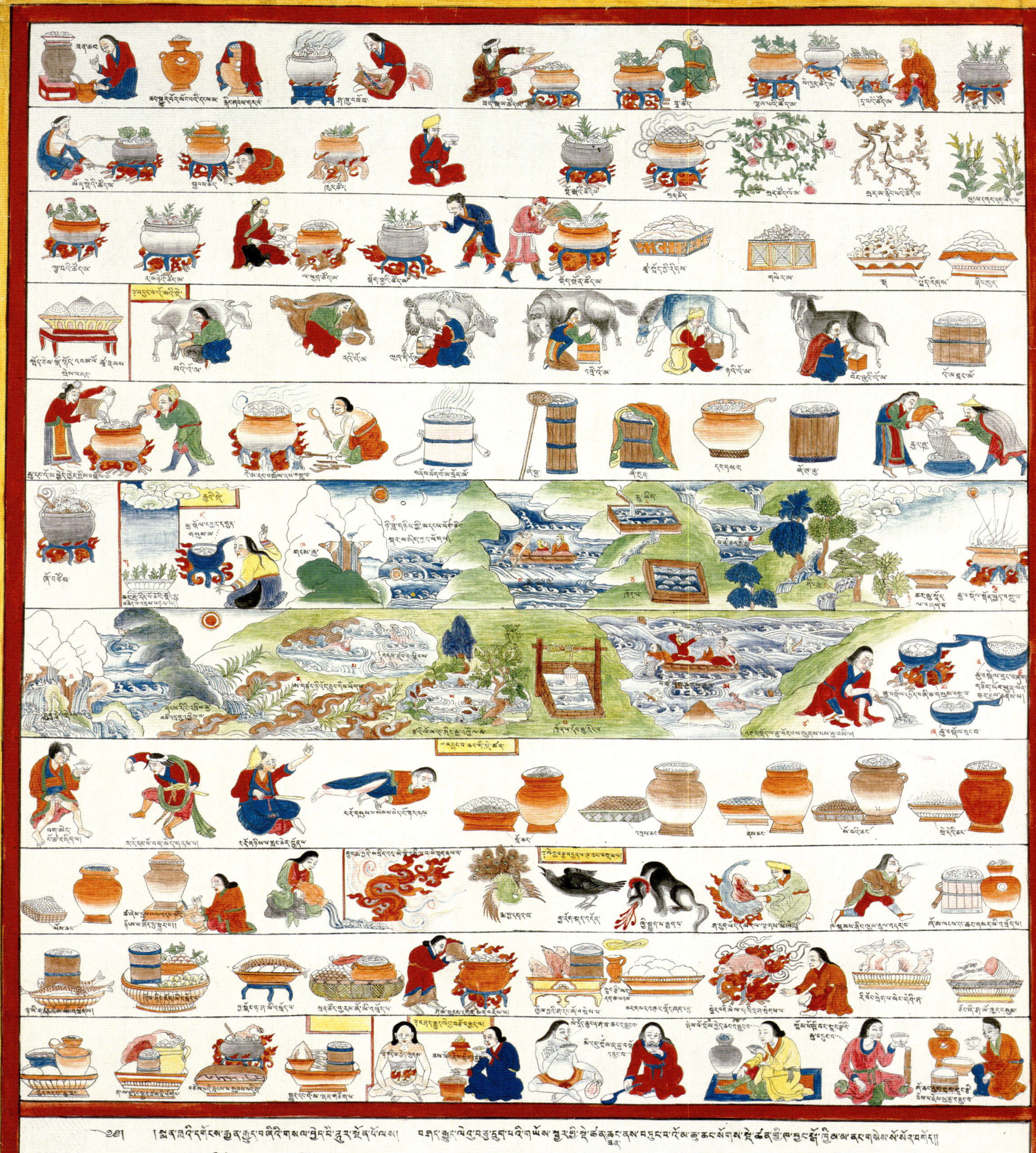

No 73

Desi Sanggye Gyatso's Medical Paintings

Lhasa, U region, central Tibet, 1687–1697

Medicine, Science, and the Everyday in Tibetan Art

THERESIA HOFER

The colorful and unique set of seventy-nine medical paintings from late seventeenth-century Lhasa depict in vivid detail and innovative form the core ideas of Sowa Rigpa, the Tibetan "science of healing," or Tibetan medicine. The mastermind behind it was Desi Sanggye Gyatso (1653–1705), the regent to the Fifth Dalai Lama (1617–1682), who unified the Tibetan regions and established Lhasa as the new capital. The painting set illustrates Desi Sanggye Gyatso's medical work *Blue Beryl*, which is his own commentary on the *Four Tantras* (*Gyuzhi*), Tibetan medicine's foundational twelfth-century text comprising overall 156 chapters in four volumes.

Both the Fifth Dalai Lama and Desi Sanggye Gyatso took a keen interest in developing academic medicine as a novel means to define, classify, and control knowledge about the body, and by extension their Tibetan subjects, in support of their political pursuits and ambitions. Another example was *The White Beryl*, a comprehensive work on the related field of divination and astrology. On a practical level, the medical set served as an indigenous mind map in aid of the memorizing of the *Four Tantras* (and the *Blue Beryl*) for ready recall in exams and during clinical and pharmacological work. For this purpose, the set was first displayed for students at Lhasa Chakpori Medical College, which opened in 1696. The college, located opposite the Potala Palace, was built around the same time the medical paintings were created. The set also helped settle medical disputes of the time.

See *The White Beryl* Illuminated Manuscript, no. 86.

See Potala Palace, no. 71.

Content and Structure of the Painting Set and Relationship to Medical Texts

The painting set maps closely onto the structure and the content of the *Blue Beryl* commentary by Desi Sanggye Gyatso on the *Four Tantras*. The *Root Tantra*, the name given to the first volume of both texts, has six chapters that cover the origins of the Tibetan medical teachings and the foundational ideas of Tibetan medicine. In the painting set, the first six paintings of the total seventy-nine illustrate the *Root Tantra*: the first plate shows an image of the Medicine Buddha in a palace teaching the *Four Tantras*; Paintings 2–4 depict the "unfolded trees" with overall nine trunks, forty-seven branches, two hundred and twenty-four leaves, and five flowers and fruits. Small paintings on each branch, leaf, and flower visually illustrate core Tibetan medical ideas—for example, related to the digestion process—or particular kinds of behaviors that are considered wholesome or unwholesome. The tree paintings in particular acted as a summary of major aspects of the medical system and a visual mind map for memorization. Painting 5 shows in descending horizontal rows the development of the fetus during pregnancy, concluding in two birthing scenes at the bottom right corner. Painting 6 describes metaphors and measurements of the body, essentially likening anatomical aspects to a Tibetan house and to elite members and functions within the Tibetan government, including a queen, a king, and their ministers.

The *Explanatory Tantra*, the name given to the second volume of the texts, has thirty-one chapters covering eleven broad themes, including the anatomy of the body, diseases, behaviors, diet, pharmacology, diagnosis, methods of healing, and medical ethics. The illustration of this volume begins with Painting 7. Paintings 7–15 show large-scale abstractions of human anatomy and physiology. Paintings 16–22 detail prognoses as well as adjustment to personal conduct and diet. The large subject of *materia medica* is covered in Paintings 23–33, including detailed drawings of stones and minerals and of primary and supplementary medicinal plants, as well as information on their pharmacological compounding. Plates 34–36 depict the external therapies of bloodletting, moxibustion, and golden-needle acupuncture,

Dietetics, Painting 22 of the Tibetan Medical Paintings, Ulan Ude Set; Lhasa, Tibet; early 20th-century copy of original from ca. 1687–1697; pigments on cloth; 33⅞ × 26¾ in. (86 × 68 cm); National Museum of the Republic of Buryatia, Ulan Ude; photograph courtesy Serindia

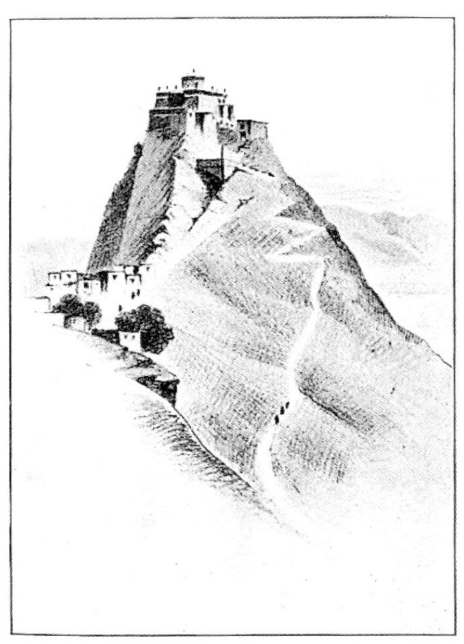

L. Austine Waddell; Chakpori Medical College; Lhasa, Tibet; 1905; pencil on paper; dimensions unknown; image after Waddell, L. A. *Lhasa and Its Mysteries: A Record of the Expedition of 1903–1904*. New York: E. P. Dutton, 1905, 376; courtesy Theresia Hofer

with the *Explanatory Tantra* concluding on the qualities of a physician and medical ethics in Painting 37.

The *Instructional Tantra*, the name given to the third volume, is the largest, with ninety-two chapters, and covers in great depth the treatment of hundreds of conditions within fifteen broad categories of diseases, for example, fevers, children's diseases, and women's diseases, including the use of elixirs for rejuvenation and long life. Illustrations of the *Instructional Tantra* are found on Paintings 38–67 and characterized by detailed drawings of varied pathology (Paintings 38–52), of the topic of virility and fertility (Painting 53), and of diagnostic methods, including tongue, pulse, and urine diagnosis (Paintings 54–67).

The *Last Tantra* and fourth volume, with twenty-seven chapters, covers the four broad divisions of pulse and urine diagnosis, pacifying medications, eliminative therapies, and external therapies (including large-scale drawings of the body with bloodletting points), illustrated on Plates 68–79. Aligned with the last two chapters of the last volume of the *Four Tantras* and the *Blue Beryl* are Plates 77 and 78, which conclude the set with a depiction of the "entrustment" of the medical tradition, that is how Tibetan medicine should be protected and safeguarded for future generations. In one early twentieth-century set, Painting 80 was added, portraying several key scholars and sponsors of medicine into the early twentieth century.

The Everyday

The detail in the paintings was unprecedented in Tibet at the time and remained unique even centuries later and across Asian scholarly medical traditions.[1] One special feature was the depiction of people not just as patients in medical consultations, but in a wide range of contexts. Seeing ordinary folk going about their lives in these paintings is delightful and also opens a unique window onto the social history of certain groups of Tibetan society in the seventeenth century not well represented in religious art. For example, on the dietetics thangka (Painting 22), we see depictions of farmers and pastoralists milking their animals, collaborative food preparations, and sources of drinking water in the high Himalayas.

Artistically, the paintings added substantially to the range of expression possible for Tibetan and Himalayan artists, who had previously focused almost entirely on the representation of extraordinary beings such as buddhas, deities, and religious teachers. Here, only few such depictions creep in. Instead we see several thousand individual paintings of people, animals, plants, concepts, and objects, many of them shown in a new format: often small and in cartoon-style, the paintings are lined up on horizontal panels. Sometimes as many as one hundred smaller paintings are found on one thangka, each with a caption. Although in a close relationship to the *Blue Beryl* text, the often lively renderings go beyond what the texts could achieve or would have required in order to conform to scholarly standards.

The content, style, and format of the paintings effectively convey original expressions of newly gained and alternative forms of authoritative visual knowledge about the world, life, and the body. While the medical scholars and artists involved in the project (including the Desi himself) operated within the cultural and religious constraints of the Buddhist religion, the medical paintings express their empirical observations, in some cases, also the result of vivid debates. For example, to settle questions about the number and exact form of bones in the human body, empirical evidence was gathered from corpses and the results were drawn on Painting 49, taking such inquiry to the greatest lengths possible. As seminal work by the scholar Janet Gyatso has shown, the team behind the medical paintings was not content simply to follow prevailing scriptural authority in medicine and religion.[2] An intriguing question remains: to what extent are these medical paintings evidence of an early scientific revolution in Tibet?

Beyond the Text

The paintings explicitly illustrate textual information of the *Blue Beryl*, yet there was also the concurrent creation of text and paintings—with a painting in the Potala Palace to prove this.[3] The influences went both ways, from texts to paintings and paintings to texts, elucidating and enhancing understanding of

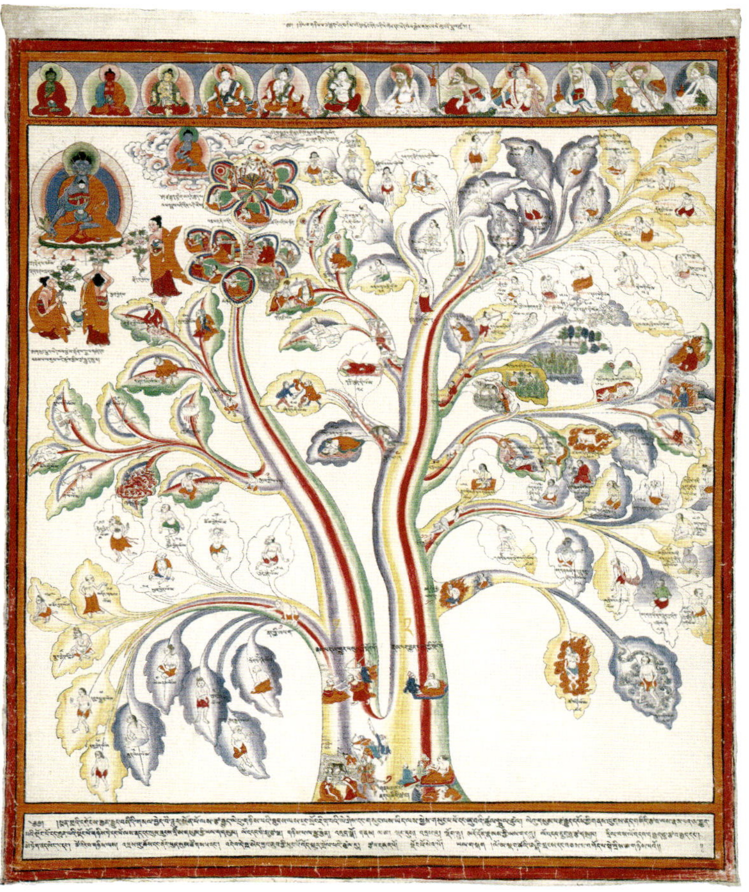

"Unfolded Tree" of the Body in Health and in Illness, Painting 2 of the Tibetan Medical Paintings; Lhasa, Tibet; 20th-century copy of the original from 1687–1697; medium unknown; dimensions unknown; Lhasa Mentsikhang; photograph by Pasang Yontan

many aspects of medicine. However, beyond sharing and explaining visually enhanced medical information, as well as feeding back new knowledge to the texts, the paintings also do something entirely new: with a sense of humor and delight in the vividness and idiosyncrasies of life, the artists provide realistic impressions of Tibetan society at the time. We even see aspects of disability and sexuality freely and seemingly nonjudgmentally (and nonreligiously) explored, a mind-boggling array of Tibetan hairstyles, animals taking thrones from human kings to explain concepts of medical lineage, and women both depicted and discredited in favor of male norms.

The sumptuous execution of the paintings, the coproduction of Desi Sanggye Gyatso's *Blue Beryl* medical work and the medical paintings by a group of artists, also shines important light on the broader political concerns of the time. Building the foundations of a more modern state, by exerting power through knowledge, and particularly by new knowledge about the body, seemed to offer an alternative to the use of brute force in geographically expanding the unified theocratic state.

The Original and Copies

Many copies have been made from the original late seventeenth-century set, the first by students and visitors to the college. Over time, the entire set and also individual paintings have been copied in a variety of media (including canvas and paper) and sizes, for use across the Himalayas and Tibetan Plateau, as well as in Buryatia and Mongolia, where Tibetan medicine also spread.[4] Copies of the set's *materia medica* drawings are often found in more portable forms, such as illustrated manuscripts and woodblock-printed books.[5] Anatomical drawings and those detailing the application of external therapies such as moxibustion and bloodletting, meanwhile, were also copied on larger sheets of paper and used to instruct students even in remote regions.[6]

A particularly beautiful set of all seventy-nine paintings was produced in Lhasa in the early twentieth century and is preserved in Buryatia.[7] As the global interest in Tibetan medicine and Himalayan art has risen steadily since the 1990s, many copies of this particular set and its individual paintings have been made, mainly in Tibetan and Nepalese thangka studios, at relatively affordable prices. They have been shipped across the world and are now displayed in diverse settings.

Further Reading

Gyatso, Janet. 2015. *Being Human in a Buddhist World: An Intellectual History of Medicine in Early Modern Tibet*. New York: Columbia University Press.

Hofer, Theresia, ed. 2014. *Bodies in Balance: The Art of Tibetan Medicine*. Exhibition catalog. New York: Rubin Museum of Art. https://issuu.com/rmanyc/docs/7._bodies_in_balance.

Parfionovich, Yuri, Gyurme Dorje, and Fernand Meyer, eds. 1992. *The Tibetan Medical Paintings: Illustrations to the Blue Beryl Treatise of Sangye Gyamtso (1653–1705)*. London: Serindia: New York: Harry N. Abrams.

Notes

1 Bates 1995.
2 Gyatso 2015.
3 Gyatso 2015.
4 Hofer 2014, 230–36, 241.
5 Hofer 2014, 227–45.
6 Hofer 2014, 42, 44, 74.
7 Parfionovich, Dorje, and Meyer 1992.

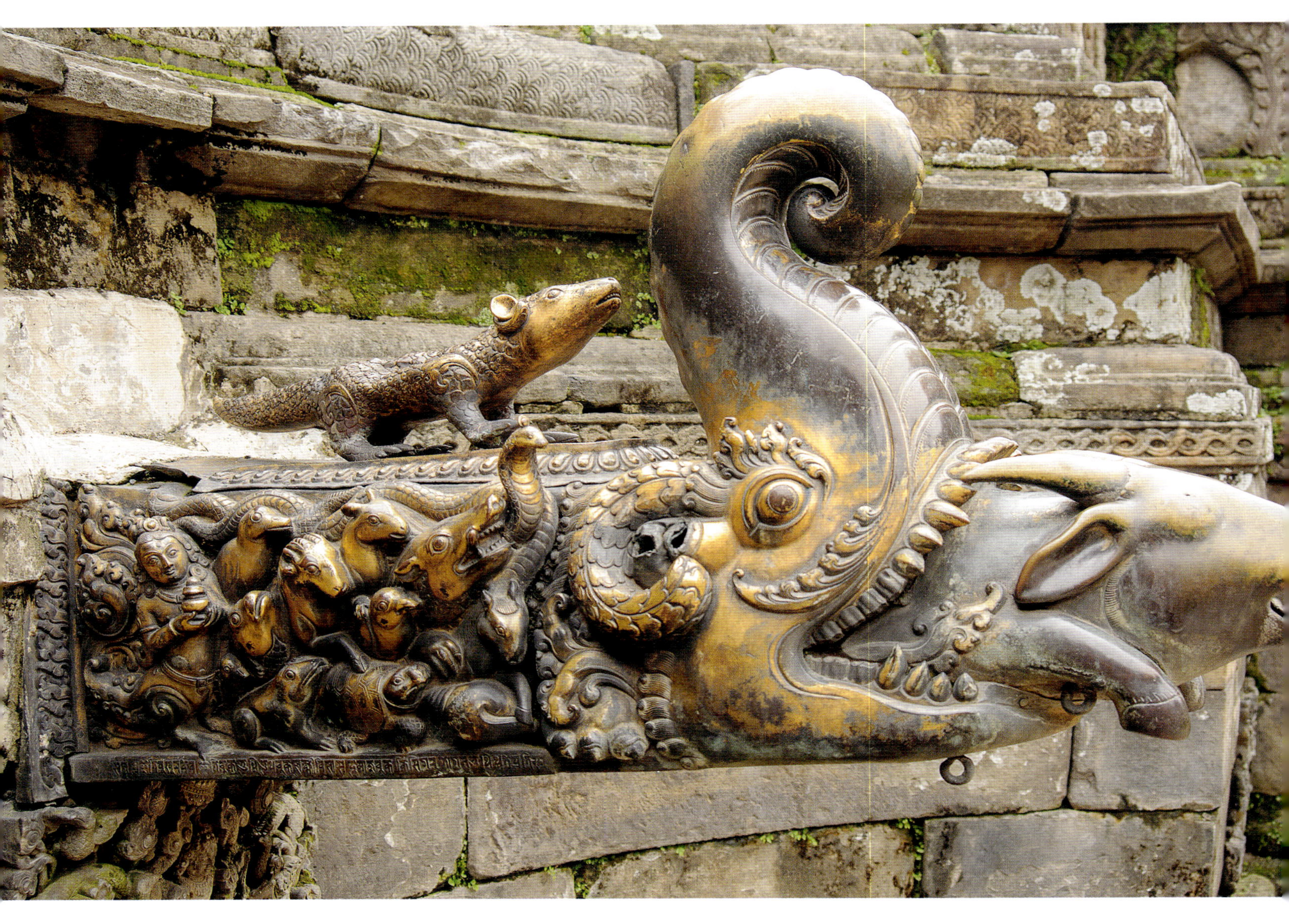

№ 74

Golden Fountain of Bhaktapur

Bhaktapur, Nepal, 1688

Architectural Expression of Monsoonal Phenomena

GAUTAMA V. VAJRACHARYA

For more on the architecture of the Kathmandu Valley, see Torana of the Main Shrine at Yetakha Baha, no. 24.

THE ART OF NEPAL is deservedly famous not only for the pagoda-like architecture of the Kathmandu Valley, site of the capital of the country, but also for the subterranean architecture that provided water through the cities of the valley. The surface fountains feature horizontally projecting spouts designed after the mythical makara, a creature that symbolizes water, both celestial (rain cloud) and terrestrial.[1] Usually, the makara spout is made from stone, but in royal palaces the stone spouts, as in this example, are often covered with tastefully designed, glittering repoussé metalwork.

The natural sources of water for all fountains in the Kathmandu Valley are the lakes situated on the slopes of the mountains surrounding the valley and fed by monsoon rains. Although the lakes are within ten or twenty miles of the cities, it was not an easy job to build subterranean brick canals with catch basins, even for short distances. The earliest, fifth-century water fountain of the valley is still functioning. The seventeenth-century golden fountains of the three royal palaces of the valley, in Bhaktapur, Patan, and Kathmandu, are examples of the continuation of the much earlier custom.

Older generations of Newars, the natives of the valley, still remember that the real name of the golden fountain of Bhaktapur is the Goat Fountain (Duguca Hiti).[2] The golden fountain of Patan palace is known as the Cow Fountain (Thusa Hiti). These names derive from the dramatic representation of animated images of a crying goat, as seen here, or a cow leaping from the mouth of the makara. Although the cow is now missing from the Patan fountain, the domesticated animal repeatedly appears in other examples. Another fascinating feature of the fountains is the three-dimensional image of a scaly creature resembling a pangolin crawling on top of the spout.[3]

The Bhaktapur fountain is highly admired for the elaborately designed scenes crowded by a variety of creatures, mostly aquatic, depicted on the panels on both sides of the spout. At the uppermost section of the scenes, male and female nagas, "divine serpents," intertwine as they mate. Below the erect head of the divine serpent, an enormous, diagonally projecting boar with sharp teeth and tusks is about to jump out of the group. The boar is trampling a running baby horse that is about to jump over a very large conch shell. Behind this scene, a baby goat, a bird, and a turtle are rendered naturalistically. They are followed by equally animated representations of a ram and a frog. Behind the ram crowd a quacking duck and the head of a large fish that appears to be about to leap out of the muddy water. At the very end of the panel, a half-bird mythical creature known to the Newars as *jalamanusha*, "aquatic man," faces the other creatures.

During the medieval period (879–1769), it was customary to place an image of Prince Bhagiratha below the fountain's spout. According to legend, the prince was responsible for bringing the atmospheric Ganga River down to the earth when all the water on earth, including the oceans, had dried up in a severe drought. Here, a stone statue of the prince occupies the wall immediately below the spout. He holds a lotus with his right hand and blows a conch shell to announce the joyful arrival of the rain river. This image of Bhagiratha conveys the message that the makara fountain symbolizes the Ganga's descent.

Spout of Golden Fountain of Bhaktapur Palace; Bhaktapur, Nepal; 1688; stone, repoussé metalwork; dimensions unknown; photograph by Christian Luczanits, 2010

The association of Bhagiratha's story with Nepalese fountains does not seem old enough to be original. During the ancient period of Nepalese history (ca. 200–ca. 879), a stone relief of one or a pair of earth spirit (*yaksha*) figures almost always occupied the wall below the spout exactly where Bhagiratha appears in later examples. They reside beneath the earth and support it; their representation is associated with the legend of the disappearance of the Sarasvati River in northwest India. During the Vedic period (1500–600 BCE) the river was still flowing, but dwindling, and eventually it vanished at a

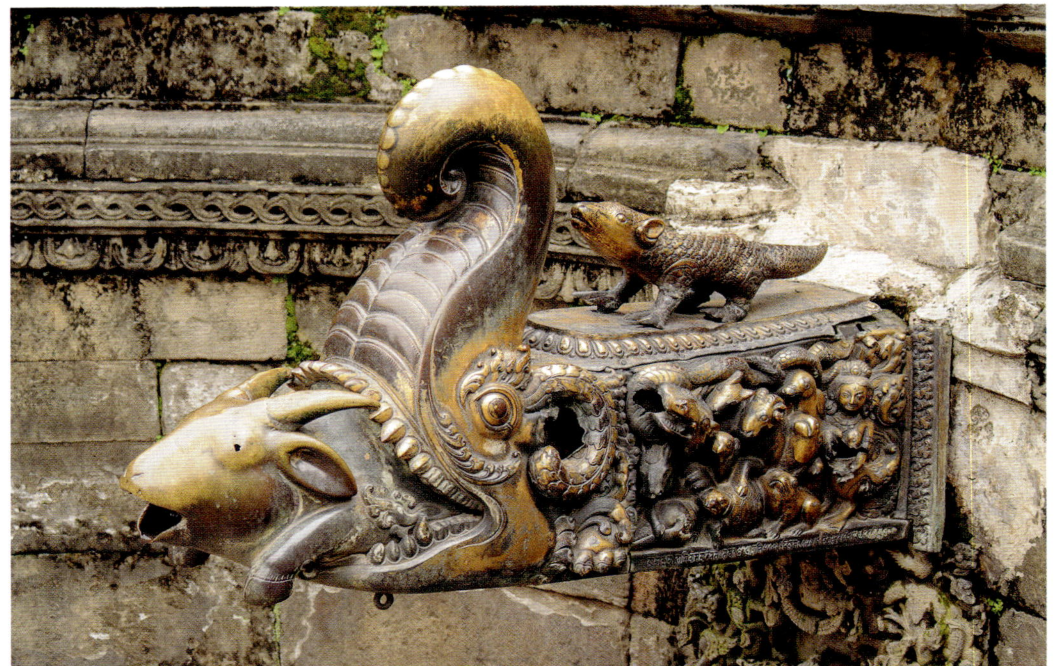

Spout of Golden Fountain of Bhaktapur Palace; Bhaktapur, Nepal; 1688; stone, repoussé metalwork; dimensions unknown; photograph by Christian Luczanits, 2010

place called Vinasana, or "disappearance." People thought that the river had emptied into the netherworld. Almost certainly, the *yakshas* below the spout symbolize the Sarasvati River rather than the Ganga.

Prominent features of the water fountain, however, such as the representations of mating serpents, a frog, and the domesticated animal coming out of the makara's mouth, do not directly relate to these rivers. A frog—shown here on the spout, but in other examples also above the spout crawling together with the pangolin-like scaly creature—holds the key to understanding the symbolism of the water fountain that developed over the millennia, some of it going back to the Vedic period or even earlier.

Divine Frogs and Other Creatures

The Vedic and pre-Vedic cowherds living near the southern slope of the Himalayas believed that frogs were divine beings capable of making rain. This belief related to an ancient technique of cow breeding. The ancient cowherds wanted their cows to conceive around autumn so that calves would be born at the beginning of the monsoon season when there is plenty of vegetation for feed. They kept bulls away from the cows and released them only after an autumnal ritual. Because frogs start croaking with the onset of the monsoon rain, their croaking coincided with the birth of the calves. The ancient people thought that it rains when frogs start croaking. In the well-known frog hymn of the *Rigveda*,[4] the frogs were prayed to in the hopes of the birth of multiple calves. According to some Vedic poets, a variety of creatures descend from heaven together with the shower of rain. The crowded scenes of creatures depicted on the spout of the golden fountain are indeed associated with this belief.

Like the Vedic people, the Newars of the Kathmandu Valley originally were cow breeders. Amazingly, they still worship the frogs and celebrate the autumnal festive days of the impregnation of cows and monsoonal birth of calves in accordance with the Vedic or pre-Vedic calendar.[5] Admittedly, the real meaning of the annual celebrations is now nearly forgotten, but the ancient Newars who adorned the water fountains with symbolic creatures certainly knew the reason for juxtaposing the image of a frog with a calf or a goat emerging from the mouth of a makara.

Makara and Monsoon Imagery

For another example of this motif, see Pitcher, no. 90.

In Sanskrit, a synonym for makara is *dhara*, which means "the shower of rain." In addition, in artworks, the lower body of the makara is carved in a popular motif known as *abhrapatra*, or "cloud foliage." In fact, the makara is an atmospheric creature visualized in the cloudscape of monsoonal rain.[6] Thus, the depiction of a frog and calves on the fountains in the valley indicates that the Nepalese water fountains are the architectural expression of monsoonal phenomena. For this reason, in the Nepalese painterly tradition, drought is symbolically depicted by a dry makara fountain with a human figure standing in front of the spout, begging for water, whereas the joyful arrival of the monsoon rain is pictured by a stream of water flowing from the mouth of the *dhara*/makara. The beginning of the monsoon is also the mating time of snakes. Like frogs, snakes aestivate in the summer and become active with the arrival of the rains. Thus, the auspicious mating serpents are shown on both sides of the spout of the Golden Fountain.

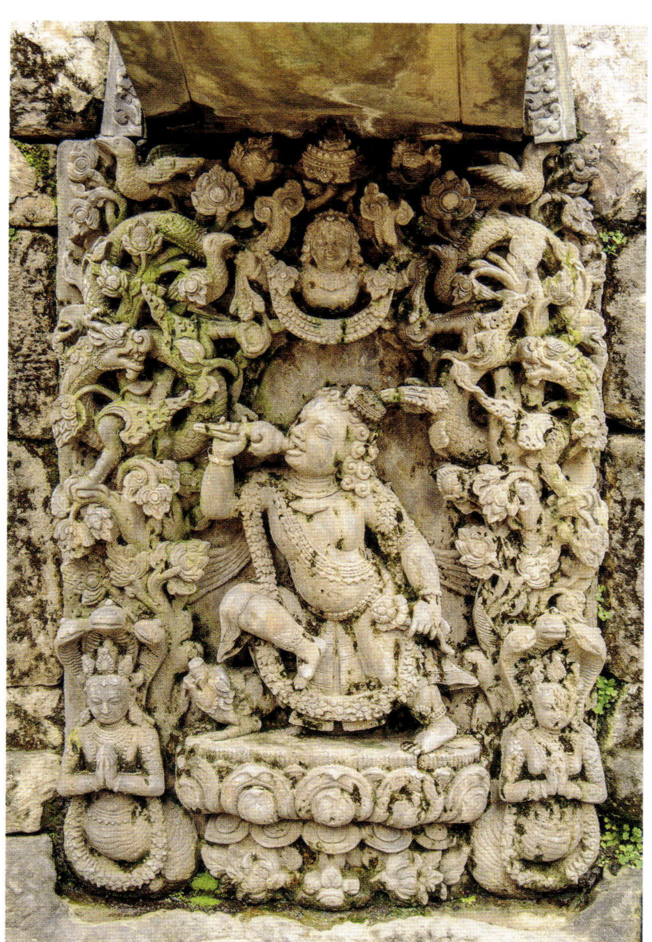

Detail of Golden Fountain of Bhaktapur Palace, showing stone statue of a prince under spout; Bhaktapur, Nepal; photograph by Christian Luczanits, 2010

Sanskrit literature tells us that the cosmos has two oceans, atmospheric and terrestrial, and that the source of water is the former. When the gods block the flow of atmospheric water, the rains stop, causing severe droughts. This view remained intact throughout the history of the ancient and medieval periods.[7] In Nepalese art, an ocean is represented by aquatic and mythical creatures, including makara-like crocodiles, serpents, conch shells, and *jalamanushas*. All these creatures flow down to the terrestrial realm when the atmospheric water descends to the earth. According to Pali literature, the rain cloud is the god Kubera's lake, which is explained as the source of rainwater. In this literature, however, *jalamanushsa* is designated as *danda-manavaka*, or "Lotus Baby."

The concept of the cloud ocean or lake intertwines with another interesting view: that just like cows, the sky conceives in autumn and gives birth to rain babies when the monsoon arrives. Astrological texts say that if aquatic and semiaquatic creatures appear in the cloudscape, it means the sky has conceived. It is this view that inspired the artists of the Ajanta ceiling painting in which aquatic and semiaquatic creatures inhabit Kubera's cloud lake and peep out of the stylized cloud (*abhrapatra*). A remarkable feature of the ceiling painting is a fully grown fetus whose lower body morphs into cloud foliage.[8] Sometimes, the umbilical cord of the fetus is depicted as a stylized lotus vine, which must be the reason that the atmospheric baby was named Lotus Baby in Pali literature.[9] It is this lotus baby that went through metamorphosis and became the *jalamanusha* in Nepalese art.

Artistically, the Golden Fountain is the epitome of both water architecture and repoussé work. Making repoussé requires a special skill and vision. The artist creates an image by hammering it into relief from the reverse side and needs to visualize the appearance of the image in negative, which seems to be why Newar artists prefer to call it *thvajya*, or "echo work." For many centuries Nepalese artists excelled in repoussé.[10]

Stylistic Observations

The unknown artist of this fountain deserves special admiration for creating a superlative composition. He understood how to exploit the play of light and shadow across the surface of the relief, which makes most of the creatures appear to emerge from an invisible deeper space. Subtle diagonal lines used for depicting the crawling pangolin on top of the spout and the dramatic projection of several creatures—the crying goat leaping out of the makara's mouth and the giant boar jumping out of the group—create animated movement. When the Malla king and members of the royal family came here for bathing, they must have enjoyed the art because all the creatures appeared to be so realistic, but they also undoubtedly appreciated the effect of the large volume of water constantly gushing with resonant sound creating a relaxing, eternal monsoonal phenomenon.

Notes

1 For recent scholarship, see Becker-Ritterspach 1995; S. S. Shrestha 1996; Bühnemann 2008; Vajracharya 2009; Vajracharya 2020.
2 Joshi 2016, 331.
3 Thanks to Kerry Lucinda Brown for identifying the creature as a pangolin.
4 An ancient Indian collection of hymns, the earliest Sanskrit text, composed around the fifteenth century BCE.
5 Vajracharya 2018.
6 Vajracharya 2013, 130.
7 Vajracharya 2020, 12.
8 Vajracharya 2013, 134–38.
9 Vajracharya 2013, 134–38.
10 Slusser 2005, 161–68.

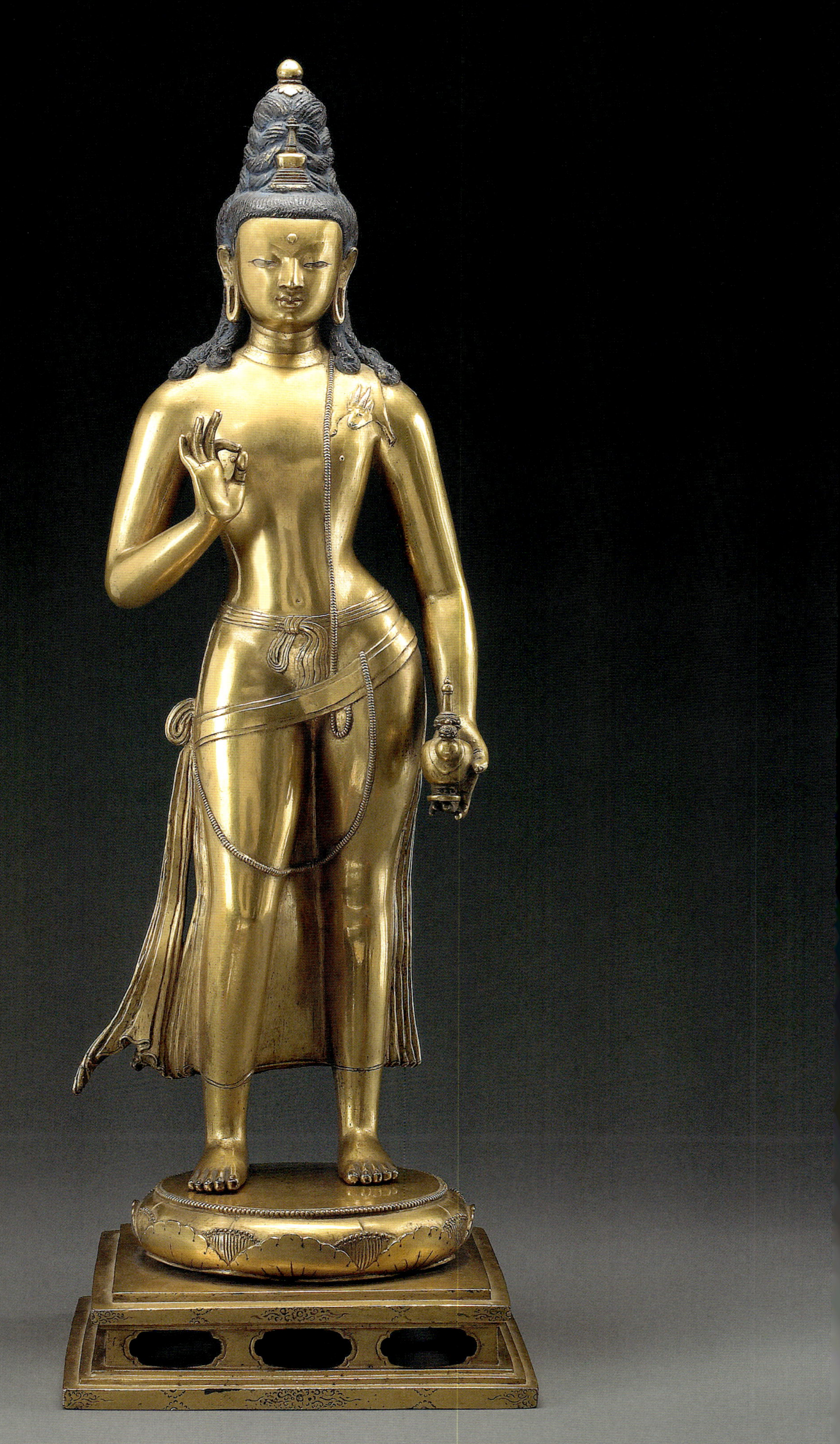

Nº 75

Maitreya

Mongolia, ca. 1680s

The Mongolian Artist Zanabazar and the Mongol Devotion to the Future Buddha Maitreya

URANCHIMEG TSULTEMIN

Attributed to Zanabazar (1635–1723); Maitreya; Mongolia; 1680s; gilt bronze with blue pigment in the hair and traces of other pigments in the eyes and mouth; 24⁹⁄₁₆ × 8⁷⁄₁₆ × 7⅝ in. (62.4 × 21.5 × 19.4 cm); Harvard Art Museums / Arthur M. Sackler Museum; Gift of John West; 1963.5; photograph © President and Fellows of Harvard College

For other images of Maitreya, see Rock Carving of Four-Armed Bodhisattva Maitreya, no. 17; Maitreya and Manjushri Mural at Dratang, no. 26; Maitreya Statue at Jampa Lhakhang, Bhutan, no. 9.

The statue of Maitreya is attributed to Zanabazar (1635–1723), an eminent Mongolian sculptor, architect, Buddhist teacher, and political leader. Maitreya, the buddha of the future, appears in a standing bodhisattva form as a slim and youthful figure holding a ritual ewer (*kundika*) in his left hand and assuming a gesture of discourse (*vitarka* mudra) with his right hand lifted to his chest. Maitreya's second main attribute, a stupa, is piled high on the hair. A deer skin, another attribute of Maitreya, is seen hanging on the left shoulder.

Maitreya displays a slight movement as he stands with his right leg forward, leaning on it and subtly shifting his weight. The lower part of the body is covered by a garment (dhoti), which is made to appear transparent to reveal the shape of the youthful figure and the legs in motion. As the sculpture is cast in bronze, it required a high level of artistry to render the translucence and lightness of the garment. The sculpture is elegant in other details as well, such as the dhoti tied in a flamboyant bow at the waist, and a broad sash that stretches diagonally across the hips, enhancing the delicate liveliness of the figure. A beaded chain that represents a Brahmanic "sacred thread" stretches from the left shoulder across the body, creating a stylish loop under the sash as a skillfully made sartorial ornament. These details augment the voluminosity of the sculpture in a visually subtle, delicate way, as they make asymmetrical linear patterns on the smooth planar surfaces.[1] As several scholars have shown, this sculpture follows an early, twelfth-century, Nepalese-inspired Maitreya in Nartang Monastery in Tibet, currently lost.[2] Lotus thrones in the sculptures by Zanabazar are distinct, their round shapes decorated with symmetrically arranged lotus leaves and accentuated with tiny beads, whereas the Newari style is seen in a suave *S* shape of the posture, the details of the jewelry, and the sartorial ornamentations. Maitreya stands on two platforms; the entire sculpture, including the pedestals, is worked all around, and the finely detailed craftsmanship continues on the back as well. All these details indicate the style of works known to be by Zanabazar. He sculpted several similar sculptures of Maitreya, two of which are currently in the Choijin Lama Temple Museum, Gandan Tegchinling Monastery, in Ulaanbaatar, Mongolia, with others located elsewhere.[3]

Zanabazar

Zanabazar was a descendant of Chinggis Khan (ca. 1162–1227) and was enthroned as the First Jibzundamba reincarnation of the Tibetan historian of the Jonang tradition, Taranatha (1575–1634), at the age of five. In 1639 two khans of Khalkha Mongolia, his own father, Tüshiyetü Khan Gombodorji (1594–1655), and his close ally, Setsen Khan (1577–1652), assembled with other Khalkha noblemen for this occasion, which is recorded in Zanabazar's first biography, written by his disciple, a learned monk, Zaya Pandita Lubsangperinlei (1642–1715).[4]

Zanabazar was the first of altogether eight historical Jibzundamba reincarnations (Khutugtus) of Khalkha Mongolia, the first two identified among the Tüshiyetü Khan's family and the remaining seven discovered in central Tibet.[5] The discovery of Tibetan reincarnations to rule in Khalkha Mongolia came about because of a shift in Inner Asian power struggles and the rise of the Qing court in Beijing, which now intervened and approved the new Jibzundamba reincarnations. Zanabazar's recognition of this new lineage connecting to Jonang tradition was a Mongol initiative and was later "confirmed" by the Fifth Dalai Lama of Tibet (1617–1682), who sent him a letter from the Potala Palace in 1645, and by the Fourth Panchen Lama (1570– 1662) in 1651.[6] Zanabazar remained active in the social and political life of the region,

See Potala Palace, no. 71.

For more on the Fourth Panchen Lama, see Nartang Woodblock Prints and Their Painted Copies, no. 81.

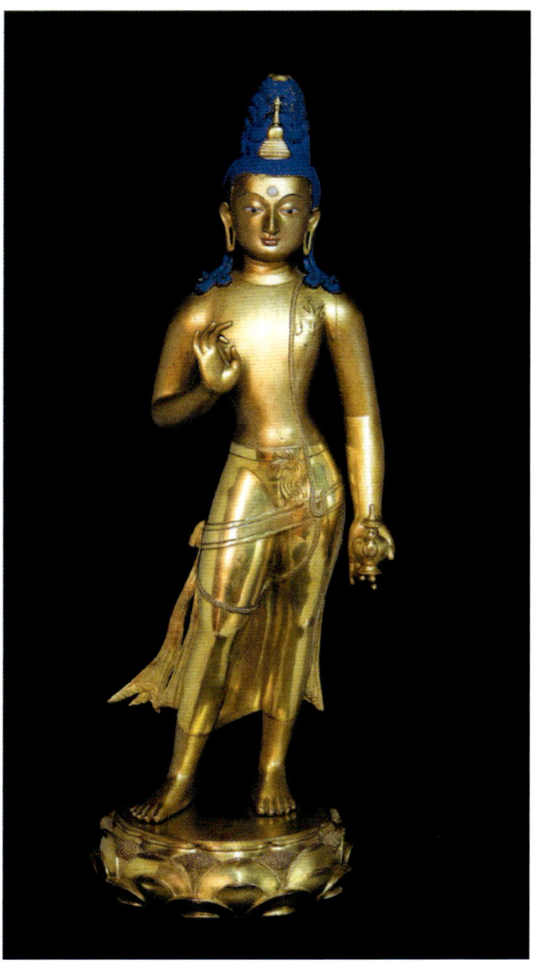

Zanabazar (1635–1723); Maitreya; Mongolia; 1680s; gilt bronze with blue pigment in the hair; 26¾ × 17¾ × 16¾ in. (68 × 45 × 42.6 cm); Choijin Lama Temple Museum, Ulaanbaatar; image after Otgonsüren, D., ed. 2015. *The Masterpieces of Undur Gegeen Zanabazar*. Ulaanbaatar: Choijin Lama Temple Museum, 12

personally visiting and establishing important alliances with the Tibetan and Qing hierarchs. Thus, he traveled to Tibet twice, visiting monasteries in eastern and central Tibet in 1649–51; in 1655 he made a shorter visit to Tashilhunpo, the main seat of the Fourth Panchen Lama. It was at Tashilhunpo where Zanabazar took his monastic novice *getsul* vows and received important teachings and initiations from the Panchen Lama, whom he considered his main teacher.

On returning home to Khalkha, Zanabazar disseminated Buddhist teachings among the Khalkha nomads, built monasteries, and created art. He was also a political leader of the Khalkha Mongols and spent many years in Beijing after the Khalkha Mongols' submission to the Qing in 1691 to become a vassal state. Zanabazar was a close friend of the Qing Kangxi emperor (1654–1722). He aided the emperor with healing rituals, consecrated and repaired sacred images, and provided empowerments and rituals for imperial family members.[7] Zanabazar died in Beijing and was later entombed in Amurbayasgalantu, a special monastery in northern Mongolia, which was built by the Qing Yongzheng emperor (1678–1735) in memory of his father.

Zanabazar's biographers describe him as an avid artist who sculpted precious Buddhist images "with his own hands."[8] Zanabazar's images suggest a pantheon of deities, including buddhas and bodhisattvas that are seminal to Buddhist practice.[9] He also made images for his foreign allies, teachers, and patrons. For instance, Zanabazar painted images of Tsongkhapa for Jakhyung Monastery in Amdo, and sculpted a buddha statue and "three gilded sculptures of Manjushri" for the Qing emperor around 1700. Some of these sculptures are still in Beijing.[10]

For more on Manjushri and the Qing emperor, see The Qianlong Emperor as Manjushri-Chakravartin, no. 84.

In his dharma seat Ribogejai-Gandan-Shaddubling in northern Mongolia, Zanabazar led a considerable sculpting workshop, creating locally an entire iconographic program with monumental buddhas, mahabodhisattvas, and over three thousand clay buddha sculptures.[11] Moreover, Zanabazar designed a new assembly hall for his monasteries based on a tent design. The development of his yurt (*ger*) into a mobile monastery in Yekhe Khüriye also began with Zanabazar.

See Mongolian Map of Capital Yekhe Khüriye, no. 96.

Zanabazar's Engagement with Maitreya

See the Maitreya Procession depicted down the middle of the Panoramic Map of Mount Wutai, no. 91.

Zanabazar had a special interest in Maitreya, as evidenced in his several sculptures of Maitreya and the rituals of Maitreya he conducted in Mongolia. Bodhisattva Maitreya sculptures were used in the annual ritual Maitreya Procession, held in Geluk monasteries in Mongolia and Tibet. During the Maitreya Procession, the image of Maitreya and Maitreya's texts are carried by the monks in a cart and followed by the lay public, a ritual particularly favored in the Geluk tradition. In Mongolia, several characteristic details in performing this ritual emerge. Unlike Tibetan monasteries, which perform the ritual during the Great Prayer Festival in the early days of the Lunar New Year, the Maitreya Procession in Mongolia is carried out in late spring or early summer. Placing the Maitreya sculpture in a green wooden horse chariot decorated with the colors of the Five Buddhas is also unique to Mongolia. Attendant monks and lay devotees accompany the cart carrying the Maitreya statue, circumambulating the monastery. Another

See Erdeni Juu Monastery, no. 65.

Mongolian hallmark, mentioned in textual records, suggests that the Jibzundamba Khutugtus' Maitreya Procession was carried out in conjunction with the long-life ritual known as *tenzhuk*. The Maitreya Procession at Erdeni Juu began in 1657, when Zanabazar's twenty-third birthday was celebrated. In 1681 it was carried out again in Erdeni Juu for Zanabazar's forty-seventh birthday.[12]

For another example of a colossal statue, see Monumental Statue of Guru Rinpoche, no. 104.

One clear source of Zanabazar's interest in Maitreya was in Tashilhunpo Monastery's Maitreya Lhakhang, where the First Dalai Lama, Gendun Drub (1391–1474), built a monumental seated Maitreya statue in 1461, and where Zanabazar's teacher, the Panchen Lama, had his artists create three monumental statues of Maitreya, inscribed in *lanydza* (Nepali: *Ranjana*) and Mongolian scripts, thereby suggesting that the patrons of the statues included Mongol noblemen.[13] Zanabazar's Maitreya statues were copied in the eighteenth century until this standing form of Maitreya Bodhisattva lost its popularity in Mongolia and was replaced by a seated form of Buddha Maitreya, which was also produced in monumental dimensions akin to monumental sculptures of Maitreya in Geluk monasteries across Inner Asia.[14] The Fifth Jibzundamba (1815–1841) initiated and supported several projects focused on Maitreya in Yekhe Khüriye. In 1833 Yekhe Khüriye's abbot Agwang Khayidub (1779–1838) built a new colossal Maitreya statue measuring about 54 feet (16.5 meters) high, which he placed in the Maitreya Temple designated specifically to house that statue and built in 1820–1822 in a Tibeto-Mongolian architectural style.[15] Agwang Khayidub wrote numerous texts about Maitreya, whereas his patron, the Fifth Jibzundamba, built a new Gandan (Maitreya's Heaven) Monastery in Yekhe Khüriye in 1838. The Mongolian interest in Maitreya continues to this day, as Zanabazar's Maitreya sculpture is now developed into a new monumental statue for a state-of-the-art satellite town on the outskirts of Ulaanbaatar.[16] When completed, the new colossal Maitreya will measure 177 feet (54 meters) in height.

Further Reading

Chuluun, S. 2019. "In Search of the Khutugtu's Monastery: The Site and Its Heritage." Translated by Uranchimeg Tsultemin. In "Buddhist Art of Mongolia: Cross-Cultural Connections, Discoveries and Interpretations," edited by Uranchimeg Tsultemin, special issue, *Cross-Currents: East Asian History and Culture Review* 8, no. 2 (June): 244–56. https://cross-currents.berkeley.edu/e-journal/issue-31/chuluun.

Tsultem, Nyam-Osoryn. 1982. *The Eminent Mongolian Sculptor—G. Zanabazar.* Ulaanbaatar: Gosizdatel'stvo.

Tsultemin, Uranchimeg. 2015. "The Power and Authority of Maitreya in Mongolia." In *Buddhism in Mongolian History, Culture, and Society*, edited by Vesna Wallace, 137–59. Oxford: Oxford University Press.

Notes

1 For more on the sculpture, see Rhie and Thurman 1996, 141.
2 Berger and Bartholomew 1995, 281.
3 Tsultem 1989, figs. 78, 79, show two other sculptures similar to this Maitreya. The current location of these sculptures is unknown.
4 See the annotated translation in Bareja-Starzyńska 2015.
5 During the Qing dynasty (1644–1911), Mongolia was divided into Outer Mongolia, which is the modern-day independent state of Mongolia, and Inner Mongolia, today the Inner Mongolian Autonomous Region of the People's Republic of China. The Khalkha are the major ethnic group in (Outer) Mongolia to this day. See Atwood 2004a, 299.
6 See S. Karmay 2014, 10. Tsultemin 2020, 87–89, translates and discusses a letter the Dalai Lama sent to the ten-year-old Zanabazar. See also Lubsangperinlei, fol. 430, in Bareja-Starzyńska 2015, 118.
7 Tsultemin 2020, 99, referring to Lubsangperinlei, fols. 495, 517, in Bareja-Starzyńska 2015, 161, 173.
8 Lubsangperinlei, fols. 453–56, in Bareja-Starzyńska 2015, 135–37.
9 Tsultemin 2020, 52–65.
10 Lubsangperinlei, fol. 454, in Bareja-Starzyńska 2015, 135, 214; Ngag dbang ye shes thub bstan rab 'byams pa (Agwang Ishitübden Rabjamba) 1982a, fols. 112–13. On Zanabazar's works in the National Palace Museum, see Luo 1999, 81–87. See also images in Tsultemin 2020, 53.
11 See Chuluun 2019, which includes images of works excavated recently in northern Mongolia.
12 Tsendina 1999, fols. 15r, 16r; Bareja-Starzyńska 2015, 132.
13 See Demo 1969, fols. 413–14.
14 Colossal Maitreya statues were built in Urga, Yonghegong, Tashilhunpo, and Lhasa, among other places. See Tsultemin 2020, 176–86; Greenwood 2013.
15 Tsultemin 2015; Ngag dbang mkhas grub (Agwang Khayidub) 1972–74a, vol. 1, fols. 175–273; Ngag dbang mkhas grub (Agwang Khayidub). 1972–74b, vol. 1, fols. 155-65. TBRC W16912–0588.
16 See Charleux 2020.

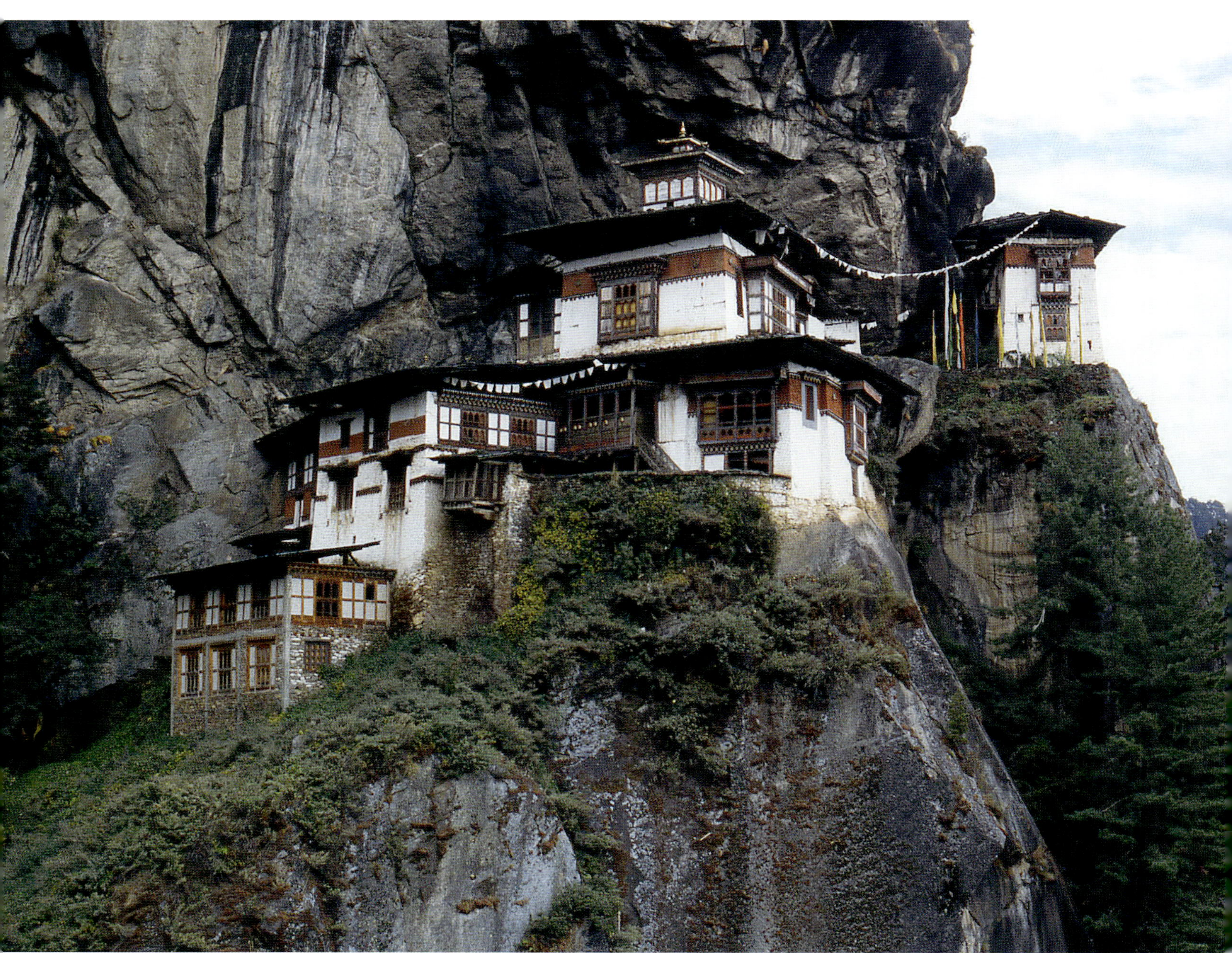

№ 76

Taktsang, the Tiger's Lair

Paro District, western Bhutan, founded 1692–1694

Bhutan's Most Acclaimed Religious Sanctuary

JOHN A. ARDUSSI

TEN MILES NORTH of modern Bhutan's Paro Airport can be found Taktsang (Taktshang), "The Tiger's Lair," one of the most profoundly spiritual Himalayan temples known from early Tibetan Buddhist lore. Prior to a destructive fire of 1998, the original Taktsang temple complex dating from the late seventeenth century was ledged across a massive cliff, along an ancient pilgrimage and trade route connecting Tibet with India. Traders and pilgrims from Tibet would have crossed into Bhutan at Trinme La (Cloudy Pass), descending a narrow, rocky gorge opening into the forested valleys of upper Paro Valley, where soon they would encounter on their left the dramatic cliffs of Taktsang.

For more on treasure revealers, see *Dorje* Discovered by Dorje Lingpa, no. 51.

The early history of Taktsang is clouded in legend. Its famous cliffside caves host meditation sites where Buddhist revelation texts called treasure literature were allegedly first deposited during the ninth century and later recovered by treasure revealers, or *terton*. The most famous are Lion Cave or Sengge Phug, and Splendor Cave, or Palphug.

The Role of Padmasambhava in the Opening of Taktsang

See Padmasambhava and His Manifestations, no. 43.

See Ritual Dance Mask of Guru Dorje Drolo, no. 94.

The most prominent religious figure associated with Taktsang is the legendary Indian master Padmasambhava, the "Lotus-born" Guru Rinpoche (eighth–ninth century), revered as the bringer of Tantric Buddhism from India to Tibet and Bhutan. His twelfth-century biography *Namtar zanglingma* (*The Copper Island Biography*), attributed to the Tibetan historian Nyangrel Nyima Wozer (1124–1192), is the earliest text dealing with his life. Consistent with his persona, Padmasambhava's dual motivation was the conquest of local deities opposed to Buddhism, and meditation in sacred spaces controlled by them, including Taktsang and other ancient sites along the Himalayas. Reflecting this tradition is the popular story that Padmasambhava flew to Taktsang riding on the back of a tiger, a theme often rendered in artistic works. It was the eighth and last of his ritualistic manifestations, that of Dorje Drolo, a fierce aspect in which Padmasambhava rides on the back of a tiger, defeating enemies of the Buddhist Dharma.[1]

The Modern History of Taktsang

The story of Taktsang shifts from the ninth to later centuries. Nyangrel's accounts of Taktsang's caves induced later generations of Tibetan monks to follow the clues in his writings, in search of meditation sites and Buddhist texts said to have been hidden in the Tibetan southlands during Tibet's royal dynastic era from the eighth to the ninth century.[2]

The earliest datable monasteries in the Taktsang complex are located not on the face of the cliff, however, but on the ridge above, where they were founded in the sixteenth century by Nyingma and Katok monks from eastern Tibet. These include Orgyen Tsemo and Zangdok Pelri. From the fifteenth to the seventeenth century, monks from these affiliated monasteries, and other Drukpa Kagyu monasteries on the valley floor, jointly cared for the sacred meditation cave sites on the cliff itself. From this pre-seventeenth-century era can also be tentatively dated a Buddhist painting on the rock wall where Taktsang is now located, before the painting's destruction in the tragic 1998 fire.

Taktsang Lhakhang; Upper Paro Valley, western Bhutan; constructed 1692–1694 by command of Desi Tenzin Rabgye (1638–1696); photograph © John A. Ardussi, 1995

The Founding of Taktsang Lhakhang and Its Enduring Legacy

The famous Taktsang Lhakhang that we see today, clinging to the face of the cliff, was originally con-

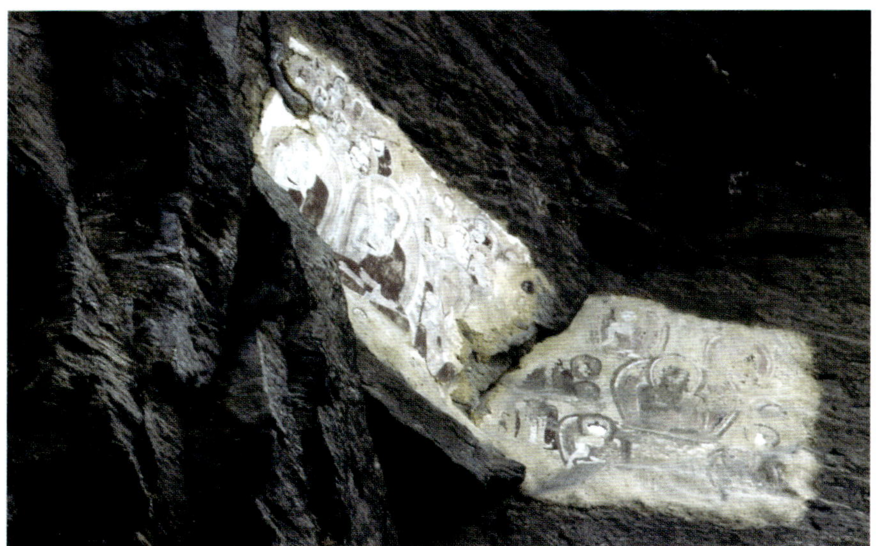

Rock Painting (no longer extant); Taktsang, Upper Paro Valley, western Bhutan; ca. 14th–15th century; photograph by Brian Shaw, 1980, courtesy Brian & Felicity Shaw Photo Archive, Centre for Bhutan Studies, Thimphu (bcs 1980 0404 [324])

For more on Tenzin Rabgye's role in the arts, see Maitreya Statue at Jampa Lhakhang, Bhutan, no. 9.

For more on the emergence of Geluk-led government and the Fifth Dalai Lama, see Potala Palace, no. 71.

See Arhats Viewing a Painting of Birds by the Tenth Karmapa, no. 72.

structed in 1692–1694 by the Fourth Druk Desi or civil ruler of Bhutan, Tenzin Rabgye (r. 1680–1694). He was a nephew of the founder of the Bhutan state, Zhabdrung Rinpoche Ngawang Namgyel (1594–1651), at whose behest the temple was constructed. As reflected in its artworks and legendary history, Taktsang represents a fusion in Bhutan of Kagyu and Nyingma sectarian traditions that continues to this day. Tenzin Rabgye came to be revered both as heir to the Zhabdrung's Drukpa doctrinal and family legacy, and as a re-embodiment of Padmasambhava.

The Paro Tshechu Festival of 1692

In the same year as Taktsang's founding, Tenzin Rabgye staged the first-ever enactment at Paro of Tshechu or "tenth-day" rites and public festivities honoring Padmasambhava, following an inaugural performance two years earlier at the Bhutanese capital in Thimphu. Tshechu is typically staged as a three-day monastic prayer event, ending with the public performance of costumed dances by monk-actors, overseen by a prominent monk garbed as Padmasambhava. For the Paro performance in 1692, Tenzin Rabgye himself led the ceremonies while standing at the entrance of Palphug Cave on the cliffside above. Culminating his performance, auspicious omens are said to have appeared in the sky, visible to the crowd of spectators on the valley floor below. The detailed account of these events was recorded by an eyewitness, Tenzin Rabgye's biographer, the Sixth Je Khenpo of Bhutan Ngawang Lhundrub (1670–1730).[3]

The Artists of Taktsang and Their Artworks

The original mural artwork within Taktsang was created by Bhutanese students of the Tibetan master artist Tsang Khenchen (1610–1684), who took refuge in seventeenth-century Bhutan during the later years of Zhabdrung Rinpoche, faced with sectarian opposition from the emergent Geluk government of the Fifth Dalai Lama. He was a master of the so-called Tsangri and Menri styles of painting, which he studied in Tibet under the Tenth Karmapa Hierarch, Choying Dorje (1604–1674), who was also an acknowledged artist.[4] Tsang Khenchen spent many years in Bhutan, where he trained a group of talented art students. Thus, the chief artisan assigned by Tenzin Rabgye to lead the Taktsang project was a Bhutanese monk named Drakpa Gyatso (1646–1719), Tsang Khenchen's most accomplished student. Drakpa Gyatso's autobiography describes in some detail how the work proceeded. Complementary information is found in the catalog of the 1688–1690 renovation of Tango Monastery, another major restoration sponsored by Tenzin Rabgye, which names the artists and lists all the murals and sculptures on each floor and wall of the building that were part of the project.[5]

Taktsang is actually a series of connected sanctuaries on the same cliff, several of which enclose the ancient meditation caves referred to earlier. Although there exists no contemporary catalog for Taktsang similar to that of Tango, a few scholars of Himalayan art were permitted by Bhutanese authorities to photograph several of Taktsang's temples, in the years prior to the 1998 fire. Based on style and level of artistry, we can with some certainty date many of the murals to the seventeenth century, and perhaps personally to the founding work of Drakpa Gyatso and other artists trained by Tsang Khenchen.

Whereas most of the Tango murals focus on members of the Drukpa lineage of Zhabdrung Rinpoche and Tenzin Rabgye,[6] Taktsang is principally a shrine to Padmasambhava in his eight manifestations, first enumerated in historical works from the era of Nyangrel Nyima Wozer. The main Taktsang temple is itself named Guru Tsengye Lhakhang, "The Temple of the Guru with Eight Names." The central portion of a vast mural from the upper level of Taktsang illustrates the main image of Padmasambhava seated on a throne within his celestial and worldly realm. He is surrounded by other images of himself, his attendants, worshippers, and fierce protectors of the dharma.[7]

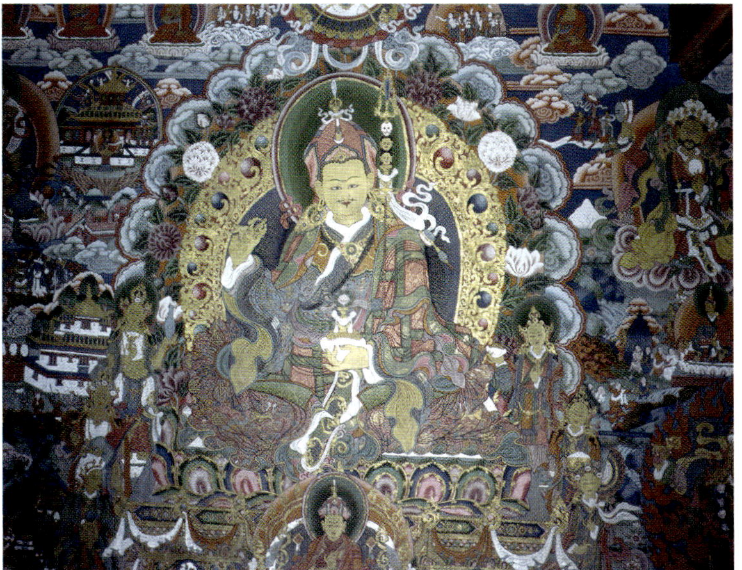

Detail of Padmasambhava Mural, showing central portion; Taktsang, Upper Paro Valley, western Bhutan; ca. 1692–1693; pigment on canvas; photograph by Brian Shaw, 1980, courtesy Brian & Felicity Shaw Photo Archive, Centre for Bhutan Studies, Thimphu (bcs 1980 0404 [323])

Visual Documentation of the Temple

We are fortunate to have photographs of the Padmasambhava mural taken separately by two European visitors, Jürgen Schick and Brian Shaw. The Huntington Archive of Buddhist and Asian Art at Ohio State University is the repository for over four hundred digital images of artwork from Bhutan, including a collection of fifty-three photographs taken at Taktsang circa 1980 by the German scholar Jürgen Schick.[8] The images come from different areas within the temple complex. By careful comparison, we now know that some are close-up photos of sections from the same mural, a fact not explained in Schick's notes, but which can be confirmed by comparison with an image taken by Brian Shaw. For example, Schick scan no. 35528 is actually a portion of the mural shown in scan no. 32888.

The close-up photos by Schick are high enough in resolution to reveal several important inscriptions in Tibetan. For example, scan no. 35528 bears a legend in Tibetan, *Pema Gyelpo* (Tibetan: *pad ma rgyal po*), "The Lotus King," one of the Eight Manifestations of Padmasambhava. Other scenes in Schick's photos bear Tibetan legends describing the physical location where Padmasambhava taught.

Further Research

There is clearly more opportunity to analyze the surviving artworks of Taktsang. Once the murals being restored at Tango are available for academic study, art specialists will be in a better position to compare them with those from Taktsang. A common thread connecting them is the person of Gyelse Tenzin Rabgye, who recruited the artists trained under Tsang Khenchen, who brought his artistic skills from Tibet to Bhutan. A significant portion of Tenzin Rabgye's biography describes temple restorations that he sponsored, showing his devotion to the painting, sculpture, and spiritual dance traditions of Bhutan.

Further Reading

Ardussi, John A. 1999. "Gyalse Tenzin Rabgye and the Founding of Taktsang Lhakhang." *Journal of Bhutan Studies* 1, no. 1, 36–63.

Ardussi, John A. 2008a. "Gyalse Tenzin Rabgye (1638–1696), Artist Ruler of 17th-Century Bhutan." In *The Dragon's Gift: The Sacred Arts of Bhutan*, edited by Therese Tse Bartholomew and John Johnston, 88–89. Exhibition catalog. Honolulu and Chicago: Honolulu Academy of Arts in association with Serindia.

Ardussi, John A. 2008b. "Gyalse Tenzin Rabgye and the Celebration of Tshechu in Bhutan." In *Written Treasures of Bhutan: Mirror of the Past and Bridge to the Future*, edited by John A. Ardussi and Sonam Tobgay, 1–24. Thimphu: National Library of Bhutan.

Notes

1. The classic work on the Eight Manifestations (*mtshan brgyad*) is the *Pema Thangyik* [Lotus Chronicle]. A mandala of these eight manifestations was once painted inside the Taktsang temple, which was destroyed by fire in 1998, and in many other locales. For background on Padmasambhava and earlier versions of the theme, see Hirshberg 2016.
2. See Quintman 2014a, 81–83, for details on several of these monks, including Kathok Sonam Gyeltsen (kaH thog bsod nams rgyal mtshan), though possibly not the Tibetan mystic Milarepa.
3. A complete translation of the account, presented in Tenzin Rabgye's Tibetan biography, is in Ardussi 1999 and Ardussi 2008b.
4. On Tsang Khenchen's work in Bhutan and examples from his artistic atelier, see Maki 2017.
5. The restoration of Tango Monastery is described in some detail in Ardussi 2008a, 93–97, based on chapter 18 of Tenzin Rabgye's biography.
6. There is, however, at least one entire temple wing within Tango dedicated to Guru Rinpoche, containing exquisite murals that likely date from the restoration of 1688–90. These artworks are currently being restored by trained personnel of the Bhutan Ministry of Culture, and should appear in a future exhibition.
7. A photograph by Jürgen Schick of the same mural can be viewed in a collection of his images at the Huntington Archive, scan no. 32888.
8. See "The Huntington Archive," http://dsal.uchicago.edu/huntington/database.php.

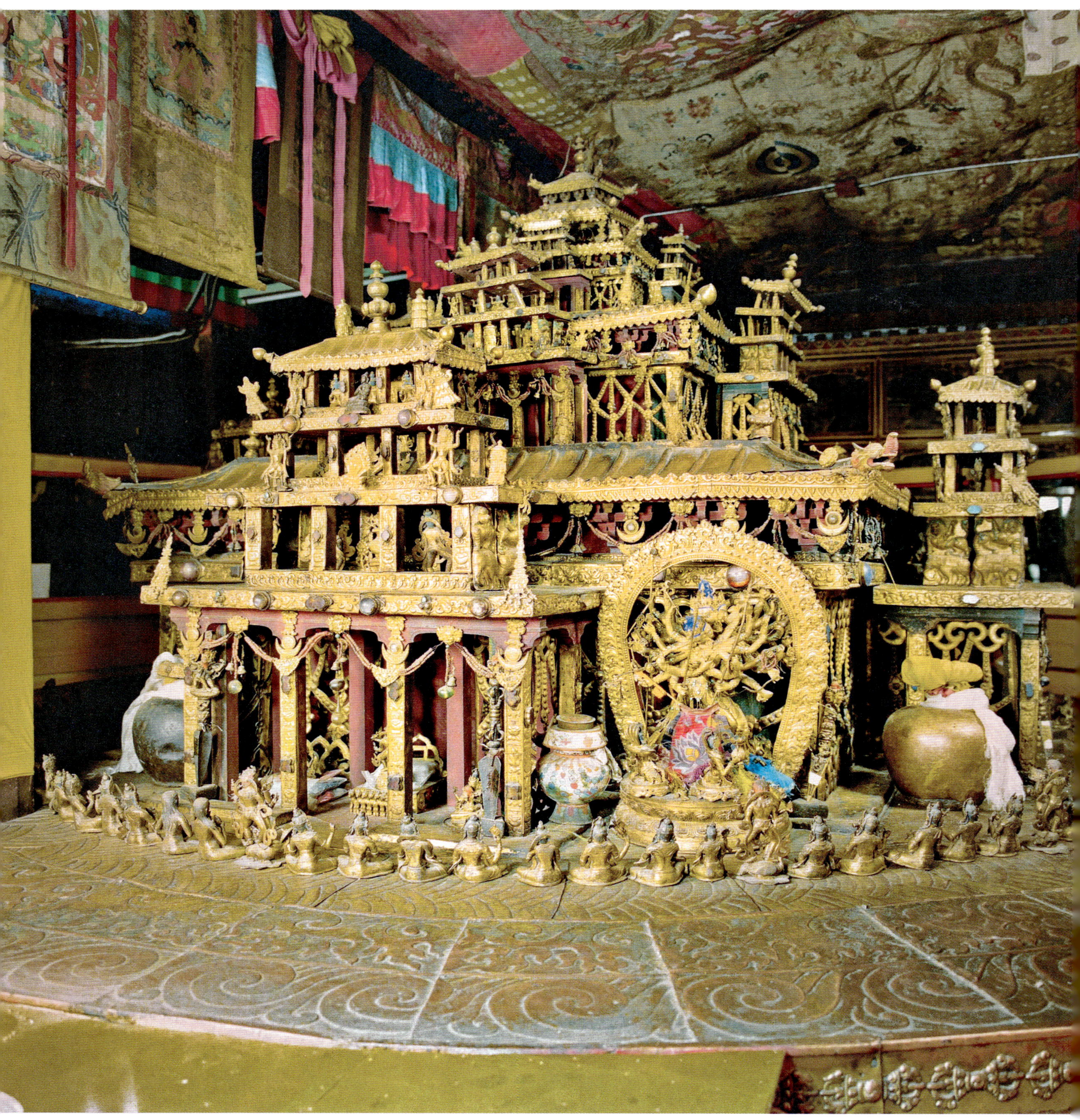

No 77

The Kalachakra Mandala in the Potala Palace

Lhasa, U region, central Tibet, late 17th century

Ritual Symbolism and Artistic Aspects of Three-Dimensional Mandalas in Tantric Tibetan Buddhism

MICHAEL HENSS WITH CONTRIBUTIONS FROM PEMA NAMDOL THAYE

For more on mandalas, see Chakrasamvara Mandala with Newar Donors, no. 29.

THE SANSKRIT WORD MANDALA (Tibetan: *kyilkhor*) can be translated as "a circle around a central point." The three-dimensional mandala is a visual cosmogram, combining the square concept of this world and the circular transcendental spheres of the macrocosmic universe. As a meditational instrument it is visualized when presented during an initiation ceremony by an authorized lama and introduced to the practitioner as a microcosmic offering of himself and of this world to the specific deity in the center and to the entire macrocosm. This celestial edifice is understood as a model of the interrelations between human and universe, representing the visualized way to the central deity in its interior with which the adept becomes finally identical.

Mandala Typology

Mandala images and objects in esoteric Tibetan Buddhism can be classified into eight types: two-dimensional sand mandalas; two-dimensional painted mandalas on cloth (thangkas) or temple walls; painted or drawn "table mandalas" on cloth or wood; three-dimensional square *torma* mandalas with multistory wooden armatures; three-dimensional Mount Meru (World Mountain) cosmos mandalas, usually small and thus portable, in gilt repoussé metal with engraved or sculptural symbolic decoration; the three-dimensional, geometric *yantras* of Newar Buddhism, with cast-metal or painted or diagrammatic patterns around a central Sanskrit root syllable; cast-metal lotus mandalas in the form of an eight-petaled bud to be opened in ritual; and large-scale three-dimensional palace mandalas, such as the main object shown here.

See Potala Palace, no. 71; Gyantse Kumbum, no. 55.

A large palace mandala has central structures in gilt metal on a wooden armature, with elaborate ornamental and figural details representing the cosmic and divine universe as described in tantric texts and visualized in mandala ritual. It is installed in a separate temple sanctuary. Some early examples survive, such as those in the Lhasa Potala Palace, the Drepung and Gyantse Monasteries, and the Buddhist sanctuaries of the former Imperial Palace in Beijing.[1]

Little attention has been paid beyond general visual concepts to the three-dimensional Mount Meru and palace mandalas. The former, with diameters of about 12 to 16 inches (30–40 centimeters), are usually accessible only in public and private collections, removed from their original ritual and historical contexts. The large palace mandalas transform the plan of the painted mandalas into larger structures such as the one here, which measures over 20 feet (6.2 meters) in diameter and over 5 feet (1.5 meters) in height.

The Mandala Palace: Construction and Symbolism

Kalachakra Palace Mandala; Potala Palace, Dukhor Lhakhang, Lhasa, U region, central Tibet; 1690s; gilt-brass repoussé, with cast figures, on wooden armature, with precious stone, crystal, and glass inlays; diam. 20 ft. 4 in. (6.2 m), height approx. 63 in. (1.6 m); Potala Palace, Lhasa; photograph by Walter Gross, 1997

The term "palace" is mentioned in the tantras and in the Tibetan Tengyur, the "translated doctrine" of the Buddhist Dharma, first compiled as the Buddhist canon in the eleventh and twelfth centuries, when the earliest three-dimensional mandalas probably existed. As noted in the contemporary *Sadhanamala* scriptures, an iconographic and ritualistic collection for visualizing and worshipping deities, "In the midst (of the outer diamond enclosure) one can see a palace with four arches."[2]

The architectural structure of three stories rises from the wavy circular platform of the World Ocean, surrounded by a lotus fence, a vajra diamond enclosure, and a fiery wall—powerful symbols of creation, purity, and rebirth, of burning and destroying all kind of samsaric ignorances, illusions, and attachments, of the indestructible Buddha nature, and of supreme wisdom and enlightenment. The three stories, partially hidden by the four-tiered portico gates oriented to the four directions, are related to the Three Realms of Existence: desire on the ground floor, the world of phenomena and forms in the middle

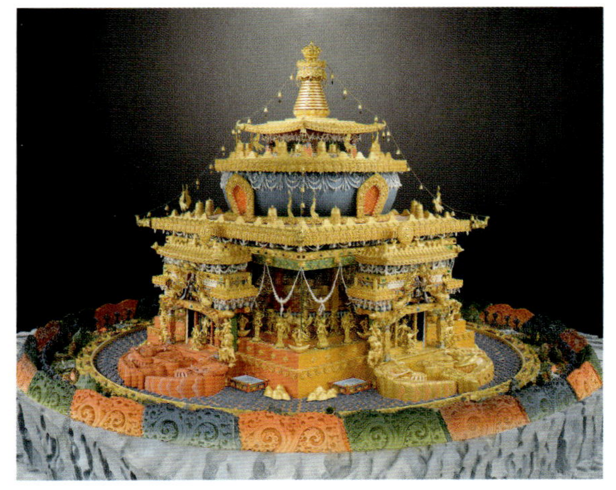

section, and the formless spheres of the divine Meru temple palace on top. According to the Mahayana Three Bodies (*trikaya*) doctrine, they may also be associated, like the 722 Kalachakra deities, with the three emanations or bodies of the Buddha: his physical human form; his transcendental, glorified enjoyment body; and his formless, absolute dharma or truth body, which is beyond representation. Another symbolic context might be the tantric concept of the Three Receptacles or "supports" of the Buddha and his teachings: his outer visible body, his inner, visually imperceptible mental body, and his secret diamond body, accessible only to the initiated.

The four-tiered portico sections and with four pillars on each tier are also associated with the Four Noble Truths in Buddhism as well as with the enlightened pacifying, increasing, conquering, and subjugating activities of the tantric practitioner, and, when double, with the Eightfold Noble Path.

Pema Namdol Thaye (American, b. 1967, Bhutan); *Zhitro Mandala*; 2000; gilt metal on wooden armature, polymeric resin compound (for minor decorative caste motifs such as animals, tassels, banners, and Buddhist emblems), semiprecious stone inlays, pearls, colored glass, and more; diam. 10 ft. 10 in. (3.3 m), height 65 in. (1.65 m); © Pema Namdol Thaye, photograph by Padma Studios

Iconography

As in a sand mandala, not all 722 Kalachakra deities can be represented figurally even in a large three-dimensional mandala; few of the many seated miniature statuettes on the outer platform are identifiable, except the large Kalachakra *yidam* with his female consort Vishvamata, surrounded by a full-body nimbus. The deities on the three terraces refer to the body mandala (536 deities) on the ground floor, to the speech mandala (of the Buddha's Word, 116 deities) on the intermediate section, and to the mind mandala (seventy deities) on the topmost divine palace level amid the celestial spheres of thirty-three gods, here in two groups associated with Great Bliss and Profound Awareness, with male and female buddhas and bodhisattvas, and wrathful and offering deities around the central main divinity. Other iconographic motifs are the offering goddesses of the five senses, the Eight Auspicious Symbols, the seven jewels of royal power, ritual offering vases filled with consecrated water or the *amrita* nectar of immortality, magic *purba* daggers protecting the sacred space, and decorative precious stone and crystal inlays.

Cosmology: The Square and the Circle

Beyond its cosmological symbolism, the basic square mandala plan, with four sides around a central point and vertical axis surrounded by a circular outer enclosure, is a five-fold manifestation of the Buddha and the Five Tathagatas mandala. The practitioner ritually circumambulates and visualizes the mandala palace in different initiation stages. Other monumental mandalas of the Highest Anuttarayoga Tantra systems are based on a crossed double vajra oriented to the four cardinal directions, a cosmic world plan, and a symbol of the clear and indestructible diamond nature of the Buddha wisdom, associated with the Diamond Throne (*vajrasana*) of Buddha's enlightenment at Bodhgaya.

For more on Vajrasana, see Mahabodi Temple Model, no. 25.

The square oriented to the four directions and the circle of the universe with no beginning or end are formulas of space and time, representing a world view and a model of the interrelated human and divine worlds, the harmony of the cosmic order, and the perfect Buddha nature.

On the process of visualizing a mandala, see The All-Knowing Buddha Vairochana Visualization Album, no. 87.

The visualized path into the mandala transforms the mind, purifies it from mental defilements, and empowers and authorizes it to practice the tantric teachings.

The cosmological symbolism can be associated with Brahmanic concepts of primordial creative energies (*prajapati*) and with the origins of the world illustrated by the dancing god Shiva, with his fire-flaming circular body nimbus, or with Vedic fire altars, as well as with later Hindu temples. The prototype of Indian sacred shrines is the square Vastupurusha mandala plan mentioned in the *Rigvedas* as many as three thousand years ago, an archetypical mandala-like building plan (*vastu*) divided into several square sections and related to an ideal cosmogonic human figure (*purusha*, "man" or "mankind"), a primordial plan of macro- and microcosmic existence.

Said to have been taught first by the Buddha Shakyamuni, the Kalachakra mandala can be traced back to the *Abhidharmakosha* scriptures on the concept of the cosmic world system by the fifth-century Indian Mahayana scholar Vasubandhu. The relevant tantric teachings were introduced to Tibet in the eleventh and twelfth centuries. Large palace mandalas existed by the fourteenth century at the Drigung, Sakya, and Ganden Monasteries.[3] Some mandalas from the fifteenth through eighteenth centuries have survived in the monasteries at Gyantse (one) and Drepung (three), in the Potala Palace (four), and in the former Imperial Palace in Beijing.[4]

A few Meru and palace mandalas were newly constructed between 1995 and 2015 at Tashilhunpo Monastery, in the Lhasa Jokhang, and a huge Meru *torma* mandala at Yachengar Monastery in eastern Tibet.

Contemporary Three-Dimensional Mandalas

The highly accomplished artist Pema Namdol Thaye, born in Bhutan in 1967 and since 2008 a permanent resident of the United States, has for this essay provided further insights on the making and meaning of three-dimensional palace mandalas.[5] In his works, he combines painting, statuary, and architecture, often on a scale comparable to the palace mandalas of centuries past. Concerned that the tradition of meditational architectures could become extinct, Thaye is, in his own words, "bringing the celestial vision into life," furthering the art of mandalas he learned as a child from his uncle, Lama Gonpo Tenzing Rinpoche.[6] Recently, Thaye completed a *Zhitro Mandala*, a colorful three-dimensional mandala of the peaceful and fear-inspiring (*zhitro*) deities of the bardo;[7] and *Zangdok Pelri Mandala*, "Copper-Colored Mountain of Glory," a palace mandala representing the celestial mansion of Padmasambhava. Both works are based on texts closely associated with Padmasambhava.

See Padmasambhava and His Manifestations, no. 43; Ritual Dance Mask of Guru Dorje Drolo, no. 94.

Zhitro is a tantric Nyingma "Great Perfection," or Integration, Awakening (Dzogchen) praxis based on once hidden and later rediscovered treasure texts *(terma)*. It visualizes the human body mandala during the transitional phase between death and rebirth as consisting of and manifested by one hundred peaceful (*zhi*) and wrathful (*tro*) deities representing the purified body, speech (teachings), and mind. Two extraordinarily large and unique mandalas of this iconography, with life-size figures, designed by Thaye as temple buildings that can be entered physically by the practitioner, are presently under construction.

After studying the tantra texts related to a specific mandala, one would visualize the relevant deities and the entire mandala before the actual meditation. The artistic process requires, as Thaye notes, many stages of visualization. The next steps in creating the cosmic palace are cleaning the site and protecting it against evil influences, asking permission of local spirits and demi-gods to build the mandala, and paying homage to the central deity through meditation and prayers requesting its blessings. As in a sand mandala, each divine figure is ritually consecrated for the empowerment conferred on the participating practitioners.

The Rubin Museum of Art, designed to some extent on circular and square mandala-like concepts, has organized its third floor as a Mandala Lab for a physical and mental journey on the path to the center, through cosmic realms and inner experiences. It is designed to focus the viewer's awareness and multiple senses, inspiring empathy and transforming emotions or mental afflictions into wisdom, so that viewers may better navigate their lives. In a wider sense, then, the museum becomes a three-dimensional mandala palace.

Further Reading

Brauen, Martin. 2009. *Mandala: Sacred Circle in Tibetan Buddhism*. Exhibition catalog. New York: Rubin Museum of Art. https://issuu.com/rmanyc/docs/2._mandala.

Henss, Michael. 2014. *The Cultural Monuments of Tibet*. 2 vols. Munich: Prestel.

Henss, Michael. 2020. *Buddhist Ritual Art of Tibet: A Handbook on Ceremonial Objects and Ritual Furnishings in the Tibetan Temple*. Stuttgart: Arnoldsche.

Notes

1 We exclude here, due to different iconographies, forms, and functions, some mandala-like thread-cross "palaces," with multicolored thread designs; see Henss 2020, figs. 103–105. For a survey of three-dimensional mandalas and further references, see Henss 2020, figs. 68–102 (Beijing, fig. 83b), *yantras*, figs. 103–5; Henss 2014, figs. 112, 172–78, 327, 328, 757b, 758, 953b, and 746nn77–78 (Sakya, no longer extant). On concepts and symbolism in mandalas, see Brauen 2009; for text sources, symbolism, and rituals unrelated to specific mandala objects and images, see Wayman 1973.

2 Wayman 1973, 88ff.

3 Henss 2014, figs. 112, 172–78, 757b, 758, 953b, and p. 217 (Ganden, erected under Tsongkhapa in 1417; compare Roerich (1949) 1976, 1078); Henss 2020, 91–95. For the former Sakya mandala, compare Tucci 1973, fig. 170, described in Butön's (Bu ston) biography "with pagoda roofs, on top of the other like a royal palace"; Henss 2020, 116n8; for Drigung, see Liu Yisi 1957, pl. 10.

4 Henss 2014, figs. 327, 328; Henss 2020, figs. 81 (Gyantse, datable to 1425), 82, 83a, 83b.

5 See also Thaye 2021; Kaplan 2021. I thank Pema Namdol Thaye very much for useful information about his mandala work.

6 Thaye 2021.

7 For the painted (*zhitro*) mandala iconography of the forty-two peaceful and fifty-eight wrathful deities, see Herrmann-Pfandt, 2018, 127–290. While historical mandalas are largely gilt, contemporary examples are more distinctively polychromed in the traditional "cosmic colors" of blue in the east, yellow in the south, red in the west, and green in the north.

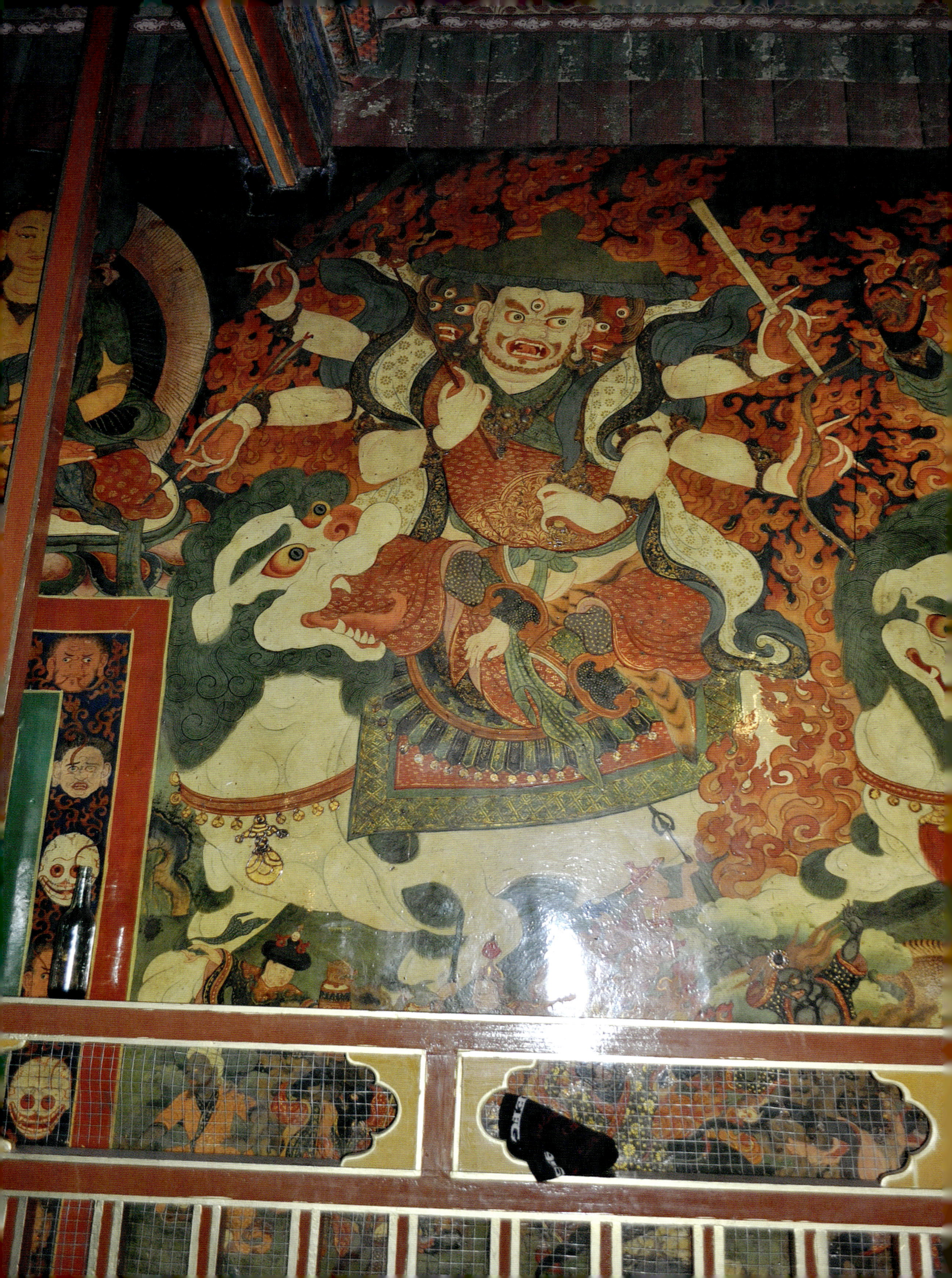

№ 78

Nechung Monastery Murals

Nechung Monastery, Lhasa, U region, central Tibet (present-day TAR, China), ca. 1682

Wrathful Tantric Imagery at the Seat of the Tibetan State Oracle

CHRISTOPHER BELL

Nechung monastery lies on the outskirts of Lhasa, halfway up to the sprawling monastery of Drepung that dominates the face of Gepel Utse Mountain. While not as large as Drepung or the other major monasteries of the Geluk tradition,[1] Nechung is home to a unique and evocative collection of murals portraying wrathful figures that cover the walls of its courtyard and assembly hall. The content of these paintings includes numerous fierce protector deities and wrathful tantric tutelary divinities. While all Tibetan monasteries have their assortment of murals and paintings, Nechung's stand out for the extensiveness of their graphic and fierce images, as well as their gruesome nature and connection to the Nechung Oracle.

These expansive murals ultimately center on a Tibetan Buddhist protector deity named Pehar, who has an important place in Tibetan mythic history overall, but who came to be housed at Nechung, where he and his various forms have taken oracular possession of a human medium for almost five hundred years. This famous medium, known as the Nechung Oracle, has had a close connection to the lineage of the Dalai Lamas since the turn of the sixteenth century. Under the auspices of the Great Fifth Dalai Lama (1617–1682), the Nechung Oracle became the main state oracle of Tibet and has since been consistently providing clairvoyant advice to the Dalai Lama and the Tibetan government up to the present day.

For more on the Fifth Dalai Lama and his government, see Potala Palace, no. 71.

Mythology and the Nechung Oracle

Nechung represents a confluence of rich mythologies and important institutions, both of which are embodied in the vast imagery of its murals. As the monastery's central protector of the Buddhist teachings, Pehar has a rich pedigree that traces back to Tibet's first Buddhist monastery of Samye, and further still into the legendary past. Elements of this mythos can be found in ritual manuals, biographies, and histories that span the major Buddhist sectarian traditions. Fittingly, however, a summary of the deity's past can be found at Nechung itself, where a late seventeenth-century monastic record is inscribed on the southern wall of the complex's courtyard.[2]

In brief, many eons ago Pehar had been a religious king who took on monastic vows with his equally devout friend and minister. Unfortunately, the king misunderstood the teachings while the minister excelled, and this resulted in the king regressing in his vows. Out of envy and anger over his former friend's progress, the king proceeded to torment the minister in different animal forms over several lifetimes, until the wrathful being was finally subdued by the great tantric deity Vajrapani. After more lifetimes spent in Buddhist Hell, the king's spirit eventually arrived at a meditation center in Mongolia, near modern-day Lake Kokonor (Qinghai), where he acted as the local deity. He was then captured by the army of the Tibetan king Tri Songdetsen (742–ca. 800) and brought back to central Tibet. The great tantric master Padmasambhava tamed and named the spirit Pehar and entrusted him with guarding Samye Monastery's treasures. Eventually Pehar migrated to Tsel, a region southeast of Lhasa, and became a protector deity for the Tselpa Kagyu hierarchs. In the sixteenth century, Pehar made his way to the vicinity of Drepung Monastery, where an abbot there predicted the deity's arrival and built for him a "small abode"—the literal meaning of *nechung*.[3]

See Vajrapani, no. 82.

See Padmasambhava and His Manifestations, no. 43.

Mural of Pehar; Assembly Hall, Nechung Monastery, Lhasa, U region, central Tibet (present-day TAR, China); ca. 1900, restored ca. 1996; materials unknown; height approx. 13 ft. (4 m); photograph by Cecilia Haynes, 2011

Once established at Nechung, Pehar began to periodically possess a monk of the monastery every generation to provide clairvoyant advice to the Dalai Lama and Tibetan officials. Oracular possession is

For more on astrological divination, see *The White Beryl Illuminated Manuscript*, no. 86.

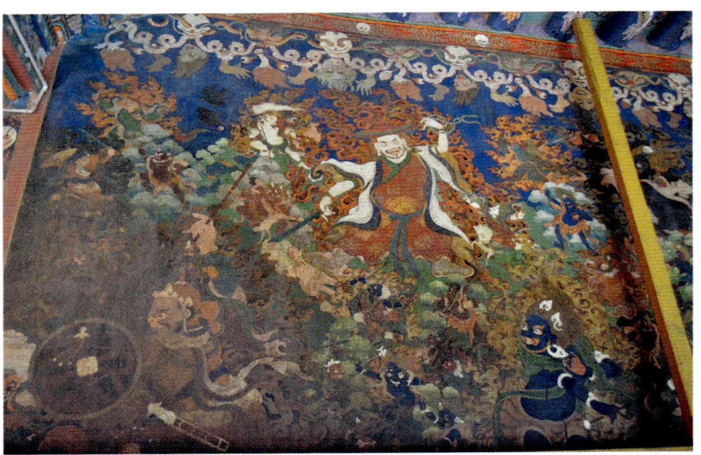

Murals of Pehar's Retinue; courtyard, Nechung Monastery, Lhasa, U region, central Tibet (present-day TAR, China); ca. 1900, restored ca. 1996; materials unknown; height approx. 13 ft. (4 m); photograph by Cecilia Haynes, 2011

one of numerous forms of divination and prognostication found in Tibetan culture, which also include astrology, geomancy, interpreting dreams, reading omens or signs, using dice or dough balls, counting rosary beads, interpreting the pulse for health concerns, and so on.[4] When a human oracle falls into a trance state, the particular possessing deity or related divine emissaries take over, causing the oracle to hiss and dance wildly before making strained and often cryptic prophetic proclamations. In preparation for such intense ceremonies, the oracle is dressed in special attire and wears a ritual mirror over his chest while monks chant and play various instruments to assist the deity's descent into the human vessel. Sometimes an oracle brandishes the weapons associated with the deity during these ritual exercises, such as the oracle of Nechung wielding Pehar's sword, bow, and arrow.

Numerous oracles in Tibetan history have served patrons on village, monastic, and government levels. While there have been several state oracles—oracles that exclusively serve the Dalai Lama, his ministers, government officials, or powerful members of the aristocracy—the Nechung Oracle has been the highest and most important of these since the seventeenth century. During such divinatory consultations, the Nechung Oracle offers insight into concerns over the Dalai Lama's well-being or next rebirth, any domestic conflicts, war and other foreign policy issues, and important matters of state overall.[5] While the oracle now resides outside Tibet and the institution of Nechung has been reestablished in Dharamsala, India, such ritual services are still performed today for the Dalai Lama and members of the Tibetan Government-in-Exile. It is in the oracle and his activities that Pehar's robust mythos and Nechung's prophetic significance intersect.

Murals and Tantric Power

See Desi Sanggye Gyatso's Medical Paintings, no. 73.

The late seventeenth century was the watershed moment for Nechung, because the monastery was extensively renovated and expanded under the auspices of the Fifth Dalai Lama and his regents, particularly his final regent, Sanggye Gyatso (1653–1705). It was at this time that the monastery structure reached its current extent, the Nechung Oracle was established as the main state oracle, and Nechung became intimately linked to the Dalai Lama's burgeoning government. The monastic record inscribed in its courtyard was also composed by the Great Fifth and Sanggye Gyatso, and it further provides descriptions of the murals the latter had commissioned, which match those still visible today.[6] While the images have been repainted and touched up over the centuries—most recently in the 1990s[7]—the figures and configurations date to the turn of the eighteenth century. For this reason, the exact artists are unknown, but the visual architectonics of the Nechung murals reveal a great deal about the tantric power represented within the monastery.

Upon entering Nechung's western gate, the visitor is immediately greeted by images of two large wrathful door guardians—the Red and Black Butchers —before arriving inside the open and expansive courtyard. Along every wall of the courtyard are vividly detailed and extensive murals of Pehar's retinue, an amazing assortment of fierce spirits of all sizes and colors riding various animals, brandishing weapons, and wearing armor or draped in human and animal skins.[8] Paintings of human skins in different states of putrefaction cover the top register of the walls, as if hanging from the rafters. Along the lower register circling the courtyard, the red waves of a painted ocean of blood churn around decapitated heads, decaying skulls, and other dismembered body parts. This frightening scene surrounds viewers as they make their way toward the main entrance of the monastery's assembly hall, where more hanging human skins are painted on the central doors. Such wrathful imagery along doors, beams, and other architectural features is typical of protector chapels at Tibetan monasteries.

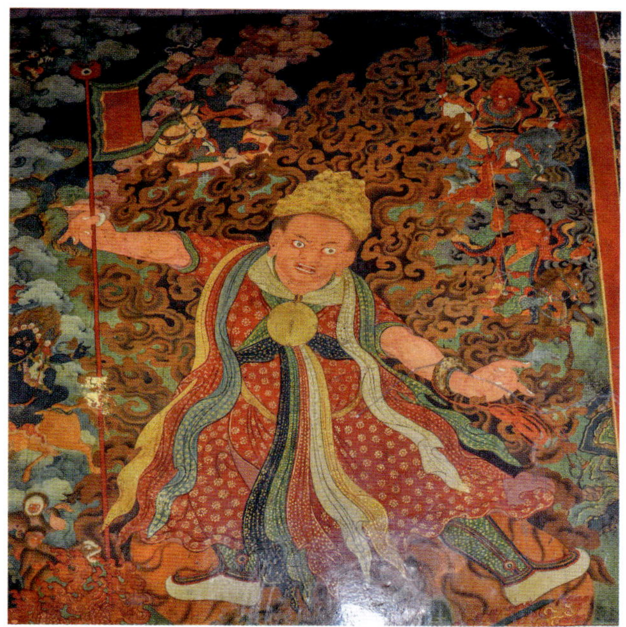

Mural of the Nechung Oracle Shakya Yarpel (fl. 1856–1900); Assembly Hall, Nechung Monastery, Lhasa, U region, central Tibet (present-day TAR, China); ca. 1900, restored ca. 1996; materials unknown; height approx. 13 ft. (4 m); photograph by Christopher Bell, 2011

After the pandemonium of the courtyard, Nechung's tantric cosmology becomes more evident inside the assembly hall. The movement from the front entrance to the back of the hall where the rear shrine rooms are found reflects the movement from the mundane to the transcendent through the murals that cover the walls of this interior space. On the walls abutting the main doors, two murals depict past Nechung Oracles in trance states. One portrays the oracle Lobzang Lekjor, who was installed as the medium of Nechung in 1690 when the monastery's major renovations were nearly complete;[9] the other image is of Shakya Yarpel, who acted as the Nechung Oracle from 1856 to 1900.[10] These figures embody the mundane world most overtly, as human beings possessed by protector deities. Moving further into the hall, on both the east and west walls, one first encounters the Five King Spirits—Pehar with the four protectors that emanate from him—before advancing to the higher enlightened tantric divinities of the Eight Sadhana Teaching Deities. Finally, near the back of the assembly hall before the rear shrine entrances, representing the height of tantric power and control, one finds on walls opposite one another murals of Padmasambhava and Hayagriva—the very tutelary deity that the tantric master embodied to tame Pehar in the eighth century.

These murals thus display a spectrum of mundane and transcendent power that moves along the north-south axis of the assembly hall.[11] Devotees who circumambulate the space clockwise along the walls move from the historic worldly entrance to the heightened mythic and timeless arena at the back, before returning once again to the front doors and the temporal present. In the central rear chapel at the back of the assembly hall, amid statues of the Five King Spirits and various goddesses, there now stands a life-size statue of the Nechung Oracle in trance, specifically Shakya Yarpel. In premodern Tibet, however, this space was where the oracle's throne was located and where he would fall into trance during special occasions and annual ceremonies. Nechung is Pehar's palace, and it places the deity at its center—represented by the oracle. The visitor must pass through the encampment of the deity's ferocious entourage, which fills the courtyard, before propitiating his emanations in the assembly hall and approaching his oracle in the central chapel beyond. Powerful tantric divinities, headed by Padmasambhava and Hayagriva, watch over the whole miraculous encounter, illustrating the rich dynamism of the murals that permeate Nechung Monastery and fill it with a unique cosmic drama.

Further Reading

Bell, Christopher. 2021. *The Dalai Lama and the Nechung Oracle*. New York: Oxford University Press.

Heller, Amy. 2003a. "The Great Protector Deities of the Dalai Lamas." In *Lhasa in the Seventeenth Century: The Capital of the Dalai Lamas*, edited by Françoise Pommaret, 81–98. Leiden: Brill.

Nebesky-Wojkowitz, René de. (1956) 1998. *Oracles and Demons of Tibet: The Cult and Iconography of the Tibetan Protective Deities*, 94–133, 409–66. Reprint, New Delhi: Paljor.

Notes

1 Nechung itself is an ecumenical monastery, with its ritual and scholastic corpus drawing from the Geluk, Nyingma, and Sakya traditions.
2 For a complete translation and transcription of this Nechung record, see Christopher Bell 2016.
3 For other variant accounts of Pehar's arrival at Nechung, see Nebesky-Wojkowitz (1956) 1998, 104–7.
4 See Maurer, Rossi, and Scheuermann 2020, vii–xx.
5 See Maurer 2010.
6 See Christopher Bell 2016, 168–69.
7 See Ricca 1999, 7.
8 For a complete list of these deities, see Ricca 1999, 95–97.
9 See Thub bstan phun tshogs 2007, 84.
10 See Thub bstan phun tshogs 2007, 138.
11 While drawing from a Ladakhi context, Martin Mills discusses in greater depth the Tibetan understanding of such axes of mundane and transcendent power. Mills 2003, 48–52, 153–64.

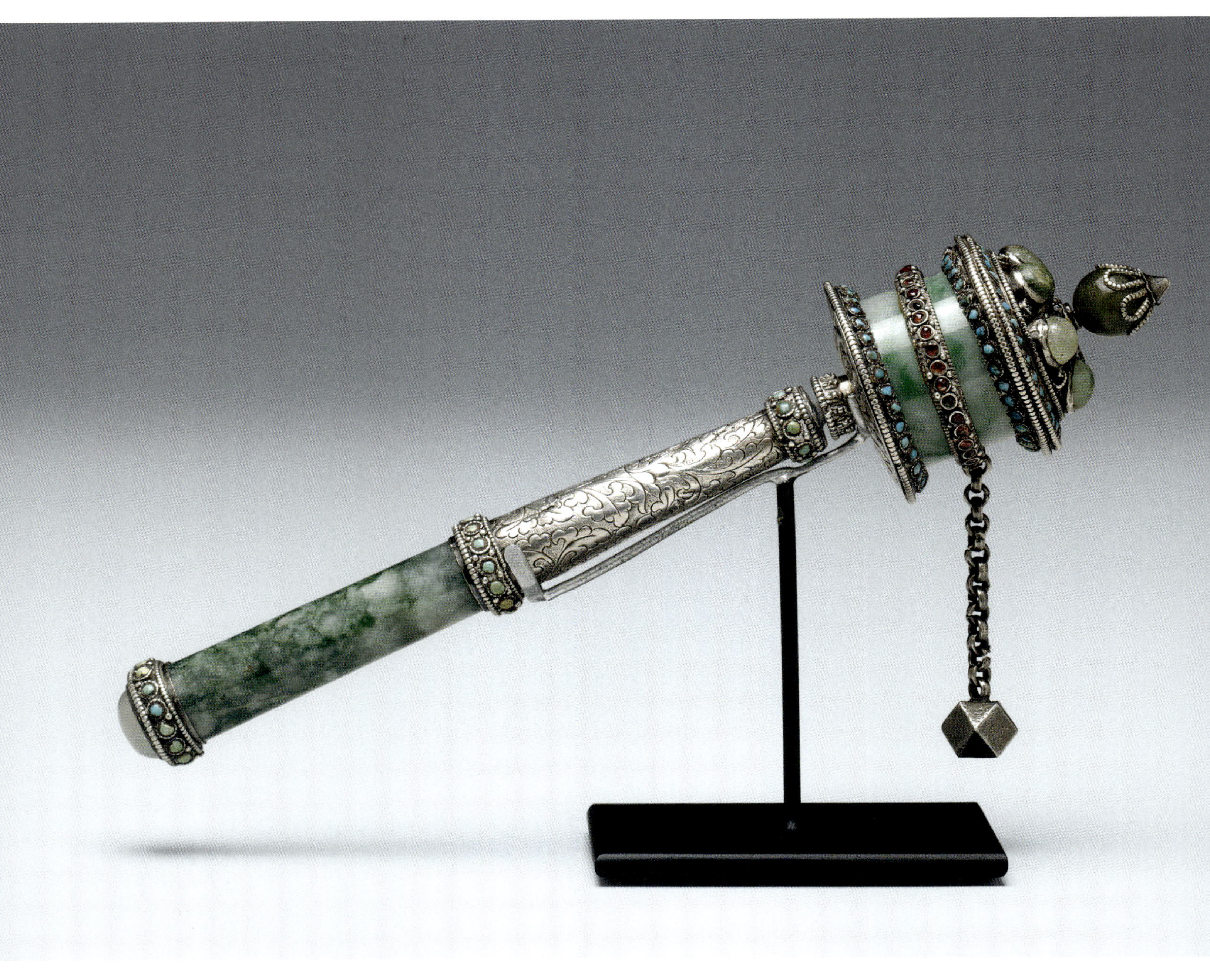

№ 79

Prayer Wheel

Tibet or Mongolia, 17th–18th century

Accumulating Merit Every Day

ELENA PAKHOUTOVA

Prayer Wheel; Tibet or Mongolia; 17th–18th century; silver, green jadeite, rubies (or spinels), turquoise, semiprecious stones; 8¾ × 1¾ × 3¾ in. (22 × 4.5 × 9.5 cm); The Walters Art Museum, Baltimore; Gift of John and Berthe Ford, 2002; 57.2285; photograph by Alain Jaramillo, courtesy The Walters Art Museum

PRAYER WHEELS ARE RITUAL OBJECTS that are ubiquitous in Tibetan Buddhist culture.[1] A cylinder contains a tight roll of paper filled with written mantras that rotates around a central axis when turned clockwise using the spindle. The simple recurring action of turning a prayer wheel with conscious intent is believed to "recite" or "read" the mantras, activating and releasing them into the world for the benefit of all.[2] Depending on the size, prayer wheels can enclose anywhere from several thousand to millions of written mantras. Lay and ordained people alike spin handheld prayer wheels, called *lakkhor*, like the one from the Walters Art Museum featured here, while going about their daily tasks. When visiting temples or pilgrimage sites, people turn larger wheels, commonly known as *mani khorlo*, combining this practice with circumambulation and mantra recitations. It takes several people working together with effort to rotate monumental prayer wheels, called *chokhor*.

The most popular mantra used in Tibetan prayer wheels is the six-syllable *Om mani padme hum*, which is the mantra of the bodhisattva of compassion Avalokiteshvara, the most popular deity in Tibetan culture. Each mantra is believed to benefit the person who both recites and turns the wheel, and once released into the world through these actions, the mantra benefits countless others. Prayer wheels are designed for purposeful use, and their structure underscores the power of intention along with repetition of the mantras and visualization.[3] The rolls of paper filled with written or printed mantras hold the potential for each individual mantra to be repeated thousands or millions of times, essentially acting as the "power cells" of the wheels.

The Power of Mantras and Merit

According to Tibetan sources, the power and efficacy of these objects are tied to internal meditational practices and to ancient Indian reverence for sound and its symbolic rendering in syllables (mantras), which are recited to invoke and bring forth inner experiences.[4] Buddhist practitioners use mantras to focus their visualization, envisioning mantras rotating in the heart center, or heart chakra.[5] Imagined in a similar way, the mantras spin outward from the center of the prayer wheel, coming forth and emitting blessings.[6]

Tibetan sources explain that the fundamental benefit of spinning a prayer wheel with proper intention is the accumulation of merit. It ensures the removal of obstacles and offers protections, freedom from bad rebirths, worldly gains, advancement in Buddhist practices, and more.[7]

Forms and Structure of Prayer Wheels

The physical form of Tibetan prayer wheels is thought to have originated in the revolving bookcases first documented in Chinese Buddhist monasteries and Japanese Buddhist temples.[8] These octagonal bookcases spun around a central axis and were first used as repositories for scriptures. Over time they developed into a means to increase, with each rotation, the merit equal to reading the whole Buddhist canon. They also symbolically referenced the Buddha's first sermon, known as the Turning of the Wheel of the Dharma.

See A Monumental Life of the Buddha Mural, no. 69.

Tibetan prayer wheels retain the general purpose of the revolving scripture repositories to generate merit, as well as the functionality of rotating around the central pole, but they diverge in their

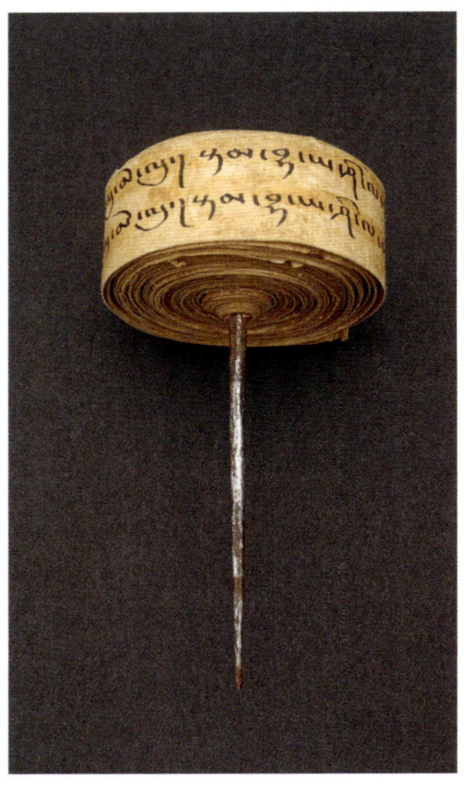

Roll of Mantras for a Prayer Wheel and Its Spindle; Tibet; ca. 12–13th century; black ink on paper with metal spindle; 3³⁄₁₆ × 1⅝ in. (8 × 4.2 cm); Private collection; photograph courtesy Scientific Analysis of Fine Art, LLC

structure and variable sizes. Furthermore, not only people but also wind, hot air from fire, and water have the power to activate them. Contemporary versions of Tibetan prayer wheels include solar-powered wheels, electricity-powered computer screen savers, compact disc–based ones, and mobile phone apps.

Essential elements of the Tibetan prayer wheel forms are the same regardless of size—a cylindrical container houses prayers and mantras written or printed on paper wound around a central axle. A handheld prayer wheel has a handle that extends into the axle inserted into the cylinder, which has an attached counterweight to help perpetuate rotation. This form seems to be a Tibetan invention. Italians may have adopted it in the fifteenth century for their mechanical designs.[9] The drum-shaped container can be made of wood, sheet metal, conch, hollowed-out bone, or stone, as in this example from the Walters Art Museum.

The creator of this prayer wheel may have used an existing cylinder of jadeite, which would explain the small size of the container. The object is similar to another prayer wheel in the Metropolitan Museum of Art, New York, which features a stone container formed by a repurposed jade archer's ring fitted with an outer decorative band, inset with semiprecious stones, and capped at the top and bottom. The tubular glass pipe that covers the axle appears to be adapted from a cigarette holder.[10] The object's unusual, innovative construction is unsurprising, given the widespread use of prayer wheels in Tibetan culture. It is possible that the Walters Museum prayer wheel, too, was made using an archer's ring, as the dimensions of both drums are almost identical.[11] Whatever the case, the materials of the Walters Art Museum prayer wheel suggest a lavish taste, as jade, silver, and precious stones indicate status and imply a wealthy owner. The use of it in public would be a conspicuous display of wealth.

For comparison with an Indian Pala period manuscript, see Illuminated Pages of the *Prajnaparamita Sutra* Manuscript, no. 23.

See Kalachakra Mantra ceiling of Dabaojigong Temple, no. 64, p. 282; Kalachakra Mandala in the Potala Palace, no. 77.

The containers of Tibetan prayer wheels are often decorated with mantras in Lantsa (Ranjana) script in relief. This script is thought to have originated in the Bengal region of eastern India at the end of the first millennium, and it became widespread during the Pala dynasty (eighth to twelfth century);[12] it reached Newar Buddhist communities of the Kathmandu Valley and was used for Nepalese Buddhist manuscripts. Tibetans embraced it as their preferred script for rendering Sanskrit titles of sutras and tantras in their books, writing mantras in decorative and symbolic composite forms (the Kalachakra mantra is the best known of such symbols), representing seed syllables in mandalas, and marking relief carvings on architectural monuments.

For another example of contained mantras, see Amulet Box (*Gau*) with Its Contents, no. 107.

For examples of stupas and related practices, see the Svayambhu Chaitya of Kathmandu, no. 4; Stupa at Toling Monastery, no. 19; White Stupa, no. 40; Chorten Cave of Luri, no. 44; Densatil Monastery, no. 30.

Relationship to Relics, Consecration, and Circumambulation

The mantras within the containers, which are also called reliquaries, relate to rituals of consecration. When Buddhist statues are consecrated to embody the Buddha or deities, they are filled with mantras and prayers in a manner similar to the prayer wheels. In this context the mantras are also the Dharma relics or Dharmakaya relics, which represent the sacred words of the Buddha. For this reason, prayer wheels conceptually connect to stupas, the ultimate and often largest repositories of these and other types of relics, as well as to the practice of circumambulation, or walking around stupas and sacred sites.

Prayer Beads and Prayer Flags

Prayer beads, *mala* in Sanskrit or *trengwa* in Tibetan, are implements that aid personal devotional practices related to prayer and mantra recitation. Just like prayer wheels, they are used in the context of accumulation of merit. More recitations accrue more merit, while the beads ensure the proper accounting of

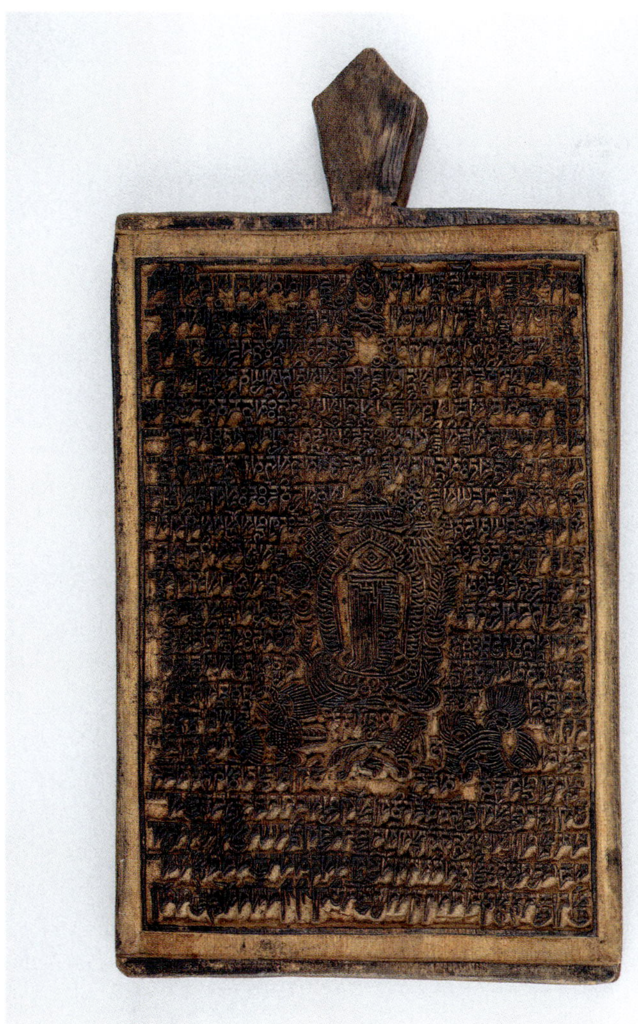

Woodblock for Printing Prayer Flags; Himalayan region; 15th–19th century; pigments on wood; 14 × 7⅞ × 1 in. (35.6 × 20 × 2.5 cm); Rubin Museum of Art; C2006.75.20 (HAR 68949)

the chanted words and are believed to take on the accumulated power of the practice.

Mantras are also employed in Tibetan prayer flags, which are variously colored cloths imprinted in ink with mantras and images from carved woodblocks.[13] The flags are hung on high grounds and around sacred sites, temples, and mountain passes. They are believed to disseminate the mantras with the wind to pacify local gods and bring about luck and fortune to benefit all, in a manner similar to the prayer wheels.

The practice of printing mantras on textiles and openly hanging them as flags does not appear to be adopted from India, and a practice of raising prayer flags may have predated Buddhism in Tibetan cultural areas.[14] The use of prayer flags is as universal as that of prayer wheels in the region. It equally reflects complex cultural practices that address worldly and religious concerns and often serves as part of formal rituals and activities that support and promote participants' harmonious existence in the larger, interdependent world.

Further Reading

Clayton, Lori, and Lama Thubten Zopa Rinpoche. 2000. *Wheel of Great Compassion: The Practice of the Prayer Wheel in Tibetan Buddhism.* Cambridge, MA: Wisdom.

Jayarava. 2011. *Visible Mantras: Visualizing and Writing Buddhist Mantras.* Cambridge: Visible Mantras Press.

Studholme, Alexander. 2012. *The Origins of Oṃ Maṇipadme Hūṃ: A Study of the Kāraṇḍavyūha Sūtra.* Albany: SUNY Press.

Notes

1 The term "prayer wheel," along with "prayer mill," is not a translation of Tibetan words and reflects similarities to ordinary objects found in Western culture. See Winder 1992, 25; Simpson 2001.

2 Karma chags med 2010, 597–600.

3 *'Khor lo dang jo dar gyi phan yon*, n.d., 3; *Ma Ni 'khor lo'i phan yon* 1985, 3–13.

4 D. Martin 1987, 16–18; *'Khor lo dang jo dar gyi phan yon*, n.d., 2.

5 D. Martin 1987, 17.

6 *Ma Ni 'khor lo'i phan yon* 1985, 13–14.

7 D. Martin 1987, 16, 18; *'Khor lo dang jo dar gyi phan yon*, n.d., 4–12.

8 Goodrich 1942–43.

9 In addition to the vertical axis windmill and the hot air turbine, thought to be inspired by Tibetan prayer wheel technologies, the ball and chain counterweight/governor design directly references Tibetan construction. L. White 2018, 47–50.

10 La Rocca 2014b, 195.

11 Each is about 1⅜ inches (3.5 cm) in diameter. Email communications with the Walters Art Museum's Curator of Asian Art Adriana Proser and the Metropolitan Museum of Art's Armorer and Conservator Edward Hunter, May 19, 2021.

12 Hartmann 1998, 37.

13 The term "prayer flag," like "prayer wheel," is an English invention that emphasizes prayer over the meaning, intent, and ritual function of these objects and their indigenous terms. See Paul 2003, xvii–xix.

14 Paul 2003, 226–30.

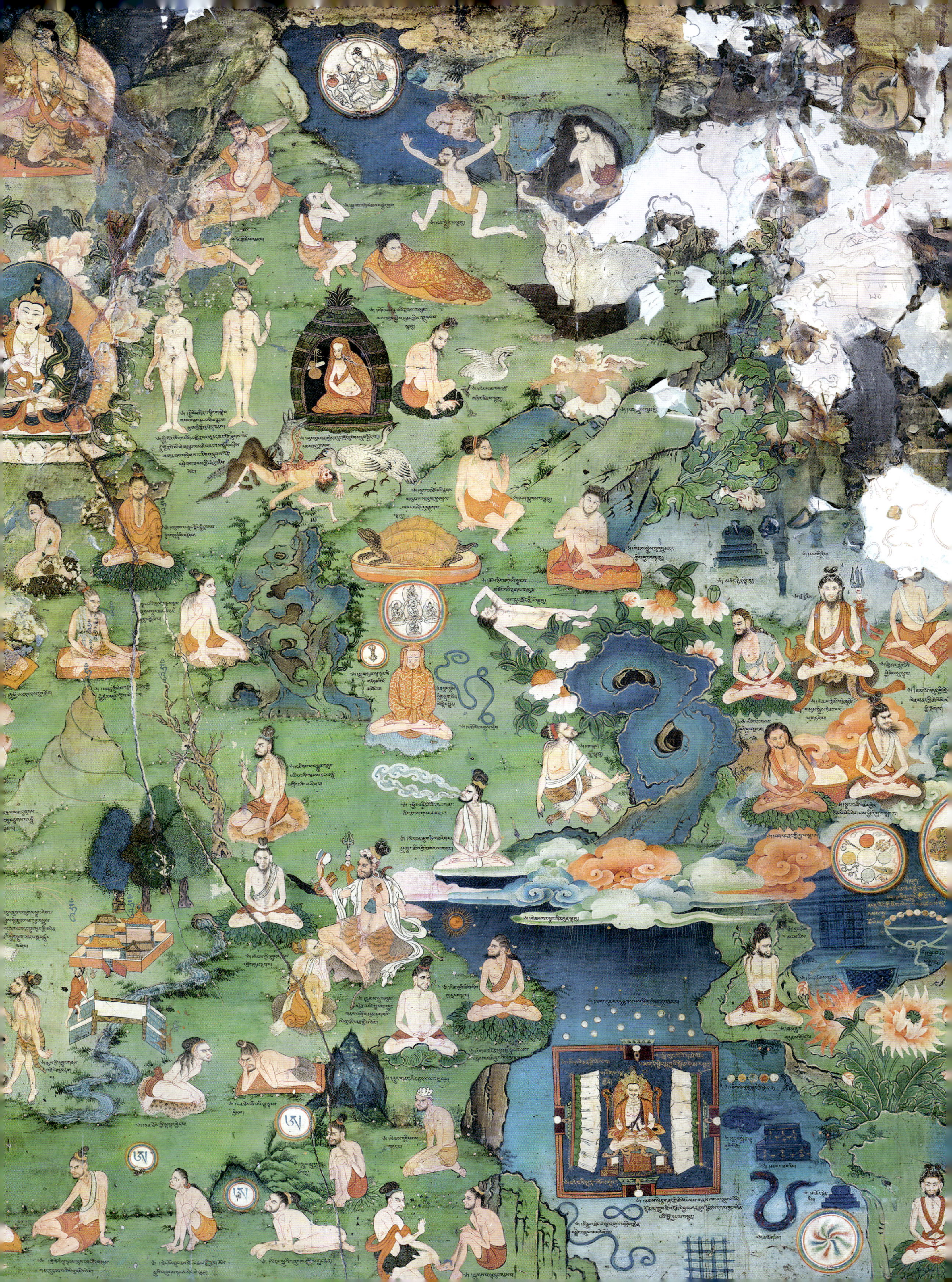

No 80

Lukhang Murals

Lhasa, U region, central Tibet (present-day TAR, China), ca. 1700 and later

Illustrating the Dzogchen Teachings through Murals

JAKOB WINKLER

See Potala Palace, no. 71.

THESE EXCEPTIONAL MURALS, which illustrate the Dzogchen teachings, are found in an enchanting temple on a small island in the middle of a small lake behind the mighty fortress of the Potala.

Accordingly, it is called the Naga Palace behind the Fortress: Dzonggyab Lui Podrang or, in short, Lukhang, literally meaning the House of the Serpents. The picturesque building is famous for its unique and exquisite paintings depicting the most secret meditation practices.[1] The pond was created by extracting earth for building the Potala Palace in the seventeenth century under the Fifth Dalai Lama (1617–1682). According to legend, the local *lu* (Sanskrit: naga), powerful serpentlike beings who inhabit bodies of water, belonging half to the animal realm and half to the god realm, and whose wrath brings disease and drought, appeared to the Great Fifth Dalai Lama during meditation and complained about the disturbance caused by the earthworks. To appease the *lu*, they were promised that a temple would be built in their honor for regular worship, thereby ensuring timely rainfall and prosperity for Tibet. There are various assertions as to whether the present-day Lukhang, a square, three-story pavilion, covered by a hexagonal Mongolian-style roof, creating the impression of a mandala palace, was built at the time of the Fifth Dalai Lama, or whether an enlargement or a new building was erected on the same site in the time of the Sixth Dalai Lama (1683–1706) in 1700. Some sources see it as a work of the Eighth Dalai Lama (1758–1804) from the year 1791.[2] Much of the thematic material of the wall paintings indicates a close connection to the Sixth Dalai Lama, for example, a detail showing a descendant of Pema Lingpa.

The First and Second Floors with Kalachakra and Narrative Murals

See the Kalachakra Mandala in the Potala Palace, no. 77.

See Shambhala Kings Mural, no. 99.

In only one of the rooms on the first floor have the murals survived to the present day. They are dedicated to the tantric teachings of Kalachakra and to the regents of the mystical land of Shambhala.

In the single room of the middle second floor, nine panels illustrate two popular stories, which are also performed by Tibetan opera (*ache lhamo*) troupes: the story of the previous incarnation of Padmasambhava as Pema Wobar, and the story of a legendary virtuous woman and *dakini*, Drowa Zangmo.[3]

The Third Floor with Mahasiddhas and Dzogchen Murals

For more on mahasiddhas, see Virupa, no. 37.

See Padmasambhava and His Manifestations, no. 43.

The top floor, with an area of less than 550 square feet (50 square meters), is the private chamber of the Dalai Lamas to which they resorted for private meditation retreats. Here we find the murals that have made the Lukhang so famous. To the left of the entrance are the guardians, or *dharmapalas*; one of the three is a *lu*. The eastern wall shows the eighty-four Indian "great accomplished ones," or mahasiddhas, and below them are Padmasambhava and his twenty-five main students. The southeastern corner murals depict historic episodes from the lives of important Tibetan masters over the centuries, including several associated with Dzogchen teachings.

The west and north walls are dedicated to the "Great Perfection," *Dzogchen* in Tibetan, considered the very essence of all Buddhist teachings. It is called the Great Perfection because it states that enlightenment is already perfectly present in all beings and only needs to be recognized.[4] Thus, awakening is based not on renunciation, as in monastic Buddhism, or on transformation of the impure into the pure, as in tantric Vajrayana teachings and practices, but on the principle of spontaneous liberation through being in our clear and empty nature.

Lukhang Murals, detail of western wall mural showing yogis applying Dzogchen practices; Lukhang, Lhasa; 17th century or later; photograph © Thomas Laird, 2018, from *Murals of Tibet*, TASCHEN

The Dzogchen teachings are illustrated according to the treasure, or *terma*, of Pema Lingpa (1450–1521). The underlying cycle of teachings is called "The Union of Samantabhadra's Knowledge" (*Kunzang Gongdu*);[5] at least eight texts from it serve as the bases for the illustrations, and passages of the text can be clearly assigned to the inscriptions, thus opening up invaluable additional information about what is depicted.[6]

Significantly, a *lu* king, or *nagaraja*, Nele Tokar, is one of the main protectors of this cycle of teachings. Pema Lingpa, who hailed from the area that today is Bhutan, is an ancestor of and in the same lineage as the Sixth Dalai Lama, which could explain why his texts were chosen as the source for the images.

For more on Pema Lingpa, see Tamshing Temple, no. 61.

The Cycle of Life, Death, Bardo, and Rebirth

The northern mural provides an overview of the Dzogchen teachings in relation to cosmology, delusion and awakening, and cyclic existence, as well as life itself, with its embryonic development, birth, death, and the intermediate state (bardo).

The left half shows the retaking of a physical form, the following details the embryonic development, and it ends with the mortal beings washed away in the "rivers" of samsara.

In the clouds sits a buddha who sends down a fine ray of light to a couple of lovers. The textual source for the left half of the detail, "Closing of the Six Classes: The Tantra of Liberation into the Dimension of Instant Presence [*rigpa*]," states

> Concerning the manner of arising of the compound body, there are two: the ones who transmigrate with control and the others without. Those who migrate in cyclic existence with control are conscious while taking rebirth. Being conscious while entering the womb, yet they incarnate [into samsara] for taming the beings of the six classes [gods, humans, animals, and so forth] in whatever form needed. Those who are transmigrating in cyclic existence without control will either descend downward due to their ten nonvirtuous actions or progress upward due to the ten virtuous actions.[7]

Below these two couples the gestational process of a human fetus is illustrated. The first four weeks are rendered in the form of white, round droplets dividing themselves into more and more segments. Below are three reddish images for the sixth, seventh, and eighth weeks. The remaining weeks are illustrated with twenty-six standing figures, each representing a different stage of embryonic development. At the lower right end of the embryos is the mother giving birth.

The buddhas, blue Samantabhadra and white Vajrasattva, who appear in light spheres, illustrate the narrative structure of the literary source: Vajrasattva asks a question to the primordial Buddha Samantabhadra at the start of each chapter.

In each chapter the reader is prompted to discover one's primordial nature in order to overcome the cycle of permanent rebirth in suffering.

For another representation of the six realms of existence, see Wheel of Existence, no. 97.

> Being swept away by these four great rivers: of existence, of desire, of karma, and the river of unawareness [*ma rigpa*]; [one] sinks into the great ocean of the six destinies of the three realms. It is like the sun covered by the clouds, if one has not distinguished between ordinary mind and primordial awareness. Thus, the primordial awareness is covered by the ordinary deluded mind and has no possibility to shine through.[8]

If the primordial state or true nature of being is not realized while the dying person is alive, that person enters the bardo. Here the luminous bardo of experiencing the nature of reality is represented in the right half of the detail of the wall painting. There are the One Hundred Peaceful and Wrathful Deities symbolically representing aspects of human existence in their primordial, enlightened form. Accordingly, in the upper center, five buddhas in union are seen; the five male ones represent the psychophysical aggregates (form, consciousness, perception, sensation, karmic formation), and the female buddhas represent the five elements (space, air, fire, water, earth). By familiarization with the process of dying and the bardo experiences through specific practices during life, the practitioner may use the moment of death for complete awakening. This corresponds to the Liberation upon Hearing teachings (*Bardo Todrol*), known in the West as the *Tibetan Book of the Dead*.[9]

The Path of Complete Liberation

The path to liberation is delineated on the western wall. Four texts of Pema Lingpa are illustrated, and the most extensive, "The Essential Instruction Known as the Illuminating Lamp, Composed by Padmasambhava," describes the start of the path.[10] Here, yogis are shown engaged in various practices. One important category of meditative practice is called *khorde rushen*, literally, discerning samsara and nirvana, that is, the ordinary mind from the nature of mind. We thus see a yogi (in the lower center) doing a visualization exercise in front of a barren tree on which the blue Tibetan syllable HUM meanders. The same Tibetan syllable HUM is depicted in the green-blue rock above him. Below him is a lama wearing a tiger skin lower garment (dhoti) and a white scarf. He plays a bell and a *damaru* drum, which he uses for the direct introduction to the nature of the mind. In this initiation, the teacher guides the student to discover within himself, through his own experience, the unchanging, pure, and spontaneously perfect nature of mind. Once the student recognizes this fundamental state of being, the next step is the continuous deepening of relaxation into this "naked" awareness. For this purpose, practitioners use different postures, as can be seen in the yogis (lower left margin) looking at spheres of light with the Tibetan letter pronounced Ah.

See Double-Sided Skull Drum, no. 93.

After the yogini has stabilized being in the primordial state, undistracted by rising thoughts, feelings, and perceptions, the practice of the release of tensions, *trekcho*, is accomplished. The last step is the practice of direct crossing, *togel*, that makes use of the spontaneous visions of clarity by integrating them in a nondual way. In summary: being in the indivisibility of awareness and emptiness is the practice of *trekcho*. Appearances and emptiness indivisible is the practice of *togel*.

The lower middle and right part of the detail of the western mural are based on the text "The Mirror of the Key Points of Practice—Teaching by Experiential Instructions."[11] We see a practitioner sitting in a retreat hut applying *togel*. Around the hut various apparitions are portrayed. On the right side we see various yogis who practice *togel* by looking at the rays of sun or moon; through these visions, which appear spontaneously and in a process of development from simple light spheres and apparitions, more and more complex spheres develop, containing symbols, buddhas, and mandalas. Finally, all these visions dissolve again. In this way the yogi experiences directly the mode of how perception and appearance manifest; he realizes experientially the dreamlike quality of all appearance as mere empty forms. Thus, the attachment to a solid self and phenomena dissolves, like recognizing the true nature of a dream, as just what it is, apparent but not real.

Further Reading

Luczanits, Christian. 2011. "Locating Great Perfection: The Murals of the Lhasa Lukhang." *Orientations* 42, no. 2 (March): 102–11.

Winkler, Jakob. 2002. "The rDzogs Chen Murals of the Klu-khang in Lhasa." In *Religion and Secular Culture of Tibet: Tibetan Studies II. PIATS 2000: Proceedings of the Ninth Seminar of the International Association for Tibetan Studies, Leiden 2000*, edited by Henk Blezer with Abel Zadoks, 321–43. Brill's Tibetan Studies Library 2/7. Leiden: Brill.

Winkler, Jakob. 2016. "The Literary Sources of the Klu-Khang Murals." In *Sharro: Festschrift for Chögyal Namkhai Norbu*, edited by Donatella Rossi and Charles Jamyang Oliphant of Rossie, 319–39. Rudolfstetten: Garuda Verlag.

Notes

1 See the copiously illustrated Laird 2018, vol. 1, and its companion volume of explanatory texts, vol. 2.
2 On the dating, see Winkler 2002.
3 Pakhoutova 2021.
4 For a simple but profound explanation of Dzogchen, see Chögyal Namkhai Norbu 2000.
5 Pema Lingpa (Padma gling pa) 1975–76c, 4, 15.
6 Winkler 2016.
7 Pema Lingpa (Padma gling pa) 1975–76d, 167, translation by the author.
8 Pema Lingpa (Padma gling pa) 1975–76d, 182, translation by the author.
9 The book contains instructions for the moment of death and the intermediate state thereafter (*bar do*) to achieve liberation from the cyclic existence.
10 Pema Lingpa (Padma gling pa) 1975–76a, 5–31.
11 Pema Lingpa (Padma gling pa) 1975–76b, 33–40.

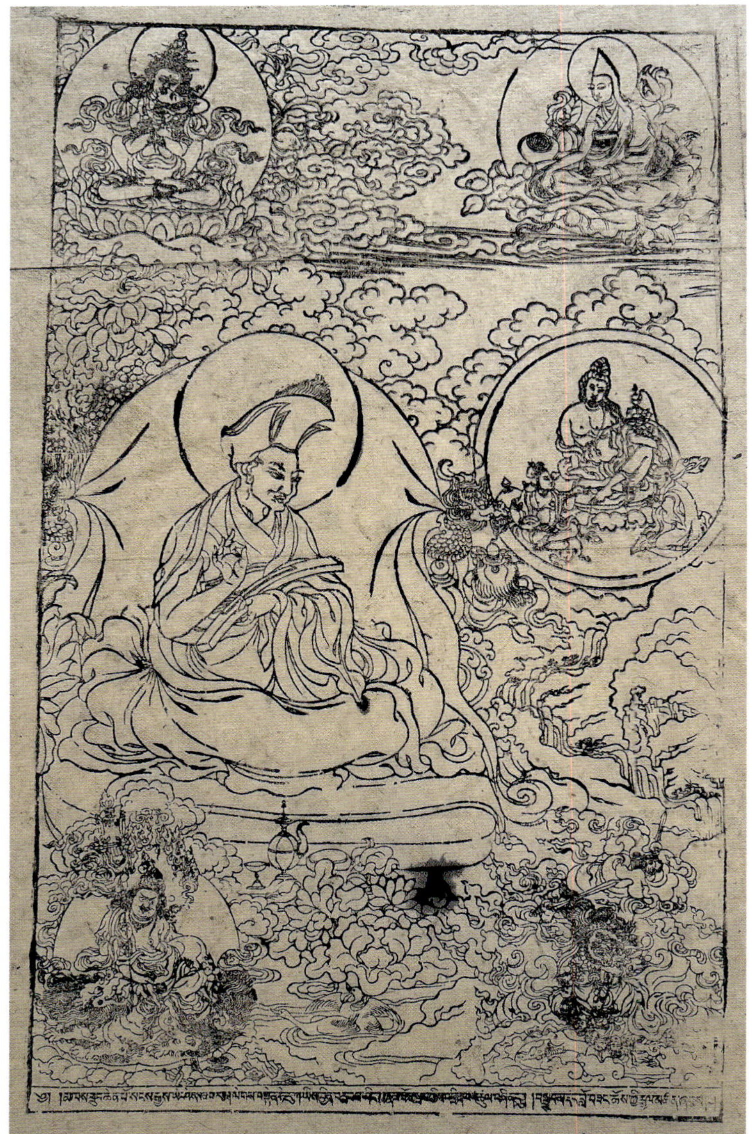

Fourth Panchen Lobzang Chokyi Gyeltsen (1570–1662), after Choying Gyatso's (act. 17th century) set of preincarnations of the Panchen Lamas; eleventh portrait in xylographic series of the Panchen rebirth lineage; Nartang printing house, Tsang region, central Tibet; second quarter of 18th century; woodblock print, ink on paper; printed area: 26³⁄₁₆ × 16⅛ in. (66.5 × 40.9 cm); Tucci Collection of the "Biblioteca IsIAO" - Sala delle collezioni africane e orientali, Biblioteca Nazionale Centrale "Vittorio Emanuele II" di Roma; inv. no. 8155/92; photograph by Nancy G. Lin

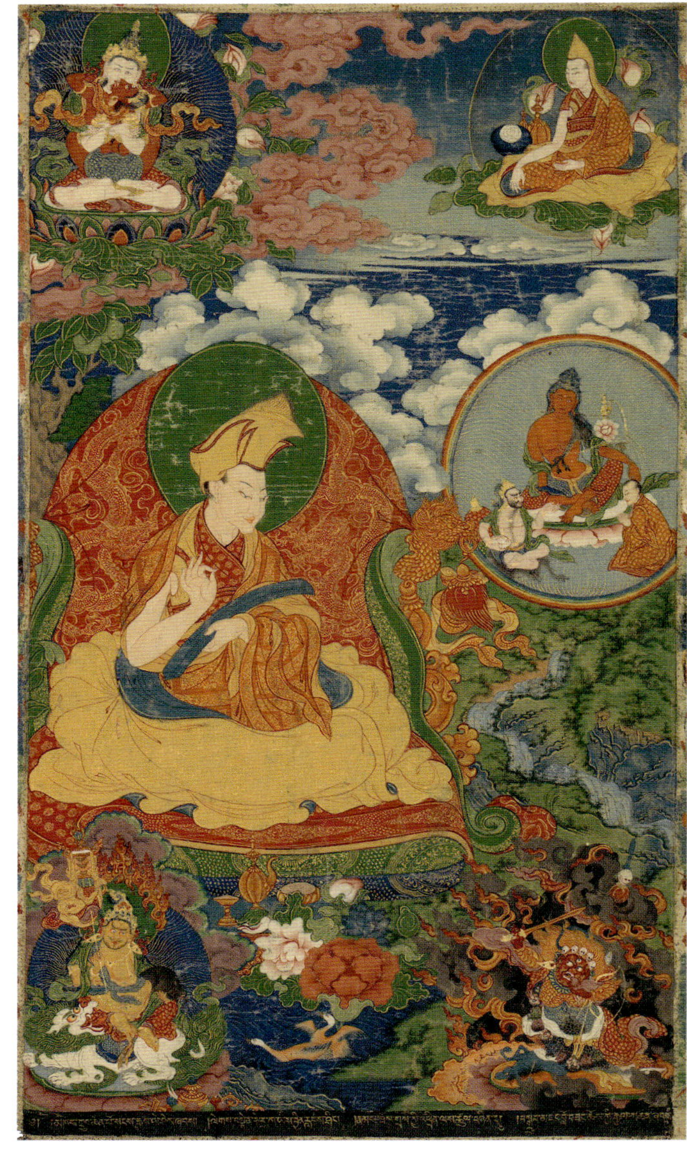

Fourth Panchen Lobzang Chokyi Gyeltsen (1570–1662), after Choying Gyatso's (act. 17th century) set of preincarnations of the Panchen Lamas; eleventh portrait in series of the Panchen rebirth lineage, copied from Nartang xylographic design; Tsang region, central Tibet; 18th century; pigment on cloth; 27 × 15½ in. (68.6 × 39.4 cm); Rubin Museum of Art; Gift of the Shelley & Donald Rubin Foundation; F1996.21.2 (HAR 477)

No 81

Nartang Woodblock Prints and Their Painted Copies: Previous Lives of the Panchen Lamas

Nartang printing house, Tsang region, central Tibet, second quarter of 18th century (and a painted copy)

Abounding Visions of Eminent Lives

NANCY G. LIN

DURING THE SECOND QUARTER OF THE EIGHTEENTH CENTURY, the Nartang printing house began issuing a series of block print portraits of the Panchen Lama rebirth lineage. Painstakingly carved in relief on large wooden blocks, then inked and applied to paper or cloth, the xylographic thangka designs enabled the creation of portrait copies and adaptations in painting or other media. The use of woodblock printing technology to make Buddhist texts and images had begun much earlier, with Tibetan-language texts printed by the mid-twelfth century in Khara-Khoto.[1] Among Tibetans, the practice of recognizing the rebirth lineage (*trungrab*) or chain of incarnations (*kutreng*) of an eminent lama was nothing new either. Dating to the twelfth century, it was roughly as old as the practice of identifying reincarnating lamas, or *tulkus*, itself.[2] Yet it was not until the golden age of woodblock printing in Tibet in the seventeenth and eighteenth centuries that rebirth lineage portraits appear to have been adapted into serial xylographic designs, thereby tapping the potential for proliferation, iteration, and authoritative ordering that the technology affords. The Nartang series of Panchen Lama portraits thus abounded in current and older senses of "abounding," by prevailing widely through circulated copies, bearing a plenitude of magnificent lives and qualities, and setting limits on how those lives were represented.

For an example of woodblock printing from Khara-Khoto, see A *Pancharaksha* Print from Khara-Khoto, no. 32.

For other *tulku* portraits, see Portrait of the Ninth Karmapa, no. 66; Portrait of Situ Panchen, no. 83.

Iterating through Rebirth and Portraiture

As one of the most eminent and powerful *tulkus* of the Geluk monastic order, the Panchen Lama was a prime subject for a rebirth lineage portrait series. The Panchens are considered emanations of Buddha Amitabha; their lineage has been widely regarded as second in importance only to the Dalai Lamas, and their sphere of authority has extended from Tsang region to the Qing imperial court and beyond. The Fourth Panchen Lama, Lobzang Chokyi Gyeltsen (1570–1662), was recognized at an early age as the rebirth of the accomplished scholar Wensapa Lobzang Dondrub.[3] After achieving scholarly fame, he served as abbot of Tashilhunpo Monastery, tutored the Fourth and Fifth Dalai Lamas, and was the first in his rebirth lineage to receive the title of Panchen ("greatly learned one"). The Nartang portrait of the Fourth Panchen emphasizes his scholarly accomplishments: he wears a *pandita*'s hat, his right hand performing the gesture (mudra) of explication and his left cradling a book. It also attests to key figures in his life, such as his root teacher (lama) Khedrub Chenpo Sanggye Yeshe at his upper left, along with three deities—white Chakrasamvara, Begtse Chen, and Vaishravana—who are praised in the verse inscription below, together with the Panchen himself. The bodhisattva Maitreya, whom the Panchen reportedly encountered in a vision, floats in a sphere just above his line of sight.

For another image of Begtse, see Monumental Appliqué of Begtse, no. 95.

For a contemporaneous image of this deity by the Panchen Lama's student, see Maitreya, no. 75.

A painted copy in the Rubin Museum collection retains the block print's figures and design details while skillfully executing line, pattern, color, and shading for a vivid and legible effect. Other copies demonstrate that the Nartang designs were accepted as authoritative visual representations of the Panchen's lives and their social networks. In some cases, painters applied color directly to the xylographic design printed onto the prepared cotton ground of a thangka; in others, a combination of tracing, stenciling, and pouncing techniques may have been employed in order to preserve the xylograph print.[4]

While spiritually advanced *tulkus* were considered capable of emanating in myriad forms, rebirth lineages highlighted and fixed their most noteworthy past lives. A lineage could emphasize aspects of the *tulku*'s personality, physical appearance, abilities, and fields of activity, as well as networks and relations with human and nonhuman beings.[5] The first eleven members of the Panchen rebirth lineage portrayed

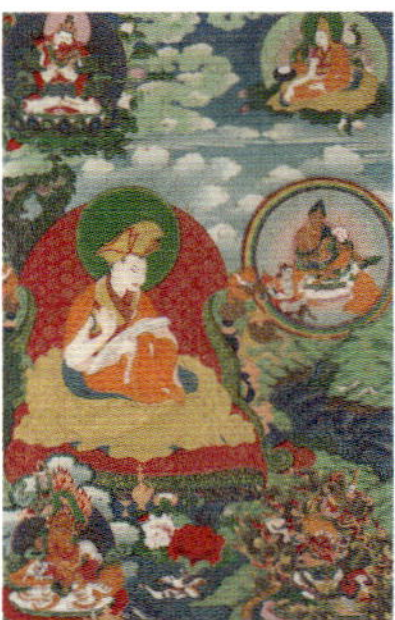
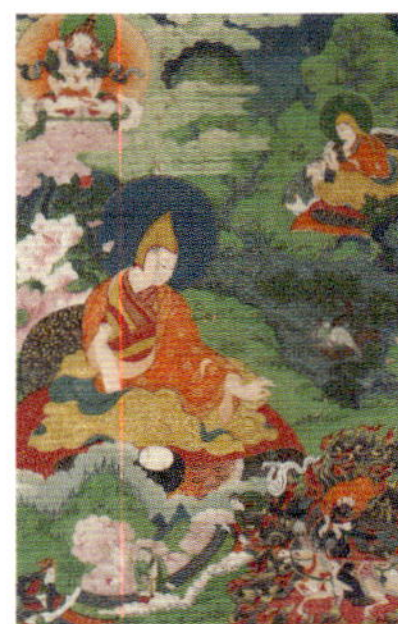
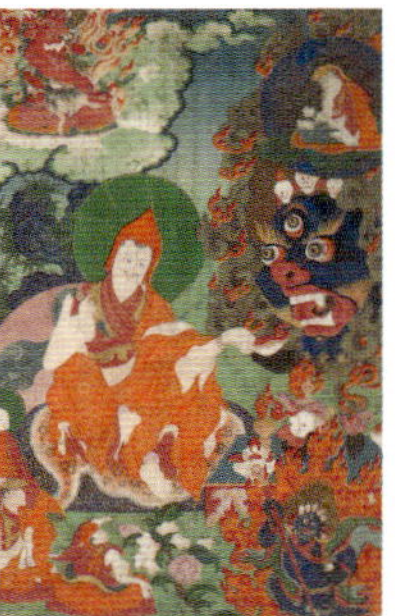
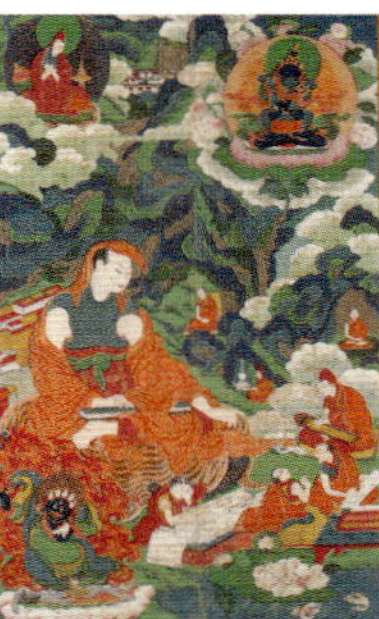
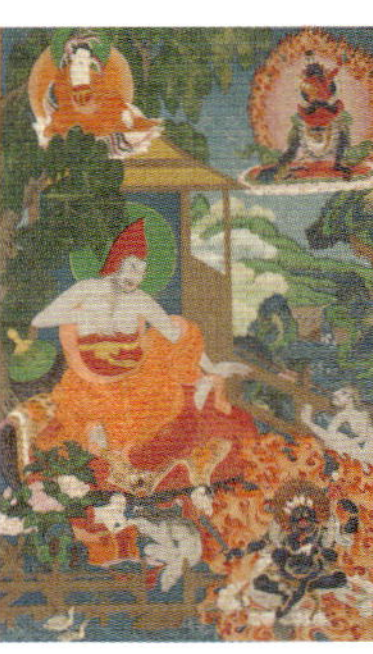
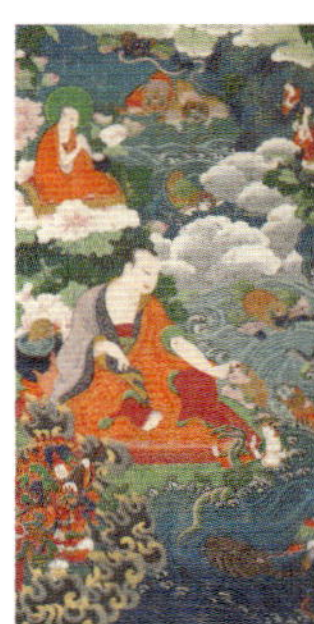

Prescribed arrangement for Panchen Lama rebirth lineage portraits, set of thirteen thangkas copied from Nartang xylographic designs; Tibet; 19th century; ground mineral pigment on cotton; dimensions vary, painted area of central thangka (Sixth Panchen) 26⅞ × 16¼ in. (68.3 × 41.2 cm); American Museum of Natural History, New York; 70.2/1216–1228; photograph courtesy the Division of Anthropology, American Museum of Natural History; design courtesy Wen-shing Chou

in the Nartang series appear to have been set during the Fourth Panchen's lifetime.[6] Like other rebirth lineages, his is traced back to the time and place of Buddha Shakyamuni, with the arhat Subhuti as the Panchen's earliest named preincarnation. Other preincarnations include Manjushriyashas, a mythical Kalki king of Shambhala; Bhaviveka, a distinguished Indic Madhyamika philosopher; Go Lotsawa Khukpa Lhetse (ca. eleventh century), a Tibetan translator and disciple of Atisha; and Sakya Pandita, the eminent monastic scholar whose relations with the Mongol prince Köten (Godan, fl. 1235–1247) set the precedent for preceptor-almsgiver (*choyon*) relations. By appearing in the Panchen's rebirth lineage, such figures resonate with elements for which the Fourth and other Panchens are renowned, including intellectual brilliance, relations with Mongols and other Buddhist patrons outside Tibet, and a predicted future rebirth as a millenarian king of Shambhala who will restore the buddhas' teachings.

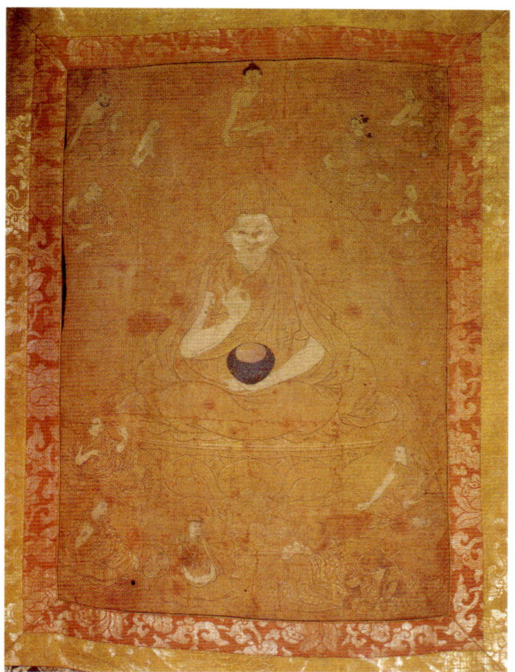

Attributed by inscription to Choying Gyatso (act. 17th century); Fourth Panchen Lobzang Chokyi Gyeltsen (1570–1662), with previous incarnations; Tsang region, central Tibet; mid-17th century; gold thangka; ground mineral pigment on cotton; 27½ × 16⅛ in. (70 × 41 cm); Tashilhunpo Monastery, Shigatse, Tibet; image after Xizang zizhiqu wenwu guanli weiyuan hui 2007 [1985], pl. 75

Serial Modeling and Proliferation

A golden thangka (*sertang*) portraying the Fourth Panchen as its main subject surrounded by smaller portraits of his ten preincarnations is attributed by handwritten inscription to Choying Gyatso (act. seventeenth century), a master painter who carried out many artistic commissions on behalf of the Fourth Panchen. According to a later source, Choying Gyatso also designed a series of portraits of the Fourth Panchen's chain of incarnations; these likely served as models for the Nartang xylographic designs.[7] His virtuosic work is marked by energetic and variegated displays that feature emotionally expressive and dynamically postured figures. The Nartang designs of the first eleven Panchen lineage members evince these interests, rendering most of the main portrait subjects in a three-quarter pose facing the thangka placed in the center. Even Sakya Pandita and Yungton Dorje Pel, who face the viewer directly, strike dramatically animated poses.[8]

The initial set of Nartang designs most likely concluded with a stiffer *en face* portrait of the Fifth Panchen placed in the central position for mounted display, with the others radiating outward in an alternating right and left pattern. The set was sponsored by his students, as the inscription notes, and may have been carved either before or after his death in 1737.[9] The next iteration of the Nartang series was produced after the Sixth Panchen's death in Beijing in 1780, borrowing elements of Qing imperial court portraits made during his visit to design his *en face* portrait, and adding a portrait of the Fifth Panchen in three-quarter pose that could be shifted to the outer edge of the arrangement.[10] The process was repeated once more with the Seventh Panchen Tenpai Nyima in about 1853.

Infinitely reproducible and extendable, the Nartang Panchen series proliferated through copies and adaptations, perpetuating traditions and creating opportunities for media adaptation, display, and diplomatic and karmic relations. Many copies are painted in the Tsangri style, one of the regionally based successors of the new Menri painting tradition that Choying Gyatso founded. The Rubin thangka is a fine example, featuring sinuous pink clouds and distinctively shaded white clouds against a mostly dark blue sky.[11] The Sixth Panchen sent a painted set to the Qing court in 1770, which was adapted into different media, including multiple sets of engravings (*moke*) that outfitted the walls of various sites in Beijing and Rehe (present-day Chengde).[12] Another unusual adaptation of the Nartang Panchen lineage portraits in about 1780 utilized the painting and poetry format of classical Chinese album leaves. In concert with two other albums portraying rebirth lineages of the Third Changkya Rolpai Dorje (1717–1786) and the

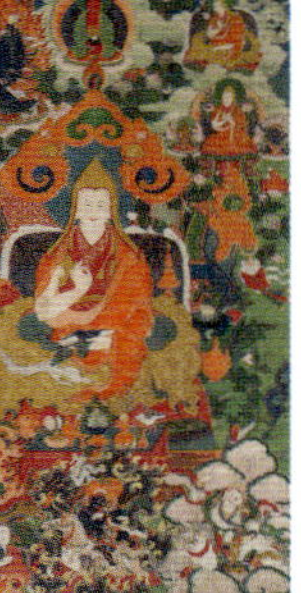 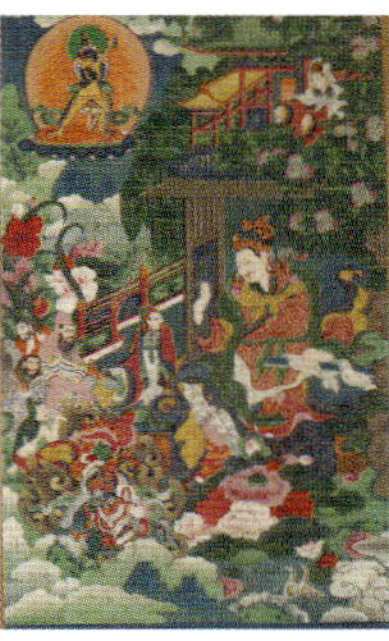 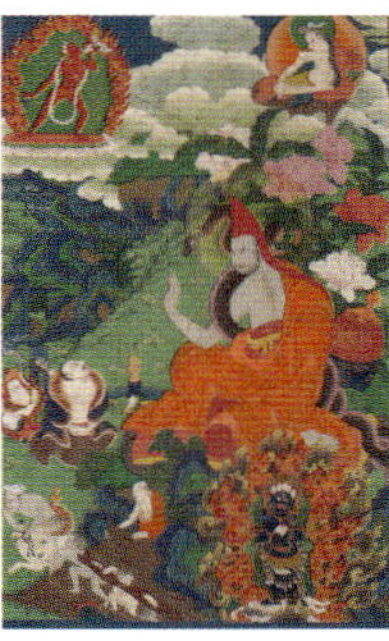 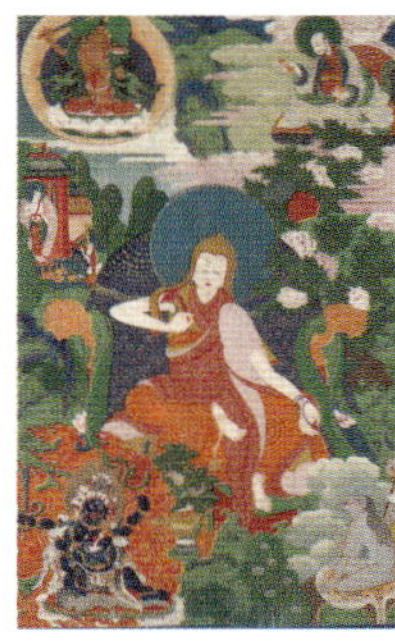 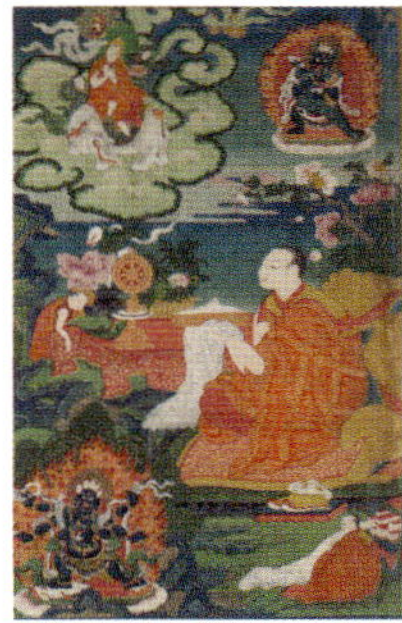 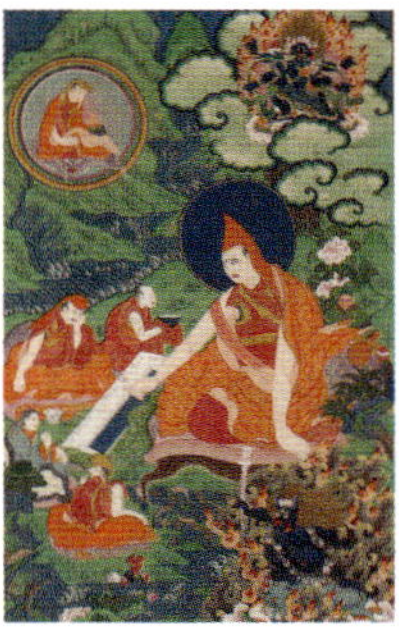 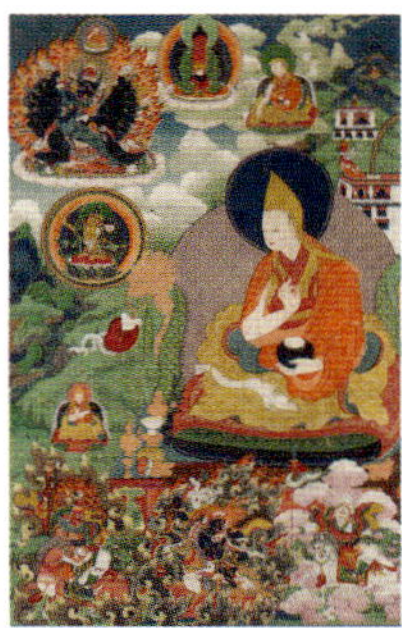

For a portrait of the emperor framed in Tibetan Buddhist terms, see The Qianlong Emperor as Manjushri-Chakravartin, no. 84.

On photographic portraits of lamas, see Photograph of the Thirteenth Dalai Lama, no. 98.

Qianlong emperor (1711–1799), the Panchen album worked to recall, articulate, and strengthen karmic affinities among these three prominent figures of Inner Asia and China and their wider networks.[13] In 1934 a Chinese Republican government representative gave a set of scrolls based on the Nartang designs, woven at a silk factory in Hangzhou, to the Ninth Panchen during one of his visits to China. This set was displayed at the controversial 1995 enthronement of Gyeltsen Norbu as the Eleventh Panchen at Tashilhunpo, alongside a photographic head shot of the Tenth Panchen.[14]

See Arhats Viewing a Painting of Birds by the Tenth Karmapa, no. 72.

For another important case of Geluk woodblock printing, see Panoramic Map of Mount Wutai, no. 91.

The Panchen series was but one of numerous important projects issued by the Nartang printing house in the eighteenth century. In 1742 an edition of the Tibetan Buddhist canon was completed there, followed in 1747 by xylographic sets of the *Wish-Fulfilling Vine of Bodhisattva Legends* (*Bodhisattvavadanakalpalata*) of Kshemendra in thirty-one thangkas, the life of Tsongkhapa in fifteen thangkas, and the sixteen arhats in seven thangkas. These large-scale projects were sponsored by the family of Miwang Polhane Sonam Tobgye, who ruled central and western Tibet from 1728 to 1750.[15] As their visual authority has only been enhanced through prodigious reproduction, circulation, and adaptation, the appeal of such woodblock prints has endured for patrons, makers, and users who wish to claim or partake in the authority, charisma, and technical and aesthetic mastery these works embody.

Further Reading

Berger, Patricia. 2008. "Reincarnation in an Age of Mechanical Reproduction: The Career of the Narthang Panchen Lama Portraits." In *Images of Tibet in the 19th and 20th Centuries*, edited by Monica Esposito, vol. 2, 727–45. Études thématiques 22. Paris: École française d'Extrême-Orient.

Chou, Wen-shing, and Nancy G. Lin. 2021. "Karmic Affinities: Rethinking Relations among Tibetan Lamas and the Qing Emperor." In *Water Moon Reflections: Essays in Honor of Patricia Berger*, edited by Ellen Huang, Nancy G. Lin, Michelle McCoy, and Michelle H. Wang. Berkeley: Institute of East Asian Studies.

Jackson, David P. 1996. "gTsang-pa Chos-dbyings-rgya-mtsho and His New sMan-ris." In *A History of Tibetan Painting: The Great Tibetan Painters and Their Traditions*. Österreichische Akademie der Wissenschaften Philosophisch-Historische Klasse Denkschriften 242. Vienna: Verlag der Österreichischen Akademie der Wissenschaften.

Notes

1 Helman-Ważny 2014, 121–23, 68, fig. 28.
2 Cabezón 2017, 4–6, 14–16.
3 Because the "Panchen" title was first applied to his *tulku* lineage during his lifetime, Lobzang Chokyi Gyeltsen is numbered as the first Panchen in an alternative system. This essay follows the numeration of Tashilhunpo, which retroactively added the Panchen title to three prior incarnations.
4 See, for example, Jagou 2005, fig. 199; Wang Jiapeng 2010, pl. 30; D. Jackson 1996, 375, 378–79n853; Jackson and Jackson 1988, 71–73.
5 Cabezón 2017, 9–11; N. Lin 2017, 144–45; Chou and Lin 2021.
6 Blo bzang chos kyi rgyal mtshan 2009, 1:337–39; cf. 1:428–59. The lineage members from Khedrubje Geluk Pelzang to Wensapa Lobzang Dondrub may have been recognized as a chain of incarnations before the Fourth Panchen's lifetime; see Schwieger 2015, 24.
7 D. Jackson 1996, 233–34, pl. 45.
8 Berger 2003, 172–76.
9 D. Jackson 1996, 234–43; cf. Tucci 1949, 2:416.
10 Berger 2003, pl. 16; figs. 57, 60; 176–77.
11 D. Jackson 2012b, 62–64.
12 Berger 2008, 736; Chou 2018, 82, 95–96; Wang Jiapeng 2010, pls. 21–30.
13 Chou 2018, 94–119; Chou and Lin 2021.
14 Berger 2008, 738–45.
15 N. Lin 2011, 68–72.

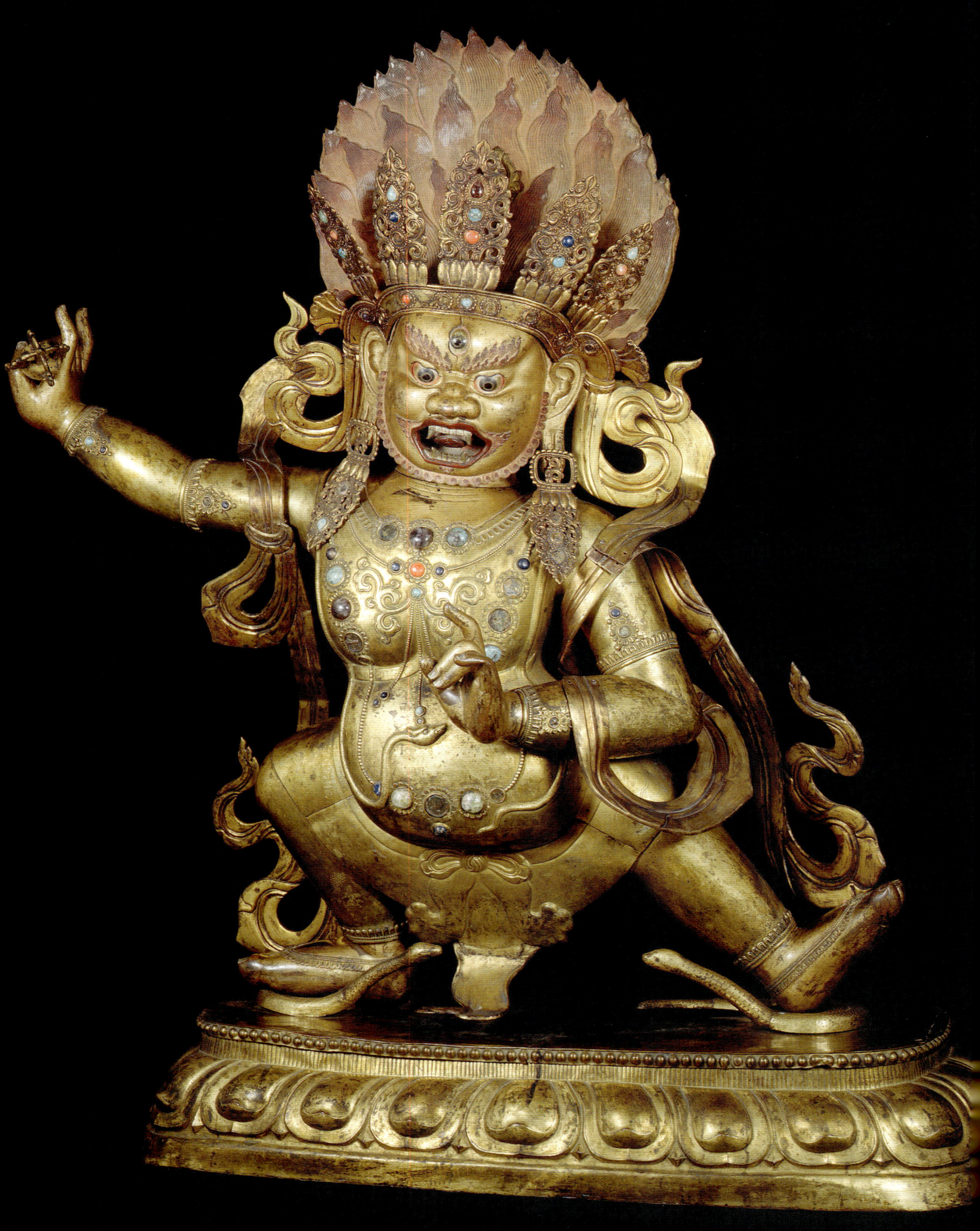

№ 82

Vajrapani

Dolonnuur, Inner Mongolia, mid-18th century

The Statuary of Dolonnuur, Inner Mongolia, and Its Impact across the Tibetan Buddhist World

ISABELLE CHARLEUX

VAJRAPANI, THE "VAJRA HOLDER," is a martial bodhisattva deriving from Indra, the Indian god of thunder. While he is portrayed in a peaceful appearance in Mahayana Buddhism, Tibetan Buddhists usually depict him in his wrathful form.

This statue, nearly six feet (two meters) high, presents mighty Vajrapani in the warrior posture (*alidha*) on a lotus seat. He crushes a snake under each foot, symbolizing obstacles he overcomes. His head has flamelike eyebrows, three bulging eyes, and a curled beard. His open mouth with lacquered red lips shows his fangs. His hair flows upward like flames, decorated with a half vajra (thunderbolt). In his stretched right hand, Vajrapani holds a vajra scepter to enforce religious and state laws, and to tame and forcefully convert demons and heretics; with his left hand, he makes a threatening gesture (*karana* mudra).

For typical attributes of protector deities, see Mahakala Stone Sculpture, no. 39; Monumental Appliqué of Begtse, no. 95.

Vajrapani wears some of the attributes of protective deities (*dharmapala*), such as the long snake necklace and the tiger-skin loincloth, but the macabre attributes of other *dharmapalas* are replaced by bodhisattva's ornaments: the five-leaf crown representing the Five Buddha Families, earrings, armbands, bracelets, necklaces, and anklets. Long swirling scarves around his shoulders and ribbons from his crown create a sense of movement.

Vajrapani, Mongolia's Tutelary Deity

Vajrapani is one of the main deities of the Mongols, who commonly believe that Mongolia is the land of Vajrapani, Tibet is the land of Avalokiteshvara, and China is the land of Manjushri; these three figures respectively represent power, compassion, and wisdom.

When Mongols reconverted to Buddhism in the sixteenth century, the Third Dalai Lama proclaimed Vajrapani as their special protector. In 1586 or 1587, he recognized Abatai Khan (1554–1588) as an emanation of Vajrapani and offered him a statue of Vajrapani indestructible by fire. Several Mongol rulers—including Chinggis Khan—were subsequently recognized as the worldly emanation of this bodhisattva.

Since the end of the eighteenth century, Mount Otgontenger, the highest peak of the Khangai Range, is said to be Vajrapani's abode in Mongolia. The mountain itself is identified with Vajrapani's body.[1]

After the fall of the Communist regime in 1990, Vajrapani was reinstated as the protector of the Mongolian state. In 2007 President Enkhbayar commissioned a giant appliqué depicting Vajrapani above Chinggis Khan and two of his successors, Ögedei and Qubilai (Kubilai), to be displayed on Otgontenger during ceremonial offerings to the mountain.

Mongol herders pray to Vajrapani to protect their livestock from thieves and wolves, to retrieve stolen or lost animals, and to protect them from gossip, harm caused by snake spirits (nagas), and sickness.

Vajrapani; Efi (efü?) khalkha süme, Shiliin Gol League (formerly in Chakhar), Inner Mongolia, China; mid-18th century; gilt-copper alloy with lacquer and pigments, inset with gems; height 73 in. (185.4 cm); Stockholm Ethnographical Museum (Folkens Museum Ethnografiska); 1935.50.1714; photograph by John B. Taylor

The Bronze Workshops of Dolonnuur in Inner Mongolia

Every region of Mongolia preserved names of famous Mongol smiths, and a few lamas were eminent sculptors, the most famous being Zanabazar, the First Jibzundamba Khutugtu (1635–1723).[2] Itinerant Chinese smiths also crisscrossed Mongolia to offer their services. In the eighteenth century, the growing demand for large-scale statues that required a high degree of specialization and a large workforce caused the progressive sedentarization of metalwork, as smiths established workshops in settlements. The main center of production in the early Qing dynasty (1644–1911) was Hohhot in Inner Mongolia. After 1850, the quality and quantity of metalwork produced in Hohhot declined because commissions moved to the famous workshops of Dolonnuur.

The Vajrapani statue belongs to a set of six sculptures brought from an abandoned monastery near Dolonnuur, Inner Mongolia, by the geographer and explorer Sven Hedin in 1930. Dolonnuur (formerly in Chakhar Province, now in Shiliin Gol League), on the southeast edge of the Mongol steppe, developed as a satellite of two large imperial monasteries, the Blue Monastery (Khökhe süme, Chinese: Huizongsi, founded in 1691 at the place where the Khalkha Mongol leaders swore allegiance to Qing emperor Kangxi [r. 1661–1722] in 1691), and the Yellow Monastery (Shira süme, Chinese: Shanyinsi, founded by Emperor Yongzheng [r. 1722–1735] in 1727).[3] After 1732, when the Qing established an office to rule Inner Mongol Buddhist affairs there, Dolonnuur became a commercial and religious hub. Located on the roads from China and Tibet to Urga/Yekhe Khüriye and Central Asia, it attracted a great number of monks and pilgrims, traders, and artisans. Although the imperial monasteries encountered economic difficulties in the late Qing period, trade and metalwork continued to prosper up to the early twentieth century.

Dolonnuur's trade and workshop center, known as Maimaicheng (a generic name for trade cities settled near large monasteries), spontaneously developed in the eighteenth century a little less than one mile (one and a half kilometers) south of the monasteries.[4] In the late nineteenth century, it counted four thousand shops and workshops, including workshops of thangkas, carpets, and metal artifacts of daily life, and was the biggest production center for Mongol Tibetan Buddhist metal statues.[5] The two main foundries were Ayushi Tunjan (*tunjan*, Chinese: *tongjiang*, metallurgists) and Khaisandai; the four others were Öntsög Tunjan, Öntsögön Nomtu, Bayantai Tunjan, and Khuuchin Nomtu. They employed from a hundred up to several hundred craftsmen.[6] They were initially run by both Chinese and Mongols, and fell entirely into the hands of Chinese in the late nineteenth century.

For paintings from Inner Mongolia from this period, see The All-Knowing Buddha Vairochana Visualization Album, no. 87.

Assimilated Chinese smiths from Dolonnuur also established bronze workshops in the Chinese settlement (Maimaicheng) east of Urga monastic city. They probably first opened branch shops to receive and assemble statues created in parts at a Dolonnuur workshop, to be assembled after delivery, and later established their own workshops. In the late nineteenth century, with twenty workshops of blacksmiths, bronze smiths, and silversmiths, Urga became the third main fabrication center for metal statues, after Dolonnuur and Beijing.

For more on Urga, see Mongolian Map of Capital Yekhe Khüriye, no. 96.

The purchase of large statues represented, with Buddhist scriptures, a major part of a monastery's budget. In the nineteenth century, large-scale statues from Dolonnuur were sold for between 700 and 6,000 taels of silver, and up to 20,000 taels, at a time when the construction of an average-size monastery cost about 10,000 taels.[7] The prices of statues made in Urga were higher than those made in Dolonnuur and Beijing.[8]

Dolonnuur exported its production by camel caravans all over the Tibetan Buddhist world. In the nineteenth century most of the metal statues of Mongolia and the northeastern province of Tibet (Amdo) came from Dolonnuur. In 1844 Fathers Huc and Gabet encountered a caravan of eighty-four camels carrying different parts of a statue to be offered to the Dalai Lama. The statue of Maitreya of Urga, almost fifty feet (fifteen meters) in height and made in seven parts in Dolonnuur by twelve Chinese artists of the Ayushi Tunjan foundry, was shipped to Urga in 1833 (it was destroyed in 1939). The Buddhist temple founded in Saint Petersburg in 1913–1915 commissioned its statues from Dolonnuur foundries.

The Techniques of the Dolonnuur Foundries

As with other Dolonnuur statues, the Vajrapani statue combined the repoussé method (hammered metal) for the body and the base, and the lost-wax technique for the arms and legs, and perhaps for the head. The decorative parts, such as the crown, attributes, and scarves, were made separately from a thinner sheet by hammering and were inlaid with turquoise, coral, and lapis lazuli. The repoussé technique is less complex and uses less metal and fuel than the lost-wax technique; it permits a mass, standardized, and cheaper production, since a single mold could be used for making several sculptures. Different metal alloys were used for different parts of the body and ornaments of a single sculpture. The Dolonnuur workshops also produced a few silver statues.[9]

For other examples in the repoussé technique, see Vishnu Riding on Garuda, no. 18; Plaque Commemorating the *Bhimaratha* Old Age Ritual, no. 85.

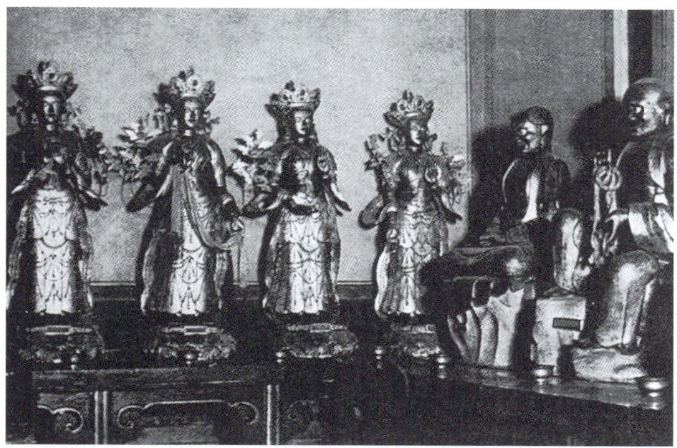

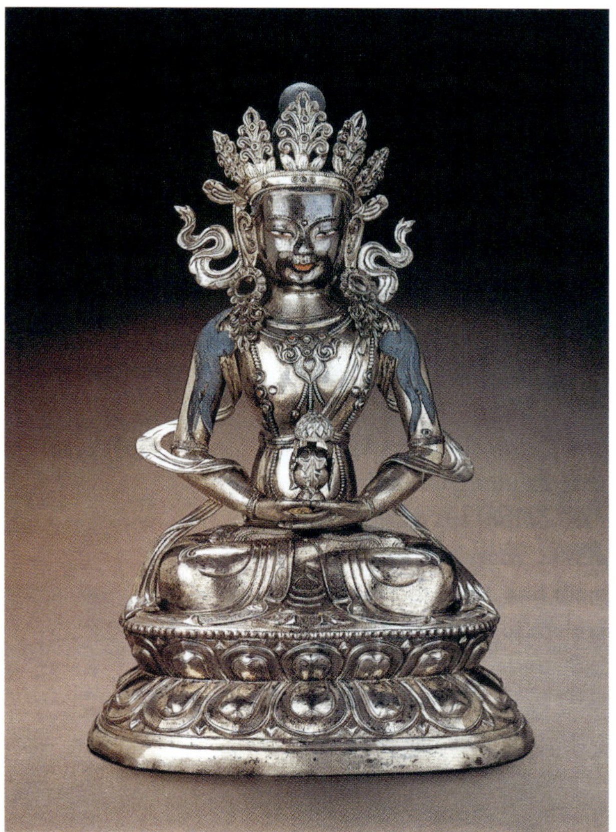

(top) A back chapel, Yellow Monastery; Dolonnuur, Inner Mongolia, China; photographed in the 1930s; image after Berger and Bartholomew 1995, 82, fig. 8

(above) Statue of Amitayus, Dolonnuur style; 19th century; silver with colors; 10⅞ × 6⅞ × 7⅛ in. (27.5 × 17.5 × 18.2 cm); Bogd Khan Palace Museum, Ulaanbaatar; image after Berger and Bartholomew 1995, 219, cat. no. 67

The different parts of large statues were delivered separately; once they arrived at a temple, they were fitted together with rivets, dovetail joints, and clasps, and were gilded (using the amalgam gilding process) and painted (they could be lacquered before the gilding).

The Style of Dolonnuur

The Chinese artisans strictly executed the will of their patrons and followed prescribed iconometry. Mongol lamas told the Russian explorer Aleksei M. Pozdneev that they preferred Dolonnuur statues to Beijing statues, because Dolonnuur craftsmen were more respectful of iconographic canons and their gilding lasted longer.[10]

Statues at the Stockholm Ethnographical Museum and the Hermitage Museum are the rare images whose provenance is firmly attested. Together with photographs taken by a Japanese scholar inside the Shira süme in the 1930s, they allow us to distinguish a few characteristics of the Dolonnuur style: big crowns with large, flat leaves, scarves billowing behind the ears and at the elbows, long, flat ear pendants, arching eyebrows meeting above the nose, inlaid semiprecious stones, and a base plate held in place by small clamps—as seen in the Vajrapani sculpture under discussion. Stylistic study combined with X-ray spectral analysis helps scholars define this style in spite of its many variations. It has so far been impossible to distinguish statues produced in Dolonnuur from statues made by craftsmen from Dolonnuur established in Urga. Besides the Urga production, hundreds of statues from China, Russia (especially Buryatia), and even Europe also imitated the Dolonnuur style.[11]

Further Reading

Charleux, Isabelle. 2010b. "The Making of Mongol Buddhist Art and Architecture: Artisans in Mongolia from the Sixteenth to the Twentieth Century." In *Meditation: The Art of Zanabazar and His School*, edited by Elvira Eevr Djaltchinova-Malets, 59–105. Warsaw: Asia and Pacific Museum.

Elikhina, Yulia, and Victoria Demenova. 2020. "A Study of Stylistic Features and Metal Composition of the Buddhist Sculpture from Inner Mongolia (Dolonnor)." *Artibus Asiae* 80, no. 2, 145–66.

Notes

1 Wallace 2015.
2 Charleux 2010b.
3 Charleux 2006, CD-ROM "Dolonnor."
4 Huc 1857, 35; Pozdneev (1896–98) 1977, 182–83. See Charleux 2006, CD-ROM "Dolonnor."
5 Yang Pu 1933, 34.
6 Pozdneev (1896–98) 1977, 179–82; Ren 2008, 221; Hua 1986, 241 (quoted by L. Wu 2017) identifies five foundries by their Chinese names.
7 Charleux 2010b, 88.
8 Charleux 2010b, 88; Pozdneev (1896) 1971, 69. On the Buddhist workshops of Beijing, see Montell 1954; Lipton and Nima Dorjee Ragnubs 1996, 268–71.
9 Elikhina and Demenova 2020 analyzes the metal composition of fifty-three sculptures from two Russian museums. See also Béguin 1993, 159; Bartholomew and Berger 1995, 82.
10 Pozdneev (1896–98) 1977, 179–82.
11 Some examples are: Béguin 1993, 158, ill. 4, and 159; Bartholomew and Berger 1995, 83, cat. no. 67, 83, 84, fig. 1, and 220; Deimel and Freiherr Speck von Sternburg 2008, 1:62–63 and 1:113–17; Rhie and Thurman 2009; Watts 2019.

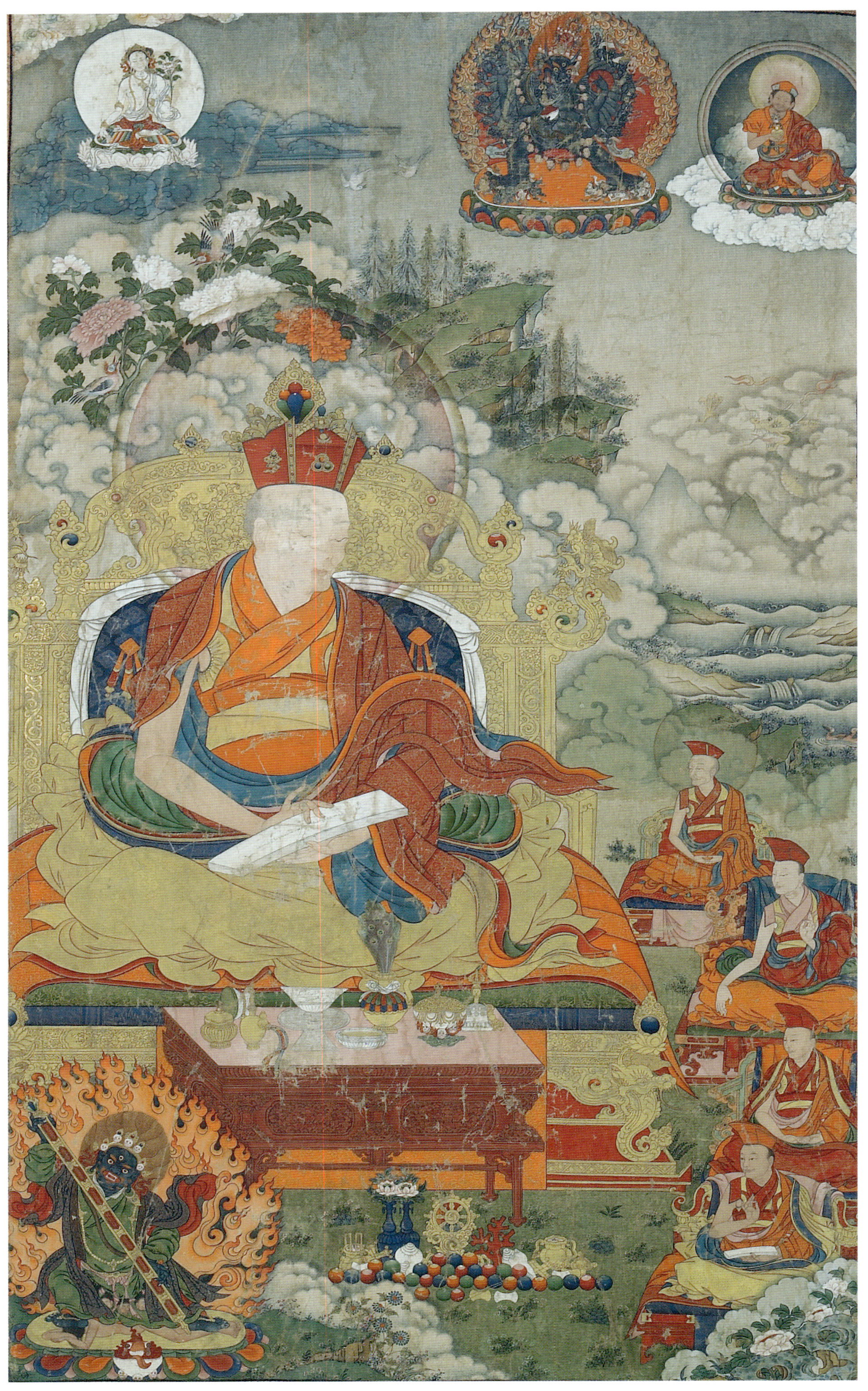

Nº 83

Portrait of Situ Panchen

Pelpung Monastery, Derge, Kham region, eastern Tibet, ca. 1760s

Great Tibetan Patron and Designer of Buddhist Art in Kham

DAVID JACKSON AND KARL DEBRECZENY

Situ Panchen (1700–1774) was both a hierarch of the Karma Kagyu tradition of Tibetan Buddhism and an important patron and artist, credited with reviving the court style of the Karmapas known as the Encampment style (Gardri), which quickly became popular in his native Kham region in southeastern Tibet. This style is characterized by figures based on Indian aesthetic models of proportion placed in open, airy, blue-green landscapes largely inspired by Chinese court painting.

As Situ worked directly with artists, the painters of this work would have known him well enough to create an accurate likeness. The physical appearance of Situ Panchen in this painting, as a venerable gray-haired master with sunken features, tends to support a dating to the 1760s. The long-life goddess White Tara above, with whom Situ had a special connection, was also included as a wish for the aged Situ Panchen's continued longevity.

Situ sits on an elaborately carved Chinese-inspired throne, wearing the badge of his office, a notched red hat emblazoned with three jewels. Behind Situ lies an open landscape with a minimally pigmented light-blue sky, featuring a flowing river, and two distant cloud-wreathed peaks, suggesting receding space. Above, a dragon emerges from the clouds. Craggy cliffs festooned with pine trees evoke the landscape of Situ's home in Derge.

Situ Panchen and the Revival of the Encampment Style

On the early Encampment style, see Portrait of the Ninth Karmapa, no. 66.

While the Encampment style was founded in the court of the Ninth Karmapa in the sixteenth century in central Tibet, most of what we know of this painting tradition belongs to its eighteenth-century revival fostered by Situ Panchen in eastern Tibet. Even more important to the history of Tibetan art than Situ Panchen's role as a painter is his role as a patron and designer of paintings, many of which continue to be copied to this day. Situ's tradition is one of the best documented of the major Tibetan painting traditions, in part because of the extensive writings that he left, including his autobiography and diaries, rare windows into his artistic intentions that detail the paintings he designed and commissioned, the names of the artists he worked with, and his iconographic and artistic sources.[1]

The Life of Situ Panchen

For more about the Ganden Podrang government, see Potala Palace, no. 71.

Situ Panchen was born in Derge, a small but culturally significant kingdom at the heart of the southeastern Tibetan region of Kham. Situ was born during a particularly volatile period in Tibet's history. Several generations of inter-sectarian warfare had left his Karma Kagyu tradition in shambles, and in central Tibet the Ganden Podrang government was suppressing Karma Kagyu monasteries. However, some areas of eastern Tibet, like Derge, lay beyond the reach of central Tibetan rule and remained relatively open to other religious traditions and artistic developments.

In 1732 the two top hierarchs of the Karma Kagyu tradition suddenly died, and Situ Panchen was thrust at the age of thirty-three into the role of de facto regent of his tradition. Situ proved to be a brilliant polymath and charismatic leader, influential in many areas of cultural and institutional life in eighteenth-century Tibet. He made major contributions to the fields of painting, religion, literature, and medicine.[2]

A watershed in Situ's religious, artistic, and political career took place in 1729 with the founding of his new monastic seat, Pelpung Monastery, in his birthplace of Derge, which became the artistic hub

Portrait of Situ Panchen (1700–1774), from a Pelpung set of Masters of the Combined Kagyu Lineages; Pelpung Monastery, Derge, Kham region, eastern Tibet; ca. 1760s; pigments on cotton; 38½ × 23½ in. (97.8 × 59.7 cm); Rubin Museum of Art; C2003.29.2 (HAR 65279)

for the revival of the Encampment style. In 1726, as part of his request for permission to build this new monastery, he offered a set of paintings of the Eight Great Tantric Adepts (mahasiddhas) to the Derge ruler Tenpa Tsering (1678–1738). It is the first set that Situ is recorded to have painted and in many ways marks the beginning of his public life as an artistic and religious leader.

Situ the Artist

Situ first learned iconographic proportions at age fifteen and soon thereafter was shown old Indian cast-metal figures by a temple steward, who introduced him to the traditional stylistic classifications of Buddhist metal sculpture. The steward pointed out different types of metal and characteristic shapes as he referenced one of the classic manuals on the evaluation of objects. Situ was thus initiated at a very young age into a Tibetan tradition of connoisseurship. From that time on he was able to evaluate the styles and quality of sacred objects, took pains to investigate the paintings and statues he came upon, and collected art.[3] Situ could paint in at least two different styles—Menri and the Encampment style—and was a keen observer of early masterpieces and different styles of painting.

Sets: Situ's Greatest Legacy

Painting sets often depict iconographic themes far too complicated to fit into a single work. Some of Situ Panchen's most important and prominent artistic legacies are the multi-painting sets that he designed, many of which are still copied to this day. Indeed, most of Situ's compositions are known to us through these later copies. Among these only six were mentioned in Situ Panchen's autobiography as his own commissions:

1. Eight Great Tantric Adepts (mahasiddhas), painted in 1726;[4]
2. The Previous Lives of Buddha Shakyamuni (jatakas), sketched in 1726;[5]
3. The Six Ornaments and Two Excellent Ones (eight greatest scholastic authorities of Indian Buddhism), painted in 1730;[6]
4. Eight Great Bodhisattvas (based on a sixteenth-century model), commissioned in 1732;[7]
5. Kshemendra's *Wish-Granting Vine* Series of One Hundred and Eight Morality Tales (Avadanas), designed in 1733;[8]
6. Twenty-Seven Tantric Deities, designed and commissioned in 1750.[9]

Situ would often set up workshops of painters he had trained, such as for the Morality Tales set, the compositions of which he sketched himself, and he personally directed the entire process, from the initial coloring to the finishing details. In an inscription Situ composed for a final painting portraying himself as patron, he outlines his all-encompassing artistic vision:

> I have followed the Chinese masters in color, in mood expressed, and form, and I have depicted lands, dress, palaces, and so forth as [I have] actually seen in India. Even though all the discriminating skill of Mentang—[both] New and Old—and the Khyen [ri] tradition followers, Jeugangpa and the Encampment (Gardri) masters are present here, I have made [these paintings] different in a hundred thousand [particulars of] style.[10]

His mention of things he had "actually seen in India" refers to his first pilgrimage to Nepal in 1723.[11]

Situ's designs became important templates for art production at Pelpung Monastery, and more widely in eastern Tibet, having a major impact on other local painting traditions.[12] Situ's compositions have some distinctive features, including the unusually diminutive rendering of figures in open, airy landscapes, contrasted with miniaturist treatments of trees, buildings, palaces, and courtyards depicted in precise detail, with every leaf and brick delineated. This is a clever visual strategy to draw the eye into each vignette. Landscapes are especially distinctive due to the layering of blue and green pigment in dots with the tip of a dry brush. This technique builds up the landscape, from blank canvas to deep color, giving paintings the airy, yet intensely bright quality for which the style became famous.

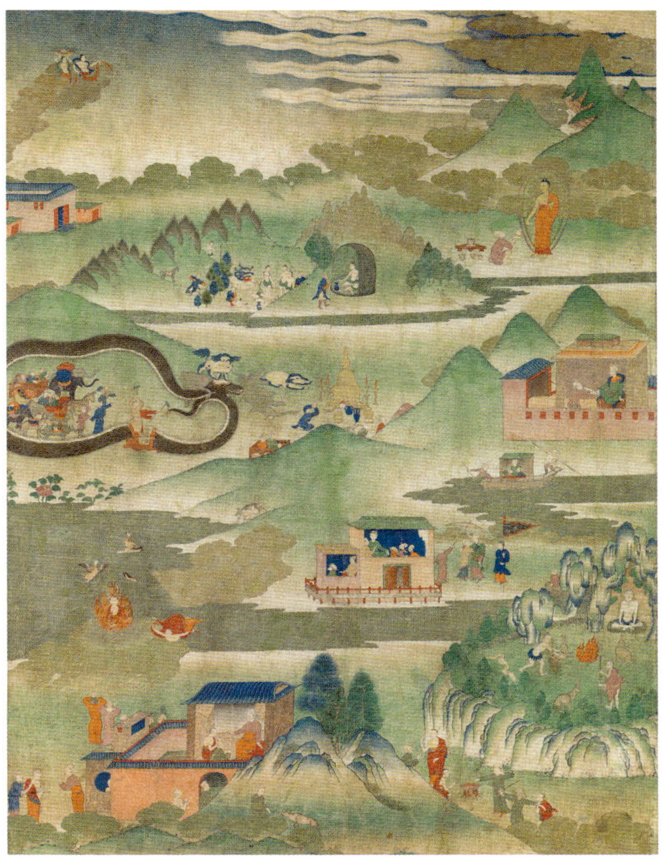

The Wish-Granting Vine Series of One Hundred and Eight Morality Tales, twenty-first painting after Situ's set; Kham region, eastern Tibet; 19th century; pigments on cotton; 33 × 24 in. (83.8 × 61 cm); Shelley and Donald Rubin Private Collection; P1996.9.5 (HAR 247); photograph by Adam Reich, courtesy the Shelley and Donald Rubin Private Collection

Related Pelpung Monastery Sets

Six other main sets of paintings have been identified as coming from Situ's monastic seat, Pelpung, using other written sources or on the basis of stylistic similarities with those sets identified in Situ's biographies.[13] The portrait of Situ Panchen under consideration belongs to one such well-known set, featuring masters of the combined lineages of the Mahamudra and Six Dharmas of Naropa, the two main teachings of the Karma Kagyu tradition. Later generations would commission paintings to bring the set up to date by adding their own gurus.

Though oral tradition by such well-informed Karma Kagyu masters as Thrangu Rinpoche (b. 1933) and Tenga Rinpoche (1932–2012) links Situ Panchen to this set, and even maintains that it was designed by him, it is not documented in Situ's autobiographies. The modern Pelpung historian Karma Gyeltsen clarifies its origins, stating that while the set does indeed date to the time of Situ, Situ was *not* the patron. Its actual patron was Situ's nephew and disciple, Won Sampel, who acted as Situ's treasurer.[14] The main painter of this set was one of Situ's chief artistic disciples in his later years, Karsho Karma Tashi, as indicated by his tiny self-portrait, identified by inscription, in the foreground of the final painting.[15] Karma Tashi was from Karsho, one of the significant centers of painting in northwestern Kham, near Karma Monastery, Situ's previous seat before he founded Pelpung.[16]

Late in his life, Situ reminisced that through the paintings that he designed and commissioned, the artistic traditions of his native Kham were beginning to shine again.[17]

Further Reading

Jackson, David P. 2009. *Patron and Painter: Situ Panchen and the Revival of the Encampment Style*. Masterworks of Tibetan Painting Series 1. Exhibition catalog. New York: Rubin Museum of Art, 2009. https://issuu.com/rmanyc/docs/patron_and_patron_96.

Tashi Tsering, ed. 2000. "Situ Panchen: His Contribution and Legacy." Special issue, *Lungta* 13 (Winter). Dharamsala: Amnye Machen Institute.

Debreczeny, Karl, ed. 2013b. "Situ Panchen: Creation and Cultural Engagement in Eighteenth-Century Tibet." Special issue, *Journal of the International Association of Tibetan Studies* 7 (August), esp. 125–92. http://www.thlib.org/collections/texts/jiats/#!jiats=/current/.

Notes

1 Si tu Pan chen 1968; D. Jackson 1996, 259–87; D. Jackson 2009, 3–19; Tashi Tsering 2013, 129–33.
2 Tashi Tsering 2000; Debreczeny 2013b.
3 Si tu Pan chen 1968, 42–47; Si tu and 'Be lo (1775) 1972, 458–59. On Situ's early life, see D. Jackson 2009, 3–6.
4 D. Jackson 2009, 118–19, 137–52.
5 D. Jackson 2009, 120–21.
6 D. Jackson 2009, 121.
7 D. Jackson 2009, 121–22; Debreczeny 2013c.
8 D. Jackson 2009, 122; Tashi Tsering 2013, 130–33, 140, 152, 162–63.
9 D. Jackson 2009, 125.
10 D. Jackson 2009, 12; see also Tashi Tsering 2013, 131, 162–63.
11 On Situ's pilgrimage to Nepal, see Decleer 2000.
12 D. Jackson 2012b, 87–116.
13 D. Jackson 2009, 125–35.
14 D. Jackson 2009, 169 and n418; Karma rgyal mtshan 1997, 231.
15 The inscription reads *ri mo'i byed po mang ga'i ming/.* D. Jackson 2009, 21–22, 168; D. Jackson 2012, 90.
16 D. Jackson 2012b, 87–88, 167–69.
17 *mdo khams kyi phyogs 'di'i bzo rigs bris 'bur gyi srol yang gsal bar gyur*: Si tu Pan chen 1968, 158.1; D. Jackson 2009, 12, 122, and 266n349; Debreczeny 2013c, 194.

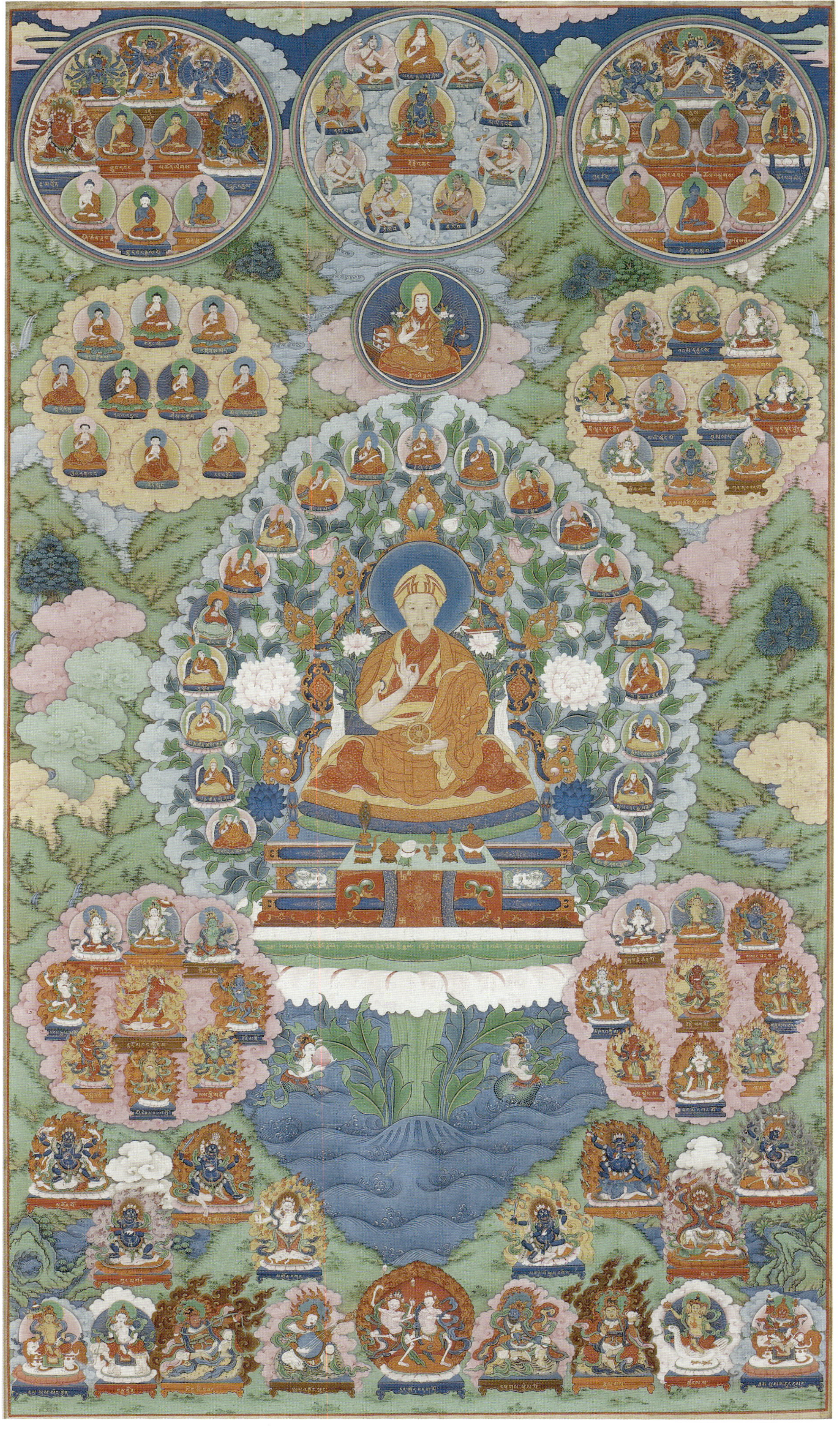

№ 84

The Qianlong Emperor as Manjushri-Chakravartin

Imperial workshop in Beijing, China, with face by Giuseppe Castiglione, mid-18th century

Tibetan Buddhism at the Qing Court

WEN-SHING CHOU

THIS PAINTING AT THE FREER GALLERY OF ART depicts the Qianlong emperor (1711–1799) of the Manchu Qing dynasty (1644–1912) as a kingly embodiment of the Bodhisattva of Wisdom Manjushri at the center of an Indo-Tibetan Buddhist cosmos. Presented in the format of a thangka, a traditional Tibetan religious hanging scroll, the painting is an unprecedented visual articulation of religious kingship. The Manchus were a people from northeast Asia who conquered China from the north side of the Great Wall. When they established the Qing dynasty, they also adopted Tibetan Buddhism as means of uniting diverse Mongol and Tibetan groups and incorporating them into their expanding empire. Qianlong was an avid supporter and practitioner of Tibetan Buddhism. He oversaw the creation of a vast array of Tibetan Buddhist art and architecture. These works were made as gifts to high lamas and for imperial monasteries, the emperor's private domains, and the interiors of his own mausoleum.[1] Among them, the portrait thangka stands as the most direct and inventive expression of Qianlong's extraordinary engagement with Tibetan Buddhism and his court's creative adaptation of Tibetan Buddhist visual and material culture.

Major Figures and Themes

The double-flapped hat is most commonly associated with the Fourth Panchen Lama. See Nartang Woodblock Prints and Their Painted Copies, no. 81.

For another example of kings as chakravartins, see Erdeni Juu Monastery, no. 65.

See Panoramic Map of Mount Wutai, no. 91.

Qianlong appears in the center wearing monk's robes and the folded hat of a Tibetan Buddhist patriarch. Seated on the diamond throne of a high lama atop a lotus blossom rising from a pond, he raises his right hand in the teaching gesture (*vitarka* mudra), while holding in his left palm a jeweled wheel of law, the Indic emblem of a universal ruler (chakravartin). He also carries in his hands the stems of two flanking lotus blossoms, above which rest a sword and a book—attributes of Manjushri. The figure presides over a pantheon of 108 figures, each labeled with gold-lettered Tibetan inscription, in a paradisiacal landscape allusive of Mount Wutai, the earthly abode of Manjushri in northern China. A verse inscription above the stem of the lotus below the throne invokes Qianlong's layered associations with monastic authority, Manjushri, and universal rulership. It reads:

> Sharp-witted Manjushri, king of men,
> Playful, unexcelled, great dharma king,
> On the diamond seat, feet firm.
> May your wishes spontaneously meet good fortune![2]

The Qianlong Emperor as Manjushri-Chakravartin; Beijing; Qianlong period (1735–1796), mid-18th century; thangka, color on silk; 44¾ × 25⁵⁄₁₆ in. (113.7 × 64.3 cm); Freer Gallery of Art, National Museum of Asian Art, Smithsonian Institutions; F2000.4; photograph courtesy Freer Gallery of Art, Smithsonian Institution, Washington, D.C.

In contrast to the Tibetan Buddhist religious language and iconography that dictate most of the composition, Qianlong's face is rendered in an empirically descriptive manner. This subdued form of Baroque realism is attributed to the emperor's favorite court painter, the Milanese Jesuit lay brother Giuseppe Castiglione (1688–1766). Likely a collaboration between lama painters of the palace workshops and the Jesuit painter, the thangka exemplifies the hybridized nature of Qing imperial production and the cultural pluralism of the Pan-Asian empire.[3]

The pantheon of figures surrounding Qianlong represents the major teachings and practices under the framework of Gelukpa Buddhism—the dominant religious institution in seventeenth- and eighteenth-century Tibet and Mongolia. Immediately surrounding Qianlong is a garland of nineteen eminent Indian and Tibetan masters of important transmission lineages. Directly above Qianlong, in a

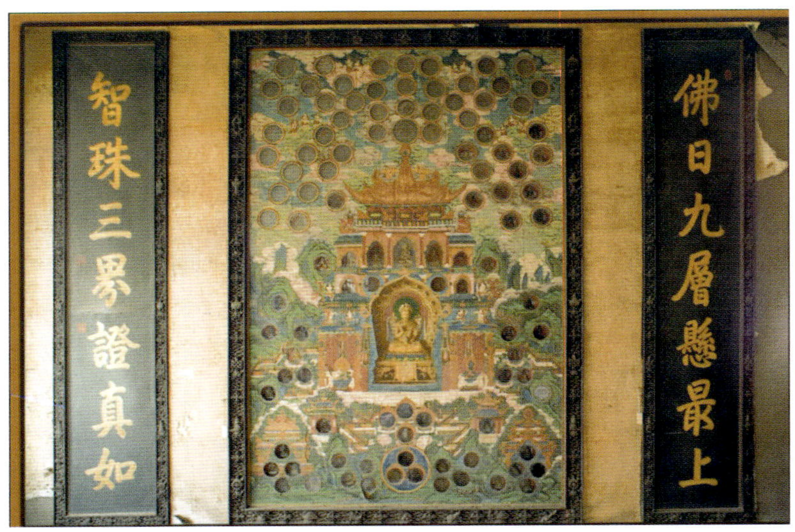

Manjughosha Emperor, niched hanging shrine panel, Eastern Side Hall, Pavilion of Raining Flowers, Palace Museum, Beijing; image courtesy Palace Museum

separate roundel, is the emperor's root teacher (Tibetan: *tsawai lama*; Sanskrit: *guru*; or main spiritual teacher), the Imperial Preceptor Changkya Rolpai Dorje (1717–1786), shown with a bell and vajra, iconographic attributes of his personal meditational deity Chakrasamvara. Rolpai Dorje was a Tibetan Buddhist polymath of ethnic Monguor origin who spent his career in the service of Qianlong.[4] As the most important reincarnate lama at the Manchu court, he played a decisive role in Qing policies toward Tibet and Mongolia, as well as in the design, translation, and production of Buddhist scriptures, art, and architecture at the Qing court. Rolpai Dorje is known to have given Qianlong initiation into many tantric teachings, which are also represented in the thangka. Tutelary deities of major Gelukpa practices, along with buddhas, bodhisattvas, mahasiddhas, disciples, and protector deities associated with major Gelukpa lineages, populate the rainbow and cloud roundels above, while the assemblies below the throne include various bodhisattvas and wrathful deities offering protection.

Related Objects and Source Imageries

The thangka is one of seven extant paintings on silk of the same subject matter in a variety of symmetrical compositions.[5] Most of them were originally hung in major imperial monasteries in and around the Qing court. But similar thangkas were known to have been sent as gifts to Tibetan Buddhist hierarchs. These thangkas therefore played a crucial role in communicating Qianlong's religio-political identity to his Tibetan and Mongol constituents. One of the earliest thangkas was likely sent to Lhasa in 1757 during a Qing imperial mission to oversee the selection of the reincarnation of the recently deceased Seventh Dalai Lama (1708–1757). According to records, thousands of monks and laymen came to the gathering during which the image of Qianlong was unveiled.[6] A decree from Qianlong instructed that the image serve as his surrogate for visiting the sacred icons of Tibet *and* for receiving veneration from the lay and monastic communities. Qianlong's decree from 1757 reads:

See Jowo Shakyamuni, no. 8.

> Tibet has been the pure and clear sacred land of my utmost aspiration. However, the journey is long, preventing me from visiting in person. Today I send my portrait with Changkya, which is just like my paying homage to the Jowo Buddha in person. Therefore, do not prevent any lay or official ministers who wish to admire the portrait. [I use this] to display my pious devotion to the Jowo Sakyamuni Buddha and my sincere intention to spread the teachings of the dharma.[7]

See Potala Palace, no. 71.

Sure enough, the thangka later became an important object of ritual veneration in the Hall of Victory over Three Realms in the Potala Palace, home of the Dalai Lamas and seat of the Tibetan government, where it remains today.[8] It also came to serve as a substitute for the Qing emperors' presence during the ritual of the Golden Urn, a ceremony Qianlong had implemented for the selection of reincarnate lamas.[9]

An eighth thangka, now in the collection of the Palace Museum, Beijing, is virtually identical in composition to two of the extant thangkas of Qianlong, but instead features Rolpai Dorje at the center, with his iconographic attributes of bell and vajra, and holding a long-life vase. It remains unclear if this was a singular experiment or a more established convention. What is palpable is a fluid and playful interchangeability between the lama and the disciple, alternately placed in the center of a deity pantheon. In addition, at least nine three-dimensional shrine panels of varying sizes and composition also feature a sculptural image of Qianlong as an ordained monk and Manjushri-Chakravartin at the center of a niched pantheon, as seen in the image above. The panels are still preserved from the inner palaces of the Forbidden City for which they were specifically designed. Given the prominence of his role in all aspects of Tibetan art and ritual, Rolpai Dorje was most likely also behind the design of these thangkas and shrine panels.

Extant thangkas and shrine panels reflect borrowings from an array of Buddhist imageries that would have been recognizable and meaningful to their viewers. An apparent inspiration for the composition and iconography is the Refuge Field (*tsok zhing*) paintings of the Gelukpa tradition, the only type of contemporaneous Tibetan Buddhist imagery that approaches the comprehensive and pluralistic display of the Qianlong images.[10] A Refuge Field painting pictorializes what the practitioner is asked to generate and invite to their world through a practice of meditative visualization (*sadhana*) in a liturgy that pays homage to their teachers (Sanskrit: *guru puja*; Tibetan: *lama chopa*), the most universally practiced liturgy for every Gelukpa practitioner. The painting thus depicts a main teacher surrounded by other teachers, deities, and protectors.[11] Not only does the painting function as a support for the practice of meditative visualization and for the longer liturgy, but it also serves as the most defining representation for the universal authority of Gelukpa Buddhism at the time.[12] The portrayal of Qianlong as an ordained Gelukpa patriarch invokes the Gelukpa Refuge Field painting's central figure Tsongkhapa (1357–1419), the fourteenth-century founder of the Gelukpa school of Tibetan Buddhism, while many of the subsidiary figures also overlap. By replacing Tsongkhapa, who was also known as an emanation of Manjushri, Qianlong is thus positioned as the source and center of Gelukpa teachings and genealogies. Borrowing the form and compositional logic of Refuge Field paintings, the Qianlong thangkas harnessed the power and authority of a Tibetan liturgical object to advance a new Qing-centered religious orthodoxy. Other pictorial sources include liturgically prescribed icons and relics, deity mandalas, and paintings of teaching transmission and incarnation lineages, as well as Buddhist paradises and cosmos. The many layers of references point to the creativity and resourcefulness with which the Qing court artists created images of the Manjushri-Chakravartin emperor.

Further Reading

Henss, Michael. 2001. "The Bodhisattva-Emperor: Tibeto-Chinese Portraits of Sacred and Secular Rule in the Qing Dynasty." Pts. 1 and 2. *Oriental Art* 47, no. 3, 2–26; 47, no. 5, 71–83.

Berger, Patricia. 2003. *Empire of Emptiness: Buddhist Art and Political Authority in Qing China*. Honolulu: University of Hawai'i Press.

Chou, Wen-shing. 2019. "Bodhisattva Emperors of the Manchu Qing Dynasty." In *Faith and Empire: Art and Politics in Tibetan Buddhism*, edited by Karl Debreczeny, 190–211. Exhibition catalog. New York: Rubin Museum of Art. https://issuu.com/rmanyc/docs/faith_and_empire.

Notes

1 For a comprehensive study of Qianlong's mausoleum, which is entirely covered in relief carvings of Sanskrit dharanis, or protective incantations, see Wang-Toutain 2017.

2 *'jam dpal rnon po mi'i rje bor/ rol pa'i bdag chen chos kyi rgyal/ rdo rje khri la zhabs brtan cing/ bzhed don lhun grub skal ba bzang//*

3 On Qing imperial production, see Berger 2003, 55. On Qing multilingualism and multiculturalism, see Hevia 1995; Rawski 1998; Crossley 1999; M. Elliott 2001.

4 See X. Wang 1995; Berger 2003.

5 Ishihama has classified the extant seven thangkas into three major compositional types as a way to account for their similarity and variation; Ishihama 2011, 209. For published images of extant thangkas, see Bruckner 1998.

6 X. Wang 1995, 228.

7 Zhongguo Zangxue yanjiu zhongxin 1995, 264.

8 See De mo 08 Ngag dbang thub bstan 'jigs med rgya mtsho 1811, 269a:2–269b:3; partially cited in Oidtmann 2018, 140. The Eighth Demo *khutugtu* served as a regent in Tibet between 1810 and 1819. For specific occasions in the nineteenth century when the portrait thangka was the object of ritual devotion, see Henss 2001, 6.

9 For a recent study of the Golden Urn, see Oidtmann 2018.

10 Henss 2001, 2–4; Berger 2003, 60; Luo 2005, 539–44; Ishihama 2011, 215–18.

11 R. Jackson 1992, 159.

12 R. Jackson 2019, 219–26.

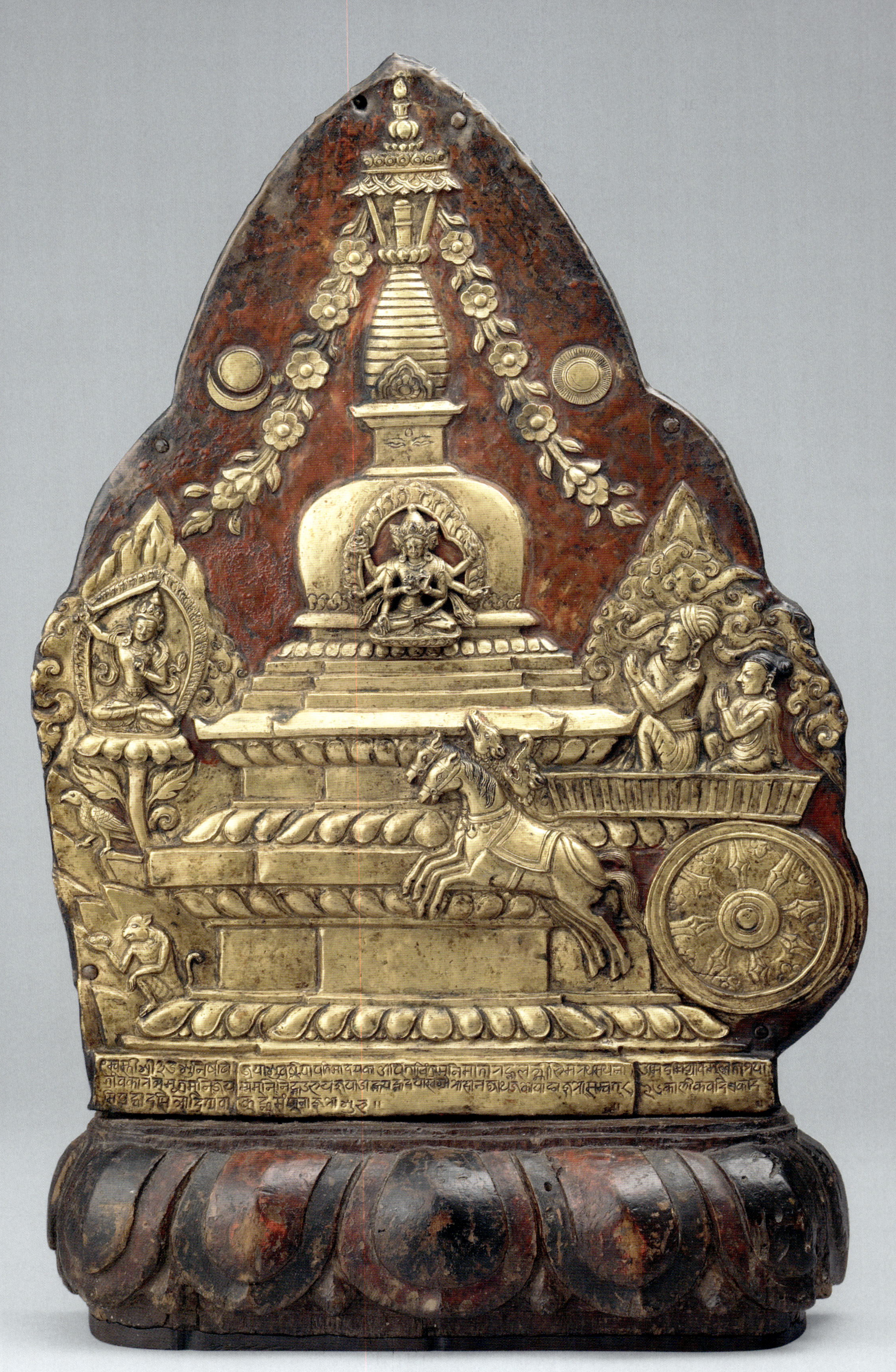

Nº 85

Plaque Commemorating the *Bhimaratha* Old Age Ritual

Kathmandu, Nepal, November 1775

Icons Marking the Communal Performance of Buddhist Rituals

ALEXANDER VON ROSPATT

Commemorative Icons

ICONS IN THE NEPALESE TRADITION OF KATHMANDU, mainly scroll paintings, more rarely metal objects such as the plaque described here, commemorate the performance of a particular ritual. Typically, such objects depict the principal deity to whom the ritual is dedicated and the main scenes of the ritual. Particularly prominent is the commemoration and depiction of the *bhimaratha* ritual, as in the gilded-copper plaque here. This ritual is celebrated when the elder has become seven decades, seven years, seven months, and seven days old. Husbands celebrate this ritual with their wives as a couple, irrespective of their spouses' age. However, women, if widowed or unmarried, celebrate this ritual on their own when they themselves reach this age. The elaborate ceremonies include apotropaic rites of appeasement (*shanti*), ensuring that the elder lives beyond the completion of seven "extended" decades as he (or she) enters (by Nepalese counting) the potentially calamitous eighth decade. At the same time, the ceremonies serve to sacralize and venerate the elder alongside his wife, with whom he is celebrated and mounts the *bhima* chariot (*ratha*) so as to be conveyed around town by his family, just as deities are.[1]

As we learn from the inscription at the bottom of the plaque here, the elders on the chariots are a certain Chintamuni and his wife Ratnalakshmi, coppersmiths from the quarter of Madu (in Kathmandu). The "old age ritual [Newari: *jyatha jako*] of ascending to heaven [*svargarohana*] [when reaching] seventy-seven years" was performed for them by their "two [sons], Amritamuni and Jayadharmamuni," on Sunday, November 11, 1775. The horses pulling the chariot—in ritual practice they are represented in wood or drawings on paper—suggest that it is equated with the sun, whom horses pull across the firmament.

See Relief Carving of a Nine-Deity Ushnishavijaya Composition, no. 41.

See the Svayambhu Chaitya of Kathmandu, no. 4.

The inscription identifies the plaque as a "golden image of the thrice-illustrious Ushnishavijaya," the Buddhist deity of longevity. In accordance with her standard iconography, she is portrayed as eight-armed and multifaced, and set in the dome of a stupa. The stupa here is executed in the likeness of the Svayambhu chaitya, because this is the archetypical stupa in the Nepalese tradition. The point is not to represent Svayambhu per se, but to appropriately render Ushnishavijaya, who is propitiated here as part of the *bhimaratha* ritual to prolong the life of the celebrated elders. However, not only is Svayambhu depicted as a backdrop for Ushnishavijaya, but the artist also took great care to render faithfully the details of the chaitya, particularly its crowning superstructure. For this, he clearly drew upon an architectural drawing (or on a shared source) that had been made on the occasion of the chaitya's renovation some twenty years earlier.[2] Additionally, tied to the mythology of Svayambhu, on the left Manjushri is rendered with his emblematic raised sword and the equally emblematic monkey offering a jackfruit.

Plaque Commemorating the Celebration of the *Bhimaratha* Old Age Ritual; Kathmandu, Nepal; dated by inscription 1775; copper repoussé; 17½ × 11⅛ × 3⅝ in. (44.5 × 28.3 × 9.2 cm); Rubin Museum of Art; Gift of Shelley and Donald Rubin; C2006.66.63 (HAR 700095)

Painted Scrolls Commemorating the *Bhimaratha* Old Age Rituals

The performance of the *bhimaratha* is commemorated most often with painted scrolls (*paubha*). Typically, their iconography accords with the plaque here, but is more complex, and the depiction of the ceremony is more detailed. An exquisite example is a painted scroll from 1830, formerly in the Jucker Collection.[3] Ushnishavijaya is seen in the dome of a chaitya that again resembles Svayambhu. The painter was careful to render the chaitya in its mythological context as resting upon a lotus blossom rising above the waters that once covered the Nepal Valley. The chaitya is flanked by a set of large fearsome (*krodha*) deities

Painted Scroll of *Bhimaratha* Ritual; Hāku Bāhāḥ, Kathmandu, Nepal; dated by inscription January 1830; distemper and gold on cloth; 35 × 23 in. (89 × 58.5 cm); Private collection; photograph by Alexander von Rospatt, December 20, 2003, in home of Mischa Jucker, Basel, Switzerland

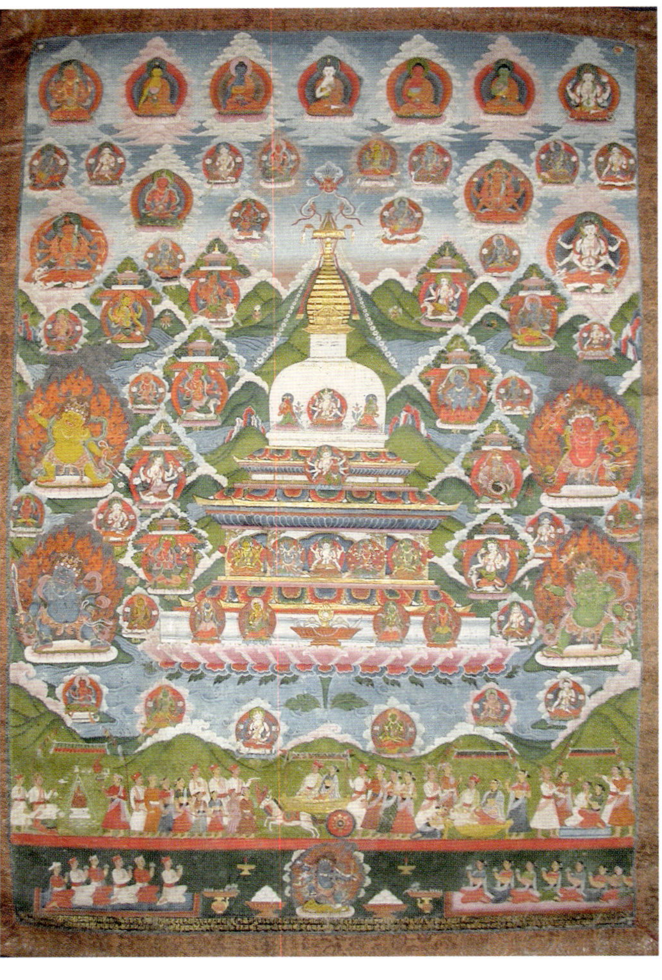

encircling and protecting Ushnishavijaya in the center—on the left, the blue Achala and the yellow Takkiraja, and on the right, red Niladanda and green Mahabala. In addition, the nine planetary deities (*navagraha*) are distributed around the chaitya, at left from the bottom, Aditya, Soma, Mangala, and Budha up to Brihaspati, and at right from the top, Shukra, Sani, Rahu, and Ketu, up to the deity standing for the configuration under which the elder was born (*janman*). They are included because as part of the *bhimaratha* ritual the celebrants propitiate the planets to ward off their potentially malign influences. Folded into their propitiation, the elders also worship the Five Protector Goddesses (*pancharaksha*), who are placed here in the socle of the chaitya.

For other examples of *pancharaksha* goddesses from different traditions, see A *Pancharaksha* Print from Khara-Khoto, no. 32; Dabaojigong Temple, no. 64.

In the register below the chaitya and the attending deities are depicted the main scenes of the *bhimaratha* ritual. First the elders are ritually bathed with blessed waters sprinkled by their sons, assisted by the Vajracharya priest, dressed in white with a reddish shawl draped over his left and adorned with the crown characteristically worn by tantric officiants in the Nepalese Buddhist tradition.[4] The celebrants then mount the chariot or palanquin (*ratha-arohana*) or a throne prepared for the occasion, thereby enacting their deification. They are now worshipped by their children and other kin, who pour water from a conch shell onto their feet (*padargha*) and bow to them with their foreheads. Having been worshipped in this manner, the elders are conveyed around town in carts (*ratha*) pulled by family members, just as deities are conveyed around town on the occasion of their annual chariot *yatra*. On the far left of the register, the family priest can be seen performing the fire ritual (*yagnya*), in which complex tantric rituals are typically embedded in this tradition.

See Vajracharya Priest's Crown, no. 38.

For more on chariot festivals, see Bunga Dya, no. 6.

Below these scenes of the *bhimaratha* ceremony, the family members sponsoring this ritual—that is, the sons and grandsons of the celebrants along with their wives, children, and grandchildren, separated according to gender—are depicted as worshipping a tantric (esoteric) deity, maybe a form of Heruka. The elders are not portrayed here because the ritual is performed for them, and hence they are not treated as sponsors who have instigated and sponsored its performance. Just as in the case of the plaque, at the very bottom a commemorative inscription records the date (January 20, 1830) and the names of the celebrated elders and their kin sponsoring the rite. In addition to the uncounted scroll paintings kept and worshipped by the Buddhists of Kathmandu in their homes, a considerable number of such scroll paintings, some of them magnificently executed, dating back to the eighteenth and nineteenth centuries, survive in art collections around the world.

For a Nepalese depiction of a tantric deity, see Chakrasamvara Mandala with Newar Donors, no. 29.

These icons are not just commemorative objects, but also play an important role in the ceremony they record. That is, alongside the sacralization of the elders they are consecrated in a complex series of tantric rituals so as to imbue them with the presence of Ushnishavijaya and of the other deities depicted. As consecrated icons, they are subsequently kept in a dedicated chamber in the home of the elders, who worship them daily (*nitya puja*) so as so to ensure longevity and ensure a good rebirth, ideally in Sukhavati, the heavenly realm of Buddha Amitabha, where they may proceed effortlessly on their path to Buddhahood.

See Goddess of Prosperity, Vasudhara, no. 34.

See Molded Clay Image (*Tsatsa*) of Amoghapasha, no. 28.

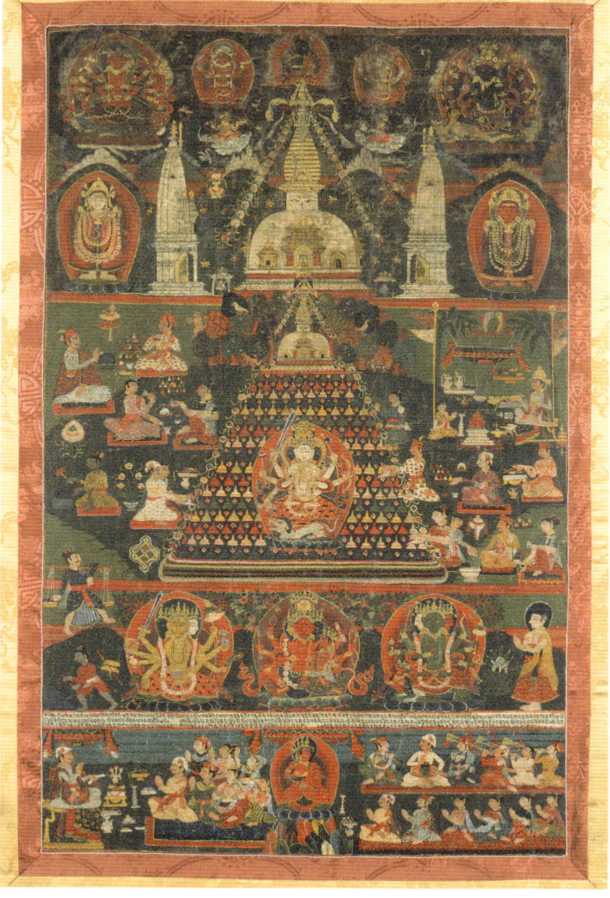

Painted Scroll of *Laksha Chaitya* Ritual; Kathmandu, Nepal; dated by inscription January 1808; opaque watercolor on cotton cloth; 38 × 24 in. (96.5 × 61 cm); Asian Art Museum of San Francisco, The Avery Brundage Collection; B61 D10+; photograph © Asian Art Museum of San Francisco

Icons Commemorating Other Rituals

Such commemorative icons are characteristic of Nepalese Buddhism. Some also record public vow practices (*vrata*) dedicated to Vasudhara, and others record the performance of the so-called *laksha chaitya* ritual devoted to the production of one hundred thousand (*laksha*) miniature clay chaityas, resembling *tsatsa*s in the Tibetan tradition. Collectively performed by a family or local community during the so-called month of virtue (Gunla), which coincides largely with July–August, participants gather each day in the early hours, fasting, to make clay chaityas one inch in height with the help of metal molds. In the process they consecrate the chaityas by inserting a rice grain (or grains) empowered by mantra recitation. Upon the conclusion of the month, all the clay chaityas thus produced are either inserted in the socle of a new chaitya erected at the time, or they are piled up on the riverbank in the shape of a chaitya and worshipped, and then consigned to the waters. Paintings commemorating this ritual typically display a chaitya in the style of Svayambhu with a socle replete with such clay chaityas. One exquisite example records the different steps in the production of the clay chaityas in vignettes distributed around the chaitya in the center, executed in the likeness of Svayambhu placed upon a base made of painted clay chaityas.[5] The top register shows again the Svayambhu chaitya, here flanked by the white and red Lokeshvara of Kathmandu and Bungamati respectively.

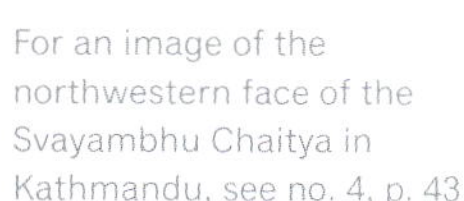

For an image of the northwestern face of the Svayambhu Chaitya in Kathmandu, see no. 4, p. 43.

On Red Lokeshvara and Bungamati, see Bunga Dya, no. 6.

The commemorative plaque and painted icons discussed here attest to the important role rituals and artworks play in Nepalese Buddhism. They also demonstrate how performances of complex rituals can become family affairs, bearing out how in this tradition the practice of Buddhism is a collective endeavor undertaken within society, rather than the quest for the liberation pursued by individual practitioners who have renounced their ties with society.

Further Reading

Huntington, John C., and Dina Bangdel. 2003. *The Circle of Bliss: Buddhist Meditational Art.* Exhibition catalog. Columbus, OH: Columbus Museum of Art; Chicago: Serindia.

Kreijger, Hugo E. 1999. *Kathmandu Valley Painting: The Jucker Collection*. Boston: Shambhala.

Rospatt, Alexander von. 2014b. "Negotiating the Passage beyond a Full Span of Life: Old Age Rituals among the Newars." *South Asia: Journal of South Asian Studies* 37, no. 1, 104–29.

Notes

1 Rospatt 2014b, 104–29.
2 This drawing (19¾ x 26¾ in., or 50.3 x 68 cm) of the Svayambhu chaitya, which records in all details its measurements after the completion of the extensive rebuilding in 1757, has been published as manuscript C in Kölver 1992. See also Rospatt 2011, 157–206.
3 See Kreijger 1999, 82, no. 28.
4 Rospatt 2019, 170–79.
5 See Huntington and Bangdel 2003, 116, cat. no. 20.

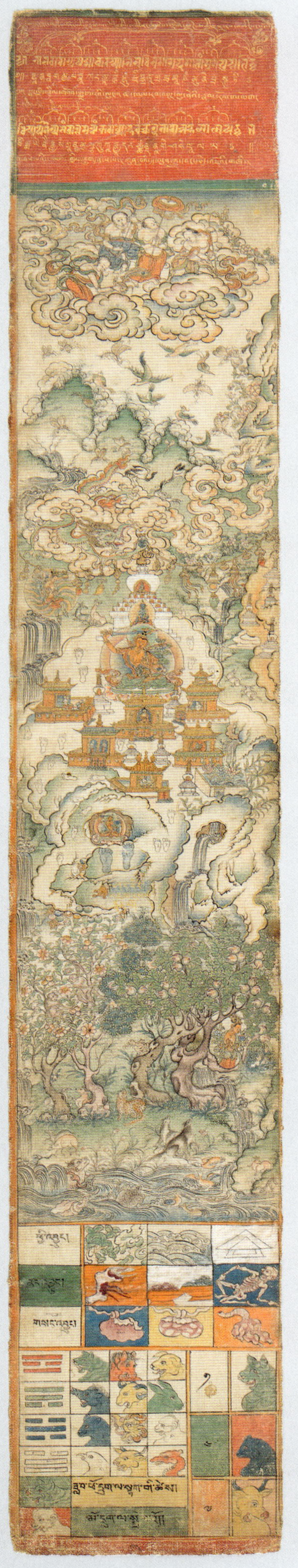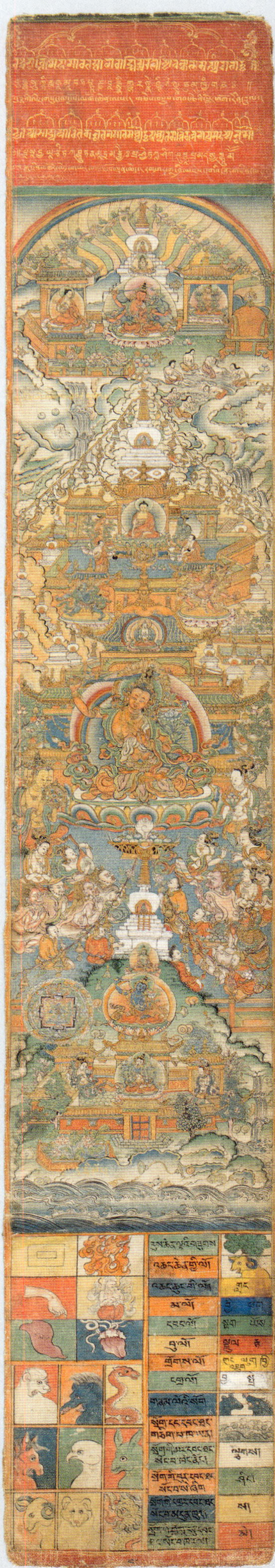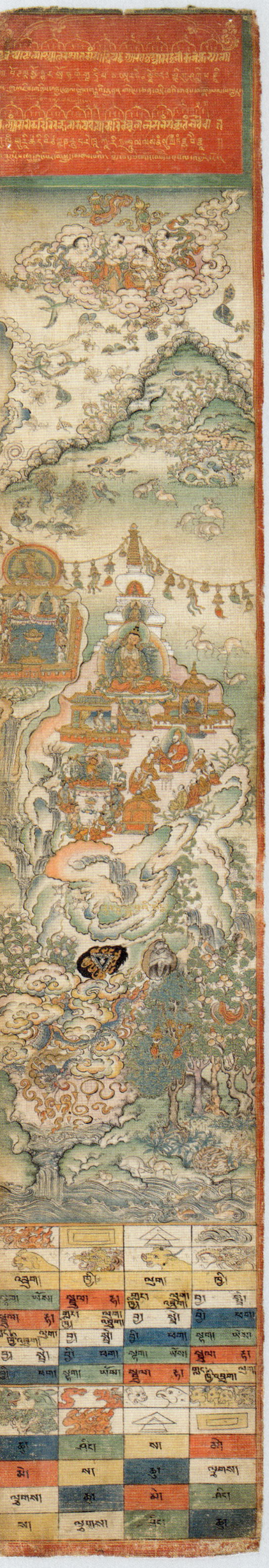

№ 86

The White Beryl Illuminated Manuscript

Sakya Monastery, Tsang region, central Tibet, 18th century

Tibetan Divination

RONIT YOELI-TLALIM

THESE PAINTINGS are illustrations of the seminal text on Tibetan divination, *The White Beryl* (*Vaidurya Karpo*), composed by Sanggye Gyatso (1653–1705). The paintings were commissioned by the Sakya court in the early to mid-eighteenth century and were painted by the Tibetan artist Sonam Peljor. The paintings were prepared to serve as illustrations for the intricate computation of divinations described in *The White Beryl.*

For another example of Tibetan divination, see Nechung Monastery Murals, no. 78.

Divination has played—and still does—a significant role in all levels of Tibetan society. Divinations and various astrological calculations are frequently applied in all parts of life, such as birth, marriage, detecting obstacles, analyzing disease, assessing spiritual progress, and foretelling death. There are various types of auspicious and inauspicious dates, which are marked on every Tibetan calendar, and they are important to know before embarking on significant events or tasks, such as moving to a new house, starting a business, or finding a date for an important event, such as a marriage. The waxing half of Tibetan lunar months is considered in general more auspicious than the waning. Therefore, constructive, positive practices are commonly performed during the first half of the lunar month.

In Tibetan, the term *tsi*, which is usually translated as "astrology," refers to astronomy, time calculation, and divination. Tibetan astral sciences are further divided into what is usually translated as "elemental astrology," or *jungtsi*, and astronomy/astrology, or *kartsi*. *Jungtsi* is also known as Chinese divination, or *naktsi*, which refers to the system of divination based on primary concepts found in Chinese divination: the relationships formed between the five phases (wood, fire, earth, metal, and water) and their various representations, the twelve animal signs (rat, ox, tiger, hare, dragon, snake, horse, sheep, monkey, bird, dog, and pig), the trigrams (*parkha*), and numeric squares (*mewa*).

The corpus of astrological and divinatory sciences is furthermore referred to as *tsuklak,* a term that also denotes the sciences as a whole. The word *tsuklak* covers a broad range of meanings, but most generally it refers to treatises (*shastra*) of techniques, sciences, morality, and the art of governance.

Origins of Tibetan Divination

Tibetan sciences of the stars are derived from several theoretical contexts. One is the *Kalachakra Tantra*, an Indian Buddhist tantra that reached Tibet in the eleventh century and which describes the association between the human body and the external world. In the Kalachakra tradition, integrating astronomical and medical knowledge is perceived as facilitating the flourishing of human potential and attainment of well-being. It focuses on the ways in which celestial bodies correlate with and influence the human body. This in turn is based on two fundamental premises. The first is that both the human body and the cosmos are of the nature of time: they are impermanent, and follow cyclical processes of origination, duration, and destruction. The second is that both the human body and the cosmos are composed of the same particles that make up the elements of earth, fire, water, wind, space, and gnosis.[1]

Sonam Peljor (act. 18th century); Detail of *The White Beryl* Illuminated Manuscript, illustrated edition of Sanggye Gyatso's *The White Beryl*, with three folios showing Manjushri on Mount Wutai; Sakya Monastery, Tsang region, central Tibet; mid-18th century; pigments on cloth and lacquered wood covers; each 23⅞ × 4¼ in. (60.7 × 10.8 cm); Rubin Museum of Art; C2015.7.1–59 (C2015.7.4–.6)

The first two chapters of the *Kalachakra*, dealing respectively with the universe (*lokadhatu* in Sanskrit) and the individual (*adhyatma* in Sanskrit), demonstrate the Buddhist tantric view of the universe as macrocosm and the individual as its microcosm. The *Kalachakra* inquiry into the nature of the external world and the individual applies various disciplines such as Buddhist cosmology, astronomy, time measurement, embryology, physiology, botany, psychology, and pharmacology. The *Kalachakra Tantra* demonstrates the correspondences between the universe and the individual by identifying the

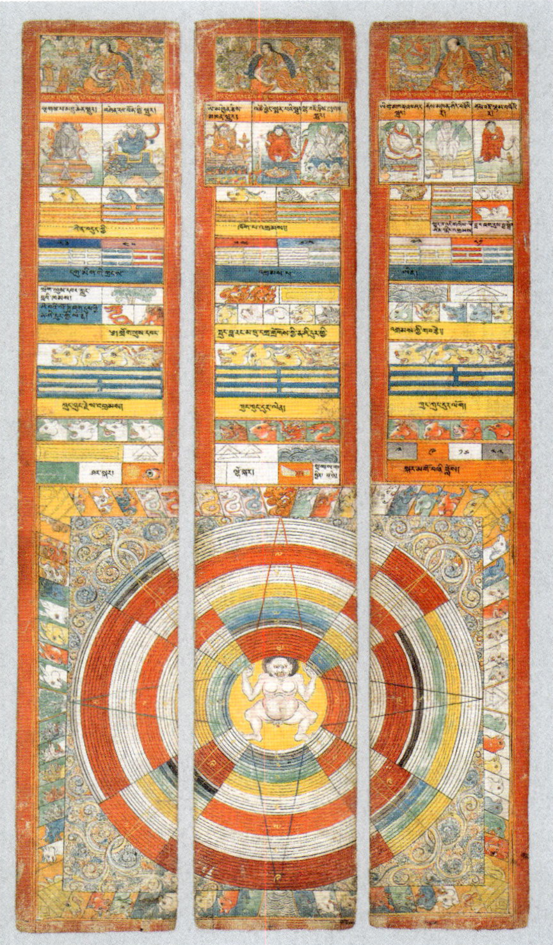

Sonam Peljor (act. 18th century); Detail of *The White Beryl* Illuminated Manuscript, illustrated edition of Sanggye Gyatso's *The White Beryl*, with three folios showing patron and painter; Sakya Monastery, Tsang region, central Tibet; mid-18th century; pigments on cloth and lacquered wood covers; each 23⅞ × 4¼ in. (60.7 × 10.8 cm); Rubin Museum of Art; C2015.7.1–59 (C2015.7.57–.59)

For an object from the Dunhuang cave complex, see Bhaishajyaguru, no. 14.

properties of the external physical universe in the body of the individual. The aim is to provide an analysis of the natural world, which is viewed as an object of purification and ultimately as a manifestation of the Buddha's mind.

In addition to the Indian cultural sphere of influence, Chinese influence on Tibetan divination has also been significant. Tibetan sources often refer to China as the "land of divination." A popular saying in Tibet maintains this connection: "Religious doctrine [*cho*]) came from India and astrology [*tsi*] from China."[2]

The association between China and divination is documented already in the Tibetan Dunhuang manuscripts, which are among the earliest extant Tibetan manuscripts, dating from the ninth and tenth centuries, where we find several Tibetan divination texts referring to Confucius (551–479 BCE) as their author. Tibetan sources also present legendary Chinese accounts regarding the origins of divination. According to these legends, as they are redacted in Tibetan sources, the mythical Chinese emperor Fu Xi saw a gold-colored turtle (*rubel*), which was offered to him by a subject from the coastal region. Upon inspecting it, the patterns of the eight trigrams (*parkha* in Tibetan, *ba gua* in Chinese) first arose in his mind. Consequently, the divination system based on the elemental relationships formed by the eight trigrams, the nine numeric squares (*mewa*), and the twelve-year cycle (*lokor junyi*) were devised, and treatises were gradually composed by kings, ministers, and learned scholars who had mastered these systems.[3]

Adaptation into a Buddhist Context

As it adapted into a Tibetan context, Tibetan divination—as well as its visual representations—underwent a process of "Buddhization." Tibetan Buddhist accounts maintain that medicine as well as astrology were taught by Buddha Shakyamuni, the founder of Buddhism. The astral sciences have been categorized as one of the Buddhist classical sciences, or *rikne*, specifically, one of the five minor sciences (*rikne chungwa*)—along with poetry (*nyenngak*), metrics (*debjor*), lexicography (*ngonjo*), and drama (*dogar*).

It is worth noting that the Tibetan term *rikne*, which is usually translated as "science," also means art, culture, or, more generally, a field of knowledge. As described in the Buddhist Mahayana traditions, the study of these fields of knowledge is essential in the path of the bodhisattva's striving toward omniscience. This omniscience is considered in Buddhist literature both as a means of helping others and a way of knowing oneself.

Tibetan sources distinguish between two strands of Chinese divination teachings: an older strand of Chinese divination (*gyatsi nyingma*) and a more recent one (*gyatsi sarma*), which was propagated from the seventeenth century onward.[4] In the seventeenth century, during the reign of the Fifth Dalai Lama and his regent, Sanggye Gyatso, notions taken from Chinese divination as well as from other traditions were synthesized and fully incorporated into a coherent whole consistent with the Tibetan Buddhist worldview. The manuscript examined here is a product of this strand. Sanggye Gyatso notes, however, that the so-called astrological texts from China in general use in Tibet were in fact not written in China, and in all probability were written by Tibetans. Whatever the case may be, the Tibetan texts are often unique variations of Chinese divination.

On the systemization and codification of knowledge in this period, see Desi Sanggye Gyatso's Medical Paintings, no. 73.

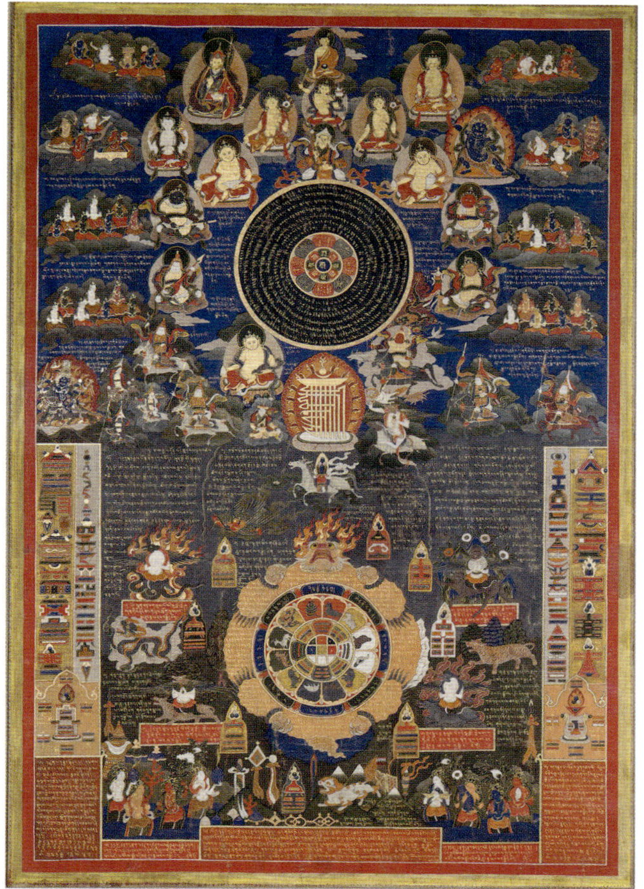

Protective Astrological Chart; Tibet; late 18th or early 19th century; pigments on cloth; 49¼ × 36¼ × 2¼ in. (125.1 × 92.1 × 5.7 cm); Rubin Museum of Art; Gift of Namkha Dorjee/Bodhicitta Art; C2006.71.11 (HAR 65764)

The categories dealt with are, for example, vitality (*sok*), body (*lu*), destiny (*wangtang*), and luck (*lungta*). The vitality aspect is the life essence present in the heart of beings; the body element determines physical health; the destiny element governs personal spheres of influence, wealth, property, food, clothing, and descendants; the luck refers to good fortune and good reputation. Some of these categories are closely linked to various healing practices, and indeed, a close connection between healing and divination practices is observable throughout the history of both. Medicine and astrology have been closely interlinked in Tibet theoretically, practically, and institutionally. Both medicine and astrology have been taught together at medical colleges. To this day, Tibetan doctors are required to study astrology as part of their training. The two main Tibetan medical colleges, in Lhasa and Dharamsala, are both called Mentsikhang (Institute of Medicine and Astrology).[5]

Like Tibetan medicine in general, Tibetan astro-medicine has synthesized elements from a number of different cultures. Yet its vividness seems to be unique. In attempting to explain this vividness, one can perhaps point out the implications of the Buddhist notion of karma. In addition to any deterministic readings into one's constitution, links with particular heavenly bodies, or any other calculation, it is the karmic factor that may alter, in one way or another, a basic proscribed tendency. At the heart of this mode of understanding lies the notion of "auspicious coincidence" (*tendrel*), which is connected to the Buddhist notion of the twelve links of dependent origination (Sanskrit: *pratityasamutpada*) through which past actions influence present and future conditions. Buddhist simultaneous acceptance of medical or astrological determinism, alongside the possibility of humans to alter this given state through positive actions, might be one explanation of the ongoing coexistence of medicine and astrology in Tibetan cultures and Tibetan people's lives. In the context of Tibetan divinations, predictions are not considered to be deterministic, but cautionary and prescriptive.[6] If the outcome is auspicious, no action needs to be taken. If, however, the outcome is negative—cautionary steps are to be taken in order to alleviate the prediction.

Further Reading

Cornu, Philippe. 1997. *Tibetan Astrology*. Boston: Shambhala.

Dorje, Gyurme, trans. 2001. *Tibetan Elemental Divination Paintings: Illuminated Manuscripts from* The White Beryl of Sangs-rgyas rGya-mtsho: *With the Moonbeams Treatise of Lo-chen Dharmaśri*. London: John Eskenazi in association with Sam Fogg.

Kalsang, Jhampa. 1999. *Tibet Astro Science*. Rome: Tibet Domani.

Notes

1 Wallace 2001.
2 Lama Chime Radha Rinpoche 1981, 6–7.
3 G. Dorje 2001, 16; Kelényi 2002, 69–90.
4 G. Dorje 2001, 16–17.
5 Yoeli-Tlalim 2014, 90–104.
6 See G. Dorje 2001, 21.

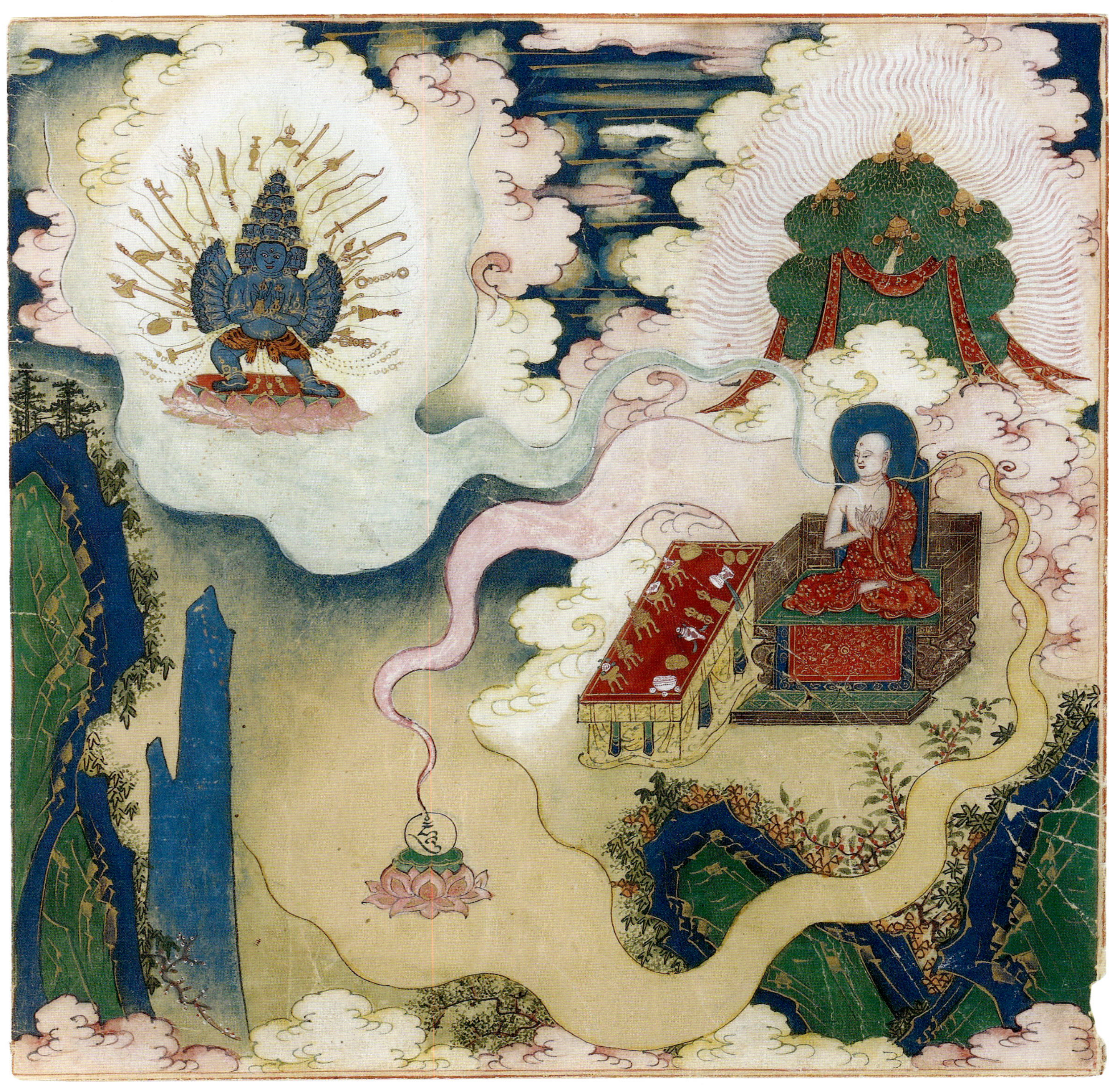

Visualization Practice (*Sadhana*), leaf 10 from the Sarvavid Vairochana Visualization Album; Wangzimiao, Aokhan Banner, Inner Mongolia; ca. late 18th–19th century; pigments on paper; 10⅜ × 10⅝ in. (26.3 × 27 cm); Museum aan de Stroom (MAS), Antwerp, Belgium; AE.1977.0026.13-54; photograph by Bart Huysmans and Michel Wuyts, courtesy Collection City of Antwerp – MAS

№ 87

The All-Knowing Buddha Vairochana Visualization Album

Wangzimiao Temple, Aokhan Banner, Inner Mongolia, ca. 18th–19th century

Cultural Translation of a Tantric Visualization Practice

ELENA PAKHOUTOVA AND KARL DEBRECZENY

USING ONE'S IMAGINATION TO TRANSFORM REALITY, a process known as visualization, is central to Tibetan Buddhist practice. The instructions for this type of meditation are shared by a teacher with a qualified student, and the process is almost never depicted. Yet a set of fifty-four paintings from Inner Mongolia illustrates such a practice, step by step. The paintings constitute a detailed visual guide to an imaginative and secret practice centered on the All-Knowing Buddha (Sanskrit: Sarvavid, Tibetan: Kunrik) Vairochana. The cleverly composed illustrations provide a rare glimpse into a meditative process that occurs only in the mind's eye. The remarkable form of these works, driven by Mongolian patronage, displays layers of cultural conventions, in which the Tibetan Buddhist content is filtered through a Chinese visual translation.

Origin of the Paintings

Aside from a few mantras, the paintings contain no other text, colophons, or identifying inscriptions. Who painted them, where, when, for whom, and even the order of the paintings are not known. In 1923 a Buddhist monk gave the paintings to the Belgian missionary Father Rafael Verbois (1885–1979) at what he referred to as Wangzimiao ("the Prince's Temple"), in eastern Mongolia.[1] It seems the Prince's Temple was a Mongolian monastery called Khoshuun Süme (known in Chinese as Hongcisi) located on Mount Gurban Tulguuri;[2] it was founded in Aokhan Banner, Inner Mongolia, in 1707 by the local Mongolian ruler Jamsu (d. 1708) as a family temple where Mongolian princes of Aokhan went to study Tibetan Buddhism.[3]

During the Qing dynasty (1644–1911), the Manchus—a people from north of the Great Wall—conquered and ruled China. They established Tibetan Buddhism as one of the official religions of the empire, and production of Tibetan Buddhist art flourished at court. The Prince's Temple, situated close to the major Qing art production centers of Beijing, Jehol, and Dolonnuur, was subsidized by the Qing court, and the Aokhan princes intermarried with the Manchu imperial family.

On Dolonnuur artistic production, see Vajrapani, no. 82.

According to local gazetteers, one of the Manchu princesses who married the local prince's son brought artisans from Beijing to Aokhan in 1729.[4] Later, the fifteenth prince, Gombojab (r. 1895–1924), himself a monk known as the lama prince, brought many artisans from Beijing and other areas to renovate the monastery.[5] While these accounts cannot be tied directly to the Album's paintings they suggest possible scenarios for its creation. Given this aristocratic association with the temple and the high quality of the paintings, it is likely the album was made for a prince of Aokhan who studied at the Prince's Temple, to aid his visualization practice.

A Guide to Visualization

Visualization is a process intended to create a different reality using one's imagination. It is a fundamental element of tantra, a system of meditation and ritual meant to transform the mind and body. When focused on a specific deity, such as Vairochana, visualization and related ritual practices are called deity yoga. In deity yoga practitioners contemplate the nature of the mind. Then they gradually imagine themselves as a deity and recite prayers, perform gestures (mudras), and use ritual implements, all of which are depicted in detail in these paintings. Through repetition the practitioners strive to become the enlightened deity they imagine, taking on the qualities the deity represents.

For more about ritual implements, see *Dorje* Discovered by Dorje Lingpa, no. 51; Double-Sided Skull Drum, no. 93.

Vairochana

According to the tantric teachings that developed in India and spread through Asia around the eighth century, Buddha Vairochana signifies the fullest awakening of human potential. This tantric interpretation linked Vairochana to Buddha Shakyamuni's enlightenment, and Vairochana was considered the center of the Buddhist universe. Vairochana has several forms, all of which symbolize his enlightened nature. Embraced by rulers as the embodiment of divine kingship, he was fundamental to the establishment of Buddhism in Tibet. As Sarvavid, he is believed to remove all obstacles to a good rebirth, which is especially important in funerary contexts.[6]

For an example of divine kingship, see Imperial Rock Carvings of Vairochana, no. 13.

The Album's Ritual Narrative

The paintings' original owner would have received an initiation and oral instructions from a qualified teacher before using these images for his visualization practice. The paintings illustrate a ritual from a system of teachings called the *Purification of All Bad Rebirths Tantra* (*Sarvadurgatiparishodana Tantra*).[7] Using the general outline, we distinguish six specific practices.

For more on mandalas, see Chakrasamvara Mandala with Newar Donors, no. 29.

The practitioner begins with the preliminary practices, taking refuge in the Three Jewels of Buddhism—the Buddha, his teachings, and the religious community—generating the wish to become enlightened (*bodhicitta*), and takes vows. He practices visualization with ritual, using implements, reciting mantras, making symbolic offerings, and performing hand gestures. Then he gradually creates the palace, or mandala, of Sarvavid Vairochana, imagining himself as the central deity of this divine realm in the practice of deity yoga. He pictures the deity Trailokyavijaya, the Conqueror of the Three Realms, to remove obstacles to the accomplishment of this practice. He envisions a red lotus with Hum, the seed syllable of the deity, resting on it. He absorbs the syllable into his heart and then manifests himself as the blue wrathful deity Trailokyavijaya. The featured painting, leaf 10, depicts the deity in front of the meditator, in his mind's eye in a typical stance with multiple heads, arms, and legs. An extra, larger set of arrayed implements provides a clearer view of each object. Color-coded, undulating ribbons of light indicate the order of the visualization. This spelled-out rendering of the practice is not the norm in Tibetan painting and suggests the album was made for someone raised outside the Tibetan tradition.

Then the practitioner imagines himself as Sarvavid Vairochana to cultivate the qualities of this buddha. The shift in leaf 17 from a three-quarter to a frontal view implies that the practitioner is assuming the qualities of the deity.[8] He sits on a blue lotus amid a limitless ocean suggestive of "the ocean of suffering," a metaphor for the cyclical existence of death and rebirth known as samsara.

For more on cyclical existence, see Wheel of Existence, no. 97.

Contemplating the Life of a Buddha

Having established himself as Sarvavid Vairochana, the practitioner contemplates the typical life of a buddha, exemplified by the story of Buddha Shakyamuni, the buddha of our time. In this album the unusual depictions of the legendary deeds of the Buddha illustrate two types of enlightenment. Following the non-tantric enlightenment shown in leaf 34, leaf 36 presents the full and complete awakening, according to the texts of the Yogatantras, and visually states the superiority of the tantric enlightenment. A moon disk symbolizing the nature of ultimate reality surmounts an enthroned blue lotus, representative of Vairochana, with rainbow-colored light emanating from it.

For other depictions of the life of the Buddha, see Murals of Gongkar Chode, no. 58; A Monumental Life of the Buddha Mural, no. 69.

The practitioners can also practice Visualizing the Deity in Front of Oneself, imagining Sarvavid's blessings as rays of light liberating all beings from unfortunate rebirths.

The last group of paintings illustrates the Ritual for Deceased and Concluding Rites to purify all negativities of the deceased and ensure a better rebirth. In leaf 53, one visualizes that with this ritual, not only the deceased but all beings are freed from the hell realm and unfortunate rebirths. The light emanating from the Buddha Vairochana's hand bathes the hell realms, releasing the beings who burst out of the gates of hell. A thanksgiving feast concludes the celebrations.

Cultural Translation

The visual language of the album is an interesting blend of Tibetan Buddhist content expressed in a markedly Chinese aesthetic with imagery quite outside the Tibetan tradition. For instance, the square format of the paper is a typical Chinese album form not used by Tibetans. The leaves illustrating the

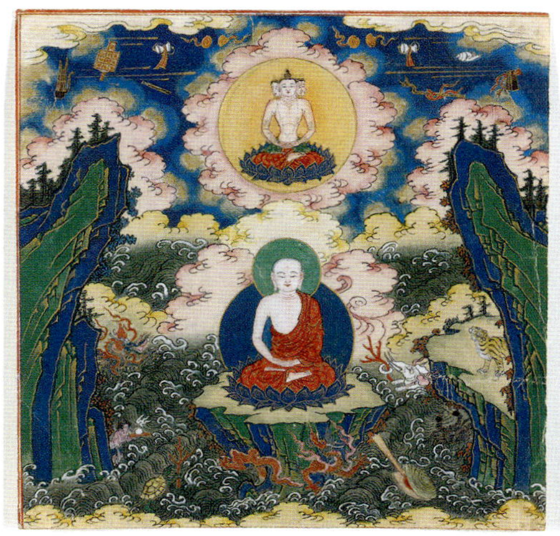

section on Contemplating the Life of the Buddha reimagine him as a Chinese prince, and buildings throughout are modeled on Chinese palace architecture. The stylized green and blue landscape, as well as the distinctive imagery of visionary experience in the form of radiating rainbow light, with pale pink and yellow multicolored clouds, can both be traced to fifteenth-century Chinese models.

Stylistic variations suggest the hands of different artists and indicate production in an atelier. Fundamental mistakes due to unfamiliarity with Tibetan Buddhist content preclude Tibetan artists.[9] Rather, the seemingly ancillary embellishments that indicate multiple cultural references hint at a Chinese identity for the artists. For instance, Daoist-inspired content, including the pairing of tigers and dragons, dragon kings, sages, and heavenly officials, foreign to Tibetan cultural or ritual context, is an indication of Chinese artists falling back on familiar forms.[10] The content of these paintings, however, is clearly Tibetan Buddhist; Daoist-inspired imagery appears as supplemental, a result of an artistic process of convergence, and is not a reflection of religious syncretism often found in Chinese art.[11]

For an example of Buddhist-Daoist religious syncretism, see Dabaojigong Temple, no. 64.

(top) Self-Generation (Imagining Oneself as the Deity), leaf 17 from the Sarvavid Vairochana Visualization Album; Wangzimiao, Aokhan Banner, Inner Mongolia; ca. late 18th–19th century; pigments on paper; 10⅜ × 10⅝ in. (26.3 × 27 cm); Museum aan de Stroom (MAS), Antwerp, Belgium; AE.1977.0026.35-54; photograph by Bart Huysmans and Michel Wuyts, courtesy Collection City of Antwerp – MAS

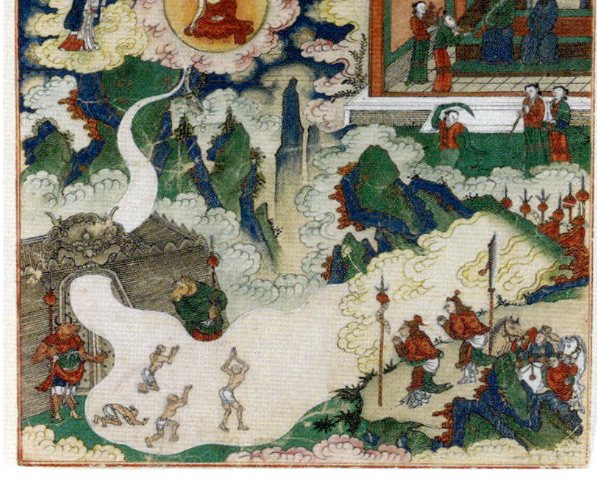

In leaf 17 the artists reveal their cultural and geographic origins in the depiction of aquatic creatures, the crab and clam in particular, not mentioned in the ritual texts. The gray crab with black claws complete with tiny hairs appears to be a detailed image of a hairy crab, and the clam with red flesh is a blood clam, both freshwater delicacies of the Jiangsu area of Zhejiang on the southeast coast of China. Such specific cultural references, so outside Tibetan and Mongolian cultural experiences (neither traditionally includes seafood), are extremely telling, and suggest the artists who created these paintings probably came from this region of China.[12] Painters from Zhejiang were quite famous, often recruited from the north to serve the imperial court.

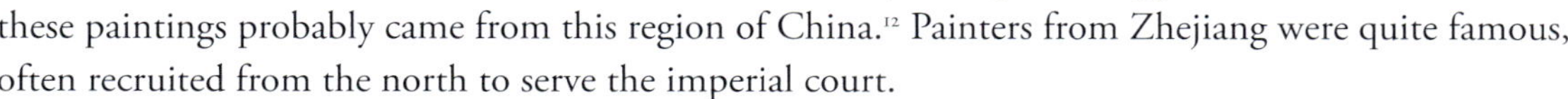

The album's many visual idiosyncrasies, such as the awkward rendering of the Tibetan Buddhist content, would be hard to imagine in the Qianlong period (1735–1796), when such imagery was strictly regulated. It is likely a product of the late eighteenth or early nineteenth century, when many of the patterns related to Tibetan Buddhism established by the Qianlong emperor were still followed, with relaxed imperial scrutiny.

On Qianlong and Tibetan Buddhist art, see The Qianlong Emperor as Manjushri-Chakravartin, no. 84.

Ritual for Deceased and Concluding Rites, Contemplating the Life of a Buddha, leaf 53 from the Sarvavid Vairochana Visualization Album; Wangzimiao, Aokhan Banner, Inner Mongolia; ca. late 18th–19th century; pigments on paper; 10⅜ × 10⅝ in. (26.3 × 27 cm); Museum aan de Stroom (MAS), Antwerp, Belgium; AE.1977.0026.41-54; photograph by Bart Huysmans and Michel Wuyts, courtesy Collection City of Antwerp – MAS

Further Reading

Van Alphen, Jan, ed. 2013. *The All-Knowing Buddha: A Secret Guide*. With essays by Christian Luczanits, Elena Pakhoutova, and Karl Debreczeny. Exhibition catalog. Antwerp: BAI; New York: Rubin Museum of Art. https://issuu.com/rmanyc/docs/all_knowing_buddha_online.

Wayman, Alex, and Ryujun Tajima. 1998. *The Enlightenment of Vairocana*. Delhi: Motilal Banarsidass.

Notes

1. Van Alphen 2013, 7–10.
2. Charleux 2006b, monastery no. 123; Debreczeny 2013a, 166n4.
3. *Aohan wenshi ziliao* 1984–86, 3:85; 1:50–58; 4:29; 4:101–16.
4. *Aohan wenshi ziliao* 1984–86, 4:36–37.
5. *Aohan wenshi ziliao* 1984–86, 4:32–33.
6. For more on Vairochana practices, see Pakhoutova 2013, 39–45.
7. Commonly referred to as Yogatantra, but given a lack of identifying captions, the exact text is unknown.
8. Pakhoutova 2013, 45; depicted in Van Alphen 2013, 80–105.
9. See, for example, Van Alphen 2013, 121.
10. Debreczeny 2013a, 27.
11. Debreczeny 2013a, 30.
12. Debreczeny 2013a, 27.

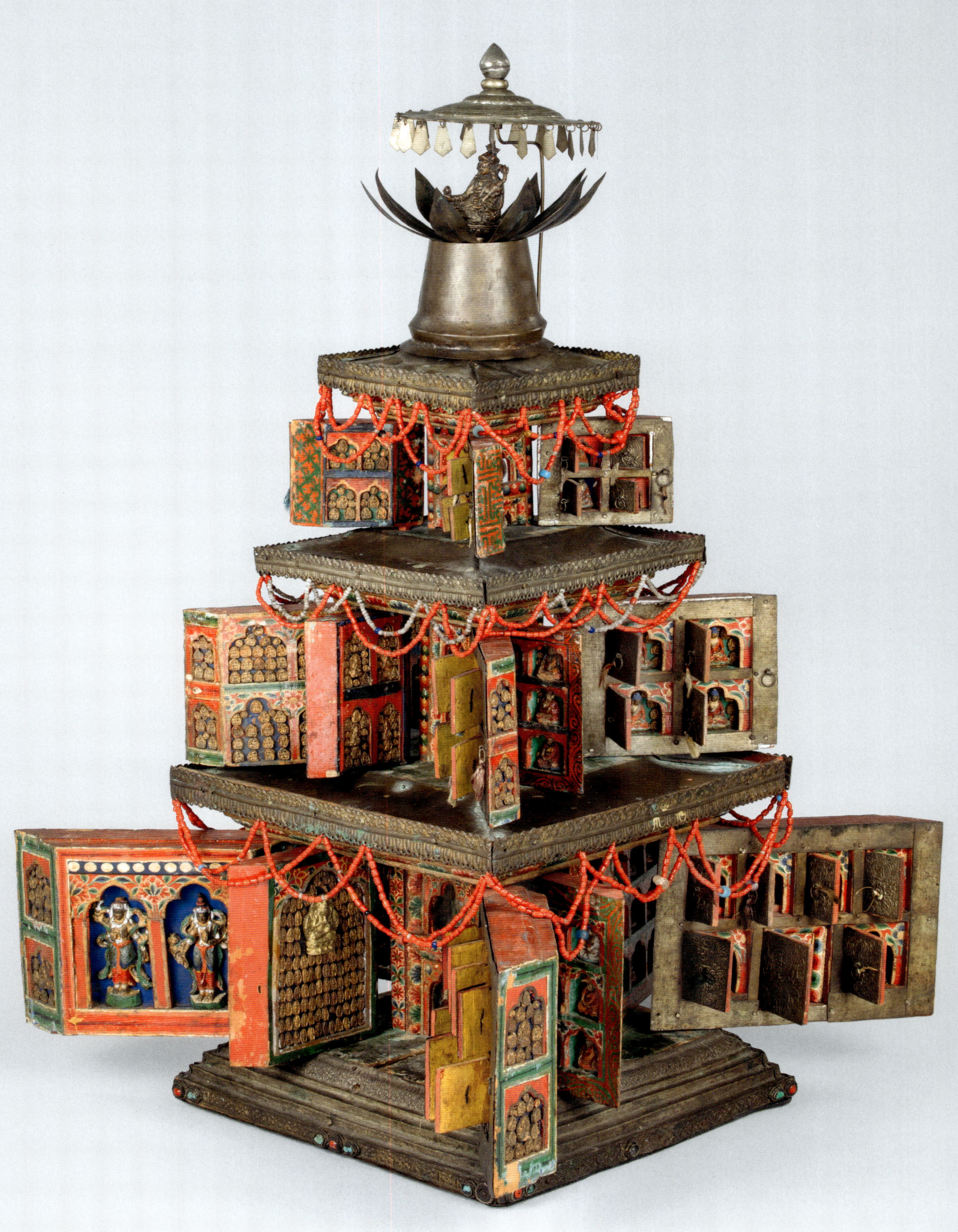

№ 88

Portable Shrine (*Tashi Gomang*)

Bhutan, 18th–19th century

Devotion in Motion, Featuring a National Treasure of Bhutan

THIERRY MATHOU

For more on three-dimensional mandalas, see the Kalachakra Mandala in the Potala Palace, no. 77.

This miniature portable shrine is one of the rare examples of *tashi gomang* to be seen outside Bhutan, where until the mid-1980s this type of three-dimensional mandala was displayed during religious festivals or weekly markets as an instrument of worship.

An Indigenous Bhutanese Tradition with Tibetan Connections

For more about stupas, see the Svayambhu Chaitya of Kathmandu, no. 4. On the life of the Buddha, see Mayadevi Giving Birth to Siddhartha, no. 3; A Monumental Life of the Buddha Mural, no. 69.

See Gyantse Kumbum, no. 55.

In the Vajrayana Buddhist tradition, the term *tashi gomang*—literally meaning "many auspicious doors"— designates the third of the eight types of stupas that present the most important events in the life of the Buddha. Also known as the "one hundred thousand images" (*kumbum*), it commemorates the Buddha's first discourse in Sarnath. It is characterized by a distinctive design: a square structure featuring a three-dimensional mandala with many tiers and multilayered niches crowded with deities. The most significant examples can be found in Tibet, such as the Gyantse Kumbum. Some are relevant to the religious history of Bhutan, as shown by the stupa built in Ralung on the relics of the founder of the Drukpa Kagyu, the dominant Buddhist tradition in Bhutan, which probably inspired Zhabdrung Ngawang Namgyel (1594–1651), the Tibetan Buddhist master who unified Bhutan as a nation-state and who is credited with the fatherhood of the *tashi gomang* tradition in the country. Also relevant to the Bhutanese tradition is the Chung Riwoche Kumbum near Lhatse, Tibet, constructed by Tangtong Gyelpo (1385–1464), a Buddhist master who had a prominent role in the development of this type of stupa and is highly revered in Bhutan.[1]

Tashi gomang stupas are rather rare in Bhutan, where the term designates portable shrines whose design is based on that of the eponymous stupa. These multitiered shrines feature dozens of small doors that open to reveal hundreds of painted images and niches containing statues of deities. They were once carried around by wandering bards, the *manips*, to confer the Buddhist teachings on the masses at public gatherings, especially in remote rural areas. Sometimes designated by other names,[2] depending on the region in the Tibetan world, *manips*—literally, "those who chant prayers"— have roamed the countryside for centuries, but it is only in Bhutan that they carry portable shrines.[3] Although accounts have attested to the presence of this tradition in ancient times in Tibet, it has been gradually replaced by the use of thangkas, as wood is particularly scarce there, while it flourished in Bhutan, where it is considered an indigenous tradition and a component of the local Drukpa Kagyu legacy.[4]

Oral Tradition

Portable Shrine (*Tashi Gomang*) of Padmasambhava's Copper-Colored Mountain Palace; Bhutan; 18th–19th century; painted and gilded wood with sun-dried clay figures, brass roof, coral beads; 30⅛ × 12 × 12 in. (76.5 × 30.5 × 30.5 cm); The Ajana Foundation

In the absence of known ancient written records, oral sources provide an alternative literature about the origin of the *tashi gomang* tradition in Bhutan. Its introduction is attributed to the First Zhabdrung and is related to the building of Punakha Dzong, the second-oldest monastery-fortress in Bhutan, which is considered the mother of all *dzongs* because it was built under his command around 1637 to house the precious relics he brought from Ralung. Also involved was a master carpenter known as Zow Balep, often presented as the incarnation of the divine craftsman Vishvakarma, a Hindu deity, believed to be the presiding god of all architects and craftsmen, who is also venerated by Buddhists, especially in Bhutan, where master builders feel associated with his tradition.

According to the most popular story, the Zhabdrung had started to build Punakha Dzong to

See Padmasambhava and His Manifestations, no. 43.

fulfill a prediction made in the eighth century by the great Buddhist Indian master Padmasambhava, when several magical events happened. While protecting deities helped him to get wood and stones in large quantities, evil forces would demolish at night the structures built during the daytime. While the Zhabdrung was meditating to find a solution, a *dakini* (sky dancer) appeared to him and told him that using a *tashi gomang* was the solution to subdue these forces. He immediately summoned Zow Balep and had him sleep beside him. Through his spiritual powers he brought him into his dreams. On the second night he entrusted protecting deities to take the dreaming consciousness of Zow Balep to Ralung Monastery. On the third night he visited Zangdok Pelri, the Copper-Colored Mountain Palace of Padmasambhava, in order to see the architectural designs of the site. On the morning of the fourth day, the Zhabdrung asked Zow Balep to recount his dream. Based on his descriptions, the Zhabdrung asked the master carpenter to build a replica of the *tashi gomang* stupa he saw in Ralung in a miniature version. Zow Balep first made a prototype from a radish. As the Zhabdrung was satisfied with his skill, he told Zow Balep to carve it in wood. When the structure of the *tashi gomang* was built, the Zhabdrung added his touch. As he was capable of instantly carving Buddhist figures with his thumb, he imprinted several of them on clay molds (*tsatsa*), which were then installed in the miniature shrine. The following day, he summoned painters to decorate the wooden structure. Blacksmiths were also asked to make engravings. A *dorje* was put inside as its major sacred relic. The Zhabdrung personally presided over the consecration of the shrine, which was installed in the *utse* (tower) of Punakha Dzong. Upon completion of the *tashi gomang*, the building of the *dzong* resumed swiftly. Based on this experience, the Zhabdrung thought that *tashi gomangs* could be used as instruments for preaching the teachings of Buddha to the masses. Therefore, he and his successors are believed to have commissioned the making of several other miniature portable shrines.

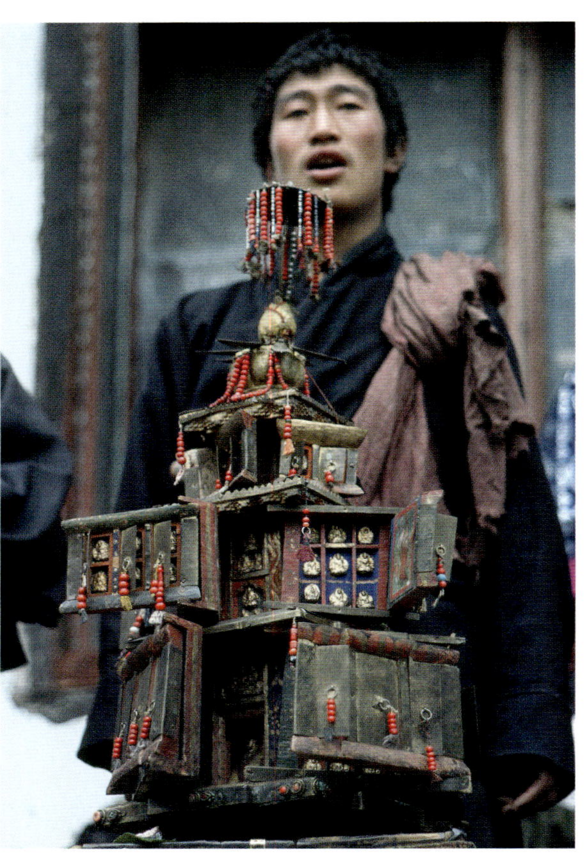

Manip displaying *tashi gomang* during a Buddhist festival; Punakha, Bhutan; 1981; photograph courtesy B&F Shaw Collection

See Molded Clay Image (*Tsatsa*) of Amoghapasha, no. 28.

See *Dorje* Discovered by Dorje Lingpa, no. 51.

Structure and Symbolism

A *tashi gomang* is a mandala involving a complex symbolism. It usually measures between twenty and twenty-four inches in height (fifty and sixty centimeters) and about twelve inches in width (thirty centimeters), and has a maximum of 108 doors. Since the demise of the Zhabdrung political system in 1907, only the king has the power to commission a *tashi gomang*.[5] When not in use, the shrine is stored in a wood transportation box that is often painted and decorated with brass ornaments. It is wrapped in several layers of five-colored brocade. Only the *manip* can unfold the shrine.

He first pulls out its four corners, which causes the *tashi gomang* to open into the shape of a swastika. The shrine is then mounted on top of its box and can be rotated clockwise. With the help of a special stick, the *manip* opens the doors to expose the deities inhabiting the niches and chants the appropriate prayers. He usually raises his left hand to his ear in the classical attitude of divine inspiration, turning his prayer wheel with the other. According to popular belief, the *tashi gomang* is an amalgamation of sacred holy sites (*ne*), brought together by Buddha for the benefit of the people. Looking at a *tashi gomang* is believed to be equivalent to seeing all the *ne*.

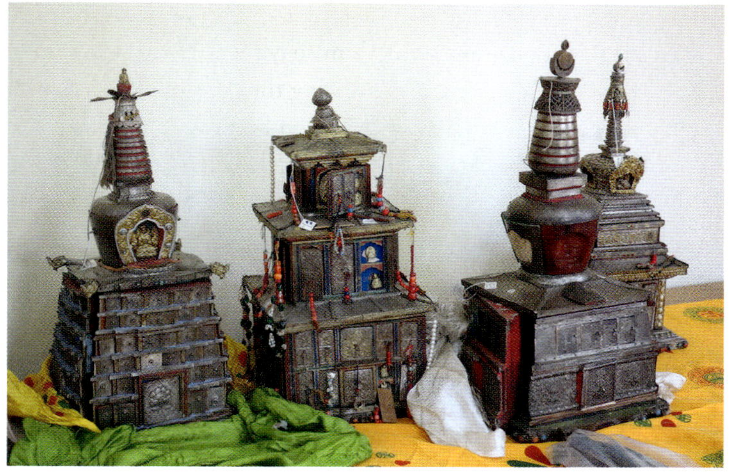

Four types of *tashi gomang*; Thimphu, Bhutan; 2016; photograph by Thierry Mathou

Types of *Tashi Gomang*

There are four types of *tashi gomangs*.[6] Each corresponds to a particular realm in the Buddhist cosmogony. The most popular is the Zangdok Pelri type. The roof of the *tashi gomang* is usually mounted with an ornamental pinnacle. When the shrine is displayed, a lotus flower appears on its top. When pulled with a thread, a figurine pops up in the center of the flower. It often represents Padmasambhava himself. Although *tashi gomangs* are all hardwood, nail-less objects, some are metal plated. They all include a central axis, but their structures may differ. In some cases, a chapel has been carved at the base to house deities. The number of folding panels, doors, clay images, statues, and paintings also varies. The pantheon represented in each type of *tashi gomang* is diverse. Ornamental features such as turquoise and coral beads, painted auspicious symbols, and engraved mantras also constitute elements of differentiation.

Reviving a Vanishing Tradition

The tradition of *manips* carrying *tashi gomangs* throughout the country to display them has declined. Until recently, there were only two surviving professional *manips*, and the number of *tashi gomangs* remaining in Bhutan, where they were kept in secluded places, was unknown. A project was initiated in 2015 to record, conserve, and revive the tradition.[7] Thirty-five *tashi gomangs* were found and brought to Thimphu for restoration and a temporary exhibition. Four young *gomchens* (lay priests) have been trained as *manips*. Now designated as national treasures, *tashi gomangs* are sometimes used by the monastic body to perform rituals on exceptional occasions. Although the display of a *tashi gomang* has become a rarity, it is still considered highly auspicious to have the opportunity to see one. Making one involves no less than nine of the thirteen traditional arts and crafts of Bhutan. A new *tashi gomang* was manufactured in 2015 at the command of the king, signaling the state's intention of reviving the tradition.

For more on traditional crafts of Bhutan, see Maitreya Statue at Jampa Lhakhang, no. 9; Bhutanese Men's Garment, no. 103.

Further Reading

Aris, Michael. 1979. *Bhutan: The Early History of a Himalayan Kingdom*. Warminster: Aris and Phillips.

Phuntsho, Karma. 2013. *The History of Bhutan*. London and Noida Random House.

Wangchuck, Ashi Kesang Choden T., ed. 2016. *Tashi Gomang: A National Treasure of Bhutan*. With contributions by Thierry Mathou, Tshering Tashi, and Lam Kezang Chhoephel. Exhibition catalog. Thimphu Royal Textile Academy.

Notes

1 Gerner 2007.
2 Origin narratives concerning the *manip* tradition, usually called *buchen* (great sons), refer to the great Tangtong Gyelpo, who is considered the founding father of the wandering bards.
3 Tashi Tsering 2011, 79–107.
4 De Montmollin 1992, 606.
5 The Zhabdrung was the head of a theocratic state, wielding both the religious and secular power, at least theoretically.
6 Imaeda and Doffu 1982.
7 Mathou 2016.

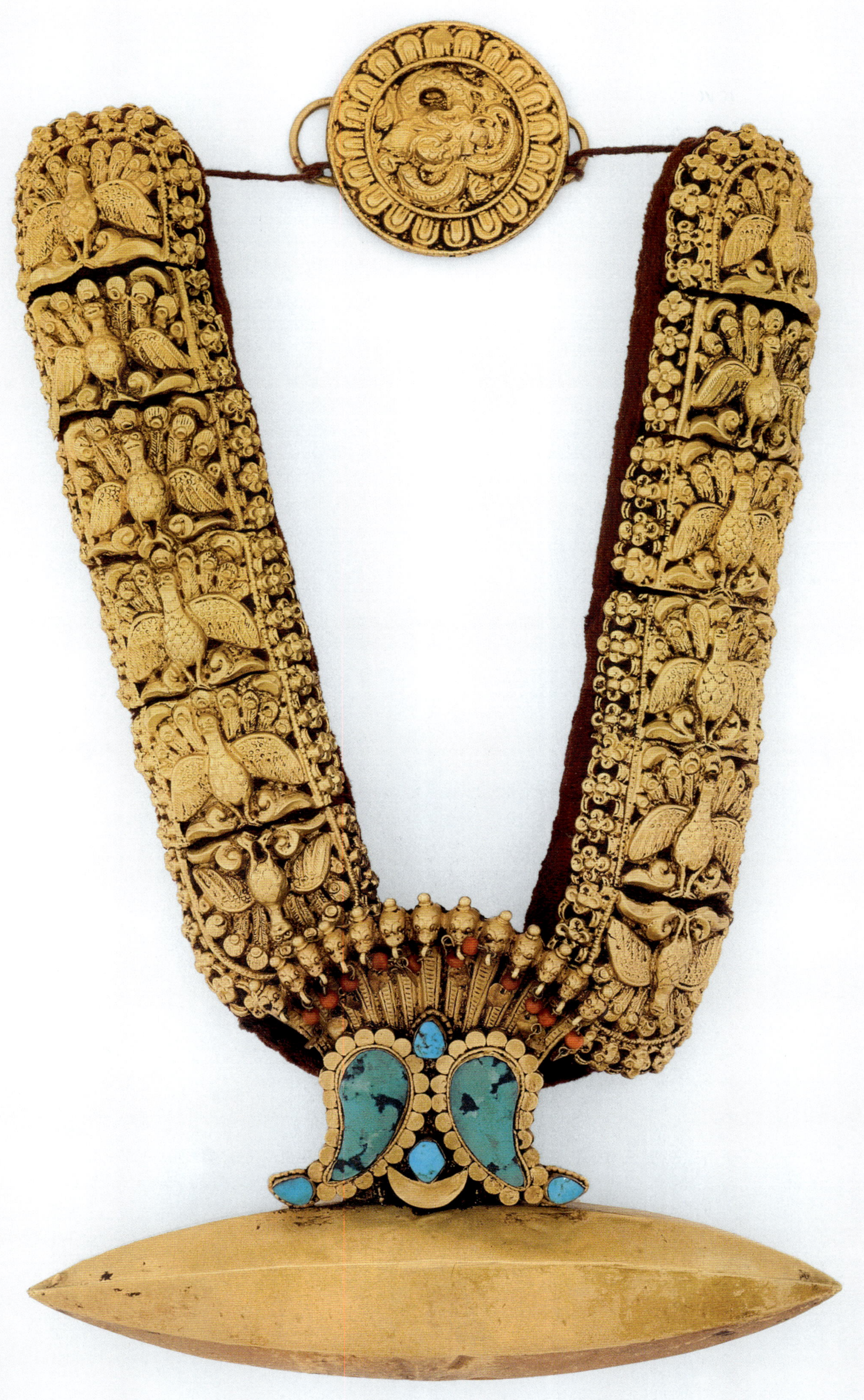

No 89

Tayo-bizakani Ritual Necklace with Naga, Peacock, and Dragon Motifs

Nepal, ca. 19th century

The Multifaceted Power of Ornament

KATHERINE ANNE PAUL

Tayo-bizakani Ritual Necklace with Naga, Peacock, and Dragon Motifs; Nepal; ca. 19th century; mercury gilded repoussé copper alloy with turquoise and coral beads, padded cloth backing; 13½ × 6¾ × 2 in. (34.3 × 17.1 × 5 cm); Los Angeles County Museum of Art; Purchased with funds provided by Camilla Chandler Frost; M.79.242; photograph © Museum Associates/LACMA, www.lacma.org

THIS DISTINCTIVE *tayo-bizakani* necklace is unique to the Newar people of Nepal. Newar forms of worship may embrace both Hindu and Buddhist scriptures, rituals, festivals, and divinities, as is evidenced in the potential special occasions when this necklace may be worn as well as how the symbolism of the necklace is interpreted. In this context, multiple—even divergent—interpretations of the same items should be embraced.

Physical Construction

Multiple hands created and assembled the necklace.[1] Ideally fashioned from high-carat gold, but usually created by fire gilding to a stronger base metal, the hollow hexagonal pendant (reminiscent of a banana) is called a *tayo* in Newari.

Thirteen snake heads (*nagpas* in Newari) are each crowned by a golden gem, while a coral bead dangles below—demonstrating they are guardians of riches.[2] Sheltered by the snakes are two greenish-turquoise pieces inset into inverted tear-drop shapes. Called *paleswan-ha* in Newari, they have been interpreted as lotus leaves or mangoes.[3]

Four smaller, light-blue turquoise pieces are set into individual beaded borders produced by the granulation technique.[4] The gem nestled between the wider portions of the *paleswan-ha* signifies a sacred five equated with five directions, five colors, five gems, and Five Tathagata Buddhas (*pancha-rashmee* in Newari).[5] Another gem is placed between the narrower ends of the *paleswan-ha* above a crescent inset with crystal—a typical sun and crescent moon motif, a feature not present in all *tayo-bizakani* examples.

For more about the repoussé technique, see Plaque Commemorating the *Bhimaratha* Old Age Ritual, no. 85; Vajrapani, no. 82; Pitcher, no. 90.

The necklace support, called *biza* in Newari, is here made of twelve repoussé panels, each displaying a peacock with fanned tail feathers.[6] The two rounded end panels that join the front pendant are inverted to visually connect the floral border. All are sewn to a red-cloth-covered support.

The circular clasp, called *paka* in Newari, features a twenty-petal flower with an undulating single dragon poised in its pericarp.[7] The double-ring fastening allows flexibility in fit—from the neck of a small child to a larger-than-life statue.

Conceptual Construction

The scholar P. Bajracharya describes the symbolism of the necklace in relation to the founding legend of the Kathmandu Valley, citing the famed Newari text *Svayambhu Purana*, in which Bipawsi Buddha planted a lotus seed in the great lake of Nag-daha.[8] The lotus blossom emanated the five colors (*pancha-rashmee*) of the Five Tathagata Buddhas: Vairochana, Akshobhya, Amitabha, Amoghasiddhi, and Ratnasambhava. The bodhisattva Manjushri sliced open a valley to release the lake's waters. The wise Shantikaracharya constructed Svayambhu stupa to enshrine the *pancha-rashmee* of the lotus. While the *tayo* illustrated here is hexagonal (as are many), Bajracharya describes octagonal *tayo* that correlate to the four sides and four corners of the Kathmandu Valley. Furthermore, Bajracharya notes that the *tayo*'s hollow body may contain *ankhe* (five unbroken rice grains to represent the Five Tathagata Buddhas) or Navaratna—nine gems—representing the Five Tathagata Buddhas and the Four Taras (Arya Tara, Saptalochani Tara, Mamaki Tara, and Padhmani Tara) of Svayambhu stupa.[9]

For more on the Five Tathagata Buddhas, see Vajracharya Priest's Crown, no. 38.

See the Svayambhu Chaitya of Kathmandu, no. 4.

For an image of Tara, see Tara Who Protects from the Eight Great Fears, no. 27.

Although the décor of the lappets (the paired sides of the necklace) varies among *tayo-bizakani*, the peacocks featured here have multivalent affiliations. Viewed through a Mahayana Buddhist lens, the peacock is paired with Buddha Amitabha. The peacock is also the animal affiliated with the goddess Kumari (popularly worshipped by Buddhists and Hindus in Nepal through Navadurga celebrations, where Kumari is one of nine goddesses embodied in masked dance festivals).[10] Similarly, the popular Newar deity Kumar (also known as Kartikeya) rides a peacock. The dancing peacock (preening for a mate) is affiliated with love. Finally, peacock feathers are also emblems of Vishnu—particularly in his form as Krishna. All these associations are relevant to the cultural uses of the necklace.

See Vishnu Riding on Garuda, no. 18.

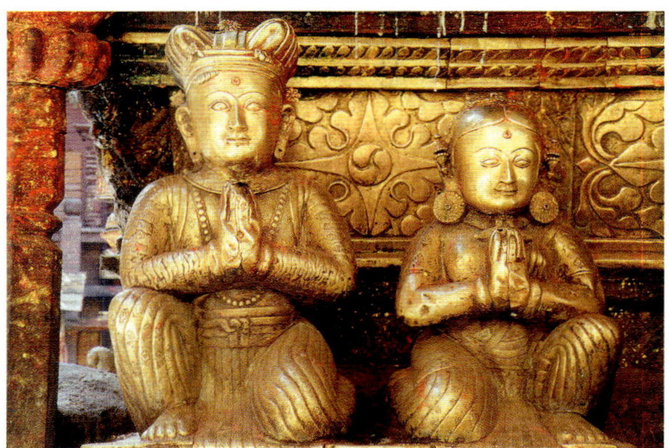

King Bhaskara Deva Varma (12th century) and Woman Donor Wearing *Tayo-bizakani*; 1804; gilt statue; including base, approx. 46 × 36 × 24 in. (117 × 91 × 61 cm); Hiranyavarna Mahavihara, "Golden Temple," Kwa Baha, Patan, Nepal; photograph by CPA Media Pte Ltd/Alamy Stock Photo/2B02XY4

Cultural Constructions

Two broad categories of wearers are adorned with *tayo-bizakani*: people and statuary. Perhaps the most familiar individuals wearing *tayo-bizakani* are the prepubescent girls who are elevated as the living goddess Kumari until their first menstruation.[11] As befits a deity, when appearing in public, Kumari is adorned with many pieces of jewelry, including this distinctive *tayo-bizakani*. This has misled some to title the necklace as a Kumari necklace. But it is only one facet of use for the distinctive necklace. Young Newar girls of appropriate social caste ritually marry the god Vishnu, called Ihi in Newari.[12] Wealthy girl brides wear distinctive hair ornaments, earrings, and necklaces that many include but are not limited to the *tayo-bizakani*. The *tayo-bizakani* may also be worn by the girls to celebrate *barha tayegu*, their first menstruation.[13] Later, *tayo-bizakani* may adorn brides for their marriage to a human bridegroom. When individuals reach the auspicious age of seventy-seven years, seven months, and seven days, both men and women may celebrate with the rite called *jyatha jako* in Newari (*bhimaratha* in Sanskrit) that provides passage to the land of the gods. Women may wear *tayo-bizakani* for this rite, but not men.[14] It is intriguing to think that the portrait statues of a mature donor couple dating to 1804 at Kwa Baha in Patan, in which the woman is portrayed wearing a *tayo-bizakani*, may celebrate the couple's Jya Jhanko.

See Plaque Commemorating the *Bhimaratha* Old Age Ritual, no. 85.

See Central Shrine Image of Kwa Baha, no. 22.

Boys also wear *tayo-bizakani* when dressed to process in public parades for Gai Jatra or Krishna Janashtami. Celebrated in the month of Gunla (August–September), the festival of Gai Jatra commemorates life-giving cows while memorializing recent family deaths.[15] The festival of Krishna Janmashtami honors Krishna's birth (an avatar of Vishnu) on the eighth day of the dark fortnight (Krishna Paksha) in the month of Shraavana or Bhadrapad (around August or September), when boys are adorned as princely Krishna.[16]

In all these celebrations, wearing *tayo-bizakani* marks moments where humans are temporarily spiritually elevated—as the goddess Kumari, to mark the life rite of menstruating, in becoming a bride, as promised access to the gods for the aged, to mourn the dead, and to celebrate life, including a divine birth. The elevation is a complement to employing the *tayo-bizakani* to adorn the divine that is consecrated within statuary.

At least six different divinities consecrated within statuary are documented wearing *tayo-bizakani*. Chandra B. Shakya's excellent study of Buddha Dipankara and the Samyak Mahadan festival in Bhaktapur illustrates that four of the Five Tathagata Buddha images featured in the ritual celebration are adorned with a *tayo-bizakani*.[17] This specificity underscores Bajracharya's discussion of the necklace's affiliation with the Five Tathagata Buddhas. Many examples display *tayo-bizakani* on statues of Buddha Dipankara, when processed in celebration of the Pancha Dan (Five Gifts Festival) celebrated during the month of Gunla (August–September), when Dipankara is worshipped as a previous buddha and patron of merchants and traders.[18] The goddess Vajrayogini embodied in statuary within Sankhu Temple has also been dressed with a *tayo-bizakani*.[19]

In temple sanctums, other deities consecrated within statuary are adorned with *tayo-bizakani*. Bajracharya's own family commissioned an inscribed *tayo-bizakani* in 1939 that beautifies Lokeshvara of Madhypur Thimi, Nepal, and is removed annually when Lokeshvara is ritually bathed.[20] Although not all are photo-documented in his article, Bajracharya lists Rato Macchendranath (Bunga Dya in

See Bunga Dya, no. 6.

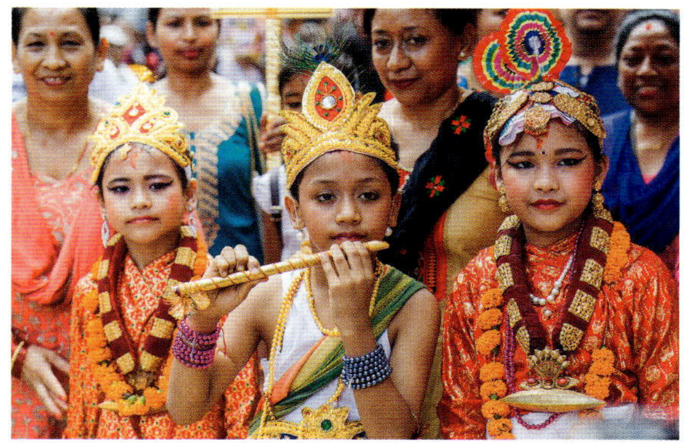

Children Wearing *Tayo-bizakani* for Gai Jatra; Kathmandu, Nepal; August 27, 2018; photograph by Nabaraj Regmi/ Alamy Stock Photo/ PGPHTB

On the ornamentation of consecrated sculpture with jewelry in a Tibetan context, see Jowo Shakyamuni, no. 8.

Newari), Seto Macchendranath, and Mina Nath, as well as the Lokeshvara of the cities of Chobhar, Bhaktapur, Madhypur, and Nala, as all wearing *tayo-bizakani*.

The Newar *tayo-bizakani* may be interpreted as a profound representation of the Kathmandu Valley intended to connect wearers to the significance of this physical and spiritual site. Particularly for important life-cycle celebrations, there are numerous Hindu-Buddhist occasions for which a *tayo-bizakani* may be worn by both girls and women, as well as young boys, ranging from the Ihi divine-marriage ceremony, *barha tayegu* menstruation celebration, weddings, Jya Jhanko marking of significant auspicious age, Gai Jatra cow procession and memorial for the recently deceased, and the birth of Krishna. There are also numerous Hindu-Buddhist occasions when a *tayo-bizakani* adorns a range of deities of both genders in their human and sculptural forms, such as Kumari, Vajrayogini, the Five Tathagata Buddhas, and Dipankara. Particularly for special occasions, when the deities are either formally worshipped in their stationary temples or processed outside, *tayo-bizakani* may be featured. The creation and donation of a *tayo-bizakani,* like other items of ornament and dress, to adorn consecrated statuary may be understood as a merit-making activity for the donors. Dressing the divine is a repeated act that provides multiple opportunities to make slight or great variations in selecting adornments. Re-dressing for ritual viewing at astrologically and liturgically significant times heightens the volume of merit accrued to the donors while simultaneously benefiting all viewers whose ritual viewing (*darshan*) is enhanced through such brilliance.

Further Reading

Gabriel, Hannelore. 1999. *Jewelry of Nepal.* London: Thames and Hudson.

Ghose, Madhuvanti. 2016. *Vanishing Beauty: Asian Jewelry and Ritual Objects from the Barbara and David Kipper Collection.* Exhibition catalog. Chicago: Art Institute of Chicago.

Xu, Xiaodong. 2018. *Xue mo ling long/Jewels of Transcendence: Himalayan and Mongolian Treasures.* Exhibition catalog. [In Chinese with some English.] Hong Kong: Art Museum, Chinese University of Hong Kong.

Notes

1 For a larger discussion of Newar jewelry artists that illustrates the creation in 2000 by Astaman Sakya of a *tayo-bizakani* prior to fire gilding, see Clarke 2004, 60, fig. 42.
2 The number of snake heads may vary in such works but is always an odd number, typically ranging from five to thirteen.
3 For the lotus leaf interpretation and Newari terminology, see Bajracharya 2001, 70. For the mango interpretation, see Pal 1985, 140.
4 For a detailed description of granulation in South Asia, see Untracht 1997, 286–95.
5 Bajracharya 2001, 76.
6 The number of panels may vary. For more about the *biza* term, see Bajracharya 2001, 76.
7 Decorations for the *paka* vary, including motifs like dragons, butterflies, lions, and flowers. Other published examples of *tayo-bizakani* may be found in the Hong Kong collections Chengxuntang (cat. no. 21, pp. 46–47) and Mengdiexuan (cat. nos. 18–19, 44–47), as well as in the collection of the Seattle Art Museum.
8 Bajracharya 2001, 70.
9 Bajracharya 2001, 70.
10 For more about Navadurga masked dances in Nepal, see Vergati 2000, 66–110.
11 For a detailed study of Kumari, see Allen 1996.
12 For more about Ihi, see Vergati 1995, 62–84.
13 Bajracharya 2001, 76.
14 Vajrācārya, Liebman, and Wein 2016, 106–7; Bajracharya 2001, 77.
15 For images of Gai Jatra, see Bajracharya 2001, 77. On Gai Jatra in Nepal, see Anderson 1988, 99–104.
16 For a description of Krishna Janmashtami, see Anderson 1988, 105–11. Gabriel's photograph of a boy Krishna wearing *tayo-bizakani*, Gabriel 1999, 65, is reused in Clarke 2004, 109, and Ghose 2016, 32.
17 C. Shakya 2014, 75–77, provides images of the Buddha from Prasannasil Mahavihara, Chaturbrahma Mahavihara (Balachhe), Mangal Dharmadip Mahavihara (Jhorbahi), and Sukravarna Mahavihara (Kothubahi).
18 For Dipankara worship, see C. Shakya 2014, 76–77; Vergati 2000, 111–21. For Pancha Dan, see Anderson 1988, 80–81.
19 Bajracharya 2001, 77.
20 Bajracharya 2001, 72–75.

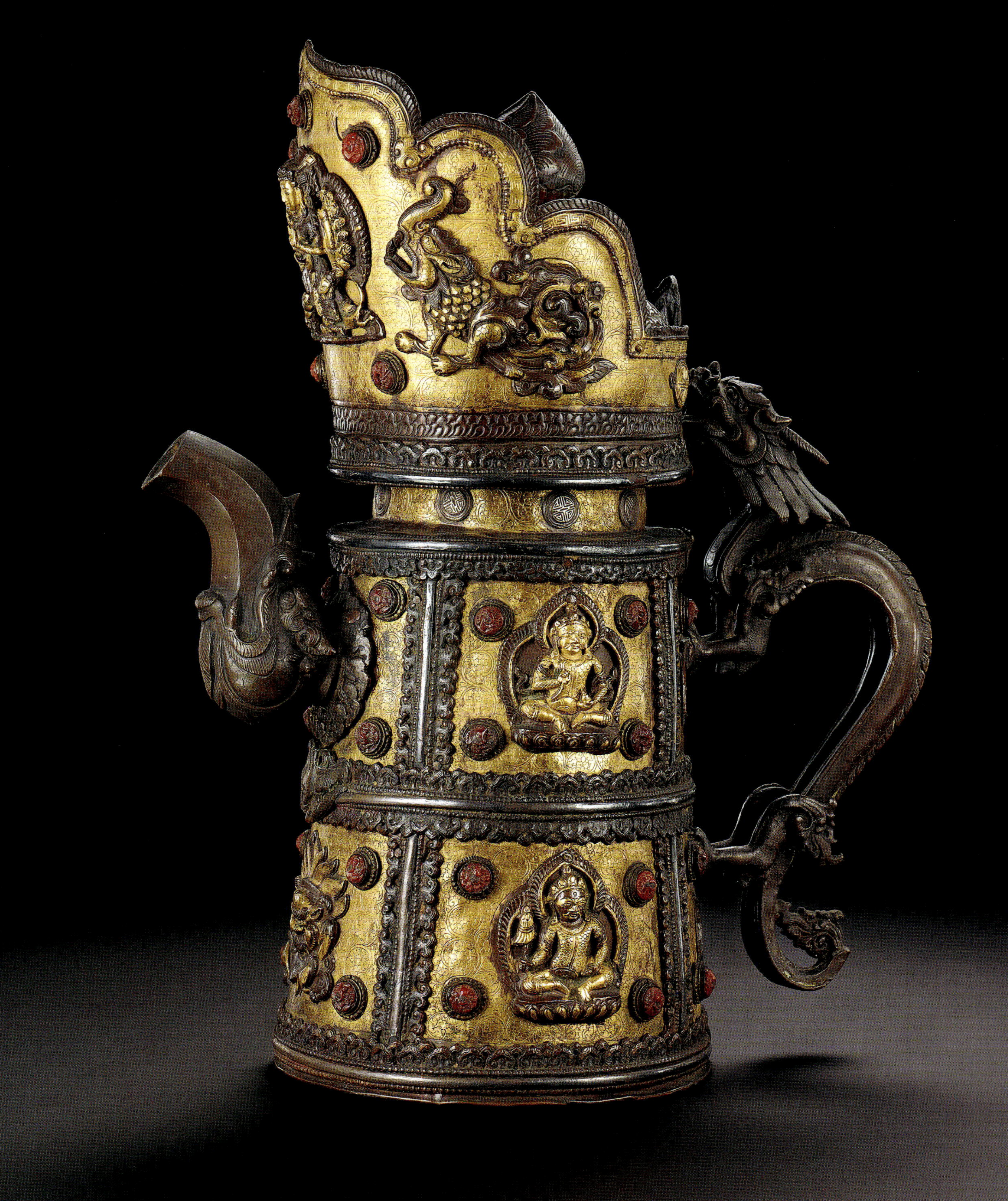

№ 90

Pitcher

Nepal, ca. 19th century

Vessels as Containers of Potential

KATHERINE ANNE PAUL

For paintings of masters with ritual vessels before them, see Portrait of the Ninth Karmapa, no. 66; Nartang Woodblock Prints and Their Painted Copies, no. 81; Portrait of Situ Panchen, no. 83; The Qianlong Emperor as Manjushri-Chakravartin, no. 84; The All-Knowing Buddha Vairochana Visualization Album, no. 87.

For an example of a medical treatise depicting daily life, see Desi Sanggye Gyatso's Medical Paintings, no. 73.

SINGLE VESSELS ARE FRAGMENTS OF GREATER STORIES. Such single objects and suites of ritual vessels feature in paintings as significant components of the ritual invocation of the divine and are status markers of ritual masters. Because of the specificity of their use, single vessels and suites of formal ritual vessels are discussed in Sanskrit, Newari, and Tibetan ritual manuals.[1] By contrast, domestic vessels are rarely seen in other art forms and are hardly mentioned in historic or even modern literature.[2] When vessels are depicted, they appear as small details in murals, on painted furniture, as components of medical treatises, and (more rarely) in thangkas. The dearth of publications featuring contextual images of domestic vessels contrasts with the volume of vessels that exist and are illustrated in recent publications. These vessels, employed in daily use and for special occasions, continue to be produced today. Some of the materials and fabrication techniques of two particular pitcher forms are described here, along with how they function in a wider cultural context and ultimately transform from utilitarian ewers into prestige objects through international diplomatic gifts desired by collectors, historically and currently.

Fabrication

Pitcher with Makara Spout and Dragon Handle Adorned by Durga, Makara, Kirtimukha, and Dikpala; Nepal; ca. 19th century; mercury gilded repoussé copper alloy with carnelian carved beads; 12⅜ × 13¾ × 6¾ in. (31.5 × 35 × 17 cm); Mengdiexuan Collection, Hong Kong; photograph courtesy Mengdiexuan Collection, Hong Kong

Unlike in neighboring regions where large numbers of sunbaked-clay or fired ceramic vessels were produced, throughout the Himalayas, Tibetan Plateau, and Mongolian steppe the primary materials of such vessels were historically leather, wood, and metal. Leather was the most abundant. Both its animal origins and its lack of rarity branded leather as a quotidian material, less suitable as an elite marker unless elaborately painted, tooled, or gilded. In many regions of Tibet and the Mongolian steppes, wood was (and continues to be) relatively scarce. Thus, wooden vessels, frequently adorned with metal, became highly valued.

Carvers hollow wood burls to produce rounded vessels prized for the wood's beauty. The contorted grain of wood burls creates durability beyond straight-growth wood. To compensate for the lack of multidirectional strength, vessels that feature vertical rather than rounded sides are pieced from flat or slightly curved wooden sections that are fastened together, barrel-like, with reed, wood, cloth, or metal bands.[3]

Traditional wooden butter churns retain this long, tubular form, relatively narrow in circumference, that enables the transformation of milk into more stable food products such as butter, ghee, and cheese—vital to contemporary and historic survival among nomadic pastoralists the world over. The significance of the butter-churn form elevates a straight-sided silhouette to one with greater epicurean and social meaning. The originally functional fastening bands have evolved into decorative elements retained in other materials.

Throughout the Himalayas, Tibetan Plateau, and Mongolian steppe, metal vessels are made using pliable metal alloys that have been hammered into sheets and formed around a mold. Called repoussé, this hammering technique can produce smooth surfaces, raised relief, and pierced open work. Metal surfaces may be embellished with incising, true and false damascening, appliquéd metal, and inset stones.[4]

For more on makaras, see Golden Fountain of Bhaktapur, no. 74.

The pitcher shown here showcases an incised scrolling foliate pattern on the vessel's body. Appliquéd plaques feature the goddess Durga with her lion mount, flanked by two makaras (the mythical hybrid elephant-crocodile form that signals the importance of celestial and terrestrial waters). Below Durga is a *kirtimukha* "face-of-glory" (symbolizing celestial waters), surrounded by the *dikpala* (guardians of the four cardinal directions). Appliquéd metal roundels featuring the Chinese character *shou*

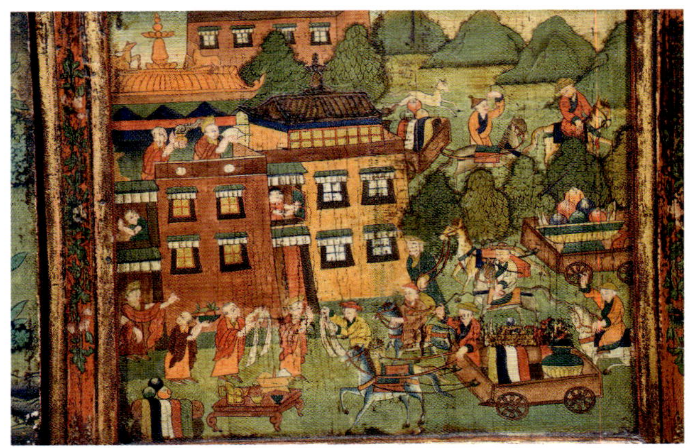

Detail of *pegam* chest showing pitcher and *chemar bo* grain vessel on the central table as greeting offerings; 19th century; colors on wood; Private collection of Jerry Teo and Sandy Song Yan, Singapore; photograph courtesy Spiritual Antique Land, Singapore

(signaling longevity), bands of lotus petals (representing purity), and *ruyi* wish-granting clouds circle the vessel, along with carved and inset carnelian beads.

Fanciful Forms: *Dombo* and *Sengmao hu*

The scalloped flange at its front is a distinctive feature of this pitcher. The front-flange model typically has vertical sides and may lack an applied spout.[5] In Mongolian, this model is called *dombo*.[6] Variations on the *dombo* include both the addition or elimination of either a spout or handle. Spouts may be plain, but if ornamented are typically modeled as makara. The handle may be a decorative dragon, a plain fixed or hinged metal handle, or a flexible chain or cord.[7] These two paintings illustrate rear-flange forms, which here is designated by the Chinese term *sengmao hu* (literally "monk's cap vessel"). It may have a spout or only a pulled lip to narrow the stream. Rear-flange pitchers always feature a handle, which may be modeled as a dragon or foliate shape, or remain unadorned. Rear-flange pitchers may have relatively vertical sides or a swollen, rounded belly.

Both front- and rear-flange forms are sometimes termed monk's cap pitchers. This silhouette references hats worn both by the Nyingma and the Kagyu religious orders, including the *pezha* (a type worn by Padmasambhava and the highest Nyingma hierarchs), *rigdzin chinzha* (worn by Nyingmapa with a ranking of *drubdra, drubla,* or *densa*), and the *zhanak* and *zhamar* (worn respectively by the black- and red-hat religious orders of the Karmapa).[8] How might this model inform its function?

Functions

Popular drinks potentially poured from these pitchers include fermented beverages of a range of beers (*chang*) or liquor (Mongolian: *araki*; Tibetan: *arak*).[9] Historically, unornamented versions of front- and rear-flange pitchers were used on a daily basis. But what were the celebratory occasions when these ornate forms would be employed?

A *pegam* chest displays a rear-flange monk's cap pitcher included as part of a greeting in which Geluk religious order monks (distinguished by their yellow crested hats) exit a building while holding up welcoming *jeldar* scarves and a fruit-filled bowl to greet a group of laymen. The front layman offers a *jeldar* scarf leading a riches-laden carriage. The rear-flange monk's cap pitcher is placed on a table next to the bifurcated *chemar bo* offering vessel.[10] The cart's riches include cloth bolts and vessels filled with coral and ivory, illustrating economic exchanges.

Seasonal celebrations—specific to particular regions—such as New Year (*losar*) and summer festivals are convened when the weather is best and foodstuffs are plentiful. Festivals often include archery, horse racing, gambling, dancing, wrestling, and feasting.[11] For example, the Mongolian Naadam festival showcases summer games and includes brewing *araki* alcohol.[12] The Durga ornament on the front-flange pitcher suggests the vessel featured here would be used for rites specific to Durga, such as the annual festival of Dashain, celebrated by many in Nepal during the lunar months of Aswin or Kartik (corresponding to the solar months of September or October).

Monk's cap pitchers also are employed in worship of fierce deities, like Palden Lhamo. In a painting of Makzor Gyelmo, a monk's cap pitcher is placed next to a blue-footed platter containing white foodstuffs. A wide variety of vessels are included, such as a vaselike pot (*bumpa* or *kalasha*) in the lap of the woman at middle left.[13] Sometimes these pitchers are called "alcohol vessels" (*chang zhi gangpa*). Note that alcohol is preferred by fierce deities, such as Durga and Palden Lhamo.[14]

Transformations

The value of front- and rear-flange domestic pitchers is recognized both by individuals within their originating traditions and by ruling elites of neighboring powers. Both rudimentary and elaborate customized cases nestle these treasures to protect them when stored and encase them for travel.[15] Another

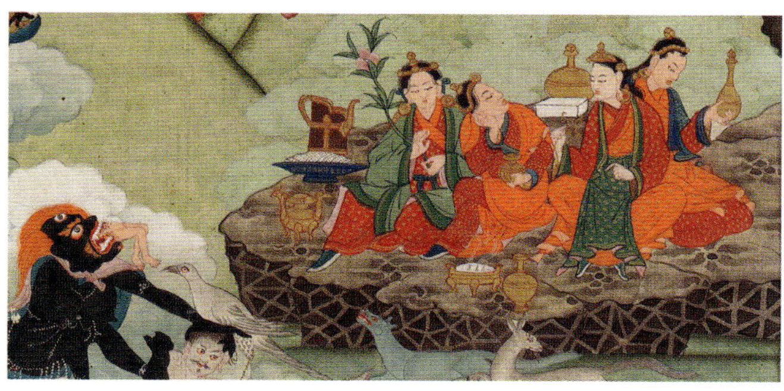

Detail of Makzor Gyelmo, Queen Who Repels Armies, from lower right of painting, showing four ladies with a range of vessels including a two-toned, open-top pitcher with spout and handle; Amdo region, eastern Tibet; 19th century; pigments on cloth; 45⅞ × 27 × ¼ in. (116.5 × 68.6 × .6 cm); Rubin Museum of Art; C2009.7 (HAR 65849)

measure of their value is the transformation of their form into rarified materials not available within the Himalayas, Tibetan Plateau, and Mongolian steppe.

Both front- and rear-flange monk's cap pitchers were created in porcelain, cloisonné, lacquer, and jade in Imperial Chinese workshops.[16] Some were made for use within the Ming and Qing courts of China, while others were intended gifts to elite Tibetans and Mongolians, as was the case with two *dombo* examples, one in gilded silver and the other a Kangxi-period *sancai* (three-color) now in the Tibet Museum, Lhasa.[17] Ming dynasty rear-flange monk's cap pitchers are found in the collection of the former summer palace of the Dalai Lama, Norbulingka, in cloisonné and blue-and-white porcelain.[18] Even if the earliest known forms of this type of vessel remain a mystery, by the Yongle period (1403–1424) rear-flange monk's cap pitchers had gained attention at the highest levels of Imperial China.[19] Farther afield, the Mughal emperor Shah Jahan (r. 1628–1658) so valued a Yongle-period Jingdezhen white porcelain monk's cap pitcher that he incised the work with the date 1053 AH (or 1643–1644 CE), demonstrating the potential of this form as a highly valued collectible—possibly acquired through diplomatic exchanges of gifts. It is intriguing to consider the shared Mongolian ancestry of the Mughals in India and several significant Qing emperors as part of this story.

For more about production in the Yongle court, see Pensive Bodhisattva Avalokiteshvara, no. 53.

Grossly underresearched, historical clues as to the forms and functions of elevated domestic vessels offer tantalizing glimpses into the constantly evolving nature of humanity's development. Celebrations of individual life rites such as birth, marriage, death, and graduations are other moments when front- or rear-flange monk's cap vessels may be employed in Himalayan life, for example for the presentation of "proposal alcohol" (*longchang*). Alternatively, communal occasions like welcoming the New Year, summer tournaments, and even political exchanges at the highest levels may also be appropriate moments to bring forth glorious monk's cap vessels. It is fascinating that this functionality connects the most concrete necessities of survival (such as eating or invoking fierce deities for protection) with the most abstract social aspirations (brokering of interfamilial, interregional, and international relationships) that transcend surviving to signal thriving.

Further Reading

Ghose, Madhuvanti. 2016. *Vanishing Beauty: Asian Jewelry and Ritual Objects from the Barbara and David Kipper Collection.* Exhibition catalog. Chicago: Art Institute of Chicago.

Tsultem, Nyam-Osoryn. 1987. *Dekorativno-prikladnoe iskusstvo Mongolii / Mongolian Arts and Crafts / Arts artisanaux de la Mongolie.* [In Russian, English, French, and Spanish.] Ulaanbaatar: Gosizdatel'stvo.

Xu Xiaodong. 2018. *Xue mo ling long / Jewels of Transcendence: Himalayan and Mongolian Treasures.* Exhibition catalog. [In Chinese with some English.] Hong Kong: Art Museum, Chinese University of Hong Kong.

Notes

1 Tucci 1988a, 116–21.
2 Exceptions include Clarke 1995, 2002, 2011.
3 Reynolds 1999, 71, pl. 22.
4 Clare and Lins 2008, 16–27.
5 Tsultem 1987, cat. nos. 27, 28, 29.
6 Transliterated into Latin script as *duomu* in Xu 2018, 216.
7 For comparable Vietnamese ceramics, see Stevenson, Wood, and Truong 2011, 65–69, 134.
8 Tucci 1988a, 124–25.
9 Avedon 1998, 100–101, fig. 14.
10 https://highpeakspureearth.com/chemar-the-auspicious-offering-of-roasted-barley-and-butter/.
11 *Unveiling Our Sacred Tibetan Treasures*, 20–21; Clarke 2011, 70–71.
12 Tsultem 1986, 161–68.
13 Tucci 1988a, 119, 148, 182.
14 Paul 2019, 159–61.
15 Lee-Kalisch 2006, 459–61; Reynolds 1999, 115, 155.
16 Xu 2018, 216–17, cat. no. 147.
17 Byrd 2003, 248–49.
18 Byrd 2003, 106–7.
19 Watt and Leidy 2005, 35.

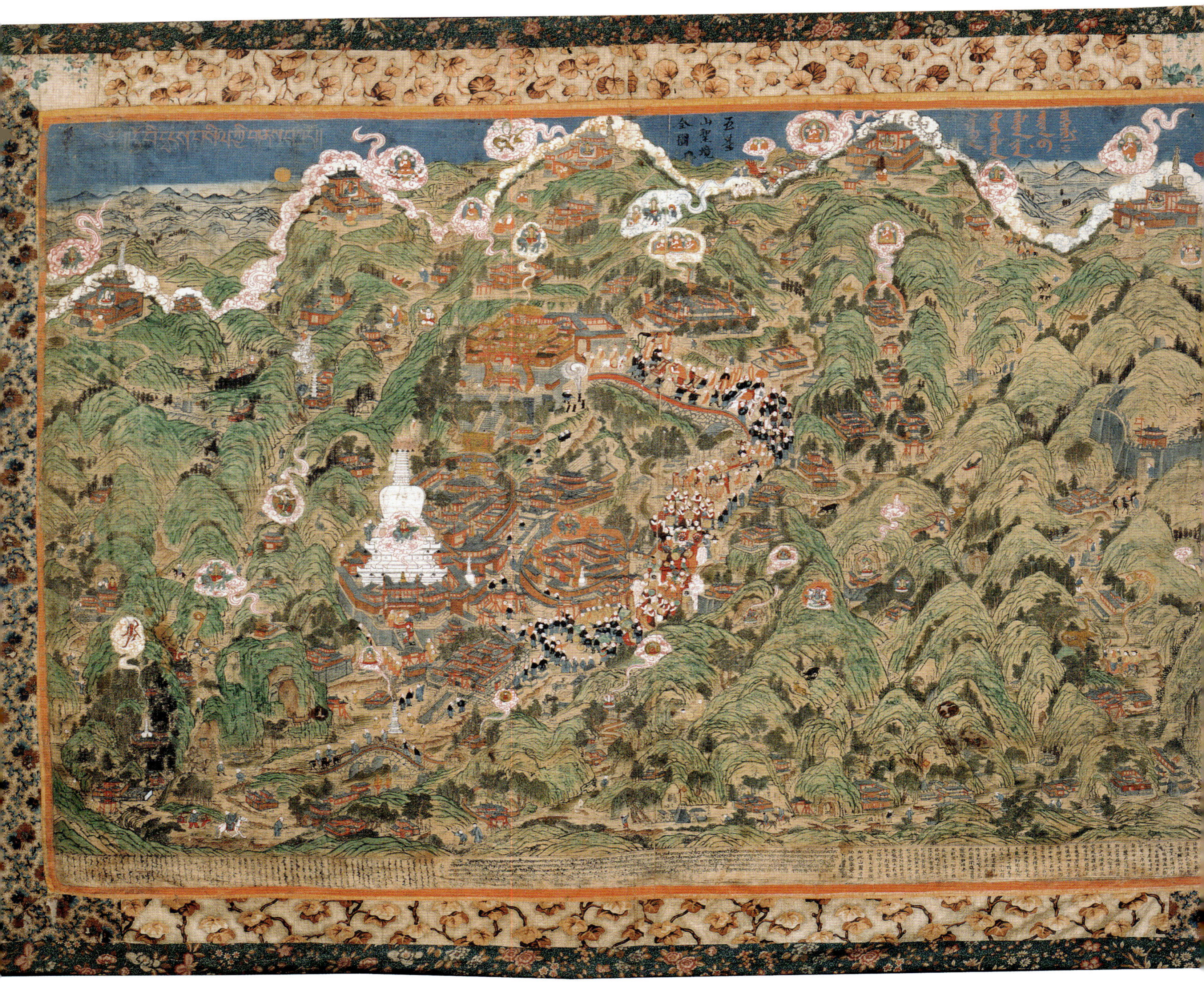

Monk Lhundrub, engraver of Sanggai Aimag (Ulaanbaatar, Mongolia); Panoramic Map of Mount Wutai; Cifu Temple, Mount Wutai, China; 1846; woodblock print on linen, hand colored; 47⅛ × 68 in. (119.7 × 172.7 cm); Rubin Museum of Art, New York; Gift of Deborah Ashencaen; C2004.29.1 (HAR 65371)

No 91

Panoramic Map of Mount Wutai

Cifu Temple, Mount Wutai, China, 1846

Transcultural Visions of a Buddhist Mountain

WEN-SHING CHOU

This panoramic map depicts the sacred Mount Wutai (Wutai Shan, literally the Five-Terraced Mountains) in Shanxi Province in northern China. The map is a six-foot-wide print on linen that has been hand colored. It contains some one hundred and fifty sites in a mountain range filled with travelers, festivities, flora and fauna, and cloud-borne deities. The woodblock panel was carved in 1846 by a Khalkha Mongol lama named Lhundrub at Mount Wutai's Cifu Temple (Benevolent Virtues Temple). The hand-colored print is among numerous examples from the same woodblock panel in collections around the world. A trilingual title, "The Panoramic Picture of the Sacred Realm of the Mountain of Five Terraces" in Tibetan, Chinese, and Mongolian, runs across the top register of the composition, and a trilingual donative inscription at the bottom of the composition details the purpose of the mapping project. The map encapsulates the cosmopolitan reality of Mount Wutai in the nineteenth century as a vibrant center of economic trade and religious devotion for different groups of people in Inner Asia, including Manchus, Tibetans, and Mongols above all. As a depiction of holy landscape and architecture, it bears witness to a millennium-old, pan-Asian practice of picturing the sacred mountain. The map's global circulation attests to the efficacy of the woodblock medium in disseminating knowledge, mediating pilgrimage experience, and redefining sacred geography.

For an early twentieth-century Mongolian representation of sacred landscape and architecture, see Mongolian Map of Capital Yekhe Khüriye, no. 96.

For an earlier example of the use of woodblocks for the dissemination of Buddhist images, see A *Pancharaksha* Print from Khara-Khoto, no. 32. For another instance of Gelukpa woodblock printing, see Nartang Woodblock Prints and Their Painted Copies, no. 81.

Tibetan Buddhism on Mount Wutai

Located in Shanxi Province in northern China, Mount Wutai was recognized as early as the fifth century as the earthly residence of the Bodhisattva of Wisdom Manjushri, one of the most important deities of Mahayana Buddhism.[1] By the early eighth century, Mount Wutai rose to prominence as a center of monastic learning, royal patronage, and Pan-Asian international pilgrimage.[2] Tibetan Buddhism was first established on Mount Wutai during the Yuan dynasty (1271–1368), when Mongol emperors invited Buddhist ritual masters from Tibet to the mountain. Mount Wutai developed into a center of Tibetan Buddhist pilgrimage and monasticism in the Qing dynasty (1644–1911).[3] The early Manchu emperors, who fashioned themselves as kingly emanations of Manjushri, promoted Mount Wutai through the production of mountain gazetteers, imperial tours to the mountain, and patronage of its monasteries. As a result of the Qing support of the Gelukpa monastic order of Tibetan Buddhism, monks and pilgrims from Tibet and Mongolia populated the mountain. Their presence continued in the nineteenth century even as imperial support waned, earning Mount Wutai the appellation "China's Tibet."[4]

For a representation, see The Qianlong Emperor as Manjushri-Chakravartin, no. 84.

On the Gelukpa order of the Dalai Lamas and for an example of Gelukpa topographical painting of famous monasteries, see Potala Palace, no. 71.

Mount Wutai's Tibetan Buddhist transformation is nowhere more evident than in the map in the Rubin Museum collection. The sites and miracles depicted on the map are predominantly associated with the Gelukpa tradition of Tibetan Buddhism through the display of apparitions, such as that of the Gelukpa founder Tsongkhapa on each of the five peaks and elsewhere on the mountain. The yellow-roofed monastery just to the left of the center of the map represents Bodhisattva's Peak (Pusa Ding).[5] As the unchanged center of worship and imperial sponsorship since the Tang dynasty (618–907), Bodhisattva's Peak was extensively renovated into the chief Gelukpa monastery and official imperial establishment (with yellow-glazed tiles) to house Mount Wutai's *jasag* lamas, the highest religious officials of the mountain.[6] The monastery also included an imperial traveling palace (*xinggong*) for the visiting Qing emperors. During the Qianlong reign, Bodhisattva's Peak housed approximately one-third of the three thousand lamas (with Tibetan, Mongol, Manchu, and Chinese ethnic markers) residing at

For more on *tsam* dance, see Ritual Dance Mask of Guru Dorje Drolo, no. 94.

For more on the sister stupa built in Beijing twenty years prior, see White Stupa, no. 40.

Mount Wutai. A Maitreya procession and a masked ritual dance (*tsam*) descend from the Bodhisattva's Peak and wind their way down to the mountain's most prominent landmark of Tibetan Buddhism, the White Stupa. It was first built by the famous Nepalese artist Anige (1245–1306) in 1301 at the behest of the Mongol Yuan emperor Temür (r. 1294–1307). The White Stupa's striking new Himalayan architectural form towered over existing Chinese-style architecture and remains the most iconic monument on the mountain today.

The Practice of Picturing Mount Wutai

For another example of portable models, see Mahabodi Temple Model, no. 25.

For as long as Mount Wutai has been a pilgrimage destination, its pictures and models circulated all over the Buddhist world, serving variously as surrogates, souvenirs, and guides for pilgrims and devotees.[7] The Rubin map descends from a long-standing tradition of imageries combining landscape elements, miraculous apparitions, and the built environment of majestic monasteries and stupas to highlight the numinous quality of Manjushri's earthly abode. The Chinese Central Asian desert oasis of Dunhuang contains a large cache of paintings of and texts on Mount Wutai. Among them, a monumental mural stretching the entire forty-five-foot (fourteen-meter) span of the west wall of a cave shrine (Mogao Cave 61), which was dedicated to Manjushri between 947 and 951, simulates the experience of pilgrimage to the mountain.[8] The Cave 61 mural from Dunhuang and the Rubin map, created more than a thousand years apart and more than a thousand miles from each other, share remarkable similarities. Their composition of a mountain range filled with apparitions, auspicious clouds, prominent temples, stupas, and miraculous sites, their comparable positioning of the terraces (from left to right, following the same order of south, west, central, north, and east) and mountain gates, and their details of tireless travelers all point to an enduring vision of the mountain as the abode of Manjushri's enlightened activities regardless of the changing cultural and sectarian affiliations.

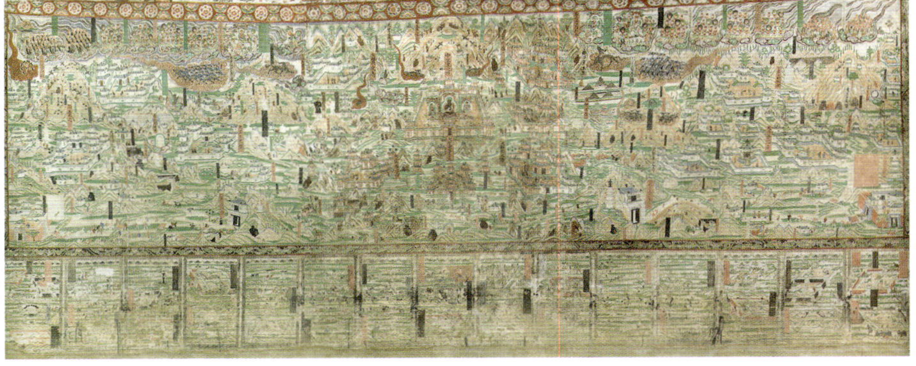

Panoramic View of Mount Wutai; Mogao Cave 61, Dunhuang, northwestern Gansu Province, China; ca. 948; ink and pigments on earthen plaster; 42 ft. 7¾ in. × 11 ft. 9⅝ in. (13 × 3.6 m); photograph courtesy Dunhuang Research Academy

Yet despite these similarities, what makes the Rubin map unique, and its woodblock carvings a particularly widespread source of influence, is that the image was created from the mapmaker's firsthand knowledge of the mountain range, rather than based on earlier pictorial models or textual sources, as scholars believe to have been the case for many images from Dunhuang.[9] From the delineation of the precise number of bays and halls of temples, and the inclusion of otherwise little-known hamlets and villages around the mountain, to the lively and often humorous depictions of popular pilgrimage activities and local legends, elements of the map display an intimate knowledge of Mount Wutai from the unique perspective of the mapmaker that is not seen in any other extant visual or textual materials. The woodblock carver's home monastery of Cifu Temple, built only thirty years before the block panel was carved, is prominently situated just to the right of the central dividing line, in a position that counterbalances Bodhisattva's Peak, the millennium-old locus of pilgrimage and imperial authority at Mount Wutai.[10] In addition, many Daoist (non-Buddhist), Tibetan Buddhist (non-Chinese), and nonreligious sites (out-of-the-way hamlets and villages), which did not appear in Chinese-language mountain gazetteers because of their lack of proper religious affiliation or significance, are included on the map, and each site is carefully labeled with a bilingual inscription in Chinese and Tibetan. The map's inclusive view of the mountain contrasts sharply with purely Buddhist portrayals of the mountain by Buddhist authorities and imperial officials from the outside.

Efficacy of the Map Image

The carver's comprehensive and inclusive approach speaks to the use of the map as a surrogate for the experience of a pilgrimage to the mountain. The trilingual donative inscription on the bottom spells out the efficacy of the map, but differs slightly in the three languages.[11] The Tibetan and Mongolian

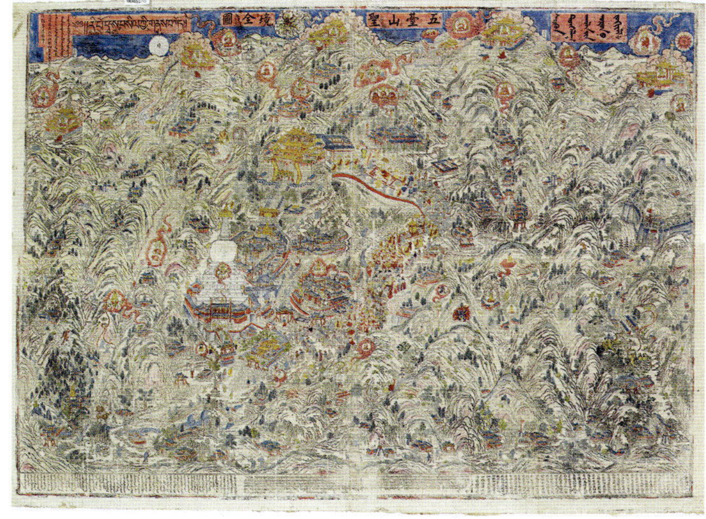

Monk Lhundrub, engraver of Sanggai Aimag (Ulaanbaatar, Mongolia); Panoramic Map of Mount Wutai; Cifu Temple, Wutaishan, China; 1846; woodblock print on linen, hand colored; 47⅛ × 68 in. (119.7 × 172.7 cm); National Museum of Finland, Helsinki, VK4851:95; photograph by Markku Haverinen, Antell Collection, National Museum of Finland

inscriptions, which parallel each other, stress the efficacy of coming into sensory contact with the map through "seeing, hearing, touching, and remembering" as means to receive the bodhisattva's blessing, while the Chinese version elaborates on the benefits from peregrinating the mountain and proliferating the image:

> Benefactors everywhere who make a pilgrimage to the sacred realm of Clear and Cool [alternate name for Mount Wutai], who view this picture of the mountain in order to listen to and recount the numinous efficacy and wondrous Dharma of the bodhisattva, will in this life be free from all calamities and diseases, and enjoy boundless blessings, happiness and longevity. After this life, they will be reborn in a land of fortune. . . . Should a person make the vow to print this image, they will accumulate immeasurable merit.

The map image proliferated just as the inscription had encouraged. While the woodblock panel remained at Cifu Temple until the early part of the twentieth century, prints of it were hand-colored, collected, and sold by artisans, pilgrims, and merchants, and widely circulated around the globe. As many as thirty separate impressions from the same carving and later copies in a variety of mediums present different schemes and styles of coloration, selective highlighting of sites, figures, narratives, and languages, and various modes of display and usage.[12] An impression of the same woodblock panel now in the National Museum of Finland, Helsinki, exemplifies a contrasting afterlife of the carved image.[13] While the Rubin print is mounted with brocades in the format of a thangka painting that was likely hung as an object of veneration, the Helsinki print exhibits multiple traces of creases, indicating that it was folded up for prolonged periods and may have been stored in a pilgrim's amulet box. The difference in the coloration, physical condition, and handling of the maps suggests divergent uses, one as an iconic image of the holy mountain to be venerated as a surrogate of the mountain itself, and the other as a guide for actual pilgrimages. In sum, each act of carving, printing, coloring, framing, copying, and circulating the map image presented a new vision of the mountain. The collaborative and accretive process of mapmaking highlights the roles maps and their makers and users play in Mount Wutai's transcultural place making.

Further Reading

Charleux, Isabelle. 2015. *Nomads on Pilgrimage: Mongols on Wutaishan (China), 1800–1940*. Leiden: Brill.

Chou, Wen-shing. 2018. *Mount Wutai: Visions of a Sacred Buddhist Mountain*. Princeton, NJ: Princeton University Press.

Debreczeny, Karl. 2011. "Wutai Shan: Pilgrimage to Five-Peak Mountain." *Journal of the International Association of Tibetan Studies* 6 (December): 30–39. http://www.thlib.org?tid=T5714.

Notes

1 For Buddhist scriptural justification of Manjushri's presence on Mount Wutai, see Lamotte 1960.
2 See Birnbaum 1986 and 1989; Gimello 1992; D. Stevenson 1996.
3 For more on Mount Wutai in the Qing, see Tuttle and Elverskog 2011; Charleux 2015; Chou 2018.
4 See the imperial stele Qingliangshan ji by the Qing Jiaqing emperor (1760–1820, r. 1796–1820), compiled in Zhou Zhenhua 1998, 81; cited and translated in Charleux 2015, 110. See also Lin Shi-hsuan 2010.
5 Chou 2018, 20.
6 Tuttle 2005, 22.
7 N. Heller 2008; Wong 1993.
8 See W-C Lin 2014, 18; Marchand 1976; Wong 1993; Zhao Shengliang 1995; N. Heller 2008.
9 Su 1951; Zhang Huiming 2000, 1; Cartelli 2012, 180–91.
10 Chou 2018, 153–55.
11 On the trilingual donative inscriptions, see Chou 2018, 156. For their transcription and translation, see Debreczeny 2011, 52–26; Charleux 2015, online appendices, 152–53; Chou 2018, 177.
12 Chou 2018.
13 For more on the comparison, see Chou 2018, 155–64.

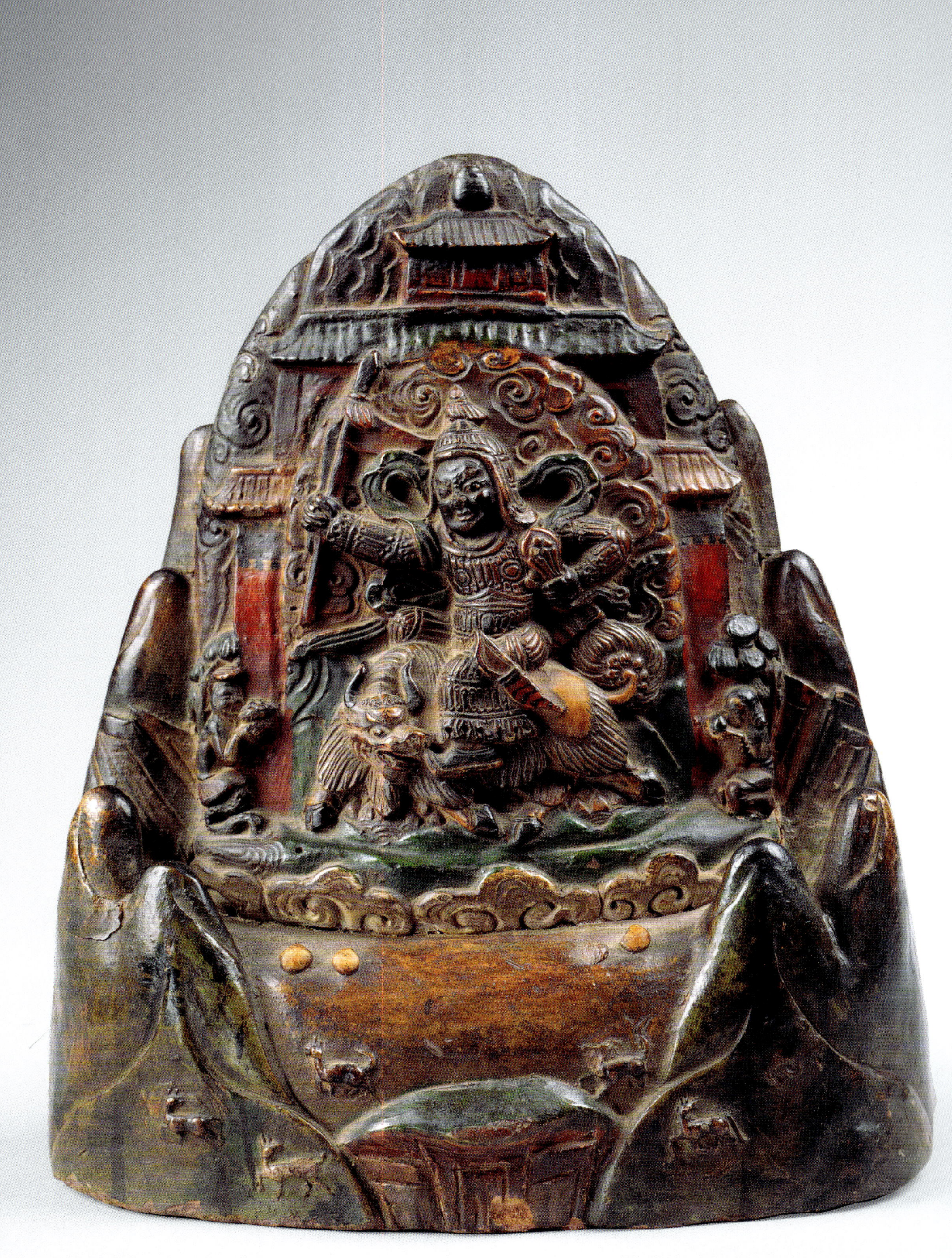

№ 92

Mountain God Kula Khari

Tibet, 19th century

The Mountain Palace of a Worldly Divinity

CHARLES RAMBLE

Mountain God Kula Khari; Tibet; 19th century; painted terracotta; 9⅞ × 8¼ × 4⅝ in. (25.1 × 21 × 11.7 cm); Rubin Museum of Art; C2002.7.3 (HAR 65079)

Portable Places

Mount kula khari stands just north of the border between Bhutan and Tibet, rising above surrounding peaks to a majestic 24,731 feet (7,538 meters) above sea level. The sculpture featured here would have been set on the altar of a shrine room in a private house, or perhaps in a temple. Such replicas of natural sites are widespread in Tibetan Buddhism: an image of another such sculpture, which appears on the following page, represents Mount Gaurishankar.[1]

For a portable representation of a sacred site, see Mahabodhi Temple Model, no. 25.

Portable representations of sacred sites are well known in other parts of the world, too. During the Liao Empire (907–1125) miniature stone replicas of the stupas at the Eight Great Sites of India were assembled in China as a virtual pilgrimage of the Holy Land of Buddhism.[2] In the Christian world, from late antiquity on, images of Jerusalem's Holy Sepulchre were depicted on metal ampullae containing sacred oil.[3] Tibetans who go on pilgrimage generally return with whatever substances the sites they visit are known for—water from Lake Manasarovar, or small stones from Pretapuri—which they place on their shrines and give to friends and family. These substances are fragments of the place that embody the whole—*pars pro toto*. Miniatures also represent the original, not as fragments but as scaled-down holograms. It is possible to combine the two ideas: scroll paintings (thangkas) of lamas often bear the imprints of their hands or feet; the ampullae decorated with images of the Holy Sepulchre contained sacred oil from the temple; and an image of a mountain may contain earth collected from its vicinity.

For an example of a footprint painting, see Bodhisattva Avalokiteshvara and the Buddha's Footprints, no. 33.

Sacred Places in the Natural World

There is one obvious difference between the Mahabodhi Temple and the Holy Sepulchre on the one hand and Kula Khari on the other: The first two are manmade monuments, while Kula Khari is a natural feature. In fact, natural sites are often considered holy places by Tibetans and form major nodes in the itineraries of pilgrims. Such mountains, known as *neri* in Tibetan, are envisaged as mandalas of the great tantric divinities. They often feature in thangkas and block prints. Examples include Mount Kailash in Tibet, Mount Wutai in China, and Kongpo Bonri, the most sacred mountain for the Bonpos, located in southeastern Tibet. This mountain is seen as a mandala of the Bonpo divinity Tsochok Khagying. Another common candidate for depiction is Zangdok Pelri, the Copper-Colored Mountain of the Buddhist master Padmasambhava: that mountain is located in a mythical land, but certain earthly mountains, notably Mount Dhaulagiri in Nepal, are revered as its terrestrial manifestations.

See Panoramic Map of Mount Wutai, no. 91.

See Bon Deity Trowo Tsochok Khagying, no. 60.

For more on Zangdok Pelri, see Portable Shrine, no. 88.

The main factors that distinguish Kula Khari from these mountains are that it is not the abode of an enlightened divinity, and it is not represented as a mandala. Kula Khari is a mountain god of the kind that are believed to have sworn an oath to protect Buddhism. In the context of the establishment of Buddhism in the country, Tibetan uses the term *dulwa*, which has a wide semantic range analagous to the English "pacify": it may denote the transformation of wilderness into farmland, or the gentle guidance of the ignorant to virtuous ways, or the forceful subjugation of humans or demons that might offer resistance to political or religious expansion. In the dominant conversion narrative, the gods of Tibet were coerced by Padmasambhava into promising to serve the doctrine, and have henceforth been known as *damchen*, "oath-bound." Territorial gods may be the object of two quite different cults: they may be revered for their native power, either as solitary local gods or as members of a group; alternatively—or additionally—they may be venerated as minor Buddhist protectors in the entourage of a tantric divinity.

For more on Padmasambhava, see Monumental Statue of Guru Rinpoche, no. 104; Padmasambhava and His Manifestations, no. 43; Ritual Dance Mask of Guru Dorje Drolo, no. 94.

Icon of the Five Auspicious Long Life Sisters; Bhutan; date unknown; clay; 12⅛ × 12¼ × ⅜ in. (30.8 × 31 × 0.8 cm); Ethnographic Museum at the University of Zurich; 20681; photograph by Tashi Brauen

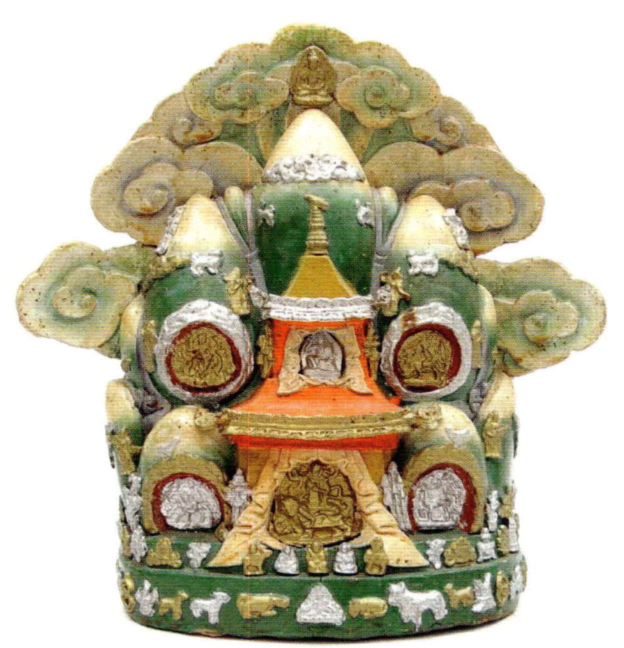

Historically, tantric divinities are projected onto the landscape by lamas who record their visions in pilgrimage guides. These works are both descriptive and prescriptive, presenting the historical and topographical aspects of the place, but also specifying the activities pilgrims should perform there, and explaining how a terrain should be perceived. Seen with such spiritual clarity, a mountain is presented as a stupa or citadel at the center of a mandala with a tantric divinity at its heart, and this vision becomes the dominant scheme for observant Buddhists or Bonpos.[4]

A Mountain without a Mandala

In the case of Kula Khari, this transformation has not taken place. Center stage in the sculpture is occupied by a divinity framed by his mansion, but the mountain is a mountain, not a mandala, and there are natural features such as rocks, clouds, a lake, and meadows with frolicking deer. The following is a paraphrase of part of a prayer to Khari:

> His father was Gangri Gauje, the king of Sheu in Lhoto, and his mother Menchen Pura Changmo. He has the body of a great crystal snow-mountain, with the sun and moon at its peak, clouds swirling around it, and a lake below. Surrounded with a fiery rainbow spitting sparks, he wears a white cloak, white armor, a crystal helmet with white silk pennants. In his right hand he holds a crystal spear, and in his left a receptacle for imprisoning enemies. His mount is a flying horse, with a crystal saddle, golden armor, and a turquoise harness, that takes the form of a crystal yak bestriding earth and sky. He is accompanied by myriad riders wearing quivers and brandishing weapons. His consort is Chammo Shelza (Crystal Lady), who belongs to the *men* class of goddesses. Adorned with jewelry and gold, she holds a conch-shell parasol, and rides a flying *dzo* (yak-cow crossbreed). She sits on a brocade saddle, wearing a white dress like a goddess, with a magical mirror on her head, and she leads a female deer decorated with jewelry.[5]

Descriptions such as these vary. For example, the attributes Khari holds are not always the same, and his consort—who goes by different names—sometimes rides the deer and leads the *dzo*.

Kula Khari was subjugated when Padmasambhava summoned all the powers of Tibet before him at Mount Nyenchen Tanglha, north of Lhasa. One account maintains that Padmasambhava repeated this exercise from a temple that had been built by Emperor Songtsen Gampo (ca. 605–649) in what would later become Bhutan.[6] The Bhutanese saint Pema Lingpa (1450–1521) recounts an episode at a monastery where he was staying in southern Tibet. In this story, he receives a visit from an old man riding a white wolf, who invites him on a journey. Pema Lingpa is borne away to a mansion on the heights of Kula Khari, where the old man reveals that he is none other than the mountain god Khari himself. Pema Lingpa is then invited to the roof of the mansion, from where he is shown various sacred mountains and paradises.[7]

For more on Pema Lingpa, see Tamshing Temple, no. 61.

Kula Khari's association with mountains is explicit in the second part of his name, Khari, "Sky Mountain," and some texts identify him as the southernmost member of a quartet of mountain gods, the others being Yarlha Shampo (east), Nojin Gangzang (west), and Nyenchen Tanglha (north).[8] The first part of his name, Kula, has been the subject of lively debate. The name has two forms, *kulha* and *kubla*, both pronounced indistinguishably as *kula* in modern Tibetan dialects. *Ku* is an honorific term

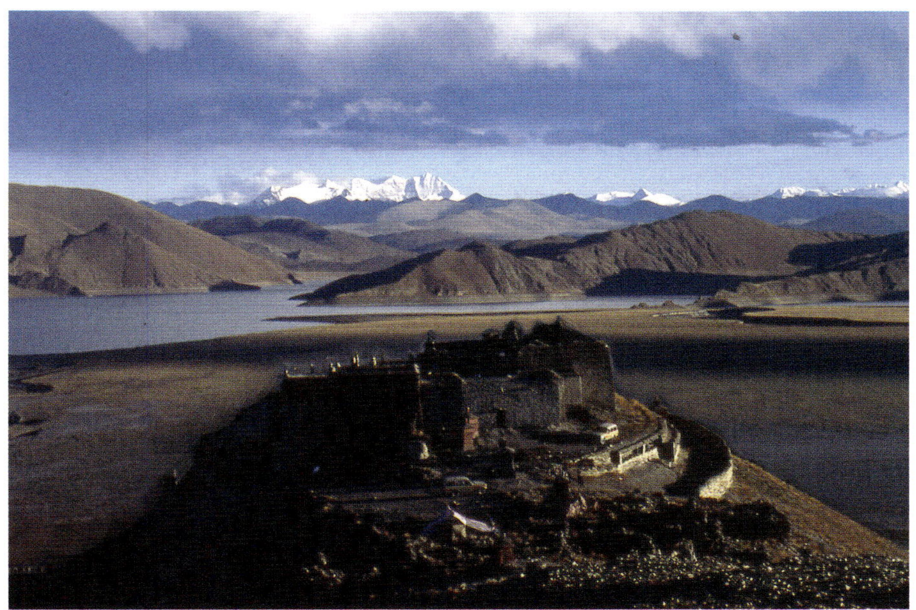

Kula Khari, seen from the north, with Samding Monastery in the foreground and Yamdrok Tso, the "Scorpion Lake," in the middle distance; photograph by Charles Ramble

for "body," while *lha* and *bla* mean respectively "god" and "soul." In early Tibet, the original form of *kubla* may have been *kulha*, but after imperial times the term reverted to *kulha* and acquired a different meaning.[9] The *kubla* had been the divine manifestation of the Tibetan emperor; there was only one (though other realms had their own),[10] and it is uncertain whether there was any association with a specific mountain. In postimperial times, the term *kubla* may have acquired a new form, *gurlha*, the title of a group of thirteen gods.[11] The term *kulha*, corresponding to the usual spelling of Kula, came to be associated with mountain gods. However, the distinction between *gurlha* and *kulha* is blurred in later Tibetan sources: one list of *gurlha* in a Bonpo text includes the name Sheu Kharing, a clear reference to Kula Khari, Shewu being a toponym that is often attached to his name. According to a recent compilation, as Shewu Khari he is also one of the "The Nine Gods of the Coming into Being of the Phenomenal World," composed of the ancient god Wode Gunggyel and his eight sons, and one of twenty-one gods who took lay-follower's vows from Padmasambhava.[12] While invocations to Khari habitually remind him of the oath he swore to protect the doctrine and to destroy its enemies, he is also associated with well-being. Among the people of the Tibet-Bhutan borderland who live in his vicinity, Khari features (as Kubla Gangri) in a group of thirteen gods called the Sipa Lha, who are entreated for benefits such as the mysterious essence of prosperity known as *yang*.[13] This same quality of *yang*, together with its associated property *cha*, is also what is primarily requested from Khari in a Buddhist prayer that is addressed to him.[14]

Further Reading

Hill, Nathan W. 2015. "The *sku bla* Rite in Imperial Tibetan Religion." In "Kingship, Ritual, and Narrative in Tibet and the Surrounding Cultural Area / Royauté, rituel et narration au Tibet et dans l'aire culturelle alentour," special issue, *Cahiers d'Extrême-Asie* 24, 49–58.

Huber, Toni, ed. 2001. *Sacred Spaces and Powerful Spaces in Tibetan Culture.* Dharamsala: Library of Tibetan Works and Archives.

Ramble, Charles. 1997. "The Creation of the Bon Mountain of Kongpo." In *Mandala and Landscape*, edited by Alexander W. Macdonald, 133–232. Delhi: D. K. Printworld.

Notes

1 This image is also on the front cover of Huber 2001.
2 Y. Kim 2017.
3 Boertjes 2014.
4 For a description of the process by which a mountain is transformed into a pilgrimage site, see Ramble 1997.
5 "Mkha' ri'i gsol kha," 1283–86 (paraphrase by the present author).
6 Pommaret 2002, 43.
7 For a more extensive summary of this episode, see Aris 1989, 54–58.
8 Nebesky-Wojkowitz 1975, 203.
9 Bialek 2018, 296–301.
10 For a recent discussion of the cult of the *kula* in imperial Tibet, see Hill 2015.
11 Kvaerne 2021, which also provides a succinct summary of the debate surrounding the *kula* class of divinities.
12 'Jam dpal brtson 'grus 2010, 215.
13 Huber 2020, 1:402.
14 Rdzong gsar mkhyen brtse 02 'jam dbyangs chos kyi blo gros 2012, 511.

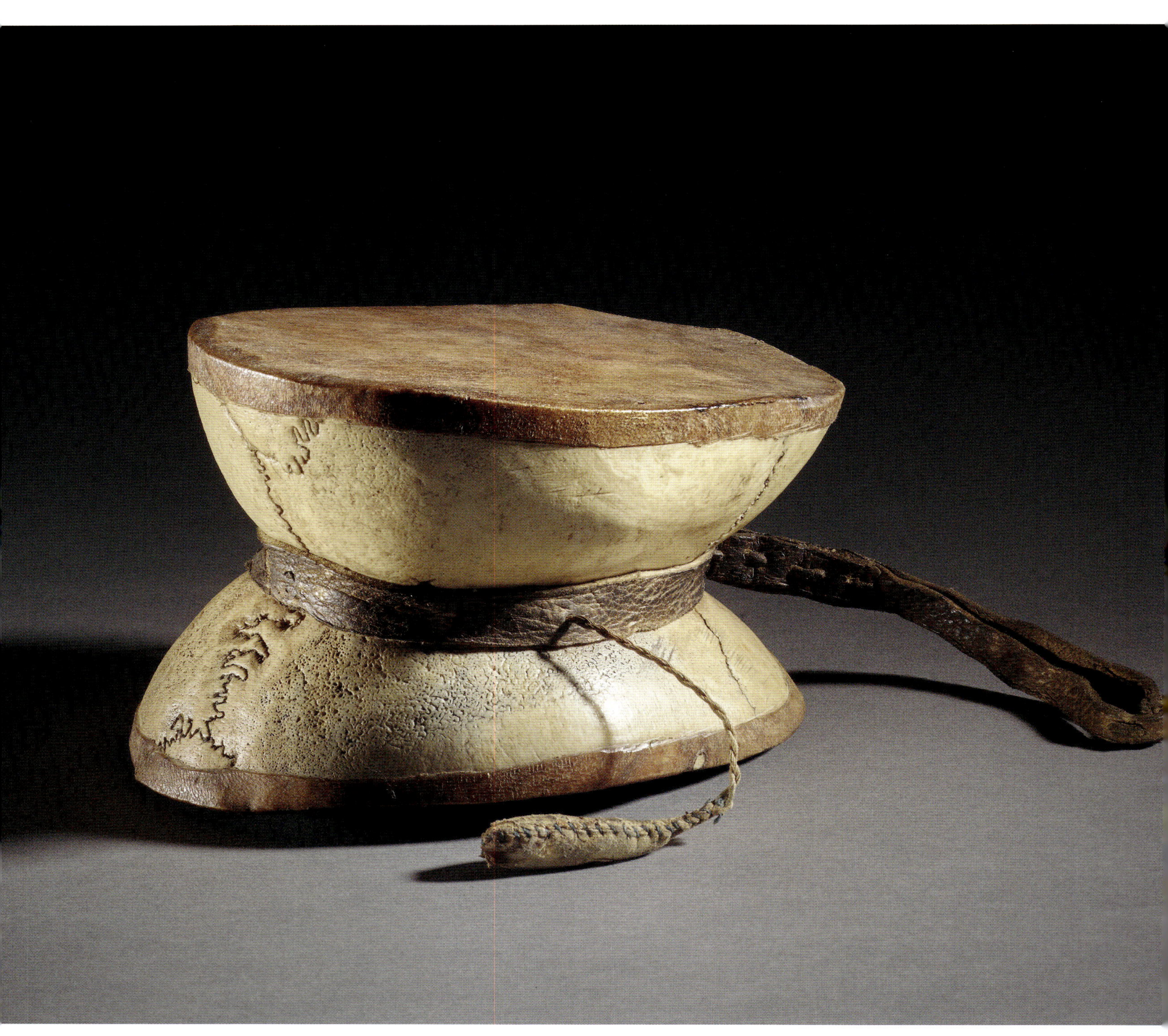

Nº 93

Double-Sided Skull Drum

Tibet, probably 19th century

The Knell of Impermanence

DAVID M. DIVALERIO

A DOUBLE-HEADED PERCUSSION INSTRUMENT fashioned from the tops of human skulls joined at their apexes has been a part of the standard ritual paraphernalia for practitioners of the later forms of tantric Buddhism since the time of their rise in India. The skull drum falls under the broader category of double-sided hand drum, or *damaru*, which are most commonly made of wood, and whose heads may be round or in an elongated shape that approximates that of a skull. These drums may be festooned with ribbons, tassels, bells, and other adornments.

The drum is held in the practitioner's right hand, between the extended index finger and thumb, with the long strap grasped between the palm and the remaining fingers. When held upright and rotated back and forth in a semicircle, the two pellets at the ends of the strings extending from opposite sides of the drum's waist hit the drumheads simultaneously. With just a little practice one can produce a variety of rhythms, or make a continuous sound by quickly spinning the drum back and forth. Meanwhile, the practitioner's left hand remains free to take up other ritual implements, such as a handbell or a rudimentary trumpet fashioned from a human leg bone, as the liturgy may call for.[1]

Human Remains as Ritual Implements

For more on tantric deities, see Chakrasamvara Mandala with Newar Donors, no. 29.

For prominent imagery of skulls (skull crown), see Ritual Dance Mask of Guru Dorje Drolo, no. 94.

To begin to understand why human remains are used in this manner in Tibetan Buddhist ritual, we must consider ourselves from two opposite perspectives, by which our paradoxical standing in the universe is established. For one, these items serve as a reminder of our mortality and the broader impermanence of all things—the central truth of all of Buddhism. At the same time, the items are emblematic of supreme tantric deities, who represent power and enlightenment, and therefore, according to late tantric theory, our own true nature. These buddhas and the members of their retinues are commonly depicted holding musical instruments made of human bone and cups made from skulls, while sporting garlands of heads, bone aprons, and capes made of flayed corpses. These emblems of death are mixed among an imaginative array of menacing weapons and suggestions of sensuality. The frightening adornments serve as analogues to the flowers, jewels, and emblems of royalty that surround Buddhist divinities of a more pacific nature. The presence of these objects as the paraphernalia of these supreme tantric deities speaks to the tantric worldview as a system that sees the inversion of norms as a source of power. Impurity is therefore to be embraced, and in the ancient Indian worldview, death, violence, and sex were the pathways to such impurity. In light of these associations, ritual implements fashioned from human remains play a central role in the Tibetan Buddhist practitioner's cultivation of a multisensory, multidimensional self-identification with the supreme tantric deity—while simultaneously reminding them of her ultimate insubstantiality. Tibetan ritual thinking and practice grows out of a dense matrix of such paradoxes.

Double-Sided Skull Drum; Tibet; probably 19th century; human bone, leather, clappers attached with string; 4½ × 12¼ × 5½ in. (11.3 × 31 × 14 cm); The British Museum; Mrs. Herbert Godsal; 1919,-.473; image

These are far from the only ways of thinking about such objects. For one, there is a tradition of expounding upon the symbolic meaning of the many facets of a ritual implement like the skull drum. One Tibetan author directs the practitioner to understand the empty space inside the skull drum as representing the true nature of all the buddhas and of reality itself (*dharmakaya*), while the skins of the drumheads represent the unity of apparent phenomena and emptiness. The two pellets represent the unification of method and wisdom, which together make liberation possible. Ribbons in five colors hanging from the drum represent the five buddha families. The different sounds produced by the drum are said to represent the emptiness of the self, offerings to the deities, and the subjugation of the different realms

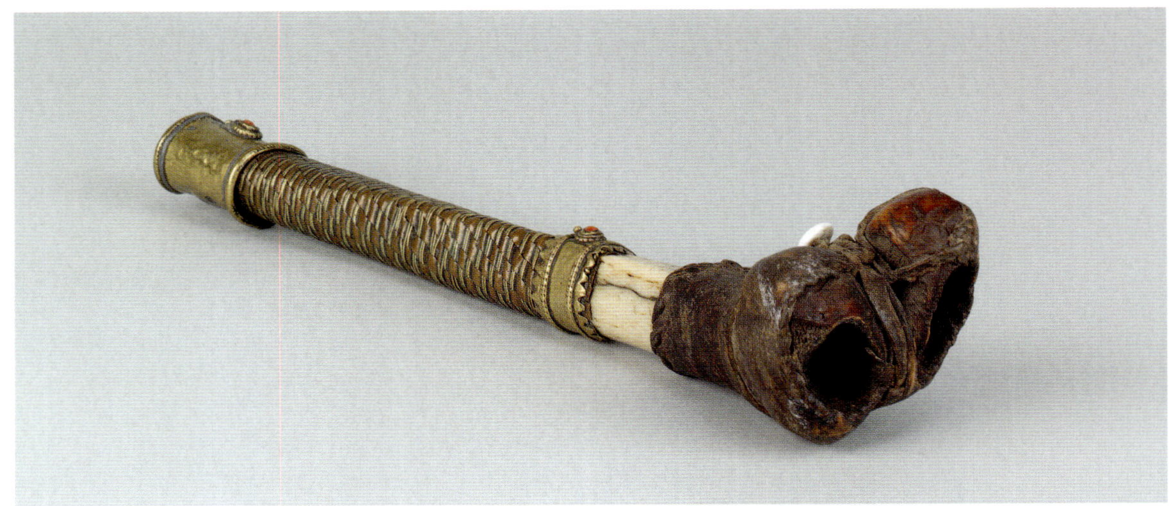

Leg Bone Trumpet (*Kang Ling*); Tibet; 18th–19th century; human bone, copper, coral, leather; 14¼ × 3 × 3½ in. (36.2 × 7.6 × 8.9 cm); Rubin Museum of Art; Gift of Robert and Lois Baylis; SC2019.3.2

of existence, among other things. Meanwhile, it is pointed out that the drum, its user, and the sounds produced all obtain their identities as such only through their dependence upon one another. This kind of interdependence defines all phenomena, which are therefore said to be empty of their own inherent existence. In this strain of native Tibetan interpretation, the object itself becomes a matrix of ritual and philosophical thought.[2]

The Practice of Cutting

The ritual and meditative practice of Cutting (*chod*) exemplifies how these hand drums have traditionally been used, while providing us with a glimpse of the Tibetan religious worldview from which such practices arise. Cutting was first widely propagated by a female Tibetan tantric practitioner known as Machik Labdron (1055–1153), who had received a basal form of the practice from her teacher, the Indian yogin Padampa Sanggye. Since Machik's time, Cutting has proliferated throughout the Tibetan religious world and is today practiced within the Geluk, Kagyu, and Nyingma traditions of Buddhism, as well as in Bon. While sharing much in common with the most elite and secretive forms of tantric practice, Cutting has traditionally been practiced widely in Tibet, by both women and men, clerical and lay, individually or in groups. Although traditional texts prescribe doing Cutting in potentially haunted places like charnel grounds, crossroads, or riverbanks, as part of a demanding ascetic trial, it is more commonly performed at one's home or in a monastery or temple as part of a quotidian cycle of practice. While itself a tantric practice, Cutting is believed to have roots in the ideology of the *Perfection of Wisdom* (*Prajnaparamita*) *Sutra*.[3]

See Illuminated Pages of the *Prajnaparamita Sutra* Manuscript, no. 23.

The practice of Cutting involves the practitioner's chanting or singing a liturgy that details a series of visualizations, while simultaneously generating those visualizations and associated attitudes—and at the same time playing the hand drum, leg bone trumpet, or manipulating other ritual items according to a received script (all done in unison with others, if performed in a group setting). Practitioners of Cutting typically use a particularly large drum with round heads made from acacia wood. Cutting practice begins with playing the drum and thigh bone trumpet, which calls into the meditator's presence malevolent as well as more positive types of spirit beings. The main part of the practice entails visualizing a wrathful tantric goddess as she uses a hooked knife to lop off the top of one's own skull, and then proceeds to chop the rest of one's body to bits, which are held within that skull cup. This mass of one's flesh, bones, and blood is imagined to be purified, and then offered to the different classes of beings who inhabit the universe, first the malevolent and then the sympathetic. This satisfies their desires utterly, and also relieves the practitioner of all karmic debts.

Cutting is believed to be effective in overcoming the demonic entities that exist in the world. Traditional histories relate how its practice has been used by individuals to make forlorn places habitable for humans, to halt outbreaks of communicable diseases, and even to cure oneself of tuberculosis or leprosy.[4] Most important, Cutting provides the means to defeat the most omnipresent and formidable demon of all: attachment to one's own being, which is the root of all ignorance and the reason behind our continually taking rebirth in flesh and bone within the realm of suffering we inhabit.

Detail of painting of Machik Labdron (1055–1153); Kham region, eastern Tibet; 19th century; pigments on cloth; 24⅜ × 15¾ in. (61.9 × 40 cm); Rubin Museum of Art; C2010.3 (HAR 57037)

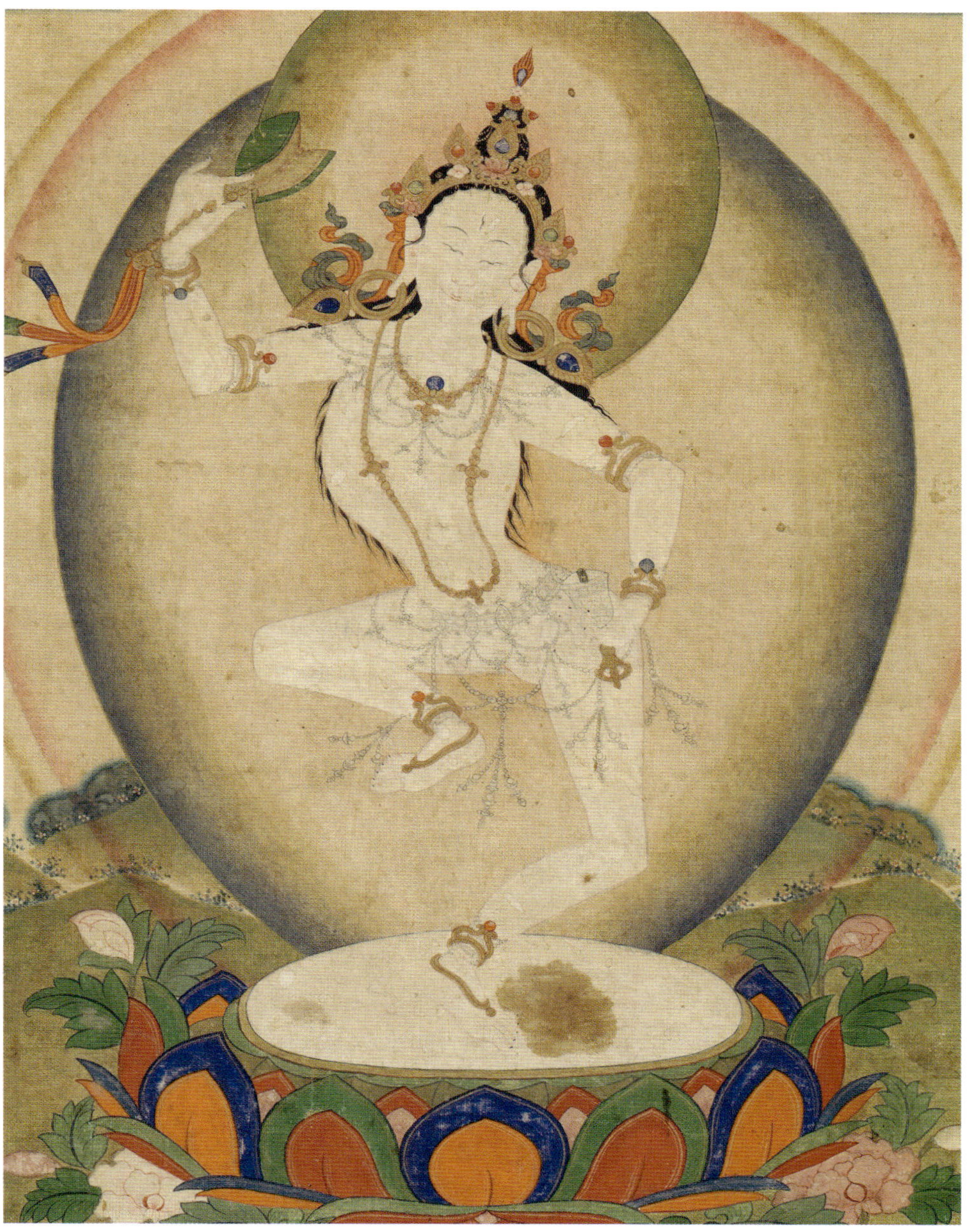

Further Reading

Cupchik, Jeffrey W. 2021. *The Sound of Vultures' Wings: The Tibetan Buddhist Chöd Ritual Practice of the Female Buddha Machik Labdrön*. Albany: SUNY Press.

Edou, Jerome. 1996. *Machig Labdron and the Foundations of Chod*. Ithaca, NY: Snow Lion.

Orofino, Giacomella. 2000. "The Great Wisdom Mother and the Gcod Tradition." In *Tantra in Practice*, edited by David Gordon White. Princeton, NJ: Princeton University Press.

Notes

1 See Fuentes 2020 for a detailed study of the use of human remains in Tibetan ritual objects, including as musical instruments, with particular attention to South Asian precedents.

2 These statements are drawn from a translation by Rinjing Dorje and Ter Ellingson of a brief exposition on the symbolic meanings to be found in the *damaru* as used in Cutting practice, written by one Gyuerme Losel ('Gyur med blo gsal), a Nyingmapa practitioner of uncertain date. The translators conclude that in his view, "The damaru is a microcosmic embodiment of the basic structure of the universe and of sentient life, and a thorough examination of it encompasses the entire scope of Buddhist philosophy and meditation," Dorje and Ellingson 1979, 63. Cupchik 2013 expands upon Dorje and Ellingson's work by exploring variations in interpretation of different aspects of the *damaru* in a living tradition of Cutting practice.

3 See Sorenson 2013 for a comprehensive history of the Cutting tradition.

4 The chapter on Cutting contained in the traditional Tibetan history the *Blue Annals* is a wellspring of such lore. See Roerich 1949, 980–1005.

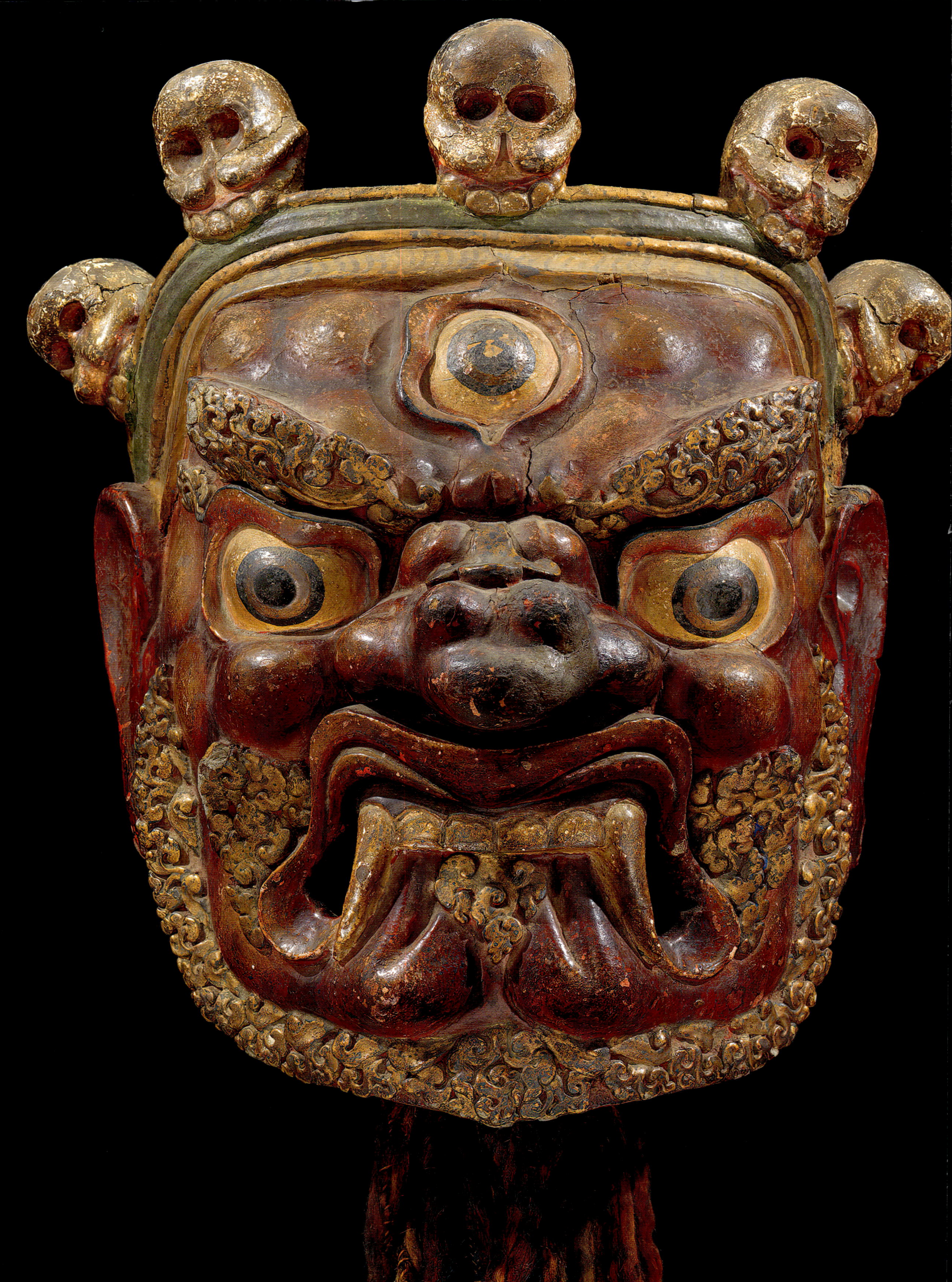

Nº 94

Ritual Dance Mask of Guru Dorje Drolo

Bhutan or southern Tibet, ca. 19th century

Reenacting Foundational Stories as Communal Performance

FRANÇOISE POMMARET

Ritual Dance (*Cham*)

THIS MASK OF GURU DORJE DROLO is one of the most important manifestations of the legendary master Padmasambhava. It belongs to a set of seven other manifestations who are represented during the dance of the Eight Manifestations of Guru Padmasambhava (Guru Tsengye).

Ritual dances, called *cham*, are an essential component of Himalayan Buddhism. They are performed during festivals, in a courtyard or indoors. Danced by monks or laymen, they can involve the wearing of masks. Their choreography and names vary according to the Buddhist sects and the regions, but their aims are broadly the same: celebration of Buddhism or a great saint, subjugation of evil spirits, teaching of Buddhist principles, liberating the faithful from their negative karma, and blessings. Dancers follow a strict practice under a dance master, who has a dance guide with steps and musical notations. The dancers must become the deities they represent. The spectacular dance costumes, made of colorful heavy brocades, are kept during the year with the masks in a specific room of the monastery. The dances form a very important part of the socioreligious binding of a community. At the time of the year when they are performed, the community comes together for religious purposes, but also for social interaction and enjoyment. From Mongolia to Ladakh, Tibet, Bhutan, and all the other Buddhist parts of the Himalayas, ritual dances constitute the apex of the year.

Who Is Padmasambhava?

Padmasambhava, also called Guru Rinpoche "the precious master" or the second buddha in the Himalayan world, is a religious hero who has attained an iconic status, difficult for a Westerner to measure. His life, of which few historical details remain, has been embellished and transformed, and the resulting account is full of great deeds, transformations, and miracles. It is believed that there is hardly any place in the Himalayan world, from Mongolia to Bhutan, through Tibet, Sikkim, and Nepal, which has not been blessed by his presence. He is the protagonist of ritual dances, the subject of paintings, large appliqués and embroidered thangkas, statues and biographies.

The places that he has blessed by his visit retain physical marks in the landscape. Over time they have become important pilgrimage places, such as Yanglesho and Halasi Maratika Caves in Nepal, Samye Monastery and Chimpu Mountain in Tibet, and Taktsang and Senge Dzong in Bhutan, to name some of the most important.

See Taktsang, the Tiger's Lair, no. 76.

According to his biographies, Padmasambhava, or "born from the lotus," was born in Oddiyana, today Swat region in Pakistan, in the eighth century and was a Buddhist tantric master with extraordinary powers. King Tri Songdetsen (742–ca. 800), unable to build the first Buddhist monastery in Samye because of interference from local deities, invited Padmasambhava to Tibet. Through his magical powers, Padmasambhava subdued them and the monastery was completed. He went on to tame most of the local deities throughout Tibet and the Himalayas, and converted the whole region to Buddhism. He became the patron saint of the first religious tradition of Tibetan Buddhism, known as the Ancient (Nyingma) tradition.

Ritual Dance Mask of Guru Dorje Drolo; Bhutan or southern Tibet; ca. 19th century; papier-mâché, polychrome, fabric; 14½ × 13½ × 10⅛ in. (36.8 × 34.3 × 25.7 cm); Bruce Miller Collection; photograph by John Bigelow Taylor

The first historical text to mention the master comes from Dunhuang manuscripts dating from the tenth century. In particular, Pelliot tibétain 44, a text devoted to the deity Vajrakila, describes Padmasambhava's time in India and Nepal before he went to Tibet.[1] Another Dunhuang manuscript,

Pelliot tibétain 307, relates how he subjugated local female deities in Tibet and bound them by oath to protect Buddhism.[2] Some texts are even attributed directly to the master.

Taming local deities and binding them to protect Buddhism is a trope that would become prevalent in the later texts and biographies of the master. The story of the construction of Samye is found in a historical text of the tenth to eleventh century, *The Testament of Ba* (Tibetan: *Bazhe/Wazhe*), and then full-blown biographies were devoted to him, the *Zanglingma* in the twelfth century, followed by the *Padma Katang* in the fourteenth century. These texts have legitimacy in the Tibetan Buddhist world because their origin is linked to Padmasambhava. They were discovered by treasure revealers (*terton*) and therefore belong to the treasure texts (*terma*) that are supposed to have been hidden by Padmasambhava himself to be rediscovered later by predestined masters and propagated among the people. The *terma* texts, which also include numerous religious texts and objects, constituted a large, revelatory genre particularly associated with the Nyingma tradition, and new *termas* are still being discovered today. Each time a *terma* was discovered, the place became a holy place because it had been blessed by Padmasambhava; such places are strewn throughout the Himalayan world.

For more about *terma*, see *Dorje* Discovered by Dorje Lingpa, no. 51.

The figure of Padmasambhava has also developed a number of manifestations related to specific liturgical texts, generally focused on the taming of obstacles and demons. The iconography of these manifestations is incredibly rich and varied, and contributes to the incredible popularity of the master and his status as not only a religious but also a cultural hero.

The most popular of these manifestations are a series of eight that correspond to eight miraculous activities of his life.[3]

The Eight Manifestations of Padmasambhava and the Ritual Dance Tradition

See Padmasambhava and His Manifestations, no. 43.

Although the treasure revealer Nyangrel (1124–1192) had visions of several Padmasambhava manifestations, it was his incarnation, Guru Chowang (1212–1270), himself a treasure revealer of the thirteenth century, who first codified Padmasambhava in eight manifestations (Guru Tsengye): Shakya Sengge, Pema Jungne (Padmasambhava), Nyima Wozer, Sengge Dradrok, Dorje Drolo, Tsokye Dorje, Pema Gyelpo, and Loden Chokse. These manifestations are ubiquitous in the temples of the Nyingma tradition, and they have their own ritual dance, an elaborate choreography.

For more on the Copper-Colored Mountain, see Portable Shrine, no. 88.

The origin of the dance is also attributed to Guru Chowang,[4] who while meditating is said to have visited the Copper-Colored Mountain (Zangdok Pelri), the paradise of Guru Rinpoche, and observed the dance there. An important text he discovered, the *Lama Sangdu*, a *sadhana* and practice on Padmasambhava, was the basis for this dance, which became very popular in Nyingma and Kagyu monasteries in the Himalayan world.[5]

The dance is usually performed during the religious festivals dedicated to Guru Rinpoche, which fall on the tenth day of a lunar month. Called Tshechu, or "tenth day," the festival corresponds to an important date in the life of the master, especially the tenth day of the fifth month of the year, which is his birthday. In Bhutanese sites such as the Paro Dzong Monastery, the festival can last several days, up to the fifteenth of the second lunar month. According to John Ardussi, it was the Fourth Temporal Ruler of Bhutan, the great Tenzin Rabgye (1638–1696), who introduced the Tshechu tradition and this dance to the Drukpa Kagyu monasteries of western Bhutan in the late seventeenth century, after sending a monk to observe the Tshechu in Tibetan monasteries.[6]

The ritual space is considered a purified place cleansed by the tantric dances, and the dance of the Eight Manifestations of Padmasambhava (Guru Tsengye) is usually performed at the end of the day, once the space has been cleansed by other dances. In Bhutan the Eight Manifestations under which Guru Rinpoche manifested himself on various occasions enter the dance space in a procession with the principal aspect of Guru Rinpoche, shaded by a parasol. Certain other aspects are accompanied by their retinues and small celestial beings.

The principal aspect of Guru Rinpoche is seated, whereas each of the other aspects, with the exception of Padmasambhava, dances before sitting next to the principal aspect. Then a public blessing takes place, and the fervor of the people is fully demonstrated: the faithful press forward to receive a thread of blessing, not from a monk who represents Guru Rinpoche but from Guru Rinpoche himself, incarnated as a human being. The dance area is transformed into his paradise, and celestial beings adorned with bone ornaments dance and sing his praises. The dance concludes with a final procession and the exit of all the aspects of Guru Rinpoche.

The dance, like others associated with Guru Rinpoche, brings "liberation through seeing" (*tongdrol*). It is considered a great blessing to watch the dance, but it is important to do so with an active mind and the aspiration of being reborn in the paradise of Guru Rinpoche. It is so powerful that today in Bhutan, elderly people watch the Tshechus live on television while praying.

The Guru Dorje Drolo's Mask

The mask shown here belongs to a series of eight; another example is the mask of Nyima Wozer, from the same collection.[7] Dorjo Drolo, the "Liberated Diamond Thunderbolt," wears a wrathful dark red mask, a garland of skulls around his body, and a long reddish garment made of heavy brocade. He holds a diamond-thunderbolt (*dorje*) and a ritual dagger (*purba*).[8] He earned this name after vanquishing evil spirits, especially the Drekpa "arrogant ones" who were creating obstacles to Buddhism at Taktsang Temple in Paro and Senge Dzong in Kurtoe, both in Bhutan. Dorje Drolo is followed by an entourage of fearsome deities. His movements are powerful, and his whirling and stomping evoke strong subduing actions and inspire fear.

This exceptional varnished polychrome mask in papier-mâché and fabric could be from Bhutan or southern Tibet and dates to the nineteenth century. Making such a mask would be a painstaking task, starting with the preparation of the papier-mâché support, composed of pulped paper, generally from the plants in the genus *Daphne* or *Edgeworthia*, and glue obtained from animal hooves. This would be followed by carving, painting with pigments extracted from leaves or minerals, and varnishing with the shellac resin (the secretion of an insect, *Laccifer lacca*).

Dorje Drolo has a maroon face made dramatic by a crown of five skulls, which represent the transmutation of five negative afflictions of human nature into five wisdoms; three protruding eyes; a bulbous large nose; beautifully carved eyebrows; and a short beard made of little flames. The mouth is the focal point of the mask, as it is opened wide in rictus, the canine teeth transformed into fangs and the upward-curving tongue ornamented with flames. With the mask sitting elevated on his head, the dancer sees through the mouth. At the back of the mask, threads fasten it onto the head, which is protected by several layers of cloth. Several thick, colored strands of fabric are attached at the top of the mask. They symbolize the hair, and the dancer deploys them like a mane by shaking his head vigorously.

Every feature of the mask, from its color to its facial expressions, is meant to inspire fear and awe, not to the devotees, but to the spirits that Guru Dorje Drolo subjugates. To a Buddhist from the Himalayas, the mask of Guru Dorje Drolo immediately evokes not only Padmasambhava in his most wrathful manifestation, but also several cultural and religious layers or meaning, forming a specific religious landscape in the mind of the devotee. The mask is not a work of art in the Western sense, but an object of devotion.

Further Reading

Ardussi, John A. 1999. "Gyalse Tenzin Rabgye and the Founding of Taktsang Lhakhang." *Journal of Bhutan Studies* 1, no. 1, 36–63.

Cantwell, Cathy. 1995. "The Dance of the Guru's Eight Aspects." *Tibet Journal* 20, no. 4, 47–63.

Pakhoutova, Elena, ed. 2018. *The Second Buddha: Master of Time*. Exhibition catalog. New York: Delmonico/Prestel.

Notes

1 Dalton 2015. Pelliot tibétain 44 is in the Bibliothèque nationale de France (BnF), Paris.

2 Dalton 2004. Pelliot tibétain 307 is also in the BnF.

3 For a complete overview of Padmasambhava's life and deeds, see Pakhoutova 2018.

4 Cantwell 1995.

5 Leschly 2007.

6 Ardussi 1999, 55n12: "ff. 193.b–194.a, 237.b–241.b, *Lho'i chos 'byung*, ff. 42.b, 56.b; *Lho'i chos 'byung* 2, f. 121.a; *LNDRR, Nga*, f. 133.b. In 1687 Tenzin Rabgye sent one of his Nyingmapa assistants to Tibet specifically to study the Tshechu traditions at various monasteries, particularly at Gong dkar, sNe'u dong, and Lho brag. Upon his return a book was written on the dance, music, and costumes, and the first full three-day performance of Tshechu dances took place at Tashichhodzong in 1690. It is possible that Tshechu traditions were independently introduced into central and eastern Bhutan at an earlier date."

7 Pakhoutova 2018, fig. 1.17:32.

8 For the iconography of Dorje Drolo, see Pakhoutova 2018, figs. 1.13:28, 1.21:35.

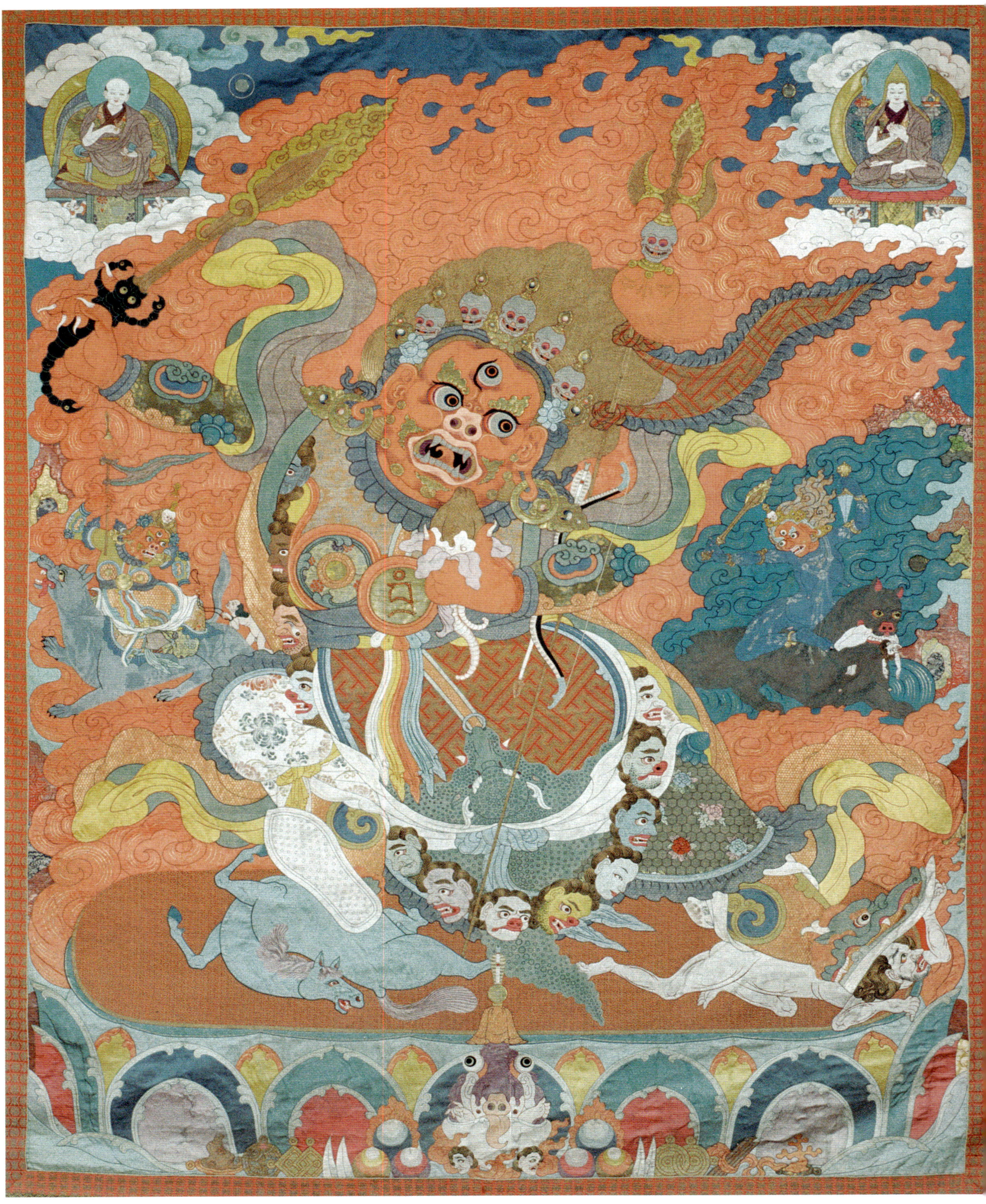

№ 95

Monumental Appliqué of Begtse

Yekhe Khüriye, Mongolia, late 19th–early 20th century

Appliqué Artistic Tradition and the War God Begtse's Significance in Mongolia

URANCHIMEG TSULTEMIN

This thangka of Begtse (also known as Jamsran) is a work by Jügdür (late 19th–early 20th century), a prominent artist of Yekhe Khüriye.[1] That city, now called Ulaanbaatar and currently Mongolia's capital, was the main seat of the ruling Jibzundamba reincarnations (Khutugtus). It was also an important cultural center and a base for many eminent artists. Jügdür was in the Zoogai *aimag* of Yekhe Khüriye's thirty *aimags* (monastic units).[2] The Eighth Jibzundamba Bogd Gegeen (1869–1924) commissioned Jügdür to paint a new map of Yekhe Khüriye; several other images by Jügdür are also extant, including a set of *Three Deities of Longevity* and some drawings.

See Mongolian Map of Capital Yekhe Khüriye, no. 96.

Begtse is a popular worldly protector deity in Tibet and Mongolia. Practices and texts including this protector date to the eleventh century in Tibet.[3] Images of Begtse are especially widespread in Mongolia. Begtse's name means "hidden coat of mail"; he is also known by the name Jamsran (from Tibetan Jamsing), meaning "brother and sister." As a worldly protector, he is worshipped as residing within this realm and occupies the position of war god.[4] He resides in his Marutse cemetery abode in the northeast and is surrounded by a group of wrathful deities, known as "butchers who wield swords," who are often depicted in Begtse images, as evidenced in a contemporaneous thangka from Yekhe Khüriye. Begtse rules as lord over demons and spirits, and vanquishes all the enemies and obstacles that keep devotees away from enlightenment.

As one of ten protector deities, Begtse manifests in a wrathful form and stands on a sun disc. With two hands and one face, garbed in armor, he sports a golden mirror on his chest that displays the Sanskrit seed syllable *bram* for recitation of his mantras and prayers; he wears a garland made of fifty freshly severed human heads and a crown with five skulls, which represent the five defilements on the path to liberation. He tramples the corpse of a horse with his right foot and the corpse of a human with his left foot. His hands hold attributes: a sword with a handle in a shape of a black scorpion in his right hand, and the heart and kidneys of enemies of the faith in his left hand. He also clutches a bow and arrow, a trident, and a banner in the bend of his left elbow. As is typical for Mongolian appliqué thangkas, jewels, such as coral beads, are used extensively in this thangka. In the textual description, Begtse is standing atop a copper mountain that emerges from the "lake formed by the blood of men and horses";[5] here he is surrounded by the majestic flames dominating the entire composition.

For more about how deities are visualized from seed syllables of their mantras, see The All-Knowing Buddha Vairochana Visualization Album, no. 87.

Above Begtse, two teachers—the First Jibzundamba Zanabazar (1635–1723) and Tsongkhapa (1357–1419)—are depicted in the two corners of the top register, alluding to the importance of the Geluk tradition's teachings and the Jibzundambas in Mongolia in general, and for this production in particular, as it was most certainly made under the patronage of the Bogd Gegeen (who ruled as Bogd Khan 1911–1924). This Begtse also has attendants on both sides: to his right is his son, the Red Master of Life, holding a spear and a noose with a human corpse, and riding a gray wolf;[6] to Begtse's left is his sister and consort Rigpai Lhamo, or Goddess of Life, whose head is red and body is blue, and who holds a sword and a ritual dagger (*purba*) in her hands and rides a bear biting into a human corpse. There are auspicious symbols, such as jewels and elephant tusks symmetrically distributed on both sides of a plate with offerings of the Five Senses to Begtse.

For more about the First Jibzundamba, see Maitreya, no. 75.

Jügdür (fl. late 19th–early 20th century); *Begtse*; Yekhe Khüriye, Mongolia; early 20th century; appliqué and embroidery on cotton; 88⅛ × 69¾ in. (224 × 177 cm); Bogd Khan Palace Museum, Ulaanbaatar

Appliqué Thangka Tradition and Production

The technique of appliqué was held in special favor in Mongolia, and it has remained a favorite traditional medium used by nomadic artists and craftspeople since early times. Carpets and rugs, handmade with felt and decorated with appliqué and embroidery, were used by nomads in their portable dwellings (known as yurts), and some extant early examples date to Xiongnu nomads (third century BCE–first century CE).[7] During the Mongol imperial period, silk and appliqué were also used in making lavish tapestries, royal garments, imperial portraits, and Buddhist images, as evidenced in a splendid Vajrabhairava thangka and in recent archeological findings. In Buddhist monasteries in Inner Asia, appliqué thangkas were often made in various sizes, and remarkable examples of colossal appliqué thangkas still exist in Himalayan art.

See Vajrabhairava Mandala, no. 46.

A team of artists, including women, were involved in the production of these monumental thangka scrolls. As Yekhe Khüriye artists reminisce,[8] Jügdür was also among the artists who produced other appliqué thangkas, such as a colossal *Thirty-Five Buddhas of Confession,* one of the most ambitious projects of Yekhe Khüriye, given its grandiose dimensions.[9] The production of these monumental appliqué images typically involved a team led by a master artist.[10] The master artist, usually a male, created the drawing based on the system of proportions and iconographic details; his team, often including women, would cut Chinese silks and brocade pieces into shapes, then render them based on the drawing and stitch them to create the composition. Artists fastened gold-wrapped horsehair to the appliqué with small stitches (known as gold couching) to create the details.

In Mongolia, appliqué thangkas were lavishly encrusted with jewels, such as seed pearls, turquoise pieces, and coral beads.[11] In Mongolia, the medium of appliqué was used most exclusively for monumental thangkas, and as this image of Begtse demonstrates, the artists kept the compositions simple, with the main deity dominating the space and the top and bottom registers either absent or kept at minimum scale. Colossal appliqué tapestries were often unfolded outdoors and hung on mountain sides and exterior monastery walls during important Buddhist rituals and celebrations attended by the entire community, such as the Lunar New Year, the Great Prayer Festival, and the *tsam* masked dance ritual.

A colossal appliqué is also depicted in Portrait of the Ninth Karmapa, no. 66.

Location and the Significance of Begtse in Yekhe Khüriye

In Yekhe Khüriye, monumental thangkas, such as this *Begtse*, hung in the Jibzundamba's Batu-Tsagan Assembly Hall (Tsogchin Dugang), and other temples. According to the Mongolian art historian Nyam-Osoryn Tsultem, the *Begtse* examined here was in Kalachakra Temple within the Yellow Palace, the central compound of the main temples in Yekhe Khüriye.[12] Regular rituals for Begtse were conducted monthly here and at the symbolic *ger* (yurt) known as Baruun Örgöö, raised by Abatai Khan (1554–1588).[13] Baruun Örgöö was a large yurt, uninhabited but of a great ritual significance for the descendants of Chinggis Khan (ca. 1162–1227) (an ancestry known as the "golden kinship"), who included Zanabazar's family of Tüshiyetü Khan, Abatai's great-grandson. Initially kept at Erdeni Juu Monastery, founded by Abatai Khan in 1586, this *ger* became part of Yekhe Khüriye, where it was maintained as a sanctuary to worship the ancestors and maintain the fire for the Mongol people day and night, overseen by a group of designated monks.[14] These monks, who were themselves part of golden kinship, were appointed by Tüshiyetü Khan to conduct the rituals of Begtse three times every month in accordance with other rituals to Begtse simultaneously performed at the Jibzundamba's Assembly Hall in the Yellow Palace.

For more about the Yellow Palace, see Mongolian Map of Capital Yekhe Khüriye, no. 96.

See Erdeni Juu Monastery, no. 65.

Such devotion to Begtse's worship in Yekhe Khüriye went back to the Second Jibzundamba (1724–1757). Believed to be a special protector for the Mongols, the Second Jibzundamba, the legend goes, was miraculously saved from lightning by Jamsran, who showed himself to the reincarnation from the Baruun Örgöö.[15] Even the first Mongolian revolutionaries, who stood up to fight for Mongolia's independence from the Qing Empire in 1911, came to receive blessings from Jamsran at Baruun Örgöö. In 1912, shortly after Mongolia became independent, the Bogd Khan and the Mongol nobles performed another special ritual to Begtse, vowing their service to the newly independent state before an image of Jamsran. One wonders if this monumental appliqué thangka could be that special image of Begtse.[16]

Appliqué Cloth Thangka of Maitreya, based on sketch of Sonam Peljor; Gyantse, Tsang region, central Tibet; 1437–1439; colored silk embroidered on silk; 73 ft. 10 in. × 73 ft. 10 in. (22.5 × 22.5 m); image after Henss 2014, fig. 727

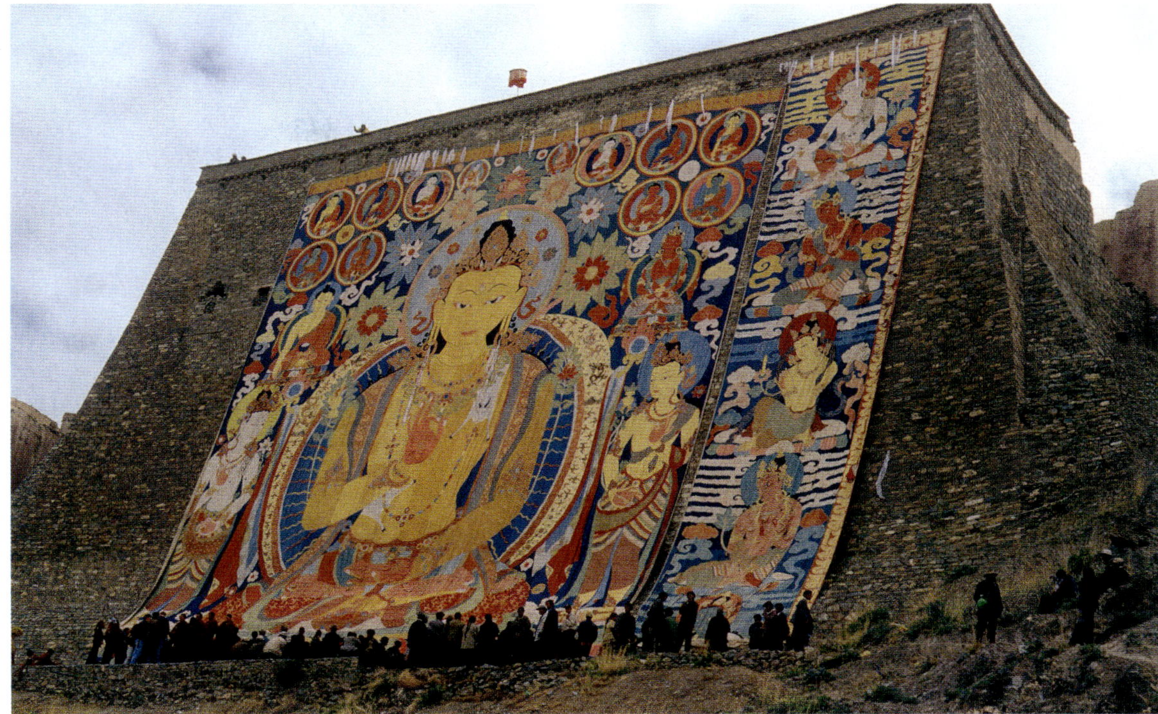

Further Reading

Berger, Patricia, and Terese Tse Bartholomew, eds. 1995. *Mongolia: The Legacy of Chinggis Khan.* Exhibition catalog. London: Thames and Hudson, 244–46.

Heller, Amy. 1988. "Early Textual Sources for the Cult of Beg-ce." In *Tibetan Studies: Proceedings of the Fourth Seminar of the International Association for Tibetan Studies, Munich 1985*, edited by Helga Uebach and Jampa L. Panglung, 185–95. Munich: Kommission für Zentralasiatische Studien Bayerische Akademie der Wissenschaften.

Tsultemin, Uranchimeg. 2020. *A Monastery on the Move: Art and Politics in Later Buddhist Mongolia.* Honolulu: University of Hawai'i Press, 130–38.

Notes

1 See also Fleming and Lkhagvademchig 2011.

2 On *aimags*, see No. 96 in this volume, 411n4.

3 Amy Heller's research has shown that Begtse first appears in eleventh-century Tibetan textual sources. He was also the personal protector of the Third Dalai Lama (1543–1588) and the guardian, together with Palden Lhamo, of Chokhorgyel Monastery, the main seat of the Second Dalai Lama (1475–1542). A. Heller 1988, 185–95; also Berger and Bartholomew 1995, 244.

4 Nebesky-Wojkowitz 1956, 88.

5 Nebesky-Wojkowitz 1956, 90.

6 Berger and Bartholomew 1995, 246.

7 There were several steppe empires prior to the rise of the Mongols in the thirteenth century. The Xiongnu, also known as Huns, established the earliest steppe empire in the territory of modern-day Mongolia.

8 Dariima 2003, 91.

9 One-fourth, measuring 76¾ × 98⅜ in. (195 × 250 cm), of this colossal appliqué thangka tapestry made for the Batu-Tsagan Assembly Hall in Yekhe Khüriye is displayed in the Fine Arts Zanabazar Museum.

10 In case of *Thirty-Five Buddhas of Confession*, which dates to 1914, head artists included Erdeni *umzad* (Tibetan: *dbu mdzad*, chant master), Chimed, Gendundamba, Jügdür, and Khasgombo. See Tsultemin 2020, 138.

11 Yekhe Khüriye's abbot Agwang Khayidub (1779–1838) mentions many artworks of his time in the city's temples. See Ngag dbang mkhas grub (Agwang Khayidub) 1972–74, vol. 5, fols. 589–618.

12 See discussion in Berger and Bartholomew 1995, 246.

13 The Russian scholar Aleksei Pozdneev visited Baruun Örgöö during his trips to Yekhe Khüriye in 1877 and in 1892. He writes about the impressive size of this yurt, which, he maintains, could easily hold three hundred people. Pozdneev (1896–98) 1977, 91–92.

14 Pürev 1994, 21.

15 Pozdneev (1896–98) 1977, 91–92.

16 See Ochir and Enkhtüvshin 2003, vol. 4.

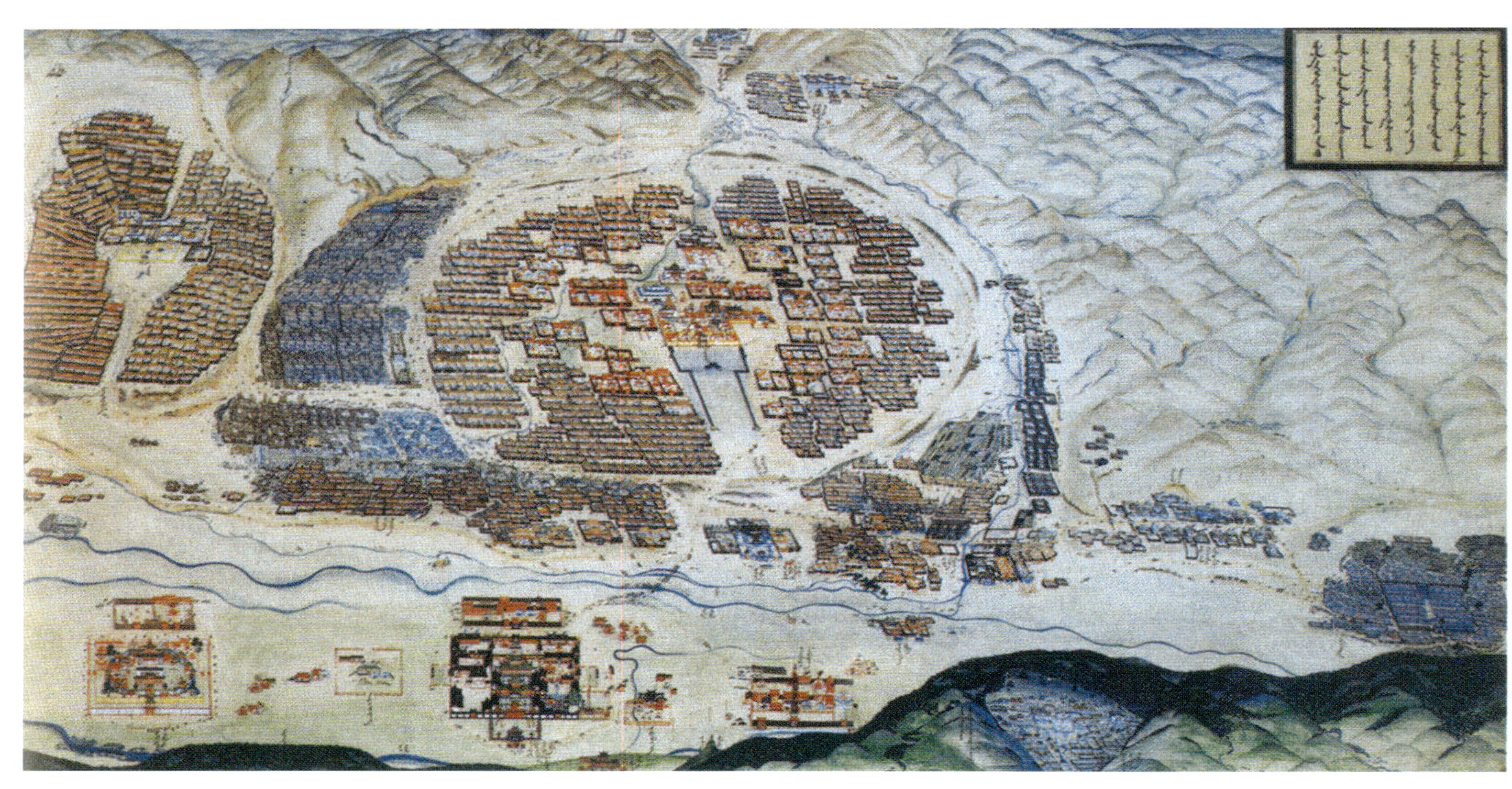

№ 96

Mongolian Map of Capital Yekhe Khüriye

Mongolia, 1912

Mapping Yekhe Khüriye's Cityscape as the "Capital City"

URANCHIMEG TSULTEMIN

Yekhe Khüriye or Urga

For more about the Jibzundamba, see Maitreya, no. 75.

THE PAINTING DEPICTS the preeminent Mongolian Buddhist monastery of the Jibzundamba reincarnate rulers (Mongolian: Khutugtu).[1] Yekhe Khüriye (Classical Mongolian: Yeke Küriy-e, also spelled Ikh Khüree; modern-day Ulaanbaatar, Mongolia), known to foreign visitors as Urga, is shown in a panoramic bird's-eye view.[2] This perspective from above is often used in depicting cityscapes and in architectural drawings in Inner and East Asia. A number of architectural representations provide specific views on the hierarchical organization of the towns.[3] Important pilgrimage sites, such as Wutaishan and Lhasa, received significant attention from the artists and their patrons. The title of this map is *Capital Yekhe Khüriye*, and as it was produced soon after Mongolia's independence from the Qing Empire in 1911, the map was a part of a larger Mongolian nation-building project, and a royal commission to promote the Khalkha Mongolian monastery as a pilgrimage site, a religious and political center of Mongolia.

See Panoramic Map of Mount Wutai, no. 91.

Jügdür, an artist from Zoogai *aimag* (monastic unit),[4] completed the painting in 1912, as the inscription in traditional Mongolian script attached to the painting attests. Jügdür was a prominent artist, as other works by him demonstrate. Among his surviving works are a remarkable appliqué of Begtse and a set of paintings of three longevity deities. Jügdür was from Setsen Khan province (modern-day Khentii *aimag*). His fame was widespread, and he spent the last years of his life working on commissions in Tibet, where he died.[5]

For more on the Mongolian artist Jügdür and his other creations, see Monumental Appliqué of Begtse, no. 95.

The inscription clarifies that the production of the map was initiated and overseen by the Eighth Jibzundamba Bogd Gegeen (1869–1924), who was proclaimed the Bogd Khan of Mongolia on December 29, 1911:

> In the second year of All-Inaugurated [1912], Lord Bogd Khan ordered Jügdür from Zoogai aimag of Züün Khüriye, who is good at and renowned for painting deities, to paint the Capital Khüriye, Gandan, and so on, the surrounding mountains, rivers, and even temples, and monasteries in the true reality of that time.[6]

The All-Inaugurated (Mahasammata) Bogd Khan of Mongolia was both political and religious head of the new state. The theocratic government under the Bogd Khan was a fragile, young state, and as part of his state-building, the Khan initiated many projects, including translations and the reprinting of old and new texts, as well as conducting new cartographic surveys.[7] This map was tantamount to his other projects to collect, systematize, and organize the information and knowledge, such as printing a new set of the Tibetan Buddhist canon (Kangyur), known as Urga Kangyur.[8] There were other paintings of various parts of Yekhe Khüriye made, and this is the second existent map of Yekhe Khüriye. Mapping the city also contributed to the status of Yekhe Khüriye as a new pilgrimage site akin to Lhasa. Yekhe Khüriye's abbot, Agwang Lubsang Khayidub (1779–1838), wrote several texts about circumambulation of Yekhe Khüriye and a ritual of mandala offerings to the Jibzundamba, thereby contributing to the elevation of Yekhe Khüriye's importance in Inner Asia.[9]

Jügdür (fl. late 19th–early 20th century); *Capital Yekhe Khüriye*; Mongolia; 1912; colors on cotton, 19⅝ × 37⅞ in. (50 × 96 cm); Bogd Khan Palace Museum, Ulaanbaatar

Jügdür depicts Yekhe Khüriye as a grandiose site with its two major components demarcated in the roughly elliptical arrangement of a traditional *khüriye* encampment. *Khüriye* encampments were in regular use among nomads, and the circular structure surrounding a chieftain in the center also had a purpose of defense. The very conception of Yekhe Khüriye begins with a yurt (Mongolian: Örgöö

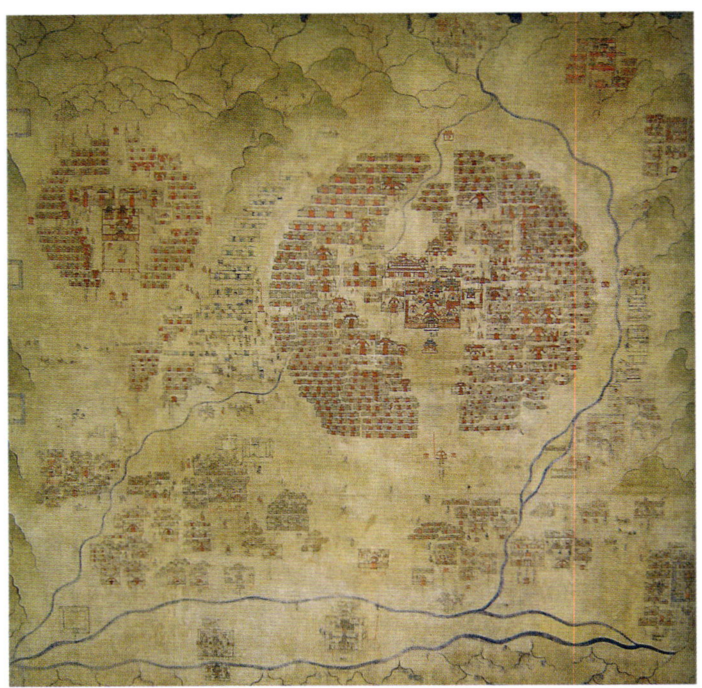

Balgan (act. late 19th century); *Yekhe Khüriye*; Mongolia, late 19th century; colors on cotton; 19⅝ × 37⅞ in. (50 × 96 cm); Fine Arts Zanabazar Museum, Ulaanbaatar

or *ger*) which was first erected for the five-year-old Zanabazar (1635–1723) in 1639 to commemorate his enthronement as the First Jibzundamba Khutugtu. Zanabazar and the succeeding Jibzundamba Khutugtus strategically developed the Örgöö (yurt) into the monastery Yekhe Khüriye. As an encampment, Yekhe Khüriye consisted of yurts, and from its early days in the 1630s until 1855, it was fully portable and mobile, traversing long distances from the southern border to the north. As the monastery grew and expanded with new temples and increased in population, its migrations became only local, along the trade route between Russia and China. The Mongolian word "Örgöö" was rendered as "Urga" by foreign visitors.

By the time Balgan in the nineteenth century and Jügdür in 1912 mapped Yekhe Khüriye's holistic structure, the monastery consisted of two major and several minor parts. As we know from later Yekhe Khüriye writers, the large circle in Yekhe Khüriye was commonly known as Züün Khüriye (Eastern Khüriye, at center in image), and the smaller oval settlement denotes Gandan Monastery (at left).[10] The core of Yekhe Khüriye was the Jibzundamba's Yellow Palace, a central compound with several buildings surrounded by a yellow fence. The Yellow Palace was the place where the Jibzundamba Khutugtus resided and where their major temples once stood. Jügdür shows the Yellow Palace annexed by a large plaza where lay festivals (such as wrestling) and Buddhist rituals (such as *tsam* ritual) took place every summer. To the north of the Yellow Palace, major temples, including Batu-Tsagan ("Firmly White") Assembly Hall (Tsogchin), Maitreya, and Dechingalba (Kalachakra) Temples also stood. This nucleus of the Jibzundamba's monastery was surrounded by thirty monastic units (*aimags*), where the monastic population was organized based on regional affiliation and relation to the Jibzundamba.

For more on *tsam* ritual dance, see Ritual Dance Mask of Guru Dorje Drolo, no. 94.

The second encampment, the Gandan Tegchinling Monastery, was built by the Fifth Jibzundamba (1815–1841) in 1838 by moving several colleges (*datsans*) from Züün Khüriye to the western hills, where new temples were additionally built to form a theological center named after Maitreya's Tushita Heaven.[11] Gandan mirrored the Züün Khüriye in the architectural design by including a central compound with the Jibzundamba's temples and another Zanabazar-designed Assembly Hall, all surrounded by monastic units (*aimags*). Yet unlike Züün Khüriye, this monastery was strictly an educational and theological center, closed and inaccessible for lay visitors, especially women and merchants.

Yekhe Khüriye was destroyed in the 1930s and later rebuilt as the modern-day capital city Ulaanbaatar ("Red Hero"). Among the surviving temples, the latest one still standing is Migjid Janraisig, or Avalokiteshvara Temple, which was built with donations from the entire Khalkha population to commemorate Khalkha Mongolia's independence from the Qing in 1911.[12] The Gandan Monastery continued to serve as the only practicing monastery and the only Buddhist educational center throughout the socialist period (1924–1992).

Yekhe Khüriye's other constituents were merchants, who occupied two streets known as Eastern and Western Porters, east and west of Züün Khüriye. Chinese merchants were settled in Maimaicheng, or Traders' Town to the southeast. Jügdür denotes all these commercial sections on the map in grayish blue color. The same color applies to the Russian settlement situated around the Russian Consulate, opened in Yekhe Khüriye in 1861, on Maakhuuz Tologai Hill to the east of Züün Khüriye, later renamed Consulate's Hill.[13] Jügdür depicts the hill, where the Russian Orthodox Holy Trinity Church was also built.

Yekhe Khüriye was located in the valley of two rivers: in the painting, the Selbe River runs in the middle of Züün Khüriye, and the Tuul River runs south of the two circles. On the bank of the Tuul River, Jügdür depicts the Bogd Khan's palaces: the largest is the Green Palace (also known as Winter Palace, Shirabpeljeiling, or Bilig Badaruulugchi süme), to the east, Norbuling süm and Khayistai Labrang; to the west, the Bogd's White Palace (also known as Güngadejidling süme) and Pandelin or

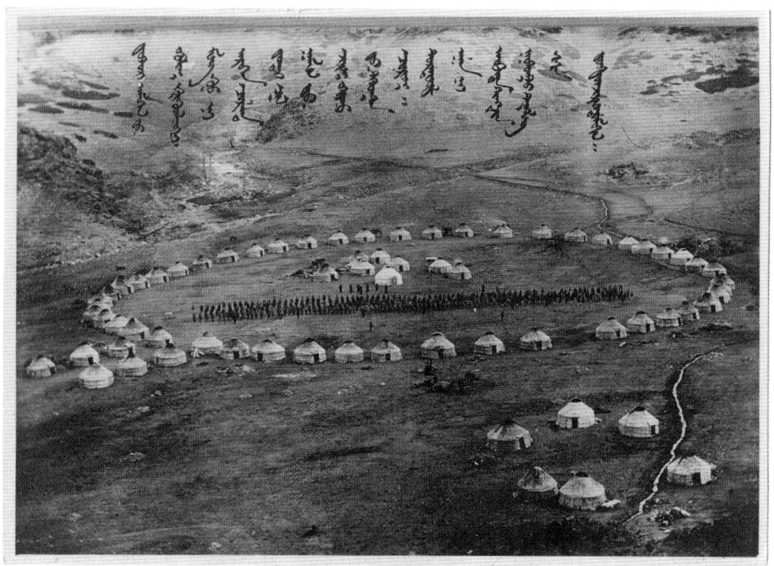

An example of a *khüriye* encampment: the Torghut Prince Sin Chin Gegeen's camp at Khara Shar, before 1927; photograph; dimensions unknown; photograph courtesy The Swedish National Museums of World Culture and Sven Hedin Foundation

Narkhajid Temple.[14] At the bottom of the painting, behind the hills, Jügdür depicts another monastery dedicated to Manjushri that was not part of Yekhe Khüriye.[15]

Yekhe Khüriye's Many Functions

While primarily a Buddhist monastery and a major pilgrimage site for the Mongols, Yekhe Khüriye served several other important functions. As the main seat of the Jibzundamba Khutugtus, Yekhe Khüriye was the political center of Mongolia, and its political importance strengthened with years. After the Bogd Khan's death and with the establishment of the new socialist government in 1924, Yekhe Khüriye was destroyed and rebuilt, and remains to this day the capital city Ulaanbaatar.

Yekhe Khüriye was also an important trade center. Several foreign businesses of large or small scale, such as the American Trading Company, operated in Yekhe Khüriye, and the important visitors to Yekhe Khüriye included a then young engineer, later the thirty-first President of the United States, Herbert Hoover (1874–1964), the paleontologist Roy Chapman Andrews (1884–1960), the Swedish missionary Frans-August Larson (1870–1957), the Thirteenth Dalai Lama (1876–1933), and the explorer Aleksei Pozdneev (1851–1920), among others.[16]

Yekhe Khüriye was an important cultural center, where many excellent artworks were produced. The city regularly hosted both secular festivals and religious ceremonies. Given textual references to the Jibzundambas as rulers who fused political and religious spheres of power (dual rulership, or Buddhist Government), these images, as well as Yekhe Khüriye itself—its structure, the activities it sponsored, roles it played, and celebrations it hosted—all were embodiments of the ruler's dual rulership.[17]

Further Reading

Teleki, Krisztina. 2011. *Monasteries and Temples of Bogdiin Khüree (1651–1938).* Ulaanbaatar: Institute of History, Mongolian Academy of Sciences.

Teleki, Krisztina. 2015. *Introduction to the Study of Urga's Heritage.* Ulaanbaatar: Mongolian Academy of Sciences.

Tsultemin, Uranchimeg. 2020. *A Monastery on the Move: Art and Politics in Later Buddhist Mongolia*, esp. 143–211. Honolulu: University of Hawai'i Press.

Notes

1 See Bawden 1961; Pozdneev (1896) 1971, 1880.
2 See Bat-Erdene, Dashdemberel, and O. Mendsaikhan 2011; Fleming, Zara, and J. Lkhagvademchig Shastri 2011.
3 See Béguin 2003; Larsen and Sinding-Larsen 2001.
4 The word *aimag* denotes two things: (1) a province in Mongolia, and there are twenty-one *aimags* in modern-day Mongolia; and (2) Geluk monasteries in Mongolia organize their monks into units called *aimags,* which often follow a model of Tibetan regional houses *khangtsen* (*khang tsan*).
5 Tsultemin 2020, 134, based on Damdinsüren 1993. On Mongolian paintings, see Tsultem 1986; Tsultem 2018.
6 The inscription added to the painting *The Capital Yekhe Khüriye.*
7 For additional historical context on the turbulent years in late and post-Qing period, see King 2019.
8 Chandra 1980. Chandra maintains Urga Kangyur was printed in 1913 to 1920.
9 Ngag dbang mkhas grub (Agwang Khayidub) 1972–74a, vol. 1, fols. 577–611. TBRC W16912–0588, vol. 3, fols. 367–472. TBRC W16912–0590.
10 For the later writers, see Dügersüren 1956; Pürevjav 1961.
11 Ngag dbang ye shes thub bstan rab 'byams pa (Agwang Ishtüvden Rabjamba) 1982b, fols. 10–11; Bstan pa 'dzin, vol. 2, fols. 416–18.
12 Sereeter 1999, 72.
13 Teleki 2011, 190.
14 See also Teleki 2011, 162–70.
15 For more about this monastery and others, see the digital database Documentation of Mongolian Monasteries, in Mongolian and English, https://www.mongoliantemples.org/en/.
16 Many of these visitors wrote articles or books about Yekhe Khüriye and Mongolia. See, for instance, Larson 1930; Korostovets 1926; Andrews 1921.
17 Tsultemin 2020, 176–211.

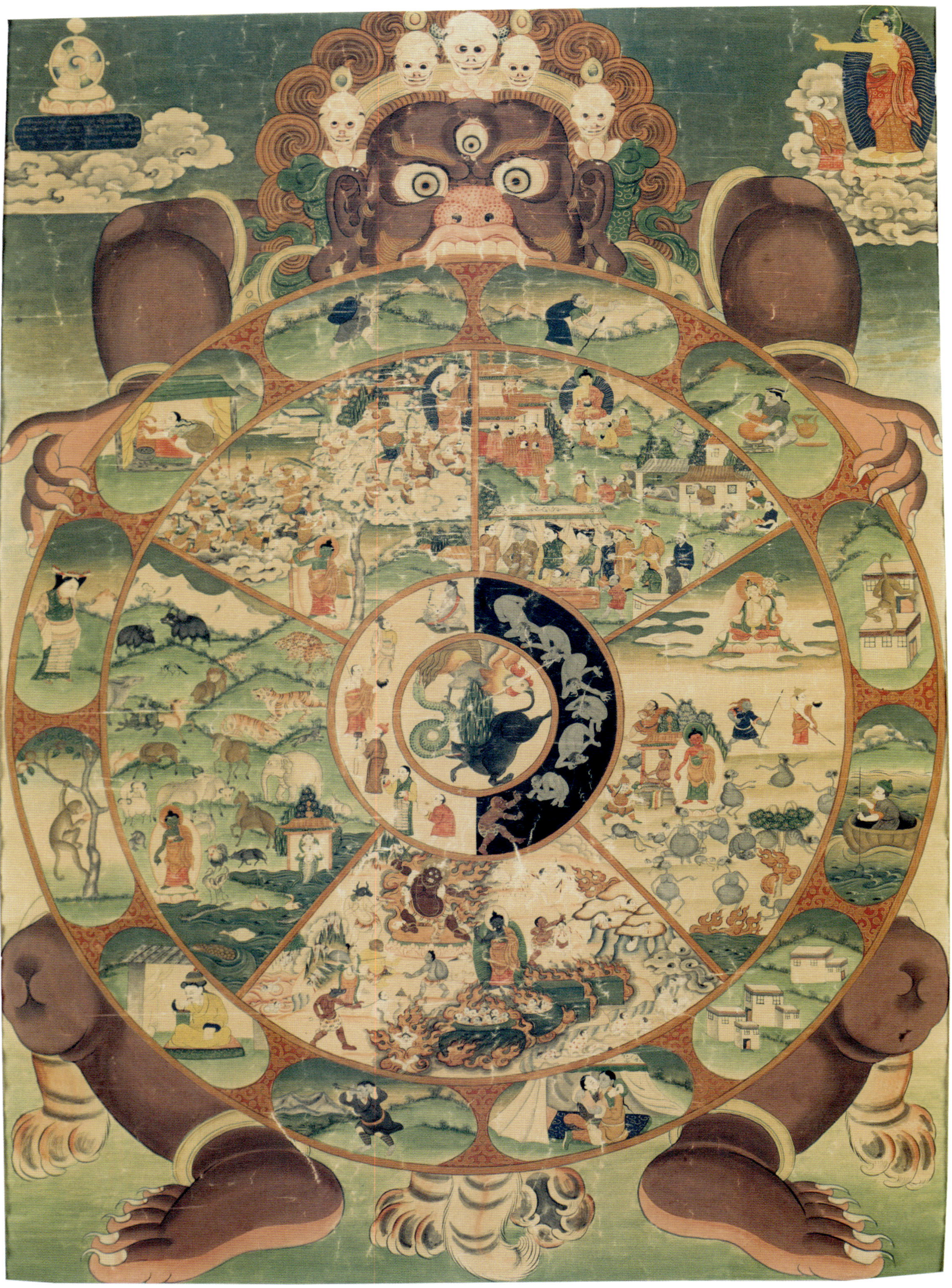

№ 97

Wheel of Existence

Central Tibet, ca. early 20th century

A Visual Explanation of Buddhist Cosmology

ERIC HUNTINGTON

Wheel of Existence; central Tibet; early 20th century; pigments on cloth; image area 31⅞ × 23⅛ in. (81 × 58.7 cm), with brocade frame 65⅝ × 40¾ × 1½ in. (166.7 × 103.5 × 3.8 cm); Rubin Museum of Art; C.2004.21.1 (HAR65356)

THE WHEEL OF EXISTENCE is one of the most recognizable and long-standing visual explanations of Buddhist conceptions of the world. It carefully diagrams the causes and conditions of life, the problems of life, and hints for how to resolve the problems. The main impact of the image is to educate viewers about the key ideas of Buddhism, and early texts even state that the wheel of existence should be displayed on exterior monastery walls with a monk posted nearby to explain it to visitors.[1] This kind of instructional art may thus be understood as distinct from other major genres, such as devotional images that relate to ritual, mandalas that suggest meditations, or portraits and narrative works that emphasize the stories of individual people.

Understanding the Cyclic Nature of Existence

The wheel of existence is depicted as a large circle that contains numerous separate vignettes, each of which characterizes something about the nature of life. The overarching lesson is provided by the demonic figure who stands outside the wheel and grasps it firmly, signifying that all forms and aspects of life are subject to death—in other words, that everything is impermanent. This demonic figure is sometimes identified with Yama, the god of death, and in this painting (although not necessarily in others), he is indeed depicted much like Yama, who also appears with similar dark-red complexion and tiger-skin clothing, dancing in flames in the realm of hells, about one-third of the way up from the bottom of the painting. The wheel itself is divided into four concentric circles of images representing, from the outside to the inside: a) the twelvefold chain of dependent origination that conditions all states of being; b) the five realms and six paths of life in the world; c) the two motions upward and downward that trap sentient beings in cyclical existence through these paths of life; and last, at the axial center, d) the three psychological poisons that drive this entrapment, an interminable cycle of suffering known as samsara.

The largest area inside the wheel is taken up by the five realms and six paths of life in the world, represented separately in complex scenes of many characters. The wedge toward the top right shows the realm and path of humans, with a formal gathering in the foreground; images of the aged, sick, and dead toward the right (recalling the four visions of the historical Buddha, Siddhartha Gautama);[2] and an assembly around yellow-skinned Buddha Shakyamuni at the top.

Clockwise from the human realm, the next wedge shows the realm and path of the hungry ghosts (*pretas*), whose small throats and distended bellies reveal their constant starvation. Here too, as in all the other realms, a buddha offers relief. In the sky above appears the bodhisattva of compassion, Avalokiteshvara, expressing the Buddhist goal to aid all sentient beings.[3] In fact, the six buddhas depicted inside the wheel of existence are sometimes said to be emanations of Avalokiteshvara intended to help beings on the six paths according to their needs.

See Avalokiteshvara at Khartse, no. 20; Bodhisattva Avalokiteshvara and the Buddha's Footprints, no. 33.

The bottom wedge of the wheel depicts scenes from hell realms, with Yama overseeing various tortures of cutting, boiling, freezing, and so on that are partially alleviated by a dark blue buddha.

Continuing clockwise, the realm of animals holds creatures of the land, sea, and sky, including a human-serpent naga in a small palace, and a dark green buddha. At the top left, the final wedge depicts the paths of gods (devas, top) and anti-gods (Asuras, left) battling for dominion over the world, along with the two buddhas dedicated to their aid.

For more on nagas, see Golden Fountain of Bhaktapur, no. 74.

The next interior ring is divided in two, with pious figures climbing to better existences in the white half (on the left) and miserable figures crawling downward to worse ones in the black half (on the right). The key message here is again one of impermanence, that all states of existence end. One's good or bad actions (karmas) have consequences, creating new states of existence that are better or worse, respectively. One may experience starvation as a hungry ghost due to previous gluttony, violence as an anti-god due to previous jealousy, or pleasure as a god due to previous generosity. Crucially, these new states are also impermanent, so that even someone experiencing hellish sufferings or heavenly pleasures will move on to new experiences resulting from their continued actions. All beings are thus subject both to the worst torments and to the loss of the best pleasures, meaning that all states of existence, good or bad, ultimately cause misery. The only true release from suffering is thus not a state of pleasure but rather an escape from the cycle of action-and-consequence altogether. Luckily, the very fact of impermanence allows the possibility of escape, since, unlike in some other religious traditions, even heaven and hell are not eternal destinations.

Escape from Suffering

In order to understand the means of escape, one must first grasp the mechanism of imprisonment, as depicted in the two remaining rings of the wheel. At the center, a rooster, a snake, and a pig represent the three psychological factors that drive the cyclical motion: attraction, aversion, and delusion or ignorance. It is because of desire for more pleasure, repulsion from displeasure, and ignorance of the consequences of their actions that sentient beings become trapped in this wheel. Overcoming these negative factors means that one can avoid the sufferings they cause.

The outermost circle reveals in more detail how ignorance (represented by a blind person with a cane, top right) is the ultimate cause of desire (which includes repulsion) and therefore also the cause of all suffering.[4] The cure for suffering is thus the overcoming of ignorance by correctly understanding the very lessons conveyed in the diagram. With proper insight into one's motivations, one can become liberated from the traps of desire and thus the cycle of causation altogether.

This possibility of escape is visually embodied by a buddha standing entirely outside the wheel, at the top right of the painting. He points to an inscription (in a dark-blue cartouche) and set of symbols at the top left, indicating that the teachings of Buddhism are the means of escape.

The Inscription

The inscription in this painting includes four passages that convey slightly different meanings. It begins with the first of two verses that commentaries say should be inscribed on the wheel of existence to motivate adoption of the Buddhist path.[5] A second short verse summarizes the idea of dependent origination as the crux of the Buddha's teachings. This verse also appears commonly elsewhere in Buddhist art and ritual to consecrate images and objects, making them efficacious.[6] The third passage exhorts sentient beings to do good deeds and is sometimes also recited to pacify the deceased.[7] The last phrase is a mantra used to ritualize the completion of the image after artists have finished painting it. The combination of these different passages reveals that the wheel of existence, though ostensibly educational in its diagrammatic form, also has connections to ethical directives, ritual interactions, and perceptions of art as sacred. Above the inscription appears an eight-spoked wheel (*dharmachakra*) on a lotus, designating the teachings of the Buddha, and a small white circle, representing the liberation of nirvana.[8]

Format, History, and Transformation

Even this single painting reveals something of the adaptability of the wheel of existence to various circumstances. For example, it unusually depicts a figure in Western clothing and a pith helmet in the foreground of the human realm, exemplifying the cross-cultural interactions of its time. It is also painted on cloth and framed by multicolored brocade, in the format of a portable hanging scroll known as a thangka, even though the wheel of existence would more paradigmatically appear in murals on the entrance walls of monasteries or temples. Indeed, the earliest extant wheel of existence dates from the

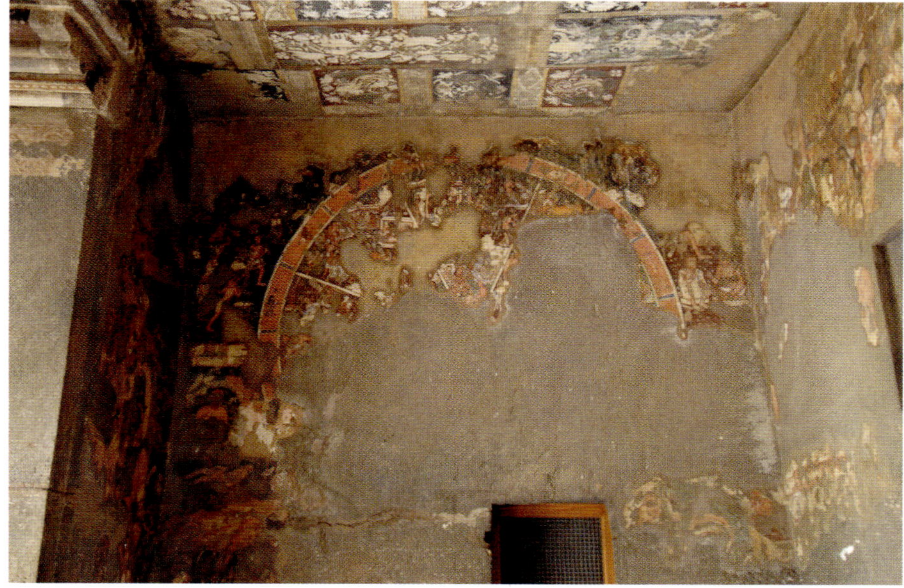

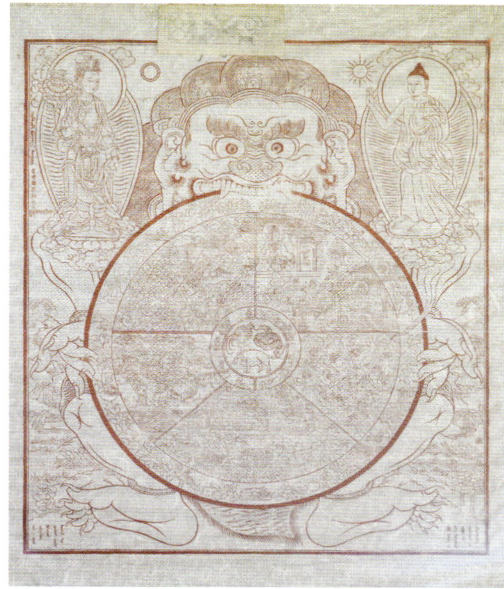

Wheel of Existence; Cave 17, Ajanta, India; 5th century; mural; photograph by Eric Huntington

Wheel of Existence; Tashicholing Temple, Ulaanbaatar, Mongolia; 20th or 21st century; block print; height approx. 24 in. (61 cm); photograph by Eric Huntington

For more on contemporary art, see Ice Buddha, no. 108.

fifth century and remains, albeit fragmented, on the walls of the exterior entranceway of Cave 17 at Ajanta, India. While many characteristics of this image differ from more recent versions, the overall message seems similar.[9] Such large, public images may help spread the ideas of Buddhism, just as the earliest textual sources describe the wheel of existence as a lasting record of the stories of the Buddha's disciple Maudgalyayana, who had visited all the realms of existence to witness for himself the consequences of good and bad actions.[10] In East Asia and Mongolia, Maudgalyayana's travels became a popular subject of narrative art,[11] although versions of the wheel of existence also appear in various forms, including a relief sculpture at Baodingshan in China[12] and a frontispiece illustration for the *Avatamsaka Sutra* (*Flower Garland Sutra*) in Korea. More recently, imagery of the wheel of existence has also been disseminated through the traditional medium of woodblock printing. Perhaps in part because of the didactic elegance of the imagery, the wheel of existence has also been reinterpreted by a variety of contemporary artists and authors to express views about the modern world, including themes of capitalism, social dysfunction, the relevance of Buddhism, and more.

Further Reading

O rgyan 'jigs med chos kyi dbang po (Patrul). 1988. *Kunzang Lama'i Shelung / The Words of My Perfect Teacher*. Translated by the Padmakara Translation Group. Boston: Shambhala.

Teiser, Stephen F. 2006. *Reinventing the Wheel: Paintings of Rebirth in Medieval Buddhist Temples*. Seattle: University of Washington Press.

Tharchin, Lobsang. 1984. *King Udrayana and the Wheel of Life: The History and Meaning of the Buddhist Teaching of Dependent Origination*. Howell, NJ: Mahayana Sutra and Tantra Press.

Notes

1 Teiser 2006, 56.
2 See, for example, Lopez 2004a, 119.
3 See, for example, Roberts and Yeshi 2019, 1.18.
4 For more on this subject, see Tharchin 1984, 83–143.
5 Sopa 1984, 128–32, 143n12.
6 Berounsky and Sklenka 2005, 69n25, 70.
7 Śāntideva, Kunpal, and Chöga 2003, 522.
8 See for example Mejor 2010, 678.
9 Teiser 2006, 79–100.
10 Teiser 2006, 53–56.
11 Kollmar-Paulenz 2010.
12 See for example Kucera 2016, fig. 18; Teiser 2006, chap. 9.

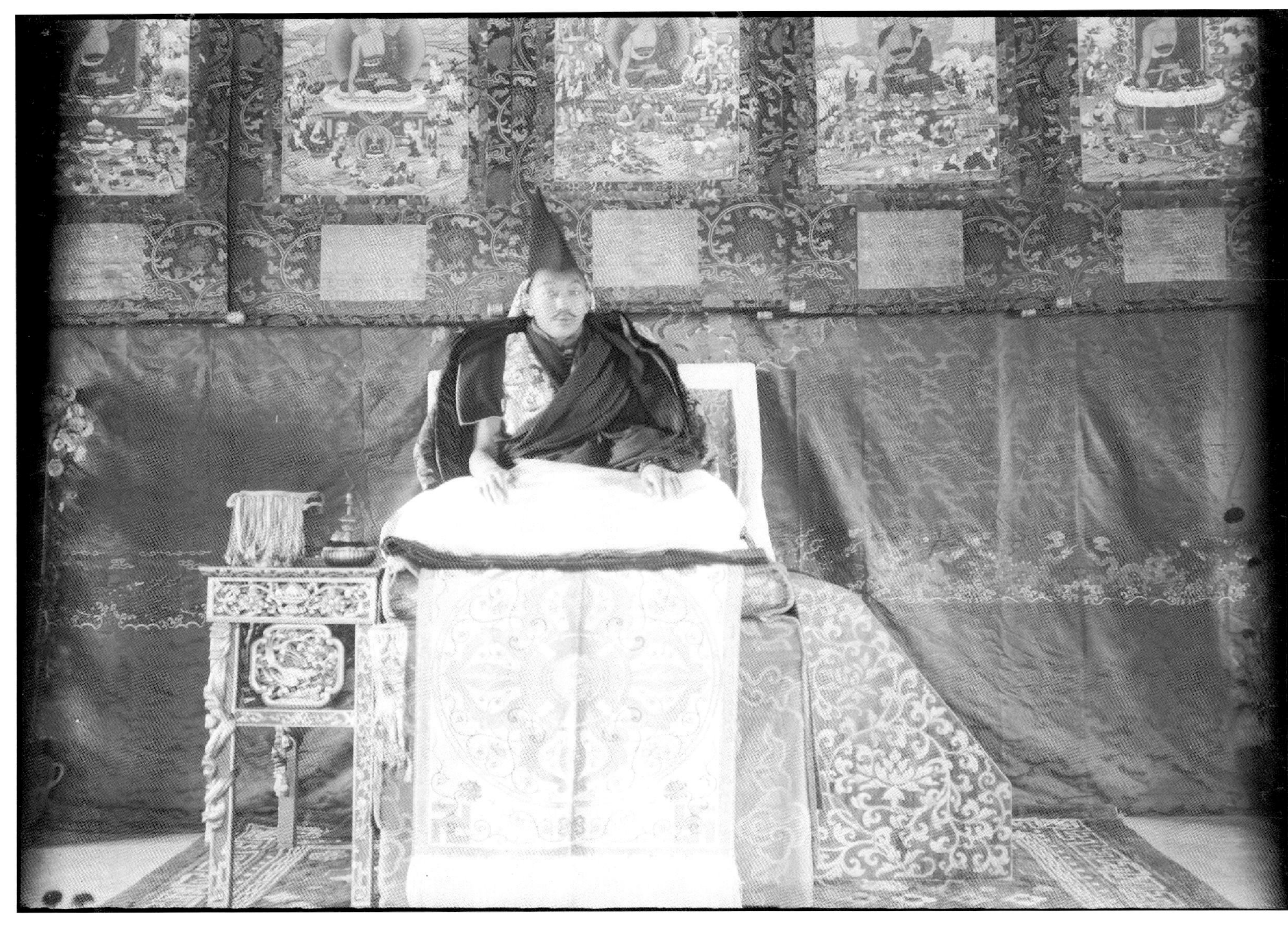

Sir Charles Bell (British, 1870–1945) and Rabden Lepcha (Sikkimese, act. early 20th century); The Thirteenth Dalai Lama on Throne in Norbulingka; Norbulingka, Lhasa; October 14, 1921; lantern slide from negative; 3³⁄₁₆ × 3³⁄₁₆ in. (8.1 × 8.1 cm); Pitt Rivers Museum, University of Oxford; 1998.285.88.2; photograph

Nº 98

Photograph of the Thirteenth Dalai Lama

Lhasa, U region, central Tibet, 1921

Lenses of Modernity: Photography in Tibet and the Himalayas

RIGA SHAKYA

For other objects related to Dalai Lamas, see Desi Sanggye Gyatso's Medical Paintings, no. 73; Potala Palace, no. 71.

PHOTOGRAPHY IS CONSIDERED ONE OF THE MOST TRANSFORMATIVE TECHNOLOGIES of the twentieth century. At the turn of the century, visual representations of Tibet were relatively rare. This black-and-white photograph depicts the Thirteenth Dalai Lama Tubten Gyatso (1876–1933) sitting on a ceremonial throne atop an ornate, multicolored dais at Norbulingka, his summer palace. The Dalai Lama is the highest-ranking lineage in the Geluk Tibetan Buddhist tradition, and successive reincarnations have served as the spiritual and political leaders of Tibet since the seventeenth century. The Thirteenth Dalai Lama ruled during a period of tremendous change in the greater world and across the Tibetan Plateau.[1] In the face of invasions by both the Qing and British Empires, he traveled across Asia, declared Tibetan independence in 1913, and implemented printing, military, and infrastructural reforms to attempt to modernize Tibet.[2]

Taken by British colonial officer Sir Charles Bell (1870–1945) and his Sikkimese orderly Rabden Lepcha on the morning of October 14, 1921, during the 1920–1921 British mission to Lhasa, the photograph is possibly the first taken of the Tibetan ruler in Lhasa. Bell, who served as political officer in Bhutan, Sikkim, and Tibet, writes in his diary that the Dalai Lama was particularly attentive to the staging of the photograph, "giving an order here, making a slight change there."[3] Developments in photographic technology and the Tibetan experience of British colonialism meant that the "Great Thirteenth" was the first Dalai Lama to be photographed. Tubten Gyatso's embrace of the photographic medium is emblematic of Tibet's encounter with modernity, and the photograph reveals how the history of photography in Tibet and the Himalayan region is entangled with that of colonialism and nation-building.

Empire, Nation, and the Photographic Archive

The visual history of modern Tibet is often thought of as the opposition between colonial stereotypes and indigenous visions. Yet the relationship between these impulses was often fraught and blurry. As scholar-soldiers, British colonial photographers were engaged in the production of useful knowledge about the region for the benefit of the empire. Following the British invasion of Tibet in 1904, photographers like Bell also saw their work as dislodging the existing cachet of exotic images that contributed to Orientalist visions of Tibet as Shangri-la.[4] They did so by embedding themselves in the highest echelons of society and building intimate relations with Tibetan aristocrats and lamas who would provide them unprecedented access to private and public life in Lhasa.[5]

The photographic records of this encounter consist of portraits of the Tibetan elite at work and play, as well as detailed ethnographic photographs of rituals, festivals, and scenes of daily life.[6] Rather than reproducing an unequal relationship of power, these photographs reveal a relationship that depended on intimacy, intermingling, and mutual accommodation. The institutional and informal afterlives of the colonial photographic archive, created in part with the collaboration of indigenous image-makers—such as Rabden Lepcha—would establish visual tropes, such as the portrait, the "Potala shot," and the ritualized scene, which would come to represent "the historical and political image of Tibet."[7] Such tropes were reproduced in the ethnographic photography of the Tibetan borderlands by and during the nation-building projects of republican and later Communist China.[8]

Coupled with the flow of trade into Lhasa from India, Western fashions and commodities—including cameras—became popular with progressive members of the Tibetan and Himalayan elite who were

(left) Sir Charles Bell (British, 1870–1945); Rabden Lepcha in Delhi; ca. 1915; glass negative; 5⅜ × 3 ½ in. (13.8 cm × 8.8 cm); Pitt Rivers Museum, University of Oxford; 1998.285.603; photograph © Pitt Rivers Museum, University of Oxford

(right) Chen Zonglie (Chinese; b. 1932); Jigme Tariṅg, Tibetan noblemen and official, holding cine camera with still camera hanging at his side; Lhasa, Tibet; possibly 1958; dimensions unknown; photograph from Xinhua News Agency

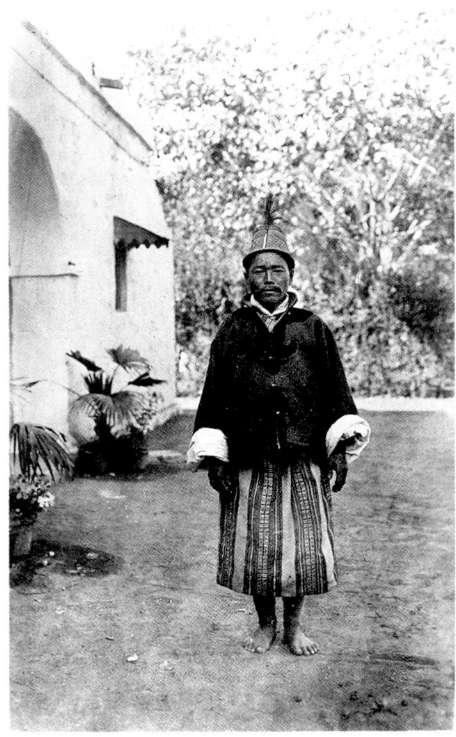

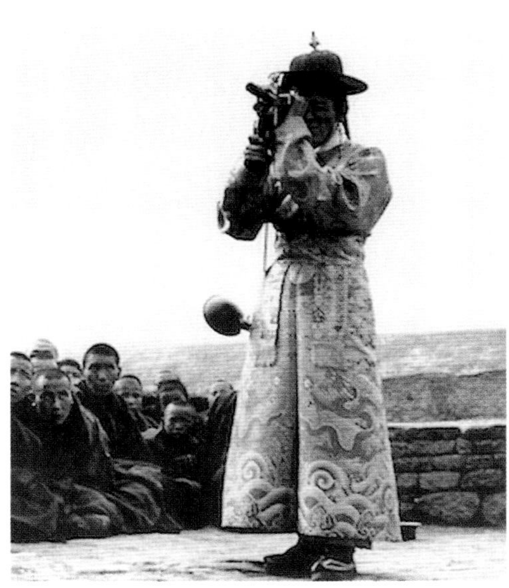

sympathetic to modernizing reforms. This would result in a generation of Tibetan photographers, such as the politician and general Dasang Damdul Tsarong (1888–1959), who used the name George, and Demo Rinpoche, the nephew of the Thirteenth Dalai Lama. These indigenous photographers were early adopters who began to realize the power of the lens as a tool of self-representation.

Shutters and Selves

For examples of traditional portraiture, see Portrait of Lowo Khenchen Sonam Lhundrub, no. 63; Portrait of the Ninth Karmapa, no. 66; Portrait of Ngadak Puntsok Rigdzin, no. 70; Portrait of Situ Panchen, no. 83.

Historically, the only visual representations of Tibetan religious leaders took the form of thangkas or devotional tapestries and gilt statues that captured idealized images of the subject based on Buddhist aesthetics. The reproducibility of the photographic image meant that Buddhist rulers like the Thirteenth Dalai Lama, the Eighth Jibzundamba in Mongolia, and the monarchs of Bhutan and Sikkim would begin to be seen in a new light by audiences at home and abroad. The legitimacy of sovereign Himalayan nations would be confirmed by the photographic record.[9] At the same time, subjects across the Himalayas would be able to visualize their rulers and religious leaders beyond fleeting glances at state and religious ceremonies, arousing feelings of national belonging and devotion in a distinctly modern way.

While the image-making practices of British colonial missions would popularize photography among the indigenous elite across the Himalayas, it was merchant communities such as the Lhasa Newars and Kashmiri Muslims who would ensure its popularity among the local populace. Newar and Kashmiri traders had been living in the urban centers of Lhasa and Shigatse since the seventeenth century. Following the enthronement of the Fourteenth Dalai Lama in 1940, these transnational communities capitalized on their access to camera equipment and chemicals and opened the first photography studios in urban centers like Lhasa and Darjeeling. Middle-class families began to sit for staged portraits and family photographs in front of scenic backdrops, holding props like bicycles and radios, or dressed in Western clothing to reflect their status as modern subjects.[10]

For more about the development of modern art, see Gendun Chopel's Woman Applying Kohl, no. 102.

Changing notions of selfhood under the influence of the camera lens were also reflected in the fine arts. Painters like Amdo Jampa (1911–2002), a pivotal figure in the development of modern Tibetan art, were inspired by the ability of the camera to capture the likeness of the subject. While he began his training in thangka painting, Amdo Jampa would go on to study Chinese classical panting, and Western classical and modernist art, as well socialist realism, through a remarkable career that spanned the best part of the twentieth century.[11] Appointed court painter to the Fourteenth Dalai Lama, he worked from photographs and incorporated photorealistic portraiture techniques into traditional Tibetan forms, typified by his murals at the Norbulingka. His mural painting of the Fourteenth Dalai Lama's enthronement

Amdo Jampa (Tibetan, 1911–2002); Detail of Mural of Fourteenth Dalai Lama Receiving International Dignitaries; Norbulingka, Lhasa, Tibet; 1956; photograph © Thomas Laird, 2018 from *Murals of Tibet*, TASCHEN

On later generations of Tibetan contemporary artists, see Ice Buddha, no. 108.

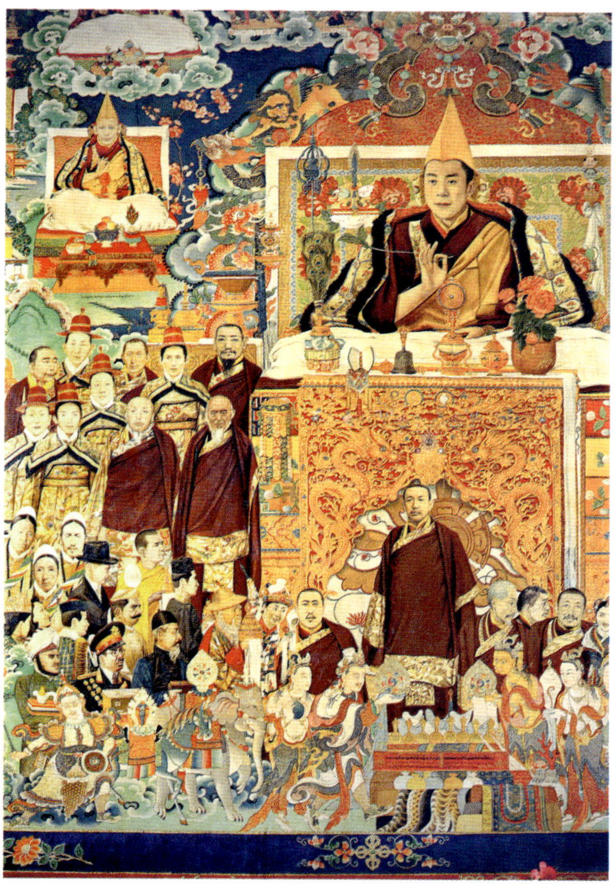

ceremony marks the first realist depiction of the Dalai Lama's personage, and its creation is considered "a remarkable event in Tibetan art history."[12] Amdo Jampa's openness to new forms of expression served as an inspiration to a later generation of Tibetan contemporary artists who came to prominence in the post–Cultural Revolution era and created their own forms of visual culture.[13]

Camera Tibetica

Photography has long been privileged as a historical source due to the tangible and visceral encounter with the past that it offers, a lens more conducive to a subjective reframing of the history than that of text. Yet historical photographs of Tibet often raise more questions than they provide answers, for as Roland Barthes observed, these images only contain traces of things past.[14] Today, galvanized by social media, more photographs of the Tibetann Plateau and the greater Himalayan region circulate than ever before. Thinking about photography in Tibet and the Himalayas as a practice with a distinct history allows us to see the diverse ways in which local visual cultures responded to and were shaped by the encounter with modernity.

Further Reading

Harris, Clare, and Tsering Shakya. 2003. *Seeing Lhasa: British Depictions of the Tibetan Capital, 1936–1947*. Exhibition catalog. Chicago: Serindia.

Harris, Clare. 2016. *Photography and Tibet*. London: Reaktion.

Tashi, Tsewang. 2014. "Modernism in Tibetan Art: The Creative Journey of Four Artists." PhD diss., Norwegian University of Science and Technology.

Notes

1 'Jigs med bsam grub 2000.
2 See Goldstein 1989.
3 Charles Bell 1946, 336.
4 For more on the British invasion of Tibet, see McKay 2012.
5 Harris and Tsering Shakya 2003.
6 H. Richardson 1993.
7 H. Richardson 1993, 24.
8 See Tsomu 2013; Y. Liu 2021; Aris 1992.
9 For example, the British political officer John Claude White photographed the 1907 coronation of the first Bhutanese king Ugyen Wangchuck. J. C. White 1909.
10 The most famous of these studios is Das Studio founded by Newari merchant Thakur Das Pradhan, which remains open today in Darjeeling. Unnamed photography studios in Lhasa are mentioned in Harris and Shakya 2003, 102. For more on the Nepalese and Muslim communities of Tibet, see Atwill 2018.
11 See Khri gong o rgyan tshe ring 2017.
12 Tsewang Tashi 2014.
13 This is attested to by prominent contemporary Tibetan artists such as Gonkar Gyatso and Tsewang Tashi. The latter recently gave a talk at Columbia University about the intersecting lives of Amdo Jampa and Gendun Chopel; see Tsewang Tashi 2020.
14 Barthes 1981.

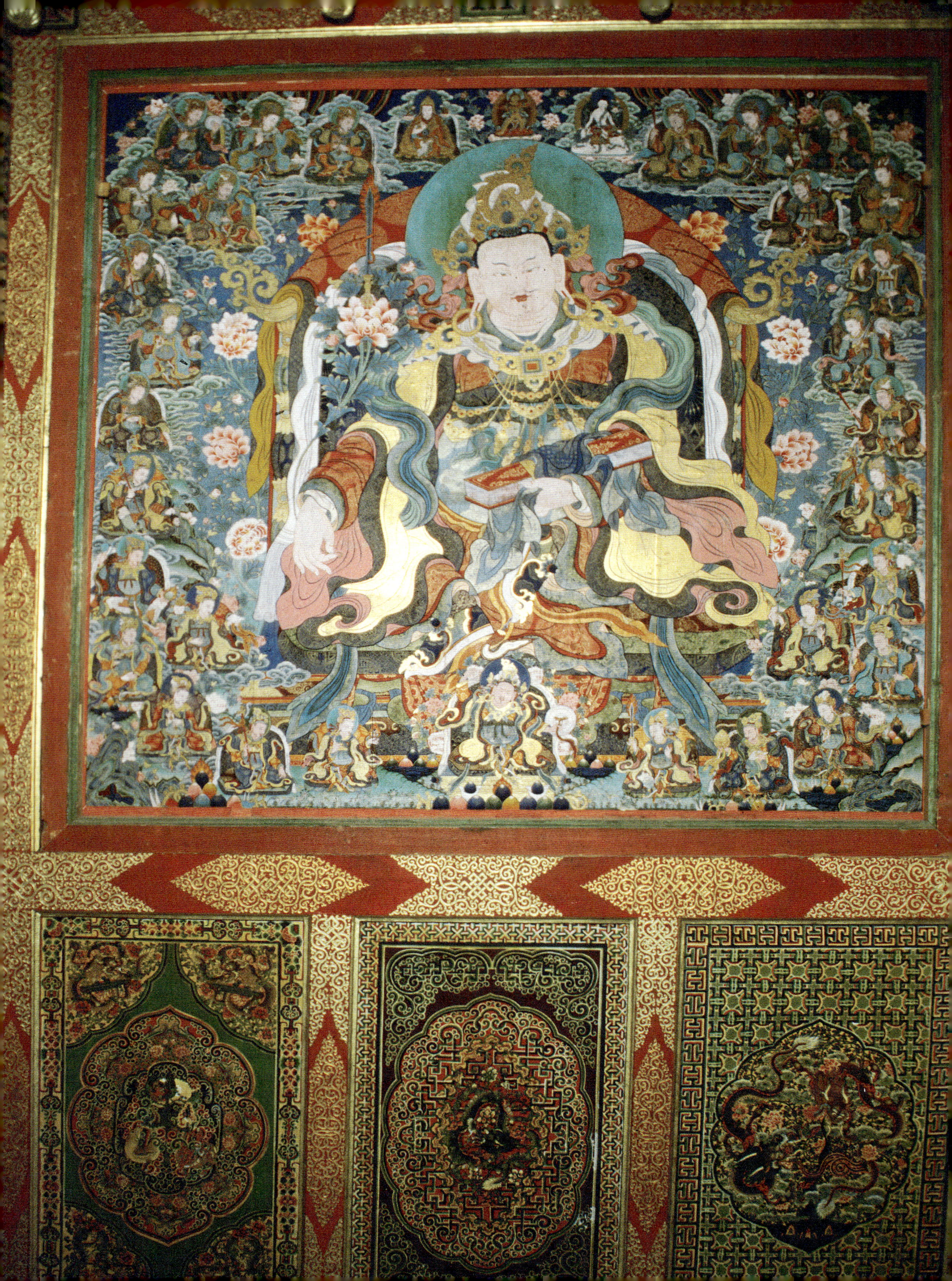

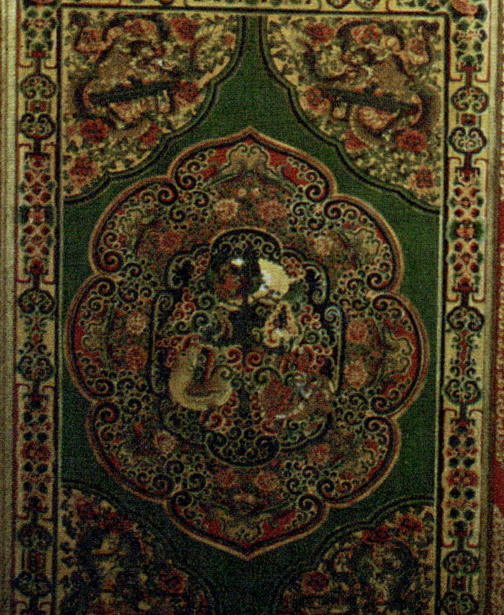
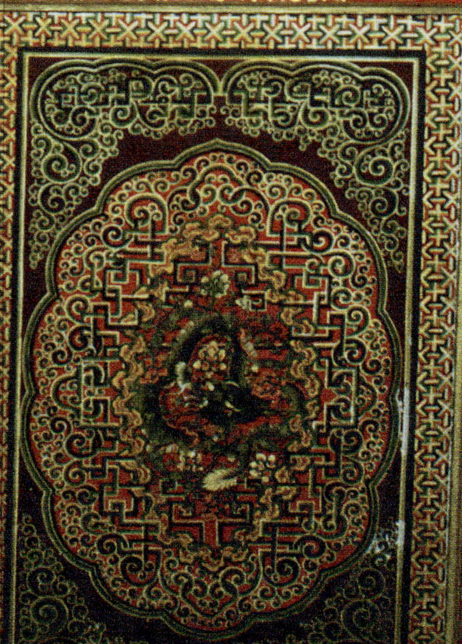
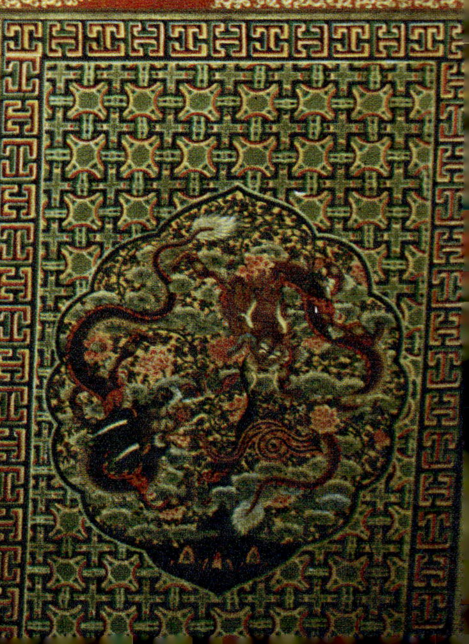

№ 99

Shambhala Kings Mural

Sengge Shong Mago Monastery, Rebkong, Amdo region, eastern Tibet (Qinghai Province, China), ca. 1935

Recognizing Rebkong's Regional Painting Contributions

ROB LINROTHE

THIS MURAL ON THE PORCH OF THE JAMPA LHAKHANG (Maitreya Shrine) of Sengge Shong Mago Monastery, Ganden Puntsok Ling, is among a handful of large-scale, pre-1950 paintings to survive in place and in good condition in Amdo Rebkong.[1] The shuttering of Buddhist institutions, the disruption of the social system that supported them, and the widespread destruction of Buddhist visual culture in the Rebkong area began with the Chinese takeover in the early 1950s. It intensified with the suppression of the late 1950s and culminated with the Cultural Revolution in the mid-1960s.[2] Along with five other paintings on the porch done at the same time, around 1935, this mural is a datable benchmark documenting the development of both twentieth-century and contemporary Rebkong art. On the one hand, the murals bear witness to the highly prized modes of painting associated with Amdo artists who worked in central Tibetan centers such as Lhasa and Shigatse in the first half of the twentieth century, the so-called first modern Tibetan artists, such as Gendun Chopel (1903–1951) and Jampa Tseten ("Amdo Jampa," 1911–2002).[3] On the other hand, it is possible to see continuities between these paintings and the resurgent, distinctively Rebkong Buddhist art after the 1980s, which has become well known and commercially successful in such metropolitan areas as Shanghai, Beijing, and Taipei.

See Gendun Chopel's Woman Applying Kohl, no. 102.

The mural is painted on cloth and then mounted and framed by painted wooden boards with dense gold patterning, supported by new colorful dragon-medallion panels below. Elaborately carved and gilded pillars support a roof over the porch. As with most Himalayan porch-entrances to shrines, the Jampa Lhakhang mural depicts the guardian generals of the four directions (*lokapalas*) in pairs on either side of the doorway. At the right end is a lovely depiction of the protectress Lakshmi Pal Lhamo surrounded by a large number of local mountain gods and with Tseringma of the Five Long-Life Sisters directly below her. At the other end of the vestibule is the mural portraying the Shambhala Kings.

For an example of the four generals in a different context, see Jivarama's Sketchbook, no. 56.

See Mountain God Kula Khari, no. 92.

Shambhala is a hidden Buddhist Pure Land somewhere in the north and ruled by a succession of bodhisattva-kings.[4] As articulated in the Tibetan literature surrounding the late Indian tantra, the *Kalachakra*, at some future date a millenarian army will emerge to confront the forces of darkness that oppose Buddhism and establish a new age of enlightenment. The mural depicts the Seven Dharma Kings (Rigden) of Shambhala and the Twenty-five Vidyadhara (knowledge-holder; also known as Kalki) Kings.[5] The large king at the center of the composition is Yashas or Manjushrikirti (Jampel Drakpa) who is also recognized as the second preincarnation of the Panchen Lama.[6] Wearing a crisply folded white turban like those in images of the early Tibetan emperors of the seventh through the ninth century, Manjushrikirti holds a book in his left hand, and in his right the stem of a pink lotus bearing a vertical sword with a blue blade and flaming tip. These attributes reinforce his connection to his namesake, the bodhisattva Manjushri. The other thirty-one kings surrounding Yashas are identified by gold inscriptions on the light azure background. The second-largest king, directly below Yashas, is another emanation of Manjushri, the warrior Rudrachakra (Drakpo Khorlo Chen), who holds a spear and a sword. He is the twenty-fifth Vidyadhara who will lead the final battle against the forces of darkness.

See the Kalachakra Mandala in the Potala Palace, no. 77.

For more on the Panchen Lama and their pre-incarnations, see Nartang Woodblock Prints and Their Painted Copies, no. 81.

Kunga Shawo (fl. early 20th century); Shambhala Kings Mural; porch of the Jampa Lhakhang (Maitreya Temple), Sengge Shong Mago Monastery, Ganden Puntsok Ling, Lower Sengge Shong Village, Rebkong, Amdo region, eastern Tibet (Qinghai Province, China); ca. 1935; pigments on cloth; dimensions unknown; photograph by R. Linrothe

In 2002, with a learned and devout local monk, Gendun Akhu Pelzang,[7] we explored many of the prominent monasteries in the area, among them Sengge Shong Mago. We learned that during preceding decades the Jampa Lhakhang had been turned into a granary for the village by its Chinese overseers. Although the sculpture and paintings inside the shrine were destroyed, the porch murals, with their high quality and subtle shades of the pigments, had somehow survived. We were able to locate an elderly monk who as an apprentice painter at age sixteen had assisted two master painters in their thirties in

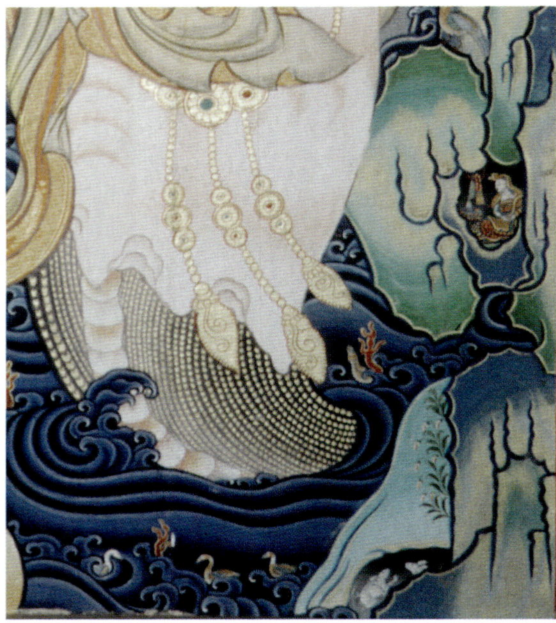

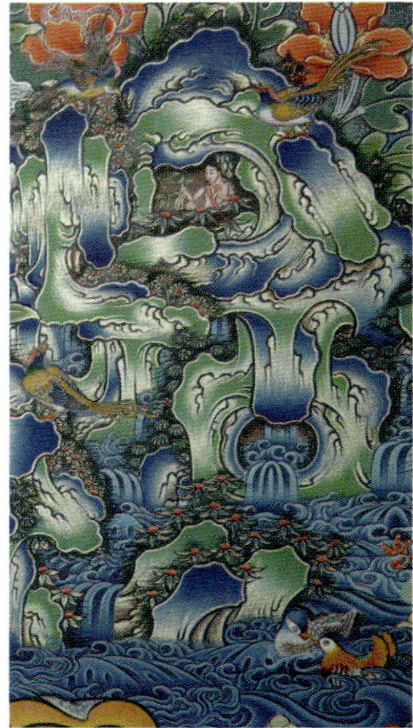

Kunga Shawo (fl. early 20th century); Detail of Virupaksha Lokapala Mural, right edge; porch of Lower Sengge Shong Jampa Lhakhang; ca. 1935; photograph by R. Linrothe

Sengge Shong artists (act. early 2000s); Detail of Vaishravana Lokapala Mural, right edge; Rongwo Gonchen Monastery shrine to Kelden Gyatso; 2006; photograph by R. Linrothe

creating the murals in about 1935. The eighty-three-year-old monk, Nyingben, recalled that one artist was named Kunga Shawo, and the other, the monk Kelzang. Kunga Shawo painted the four *lokapalas* and the Shambhala Kings on the porch, which would leave Kelzang as primarily responsible for the Lakshmi mural.[8]

These paintings establish a relatively rare datable point in the evolution of Rebkong painting in the second quarter of the twentieth century. Between 1950 and 1980, local Buddhist painting was curtailed and its development suspended. In the late 1980s and 1990s, when painting of Buddhist subject matter resumed as part of the general relaxing of restrictions on religious practice, it was fueled by pent-up demand to replace or refurbish dozens of shrines and monasteries in the region damaged or destroyed during the Cultural Revolution. A few artists who like Nyingben were trained in the 1930s and 1940s transmitted the earlier mode of painting to the younger generation; the older artists included Nyingben, Shawo Tsering, Jyamsho, and others.[9] Many of the particular characteristics represented in the 1930s painting are visible in the revival style, demonstrating the fidelity of many recent painters to former painting practices.

Contemporary continuities from the foundational inheritance as well as further developments can be illustrated by comparing details from *lokapala* compositions on both the porch of the Jampa Lhakang in Lower Sengge Shong and in a shrine at the largest monastery of Rebkong, the Rongwo Gonchen Monastery. The latter shrine was dedicated to Kelden Gyatso (1607–1677), the first in the Rongwo Drubchen Tulku lineage, and was completed around 2006 by painters familiar with the 1935 Jampa Lhakhang paintings; indeed, the murals were created by painters from Sengge Shong Village. In a detail from the circa 1935 Virupaksha Lokapala of Sengge Shong, blue-green rock formations with sharply cusped outlines edged in gold feature two cave-like cavities. In one, a tiny recluse sits in meditation, and in the other (at the bottom), two diminutive white rabbits frolic. A pair of colorful birds perch on the rocks above the meditator and call to each other. Ducks, fish, and coral trees emerge from the dark blue foamy lake.

Nearly identical forms appear in the Vaishravana Lokapala of circa 2006 at the Kelden Gyatso Shrine, though with more insistence, detail, and density. The biggest difference is accounted for by the colors. Interviews with older painters in Rebkong made it clear that previously they used stone-ground pigments, which allow lighter, subtler, and softer hues. Post-1980, all the Rebkong painters embraced standardized, prefabricated, industrial paints with harsher but brighter colors. In both the pre-1950 paintings and the twenty-first-century murals, there is a willingness to incorporate extreme differences of scale, from the gigantic to the minuscule, and to seed all areas of the surface with elaborate detail work and surprising elements that reward close looking. The elaborate textile and serpent patterns of the *nagini* at the right edge of the Virupaksha Lokapala mural are examples of the latter, and the huge

Dondrub Gyatso (act. 1990s); Detail of Buddha Nageshvara Raja Mural; Lower Sengge Shong Jampa Lhakhang; late 1990s; photograph by R. Linrothe

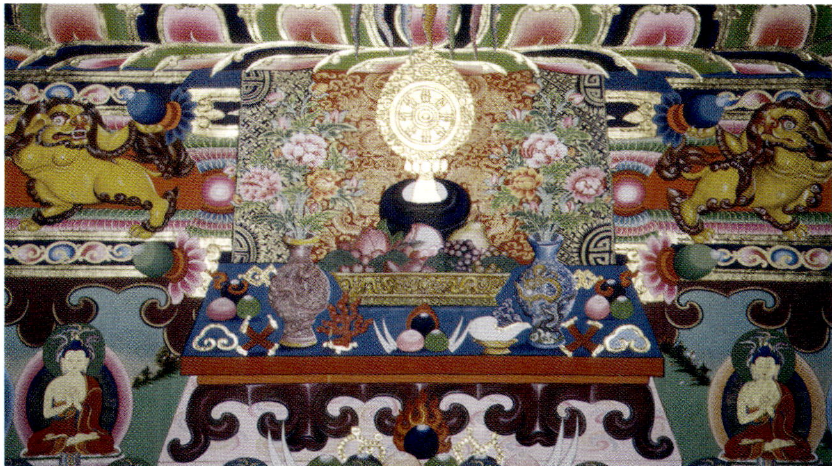

hibiscus flowers on the right edge, larger than the cave's mahasiddha with his ritual drum (*damaru*) in the 2006 painting, illustrate the former.

Another tendency incipient in the 1930s paintings but more highly developed among contemporary painters is what can be called selective naturalism.[10] In the 1990s a young artist named Dondrub Gyatso painted a mural of Buddha Nageshvara Raja inside the Sengge Shong Mago Jampa Lhakhang, a detail of which is included here. While the buddhas in the corners of the detail are in a traditional mode, the altar table is in one-point perspective, the vases and other objects on the table cast shadows, and the two lions on the throne are in an aggressively "plastic" mode (in the senses both of fully moldable and of a synthetic polymer material), with glinting highlights accentuating the illusory roundness of their forms. The lessons of artists such as Gendun Chopel and Jampa Tseten, famous for incorporating photographic effects and selective aspects of Western painting traditions, increasingly make their appearance in contemporary Rebkong painting.[11] It is no surprise that both of these renowned artists, who worked in central Tibet as well as India, are celebrated native sons of Amdo.

Further Reading

Linrothe, Rob. 2001a. "Creativity, Freedom and Control: The Renaissance of Tibetan Buddhist Painting in Rebgong." *Tibet Journal* 26, no. 3–4, 9–50.

Stevenson, Mark. 2005. *Many Paths: Searching for Old Tibet in New China*. Melbourne: Lothian Books.

Weiner, Benno. 2020. *The Chinese Revolution on the Tibetan Frontier*. Ithaca, NY: Cornell University Press.

Notes

1 Amdo is the Tibetan name for a dominantly Tibetan cultural region situated north of central and western Tibet (now known as the Tibetan Autonomous Region of the People's Republic of China [PRC]), and on the southern border of Mongol cultural spaces. After 1949, areas of Amdo were carved by the PRC into parts of Qinghai, Gansu, and Sichuan Provinces. Rebkong, now in Qinghai Province, was an important artistic center of long standing and enduring connections to the Buddhist institutions of Lhasa and Shigatse. See Gruschke 2001; Smith 2013.

2 Weiner 2020; M. Stevenson 2005; Linrothe 2001a.

3 Harris 1999, 50–56, 165–67; Tsewang Tashi 2018, 7–26, 39–56; Wen Pulin 2002; Lopez 2013.

4 Kollmar-Paulenz 1992–93; Lo Bue 2010a.

5 For their names and primary attributes, see Himalayan Art Resources, https://www.himalayanart.org/search/set.cfm?setID=1964.

6 Complete sets of preincarnations are included on Himalayan Art Resources, http://www.himalayanart.org/search/set.cfm?setID=72.

7 Pelzang later produced a study of the monasteries of Rebkong (Reb gong), their histories and holdings: Chu skyes Dge 'dun dpal bzang 2007.

8 A fuller account of our interviews with Nyingben and several locally esteemed painters is found in Linrothe 2015.

9 Linrothe 2001a; M. Stevenson 2005; Fraser 2010, 363–64; Fraser 2011.

10 Linrothe 2001a, 21–22.

11 Harris 1999, 50–56, 165–67; Tsewang Tashi 2018, 7–26, 39–56; Wen Pulin 2002; Lopez 2013.

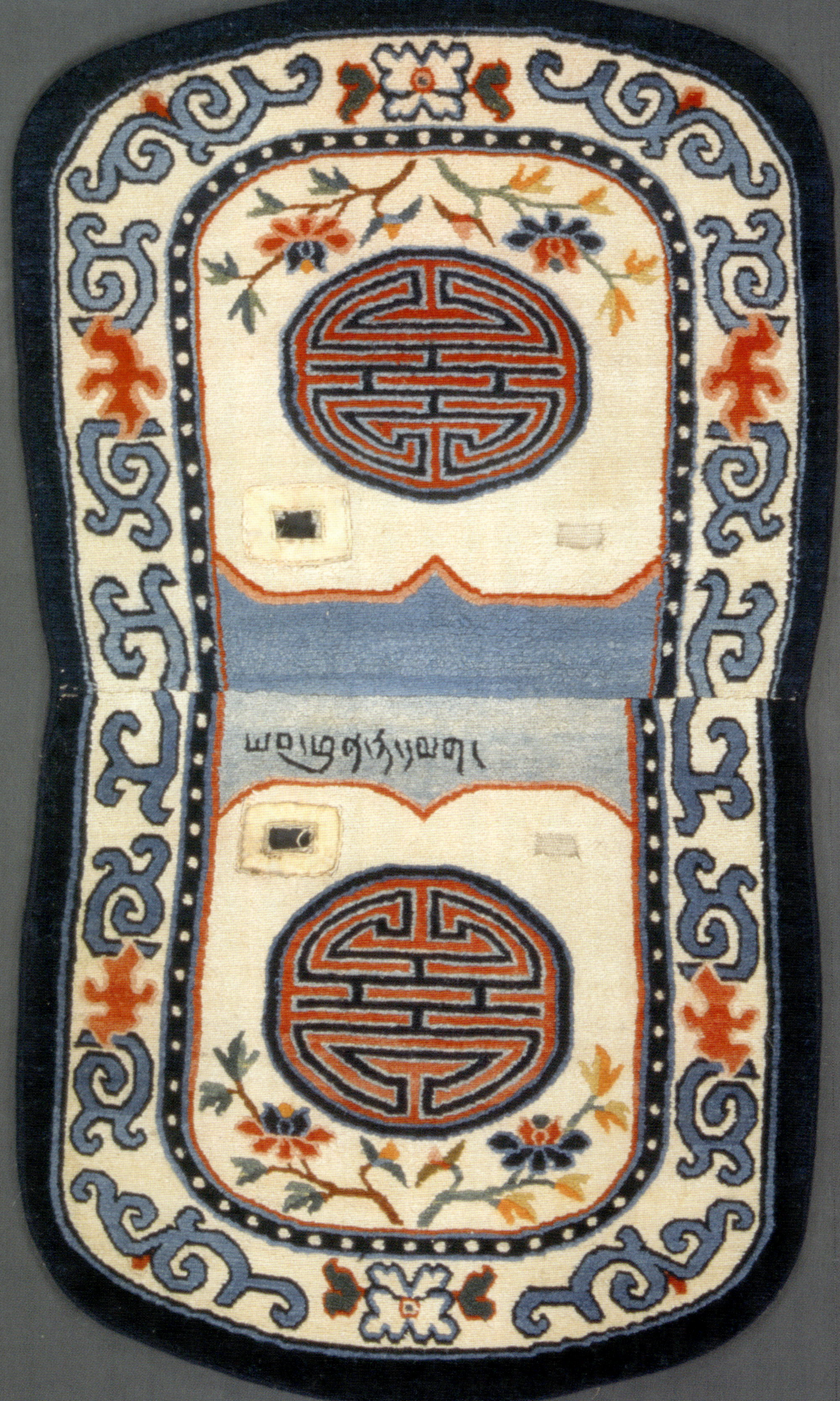

№ 100 Saddle Carpet for the Yabzhi Punkhang Ceremonial Cavalry

Gyantse, Tsang region, central Tibet, 1930s

A Mundane Craft Elevated for a Commemorative Parade

ALICE TRAVERS

PILE WEAVING IS AN ANCIENT TRADITION among the populations of Central and North Asia. In Tibet, it dates back at least to the period of the early kings (7th–9th centuries).[1] These carpets (*den*, a generic word meaning seat, cushion, or mattress) were made mainly of the abundantly available highland sheep's wool, which, despite its somewhat rough quality, is ideal for pile rugs due to its flexibility and luster.[2] Tibetan carpet production can be divided into two main categories: the primitive planted-pile carpet (*tsukden*), which is still woven by nomads and farmers on horizontal frames and back-strap looms, and the knotted-pile carpet (*drumtse* or *rumden*), thought to have appeared later, which is woven on a stationary vertical loom (*taktri*) and involves an archaic method of tying multiple knots around a continuous warp (*gyu*) thread. The Tibetan pile-weaving tradition is based on a unique cut-loop weaving technique that is distinct from all others worldwide, but that also reflects centuries of cultural exchange.[3]

Saddle Rugs

For a Tibetan wooden saddle, see Saddle Made for Yuthok Tashi Dhondup, no. 101.

Saddle rugs (*taden* or *gaden*) and other woven equestrian decorative elements like forehead trappings composed a ubiquitous category of knotted, pile-woven carpets. Because Tibetan wooden saddles required a lot of padding for both horse and rider, saddle carpets usually came in pairs: a larger one placed under the saddle and a smaller one on top, which served as a cushion to provide warmth and comfort to the rider.[4]

The top saddle carpet presented here has a wool weft (*pun*) and a cotton warp and is made, like most others, of two parts woven separately and then sewn together, with visible holes bordered in leather to accommodate straps. It has been identified by the Tibetan scholar Kesang Tashi as belonging to a set of twenty-four pieces woven in the 1930s for the ceremonial cavalry of Yabzhi Punkhang; all these carpets are recognizable not only in their identical structure and design, but also because they display an inscription (a rare feature on carpets) allowing us to contextualize the object: "*yab phun rta dmag*," that is, "cavalry of the yab [gzhis] phun [khang family]."[5] The Punkhang noble house goes back to the Eleventh Dalai Lama (1838–1856), whose family entered one of the most prestigious subgroups of the Lhasa aristocracy (*kudrak*), the *yabzhi* (literally, "the estate of the father"), which comprises six ennobled families of former Dalai Lamas.[6]

The Ceremonial Cavalry of the New Year State Ceremonies

Saddle Carpet; presumably Punkhang family estate, Gyantse, Tsang region, central Tibet; 1930s; wool pile and weft, cotton warp; 25¼ × 48½ in. (64 × 123 cm); The Newark Museum of Art; Purchase 2002 Helen McMahon Brady Cutting Fund 2002.1.40; photograph courtesy The Newark Museum of Art

The ceremonial cavalry of Yabzhi Punkhang took part in the commemorative parade of Güüshi Khan's troops in and around Lhasa, which was part of the annual Great Prayer (*monlam*) Festival, instituted by the Fifth Dalai Lama (1617–1682).[7] The military parade was supervised by two Yasor commanders (Yasor *chikhyab* or Yasor *tripa*), government lay officials (*drungkhor*) of the fourth rank appointed every year to the task of embodying the Mongol general of one of the two wings (*yeru* and *yonru*). The parade of the cavalry started on the twenty-second day of the first month with the "preparation of the camp at Lubu" (Lubu *gardrik*), followed by the "review of the troops at Trapchi (or Drachi)" (Trapchi *tsisher*) held on the twenty-third day, and the "gallop behind the fort" (*dzonggyab zhambel*) in a meadow north of the Potala Palace on the twenty-sixth day, when cavalrymen competed in marksmanship while galloping.[8]

High-ranking aristocratic lay officials had to provide around five hundred troops for the events, adorned in ancient military costumes and with their horses decorated with pomp. They were chosen from

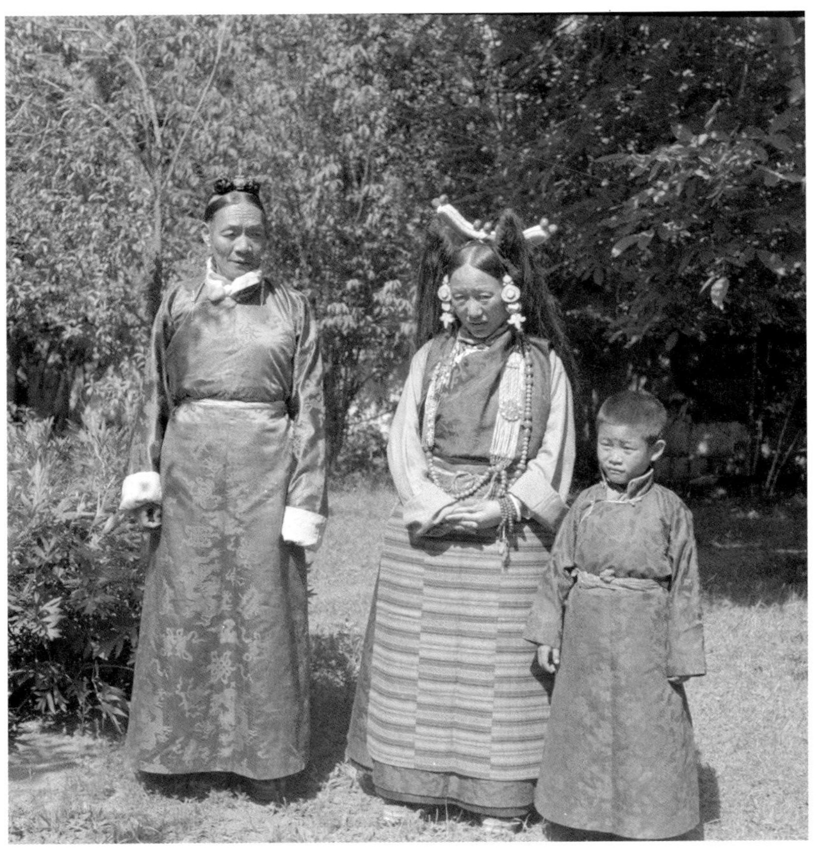

Hugh E. Richardson (British, 1905–2000); *Phunkhang Yabshi Kung, His Wife and Son*; Tibet; 1948; negative film nitrate; Pitt Rivers Museum, University of Oxford, 2001.59.7.7.1; image © Pitt Rivers Museum, University of Oxford, 2001.59.7.7.1

the servants of their domains: the Doring noble house had to provide twenty-five men; the two Yasor commanders and each lay minister had to provide twenty-four men; the regular army generals (*dapon*) thirteen men; the aristocratic sons seven men, and so forth.[9]

Yabzhi Punkhang *kung* (or duke) Tashi Dorje (b. 1888) was appointed a minister (*kalon*) from 1938 to 1946, and his son Gonpo Tsering (b. 1918) was nominated as Yasor commander in 1940.[10] Consequently, the Punkhang family had to provide for the festivities, depending on the year, between seven and twenty-four fully equipped cavalrymen, including their saddle carpets.

In pre-1959 Tibet the finest carpets were woven in small workshops in the area of Gyantse and were sold for domestic use or export. From the 1920s, carpets were produced either by a guild created by the Thirteenth Dalai Lama in Gyantse or in workshops located on the aristocratic estates of the Palha, Doring or Gabzhi, and the Langtong and Changra houses, all located near Gyantse, as well as on the Gyantse estate of the Punkhang family to which this set of saddle carpets belongs.[11]

The Punkhang Ceremonial Cavalry's Saddle Rug: A Twentieth-Century Imitation of an Ancient Model

Because carpets represent a mundane craft, by comparison with the Tibetan sacred arts, they display an overall striking level of diversity resulting from unconstrained artistic creativity.[12] The decoration of saddle rugs is based on that of larger, rectangular bed-size rugs (*khaden,* roughly three by six feet); they display the usual border strip, elaborate designs allowed by the pile-weaving technique, and similar colors adapted to their particular dimensions, for instance, with only one medallion or round-shaped flower on each side.[13] The top saddle carpets considered here have an oblong shape resembling the Mongol saddle, which is considered the oldest model. (Top saddle carpets came in two other shapes, namely, a distinctly Tibetan rectangular shape, sometimes with notched ends, and the "butterfly" shape replicating the shape of British saddle cloths, favored in later times.)[14]

This saddle carpet is executed in predominantly blue, red, and white. The border strip is filled with scrolling foliate forms, and each field contains shrubs with lotus flowers. The center of each field is occupied by one medallion, the Chinese symbol of longevity *shou*, which appears quite frequently in Tibetan ornamentation and was probably chosen to match the trousers of the cavalrymen's costumes, which also displayed a red (and sometimes blue) longevity symbol. Since the set of saddle carpets was meant for ceremonial use to commemorate the seventeenth-century Mongol cavalry, the oblong Mongolian shape and parts of the decorative elements of this saddle carpet point to a fashion of older times, while other elements clearly indicate the twentieth-century context of production.[15]

To the memory of Kesang Tashi (1943–2021)

Further Reading

Chodrak, Trinley, and Kesang G. Tashi. 2000. *Of Wool and Loom: The Tradition of Tibetan Rugs*. Edited by Kesang G. Tseten. Trumbull, CT: Weatherhill in cooperation with Orchid Press.

Cole, Thomas. 2011. *Patterns of Life: The Art of Tibetan Carpets*. With an introduction by Diana K. Myers. New York: Rubin Museum of Art. https://issuu.com/rmanyc/docs/4._patterns_of_life_96.

Richardson, Hugh E. 1993. *Ceremonies of the Lhasa Year*. London: Serindia.

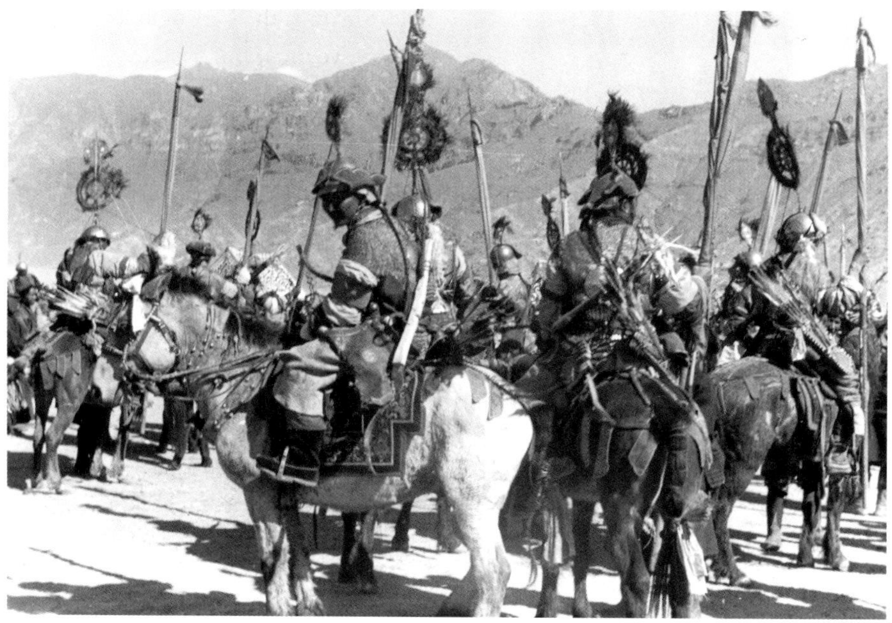

Ernst Schäfer (German, 1910–1992); A cavalryman with another style of saddle rug (rectangular shape with notched ends) in *Lhasa, die große Neujahrsparade* (Lhasa, the great New Year's parade); Lhasa; 1938 or 1939; photograph; 7 × 9½ in. (18 × 24 cm); Sven-Hedin-Institut für Innerasienforschung, Bundesarchiv, Berlin; Bild 135-S-16-18-03

Notes

1 Diana K. Myers, introduction to Cole 2011, 12; Chodrak and Tashi 2000, 17.
2 Chodrak and Tashi 2000; Cole 2011, 22.
3 Denwood 1974, 82; Chodrak and Tashi 2000, 18; Cole 2011, 20.
4 Denwood 1974, 71–72. See Chodrak and Tashi 2000, 59, and Cole 2011, 90–91, for two examples of intact sets.
5 As emphasized in Chodrak and Tashi 2000, 124, it is rare to find written evidence of the provenance of a rug incorporated into the object itself. Regarding the dating of the set, the authors have written that the set was originally produced as a result of the nomination of Punkhang as minister in the 1930s (Chodrak and Tashi 2000, 57), based on Punkhang Diki Dolma's oral account. Thus, their mention of the 1920s as the period of production of the saddle rug in their caption (124) is certainly erroneous; also, it is probable that the set initially comprised twenty-four items (57) instead of twenty (124). These saddle rugs have reached us today after being sold at some point by the Tsunmo Khangsar family of Lhasa, into which a younger son of the Punkhang family had been married (59). A fourth saddle rug of the same set has been published in Cole 2011, 95.
6 The Lhasa aristocracy comprised around 213 families and was internally divided into four subgroups, three of which (*sde dpon*, *yab gzhis*, and *mi drag*) formed a higher-ranking minority of twenty-seven families, while the majority of the noble houses were referred to simply in their capacity of private land owners (*sger pa*). Travers 2011a, 156–57.
7 A 1943 photograph by Ilia Tolstoy and Brooke Dolan of this saddle carpet, used by the Punkhang Cavalry during the New Year festivities, is reproduced in Tung 1996, pl. 112, with the caption "Horsemen dressed in the uniforms of Mongolian cavalry ride out to the Trapchi Plain."
8 On these ceremonies, see Karsten 1983; H. Richardson 1993, 31–57; Chodrak and Tashi 2000, 56.
9 For a discussion of the total number of the troops, see Karsten 1983, 136.
10 At that time, in 1939 through 1947, Gonpo Tsering was western governor of Gyantse (*rgyal rtse rdzong sdod nub pa*), and in the same year, 1940, he married the princess of Sikkim Kumari Pema Choden (Kukula). For biographies of Yabzhi Punkhang father and son, see Petech 1973, 27, and Karsten 1983, 129n71. For 1947 as the year of end of charge as Gyantse governor for Punkhang Se (*sras*), see Government of India Press 1949, 141, and H. Richardson 1947.
11 Chodrak and Tashi 2000, 40.
12 Chodrak and Tashi 2000, 51; Myers, introduction to Cole 2011, 12.
13 Chodrak and Tashi 2000, 26.
14 Cole 2011, 90–91; Chodrak and Tashi 2000, 59. For an example of a butterfly shape, see Cole 2011, 40, 57.
15 Though the identical top saddle rug reproduced in Cole 2011, 95, has not been identified by the author as belonging to the Punkhang cavalry set, the analysis concerning its dating is most interesting, as it points to the presence of contradictory elements: the oblong shape of the saddle carpet and its border design (the scrolling foliate forms) indicate a piece of the mid-nineteenth century or even earlier, while the angularity of the foliage, the longevity symbol, and the lotus flower in the field all point to a later production.

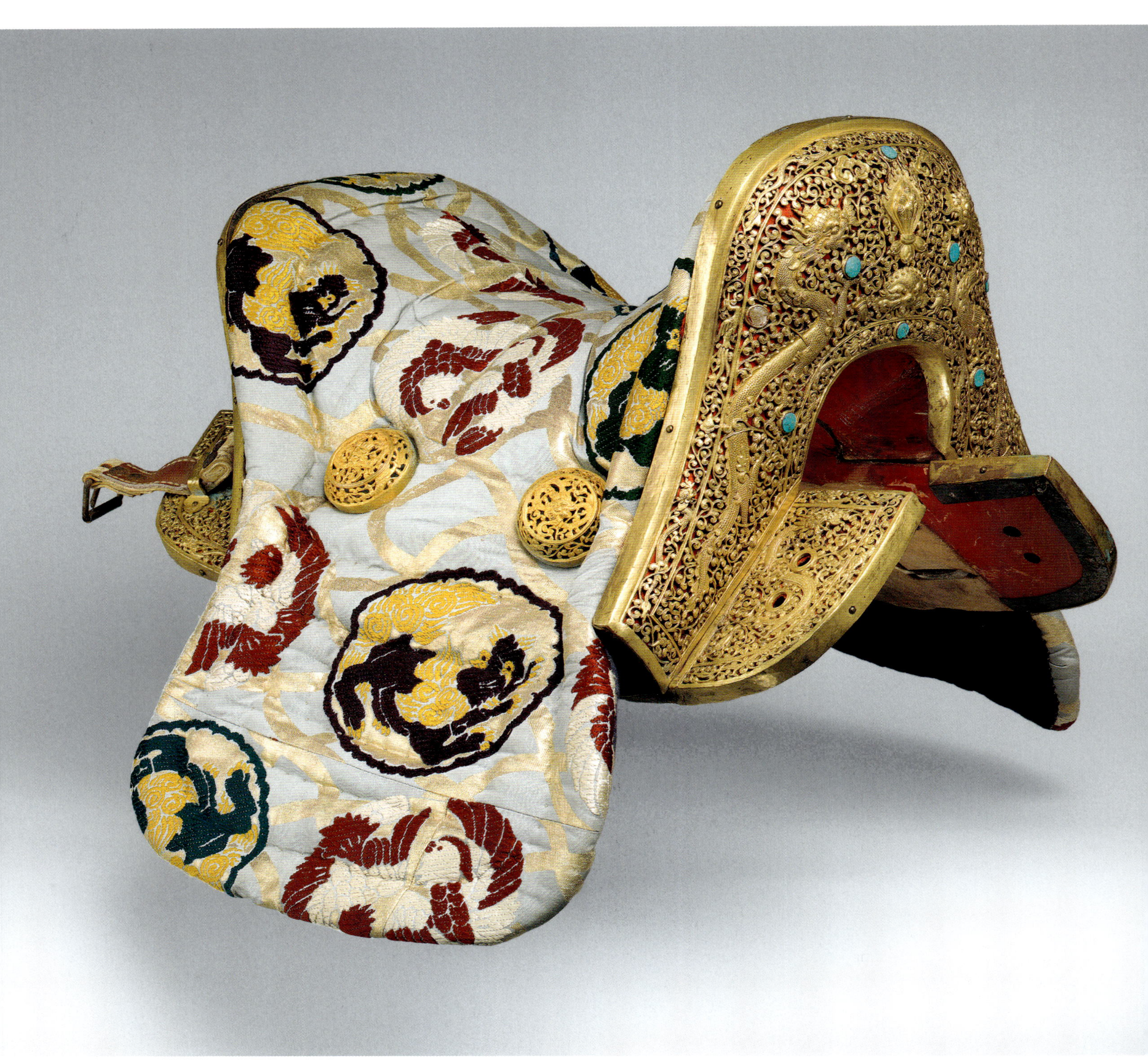

№ 101 Saddle Made for Yuthok Tashi Dhondup

Derge, Kham region, southeastern Tibet, ca. 1943–1947

A Progressive Tibetan Aristocrat's Traditional Equestrian Equipment

DONALD J. LA ROCCA AND ALICE TRAVERS

Saddles with Ornate Metalwork as Objects of Rank and Status

THIS LUXURIOUS SADDLE was among the ceremonial trappings of Yuthok Tashi Dhondup when he was governor general (*dochi*) of eastern Tibet, or Kham. Tibetan horses were prized for their strength, endurance, and agility since at least the seventh century and continued to be utilized for transportation, agriculture, and warfare into the modern era. The practice of adorning saddles with ornamental plates of gold, silver, or gilt copper occurred among the nomadic cultures of Central Asia by the fourth century.[1] Saddles clad with plates of pierced and chiseled iron and decorated with gold or silver damascening, a distinctive feature of fine Tibetan saddles (*serga*), existed by the late fourteenth to the early fifteenth century.[2] These and other types of pierced ironwork—censers, cup cases, pen cases, and certain ritual objects—are found from then onward mainly in Tibet, and to a lesser extent in China, suggesting that this style of ironwork was an innovation of Tibetan or Mongolian artisans, possibly originating in the late Yuan dynasty (1271–1368). Ornate ceremonial saddles were included among the valued possessions of Tibetan monasteries and aristocratic households, and even accorded a designated saddle storeroom (*chibga khang*) in the Potala Palace.[3] Their use as important signifiers of both secular and religious rank and status continued in Tibet until the mid-twentieth century.

See Potala Palace, no. 71.

Yuthok Tashi Dhondup: Aristocrat, Government Official, and Military Officer

One of the latest, possibly the very latest, complete example in this long tradition is the saddle and tack (including bridle, crupper, and stirrups) of Yuthok Tashi Dhondup (1906–1983), a Tibetan nobleman and government official (*zhungzhab*). The Lhasa aristocracy (*kudrak*) encompassed more than two hundred families, who owned hereditary estates across central Tibet and were obligated to serve as officials in the Tibetan government, called Ganden Podrang (1642–1959). This aristocratic elite was divided into a hierarchy of four subgroups, among the most prestigious of which were the *yabzhi* families, comprising the six ennobled families of former Dalai Lamas. One of them, the Yuthok, stems from the Tenth Dalai Lama in the early nineteenth century. The name references a famous Lhasa bridge covered with turquoise-hued roof (*thok*) tiles,[4] located near the family's house. The prominent use of turquoise (*yu*) on Yuthok Tashi Dhondup's saddle likely alludes to the name Yuthok, literally, "turquoise roof."

Saddle (*serga*) made for Yuthok Tashi Dhondup (1906–1983); Kham region, southeastern Tibet; ca. 1943–1947; copper alloy, iron, gold, turquoise, wood, leather, textile (silk, cotton); 18½ × 24 × 17 in. (47 × 61 × 43.2 cm); The Metropolitan Museum of Art, New York; Purchase, Arthur Ochs Sulzberger and Kenneth and Vivian Lam Gifts; funds from various donors, by exchange; Laird and Kathleen Landmann and Bernice and Jerome Zwanger Gifts; and funds from various donors, 2008; 2008.81a; image © The Metropolitan Museum of Art, image source: Art Resource, NY

Yuthok Tashi Dhondup entered government service as a lay official (*drungkhor*) in 1924.[5] Like many other lay officials during this period, when the Tibetan army was being strengthened and modernized, he alternated between holding civil and military positions. The latter represented a significant part of his career; the British considered him one of the best military officers in Tibet.[6] In 1926, he became a secretary of the Cabinet of Ministers (*kadrung*).[7] Returning to the army in 1932, Yuthok was promoted to general (*dapon*), fourth rank. Early in 1933 he was appointed senior general (with Taring Jigme as junior general) of a new elite regiment (*drongdrak makgar*), colloquially called the Trapchi regiment. After the regiment was disbanded in 1934, Yuthok remained a general, commanding the Dalai Lama's bodyguard (*kusung makgar*), again with Taring Jigme as his junior commander, from 1935 to 1938. He was removed by Regent Reting from active army service in September 1938 and granted the honorific title of *taiji*, which elevated him to the third rank of government officials. Along with other military and civil posts that followed, Yuthok captained Tibet's first football team, Lhasa United. In 1942 he was again promoted, receiving the honorific title of *dzasak*,[8] and appointed governor general of eastern Tibet (*dochi*), a

Set of Saddle Plates; Tibetan or Chinese, ca. 1400; iron, gold, lapis lazuli, turquoise; 10⅞ × 23½ × 13¾ in. (27.6 × 59.7 × 43.9 cm); The Metropolitan Museum of Art, New York; Purchase, Gift of William H. Riggs, by exchange, and Kenneth and Vivian Lam Gift, 1999; 1999.118a–g;

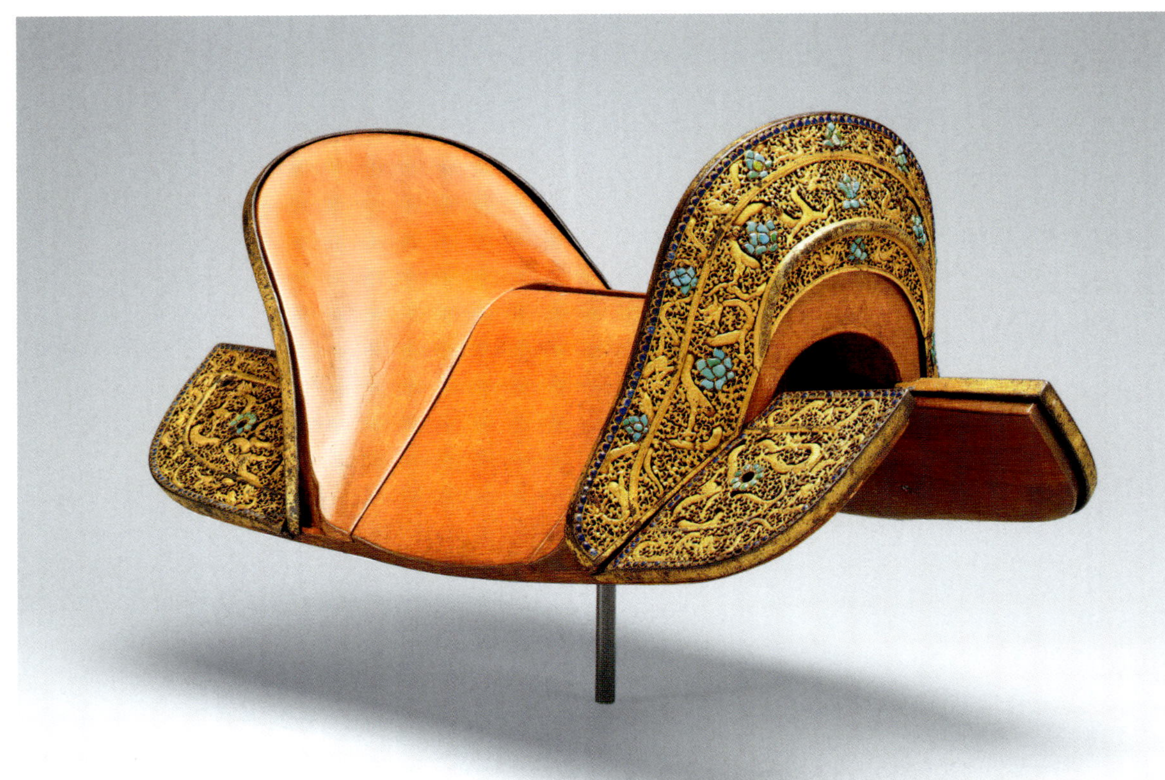

position carrying both civil and military responsibilities. He left Lhasa to take up residence in Chamdo, capital of Kham region, arriving in April 1943, and returning to Lhasa in October 1947.

The Creation of the Yuthok Saddle

During his sojourn in Kham, Yuthok commissioned the saddle and equestrian equipment discussed here[9] from artisans in Derge (present-day Ganzi Tibetan Autonomous Prefecture, Sichuan Province, China), a renowned center for decorative metalwork.[10] The saddle is distinguished by elaborate mounts comprising intricately pierced, embossed, and gilt copper plates set with turquoise.[11] It is exceptional for its fine craftsmanship and artistic excellence; for being one of the few extant Tibetan ceremonial saddles of which the original patron is identifiable; and as a documented example of the late "Derge pierced-gold" (*derge sertsak*) metalworking style.[12]

Ceremonial Trappings and Luxury Objects in Traditional Aristocratic Life

For more on equestrian equipment ordered by Tibetan aristocrats for use in processions and state functions, see Saddle Carpet for the Yabzhi Punkhang Ceremonial Cavalry, no. 100.

In traditional Tibet, aristocrats from prestigious families displayed their social standing through material possessions of great quality that were used both in everyday life and on ceremonial occasions, such as their official's robes, headdresses, and jewelry, as well as elaborate equestrian equipment. Lay officials above the fourth rank regularly took part in festivities and processions and attended state functions, in which they would ride magnificently caparisoned horses. The principal events in which saddles such as the one presented here were employed included the ceremonies of the New Year, or Great Prayer Festival in Lhasa, and the compulsory horse-riding and target-shooting contests for lay officials (*drungkhor tselgyuk*).[13] The opulent costumes and trappings that often accompanied these saddles are documented in a photograph of the Tibetan aristocrat and government official "George" Dundul Namgyal Tsarong, who can be seen sitting astride a very similar saddle while taking part in the New Year Festival in 1950.[14] Another rare example of an elaborate ceremonial saddle with a known owner is that of Surkhang Wangchen Tseten, Yuthok Tashi Dhondup's relative (through the family of his second wife),[15] which was also made in Derge. It was commissioned by Surkhang Wangchen Tseten when he served as governor general of eastern Tibet in the 1930s.[16]

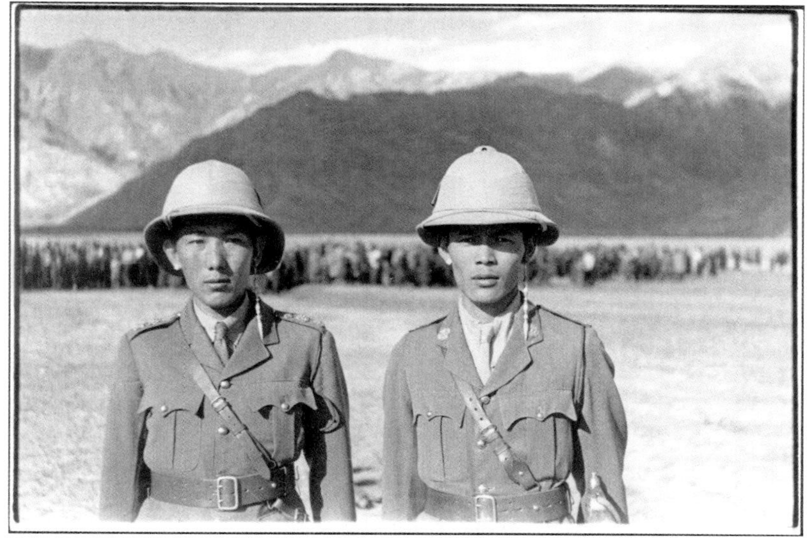

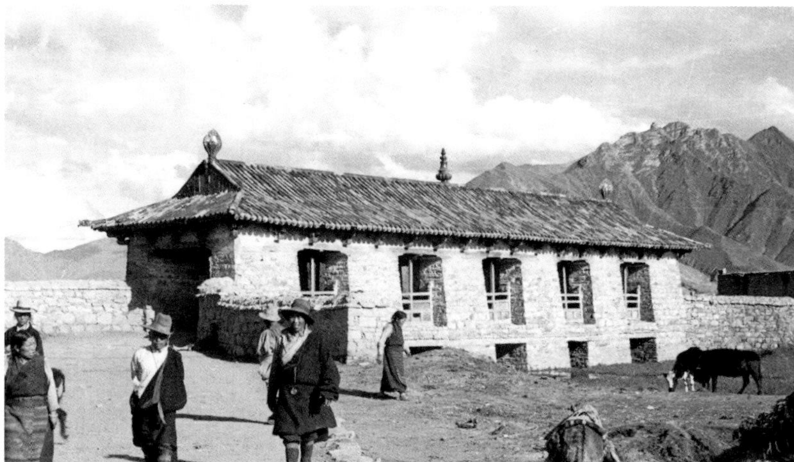

(top) Frederick Spencer Chapman (British, 1907–1971); *Yuthok Tashi Dhondup (left) and Taring Jigme (right) in Military Uniform;* September 7, 1936; photograph; Pitt Rivers Museum, Oxford; 1998.131.501; image © Pitt Rivers Museum, University of Oxford, 1998.131.501

(bottom) Tse Ten Tashi; *Turquoise Bridge, Lhasa;* 1951; photograph; The Newark Museum of Art, Newark, NJ; 2000.36.2.13; image courtesy The Newark Museum of Art

Further Reading

La Rocca, Donald J. 2006. *Warriors of the Himalayas: Rediscovering the Arms and Armor of Tibet.* With essays by John Clarke, Amy Heller, and Lozang Jamspal. Exhibition catalog. New York: The Metropolitan Museum of Art.

Richardson, Hugh E. 1993. *Ceremonies of the Lhasa Year.* London: Serindia.

Yutok, Dorje Yudon. (1990) 1995. *The House of the Turquoise Roof.* Ithaca, NY: Snow Lion.

Notes

1 For a fourth-century Xianbei example, see Desroches 2000, 163, cat. no. 152; Watt et al. 2005, 124–25, cat. no. 25.
2 La Rocca et al. 2006, 214–51.
3 Jiang Huaiying 1996, 1:15.
4 Petech 1973, 28; Yuthok (1990) 1995, 154.
5 Government of India Press 1949, 146; see also the government list of lay officials entitled "Shing byi [Wood bird year, i.e., 1924] roll," reproduced in Petech 1973, 248. In this list, G.yu thog *sras* Bkra shis don grub is mentioned in the following way (our translation): "G.yu thog sras Bkra shis don grub, aged 19 [*tibetico more*, that is, eighteen years old according to Western reckoning], entered government service in 1924, currently has no government position."
6 Government of India Press 1938, 79.
7 This biographical account is based on the following secondary sources: Petech 1973, 31; Taring (1970) 1986, 132; Yuthok (1990) 1995, 180, 242; G.yu thog 2002, 14; Goldstein 1989; and on the following primary sources: Caccia 1935, 6; Norbu Dhondup 1937; Norbu Dhondup 1938; Tsering 1947; Government of India Press 1938, 79; Government of India Press 1949, 146. See Tenzin Dickie 2016 for a presentation of his later career, including while in exile.
8 This title of Mongol origin, referring to both lay and monk officials, bestows the third rank in the government officials' rank ladder.
9 For a more detailed discussion of the construction, materials, and iconography of the saddle and its tack, see La Rocca 2014b, 201–3. Yuthok Tsering Dolkar and her daughter Yuthok Tsezom very kindly confirmed many facts about the history of the saddle, and Yangchen Lakar provided additional useful information (via letters, emails, and verbal communications, 2007–8).
10 Concerning the reputation of Derge as a center for fine metalwork, see Clarke 2006, 29; Rockhill 1895, esp. 692, 695–96, 705, 712–13, 716–17, 740.
11 Perhaps because the craft of fine ironworking was in decline, plates of nonferrous metal, particularly embossed copper, rather than pierced iron became more typical for ceremonial saddles from some point in the nineteenth century on. A notable exception is the late saddle with tack and matching sword in the Metropolitan Museum of Art, New York, 2003.230.1–.3a–e, for which see La Rocca 2006, 234–39.
12 Literally "Derge pierced gold," usually referring to pierced, chiseled, and gilt ironwork, or, as in this case, gilt copper. This term, as it relates to the saddle, was pointed out by Yangchen Lakar (written communication, December 3, 2007).
13 Travers 2011.
14 H. Richardson 1993, 31–59; Karsten 1983, 131.
15 His first wife was from the Langdun (glang mdun) family but passed away after childbirth while he was undergoing military training in Gyantse in 1932; see Taring (1970) 1986, 132. For information on his other marriages, see his second wife's autobiography, Yuthok (1990) 1995, 313; Tenzin Dickie 2016.
16 The Metropolitan Museum of Art, 2005.427.1 (published in La Rocca 2006, 242–43, cat. no. 126).

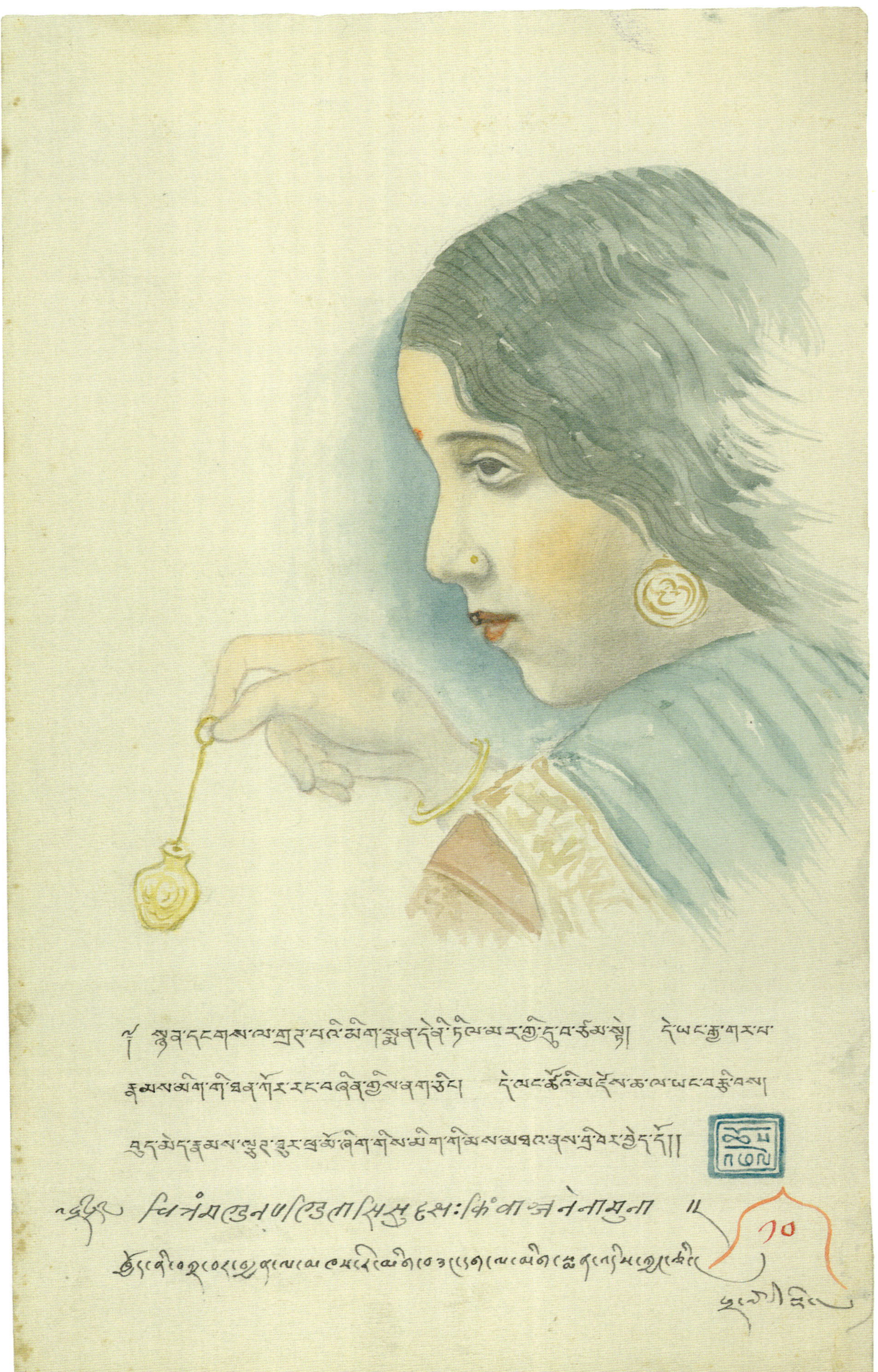

༄། སྙན་དངགས་ལ་གྲགས་པའི་མིག་སྨན་དེའི་ཏི་ལ་མ་ར་གྱི་དུ་བ་ཙམ་སྟེ། དེ་ཡང་རྒྱ་གར་བ
རྣམས་མིག་གི་ཐན་ཀོར་རང་བཞིན་གྱིས་ནག་ཅིང་། དེ་ལ་ང་ཚོའི་མཛེས་ཆ་ལ་ཡང་བསྐྱེད་ནས།
བུད་མེད་རྣམས་ལྷུར་བྱུར་ཐྲ་མོ་ཞིག་གིས་མིག་གི་མིས་མཐའ་ནས་བྱུ་བར་བྱེད་དོ།།
10

No 102 Gendun Chopel's Woman Applying Kohl

India, ca. 1940

Tibet's First Modern Artist

DONALD S. LOPEZ JR.

THIS WATERCOLOR, UNTITLED BY THE ARTIST, is the work of Gendun Chopel (1903–1951), one of the most important Tibetan cultural figures of the first half of the twentieth century, renowned as a poet, painter, philosopher, and historian.[1] Born in Amdo, the northeastern region of Tibet, he was the son of a prominent lama of the Nyingma tradition and was himself identified as the incarnation of a famous Nyingma teacher. His father died when he was a young boy, after which he became a monk of the Geluk tradition, distinguishing himself as a debater at Labrang Monastery. He was expelled from the monastery for reasons that are unclear; his unorthodox philosophical views may have been one factor. In 1928 he traveled to Lhasa and enrolled in Drepung Monastery to continue his studies. During his time in the monastery, he supported himself as a painter, producing works in the traditional Tibetan style.

In 1934, as he was completing the monastic curriculum, he was asked by his teacher Sherab Gyatso (1884–1968) to serve as the guide to the Indian scholar and political activist Rahul Sankrityayan (1893–1963), who had come to Tibet in search of Sanskrit manuscripts. At the end of their tour of monasteries in central Tibet, Sankrityayan invited Gendun Chopel to go back with him to India. He accepted the invitation, not returning to Tibet until 1945, traveling extensively through India and Sri Lanka and writing his two most famous works. The first was a verse work on erotica (he had given up his monk's vows by this point) called *Treatise on Passion*.[2] The second is what he considered his most important work, an account of his travels, with essays on South Asian and Tibetan history and culture, entitled *Grains of Gold: Tales of a Cosmopolitan Traveler*.[3] The painting here was intended as an illustration for this book. He also contributed essays and poems to *Melong* ("Mirror"), the only Tibetan-language newspaper of the day, published in Kalimpong, India, including an essay in 1938 explaining that the world is round, rather than flat, as it is described in Buddhist texts.[4]

Gendun Chopel returned to Tibet in 1945. The following year he was arrested on trumped-up charges of counterfeiting currency and sentenced to three years in prison. Numerous theories have been put forth for his arrest. His involvement with a group called the Tibet Improvement Party (whose logo he designed) was likely one factor. He emerged from prison a broken man and died two years later, in 1951, as troops of the Chinese People's Liberation Army marched into Lhasa.

Gendun Chopel made numerous illustrations for *Grains of Gold*, both in pen and ink and in watercolor. The majority of these works have been lost. Among those that survive, each is numbered in Gendun Chopel's own hand, with the highest number being 178, giving some sense of how richly illustrated he intended his book to be. Twenty-seven paintings survive, together with a sketchbook.[5] The paintings present a wide range of subjects in a number of styles. Some reproduce famous Buddhist works, while others are more scientific, portraying archaeological artifacts and Indian plants, providing dimensions. Yet others might be called ethnographic, depicting for his Tibetan audience a Brahman, a devotee of Shiva, a group of Indians bathing, and a Hindu ascetic lying on a bed of nails.

Gendun Chopel is said to have supported himself as a painter during his years as a monk in Lhasa. Unfortunately, no works from this period can be confidently attributed to him. He is said to have been employed by Denchen Nyingpo, Second Pabongkha (1878–1941), the most powerful Geluk monk of the day. That he was asked to work for a figure of such renown suggests that he was considered highly skilled and that he painted in the traditional style. This makes his paintings from his time in South Asia all the more fascinating; they are unlike anything previously produced by a Tibetan artist. There are works in pen and ink, pencil, and, as in the example here, watercolor. These media, and his use of techniques such as

Gendun Chopel (Tibetan, 1903–1951); Woman Applying Kohl; India; ca. 1940; watercolor; 10 × 6 in. (25.5 × 15.4 cm); Private collection; image after Xiong Wenbin and Zhang Chunyan, eds. 2012. *2012 nian de zhui xun: Xizang wen hua bo wu guan Gendunqunpei sheng ping xue shu zhan 2012* 年的追寻: 西藏文化博物馆根敦群培生平学术展. Beijing: Zhongguo Zang xue chu ban she; photograph courtesy Latse Library

Photographer unknown; Gendun Chopel (Tibetan, 1903–1951); India; 1935; photograph; Private collection; photograph courtesy Donald Lopez

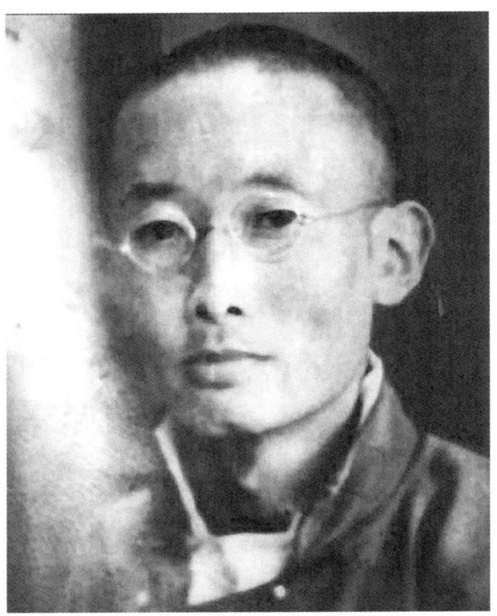

single-point perspective, were not practiced in traditional Tibetan painting. He therefore must have learned them in India, where they had been brought by the British. It is not known where Gendun Chopel learned these techniques, from whom, and how he mastered them so quickly. We do know that he brought some of them back to Tibet when he returned in 1945; there is some evidence of his influence in the works of his friend and compatriot Amdo Jampa (1911–2002). In the decades after his death and continuing to the present day, he has been an important inspiration for Tibetan artists, both in Tibet and in exile.

The painting here offers a perfect example of the things he learned in India. Despite appearing to be a portrait of an Indian beauty, the watercolor also falls into the ethnographic category. This is not apparent from the painting itself, which may be based on a magazine advertisement for eye makeup. In the lower right-hand corner, in red, is the number "10" in Tibetan, indicating that this was intended as the tenth illustration in *Grains of Gold*. The writing below the painting, in two different languages and four different scripts, tells us much about Gendun Chopel's interests. The text directly below the painting is in Tibetan, written in the capital script that is used in printed texts. It reads, "The famous eye ointment from the poems is just the smoke of red lac. The skin around the eyes of Indians is naturally dark and they consider this a mark of youthful beauty. Thus, women use a small spoon to paint around their eyes."

Sanskrit poems often speak of the dark eyes of Indian women, who would apply kohl as eye makeup. Sanskrit poetry, especially Buddhist Sanskrit poetry, was well known to learned Tibetans, but the application of kohl would have been quite exotic. Thus, in this painting, Gendun Chopel illustrates a woman applying kohl, making the painting as much an illustration of the text as the text is a caption for the painting.

Sanskrit poetics, and belles lettres in general, were highly valued in Tibet, with many learned authors, both monastic and lay, studying Dandin's *Mirror of Poetry* (*Kavyadarsha*), an eighth-century work on poetic forms. Gendun Chopel himself studied the text as a boy. While in India, he learned Sanskrit well and is said to have read the text in the original. Indeed, he was rightfully proud of his knowledge of Sanskrit, reading many works on erotica, including the *Kama Sutra* in the original, not only for the expected purposes but because erotica was one genre of Sanskrit literature that did not exist in Tibet; his *Treatise on Passion* was intended to fill that lacuna.

Thus, the next element of the text below the painting is in Sanskrit, written in a somewhat stylized script. It is a passage from a famous Buddhist text called the *Heavenly Vine of the Deeds of the Bodhisattva* (*Bodhisattvavadanakalpalata*), a collection of one hundred and eight stories of the Buddha's past lives, in verse, by the eleventh-century Kashmiri poet Kshemendra. To indicate this source to a well-read Tibetan reader, he simply writes "vine" in cursive Tibetan to the left of the Sanskrit inscription. After the original Sanskrit, Gendun Chopel provides his translation of the passage into Tibetan, written in cursive Tibetan script:

For a painting illustrating scenes from this text, see the image on p. 359 in Portrait of Situ Panchen, no. 83.

> You are skilled in the arts of beauty.
> Why do you put eye ointment on your beautiful eyes?[6]

The speaker, praising the beauty of a woman's eyes, tells her that she does not need to apply kohl. This single passage immediately changes the painting from an ethnographic illustration to an illustration from a scene in a previous life of the Buddha, as the woman in the watercolor, upon hearing this verse while looking at the speaker to her left, stops just as she is about to put kohl on her eyes. To demonstrate his knowledge of Dandin's *Mirror of Poetry*, Gendun Chopel adds a note in cursive Tibetan that says, "subtle category," referring to the *sukshma* rhetorical form in Sanskrit poetics.

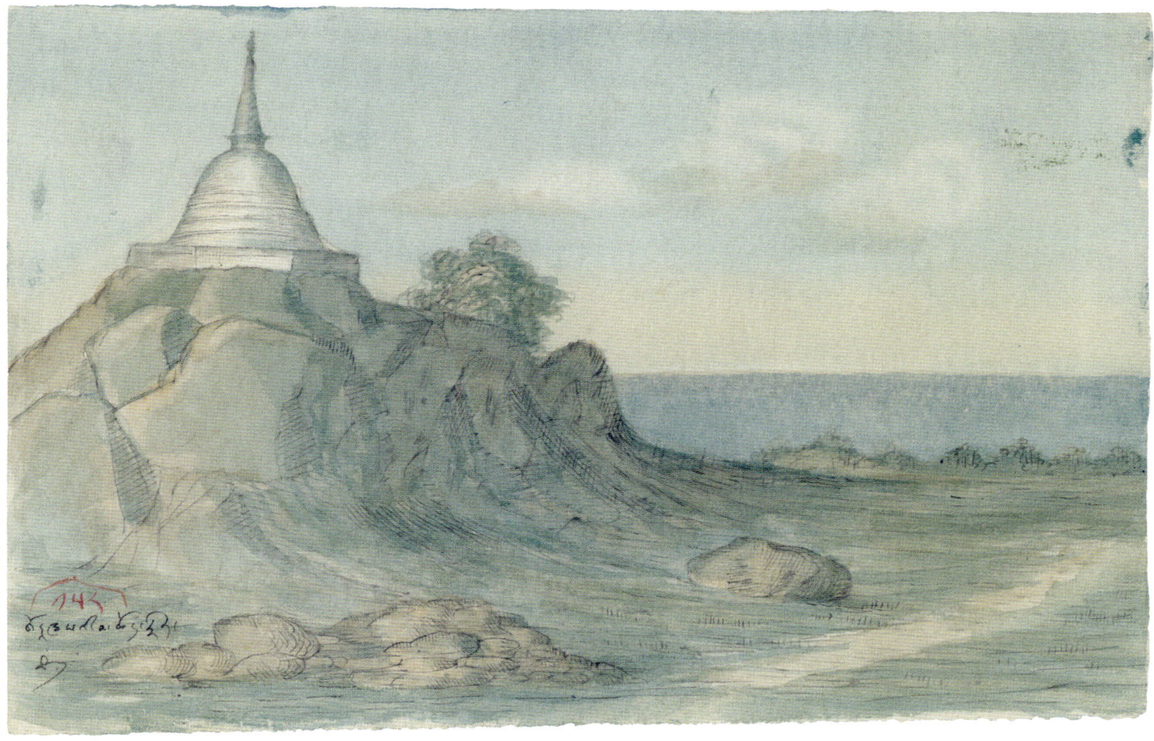

Gendun Chopel (Tibetan, 1903–1951); *Godāvapa Stūpa*; Sri Lanka; 1941; watercolor; 6⅝ × 10 in. (16.8 × 25.5 cm); Private collection; image after Xiong Wenbin and Zhang Chunyan, eds. 2012. *2012 nian de zhui xun: Xizang wen hua bo wu guan Gendunqunpei sheng ping xue shu zhan 2012* 年的追寻: 西藏文化博物馆根敦群培生平学术展. Beijing: Zhongguo Zang xue chu ban she; photograph courtesy Latse Library

As we see, the Tibetan artist thus displays many skills on a single page, as a painter, an ethnographer, a scholar of Sanskrit literature, a translator, and a poet. Clearly proud of his achievement, he designs a stamp for the painting to identify its author. The blue square in the lower right says "Chopel."

Further Reading

Gendun Chopel. 2009. *In the Forest of Faded Wisdom: 104 Poems by Gendun Chopel; A Bilingual Edition*. Edited and translated by Donald S. Lopez Jr. Chicago: University of Chicago Press.

Lopez, Donald S., Jr. 2018. *Gendun Chopel: Tibet's Modern Visionary*. Boulder, CO: Shambhala.

Stoddard, Heather. 1985b. *Le mendiant de l'Amdo.* Paris: Société d'ethnographie.

Notes

1 For a documentary film on Gendun Chopel, see Schaedler 2005.
2 *'Dod pa'i bstan bcos*. For a full translation, see Gendun Chopel 2018.
3 *Rgyal khams rig pas bskor ba'i gtam rgyud gser gyi thang ma.* For a full translation, see Gendun Chopel 2014.
4 For a translation of all of Gendun Chopel's extant poetry, see Gendun Chopel 2009. For a translation of his essay on the round earth, see Lopez 2018, 134–37.
5 Gendun Chopel's surviving paintings from *Grains of Gold* and his sketchbook have been published in Lopez 2013.
6 My translation, in Lopez 2013.

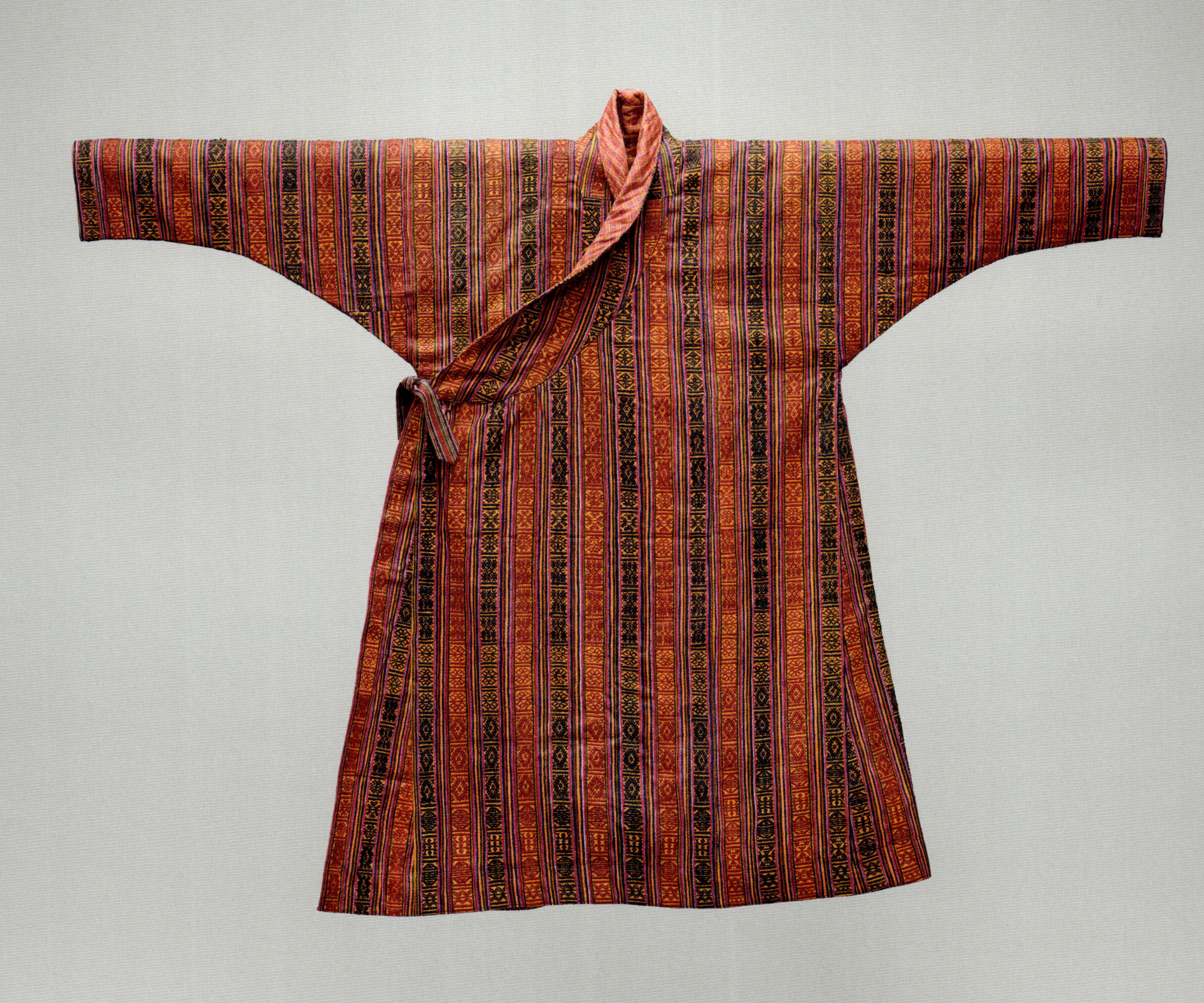

№ 103 Bhutanese Men's Garment (*Gho*)

Bhutan, 1970–1980

Precious Fabrics in the Buddhist Himalayan Kingdom of Bhutan: Symbols of Identity, Prestige, and Prosperity

KARIN ALTMANN

THE *GHO* IS A TRADITIONAL GARMENT worn by Bhutanese laymen. It consists of three to four lengths of cloth that are sewn together to form a floor-length, left-crossing, loose robe with long sleeves. The robe overlaps in front, folds into two wide pleats at the back, and is held in place with a belt; it is then drawn up to achieve the desired length. The lengths of cloth are vertical; the *gho* is generally woven in silk or cotton in a variety of patterns.

This hand-woven *gho* is made of raw silk (*bura*) with supplementary-warp patterns, called *aikapur*, which originated in eastern Bhutan. Aikapur can entail a variety of color combinations. The combination in the *gho* featured here shows red and green supplementary-warp pattern bands on an orange-yellow ground *(lungserma),* with alternating rainbow stripes *(jadrima*). It belonged to Dasho Ugyen Dorji, a high-ranking official to whom the king of Bhutan awarded the title *dasho* ("excellent one") in recognition of his services. Bhutanese etiquette requires such an officer to wear his *gho* with a scarf in dark red wild silk (*bura map* or *kabne map*) over his left shoulder and a sword on formal occasions.

See Sword, Scabbard, and Sword Belt, no. 68.

National Dress as a Mark of Bhutanese Identity

For more on the Buddhist kingdom, see Taktsang, the Tiger's Lair, no. 76.

The invention of the Bhutanese *gho* is attributed to the cleric Zhabdrung Ngawang Namgyel (1594–1651), who unified Bhutan in the seventeenth century, forming a Buddhist kingdom.[1] The Zhabdrung developed the *gho* as a mark of Bhutanese identity, to distinguish Bhutan from Tibet. Considering the small size of the country and the hostile and hegemonic attitude of the rulers of Tibet, the Zhabdrung felt it was necessary to promote a separate cultural identity for Bhutan, including different Bhutanese characteristics of dress. For this purpose, he altered the Tibetan costume (*chuba*) and adapted it to the somewhat warmer and more humid climate of Bhutan.[2] Consequently, the Bhutanese *gho* is worn drawn up to the knees. The shorter the *gho*, the more voluminous is the front pouch resulting from the overhanging material, which offers space to carry all sorts of objects. Traditionally, it was used to hold wooden drinking cups for tea or home-brewed alcohol (*ara*), dried cheese (*chugo*) to chew on one's travels, silver boxes (*chaka/timi*) containing the ingredients for chewing betel nuts (*doma*), or even babies. Nowadays, it is more likely to hold wallets, sunglasses, and car keys. In the Zhabdrung's time, the *gho* was mandatory only for members of the elite, but over time, it was gradually adopted by the whole male population; since 1989 the *gho* has been the national dress for Bhutanese men.

The Bhutanese garment for women is called the *kira* and was also established as the official national dress in 1989. It consists of a large square cloth that is wrapped tightly around the body, fixed at the shoulders with two brooches (*koma*) and held in place at the waist with a belt (*kera*). It is generally believed that the *kira* was already worn long before the Zhabdrung's time, and that before that, Bhutanese women wore a tunic-style garment made of nettle, cotton, or wool (*kushung* or *shingkha*).

Men's Robe *(bura lungserma gho)*; Bhutan; 1970–1980; raw silk and cotton lining; 55¾ × 69¼ in. (141.5 × 175.5 cm); Asian Art Museum of San Francisco; Himalayan Art Collection; Gift of Dasho Ugyen Dorji; 1993.17; photograph © Asian Art Museum of San Francisco

In addition to the introduction of the *gho*, the Zhabdrung codified a system of rules of etiquette in the form of *driglam namzhag* ("Code of Disciplined Behavior").[3] Before *driglam namzhag* became law in 1989, many Bhutanese people could be seen wearing Western clothes, mainly in the towns, and especially in Bhutan's capital, Thimphu. With the opening-up of Bhutan, Western fashions became status symbols that were displayed, for instance, by wearing sneakers, which were adopted by court ladies and later by many other Bhutanese women, and by the fashion for denim jeans, which developed in Bhutan in the 1990s. The Royal Government of Bhutan tried to put a stop to the trend, strengthen Bhutan's national

Aikapur in Different Color Combinations; 2007; white and yellow warp pattern bands on a red ground with alternating rainbow stripes (*jadrima*), and yellow warp pattern bands on a red ground (*mense*); photograph by Karin Altmann, 2007

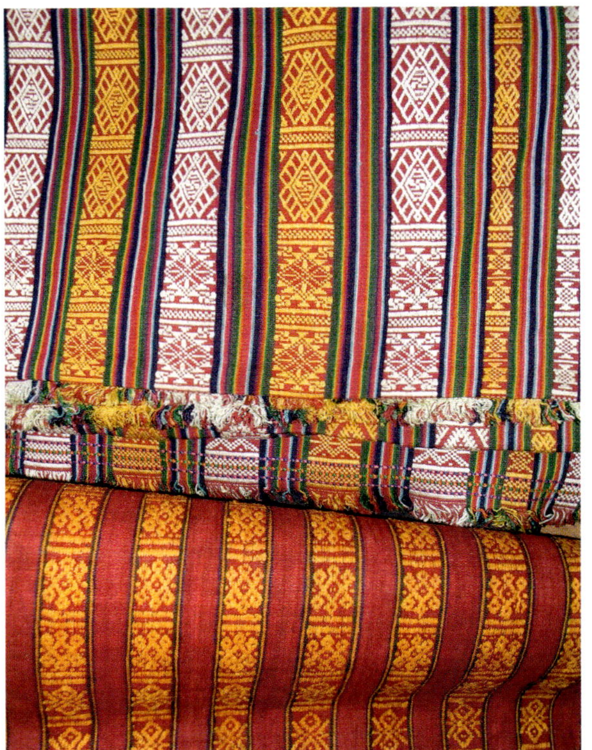

identity, and prevent its culture from disappearing by establishing the traditional costume of the Drupka, the largest ethnic group in Bhutan, as its national dress.[4]

Hand-Woven Treasures—Symbols of Prestige and Prosperity

Due to Bhutan's remote mountainous location with its natural borders, a deliberate foreign policy, and the basic principles of Buddhist ethics, the Himalayan kingdom has been able to preserve a remarkable textile art, which is both a symbol of national identity and evidence of the regional diversity within the country.

Textiles are present in all aspects of Bhutanese life and have always functioned as indicators of prestige and prosperity. Cloth circulated as currency in society, and hand-woven fabrics were presented as gifts to neighboring states and for state distributions to officials and monasteries, or to pay family and community taxes to the monastic fortress (*dzong*), the district's seat of secular and religious power.[5]

To this day, hand-woven textiles are present on an everyday basis in the form of garments, bags, and covers, and although they no longer function as taxes and currency, they still play an important part in the local economy as commercial wares, prestige items, and gifts for marking important events in the course of a life.

Arranging cloth gifts requires a precise knowledge of etiquette, particularly with regard to gifts to members of the royal family or other high-ranking persons. For instance, if the set includes a fabric made with supplementary-warp patterns (*aikapur*), attention should be focused on the bands of supplementary-warp patterns, which are distinguished by the number of "legs" *(kang/be)*, cross-hatched bars that run at right angles between the individual patterns. The legs always occur as odd numbers, which are considered auspicious in the Buddhist context. The more legs a supplementary-warp pattern band presents, the greater its value, as wider patterns are more complicated to weave. Consequently, a person of higher rank is presented with an *aikapur* with a significant number of legs.

The value of a Bhutanese hand-woven cloth depends on many factors: the selection and quality of the materials, the type and quality of the dyes, the quality of the weaving—which requires that the ground and patterns are even and tightly woven—the complexity and number of patterns, and the creativity of the pattern and color combinations. A distinction is made between textiles that the weavers make for themselves and their loved ones, which are called "heart weaving" (*hingtham*), and those for commercial purposes, called "commercial weaving" (*tshongtham*). Heart weaving is characterized by its very fine quality and careful work with elaborate patterns and harmonious colors.

Weaving and Creativity: The Domain of Women

Weaving (*thagzo*) is the preserve of women, and involves many different stages, from obtaining the fibers, to producing and dyeing the yarn, right up to the finished woven textiles.[6] The entire weaving process can require any length of time, from a week to a whole year, depending on the materials, the dyeing methods, and the type of textile woven. Bhutanese textiles are woven from nettle fibers, cotton, silk, sheep's wool, yak hair, and yak wool, using three kinds of looms: the backstrap loom (*pangthag*), the card loom (*shogu thagshing*), and the horizontal frame loom (*thrithag*), all of which made their way from Tibet to Bhutan.

Zhabdrung Ngawang Namgyel (1594–1651), who unified Bhutan in the seventeenth century, developed the *gho* as a mark of Bhutanese identity, to distinguish Bhutan from Tibet; photograph by Karin Altmann, 2006

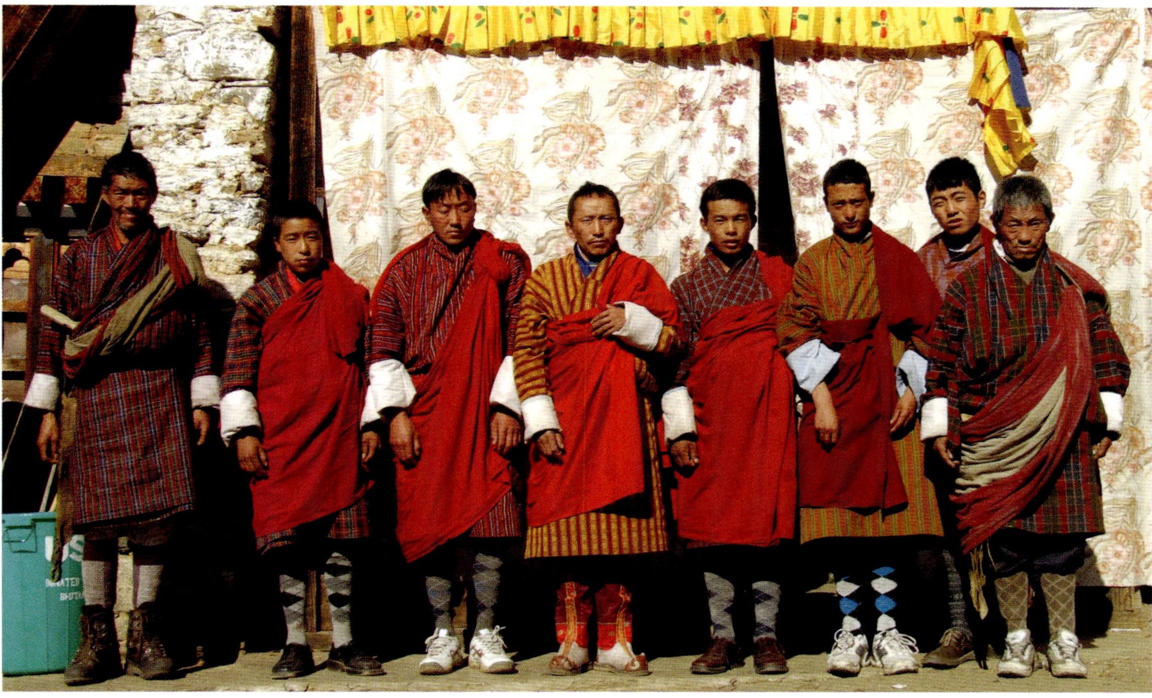

Eastern and central Bhutan in particular can look back on a long tradition of weaving. In the old days, local nobles employed several weavers within their own establishments; currently, many households in these regions still have their own looms. While Bumthang in central Bhutan is well known for its patterned woolen cloths (*yathra*) made of yak and sheep's wool on horizontal frame looms, women in eastern Bhutan specialize in silk fabrics with elaborate patterns (*kushu*), woven on backstrap looms.

Today, women all over Bhutan compete to produce the finest fabrics and to develop new patterns and color combinations. While many traditional patterns continue to be produced, at the same time new ones are being created—some inspired by foreign designs—so the number of patterns is constantly growing. The patterns reflect the diversity of Bhutan's landscape by presenting its mountains, valleys, rivers, and rich flora in a simplified way. They are further characterized by the country's Buddhist and pre-Buddhist traditions, and may refer to religious objects and symbols in stylized forms.

For more on a common religious object, the vajra, see *Dorje* Discovered by Dorje Lingpa, no. 51.

While men, insofar as they produce textiles for the sacred sphere, adhere strictly to Buddhist iconography and are honored for their exact observance of the rules and for their precision, women are praised above all for individual creativity in the art of weaving. Since weaving has been established as an elevated art form in Bhutan, while also making an important contribution to the culture and economy of the country, weavers of Bhutan enjoy their freedom of artistic expression and a well-regarded position in society to this day.

For more on Buddhist iconography, see Maitreya Statue at Jampa Lhakhang, Bhutan, no. 9. For depictions of Tibetan clothing, see Desi Sanggye Gyatso's Medical Paintings, no. 73.

Further Reading

Altmann, Karin. 2016. *Fabric of Life: Textile Arts in Bhutan—Culture, Tradition and Transformation*. Berlin: De Gruyter.

Aris, Michael. 1994. *The Raven Crown: The Origins of Buddhist Monarchy in Bhutan*. London: Serindia.

Myers, Diana K., and Susan S. Bean. 1994. *From the Land of the Thunder Dragon: Textile Arts of Bhutan*. Exhibition catalog. London: Serindia.

Notes

1 See Aris 1994.
2 On Tibetan dress, see Corrigan 2017.
3 On *driglam namzhag*, see Wangchuk et al. 1999.
4 Besides the Drukpa, there are several ethnic groups in Bhutan with local languages and distinct cultural features, among them the Ngalong, Sharchopa, and Lhotshampa, as well as small communities such as the Layap and Brokpa, who are yak herders, and the Monpa, who are considered an indigenous ethnic group.
5 Myers and Pommaret 1994, 71.
6 While weaving is the preserve of women, fabric processing, such as sewing garments, making traditional boots, and creating elaborate embroidery and appliqué work, is primarily done by men.

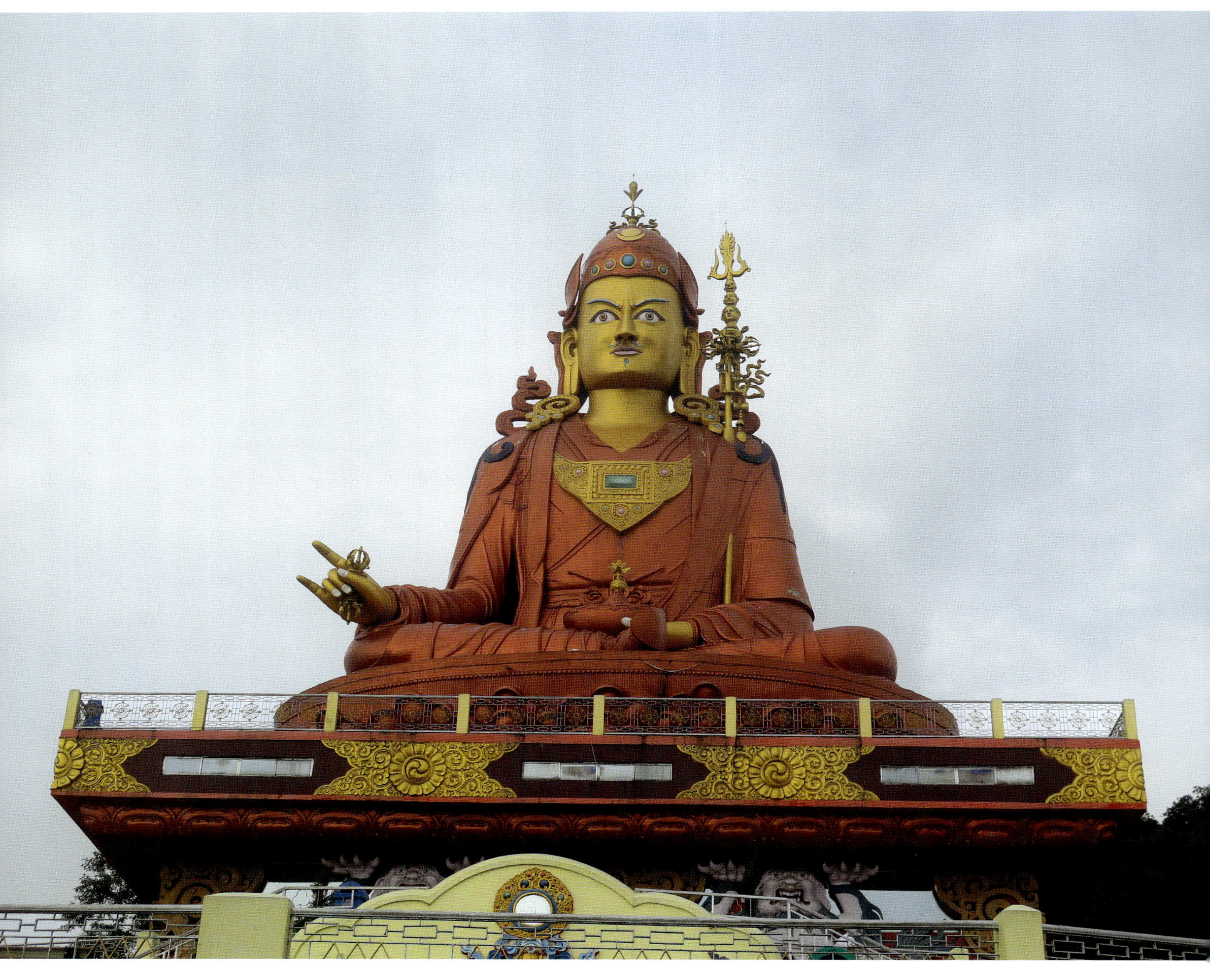

Naresh Kumar Verma (Indian), design, and Lopon Lhundrup (Bhutanese), construction; Statue of Guru Rinpoche; Samdruptse, Namchi, Sikkim, India; 2004; concrete base with gilded bronze and copper body; height 135 ft. (41.1 m); photograph by Amy Holmes-Tagchungdarpa

№ 104 Monumental Statue of Guru Rinpoche

Samdruptse, Namchi, Sikkim, India, 2004

The Mega-Sized Guru that Presides over the Hidden Land

KALZANG DORJEE BHUTIA AND AMY HOLMES-TAGCHUNGDARPA

THIS LARGE-SCALE REPRESENTATION of Guru Rinpoche, also known as Padmasambhava, is one of many enormous statues built in the Himalayan region since the turn of the millennium. At the time of its completion in 2004, it was considered the largest statue of Guru Rinpoche in the world. While, historically, a number of Buddhist communities built large statues of other popular buddhas, this particular statue held special significance for Sikkim, the small northeast Indian state where it was constructed. Local Buddhist communities trace the beginning of Buddhist history in Sikkim to the eighth century, with the visit of the legendary tantric teacher described in Tibetan and Himalayan narratives.

For more on Guru Rinpoche, see Padmasambhava and His Manifestations, no. 43; Ritual Dance Mask of Guru Dorje Drolo, no. 94.

For more on places associated with Padmasambhava, see Taktsang, the Tiger's Lair, no. 76.

For more on *terma*, see *Dorje* Discovered by Dorje Lingpa, no. 51.

Guru Rinpoche is venerated throughout Inner Asia and the Himalayas as the figure who introduced Tantric Buddhism to the region after he was invited from India to Tibet by the Tibetan king Tri Songdetsen (742–ca. 800).[1] His activities are held to have assisted in the consolidation of Buddhism on the Tibetan Plateau, including the conversion of local deities into protectors of Buddhism. He is also believed to have visited other areas of the Himalayas, including parts of present-day Ladakh, Sikkim, Himachal Pradesh, and Arunachal Pradesh in India, and Nepal and Bhutan. While Guru Rinpoche's fame has been promulgated through his biographies and association with ritual and institutional traditions, there are also rich repositories of local written and oral traditions that discuss his visits to different regions. He also left behind teachings to inspire later Buddhist practices in these regions. These teachings have been recovered as objects and texts, known as treasures (*terma*), from the landscape and in visionary episodes by Buddhist practitioners with karmic connections to the guru, who are known as treasure revealers (*terton*).

For one of the teachers who is said to have opened the Hidden Land of Sikkim, see Portrait of Ngadak Puntsok Rigdzin, no. 70.

In a number of places that he visited, Guru Rinpoche designated particular locations as Hidden Lands (*beyul*) that would function as safe havens for Buddhist communities in times of need.[2] In treasure literature and traditions, Sikkim was known as the Beyul Dremojong, or the Hidden Land of Rice, and it was "opened" in several stages by treasure revealers fleeing civil strife on the Tibetan Plateau. The treasure revealers inspired waves of Tibetan migrants to relocate to Sikkim. The migrants became known as the Lhopo community, and in Sikkim, they lived together with a number of ethnic groups, including Lepchas (also known as the Rong in their own language, the first indigenous people of the region). In the seventeenth century, a treasure revealer named Lhatsun Namkha Jigme (1597–1650) visited Sikkim where he supported the enthronement of local chieftain Puntsok Namgyel (1604–1670) as the first dharma king (*choygel*) of the Namgyal dynasty that nominally ruled Sikkim until 1975, when Sikkim became part of India.[3]

Today, Sikkim is a culturally diverse state that is famed for its mountain vistas and pristine natural sites. Demographic change has rendered Buddhists a minority in the state, as Hindus now make up the majority of the population, along with practitioners of a diverse variety of other religions, including indigenous religions, Christianity, Islam, and new religious movements. Despite this, Buddhism continues to be overrepresented in tourist marketing materials and in state-sponsored tourist sites.[4] Many of these sites overlap with traditional pilgrimage routes that include historically significant monasteries and temples, as well as caves, rivers, and lakes that make up the sacred landscape of the Hidden Land that is presided over by Kanchendzonga, the world's third-highest mountain, seen as the protector deity of the state.[5] The monumental Guru Rinpoche statue represents a new type of Buddhist tourist site in the state; political and business groups have built such sites in consultation with Buddhist authorities, with emphases on profit, leisure, and marketability as well as piety, for Buddhist and non-Buddhist visitors alike.[6]

For more on mountain gods, see Mountain God Kula Khari, no. 92.

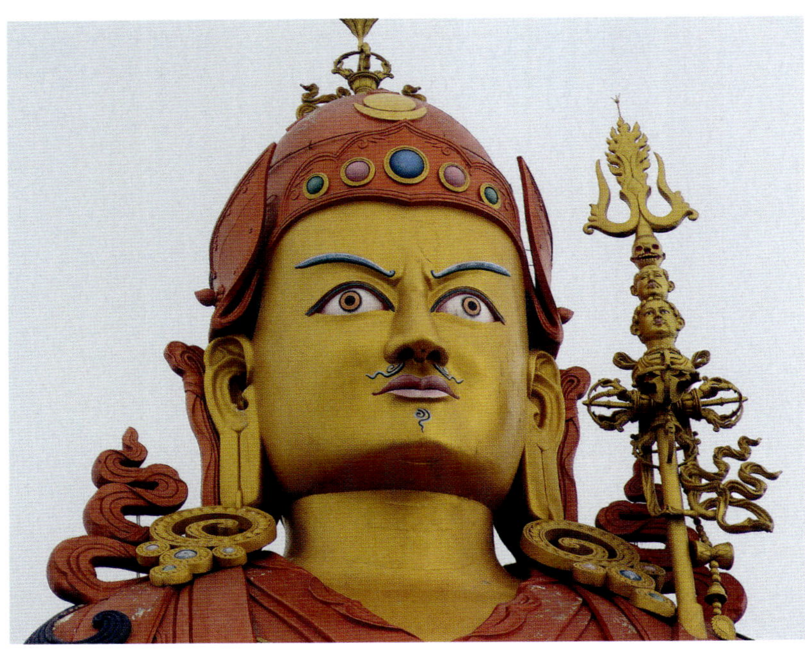

Naresh Kumar Verma (Indian), design, and Lopon Lhundrup (Bhutanese), construction; Detail of Statue of Guru Rinpoche showing face; Samdruptse, Namchi, Sikkim, India; photograph by Amy Holmes-Tagchungdarpa

Tradition and Modernity in Presenting the Guru

Part of what allows for the giant Guru Rinpoche statue at Namchi to appeal to multiple audiences, including pilgrims, tourists, and those in-between, is its style. The 135-foot statue is enormous and looms over visitors. Made from concrete and painted with rose-gold and golden paint, it is visible from hilltops throughout Sikkim, standing as a grand invocation of the continued blessings of Guru Rinpoche in the Hidden Land of Rice.

The design of the statue incorporates traditional stylistic elements with modern fabrication technology. Guru Rinpoche is often represented in this position in Buddhist art, sitting cross-legged, with a vajra in his right hand, representing his indestructible wisdom, and a skull cup, or *kapala*, or bowl, on his lap, holding the *amrita* of wisdom. On his right shoulder rests a trident, or *khatvanga*, and he is wearing his famous lotus-shaped hat, his long ears decorated with round shell earrings. Guru Rinpoche's facial expression is strong and wide-eyed, representing his attention to and awareness of everything taking place around him. He is seated on a lotus throne, atop a base that contains a meeting hall.

The inclusion of the traditional elements in the design of the statue stemmed from the participation of Buddhist authorities from the beginning of the design process. In Sikkim, popular oral lore attributes the original idea for the Guru Rinpoche statue to Dodrupchen Rinpoche (1927–2022), a widely respected Tibetan lama who resided in Gangtok. Building large statues has long been seen as meritorious in Buddhism; important examples include the giant Buddha statues of Bamiyan Valley in Afghanistan, dated to the first century, and the Leshan Giant Buddha of Sichuan, China, which dates to the eighth century. Dodrupchen Rinpoche had told his students that a statue of Guru Rinpoche would bring auspicious results for the state, along with protection from negative forces. In Buddhist traditions, statues are often attributed with the agency of the divine beings that they represent, particularly if they are constructed with appropriate ritual processes, especially consecrations (*rabne*) that are considered to awaken the statue.[7]

Shifting Scales of Intention in the Making of Guru Rinpoche

Other elements of the construction of Guru Rinpoche, however, were far from traditional. The original design of the statue was undertaken in the late 1990s by Naresh Kumar Verma, an Indian statue designer based in Gurugram who specializes in large statues built from contemporary materials.[8] Although the construction was supervised by Lopon Lhundrup, a Bhutanese statue maker, and undertaken by Sikkimese contractors, the original idea of making an enormous statue from concrete resonated with similar projects appearing throughout Asia starting in the 1970s.[9] The trend began due to the availability of concrete and fiberglass, and developments in Asian industries and local economies that allowed for the construction of massive projects.[10] In India, such projects have been supported by industrialists and entrepreneurs as well as politicians; they reflect new modes for the deployment of nationalist aspirations and entanglements between religion and secularism.[11] Elsewhere in the Himalayas, in the Indian states of Ladakh and Arunachal Pradesh and the nations of Nepal and Bhutan, giant statues of Guru Rinpoche and other Buddhist figures have also been constructed as monuments to both traditional Buddhism and modernity.

On a local level, many Sikkimese people also connect the building of Guru Rinpoche to the long-reigning chief minister of Sikkim, Pawan Kumar Chamling, who was in office from 1994 until 2019. Chamling supported the building of Guru Rinpoche near his home constituency in order to promote tourism in Namchi, but he was also aware of the significance of the historical precedents of

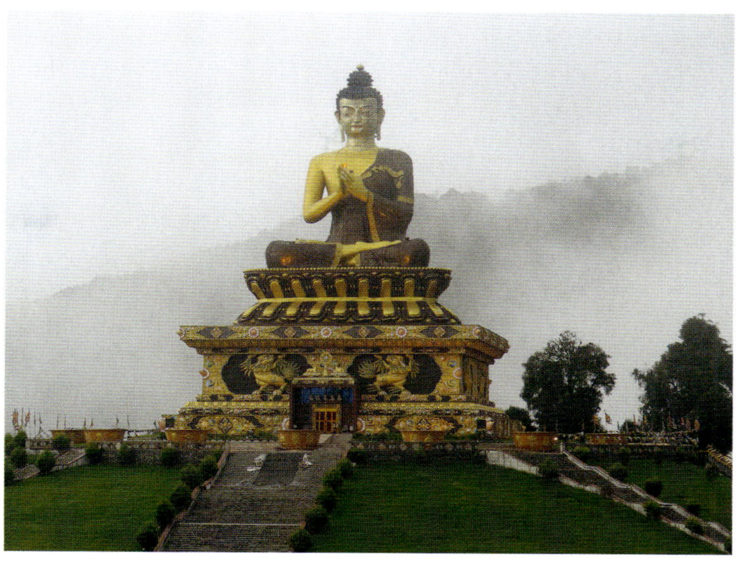

Statue of Shakyamuni Buddha; Ravangla, Sikkim, India; 2013; concrete base with gilded bronze body; height 130 ft. (39.6 m); photograph by Amy Holmes-Tagchungdarpa

political leaders who promoted Buddhism, and religion more generally, as ways to be perceived as meritorious and concerned about the spiritual, as well as physical, welfare of their subjects.[12] Chamling and his government invited the Dalai Lama to inaugurate the statue in 2004, and afterwards also supported the building of a 130-foot (39.6-meter) Shakyamuni Buddha statue in Ravangla, South Sikkim, that was completed in 2013,[13] and a 137-foot (41.8-meter) statue of Avalokiteshvara in Pelling, West Sikkim, that was completed in 2018.[14] Besides the construction of this statue geared toward his Buddhist constituents, Chamling's Sikkim Democratic Front Government presided over the building of a 108-foot (32.9-meter) statue of Shiva at Solophok Hill, near Namchi, that was completed in 2011.[15]

The political patronage behind these projects has led to discussions about intention, since historically, intention was important for ensuring good results from undertaking religiously motivated projects in Buddhist communities. However, connections between politics and economics in the making of Guru Rinpoche and other large-scale statues in Sikkim have not stopped local communities, Buddhist and otherwise, from developing a genuine appreciation and even affection for these astounding concrete interventions in the landscape. Local visitors bring offerings to the statues, including scarves, incense, and prostrations, and hold these statues as capable of bringing about spiritual transformation, just as other historically significant empowered sites and objects do in the Hidden Land.

Further Reading

Becker, Catherine. 2015. *Shifting Stones, Shaping the Past: Sculpture from the Buddhist Stupas of Andhra Pradesh.* New York: Oxford University Press.

Bruntz, Courtney, and Brooke Schedneck, eds. 2020. *Buddhist Tourism in Asia.* Honolulu: University of Hawai'i Press.

Falcone, Jessica. 2018. *Battling the Buddha of Love.* Ithaca, NY: Cornell University Press.

Notes

1 For more on Guru Rinpoche, see Pakhoutova 2018.
2 Samuel 2020.
3 Mkhan po lha tshe ring 2002.
4 Arora 2010; Chettri 2015.
5 See Balikci-Denjongpa 2001 on Kanchendzonga, and Bkra shis tshe ring 2008 for a compilation of historical pilgrimage guides about Sikkim.
6 McDaniel 2017; Shangderpa 2004.
7 Bentor 1996.
8 Jain 2021.
9 Information from Jain 2021, pl. 3; Irons 2020.
10 McDaniel 2017; McDuie-Ra and Chettri 2020.
11 Jain 2021.
12 Chettri 2015; Jain 2021.
13 Jain 2021.
14 Press Trust of India 2018.
15 Chettri 2015; Jain 2021.

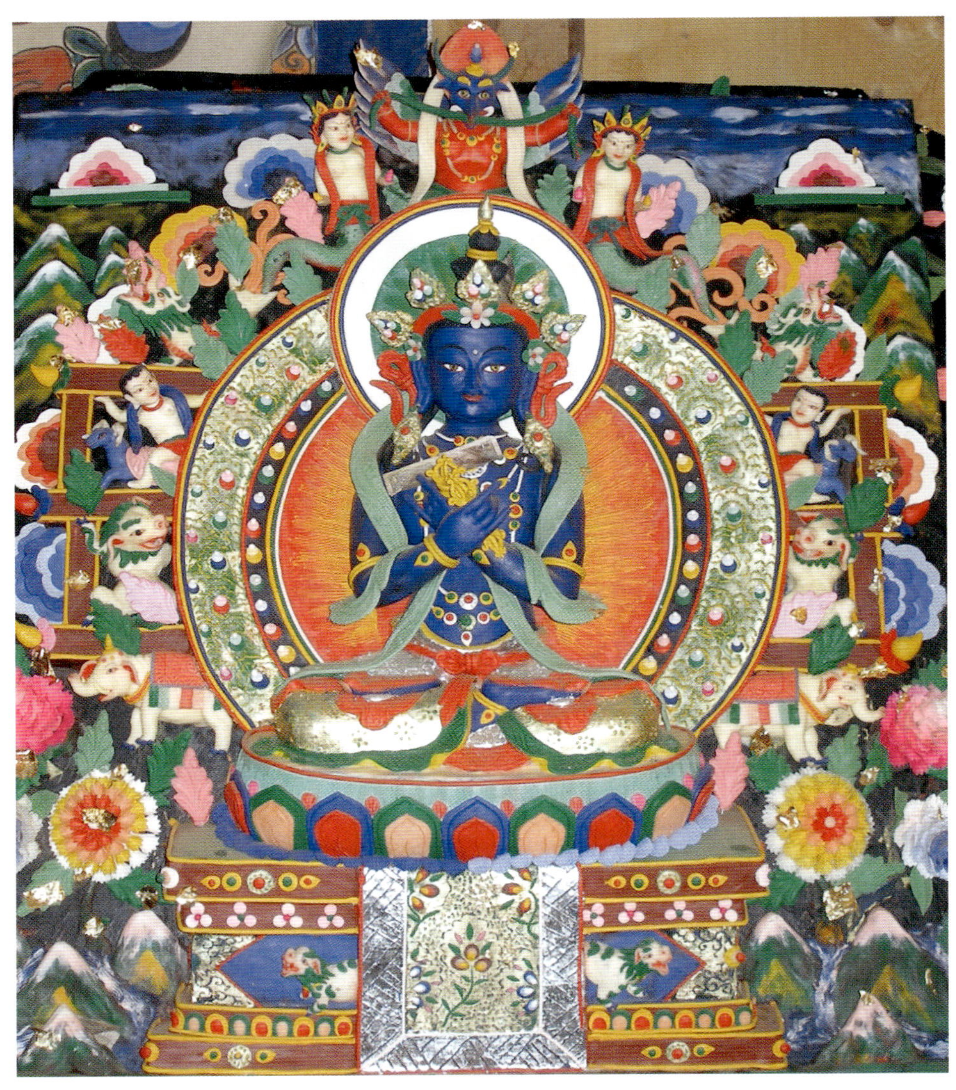

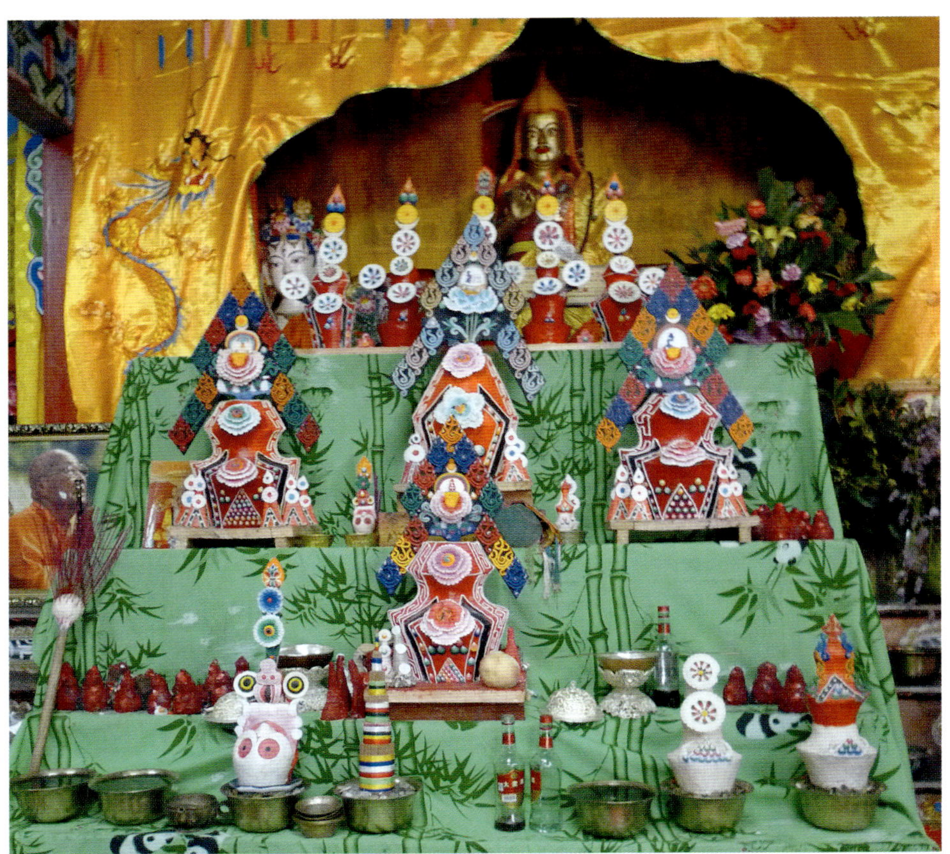

№ 105 *Tormas*

Labrang Monastery, Amdo region, eastern Tibet (Gansu Province, China), 2006

Ritual Offerings Connecting Humans and Deities

PAUL KOCOT NIETUPSKI

(top) Vajradhara, *torma* butter sculpture; Labrang Monastery, Amdo region, eastern Tibet (Gansu Province, China); 2006; flour, butter, natural pigments; height of figure approx. 12 in. (30.5 cm); photograph by Sandar Aung

(bottom) Aniconic *torma* butter sculptures; Wenfengsi, Lijiang, Yunnan Province, China; photograph by Karl Debreczeny, 2009

TORMAS, AS THEY ARE KNOWN IN TIBETAN (*bali* in Sanskrit), are ritual sculptures made of flour, butter, and decorative materials and are used in Tibetan, Indian, and other Asian religious traditions as conduits to a range of divinities.[1] The most common *tormas* are made of roasted barley flour and butter—two important staples of the Himalayan diet—and are intended as offerings of food to deities.[2] In addition, humans can participate in *torma* functions, for example in the *lu* ransom *torma* (*ludzong*), in ritualized medicine (*lutor*), projecting or "throwing" a prayer, a request, or a compelling command to a deity, and in return receiving a substantive response from the deity.[3] *Tormas* are intended to be attractive art objects and appetizing foods for communities of divinities and of humans.[4] They are also intended to be effective tools for use in a broad range of functions, including protection, Buddhist insight, tantric rituals, for good luck on auspicious holidays, and for community needs in general.[5] *Torma* rituals vary, from long, detailed liturgies to brief recitations.

Practical Uses of *Tormas*

For more about the arts of Sengge Shong, see Shambhala Kings Mural, no. 99.

Torma offering rituals can be expressions of local identity and used to build bonds between religious communities. For instance, group belief in and worship of a bright blue *torma* of Vajradhara, a transcendent buddha and source of all elements of existence, can enhance regional community religious identity. Worship of Tibetan Buddhist iconic *tormas* of the famous eighteenth-century Tibetan Buddhist Gelukpa scholar, the Second Jamyang Zhepa (1728–1791), can enhance commitments to the regional political and religious institutions, in this case the Gelukpa Labrang Monastery and its branch communities. In this respect the ostensibly religious *tormas* serve social and political purposes.[6] Further, as with other art objects, one can recognize the sources of distinctively sculpted *tormas* and works of prominent artists from different regions. For example, in Amdo, one can see the differences between artworks made by Labrang artists and by those from nearby Sengge Shong. This recognition likewise generates a sense of community definition.

Types of *Torma*

For more about regional deities, see Mountain God Kula Khari, no. 92.

Tormas are often at the center of Tibetan Buddhist ritual practices and used to engage Buddhist and non-Buddhist deities, tantric protectors, bodhisattvas, and historically prominent scholars. Local Tibetan deities include, among others, *yul lha* (regional deities), *zhi dak* (local lords), *nyen* (local tutelary deities), *don* (local spirits), *gek* (demons), and *lu* (nagas, semidivine aquatic creatures). The deities often play specific roles in communities and homelands, and require specialized recognition and offerings, often communicated by *tormas*.

Iconic *Tormas*

There are accordingly many types of *tormas*, among them iconic *tormas* with a deity or historical figure carved, painted, or imagined.[7] Iconic *tormas* often depict brightly colored Buddhist divinities or saints, and are used in a wide range of rituals. Works portraying Vajradhara and the Second Jamyang Zhepa are examples of iconic *tormas*. The iconic *torma* for Avalokiteshvara and details of the ritual process for invoking him are described in text excerpts from the "One Hundred *Tormas*" (*Torma gya tsa*), a relatively

For more on the Panchen Lamas, see in Nartang Woodblock Prints and Their Painted Copies, no. 81.

long *torma* liturgy composed by the Fourth Panchen Lama Lobzang Chokyi Gyeltsen (1570–1662). This document contextualizes *tormas* with ancient Buddhist teachings on dependent origination and goes on to assert that the fundamental mode of being of all elements of existence is emptiness.[8] It includes a statement of the Mahayana commitment to the speedy attainment of Buddhist enlightenment by all living beings. The text provides a description and liturgy of an "offering *torma*" to Avalokiteshvara, for visualization and recitation (excerpts paraphrased in English as follow):

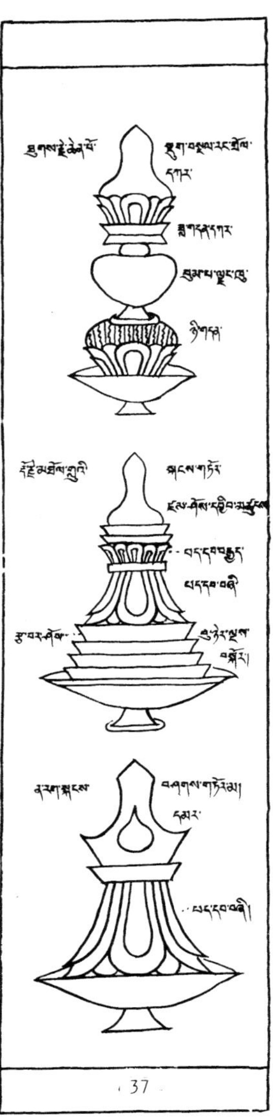

Jigme Lingpa (Tibetan, 1730–1798); Three Illustrations of Aniconic *Tormas*, from "Klong chen snying thig gi bla ma rig 'dzin 'dus pa'i gdang rol nyung ngu blo gsal mgul rgyan gtor ma'i dpe'u ris bcas dang pad gling gi dbyangs yig" [Chanting and musical notations for the performance of the bla ma rig 'dzin 'dus pa practice from the klon chen snying thig cycle of visions of 'jigs-med-gling-pa, with the illustrations of the gtor-ma cakes and chanting notations for the rituals]; late 18th century; image from Pema Kunkhyab, 1985, *Buddhist Digital Resource Center (BDRC)*, purl.bdrc.io/resource/MW23624

> This *torma* is offered to appease the leader of demons, to appease spirits that afflict children, and others, nonhumans and powerful beings visible and invisible. It is offered to protectors of the teachings and to those who generate unchanging love, especially to those who eliminate negative and generate positive circumstances, to the one thousand eight hundred classes of demons, the three hundred and sixty devils, the fifteen ghosts above, in between, and below, the demons and elementals. This offering *torma* will satisfy and counteract disease, epidemic, famine, frost and hail, drought, and will bring mental and physical benefit to all living beings who have been our parents.
>
> This *torma* purifies all of the retributive causes of rebirth—killing, capturing, beating, stealing, robbing, and all that lead one to bondage. Eliminating causes of rebirth, one will quickly attain the best goal, enlightenment.[9]

Aniconic *Tormas*

Aniconic flour-and-butter *tormas* serve as receptacles and food for ephemeral deities invoked to receive and consume the *torma* offerings. The deities reciprocate by granting the wishes of the supplicants. The topmost *torma* in the diagram at left is designated as white in color, on a white moon disk, both on a green vase, and both of these on a sun disk. The middle aniconic *torma* is a healing *torma* with a tantric song.[10] The lower *torma* is a confessional instrument for beings in hell. The top is red in color and the base has four lotus petals.

Iconic and aniconic *tormas* serve a broad range of purposes. The bright blue transcendent Buddha Vajradhara identifies the community's visionary origins, the crowned and richly ornamented Buddha Shakyamuni asserts the historical Buddha's pedigree,[11] the presence of the Palden Lhamo *torma* signals her protection of the Tibetan Buddhist Gelukpa order, Buddha Amitayus holds promise of longevity, and Manjushri cuts through ignorance. When the *tormas* are produced according to the standards for construction and invocation, with correct appearance and implementation, they are believed to be effective, functional devices.

Torma Rituals

On *cham* dance, see Ritual Dance Mask of Guru Dorje Drolo, no. 94.

The *torgyak* (*gtor rgyag*) ritual is shown in a community procession following a *cham* dance at Labrang Monastery in Amdo. The image shows a vajra and stylized skull on top of the conical *zor* weapon. The leader carries an aniconic butter-flour *torma* in front. The dance and *torma* ritual are performed. The ritual is intended to absorb and eliminate the negative forces accumulated in the preceding months. After the dance the community proceeds to the outer wall of the monastery, and the event culminates in the burning of the *torma* and the *zor* weapon.

Another ritual figure from a New Year festival in about 1932 at Labrang Monastery is a *ludzong*, the *lu* ransom *torma*. This person and his costume express the function of a *torma* (*dzong*) and an effigy (*lu*),

Torgyak, a vajra and stylized skull on top of the conical *zor* weapon, aniconic butter-flour *torma* carried in front; Labrang Monastery, Amdo region, Gansu Province, China; procession after a *cham* dance; November 3, 2002; photograph by Paul Nietupski

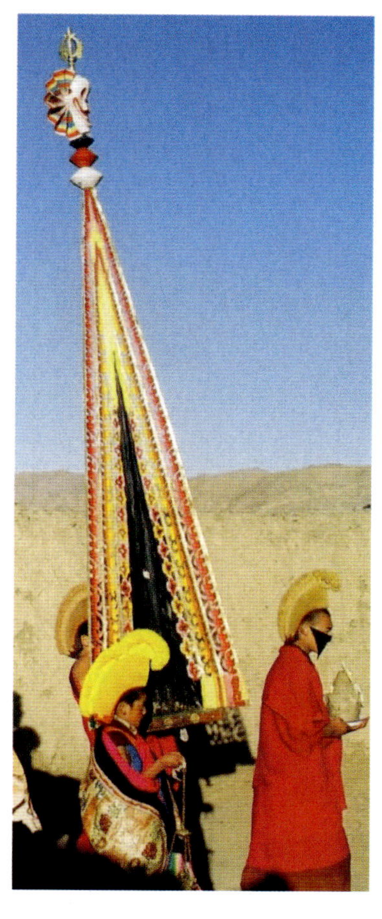

For another kind of impermanent ritual sculpture used in ransom, protection, and offerings, and sometimes used with *torma*, see Thread Crosses, no. 106.

which absorbs all of the positive and negative influences on the monastery and community accumulated over the past year. The *torma* function is embodied here, and the figure is named as a *torma*. The figure circulates through the monastery and is eventually chased out, taking with him all of the year's negativity.

Ransom medical therapy (*lutor*) is another *torma* function. In Paro, Bhutan, the officiant uses herbs, wool, a live chicken, foods, a bell, and a drum to perform a *torma* ritual, invoking and compelling a malignant deity to leave a sick person, for instance a teenage boy with a respiratory disease.

Contacts and communications between humans and deities are important parts of the Tibetan and Indian religious worldview. Tibetans and Indians share a world densely populated by deities of broad description, and the boundaries between human and deity are very porous. *Tormas* and ritual objects are vehicles for interaction between the two realms. In this vision humans and deities can interact with stylized *torma* gifts of foods often made of roasted barley flour and butter that compel deities to grant their wishes. *Torma* gifts can be iconic, with distinctive images of deities and humans who have places of prestige and power in the community legacy. *Tormas* can also be aniconic, exquisitely crafted with no anthropomorphic or divine shape of any kind. When accompanied by proper invocations, *torma* foods, and musical performances, deities are compelled to respond to human requests.

Further Reading

Barnett, Robert. 2012. "Notes on Contemporary Ransom Rituals in Lhasa." In *Revisiting Rituals in a Changing Tibetan World*, edited by Katia Buffetrille, 273–374. Leiden: Brill.

Eck, Diana L. 1998. *Darśan: Seeing the Divine Image in India*. 3rd ed. New York: Columbia University Press.

Harrison, Paul. 1992. "Commemoration and Identification in Buddhānusmṛti." In *In the Mirror of Memory: Reflections on Mindfulness and Remembrance in Indian and Tibetan Buddhism*, edited by Janet Gyatso, 215–338. Albany: SUNY Press.

Notes

1 "The word *bali* occurs several times in the *Rigveda* and often later in the sense of tribute to a king or offering to a god. . . . The attitude of the Vedic Indian to his gods was at least as compatible with tribute as with voluntary gifts." Monier Monier-Williams, Sanskrit Dictionary. Accessed May 25, 2021. https://sanskritdictionary.com/?iencoding=iast&q=bali&lang=sans&action=Search. For dyes and pigments used in *tormas*, see J. Watt 2017.

2 See Garrett 2010a.

3 See Tibetan and Himalayan Library 2019. The entry for "*gtor ma* (*torma*)" lists tantric ceremonies, protection of the Buddhist Dharma, daily *tormas*, occasional *tormas*, and types mentioned by Künkhyen Tenpey Nyima: shrine *torma* (*rten gtor*), perpetual *torma* (*rtag gtor*), *sadhana torma* (*sgrub gtor*), offering *torma* (*mchod gtor*), mending *torma* (*skang gtor*), session *torma* (*thun gtor*), daily *torma* (*rgyun gtor*), captured *torma* (*gta' gtor*), and food *torma*.

4 J. Watt 2017.

5 For medical applications, see Garrett 2010a.

6 For a concise statement of community bonding mechanisms, see Wiltermuth and Heath 2009.

7 Blo bzang chos kyi rgyal mtshan, n.d.; Butler 1996.

8 On dependent origination, the document says, "Ye dharmā hetuprabhavā hetuṃ teṣāṃ tathāgato hy avadat, teṣāṃ ca yo nirodha evaṃvādī mahāśramaṇaḥ" [The great ascetic explained that all elements of existence are causally produced and causally destroyed]. Jayarava 2009.

9 Blo bzang chos kyi rgyal mtshan, n.d., translation by Paul Nietupski.

10 The title of the song is "*rdo rje mthol glu skangs gtor*."

11 Twist 2018.

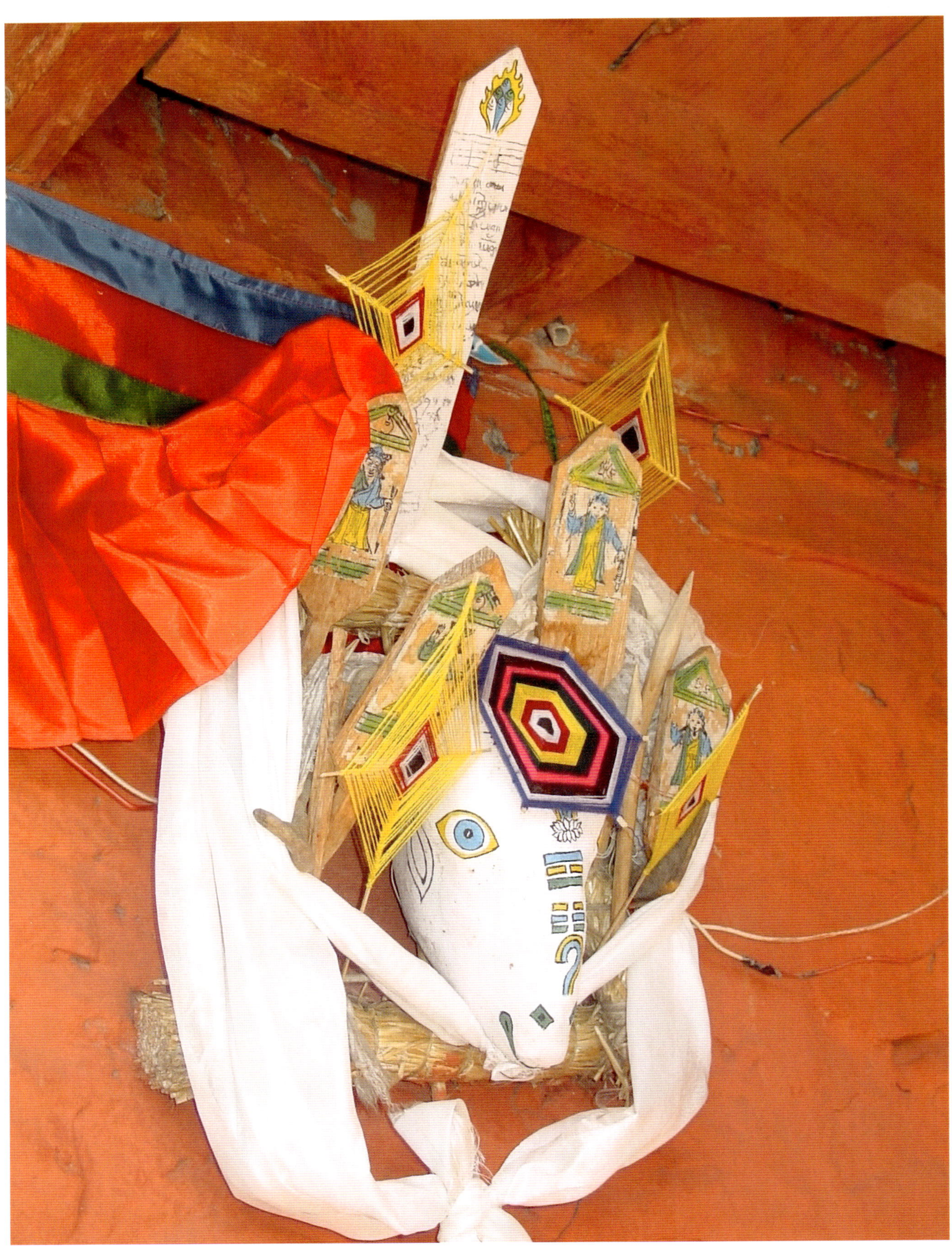

№ 106 Thread Crosses

Kagbeni, Mustang, Nepal, 2007

Sky Symbols of Divine and Cosmic Forces

CHARLES RAMBLE

Lama Tshultrim of Lubrak (b. 1949, Lubrak, Mustang, Nepal); Sky Door (*Namgo*); house of Pema Dolkar, Kagbeni, Mustang, Nepal; 21st century, restored 2007; sheep's skull, cotton cloth, wood, barley straw, bamboo, woolen yarn; 17¾ × 9 × 6¾ in. (45 × 23 × 17 cm); photograph by Charles Ramble

For more on astrology, see *The White Beryl* Illuminated Manuscript, no. 86.

In any culturally Tibetan area, it is common to encounter a distinctive type of discarded ritual waste, at the edges of remote villages or at busy intersections in urban Lhasa. The debris usually consists of the dough figurines of a man or woman, wooden tablets with arcane symbols, and other items of ritual paraphernalia. Among these items will be one or more small bamboo crosses strung with yarn to form a brightly colored web. Foreign travelers frequently collect these discarded objects as souvenirs, little knowing that the effigies are dangerously polluted representations of sick people, intended as offerings to demons as ransoms for their stolen souls. Another common sight is the object featured in this essay: the cloth-wrapped skull of a dog or sheep, festooned with items that include several small thread crosses, positioned over the doorways of village houses. The construction based on the sheep skull, shown here, is known as a "Sky Door" (*namgo*), and that based on the dog skull as an "Earth Door" (*sago*). Both terms denote inauspicious astrological configurations, and the purpose of these effigies is to protect the household from their effects.

Namkhas, Dreamcatchers, and God's Eyes

Thread crosses feature in many cultures around the world, and English-language accounts often refer to the Tibetan variants as "dreamcatchers," after the well-known Native American constructions that they resemble, even to the extent of including feathers in their composition. The principle of the dreamcatcher is that the meshes form a barrier to hostile forces that become entangled in them. This, however, is an erroneous interpretation of Tibetan thread crosses. While we should certainly keep open the possibility that Tibetan thread crosses, like other sacred motifs, once had a significance that has been transformed in a different ideological climate (by way of a parallel, one has only to think of the fate of the swastika), the orthodox understanding of their meaning is both precise and elaborate, and, perhaps surprisingly, has little to do with ensnaring spirits. Tibetan thread crosses are, if anything, more reminiscent in both form and function to Latin American *ojos de Dios*, "God's eyes."

For more about Bon, see Bon Deity Trowo Tsochok Khagying, no. 60.

The Tibetan term for a thread cross is *namkha*, meaning "sky." *Namkhas* feature in both Bon and Buddhist rituals, but may once have been part of an archaic repertoire of ritual practices that were appropriated by both religions and endowed with new meanings. For the Bonpos (the followers of Bon), the use of *namkhas* was first taught by the legendary founder of their religion, Shenrab Miwo. *Namkhas* appear in the first of the *Nine Ways of Bon, the Way of the System of Prediction*, when Shenrab explains the procedure for performing ransom rituals. This ritual, described as the "'Exchange' Rite for transposing two equal things," requires "the right sized figurine as ransom for the [patient's] body, a *namkha*, a wool-wrapped splint, an arrow [for a man], a spindle [for a woman] . . ."[1] The purpose of the *namkha*, however, is not explained. In chapter 39 of the *Ziji*, the twelve-volume biography of Shenrab, the master instructs the Bon priests of the land of Zhangzhung in a variety of procedures, including the use of "black and white *namkhas*." Again, we are given no details about their significance.

The Basic Construction

See *Tormas*, no. 105.

Namkhas have a similar function to the dough-and-butter effigies known as *tormas*, in that they may represent either offerings to divinities or the divinities themselves, as well as certain other functions, some listed below. *Namkhas* that represent divinities are called *zhelnam*, "face *namkhas*." Like *tormas*,

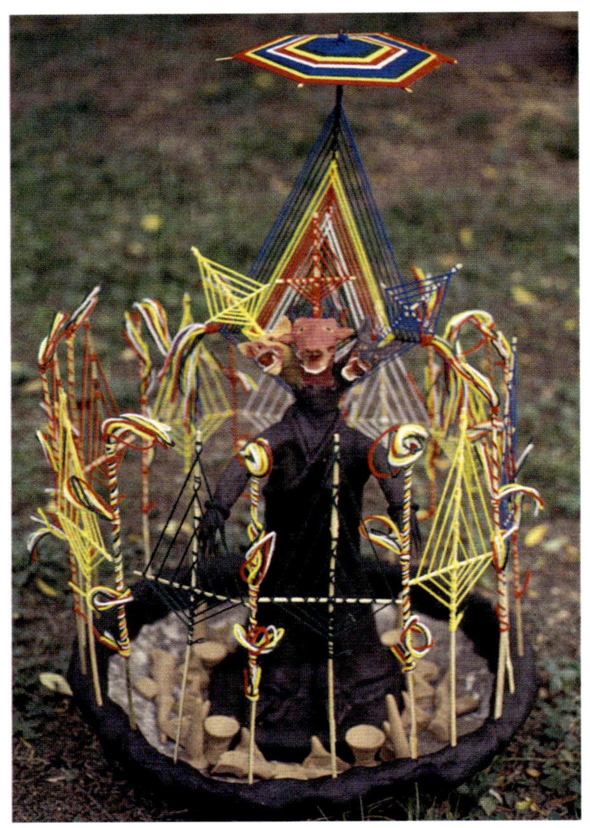

Lama Karma Tshering of Tshognam (b. 1951, Tetang, Mustang, Nepal); Three-Headed One of the Black Rituals, Nyingma Buddhist version of a ritual effigy; Sanepa, Kathmandu, Nepal; 1995; clay, wood, iron, barley dough, bamboo, woolen yarn, chemical dyes; 18½ × 12¼ in. (47 × 31 cm); photograph by Charles Ramble

namkhas are used not alone, but in an assemblage of objects. Some are simple, but others may be highly elaborate, such as the construction known as the *namkha khangzang*, a "*namkha* mansion." Most ritual texts give only brief instructions about any *namkhas* that are to be made for the performance, but a few works, such as the following, provide systematic details: "The thread where the two sticks cross should be black. Outside that there should be a ring of white thread, then one of red thread, and after that there should be a gap, called 'the space between the eyes.' Outside this one may string whatever 'changing eye' is required."[2] Changing eye refers to the fact that the colors in this ring vary according to the identity of the divinity represented. Thus the goddess Sipai Gyelmo, whose three faces are white, blue, and red, is represented by woolen rings of these colors. The text continues: "Beyond this, there should be a gap called the 'hollow space,' and then [three rings] called the *dabgyur*, the *tragyur*, and the *khatun*, that together constitute the 'perimeter wall.' . . . Generally speaking, at the crossing point of the sticks, the 'pupil of the eye,' the thread should be black; the next band white, and the third red; there are usually three rings of threads, separated by two gaps."

This central "eye" is a widespread feature of Bonpo *namkhas*, and the text's injunction that *namkhas* "should not be blind" underscores its significance. Buddhist *namkhas*, by contrast, seem not to require it, as seen in a partially completed Bonpo version and a Buddhist equivalent of an effigy known as *tonak gosum*, the "Three-Headed One of the Black Rituals." According to a myth, this fearsome monster was tamed by the Buddhist or Bonpo hero and commissioned to destroy enemies of the doctrine and of sentient beings. Its three animal heads have different colors, and the Bonpo text specifies simply that the *namkhas* surmounting them "should be of the corresponding colors." Even here, however, while the *namkhas* in the Buddhist effigy are uniformly colored, the Bonpo *namkhas* feature the ubiquitous central eye.[3]

Certain pioneering studies of Tibetan ritual refer to thread crosses not as *namkha* but as *do* (Tibetan: *mdos*).[4] While this appellation is technically incorrect, the usage is metonymic insofar as the *namkha* is the most conspicuous component of *do* constructions. *Do* are microcosms of the universe, varying in complexity and with multiple functions, such as offerings to the higher gods and ransom effigies for earthly powers. Both the Sky Door/Earth Door and the Three-Headed One are classified as *do*. In the *Nobeka*, a Bon treatise on *do* rituals, the *namkha* is the first component to be described and discussed. The following is a selection of some of the features of *namkhas* that this treatise presents.

Features Related to Specific Objectives of *Namkhas*

There are eighty kinds of *namkha*, subdivided into different categories. The first comprises "wisdom" *namkhas*, representing the wisdom deities. Since these gods are indistinguishable with respect to front and back, their *namkhas* should also not exhibit such a distinction; they should be resistant to water and wind, and the gaps should be such that one's finger can pass through them. They should be constructed with the idea that they emit light for the benefit of living beings. "Action" *namkhas* should be flexible, as if they were able to walk. Each of the four kinds of virtuous action, too, has its appropriate characteristics; thus "benign" *namkhas* should have a "smiling" appearance, "subjugating" *namkhas* should exhibit the power known as *jin*, while "increasing" and "wrathful" *namkhas* should likewise express their natures.

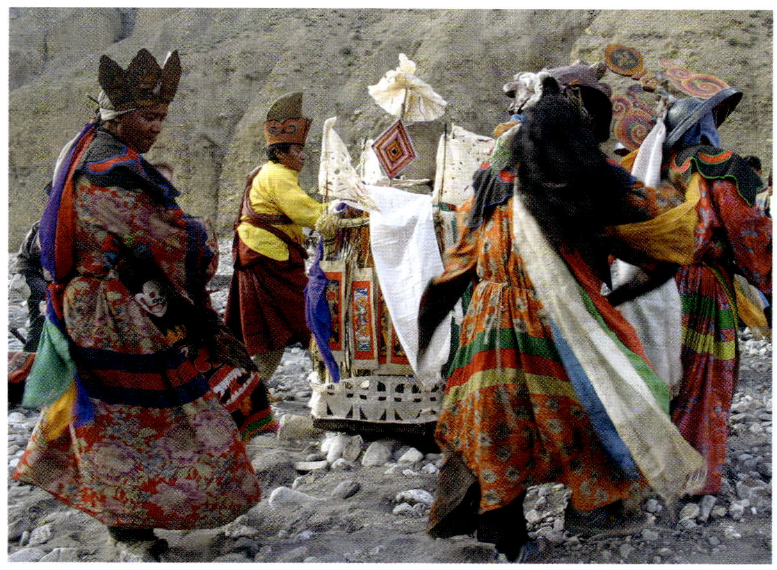

Bonpo lamas dance around a *do* effigy, surmounted by a *namkha*, shortly before its immolation by fire. The ceremony, called *dogyab* ("casting out the *do*") assures the annual purification of the community; Lubrak, Mustang, Nepal; 2008; photograph by Charles Ramble

Three inversions should be avoided: the vertical stick should respect the direction of the bamboo's growth; front and back should not be confused (except of course in the case of wisdom *namkhas*); and if feathers are used, care should be taken to ensure that their outer surface faces forward. *Namkhas* of appeasement (*kangnam*) should be tall, to "reach up to the sky," while *namkhas* for repulsion (*doknam*) should have a large number of gaps.

Certain defects in the construction are to be avoided; the bamboo joints should be neither too small nor too big, and the bamboo itself should be straight. Hexagonal "parasol" *namkhas* should not be concave or flat, nor too closed, but gently convex. The threads should be taut and evenly spaced: they should not resemble an avalanche, a torrent of water, or "a pair of sagging breeches."

The size of the *namkha* should be determined by various factors: the scale of the *do* that they ornament, the height of the room in which the ritual is performed, and the patron's resources. Generally, they should range in height from one cubit to one fathom (though in practice smaller *namkha* are commonly used).

Namkhas for wisdom beings should use fine silk; those for beings that are manifested in the physical world should use woolen yarn; for haughty demons, yarn made from the fur of tigers, bears, or other carnivores; for worldly people, the wool of antelopes and gazelles; for various categories of obstructive demons, the wool of yaks and yak-cow crossbreeds; and finally, for certain classes of harmful spirits, yarn made from the fur of dogs, goats, and pigs.

Finally, the text notes that *namkhas* may be used to represent any of the auspicious symbols required by the instructions for a *do* ritual, such as swastikas, vases, conches, and the *patra,* or "knot of eternity."

Further Reading

Blondeau, Anne-Marie. 2000. "The *mKha' klong gsang mdos*: Some Questions on Ritual Structure and Cosmology." In *New Horizons in Bon Studies: Proceedings of a Conference in Osaka, August 1999*, edited by Samten Karmay and Yasuhiko Nagano, 249–87. Osaka: National Museum of Ethnology.

Namkhai Norbu, Chögyal. 2021. *Namkha: Harmonizing the Energy of the Elements.* Merigar: Shang Shung Publications. (Restricted access.)

Nebesky-Wojkowitz, R. de. (1956) 1975. *Oracles and Demons of Tibet: The Cult and Iconography of the Tibetan Protective Deities.* Reprint, Graz: Akademische Druck- u. Verlagsanstalt.

Notes

1 Snellgrove (1967) 1980, 37; the translation has been modified for consistency with the terminology in the present essay.

2 *Bonkyong*, fol. 1v. I am indebted to Geshe Tri Kalsang of Menri Monastery, Dolanji, India, for kindly making available to me both this text and the other, *Nobeka*, on which the present essay is based. Geshe Tri Kalsang is currently preparing a book-length study of *namkhas*.

3 For a fifteen-part video entitled *Soul, Fortune, and the Three-Headed Man*, documenting a ceremony in which this ritual is performed, see http://kalpa-bon.com/performances; the process of making the effigy of the Three-Headed One, including the three *namkhas*, appears in Part 2, 30 min. 10 sec. before the end, and in Part 3, beginning at 22 min. 5 sec.

4 See, for example, Nebesky-Wojkowitz (1956) 1975. The history of this confusion is traced in Blondeau 1990, which remains the single most important source concerning both *do* and *namkhas*. For a study of a particular Bonpo *do* ritual, see Blondeau 2000; photographs by Yoshiro Imaeda of the *namkhas* for this *do* appear on 278–84. For video documentation of the construction of a *do* effigy and associated *namkhas*, see *Between the Lines: Exorcising the Old Year in a Himalaya Bonpo Village*, https://youtu.be/SqjN_owRXls, 22 min. 50 sec. to 26 min. 52 sec.

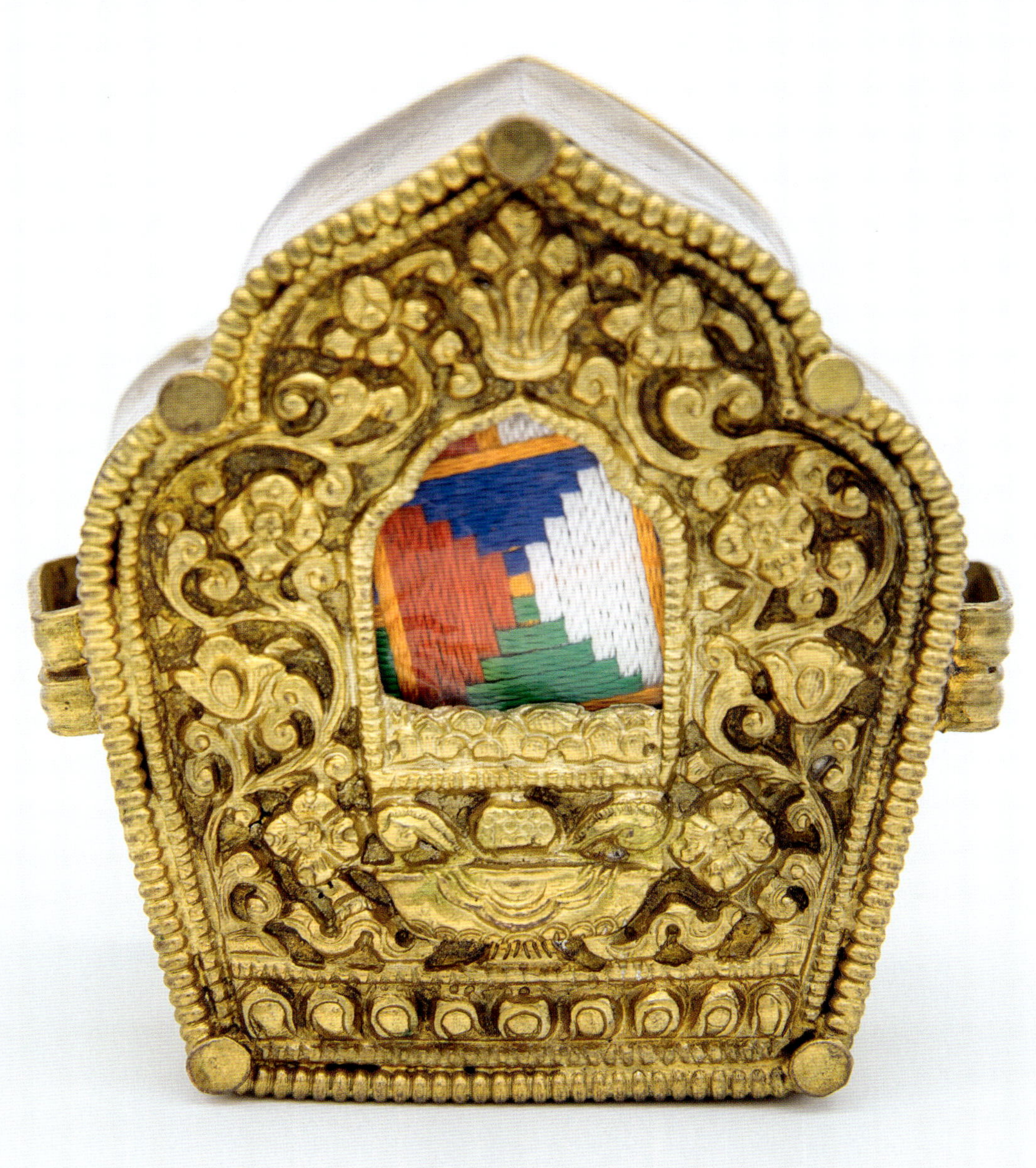

Amulet Box (*Gau*) and Its Contents; Kathmandu, Nepal; first decade of the 21st century; metal alloy; 3½ × 3⅛ × 1½ in. (9 × 8 × 4 cm); Private collection, Central Europe; photograph by Chris Zvitkovits

№ 107 Amulet Box (*Gau*) with Its Contents

Kathmandu, Nepal, first decade of the 21st century

Portable Sacred Items for Pragmatic and Transcendent Goals

JAMES GENTRY

PORTABLE AMULET BOXES FILLED WITH SACRED OBJECTS, or *gau* in Tibetan, such as the one pictured here with its contents, are among the most ubiquitous features of Tibetan Buddhist culture. The contents of amulet boxes are referred to in Tibetan as *ten*, meaning "receptacle," for their role in encapsulating the "blessings" (*jinlab*) and "power" (*tu*) of buddhas, bodhisattvas, and revered lamas.[1] *Gaus* come in a wide variety of shapes and sizes, ranging from tiny pendants to larger miniature reliquaries.[2] Their materials and decorations also vary considerably, reflecting the social status, religious role, and gender of their owners, and sometimes the region of their origin.[3]

The *gau* pictured here was a personal gift from the Tsike Chokling, Fourth Karma Mingyur Dewe Dorje (1953–2020), known as Chokling Rinpoche, to two of his students.[4] Judging by its size and shape, fashioned in imitation of a Buddhist reliquary or chorten (Sanskrit: stupa), this is a men's *gau*. Men's *gaus* can range in size from an inch (two and a half centimeters) to over fourteen inches (thirty-five centimeters) in height. Smaller *gaus* like this one are worn around the neck, while larger *gaus* are hung over the chest or under the arm, suspended from a leather strap or cloth band.[5] The flat base enables them also to function as makeshift shrines when traveling, and as centerpieces for home or temple shrines, where they can house especially revered objects in initiations and other tantric Buddhist rituals.

For more about stupas, see the Svayambhu Chaitya of Kathmandu, no. 4 and White Stupa, no. 40.

The contents of *gaus* vary widely, depending on their owner and function, but they typically house an assortment of *sacra* collected over time, such as miniature statues; photographs of lamas; votive plaques; amulets; Sanskrit mantras or sacred incantations written on small pieces of paper; relic pills; materials from sacred sites; and fragments of silk scarves, fabrics, strands of hair, or anything else once in contact with a revered person, place, or thing.[6] *Gaus* used in initiation rituals might house only a single object, such as a miniature statue or ritual object associated with a famous tantric master from the past.

For more about relics and votive plaques, see Molded Clay Image (*Tsatsa*) of Amoghapasha, no. 28.

The *gau* pictured here was handselected by Chokling Rinpoche, who specially prepared its contents and consecrated it in Kathmandu, Nepal, during the first decade of the twenty-first century. Its metal surface is decorated with the Wish-Fulfilling Jewel above the window and offerings below it, flanked on the right and left by a pattern vaguely suggestive of the Eight Auspicious Symbols, the *gau*'s most common decorative motif.[7] Its contents include 1) an amulet diagram encased in cords of five colors, together with three dark brown pills of unknown origin and constitution; 2) two reddish brown pills composed of relics said to be from the eighth-century Indian tantric master Padmasambhava and his core group of disciples in the Tibetan imperial court known as the Twenty-Five Figures of King Tri Songdetsen (742–ca. 800) and his subjects (*Orgyen jebang nyernga*), which belonged to the late Dudjom Rinpoche, Jikdrel Yeshe Dorje (1904–1987);[8] and 3) two small golden pills of unknown origin and constitution. Unlike most *gaus*, which display in their window an enclosed image, such as the statue of a buddha or the photograph of a lama, this one displays through its window the amulet, with its other contents concealed behind it.

See Padmasambhava and His Manifestations, no. 43; Ritual Dance Mask of Guru Dorje Drolo, no. 94.

Amulets and Their Purpose

The owners of this *gau* report that Chokling Rinpoche gave it to them for the express purpose of protection. Protective amulets (*sungwa, sungkhor*) like this one are geometric diagrams drawn on paper with a combination of mantra formulas and images, and consecrated through contemplative ritual proceedings, before being folded up, wrapped in cords of five colors with sacred substances, and

Amulet Box (*Gau*) and Its Contents (amulet and assorted relic pills); Kathmandu, Nepal; first decade of the 21st century; Private collection, Central Europe; photograph by Chris Zvitkovits

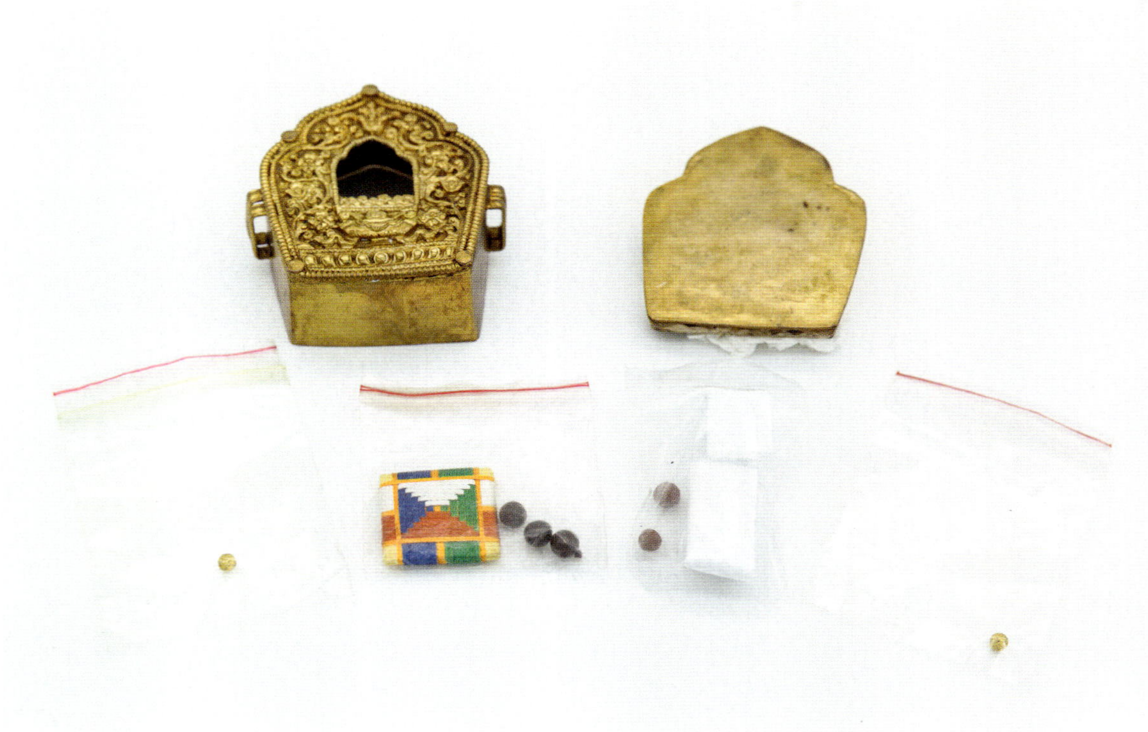

distributed for use. They can be included among the contents of amulet boxes or worn separately. Tibetans have used them to protect against misfortune during travel, injury during battle, illness, harmful spirits, and any other potential calamity.[9] The manufacture of such protective amulets has been so prevalent among Buddhists in Tibet through the ages that it might have influenced the advent of Muslim amulet use in the twelfth century.[10]

Gaus and the amulets they house have a range of other functions, too. They can be worn to extend longevity, personal power (*wangtang*), and good fortune (*lungta*), and to enhance wealth and intelligence, among other desirable aims. Their functions can also be coercive or destructive. They can be made to seduce a potential partner, influence a powerful political leader, or destroy an enemy.[11] In the latter instances, the charm would not be worn by the owner but secretly placed close to the intended target.

On astrological calculations, see *The White Beryl* Illuminated Manuscript, no. 86.

Amulets are sometimes made using astrological calculations to tailor them to specific individuals and functions. In such instances, the date of birth of the wearer or target is tallied according to the sixty-year astrological cycle of the various combinations of twelve animals and five elements. An amulet is then specially produced to manipulate negative and positive influences according to personal and temporal specifications.[12]

Tibetan Buddhist ritual experts who produce amulets tend to frame their diversity of aims according to the rubric of the "four tantric activities" of pacifying (Tibetan: *zhiwa*; Sanskrit: *shantika*), enriching (Tibetan: *gyepa*; Sanskrit: *paushtika*), subjugating (Tibetan: *wangwa*; Sanskrit: *vashikarana*), and destroying (Tibetan: *ngoncho*; Sanskrit: *abhichara*), whereby protection figures primarily as an act of quelling potential adversities.[13] Moreover, these categories are often understood as multivalent, so that the notion of protection partakes of a broader doctrinal understanding, extending also to protection against karmic obstacles that thwart positive rebirth and spiritual obstructions that interfere with the attainment of awakening. The tendency to intertwine these three orientations—the pragmatic, karmic, and transcendent—in one and the same object and practice has been highlighted as a unique feature of tantric Buddhist traditions.[14]

Sacred Pills and Their Purpose

Sacred pills like the ones pictured here are as commonplace in Tibetan Buddhist cultural regions as amulets. The Tibetan practice of concocting, consecrating, consuming, and wearing sacred pills in *gaus* originates from Indian Buddhist tantric traditions brought to Tibet beginning in the eighth century that had integrated Buddhist relic veneration with pan-Indian medical and alchemical practices.[15]

Dudjom Rinpoche, from whom the relic pills in this *gau* originate, composed a short text for the production and consecration of pills that includes compounds consecrated previously by Padmasambhava and his twenty-five disciples of King Tri Songdetsen and subjects, and by the first Chokling Rinpoche, Chokgyur Dechen Zhikpo Lingpa (1829–1870). This might very well describe the pills housed in this *gau*.

As Dudjom describes, his pills need not be consumed to bring about effects. Like amulets, their governing principle of efficacy is physical contact, and they protect not only against mundane dangers, but also against rebirth as an animal, anguished spirit, or hell being.[16] Ultimately, Dudjom promises, his pill concoction can confer awakening in this very lifetime, without the need even to cultivate it but through just tasting or coming into contact with the minutest trace of a single pill.[17] To help reach this goal, he adds, practitioners are advised to connect with it devoutly by means of contemplative practice. While eating it, for example, the consumer visualizes herself as a tantric deity and the pill as flowing from the sexual union of two buddhas to pervade her subtle body with the immaculate great bliss of awakening.[18] In this and other ways, Dudjom insists, interacting with such pills should not be disregarded as a palliative done in lieu of genuine Buddhist practice, but as part of a rich contemplative tradition connected with the loftiest goals of Vajrayana Buddhism.

This *gau* and its contents thus serve as a powerful illustration of the Tibetan Buddhist penchant for integrating mundane pragmatic concerns with the aspiration for ultimate awakening. Here they are combined in a single portable box.

Further Reading

Clarke, John. 2001. "Ga'u—The Tibetan Amulet Box." *Arts of Asia* 31, no. 1 (May–June): 45–67.

Gentry, James. 2019b. "Tibetan Buddhist Power Objects." In *Oxford Research Encyclopedia of Religion*. Oxford University Press. doi: http://dx.doi.org/10.1093/acrefore/9780199340378.013.657.

Skorupski, Tadeusz. 1983. *Tibetan Amulets*. Bangkok: White Orchid Books.

Notes

1 Gentry 2019b.
2 Clarke 2001.
3 See Clarke 2001, 46–47, for details regarding the history of amulet box use in Tibet and across Asia.
4 For more on this incarnation line, and particularly the life of the first Chokling Rinpoche, Chokgyur Dechen Zhikpo Lingpa, see Gardner 2009; Guru Padmasambhava, Lingpa, and Wangpo 2016.
5 On the size of *gaus* and how they are worn, see Clarke 2001, 54–55.
6 Clarke 2001, 46.
7 Clarke 2001, 50. The Eight Auspicious Substances are the mirror, *ghiwang* medicine, yogurt, *durva* grass, *bilva* fruit, conch shell, cinnabar, and mustard seeds.
8 For a traditional narrative about Padmasambhava and his relationship with the Tibetan imperial court, see Dudjom 1991, 512–21. See Dalton 2015 for a brief biography of Padmasambhava, and Samuel and Oliphant of Rossie 2020 for a collected volume of the latest scholarship about him. For a biography of Dudjom Rinpoche, see Tsewang Dongyal 2008.
9 Skorupski 1983, 15–45.
10 Elverskog 2010, 104–16.
11 Elverskog 2010, 46–49, x–xii, 11.
12 Elverskog 2010, 53–54.
13 Skorupski 1983, 11. Kuranishi 2013, 269–72, describes nine functions in the *Krishnayamari Tantra*, including the first three and six others, most of which Tibetans tend to group under the function of "destroying." For more on pan-Indian uses of amulets (*chakras* and *yantras*), see Bühnemann 2003.
14 For a discussion of this tripartite distinction, drawn from the Spiro 1982 study of Burmese Theravada Buddhist society, and how it compares to Tibetan Buddhism, see Samuel 1993, 27–38.
15 Gayley 2007b; Garrett 2010b; Gentry 2017, 259–84, 296–332; Gentry 2019a, 88–95.
16 Gentry 2017, 259–84, 296–332; Gentry 2019a, 88–95.
17 For more on the Tibetan Buddhist tradition of liberation through sensory contact, see Gayley 2007b; Gentry 2017, 171–290; Gentry 2019a; Gentry 2019b.
18 Bdud 'joms 'Jigs bral ye shes rdo rje, n.d., 9a.6–12b.5, 11a.4–11a.5, 11a.5–11b.2

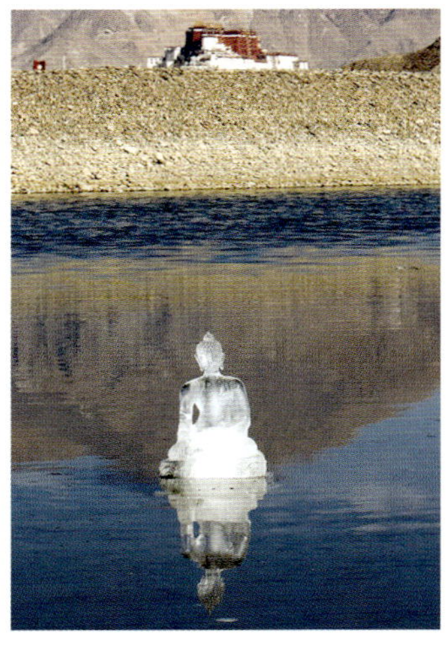
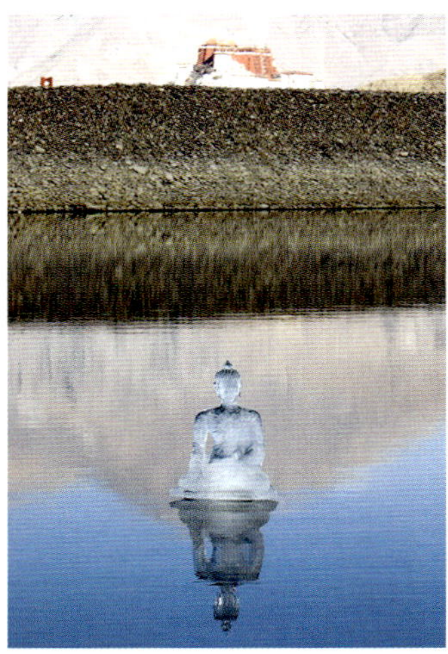
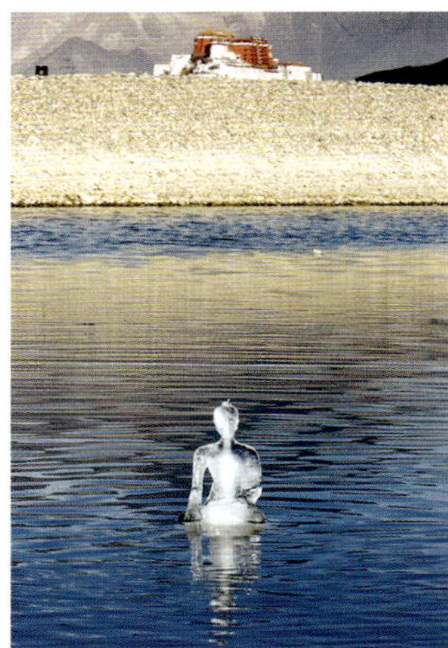
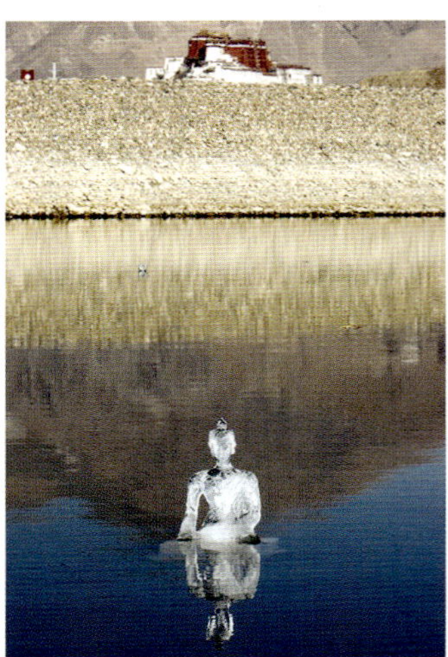

№ 108 Ice Buddha

Lhasa, U region, central Tibet (TAR, China), 2006

Tibetan Artists' Contemporary Practices

YANGLA GESANG, YUYUAN (VICTORIA) LIU, AND ELENA PAKHOUTOVA

See Potala Palace, no. 71.

On the placid and reflective surface of the water sits a glittering, translucent statue of a buddha made of ice, with the Potala Palace in the background. Under the scorching sunlight, *Ice Buddha* gradually melts and sinks into the river.

Eight photographs document the 2006 conceptual installation by the artist Gade. He collected water from the Kyichu River, which flows through the city of Lhasa, froze the water, and, following traditional proportions and visual conventions, sculpted the ice into a statue of Buddha Shakyamuni. As the statue melted, the river's own water returned to its source, which flows through India—where Buddhism originated before it was introduced to Tibet—eventually reaching the Indian Ocean.[1]

See Wheel of Existence, no. 97.

For a similarly impermanent medium, see *Tormas*, no. 105.

In *Ice Buddha* Gade uses the most recognizable Buddhist symbol and the temporality of water as his medium. He connects the water's changing forms, from liquid to solid ice and back to water, with the Buddhist philosophical concepts of impermanence and reincarnation in the karmically driven cycle of successive existences (samsara). The artist preserves the essence of the Buddha's form, but moves away from the traditional formats of two-dimensional painting and static metal sculpture to performative aspects and installation in nature, using impermanent media not previously explored in emerging Tibetan contemporary art.[2]

Gade (b. 1971, Lhasa); *Ice Buddha No. 1* (8 photographs); Lhasa; 2006; chromogenic prints; each 31½ × 19⅝ in. (80 × 50 cm); photographs by Jason Sangster, courtesy Gade

Viewers can read much into this work's multilayered meaning. The connotations it evokes range from the purely philosophical to the culturally astute, socially relevant, and personally evocative. To name a few: impermanence, the cyclical nature of existence and reincarnation; the fragility of traditional cultural values; the dissolution of Tibetan Buddhist culture; change; and reflections on the passage of time.

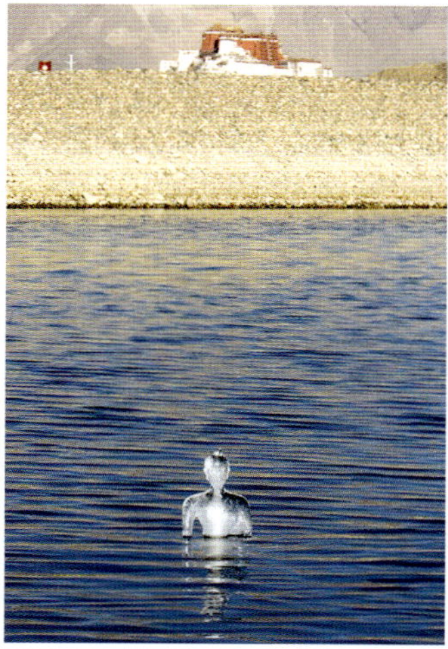
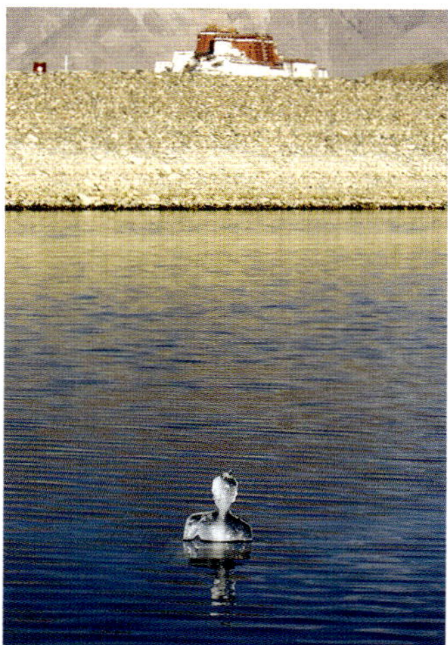
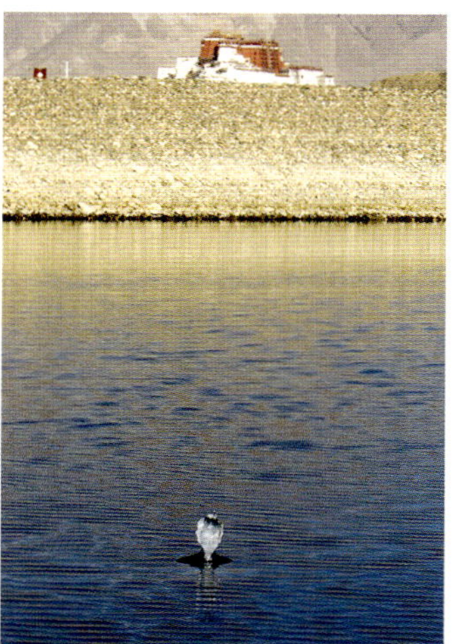
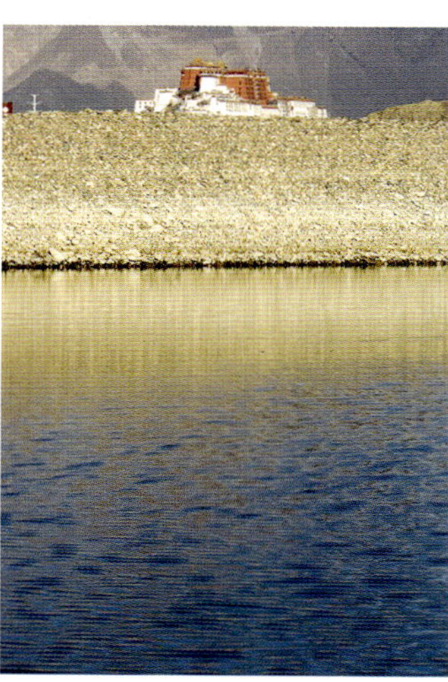

Interpretations of Traditional Forms

For other buddha images, see Buddha on the Cosmic Mountain, no. 10; Central Shrine Image of Kwa Baha, no. 22; Crowned Buddha, no. 16; Jowo Shakyamuni, no. 8.

The buddha image is the most representative visual form and religious symbol associated with contemplative qualities. A buddha's form embodies Buddhist teachings on the nature of reality, and universal philosophical notions of impermanence and emptiness,[3] as well as cultural practices and personal connections to the teachings (dharma). Contemporary Tibetan artists explore and often contest the richly symbolic religious and cultural associations of this form.

Around the turn of the twenty-first century, several artists engaged the buddha's form in ways that challenged assumptions and preconceptions about Tibetan Buddhist culture. Their work addressed on the one hand, the loss of traditional culture and the pervasiveness of popular culture with its new icons,[4] and on the other hand, consumption of Buddhist images and the "commercialization" of Tibetan Buddhism. In his earlier works, Gonkar Gyatso, an artist based in the United Kingdom and China, used colorful stickers and commercial logos to fill an outlined buddha's head, replacing the buddha's features.[5] For a 2010 work titled *Do What You Love*, he made a three-dimensional scan of a traditionally cast fourteenth-century sculpture, digitally manipulated the image, and mass-produced buddha figures, positioning them with their heads stuck in the wall and their backs toward the viewer. Other artists, including the Lhasa-based Nortse and Angsang, and the US-based Ang Tsherin Sherpa and Tenzing Rigdol, have addressed various aspects of their present-day lives through the images of the buddha's form.[6]

For historical examples, see the Svayambhu Chaitya of Kathmandu, no. 4; Stupa at Toling Monastery, no. 19; White Stupa, no. 40.

Artists have also reinterpreted another recognizable Buddhist symbol that represents the Buddha's mind, the stupa. The US-based Palden Weinreb, in his *Untitled* (*Stupa*), created in encaustic wax and made luminous from within by LED lights, reaffirms the traditional symbolic power of the stupa, but reconsiders its form as both solid and illusory. Yak Tseten took a very different medium—beer bottles—to fashion a large stupa in Tibetan grasslands and then reassembled it at an exhibition space in Beijing several months later.

For traditional examples, see Illuminated Pages of the *Prajnaparamita Sutra* Manuscript, no. 23; Earliest Extant Printed Edition of Milarepa's Life Story, no. 62.

Tibetan artists have also employed Buddhist texts (*pecha*), important objects of Tibetan Buddhist culture. Tenzing Rigdol's radical engagement with Tibetan Buddhist texts in his 2009 performance work *Scripture Noodles* is documented in a video.[7] He sliced up pages of Tibetan Buddhist texts as noodles, stir-fried them with vegetables, and consumed this dish, disposing of the leftovers in a trash bin. The video caused a considerable backlash from some Tibetans, who felt the artist disrespected Tibetan culture and Buddhist teachings, which the pages literally represent.

Contemporary artists often intentionally combine religious forms with the profane or mundane. Kesang Lamdark, based in Switzerland, uses found ordinary objects in mandala-like installations and tantric montages, and includes depictions of sex in his light boxes, needle-pierced metallic surfaces, and mirrors.[8] An apparent freedom in modifying the sacred images often raises fiercely protective and angry feelings in some viewers. This sort of religious "censorship" may be expected and extends to the works that use images considered sacred in mundane contexts, as traditionally these were separate areas of human experience. For Tibetan artists, no matter where they practice, such explorations often relate to the notion of cultural identity.

Exploring Identity, Collectively and Individually

Like-minded artists working in Lhasa have organized collectives to explore their identity as Tibetan contemporary artists, to share and grow in their individual practices while jointly experimenting with contemporary art forms.

The Sweet Tea House movement grew out of the first exhibition of modern Tibetan painting, presented in a tea house in 1985. The pioneering work of its organizers—Gonkar Gyatso, Angsang, Angqing, and Aibu—and others, shown in several exhibitions in Lhasa, had a profound impact on the development of contemporary Tibetan art.[9]

Another group of artists established the Gedun Choephel Artists' Guild in response to formulaic state-sponsored exhibitions in Lhasa in the late twentieth century and to mark the one-hundredth birth anniversary of the renowned Tibetan intellectual and self-taught painter Gendun Chopel (1903–1951) in 2003.[10] It became a platform for free creative expression and artistic dialogue. In their statement, the artists declare their respect for traditional Tibetan art and culture and a desire to express themselves in whatever medium they choose as contemporary artists in a changing modern world.[11] Gade's *Ice Buddha* is one manifestation of such work.

For more on the artist and his work, see Gendun Chopel's Woman Applying Kohl, no. 102.

Navigating complexities of contemporary life, responding to cultural changes while communicating the sense of being through their art—these are constants among many artists who create in Tibetan areas and around the world.[12] A momentous event in 2006—the arrival of Beijing-Lhasa railway service—has altered the city of Lhasa, bringing more visitors from mainland China and foreign tourists.[13] In this changed reality, in 2007 a few artists established the Melong (Mirror) group. In 2009 another eight Tibetan painters founded Botson (Tibetan paint); they hold annual exhibitions in Lhasa and participate in shows elsewhere in China and abroad.

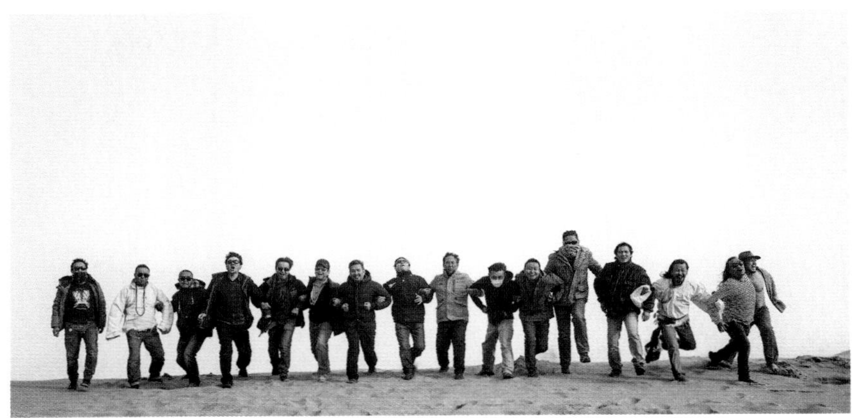

Jiang Hailong (b. 1974, China); Group Portrait of Gedun Choephel Artists' Guild; 2017; from left: Tenchoe, Weidong (Yak Tseten), Tse Kal, Tsewang Tashi, Angsang, Lu Zungde, Gade, Tserang Dhandrup, Nortse, Tsering Nyandak, Somani, Jhamsang, Huang Zhaji (Huang Yaohong), Huang Jialin, Penpa, Anu Shelkawa (not all Guild members are featured); photograph courtesy Jiang Hailong

Many address in their art the importance of Tibetan language and cultural history. Sodhon's use of Tibetan letters as major elements in his painting and Nortse's installation *30 Letters* of the Tibetan alphabet made out of rusting iron[14] comment on the fragility and erosion of their native language. Some artists explore the art of calligraphy, using flowing lines of Tibetan script to deliver meaning or form abstract images. In recent work, the artist Penpa created rubbings of windows from demolished traditional buildings in Lhasa's Tolung neighborhood as tactile memories of the lives lived in those buildings.

Scorching Sun of Tibet, a 2010 exhibition at the Songzhuang Art Museum in Beijing, displayed a broad range of artistic sensibilities in diverse forms and mediums.[15] Cocurated by Gade and Li Xianting, a well-known art critic, with attention to the works' contemporary significance, it is the most comprehensive, self-reflexive exhibition of contemporary Tibetan art to date.[16] In 2016 Gade and Nortse opened the Scorching Sun Art Lab in Lhasa to provide a platform for local groups and young artists to show their work. The Lab cooperated with galleries in mainland China running an artist-in-residence exchange program until its closure in 2019.

Many exhibitions organized in the West and India, in commercial galleries and public spaces, continue to be curated with formulaic notions of Tibetan contemporary art as juxtaposed with traditional art and as seen through the lens of Tibetan identity.[17]

Tibetan artists who are internationally active are aware of and critically responsive to external expectations of spirituality and "Tibetan-ness" in their art.[18] Their work often focuses on the complexity

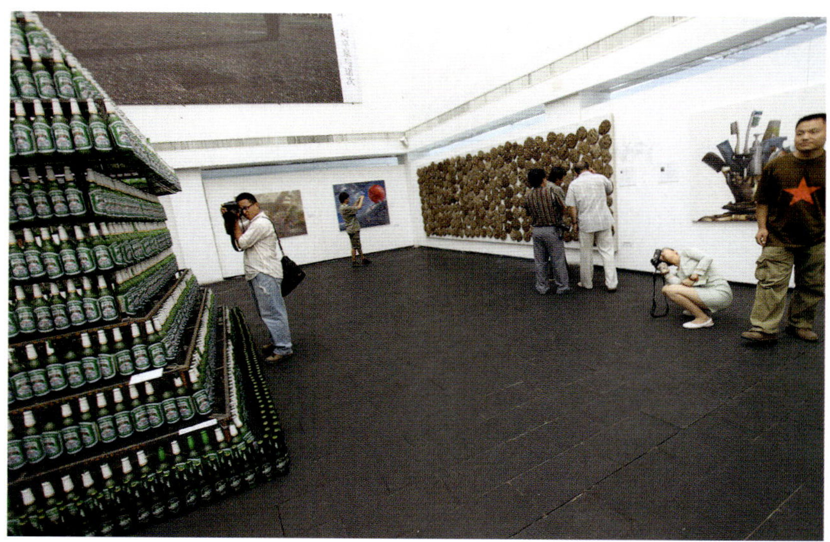

Installation view of the exhibition *Scorching Sun of Tibet*, Beijing, 2010; photograph courtesy Gade

and realness of their experiences. Tenzing Rigdol, based in the United States and India, in his *Our Land, Our People* (2011), experimented with a site-specific installation. Soil from Tibet was secretly brought to India for Tibetans living in exile to stand on, symbolically and physically connecting them with their land. Rigdol's communal and interactive project is a social commentary that also reflects the artist's own examination of identity.[19] Gonkar Gyatso's *Family Album* (2016) shows the multiple identities of his family members, who include a member of the Communist Party, a Buddhist nun, an artist, and others. He questions the monolithic view of Tibetan-ness in the multilayered and complex contemporary Tibetan world. Photographs by Nyema Droma (Nyedron) of young international Tibetans at the Pitt Rivers Museum at the University of Oxford in 2019, created in response to the early twentieth-century photographs of Tibet and Tibetans by the British, showed very different but "just as cool" Tibetans.[20]

A Different Kind of Identity

In 2003 Lhasa witnessed the first exhibition dedicated to paintings and ideas of six women artists, Dedron, Chime Dolkar, Tsering Lhamo, Tsering Dolma, Zhang Linhong, and Zhang Ping. In 2017 Gade curated the exhibition *Her* in Lhasa, intended as the first in a series of shows to highlight women in different creative fields—visual art, literature, music, film, dance, and fashion. It included photographs by Nyema Droma and paintings of Dedron, Tsering Lhamo, Tsering Dolma, and Dangsel Dawa. In 2020 the first solo exhibition in Lhasa of a Tibetan woman painter, Tsering Dolma's *Dance! Dance! Dance!*, traced her creative journey from the 1980s to the present and introduced younger viewers to contemporary work by women artists in Tibet.

Beyond the "Identity Box," Belonging to the Larger World

Identity has never been the only framework for Tibetan artists; they have assembled for other reasons and causes, such as the collaborative ecological project *Keepers of the Water* organized by Betsy Damon in Chengdu (1995) and Lhasa (1996). A series of art events revealing the interconnectedness of humans and environment, the Lhasa presentation of *Keepers of the Water* took place along the Kyichu River in August–September 1996. Artists from Beijing, Shanghai, Chengdu, Xi'an, Tibet, Switzerland, and the United States came together to raise awareness about water protection through installation and performance art. The Lhasa-based artists engaged the local community to make art as an embodied practice of awareness about ecology. Much of their work was inspired by Tibetan culture, land, and environment.[21]

Tibetan artists around the world continue exploring these notions. Sonam Dolma Brauen, unlike most Tibetan artists, does not generally employ traditional Tibetan cultural markers in her work. She uses the language of modern art to address themes that are informed by her worldview. Her installation works, such as *My Father's Death* (2010), *Boomerang* (2010), and *DNA* (2013), are deeply personal and universal in their themes.[22] Marie-Dolma Chophel's paintings map and relate micro- and macrocosmic terrains, from a single atom to distant galaxies—atmospheric depictions of landscape and the cosmos, or a flux of the concrete and the abstract, natural and artificial, real and virtual, personal and shared. Palden Weinreb's works—in delicate pencil drawing or large, glowing sculptures—embrace and mine diverse cultural and collective ideas and forms. Tsherin Sherpa's *Wish-Fulfilling Tree* (2016), is a response to the devastating 2015 earthquake in Nepal, but also a communal acknowledgement of universal human suffering caused by a natural disaster. Nortse's work, *2020*, created in response to the COVID-19 pandemic, is an overwhelming, looming sphere that seems to represent the globe and the virus; it conveys the sense of tangled lives, broken structures, and emergency.

Changing Realities and New Practices

Although commercial galleries no longer play a dominant role in commissioning Tibetan artists, less representation does not affect the younger generation of artists and curators engaging with global trends in the digital age. Lhasa remains a cultural center for contemporary artists of different generations from within and without the Tibet Autonomous Region. An alternative art space founded in 2021, Lhasa Art Box (LAB), is a platform for diverse local artists to present their work and communicate with the outside world. In October 2021 LAB organized the citywide Sweet Tea House Art Festival, focused on the works of young artists and creatives.

All generations of Tibetan artists actively respond to the realities in which they live with distinct creative expressions, experimenting in new media and formats, and seek to engage in global discourse. Artists in Bhutan, Nepal, and Mongolia create in their own artistic spheres and in recent years have expanded into the global art scene.[23]

Further Reading

Brauen, Martin. 2015. "The Buddha in a Shopping Bag." In Trace Foundation, *Transcending Tibet: 30 Contemporary Artists Explore What It Means to Be Tibetan Today,* 66–79. Exhibition catalog. New York: Trace Foundation.

Kesang Lamdark with contributions by David Elliott, Regina Höfer, Andy Cohen, and A. C. Kupper. 2021. *Kesang Lamdark.* Milan: Skira.

Gade. 2016. "A Broken Flower Blossoming in the Cracks: Tibetan Artist Gade Talks about Contemporary Tibetan Art." Interview by Tsesung Lhamo, translated by High Peaks Pure Earth. High Peaks Pure Earth website. https://highpeakspureearth.com/a-broken-flower-blossoming-in-the-cracks-tibetan-artist-gade-talks-about-contemporary-tibetan-art/.

Notes

1 The Kyichu is a tributary of the Yarlung Tsangpo River, which becomes the Brahmaputra upon reaching India.

2 The use of ephemeral mediums in Tibetan Buddhist culture directly relates to Buddhist notions of impermanence and performative aspects of offerings, such as *torma* offerings.

3 We perceive objects, forms, sensations, and thoughts as real in a relative sense, but ultimately everything is nondual and empty of unchanging, independent existence. See Lopez 2002, 27–30, 37–129.

4 See Miller 2016, 163–64.

5 Harris 2012a, 154–58.

6 For more examples of the buddha's form in contemporary Tibetan art, see Masters and Ng 2013, 45, 59, 91, 104, 124, 144–45; Trace Foundation 2015, 120–21, 164; Brauen 2015, 66–77.

7 For still photographs, see D. Elliott 2013, 30; Masters and Ng 2013, 160–61.

8 For more on his diverse work, see Kesang Lamdark et al. 2021.

9 Conversation with Gade, October 1, 2019.

10 Beginning with state-sponsored exhibitions in the 1970s, Tibet and Tibetans have been frequent subjects of realist oil paintings by Chinese artists who explored regions new to them for artistic inspiration; some Tibetan artists were also trained in this mode of painting and have followed similar formulas for depicting Tibet, resulting in stereotypical representations of Tibet in visual art. On Gendun Chopel and his role in Tibetan modern art, see Lopez 2013.

11 See Salviati 2012, 159; Gade 2003.

12 In addition to the artists' self-organizing movements and their exhibitions, commercial galleries, such as Rossi and Rossi in the United Kingdom and Peaceful Wind in the United States, have represented Tibetan artists since the early years of the twenty-first century.

13 *Lhasa Train* exhibition at the Peaceful Wind Gallery in Santa Fe, New Mexico (September–October 2006), marked this occasion. The paintings commissioned in advance from the artists of the Gedun Choephel Artists' Guild demonstrated the anticipation, hopes, and imaginings of how this new reality would change Lhasa.

14 See also Harris 2012a, 160–61.

15 In addition, the early 2010 exhibition *Tradition Transformed: Tibetan Artists Respond,* hosted at the Rubin Museum of Art in New York, attempted to gather works by Tibetan artists active in the West, a few Tibetan artists from Lhasa, and Nepal.

16 Li Xianting 2010.

17 For instance, *Tibetan Encounters: Contemporary Meets Tradition* (London, 2007), *Beyond the Mandala: Contemporary Art from Tibet* (Mumbai, 2011), *Tradition Transformed: Tibetan Artists Respond* (New York, 2010); and *Boundless: Contemporary Tibetan Artists at Home and Abroad* (San Francisco, 2018). Identity-focused exhibitions include *Anonymous: Contemporary Tibetan Art* (New Paltz, NY, 2013) and *Transcending Tibet: 30 Contemporary Artists Explore What It Means to Be Tibetan Today* (New York, 2015). See Masters and Ng 2013; Trace Foundation 2015.

18 For more on complex preconceptions about Tibetan culture, see Brauen 2004.

19 A film made in 2013 about this project, *Bringing Tibet Home,* is available on streaming platforms. Rigdol has also established an artist residency program in Dharamsala, India.

20 Nyedron in conversation, May 24, 2019.

21 For instance, Tsewang Tashi's *Liberation,* saving fish by releasing them into the river, was based in Buddhist practice, as was *Water Burial* by Tsering Lhamo.

22 See R. Höfer 2011.

23 For more on contemporary art in these countries, see the Project Himalayan Art digital platform, https://rubinmuseum.org/projecthimalayanart.

Bibliography

Agrawal, Om Prakash. 1984. *Conservation of Manuscripts and Paintings of South-East Asia.* Butterworth-Heinemann series in Conservation and Museology. London: Butterworth-Heinemann in association with the International Institute for Conservation of Historic and Artistic Works.

Akester, Matthew. 2016. *Jamyang Khyentsé Wangpo's Guide to Central Tibet.* Chicago: Serindia.

Alexander, André. 2007. *The Temples of Lhasa: Tibetan Buddhist Architecture from the 7th to the 21st Centuries.* Chicago: Serindia.

_____. 2008. *Empire road: Design and positioning of cultural monuments of the early Tibetan empire.* Unpublished manuscript.

Alexander, André, and Sam van Schaik. 2011. "The Stone Maitreya of Leh: The Rediscovery and Recovery of an Early Tibetan Monument." *Journal of the Royal Asiatic Society* 21, no. 4, 421–39.

Allen, Michael. 1996. *The Cult of Kumārī: Virgin Worship in Nepal.* Kathmandu: Mandhab Lal Maharjan.

Allinger, Eva. 1995. "The Green Tārā in the Ford Collection: Some Iconographical Remarks." In *South Asian Archaelogy, 1995: Proceedings of the Thirteenth International Conference of the European Association of South Asian Archaeologists, Cambridge, 5–9, 1995*, edited by F. Raymond Allchin and Bridget Allchin, vol. 2, 666–71. New Delhi: Science Publications.

_____. 2001. "Narrative Paintings in 12th–13th Century Manuscripts: An Examination of Photographs Taken by Rahula Sankrtyayana at the Ngor Monastery, Tibet." *Journal of Bengal Art* 6, 101–15.

Allsen, Thomas. 1997. *Commodity and Exchange in the Mongol Empire: A Cultural History of Islamic Textiles.* Cambridge: Cambridge University Press.

Alsop, Ian. 1990. "Phagpa Lokeśvara of the Potala." *Orientations* 21, no. 4 (April): 51–61.

_____. 1994. "The Metal Sculpture of the Khasa Malla Kingdom." *Orientations* 25, no. 6 (June): 61–68.

_____. 1997. "Metal Sculpture of the Khasa Mallas." In Singer and Denwood 1997, 68–79.

_____. 2004. "The Wall Paintings of Mustang." In Pal 2004b, 128–39.

_____. 2005. "The Metal Sculpture of the Khasa Mallas of West Nepal/West Tibet." Asianart.com. Published August 26, 2005. https://www.asianart.com/articles/khasa/index.html.

_____. 2012. "Sculpture." In Debreczeny 2012, 215–77. New York: Rubin Museum of Art.

Alsop, Ian, and Jill Charlton. 1973, "Image Casting in Oku Bahal," *Contributions to Nepalese Studies* 1, no. 1, 22–49. Also Asianart.com. Published March 2, 2022. https://asianart.com/articles/oku_bahal/.

Altmann, Karin. 2016. *Fabric of Life: Textile Arts in Bhutan—Culture, Tradition and Transformation.* Translated by Sarah Tolley. Berlin: De Gruyter.

Anderson, Mary M. 1988. *The Festivals of Nepal.* Calcutta: Rupa.

Andolfatto, David C. 2021. "Ripu Malla, a Buddhist Emperor from Western Nepal." *Orientations* 52, no. 3 (May/June): 69–76.

Andrews, Roy Chapman. 1921. *Across Mongolian Plains: A Naturalist's Account of China's "Great Northwest."* New York: Blue Ribbon Books.

Appleton, Naomi. 2011. "In the Footsteps of the Buddha? Women and the Bodhisattva Path in Theravada Buddhism." *Journal of Feminist Studies in Religion* 27, no. 1 (Sprng): 33–51.

Ardussi, John A. 1999. "Gyalse Tenzin Rabgye and the Founding of Taktsang Lhakhang." *Journal of Bhutan Studies* 1, no. 1, 36–63.

_____. 2008a. "Gyalse Tenzin Rabgye (1638–1696), Artist Ruler of 17th-Century Bhutan." In Bartholomew and Johnston 2008, 88–99.

_____. 2008b. "Gyalse Tenzin Rabgye and the Celebration of Tshechu in Bhutan." In *Written Treasures of Bhutan: Mirror of the Past and Bridge to the Future*, edited by John A. Ardussi and Sonam Tobgay, 1–24. Thimphu: National Library of Bhutan.

Aris, Michael. 1979. *Bhutan: The Early History of a Himalayan Kingdom.* Warminster: Aris and Phillips.

_____. 1988. "The Temple-palace of gTam-zhing as Described by Its Founder." In *Arts asiatiques* 43, 33–39.

_____. 1989. *Hidden Treasures and Secret Lives: A Study of Pemalingpa (1450–1521) and the Sixth Dalai Lama (1683–1706).* London and New York: Kegan Paul International.

_____. 1994. *The Raven Crown: The Origins of Buddhist Monarchy in Bhutan.* London: Serindia.

Aris, Michael, Patrick Booz, S. B. Sutton, and Jeffery Wagner. 1992. *Lamas, Princes, and Brigands: Joseph Rock's Photographs of the Tibetan Borderlands of China.* Exhibition catalog. New York: China Institute in America.

Arora, Vibha. 2010. "Framing the Image of Sikkim." *Visual Studies* 24, no. 1, 54–64. https://doi.org/10.1080/14725860902732710.

Arthur, Bríd. 2015. "Envisioning Lhasa: 17th–20th Century Paintings of Tibet's Sacred City." PhD diss., Ohio State University.

_____. 2016. "Visions of Lhasa: Exploring Tibetan Monument Paintings." *Orientations* 47, no. 7 (October): 49–55.

Asher, Frederick M. 2008. *Bodh Gaya.* Oxford: Oxford University Press.

Atwill, David G. 2018. *Islamic Shangri-La: Inter-Asian Relations and Lhasa's Muslim Communities, 1600 to 1960.* Oakland: University of California Press.

Atwood, Christopher P. 2004a. *Encyclopedia of Mongolia and the Mongol Empire*, 258–59, 519–20. New York: Facts on File.

_____. 2004b. "Validation by Holiness or Sovereignty: Religious Toleration as Political Theology in the Mongol World Empire of the Thirteenth Century." *The International History Review*, vol. 26, no. 2, 237–56.

Atwood, Christopher P., with Lynn Struve. 2021. *The Rise of the Mongols: Five Chinese Sources.* Indianapolis, IN: Hackett Publishing.

Auboyer, Jeannine, and Gilles Béguin. 1977. *Dieux et démons de l'Himâlaya.* Paris: Éditions des musées nationaux.

Avedon, John F. 1998. *The Buddha's Art of Healing: Tibetan Paintings Rediscovered.* New York: Rizzoli.

Bacot, Jacques, F. W. Thomas and Gustave Charles Toussaint. 1940. *Documents de Touen-houang relatifs à l'histoire du Tibet.* Paris: Paul Geuthner.

Bagchi, Prabodh Chandra. 1941. "The Eight Great Caityas and their Cult." *Indian Historical Quarterly* 17, 223–35.

Bailey, H. W. 1936. "An Itinerary in Khotanese Saka." *Acta Orientalia* 14, no. 4, 258–67.

Bajracharya, P. 2001. "Tayo-bizakani: A Newari Ceremonial Necklace." *Arts of Asia* 31, 69–77.

Balikci-Denjongpa, Anna. 2001. "Kangchendzönga: Secular and Buddhist Perceptions of the Mountain Deity of Sikkim among the Lhopos." *Bulletin of Tibetology* 38, no. 2, 5–37.

Bangdel, Dina. 1999. *Manifesting the Mandala: A Study of the Core Iconographic Program of Newar Buddhist Monasteries in Nepal.* PhD diss., Ohio State University.

_____. 2011. "Visual Histories of Svayambhu Mahacaitya." In Gellek and Maitland 2011. 272–85.

Bangdel, Lain S. 1982. *The Early Sculptures of Nepal.* New Delhi: Vikas.

_____. 1995. *Inventory of Stone Sculptures of the Kathmandu Valley.* Kathmandu: Royal Nepal Academy.

Bangdel, Lain Singh, and Mukunda Raj Aryal. 1996. *A Report on the Study of Iconography of Kathmandu Valley and Their Preservation and Protection.* Kathmandu: Ministry of Youth, Sports and Culture, Department of Archeology.

Bareja-Starzyńska, Agata. 2015. *The Biography of the First Khalkha Jetsundampa Zanabazar by Zaya Paṇḍita Luvsanprinlei: Studies, Annotated Translation, Transliteration and Facsimile.* Warsaw: Faculty of Oriental Studies, University of Warsaw.

Barkmann, Udo B. 2010. "Die Geschichte des Klosters Erdeni Joo oder das Prinzip der Verflechtung von Staat und Religion." In *Mongolian-German Karakorum Expedition*, vol. 1, *Excavations in the Craftsmen Quarter at the Main Road*, edited by Jan Bemmann, Ulambayar Erdenebat, and Ernst Pohl, 321–50. Forschungen zur Archäologie außereuropäischer Kulturen 8. Wiesbaden: Reichert.

Barnett, Robert. 2012. "Notes on Contemporary Ransom Rituals in Lhasa." In *Revisiting Rituals in a Changing Tibetan World*, edited by Katia Buffetrille, 273–374. Leiden: Brill.

Barrett, David. 1962. "Bronzes from Northwest India and Western Pakistan." *Lalit Kala: A Journal of Oriental Art, Chiefly Indian*, no. 11 (April): 35–44.

Barthes, Roland. 1981. *Camera Lucida: Reflections on Photography*. Translated by Richard Howard. New York: Hill and Wang.

Bartholomew, Terese Tse, and John Johnston, eds. 2008. *The Dragon's Gift: The Sacred Arts of Bhutan*. Exhibition catalog. Honolulu and Chicago: Honolulu Academy of Arts in association with Serindia.

Bat-Erdene, Dashdemberel, and O. Mendsaikhan, eds. 2011. *Masterpieces of Bogd Khan Palace Museum*. Ulaanbaatar: Bogd Khan Palace Museum.

Bates, Don. 1995. *Knowledge and the Scholarly Medical Traditions*. Cambridge: Cambridge University Press.

Bautze-Picron, Claudine. 1995–96. "Śākyamuni in Eastern India and Tibet in the 11th to the 13th Centuries." *Silk Road Art and Archaeology: Journal of the Institute of Silk Road Studies* 4, 355–408.

_____. 1998. "The Elaboration of a Style: Eastern Indian Motifs and Forms in Early Tibetan (?) and Burmese Painting." In *The Inner Asian International Style, 12th–14th Centuries: Papers Presented at a Panel of the 7th Seminar of the International Association for Tibetan Studies, Graz 1995*, edited by Deborah E. Klimburg-Salter and Eva Allinger, 15–65. Vienna: Verlag der Österreichischen Akademie der Wissenschaften.

_____. 1999. "Between India and Burma: The 'Andagu' Stelae." *Marg* 50, no. 4, 37–52.

_____. 2014. *The Forgotten Place: Stone Images from Kurkihar, Bihar*. New Delhi: Archaeological Survey of India.

Bautze-Picron, Claudine, and J. Bautze. 2003. *The Buddhist Murals of Pagan: Timeless Vistas of the Cosmos*. Trumbull, CT: Weatherhill Inc.

Bawden, Charles. 1961. *The Jebtsundamba Khutukhtus of Urga*. Wiesbaden: Harrassowitz.

Becker, Catherine. 2015. *Shifting Stones, Shaping the Past: Sculpture from the Buddhist Stupas of Andhra Pradesh*. New York: Oxford University Press.

Becker-Ritterspach, Raimund O. A. 1995. *Water Conduits in the Kathmandu Valley*. New Delhi: Munshiram Manoharlal.

Béguin, Gilles. 1977. *Dieux et Demons de l'Himalaya: Art du Bouddhisme lamaique*. Exhibition catalog. Paris: Editions des musées nationaux

_____. 1990. *Art ésoterique de l'Himalaya: Catalogue de la donation Lionel Fournier au Musée national des arts asiatiques*. Paris: Réunion des musées nationaux.

_____. 1993. "La statuaire mongole." In Béguin and Dashbaldan 1993, 156–61.

_____. 2003. "The Great Monuments of Lhasa as Presented in the Architectural Paintings of the Musée Guimet." In Pommaret 2002, 53–63. Brill's Tibetan Studies Library 3. Leiden: Brill.

Béguin, Gilles, and Dorjiin Dashbaldan, eds. 1993. *Trésors de Mongolie : XVIIe–XIXe siècles*. Exhibition catalog. Paris: Réunion des musées nationaux.

Bell, Charles. 1946. *Portrait of the Dalai Lama*. London: Collins.

Bell, Christopher. 2016. "The Nechung Record." *Revue d'Etudes Tibétaines* 36 (October): 143–249.

_____. 2021. *The Dalai Lama and the Nechung Oracle*. New York: Oxford University Press.

Bellezza, John V. 2000. "Bon Rock Paintings at gNam mtsho: Glimpses of the Ancient Religion of Northern Tibet." *Rock Art Research* 17, no. 1, 35–55.

_____. 2002a. *Antiquities of Upper Tibet: Pre-Buddhist Archaeological Sites on the High Plateau; Findings of the Upper Tibet Circumnavigation Expedition, 2000*. Delhi: Adroit.

_____. 2002b. "Gods, Hunting and Society: Animals in the Ancient Cave Paintings of Celestial Lake in Northern Tibet." *East and West* 52, no. 1/4: 347–96.

_____. 2008. *Zhang Zhung: Foundations of Civilization in Tibet. A Historical and Ethnoarchaeological Study of the Monuments, Rock Art, Texts and Oral Tradition of the Ancient Tibetan Upland*. Philosophisch-Historische Klasse Denkschriften 368. Vienna: Verlag der Österreichischen Akademie der Wissenschaften.

_____. 2011–17. *Flight of the Khyung* (newsletters), Tibet Archaeology. http://www.tibetarchaeology.com.

_____. 2013. *Death and Beyond in Ancient Tibet: Archaic Concepts and Practices in a Thousand-Year-Old Illuminated Funerary Manuscript and Old Tibetan Funerary Documents of Gathang Bumpa and Dunhuang*. Philosophisch-Historische Klasse Denkschriften 454. Vienna: Verlag der Österreichischen Akademie der Wissenschaften.

_____. 2014a. *Antiquities of Zhang Zhung: A Comprehensive Inventory of Pre-Buddhist Sites on the Tibetan Upland, Residential Monuments*, vol. 1. Miscellaneous Series–28. Sarnath: Central University of Tibetan Studies. Online version, 2011. Tibetan & Himalayan Library. https://texts.mandala.library.virginia.edu/thl/zhangzhung/antiquities/vol1.

_____. 2014b. *Antiquities of Zhang Zhung: A Comprehensive Inventory of Pre-Buddhist Sites on the Tibetan Upland, Ceremonial Monuments*, vol. 2. Miscellaneous Series–29. Sarnath: Central University of Tibetan Studies. Online version, 2011. Tibetan & Himalayan Library. https://texts.mandala.library.virginia.edu/thl/zhangzhung/antiquities/vol2.

_____. 2017. "The Swastika, Stepped Shrine, Priest, Horned Eagle, and Wild Yak Rider: Prominent Antecedents of Bon Figurative and Symbolic Traditions in the Rock Art of Upper Tibet." *Revue d'Etudes Tibétaines*, 42 (October): 5–38. http://himalaya.socanth.cam.ac.uk/collections/journals/ret/pdf/ret_42_01.pdf.

_____. 2018. "Discerning Bon and Zhang Zhung on the Western Tibetan Plateau: Designing an Archaeological Nomenclature for Upper Tibet, Ladakh and Spiti Based on a Study of Cognate Rock Art." In *Ancient Civilization of Tibetan Plateau: Proceedings of the First Beijing International Conference on Shang Shung Cultural Studies*, edited by Tsering Thar Tongkor and Tsering Dawa Sharshon, 49–112. Xining: Qinghai Ethnic Publishing House.

_____. 2020a. *Besting the Best: Warriors and War in the Religious and Cultural Traditions of Tibet; A Historical, Ethnographic and Archaeological Study on the Nature of Martial Activities over the Last Three Millennia*. Lumbini: Lumbini International Research Institute.

_____. 2020b. *Drawn and Written in Stone: An Inventory of Stepped Structures and Early Rock Inscriptions in Upper Tibet (ca. 100 BCE to 1400 CE)*. British Archaeological Reports International Series 2995. Oxford: BAR.

_____. 2020c. *Tibetan Silver, Gold and Bronze Objects and the Aesthetics of Animals in the Era before Empire: Cross-Cultural Reverberations on the Tibetan Plateau and Soundings from other Parts of Eurasia*. British Archaeological Reports International Series 2984. Oxford: BAR.

Bentor, Yael. 1995a. "In Praise of Stūpas: The Tibet Eulogy at Chu-Yung-Kuan Reconsidered." *Indo-Iranian Journal* 38, 31–54.

_____. 1995b. "On the Indian Origins of the Tibetan Practice of Depositing Relics and *Dhāraṇīs* in Stūpas and Images." *Journal of the American Oriental Society*, 115, no. 2, 248–61.

_____. 1996. *Consecration of Images and Stupas in Indo-Tibetan Tantric Buddhism*. Leiden: Brill.

Berger, Patricia. 1994. "Preserving the Nation: The Political Uses of Tantric Art in China." In *Latter Days of the Law: Images of Chinese Buddhism, 850–1850*, edited by Marsha Weidner, 89–124. Exhibition catalog. Lawrence: Spencer Museum of Art, University of Kansas.

_____. 2003. *Empire of Emptiness: Buddhist Art and Political Authority in Qing China*. Honolulu: University of Hawai'i Press.

_____. 2008. "Reincarnation in an Age of Mechanical Reproduction: The Career of the Narthang Panchen Lama Portraits." In *Images of Tibet in the 19th and 20th Centuries*, edited by Monica Esposito, vol. 2, 727–45. Études thématiques 22. Paris: École française d'Extrême-Orient.

Berger, Patricia, and Terese Tse Bartholomew, eds. 1995. *Mongolia: The Legacy of Chinggis Khan*. Exhibition catalog. London and New York: Thames and Hudson; San Francisco: Asian Art Museum of San Francisco.

Berounsky, Daniel, and Lubomir Sklenka. 2005. "Tibetan Tsha-Tsha." *Annals of the Náprstek Muzeum* 26, 59–72.

Bhattacharyya, Benoytosh. (1928) 2017. *Sadhanamala*, vol. 2. Facsimile, New Delhi: Gyan Books.

_____. 1958. *The Indian Buddhist Iconography*. Calcutta: K. L. Mukhopadhyay.

Bhattarai, Bidur. 2020. *Dividing Texts: Conventions of Visual Text-Organization in Nepalese and North Indian Manuscripts*. Berlin: De Gruyter.

Bialek, Joanna. 2018. *Compounds and Compounding in Old Tibetan: A Corpus Based Approach*. Marburg: Indica et Tibetica Verlag.

Birnbaum, Raoul. 1986. "The Manifestation of a Monastery: Shen-Ying's Experiences on Mount Wu-t'ai in T'ang Context." *Journal of the American Oriental Society* 106, no. 1, 110–37.

_____. 1989. "Secret Halls of the Mountain Lords: The Caves of Wu-t'ai Shan." *Cahiers d'Extrême-Asie* 5, 116–40.

Bishop, Peter. 1994. "The Potala and Western Place Making." *Tibet Journal* 19, 5–22.

Blezer, Henk. 2000. "The '*Bon*' *dBal-mo Nyer-bdun* (/ *brgyad*) and the Buddhist *dBang-phyug-ma Nyer-brgyad*." In *New Horizons in Bon Studies: Proceedings of a Conference Held in Osaka, August 1999*, edited by Samten Karmay and Yasuhiko Nagano, 117–80. Osaka: National Museum of Ethnology.

_____. 2015. "Notes on an Unidentified Thangka of the Black-Cloak Mahākāla." In *From Bhakti to Bon: Festschrift for Per Kvaerne*, edited by Hannah Havnevik and Charles Ramble, 113–31. Oslo: Novus Press.

Blondeau, Anne-Marie. 1990. "Questions préliminaires sur les rituels *mdos*." In *Tibet: Civilisation et société*, edited by F. Meyer, 91–107. Paris: Éditions de la Fondation Singer-Polignac.

_____. 2000. "The *mKha' klong gsang mdos*: Some Questions on Ritual Structure and Cosmology." In *New Horizons in Bon Studies: Proceedings of a Conference Held in Osaka, August 1999*, edited by Samten Karmay and Yasuhiko Nagano, 249–87. Osaka: National Museum of Ethnology.

Bloom, Rebecca, Kevin Carr, Chun Wa Chan, Donald S. Lopez, Carla Sinopoli, and Keiko Yokota-Carter. 2018. "Hyecho's Journey." http://hyecho-buddhist-pilgrim.asian.lsa.umich.edu/index.php.

Boerschmann, Ernst. 1937. "Die grosse Gebetmühle im Kloster Ta Yüan Sï auf dem Wu Tai Schan." *Sinica-Sonderausgabe*, 35–43. Frankfurt.

Boertjes, Katja. 2014. "The Reconquered Jerusalem Represented. Tradition and Renewal on Pilgrimage Ampullae from the Crusader Period." In *The Imagined and Real Jerusalem in Art and Architecture*, edited by Jeroen Goudeau, Mariëtte Verhoeven, and Wouter Weijers, 169–89. Leiden: Brill.

Bogdanov, K. M. 2012. "Nekotorye Otogi i Perspectivy issledovania materialov Tangutskogo fonda" [Some Results and Perspectives of Research of the Tangut Collection]. In *Tanguty v Tsentralnoi Asii* [Tanguts in Central Asia], edited by I. F. Popova, 72–83. Moscow: GRVL.

Booz, Patrick. 2011. "Tea, Trade and Transport in the Sino-Tibetan Borderlands." PhD diss., University of Oxford.

_____. 2016. "'To Control Tibet, First Pacify Kham': Trade Routes and 'Official Routes' (Guandao) in Easternmost Kham." *Cross-Currents: East Asian History and Culture Review* 19 (June): 27–47. https://cross-currents.berkeley.edu/e-journal/issue-19/booz.

_____. 2018. "Tibet and Tea: A Summary of Trade, Social Customs and Sino-Tibetan Relations Dealing with Ja/Cha." In *Commerce and Communities: Social Status and Political Status and the Exchange of Goods in Tibetan Societies*, edited by Jeannine Bischoff, 127–60. Berlin: EB Verlag.

Bowring, Richard, Richard McBride II, Miyaji Akira, and Jonathan Silk. n.d. "Maitreya," *Encyclopedia of Buddhism Online*, 2.302–324. Edited by Jonathan A. Silk, Oskar von Hinüber, Vincent Eltschinger. Accessed June 24, 2021 http://dx.doi.org/10.1163/2467-9666_enbo_COM_2044; first print edition: 20190619: 302–24.

Brandt, Andreas, and Niels Gutschow. 2003. "Erdene Zuu: Zur Baugeschichte der Klosteranlage auf dem Gebiet von Karakorum, Mongolei." *Beiträge zur allgemeinen und vergleichenden Archäologie* 23, 21–48.

Brauen, Martin. 2004. *Dreamworld Tibet: Western Illusions*. Translated by Martin Willson. Boston: Weatherhill.

_____, ed. 2005. *The Dalai Lamas: A Visual History*. Chicago: Serindia.

_____. 2009. *Mandala: Sacred Circle in Tibetan Buddhism*. Exhibition catalog. New York: Rubin Museum of Art. https://issuu.com/rmanyc/docs/2._mandala.

_____. 2015. "The Buddha in a Shopping Bag." In Trace Foundation 2015, 66–79.

Broeskamp, Bernadette. 2009. "Dating the kesi-Thangka of Acala in the Tibet Museum, Lhasa." In *Han Zang Fojiao meishu yanjiu—di san jie Xizang kaogu yu yishu guoji xueshu taolun hui lunwen ji 漢藏佛教美術 研究—第三屆西藏考古與藝術國際學術討論會論文集 / Studies on Sino-Tibetan Buddhist Art, Proceedings of the Third International Conference on Tibetan Archaeology and Art*, edited by Xie Jisheng 謝繼勝 and Luo Wenhua 羅文華, 185–97. Beijing: Shanghai guji chubanshe.

Brown, Kerry Lucinda. 2017. "Adorning the Buddhas: The Ceremonial Regalia of the Daśa Sthavira Ājus from Kwā Bahā, Nepal." *Ars Orientalis* 47, 266–302. https://doi.org/10.3998/ars.13441566.0047.012.

Bruckner, Christopher, ed. 1998. *Chinese Imperial Patronage: Treasures from Temples and Palaces*. Exhibition catalog. London: Christopher Bruckner Asian Art Gallery.

Bruneau, Laurianne. 2010. "Le Ladakh (Jammu & Cachemire, Indie) de l'âge du Bronze à l'introduction du Bouddhisme: une étude de l'art rupestre." PhD diss., Université Paris 1 Panthéon-Sorbonne.

Bruneau, Laurianne, and John V. Bellezza. 2013. "The Rock Art of Upper Tibet and Ladakh: Inner Asian Cultural Adaptation, Regional Differentiation and the 'Western Tibetan Plateau Style.'" *Revue d'Etudes Tibétaines* 28 (December): 5–161. http://himalaya.socanth.cam.ac.uk/collections/journals/ret/pdf/ret_28.pdf.

Bruntz, Courtney, and Brooke Schedneck, eds. 2020. *Buddhist Tourism in Asia*. Honolulu: University of Hawai'i Press.

Bsod nams rgya mtsho. 1991. *The Ngor Mandalas of Tibet: Listings of the Mandala Deities*. Revised by Tachikawa Musashi, Onoda Shunzo, Noguchi Keiya, and Tanaka Kimiaki. Tokyo: Centre for East Asian Cultural Studies.

Bühnemann, Gudrun. 1992. "Some Remarks on the Date of Abhayākaragupta and the Chronology of His Work." *Zeitschrift der Deutschen Morgenländischen Gesellschaft* 142, no. 1, 120–27.

_____. 2003. "Maṇḍala, Yantra and Cakra: Some Observations." In *Maṇḍalas and Yantras in the Hindu Traditions*, edited by Gudrun Bühnemann, 1–56. Brill's Indological Library 18. Leiden: Brill.

_____. 2008. "17th Century Tantric Iconography of Nepal: New Research on the 'Royal Bath' in Patan," *Orientations* 39, no. 6 (September): 88–95.

Bussagli, Mario. 1963. *Painting of Central Asia*. Translated by Lothian Small. Geneva: Skira.

Buswell, Robert E., Jr., and Donald S. Lopez, Jr. 2014. *The Princeton Dictionary of Buddhism*. Princeton, NJ: Princeton University Press.

Butler, Claudia. 1996. "Torma: The Tibetan Ritual Cake." *Chö Yang (chos dbyangs): The Voice of Tibetan Religion and Culture* 7, 38–52.

Byrd, Vickie C. 2003. *Tibet: Treasures from the Roof of the World*. Exhibition catalog. Santa Ana, CA: Bowers Museum of Cultural Art.

Cabezón, José Ignacio. 2017. "On Tulku Lineages." *Revue d'Etudes Tibétaines* 38 (February): 1–28.

Caccia. 1935. *Notes on Tibetan Institutions and Personalities*, confidential document prepared by Mr. Caccia (Peking), transmitted to FO by E. Teichman the 1st July 1935. British National Archives, FO/371/19254.

Campbell, Aurelia. 2020. "From Mandala to Palace: Transforming Space and Site at Gautama Monastery." In *What the Emperor Built: Architecture and Empire in the Early Ming*, 127–64. Seattle: University of Washington Press.

_____. 2022. "Consecrating the Imperial City: Tibetan Stupas in Yuan Dadu." *Journal of Song and Yüan Studies* 51, 207–43.

Cantwell, Cathy. 1995. "The Dance of the Guru's Eight Aspects." *Tibet Journal* 20, no. 4, 47–63.

Cartelli, Mary Anne. 2012. *The Five-Colored Clouds of Mount Wutai: Poems from Dunhuang*. Leiden: Brill.

Carter, Martha L. 1990. *The Mystery of the Udayana Buddha*. Naples: Istituto universitario orientale.

Casey, Jane. Forthcoming. *Taklung Painting: A Study in Chronology*. Chicago: Serindia.

Chan, Victor. 1994. *Tibet Handbook. A Pilgrimage Guide*. Chico, CA: Moon Publications.

Chandra, Lokesh, ed. 1980. *Urga Kanjur*. Śata-piṭaka series nos. 396–500. Delhi: Sata-pitaka.

_____. 1999. *Dictionary of Buddhist Iconography*, vol. 1. Śata-piṭaka series. New Delhi: International Academy of Indian Culture and Aditya Prakashan.

Chandra, Lokesh, and Nirmala Sharma. 2015. *Nispanna-Yogāvalī: Sanskrit and Tibetan Texts with English Translation*. New Delhi: International Academy of Indian Culture and Aditya Prakashan.

Chaoul, Alejandro. 2009. *Chöd Practice in the Bön Tradition*. Ithaca, NY: Snow Lion.

Charleux, Isabelle. 2006a. "Copies de Bodhgayā en Asie orientale: Les stūpas de type Wuta à Pékin et Kökeqota (Mongolie-Intérieure)." *Arts asiatiques* 61, 120–42.

_____. 2006b. *Temples et monastères de Mongolie-Intérieur*. Paris: Éditions du Comité des travaux historiques et scientifiques and Institut national d'histoire de l'art (with CD-ROM).

_____. 2008. "From the Yuan to the Qing Dynasty: The Career of a Famous Statue of Mahākāla, Lord of the Cemeteries." In *Han Zang Fojiao Meishu Yanjiu 汉藏佛教美术研究 / Studies in Sino-Tibetan Buddhist Art*, edited by Xie Jisheng 谢继胜, 183–207. Beijing: Shoudu shifan daxue chubanshe.

_____. 2010a. "From Ongon to Icon: Legitimization, Glorification and Divinization of Power in Some Examples of Mongol Portraits." In *Representing Power in Ancient Inner Asia: Legitimacy, Transmission and the Sacred*, ed. Isabelle Charleux and Grégory Delaplace, Roberte Hamayon, and Scott Pearce, 209–60. Bellingham: Center for East Asian Studies, Western Washington University.

_____. 2010b. "The Making of Mongol Buddhist Art and Architecture: Artisans in Mongolia from the Sixteenth to the Twentieth Century." In *Meditation: The Art of Zanabazar and His School*, edited by Elvira Eevr Djaltchinova-Malets, 59–105. Warsaw: Asia and Pacific Museum.

_____. 2014. "Recent Research on the Maitreya Monastery in Inner Mongolia (China)." *Asiatische Studien—Études Asiatiques* 68, no. 1, 1–64. https://doi.org/10.1515/asia-2014-0001.

_____. 2015. *Nomads on Pilgrimage. Mongols on Wutaishan (China), 1800–1940*. Brill's Inner Asian Library 33. Leiden: Brill; with online appendices: https://halshs.archives-ouvertes.fr/halshs-01175826/document.

_____. 2017. "Circumambulating the Jowo in Mongolia: Why 'Erdeni juu' Must Be Translated as 'Jowo Rinpoche.'" In *Interaction in the Himalayas and Central Asia: Processes of Transfer, Translation and Transformation in Art, Archaeology, Religion and Polity; Proceedings of the Third International SEECHAC Colloquium, 25–27 Nov. 2013, Austrian Academy of Sciences, Vienna*, edited by Eva Allinger, Frantz Grenet, Christian Jahoda, Maria-Katharina Lang, and Anne Vergati, 357–74. Vienna: Verlag der Österreichischen Akademie der Wissenschaften.

_____. 2020. "The Grand Maitreya Project of Mongolia: A Colossal Statue-cum-Stupa for a Happy Future of 'Loving ♡ Kindness.'" *Contemporary Buddhism* 21, no. 1–2, 73–132. https://doi.org/10.1080/14639947.2021.1985352.

Chayet, Anne. 1985a. *Art et archéologie du Tibet*. Paris: Picard.

_____. 1985b. *Les temples de Jehol et leurs modèles tibétains*. Paris: Éditions Recherche sur les Civilisations.

Chettri, Mona. 2015. "Engaging the State: Ethnic Patronage and Cultural Politics in the Eastern Himalayan Borderland." *South Asia: Journal of South Asian Studies* 38, no. 4, 558–73. https://doi.org/10.1080/00856401.2015.1070236.

Cho, Yong. 2020. "The Mongol Impact: Rebuilding the Arts System in Yuan China (1271–1368)." PhD diss., Yale University.

Chodrak, Trinley, and Kesang G. Tashi. 2000. *Of Wool and Loom: The Tradition of Tibetan Rugs*. Edited by Kesang G. Tseten. Trumbull, CT: Weatherhill in cooperation with Orchid Press.

Chögyal Namkhai Norbu. 2000. *The Crystal and the Way of Light: Sutra, Tantra, and Dzogchen*, edited by John Shane. Ithaca, NY: Snow Lion.

_____. 2021. *Namkha: Harmonizing the Energy of the Elements*. Merigar: Shang Shung.

Chogye Trichen Rinpoche. 2021. *Fortunate to Behold: A History of the Birth of the Blessed One Śākyamuni Buddha at Lumbini*. Translated by David P. Jackson. Kathmandu: Vajra Publications.

Chou, Wen-shing. 2018. *Mount Wutai: Visions of a Sacred Buddhist Mountain*. Princeton, NJ: Princeton University Press.

Chou, Wen-shing, and Nancy G. Lin. 2021. "Karmic Affinities: Rethinking Relations among Tibetan Lamas and the Qing Emperor." In *Water Moon Reflections: Essays in Honor of Patricia Berger*, edited by Ellen Huang, Nancy G. Lin, Michelle McCoy, and Michelle H. Wang. Berkeley: Institute of East Asian Studies.

Chuluun, S. 2019. "In Search of the Khutugtu's Monastery: The Site and Its Heritage." Translated by Uranchimeg Tsultemin. In "Buddhist Art of Mongolia: Cross-Cultural Connections, Discoveries and Interpretations," edited by Uranchimeg Tsultemin, special issue, *Cross-Currents: East Asian History and Culture Review* 8, no. 2 (June): 244–56. https://cross-currents.berkeley.edu/e-journal/issue-31/chuluun.

Clare, Tami Lasseter, and P. Andrew Lins. 2008. *Finishing Techniques in Metalwork: An Introduction to the History and Methods of Decorating Metal*. Philadelphia: Philadelphia Museum of Art.

Clarke, John. 1995. "A Survey of Metalwork in Ladkah." In *Recent Research on Ladakh 4 & 5: Proceedings of the Fourth and Fifth International Colloquia on Ladakh, Bristol 1989 and London 1992*, edited by Henry Osmaston and Philip Denwood, 10–17. London: SOAS University of London.

_____. 2001. "Ga'u–The Tibetan Amulet Box." *Arts of Asia* 31, no. 1 (May–June): 45–67.

_____. 2002. "Metalworking in dBus and gTsang 1930–1977." *Tibet Journal*, 27, nos. 1–2 (Spring–Summer): 113–52.

_____. 2004. *Jewellery of Tibet and the Himalayas*. London: V&A Publications.

_____. 2006. "A History of Ironworking in Tibet: Centers of Production, Styles, and Techniques." In La Rocca 2006, 21–33.

_____. 2011. "Non-Sculptural Metalworking in Eastern Tibet 1930–2003." In Lo Bue 2011b, 171–91.

Clayton, Lori, and Lama Thubten Zopa Rinpoche. 2000. *Wheel of Great Compassion: The Practice of the Prayer Wheel in Tibetan Buddhism*. Cambridge, MA: Wisdom.

Cleaves, Francis Woodman. 1953. "Daruγa and Gerege," *Harvard Journal of Asiatic Studies* 16, no. 1/2 (June): 237–59.

Cohen, Richard S. 2012. *The Splendid Vision: Reading a Buddhist Sutra*. New York: Columbia University Press.

Cole, Thomas. 2011. *Patterns of Life: The Art of Tibetan Carpets*. With an introduction by Diana K. Myers. Exhibition catalog. New York: Rubin Museum of Art. https://issuu.com/rmanyc/docs/4.patterns_of_life_96.

Cook, Lowell. 2018. "Lha Lama Yeshe Wo." Treasury of Lives. https://treasuryoflives.org/biographies/view/Lha-Lama-Yeshe-O/11056.

Copp, Paul. 2008. "Altar, Amulet, Icon. Transformations in *Dhāraṇī* Amulet Culture, 740–980." *Cahiers d'Extrême-Asie* 17, 239–64.

Cornu, Philippe. 1997. *Tibetan Astrology*. Boston: Shambhala.

_____. 2001. *Dictionnaire Encyclopédique du Bouddhisme*. Paris: Éditions du Seuil.

Corrigan, Gina. 2017. *Tibetan Dress in Amdo & Kham: Nomads and Farmers of Amdo and Kham*. London: Hali Publications.

Coyle, Leiko. 2004–5. "The Karmacharyas of Bhaktapur and Tantric Tradition in Nepal." *Newāh Vijñāna: Journal of Newar Studies* 5, 12–21.

Crossley, Pamela. 1999. *A Translucent Mirror: History and Identity in Qing Imperial Ideology* Berkeley: University of California Press.

Cuevas, Bryan J. 2019. "The Politics of Magical Warfare." In Debreczeny 2019a, 170–89.

Cunningham, Alexander. (1892) 1961. *Mahābodhi, or The Great Buddhist Temple under the Bodhi Tree at Buddha-Gaya*. London: W. H. Allen. Reprint, Varanasi: Indological Book House.

Cupchik, Jeffrey W. 2013. "The Tibetan *gCod Ḍamaru*—A Reprise: Symbolism, Function, and Difference in a Tibetan Adept's Interpretative Community." *Asian Music* 44, no. 1, 113–39.

_____. 2021. *The Sound of Vultures' Wings: The Tibetan Buddhist Chöd Ritual Practice of the Female Buddha Machik Labdrön*. Albany: SUNY Press.

Cüppers, Christoph, Leonard van der Kuijp, and Ulrich Pagel. 2012. *Handbook of Tibetan Iconometry: A Guide to the Arts of the 17th Century*. Introduction in Chinese by Dobis Tsering Gyal. Brill's Tibetan Studies Library 16/4. Leiden: Brill.

Czaja, Olaf. 2014. *Medieval Rule in Tibet: The Rlangs Clan and the Political and Religious History of the Ruling House of Phag mo gru pa*. Vienna: Verlag der Österreichischen Akademie der Wissenschaften.

Czaja, Olaf, and Adriana G. Proser. 2014. *Golden Visions of Densatil: A Tibetan Buddhist Monastery*. Exhibition catalog. New York: Asia Society.

Dalton, Jacob. 2004. "The Early Development of the Padmasambhava Legend in Tibet: A Study of IOL Tib J 644 and Pelliot tibétain 307." *Journal of the American Oriental Society* 124, no. 4 (October–December): 759–72.

_____. 2015. "Padmasambhava." Treasury of Lives. https://treasuryoflives.org/biographies/view/Padmasambhava/7442.

Dalton, Jacob P. 2020. "The Early Development of the Padmasambhava Legend in Tibet: A Second Look at the Evidence from Dunhuang." In Samuel and Oliphant of Rossie 2020, 29–64.

Damron, Ryan C. 2021. "Deyadharma—A Gift of the Dharma: The Life and Works of Vanaratna (1384–1468)." PhD diss., University of California, Berkeley.

Dang, Baohai. 2001–3. "The Paizi of the Mongol Empire." *Zentralasiatische Studien* 30, 31–62; 32, 7–10.

Dar, Saifur Rahman. 1985. "Rock-cut Standing Figure at Kargah, near Gilgit: Some Thoughts on Its Identification, Origin and Date." *Journal of Central Asia* 8, no. 2, 191–211.

Davidson, Ronald M. 1995. "The Litany of Names of Mañjuśrī." In *Religions of India in Practice*, edited by Donald S. Lopez, 104–25. Princeton, NJ: Princeton University Press.

_____. 2002. *Indian Esoteric Buddhism: A Social History of the Tantric Movement*. New York: Columbia University Press.

_____. 2005. *Tibetan Renaissance: Tantric Buddhism in the Rebirth of Tibetan Culture*. New York: Columbia University Press.

De Antoni, Désirée, Hilde Vets, and Nils Martin. 2021. "On Top of the Chiefdom: The Three-Storey Tower in Wanla." In *Against Forgetting: Investigating and Preserving Historic Buildings in a Himalayan Village*, edited by Alexandra Skedzuhn-Safir, Martina Oeter, Hilde Vets, and Heike Pfund, 211–36. Cottbus-Senftenberg: Brandenburgische Technische Universität.

De Montmollin, Marceline. 1992. "bKra shis sgo mang of Bhutan: On a Specific Tradition of Shrines and Its Prolongation in the Museum of Ethnography in Neuchâtel." In *Tibetan Studies: Proceedings of the Fifth Seminar of the International Association for Tibetan Studies, Narita 1989*, vol. 2, edited by Ihara Shoren and Yamaguchi Zuiho. Narita: Naritasan Shinshoji.

Debreczeny, Karl. 2007. "Ethnicity and Esoteric Power: Negotiating the Sino-Tibetan Synthesis in Ming Buddhist Painting." PhD diss., University of Chicago.

_____. 2009. "Dabaojigong and the Regional Tradition of Ming Sino-Tibetan Painting in Lijiang." In Kapstein 2009a, 97–152.

_____. 2011. "Wutai Shan: Pilgrimage to Five-Peak Mountain." *Journal of the International Association of Tibetan Studies* 6 (December): 30–39. https://www.thlib.org/collections/texts/jiats/#!jiats=/06/debreczeny/.

_____. 2012. *The Black Hat Eccentric: Artistic Visions of the Tenth Karmapa*. Exhibition catalog. New York: Rubin Museum of Art. https://issuu.com/rmanyc/docs/6._black_hat_eccentric_96.

_____. 2013a. "The Art Historical Context of Antwerp's Vairocana Album." In Van Alphen 2013, 25–37.

_____, ed. 2013b. "Situ Panchen: Creation and Cultural Engagement in Eighteenth-Century Tibet." Special issue, *Journal of the International Association of Tibetan Studies* 7 (August). http://www.thlib.org/collections/texts/jiats/#!jiats=/current/.

_____. 2013c. "Situ Penchen's Artistic Legacy in 'Jang." *Journal of the International Association of Tibetan Studies* 7 (August): 193–276. http://www.thlib.org/collections/texts/jiats/#!jiats=/07/debreczeny/.

_____. 2015. "Imperial Interest Made Manifest: sGa A gnyan dam pa's Mahākāla Protector Chapel of the Tre shod *Maṇḍala* Plain." *Revue d'Etudes Tibétaines* 31, no. 10 (February). http://himalaya.socanth.cam.ac.uk/collections/journals/ret/pdf/ret_31_10.pdf. Originally published in *Trails of the Tibetan Tradition: Papers for Elliot Sperling*, edited by Roberto Vitali, 129–66. Dharamshala: Amnye Machen Institute, 2014.

_____. 2016a. "The Early Ming Imperial Atelier on the Tibetan Frontier." In *Ming China: Courts and Contacts, 1400–1450,* edited by Craig Clunas, Jessica Harrison-Hall, and Yu-ping Luk, 152–62. London: British Museum Press.

_____. 2016b. "From Hand of the Master to Workshop Production: Paintings Attributed to the Tenth Karmapa." In Debreczeny and Tuttle 2016, 195–233.

_____, ed. 2019a. *Faith and Empire: Art and Politics in Tibetan Buddhism*. Exhibition catalog. New York: Rubin Museum of Art. http://issuu.com/rmanyc/docs/faith_and_empire.

_____. 2019b. "Faith and Empire: An Overview." In Debreczeny 2019a, 19–51. Also Asianart.com. Published May 30, 2019. http://asianart.com/articles/faith-empire/index.html.

_____. 2020. "Recrafting Remote Antiquity: Art of the Tenth Karmapa." *Arts of Asia* 50, no. 6 (November–December): 72–87.

_____.2021. "Of Bird and Brush: A Preliminary Discussion of a *parinirvāṇa* Painting in the Distinctive Idiom of the Tenth Karmapa Recently Come to Light." In *Gateways to Tibetan Studies: A Collection of Essays in Honour of David P. Jackson on the Occasion of his 70th Birthday*, edited by Volker Caumanns, Jörg Heimbel, Kazuo Kano, and Alexander Schiller, 1:161–88. Indian and Tibetan Studies 12.1. Hamburg: Department of Indian and Tibetan Studies, University of Hamburg.

_____. Forthcoming. "Patronage of the Musée Guimet Mahākāla Sculpture Dated 1292 Revisited." In *New Directions in the Study of Tibetan Buddhist Art History*, edited by Zhang Changhong et al. Cambridge, MA: Harvard-Yenching Institute.

Debreczeny, Karl and Gray Tuttle, eds. 2016. *The Tenth Karmapa and Tibet's Turbulent Seventeenth Century*. Chicago: Serindia.

Decleer, Hubert. 2000. "Si tu Paṇchen's Translation of the Svayambhu Purana and His Role in the Development of the Kathmandu Valley Pilgrimage Guide (*gnas yig*) Literature." *Lungta* 13 (Summer): 33–64.

_____. 2005. Review of *Sacred Visions: Early Paintings from Central Tibet* by Steven M. Kosssak and Jane Casey Singer. *Tibet Journal* 30, no. 1 (Spring 2005): 73–114.

Deeg, Max. 2010. "Has Huichao Been Back to India? On a Chinese Inscription on the Back of a Pāla Bronze and the Chronology of Indian Esoteric Buddhism." In *From Turfan to Ajanta: Festschrift for Dieter Schlingloff on the Occasion of His Eightieth Birthday*, edited by Eli Franco and Monika Zin, 197–213. Lumbini: Lumbini International Research Institute.

Deimel, Claus, and Wolf-Dietrich Freiherr Speck von Sternburg. 2008. *Buddhas Leuchten und Kaisers Pracht: Die Pekinger Sammlung Hermann Speck von Sternburg*, 2 vols. Leipzig: Staatliche Ethnographische Sammlungen Sachen, Grassi Museum für Völkerkunde zu Leipzig.

Demiéville, Paul. (1952) 2006. *Le Concile de Lhasa*. Paris: Imprimerie Nationale de France, Presses Universitaires de France. Reprint with corrections, Bibliothèque de l'Institutes hautes études chinoises 7. Paris: Collège de France, Institut des hautes études chinoises.

Denwood, Philip. 1974. *The Tibetan Carpet*. Warminster: Aris and Phillips.

_____. 1980. "Temple and Rock Inscriptions at Alchi." In Snellgrove and Skorupski 1980, 117–63.

_____. 2007. "The Tibetans in the Western Himalayas and Karakoram, Seventh-Eleventh Centuries: Rock Art and Inscriptions." *Journal of Inner Asian Art and Archaeology* 2, 49–58. https://doi.org/10.1484/J.JIAAA.2.302546.

_____. 2008. "The Tibetans in the West, Part I." *Journal of Inner Asian Art and Archaeology* 3, 7–21. https://doi.org/10.1484/J.JIAA.3.1.

_____. 2009. "The Tibetans in the West, Part II." *Journal of Inner Asian Art and Archaeology* 4, 149–60. https://doi.org/10.1484/J.JIAA.3.27.

Desroches, Jean-Paul. 2000. *L'Asie des steppes: d'Alexandre le Grand à Gengis Khan.* Paris: Réunion des musées nationaux; Barcelona: Fundació la Caxia.

Devers, Quentin, Laurianne Bruneau, and Martin Vernier. 2014. "An Archaeological Account of Ten Ancient Painted Chortens in Ladakh and Zanskar." In *Art and Architecture in Ladakh: Cross-Cultural Transmissions in the Himalayas and Karakoram*, edited by Erberto Lo Bue and John Bray, 100–140. Brill's Tibetan Studies Library 35. Leiden: Brill.

Diemberger, Hildegard, Franz-Karl Ehrhard, and Peter F. Kornicki, eds. 2016. *Tibetan Printing: Comparisons, Continuities, and Change*. Brill's Tibetan Studies Library 39. Leiden: Brill.

Dinwiddie, Donald, ed. 2003. *Portraits of the Masters: Bronze Sculptures of the Tibetan Buddhist Lineages*. Chicago: Serindia.

Doctor, Andreas. 2005. *Tibetan Treasure Literature: Revelation, Tradition, and Accomplishment in Visionary Buddhism*. Boulder, CO: Shambhala.

Doerfer, Gerhard. 1965. *Türkische und mongolische Elemente in Neupersischen*, vol. 2. Wiesbaden: Harrassowitz.

Donaldson, Thomas E. 2001. *Iconography of the Buddhist Sculpture of Orissa*. New Delhi: Indira Gandhi National Centre for the Arts and Abhinav Publications.

Dorje, Gyurme, trans. 2001. *Tibetan Elemental Divination Paintings: Illuminated Manuscripts from the White Beryl of Sangs-rgyas rGya-mtsho with the Moonbeams Treatise of Lo-chen Dharmaśri*. London: John Eskenazi in association with Sam Fogg.

_____. 2010. "Introduction." "Shakabpa's Inventory." In Dorje et al. 2010, 7–30; 47–123.

Dorje, Gyurme, and Matthew Kapstein. 1991. *The Nyingma School of Tibetan Buddhism: Its Fundamentals and History*. Boston: Wisdom.

Dorje, Gyurme, Tashi Tsering, Heather Stoddard, and André Alexander. 2010. *Jokhang: Tibet's Most Sacred Buddhist Temple*. London: Hans-Jörg Mayer.

Dorje, Rinjing, and Ter Ellingson. 1979. "'Explanation of the Secret *Gcod Ḍa ma ru*': An Exploration of Musical Instrument Symbolism." In "Tibet Issue," special issue, *Asian Music* 10, no. 2, 63–91.

Dotson, Brandon. 2009. *The Old Tibetan Annals: An Annotated Translation of Tibet's First History*. Vienna: Verlag der Österreichischen Akademie der Wissenschaften.

_____. 2019. "The Emanated Emperor and His Cosmopolitan Contradictions." In Debreczeny 2019a, 69–81.

Dowman, Keith. 1985. *Masters of Mahamudra: Songs and Histories of the Eighty-Four Buddhist Siddhas*. Albany: SUNY Press.

Dudjom Rinpoche Jikdrel Yeshe Dorje. 1991. *The Nyingma School of Tibetan Buddhism: Its Fundamentals and History*. Edited and translated by Gyurme Dorje, with Matthew Kapstein, 2 vols. Boston: Wisdom.

Dungkar Lobzang Trinlé and Tsering Dhundup Gonkatsang. 2014. "Tibetan Woodblock Printing: An Ancient Art and Craft." *Himalaya* 36, no. 1, 163–77.

Dunnell, Ruth. 1992. "The Hsia Origins of the Yüan Institution of Imperial Preceptor." *Asia Major* 5, no. 1, 85–111.

_____. 1996. *The Great State of White and High: Buddhism and State Formation in Eleventh-Century Xia*. Honolulu: University of Hawai'i Press.

Dy-Liacco, Kristina. 2005. "The Victorious Karma-pa Has Come to 'Jang: An Examination of Naxi Patronage of the Bka'-brgyud-pa in the Fifteenth to Seventeenth Centuries." Master's thesis, Indiana University.

Eck, Diana L. 1998. *Darśan: Seeing the Divine Image in India*, 3rd ed. New York: Columbia University Press.

Edou, Jerome. 1996. *Machig Labdron and the Foundations of Chod*. Ithaca, NY: Snow Lion.

Edwards, Richard. 1984. "Pu-tai-Maitreya and a Reintroduction to Hangchou's Fei-lai-Feng." *Art Orientalis* 14, 5–50.

Ehrhard, Franz-Karl. 2005. "The mNga' bdag Family and the Tradition of Rig 'dzin Zhig po gling pa (1524–1583) in Sikkim." *Bulletin of Tibetology* 41, no. 2, 11–29.

Ehrhard, Franz-Karl, and Marta Sernesi. 2019. "Apropos a Recent Collection of Tibetan Xylographs from the 15th to the 17th Centuries." In *Perspectives on Tibetan Culture: A Small Garland of Forget-Me-Nots Offered to Elena De Rossi Filibeck*, edited by Michela Clemente, Oscar Nalesini, and Federica Venturi, 119–40. Paris: Centre de recherche sur les civilisations de l'Asie orientale. Reprinted from *Revue d'Etudes Tibétaines* 51 (July 2019).

Erhard, Franz Xaver, and Thomas Wild. 2021. *Drumze: Metamorphosen des tibetischen Teppichs*. Exhibition catalog. Potsdam: Edition Tethys.

Elikhina, Yulia, and Victoria Demenova. 2020. "A Study of Stylistic Features and Metal Composition of the Buddhist Sculpture from Inner Mongolia (Dolonnor)." *Artibus Asiae* 80, no. 2, 145–66.

Elliott, David. 2013. "What Is . . . ? Pitfalls of Identity in a Slippery Age." In Masters and Ng 2013, 19–30.

Elliott, Mark. 2001. *The Manchu Way: The Eight Banners and Ethnic Identity in Late Imperial China*. Stanford, CA: Stanford University Press.

Elverskog, Johan. 2006. *Our Great Qing: The Mongols, Buddhism and the State in Late Imperial China*. Honolulu: University of Hawai'i Press.

_____. 2010. *Buddhism and Islam on the Silk Road*. Philadelphia: University of Pennsylvania Press.

Estournel, Jean-Luc. 2020. "About the 18 Stupas and Other Treasures Once at the Densatil Monastery." Asianart.com. Published September 29, 2010. https://www.asianart.com/articles/densatil/index.html.

_____. 2021. "About the Portraits of Tibetan Masters." Asianart.com. Published February 28, 2021. https://www.asianart.com/articles/tibetan_masters/index.html.

Evans-Wentz, W. Y. (1954) 2000. *The Tibetan Book of the Great Liberation*. Reprint, New York: Oxford University Press.

Everding, Karl-Heinz. 2017. "Gyantse: Rise, Prime and Decline of a Tibetan Principality in the 14th–16th Centuries." In *Fifteenth Century Tibet: Cultural Blossoming and Political Unrest. Proceedings of a Conference Held in Lumbini, Nepal, March 2015*, edited by Volker Caumanns and Marta Sernesi, 33–62. Lumbini: Lumbini International Research Institute.

Falcone, Jessica. 2018. *Battling the Buddha of Love*. Ithaca, NY: Cornell University Press.

Farquhar, David. 1978. "Emperor as Bodhisattva in the Governance of the Ch'ing Empire." *Harvard Journal of Asiatic Studies* 38, no. 1, 5–34.

Filigenzi, Anna. 2015. *Art and Landscape: Buddhist Rock Sculptures of Late Antique Swat/Uḍḍiyāna*. Vienna: Verlag der Österreichischen Akademie der Wissenschaften.

Finnegan, Damchö Diana, trans. 2006. *Ārya Saṅghāṭasūtra Dharmaparyāya*. https://fpmt.org/wpcontent/uploads/teachers/zopa/advice/sutras/sanghata_sutra_c5_0411.pdf.

Fleming, Zara, and J. Lkhagvademchig Shastri, eds. 2011. *Mongolian Buddhist Art: Masterpieces from the Museums of Mongolia*, vol. 1, *Thangkas, Appliqués and Embroideries*, part 2. Chicago: Serindia.

Formigatti, Camillo A. 2016. "A Forgotten Chapter in South Asian Book History? A Bird's Eye View of Sanskrit Print Culture." In Diemberger, Ehrhard, and Kornicki 2016, 72–134.

Foucher, Alfred. 1900. *Étude sur l'iconographie bouddhique de l'Inde après des documents nouveaux*. Paris: Ernest Leroux.

Francfort, Henri-Paul, Daniel Klodzinski, and Georges Mascle. 1992. "Archaic Petroglyphs of Ladakh and Zanskar." In *Rock Art in the Old World: Papers Presented in Symposium A of the AURA Congress, Darwin Australia, 1988*, edited by Michel Lorblanchet, 147–92. Delhi: Indira Gandhi National Centre for the Arts.

Francke, A. H. 1906. "The Rock Inscriptions at Mulbe." *Indian Antiquary* 25, 72–81.

Franke, Herbert. 1978. *From Tribal Chieftain to Universal Emperor and God: The Legitimation of the Yuan Dynasty*. Munich: Verlag der Bayerischen Akademie der Wissenschaften.

_____. 1984. "Tan-pa, a Tibetan Lama at the Court of the Great Khans." *Orientalia Venetiana I*, edited by Merio Sabatini, 157–80. Florence: Leo S. Olschki.

_____. 1994. "Consecration of the 'White Stupa' in 1279." *Asia Major*, third ser., 7, no. 1, 15–183.

_____. 1996. *Chinesischer und Tibetischer Buddhismus im China der Yuanzeit*. Munich: Kommission für Zentralasiatische Studien, Bayerische Akademie der Wissenschaften.

_____. 2014. "Tibetans in Yuan China." In *China under Mongol Rule*, edited by John D. Langlois, 296–328. Princeton, NJ: Princeton University Press.

Fraser, Sarah E. 2010. "'Antiquarianism or Primitivism': The Edge of History in the Modern Chinese Imagination." In *Reinventing the Past: Archaism and Antiquarianism in Chinese Art and Visual Culture*, edited by Wu Hung, 342–67. Chicago: Art Media Resources.

_____. 2011. "Sha Bo Tsh Ring, Zhang Daqian and Sino-Tibetan Cultural Exchange, 1941–43: Defining Research Methods for A mdo Regional Painting Workshops in the Medieval and Modern Periods." In Lo Bue 2011b, 115–36, pls. 73–80.

Fuentes, Ayesha. 2020. "On the Use of Human Remains in Tibetan Ritual Objects." PhD diss., SOAS University of London.

Fussman, Gerard. 1993. "Chilas, Hatun et les bronzes bouddhiques du Cachemire." In *Antiquities of Northern Pakistan. Reports and Studies*, edited by K. Jettmar, 2, 1–60. Mainz: Philip von Zabern.

Gabriel, Hannelore. 1999. *Jewelry of Nepal*. London: Thames and Hudson.

Gade. 2003. Quoted in "Gedun Choephel Artists' Guild." Asianart.com. https://www.asianart.com/gendun/about.html.

_____. 2016. "A Broken Flower Blossoming in the Cracks: Tibetan Artist Gade Talks about Contemporary Tibetan Art." Interview by Tsesung Lhamo, translated by High Peaks Pure Earth. High Peaks Pure Earth website. https://highpeakspureearth.com/a-broken-flower-blossoming-in-the-cracks-tibetan-artist-gade-talks-about-contemporary-tibetan-art/.

Gail, Adalbert J. 2004. "Nagas of Kathmandu Valley, with Special Reference to the Lichchhavi Period." In Pal 2004b, 37–45.

Galambos, Imre. 2015. *Translating Chinese Tradition and Teaching Tangut Culture: Manuscripts and Printed Books from Khara-Khoto*. Berlin: De Gruyter.

Gamble, Ruth. 2013. "The View from Nowhere: The Travels of the Third Karmapa, Rang Byung Rdo Rje in Story and Songs." PhD diss., Australian National University.

_____. 2018. *Reincarnation in Tibetan Buddhism: The Third Karmapa and the Invention of a Tradition*. New York: Oxford University Press.

Gardner, Alexander. 2009. "Chokgyur Lingpa." Treasury of Lives. https://treasuryoflives.org/biographies/view/Chokgyur-Lingpa/8181.

Garrett, Frances. 2010a. "Shaping the Illness of Hunger: A Culinary Aesthetics of Food and Healing in Tibet." *Asian Medicine* 6, no. 1, 33–54.

_____. 2010b. "Tapping the Body's Nectar: Gastronomy and Incorporation in Tibetan Literature." *History of Religions* 49, no. 3, 300–26.

Gayley, Holley. 2007a. "Patterns in the Ritual Dissemination of Padma Gling pa's Treasures." In *Bhutan: Traditions and Changes. PIATS 2003: Proceedings of the Tenth Seminar of the International Association for Tibetan Studies, Oxford 2003*, edited by John Ardussi and Françoise Pommaret, 97–120. Brill's Tibetan Studies Library 10/5. Leiden: Brill.

_____. 2007b. "Soteriology of the Senses in Tibetan Buddhism." *Numen* 54, 459–99.

Geary, David. 2017. *The Rebirth of Bodh Gaya: Buddhism and the Making of a World Heritage Site*. Seattle: University of Washington Press.

Gega Lama. 1983. *Principles of Tibetan Art: Illustrations and Explanations of Buddhist Iconography and Iconometry according to the Karma Gardri School*, 2 vols. Translated by Karma Chochi Nyima (Richard Barron). Darjeeling: Jamyang Singe.

Giès, Jacques. 1995. *Les arts de l'Asie centrale: la collection Paul Pelliot du Musée national des arts asiatiques—Guimet*. Paris: Réunion des musées nationaux.

Gellek, Tsering Palmo, and Padma Dorje Maitland, eds. 2011. *Light of the Valley: Renewing the Sacred Art and Traditions of Svayambhu*. Cazadero, CA: Dharma Publishing.

Gellner, David N. 1989. "Buddhist Monks or Kinsmen of the Buddha? Reflections on the Titles Traditionally Used by Śākyas in the Kathmandu Valley." *Kailash* 15, nos. 1–2, 5–20.

_____. 1992. *Monk, Householder, and Tantric Priest: Newar Buddhism and its Hierarchy of Ritual*. Cambridge: Cambridge University Press.

_____. 1997. "The Consecration of a Vajra Master in Newar Buddhism." In *Les habitants du toit du monde: Etudes recueillies en hommage à Alexander W. MacDonald*, edited by Samten Gyaltsen Karmay and Philippe Sagant, 659–75. Nanterre: Publications de la Société d'ethnologie.

Gendun Chopel. 2009. *In the Forest of Faded Wisdom: 104 Poems by Gendun Chopel; A Bilingual Edition*. Edited and translated by Donald S. Lopez Jr. Chicago: University of Chicago Press.

_____. 2014. *Grains of Gold: Tales of a Cosmopolitan Traveler*. Translated by Thupten Jinpa and Donald S. Lopez Jr. Chicago: University of Chicago Press.

_____. 2018. *The Passion Book: A Tibetan Guide to Love and Sex*. Translated by Donald S. Lopez Jr. and Thupten Jinpa. Chicago: University of Chicago Press.

Gentry, James. 2017. *Power Objects in Tibetan Buddhism: The Life, Writings, and Legacy of Sokdokpa Lodrö Gyeltsen*. Leiden: Brill.

_____. 2019a. "Liberation through Sensory Encounters in Tibetan Buddhist Practice." *Revue d'Etudes Tibétaines* 50 (October): 73–131.

_____. 2019b. "Tibetan Buddhist Power Objects." In *Oxford Research Encyclopedia of Religion*, edited by John Barton. Oxford: Oxford University Press. https://doi.org/10.1093/acrefore/9780199340378.013.657

Gerner, Manfred. 2007. *Chakzampa Thangtong Gyalpo: Architect, Philosopher and Iron Chain Bridge Builder*. Thimphu: Centre for Bhutan Studies. https://fid4sa-repository.ub.uni-heidelberg.de/311/.

Ghose, Madhuvanti. 2016. *Vanishing Beauty: Asian Jewelry and Ritual Objects from the Barbara and David Kipper Collection*. Exhibition catalog. Chicago: Art Institute of Chicago.

Ghosh, Bhajagovinda. 1997. "The Concept of Vajra and Its Symbolic Transformation," *Bulletin of Tibetology* 33, no. 2, 25–43.

Giès, Jacques, ed. 1995–96. *Les arts de l'Asie centrale: la collection Paul Pelliot du Musée national des arts asiatiques-Guimet*. 2 vols. Paris: Réunion des musées nationaux.

Giès, Jacques, and Monique Cohen. 1995. *Sérinde, Terre de Bouddha: Dix siècles d'art sur la Route de la Soie*. Exhibition catalog. Paris: Réunion des musées nationaux.

Gimello, Robert. 1992. "Chang Shang-ying on Wu-t'ai Shan." In *Pilgrims and Sacred Sites in China*, edited by Susan Naquin and Chünfang Yü, 89–149. Berkeley: University of California Press.

Goepper, Roger, and Jaroslav Poncar. 1996. *Alchi: Ladakh's Hidden Buddhist Sanctuary. The Sumtsek*. London: Serindia.

Goldstein, Melvyn C. 1989. *A History of Modern Tibet, 1913–1959: The Demise of the Lamaist State*. Berkeley: University of California Press.

Gonkatsang, Tsering, and Michael Willis. 2013. "Tibetan, Burmese and Chinese Inscriptions from Bodhgayā in the British Museum." *Journal of the Royal Asiatic Society* 23, 429–39.

_____. 2021. "Text and Translation." In *Bringing Buddhism to Tibet: History and Narrative in the Dba' bzhed Manuscript*, edited by Lewis Doney, 102–57. Berlin: De Gruyter.

Goodrich, L. C. 1942–43. "The Revolving Book-case in China." *Harvard Journal of Asiatic Studies* 7, 130–61.

Government of India Press. 1938. *Who's Who in Tibet, Corrected to the Autumn of 1937, with a few subsequent additions up to February 1938 (plus addenda)*. Calcutta: Government of India Press. British Library, India Office Records L/P&S/12/4185.

Government of India Press. 1949. *Who's Who in Tibet, Corrected with a few subsequent additions up to 30th September 1948*. Calcutta: Government of India Press. British Library, India Office Records, L/P&S/20 D 220/2.

Gray, David. 2005. "Disclosing the Empty Secret: Textuality and Embodiment in the Cakrasamvara Tantra." *Numen* 52, no. 4, 417–44. https://doi.org/10.1163/1568527057775220017.

_____. 2007. *The Cakrasamvara Tantra: the Discourse of Śrī Heruka (Śrīherukābhidhāna)*. New York: American Institute of Buddhist Studies at Columbia University.

Greenwood, Kevin. 2013. "Yonghegong: Imperial Universalism and the Art and Architecture of Beijing's 'Lama Temple.'" PhD diss., University of Kansas.

Grunwëdel, Alfred. 1912. *Altebuddhische Kultstätten in Chinesisch-Turkistan*. Berlin: G. Reimer.

Grupper, Samuel M. 1984. "Manchu Patronage and Tibetan Buddhism during the First Half of the Ch'ing Dynasty: A Review Article." *Journal of the Tibet Society* 4, 47–75.

Gruschke, Andreas. 2001. *The Cultural Monuments of Tibet's Outer Provinces*, vol. 1, *The Qinghai Part of Amdo*. Bangkok: White Lotus.

Guru Padmasambhava, Chokgyur Lingpa, Jamyang Khyentsé Wangpo, Jamgön Kongtrül Lodrö Thayé, Orgyen Tobgyal Rinpoché, and Phakchok Rinpoché. 2016. *The Great Tertön: The Life and Activities of Chokgyur Lingpa*. Translated by Lhasey Lotsawa Translations. Kathmandu: Lhasey Lotsawa Publications.

Gurung, Kalsang Norbu. 2009. "The Role of Confucius in Bon Sources: Kong tse and His Attribution in the Ritual of Three-Headed Black Man." In *Contemporary Visions in Tibetan Studies: Proceedings of the First International Seminar of Young Tibetologists*, edited by B. Dotson, K. N. Gurung, G. Halkias, and T. Myatt, 257–79. Chicago: Serindia.

Gutschow, Niels. 1994. "The Chörten of the Cave at Luri." In Mustang special issue, *Ancient Nepal* 136, 137–45.

_____. 1997. *The Nepalese* Caitya: *1500 Years of Buddhist Votive Architecture in the Kathmandu Valley.* Stuttgart and London: Edition Axel Menges.

_____. 2011. *Architecture of the Newars: A History of Building Typologies and Details in Nepal.* Chicago: Serindia.

Gutschow, Niels, and Andreas Brandt. 2005. "Die Baugeschichte der Klosteranlage von Erdeni Joo (Erdenezuu)." In *Dschingis Khan und seine Erben: Das Weltreich der Mongolen*, edited by Claudius Müller and Henriette Pleiger, 352–56. Munich Hirmer Verlag.

Guy, John. 1991. "The Mahābodhi Temple: Pilgrim Souvenirs of Buddhist India." *Burlington Magazine* 133, no. 1059, 356–67.

_____. 2018. "Crowns of the Vajra Masters: Tracing Nepalese Buddhist Ritual Art." *Orientations* 49, no. 2 (March/April): 90–101.

Gyatso, Janet. 1987. "Down with the Demoness: Reflections on a Feminine Ground in Tibet." *Tibet Journal* 12, no. 4, 38–53.

_____. 2015. *Being Human in a Buddhist World: An Intellectual History of Medicine in Early Modern Tibet*. New York: Columbia University Press.

György Kara. 2005. *Books of the Mongolian Nomads: More than Eight Centuries of Writing Mongolian*. Translated by John R. Krueger. Bloomington: Research Institute for Inner Asian Studies Indiana University Press.

Halkias, Georgios T. 2017. "The Mirror and the Palimpsest: The Myth of Buddhist Kingship in Imperial Tibet." In *Locating Religions: Contact, Diversity, and Translocality*, edited by Reinhold Glei and Nikolas Jaspert, 123–50. Leiden: Brill.

Hambis, Louis. 1976. *Bannières et Peintures de Touen-Houang conservées au Musée Guimet*. Mission Paul Pelliot, documents archaeologiques publiés sous les auspices de l'Académie des Inscriptions et Belles-Lettres 15. Paris: Imprimerie Nationale.

Harding, Sarah, trans. 2003. *The Life and Revelations of Pema Lingpa*. Ithaca, NY: Snow Lion.

Harimoto, Kengo. 2017. "The Dating of the Cambridge Bodhisattvabhūmi Manuscript Add. 1702." In *Indic Manuscript Cultures through the Ages: Material, Textual, and Historical Investigations*, edited by Vincenzo Vergiani, Daniele Cuneo, and Camillo A. Formigatti, 355–76. Studies in Manuscript Cultures 14. Berlin: De Gruyter.

Harris, Clare. 1999. *In the Image of Tibet: Tibetan Painting after 1959*. London: Reaktion.

_____. 2005. "Tibet: Photography and the Construction of Place." In *The Oxford Companion to the Photograph*, edited by Robin Lenman, 626. Oxford: Oxford University Press.

_____. 2007. "British and German Photography in Tibet in the 1930s: The Diplomatic, the Ethnographic, and Other Modes." In *Tibet in 1938–1939: Photographs from the Ernst Schäfer Expedition to Tibet*, edited by Isrun Engelhardt, 73–90. Chicago: Serindia.

_____. 2012a. "In and Out of Place: Tibetan Artists' Travels in the Contemporary Art World." *Visual Anthropology Review* 28, no. 2, 152–63.

_____. 2012b. *The Museum on the Roof of the World: Art, Politics, and the Representation of Tibet*. Chicago: University of Chicago Press.

_____. 2016. *Photography and Tibet*. London: Reaktion.

Harris, Clare, and Tsering Shakya. 2003. *Seeing Lhasa: British Depictions of the Tibetan Capital 1936–1947*. Exhibition catalog. Chicago: Serindia.

Harrison, John, Christian Luczanits, Charles Ramble, and Nyima Drandul, eds. 2018. *A Blessing for the Land: The Architecture, Art and History of a Buddhist Nunnery in Mustang, Nepal*. Kathmandu: Vajra.

Harrison, Paul. 1992. "Commemoration and Identification in Buddhānusmṛti." In *In the Mirror of Memory: Reflections on Mindfulness and Remembrance in Indian and Tibetan Buddhism*, edited by Janet Gyatso, 215–338. Albany: SUNY Press.

_____. 1996. "A Brief History of the Tibetan bKa' 'gyur." In *Tibetan Literature: Studies in Genre*, edited by José Ignacio Cabezón and Roger R. Jackson, 70–94. Ithaca, NY: Snow Lion.

_____. 2007. "Notes on some West Tibetan manuscript folios in the Los Angeles County Museum of Art." In *Pramāṇakīrtiḥ: Papers Dedicated to Ernst Steinkellner on the Occasion of his 70th Birthday, Part I*, edited by Birgit Kellner, Helmut Krassner, Horst Lasic, Michael Torsten Much, and Helmut Tauscher, 229–45. Wiener Studien zur Tibetologie und Buddhismuskunde, 70.1. Vienna: Arbeitskreis für tibetische und buddhistische Studien Universität Wien.

Hartmann, Jens-Uwe. 1998. "The Rañjanā Script." In *The Fifth Seal: Calligraphic Icons*, edited by Andreas Kretschmar, 37–39. Kathmandu: Radheshyam Saraf Art Collection.

Hatt, Robert T. 1980. "A Thirteenth Century Tibetan Reliquary." *Artibus Asiae* 42, nos. 2–3, 175–220.

Hazod, Guntram. 2022. "The 'Stranger-King' and the Temple: The Tibetan Ruler Image Retained in Post-imperial Environments—the Example of the *lha* of Khra 'brug." In Hazod, Fermer, and Jahoda 2022, 59–92.

Hazod, Guntram, Mathias Fermer, and Christian Jahoda. 2022. *The Social and the Religious in the Making of Tibetan Societies: New Perspectives on Imperial Tibet.* Veröffentlichungen zur Sozialanthropologie 30. Vienna: Verlag der Österreichischen Akademie der Wissenschaften.

Heimbel, Jörg. 2017. *Vajradhara in Human Form. The Life and Times of Ngor chen Kun dga' bzang po*. Lumbini: Lumbini International Research Institute.

Heller, Amy. 1988. "Early Textual Sources for the Cult of Beg-ce." In *Tibetan Studies: Proceedings of the Fourth Seminar of the International Association for Tibetan Studies, Schloss Hohenkammer, Munich 1985*, edited by Helga Uebach and Jampa L. Panglung, 185–95. Munich: Kommission für Zentralasiatische Studien Bayerische Akademie der Wissenschaften.

_____. 1994a. "Early Ninth Century Images of Vairochana from Eastern Tibet," *Orientations* 25, no. 6 (June): 74–79.

_____. 1994b. "Ninth-century Buddhist images carved at lDan-ma-brag to commemorate Tibeto-Chinese negotiations." In *Tibetan Studies: Proceedings of the Sixth Seminar of the International Association for Tibetan Studies, Fagernes 1992*, edited by P. Kvaerne, 335–49; (separatum) Appendix, 12–19. Oslo: The Institute for Comparative Research in Human Culture.

_____. 1997. "Buddhist images and rock inscriptions from Eastern Tibet, Part IV." In *Proceedings of the Seventh Seminar of the International Association for Tibetan Studies, Graz 1995*, edited by H. Krasser, M. T. Much, E. Steinkellner, and H. Tauscher, 385–403. Vienna: Verlag der Österreichischen Akademie der Wissenschaften.

_____. 1998. "Two Inscribed Fabrics and their Historical Context: Some Observations on Esthetics and Silk Trade in Tibet, 7th to 9th century." In *Entlang der Seidenstrasse: Frühmittelalterliche Kunst zwischen Persien und China in der Abegg-Stiftung*, edited by Karel Otavsky, 95–118. Riggisberg: Abegg-Stiftung.

_____. 1999. *Tibetan Art: Tracing the Development of Spiritual Ideals and Art in Tibet, 600–2000 A.D.* Milan: Jaca Book.

_____. 2003a. "The Great Protector Deities of the Dalai Lamas." In Pommaret 2002, 81–98. Leiden: Brill.

_____. 2003b. "The Silver Jug of the Lhasa Jokhang: Some Observations on silver objects and costumes from the Tibetan Empire (7th–9th century)." *Silk Road Art and Archaeology* 29, no. 3, 213–38.

_____. 2007. "P.T. 7a, P.T. 108, P.T. 240 and Beijing bsTan 'gyur 3489: Ancient Tibetan rituals dedicated to Vairocana." In *The Pandita and the Siddha: Tibetan Studies in Honor of E. Gene Smith*, edited by R. Vitali, 85–91. Dharamsala: Library of Tibetan Works and Archives.

_____. 2008. "The Ramoche Restoration Project, Lhasa." *Orientations* 39, no. 6 (September): 85–87.

_____. 2010a. "Portable Buddhist Sculptures of Lo: A Chronological Selection, 15th through 17th Centuries." In Lo Bue 2010b, 90–105.

_____. 2010b. "Preliminary Remarks on the Donor Inscriptions and Iconography of an 11th-Century Mchod rten at Tholing." In Lo Bue and Luczanits 2010, 43–74.

_____. 2013a. "A Sculpture of Avalokiteśvara Donated by the Ruler of Ya tse." In *Nepalica-Tibetica Festgabe for Christoph Cüppers*, edited by Franz-Karl Ehrhard and Petra Maurer, 1:243–48. Andiast: International Institute for Tibetan and Buddhist Studies.

_____. 2013b. "Tibetan Inscriptions on Ancient Silver and Gold Vessels and Artefacts." *Journal of the International Association for Bon Research* 1, 259–91.

_____. 2015. "Three Early Bonpo Thangka and their Consecration Inscriptions." In *Tibetan and Himalayan Healing: An Anthology for Anthony Aris*, edited by Charles Ramble and Ulrike Roesler, 225–40. Kathmandu: Vajra Books.

_____. 2016a. "Observations on Painted Coffin Panels of the Tibetan Empire." *Zentralasiatische Studien* 45, 147–202.

_____. 2016b. "Three Ancient Manuscripts from Tholing in the Tucci collection, IsIAO, Roma, Part I. Manuscript 1329 E." *Studi in Onore di Luciano Petech, Rivista degli Studi Orientali* 89, 125–32.

_____. 2018. "Preliminary Remarks on Birds and Deer in Shang Shung and Early Tibet." In *Ancient Civilization of Tibetan Plateau: Proceedings of the First Beijing International Conference on Shang Shung Cultural Studies*, edited by Tsering Thar Tongkor and Tsering Dawa Sharshon, 1:3–37. Xining: Qinghai Ethnic Publishing House.

Heller, Natasha. 2008. "Visualizing Pilgrimage and Mapping Experience: Mount Wutai on the Silk Road." In *The Journey of Maps and Images on the Silk Road*, edited by Philippe Forêt and Andreas Kaplony, 29–50. Leiden: Brill.

Helman-Ważny, Agnieszka. 2014. *The Archaeology of Tibetan Books*. Brill's Tibetan Studies Library 36. Leiden: Brill.

Hemis Museum, with photography by Ravinder Kalra. 2011. *Hemis Museum* (*Sku-rten Khang*). Ladakh: Hemis Museum.

Henss, Michael. 2001. "The Bodhisattva-Emperor: Tibeto-Chinese Portraits of Sacred and Secular Rule in the Qing Dynasty." Pts. 1 and 2. *Oriental Art* 47 no. 3, 2–26; 47, no. 5, 71–83.

_____. 2008. *Buddhist Art in Tibet: New Insights on Ancient Treasures; A Study of Paintings and Sculptures from 8th to 18th century*. Ulm: Fabri Verlag.

_____. 2011. "Liberation from the Pain of Evil Destinies: The Giant Appliqué Thang Kas (Gos Sku) at Gyantse (Rgyal Rtse Dpal 'Khor Chos Sde)." In Lo Bue. 2011b, 73–90.

_____. 2014. *The Cultural Monuments of Tibet: The Central Regions*, 2 vols. Munich: Prestel.

_____. 2020. *Buddhist Ritual Art of Tibet: A Handbook on Ceremonial Objects and Ritual Furnishings in the Tibetan Temple*. Stuttgart: Arnoldsche.

Herrmann-Pfandt, Adelheid. 2018. *The Copper-Coloured Palace: Iconography of the rNyingma School of Tibetan Buddhism*. Vol. 1, *Buddha and Buddha Worlds*. Delhi: Agam Kala Prakashan.

Hevia, James. 1995. *Cherishing Men from Afar: Qing Guest Ritual and the Macartney Embassy of 1793*. Durham, NC: Duke University Press.

Hidas, Gergely. 2013. "Rituals in the *Mahāsāhasrapramardanasūtra*." In *Puṣpikā: Tracing Ancient India through Texts and Traditions*, edited by Nina Mirnig et al., 225–40. Oxford: Oxbow Books.

_____. 2020. "Buddhism, Kingship and the Protection of the State: The *Suvarṇaprabhāsottamasūtra* and *Dhāraṇī* Literature." In *Śaivism and the Tantric Traditions: Essays in Honour of Alexis G. J. S. Sanderson*, edited by Dominic Goodall et al., 235–48. Gonda Indological Studies 22. Leiden: Brill.

Hill, Nathan W. 2015. "The *sku bla* Rite in Imperial Tibetan Religion." In "Kingship, Ritual, and Narrative in Tibet and the Surrounding Cultural Area / Royauté, rituel et narration au Tibet et dans l'aire culturelle alentour," special issue, *Cahiers d'Extrême-Asie* 24, 49–58.

Hinüber, Oskar von. 2005. *Die Palola Ṣāhis. Ihre Steininschriften, Inschriften auf Bronzen, Handschriftenkolophone und Schutzzauber. Materialien zur Geschichte von Gilgit und Chilas*. Antiquities of Northern Pakistan. Reports and Studies Vol. 5. Mainz: Philip von Zabern.

Hirshberg, Daniel A. 2016. *Remembering the Lotus-Born: Padmasambhava in the History of Tibet's Golden Age*. Somerville, MA: Wisdom.

"History of Erdeni Juu" (Erdeni juu-yin teüke). (1803) 1999. In *Istoriya Erdeni-dzu: Faksimile rukopisi; Perevod s mongol'skogo, kommentarii i prilojeniya*. Translated by Anna Damdinovna Tsendina. Reprint, Moscow: Vostočnaya literatura RAN.

Hitchcock, John T. 1978. "An Additional Perspective on the Nepali Caste System." In *Himalayan Anthropology: The Indo-Tibetan Interface*, edited by James F. Fisher, 111–20. The Hague: Mouton.

Hodge, Stephen, trans. 2003. *The Mahā-Vairocana-Abhisaṃbodhi-Tantra with Buddhaguhya's Commentary*. London: Routledge Curzon.

Höfer, András. 1978. "A New Rural Elite in Central Nepal." In *Himalayan Anthropology: The Indo–Tibetan Interface*, edited by James F. Fisher, 179–86. The Hague: Mouton.

Höfer, Regina. 2011. "Sichtbarmachung der Leerheit: Sonam Dolma und die zeitgenössische tibetische Abstraktion" (Making emptiness visible: Sonam Dolma and contemporary Tibetan abstraction). *Masala Newsletter: Virtuelle Fachbibliotek Südasien* 6, no. 2, 9–16. https://journals.ub.uni-heidelberg.de/index.php/masala/article/view/19289/13081.

Hofer, Theresia, ed. 2014. *Bodies in Balance: The Art of Tibetan Medicine*. Exhibition catalog. New York: Rubin Museum of Art. https://issuu.com/rmanyc/docs/7._bodies_in_balance.

Hoffmann, Helmut. 1973. "Buddha's Preaching of the Kalacakra Tantra at the Stupa of Dhanyakataka." In *German Scholars on India*, edited by Cultural Dept. of the Embassy of the Federal Republic of Germany, New Delhi, vol. 1, 136–40. Varanasi: Chowkhamba Sanskrit Series Office.

Howard, Neil. 1989. "The Development of the Fortresses of Ladakh c. 950 to c. 1650 A.D." *East and West* 39, no. 1, 217–88.

Hsiao, Ch'i-Ch'ing. 1994. "Mid-Yüan Politics." In *The Cambridge History of China, Volume 6: Alien Regimes and Border States, 907–1368*, edited by Herbert Franke and Denis Twitchett, 490–560. Cambridge: Cambridge University Press.

Huang, Shih-shan Susan. 2014. "Reassessing Printed Buddhist Frontispieces from Xi Xia." *Zhejiang University Journal of Art and Archaeology* 1, 129–81.

Huber, Tony. 1992. "Some 11th Century Indian Buddhist Clay Tablets (*tsha tsha*) from Central Tibet." In *Tibetan Studies: Proceedings of the Fifth Seminar of the International Association for Tibetan Studies, Narita, 1989*, edited by Shoren Ihara and Zuiho Yamaguchi, 493–96. Narita: Naritasan Shinshoji.

_____, ed. 2001. *Sacred Spaces and Powerful Spaces in Tibetan Culture*. Dharamsala: Library of Tibetan Works and Archives.

_____. 2008. *The Holy Land Reborn: Pilgrimage and the Tibetan Reinvention of Buddhist India*. Chicago: University of Chicago Press.

_____. 2020. *Source of Life: Revitalisation Rites and Bon Shamans in Bhutan and the Eastern Himalayas*, vol. 1. Vienna: Verlag der Österreichischen Akademie der Wissenschaften.

Huc, Regis Évariste. 1857. *Travels in Tartary, Tibet, and China during the Years 1844–46*. Translated by W. Hazlitt. London: Vizetelly.

Huntington, John. 2006. "Nevar Artist Jīvarāma's Sketchbook." In *Indian Art Treasures: Suresh Neotia Collection*, edited by R. C. Sharma, Kamal Giri, and Anjan Chakraverty, 76–85. New Delhi: Mosaic Books.

Huntington, John, and Dina Bangdel. 2003. *The Circle of Bliss: Buddhist Meditational Art*. Exhibition catalog. Columbus, OH: Columbus Museum of Art; Chicago: Serindia.

Huntington, Susan L., and John C. Huntington. 1990. *Leaves from the Bodhi Tree: The Art of Pala India (8th–12th Centuries) and Its International Legacy*. Dayton, OH, and Seattle: Dayton Art Institute in association with the University of Washington Press.

Huo, Wei. 2012. "A Study of Ancient Tibetan Gold and Silver Ware," translated by Suzanne Cahill and Ye Wa. *Chinese Archeology* 12, no. 1, 165–74. https://doi.org/10.1515/char-2012-0020.

Hutt, Michael. 2010. *Nepal: A Guide to the Art and Architecture of the Kathmandu Valley*, 178, image of Shakyamuni. New Delhi: Adroit Publishers.

Imaeda, Yoshiro. 1977. "Mise au point concernant les éditions chinoises du Kanjur et du Tanjur tibéains." In Macdonald and Imaeda 1977, 23–51.

_____. 1982. "L'édition du kanjur Tibétain de 'Jang sa-tham." *Journal asiatique* 270, 173–89.

_____. 2012. "Re-examination of the 9th-Century Inscription at Ldan ma brag (II) in Eastern Tibet." In *Old Tibetan Studies: Dedicated to the Memory of R. E. Emmerick. Proceedings of the Tenth Seminar of the International Association for Tibetan Studies, Oxford 2003*, edited by Cristina Scherrer-Schaub, 113–18. Brill's Tibetan Studies Library 10/14. Leiden: Brill.

Imaeda, Yoshiro and Drukpa Doffu. 1982. "Bhûtan no Tashi goman/Tashigomang of Bhutan." Exhibition brochure for *Asian Concepts of the Cosmos*. Tokyo: Laforet Museum.

Irons, Edward. 2020. "Under the Gaze of the Buddha Mega-Statue: Commodification and Humanistic Buddhism in Fo Guang Shan." *Journal of the Oxford Centre for Buddhist Studies* 18, 96–122. http://jocbs.org/index.php/jocbs/article/view/214.

Isaacson, Harunaga. 1998. "Tantric Buddhism in India (From A.D. 800 to A.D. 1200)." *Buddhismus in Geschichte und Gegenwart* 2, 23–49.

Jackson, David P. 1984. *The Mollas of Mustang: Historical, Religious, and Oratorical Traditions of the Nepalese-Tibetan Borderland*. Dharamsala: Library of Tibetan Works and Archives.

_____. 1996. *A History of Tibetan Painting: The Great Tibetan Painters and Their Traditions*. Österreichische Akademie der Wissenschaften Philosophisch-Historische Klasse Denkschriften 242. Vienna: Verlag der Österreichischen Akademie der Wissenschaften.

_____. 2009. *Patron and Painter: Situ Panchen and the Revival of the Encampment Style*. Masterworks of Tibetan Painting Series 1. Exhibition catalog. New York: Rubin Museum of Art. https://issuu.com/rmanyc/docs/patron_and_patron_96.

_____. 2010. *The Nepalese Legacy in Tibetan Painting: Early Beri to Ngor*. Masterworks of Tibetan Painting Series 2. Exhibition catalog. New York: Rubin Museum of Art. https://issuu.com/rmanyc/docs/nepalese_legacy_96.

_____. 2011. *Mirror of the Buddha: Early Portraits from Tibet*. Masterworks of Tibetan Painting Series 3. Exhibition catalog. New York: Rubin Museum of Art. https://issuu.com/rmanyc/docs/mirror_of_the_buddha_96.

_____. 2012a. "The Language of Art: The Challenge of Translating Art Historical Terms from the Biography of the Tenth Karmapa." In Debreczeny 2012, 279–89.

_____. 2012b. *The Place of Provenance: Regional Styles in Tibetan Painting*. Masterworks of Tibetan Painting Series 4. Exhibition catalog. New York: Rubin Museum of Art. https://issuu.com/rmanyc/docs/place_of_provenance_96.

_____. 2015a. "Early Drigung Kagyu Painting." In Jackson 2015b, 75–99.

_____. 2015b. *Painting Traditions of the Drigung Kagyu School*. Masterworks of Tibetan Painting Series 5. New York: Rubin Museum of Art. https://issuu.com/rmanyc/docs/drigung_96.

_____. 2016. *A Revolutionary Artist of Tibet: Khyentse Chenmo of Gongkar*. Masterworks of Tibetan Painting Series 6. New York: Rubin Museum of Art. https://issuu.com/rmanyc/docs/a_revolutionary_artist_96.

Jackson, David, and Janice A. Jackson. 1988. *Tibetan Thangka Painting: Methods and Materials*, 2nd ed. London: Serindia.

Jackson, Roger R. 1992. "The Tibetan Tshogs Zhing (Field of Assembly): General Notes on Its Function, Structure, and Contents." *Asian Philosophy* 2, no. 2, 157–72.

____. 2019. *Mind Seeing Mind: Mahāmudrā and the Geluk Tradition of Tibetan Buddhism*. Somerville, MA: Wisdom.

Jagou, Fabienne. 2005. "The Panchen Lamas and the Dalai Lamas: A Questionable Master-Disciple Relationship." In Brauen 2005, 202–11.

Jahn, Karl. 1956. "A Note on Kashmīr and the Mongols." *Central Asiatic Journal* 2, no. 3, 176–80.

Jahoda, Christian. 2022. "The Social and the Religious in Early Post-Imperial Tibet: The Case of 10th–11th Century Western Tibet and Its Antecedents." In Hazod, Fermer, and Jahoda 2022, 149–88.

Jahoda, Christian, and Christiane Kalantari. 2015. "Kingship in Western Tibet in the 10th and 11th Centuries." *Cahiers d'Extrême Asie* 24, 77–103.

Jahoda, Christian, Tsering Gyalpo, Christiane Papa-Kalantari, and Patrick Sutherland. 2012. *'Khor chags / Khorchag / Kuojia si wenshi daguan* 廓迦寺文史大观 [Kuojia Monastery: An overview of its history and culture]. [In Tibetan, English, and Chinese.] Lhasa: Bod ljongs bod yig dpe rnying dpe skrun khang.

Jain, Kajri. 2021. *Gods in the Time of Democracy*. Durham, NC: Duke University Press.

Jamieson, R. C. 2000. *The Perfection of Wisdom: Extracts from the Aṣtasāhasrikāprajñapāramitā*. New York: Viking Studio.

Jamtsarano, Ts. 2012. "Description of the Three "Dzū" and the "Lavran" in the Erdene Zuu Monastery by Ts. Jamtsarano." Translated by Jerzy Tulisow, Agata Bareja-Starzyńska, and Filip Majkowski. In Tulisow et al. 2012, 333–63.

Jayarava, trans. 2009. "Ye dharmā hetuprabhavā—Causation." Visible Mantra Press. http://www.visiblemantra.org/dharma-hetuprabhava.html.

_____. 2011. *Visible Mantras: Visualizing and Writing Buddhist Mantras*. Cambridge: Visible Mantra Press.

Jing, Anning. 1994. "The Portraits of Khubilai Khan and Chabi by Anige (1245–1306), a Nepali Artist at the Yuan Court." *Artibus Asiae* 54, no. 1/2, 40–86.

_____. 1996. "Anige, Himalayan Artist in Khubilai Khan's Court." *Asian Art and Culture* 9, no. 3 (Fall): 31–44.

_____. 2004. "Financial and Material Aspects of Tibetan Art under the Yuan Dynasty." *Artibus Asiae* 64, no. 2, 213–41.

John, Gudrun. 2006. *Tibetische Amulette aus Himmels-Eisen*. Rahden: Verlag Marie.

Johne, Isabell. 2014. *Vasudhārā: A Study of the Origin, Development, and Diffusion of Artistic Representations of the Buddhist Goddess of Prosperity in Their Cultural Contexts*. Translated by Rachel Marks-Ritzenhoff. Aachen: Shaker Verlag.

Juvaini, 'Ala' al-Din 'Aṭa Malik. 1958. *The History of the World Conqueror*, 2 vols. Translated by John Andrew Boyle. Cambridge, MA: Harvard University Press.

Kagyu Monlam. 2020. "Junior Torma Makers Extend Their Skills." Kagyu Monlam. http://www.kagyumonlam.org/index.php/en/component/content/article/256-kagyu-monlam/in-pictures/2020/1609-junior-torma-makers-extend-their-skills.

Kalantari, Christiane, and Tsering Gyalpo. 2011. "On Ornament, Textiles and Baldachins Depicted on the Deilings of Buddhist Cave Temples in Khartse Valley, Western Tibet: Form, Function and Meaning." Kunstgeschichte. http://www.kunstgeschichte-ejournal.net.

Kalsang, Jhampa. 1999. *Tibet Astro Science*. Rome: Tibet Domani.

Kaplan, Howard. 2021. "Circle in the Square: How the Mandala Lab Builds on the Rubin Museum of Art's Storied Architecture." In *Spiral Magazine*, 41–42. New York: Rubin Museum of Art. https://rubinmuseum.org/spiral/circle-in-the-square.

Kapstein, Matthew T., ed. 2009a. *Buddhism Between Tibet and China*. Boston: Wisdom.

_____. 2009b. "The Treaty Temple of the Turquoise Grove." In Kapstein 2009a, 21–72.

_____. 2015. "Textualizing the Icon: The Three Deities of Longevity in Art and Ritual." In *Tibetan and Himalayan Healing: An Anthology for Anthony Aris*, edited by Charles Ramble and Ulrike Roesler, 383–403. Kathmandu: Vajra Publications.

Karmay, Heather. 1975. *Early Sino-Tibetan Art*. Warminster: Aris and Phillips.

_____. 1977. "Tibetan Costume, Seventh to Eleventh Centuries." In *Essais sur l'Art du Tibet*, edited by Ariane Macdonald and Yoshiro Imaeda, 64–81. Paris: Jean Maisonneuve.

Karmay, Samten G. 1997. "Inscriptions Dating from the Reign of Btsan po Khri lde-srong-btsan." In *Tibetan Studies: Proceedings of the Seventh Seminar of the International Association for Tibetan Studies, Graz 1995*, edited by Helmut Krasser, M. Much, E. Steinkellner, and H. Tauscher, 477–86. Vienna: Verlag der Österreichischen Akademie der Wissenschaften.

_____. 2005. "The Mural Paintings in the Red Palace of the Potala." In *The Arrow and the Spindle: Studies in History, Myths, Rituals and Beliefs in Tibet*, edited by Samten G. Karmay, 2:109–18. Kathmandu: Mandala Book Point.

_____. 2009a. "An Open Letter by Pho-brang Zhi-ba-'od." In *The Arrow and the Spindle: Studies in History, Myths, Rituals and Beliefs in Tibet*, rev. ed, 17–40. Kathmandu: Mandala Book Point.

_____. 2009b. "The Ordinance of lHa Bla-ma Ye-shes-'od." In *The Arrow and the Spindle: Studies in History, Myths, Rituals and Beliefs in Tibet*, rev. ed, 3–16. Kathmandu: Mandala Book Point.

_____. 2014. *The Illusive Play: The Autobiography of the Fifth Dalai Lama*. Chicago: Serindia.

_____. 2018. "The Gold Masks Found in Shang Shung and the 'Five Supports of the Soul *(rten lnga)*' of the Bon Funerary Tradition." In *Ancient Civilization of Tibetan Plateau: Proceedings of the First Beijing International Conference on Shang Shung Cultural Studies*, edited by Tsering Thar Tongkor and Tsering Dawa Sharshon, 330–44. Xining: Qinghai Ethnic Publishing House.

Karsten, Joachim. 1983. "A Note on *ya sor* and the Secular Festivals following the Smon lam chen mo." In *Contributions on Tibetan Language, History, and Culture: Proceedings of the Csoma de Körös Symposium Held at Velm-Vienna, Austria, 13–19 September 1981*, edited by Ernst Steinkellner, 1:117–48. Vienna: Arbeitskreis für Tibetische und Buddhistische Studien, Universität Wien.

Kesang Landark with contributions by David Elliott, Regina Höfer, Andy Cohen, and A. C. Kupper. 2021. *Kesang Lamdark*. Milan: Skira.

Kelényi, Béla. 2002. "The Myth of the Cosmic Turtle according to the Late Astrological Tradition." In *Impressions of Bhutan and Tibetan Art: Tibetan Studies III. PIATS 2000: Proceedings of the Ninth Seminar of the International Association for Tibetan Studies, Leiden 2000*, edited by John Ardussi and Henk Blezer, 69–90. Brill's Tibetan Studies Library 2/3. Leiden: Brill.

Khanchen Tsewang Rigzin, ed. n.d. *Hemis Museum*. Exhibition catalog. Leh: Hemis Monastery.

Khokhlov, Yury. 2016. "The Xi Xia Legacy in Sino-Tibetan Art of the Yuan Dynasty." Asianart.com. Published September 15, 2016. https://www.asianart.com/articles/xi-xia/.

Khokhlov, Yury, and Yannick Laurent. 2020. "Nam mkha' grags and the Three Silver Brothers: A Sixteenth-Century 'Divine Artist' from Western Tibet and His Artistic Legacy." *Journal of Tibetology* 22, 236–74.

Kim, Jinah. 2010. "A Book of Buddhist Goddesses: Illustrated Manuscripts of the *Pañcarakṣā sūtra* and Their Ritual Use." *Artibus Asiae* 70, no. 2, 259–329.

_____. 2013. *Receptacle of the Sacred: Illustrated Manuscripts and the Buddhist Book Cult in South Asia*. Berkeley: University of California Press.

_____. 2020. "Women in Action: Images of Women in the Buddhist Art of Medieval Eastern India and Nepal." *Orientations* 51, no. 6 (November/December): 2–13.

_____. 2021. *Garland of Visions: Color, Tantra, and a Material History of Indian Painting*. Oakland: University of California Press.

Kim, Jinah, and Todd Lewis. 2019. *Dharma and Puṇya. Buddhist Meditational Art*. Leiden: Hotei.

Kim, Youn-mi. 2017. "Virtual Pilgrimage and Virtual Geography: Power of Liao Miniature Pagodas (907–1125)." *Religions* 8, no. 10, 206–35.

Kimmet, Natasha N. 2016. "Anchored in Architecture: 'Monumental Lhasa' at the Rubin Museum of Art." *Orientations* 47, no. 7 (October): 40–48.

_____. 2018. "Nako—The Village 'Adorned with Temples': Residential Architecture on the West Tibetan Frontier (c. 18th to 21st Centuries)." PhD diss., University of Vienna.

King, Matthew. 2019. *Ocean of Milk, Ocean of Blood: A Mongolian Monk in the Ruins of the Qing Empire*. New York: Columbia University Press.

Klimburg-Salter, Deborah E., ed. 1982. *The Silk Route and the Diamond Path: Esoteric Buddhist Art on the Trans-Himalayan Trade Routes*. Los Angeles: UCLA Art Council.

_____. 1997. *Tabo: A Lamp for the Kingdom: Early Indo-Tibetan Buddhist Art in the Western Himalaya*. Milan: Skira; New York: Thames and Hudson.

_____. 2001. "Dung Dkhar/Phyi Dbang, West Tibet, and the Influence of Tangut Buddhist Art." *East and West* 51, nos. 3–4, 323–48.

_____. 2015. "Along the Pilgrimage Routes between Uḍḍiyāṇa and Tibet: The Gilgit MSS Covers and the Tibetan Decorated Book Cover." In *Tibet in Dialogue with Its Neighbors: History, Culture and Art of Central and Western Tibet, 8th to 15th Century*, edited by Erica Forte, Liang Junyan, Deborah Klimburg-Salter, Zhang Yun, and Helmut Tauscher, 392–406. Vienna: China Tibetology Research Center and Arbeitskreis für Tibetische und Buddistische Studien, Universität Wien.

Kollmar-Paulenz, Karénina. 1992–93. "Utopian Thought in Tibetan Buddhism: A Survey of the Śambhala Concept and its Sources." *Studies in Central and East Asian Religions* 5–6, 78–96.

_____. 2010. "Teaching the Dharma in Pictures: Illustrated Mongolian Books in the Ernst Collection in Switzerland." In *The Arts of Tibetan Painting: Recent Research on Manuscripts, Murals and Thangkas of Tibet, the Himalayas and Mongolia (11th–19th Century). Proceedings of the Twelfth Seminar of the International Association for Tibetan Studies, Vancouver, 2010*, edited by Amy Heller. Asianart.com. http://asianart.com/articles/paulenz/index.html.

Kölver, Bernhard. 1992. *Re-Building a Stūpa: Architectural Drawings of the Svayaṃbhūnāth*. Bonn: VGH Wissenschaftsverlag.

Konishi, Masatoshi. 2013. *Hāth-Kāghaz: History of Handmade Paper in South Asia*. Shimla and New Delhi: Indian Institute of Advanced Study and Arya Books International.

Kornicki, Peter. 2012. "Steps Towards a History of the Tangut Book: Some Recent Publications." *East Asian Publishing and Society* 2, 83–91.

Korostovets, Ivan. 1926. *Von Cinggis Khan zur Sowjetrepublik: Eine kurze Geschichte der Mongolei unter besonderer Berücksichtigung der neuesten Zeit*. Berlin: De Gruyter.

Kossak, Steven M. 1997. "Sakya Patrons and Nepalese Artists in Thirteenth-Century Tibet." In Singer and Denwood 1997, 26–37.

Kossak, Steven M., and Jane Casey Singer. 1998. *Sacred Visions: Early Paintings from Central Tibet*. Exhibition catalog. New York: The Metropolitan Museum of Art.

Kozicz, Gerald. 2017. "One *Stūpa* and Three *Lha thos*. The Monuments of Tashigang." *Revue d'Etudes Tibétaines*, no. 41 (September): 226–48.

_____. 2002. "The Wanla Temple." In *Buddhist Art and Tibetan Patronage, Ninth to Fourteenth Centuries. PIATS 2000: Proceedings of the Ninth Seminar of the International Association for Tibetan Studies, Leiden 2000*, edited by Deborah Klimburg-Salter and Eva Allinger, 127–36. Brill's Tibetan Studies Library 2/7. Leiden: Brill.

Kramer, Jowita. 2008. *A Noble Abbot from Mustang: Life and Works of Glo-bo mKhan-chen (1456–1532)*. Vienna: Arbeitskreis für Tibetische und Buddhistische Studien, Universität Wien.

Kreijger, Hugo E. 1999. *Kathmandu Valley Painting: The Jucker Collection*. Boston: Shambhala.

Kucera, Karil J. 2016. *Ritual and Representation in Chinese Buddhism: Visualizing Enlightenment at Baodingshan from the 12th to 21st Centuries*. Amherst, NY: Cambria.

Kuløy, Hallvard Kåre. 1985. *Tibetan Rugs*. Bangkok: White Orchid Press.

Kuranishi, Ken'ichi. 2013. "Yantras in the Buddhist Tantras: Yamāritantras and Related Literature." In *Proceedings of the First International Indology Graduate Research Symposium (September 2009, Oxford)*, vol. 1, *Puṣpikā: Tracing Ancient India through Texts and Traditions*, edited by Nina Mirnig, Péter-Dániel Szántó, and Michael Williams, 265–81. Oxford: Oxbow Books.

Kvaerne, Per. 1990. "A Preliminary Study of the Bonpo Divinity Khro bo gTso mchog mkha' 'gying." In *Reflections on Tibetan Culture: Essays in Memory of Turrell V. Wylie*, edited by Lawrence Epstein and Richard F. Sherburne, 117–25. Lewiston, NY: Edwin Mellen Press.

_____. 1995. *The Bon Religion of Tibet: The Iconography of a Living Tradition*. London: Serindia.

_____. 2021. "The *sku bla* of the Tibetan Emperors—Metamorphosed in Yungdrung Bon?" In *Crossing Boundaries: Tibetan Studies Unlimited*, edited by Diana Lange, Jarmila Ptáčková, Marion Wettstein, and Mareike Wulff, 32–44. Prague: Academia Publishing House.

Kychanov E. I., trans. 2013. *"Novye zakony" tangutskogo gosudarstva* ["New Laws" of the Tangut State]. Moscow: GRVL.

La Rocca, Donald J. 2006. *Warriors of the Himalayas: Rediscovering the Arms and Armor of Tibet*. With essays by John Clarke, Amy Heller, and Lozang Jamspal. Exhibition catalog. New York: The Metropolitan Museum of Art.

_____. 2014a. "An Early Tibetan Text on the Connoisseurship of Swords." In *The Armorer's Art: Essays in Honor of Stuart Pyhrr*, edited by Donald J. La Rocca, 89–105. Woonsocket, RI: Mowbray Publishing.

_____. 2014b. "Recent Acquisitions of Tibetan and Mongolian Arms and Armor in the Metropolitan Museum of Art. Part 2." *Waffen-und Kostümkunde: Zeitschrift der Gesellschaft für Historische Waffen-und Kostükunde* 56, no. 2, 187–210.

Laird, Thomas. 2018. *Murals of Tibet*, vol. 1, collector's edition of photographs by Laird; vol. 2, edited by Florian Kobler. Cologne: Taschen.

Laird, Thomas, Robert A. F. Thurman, Heather Stoddard, Cameron Bailey, Jakob Winkler, Shigeru Ban, and Bstan-'dzin-rgya-mtsho. 2018. *Murals of Tibet*. Cologne: Taschen.

Lalou, Marcelle. 1939. *Inventaire des manuscrits tibétains de Touen-Houang conservés à la Bibliothèque nationale (fonds Pelliot tibétain)*, vol. 1. Paris: Adrien Maisonneuve.

Lama Chime Radha Rinpoche. 1981. "Tibet." In *Divination and Oracles*, edited by Michael Loewe and Carmen Blacker, 3–37. London: Allen and Unwin.

Lamotte, Étienne. 1960. "Mañjuśrī." *T'oung Pao* 48, 1–96.

Larsen, Knud, and Amund Sinding-Larsen. 2001. *The Lhasa Atlas: Traditional Tibetan Architecture and Townscape*. Boston: Shambhala.

Larson, Frans-August. 1930. *Larson, Duke of Mongolia*. Boston: Little Brown & Co.

Lee-Kalisch, Jeong-hee. 2006. *Tibet: Klöster öffnen ihre Schatzkammern*. Exhibition catalog. Essen: Kulturstiftung Ruhr.

Leidy, Denise Patry. 1997. "Kashmir and China: A Note about Styles and Dates." *Orientations* 28, no. 2 (February): 66–70.

_____. 2010. "Buddhism and Other 'Foreign' Practices in Yuan China." In Watt 2010, 87–128.

Leidy, Denise Patry, and Sherman E. Lee. 1994. *Treasures of Asian Art: The Asia Society's Mr. and Mrs. John D. Rockefeller 3rd Collection*. New York: Asia Society Galleries; Abbeville Press.

Leoshko, Janice. 1988. *Bodhgaya: The Site of Enlightenment*. Bombay: Marg Publications.

_____. 1993–94. "Scenes of the Buddha's Life in Pāla-Period Art." *Silk Road Art and Archaeology* 3, 251–76.

_____. 1996. "On the Construction of a Buddhist Pilgrimage Site." *Art History* 19, 573–97.

_____. 2003. *Sacred Traces: British Explorations of Buddhism in South Asia*. Aldershot: Ashgate.

_____. 2020. "Time and Time Again: Finding Perspective for Bodhgayā Buddha Imagery." *Ars Orientalis* 50. https://doi.org/10.3998/ars.13441566.0050.013.

Leschly, Jakob. 2007. "Guru Chowang." Treasury of Lives. Treasuryoflives.org/biographies/view/Guru-Chowang/5588.

Lewis, Todd T. 1994. "A modern Guide for Mahāyāna Buddhist Life-Cycle Rites: The Nepāl Jana Jīvan Kriyā Paddhati." *Indo-Iranian Journal* 37, 1–46.

_____. 2000. *Popular Buddhist Texts from Nepal: Narratives and Rituals of Newar Buddhism*. Albany: SUNY Press.

Li, Brenda W. L. 2011. "A Critical Study of the Life of the 13th-Century Tibetan Monk U rgyan pa Rin chen dpal Based on his Biographies." PhD diss., University of Oxford.

Lidke, Jeffrey S. 2017. *The Goddess Within and Beyond the Three Cities: Śākta Tantra and the Paradox of Power in Nepāla-maṇḍala*. New Delhi: DK Printworld.

Lin, Nancy G. 2011. "Adapting the Buddha's Biographies: A Cultural History of the *Wish-Fulfilling Vine* in Tibet, Seventeenth to Eighteenth Centuries." PhD diss., University of California, Berkeley.

_____. 2017. "Recounting the Fifth Dalai Lama's Rebirth Lineage." *Revue d'Etudes Tibétaines* 38 (February): 119–56.

Lin, Wei-Cheng. 2014. *Building a Sacred Mountain: The Buddhist Architecture of China's Mount Wutai*. Seattle: University of Washington Press.

Linrothe, Rob. 1996. "Usnīsavijaya and the Tangut Cult of the Stūpa at Yu-lin Cave 3." *National Palace Museum Bulletin* 31, nos. 4–5, 1–24.

_____. 1998. "Xia Renzong and the Patronage of Tangut Buddhist Art: The Stūpa and Ushnīsavijayā Cult." *Journal of Sung-Yuan Studies* 28, 91–121.

_____. 2001a. "Creativity, Freedom and Control: The Renaissance of Tibetan Buddhist Painting in Rebgong." *Tibet Journal* 26, nos. 3–4, 9–50.

_____. 2001b. "Group Portrait: Mahāsiddhas in the Alchi Sumtsek." In *Embodying Wisdom. Art, Text and Interpretation in the History of Esoteric Buddhism*, edited by Rob Linrothe and Henrik H. Sørensen, 185–208. Copenhagen: Seminar for Buddhist Studies.

_____. 2006a. *Holy Madness: Portraits of Tantric Siddhas*. New York: Rubin Museum of Art.

_____. 2006b. "Two Fieldnotes from Zangskar: A Kashmiri Sculpture in a Personal Shrine and an Etymology of 'Kankani' Chorten." In *Long Life: Festschrift in Honour of Roger Goepper*, edited by Jeong-hee Lee-Kalisch et al., 167–79. Frankfurt: Peter Lang.

_____. 2009. "The Commissioner's Commissions: Late-Thirteenth-Century Tibetan and Chinese Buddhist Art in Hangzhou Under the Mongols." In Kapstein 2009a, 73–96.

_____. 2015a. *Collecting Paradise: Buddhist Art of Kashmir and Its Legacies*. With essays by Melissa R. Kerin and Christian Luczanits. Exhibition catalog. New York: Rubin Museum of Art.

_____. 2015b. "Introduction." In Linrothe 2015a, 1–27.

_____. 2015c. "A Group of Mural Paintings from the 1930s in A mdo Reb gong." In *Centering the Local: A Festschrift for Dr. Charles Kevin Stuart on the Occasion of his Sixtieth Birthday*, edited by Gerald Roche, Keith Dede, Fernanda Pirie, and Benedict Copps, 283–95. Asian Highlands Perspectives 37. Morrisville, NJ: Asian Highlands Perspectives.

_____. 2016a. "Origins of the Kashmiri Style in the Western Himalayas: Sculpture of the 7th–11th Centuries." In *Transfer of Buddhism across Central Asian Networks (7th to 13th Centuries)*, edited by Carmen Meinert, 147–88. Dynamics in the History of Religions 8. Leiden: Brill.

_____. 2016b. *Seeing into Stone: Pre-Buddhist Petroglyphs and Zangskar's Early Inhabitants*. Berlin: Studio Orientalia.

Lipton, Barbara, and Nima Dorjee Ragnubs. 1996. *Treasures of Tibetan Art: Collections of the Jacques Marchais Museum of Tibetan Art*. Staten Island, NY: Jacques Marchais Museum of Tibetan Art; New York: Oxford University Press.

Liu, Yuyuan (Victoria). 2021. "Exhibition Review of the *Story of Light and Shadow: 20th Century Chinese Photography from Huang Jianpeng's Collection*." *Waxing Moon* 1, no. 1, 131–39.

Lo Bue, Erberto. 1992. "The Princes of Gyantse and Their Role as Builders and Patrons of Arts." In *Proceedings of the Fifth Seminar of the International Association of Tibetan Studies, Narita 1989*, edited by Ihara Shoren and Yamaguchi Zuiho, 2:559–73. Narita: Naritasan Shinshoji.

_____. 2000. "On Some Inscriptions in the Temples of the 'bum-pa' of the Great Stupa at Gyantse." *East and West* 50, no. 1/4, 387–437.

_____. 2007. "The Gu ru lha khang at Phyi dbang: A Mid-15th Century Temple in Central Ladakh." In *Discoveries in Western Tibet and the Western Himalayas: Essays on History, Literature, Archaelogy and Art. PIATS 2003: Proceedings of the Tenth Seminar of the International Association for Tibetan Studies, Oxford 2003*, edited by Amy Heller and Giacomella Orofino, 175–96. Brill's Tibetan Studies Library 8/13. Leiden: Brill.

_____. 2010a. "The Śambhala Murals in the Klu khang and Their Historical Context: A Preliminary Report." In Lo Bue and Luczanits 2010, 353–74.

_____, ed. 2010b. *Wonders of Lo: The Artistic Heritage of Mustang*. Mumbai: Marg Foundation.

_____. 2011a. "Newar Artistic Influence in Tibet and China between the 7th and the 15th Century." *Rivista degli Studi Orientali* 84, supplemento 1, 25–62.

_____, ed. 2011b. *Art in Tibet: Issues in Traditional Tibetan Art from the Seventh to the Twentieth Century. PIATS 2003: Proceedings of the Tenth Seminar of the International Association for Tibetan Studies, Oxford 2003*. Brill's Tibetan Studies Library 10/13. Leiden: Brill.

Lo Bue, Erberto, and Christian Luczanits, eds. 2010. *Tibetan Art and Architecture in Context: Tibetan Studies. PIATS 2006: Proceedings of the Eleventh Seminar of the International Association for Tibetan Studies, Königswinter 2006*. Andiast: International Institute for Tibetan and Buddhist Studies.

Lo Bue, Erberto, and Franco Ricca. 1990. *Gyantse Revisited*. Florence: Le Lettere.

Locke, John K. 1973. *Rato Matsyendranath of Patan and Bungamati*. Kirtipur: Tribhuvan University Press.

_____. 1980. *Karunamaya: The Cult of Avalokitesvara-Matsyendranath in the Valley of Nepal*. Kathmandu: Sahayogi Prakashan.

_____. 1985. *Buddhist Monasteries of Nepal: A Survey of the Bāhās and Bahīs of the Kathmandu Valley*. Kathmandu: Sahayogi Prakashan.

Lopez, Donald S, Jr. 1998. *Prisoners of Shangri-La*. Chicago: University of Chicago Press.

_____. 2002. *The Story of Buddhism: A Concise Guide to Its History and Teachings*. San Francisco: HarperSanFrancisco.

_____. 2004a. *Buddhist Scriptures*. London: Penguin Books.

_____. 2004b. "Limbs of Enlightenment." In Selig Brown 2004, 9–11.

_____. 2006. *The Madman's Middle Way: Reflections on Reality of the Tibetan Monk Gendun Chopel*. Chicago: University of Chicago Press.

_____. 2013. *Gendun Chopel: Tibet's First Modern Artist*. New York: Trace Foundation's Latse Library; Chicago: Serindia.

_____. 2018. *Gendun Chopel: Tibet's Modern Visionary*. Boulder, CO: Shambhala.

Losty, Jeremiah P. 1982. *The Art of the Book in India*. London: British Library.

Lowry, John. 1977. "A Fifteenth Century Sketchbook (Preliminary Study)." In Macdonald and Imaeda 1977, 83–118.

Luczanits, Christian. 2002. "The Wanla bKra shis gsum brtsegs." In *Buddhist Art and Tibetan Patronage, Ninth to Fourteenth Centuries. PIATS 2000: Proceedings of the Ninth Seminar of the International Assocation for Tibetan Studies, Leiden 2000*, edited by Deborah Klimburg-Salter and Eva Allinger, 115–26. Brill's Tibetan Studies Library 2/7. Leiden: Brill.

_____. 2003. "Early Tibetan Clay Sculpture." *Aziatische Kunst* 33, no. 2, 2–15.

_____. 2004. *Buddhist Sculpture in Clay: Early Western Himalayan Art, Late 10th to Early 13th Centuries*. Chicago: Serindia.

_____. 2006a. "Alchi and the Drigungpa School of Tibetan Buddhism: The Teacher Depiction in the Small Chörten at Alchi." In *Mei shou wan nian–Long Life Without End: Festschrift in Honor of Roger Goepper*, edited by Jeong-hee Lee-Kalisch, Antje Papist-Matsuo, and Willibald Veit, 181–96. Frankfurt: Peter Lang.

_____. 2006b. "The Eight Great Siddhas in Early Tibetan Painting from c. 1200 to c. 1350." In Linrothe 2006a, 76–91.

_____, ed. 2008. *Gandhara, The Buddhist Heritage of Pakistan: Legends, Monasteries, and Paradise*. Exhibition catalog. Mainz: Phillip van Zabern.

_____. 2010. "Mandalas of Mandalas: The Iconography of a Stupa of Many Auspicious Doors for Phagmodrupa." In Lo Bue and Luczanits 2010, 281–310.

_____. 2011. "Locating Great Perfection: The Murals of the Lhasa Lukhang." *Orientations* 42, no. 2 (March): 102–11.

_____. 2015a. "Beneficial to See: Early Drigung Painting." In *Painting Traditions of the Drigung Kagyu School*, edited by David P. Jackson, 214–59. Masterworks of Tibetan Painting Series 5. New York: Rubin Museum of Art.

_____. 2015b. "From Kashmir to Western Tibet: The Many Faces of a Regional Style." In Linrothe 2015a, 108–49.

_____. 2015c. "The Interior Decoration of Wanla." Homepage of Christian Luczanits. https://luczanits.net/sites/Wanla.html

_____. 2016a. "Inspired by the Past: The Art of Chöying Dorjé and Western Himalayan Sculpture." In Debreczeny and Tuttle 2016, 107–51.

_____. 2016b. "Portable Heritage in the Himalayas: The Example of Namgyal Monastery, Mustang: Part 1, Sculpture." *Orientations* 47, no. 2 (March): 120–30.

_____. 2016c. "Portable Heritage in the Himalayas: The Example of Namgyal Monastery, Mustang: Part 2, Books and Stupas." *Orientations* 47, no. 5 (June): 22–32.

_____. 2021. "Illumination Programs: The Visual Subtext of Two Text Collections." In *Two Illuminated Text Collections of Namgyal Monastery. A Study of Early Buddhist Art and Literature in Mustang*, edited by Christian Luczanits and Markus Viehbeck, 92–143. Kathmandu: Vajra.

_____. 2023. *Alchi: Ladakh's Hidden Buddhist Sanctuary*. Chicago: Serindia.

_____. n.d. "Alchi, Ladakh." Accessed December 7, 2022. http://www.luczanits.net/sites/Alchi.html.

_____. n.d. "Tabo Main Temple." Accessed December 7, 2022. http://www.luczanits.net/sites/Tabo/MainTemple.html.

_____. Forthcoming(a). "Mandalas Intertwined—Why Minor Goddesses in the Tabo Main Temple Matter."

_____. Forthcoming(b). "The Pearl Garland Composition. The Main Inscription of the Palden Drepung Chörten at Alchi." In *Buddhist Heritage in the Western Himalayas: Essays on the Art, Architecture and History of Ladakh*, edited by Christian Luczanits and Heinrich Poell.

Luczanits, Christian, and Jaroslav Poncar, eds. 2023. *Alchi: The Choskhor*. Chicago: Serindia.

Luo Wenhua. 2016. "A Survey of a Willow-Branch Guanyin Attributed to the Tenth Karmapa in the Palace Museum and Related Questions." In Debreczeny and Tuttle 2016, 153–83.

Macdonald, Ariane. 1970. "Le Dhānyakataka de Man-Luns guru." *Bulletin de l'Ecole Française d'Extrême-Orient* 57, 169–213.

Macdonald, Ariane, and Yoshiko Imaeda, eds. 1977. *Essais sur l'Art du Tibet*. Paris: Librairie d'Amérique et d'Oriente.

Mahler, Jane Gaston. 1959. *The Westerners among the Figurines of the Tang Dynasty of China*. Serie Orientale Roma. Rome: Istituto Italiano per Il Medio ed Estremo Oriente.

Maki, Ariana. 2012. "The Temple of Tamzhing Lhundrup Choling and the Legacy of Pema Lingpa (1450–1521): An Iconological Study." PhD diss., Ohio State University.

_____. 2017. "Tracing the Legacy of Tsang Khenchen Penden Gyatso (1610–84) in Bhutanese Art." *Orientations* 48, no. 3 (May/June): 108–17.

Malagò, Amina. 1988. "The Origin of Kesi, the Chinese Silk Tapestry." *Annali di Ca 'Foscari* 27, no. 3, 279–97.

_____. 1991. "*Kesi*, Chinese Literary Sources in the Study of Silk Tapestry." *Annali di Ca 'Foscari* 3, 244–57.

Mallinson, James, and Péter-Dániel Szántó. 2021. *The Amṛtasiddhi and Amṛtasiddhimūla: The Earliest Texts of the Haṭhayoga Tradition*. Pondichery: Institut Français de Pondichéry, École Française d'Extrême-Orient.

Mallmann, Marie-Thérèse de. 1975. *Introduction à l'iconographie du tântrisme bouddhique*. Paris: Centre de recherches sur l'Asie centrale et la Haute Asie.

_____. 1986. *Introduction à l'iconographie du Tântrisme Bouddhique*. Paris: Maisonneuve.

Marchand, Ernesta. 1976. "The Panorama of Wutaishan as an Example of Tenth Century Cartography." *Oriental Art* 22, no. 2, 158–73.

Marshak, Boris. 2002. "La thématique sogdienne dans l'art de la Chine de la seconde moitié du Vie siècle." *Comptes-rendus des séances de l'Académie des Inscriptions et Belles-Lettres*, no. 1, séances de l'année 2001, 227–64. Paris: Academie des Belles-Lettres.

Martin, Dan. 1987. "On the Origin and Significance of the Prayer Wheel according to Two Nineteenth-Century Tibetan Literary Sources." *Journal of the Tibet Society* 7, 13–29.

_____. 2001a. "Painters, Patrons and Paintings of Patrons in Early Tibetan Art." In *Embodying Wisdom. Art, Text, and Interpretation in the History of Esoteric Buddhism*, edited by Rob Linrothe and Henrik H. Sørensen, 139–84. Copenhagen: Seminar for Buddhist Studies.

_____. 2001b. "Painters, Patrons and Paintings of Patrons in Early Tibetan Art." Tiblical. https://sites.google.com/site/ tiblical/painters-patrons-and-paintings-of-patrons-in-early-tibetan-art.

_____. 2006. "Padampa Sangye: A History of Representation of a South Indian Siddha in Tibet." In Linrothe 2006a, 108–23.

_____. 2018. "Art in the Life of Atiśa with Emphasis on the Question of 11th-Century Pāla Art in Tibet." Lecture, Hong Kong, May 13, 2018.

Martin, Nils. 2022. "The Wanla Group of Monuments: 14th-century Tibetan Buddhist Murals in Ladakh." PhD diss., Ecole Pratique des Hautes Etudes.

_____. 2023. "The Foundation Inscription of the Sumtsek." In Luczanits and Poncar 2023, 781–89.

Massa, Giovanni, Mark Aldenderfer, and Marcos Martinón-Torres. 2019. "Of Gold Masks, Bronze Mirrors and Brass Bracelets: Analyses of Metallic Artefacts from Samdzong, Upper Mustang, Nepal 450–650 CE." *Archaeological Research in Asia* 18, 68–81.

Masters, H. G., and Elaine W. Ng, eds. 2013. *Anonymous: Contemporary Tibetan Art*. Exhibition catalog. Hong Kong: ArtsAsiaPacific.

Mathieu, Christine, and Cindy Ho, eds. 2011. *Ancestral Realms of the Naxi: Quentin Roosevelt's China*. New York: Rubin Museum of Art; Stuttgart: Arnoldsche Art Publishers.

Mathou, Thierry. 2016. "The Tashi Gomang Project: Preserving a National Treasure of Bhutan" and "The Tradition of Miniature Portable Shrines in Bhutan." In Wangchuck 2016.

Matsukawa Takashi and Ayudai Ochir, eds. 2011. *The International Conference on "Erdene-Zuu: Past, Present and Future."* Ulaanbaatar: International Institute for the Study of Nomadic Civilizations.

Maurer, Petra. 2010. "Das tibetische Staatsorakel (sku-rten) des Klosters Nechung (gNas-chung)." In *Tibet-Encyclopaedia*, edited by Dieter Schuh, Christoph Cüppers, Wolfgang Bertsch, Franz-Karl Ehrhard, Karl-Heinz Everding, Petra H. Maurer, and Peter Schwieger. Andiast: International Institute for Tibetan and Buddhist Studies. http://www.tibet-encyclopaedia.de/staatsorakel.html.

Maurer, Petra, Donatella Rossi, and Rolf Scheuermann. 2020. *Glimpses of Tibetan Divination: Past and Present*. Leiden: Brill.

McCausland, Shane. 2014 (2015). *The Mongol Century: Visual Cultures of Yuan China (1271–1368)*. London: Reaktion.

McDaniel, Justin. 2017. *Architects of Buddhist Leisure*. Honolulu: University of Hawai'i Press.

McDuie-Ra, Duncan, and Mona Chettri. 2020. "Concreting the Frontier: Modernity and Its Entanglements in Sikkim, India." *Political Geography* 76. https://doi.org/10.1016/j.polgeo.2019.102089.

McKay, Alex. 2014. "The British Invasion of Tibet, 1903–4." In "The Younghusband 'Mission' to Tibet," special issue, *Inner Asia* 14, no. 1, 5–25.

Mejor, Marek. 2010. "Painting the 'Wheel of Transmigration' (Saṃsāra-Cakra): A Note on the Textual Transmission." In *From Turfan to Ajanta: Festschrift for Dieter Schlingloff on the Occasion of His Eightieth Birthday*, edited by Eli Franco and Monika Zin, 2, 671–90. Lumbini: Lumbini International Research Institute.

Melikian-Chirvani, A. Souren. 2011. "Iran to Tibet." In *Islam and Tibet*, edited by Anna Akasoy, Charles Burnett, and Ronit Yoeli-Tlalim, 89–116. Farnham: Ashgate Publishing.

Mengele, Irmgard. 2012. *Riding a Huge Wave of Karma: The Turbulent Life of the Tenth Karma-pa*. Kathmandu: Vajra Publications.

The Metropolitan Museum of Art. 2017. "Crowns of the Vajra Masters: Ritual Art of Nepal." https://www.metmuseum.org/exhibitions/listings/2017/crowns-of-vajra-masters.

The Metropolitan Museum of Art. n.d. "Vishnu Riding on Garuda." Accessed July 4, 2022. https://www.metmuseum.org/art/collection/search/78185.

Meyer, Fernand. 1987. "The Potala Palace of the Dalai Lamas in Lhasa." *Orientations* 18, no. 7 (July): 14–33.

Miller, Leigh. 2014. "Contemporary Tibetan Art and Cultural Sustainability in Lhasa, Tibet." PhD diss., Emory University.

_____. 2016. "A Buddhist Mickey Mouse." In *Figures of Buddhist Modernity in Asia*, edited by Jeffrey Samuels, Justin McDaniel, and Mark Rowe, 163–64. Honolulu: University of Hawai'i Press.

_____. 2022. "Tibet: Dratang Monastery." HAR: Himalayan Art Resources. https://www.himalayanart.org/search/set.cfm?setID=1669.

Mills, Martin. 2003. *Identity, Ritual and State in Tibetan Buddhism: The Foundations of Authority in Gelukpa Monasticism*. London: Routledge Curzon.

Miyaji, Akira. 2004. "Maitreya and the Colossal Buddha Images." *Sites: Journal of Studies for the Integrated Text Science* 2, no. 1, 87–110.

Mocko, Anne. 2017. "Tolerance in Nepal Mandala: Communal Relations and Royal Religious Patronage in Malla-Era Kathmandu." In *Toleration in Comparative Perspective*, edited by Vicki A. Spencer, 121–39. Lanham, MD: Lexington Books.

Montell, Gösta. (1943) 1954. "The Idol Factory of Peking." Reprint, *Ethnos* 1, no. 4, 143–56.

Mori, Masahide. 1997. "The Vajrāvalī of Abhayākaragupta. A critical study, Sanskrit edition of select chapters and complete Tibetan version." Ph.D. diss., SOAS University of London.

_____. 2008. "The Vajrāvalī Maṇḍala Series in Tibet." In *Esoteric Buddhist Studies: Identity in Diversity. Proceedings of the International Conference on Esoteric Buddhist Studies, Koyasan University, 5 Sept.-8 Sept. 2006*, edited by ICEBS Editorial Board, 223–41. Kōyasan: Kōyasan University.

Muller, F. Max, and Bunyiu Nanjio. 1884. *The Ancient Palm-Leaves: Containing the Prajñā-pāramita-hṛdaya-sūtra and the Ushnisha-vijaya-dhāranī*. Oxford: Clarendon Press.

Myers, Diana K., Arthur Alden Leeper, and Valrae Reynolds. 1984. *Temple, Household, Horseback: Rugs of the Tibetan Plateau*. Exhibition catalog. Washington, DC: Textile Museum.

Myers, Diana K., and Françoise Pommaret. 1994. "The Fabric of Life in Bhutan." In Myers and Bean 1994, 71–80.

Myers, Diana K., and Susan S. Bean, eds. 1994. *From the Land of the Thunder Dragon: Textile Arts of Bhutan*. Exhibition catalog. London: Serindia.

Nagao, Gadjin M. 1985. "The Tibetan Eulogy at Chü-yung-kuan Text and Translation." In *Tantric and Taoist Studies in Honour of R. A. Stein*, edited by M. Strickmann, 3:835–61. Bruxelles: L'Institut belge des hautes Études chinoises.

Namdak, Tenzin, Yasuhiko Nagano, and Musashi Tachikawa, eds. 2000. *Mandalas of the Bon Religion*. Senri Ethnological Reports 12. Osaka: National Museum of Ethnology.

Namgyal-Lama, Kunsang. 2013a. "Les *tsha tsha* du monde tibétain: Études de la production, de l'iconographie et des styles des moulages et estampages bouddhiques." PhD diss., University of Paris-Sorbonne.

_____. 2013b. "*Tsha tsha* Inscriptions: A Preliminary Survey." In *Tibetan Inscriptions: Proceedings of a Panel Held at the Twelfth Seminar of the International Association for Tibetan Studies, Vancouver 2010*, edited by Kurt Tropper and Cristina Scherrer-Schaub, 1–41. Brill's Tibetan Studies Library 32. Leiden: Brill.

Namkhai Norbu, Chögyal. 2021. *Namkha: Harmonizing the Energy of the Elements*. Merigar: Shang Shung Publications. (Restricted access.)

Nebesky-Wojkowitz, René de. 1956. *Oracles and Demons of Tibet: The Cult and Iconography of the Tibetan Protective Deities*. The Hague: Mouton.

_____. (1956) 1975. *Oracles and Demons of Tibet: The Cult and Iconography of the Tibetan Protective Deities*. Reprint, Graz: Akademische Druck- u. Verlagsanstalt.

_____. (1956) 1998. *Oracles and Demons of Tibet: The Cult and Iconography of the Tibetan Protective Deities*. Reprint, New Delhi: Paljor.

Neumann, Helmut F. 1994. "The Wall Paintings of the Lori Gonpa." *Orientations* 25, no. 11 (November): 79–91.

_____. 1997. "Paintings of the Lori Stūpa in Mustang." In Singer and Denwood 1997, 178–85.

Neumann, Helmut F., and Heidi A. Neumann. 2010. "Early Wall Paintings in Lo: Luri Reconsidered." In Lo Bue 2010b, 64–75.

Neuwirth, Holger. 2015. "Building description." In Neuwirth and Auer 2015, 28–55.

Neuwirth, Holger, and Carmen Auer, eds. 2015. *The Three Storied Temple of Wanla*. Graz: Verlag des Technischen Universität Graz.

Norbu Dhondup. 1937. *Lhasa Mission Diary (October to December 1937) from Norbu Dhondup British Trade Agent, Yatung and Assistant of the Political Officer in Sikkim, British Mission, Lhasa, Tibet.* British Library, India Office Records, L/P&S/12/4193.

_____. 1938. *Lhasa Mission Diary for the month of September 1938 from Norbu Dhondup, British Trade Agent, Yatung and Assistant to the Political Officer in Sikkim, British Mission, Lhasa, Tibet.* British Library, India Office Records, L/P&S/12/4193.

Norbu, Jamyang. 2014. "Tibet's First War Photographer." *Shadow Tibet*. Published November 22, 2014. https://www.jamyangnorbu.com/blog/2014/11/22/tibets-first-war-photographer/.

O rgyan 'jigs med chos kyi dbang po (Patrul). 1988. *The Words of My Perfect Teacher: Kunzang Lama'i Shelung*. Translated by the Padmakara Translation Group. Boston: Shambhala.

Oidtmann, Max. 2018. *Forging the Golden Urn: The Qing Empire and the Politics of Reincarnation in Tibet*. New York: Columbia University Press.

Olivieri, Luca Maria. 2010. "Late Historic Cultural Landscape in Swat. New data for a tentative Historical Reassessment." In *Coins, Art and Chronology II: The First Millennium C.E. in the Indo-Iranian Borderlands*, edited by M. Alram, D. Klimburg-Salter, M. Pfisterer, and I. Minoru, 357–69. Vienna: Verlag der Österreichischen Akademie der Wissenschaften.

Olschak, Blanche Christine, and Geshé Thupten Wangyal. 1973. *Mystic Art of Ancient Tibet*. London: Allen and Unwin.

Orofino, Giacomella. 1990. "A Note on Some Tibetan Petroglyphs of the Ladakh Area." *East and West* 40, no. 1/4, 173–200.

_____. 2000. "The Great Wisdom Mother and the Gcod Tradition." In *Tantra in Practice*, edited by David Gordon White. Princeton, NJ: Princeton University Press.

Orzech, Charles. 1998. *Politics and Transcendent Wisdom: The Scripture for Humane Kings in the Creation of National Protection Buddhism*. State College: Pennsylvania State University Press.

Owens, Bruce McCoy. 1989. "The Politics of Divinity in the Kathmandu Valley: The Festival of Bungadya/Rato Matsyendranath." PhD diss., Columbia University.

Pabel, Roland. 2014. "Der Wanla Tempel in Ladakh: Konstruktive Interventionen an einem buddhistischen Sakralbau." PhD diss., Graz: Institute of Architecture Technology.

Padmakara Translation Group, trans. 2018. "*The Transcendent Perfection of Wisdom in Ten Thousand Lines* (*Daśasāhasrikāprajñāpāramitā*)" 2018. 84000: Translating the Words of the Buddha. 33.70. (Toh 11. Degé Kangyur, vol. 31 [shes phyin, ga], folios 1b–91a, and vol. 32 [shes phyin, nga], fols. 92.b–397.a.). http://read.84000.co/translation/UT22084-031-002.html.

Pakhoutova, Elena. 2009. "Reproducing Sacred Places: The Eight Great Events of the Buddha's Life and Their Commemorative Stūpas in the Medieval Art of Tibet (10th–13th century)." PhD diss., University of Virginia.

_____. 2013. "Buddhist Practices and Rituals Centered on Buddha Vairocana in Tibet." In Van Alphen 2013, 39–45.

_____, ed. 2018. *The Second Buddha: Master of Time*. Exhibition catalog. New York: Delmonico/Prestel.

_____. 2021. "For One and or for Many: Affluent and Common Patronage of Narrative Art in Tibet." *Material Religion* 17, no. 1, 29–55.

Pal, Pratapaditya. 1969. *The Art of Tibet*. Exhibition catalog. New York: Asia House Gallery Publication.

_____. 1974. *The Arts of Nepal*, Part I: *Sculpture*. Leiden: Brill.

_____. 1975a. *Bronzes of Kashmir*. Graz: Akademische Druck- und Verlagsanstalt.

_____. 1975b. *Nepal Where the Gods are Young*. Exhibition catalog. New York: Asia House Gallery.

_____. 1978. *The Arts of Nepal*, Part II: *Painting*. Leiden: Brill.

_____. 1984a. *Tibetan Paintings*. Basel: Basilius Press.

_____. 1984b. *Tibetan Paintings: A Study of Tibetan Thankas, Eleventh to Nineteenth Centuries*. New York: Ravi Kumar.

_____. 1985. *Art of Nepal: A Catalogue of the Los Angeles County Museum of Art Collection*. Berkeley: Los Angeles County Museum of Art in association with University of California Press.

_____. 1989. "The Last Buddhist Pundit of Bengal." In *Studies in Art and Archaeology of Bihar and Bengal*, edited by Debala Mitra and Gouriswar Bhattacharya, 189–97. Delhi: Sri Satguru.

_____. 1990. *Art of Tibet: A Catalogue of the Los Angeles County Museum of Art Collection*. Los Angeles: LACMA.

_____. 1991. *Art of the Himalayas: Treasures from Nepal and Tibet*. Exhibition catalogue. New York: Hudson Hills Press.

_____. 1997. *Tibet: Tradition and Change*. Exhibition catalog. Albuquerque: Albuquerque Museum.

_____, ed. 2003. *Himalayas: An Aesthetic Adventure*. Exhibition catalog. Chicago: Art Institute of Chicago in association with University of California Press and Mapin Publications.

_____. 2004a. "Cosmic Forms of Hindu Divinities in Nepal." In Pal. 2004b, 46–61.

_____, ed. 2004b. *Nepal: Old Images, New Insights*. Mumbai: Marg Publications.

_____. 2007. *The Arts of Kashmir*. Exhibition catalog. Milan: 5 Continents; New York: Asia Society.

Pal, Pratapaditya and Julia Meech-Pekarik. 1988. *Buddhist Book Illuminations*. Hong Kong: Ravi Kumar.

Parfionovich, Yuri, Gyurme Dorje, and Fernand Meyer, eds. 1992. *The Tibetan Medical Paintings: Illustrations to the Blue Beryl Treatise of Sangye Gyamtso (1653–1705)*. New York: Harry N. Abrams.

Paul, Katherine Anne. 2003. "Words on the Wind: A Study of Himalayan Prayer Flags." PhD diss., University of Wisconsin–Madison.

_____. 2019. "Tools of the Trade: Implements for Enlightenment." In *Awaken: A Tibetan Buddhist Journey Toward Enlightenment*, edited by John Henry Rice and Jeffrey Durham. Exhibition catalog. Richmond: Virginia Museum of Fine Arts.

Pelliot, Paul. 1914. *Les Grottes de Touen-houang: Peintures et sculptures bouddhiques des epoques des Wei, des T'ang et des Song*. Vol. 1. Paris: Paul Geuthner.

_____, trans. 1961. *Histoire ancienne du Tibet*. Paris: Librairie d'Amérique et d'Orient Adrien Maisonneuve.

Perdue, Daniel E. 1992. *Debate in Tibetan Buddhism*. Ithaca, NY: Snow Lion.

Petech, Luciano. 1973. *Aristocracy and Government in Tibet, 1728–1959*. Serie Orientale Roma 45. Rome: Instituto Italiano per il Medio ed Estremo Oriente.

_____. 1978. "The 'Bri-guṅ-pa Sect in Western Tibet and Ladakh." In *Proceedings of the Csoma de Körös Memorial Symposium*, edited by Louis Ligeti, 313–25. Budapest: Akadémiai Kiadó.

_____. 1990. *Central Tibet and the Mongols: The Yüan-Sa-Skya Period of Tibetan History*. Serie Orientale Roma 65. Rome: Instituto Italiano per il Medio ed Estremo Oriente.

Petech, Luciano and Christian Luczanits, eds. 1999. *Inscriptions from the Tabo Main Temple: Texts and Translations*. Rome: Istituto italiano per l'Africa e l'Oriente.

Phuntsho, Karma. 2008. "Ogyen Pema Lingpa (1450–1521), His Life and Legacy." In Bartholomew and Johnston 2008, 66–77.

_____. 2013. *The History of Bhutan*. London and Noida: Random House.

Pinney, Christopher. 1997. *Camera Indica: The Social Life of Indian Photographs*. London: Reaktion.

Piotrovsky, M. B., ed. 1993. *Lost Empire of the Silk Road: Buddhist Art from Khara-Khoto (X–XIIIth Century)*. Exhibition catalog. Milan: Electa.

Pommaret, Françoise, ed. 2002. *Lhasa in the Seventeenth Century: The Capital of the Dalai Lamas*. Brill's Tibetan Studies Library 3. Leiden: Brill.

Poppe, N. N. 1957. *Mongolian Monuments in hP'ags-pa Script*, 2nd ed. Translated and edited by John R. Krueger. Wiesbaden: Harrassowitz.

Pozdneev, Aleksei M. 1880. *Goroda severnoi Mongolii* [Towns of northern Mongolia]. St. Petersburg: Tip. V. S. Balasheva.

_____. (1892, 1893) 1997. *Mongolia and the Mongols*, in one vol. Translated by J. R. Shaw and D. Plank. Reprint, London: Curzon Press.

_____. (1896) 1971. *Mongolia and the Mongols*, vol. 1. Translated by John Roger Shaw and Dale Plank. Reprint, Bloomington: Indiana University Press.

_____. (1896–98) 1977. *Mongolia and the Mongols*, vol. 2. Translated by William H. Dougherty. Reprint, Bloomington: Indiana University Press.

Press Trust of India. 2018. "137-Feet Chenrezig Statue, Sikkim's Tallest, to Be Inaugurated in November." NDTV. https://www.ndtv.com/india-news/137-feet-chenrezig-statue-sikkims-tallest-to-be-inaugurated-in-november-1940113.

Pritzker, David. 2000. "The Treasures of Par and Kha-tse." *Orientations* 31, no. 7 (September): 131–33.

_____. 2021. "Banquet Set with Ewer, Decanter and Plate." In *Masterpieces from the Al Thani Collection*, edited by Stéphane Castelluccio and Amin Jaffer, 156–59. Paris, Éditions du Patrimoine.

Quintman, Andrew, trans. 2010. *The Life of Milarepa*. New York: Penguin Classics.

_____. 2013. "Wrinkles in Time: On the Vagaries of Mi la ras pa's Dates." *Acta Orientalia* 74, 3–26.

_____. 2014a. "Redacting Sacred Landscape in Nepal: The Vicissitudes of Yolmo's Tiger Cave Lion Fortress." In *Himalayan Passages: Tibetan and Newar Studies in Honor of Hubert Decleer*, edited by Benjamin Bogin and Andrew Quintman, 69–95. Boston: Wisdom.

_____. 2014b. *The Yogin and the Madman: Reading the Biographical Corpus of Tibet's Great Saint Milarepa.* New York: Columbia University Press.

Quintman, Andrew, and Kurtis R. Schaeffer. 2016. "The Life of the Buddha at Rtag brtan Phun tshogs gling Monastery in Text, Image, and Institution: A Preliminary Overview." *Journal of Tibetology* 13, 32–73.

_____. 2022. "The Life of the Buddha." http://www.lifeofthebuddha.org.

Ra Yeshé Sengé. 2015. *The All-Pervading Melodious Drumbeat: The Life of Ra Lotsawa.* Translated by Bryan Cuevas. New York: Penguin Books.

Ramble, Charles. 1997. "The Creation of the Bon Mountain of Kongpo." In *Mandala and Landscape*, edited by Alexander W. Macdonald, 133–232. Delhi: D. K. Printworld.

_____. 1998. "The Classification of Territorial Divinities in Pagan and Buddhist Rituals in South Mustang." In *Tibetan Mountain Deities: Their Cults and Representations*, edited by Anne-Marie Blondeau, 123–44. Vienna: Verlag der Österreichischen Akademie der Wissenschaften.

Ramble, Charles, and Kemi Tshewang, directors. 2010. *Between the Lines: Exorcising the Old Year in a Himalayan Bonpo Village.* Color film, 1:20:17. Epalinges: The Kalpa Group. https://youtu.be/SqjN_owRXls.

Rawski, Evelyn. 1998. *The Last Emperors: A Social History of the Qing Imperial Institutions.* Berkeley: University of California Press.

Ray, Nihar Ranjan, Karl Khandalavala, and Sadashiv Gorakshkar. 1986. *Eastern Indian Bronzes.* New Delhi: Lalit Kalā Akademi.

Reedy, Chandra L. 1997. *Himalayan Bronzes: Technology, Style, and Choices.* Newark: University of Delaware Press.

Repo, Joona. 2011. "Tsongkhapa Lobzang Drakpa." Treasury of Lives. https://treasuryoflives.org/biographies/view/Tsongkhapa-Lobzang-Drakpa/8986.

Reynolds, Valrae. 1978. *Tibet, a Lost World: The Newark Museum Collection of Tibetan Art and Ethnography.* Exhibition catalog. New York: American Federation of Arts.

_____, ed. 1999. *From the Sacred Realm: Treasures of Tibetan Art from the Newark Museum.* Exhibition catalog. Munich: Prestel.

Rhie, Marilyn M., and Robert A. F. Thurman, eds. 1996. *Wisdom and Compassion: The Sacred Art of Tibet.* Exhibition catalog. New York: Tibet House New York in association with Harry N. Abrams.

_____. 2009. *A Shrine for Tibet: The Alice S. Kandell Collection.* New York: Tibet House US, in association with Overlook Duckworth.

Ricca, Franco. 1997. "Stylistic Features of the Pelkhor Chode at Gyantse." In Singer and Denwood 1997, 196–209.

_____. 1999. *Il tempio oracolare di gNas-chuṅ: Gli dei del Tibet più magico e segreto.* Orientalia 8. Alessandria: Edizioni dell'Orso.

Ricca, Franco, and Erberto Lo Bue. 1993. *The Great Stupa of Gyantse: A Complete Tibetan Pantheon of the Fifteenth Century.* London: Serindia.

Riccardi, Theodore. 1989. "The Inscription of King Mānadeva at Changu Narayan." *Journal of the American Oriental Society* 109, no. 4, 611–20.

Richardson, Hugh E. 1947. *Lhasa letter for the week ending the 11 May 1947 from H. E. Richardson, British Trade Agent, Gyantse and Officer in charge, British Mission, Lhasa.* British Library, India Office Records, L/P&S/12/4202.

_____. (1977) 1998. "The Jokhang 'Cathedral' of Lhasa." In Richardson 1998, 237–61.

_____. 1985. *A Corpus of Early Tibetan Inscriptions.* London: Royal Asiatic Society.

_____. 1993. *Ceremonies of the Lhasa Year.* London: Serindia.

_____, ed. 1998. *High Peaks, Pure Earth: Collected Writings on Tibetan History and Culture.* London: Serindia.

Richardson, Sarah A. 2021. "When Walls Could Talk: The Powers of Tibetan Paintings in a Buddhist Library." *Archives of Asian Art* 71, no. 2, 243–68.

Rigzin, Tsepak. 1984. "Rinchen Zangpo: The Great Tibetan Translator (958–1055 A.D.)." *Tibet Journal* 9, no. 3, 28–37.

Roberts, Peter Alan, and Tulku Yeshi, trans. 2019. "Za Ma Tog Bkod Pa/The Basket's Display/Kāraṇḍavyūha." 84000: Translating the Words of the Buddha. http://read.84000.co/translation/toh116.html.

Robinson, David M. 2009. *Empire's Twilight: Northeast Asia Under the Mongols.* Cambridge, MA: Harvard University Asia Center.

Rock, Joseph F. 1947. *The Ancient Na-khi Kingdom of Southwest China*, 2 vols. Cambridge, MA: Harvard University Press.

Rockhill, William Woodville. 1895. "Notes on the Ethnology of Tibet: Based on the Collections of the United States National Museum," *Annual Report of the Board of Regents of the Smithsonian Institution . . . for the Year Ending 1893: Report of the U.S. National Museum*, 665–747. Washington, DC: Smithsonian Institution.

Roerich, George N., trans. 1949. *The Blue Annals*, 2 vols. Calcutta: Royal Asiatic Society of Bengal.

_____. (1949) 1976 and 1979. *The Blue Annals*, 2 vols. Calcutta: Royal Asiatic Society of Bengal. Reprints, Delhi: Motilal Banarsidass. Citations refer to the Motilal Banarsidass editions.

_____, trans. 1959. *Biography of Dharmasvamin (Chag lo tsa-ba Chos-rje-dpal). A Tibetan Monk Pilgrim.* Historical Research Series 2. Patna: K. P. Jayaswal Research Institute.

Ronis, Jann. 2017. "A Letter to the Queen." In *A Gathering of Brilliant Moons: Practice Advice from the Rimé Masters of Tibet*, edited by Holly Gayley and Joshua Schapiro, 109–22. Somerville, MA: Wisdom.

Rospatt, Alexander von. 2009. "The Sacred Origins of the Svayambhūcaitya and the Nepal Valley: Foreign Speculation and Local Myth." *Journal of the Nepal Research Centre* 13, 33–91.

_____. 2010, "Remarks on the Consecration Ceremony in Kuladatta's Kriyāsaṃgrahapañjikā and its Development in Newar Buddhism." In *Hindu and Buddhist Initiations in Nepal and India*, edited by Astrid Zotter and Christof Zotter, 199–262. Wiesbaden: Harrassowitz.

_____. 2011. "The Past Renovations of the Svayambhūcaitya." In Gellek and Maitland 2011, 157–206.

_____. 2013. "Altering the Immutable. Textual Evidence in Support of an Architectural History of the Svayambhū Caitya of Kathmandu." In *Nepalica-Tibetica: Festgabe für Christoph Cüppers*, edited by Franz-Karl Ehrhard and Petra Maurer, 2:91–116. Beiträge zur Zentralasienforschung 28. Andiast: International Institute for Tibetan and Buddhist Studies.

_____. 2014a. "The Mural Paintings of the Svayambhūpurāṇa at the Shrine of Śantipur, and their Origins with Pratāpa Malla." In *Himalayan Passages: Tibetan and Newar Studies in Honor of Hubert Decleer*, edited by Benjamin Bogin and Andrew Quintman, 45–68. Somerville, MA: Wisdom.

_____. 2014b. "Negotiating the Passage beyond a Full Span of Life: Old Age Rituals among the Newars." *South Asia: Journal of South Asian Studies* 37, no. 1, 104–29.

_____. 2015. "Local Literatures: Nepal." In *Brill's Encyclopedia of Buddhism*, edited by Jonathan Silk, Oskar von Hinüber, and Vincent Eltschinger, 1:819–30. Leiden: Brill.

_____. 2019. "Vajracharya Crowns and Diadems: Structure, Iconography, and Function." In *Awaken: A Tibetan Buddhist Journey Toward Enlightenment*, edited by John Henry Rice and Jeffrey S. Durham, 171–79. Exhibition catalog. Richmond: Virginia Museum of Fine Arts.

Ruegg, David S. 1996. *The Life of Bu Ston Rin Po Che: With the Tibetan Text of the Bu Ston rNam Thar.* Rome: Istituto italiano per il Medio ed Estremo Oriente.

Salomon, Richard. 1998. *Indian Epigraphy: A Guide to the Study of Inscriptions in Sanskrit, Prakrit, and Other Indo-Aryan Languages.* Oxford: Oxford University Press.

Salviati, Filippo. 2012. "Tibetan Art between Past and Present: Dialogue with the Past; An Overview of Contemporary Tibetan Artists." In *Tibetan Art between Past and Present: Studies Dedicated to Luciano Petech, Proceedings of the Conference held in Rome on the 3rd of November 2010*, edited by Elena De Rossi Filibeck, 157–68. Pisa: Fabrizio Serra Editore.

Samuel, Geoffrey. 1993. *Civilized Shamans: Buddhism in Tibetan Societies.* Washington, DC: Smithsonian Institution Press.

_____. 2020. "Hidden Lands of Tibet in Myth and History." In *Hidden Lands in Himalayan Myth and History: Transformations of sbas yul through Time*, edited by Frances Garrett, Elizabeth McDougal, and Geoffrey Samuel, 51–91. Brill's Tibetan Studies Library 46. Leiden: Brill.

Samuel, Geoffrey, and Jamyang Oliphant of Rossie, eds. 2020. *About Padmasambhava: Historical Narratives and Later Transformations of Guru Rinpoche.* Zurich: Garuda Verlag.

Sāṅkṛityāyana, Rāhula. 1937. "Second Search of Sanskrit Palm-Leaf Mss. in Tibet." *Journal of the Bihar and Orissa Research Society* 23 (March): 1-57.

Śāntideva, Khenpo Kunpal, and Khenpo Chöga. 2003. "Shantideva's Bodhisattva-charyavatara, according to the Tradition of Paltrül Rinpoche, Commentary by Khenpo Kunpal, with Oral Explanations by Khenpo Chöga." Translated by Andreas Kretschmar. http://www.buddhism.org/Sutras/2/Shantideva.htm.

Schaedler, Luc, director. 2005. *Angry Monk: Reflections on Tibet.* Color film, 1:37. Zurich: Go Between Films.

Schaeffer, Kurtis R. 2005. "The Fifth Dalai Lama Ngawang Lopsang Gyatso." In Brauen 2005, 64–91.

_____. 2006. "Ritual, Festival and Authority Under the Fifth Dalai Lama." In *Power, Politics, and the Reinvention of Tradition: Tibet in the Seventeenth and Eighteenth Centuries. PIATS 2003: Proceedings of the Tenth Seminar of the International Assocation for Tibetan Studies, Oxford 2003*, edited by Bryan J. Cuevas and Kurtis R. Schaeffer, 187–202. Brill's Tibetan Studies Library 3/13. Leiden: Brill.

_____. 2009. *The Culture of the Book in Tibet.* New York: Columbia University Press.

Schafer, Edward. 1963. *The Golden Peaches of Samarkand: A Study of T'ang Exotics.* Berkeley and Los Angeles: University of California Press.

Schram, Louis. 1957. "The Monguors of the Kansu-Tibetan Border, Part II: Their Religious Life." *Transactions of the American Philosophical Society* 47, 1–164.

Schwieger, Peter. 2015. *The Dalai Lama and the Emperor of Tibet: A Political History of the Tibetan Institution of Reincarnation*. New York: Columbia University Press.

Sharma, Prayag Raj. 1972. *Preliminary Study of the Art and Architecture of the Karnali Basin, West Nepal.* Recherche coopérative sur programme 253. Paris: Centre national de la recherche scientifique.

Selig Brown, Kathryn. 2004. *Eternal Presence: Handprints and Footprints in Buddhist Art.* Exhibition catalog. Katonah, NY: Katonah Museum of Art.

Sernesi, Marta. 2011. "A Continuous Stream of Merit: The Early Reprints of gTsang smyon Heruka's Hagiographical Works." *Zentral-Asiatiche Studien* 40, 179–237.

Shakya, Chandra B. 2014. *Golden Faces of Dipankara Buddha, Samyak Mahadan Festival of Nepal: Excellence in Newari Arts and Crafts.* Lalitpur: Mrs. Rita Shakya.

Shakya, Hema Raj. 2004. *Svayambhū Mahācaitya: The Self-Arisen Great Caitya of Nepal*, 496–97, 499, pl. 43. Kathmandu: Swayambhu Vikash Mandal.

Shakya, Milan Ratna. 2011. *Ancient Stone Images of Buddha & Bodhisattva in Nepal.* Kathmandu: Centre for Nepal and Asian Studies.

Shakya, Min Bahadur. 1997. *Life and Contribution of the Nepalese Princess Bhrikuti Devi to Tibetan History*. Delhi: Book Faith India.

_____. 2004. *Hiranyavarṇa Mahāvihāra: A Unique Newar Buddhist Monastery.* Lalitpur: Nagarjuna Publication.

Shakya, Tsering. 2005. "The Thirteenth Dalai Lama, Thupten Gyatso." In Brauen 2005, 137–61.

Shamar Rinpoche. 2012. *A Golden Swan in Turbulent Waters: The Life and Times of the Tenth Karmapa Choying Dorje.* Lexington, VA: Bird of Paradise Press.

Shangderpa, Pema Leyda. 2004. "Blessed Land Shines in Statue Splendour." *The Telegraph*, February 18, 2004. https://www.telegraphindia.com/west-bengal/blessed-land-shines-in-statue-splendour/cid/773130.

Sharf, Robert H. 2013. "Art in the dark: the ritual context of Buddhist caves in western China." In *Art of Merit: Studies in Buddhist Art and its Conservation, Proceedings of the Buddhist Art Forum 2012*, edited by David Park, Kuenga Wangmo, and Sharon Cather, 38–65. London: Archetype.

Shaw, Julia. 1999. "Buddhist Landscapes and Monastic Planning in Eastern Malwa: The Elements of Intervisibility, Surveillance and the Protections of Relics." In *Case Studies in Archaeology and World Religion: The Proceedings of the Cambridge Conference*, edited by Timothy Insoll, 5–17. Oxford: Archaeopress.

Shaw, Miranda Eberle. 2006. *Buddhist Goddesses of India.* Princeton, NJ: Princeton University Press.

Shen Weirong. 2004. "Magic Power, Sorcery and Evil Spirit: The Image of Tibetan Monks in Chinese Literature during the Yuan Dynasty." In *The Relationship Between Religion and State (Chos srid zung 'brel) in Traditional Tibet: Proceedings of a Seminar Held in Lumbini, Nepal, March 2000*, edited by Christoph Cüppers, 189–227. LIRI Seminar Proceedings, Series 1. Lumbini: Lumbini International Research Institute.

_____. 2005. "Studies on Chinese Texts of the Yogic Practices of Tibetan Tantric Buddhism Found in Khara Khoto of Tangut Xia [I]." *Cahiers d'Extrême-Asie* 15, 187–230.

_____. 2011. "Tibetan Buddhism in Mongol-Yuan China (1206–1368)." In *Esoteric Buddhism and the Tantras in East Asia*, edited by Charles Orzech, Henrik Sørensen, and Richard Payne, 539–49. Leiden: Brill.

Sheng, Angela. 1995. "Chinese Silk Tapestry: A Brief Social Historical Perspective of Its Early Development." *Orientations* 26, no. 5 (May): 70–75.

_____. 1998. "Addendum to 'Chinese Silk Tapestry: A Brief Social Historical Perspective of Its Early Development.'" In *Chinese and Central Asian Textiles: Selected Articles from Orientations 1973–1997*, 225. Hong Kong: Orientations.

Shi Jinbo. 2021. *The Economy of Western Xia: A Study of 11th to 13th Century Tangut Records.* Leiden: Brill.

Shim, Hosung. 2014. "The Postal Roads of the Great Khans in Central Asia under the Mongol-Yuan Empire." *Journal of Song-Yuan Studies* 44, 405–69.

Shrestha, Shobha. 2000. "Purnachandi Temple of Lalitpur." *Ancient Nepal* 145, 1–6.

Shrestha, Sukra Sagar. 1996. "Tusa Hiti." *Ancient Nepal: Journal of the Department of Archaeology* 139, 1–10.

Siklós, Bulcsu. 1996. *The Vajrabhairava Tantras.* Tring: The Institute of Buddhist Studies.

Simpson, William. (1896) 2001. *The Buddhist Praying Wheel.* Reprint, London: Adamant Media.

Sinclair, Iain. 2014. "Envisioning Durjayacandra's Saptākṣarasādhana: On the Sources and Sponsors of a Twelfth-Century Painting of Seven-Syllabled Saṃvara." In *Himalayan Passages: Tibetan and Newar Studies in Honor of Hubert Decleer*, edited by Benjamin Bogin and Andrew Quintman, 205–50. Boston: Wisdom.

Singer, Jane Casey. 1994. "Painting in Central Tibet, ca. 950–1450." *Artibus Asiae* 54, nos. 1–2, 96–108.

_____. 1995. "Early Portrait Painting in Tibet." In *Function and Meaning in Buddhist Art*, edited by K. R. van Kooij, 8–99. Groningen: E. Forsten.

_____. 1998a. "The Cultural Roots of Early Tibetan Painting." In Kossak and Singer 1998, 3–24.

_____. 1998b. "An Early Tibetan Painting Revisited: The Ashtamahabhaya Tara in the Ford Collection." *Orientations* 29, no. 10 (October): 65–73.

Singer, Jane Casey, and Philip Denwood, eds. 1997. *Tibetan Art: Towards a Definition of Style.* London: Laurence King.

Singh, Madanjeet. (1968) 1971. *Himalayan Art: Wall-painting and Sculpture in Ladakh, Lahaul and Spiti, the Siwalik Ranges, Nepal, Sikkim and Bhutan.* Unesco Art Books. New York: Collier. Reprint, London: Macmillan.

Siudmak, John. 2013. *The Hindu-Buddhist Sculpture of Ancient Kashmir and Its Influences.* Leiden: Brill.

Skorupski, Tadeusz. 1983. *Tibetan Amulets.* Bangkok: White Orchid Press.

_____. 2001. "Two Eulogies of the Eight Great Caityas." In *Buddhist Forum*, edited by Tadeusz Skorupski, 37–56. Tring: The Institute of Buddhist Studies.

Slusser, Mary Shepherd. 1982. *Nepal Mandala: A Cultural Study of the Kathmandu Valley*, 2 vols. Princeton, NJ: Princeton University Press.

_____. 1988. "Bodhgaya and Nepal." In Leoshko 1988, 125–42.

_____. 1996. "Lord Vishnu and the Kings of Nepal." *Asian Art and Culture: The Himalayas* 9, no. 3, 9–29.

_____. 2005. *Art and Culture of Nepal: Selected Papers.* Kathmandu: Mandala Publication.

Slusser, Mary Shepherd, Nutan Sharma, and James A. Giambrone. 1999. "Metamorphosis: Sheet Metal to Sacred Image in Nepal." *Artibus Asiae* 58, nos. 3–4, 215–52.

Slusser, Mary Shepherd, with Paul Jett. 2010. *The Antiquity of Nepalese Wood Carving: A Reassessment.* Seattle: University of Washington Press

Smith, Stewart. 2013. *The Monasteries of Amdo: A Comprehensive Guide to the Monasteries of the Amdo Region of Tibet.* [In English and Tibetan.] Scott Valley, CA: CreateSpace Independent Publishing Platform.

Snellgrove, David, ed. and trans. (1967) 1980. *The Nine Ways of Bon: Excerpts from gZi-brjid.* Boulder, CO: Prajñā.

_____. 1982. "Buddhism in North India and the Western Himalays—Seventh to Thirteenth Centuries." In Klimburg-Salter 1982, 64–81.

_____. 1987. *Indo-Tibetan Buddhism: Indian Buddhists and Their Tibetan Successors*, 2 vols. Boston: Shambhala.

Snellgrove, David, and Hugh Richardson. 1968. *A Cultural History of Tibet.* London: Weidenfeld & Nicolson.

Snellgrove, David L., and Tadeusz Skorupski, eds. 1980. *The Cultural Heritage of Ladakh, Volume Two: Zangskar and the Cave Temples of Ladakh, with Part 4 on the Inscriptions at Alchi by Philip Denwood.* New Delhi: Vikas.

Solonin, Kirill. 2008. "The Glimpses of Tangut Buddhism." *Central Asiatic Journal* 52, no. 1, 64–127.

_____. 2013a. "Buddhist Connections between the Liao and Xixia: Preliminary Considerations." *Journal of Song-Yuan Studies* 43, 171–219.

_____. 2015. "Local Literatures: Tangut/Xixia." In *Brill's Encyclopedia of Buddhism*, edited by Jonathan A. Silk, 1: 844–59. Leiden: Brill.

_____. 2020. "The Formation of Tangut Ideology: Buddhism and Confucianism." In *Buddhism in Central Asia I: Patronage, Legitimation, Sacred Space, and Pilgrimage*, edited C. Meinert et al., 124–50. Leiden: Brill.

Sopa, Lhundup. 1984. "The Tibetan 'Wheel of Life': Iconography and Doxography." *Journal of the International Association of Buddhist Studies* 7, no. 1, 125–45.

Sørensen, Per K. 1994. *Tibetan Buddhist Historiography: The Mirror Illuminating the Royal Genealogies: An Annotated Translation of the XIVth Century Tibetan Chronicle rGyal-rabs gsal-ba'i melong.* Asiatische Forschungen 128. Wiesbaden: Harrassowitz.

_____. 2019a. "In his Name: The Fake Royal Biography—Fabricated Prophecy and Literary Imposture." *Revue d'Etudes Tibétaines* 52 (October): 284–335.

_____. 2019b. "Rise of the Dalai Lamas: Political Inheritance through Reincarnation." In Debreczeny 2019a, 151–69.

Sørensen, Per K., and Guntram Hazod, in cooperation with Tsering Gyalbo. 2005. *Thundering Falcon: An Inquiry into the History and Cult of Khra-'brug, Tibet's First Buddhist Temple.* Vienna: Verlag der Österreichischen Akademie der Wissenschaften.

_____. 2007. *Rulers on the Celestial Plain: Ecclesiastic and Secular Hegemony in Medieval Tibet: A Study of Tshal Gung-thang.* Vienna: Verlag der Österreichischen Akademie der Wissenschaften.

Sorenson, Michelle Janet. 2013. "Making the Old New Again and Again: Legitimation and Innovation in the Tibetan Buddhist Chöd Tradition." PhD diss., Columbia University.

Sperling, Elliot. 1983. "Early Ming Policy toward Tibet: An Examination of the Proposition that the Early Ming Emperors Adopted a 'Divide and Rule' Policy toward Tibet." PhD diss., Indiana University.

_____. 1987. "Lama to the King of Hsia." *Journal of the Tibet Society* 7, 32–33.

_____. 1988. "The Szechwan-Tibet Frontier in the Fifteenth Century." *Ming Studies* 26 (Fall): 37–55.

_____. 1990. "Hulegu and Tibet." *Acta Orientalia Academiae Scientiarum Hungaricae* 44, nos. 1–2, 145–57.

_____. 1991. "Some Remarks on sGa A-gnyan dam-pa and the Origins of the Hor-pa Lineage of the dKar-mdzes Region." In *Tibetan History and Language: Studies Dedicated to Uray Géza on His Seventieth Birthday*, edited by Ernst Steinkellner, 455–65. Vienna: Arbeitskreis für Tibetische und Buddhistische Studien, Universität Wien.

_____. 2003. "The 5th Karma-pa and Some Aspects of the Relationship between Tibet and the Early Ming." In *The History of Tibet*, edited by Alex McKay, *The Medieval Period, c. 850–1895: The Development of Buddhist Paramountcy*, 2:473–82. London: Routledge Curzon.

_____. 2004a. "Further Remarks Apropos of the 'Ba'-Rom-Pa and the Tanguts." *Acta Orientalia Academiae Scientiarum Hungary* 57, no. 1, 1–26.

_____. 2004b. "Karma Rol-pa'i rdo-rje and the Re-Establishment of Karma-pa Political Influence in the 14th Century." In *The Relationship between Religion and State (Chos srid zung 'brel) in Traditional Tibet: Proceedings of a Seminar Held in Lumbini, Nepal, March 2000*, edited by Christoph Cüppers, 229–44. LIRI Seminar Proceedings, Series 1. Lumbini: Lumbini International Research Institute.

_____. 2009. "Tibetan Buddhism, Perceived and Imagined, along the Ming-Era Sino-Tibetan Frontier." In Kapstein 2009a, 155–80.

Spiro, Melford. 1982. *Buddhism and Society: A Great Tradition and Its Burmese Vicissitudes*. Berkeley: University of California Press.

Stagg, Christopher, trans. 2016. *The Hundred Thousand Songs of Milarepa*. Boulder, CO: Shambhala.

Stein, R. A. 1972. *Tibetan Civilization*. Translated by J. E. Stapleton Driver. Stanford, CA: Stanford University Press.

Steinkellner, Ernst. 2004. *A Tale of Leaves: On Sanskrit Manuscripts in Tibet, Their Past and Their Future*. 2003 Gonda Lecture. Amsterdam: Royal Netherlands Academy of Arts and Sciences.

Stevenson, Daniel. 1996. "Visions of Mañjuśrī on Mount Wutai." In *Religions of China in Practice*, edited by Donald S. Lopez, 203–22. Princeton, NJ: Princeton University Press.

Stevenson, John, Donald Alan Wood, and Philippe Truong. 2011. *Dragons and Lotus Blossoms: Vietnamese Ceramics from the Birmingham Museum of Art*. Exhibition catalog. Seattle: University of Washington Press.

Stevenson, Mark. 2005. *Many Paths: Searching for Old Tibet in New China*. Melbourne: Lothian Books.

Stoddard, Heather. 1985a. "A Stone Sculpture of mGur mGon-po, Mahakala of the Tent, Dated 1292." *Oriental Art* 31, no. 3 (Autumn): 278–82.

_____. 1985b. *Le mendiant de l'Amdo*. Paris: Société d'ethnographie.

_____. 1996. "Early Tibetan Paintings: Sources and Styles (Eleventh–Fourteenth Centuries A.D.)." *Archives of Asian Art* 49, 26–50.

_____. 2003. "Fourteen Centuries of Tibetan Portraiture." In Dinwiddie 2003, 16–61.

_____. 2008. *Early Sino-Tibetan Art*, 2nd ed. Bangkok: Orchid Press. First published 1975 by Aris and Phillips (Warminster).

Studholme, Alexander. 2012. *The Origins of* Oṃ Maṇipadme Hūṃ: *A Study of the* Kāraṇḍavyūha Sūtra. Albany: SUNY Press.

Sugiki, Tsunehiko. 2003. "Five Types of Internal Maṇḍala described in the Cakrasaṃvara Buddhist Literature: Somatic Representations of One's Innate Sacredness." *Tōkyō Daigaku Tōyō Bunka Kenkyūjo*東洋文化研究所紀要 [Notes of the Institute of Oriental Culture, Tokyo University] 144, 276–202 [157–203]. Tokyo: Institute of Oriental Culture, University of Tokyo.

Sun Wenjing. 1988. "Remarks on the Cataloguing and Classification of Tibetan Classics and Literary Texts: A Preliminary Survey of the Tibetan Collection in the China Library of Nationalities in Beijing." *Studies in Central and East Asian Religions* 1 (Autumn): 88–101.

Sun, Zhixin. 1999. "A Quest for the Imperishable: Chao Meng-fu's Calligraphy for Stele Inscriptions." In *The Embodied Image: Chinese Calligraphy from the John B. Elliott Collection*, edited by Robert Harrist Jr. and Wen C. Fong, 302–19. Exhibition catalog. Princeton, NJ: The Art Museum, Princeton University.

Suolang Wangdui (Bsod nams dbang 'dus). 1994. *Art of Tibetan Rock Paintings*. Introduction by Li Yongxian and Huo Wei. Chengdu: Sichuan People's Publishing House.

Swoyambhu Stupa. 2019–22. https://swoyambhustupa.com/.

Takeuchi, Tsuguhito. 2012. "Old Tibetan Rock Inscriptions near Alchi." In *Historical Developments in Tibetan Languages: Proceedings of the Workshop B of the 17th Himalayan Languages Symposium (Kobe, 6th–9th September 2011)*, edited by Tsuguhito Takeuchi and Norihiko Hayashi, 29–70. Kobe: Kobe City University of Foreign Studies.

Tanaka, Kimiaki. 1995. "Mandala des Huit Divinités, section du Lotus." In *Sérinde, Terre de Bouddha Dix Siècles d'art sur la Route de la Soie*, edited by Jacques Giès and M. Cohen, 400–401. Exhibition catalog. Paris: Réunion des musées nationaux.

Taring, Rinchen Dolma. 1986 (1970). *Daughter of Tibet: The Autobiography of Rinchen Dolma Taring*. Reprint, Boston: Wisdom.

Tashi Tsering, ed. 2000. "Situ Panchen: His Contribution and Legacy." Special issue, *Lungta* 13 (Winter). Dharamsala: Amnye Machen Institute.

_____. 2010. "Jowo Śākyamuni: The Central Figure of the Great Temple of Magical Emanation at Rasa: A Representative Image Conferring Liberation through Sight, Which Is [recognized as] One of the Six Modes of Liberation." In Dorje et al. 2010, 122–57.

_____. 2011. "Preliminary Notes on the Origin of the Blama Nipa Storytellers and Their Fate in Exile Today." In *Disciples of a Crazy Saint: The Buchen of Spiti*, edited by Patrick Sutherland and Tashi Tsering, 77–112. Exhibition catalog. Oxford: Pitt Rivers Museum.

_____. 2013. "Si tu paṇ chen and His Painting Style: A Retrospective." In special issue, *Journal of the International Association of Tibetan Studies*, no. 7 (August), edited by Karl Debreczeny, 125–92. https://www.thlib.org/collections/texts/jiats/#!jiats=/07/tsering/.

Tashi, Tsewang. 2014. "Modernism in Tibetan Art: The Creative Journey of Four Artists." PhD diss., Norwegian University of Science and Technology.

_____. 2020. "Early Modern Art in Tibet: Gendun Chophel and Amdo Jampa." Virtual lecture, Columbia University, New York, November 19, 2020.

Teiser, Stephen F. 2006. *Reinventing the Wheel: Paintings of Rebirth in Medieval Buddhist Temples*. Seattle: University of Washington Press.

Teleki, Krisztina. 2011. *Monasteries and Temples of Bogdiin Khüree (1651–1938)*. Ulaanbaatar: Institute of History, Mongolian Academy of Sciences.

_____. 2015. *Introduction to the Study of Urga's Heritage*. Ulaanbaatar: Mongolian Academy of Sciences.

Tenzin, Acharya Kirti Tulku Lobsang. 1982. "Early Relations between Tibbet [sic] and Nepal (7th to 8th Centuries)." Translated by K. Dhondup. *Tibet Journal* 7, nos. 1–2 (Spring/Summer): 83–86.

Tenzin (Bstan 'dzin). 1992. "A Brief Description of Yumbu Lakhar Castle." *Tibet Journal* 17, no. 2 (summer): 59–64.

Tenzin Chögyel. 2015. *The Life of the Buddha*. Translated with introduction by Kurtis R. Schaeffer. New York: Penguin Classics.

Tenzin Dickie. 2016. "Yuthok Tashi Dhondup", Treasury of Lives. http://treasuryoflives.org/biographies/view/Yuthok-Tashi-Dhondup/9333.

Tsering, P. 1947. *Lhasa letter for the week ending the 19 October 1947 from P. Tsering for the Officer in charge, Indian Mission Lhasa*. British Library, India Office Records, L/P&S/12/4202.

Tharchin, Lobsang. 1984. *King Udrayana and the Wheel of Life: The History and Meaning of the Buddhist Teaching of Dependent Origination*. Howell, NJ: Mahayana Sutra and Tantra Press.

Thaye, Pema Namdol. 2021. "Celestial Visions in Three Dimensions: How Pema Namdol Thaye Builds Mandalas, Bringing Cosmic Realms to Life; Interview by Elena Pakhoutova. In *Spiral Magazine*, 8–13. New York: Rubin Museum of Art. https://rubinmuseum.org/spiral/celestial-visions-in-three-dimensions.

Thomas, F. W. 1935–63. *Tibetan Literary Texts and Documents Concerning Chinese Turkestan*. London: Royal Asiatic Society.

Tibetan and Himalayan Library. 2019. "gtor ma" entry at THL Tibetan to English Translation Tool. https://www.thlib.org/reference/dictionaries/tibetan-dictionary/translate.php.

Timalsina, Sthaneshwar. 2006. "Terrifying Beauty: Interplay of the Sanskritic and Vernacular Rituals of Siddhilakṣmī." *International Journal of Hindu Studies* 10, no. 1, 59–73.

Toffin, Gérard. 2007. *Newar Society: City, Village and Periphery*. Lalitpur: Social Science Baha; Kathmandu: Himal Books.

Tong, Tao, and Linhui Li. 2016. "The Himalayan Gold Masks from the Eurasian Perspective." *Chinese Archaeology* 16, no. 1, 85–90.

Toyka-Fuong, Ursula. 1998. "The Influence of Pāla Art on 11th-Century Wall-Paintings of Grotto 76 in Dunhuang." In *The Inner Asian International Style 12th–14th Centuries*, edited by Deborah E. Klimburg-Salter and Eva Allinger, 67–95. Vienna: Verlag der Österreichischen Akademie der Wissenschaften.

Trace Foundation. 2015. *Transcending Tibet: 30 Contemporary Artists Explore What It Means to Be Tibetan Today*. Exhibition catalog. New York: Trace Foundation.

Travers, Alice. 2011a. "The Careers of the Noble Officials of the Ganden Phodrang (1895–1959): Organisation and Hereditary Divisions within the Service of State." In *Revisiting Tibetan Culture and History. Proceedings of the Second International Seminar of Young Tibetologists, Paris, 2009*, vol. 1, edited by Kalsang Norbu Gurung, Tim Myatt, Nicola Schneider, and Alice Travers; special issue, *Revue d'Etudes Tibétaines* 21 (October): 155–74. https://himalaya.socanth.cam.ac.uk/collections/journals/ret/pdf/ret_21_08.pdf.

_____. 2011b. "The Horse-riding and Target-shooting Contest for Lay Officials (drung 'khor rtsal rgyugs): Reflections on the Military Identity of the Tibetan Aristocracy at the Beginning of the 20th Century." In *Études mongoles et sibériennes, centrasiatiques et tibétaines (EMSCAT)* 42. https://doi.org/10.4000/emscat.1850.

Trevnick, Alan. 1999. "British Archaeologists, Hindu Abbots, and Burmese Buddhists: The Mahābodhi Temple at Bodh Gaya, 1811–1877." *Modern Asian Studies* 33, 635–56.

Tropper, Kurt. 2007. "The Historical Inscription in the Gsum brtsegs Temple at Wanla, Ladakh." In *Text, Image and Song in Transdisciplinary Dialogue. PIATS 2003: Proceedings of the Tenth Seminar of the International Association for Tibetan Studies, Oxford 2003*, edited by Deborah Klimburg-Salter, Kurt Tropper, and Christian Jahoda, 105–50. Brill's Tibetan Studies Library 10/7. Leiden: Brill.

Tsangwang Gendun Tenpa. 2019. "Tibetan Buddhism and Art in the Mongol Empire According to Tibetan Sources." Translated by Eveline Washul. In Debreczeny 2019a, 105–23.

Tsewang Dongyal, Khenpo. 2008. *Light of Fearless Indestructible Wisdom: The Life and Legacy of HH Dudjom Rinpoche*. Ithaca, NY: Snow Lion.

Tsewang Tashi. 2018. *A History of Art in Twentieth Century Tibet*. Beijing: China Tibetology Publishing House.

Tsomu, Yudru. 2013. "Taming the Khampas: The Republican Construction of Eastern Tibet." *Modern China* 39, no. 3 (May): 319–44.

Tsultem, Nyam-Osoryn. 1982. *The Eminent Mongolian Sculptor–G. Zanabazar*. Ulaanbaatar: Gosizdatel'stvo.

_____. 1986. *Mongol'skaja nacional'naja živopis "mongol zurag"/Development of the Mongolian National Style Painting "Mongol Zurag" in Brief*. [In Russian, English, French, and Spanish.] Ulaanbaatar: Gosizdatel'stvo.

_____. 1987. *Dekorativno-prikladnoe iskusstvo Mongolii / Mongolian Arts and Crafts / Arts artisanaux de la Mongolie*. [In Russian, English, French, and Spanish.] Ulaanbaatar: Gosizdatel'stvo.

_____. 1988. *Mongolian Architecture*. Ulaanbaatar: Gosizdatel'stvo.

_____. 1989. *Mongolian Sculpture*. Ulaanbaatar: Gosizdatel'stvo.

Tsultemin, Uranchimeg. 2015. "The Power and Authority of Maitreya in Mongolia." In *Buddhism in Mongolian History, Culture, and Society*, edited by Vesna Wallace, 137–59. Oxford: Oxford University Press.

_____. 2018. "Mongolian Art and the Dilemma of Himalayan Affilication." *South Asian Studies* 34, no. 2, 137–53.

_____. 2020. *A Monastery on the Move: Art and Politics in Later Buddhist Mongolia*. Honolulu: University of Hawai'i Press.

Tucci, Giuseppe. 1932. *Indo-Tibetica I: "Mc'od rten" e "Ts'a ts'a" nel Tibet indiano ed occidentale, contributo allo studio dell'arte religiosa tibetana e del suo significato*. Rome: Reale accademia d'Italia.

_____. (1932) 1988. *Rin-chen-bzan-po and the Renaissance of Buddhism in Tibet around the Millenium*. Translated by Nancy Kipp Smith and edited by Lokesh Chandra. *Indo-Tibetica* 2. Reprint, New Delhi: Aditya Prakashan.

_____. (1932–41) 1989. *Gyantse and Its Monasteries*. Edited by Lokesh Chandra. Translated by Uma Marina Vesci. 3 vols. *Indo-Tibetica* 4. Reprint, New Delhi: Aditya Prakashan.

_____. 1941. *Indo-Tibetica 4: Gyantse ed i suoi monasteri*, 3 vols. Roma: Reale Accademia d'Italia.

_____. 1949. *Tibetan Painted Scrolls*, 3. vols. Roma: La Libreria dello Stato

_____. (1949) 1999. *Tibetan Painted Scrolls*, 3 vols. Reprint, Bangkok: SDI Publications.

_____. 1956a. *Preliminary Report on Two Scientific Expeditions in Nepal*. Serie Orientale Roma 10, Materials for the Study of Nepalese History and Culture 1. Rome: Istituto Italiano per il Medio ed Estremo Oriente.

_____. 1956b. *To Lhasa and Beyond: Diary of an Expedition to Tibet in the Year 1948*. Rome: Istituto Poligrafico dello Stato.

_____. 1962. *Nepal: The Discovery of the Malla*. London: Allen and Unwin.

_____. 1973. *Transhimalaya*. Geneva: Nagel.

_____. 1977. "On Swāt. The Dards and Connected Problems." *East and West* 27, nos.1–4, 9–103.

_____. 1988a. *The Religions of Tibet*. Translated by Geoffrey Samuel. Berkeley: University of California Press.

_____. 1988b. *Stupa: Art, Architectonics and Symbolism*. New Delhi: Aditya Prakashan.

Tucci, Giuseppe, and Eugenio Ghersi. (1933) 1996. *Secrets of Tibet: Being the Chronicle of the Tucci Scientific Expedition to Western Tibet (1933)*. Translated by Mary A. Johnstone. Reprint, New Delhi: Cosmo Publications.

Tuladhar-Douglas, Will. 2007. *Remaking Buddhism for Medieval Nepal: The Fifteenth-Century Reformation of Newar Buddhism*. London: Routledge.

Tulisow, Jerzy, Osamu Inoue, Agata Bareja-Starzyńska, and Ewa Dziurzyńska, eds. 2012. *In the Heart of Mongolia: 100th Anniversary of W. Kotwicz's Expedition to Mongolia in 1912*. Cracow: Polish Academy of Arts and Sciences (with DVD).

Tulku Thondup Rinpoche. 1982. *Buddhist Civilization in Tibet*. [Cambridge, MA]: Maha Siddha Nyingma Center.

_____. 1997. *Hidden Teachings of Tibet: An Explanation of the Terma Tradition of Tibetan Buddhism*. Boston: Wisdom.

Tung, Rosemary. 1996. *A Portrait of Lost Tibet*. Berkeley: University of California Press.

Tunstall, Alexandra. 2012. "Beyond Categorization: Zhu Kerou's Tapestry Painting *Butterfly and Camellia*." *East Asian Science, Technology, and Medicine* 36, no. 1, 39–76.

Tuttle, Gray. 2005. *Tibetan Buddhists in the Making of Modern China*. New York: Columbia University Press.

Tuttle, Gray, and Johan Elverskog, eds. 2011. "Wutai Shan and Qing Culture." Special issue, *Journal of the International Association of Tibetan Studies* 6.

Twist, Rebecca L. 2018. "Images of the Crowned Buddha along the Silk Road: Iconography and Ideology." *Humanities* 7, no. 4, 92. https://doi.org/10.3390/h7040092.

Untracht, Oppi. 1997. *Traditional Jewelry of India*. New York: Abrams.

Unveiling Our Sacred Tibetan Treasures. n.d. Singapore: Spiritual Antique Land.Vajrācārya, Dhanavajra, and Kamal P. Malla. 1985. *The Gopālarājavaṃśāvalī*. Nepal Research Centre Publication 9. Wiesbaden: Franz Steiner Verlag.

Vajracharya, Gautama V. 2003. "Threefold Intimacy: The Recent Discovery of an Outstanding Nepalese Portrait Painting." *Orientations* 34, no. 4 (April): 40–45.

_____. 2004a. "Crown Jewel of Newar Painting: Discovery of a Masterpiece." In Pal 2004b, 64–79.

_____. 2004b. "Elements of Newar Buddhist Art: *Circle of Bliss*—A Review Article." Asianart.com. Published December 22, 2004. https://www.asianart.com/articles/circle/index.html, search> "jivarama"

_____. 2009. "The Creatures of the Rain Rivers, Cloud Lakes: Newars Saw Them, So Did Ancient India." Asianart.com. Published January 7, 2009. https://www.asianart.com/articles/rainrivers/index.html.

_____. 2013. *Frog Hymns and Rain Babies: Monsoon Culture and the Art of Ancient South Asia*. Mumbai: Marg Foundation.

_____. 2014. "Kirtimukha, The Serpentine Motif, and Garuda: The Story of a Lion that Turned into a Big Bird." *Artibus Asiae* 74, no. 2, 311–36.

_____. 2016. *Nepalese Seasons: Rain and Ritual*. Exhibition catalog. New York: Rubin Museum of Art. https://issuu.com/rmanyc/docs/nepalase_seasons_-_combo-_96_ppi.

_____. 2018. "Nepal Samvat and Vikrama Samvat: Discerning Original Significance." Asianart.com. Published November 6, 2018. https://www.asianart.com/articles/gvv-lecture/index.html.

_____. 2020. "Sculpted Spouts of Nepalese Fountains and Vedic Evidence: Dolphin Deified—A Review Article." *Electronic Journal of Vedic Studies* 25, no. 3, 1–23. https://crossasia-journals.ub.uni-heidelberg.de/index.php/ejvs/article/view/13105/12835.

Van Alphen, Jan, ed. 2013. *The All-Knowing Buddha: A Secret Guide*. With essays by Christian Luczanits, Elena Pakhoutova, and Karl Debreczeny. Exhibition catalog. Antwerp: BAI; New York: Rubin Museum of Art. https://issuu.com/rmanyc/docs/all_knowing_buddha_online.

van der Kuijp, Leonard W. J. 1993. "Jayānanda. A Twelfth Century *Guoshi* from Kashmir Among the Tangut." *Central Asiatic Journal* 37, no. 3/4, 188–97.

_____. 1995. "'Baγši' and Baγši-s in Tibetan Historical, Biographical and Lexicographical Texts." *Central Asiatic Journal* 39, no. 2, 275–302.

_____. 2018. "The Bird-faced Monk and the Beginnings of the New Tantric Tradition, Part One." In *Tibetan Genealogies: Studies in Memorium of Guge Tsering Gyalpo (1961–2015)*, edited by Guntram Hazod and Shen Weirong, 403–50. Beijing: China Tibetology Publishing.

van Ham, Peter. 2014. "The Khawaling Chörten: A Unique Sculpted and Painted Mandala at Nyoma, Ladakh." *Orientations* 45, no. 5 (June): 28–40.

_____. 2016. Guge, *Ages of Gold: The West Tibetan Masterpieces*. Munich: Hirmer.

van Schaik, Sam. 2022. "The Advent of the Dharma: Religion and Rationality in the Coming of Buddhism to Tibet." In Hazod, Fermer, and Jahoda 2022, 153–60.

Vandier-Nicolas, Nicole. 1974. *Bannières et Peintures de Touen-Houang Conservées au Musée Guimet*. Mission Paul Pelliot, sous la direction de Louis Hambis 14. Paris: l'Académie des Inscriptions et Belles-Lettres.

Vér, Martón. 2016. "The Origins of the Postal System of the Mongol Empire." *Archivum Eurasiae Medii Aevi* 22, 221–39.

_____. 2017. "Religious Communities and the Postal System of the Mongol Empire." In *Role of Religions in the Turkic Culture*, edited by Éva Csáki, Mária Ivanics, and Zsuzsanna Olach, 291–306. Budapest: Péter Pázmány Catholic University.

Vergati, Anne. 1995. *Gods, Men, and Territory: Society and Culture in Kathmandu Valley*. New Delhi: Manohar.

_____. 2000. *Gods and Masks of the Kathmandu Valley*. New Delhi: DK Printworld.

Vitali, Roberto. 1990. *Early Temples of Central Tibet*. London: Serindia.

_____. 1996. *The Kingdoms of Gu.ge Pu.hrang According to mNga'.ris rgyal.rabs by Gu.ge mkhan.chen Ngag.dbang grags.pa*. Dharamsala: Tho ling gtsug lag khang lo gcig stong 'khor ba'i rjes dran mdzad sgo'i go sgrig tshogs chung.

_____. 1999. *Records of Tho-ling: A Literary and Visual Reconstruction of the "Mother" Monastery in Gu-ge*. New Delhi: High Asia.

_____. 2001. "Sa skya and the mNga' ris skor gsum legacy: the case of Rin chen bzang po's flying mask." *Lungta* 14 (Spring): 5–44.

_____. 2009–10. "In the Presence of the 'Diamond Throne': Tibetans at rDo rje gden (Last Quarter of the 12th Century to the Year 1300)." In "The Earth Ox Papers," special issue, *Tibet Journal* 34/35, no. 3/2, 161–208.

_____. 2012a. *The dGe lugs pa in Gu ge and the Western Himalaya*. Dharamshala: Amnye Machen Tibetan Institute for Advanced Studies.

_____. 2012b. *A Short History of Mustang (10th–15th century)*. Dharamsala: Amnye Machen Tibetan Institute for Advanced Studies.

_____. 2020. "lHa sa's Hectic Years ca. 975–1160. In *On a Day of a Month of the Fire Bird Year, Festschrift for Peter Schwieger on the Occasion of His 65th Birthday*, edited by Jeanine Bischoff, Petra Maurer, and Charles Ramble. Lumbini: Lumbini International Research Institute.

von Hinüber, Oskar. 2004. *Die Palola Ṣāhis: Ihre Steininschriften, Inschriften auf Bronzen, Handschriftenkolophone und Schutzzauber; Materialien zur Geschichte von Gilgit und Chilas*. Mainz: Philipp von Zabern.

_____. 2015. "An Inscribed Avalokiteśvara from the Hemis Monastery, Ladakh." *Annual Report of the International Research Institute for Advanced Buddhology at Soka University for the Academic Year 2014* 18, 3–9.

von Schroeder, Ulrich. 1981. *Indo-Tibetan Bronzes*. Hong Kong: Visual Dharma Publications.

_____. 2001a. *Buddhist Sculptures in Tibet*, 2 vols. Hong Kong: Visual Dharma Publications.

_____. 2001b. "Nepal: Licchavi Period; Wood Carvings of the Jokhang of Lhasa." In von Schroeder 2001a, 1:407–31.

_____. 2006. *Empowered Masters: Tibetan Wall Paintings of Mahāsiddhas at Gyantse*. Chicago: Serindia.

_____. 2008. *108 Buddhist Statues in Tibet*. Chicago: Serindia.

_____. 2019. *Nepalese Stone Sculptures*. 2 vols. Weesen: Visual Dharma Publications.

von Schroeder, Ulrich, and Heidi von Schroeder. 2009. *Tibetan Art of the Alain Bordier Foundation*. Hong Kong: Visual Dharma Publications.

von Schroeder, Ulrich, and Joachim G. Karsten. 2009. "The Silver Jug of the Lhasa Jokhang: a Reply." Asianart.com. Published July 13, 2009. https://www.asianart.com/articles/silver_jug/index.html#3.

Wallace, Vesna. 2001. *The Inner Kālacakratantra: A Buddhist Tantric View of the Individual*. Oxford: Oxford University Press.

_____. 2015. "How Vajrapāṇi Became a Mongol." In *Buddhism in Mongolian History, Culture, and Society*, edited by Vesna Wallace, 179–201. New York: Oxford University Press.

Walsh, Michael. 2020. "Reincarnation." In *Stating the Sacred: Religion, China, and the Formation of the Nation-State*, 87–108. New York: Columbia University Press.

Wang, Xiangyun. 1995. "Tibetan Buddhism at the Court of Qing." PhD diss., Harvard University.

Wang Yao. 1994. "A Cult of Mahākāla in Beijing." In *Tibetan Studies: Proceedings of the Sixth Seminar of the International Association for Tibetan Studies, Fagernes, 1992*, vol. 2, edited by Per Kvaerne, 957–64. Oslo: Institute for Comparative Research in Human Culture.

Wang-Toutain, Françoise. 2017. *Le décor de la tombe de Qianlong (r. 1735–1796): Un empereur mandchou et le bouddhisme tibétain*. Paris: Françoise Wang-Toutain.

Wangchuck, Ashi Kesang Choden T., ed. 2016. *Tashi Gomang: A National Treasure of Bhutan*. With texts by Thierry Mathou, Tshering Tashi, and Lam Kezang Chhoephel. Exhibition catalog. Thimphu: Royal Textile Academy.

Warner, Cameron David. 2008. "The Precious Lord: The History and Practice of the Cult of the Jo bo Śākyamuni in Lhasa, Tibet." PhD diss., Harvard University.

_____. 2011a. "The Genesis of Tibet's First Buddha Images: An Annotated Translation from Three Editions of the 'Vase-shaped Pillar Testament (*bka' chems ka khol ma*).'" *Light of Wisdom* 1, no. 1, 33–45.

_____. 2011b. "A Miscarriage of History: Wencheng Gongzhu and Sino-Tibetan Historiography." *Inner Asia* 13, no. 2, 239–64.

_____. 2011c. "Re/crowning the Jowo Śākyamuni: Texts, Photographs, and Memories." *History of Religions* 51, no. 1, 1–30.

Watt, James C. Y., ed. 2010. *The World of Khubilai Khan: Chinese Art in the Yuan Dynasty*. Exhibition catalog. New York: The Metropolitan Museum of Art.

Watt, James C. Y., An Jiayao, Angela F. Howard, Boris I. Marshak, Su Bai, and Zhao Feng. 2005. *China: Dawn of a Golden Age, 200–750 A.D.* Exhibition catalog. New York: The Metropolitan Museum of Art.

Watt, James C. Y., and Anne E. Wardwell, eds. 1997. *When Silk Was Gold: Central Asian and Chinese Textiles*. Exhibition catalog. New York: The Metropolitan Museum of Art in cooperation with the Cleveland Museum of Art.

Watt, James C. Y., and Denise Patry Leidy. 2005. *Defining Yongle: Imperial Art in Early Fifteenth-Century China*. Exhibition catalog. New York: The Metropolitan Museum of Art.

Watt, Jeff. 2017. "Torma Offering Main Page." HAR: Himalayan Art Resources. https://www.himalayanart.org/search/set.cfm?setID=1062&page=1.

_____. 2018–19. "Tibet: Dratang Monastery (SRG Archive)." HAR: Himalayan Art Resources. Updated September 2018, April 2019. https://www.himalayanart.org/search/set.cfm?setID=1375

_____. 2019. "Sculpture: Dolonnor Style, Inner Mongolia." HAR: Himalayan Art Resources. https://www.himalayanart.org/search/set.cfm?setID=4357.

_____. "Mandala of Hayagriva (Buddhist Deity)—Red with Consort (1 Face, 2 Hands)." n.d. HAR: Himalayan Art Resources. Accessed June 29, 2021. https://www.himalayanart.org/items/30911.

Wayman, Alex. 1973. *The Buddhist Tantras: Light on Indo-Tibetan Esotericism*. New York: S. Weiser.

Wayman, Alex, and Ryujun Tajima. 1998. *The Enlightenment of Vairocana*. Delhi: Motilal Banarsidass.

Wei, Huo (Hou Wei). 2012. "A Study of Ancient Tibetan Gold and Silver Ware." Translated by Suzanne Cahill 柯素芝 and Ye Wa 叶娃. *Chinese Archeology* 12 (2012): 165–74. https://doi.org/10.1515/char-2012-0020.

Weiner, Benno. 2020. *The Chinese Revolution on the Tibetan Frontier*. Ithaca, NY: Cornell University Press.

Weldon, David, and Jane Casey Singer. 1999. The *Sculptural Heritage of Tibet: Buddhist Art in the Nyingjei Lam Collection*. Exhibition catalog. London: Laurence King.

White, John Claude. 1909. *Sikhim & Bhutan: Twenty-One Years on the North-East Frontier, 1887–1908*. London: E. Arnold.

White, Lynn. 2018. *Medieval Religion and Technology: Collected Essays*. Berkeley: University of California Press.

Whitfield, Roderick. 1982. *The Art of Central Asia: The Stein Collection in the British Museum, Vol. 1, Paintings from Dunhuang*. Tokyo: Kodansha International.

Willson, Martin. 1986. *In Praise of Tara: Songs to the Saviouress*. London: Wisdom.

Willson, Martin, and Martin Brauen, eds. 2000. *Deities of Tibetan Buddhism: The Zürich Paintings of the Icons Worthwhile to See* (*Bris sku mthong ba don ldan*). Boston: Wisdom.

Wilson, Horace Hayman. 1841. *Travels in the Himalayan Provinces of Hindustan and the Panjab, in Ladakh and Kashmir, in Peshawar, Kabul, Kunduz and Bokhara by Mr. William Moorcroft and Mr. George Trebeck from 1819 to 1825*, 2 vols. London: John Murray.

Wiltermuth, Scott S., and Chip Heath. 2009. "Synchrony and Cooperation." *Psychological Science* 20, no. 1, 1–5.

Winder, Marianne. 1992. "Aspects of the History of the Prayer Wheel." *Journal of the Tibet Society* 28, 25–33.

Winkler, Jakob. 2002. "The rDzogs Chen Murals of the Klu-khang in Lhasa." In *Religion and Secular Culture of Tibet: Tibetan Studies II. PIATS 2000: Proceedings of the Ninth Seminar of the International Assocaition for Tibetan Studies, Leiden 2000*, edited by Henk Blezer with Abel Zadoks, 321–43. Brill's Tibetan Studies Library 2/7. Leiden: Brill.

_____. 2016. "The Literary Sources of the Klu-Khang Murals." In *Sharro: Festschrift for Chögyal Namkhai Norbu*, edited by Donatella Rossi and Charles Jamyang Oliphant of Rossie. Rudolfstetten: Garuda Verlag.

Woeser, Tsering. 2020. *Forbidden Memory: Tibet During the Cultural Revolution*. Omaha: Potomac Books.

Wong, Dorothy C. 1993. "A Reassessment of the Representation of Mt. Wutai from Dunhuang Cave 61." *Archives of Asian Art* 46, 27–52.

_____. 2002. "The Making of a Saint: Images of Xuanzang in East Asia." *Early Medieval China* 8, 43–98.

_____. 2007. "The Case of Amoghapāśa." *Journal of Inner Asian Art and Archaeology* 2, 151–58.

Wood, Christopher S. 2019. *A History of Art History.* Princeton, NJ: Princeton University Press.

Woodward, Hiram. 1981. "Burmese Sculpture and Indian Painting." In *Chhavi-2: Rai Krishnadasa Felicitation Volume*, edited by Raya Krishnadasa et al., 21–24. Banaras: Bharat Kala Bhavan.

Wu, Lan. 2017. "Crafting Buddhist Art in Qing China's Contact Zones during the Eighteenth Century." *Journal 18: A Journal of Eighteenth-Century Art and Culture* 4 (Fall). https://www.journal18.org/issue4/crafting-buddhist-art-in-qing-chinas-contact-zones-during-the-eighteenth-century/.

Wylie, Turrell V. (1979) 2003. "Lama Tribute in the Ming Dynasty." In *The History of Tibet*, edited by Alex McKay, vol. 2, *The Medieval Period, c. 850–1895: The Development of Buddhist Paramountcy*," 467–72. Reprint, London: Routledge Curzon.

_____. 1980. "Monastic Patronage in 15th Century Tibet." *Acta Orientalia Academiae Scientiarum Hungaricae* 34, nos. 1–3, 319–28.

Xie Jisheng. 2019. "Tibetan Buddhism and Tibetan Buddhist Art in the Xixia Kingdom." Translated by Michelle McCoy. In Debreczeny 2019a, 83–103.

Xuanzang. 1996. *The Great Tang Dynasty Record of the Western Regions.* Translated by Li Rongxi. Berkeley: Numata Center for Buddhist Translation and Research.

Yablonsky, Gabrielle. 2002. "Sculpture in Bhutan: The Tshogs Zhing in the Paro Museum." In *Impressions of Bhutan and Tibetan Art: Tibetan Studies III. PIATS 2000: Proceedings of the Ninth Seminar of the International Assocation for Tibetan Studies, Leiden 2000*, edited by John Ardussi and Henk Blezer, 49–67. Brill's Tibetan Studies Library 2/3. Leiden: Brill.

Yang Fuquan. 2016. "In Living Memory: The Tenth Karmapa in the Folklore of the Naxi People." In Debreczeny and Tuttle 2016, 95–106.

Yang, Han-sung, Yün-hua Jan, Shotaro Iida, and Laurence W. Preston. 1984. *The Hye Ch'o Diary: Memoir of the Pilgrimage to the Five Regions of India.* Berkeley: Asian Humanities Press; Seoul, Korea: Po Chin Chai.

Yen, Chih-hung. 1997. *Bhaiṣajyaguru at Dunhuang.* PhD diss., SOAS University of London.

Yeshe Tsogyal (Ye shes mtsho rgyal). (1978) 2007. *The Life and Liberation of Padmasambhava (Padma bka'i thang)*, 2 vols. Translated by Kenneth Douglas and Gwendolyn Bays. Reprint, Berkeley: Dharma Publishing.

_____. 1991. *The Lotus-Born: The Life-Story of Padmasambhava.* Translated by Erik Pema Kunzang. Boston: Shambhala.

Yoeli-Tlalim, Ronit. 2014. "Medicine, Astrology, and Divination." In Hofer 2014, 90–104.

Yonezawa Yoshiyasu 2020. "The Sanskrit Manuscript of the Vinayasūtravṛtti in dBu med Script." 成田山仏教研究所紀要 *Narita Sanbukyo Kenkyujo Kiyo* [Journal of Naritasan Institute for Buddhist Studies] 43, 65–84.

Young, G. M. (1918) 2007. "A Journey to Toling and Tsaparang in Western Tibet." *Journal of the Panjab Historical Society* 7, no. 2. Reprint, *Tibet Journal* 32, no. 2, 95–118.

Yutok, Dorje Yudon. (1990) 1995. *The House of the Turquoise Roof.* Reprint, Ithaca, NY: Snow Lion.

Zhiguan Museum of Fine Art. 2018. *The Light of Buddha: Buddhist Sculptures of the Palace Museum and Zhiguan Museum of Fine Art.* Exhibition catalog. [In Chinese and English.] Beijing: Wenwu.

TIBETAN AND DZONGKHA

Ārya Tārā aṣṭabhaya trāta nāma sādhanaṃ (Tib. *'Phags ma sgrol ma 'jigs pa brgyad las skyob pa zhes bya ba'i sgrub thabs*). In *The Tibetan Tripitaka*, edited by D. T. Suzuki, Peking edition, *Bstan 'gyur rgyud 'grel*, 1955–61, vol. 81, 74 1.1–5.4, DU 373a–375a. Also at https://library.bdrc.io/show/bdr:MW2KG5015_3287.

Bdud 'joms 'Jigs bral ye shes rdo rje. n.d. "Dam rdzas bdud rtsi chos sman gyi phab rgyun dkar chag dang phan yon mdor bsdus dad pa'i shing rta." In *Dung dkar chos rje'i gces nyar dpe tshogs (dum bu gsum pa)*, 4 vols. Dungkar Choji Collection, part 3, 12 ff., PDF, 316–39. Facsimile of publication by Tsering Thendup, Kalimpong: Mani Printing Works. http://purl.bdrc.io/resource/W3CN12069.

Bkra shis tshe ring, ed. 2008. *Mkha' spyod 'bras ljongs kyi gnas yig phyogs bsdebs bzhugs* [Anthology of writings by various treasure revealers on the hidden lands of Sikkim]. Gangtok: Namgyal Institute of Tibetology; Dharamsala: Amnye Machen Institute. http://purl.bdrc.io/resource/MW1KG818.

Blo bzang chos kyi rgyal mtshan, Paṇchen IV. 2009. *Paṇ chen Blo bzang chos kyi rgyal mtshan gyi gsung rtsom*, 5 vols. Beijing: Krung go'i bod rig pa dpe skrun khang. http://purl.bdrc.io/resource/MW1PD177557.

Blo bzang chos kyi rgyal mtshan. n.d. *Gtor ma brgya rtsa* [One hundred tormas]. BUDA by BDRC. Accessed January 12, 2022. http://purl.bdrc.io/resource/MW3CN1676

Bo dong paN chen phyogs las rnam rgyal (bo dong thams cad mkhyen pa). 1981. *Mkhas pa 'jug pa'i bzo rig sku gsung thugs kyi bzhengs tshul bzhugs so* [Entrance for the experts in crafting art: The way of constructing three representations of body, speech, and mind (of Tatagathas)]. In *The collected works of Bo-doṅ Pan-chen Phyogs-las-rnam-rgyal* 9, 256–60. New Delhi: Tibet House.

Bon skyong nam mkha'i lag len bzhugs pa'o. Unpublished manuscript of 6 folios. Collection of Geshe Tri Kalsang.

'Bri gung skyob pa 'jig rten gsum mgon. 1975. *'Bri gung thel chos bdud rtsi'i thigs pa.* New Delhi: Tsering Dorma Gelek. http://purl.bdrc.io/resource/W4CZ1721

Bsod nams rgya mtsho. n.d. *Chos kyi rje paṇ chen nags kyi rin po che'i zhal snga nas kyi rnam par thar pa* [The life story of the lord of dharma, the mahapandita Vanaratna as told in his own words], fols. 32r–60v. Manuscript. *Buddhist Digital Resource Center (BDRC)*, purl.bdrc.io/resource/W1CZ1887. Accessed January 10, 2023.

Bstan 'dzin chos rgyal. 1759. *Lho'i chos 'byung bstan pa rin po che'i 'phro mthud 'jam dgon smon mtha'i 'phreng ba.* Thimphu: Zab don lhun rtse. https://library.bdrc.io/show/bdr:MW1KG9413.

Bstan pa bstan 'dzin. 2003. "Rje btsun dam pa'i sgu phreng." In *Chos sde chen po dpal ldan 'bras spungs bkra shis sgo mang grwa tshang gi chos 'byung dung g.yas su 'khyil ba'i sgra dbyangs*, vol. 2. http://purl.bdrc.io/resource/W28810.

Byams pa 'phrin las. 1990. *Gangs ljongs gSo rig bstan pa'i nyin byed rnam thar* [The story of the sun of teachings of medicine in the Land of Snows]. Beijing: Mi rigs dpe skrun khang.

Chos kyi 'od zer, Myang ston Bsod nams seng ge, and Mi 'gyur rdo rje. 1978. "Sprul sku mnga' bdag chen po'i skyes rabs rnam thar dri ma med pa'i bka' rgya can la ldeb." In *Bka' brgyad bder gshegs 'dus pa'i chos skor*, 1, 1–163. Gangtok: Lama Sonam Tobgay Kazi.

Chu skyes Dge 'dun dpal bzang. 2007. *Reb gong yul skor zin tho.* Lanzhou: Kan su'u mi rigs dpe skrun khang.

De mo 08 Ngag dbang thub bstan 'jigs med rgya mtsho. 1811. *'Jam dpal rgya mtsho'i rnam thar* [Life of the Eighth Dalai Lama, Jampel Gyatso]. Bras spungs, Lhasa: Dga' ldan pho brang. http://purl.bdrc.io/resource/W2CZ7847.

Demo, Ngawang Gelek, ed. 1969. *The Autobiography of the First Panchen Lama Blo-bzang- chos-kyi-rgyal-mtshan.* New Delhi: Ngawang Gelek Demo.

Dkon mchog bstan 'dzin, Yon tan tshe ring, and Rdo dril, eds. 2006. *Thang bla tshe dbang phyag bris gces bsgrigs bzo rig mig rgyan.* Chengdu: Sichuan minzu chubanshe. http://purl.bdrc.io/resource/MW1PD82465.

Dpa' bo gtsug lag phreng ba. (1545–64). 1961. *Chos 'byung mkhas pa'i dga' ston* [Scholar's feast of religious history]. Edited by Lokesh Chandra. New Delhi: International Academy of Indian Culture.

_____. 1986. *Dam pa'i chos kyi 'khor lo bsgyur ba rnams kyi byung pa gsar bar byed pa mkhas pa'i dga ston* [Scholar's feast of religious history]. Beijing: Mi rigs dpe skrun khang. http://purl.bdrc.io/resource/MW7499.

Dpal 'byor bzang po (Stag sna rdzong pa). 1985. *Rgya bod yig tshang chen mo.* Chengdu: Si khron mi rigs dpe skrun khang.

Dpal rdo rje gdan gyi sgrub thabs. (1724). In *bsTan 'gyur (pe cing).* 73, 6–11. [Pe cing, Beijing]: [Pe cing pho brang]. http://purl.bdrc.io/resource/MW1KG13126_4127.

Gu ge Khyi thang pa Ye shes dpal. 1977. *Rin chen bzang po'i rnam thar 'bring po: Byang chub sems dpa' lo tsa ba Rin chen bzang po'i khrung rabs dka' spyad sgron ma rnam thar shel gyi phreng ba lu gu rgyud.* In *Collected Biographical Material About Lo-chen Rin-chen-Bzaṅ-po and His Subsequent Reembodiments*, edited by Dorje Tsetan. Delhi: Rdo-rje-tshe-brtan.

G.yu thog tshe ring sgrol dkar (Yutok, Tsering Dolkar). 2002. *Yab gzhis g.yu thog sa dbang dam pa Bkra shis don grub mchog gi sku tshe'i byung ba che long tsam ma bcos lhug par brjod pa bzhugs so* [Biographical account of Yabshe Yuthok Sawang Tashi Dhondup]. Rtsom rig sgyu rtsal deb phreng 6. Dharamsala: AMI.

Grags pa rgyal mtshan. 2007a. *Chos spyod rin chen phreng ba.* In *Gsung rab dpe bsdur ma pod lnga pa*, vol. 5. Pe cin: Krung go'i bod rig pa dpe skrun khang.

_____. 2007b. *Phags pa rdo rje gur gyi rgyan zhes bya ba.* In *Gsung rab dpe bsdur ma pod gnyis pa*, vol. 2. Pe cin: Krung go'i bod rig pa dpe skrun khang.

Gtsang mkhan chen 'Jam dbyangs dpal ldan rgya mtsho. 1982. "Rgyal mchog Chos dbyings rdo rje'i rnam thar mdo sde rgyan gyi lung dang sbyar ba." In *Gsung thor bu / 'Jam dbyangs dpal ldan rgya mtsho*, published as *Poetical Biographies of Dharmakirti and the Tenth Karma pa Chos dbyings rdo rje with a Collection of Instructions on Buddhist Practice.* Delhi: Lakshmi Press. http://purl.bdrc.io/resource/MW23998.

Gzhon nu dpal. n.d. *Mkhas pa chen po dpal nags kyi rin chen kyi rnam par thar pa* [The life of the great pandita, the illustrious Vanaratna]. Manuscript. https://library.bdrc.io/show/bdr:W23928.

Hor chos rje sku phreng gong rim gyi rnam thar = Hor chos rje dbyangs can snyems pa'i lang tsho. *Hor chos rje sku phreng gong rim gyi rnam thar* [The biographies of the First and Second Hor Cho-rje Ṅag-dbaṅ Phun-tshogs (1668–1746) and Skal bzaṅ Mthu-stobs Dpal-'bar (1747–1796) with sketches of the lives of their predecessors, 1849]. 1983. Delhi: Tibet House.

'Jam dpal brtson 'grus. 2010. "Sku lha mkha' ri." In *Lho brag gnas yig*, 215–16. Beijing: Mi rigs dpe skrun khang.

Jigme Lingpa. 1985. "Bla ma dgongs pa 'dus pa'i cho ga'i rnam bzhag dang 'brel ba'i bskyod rdzogs zung 'jig gi sgrom mkhyen brtse'i me long 'od zer brgya pa zhes bya ba." In *The collected works of 'jigs-med-gliṅ-pa raṅ-byuṅ-rdo-rje mkhyen-brtse'i-'od-zer*, vol. 4, 89–92. Gangtok: Pema Thinley for Dodrupchen Rinpoche; also http://purl.bdrc.io/resource/MW27300.

Jigme Thinley Özer. 2019. "Rdo rje dang dril bu'i bshad pa." [Explanation of the vajra and bell.] In *Btsan po mgar gyi dra ba*. http://www.tbmgar.com/zwndbw.asp?id=4799&Zhg=001&NdRak_ID=ZamqowLc.

'Jigs med bsam grub. 1995. Sde mgon khang gyi lo rgyus [A history of sDe mgon khang]. In *Khams phyogs dkar mdzes khul gyi dgon sde so so'i lo rgyus gsal bar bshad pa nang bstan gsal pa'i me long* [A luminous mirror of clearly explained histories of each individual monastery of Ganze County, Khams], edited by 'Jigs med bsam grub, vol. 1, 153–63. Kangding: Krung go'i bod kyi shes rig dpe skrun khang.

_____. 2000. "Rgyal ba sku phreng bcu gsum pa thub bstan rgya mtsho'i chos srid mdzad rnam." In *Gong sa tA la'i bla ma sku phreng rim byon gyi chos srid mdzad rnam*, 705–835. Beijing: Mi rigs dpe skrun khang. http://purl.bdrc.io/resource/W25268.

'Jigs med gling pa. 1985. "Klong chen snying thig gi bla ma rig 'dzin 'dus pa'i gdang rol nyung ngu blo gsal mgul rgyan gtor ma'i dpe'u ris bcas dang pad gling gi dbyangs yig" [Chanting and musical notations for the performance of the bla ma rig 'dzin 'dus pa practice from the klon chen snying thig cycle of visions of 'jigs-med-gling-pa, with the illustrations of the gtor-ma cakes and chanting notations for the rituals]. Thimphu: Pema Kunkhyab. https://library.bdrc.io/show/bdr:W23624.

'Jigs med grags pa. 1987. *Rgyal rtse chos rgyal gyi mam par thar pa dad pa'i lo thog dngos grub kyi char 'beb*. Lhasa: Bod ljongs mi dmangs dpe skrun khang.

KaH thog Si tu Chos kyi rgya mtsho. (1918–20) 2001. *Gangs ljongs dbus gtsang gnas bskor lam yig nor bu zla shel gyi se mo do / An Account of a Pilgrimage to Central Tibet during the Years 1918 to 1920*. Chengdu: Sichuan minzu chubanshe. http://purl.bdrc.io/resource/WA21611.

Karma chags med. (17th century) 2010. "Thugs rje chen po'i 'khor lo'i phan yon" [Benefits of Avalokiteshvara's prayer wheel]. In *Gsung 'bum karma chags med* [Collected works of Karma Chakme], vol. 35, 595–618. [Nang chen rdzong]: Gnas mdo gsang sngags chos 'phel gling gi dpe rnying nyams gso khang. https://library.bdrc.io/show/bdr:W1KG8321.

Karma Nges don bstan rgyas. (1891) 1973. *Chos rje karma pa sku 'phreng rim byon gyi rnam thar mdor bsdus dpag bsam 'khri shing*. Reprint, Delhi: Topden Tsering. https://library.bdrc.io/show/bdr:WA1KG3830.

Karma rgyal mtshan. 1997. *Kaṃ tshang yab sras dang dpal spungs dgon pa'i lo rgyus ngo mtshar dad pa'i padma rgyas byed* [History of the chief lamas of the Karma Kagyu tradition and of Pelpung Monastery]. Chengdu: Si khron mi rigs dpe skrun khang.

Karma rgyal mtshan (1880–1925). 1999. *Gangs ljongs dbus gtsang gnas bskor lam yig nor bu zla shel gyi se mo mdo* [The Crystal-Moon jewel discourse: Road-guide to the pilgrimage sites of U-Tsang in the Land of Snows]. Reprint, Lhasa: Bod ljongs bod yig dpe rnying dpe skrun khang.

Khang dmar pa. n.d. *Tre shod ye shes mgon po'i brnyan mthong grol chen po'i lo rgyus* [A history of the great image which liberates through sight, the Ye shes mgon po of Tre shod]. Manuscript.

'Khor lo dang jo dar gyi phan yon [Benefits of prayer wheels and prayer flags]. n.d. n.p.: 'Bum nyag chos sgar lnga rig bsam gtan chos gling. https://library.bdrc.io/show/bdr:MW1KG11869.

Khri gong o rgyan tshe ring. 2017. *A mdo byams pa dang dge 'dun chos 'phel*. Chengdu: Si khron mi rigs dpe skrun khang.

Kongtrul Lodöe Thaye. 2021. "Zab mo'i gter dang gter ston grub thob ji ltar byon pa'i lo rgyus mdor bsdus bkod pa rin chen baiDUr+Ya'i phreng ba" [The rosary of lapis lazuli: A brief account of the profound treasures and treasure revealers]. *Rinchen Terdzö*. https://rtz.tsadra.org/index.php/Terdzo-KA-006.

Lading, Quiangba Gesang (Lha sding Byams pa Skal bzang), ed. 2000. *A Mirror of the Murals in the Potala / Budala gong bihua yuanliu*. [In Tibetan, Chinese, and English.] Beijing: Jiuzhou tushu chubanshe.

Lcags mo mtsho. n.d. *Bon gyi dmangs khrod kyi cho ga bya rdang gi skor gleng ba*. Unpublished manuscript.

Lhun grub chos 'phel. 1994. *Rwa sgreng Dgon pa'i Dkar chag*. Chengdu: Si khron Mi rigs Dpe skrun khang. http://purl.bdrc.io/resource/W20838.

Ma Ni 'khor lo'i phan yon [On the benefits to be derived from the use of the prayer wheel and the recitation of the Avalokiteshvara formula]. 1985. Gangtok: Dzongsar Khyentse Labrang Palace Monastery. http://purl.bdrc.io/resource/W27609.

Mchims nam mkha' grags. 1994. *Dpal ldan a ti sha'i rnam thar rgyas pa: Jo bo rin po che dpal ldan a ti sha'i rnam thar rgyas pa yongs grags* [The extended biography of glorious Atisha]. In *Jo bo rje dpal ldan a ti sha'i rnam thar bka' gdams pha chos*, 44–228. Zi ling (Xining): Qinghai minzu chubanse. http://purl.bdrc.io/resource/MW00KG09688.

"Mkha' ri'i las byang gsol kha." In *Dro bo bla mas nyar tshags mdzad pa'i dpe rnying dpe dkon*, vol. 15, 1283–86. Accessed August 20, 2022. http://purl.bdrc.io/resource/MW4PD971_FF5d5E.

Mkhan po phun tshogs bkra shis. 2003. 'Brug gi bzo rigs bcu gsum gyi bshad pa mkhas pa'i dga' ston. SPar thengs 1 [A feast for scholars: An explanation of the thirteen crafts of Bhutan]. Thimphu: sKal bzang gzhan phan. http://purl.bdrc.io/resource/MW29220.

Mkhan po lha tshe ring. 2002. *Mkha' spyod 'Bras mo ljongs kyi gtsug nor sprul pa'i rnal 'byor mched bzhi brgyud 'dzin dang bcas pa'i byung ba brjod pa blo gsar gzhon nu'i dga ston* [A saga of Sikkim's supremely revered four pioneer Nyingmapa reincarnates and their torchbearers]. Gangtok: Khenpo Lha Tsering. http://purl.bdrc.io/resource/MW1KG5907.

Mkhar nag lo tsa ba Dpal 'byor bzang po. *Dga' ldan chos 'byung: Dga' ldan chos 'byung dPag bsam sdong po mkhas pa dgyes byed ces bya ba bzhugs so*, 102 ff. *dbu med* manuscript.

Mnga' bdag nyang ral nyi ma 'od zer (1124–1192). *Pad ma bka' chems brgyas pa*. Manuscript. Nepal-German Manuscript Cataloguing Project (NGMCP) E 2703/10.

_____. *Slob dpon padma 'byung gnas kyi skyes rabs chos 'byung nor bu'i phreng ba zhes bya ba: Rnam thar Zangs gling ma*. In *Rin chen gter mdzod chen mo*, 1:1–219. Paro: Ngodrup and Sherab Drimay.

Ne'u pandi ta. 1990. "Sngon gyi gtam me tog phreng ba" [A flower garland of ancient sayings]. In *Bod kyi lo rgyus deb ther khag lnga*, Gangs can rig mdzod 9, 3–54. Lhasa: Bod ljongs Bod yig dpe rnying dpe skrun khang.

Ngag dbang kun dga' bsod nams 1986. *Sa skya'i gdung rabs ngo mtshar bang mdzod*. Beijing: Mi rigs dpe skrun khang.

Ngag dbang mkhas grub (Agwang Khayidub). 1972–74. *Rten bzhengs kyi dkar chag mthong ba don ldan*. In *The Collected Works of Nag-dban-mkhas-grub, Kyai-rdor Mkhan-po of Urga: Reproduced under the Instructions of the Ven. Gliṅ Rin-po-che from a Set of MSS. and Xylographic Prints from the Urga Blocks*, edited by Nag-dban-mkhas-grub, vol. 5. Ladakh: S. W. Tashigangpa. TBRC W16912–0592.

_____. 1972–74a. *Khu re chen mor bzhengs pa'i byams pa'i sku brnyan gyi dkar chag dad pa'i bzhin ras gsal bar byed pa'i nor bu'i me long*. In *The Collected Works of Nag-dban-mkhas-grub, Kyai-rdor Mkhan-po of Urga: Reproduced under the Instructions of the Ven. Gliṅ Rin-po-che from a Set of MSS. and Xylographic Prints from the Urga Blocks*, edited by Nag-dban-mkhas-grub, vol. 1, fols. 175–273. Ladakh: S. W. Tashigangpa. TBRC W16912–0588.

_____. 1972–74b. *Rgyal ba byams mgon gyi dang po thugs bskyed pa nas bzung sa lam rim par bgrod de mngon par byang chub pa'i tshul las brtsams shing ma 'ongs pa na sangs rgyas lnga pa'i mdzad pa ji ltar ston tshul gsal bar brjod pa'i sgo nas bstod cing gsol ba 'debs pa'i rab tu byed pa byams mgon zhal bzang lta ba'i dga' ston*. In *The Collected Works of Nag-dban-mkhas-grub, Kyai-rdor Mkhan-po of Urga: Reproduced under the Instructions of the Ven. Gliṅ Rin-po-che from a Set of MSS. and Xylographic Prints from the Urga Blocks*, edited by Nag-dban-mkhas-grub, vol. 1, fols. 155–65. Ladakh: S. W. Tashigangpa. TBRC W16912–0588.

_____. 1972–74c. *Ri bo dge rgyas dga' ldan bshad sdrub gling gi skor tshad*. In *The Collected Works of Nag-dban-mkhas-grub, Kyai-rdor Mkhan-po of Urga: Reproduced under the Instructions of the Ven. Gliṅ Rin-po-che from a Set of MSS. and Xylographic Prints from the Urga Blocks*, edited by Nag-dban-mkhas-grub. Ladakh: S. W. Tashigangpa.

Padma rdo rje. n.d. "Dpyal gyi gdung rabs Gangga'i chu rgyun: Bla chen dPyal gyi gdung rabs rin po che'i za ra tshags zhes bya ba dang/ gDung rabs Gangga'i chu rgyun gnyis gleg bam gcig tu bris pa las/ kun gsal me long che ba bcud ldan bzhugs so." Unpublished computer edition, 33 pages.

Padma gling pa (1450–1521). 1975–76. Rig 'dzin padma gling pa'i zab gter chos mdzod rin po che. 21 vols. Thimphu: Kunsang Tobgay. http://purl.bdrc.io/resource/MW21727.

_____. 2014. *Bum thang dar rgud kyi lung bstan* [The prophecy of Bumtang's flourishing and decline]. Thimphu: KMT Press.

Pema Lingpa (Padma gling pa). 1975–76a. "Don khrid gsal ba'i sgrom me." In *Rig 'dzin padma gling pa'i zab gter chos mdzod rin po che* 15, 5–31. Thimphu: Kunsang Tobgay. http://purl.bdrc.io/resource/W21727.

_____. 1975–76b. "Nyams len gnad kyi me long nyams khrid du bstan pa ldeb" [The mirror of the key points of practice]. In *Rig 'dzin padma gling pa'i zab gter chos mdzod rin po che* 15, 33–40. Thimphu: Kunsang Tobgay. http://purl.bdrc.io/resource/W21727.

_____. 1975–76c. "rDzogs chen kun bzang dgongs 'dus." In *Rig 'dzin padma gling pa'i zab gter chos mdzod rin po che* 4 and 15. Thimphu: Kunsang Tobgay. http://purl.bdrc.io/resource/W21727.

_____. 1975–76d. "Rig pa klong grol gyi rgyud rigs drug sgo bcad." In *Rig 'dzin padma gling pa'i zab gter chos mdzod rin po che*, 4, 163–84. Thimphu: Kunsang Tobgay. http://purl.bdrc.io/resource/W21727.

Phag mo gru pa. 1997. "*Rin po che mtha'i rtsa bas mdzad pa'i zhabs rjes zhu ba'o*," five folia.

Phag mo gru pa rdo rje rgyal po'i gsung 'bum. Beijing: Mi rigs dpe skrun khang, 299–303. Also in http://purl.bdrc.io/resource/MW1KG15061.

Phun tshogs (Phuntsho), Karma. 2015. *Gter ston pad+ma gling pa'i rnam thar / The Autobiography of Terton Pema Lingpa: A Brilliant and Beautiful Rosary of Gems.* Thimphu: Shejun.

Phyi nang gsang ba'i mdos kyi byung khungs gsal byed lag khrid no bwe ka'i lag len bzhugs so. 2008. In *G.yung drung Bon gyi bka' brten dpe rnying phyogs bsgrigs bzhugs so*, vol. 64. Khyung po steng chen dgon nas bsgrigs. Lanzhou: Kan su'u mi rigs dpe skrun khang.

Rdo rje gdan gyi sgrub thabs. (1724). In *bsTan 'gyur (pe cing).* 72: 424–28; 429–31; 73: 174–78; 178–80; 180–82. (Pe cing, Beijing): (Pe cing pho brang). http://purl.bdrc.io/resource/MW1KG13126_3969; http://purl.bdrc.io/resource/MW1KG13126_3970; http://purl.bdrc.io/resource/MW1KG13126_4223; http://purl.bdrc.io/resource/MW1KG13126_4224; http://purl.bdrc.io/resource/MW1KG13126_4225.

Rin chen tshul khrims. ca. 15th century. *Lha btsun rin chen rgya mtsho'i rnam thar thun mong ma yin pa zin bris su btab pa bzhugs so* [A note of the uncommon biography of Lhatsun Rinchen Gyatso]. Manuscript.

Rdzong gsar mkhyen brtse 02 'jam dbyangs chos kyi blo gros. 2012. "Sku lha mkha' ri'i gsol mchod." In *Gsung 'bum 'jam dbyangs chos kyi blo gros* 11, 509–11. Khyentse Labrang. http://purl.bdrc.io/resource/MW1KG12986_E61BDE.

Sa chen kun dga' snying po and 'Gro mgon chos rgyal 'phags pa. 2006. "Zhe dgu'i ma'i sgrub thabs zhi khro rnam rol." In *Sa skya bka' 'bum*, 14, 612–25. Kathmandu: Sachen International. http://purl.bdrc.io/resource/W00EGS1017151.

Sa skya'i gdung rabs ngo mtshar bang mdzod (*Sajia shixi shi* 薩迦世系史). 1986. Beijing: Minzu chubanshe.

Sde mgon po'i dkar chag = Hor Chos rje ngag dbang phun tshogs, ed. 1996. *Sde mgon po'i dkar chag* [The descriptive catalog of Degonpo]. Full title: *Bla chen 'phags pas lung bstan cing/ rgya yul nas phyag nas 'thor bar grags pa'i tre'i mgon khang ngam yongs grags sde mgon po'i dkar chag hor chos rje ngag dbang phun tshogs kyis mdzad pa.* In *Dga' ldan khri pa tre hor byams pa chos grags. Rigs dang dkyil 'khor rgya mtsho'i mnga 'dbag [sic] nges pa don gyi rdo rje 'chang khang gsar skyabs mgon blo bzang tshul khrims bstan pa'i rgyal mtshan dpal bzang po'i rnam par thar pa dad pa'i pad mo bzhad pa'i nyin byed* [The biography of the First Tri hor Khang gsar Skyabs mgon Blo bzang tshul khrims bstan pa'i rgyal mtshan, 1838–1897], fols. 244r–247v. Dharamsala: Library of Tibetan Works and Archives.

Sde srid sangs rgyas rgya mtsho. 2002. *Bai DUrya g.ya' sel* (*Baiḍūrya dkar po las dris lan 'khrul snang g.ya' sel*) [Removal of the tarnish of deluded appearances: Questions and answers arising from the *White Beryl*], 2 vols. Beijing: Krung go'i bod rig pa dpe skrun khang.

Sha bo mkha' byams. 2021. "Btsan po'i skabs kyi phyogs bzhi'i rgyal po btul ba'i lo rgyus dang 'brel lha sras mu rug brtsan gyi skor la dpyad pa." In *Bod ljongs slob grwa chen mo'i rig deb* (4).

Shakabpa, W. D. 1976. *Bod kyi srid don rgyal rabs / Political History of Tibet.* Kalimpong: T. Tsepal Taikhang. http://purl.bdrc.io/resource/MW28263.

Si tu and 'Be lo = Si tu Paṇ chen Chos kyi 'byung gnas and 'Be lo Tshe dbang kun khyab. 1775 [Unpublished biography of Chos dbyings rdo rje]. Originally part of *Bsgrub rgyud karma kam tshang brgyud pa rin po che'i rnam par thar pa rab 'byams nor bu zla ba chu shel gyi phreng ba.* Republished in *Rgyal dbang Karma-pa sku phreng bcu pa Chos-dbyings-rdo-rje'i rnam thar dang Gar-dbang Chos-kyi-dbang-phyug gi rnam thar rtogs brjod 'dod 'jo'i ba mo.* 2012. Sarnath, Varanasi: Wā-ṇa Badzra-bidyā Dpe-mdzod-khang, 399–468. http://purl.bdrc.io/resource/MW4CZ294918.

_____. (1775) 1972. *Bsgrub rgyud karma kam tshang brgyud pa rin po che'i rnam par thar pa rab 'byams nor bu zla ba chu shel gyi phreng ba.* Reprint, New Delhi: D. Gyaltsan and Kesang Legshay. http://purl.bdrc.io/resource/MW23435.

Si tu chos kyi 'byung gnas, ed. 1985. "De bzhin gshegs pa thams cad kyi gtsug tor rnam par rgyal ba zhes bya ba'i gzungs rtog pa dang bcas pa." In bKa' 'gyur (sde dge'i mtshal par spus legs), 90, 474–483. sDe dge, Derge: sDe dge par khang chen mo. http://purl.bdrc.io/resource/MW3CN20612_0595.

Si tu Chos kyi rgya mtsho (1880–1925). 1999. *Dbus Gtsang gnas yig*, Gangs can rig mdzod 33. Lhasa: Bod ljongs Bod yig dpe rnying dpe skrun khang.

Si tu Paṇ chen Chos kyi 'byung gnas. 1968. *Ta'i si tur 'bod pa karma bstan pa'i nyin byed kyi rang tshul drangs por brjod pa dri bral shel gyi me long* [The autobiography and diaries of Situ Panchen]. Edited by Lokesh Chandra. Śatapitaka Series 77. New Delhi: International Academy of Indian Culture.

Sman bla don grub. 1944. *Dde bar gshegs pa'i sku gzugs kyi tshad kyi rab tu byed pa yid bzhin nor bu zhes bya ba bzhugs so* [The Wish-fulfilling jewel: A treatise on canonical proportions of Tathāgatas] 6 (folio), woodblock print. Lhasa: Zhol par khang.

Sman thang pa sman bla don grub. 1985. "Bstan bcos legs bshad nor bu'i phreng ba." In *Ri mo'i thig tshad dang tshon gyi lag len tshad ldan don du gnyer ba rnams la nye bar mkho ba mthong ba don ldan*, 177–218. [n.p.] http://purl.bdrc.io/resource/MW8LS44211.

Snying stobs rgya mtsho. 2012. *Mtho gling gSer khang gi dkar chab: Mtho gling gSer khang gi dkar chab* [sic] *dad pa'i 'dab rgyas byed pa'i nyi ma.* In *The dGe lugs pa in Gu ge and the Western Himalaya (Early 15th–late 17th Century)*, edited by Roberto Vitali. Dharamsala: Amnye Machen Tibetan Institute for Advanced Studies.

Thub bstan phun tshogs. 2007. *Gnas chung rdo rje sgra dbyangs gling gi chos 'byung kun gsal chu shel dbang po.* Dharamsala: Nechung Monastery.

Tsa mo rong pa bsod nams 'od zer. 14th century. *Rten gsum bzhugs gnas dang bcas pa'i bsgrub tshul yon ten 'byung gnas* [Source of excellent qualities: A treatise on proportions for making three representations and their abodes]. Manuscript.

Tshangs pa bstan 'dzin, Dpon slob rin po che, Dge bshes Bsam gtan gtsug phud, Shes Rab mthar phyin, and Khri gtsug bstan pa. 2014. *Bdud rtsi 'od zer 'khyil ba'i lag len skor.* Kathmandu: Triten Norbutse Monastery.

Tsechang Penba Wangdu (brtse byang spen pa dbang 'dus). 2005. "Gong dkar rdo rje gdan gyi ldebs bris kyi don snying dang da lta'i gnas babs skor la rags tsam gleng ba." In *Bod ljongs zhib 'jug* 94, no. 2, 105–9.

_____. 2010. "Gong dkar sgang stod mkhyen brtse chen mo dge bsnyen rnam par rgyal ba dang mkhyen lugs kyi khyad chos skor rags tsam gleng ba." *Journal of Tibet University* 4, 112–17. Translated by David P. Jackson as "A Recent Introduction of Khyentse Chenmo and His Art," in Jackson 2016, 67–80.

Tsering Gyalpo. 2015. "Gsar du rnyed pa'i bod btsan po'i skabs bzhengs pa'i smar khams rdzong rnam par snang mdzad kyi brag brkos snang brnyan skor la rags tsam brjod pa" / "A brief report on a rock-carve image of Vairocana, recently traced in Smar khams County and erected during the imperial period." In *The Illuminating Mirror: Tibetan Studies in Honour of Per K. Sørensen on the Occasion of his 65th Birthday*, edited by Olaf Czaja and Guntram Hazod, 181–87. Wiesbaden: Reichert.

Wangchuk, Karma, Lam Dampa, Ugyen Tenzin, and Yonten Dargye. 1999. *Driglam Namzhag (Bhutanese Etiquette): A Manual.* Thimphu: National Library of Bhutan.

NEPALI AND NEWARI

Josi, Satyamohan. 2016. *Nepali Kalako Ruparekna: Pracina Ra Madhyakalina* [An outline of Nepalese art]. [In Nepali with some English.] Kathmandu: BookArt Nepal.

Pant, Mahesraj. 2013. "Nevārarājyakā Kānūnī likhatamā sthāpita ra bārāhi." *Sthāpita Khalah* (*Souvenir*) 4, no. 4 (NS 1133/VS 2070), 61–77. [In Nepali.]

Shakya, Hemraj. 1978. *Śrī Bhāskarkīrti mahāvihāra Yeṭakhābāhāḥ chagu adhyayana.* [In Newari.] Kathmandu: Yeṭakhābāhāḥ Ārya nāmasaṃgīti guṭhī, NS 1099 Maṃsira 21 (December 6, 1978).

MONGOLIAN

Baasansüren, Khandsüren (Khambo Lama). 2011. *Enkh tunkh Erdene zuu—Erdene Zuu: The Jewel of Enlightenment.* Translated by Glenn H. Mullin. Ulaanbaatar: Pozitiv.

Changkya Khutugtu Rolpai Dorje (Lcang skya rol pa'i rdo rje). Beijing Xylograph, 1753. *Rgyal khab chen po'i mchod rten dkar po'i dkar chag dad pa rgyas byed ces bya ba bzhugs* so [Catalog of the White Stupa at the western gate of the Great Kingdom, prosperous faith].

Damdinsüren, D. 1993. *Ikh Khüreenii Nert Urchuud* [Eminent artists of Ikh Khüree]. Ulaanbaatar: Mongolpress.

Dariima, D. 2003. *Dursgakhyn buyantai burkhan zuraach* [The monk artist of praiseworthy memory]. Ulaanbaatar: BIT.

Dügersüren, L. 1956. *Ulaanbaatar khotiin tüükhees* [From the history of Ulaanbaatar]. Ulaanbaatar: Ulsyn Khevleliin Gazar.

Khatanbaatar, N., and Naigal Ye. 2005: *Erdene zuugiin tüükh, 16–20-r zuun* [History of Erdeni juu, 16th–20th centuries]. Ulaanbaatar: Soyombo Press.

Maidar, D. (1970) 1972. *Mongolyn arkhitektur ba khot baiguulalt: Toim* [Architecture and construction of cities in Mongolia: Overview]. Reprint, Ulaanbaatar: Ulsiin khevleliin gazar.

Ngag dbang ye shes thub bstan rab 'byams pa (Agwang Ishitübden Rabjamba). 1982a. Khyab bdag 'khor lo'i mgon rje btsun dam pa blo bzang bstan pa'i rgyal mtshan gyi rnam thar skal bzang dad pa'i shing rta. In *The Life and Works of Jibcundampa I*, edited by Lokesh Chandra. New Delhi: Sharada Rani.

_____. 1982b. *Skyabs mgon rje btsun dam pa rin po che'i skye khreng rim byon rnams dyi rnam thar mdo tsam bgod pa pad dgar 'phreng mjes zhes bya ba bzhugs so.* In *Life and Works of Jibcundampa I*, edited by Lokesh Chandra. [In Tibetan and Mongolian.] New Delhi: Śata-Piṭaka Series, Jayed Press.

Ochir, A., and B. Enkhtüvshin, eds. 2003. *Mongol Ulsyn Tüükh* [History of Mongolia], 5 vols. Ulaanbaatar: Academy of Sciences.

Pürev, O. 1994. *Mongolyn uls töriin töv* [Mongolian political center]. Ulaanbaatar: Mana.

Pürevjav, S. 1961. *Khuvsgaliin ömnöh Ikh Khüree* [Prerevolutionary Ikh Khüree]. Ulaanbaatar: Ulsin Khevlelin Khereg Erkhlekh Khoroo.

Sereeter, O. 1999. *Mongoliin Ikh Khüree, Gandan Khiidiin tüükhen butetsiin tovch* [Survey of historical structure of Ikh Khüree and Gandan Monastery of Mongolia]. Ulaanbaatar: Mongol Ulsyn Undesnii Tov Arkhiv.

Tsendina, A., trans. 1999. *Erdeni juu-yin teüke* [History of Erdene Zuu]. Moscow: Eastern Literature Publishing RAN.

Tsultem, Nyam-Osoryn. 2018. *Mongoliin uran zurgiin khögjij irsen toim* [Development of Mongolian painting]. Edited by Narmandakh Tsultem. Ulaanbaatar: BCI Publishing.

CHINESE

Aohan wenshi ziliao 敖汉文史资料 [Veritable records of the Aohan]. 1984–86, 4 vols. Aohan Banner, Inner Mongolia: Zhongguo renmin zhengzhi xieshang huiyi Aohanqi weiyuanhui 中国人民政治协商会议敖汉旗委员会 (*neibu* 内部 internal publication).

Cangkya Rolpal Dorje, ed. 1994. *Sanbai Foxiangji* 三百佛像集 [Three hundred icons]. Beijing: Zhongguo Zangxue chubanshe.

Cao Zhao曹昭 (ca. 13–14th century). 2012. *Gegu yaolun* 格古要論. Zhonghua shuju中華書局.

Chen Qingying 陈庆英. 2000. *Lun Ming chao dui Zang chuan fo jiao de guan li* 論明朝對藏傳佛教的管理 [Discussing the Ming court's management of Tibetan Buddhism]. *Zhongguo Zangxue* 中国藏学 / *China Tibetology* 3. 57–74.

Chen Qingying 陈庆英 and Zhou Shengwen 周生文. 1990. "Yuan dai Zangzu mingseng Danba guoshi kao" 元代藏族名僧胆巴国师考 [Textual research on Danba, a famous Tibetan monk in the Yuan dynasty]. *Zhongguo Zangxue* 中国藏学 / *China Tibetology* 1, 58–67.

Cheng Jufu 程鉅夫. (1249–1318) 1970. "Liangguo minhui gong shendao bei" 涼國敏慧公神道碑 [The spirit-way stele for Minhui, Duke of the state of Liang, 1316]. In *Cheng Xuelou wenji* 程雪樓文集 / *The Collective Works of Cheng Jufu*, edited by Cheng Jufu. Taipei: Zhongyang cushu guan.

China Cultural Heritage Information and Consulting Center, ed. 2002. *Zhongguo zangchuan fojiao jintong zaoxiang yishu* 中国藏传佛教金铜造像艺术 [Tibetan Buddhist bronze statue art in China]. Beijing: Renmin meishu chubanshe.

Chung Tzu-yin 鍾子寅. 2014. "Chongtan Qinghai Qutansi zhi Qutandian (yi): 'Pilu huanhua wangxu' 'Wenshu jingang 43 mantula' wanzheng zuo li de xin faxian ji qi yishu shi zhi yiyi" 重探青海瞿曇寺之瞿曇殿(一):《毗盧幻化網續》 '文殊金剛43尊曼荼羅' 完整作例的新發現及其藝術史之意義 [Reassessing the Gautama Hall in Gautama Monastery, Qinghai, part one: The discovery of a complete 43-deity Mañjuvajra Mandala derived from the Māyājāla-tantra (rNam snag sgyu dra'i rgyud) and its significance in Tibetan art]. *Meishu xue* 29, 161–244.

_____. 2015. "Chongtan Qinghai Qutansi zhi Qutandian (er): Zangchuan fojiao 'Jingangman' jiaofa zai Mingchu Anduo diqu chuanbo de xin faxian" 重探青海瞿曇寺之瞿曇殿(二): 藏傳佛教《金剛鬘》教法在明初安多地區傳播的新發現 [Reassessing the Qutan Hall in Qutan Monastery, Qinghai, part two: The Visual Evidence of Vajrāvali (rDo rje phreng b) in Early-Ming Amdo]. *The National Palace Museum Research Quarterly* 32, no. 4, 143–218.

Daci'ensi Sanzang fashi zhuan大慈恩寺三藏法师传 [A Biography of Master Sanzang of the Daci'en Temple]. Taishō Tripiṭaka, T.2053.

Dang Baohai 党宝海. 2006. *Meng-Yuan yizhan jiaotong yanjiu* 蒙元驿站交通研究. Beijing: Kunlun Press.

Dongyang Dehui 東陽德輝 (fl. 14th century). *Chixiu baizhang qinggui* 勅修百丈清規 [Imperial edition of Baizhang's Rules of Piety, 1338]. Taishō Tripiṭaka, T. 2025. China Buddhist Electronic Text Association. http://tripitaka.cbeta.org/T48n2025.

Dunhuang Academy, ed. 2018. *Pingshanyufu de silu shijie* 平山郁夫的丝路世界 [Hirayama Ikuo's world of the Silk Road]. Beijing: Blossom Press.

Fan Jinshi樊锦诗, ed. 1999. *Anxi: Yulin ku* 安西: 榆林窟 [The Anxi Yulin Grottoes]. Lanzhou: Gansu minzu chubanshe.

Feng Zhi 馮智. 1996. "Mingdai Lijiang mushi tusi yu Xizang Gamabapai guanxi shulue" 明代麗江木氏土司與西藏噶瑪巴派關係述略 [A brief account of the relationship between the Mu family chieftain in Lijiang and the Karmapa sect in Tibet in the Ming dynasty]. In *Zangzu lishi zongjiao yanjiu*, diyi ji 藏族歷史宗教研究, 第一辑, 46–70. Beijing: Zhongguo Zangxue chubanshe.

Fozu lidai tongzai 佛祖历代通載, chap. 22; Nian Chang 念常. *Fozu Lidai Tongzai* [A comprehensive registry of the successive ages of the Buddhas and the patriarchs]. Chap. 22 (before 1340). CBETA 電子佛典 大正新脩大藏經 Taishō Tripiṭaka大正藏第 49 冊 no. 2036 佛祖歷代通載 [0725c14] (十一). Accessed April 18, 2017. http://tripitaka.cbeta.org/ko/T49n2036_022. Also Taisho Shinshu Daizo Publishing, eds.大正新修大藏經刊行會 编. Tokyo 東京: Daizo Publishing Co., Ltd.大藏出版株式會社, 1988.

Guan Xuexuan 管学宣. (1743) 1991. *Lijiang fu zhilue* 麗江府志略, edited by Lijiang xian xianzhibian weihui 丽江县县志编委会. Reprint, Lijiang: Lijiang Naxizu zizhixian.

He Shiyong 和仕勇, ed. 2011. *Lijiang Baisha bihua tushi* 丽江白沙壁画图释 [Lijiang Baisha mural images and explanations]. Kunming: Yunnan renmin chubanshe.

Hong Hao 洪浩 (1088–1155). 2008. *Songmo jiwen* 松漠紀聞, vol. 1. In *Quansong biji*全宋筆記, vol. 7 of part 3. Zhengzhou: Daxiang chubanshe.

Hong Zaixin 洪再新. 1995. "Zhao Mengfu Hong yi Xiyu seng (juan) yanjiu 赵孟頫《红衣西域僧(卷)》研究" [Research on Zhao Mengfu's *Red-Robed Monk of the Western Regions* scroll]. In *Zhao Mengfu yanjiu lunwenji* 赵孟頫研究论文集, 519–33. Shanghai: Shanghai shuhua chubanshe.

Hua Jueming 華覺明. 1986. *Zhongguo yezhu shi lunji* 中國冶鑄史論集 [Essays on the history of metallurgy in China]. Beijing: Wenwu chubanshe.

Huang Hao 黄颢. 1993. *Zai Beijing de Zangzu wenwu* 在北京的藏族文物 [Tibetan cultural relics in Beijing]. Beijing: Minzu chubanshe.

Huo Wei 霍巍 and Li Yongxian 李永憲. 2001. *Xizang xibu fojiao yishu* 西藏. 西部佛教艺术 [Buddhist art in western Tibet]. Chengdu: Sichuan renmin chubanshe.

Jia Weiwei 贾维维 2020. *Yulin ku: Di san ku tuxiang yu wenben yanjiu* 榆林窟: 第三窟图像与文本研究 [Yulin grottoes and related textual research of Cave 3]. Hangzhou: Zhejiang University Press.

Jiang Gaochen 蔣高宸. 1997. *Yunnan minzu zhuwu wenhua* 雲南民族住屋文化 [Yunnan ethnic house culture]. Kunming: Yunnan daxue chubanshe.

Jiang Huaiying. 1996. *Xizang Budala gong* [Potala Palace in Tibet]. Beijing: Wenwu chubanshe.

Jin Weinuo 金维诺. 2001. *Zhongguo Zangchuan Fojiao diaosu quanji: caca* 中国藏传佛教雕塑全集4：擦擦卷 [Complete book of Tibetan Buddhist sculptures in China, vol. 4: *Tsatsa*]. Beijing: Beijing meishu sheying chubanshe.

Kang Gesang Yixi 康 格桑益希. 2015. *Zang chuan Gama gazi huapai tangka yishu* 藏传噶玛嘎孜画派唐卡艺术 [Tibetan Karma Gadri painting school thangka art]. Chengdu: Sichuan meishu chubanshe.

Tanaka Kimiaki. 2014. "On the So-called Garbhadhātu Maṇḍala in Cave 3 of Anxi Yulin Caves." In *Han Zang Fojiao meishu yanjiu: Disi jie Xizang kaogu yishu guoji xueshu taolun wenji* 汉藏佛教美术研究：第四届西藏考古与艺术国际学术讨论会论文集 / *Studies on Sino-Tibetan Buddhist Art: Essays of the Fourth International Conference of Tibetan Archaeology and Art*, edited by Xie Jisheng 谢继胜, Luo Wenhua 罗文华, and Shi Yangang 石岩刚, 155–60. [Primarily in Chinese, with some English.] Shanghai: Shanghai guji chubanshe.

Lading, Quiangba Gesang (Lha sding Byams pa Skal bzang), ed. 2000. *A Mirror of the Murals in the Potala / Budala gong bihua yuanliu*. [In Tibetan and Chinese.] Beijing: Jiuzhou tushu chubanshe.

Li Xianting. 2010. *Lie ri Xi zang—Xi zang dang dai yi shu zhan* 烈日西藏—西藏當代藝術展 [*Scorching Sun of Tibet:* Contemporary art show]. Exhibition catalog. Beijing: Songzhuang yishu guan.

Liao Yang 廖旸. 2014. "Feilaifeng Yuan dai shike zaoxiang neirong xu lu" 飞来峰元代石刻造像内容叙錄 [Thematic description of the Yuan dynasty stone sculptures at Feilaifeng]. In *Jiangnan Zangchuan Fojiao Yishu: Hangzhou Feilaifeng shike zaoxiang yanjiu* [Tibetan Buddhist art south of the Yangtse River: Collective research of Feilaifeng's Tibetan-style sculpture], edited by Xie Jisheng, 65–177. Beijing: Zhongguo Zangxue chubanshe.

Lijiang Naxizu zizhixian wenhuaju 丽江纳西族自治县文化局, and Lijiang Naxi Dongba wenhua bowuguan 丽江纳西东巴文化博物馆, eds. 1999. *Lijiang Baisha bihua* 丽江白沙壁画 [Lijiang Baisha murals]. Chengdu: Sichuan renmin chubanshe.

Lin Shi-hsuan. 2010. "Zhonghua Weizang: Qing Renzong xixun Wutai shan yanjiu." 中華衛藏: 清仁宗西巡五臺山研究 [Making Tibet inside the frontier: On the last western tour to Wutai Mountain of Emperor Jiaqing]. *Gugong xueshu jikan* 故宮學術季刊 28, no. 2, 147–212.

Liu Yisi 刘艺斯. 1957. *Xizang fojiao yishu* 西藏佛教艺术 [Buddhist art of Tibet]. Beijing: Wenwu chubanshe.

Lü Hongliang 吕红亮. 2015. *Kua Ximalaya de wenhua hudong: Xizang xibu shiqian kaogu yanjiu* 跨喜马拉雅的文化互动：西藏西部史前考古研究 [Trans-Himalayan interaction: An archaeological study of the prehistory of western Tibet]. Beijing: Kexue chubanshe.

Luo Wenhua 罗文华. 1999. "Gugong cang Menggu tongfo zaoxiang yanjiu" 故宮藏蒙古铜佛造像研究 *Gugong bowuyuan yuankan* 故宮博物院院刊 [Palace Museum Journal] 2, 81–87.

_____. 2005. *Longpao yu jiasha: Qinggong Zangchuan fojiao wenhua kaocha* 龙袍与袈裟: 清宮藏传佛敎文化考察 [Dragon robes and *kasaya*: An investigation of Tibetan Buddhist culture at the Qing court)]. Beijing: Zijincheng chubanshe.

_____. (2009) 2012. *Gugong jingdian: Zang chuan fojiao zaoxiang* 故宫经典: 藏传佛教造像 [Gugong classic: Tibetan Buddhist sculptures]. Reprint, Beijing.

_____. 2014. "Yongxuan zaoxiang kao" 永宣造像考 [Key issues in Yongle and Xuande sculptures]. In *Forbidden City* 5, 29–56.

———. 2020. *Zangchuan fojiao zaoxiang* 藏传佛教造像 [Tibetan Buddhist sculpture], fifth ed. Beijing: Gugong chubanshe.

Luo Wenhua 罗文华 and Gesang Qupei 格桑曲培. 2015. *Gongga Qudesi bihua: Zangchuan fojiao meishu shi de licheng bei* 贡嘎曲德寺壁画: 藏传佛教美术史的里程碑. Beijing: Gugong chubanshe.

Ma Xiaolin 马晓林. 2013. "Yuanchao taimiao yanbian kao—yi shici wei zhongxin 元朝太庙演变考—以室次为中心." *Lishi yanjiu* 5, 67–82.

Palace Museum, ed. 2010. *Yongxuan wenwu cuizhen* 永宣文物萃珍 [Splendors from the Yongle (1403–1424) and Xuande (1426–1435) reigns of China's Ming dynasty]. Beijing: Gugong chubanshe.

Ping Cuo Ci Dan, ed. 2000. *Pho brang po ta la'i ldebs bris ri mo'i 'byung khungs lo rgyus gsal ba'i me long/Budala gong bi hua yuan liu / A Mirror of the Murals in the Potala.* [In Tibetan, Chinese, and English.] Beijing: Jiuzhou tushu chubanshe.

Pritzker, David, and Wang Xudong 王旭东. 2020. *Sizhou zhi lu de wenhua jiaoliu: Tubo shiqi yishu zhenpin zhan* 丝绸之路上的文化交流—吐蕃时期艺术珍品展 / *Cultural Exchange along the Silk Road: Masterpieces of the Tubo Period (7th–9th Century).* Exhibition catalog. Beijing: Zhingguo Zangxue chubanshe. English edition forthcoming.

Qian Zhengkun 錢正坤. 1995. "Qinghai Ledu Qutansi bihua yanjiu" 青海樂都瞿曇寺壁畫研究 [Research on the wall paintings of Qutan Monastery in Ledu, Qinghai]. *Meishu shi yanjiu* 美術史研究 4, no. 80, 57–62.

Ren Yuehai 任月海. 2008. *Duolun wenshi ziliao* 多倫文史資料 [Dolonnuur historical documents], vol. 3. Hohhot: Nei Menggu daxue chubanshe.

Samghata Sutra. Taishō Tripiṭaka. (T.13.423)

Shang Gang 尚刚. 2009. "Yifu juzuo, jidian caice 一幅巨作，几点猜测." In *Hanzang fojiao meishu yanjiu* 汉藏佛教美术研究, edited by Xie Jisheng, Luo Wenhua, and Jing Anning, 261–67. Shanghai: Shanghai guji chubanshe.

Shi Jinbo 史金波. 1988. *Xixia Fojiao shilue* 西夏佛教史略 [A brief history of Buddhism in Western Xia]. Yinchuan: Ningxia renmin chubanshe.

Solonin, Kirill [Suoluoning 索羅寧]. 2013b. "Xixia fojiao xitong xing chutan" 西夏佛教系統性初探 [Sinitic Buddhism in the Tangut state]. *Shijie zongjiao yanjiu* 2013, no. 4, 22–39.

Song Lian 宋濂 (1310–1381) et al. 1976. *Yuanshi* 元史 [The history of the Yuan, 1370]. Beijing: Zhonghua shuju.

Su Bai 宿白. 1951. "Dunhuang Mogao ku zhong de 'Wutai shan tu'" 敦煌莫高窟中的"五臺山圖" [Pictures of Mount Wutai in Mogao caves of Dunhuang]. *Wenwu cankao ziliao* 文物参考資料 5, no. 2, 49–71.

———. 1996a. *Zangchuan fojiao siyuan kaogu* 藏传佛教寺院考古 [Archaeological studies on monasteries of Tibetan Buddhism]. Beijing: Wenwu chubanshe.

———. 1996b. "Yuan dai Hangzhou de Zang chuan mijiao ji qi you guan yiji" 元代杭州的藏传密教及其有关遗迹. In *Zang chuan fojiao siyuan kaogu* 藏传佛教寺院考古, 365–87. Beijing: Wenwu chubanshe.

Tong Tao 仝涛, 2021. *Qing Zang Gaoyuan sichou zhu lu de kaogu xue yanjiu*青藏高原丝绸之路的考古学 研究 [Archeological study on the Silk Roads of the Qinghai-Tibet Plateau]. Beijing: Wenwu chubanshe.

Tucci, Giuseppe. 2009. *Fan tian fo di. Di si juan. Jiangzi ji qi siyuan.* 梵天佛地. 第四卷. 江孜及其寺院. 2 vols. Edited by Wei Zhengzhong (Vignato Giuseppe) and Saerji. *Indo-Tibetica 4*, vol. 2. Shanghai: Shanghai guji chubanshe.

Wang Haitao 王海濤. 2002. *Yunnan lishi bihua yishu* 雲南歷史壁畫藝術 [The art of Yunnan historical murals]. Kunming: Yunnan renmin chubanshe.

Wang Jiapeng 王家鵬. 2010. *Gugong tangka tudian* 故宮唐卡圖典 [Thangka paintings in the collection of the Palace Museum]. Beijing: Gugong chubanshe.

Wei Wen 魏文. 2013. "Zuishang le ji benxu xianshi ji yichuan yuanliu kao" 最上樂集本續顯釋記 譯傳源流考. In *Studies on Chinese and Tibetan Buddhism, Han Zang Fojiao Yanjiu* 漢藏佛學研究 / *Sino-Tibetan Buddhist Studies*, edited by Shen Weirong, 301–31. Beijing: Zhongguo Zangxue chubanshe.

Wen Pulin 溫 普林. 2002. *Anduo Qiangba: 1914–2002: Dalai yu Xizang de hua shi* 安多 强巴: *1914–2002:* 達賴 與 西藏 的 畫師 / *Amdo Qiampa.* Taibei: Da kuai wenhua chuban gu fen you xian gongsi.

Wen Yucheng 温玉成. 2002. "Zhenjiangshi Xijindu guojieta kao" 镇江市西津渡过街塔考 [A study on Xijindu stupa gate in Zhenjiang City]. In *Su Bai xiansheng bazhi huadan jinian wenji* 宿白先生八秩华诞纪念文集 [Collected works celebrating the 80th birthday of Mr. Su Bai], 597–613. Beijing: Wenwu chubanshe.

Wu Jingshan 吳景山. 2011. "Qinghai Ledu Qutansi jianzhu yanjiu青海樂都瞿曇寺建築研究" [Research on the architecture of Qinghai Ledu Qutan Monastery]. *Zhongguo Zangxue* 中国藏学 / *China Tibetology* 1, no. 95, 106–21.

Wu Jun 吳均, Mao Jizu 毛繼祖, and Ma Shilin 馬世林, trans. 1989. *Anduo zheng jiao shi* 安多正教史 [History of the Dharma in Amdo]. Lanzhou: Gansu minzu chubanshe.

Xiangmai 祥邁 (Monk Ruyi Xiangmai 如意祥邁). 1924–32. "Shengzhi tejian Shijia sheli lingtong zhi ta beiwen" 聖旨特建釋迦舍利靈通之塔碑文 [Stele inscription of the imperially constructed efficacious stupa of Sakya relics], 13th century – Preserved in Xiangmai, *Bianwei lu* 辨偽錄 [Records of debating the false], edited by Taishō shinshū daizōkyō 大正新脩大藏經, vol. 32, ch. 5, 779B-81A. Tokyo: Taishō issaikyō kankōkai.

Xiawu Kaxian 夏吾卡先. 2015. "Shi qu Tubo mo ya ke wen de zheng li yu yan jiu" 石渠吐蕃摩崖刻文的整理与研究. *Zangxue xuekan* 藏学学刊 12, 19–35.

Xie Jisheng 谢继胜. 2001. "Tubo Xixia lishi wenhua yuan yuan yu Xixia Zang chuan huihua" 吐蕃西夏历史文化渊源与西夏藏传绘画 [Tibetan-Xixia historical and cultural origins and Xixia-Tibetan painting]. *Xizang yanjiu* 西藏研究 3, 35–48.

———. 2014. "Juyong Guan guojieta zaoxiang yiyun kao–11 zhi 14 shiji Zhongguo fojiao yishu tuxiang peizhi de chonggou" 居庸关过街塔造像意蕴考—11至14世纪中国佛教艺术图像配置的重构 [The iconography of Crossing Road Pagoda (Guojie Ta) images of JuYongGuan Pass—Reconstruction of Chinese Buddhist art images and composition from 11th to 14th centuries]." *Gugong bowuyuan yuankan* 故宮博物院院刊 [Palace Museum Journal] 5, 49–80.

Xie Jisheng 謝繼勝 and Liao Yang 廖暘. 2006. "Qinghai Ledu Qutansi Baoguangdian yu Longguodian bihua nei-rong bianshi" 青海樂都瞿曇寺寶光殿與隆國殿壁畫內容辨識 [Identifying the content of the wall paintings in Baoguang Hall and Longguo Hall of Qutan Monastery]. *Meishu shi yanjiu* 3, 23–30.

Xie Jisheng, Xiong Wenbin, Liao Yang, and Rob Linrothe. 2014. *Jiangnan Zangchuan Fojiao Yishu: Hangzhou Feilaifeng shike zaoxiang yanjiu* 江南藏传佛教艺术：杭州飞来峰石刻造研究 [Tibetan Buddhist art south of the Yangtse River: Collective research of Feilaifeng's Tibetan-style sculpture]. Beijing: Zhongguo Zangxue chubanshe.

Xie Zuo 謝佐. 1981. "Qutansi bukao" 瞿曇寺補考 [Supplementary investigation of Qutan Monastery]. *Qinghai minzu daxue xuebao* 1, 52–60.

———. 1998. *Qutansi* 瞿曇寺 [Qutan Monastery]. Xining: Qinghai renmin chubanshe.

Xiong Wenbin 熊文彬. 2003. *Yuan dai Zang Han yishu jiaoliu* 元代藏汉艺术交流 [Yuan dynasty Sino-Tibetan artistic exchanges]. Shijiazhuang: Hebei jiaoyu chubanshe.

———. 2014. "Cong Zangwen tiji he Gajupai da shouyin shang shi chuancheng tu kan Lijiang Baisha Dabaojigong bihua de chuangzuo niandai" 从藏文题记和噶举派大手印上师传承图看丽江白沙大宝积宫壁画的创作年代 [The dating of the murals of Dabaojigong Temple, Lijiang, Yunnan Province, according to the Tibetan inscription and the image of Mahamudra lineage]. In *Da xile yu da yuanman: Qingzhu Tan Xiyong xiansheng 80 huadan Han Zang Foxue yanjiu lun ji* 大喜乐与大圆满：庆祝谈锡永先生八十华诞汉藏佛学研究论集, edited by Shen Weirong 沈卫荣, 479–91. Beijing: Zhingguo Zangxue chubanshe.

Xiong Wenbin 熊文彬 and Li Yizhi 李逸之. 2016. *Xizang Guge caca yishu* 西藏古格擦擦艺术 [Art of *tsatsa* from Guge, Tibet]. Beijing: Zhongguo Zangxue chubanshe.

Xiong Wenbin 熊文彬, Shargan Wangdui 夏格旺堆, and Habibu 哈比布. 2013. "Yunnan Lijiang Baisha Dabaojigong Mingdai bihua tiji ji qi xiangguan wenti taolun" 云南丽江白沙大宝积宫明代壁画题记及其相关问题讨论 [Discussions on the Tibetan inscription on the murals created in the Ming dynasty in Dabaojigong Temple, Baisha, Lijiang, Yunnan Province and relevant questions]. *Zhongguo Zangxue* 中国藏学 / *China Tibetology* 3, 57–70.

Xixia wen fojiao bu fen 西夏文佛教部分. 2019. v. 29. *Eluosi kexueyuan dongfang wenxian yanjiu suo cang hei shuicheng wenxian: Xixia wen fojiao bufen* 俄羅斯科學院東方文獻研究所藏黑水城文獻. 29, 西夏文佛教部分 [Documents collected by the Institute of Oriental Literature of the Russian Academy of Sciences: Part of Buddhism in Western Xia]. Shanghai: Shanghai guji chubanshe.

Xizang zizhiqu wenwu guanli weiyuan hui 西藏自治区文物管理委员会, eds. (1985) 2007. *Bod kyi thang ka /Xizang tangka* 西藏唐卡. Beijing: Wenwu chubanshe.

Xu Xiaodong. 2018. *Xue mo ling long / Jewels of Transcendence: Himalayan and Mongolian Treasures.* Exhibition catalog. [In Chinese with some English.] Hong Kong: Art Museum, Chinese University of Hong Kong.

Xu Zhenghong 許正弘. 2012. "Yuan taixizongyin yuan guanshu jianzhi kaolun" 元太禧宗禋院官署建置考論. *Qinghua baogao* 42, no. 3, 443–87.

Xuanzang and Bianji. (1573). *Da Tang xi yu ji*大唐西域记 [Traveling notes of the western regions in the Great Tang dynasty], 12 vols. n.p.

Yang Pu 楊溥. 1933. *Chaha'er koubei liu xian diaocha ji* 察哈爾口北六縣調查記 [Investigation of the six Chakhar districts north of the passes]. Beijing: Jincheng yinshuju.

Yang Qingfan 杨清凡, Lu Suwen 卢素文, and Zhang Yanqing 张延清. 2017. "Xizang Mangkang ga tuo zhen xin faxian Tubo moya shike diaocha jianbao." 西藏芒康嘎托镇新发现吐蕃摩崖石刻调查简报 [Archaeological report on the newly discovered Tubo dynasty rock sculptures in the town of Sgar thog in Smar khams County, Tibet]. *Zangxue xue kan* 藏学学刊 / *Journal of Tibetology* 16, no. 1, 233–51.

Yang Xuezheng 楊學政. 1995. "Xizang fojiao zai Yunnan de chuanbo he yingxiang" 西藏佛教在雲南的傳播和影響 [The spread and influence of Tibetan Buddhism in Yunnan]. In *Yunnan Zangxue yanjiu lunwen ji* 雲南藏學研究論文集, 256–78. Kunming: Yunnan minzu chubanshe.

Yixi 一西, ed. 2013. *Foyun: Zaoxiang Yishu jicui* 佛韵: 造像艺术集粹 / *The Art of Buddhist Sculpture*. Beijing: Wenwu chubanshe.

Yu Xiaodong 于小冬. 2006. *Zang chuan fojiao huihua shi* 藏传佛教绘画史 [History of Tibetan Buddhist paintings]. Nanjing: Jiangsu meishu chubanshe.

_____. 2021. *Xizang huihua fengge shi* 西藏绘画风格史 [History of Tibetan painting styles], Part 2. Tianjin: Tianjin meishu chubanshe.

Yuandai huasu ji 佚名 元代畫塑記. (ca. 13th century) 2005. In *Sita ji. Yizhou minghua lu. Yuandai huasu ji* 寺塔記·益州名畫錄·元代畫塑記. Beijing: Renmin meishu chubanshe.

Yunnan Provincial Museum 雲南省博物館. 2001. *Mushi huanpu* 木氏宦譜 「影印本」 [The Mu family lineage]. Facsimile, Kunming: Yunnan meishu chubanshe.

Zhang Huiming 張惠明. 2000. "Dunhuang 'Wutai shan huaxian tu' zaoqi diben de tuxiang jiqi laiyuan" 敦煌'五臺山化現圖' 早期底本的圖像及其來源 [The origin and iconography of the representations of apparitions of Mount Wutai in Dunhuang]. *Dunhuang Yanjiu* 4, 1–9.

Zhang Runping 张润平, Su Hang 苏航, and Luo Zhao 罗炤, eds. 2012. *Xitian fozi yuanliu lu: Wenxian yu chubu yanjiu* 西天佛子源流录：文献与初步研究 [The Biography of Buddha's son of the Western Heaven: The literature and a preliminary study]. Beijing: Kexue chubanshe.

Zhang Shubin 张书彬. 2019. "Zhonggu Fahua xinyang xin tuxiang leixing zhi kaoshi - yi Yulin shiku 3 ku 'Tanyi gan Puxian pusa huaxian nü shen tu' (ni ti) wei zhongxin" 中古法华信仰新图像类型之考释–以榆林窟第3窟《昙翼感普贤菩萨化现女身图》(拟题) 为中心 [Textual research on new types of images related to veneration of the *Lotus Sutra* in the Middle Ages, centered on the image "Tanyi Contemplates Samantabhadra Manifesting a Female Form"]. *Xin Meishu* 新美术 [New Art] 40, no. 12, 22–30.

Zhang Yajing. 2014. "An Iconographical Study of Hari hariharivāhanodbhavalokeśvara (Hariharihari Guanyin) Image." *Palace Museum Journal* 1, 25–36 and 157.

Zhang Yisun 张怡荪, ed. 1993. *Bod rgya tshig mdzod chen mo* [Great Tibetan-Chinese dictionary]. Beijing: Minzu chubanshe.

Zhao Shengliang 赵声良. 1995. *Dunhuang shiku yishu, Mogaoku di 61 ku* 敦煌石窟艺术·莫高窟第 61 窟 [Dunhuang Cave 61]. Nanjing: Jiangsu meishu chubanshe.

Zhao Shiyan 趙世延 (1260–1336) and Yu Ji 虞集 2020. *Jingshi dadian jijiao* 经世大典輯校 [The imperial compendium for governing the world, 1330] edited by Zhou Shaochuan 周少川, Wei Xuntian 魏訓田, and Xie Hui 謝輝. Beijing: Zhonghua shuju.

Zhiguan Museum of Fine Art. 2018. *The Light of Buddha: Buddhist Sculptures of the Palace Museum and Zhiguan Museum of Fine Art*. Exhibition catalog. [In Chinese and English.] Beijing: Wenwu chushuban.

Zhongguo Zangxue yanjiu zhongxin 中国藏学研究中心, et al., eds. 1994. *Yuan yilai Xizang difang yu zhongyang zhengfu guanxi dang'an shiliao huibian* 元以来西藏地方与中央政府关系档案史料汇编, vol. 5, 2130. Beijing: Zhongguo zangxue chubanshe.

Zhou Mi 周密 (1232–1298) 2001. *Shaoxing yufu shuhuashi* 紹興御府書畫式. In *Qidong yeyu* 齊東野語, vol. 6, *Shuhua zhuangbiao jiyi jishi* 書畫裝裱技藝集釋, edited by Du Bingzhuang 杜秉莊and Du Zixiong 杜子熊. Shanghai: Shanghai shuhua chubanshe.

Zhou Qiyu 鄒啟宇, ed. 1991. *Yunnan fojiao yishu* 雲南佛教藝術 [Yunnan Buddhist art]. Kunming: Yunnan jiaoyu chubanshe.

Zhou Zhenhua 周振華. 1998. *Wutai shan beiwen, bian'e, yinglian, shifu xuan* 五臺山碑文匾額楹聯詩賦選 [Selection of stele inscriptions, placard inscriptions, couplets, and poems from Wutai Shan]. Taiyuan: Shanxi jiaoyu chubanshe.

Zhuang Chuo 莊綽. 1983. *Jilei bian* 雞肋编. Beijing: Zhonghua shuju.

JAPANESE

Ishihama, Yumiko. 2011. *Shinchō to Chibetto Bukkyō: Bosatsuō to Natta Kenryūtei* 清朝とチベット仏教: 菩薩王となった乾隆帝 [The Qing dynasty and the Tibetan Buddhist world]. Tokyo: Waseda daigaku shuppanbu.

Kychanov, E. I. 1999. *Каталог ТАнгутских Буддийских Памятников Института ВОстоковедения Российской Академии Наук*. [A catalogue of the Tangut Buddhist texts in the Institute of Oriental Studies Russian Academy of Sciences]. [In Japanese and Russian.] Kyoto: University of Kyoto.

Miyaji, Akira 宮治昭. 2010. *Indo Bukkyō bijutsu shiron* インド仏教美術史論 [Essays on Buddhist art history in India]. Tokyo: Chūō Kōron Bijutsu Shuppan.

Murata, Jirō 村田治郎, ed. 1955–58. *Kyoyōkan* 居庸關 / *Chü-Yung-Guan, The Buddhist Arch of the Fourteenth Century AD at the Pass of the Gate Wall Northeast of Peking*, 1:325–59. [In Japanese, with a summary in English.] Kyoto: Faculty of Engineering, Kyoto University.

Sato, Hisashi 佐藤长. 1986. "Eight Ecclesiastical Kings Appointed by Ming Emperors." In *Studies on the Mediaeval History of Tibet*, edited by Hisashi Sato, 173–208. Kyoto: Dohosha.

Index

Contributors

IAN ALSOP is an independent researcher into the cultural and art history of the Himalayas, with a special interest in Newar art and culture.

KARIN ALTMANN is an artist, researcher, and senior lecturer in the Department of Textile Arts at the University of Applied Arts Vienna.

JOHN A. ARDUSSI is a senior research fellow at the University of Virginia Tibet Center.

CHRISTOPHER P. ATWOOD is professor of Mongolian and Chinese frontier and ethnic history and chair of the East Asian Languages and Civilizations Department at the University of Pennsylvania.

CHRISTOPHER BELL is associate professor of religious studies at Stetson University, DeLand, Florida.

JOHN VINCENT BELLEZZA is a specialist on the cultural history and archaeology of Tibet and a senior research fellow at the University of Virginia Tibet Center.

KALZANG DORJEE BHUTIA is a visiting scholar in the East Asian Studies Center at the University of Southern California.

KERRY LUCINDA BROWN, a specialist in Nepalese art and architecture, is professor of art history at Savannah College of Art and Design.

AURELIA CAMPBELL is associate professor in the Art, Art History, and Film Department at Boston College.

JANE CASEY is an art historian specializing in Himalayan art. She is a research fellow in Tibetan art at the Palace Museum, Beijing, and guest professor at the Center for Buddhist Art, Zhejiang University, Hangzhou.

ISABELLE CHARLEUX is director of research at the French National Centre for Scientific Research, Paris.

YONG CHO is assistant professor in the Department of the History of Art at the University of California, Riverside.

WEN-SHING CHOU is associate professor of art history at Hunter College and the Graduate Center, City University of New York.

RYAN DAMRON is research editor at *The 84000: Translating the Words of the Buddha* and holds a PhD from the Department of South and Southeast Asian Studies at the University of California, Berkeley.

KARL DEBRECZENY is senior curator of collections and research at the Rubin Museum of Art, New York.

DAVID M. DIVALERIO is associate professor of history and religious studies at the University of Wisconsin-Milwaukee.

SHENGNAN DONG is a PhD candidate at SOAS University of London, specializing in Tibetan and Chinese Buddhist art and architecture.

JEAN-LUC ESTOURNEL is a research graduate of the École du Louvre/Musée Guimet, Paris, and a member of the Compagnie Nationale des Experts.

ANNA FILIGENZI is associate professor at the University of Naples "L'Orientale."

JAMES GENTRY is assistant professor of religious studies at Stanford University.

YANGLA GESANG is a PhD candidate in art history at the Tibet University.

AURORA GRALDI earned a PhD in the History of Art Department at the University of Vienna in 2019.

GUNTRAM HAZOD is a senior researcher in the Institute for Social Anthropology (ISA) at the Austrian Academy of Sciences and the director and principal investigator of the Austrian Science Fund (FWF)–financed research project on the Tibetan tumulus tradition.

AMY HELLER is an associate researcher at the Institute for the Science of Religion at the University of Berne and since 1986 has been a research collaborator of the Tibetan studies team in the East Asian Civilizations Research Centre at the French National Centre for Scientific Research, Paris.

AGNIESZKA HELMAN-WAZNY is a research professor of social sciences at the University of Warsaw.

MICHAEL HENSS is an art historian and scholar in Zurich, specializing in Buddhist art.

DANIEL A. HIRSHBERG is executive director of SŌTERIC Contemplative Training in Boulder and visiting faculty at the University of Colorado and Naropa University.

THERESIA HOFER works as senior lecturer in social anthropology at the University of Bristol.

AMY HOLMES-TAGCHUNGDARPA is associate professor of religious studies and Asian studies at Occidental College, Los Angeles.

ERIC HUNTINGTON is a T. T. and W. F. Chao Assistant Professor of Transnational Asian Studies at Rice University, Houston.

DAVID JACKSON is a retired scholar of Tibetan studies who worked at the Rubin Museum of Art for ten years, authoring the Masterworks of Tibetan Painting series.

JIA WEIWEI is an associate research fellow in the Department of Art and Archaeology at Zhejiang University, Hangzhou.

JINAH KIM is George P. Bickford Professor of Indian and South Asian Art in the Department of History of Art and Architecture at Harvard University.

NATASHA N. KIMMET is a postdoctoral researcher at the University of Vienna.

JOWITA KRAMER is professor of Indology at the Institute for South and Central Asian Studies at Leipzig University.

DONALD J. LA ROCCA is curator emeritus in the Department of Arms and Armor at the Metropolitan Museum of Art, New York.

NANCY G. LIN is the Noboru and Yaeko Hanyu Professor of Buddhist Chaplaincy at the Institute of Buddhist Studies.

ROB LINROTHE is associate professor emeritus and former department chair of art history at Northwestern University, Evanston, Illinois.

YUYUAN (VICTORIA) LIU is a PhD student of Tibetan visual culture in the History-East Asia Program at Columbia University, specializing in Tibetan art and photography.

DONALD S. LOPEZ JR. is the Arthur E. Link Distinguished University Professor of Buddhist and Tibetan Studies in the Department of Asian Languages and Cultures, University of Michigan.

CHRISTIAN LUCZANITS is David L. Snellgrove Senior Lecturer in Tibetan and Buddhist Art in the Department of History of Art and Archaeology, SOAS, University of London.

LUO WENHUA is a research fellow at the Palace Museum in Beijing and director of the Research Center for Tibetan Buddhist Heritage.

ARIANA MAKI is associate director of the University of Virginia Tibet Center and Bhutan Initiative.

NILS MARTIN is a postdoctoral researcher in Tibetan art history at the French East Asian Civilizations Research Centre (CRCAO-UMR8155), Paris.

THIERRY MATHOU is a career diplomat and an associated political scientist with the Department of Himalayan Studies of the French National Centre for Scientific Research, Paris.

KUNSANG NAMGYAL-LAMA is a lecturer in the history of Nepalese and Tibetan art at the Institut National des Langues et Civilisations Orientales, Paris, and associate researcher in the Centre for Himalayan Studies at the French National Centre for Scientific Research, Paris.

PAUL KOCOT NIETUPSKI is professor in the Department of Theology and Religious Studies at John Carroll University, University Heights, Ohio.

LUCA MARIA OLIVIERI is associate professor of archaeology and cultures of Gandhara and the Silk Roads at Ca' Foscari University of Venice, and director of the Italian Archaeological Mission in Pakistan (ISMEO - Ca' Foscari University of Venice).

ELENA PAKHOUTOVA is senior curator of Himalayan art at the Rubin Museum of Art, New York.

KATHERINE ANNE PAUL is the lead curator and Virginia and William M. Spencer III Curator of Asian Art at the Birmingham Museum of Art, Alabama.

KARMA PHUNTSHO is a Bhutanese cultural scholar and Buddhist teacher with a DPhil from the University of Oxford.

FRANÇOISE POMMARET is director of research emeritus at the French National Centre for Scientific Research, Paris.

ANDREW QUINTMAN is associate professor of religion and East Asian studies at Wesleyan University, Middletown, Connecticut.

CHARLES RAMBLE is directeur d'études (professor) in Tibetan history and philology at the École Pratique des Hautes Études, PSL University, Paris.

SARAH A. RICHARDSON is assistant professor of history of religions in the Department of Historical Studies at the University of Toronto Mississauga.

ALEXANDER VON ROSPATT the Catherine and William L. Magistretti Distinguished Professor in the Department of South and Southeast Asian Studies and the director of the Group in Buddhist Studies at the University of California, Berkeley.

KURTIS R. SCHAEFFER is the Frances Myers Ball Professor in the Department of Religious Studies at the University of Virginia.

KATHRYN SELIG BROWN is an independent curator and author specializing in Himalayan art.

RIGA SHAKYA is a historian of China, Tibet, and the Himalayas with a PhD from the Department of East Asian Languages and Cultures at Columbia University.

KIRILL SOLONIN is a professor in the Department of History and Philology of China Western Regions at Renmin University, China.

KASHINATH TAMOT is a Nepalese senior expert and researcher into the cultural history and languages of Nepal, specializing in the Newari language and historical records.

PEMA NAMDOL THAYE is a painter, sculptor, 3D mandala specialist, traditional Tibetan architect, author, and art educator.

ALICE TRAVERS is a permanent researcher at the French National Centre for Scientific Research and a member of the East Asian Civilizations Research Centre (CRCAO, UMR 8155), Paris.

TSECHANG PENBA WANGDU is a painter, professor, and PhD advisor of art and art history at the College of Fine Art, Tibet University.

URANCHIMEG TSULTEMIN is assistant professor and Edgar and Dorothy Fehnel Chair in International Studies in Herron School of Art and Design at Indiana University–Indianapolis.

GAUTAMA V. VAJRACHARYA is a distinguished Sanskritist and scholar of South Asian art and culture.

ROBERTO VITALI works on primary sources dedicated to Tibet and the Himalayas and writes on their history from the earliest time to the fifteenth century.

ULRICH VON SCHROEDER is an independent scholar specializing in Buddhist art and culture.

CAMERON DAVID WARNER is associate professor of anthropology at Aarhus University, Denmark.

JAKOB WINKLER holds an MA in Tibetology, Indian art history, and social anthropology, working as an author, editor, and proofreader for Buddhist publications and as an instructor for the International Dzogchen Community.

XIE JISHENG is professor at Zhejiang University Center for Buddhist Art, Hangzhou.

RONIT YOELI-TLALIM is a reader in the History Department at Goldsmiths, University of London.

First published in 2023 by
Scala Arts Publishers, Inc.
1301 Avenue of the Americas
10th floor
New York, NY 10019
ScalaPublishers.com
Scala – New York – London

The Rubin Museum of Art
150 West 17th Street
New York, NY 10011
RubinMuseum.org

Distributed outside of the Rubin Museum of Art in the book trade by
ACC Art Books
6 West 18th Street
4th Floor
New York, NY 10011

ISBN 978 1 78551 452 4

Editors: Karl Debreczeny and Elena Pakhoutova

Project Director: Sarah Zabrodski

Assistant Project Manager: Erin Barnett

Copyeditors: Lory Frankel and Joe Hannan

Designer: Phil Kovacevich

Cartographer: Anandaroop Roy

Printed and bound in Malaysia

Cover: No. 10 (p. 64)
Frontispiece: Detail of no. 92 (p. 392)
Page 4: No. 37 (p. 172)
Page 18: Detail of no. 66 (p. 288)
Page 20: Detail of no. 97 (p. 412)
Back cover: No. 5 (p. 44)

Library of Congress Cataloging-in-Publication Data:

Names: Karl Debreczeny and Elena Pakhoutova., editors | Rubin Museum of Art (New York N.Y.) host institution. Title. | Himalayan Art in 108 Objects / The Rubin Museum of Art | in association with Scala Arts Publishers, Inc. New York. Authors. | Ian Alsop. Karin Altmann. John A. Ardussi. Christopher Atwood. Christopher Bell. John Vincent Bellezza. Kalzang Dorjee Bhutia. Kerry Lucinda Brown. Aurelia Campbell. Jane Casey. Isabelle Charleux. Yong Cho. Wen-shing Chou. Ryan Damron. David M. DiValerio. Shengnan Dong. Jean-Luc Estournel. Anna Filigenzi. James Gentry. Yangla Gesang. Aurora Graldi. Guntram Hazod. Amy Heller. Agnieszka Helman-Wazny. Michael Henss. Daniel A. Hirshberg. Theresia Hofer. Amy Holmes-Tagchungdarpa. Eric Huntington. David Jackson. Jia Weiwei. Jinah Kim. Natasha N. Kimmet. Jowita Kramer. Donald J. LaRocca. Nancy G. Lin. Rob Linrothe. Yuyuan (Victoria) Liu. Donald S. Lopez Jr. Christian Luczanits. Luo Wenhua. Ariana Maki. Nils Martin. Thierry Mathou. Kunsang Lama Namgyal. Paul Kocot Nietupski. Luca Maria Olivieri. Katherine Anne Paul. Karma Phuntsho. Françoise Pommaret. Andrew Quintman. Charles Ramble. Sarah A. Richardson. Alexander von Rospatt. Kurtis R. Schaeffer. Kathryn Selig Brown. Riga Shakya. Kirill Solonin. Kashinath Tamot. Pema Namdol Thaye. Alice Travers. Tsechang Penba Wangdu. Uranchimeg Tsultemin. Gautama V. Vajracharya. Roberto Vitali. Ulrich von Schroeder. Cameron David Warner. Jakob Winkler. Xie Jisheng. Ronit Yoeli-Tlalim.
Description. | New York: Rubin Museum of Art, 2023 | Includes map, bibliographical references and index. Identifiers. | LCCN 2023930994| ISBN 9781785514524 (hbk.)
Subjects: Art. Artist. Himalayan Art. Buddhist Art. Religion. Buddhism. Hinduism. Bon. Material Culture. Bhutan. Mongolia. Nepal. Tibet Region. People's Republic of China.